Komm mit!®

Your passport to proficiency

Dein Pass zur Welt!

Plan your itinerary for success

What's your **Destination?**

Communication!

Komm mit! takes your classroom there.

It's even possible that **"What's next?"** becomes your students' favorite question!

Communication and culture in context

The clear structure of each chapter makes it easy t
present, practice, and apply language skills—a
in the context of the location where the chapte
takes place!

Grammar support and practice in every lesson

Komm mit! builds a proven communicativ
approach on a solid foundation o
grammar and vocabulary so student
become proficient readers, writers, an
speakers of German. With th
Grammatikheft, Grammar Tutor, an
CD-ROM Tutor, students can practice th
way they learn best.

Technology that takes you there

Bring the world into your classroom with integrated audio, video, **CD-ROM,** and Internet resources that immerse students in authentic language and culture.

Assessment for state and national standards

Every chapter features a variety of writing activities, including process writing strategies. To help you incorporate standardized test practice, the Lies mit mir! Reader and Reading Strategies and Skills Handbook offer additional reading practice and reading skills development.

Easy lesson planning for all learning styles

Planning lessons has never been easier with a Lesson Planner with Substitute Teacher Lesson Plans, an editable One-Stop Planner® CD-ROM, and a Student Make-Up Assignments with Alternative Quizzes resource.

*Travel a balanced program that's **easy to navigate.***

Die Welt erwartet dich!

Komm mit!

Program components

Texts
- Pupil's Edition
- Teacher's Edition

Middle School Resources
- Exploratory Guide
- TPR Storytelling Book

Planning and Presenting
- One-Stop Planner CD-ROM with Test Generator
- Lesson Planner with Substitute Teacher Lesson Plans
- Student Make-Up Assignments with Alternative Quizzes
- Teaching Transparencies

Grammar
- Grammatikheft
- Grammar Tutor for Students of German

Reading and Writing
- Reading Strategies and Skills Handbook
- Lies mit mir! Reader
- Übungsheft

Listening and Speaking
- Audio CD Program
- Listening Activities
- Activities for Communication
- TPR Storytelling Book (Levels 1 and 2)

Assessment
- Testing Program
- Alternative Assessment Guide
- Student Make-Up Assignments with Alternative Quizzes

Technology
- One-Stop Planner CD-ROM with Test Generator
- Audio CD Program
- Interactive CD-ROM Tutor (Levels 1 and 2)
- Video Program
- Video Guide

Internet
- go.hrw.com
- www.hrw.com
- www.hrw.com/passport

Komm mit!

HOLT GERMAN

LEVEL 1

HOLT, RINEHART AND WINSTON

A Harcourt Classroom Education Company

Austin · New York · Orlando · Atlanta · San Francisco · Boston · Dallas · Toronto · London

For permission to reprint copyrighted material in the Teacher's Edition, grateful acknowledgment is made to the following sources:
National Standards in Foreign Language Education Project: "National Standards Report" from **Standards for Foreign Language Learning:** Preparing for the 21st Century. Copyright © 1996 by National Standards in Foreign Language Education Project.

For permission to reprint copyrighted material in the Pupil's Edition and the Teacher's Edition, grateful acknowledgment is made to the following sources:
Baars Marketing GmbH: Advertisement, "Leerdammer Light: Das haben Sie jetzt davon," from Stern, no. 27, June 25, 1992.
Bauconcept: Advertisement, "Die Oase in der City!," from Südwest Presse: Schwäbisches Tagblatt, Tübingen, July 14, 1990.

ACKNOWLEDGMENTS

Cover/Photo Credits
Cover: (front cover house), Helga Lade/Peter Arnold, Inc.; (teens), Steve Ewert/HRW Photo; (back cover house), George Winkler/HRW Photo; (back cover frame), © 2003 Image Farm, Inc.

In the Annotated Teacher's Edition,
All photos by George Winkler/Holt, Rinehart and Winston, Inc. except:

Master element icons: Community Link: HBJ Photo; CD-Rom tutor: Courtesy Neel Heisel; Internet Connection computers: Digital imagery® © 2003 PhotoDisc, Inc.; Jupiter page: Digital imagery® © 2003 PhotoDisc, Inc.; Chess piece: Digital imagery® © 2003 PhotoDisc, Inc.; Clock: Digital imagery® © 2003 PhotoDisc, Inc.; Globes: Mountain High Maps® Copyright © 1997 Digital Wisdom, Inc.; Euros: © European Communities

Front Matter: T5, Steve Ewert/HRW Photo; T9, Sam Dudgeon/HRW Photo. Chapter One: 15D, Victoria Smith/HRW Photo; 15V, Courtesy of Hildegard Becker-Lipp. Chapter Two: 41T, Courtesy of Becky McQueen. Chapter Three: 67D, Victoria Smith/HRW Photo; 67S, Courtesy of Jean Brooks; 67X, Courtesy of Brenda Weimann Ludwig. Chapter Four: 99X, Courtesy of Elaine Bird. Chapter Five: 127V, Courtesy of Ingrid Langer. Chapter Six: 155V, Courtesy of Petronella Gaal; 155D (milk), Digital imagery® copyright 2003 PhotoDisc, Inc.; 155D (flour), © PhotoSpin, Inc.; 155D (salt), Corbis Images; 155D (lemon), Digital imagery® copyright 2003 PhotoDisc, Inc.; 155D (bacon), © Stockbyte. Chapter Seven: 187S, Courtesy of Lilo Townsend. Chapter Eight: 215Q, Courtesy of Kristine Conlon. Chapter Nine: 243X, Courtesy of Carolyn Ostermann-Healey; 243D, Konnie Brown/HRW Photo. Chapter Ten: 275T, Larry B. Tenbarge. Chapter Eleven: 303S, Courtesy of Alice Harrill. Chapter Twelve: 331O, Courtesy of Mary Ann R. Boyce

Art Credits
All art, unless otherwise noted, by Holt, Rinehart & Winston.

Chapter Two: Page 41O, Eduard Böhm; 41X, Holly Cooper. Chapter Three: Page 65S, George McLeod. Chapter Five: Page 127T, Tomm Rummonds. Chapter Six: Page 155U, Eduard Böhm. Chapter Seven: Page 187Q, Holly Cooper. Chapter Nine: Page 243W, Holly Cooper. Chapter Eleven: Page 303S, Mike Krone.

ACKNOWLEDGMENTS continued on page R59, which is an extension of the copyright page.

Komm mit! Level 1
Teacher's Edition

CONTRIBUTING WRITERS

Ulrike Puryear
Austin, TX
Mrs. Puryear wrote background information, activities, and teacher suggestions for all chapters of the Teacher's Edition.

Dorothea Bruschke, retired
Parkway School District
Chesterfield, MO
Mrs. Bruschke wrote activities and teacher suggestions for Chapters 1 and 6 of the Teacher's Edition.

CONSULTANTS

The consultants conferred on a regular basis with the editorial staff and reviewed all the chapters of the Teacher's Edition.

Dorothea Bruschke, retired
Parkway School District
Chesterfield, MO

Diane E. Laumer
San Marcos High School
San Marcos, TX

Patrick T. Raven
National Consultant
Holt, Rinehart and Winston

Rolf M. Schwägermann
Stuyvesant High School
New York, NY

Jim Witt
Grand Junction High School
Grand Junction, CO

TEACHER-TO-TEACHER CONTRIBUTORS

Chapter 1
Hildegard Becker-Lipp
Shawnee Heights High School
Tecumseh, KS

Chapter 2
Becky McQueen
Alexander Middle School
Nekoosa, WI

Chapter 3
Jean Brooks
Livonia High School
Livonia , MI

Brenda Weinmann Ludwig
West Milford High School
West Milford, NJ

Chapter 4
Elaine Bind
McDonogh School
Owings Mills, MD

Chapter 5
Ingrid Langer
Worthington Kilbourne High School
Columbus, OH

Chapter 6
Petronella Gaal
International School of Prague
Czech Republic

Chapter 7
Lilo Townsend
Notre Dame High School
Batavia, NY

Chapter 8
Kristine Conlon
Muscatine High School
Muscatine, IA

Chapter 9
Carolyn Ostermann-Healey
Oakton High School
Vienna, VA

Chapter 10
Larry B. Tenbarge
Forest Park High School
Ferdinand, IN

Chapter 11
Alice Harrill
Harding University High School
Charlotte, NC

Chapter 12
Mary Ann R. Boyce
Linglestown Junior High and
East Junior High
Harrisburg, PA

PROFESSIONAL ESSAYS

Bringing Standards into the Classroom
Paul Sandrock
Foreign Language Education
Department of Public Instruction
Madison, WI

Reading Strategies and Skills
Nancy A. Humbach
Miami University
Oxford, OH

Technology in the Language Classroom
Cindy A. Kendall
Williamston High School
Williamston, MI

Using Portfolios in the Language Classroom
JoAnne S. Wilson
J. Wilson Associates
Glen Arbor, MI

Teaching Culture
Nancy A. Humbach
Miami University
Oxford, OH

Dorothea Bruschke, retired
Parkway School District
Chesterfield, MO

Implementing Komm mit! in the Middle Grades
Leslie Bouton Peterson
Parkway West Middle School
Chesterfield, MO

Learning Styles and Multi-Modality Teaching
Mary B. McGehee
Louisiana State University
Laboratory School
Baton Rouge, LA

To the Teacher

Principles and Practices

As nations become increasingly interdependent, the need for effective communication and sensitivity to other cultures becomes more important. Today's youth must be culturally and linguistically prepared to participate in a global society. At Holt, Rinehart and Winston, we believe that proficiency in more than one language is essential to meeting this need.

The primary goal of the Holt, Rinehart and Winston World Languages programs is to help students develop linguistic proficiency and cultural sensitivity. By interweaving language and culture, our programs seek to broaden students' communication skills while at the same time deepening their appreciation of other cultures.

We believe that all students can benefit from foreign language instruction. We recognize that not everyone learns at the same rate or in the same way; nevertheless, we believe that all students should have the opportunity to acquire language proficiency to a degree commensurate with their individual abilities.

Holt, Rinehart and Winston's World Languages programs are designed to accommodate all students by appealing to a variety of learning styles.

We believe that effective language programs should motivate students. Students deserve an answer to the question they often ask: "Why are we doing this?" They need to have goals that are interesting, practical, clearly stated, and attainable.

Holt, Rinehart and Winston's World Languages programs promote success. They present relevant content in manageable increments that encourage students to attain achievable functional objectives.

We believe that proficiency in another language is best nurtured by programs that encourage students to think critically and to take risks when expressing themselves in the language. We also recognize that students should strive for accuracy in communication. While it is imperative that students have a knowledge of the basic structures of the language, it is also important that they go beyond the simple manipulation of forms.

Holt, Rinehart and Winston's World Languages programs reflect a careful progression of activities that guide students from comprehensible input of authentic language through structured practice to creative, personalized expression. This progression, accompanied by consistent re-entry and spiraling of functions, vocabulary, and structures, provides students with the tools and the confidence to express themselves in their new language.

Finally, we believe that a complete program of language instruction should take into account the needs of teachers in today's increasingly demanding classrooms.

At Holt, Rinehart and Winston, we have designed programs that offer practical teacher support and provide resources to meet individual learning and teaching styles.

We have seen significant advances in modern language curriculum practices:

1. a redefinition of the objectives of foreign language study involving a commitment to the development of proficiency in the four skills and in cultural awareness;

2. a recognition of the need for longer sequences of study;

3. a new student-centered approach that redefines the role of the teacher as facilitator and encourages students to take a more active role in their learning;

4. the inclusion of students of all learning abilities.

The new Holt, Rinehart and Winston World Languages programs take into account not only these advances in the field of foreign language education but also the input of teachers and students around the country.

TEACHER'S EDITION
Contents

TO THE TEACHER **T8**

TABLE OF CONTENTS **T9**

PACING GUIDE AND ARTICULATION CHART **T10**

SCOPE AND SEQUENCE, HOLT GERMAN, LEVELS 1–3 .... **T12**

OVERVIEW OF *KOMM MIT!*, LEVEL 1 .... **T24**

PUPIL'S EDITION

- Location Opener **T25**
- Chapter Opener **T25**
- Los geht's! **T26**
- Stufen **T26**
- Landeskunde **T27**
- Zum Lesen **T27**
- Mehr Grammatikübungen **T28**
- Anwendung **T28**
- Kann ich's wirklich? **T28**
- Wortschatz **T28**

TECHNOLOGY **T29**

ANCILLARY PROGRAM **T30**

TEACHER'S EDITION **T32**

PROFESSIONAL ESSAYS

- Bringing Standards into the Classroom **T36**
- Reading in the Foreign Language Classroom **T38**
- Using Portfolios in the Language Classroom **T40**
- Implementing *Komm mit!* in the Middle Grades **T42**
- Teaching Culture **T44**
- Learning Styles and Multi-Modality Teaching **T46**

PROFESSIONAL REFERENCES **T48**

A BIBLIOGRAPHY FOR THE GERMAN TEACHER **T50**

TABLE OF CONTENTS, VORSCHAU–KAPITEL 12 .... **T57**

INDEX OF CULTURAL REFERENCES **T70**

MAP **T82**

Pacing and Planning

Traditional Schedule

Days of instruction: 180

Location Opener	2 days per Location Opener x 6 Location Openers	**12 days**
Chapter	13 days per chapter x 12 chapters	**156 days**
		168 days

If you are teaching on a traditional schedule, we suggest following the plan above and spending 13 days per chapter. A complete set of lesson plans in the interleaf provides detailed suggestions for each chapter. For more suggestions, see the **Lesson Planner with Substitute Teacher Lesson Plans.**

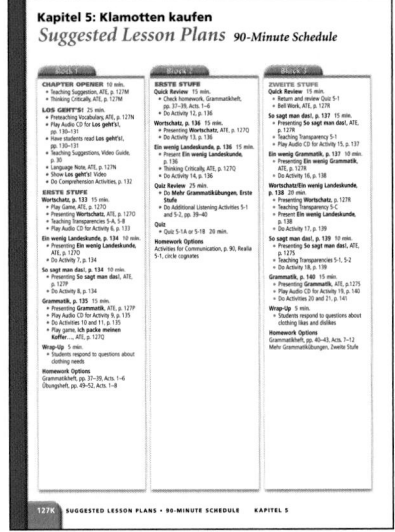

Block Schedule

Blocks of instruction: 90

Location Opener	1/2 block per Location Opener x 6 Location Openers	**3 blocks**
Chapter	7 blocks per chapter x 12 chapters	**84 blocks**
		87 blocks

If you are teaching on a block schedule, we suggest following the plan above and spending seven blocks per chapter. A complete set of lesson plans in the interleaf provides detailed suggestions for each chapter. For more suggestions, see the **Lesson Planner with Substitute Teacher Lesson Plans.**

One-Stop Planner CD-ROM

Use the **One-Stop Planner CD-ROM with Test Generator** to aid in lesson planning and pacing.

- Editable lesson plans with direct links to teaching resources
- Printable worksheets from resource books
- Direct launches to the HRW Internet activities
- Video and audio segments
- Test Generator
- Clip Art for vocabulary items

Pacing Tips

At the beginning of each chapter, you will find a Pacing Tip to help you plan your lessons.

Articulation Across Levels

CHAPTER 12
Review of Level 1

- The **möchte**-forms; **noch ein** and **kein**
- Nominative and accusative pronouns; definite and indefinite articles
- Possessive pronouns
- The verb **können**; **für**; accusative pronouns; **du**-commands
- The verb **wissen**; word order; formal commands
- The verbs **wollen** and **müssen**; word order
- Asking where something is and giving directions

The following chart shows how topics are repeated across levels in *Komm mit!* from the end of Level 1 to the beginning of Level 3.

- In each level, the last chapter is a review chapter.
- In Levels 2 and 3, the first two chapters review the previous level.

LEVEL 2

CHAPTER 1
Review of Level 1

- **Haben** and **sein**
- **Mein, dein, sein,** and **ihr**
- The **möchte**-forms and **wollen**
- The nominative and accusative forms of indefinite and definite articles
- Regular and stem-changing verbs
- Third person pronouns
- Asking for and giving information
- Describing people
- Expressing likes and dislikes
- Giving and responding to compliments; expressing wishes

CHAPTER 2

- Clauses with **weil** and **denn**
- Dative case of **mein, dein, sein,** and **ihr**
- **Du**-commands
- The interrogative **warum**
- **Kein**
- **Müssen, können, sollen,** and **mögen**
- **Noch ein**
- Personal pronouns
- Possessives
- Past tense of **sein**
- Asking and telling what to do
- Discussing gift ideas
- Expressing obligations

CHAPTER 12
Review of Level 2

- Adjective endings
- Command forms of strong verbs
- Comparative forms of adjectives
- The past tense
- Prepositions
- Questions and statements
- **Sollen; würde** forms
- Asking for and giving advice
- Asking for, making, and responding to suggestions
- Expressing hearsay; regret

LEVEL 3

CHAPTER 1
Review of Level 2

- Dative-case forms
- **Dieser** and **welcher**
- Past tense
- Prepositions followed by dative-case forms
- Reflexive and object pronouns
- Asking and telling what you may or may not do
- Asking for information
- Asking how someone liked something; expressing enthusiasm, disappointment
- Expressing hope
- Inquiring about someone's health

CHAPTER 2

- Reporting past events
- Adjective endings
- Two-way prepositions
- The verb **hatte**
- Word order in **dass**- and **ob**-clauses
- Asking for and making suggestions
- Asking for, making, and responding to suggestions
- Expressing doubt, conviction, and resignation
- Expressing hearsay
- Expressing preference and giving a reason
- Expressing wishes

CHAPTER 12
Review of Level 3

- Direct and indirect object pronouns
- Infinitive forms of verbs
- The narrative past (imperfect)
- Subjunctive
- The **würde**-forms
- Reporting past events
- Agreeing; agreeing with reservations
- Expressing determination or indecision
- Expressing surprise and disappointment
- Giving advice; reasons
- Hypothesizing

Komm mit! German Level 1
Scope and Sequence

FUNCTIONS	GRAMMAR	VOCABULARY	CULTURE	RE-ENTRY

VORSCHAU, *Pages 1–11*

		• Das Alphabet • Wie heißt du? • Im Klassenzimmer • Die Zahlen von 0 bis 20		

KAPITEL 1   Wer bist du?, *Pages 16–41*

• Saying hello and goodbye • Asking someone's name and giving yours • Asking who someone is • Asking someone's age and giving yours • Talking about places of origin • Talking about getting to school	• Forming questions • Definite articles **der, die, das** • Subject pronouns and **sein**	• Numbers 0-20 • Words to describe how students get to school	• Greetings • Using **der** and **die** in front of people's names • Map of German states and capitals • **Wie kommst du zur Schule?**	• Asking someone's name • Numbers 0–20 • Geography of German-speaking countries

KAPITEL 2   Spiel und Spaß, *Pages 42–67*

• Talking about interests • Expressing likes and dislikes • Saying when you do various activities • Asking for an opinion and expressing yours • Agreeing and disagreeing	• The singular subject pronouns and present tense verb endings • The plural subject pronouns and verb endings • Present tense of verbs • Word order • Verbs with stems ending in **d, t,** or **n**	• Sports, instruments, and games you play • Leisure activities and hobbies • Seasons of the year	• Formal and informal address • **Was machst du gern?** • German weekly planner	• Question formation • Greetings • Expressions **stimmt/ stimmt nicht** used in a new context

KAPITEL 3   Komm mit nach Hause!, *Pages 68–95*

• Talking about where you and others live • Offering something to eat and drink and responding to an offer • Saying please, thank you, you're welcome • Describing a room • Describing the family • Describing people	• The **möchte**-forms • Indefinite articles **ein, eine** • The pronouns **er, sie, es,** and **sie** • The possessive adjectives **mein, dein, sein,** and **ihr**	• Words to describe where you live • Food and drink items • Words to describe a room • Members of the family	• The German preference for **Mineralwasser** • **Wo wohnst du?**	• Definite articles **der, die, das** • Asking someone's name and age • Asking who someone is • Talking about interests

Brandenburg

KAPITEL 4   Alles für die Schule!, *Pages 100–127*

FUNCTIONS	GRAMMAR	VOCABULARY	CULTURE	RE-ENTRY
• Talking about class schedules • Using a schedule to talk about time • Sequencing events • Expressing likes, dislikes, and favorites • Responding to good news and bad news • Talking about prices • Pointing things out	• The verb **haben** • Using **Lieblings-** • Noun plurals	• Classes at school • School supplies	• The German school day • 24-hour time system • The German grading system • **Was sind deine Lieblingsfächer?** • German currency	• Numbers • Likes and dislikes: **gern** • Degrees of enthusiasm • The pronouns **er, sie, es,** and **sie** (pl)

KAPITEL 5   Klamotten kaufen, *Pages 128–155*

FUNCTIONS	GRAMMAR	VOCABULARY	CULTURE	RE-ENTRY
• Expressing wishes when shopping • Commenting on and describing clothes • Giving compliments and responding to them • Talking about trying on clothes	• Definite and indefinite articles in the accusative case • The verb **gefallen** • Direct object pronouns • Separable-prefix verbs • Stem-changing verbs **nehmen** and **aussehen**	• Clothing items • Colors • Words to describe clothing	• Exchange rates • German store hours • German clothing sizes • **Welche Klamotten sind „in"?**	• Numbers and prices • Colors • Pointing things out • Expressing likes and dislikes • Asking for and expressing opinions • The verb **aussehen**

KAPITEL 6   Pläne machen, *Pages 156–183*

FUNCTIONS	GRAMMAR	VOCABULARY	CULTURE	RE-ENTRY
• Starting a conversation • Telling time and talking about when you do things • Making plans • Ordering food and beverages • Talking about how something tastes • Paying the check	• The verb **wollen** • The stem-changing verb **essen**	• Telling time • Words used to make plans • Food and drink items in a café	• Clocks on public buildings • **Was machst du in deiner Freizeit?** • Tipping in Germany	• Expressing time when referring to schedules • Vocabulary: School and free-time activities • Inversion of time elements • Sequencing events • Accusative case • The verb **nehmen** • Using **möchte** to order food

Schleswig-Holstein

KAPITEL 7 Zu Hause helfen, *Pages 188–215*

FUNCTIONS	GRAMMAR	VOCABULARY	CULTURE	RE-ENTRY
• Extending and responding to an invitation • Expressing obligations • Talking about how often you do things • Offering help and explaining what to do • Talking about the weather	• The modals **müssen** and **können** • The separable-prefix verb **aufräumen** • The accusative pronouns • Using present tense to refer to the future	• Household chores • Words describing how often you have to do things • Words to describe the weather • Months	• **Was tust du für die Umwelt?** • German weather map and weather report • Weather in German-speaking countries	• Separable-prefix verbs • The verb **wollen** • Time expressions • Vocabulary: Free-time activities • Vocabulary: School supplies • Using numbers in a new context, temperature

KAPITEL 8 Einkaufen gehen, *Pages 216–243*

FUNCTIONS	GRAMMAR	VOCABULARY	CULTURE	RE-ENTRY
• Asking what you should do • Telling someone what to do • Talking about quantities • Saying you want something else • Giving reasons • Saying where you were and what you bought	• The modal **sollen** • The **du-** and **ihr-** commands • The conjunctions **weil** and **denn** • The past tense of **sein**	• Groceries • Weights • Time expressions	• Specialty shops and markets • **Was machst du für andere Leute?** • Weights and measures • German advertisements	• The **möchte**-forms and **können** • Numbers used in a new context, weights and measures • Expressing wishes when shopping • Responding to invitations • Vocabulary: Activities • Vocabulary: Household chores • Sequencing words • Vocabulary: Clothing

KAPITEL 9 Amerikaner in München, *Pages 244–271*

FUNCTIONS	GRAMMAR	VOCABULARY	CULTURE	RE-ENTRY
• Talking about where something is located • Asking for and giving directions • Talking about what there is to eat and drink • Saying you do/don't want more • Expressing opinions	• The verb **wissen** • The verb **fahren** • The formal commands with **Sie** • The phrase **es gibt** • Using **kein** • The conjunction **dass**	• Places in a city • Words used to give directions • Food and appetite	• The German **Innenstadt** • **Was isst du gern?** • Map of a German neighborhood • **Imbissstube** menu • **Leberkäs**	• Vocabulary: Stores and food items • **Du**-commands, **möchte**, and **zu** • Saying you want something else • Indefinite articles: accusative case • Expressing opinions • Subordinate-clause word order

München

Baden-Württemberg

KAPITEL 10   Kino und Konzerte, *Pages 276–303*

FUNCTIONS	GRAMMAR	VOCABULARY	CULTURE	RE-ENTRY
• Expressing likes and dislikes • Expressing familiarity • Expressing preferences and favorites • Talking about what you did in your free time	• **Mögen, kennen, sehen, lesen** • **Sprechen** and **sprechen über** • **Lieber, am liebsten, gern**	• Film genres • Words describing how much you do or don't like something • Entertainers and forms of entertainment • Words used to describe films • Book genres	• The German movie rating system • German movie ads • A German pop chart • **Welche kulturellen Veranstaltungen besuchst du?** • German upcoming events poster • German best-seller lists • German video hits list • Popular German novels	• Expressing likes and dislikes • Expressing opinions; giving reasons • Describing people • **Aussehen, nehmen, wissen, essen, können** • Vocabulary: Activities • Talking about when and how often you do things

KAPITEL 11   Der Geburtstag, *Pages 304–331*

FUNCTIONS	GRAMMAR	VOCABULARY	CULTURE	RE-ENTRY
• Using the telephone in Germany • Inviting someone to a party • Talking about birthdays and expressing good wishes • Discussing gift ideas	• Introduction to the dative case • Word order in the dative case	• Telephone vocabulary • Dates of the year • Holidays and holiday greetings • Gift ideas	• Using the telephone • Saints' days • German good luck symbols • **Was schenkst du zum Geburtstag?** • German gift ideas	• Numbers 0–20 • Time and days of the week • Months • Accusative case • Vocabulary: Family members

KAPITEL 12   Die Fete, *Pages 332–383*   *Review Chapter*

FUNCTIONS	GRAMMAR	VOCABULARY	CULTURE	RE-ENTRY
• Offering help and explaining what to do • Asking where something is located and giving directions • Making plans and inviting someone to come along • Talking about clothing • Discussing gift ideas • Describing people and places • Saying what you would like and whether you do or don't want more • Talking about what you did	• The verb **können**; the preposition **für**; accusative pronouns; **du**-commands • The verb **wissen** and word order following **wissen**; formal commands • The verbs **wollen** and **müssen**; word order • Nominative and accusative pronouns; definite and indefinite articles • The nominative pronouns **er, sie, es,** and **sie** (pl); possessive pronouns • The **möchte**-forms; **noch ein** and **kein**	• Ingredients • Freetime activities • Words used to describe clothing • Furniture and appliances	• **Spätzle** and **Apfelküchle** • **Musst du zu Hause helfen?** • German gift ideas • Photos from furniture ads • Menu from an **Imbissstube**	

Komm mit! German Level 2
Scope and Sequence

FUNCTIONS	GRAMMAR	VOCABULARY	CULTURE	RE-ENTRY

KAPITEL 1 Bei den Baumanns, *Pages 4–31* — *Review Chapter*

FUNCTIONS	GRAMMAR	VOCABULARY	CULTURE	RE-ENTRY
• Asking for and giving information about yourself and others; describing yourself and others; expressing likes and dislikes • Identifying people and places • Giving and responding to compliments; expressing wishes when buying things • Making plans; ordering food; talking about how something tastes	• Present tense forms of **haben** and **sein** • **Mein, dein, sein,** and **ihr** (nom.) • The nominative and accusative forms of the definite and indefinite articles • The third person pronouns • Regular and stem-changing verbs • The **möchte**-forms and **wollen**	• Personal characteristics • Sports and hobbies • Clothing accessories	• Questionnaire: **Was für eine Person bist du?** • Article: **Sebastian über seine Familie** •Article: **Popstars machen Mode** • **Und was hast du am liebsten?** • Advertisements	• Chapters 1 and 2 are a global review of *Komm mit!*, Level 1.

KAPITEL 2 Bastis Plan, *Pages 32–59* — *Review Chapter*

FUNCTIONS	GRAMMAR	VOCABULARY	CULTURE	RE-ENTRY
• Expressing obligations; extending and responding to an invitation; offering help and telling what to do • Asking and telling what to do; telling that you need something else; telling where you were and what you bought • Discussing gift ideas; expressing likes and dislikes; expressing likes, preferences, and favorites; saying you do or don't want more	• **Müssen, können, sollen,** and **mögen** • **Warum** • **Weil** and **denn** • Personal pronouns (acc.) • The possessives **mein, dein, sein, ihr** (acc.) • The **du**-commands • **Sein:** past tense • The dative case of **mein, dein, sein, ihr** • **Noch ein** (nom./acc.) • **Kein** (nom./acc.)	• Words useful for traveling • Things to take on a picnic	• **Was nimmst du mit, wenn du irgendwo eingeladen bist?** • Grocery advertisements • German gift ideas	• Chapters 1 and 2 are a global review of *Komm mit!*, Level 1.

KAPITEL 3 Wo warst du in den Ferien?, *Pages 60–89*

FUNCTIONS	GRAMMAR	VOCABULARY	CULTURE	RE-ENTRY
• Reporting past events, talking about activities • Reporting past events, talking about places • Asking how someone liked something; expressing enthusiasm or disappointment; responding enthusiastically or sympathetically	• Conversational past • Past tense of **haben** and **sein** • **An** and **in** with dative-case forms to express location • The definite article, dative plural • Personal pronouns, dative case • The dative-case forms of **ein**	• Film media • Places in Frankfurt a.M. • Time expressions • Places to eat or spend the night	• Information on Dresden and **Frankfurt am Main** • **Was hast du in den letzten Ferien gemacht?**	• Expressions of time/frequency • **Weil**-clauses • Expressing likes and dislikes (For additional Re-entry, see Ch. 3, p. 59A.)

Bayern

KAPITEL 4 Gesund leben, *Pages 94–121*

FUNCTIONS	GRAMMAR	VOCABULARY	CULTURE	RE-ENTRY
• Expressing approval and disapproval • Asking for information and responding emphatically or agreeing, with reservations • Asking and telling what you may or may not do	• The verb **schlafen (schläft)** • **Für** + accusative • Reflexive verbs (accusative) • **Jeder, jede, jedes** (nominative) • The accusative forms of **kein** • The verb **dürfen**	• Words describing healthy habits • Words for how you feel where • Fruits, vegetables, fish, meat	• Interviews of German teenagers • **Was tust du, um gesund zu leben?** • Survey on health habits • **Bioläden** and **Reformhäuser**	• **Essen, sollen** and **müssen** • **Dass**-clauses; **für**; **kein** • Conjunctions **weil** and **denn** • Expressions of place, time, frequency, and quantity • Giving reasons • Responding to an invitation (For additional Re-entry, see Ch. 4, p. 93A.)

KAPITEL 5 Gesund essen, *Pages 122–149*

FUNCTIONS	GRAMMAR	VOCABULARY	CULTURE	RE-ENTRY
• Expressing regret and downplaying; expressing skepticism and making certain • Calling someone's attention to something and responding • Expressing preference and strong preference	• **Dieser, diese, dieses** • The possessives (Summary) • Verbs used with dative case • **Welcher, welche, welches; zu**	• **Schulpause** foods • Things to put on bread • Foods from the supermarket	• **Was isst du, was nicht?** • Nutritious snacks for **Gymnasiasten** • German meals	• Talking about quantities • The possessives • Talking about how food tastes • Comparatives and superlatives • Saying you want more • The interrogative **was für** (For additional Re-entry, see Ch. 5, p. 121A.)

KAPITEL 6 Gute Besserung!, *Pages 150–177*

FUNCTIONS	GRAMMAR	VOCABULARY	CULTURE	RE-ENTRY
• Inquiring about someone's health and responding; making suggestions • Asking about and expressing pain • Asking for and giving advice; expressing hope	• Reflexive pronouns in dative • The inclusive command • Verbs used with dative case • The verbs **brechen, waschen, messen,** and **wehtun** • The dative case to express the idea of something too expensive, too large, too small for you	• Aches and pains • Body parts and injuries • Healthy habits • Toiletries	• **Was machst du, wenn dir nicht gut ist?** • **Apotheke** and **Drogerie** • Article about sun exposure	• The verb **sich fühlen** • The accusative reflexive pronouns • Expressing obligations • The conversational past • **Dass**-clauses (For additional Re-entry, see Ch. 6, p. 149A.)

Hamburg

FUNCTIONS	GRAMMAR	VOCABULARY	CULTURE	RE-ENTRY

KAPITEL 7 Stadt oder Land?, *Pages 182–209*

• Expressing preference and giving a reason • Expressing wishes • Agreeing, with reservations; justifying your answers	• Comparative forms of adjectives • The verb **sich wünschen** • Adjective endings following **ein**-words • Adjective endings of comparatives	• Places to live • Advantages and disadvantages of city and country life • Parts of a house • Wishes for the future • Noisy things	• **Wo wohnst du lieber? Auf dem Land? In der Stadt?** • **Schule im Garten** • Letter from a German pen pal	• Talking about where something is located • Reflexive dative verbs • Expressing opinions • Dative verb **gefallen** (For additional Re-entry, see Ch. 7, p. 181A.)

KAPITEL 8 Mode? Ja oder nein?, *Pages 210–237*

• Describing clothes • Expressing interest, disinterest, and indifference; making and accepting compliments • Persuading and dissuading	• Adjective endings following **der** and **dieser**-words • **Passen (zu), stehen, tragen,** and **sich interessieren** • The conjunction **wenn** • **Kaufen** with dative	• Clothing • Words to describe clothing • Fabrics	• **Was trägst du am liebsten?** • Clothes typically worn by German-speaking youths • Interviews about fashion	• Talking about what you bought • Accusative reflexive verbs • **Für** + accusative • Giving reasons • Word order with subordinate conjunctions (For additional Re-entry, see Ch. 8, p. 209A.)

KAPITEL 9 Wohin in die Ferien?, *Pages 238–265*

• Expressing indecision; asking for and making suggestions • Expressing doubt, conviction, and resignation • Asking for and giving directions	• Articles/names for mountains • **Nach, in, an,** and **auf; ob**-clauses • Expressing direction and location (Summary) • Prepositions followed by dative • **Durch, um, vor, neben,** and **zwischen**	• Means of transportation • Vacation activities • Words for giving directions in a city	• **Wohin fährst du in den nächsten Ferien?** • **Urlaub in letzter Minute** • Statistics on transportation • Students talk about vacations • **Stadtrundgang durch Bietigheim**	• Inclusive commands • **Können, fahren,** and **wissen** • Giving directions • Inviting someone and responding to an invitation (For additional Re-entry, see Ch. 9, p. 237A.)

Stuttgart

KAPITEL 10   Viele Interessen!, *Pages 270–297*

• Asking about and expressing interest • Asking for and giving permission; asking for information and expressing an assumption • Expressing surprise, agreement, and disagreement; talking about plans	• Verbs with prepositions • **Wo**-compounds and **da**-compounds • The verbs **lassen** and **laufen** • The use of **kein** to negate a noun • The future tense with **werden**	• TV programs • TV accessories • Standard and optional car equipment	• Television channels • **Was machst du, um zu relaxen?** • Statistics on television programs • Getting a driver's license in Germany • Statistics on cars	• **Weil** and **dass**, and **was für** • Word order with modals • Time expressions • Expressing future events with present tense • Making plans • Expressing interest • **Können, dürfen,** and **sich freuen** (For additional Re-entry, see Ch. 10, p. 269A.)

KAPITEL 11   Mit Oma ins Restaurant, *Pages 298–325*

• Asking for, making, and responding to suggestions • Expressing hearsay • Ordering in a restaurant; expressing good wishes	• The **würde**-forms • Unpreceded adjectives • The **hätte**-forms	• Cultural activities • Cuisine of Germany and other countries • Words to describe food • Things to order in a restaurant	• **Für welche kulturellen Veranstaltungen interessierst du dich?** • State-supported art in Germany • International cuisine • Menu	• Cultural activities and sights • The impersonal pronoun **man** • Talking about favorites • The modal **sollen** • Saying what's available • Ordering and asking for the bill (For additional Re-entry, see Ch. 11, p. 297A.)

KAPITEL 12   Die Reinickendorfer Clique, *Pages 326–353*   *Review Chapter*

• Reporting past events; asking for, making, and responding to suggestions • Ordering food; expressing hearsay and regret; persuading and dissuading • Asking for and giving advice; expressing preference, interest, disinterest, and indifference	• The past tense • **Sollen** and the **würde**-forms • Questions and statements • Prepositions • The command forms of strong verbs • Adjective endings • Comparative forms of adjectives	• Places near water • Sport sites • International cuisine • Clothing	• **Welche ausländische Küche hast du gern?** • Article on travel habits • Etiquette in German restaurants • Franziska van Almsick	• Chapter 12 is a global review of Chapters 1–11, Level 2.

Berlin

Komm mit! German Level 3
Scope and Sequence

FUNCTIONS	GRAMMAR	VOCABULARY	CULTURE	RE-ENTRY

KAPITEL 1   Das Land am Meer, *Pages 4–31*   *Review Chapter*

FUNCTIONS	GRAMMAR	VOCABULARY	CULTURE	RE-ENTRY
• Reporting past events • Asking how someone liked something; expressing enthusiasm, disappointment, and sympathy • Asking and telling what you may or may not do • Asking for information • Inquiring about someone's health and responding; expressing pain • Expressing hope	• Prepositions followed by dative-case forms • Past tense • Dative-case forms • Forms of **dieser** and **welcher** • Reflexive and object pronouns	• Time expressions • Errands • Produce and cuts of meat • Things to put on bread • Body parts and injuries	• **Insel Rügen** • **Fit ohne Fleisch** • **Währungen und Geld wechseln**	• Chapters 1 and 2 are a global review of *Komm mit!*, Levels 1 and 2.

KAPITEL 2   Auf in die Jugendherberge!, *Pages 32–59*   *Review Chapter*

FUNCTIONS	GRAMMAR	VOCABULARY	CULTURE	RE-ENTRY
• Asking for and making suggestions • Expressing preference and giving a reason • Expressing wishes • Expressing doubt, conviction, resignation • Asking for information, expressing assumptions • Expressing hearsay • Asking for, making, and responding to suggestions • Expressing wishes when shopping	• Two-way prepositions • Word order in **dass**- and **ob**-clauses • Adjective endings • The verb **hätte**	• Words useful for traveling • Things to take on a picnic	• **Jugendherbergen** • **Einkaufsliste** • **Programm für eine 6-Tage-Reise nach Weimar** • **Weimar im Blickpunkt** • Poems	• Chapters 1 and 2 are a global review of *Komm mit!*, Levels 1 and 2.

KAPITEL 3   Aussehen: wichtig oder nicht?, *Pages 60–87*

FUNCTIONS	GRAMMAR	VOCABULARY	CULTURE	RE-ENTRY
• Asking for and expressing opinions; expressing sympathy and resignation • Giving advice; giving a reason • Admitting something and expressing regret	• **Da** and **wo**-compounds (Summary) • Infinitive clauses	• Words teens use in conversation • Phrases used to express sympathy, resignation, and to give advice	• **Die deutsche Subkultur** • Teenagers talking about what they do to feel better	• Expressing interest • Sequencing events • Expressing opinions • Verbs requiring prepositional phrases • Hobby and clothing vocabulary • **Wo-** and **da**-compounds • Responding sympathetically • Asking for and giving advice • Making suggestions • Giving reasons • Infinitives • **Weil**-clauses

Die neuen Bundesländer

KAPITEL 4 Verhältnis zu anderen, *Pages 92–119*

FUNCTIONS	GRAMMAR	VOCABULARY	CULTURE	RE-ENTRY
• Agreeing; giving advice • Introducing another point of view; hypothesizing	• Ordinal numbers • Relative clauses • **Hätte** and **wäre** • The genitive case	• Words used for describing relationships • Words used for getting along with others	• Importance of **Cliquen** • **Die verschiedenen Bildungswege in Deutschland**	• Agreeing • **Wenn-, weil-,** and **dass-**clauses • Cardinal numbers • Pronouns (nom., acc., and dat.) • Giving advice • **Wenn-**phrases • Subjunctive (**würde-, hätte-, wäre-**forms) • The preposition **von** + dative

KAPITEL 5 Rechte und Pflichten, *Pages 120–147*

FUNCTIONS	GRAMMAR	VOCABULARY	CULTURE	RE-ENTRY
• Talking about what is possible • Saying what you would have liked to do • Saying that something is going on right now • Reporting past events • Expressing surprise, relief, and resignation	• The **könnte-**forms • Further uses of **wäre** and **hätte** • Verbs used as neuter nouns • The past tense of modals (the imperfect)	• Words to describe rights and responsibilities • Military terms • Time expressions	• **Artikel 38/2. Absatz des Grundgesetzes** • **Artikel 12a des Grundgesetzes** • Cartoon • **Gleichberechtigung im deutschen Militär?** • **Wehrpflicht**	• **Hätte-**forms and **wäre-**forms • **Weil-**clauses • Giving reasons • The modals **können, wollen,** and **müssen** • Reporting past events • Expressing surprise • Expressing resignation • Expressing hearsay

KAPITEL 6 Medien: stets gut informiert?, *Pages 148–175*

FUNCTIONS	GRAMMAR	VOCABULARY	CULTURE	RE-ENTRY
• Asking someone to take a position; asking for reasons; expressing opinions • Reporting past events • Agreeing or disagreeing; changing the subject; interrupting • Expressing surprise or annoyance	• Narrative past (imperfect) • Superlative forms of adjectives	• Terms used in discussions • Words related to media • Words of quantity	• **Die TV-Kids** • **Die Schülerzeitung** • **Leserbriefe an die Redaktion der Pepo**	• Talking about favorites • Leisure-time activities • Expressing opinions • The conversational past • Agreeing and disagreeing • Television vocabulary • Expressing surprise • The comparative forms of adjectives • Time expressions • Words of quantity

Würzburg

KAPITEL 7 Ohne Reklame geht es nicht!, *Pages 180–207*

FUNCTIONS	GRAMMAR	VOCABULARY	CULTURE	RE-ENTRY
• Expressing annoyance • Comparing • Eliciting agreement and agreeing • Expressing conviction, uncertainty, and what seems to be true	• **Derselbe, der gleiche** • Adjective endings following determiners of quantity • Introducing relative clauses with **was** and **wo** • **Irgendein** and **irgendwelche**	• Words used in advertising • Words preceded by **irgend**	• **Werbung—pro und contra** • **Warum so wenig Unterbrecherwerbung?** • Excerpt from *Frankfurter Allgemeine* • Cartoon	• Expressing annoyance • The conjunctions **wenn** and **dass** • Comparative and superlative • Adjective endings • Agreeing • Relative pronouns • Word order in dependent clauses • Expressing conviction • Expressing uncertainty

KAPITEL 8 Weg mit den Vorurteilen!, *Pages 208–235*

FUNCTIONS	GRAMMAR	VOCABULARY	CULTURE	RE-ENTRY
• Expressing surprise, disappointment, and annoyance • Expressing an assumption • Making suggestions and recommendations • Giving advice	• The conjunction **als** • Coordinating conjunctions (Summary) • Verbs with prefixes (Summary)	• Words used to express prejudices and clichés • Personal characteristics	• Cartoon • **Verständnis für Ausländer?** • **Der sympathische Deutsche**	• Expressing surprise • Expressing disappointment • **Dass**-clauses • Narrative past • Conversational past • Coordinating conjunctions • Expressing an assumption • Prepositions followed by dative • Separable-prefix verbs • Making suggestions • Giving advice

KAPITEL 9 Aktiv für die Umwelt!, *Pages 236–263*

FUNCTIONS	GRAMMAR	VOCABULARY	CULTURE	RE-ENTRY
• Expressing concern • Making accusations • Offering solutions • Making polite requests • Saying what is being done about a problem • Hypothesizing	• Subjunctive forms of **können, müssen, dürfen, sollen,** and **sein** • The passive voice, present tense • Use of a conjugated modal verb in the passive • Conditional sentences	• Words describing pollution and the environment	• Environmental concerns • **Ein umweltfreundlicher Einkauf**	• Adjective endings • **Dass-, wenn-** and **weil**-clauses • **Hätte-, würde-,** and **könnte**-forms • **Werden** and **sollen** • Environment vocabulary • Subjunctive forms

Frankfurt

KAPITEL 10 Die Kunst zu leben, *Pages 268–295*

FUNCTIONS	GRAMMAR	VOCABULARY	CULTURE	RE-ENTRY
• Expressing preference, given certain possibilities • Expressing envy and admiration • Expressing happiness and sadness • Saying that something is or was being done	• Prepositions with genitive • The passive voice (Summary)	• Words used in the arts and in theaters	• Film critiques • **Aphorismen** • **Kultur findet man überall!**	• Expressing preference • **Würde**-forms • Genitive case forms • Prepositions • **Da-** and **wo-** compounds • Past participles • Subjunctive forms of modals • **Von** + dative case

KAPITEL 11 Deine Welt ist deine Sache!, *Pages 296–323*

FUNCTIONS	GRAMMAR	VOCABULARY	CULTURE	RE-ENTRY
• Expressing determination or indecision • Talking about whether something is important or not important • Expressing wishes • Expressing certainty and refusing or accepting with certainty • Talking about goals for the future • Expressing relief	• The use of **wo-** compounds to ask questions • Two ways of expressing the future tense • The perfect infinitive with modals and **werden**	• Careers and occupations • Words used to talk about the future	• German universities • **Wie findet man eine Arbeitsstelle in Deutschland?** • **Umfragen und Tests**	• Reflexive verbs • Expressing indecision • Conversational past and conditional • **Ob-** and **dass-**clauses • **Um ... zu** • **Wo-**compounds • Expressing wishes • **Wäre** • Determiners of quantity • Negation with **kein** • Future tense formation

KAPITEL 12 Die Zukunft liegt in deiner Hand!, *Pages 324–351*   *Review Chapter*

FUNCTIONS	GRAMMAR	VOCABULARY	CULTURE	RE-ENTRY
• Reporting past events • Expressing surprise and disappointment • Agreeing; agreeing, with reservations • Giving advice; giving reasons • Expressing determination or indecision • Talking about what is important or not important • Hypothesizing	• The narrative past (imperfect) • The **würde**-forms • Infinitive forms of verbs • Direct and indirect object pronouns • Subjunctive	• Careers and occupations • Words used to talk about the future	• **Kummerkasten** • **Pauken allein reicht nicht** • **Claudias Pläne für die Zukunft** • **Textbilder**	• Chapter 12 is a global review of Chapters 1–11, Level 3.

Dresden

Pupil's Edition

Komm mit! offers an integrated approach to language learning. Presentation and practice of functional expressions, vocabulary, and grammar structures are interwoven with cultural information, language learning tips, and realia to facilitate both learning and teaching. The technology, audiovisual materials, and additional print resources are integrated throughout each chapter.

Komm mit! Level 1

The *Komm mit! Pupil's Edition* opens with the **Vorschau**, a preliminary chapter that invites students to explore the geography and culture of the German-speaking nations. This motivating, colorful preview of the benefits—and fun—of learning German starts the year on a positive, exciting note.

Following the **Vorschau**, Chapters 1-11 provide a carefully sequenced program of balanced skills instruction in the four key areas of listening, speaking, reading, and writing. In addition, every chapter is rich in authentic culture and language. Most chapter photographs were taken on location and reflect the characters and settings featured in the videos that accompany *Komm mit!*

Chapter 12 is a review of the first year's study of German. It provides an opportunity to reinforce skills and remediate deficiencies before the end of the school year. This opportunity to pause and reflect on what has been learned provides closure and gives students a sense of accomplishment and renewed purpose.

At the end of the *Pupil's Edition*, a Reference Section summarizes functions, grammar rules, and pronunciation features for quick reference. Additional Vocabulary as well as German>English and English>German glossaries can be found there as well. Throughout the year, students are encouraged to consult the Reference Section to review, expand their choices, and further practice functional expressions, vocabulary, and structures.

Activity-Based Instruction

In *Komm mit!,* language acquisition is an active process. From the first day, students are using German. Within each lesson, a progression of activities moves students from discrete point use of language to completely open-ended activities that promote personalized, meaningful expression. This sequence allows students to practice receptive skills before moving on to language production. It is this carefully articulated sequence that ensures success.

A Guided Tour

On the next several pages, you will find a guided tour of *Komm mit!* On these pages, we have identified for you the essential elements of the textbook and the various resources available. If, as you are using *Komm mit!,* you encounter any particular problems, please contact your regional office for information or assistance.

Starting Out...

Location Opener In *Komm mit!* chapters are arranged in groups of three, with each group set in a different German-speaking location. Each new location is introduced by four pages of colorful photos and information of the city or region presented. ·····▶

Chapter Opener These pages are a visual introduction to the theme of the chapter and include a list of objectives students will be expected to achieve.

Setting The Scene...

Los geht's! Language instruction begins with this comprehensible input that models language in a culturally authentic setting. Presented also on video, audio, and CD, the highly visual presentation allows students to practice their receptive skills and begin to recognize some of the new functions and vocabulary they will encounter in the chapter.

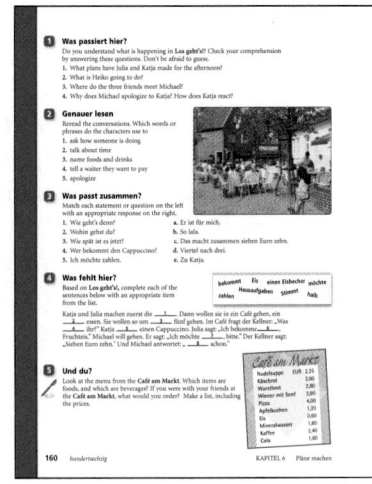

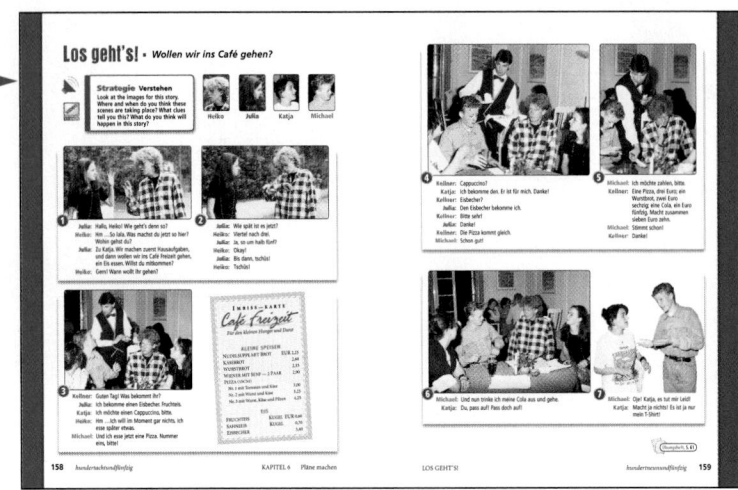

Following **Los geht's!** is a series of activities to check comprehension.

Building Proficiency Step By Step...

Erste, Zweite, and **Dritte Stufe** are the core instructional sections where language acquisition will take place. The communicative goals in each chapter center on the functional expressions presented in **So sagt man das!** boxes. These expressions are supported by material in the **Wortschatz, Grammatik,** and **Ein wenig Grammatik** sections. Activities following the above features are designed to practice recognition or to provide closed-ended practice. Activities then progress from controlled to open-ended practice where students are able to express themselves in meaningful communication.

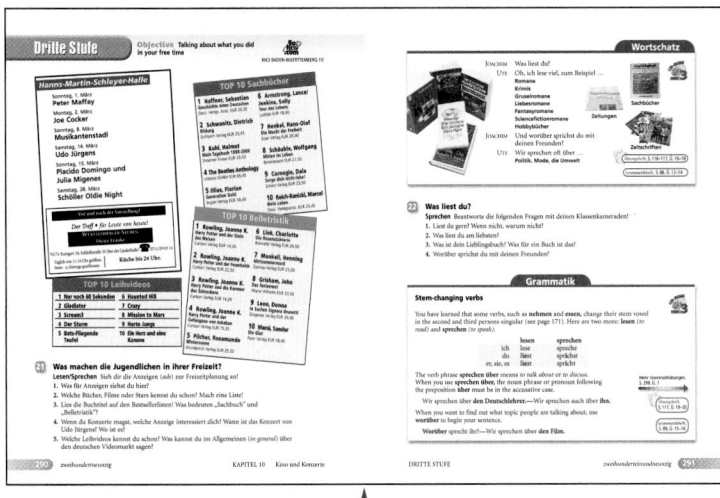

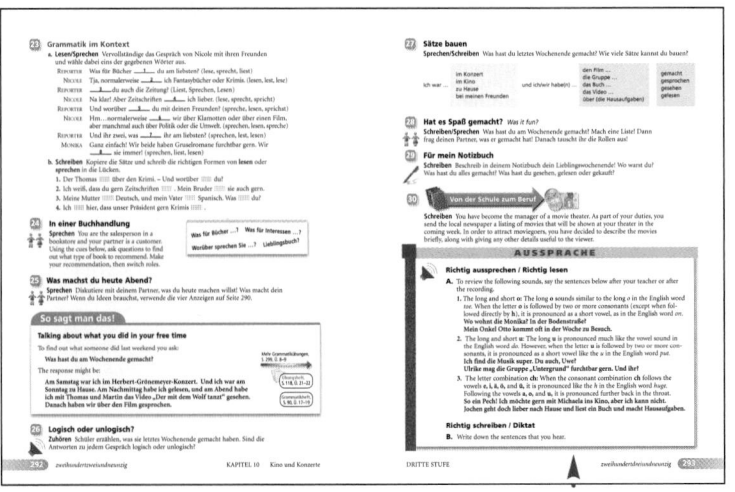

Aussprache, at the end of each **Stufe,** explains certain sounds and spelling rules. Pronunciation is practiced using vocabulary words that contain the targeted sounds. In a dictation exercise students hear and write sentences using the targeted sounds and letters.

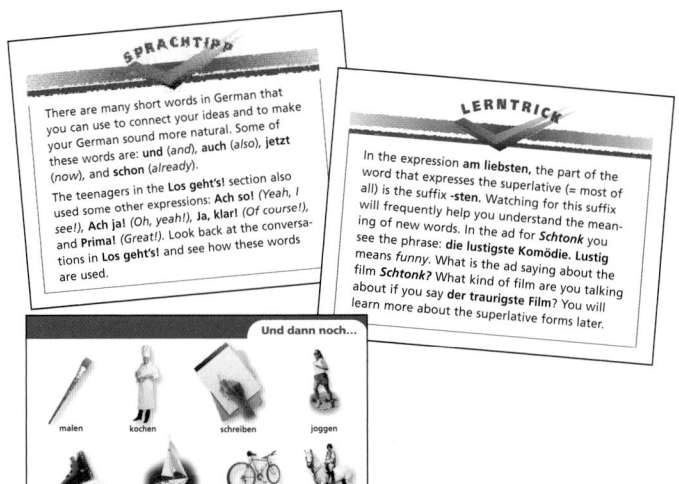

Targeting Students' Needs...

Several special features may be used to enhance language learning.

Sprachtipp provides students with tips for speaking more natural-sounding German.

Lerntrick suggests effective ways for students to learn a foreign language.

Und dann noch presents additional useful vocabulary to help students with the theme of the chapter.

Discovering the People and the Culture...

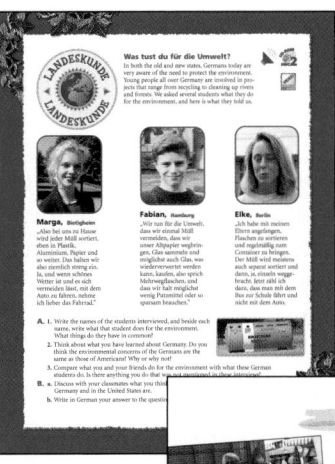

There are two major cultural features to help students develop an appreciation and understanding of the cultures of German-speaking countries.

Landeskunde presents interviews conducted throughout Germany on a topic related to the chapter theme. The interviews may be presented on video or done as a reading supplemented by the Audio CD recording. Culminating activities on this page verify comprehension and encourage students to think critically about the target culture as well as their own.

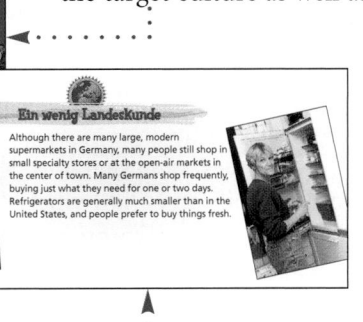

Ein wenig Landeskunde helps students gain knowledge and understanding of the other culture and can be used to enrich and enliven activities and presentations at various places throughout each chapter.

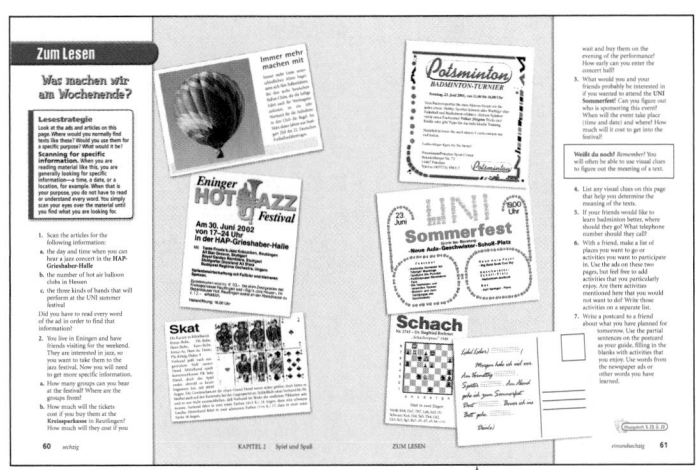

Understanding Authentic Documents...

Zum Lesen presents reading strategies that help students understand authentic German documents and literature presented in each chapter. The reading selections vary from advertisements to letters to short stories or poems in order to accommodate different interests and familiarize the students with different styles and formats. The accompanying prereading, reading, and postreading activities develop students' overall reading skills and challenge their critical thinking abilities. A **Lesestrategie** provides effective ways to enhance students' reading comprehension.

Wrapping It All Up...

Mehr Grammatikübungen provide additional practice on the grammar concepts presented in the chapter. These activities are divided by **Stufe** and may be assigned as homework or as a review for quizzes and tests.

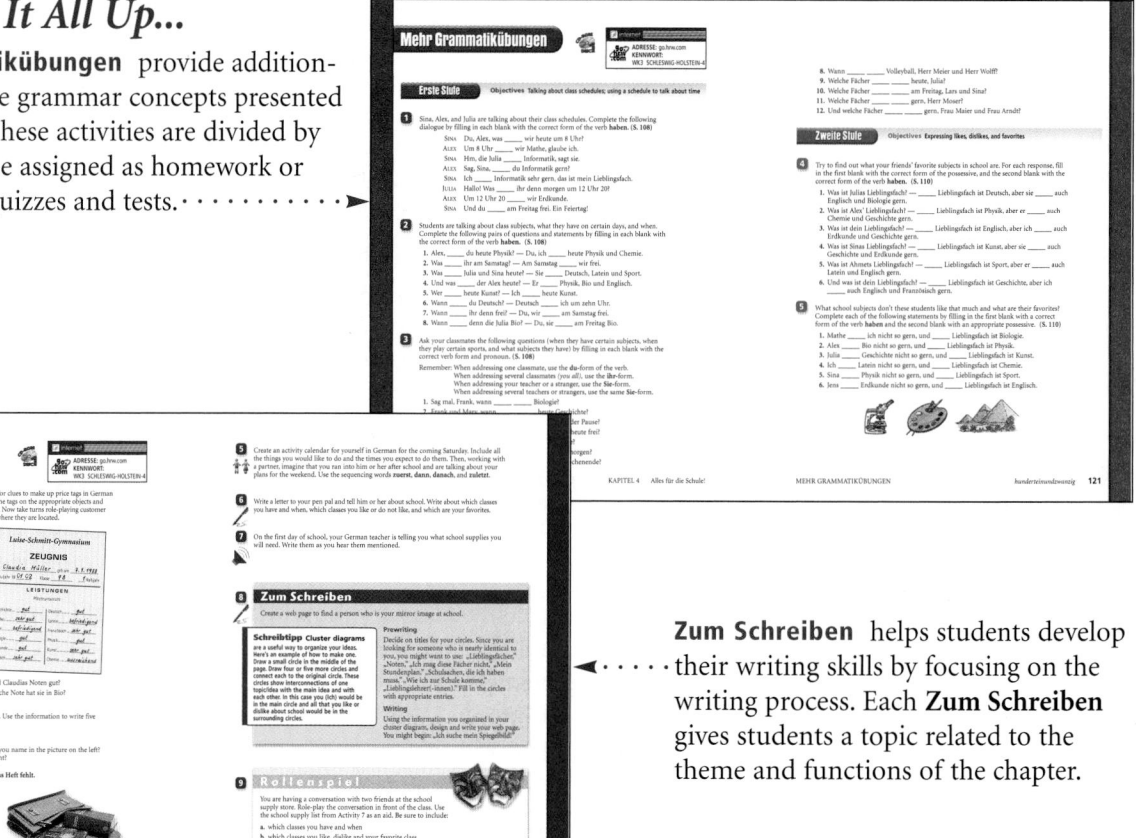

Zum Schreiben helps students develop their writing skills by focusing on the writing process. Each **Zum Schreiben** gives students a topic related to the theme and functions of the chapter.

Anwendung gives students the opportunity to review what they have learned and to apply their skills in new communicative contexts. Focusing on all four language skills as well as cultural awareness, the **Anwendung** can help you determine whether students are ready for the Chapter Test.

Kann ich's wirklich? is a checklist that students can use on their own to see if they have achieved the goals stated on the Chapter Opener page. Each communicative function is paired with one or more activities for students to use as a self-check.

Wortschatz presents the chapter vocabulary grouped by **Stufe** and arranged according to function or theme.

Technology Resources

The Video Program

The *Video Program* provides the following video support:

- **Location Opener** documentaries

- **Los geht's!** and **Fortsetzung** dramatic episodes

- **Landeskunde** interviews on a variety of cultural topics

- **Videoclips** which present authentic footage from target cultures

The *Video Guide* contains background information, suggestions for presentation, and activities for all portions of the *Video Program*.

Interactive CD-ROM Tutor

The *Interactive CD-ROM Tutor* offers:

- a variety of supporting activities correlated to the core curriculum of **Komm mit!** and targeting all five skills

- a Teacher Management System (TMS) that allows teachers to view and assess students' work, manage passwords and records, track students' progress as they complete the activities, and activate English translations

- features such as a grammar reference section and a glossary to help students complete the activities

Internet Connection

Keywords in the *Pupil's Edition* provide access to two types of online activities:

- **Interaktive Spiele** are directly correlated to the instructional material in the textbook. They can be used as homework, extra practice, or assessment.

- **Internet Aktivitäten** provide students with selected Web sites in German-speaking countries and activities related to the chapter theme. A printable worksheet in PDF format includes pre-surfing, surfing, and post-surfing activities that guide students through their research.

For easy access, see the keywords provided in the *Pupil's* and *Teacher's Editions*. For chapter-specific information, see the F page of the chapter interleaf.

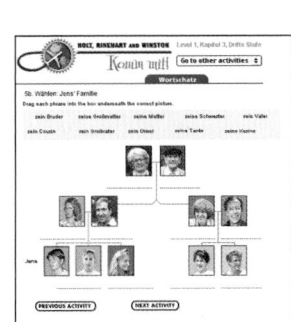

One-Stop Planner CD-ROM with Test Generator

The *One-Stop Planner CD-ROM* is a convenient tool to aid in lesson planning and pacing.

Easy navigation through menus or through lesson plans allows for a quick overview of available resources. For each chapter the *One-Stop Planner* includes:

- Editable lesson plans with direct links to teaching resources

- Printable worksheets from resource books

- Direct launches to the HRW Internet activities

- Video and audio segments

- Test Generator

- Clip Art for vocabulary items

Ancillaries

The *Komm mit!* German program offers a comprehensive ancillary package that addresses the concerns of today's teachers and is relevant to students' lives.

Lesson Planning

One-Stop Planner with Test Generator

- editable lesson plans
- printable worksheets from resource books
- direct link to HRW Internet activities
- entire video and audio programs
- Test Generator
- Clip Art

Lesson Planner with Substitute Teacher Lesson Plans

- complete lesson plans for every chapter
- block scheduling suggestions
- correlations to Standards for Foreign Language Learning
- a homework calendar
- chapter by chapter lesson plans for substitute teachers
- lesson plan forms for customizing lesson plans

Student Make-Up Assignments

- diagnostic information for students who are behind in their work
- copying masters for make-up assignments

Listening and Speaking

TPR Storytelling Book

- step-by-step explanation of the TPR Storytelling method
- illustrated stories for each **Stufe** with vocabulary lists and gestures
- teaching suggestions

Listening Activities

- print material associated with the *Audio Program*
- Student Response Forms for all *Pupil's Edition* listening activities
- Additonal Listening Activities
- scripts, answers
- lyrics to each chapter's song

Audio Compact Discs

Listening activities for the *Pupil's Edition,* the Additional Listening Activities, and the *Testing Program*

Activities for Communication

- Communicative Activities for partner work based on an information gap
- Situation Cards to practice interviews and role-plays
- Realia: reproductions of authentic documents

Grammar

Grammatikheft

- re-presentations of major grammar points
- additional focused practice
- *Teacher's Edition* with overprinted answers

Grammar Tutor for Students of German

- presentations of grammar concepts in English
- re-presentations of German grammar concepts
- discovery and application activities

Reading and Writing

Reading Strategies and Skills Handbook
- explanations of reading strategies
- copying masters for application of strategies

Lies mit mir!
- readings on familiar topics
- cultural information
- additional vocabulary
- interesting and engaging activities

Übungsheft
- activities for practice
- *Teacher's Edition* with overprinted answers

Teaching Transparencies
Colorful transparencies that help present and practice vocabulary, grammar, culture, and a variety of communicative functions

Exploratory Guide
- lessons with activity masters
- vocabulary lists
- review and assessment options

Assessment

Testing Program
- Grammar and Vocabulary quizzes
- **Stufe** quizzes that test the skills
- Chapter Tests
- Speaking Tests
- Midterm and Final Exams
- Score sheets, scripts, answers

Alternative Assessment Guide
- Suggestions for oral and written Portfolio Assessment
- Performance Assessment
- CD-ROM Assessment
- rubrics, portfolio checklists, and evaluation forms

Student Make-Up Assignments
Alternative Grammar and Vocabulary quizzes for students who missed class and have to make up the quiz

Teacher's Edition

Using the Chapter Interleaf

Each chapter of the **Komm mit!** *Teacher's Edition* includes the following interleaf pages to help you plan, teach, and expand your lessons.

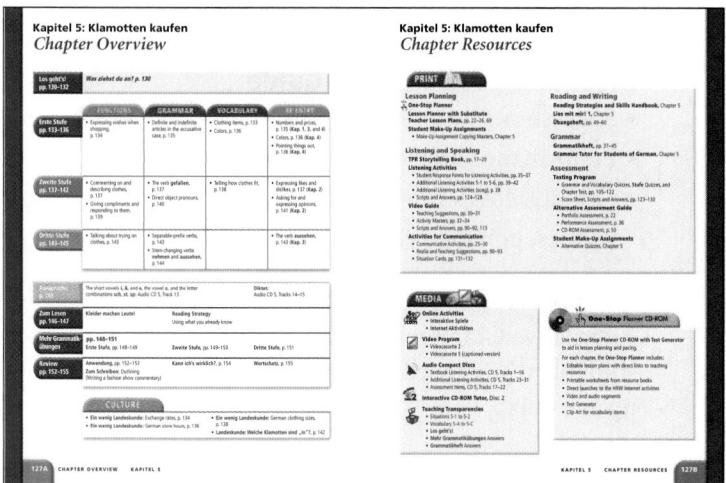

Chapter Overview

The Chapter Overview chart outlines at a glance the functions, grammar, vocabulary, re-entry, and culture featured in the chapter. You will also find a list of corresponding print and audiovisual resources organized by listening, speaking, reading, and writing skills, grammar, and assessment.

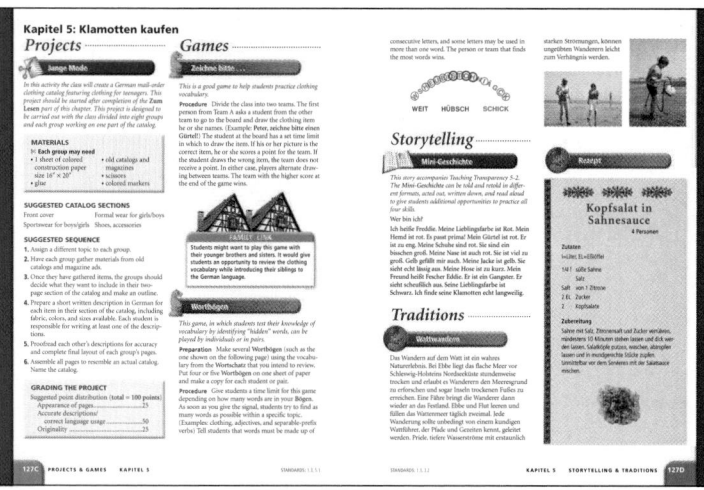

Projects/Games/ Storytelling/Traditions

Projects allow students to personalize and expand on the information from the chapter. Games reinforce the chapter content. In the Storytelling feature, you will find a story related to a *Teaching Transparency*. The Traditions feature concentrates on a unique aspect of the culture of the region. A recipe typical for the region accompanies this feature.

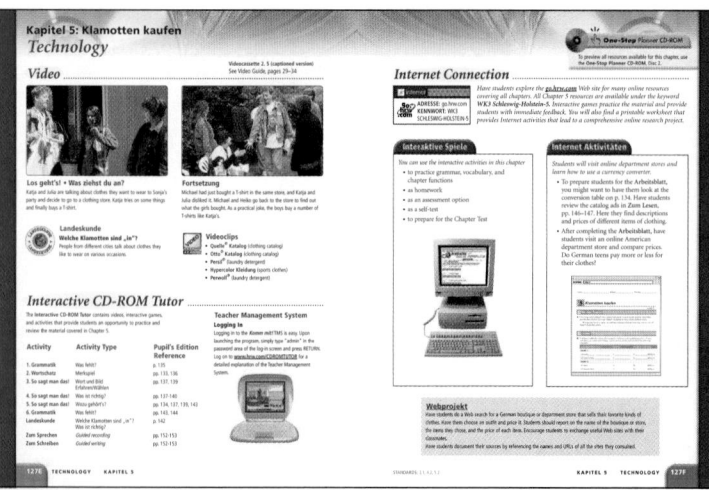

Technology

These pages assist you in integrating technology into your lesson plans. The Technology page provides a detailed list of video, CD-ROM, and Internet resources for your lesson. You will also find an Internet research project in each chapter.

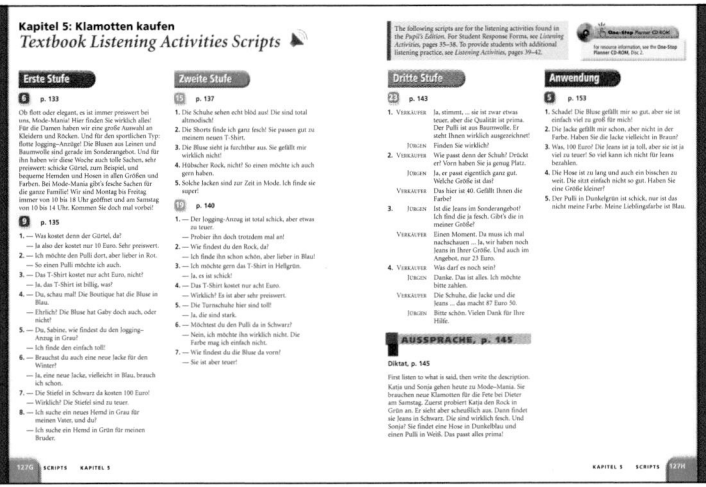

Textbook Listening Activities Scripts

Textbook Listening Activities Scripts provide the scripts of the chapter listening activities for reference or for use in class.

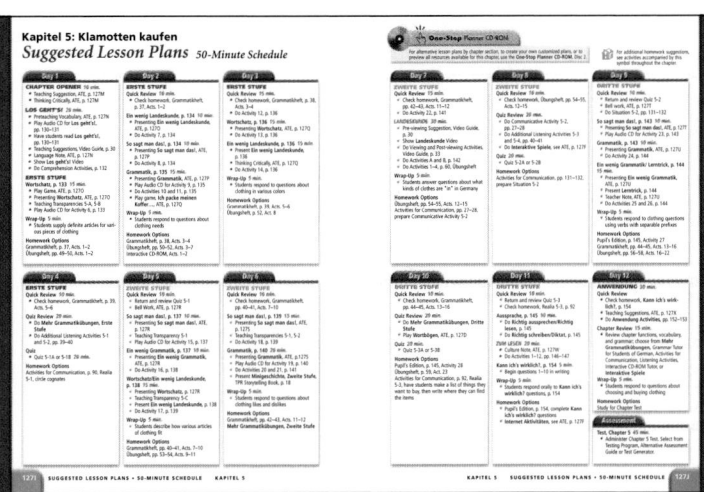

Suggested Lesson Plans—
50-Minute Schedule

This lesson plan is used for classes with 50-minute schedules. Each lesson plan provides a logical sequence of instruction along with homework suggestions.

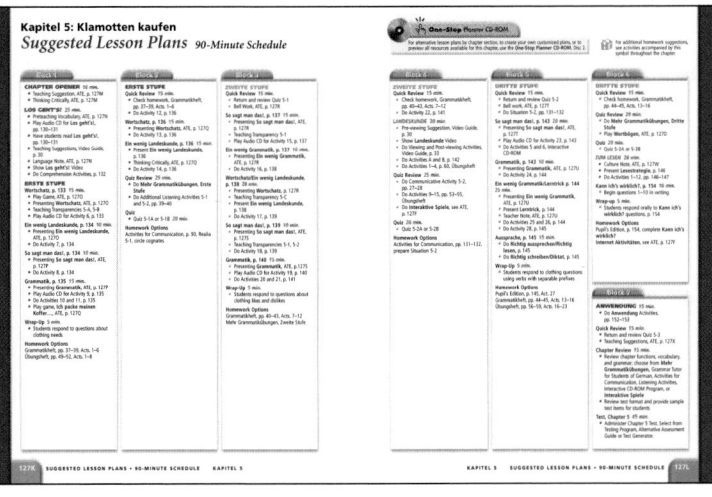

Suggested Lesson Plans—
90-Minute Schedule

This lesson plan is used for classes with 90-minute schedules. Each lesson plan provides a logical sequence of instruction along with homework suggestions.

The Annotated Teacher's Edition
Using the Interleaf Teacher Text

Connections and Comparisons
Under this head you will find connections and comparisons with other languages, cultures, and disciplines.

Resource Boxes
provide a quick list of all the resources you can use for each chapter section.

Presenting Features
offer useful suggestions for presenting new material.

ERSTE STUFE

Teaching Resources
pp. 73–77

PRINT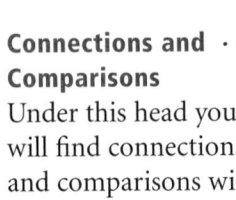
- Lesson Planner, p. 13
- TPR Storytelling Book, pp. 9, 12
- Listening Activities, pp. 19, 23
- Activities for Communication, pp. 13-14, 82, 127-128
- Grammatikheft, pp. 19-21
- Grammar Tutor for Students of German, Chapter 3
- Übungsheft, pp. 26-28
- Testing Program, pp. 53-56
- Alternative Assessment Guide, p. 34
- Student Make-Up Assignments, Chapter 3

MEDIA
- One-Stop Planner
- Audio Compact Discs, CD3, Trs. 3-4, 19, 25-26
- Teaching Transparencies
  Vocabulary 3-A
  Mehr Grammatikübungen Answers
  Grammatikheft Answers
- Interactive CD-ROM Tutor, Disc 1

PAGE 73

Bell Work
On the board or a transparency write the following: **Wo wohnst du?** Have students respond in writing.

PRESENTING: So sagt man das!
To teach the verb **wohnen**, use the verb in context as you give examples of several famous people and the places where they live. (Examples: **Der amerikanische Präsident wohnt in Washington, D.C. Steffi Graf wohnt in Deutschland.**)

PRESENTING: Wortschatz
Have students infer the meaning of this vocabulary through contextual guessing. Give examples such as: **Los Angeles ist eine große Stadt. Beverly Hills ist ein Vorort von Los Angeles. Der Rodeo Drive ist eine Straße in Beverly Hills. Old MacDonald wohnt auf dem Land.** If necessary, draw a simple map on the board or on a transparency as you present your examples.

Connections and Comparisons

Language-to-Language
Tell your students that the English verb "to live" is expressed by two different verbs in German: **leben/wohnen.** French makes the same distinction: **vivre/habiter.** Ask students what English words correspond most closely to the German **leben/wohnen.** (live/reside)

Cultures and Communities

Culture Note
Potsdam (pop. 138,000) is located on the river Havel at the site of an early settlement near the **Alter Markt** that dates back as early as 993. The settlement didn't expand until the 16th century, when it became the second residence for Prussian kings such as King Friedrich I and Friedrich Wilhelm I.

PAGE 74

Communication for All Students

Challenge
7 Put the following words on the board for the students to refer to (in addition to the **Wortschatz** on p. 73) as they work in pairs on this activity: wohnen; Vorort = Vorstadt; weit von hier; in der Nähe von; in der _____ Straße; Wohnung; Haus; Zweifamilienhaus. Quickly explain these words so students will be able to use them for the activity.

KAPITEL 3

STANDARDS: 4.1

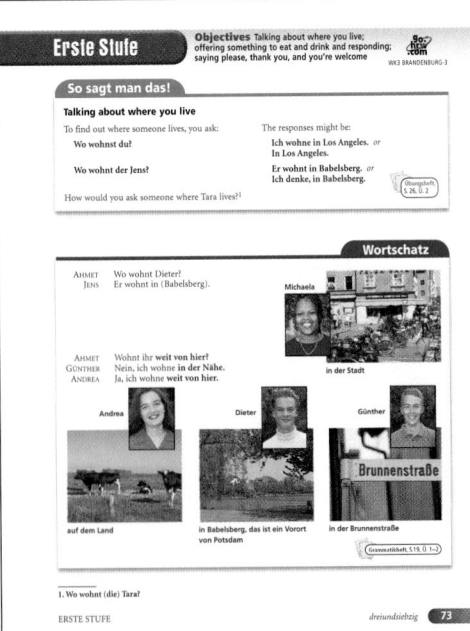

** Erste Stufe**

Objectives Talking about where you live; offering something to eat and drink and responding; saying please, thank you, and you're welcome

WK3 BRANDENBURG-3

So sagt man das!

Talking about where you live

To find out where someone lives, you ask:
Wo wohnst du?

Wo wohnt der Jens?

How would you ask someone where Tara lives?¹

The responses might be:
Ich wohne in Los Angeles. or **In Los Angeles.**

Er wohnt in Babelsberg. or **Ich denke, in Babelsberg.**

Übungsheft, S. 26, Ü. 2

Wortschatz

AHMET Wo wohnt Dieter?
JENS Er wohnt in (Babelsberg).
Michaela

AHMET Wohnt ihr **weit von hier?**
GÜNTHER Nein, ich wohne **in der Nähe.**
ANDREA Ja, ich wohne **weit von hier.**
in der Stadt

Andrea   Dieter   Günther

Brunnenstraße

auf dem Land   in Babelsberg, das ist ein Vorort   in der Brunnenstraße
                von Potsdam

Grammatikheft, S.19, Ü. 1-2

1. Wo wohnt (die) Tara?

ERSTE STUFE

dreiundsiebzig **73**

Communication for All Students
Under this head you will find helpful suggestions for students with different learning styles and abilities.

Correlations to the Standards for Foreign Language Learning
are provided for your reference.

Teacher Note

You might want to point out to students the difference between **Er hat eine Glatze** and *He is bald.*

For Additional Practice

Tell students to imagine their family is having a big family reunion where not everybody knows everybody else. Therefore, attending members are asked to give a short personal introduction. Ask students to describe themselves to the rest of the family.

PAGE 85

Cultures and Communities

Career Path

Have students work in pairs to brainstorm scenarios in law enforcement which would require knowledge of German. (Suggestions: Imagine you work for the NYPD, and the German **Kripo** [detective force] has asked you to help in its search for a convicted felon who has fled Germany and disappeared in New York; imagine you work for the customs service at the airport in Houston, and the German **Bundesgrenzschutz** [Federal Border Police] asks you to apprehend a smuggler, whom you will have to identify based on the description they faxed you.)

Game

Divide the class into two groups and, alternating between groups, choose one person to come to the front. Show this person the name of a fellow classmate, teacher, or celebrity on an index card. Alternating between teams, students will try to guess the identity of the secret person by asking yes/no questions. If the answer to a question is yes, the team gets another turn; if the answer is no, the other team gets a turn. The team that guesses the correct name wins.
Example: Boris Becker
Ist es ein Mann? Ja.
Ist er alt? Nein.

Cultures and Communities

Reteaching: Family members

Put students in small groups and have them cut out magazine pictures of famous people to create a "unique" tree showing imaginary relationships among the celebrities. Students should write sentences about the relationships they have created. Ask one or two groups to read them aloud.

Teaching Suggestion ◄ • • • • • • • • • • •

Show students pictures of famous people and ask them to describe the pictures.
or
Ask students to compare the characteristics of a young member of their family with an older member based on age, appearance, or any other relevant characteristics.

Von der Schule zum Beruf

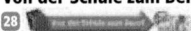

You could ask students to profile someone famous and have the rest of the class guess who it is. This activity could also be done on posterboard to be displayed in the classroom.

PRESENTING: Aussprache

Remind students that German vowels require more tension in the mouth than the English and do not glide. To illustrate this point, and as ongoing remedial work, contrast the German word **Boot** with the English *boat.*

Assess

▸ Testing Program, pp. 61–64
  Quiz 3-3A, Quiz 3-3B
  Audio CD3, Tr. 21

▸ Student Make-Up Assignments
  Chapter 3, Alternative Quiz

▸ Alternative Assessment Guide, p. 34

DRITTE STUFE

---

26 Wie sieht Steffis Familie aus?

Schreiben Referring to the chart you and your partner made for Activity 25, try to answer the following questions about Steffi's family.

1. Wer hat blaue Augen?
2. Wie alt ist Steffis Bruder? Und ihre Kusine?
3. Wie sieht Onkel Florian aus?
4. Was macht die Mutter in der Freizeit? Der Vater? Anna?
5. Wie sehen die Eltern aus?
6. Wer hat schwarze Haare?
7. Wer hat kurze Haare? Lange Haare?
8. Wie alt ist die Großmutter? Wie sieht sie aus?
9. Wer hat eine Brille?

27 Rate mal!

Sprechen Pick one person in the room and think about how you might describe him or her to someone else. Your partner will ask you questions and try to guess whom you have chosen. Then switch roles.

BEISPIEL   PARTNER   Hat diese Person blonde Haare?

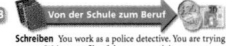
28 Von der Schule zum Beruf

Schreiben You work as a police detective. You are trying to apprehend a wanted person. Write a profile of that person, giving name, age, residence, interests, and a physical description.

AUSSPRACHE

Richtig aussprechen / Richtig lesen

A. To practice the following sounds, say the words and sentences below after your teacher or after the recording.

1. The letter **o:** The long **o** is pronounced much like the long *o* in the English word *oboe*; however, the lips are more rounded.

   Obst, Moped, schon / Wo wohnt deine Oma?

2. The letter **u:** The long **u** is similar to the vowel sound in the English word *do*; however, the lips are more rounded.

   Stuhl, super, Kuchen / Möchtest du ein Stück Kuchen?

3. The letters **s, ß, ss:** When the letter **s** begins a word or syllable and is followed by a vowel, it is pronounced like the *z* in the English word *zebra.* In the middle or final position of a syllable, the letter **s** sounds similar to the *s* in the English word *post.* The letters **ß** and **ss** are also pronounced this way.

   so, sieben, Sonja / Deine Kusine sieht sehr hübsch aus.
   aus, das, es / Die Couch ist zu groß und ganz hässlich.

Richtig schreiben / Diktat

B. Write down the sentences that you hear.
Note: You write **ß** after a long vowel (**groß**), diphthongs (**weiß**) and **ss** after a short vowel (**hässlich**). Exceptions are some short words, such as **das** and **was**, that are spelled with a single **s** after a short vowel.

DRITTE STUFE   *fünfundachtzig*   **85**

Cultures and Communities

Under this head you will find helpful cultural information and suggestions that relate the content to students' families and communities.

Teaching Suggestions

offer helpful suggestions and information at point-of-use. You will also find references to other ancillaries.

Assessment

At the end of every **Stufe** and again at the end of the chapter, you will find references to assessment material available for that section of the chapter.

Bringing Standards into the Classroom

by Paul Sandrock, Foreign Language Consultant, Wisconsin Department of Public Education

The core question that guided the development of the National Standards and their accompanying goals was simply: what matters in instruction?

Each proposed standard was evaluated. Did the standard target material that will have application beyond the classroom? Was the standard too specific or not specific enough? Teachers should be able to teach the standard and assess it in multiple ways. A standard needs to provide a target for instruction and learning throughout a student's K–12 education.

In the development of standards, foreign languages faced other unique challenges. The writers could not assume a K–12 sequence available to all students. In fact, unlike other disciplines, they could not guarantee that all students would experience even any common sequence.

From this context, the National Standards in Foreign Language Education Project's task force generated the five C's, five goals for learning languages: communication, cultures, connections, comparisons, and communities. First presented in 1995, the standards quickly became familiar to foreign language educators across the US, representing our professional consensus and capturing a broad view of the purposes for learning another language.

To implement the standards, however, requires a shift from emphasizing the means to focusing on the ends. It isn't a matter of grammar versus communication, but rather how much grammar is needed to communicate. Instead of teaching to a grammatical sequence, teaching decisions become based on what students need to know to achieve the communicative goal.

The Focus on Communication

The first standard redefined communication, making its purpose **interpersonal, interpretive,** and **presentational** communication. Teaching to the purpose of interpersonal communication takes us away from memorized dialogues to spontaneous, interactive conversation, where the message is most important and where meaning needs to be negotiated between the speakers. Interpretive communication is not an exercise in translation, but asks beginners to tell the gist of an authentic selection that is heard, read, or viewed, while increasingly advanced learners tell deeper and deeper levels of detail and can interpret based on their knowledge of the target culture. In the presentational mode of communication, the emphasis is on the audience, requiring the speaker or writer to adapt language to fit the situation and to allow for comprehension without any interactive negotiation of the meaning.

Standards challenge us to refocus many of the things we've been doing all along. The requirements of speaking and our expectation of how well students need to speak change when speaking is for a different purpose. This focus on the purpose of the communication changes the way we teach and test the skills of listening, speaking, reading, and writing.

Standards help us think about how to help students put the pieces of language to work in meaningful ways. Our stan-

Standards for Foreign Language Learning

Communication Communicate in Languages Other than English	**Standard 1.1**	Students engage in conversations, provide and obtain information, express feelings and emotions, and exchange opinions.
	Standard 1.2	Students understand and interpret written and spoken language on a variety of topics.
	Standard 1.3	Students present information, concepts, and ideas to an audience of listeners or readers on a variety of topics.
Cultures Gain knowledge and understanding of Other Cultures	**Standard 2.1**	Students demonstrate an understanding of the relationship between the practices and perspectives of the culture studied.
	Standard 2.2	Students demonstrate an understanding of the relationship between the products and perspectives of the culture studied.
Connections Connect with other disciplines and Acquire Information	**Standard 3.1**	Students reinforce and further their knowledge of other disciplines through the foreign language.
	Standard 3.2	Students acquire information and recognize the distinctive viewpoints that are only available through the foreign language and its cultures.
Comparisons Develop Insight into the Nature of Language and Culture	**Standard 4.1**	Students demonstrate understanding of the nature of language through comparisons of the language studied and their own.
	Standard 4.2	Students demonstrate understanding of the concept of culture through comparisons of the cultures studied and their own.
Communities Participate in Multilingual Communities at Home and Around the World	**Standard 5.1**	Students use the language both within and beyond the school setting.
	Standard 5.2	Students show evidence of becoming life-long learners by using the language for personal enjoyment and enrichment.

dards answer *why* we are teaching various components of language, and we select *what* we teach in order to achieve those very standards.

The 5 C's

Originally the five C's were presented as five equal circles. During the years since the national standards were printed, teachers implementing and using the standards to write curriculum, texts, and lesson plans have come to see that communication is at the core, surrounded by four C's that influence the context for teaching and assessing.

The four C's surrounding our core goal of **Communication** change our classrooms by bringing in real-life applications for the language learned:

- **Cultures:** Beyond art and literature, learning occurs in the context of the way of life, patterns of behavior, and contributions of the people speaking the language being taught.

- **Connections:** Beyond content limited to the culture of the people speaking the target language, teachers go out to other disciplines to find topics and ideas to form the context for language learning.

- **Comparisons:** Foreign language study is a great way for students to learn more about native language and universal principles of language and culture by comparing and contrasting their own to the target language and culture.

- **Communities:** This goal of the standards adds a broader motivation to the context for language learning. The teacher makes sure students use their new language beyond the class hour, seeking ways to experience the target culture.

Implementation at the Classroom Level: Assessment and Instruction

After the publication of the standards, states developed more specific performance standards that would provide evidence of the application of the national content standards. Standards provide the organizing principle for teaching and assessing. The standards-oriented teacher, when asked what she's teaching, cites the standard "students will sustain a conversation." With that clear goal in mind, she creates lessons to teach various strategies to ask for clarification and to practice asking follow-up questions that explore a topic in more depth.

Textbook writers and materials providers are responding to this shift. Standards provide our goals; the useful textbooks and materials give us an organization and a context. Standards provide the ends; textbooks and materials can help us practice the means. Textbooks can bring authentic materials into the classroom, real cultural examples that avoid stereotypes, and a broader exposure to the variety of people who speak the language being studied. Textbooks can model the kind of instruction that will lead students to successful demonstration of the knowledge and skill described in the standards.

To really know that standards are the focus, look at the assessment. If standards are the target, assessment won't consist only of evaluation of the means (grammatical structures and vocabulary) in isolation. If standards are the focus, teachers will assess students' use of the second language in context. The summative assessment of our target needs to go beyond the specific and include open-ended, personalized tasks. Regardless of how the students show what they can do, the teacher will be able to gauge each student's progress toward the goal.

Assessment is like a jigsaw puzzle. If we test students only on the means, we just keep collecting random puzzle pieces. We have to test, and students have to practice, putting the pieces together in meaningful and purposeful ways. In order to learn vocabulary that will help students "describe themselves," for example, students may have a quiz on Friday with an expectation of close to 100% accuracy. But if that is all we ever do with those ten words, they will quickly be gone from students' memory, and we will only have collected a puzzle piece from each student. It is absolutely essential to have students use those puzzle pieces to complete the puzzle to provide evidence of what they "can do" with the language.

During this period of implementing our standards, we've learned that the standards provide a global picture, the essence of our goals. But they are not curriculum, nor are they lesson plans. The standards influence how we teach, but do not dictate one content nor one methodology. How can we implement the standards in our classrooms? Think about the targets; think about how students will show achievement of those targets through our evaluation measures; then think about what we need to teach and how that will occur in our classrooms. Make it happen in your classroom to get the results we've always wanted: students who can communicate in a language other than English.

Reading Strategies and Skills

by Nancy Humbach, Miami University, Oxford, Ohio

Reading is the most enduring of the language skills. Long after a student ceases to study the language, the ability to read will continue to provide a springboard to the renewal of the other skills. We must consider all the ways in which our students will read and address the skills needed for those tasks.

How can we accomplish this goal? How can we, as teachers, present materials, encourage students to read, and at the same time foster understanding and build the student's confidence and interest in reading?

Selection of Materials

Reading material in the foreign language classroom should be relevant to students' backgrounds and at an accessible level of difficulty, i.e., at a level of difficulty only slightly above the reading ability of the student.

Authentic materials are generally a good choice. They provide cultural context and linguistic authenticity seldom found in materials created for students, and the authentic nature of the language provides a window on a new world. The problem inherent in the selection of authentic materials at early levels is obvious: the level of difficulty is frequently beyond the skill of the student. At the same time, however, readers are inspired by the fact that they can understand materials designed to be read by native speakers.

Presenting a Selection/ Reading Strategies

We assume that students of a second language already have a reading knowledge in their first language and that many of the skills they learned in their "reading readiness" days will serve them

well. Too often, however, students have forgotten such skills as activating background knowledge, skimming, scanning, and guessing content based on context clues. Helping student to reactivate these skills is part of helping them become better readers.

Teachers should not assume their students' ability to transfer a knowledge set from one reading to another. Students use these skills on a regular basis, but often do not even realize they are doing so. To help students become aware of these processes, they need to be given strategies for reading. These strategies offer students a framework for the higher level skills they need to apply when reading. Strategies also address learners of different learning styles and needs.

Advance Organizers

One way to activate the student's background knowledge is through advance organizers. They also serve to address the student's initial frustrations at encountering an unfamiliar text.

Advance organizers call up pertinent background knowledge, feelings, and experiences that can serve to focus the attention of the entire group on a given topic. In addition, they provide for a sharing of information among the students. Background information that includes cultural references and cultural information can reactivate in students skills that will help them with a text and provide for them clues to the meaning of the material.

A good advance organizer will provide some information and guide students to think about the scenarios being presented. An advance organizer might include photographs, drawings, quotations, maps, or information about the area where the story takes

place. It might also be posed as a question, for example, "What would you do if you found yourself in....?" Having students brainstorm in advance, either as a whole class or in small groups, allows them to construct a scenario which they can verify as they read.

Prereading Activities

Prereading activities remind students of how much they really know and can prepare students in a number of ways to experience the language with less frustration. While we know that we must choose a reading selection that is not far beyond students' experience and skill level, we also know that no group of students reads at the same level. In the interest of assisting students to become better language learners, we can provide them with opportunities to work with unfamiliar structures and vocabulary ahead of time.

Preparing students for a reading selection can include a number of strategies that may anticipate but not dwell on potential problems to be encountered by students. Various aspects of grammar, such as differences in the past tenses and the meanings conveyed, can also cause problems. Alerting students to some of the aspects of the language allows them to struggle less, understand more quickly, and enjoy a reading selection to a greater degree.

Grouping vocabulary by category or simply choosing a short list of critical words for a section of reading is helpful. Providing an entire list of vocabulary items at one time can be overwhelming. With a bit of organization, the task becomes manageable to the point where students begin to master words they will find repeated throughout the selection.

Teaching students to skim for a particular piece of information or to scan for words, phrases, indicators of place, time, name, and then asking them to write a sentence or two about the gist of a paragraph or story, allows them to gain a sense of independence and success before they begin to read.

Getting into the Assignment

Teachers can recount the times they have assigned a piece of reading for homework, only to find that few students even attempted the work. Therefore, many teachers choose to complete the reading in class. Homework assignments should then be structured to have the student return to the selection and complete a assignment that requires critical thinking and imagination.

During class, several techniques assist students in maintaining interest and attention to the task. By varying these techniques, the teacher can provide for a lively class, during which students realize they *are* able to read. Partners can read passages to each other or students can take turns reading in small groups. The teacher might pose a question to be answered during that reading. Groups might also begin to act out short scenes, reading only the dialogue. Student might read a description of a setting and then draw what they imagine it to be. Of course, some selections might be silent reading with a specific amount of time announced for completion.

Reading aloud for comprehension and reading aloud for pronunciation practice are two entirely unrelated tasks. We can all recount classes where someone read aloud to us from weary lecture notes. Active engagement of the readers, on the other hand, forces them to work for comprehension, for the development of thought processes, and for improvement of language skills.

Postreading Activities

It is important to provide students with an opportunity to expand the knowledge they have gained from the reading selection. Students should apply what they have learned to their own personal experiences. How we structure activities can provide students more opportunities to reflect on their reading and learn how much they have understood. We often consider a written test the best way to ensure comprehension; however, many other strategies allow students to keep oral skills active. These might include acting out impromptu scenes from the story and creating dialogues that do not exist in a story, but might be imagined, based on other information. Consider the possibility of debates, interviews, TV talk show formats, telephone dialogues, or a monologue in which the audience hears only one side of the conversation.

Written assignments are also valid assessment tools, allowing students to incorporate the vocabulary and structures they have learned in the reading. Students might be encouraged to write journal entries for a character, create a new ending, or retell the story from another point of view. Newspaper articles, advertisements, and other creations can also be a means of following up. Comparisons with other readings require students to keep active vocabulary and structures they have studied previously. Encourage students to read their creations aloud to a partner, to a group, or to the class.

Conclusion

Reading can be exciting. The combination of a good selection that is relevant and rates high on the interest scale, along with good preparation, guidance, and post-reading activities that demonstrate to the students the level of success attained, can encourage them to continue to read. These assignments also allow for the incorporation of other aspects of language learning, and incorporate the Five C's of the National Standards. Communication and culture are obvious links, but so are connections (advance organizers, settings, and so on), comparisons (with other works in the heritage or target language), and communities (learning why a type of writing is important in a culture).

Komm mit!

offers reading practice and develops reading skills and strategies in the following ways:

THE PUPIL'S EDITION

▶ Provides an extensive reading section in each chapter called **Zum Lesen**. Each **Zum Lesen** section offers a strategy students apply to an authentic text, as well as activities to guide understanding and exploration of the text.

THE TEACHER'S EDITION

▶ Provides teachers with additional activities and information in every **Zum Lesen** section. Additional suggestions are provided for Pre-reading, Reading, and Postreading activities.

THE ANCILLARY PROGRAM

▶ *Lies mit mir!* This component offers reading selections of various formats and difficulty levels. Each chapter has a prereading feature, a reading selection with comprehension questions, and two pages of activities.

▶ The *Reading Skills and Strategies Handbook* offers useful strategies that can be applied to reading selections in the *Pupil's Edition, Lies mit mir!,* or a selection of your choosing.

▶ The *Übungsheft* contains a reading selection, tied to the chapter theme, and reading activities for each chapter in *Komm mit!*

Using Portfolios in the Language Classroom

by JoAnne S. Wilson, J. Wilson Associates

Portfolios offer a more realistic and accurate way to assess the process of language teaching and learning.

The communicative, whole-language approach of today's language instruction requires assessment methods that parallel the teaching and learning strategies in the proficiency-oriented classroom. We know that language acquisition is a process. Portfolios are designed to assess the steps in that process.

What Is a Portfolio?

A portfolio is a purposeful, systematic collection of a student's work. A useful tool in developing a student profile, the portfolio shows the student's efforts, progress, and achievements for a given period of time. It may be used for periodic evaluation, as the basis for overall evaluation, or for placement. It may also be used to enhance or provide alternatives to traditional assessment measures, such as formal tests, quizzes, class participation, and homework.

Why Use Portfolios?

Portfolios benefit both students and teachers because they:

- **Are ongoing and systematic.** A portfolio reflects the real-world process of production, assessment, revision, and reassessment. It parallels the natural rhythm of learning.

- **Offer an incentive to learn.** Students have a vested interest in creating the portfolios, through which they can showcase their ongoing efforts and tangible achievements. Students select the works to be included and have a chance to revise, improve, evaluate, and explain the contents.

- **Are sensitive to individual needs.** Language learners bring varied abilities to the classroom and do not acquire skills in a uniformly neat and orderly fashion. The personalized, individualized assessment offered by portfolios responds to this diversity.

- **Provide documentation of language development.** The material in a portfolio is evidence of student progress in the language learning process. The contents of the portfolio make it easier to discuss their progress with the students as well as with parents and others.

- **Offer multiple sources of information.** A portfolio presents a way to collect and analyze information from multiple sources that reflects a student's efforts, progress, and achievements in the language.

Portfolio Components

The language portfolio should include both oral and written work, student self-evaluation, and teacher observation, usually in the form of brief, nonevaluative comments about various aspects of the student's performance.

The Oral Component

The oral component of a portfolio might be an audio- or videocassette. It may contain both rehearsed and extemporaneous monologues and conversations. For a rehearsed speaking activity, give a specific communicative task that students can personalize according to their individual interests (for example, ordering a favorite meal in a restaurant). If the speaking activity is extemporaneous, first acquaint students with possible topics for discussion or even the specific task they will be expected to perform. (For example, tell them they will be asked to discuss a picture showing a sports activity or a restaurant scene.)

The Written Component

Portfolios are excellent tools for incorporating process writing strategies into the language classroom. Documentation of various stages of the writing process—brainstorming, multiple drafts, and peer comments—may be included with the finished product.

Involve students in selecting writing tasks for the portfolio. At the beginning levels, the tasks might include some structured writing, such as labeling or listing. As students become more proficient, journals, letters, and other more complicated writing tasks are valuable ways for them to monitor their progress in using the written language.

Student Self-Evaluation

Students should be actively involved in critiquing and evaluating their portfolios and monitoring their own progress.

The process and procedure for student self-evaluation should be considered in planning the contents of the portfolio. Students should work with you and their peers to design the exact format. Self-evaluation encourages them to think about what they are learning (content), how they learn (process), why they are learning (purpose), and where they are going in their learning (goals).

Teacher Observation

Systematic, regular, and ongoing observations should be placed in the portfolio after they have been discussed with the student. These observations provide feedback on the student's progress in the language learning process.

Teacher observations should be based on an established set of criteria that has been developed earlier with input from the student. Observation techniques may include the following:

- Jotting notes in a journal to be discussed with the student and then placed in the portfolio

- Using a checklist of observable behaviors, such as the willingness to take risks when using the target language or staying on task during the lesson

- Making observations on adhesive notes that can be placed in folders

- Recording anecdotal comments, during or after class, using a cassette recorder.

Knowledge of the criteria you use in your observations gives students a framework for their performance.

Electronic Portfolios

Technology can provide help with managing student portfolios. Digital or computer-based portfolios offer a means of saving portfolios in an electronic format. Students can save text, drawings, photographs, graphics, audio or video recordings, or any combination of multimedia information. Teachers can create their own portfolio templates or consult one of the many commercial software programs available to create digital portfolios. Portfolios saved on videotapes or compact discs provide a convenient way to access and store students' work. By employing technology, this means of alternative assessment addresses the learning styles and abilities of individual students. Additionally, electronic portfolios can be shared among teachers, and parents have the ability to easily see the students' progress.

Logistically, the hypermedia equipment and software available for students' use determine what types of entries will be included in the portfolios. The teacher or a team of teachers and students may provide the computer support.

How Are Portfolios Evaluated?

The portfolio should reflect the process of student learning over a specific period of time. At the beginning of that time period, determine the criteria by which you will assess the final product and convey them to the students. Make this evaluation a collaborative effort by seeking students' input as you formulate these criteria and your instructional goals.

Students need to understand that evaluation based on a predetermined standard is but one phase of the assessment process; demonstrated effort and growth are just as important. As you consider correctness and accuracy in both oral and written work, also consider the organization, creativity, and improvement revealed by the student's portfolio over the time period. The portfolio provides a way to monitor the growth of a student's knowledge, skills, and attitudes and shows the student's efforts, progress, and achievements.

How to Implement Portfolios

Teacher-teacher collaboration is as important to the implementation of portfolios as teacher-student collaboration. Confer with your colleagues to determine, for example, what kinds of information you want to see in the student portfolio, how the information will be presented, the purpose of the portfolio, the intended purposes (grading, placement, or a combination of the two), and criteria for evaluating the portfolio. Conferring among colleagues helps foster a departmental cohesiveness and consistency that will ultimately benefit the students.

The Promise of Portfolios

The high degree of student involvement in developing portfolios and deciding how they will be used generally results in renewed student enthusiasm for learning and improved achievement. As students compare portfolio pieces done early in the year with work produced later, they can take pride in their progress as well as reassess their motivation and work habits.

Komm mit!

supports the use of portfolios in the following ways:

THE PUPIL'S EDITION

▸ Includes numerous oral and written activities that can be easily adapted for student portfolios, such as **Notizbuch, Zum Schreiben,** and **Rollenspiel.**

THE TEACHER'S EDITION

▸ Suggests activities in the Portfolio Assessment feature that may serve as portfolio items.

THE ANCILLARY PROGRAM

▸ Includes criteria in the *Alternative Assessment Guide* for evaluating portfolios.

▸ Provides Speaking Tests in the *Testing Program* for each chapter that can be adapted for use as portfolio assessment items.

▸ Offers several oral and written scenarios on the *Interactive CD-ROM Tutor* that students can develop and include in their portfolios.

Komm mit! in the Middle Grades

Remember that planning a variety of tactile, kinesthetic, and visual activities that invite participation will help students be successful.

Students in the middle grades are at different levels of cognitive development than are high school and elementary students. In addition, middle school students are at markedly different levels of development from one another and have many different learning styles. Many sixth and seventh graders, especially, are tactile and kinesthetic, with a particular need for opportunities for movement. Seventh and eighth graders are more capable of formal cognitive operations and are increasingly preoccupied with social issues. They need and demand to know that what they learn in school relates to their lives. For all middle school students, self-esteem can be particularly fragile because of the many developmental changes they are undergoing.

The wide variety of activities in the various components of *Komm mit!* Level 1 enables teachers to adapt the many materials to their students' needs.

Scheduling

Komm mit! Level 1 can best be taught as a two-year program in the middle grades. Covering six chapters and two Location Openers each year allows five to six weeks for each chapter. This scheduling affords ample time to include varied activities that the diversity of the students demands.

Instruction

A number of proposals for teaching **Kapitel 3** are presented below as examples of activities especially well suited to middle school students. Many of these suggestions are either directly excerpted or adapted from those in the Teacher's Edition and ancillary materials. As you plan your own lessons, remember that planning a variety of tactile, kinesthetic, and visual activities that invite participation will help students be successful. Remember, too, that varying the type of activity often within each class and offering students choices will augment enthusiasm and motivation.

Los geht's!

Visual and concrete learners enjoy and learn from the videos. Show them the video segment **Los geht's!** without sound and ask them to watch for things that seem to be different in Germany.

- After briefly discussing what they think happened in the segment, write the title **Nach der Schule** on the board, and then draw three sets of spokes branching from the themes **Was wir tun, Was wir essen,** and **Was wir trinken.** Ask the students in English about what they like to do after school, and put their answers into German in the word webs on the board. Creating the web personalizes the material, makes it visual, and also helps students anticipate what they are about to see and hear as the video is presented a second time.

- Occasionally, have groups briefly speculate about what will happen in the **Fortsetzung** before showing it. This activity is fun and encourages the students to anticipate what they may see and hear.

Erste Stufe

Before beginning the **Erste Stufe,** offer students a concrete, hands-on project. For example, share with them a list of foods and beverages that you would like to have as props in the classroom for presentations and role-playing, and have them sign up to make the life-size prop of their choice, using chenille stems, construction paper, fabric, papier-maché, plastic cups, and more. Have them make more than one of whatever they choose so that you will have props for all of the cooperative learning groups.

- To introduce the **Wortschatz** give each group a basket full of props, and then use TPR. Call on one student from each group as you request each prop.

- The **möchte**-forms are introduced on p. 76; Activity 11 on p. 76 provides a brief opportunity to practice them. Another opportunity particularly suited to visual, kinesthetic, and social learners is a team game requiring dry erase boards, dry erase markers preferably of the low odor variety, and rags. Show a glass of mineral water and ask **Was möchtet ihr trinken?** The cooperative learning groups work silently as teams to write **Wir möchten ein Glas Mineralwasser, bitte.,** or **Wir möchten ein Mineralwasser.** The student in each group who has possession of the board when the question is given should write the first word of an appropriate response and then pass the materials to the next person. That person can choose either to correct the one word that has been written or to add the word that should follow. The third student, in turn, may choose either to correct a word or to add the word that should follow. Allow a designated amount of time to pass, and then award each group a point for each word correctly written.

- Have students use the props they made to do Activity 12 on p. 76.

- The students very much enjoy seeing and hearing kids close to their own ages in the **Landeskunde** segments. The activities in the Activity Masters and in the CD-ROM define clear tasks for them to accomplish as they listen.

Zweite Stufe

In the *Zweite Stufe,* students learn to describe bedrooms and the furniture in them; personalize the material by asking students how they would like to furnish their bedrooms if money were no object.

- Presenting the grammar introduced on p. 79 and elsewhere in the book in the way suggested on p. 67R encourages students to draw their own inferences, and this process promotes self-esteem as it encourages students to use higher-order thinking skills and empowers them to construct their own knowledge.

- Many learners in the middle grades especially enjoy games involving movement, such as the opposites game suggested on p. 67R and **Was ist richtig?** in Level 1 CD-ROM, Chapter 3.

- A number of activities presented in the teacher's suggestions such as Activity 15 on p. 67R, Activity 18 on p. 67S, and the Suggested Project on p. 67C, are suitable for middle school students.

Dritte Stufe

In the **Dritte Stufe,** students learn to describe people and talk about family members. To introduce the new vocabulary, talk about and show pictures of your own family as you put the words for relations onto the board in a family tree. Instead of simply using chalk, color code the new words according to whether they refer to male or female relations.

- Have students work in groups to ask one another about their families using possessives, pronouns, and the new vocabulary for describing people.

- The numbers 21–100 are introduced on p. 83, and p. 67U suggests playing Bingo. Model the game by playing as a class, then break into small groups to

allow more students to be callers and thus practice pronouncing the new vocabulary.

- Seventh grade students especially enjoy playing Buzz when they can stand at their desks until they are eliminated, and addition games such as the one on p. 67U can also be good fun.

- A number of activities presented in the teacher's suggestions, such as the TPR game and the game of *Twenty Questions* on p. 67V, or Activity 20 on p. 82 of the Pupil's Edition, are suitable for the middle school students.

- Middle school students will also enjoy the kinesthetic aspect of the CD-ROM games **Wort und Bild** and **Wozu gehört's?** in Level 1 CD-ROM, Chapter 3 and the **Interaktive Spiele** at WK3 Brandenburg-3 at **go.hrw.com.**

Komm mit!

addresses the needs of learners in the middle grades in the following ways:

THE PUPIL'S EDITION

▶ Offers a sequence of activities in each **Stufe** that guides students from structured practice to open-ended activities promoting personalized, meaningful expression.

▶ Provides tips in the **Lerntrick** and **Lesestrategie** features that help students become autonomous learners.

▶ Includes a **Zum Lesen** section in each chapter that offers Prereading, Reading, and Postreading activities to help students develop reading strategies.

▶ Features many photos and drawings.

THE TEACHER'S EDITION

▶ Proposes a variety of activities that target auditory, kinesthetic, tactile, and visual learners; features many cooperative learning activities.

▶ Offers Family Link suggestions that younger students enjoy.

▶ Presents game ideas at the beginning of each chapter that can easily be made active and can often be used just as well with other chapters.

THE ANCILLARY PROGRAM

▶ The extensive ancillary program provides both extensive auditory and visual exposure to the language and many activities that help learners simplify complex learning tasks.

Teaching Culture

by Nancy A. Humbach, Miami University, and Dorothea Bruschke, Parkway School District

We must integrate culture and language in a way that encourages curiosity, stimulates analysis, and teaches students to hypothesize.

The teaching of culture has undergone some important and welcome changes in recent years. Instead of teaching the standard notions of cultures, language and regions, we now stress the teaching of analysis and the critical thinking skills required to evaluate a culture, not by comparing it to one's own, but within its own setting. The setting includes the geography, climate, history, and influences of peoples who have interacted within that cultural group.

The National Standards for the Teaching of Foreign Languages suggests organizing the teaching of culture into three categories: products, practices, and perspectives. Through the presentation of these aspects of culture, students should gain the skill to analyze the culture, evaluate it within its context, compare it to their culture and develop the ability to function comfortably in that culture.

Skill and practice in the analysis of cultural phenomena equip students to enter a cultural situation, assess it, create strategies for dealing with it and accepting it as a natural part of the people. The ultimate goal of this philosophy is to reduce the "we vs. they" approach to culture. If students are encouraged to accept and appreciate the diversity of other cultures, they will be more willing and better able to develop the risk-taking strategies necessary to learn a language and to interact with people of different cultures.

There are many ways to help students become culturally knowledgeable and to assist them in developing an awareness of differences and similarities between the target culture and their own. Two of these approaches involve critical thinking, that is, trying to find reasons for a certain behavior through observation and analysis, and putting individual observations into larger cultural patterns. We must integrate culture and language in a way that encourages curiosity, stimutates analysis, and teaches students to hypothesize.

First Approach: Questioning

The first approach involves *questioning* as the key strategy. At the earliest stages of language learning, students learn ways to greet peers, elders, strangers, as well as the use of **du, ihr,** and **Sie.** Students need to consider questions such as: How do German-speaking people greet each other? Are there different levels of formality? Who initiates a handshake? What's considered a good handshake? Each of these questions leads students to think about the values that are expressed through words and gestures. They start to "feel" the other culture, and at the same time, understand how much of their own behavior is rooted in their cultural background.

Magazines, newspapers, advertisements, and television commercials are all excellent sources of cultural material. For example, browsing through a German magazine, one finds an extraordinary number of advertisements for health-related products. Could this indicate a great interest in staying healthy? To learn about customs involving health, reading advertisements can be followed up with viewing videos and films, or by interviewing native speakers or people who have lived in German-speaking countries. Students might want to find answers to questions such as: "How do Germans treat a cold? What is their attitude toward fresh air? Toward exercise?" This type of questioning might lead students to discover that some of the popular leisure-time activities, such as **einen Spaziergang machen** or **eine Wanderung machen,** are related to health consciousness.

An advertisement for a refrigerator or a picture of a German kitchen can provide an insight into practices of shopping for food. Students first need to think about the refrigerator at home, take an inventory of what is kept in it, and consider when and where their family shops. Next, students should look closely at a German refrigerator. What is its size? What could that mean? (Smaller refrigerators might mean that shopping takes place more often, stores are within walking distance, and people eat more fresh foods.)

Food wrappers and containers also provide cultural insight. For example, in German-speaking countries, bottled water is preferred to tap water even though tap water is safe to drink in most places. Why, then, is the rather expensive bottled water still preferred? Is it a tradition stemming from a time when tap water was not pure? Does it relate to the Germans' fondness of "taking the waters," i.e., drinking fresh spring water at a spa?

Second Approach: Associating Words with Images

The second approach for developing cultural understanding involves *forming associations of words with the cultural images they suggest.* Language and culture are so closely related that one might actually say that language is culture. Most words, especially nouns, carry a cultural connotation. Knowing the literal equivalent of a word in another language is of little use to students in understanding this connotation. For example, **Freund** cannot be translated simply as *friend,* **Brot** as *bread,* or **Straße** as *street.* The German word **Straße,** for instance, carries with it such images as people walking, sitting in a sidewalk café, riding bicycles, or shopping in specialty stores, and cars parked partly over the curb amid dense traffic. There is also the image of **Fußgängerzone,** a street for pedestrians only.

When students have acquired some sense of the cultural connotation of words—not only through explanations but, more importantly, through observation of visual images—they start to discover the larger underlying cultural themes, or what is often called deep culture.

These larger cultural themes serve as organizing categories into which individual cultural phenomena fit to form a pattern. Students might discover, for example, that Germans, because they live in much more crowded conditions, have a great need for privacy (cultural theme), as reflected in such phenomena as closed doors, fences or walls around property, and shutters on windows. Students might also discover that love of nature and the outdoors is an important cultural theme as indicated by such phenomena as flower boxes and planters in public places, well-kept public parks in every town, and people going for a walk or hiking.

As we teach culture, students learn to recognize elements not only of the target culture but also of their American cultural heritage. They see how elements of culture reflect larger themes or patterns. Learning what makes us Americans and how that information relates to other people throughout the world can be an exciting discovery for a young person.

As language teachers, we are able to facilitate this discovery of our similarities with others as well as our differences. We do not encourage value judgments about others and their culture, nor do we recommend adopting other ways. We simply say to students, "Other ways exist. They exist, just as our ways exist, due to our history, geography, and what our ancestors have passed on to us through traditions and values."

Komm mit!

develops *cultural understanding and cultural awareness* in the following ways:

THE PUPIL'S EDITION

▶ Informs students about daily life in German-speaking countries through culture notes.

▶ Provides deeper insight into cultural phenomena through personal interviews in the **Landeskunde** section.

▶ Helps students associate language and its cultural connotations through authentic art and photos.

THE TEACHER'S EDITION

▶ Provides additional cultural and language notes and background information.

▶ Suggests critical thinking strategies that encourage students to hypothesize, analyze, and discover larger underlying cultural themes.

THE ANCILLARY PROGRAM

▶ Includes realia to develop cultural insight by serving as catalyst for questioning and discovery.

▶ Offers activities that require students to compare and contrast cultures.

▶ Provides songs, short readings, and poems, as well as many opportunities for students to experience regional variation and idioms in the video, audio, and CD-ROM programs.

Learning Styles and Multi-Modality Teaching

by Mary B. McGehee, Louisiana State University

Incorporating a greater variety of activities to accommodate the learning styles of all students can make the difference between struggle and pleasure in the foreign language classroom.

The larger and broader population of students who are enrolling in foreign language classes brings a new challenge to foreign language educators, calling forth an evolution in teaching methods to enhance learning for all our students. Educational experts now recognize that every student has a preferred sense for learning and retrieving information: visual, auditory, or kinesthetic. Incorporating a greater variety of activities to accommodate the learning styles of all students can make the difference between struggle and pleasure in the foreign language classroom.

Accommodating Different Learning Styles

A modified arrangement of the classroom is one way to provide more effective and enjoyable learning for all students. Rows of chairs and desks must give way at times to circles, semicircles, or small clusters. Students may be grouped in fours or in pairs for cooperative work or peer teaching. It is important to find a balance of arrangements, thereby providing the most comfort in varied situations.

Since visual, auditory, and kinesthetic learners will be in the class, and because every student's learning will be enhanced by a multi-sensory approach, lessons must be directed toward all three learning styles. Any language lesson content may be presented visually, aurally, or kinesthetically.

Visual presentations and practice may include the chalkboard, charts, posters, television, overhead projectors, books, magazines, picture diagrams, flash cards, bulletin boards, films, slides, or videos. Visual learners need to see what they are to learn. Lest the teacher think he or she will never have the time to prepare all those visuals, Dickel and Slak (1983) found that visual aids generated by students are more effective than ready-made ones.

Auditory presentations and practice may include stating aloud the requirements of the lesson, oral questions and answers, paired or group work on a progression of oral exercises from repetition to communication, tapes, CDs, dialogues, and role-playing. Jingles, catchy stories, and memory devices using songs and rhymes are good learning aids. Having students record themselves and then listen as they play back the cassette allows them to practice in the auditory mode.

Kinesthetic presentations entail the students' use of manipulatives, chart materials, gestures, signals, typing, songs, games, and role-playing. These lead the students to associate sentence constructions with meaningful movements.

A Sample Lesson Using Multi-Modality Teaching

A multi-sensory presentation on greetings might proceed as follows:

For Visual Learners

As the teacher begins oral presentation of greetings and introductions, he or she simultaneously shows the written forms on transparencies, with the formal expressions marked with an adult's hat, and the informal expressions marked with a baseball cap.

The teacher then distributes cards with the hat and cap symbols representing the formal and informal expressions. As the students hear taped mini-dialogues, they hold up the appropriate card to indicate whether the dialogues are formal or informal. On the next listening, the students repeat the sentences they hear.

For Auditory Learners

A longer taped dialogue follows, allowing the students to hear the new expressions a number of times. They write from dictation several sentences containing the new expressions. They may work in pairs, correcting each other's work as they "test" their own understanding of the lesson at hand. Finally, students respond to simple questions using the appropriate formal and informal responses cued by the cards they hold.

For Kinesthetic Learners

For additional kinesthetic input, members of the class come to the front of the room, each holding a hat or cap symbol. As the teacher calls out situations, the students play the roles, using gestures and props appropriate to the age group they are portraying. Non-cued, communicative role-playing with props further enables the students to "feel" the differences between formal and informal expressions.

Helping Students Learn How to Use Their Preferred Mode

Since we require all students to perform in all language skills, part of the assistance we must render is to help them develop strategies within their preferred learning modes to carry out an assignment in another mode. For example, visual students hear the teacher assign an oral exercise and visualize what they must do. They must see themselves carrying out the assignment, in effect watching themselves as if there were a movie going on in their heads. Only then can they also hear themselves saying the right things. Thus, this assignment will be much easier for the visual learners who have been taught this process, if they have not already figured it out for themselves. Likewise, true auditory students, confronted with a reading/writing assignment, must talk themselves through it, converting the entire process into sound as they plan and prepare their work. Kinesthetic students presented with a visual or auditory task must first break the assignment into tasks and then work their way through them.

Students who experience difficulty because of a strong preference for one mode of learning are often unaware of the degree of preference. In working with these students, I prefer the simple and direct assessment of learning styles offered by Richard Bandler and John Grinder in their book *Frogs into Princes,* which allows the teacher and student to quickly determine how the student learns. In an interview with the student, I follow the assessment with certain specific recommendations of techniques to make the student's study time more effective.

It is important to note here that teaching students to maximize their study does not require that the teacher give each student an individualized assignment. It does require that each student who needs it be taught how to prepare the assignment using his or her own talents and strengths. This communication between teacher and student, combined with teaching techniques that reinforce learning in all modes, can only maximize pleasure and success in learning a foreign language.

References

Dickel, M.J. and S. Slak. "Imaging Vividness and Memory for Verbal Material." *Journal of Mental Imagery* 7, i (1983):121–126.

Bandler, Richard, and John Grinder. *Frogs into Princes.* Real People Press, Moab, UT. 1978.

Komm mit!

accommodates different learning styles in the following ways:

THE PUPIL'S EDITION

▸ Presents basic material in audio, video, print, and online formats.

▸ Includes role-playing activities and a variety of multi-modal activities, including an extensive listening strand and many art-based activities.

THE TEACHER'S EDITION

▸ Provides suggested activities for visual, auditory, and kinesthetic learners as well as suggestions for slower-paced learning and challenge activities.

▸ Includes Total Physical Response activities.

THE ANCILLARY PROGRAM

▸ Provides additional reinforcement activities for a variety of learning styles.

▸ Presents a rich blend of audiovisual input through the video program, audio program, CD-ROM Tutor, transparencies, blackline masters, and Internet activities.

Professional References

The Professional References section provides you with information about many resources that can enrich your German class. Included are addresses of German government and tourist offices, pen pal organizations, subscription agencies, and many others. Since addresses change frequently, you may want to verify them before you send your requests.

PEN PAL ORGANIZATIONS

The Student Letter Exchange will arrange pen pals for your students. For the names of other pen pal groups, contact your local chapter of AATG. There are fees involved, so be sure to write for information.

**Student Letter Exchange
(League of Friendship)**
211 Broadway, Suite 201
Lynbrook, NY 11563
(516) 887-8628

EMBASSIES AND CONSULATES

Embassy of the Federal Republic of Germany
4645 Reservoir Rd. N.W.
Washington, D.C. 20007-1998
(202) 298-4000

Consulate General of the Federal Republic of Germany
460 Park Avenue
New York, NY 10022-1971
(212) 308-8700
(also in Atlanta, Boston, Chicago, Detroit, Houston, Los Angeles, San Francisco, Seattle)

Embassy of Austria
3524 International Court N.W.
Washington, D.C. 20008
(202) 895-6700

Austrian Consulate General
31 East 69th Street
New York, NY 10021
(212) 737-6400
(also in Los Angeles and Chicago)

Embassy of Switzerland
2900 Cathedral Ave. NW
Washington, DC 20008
(202) 745-7900

Consulate General of Switzerland
665 5th Av. 8th Floor
New York, NY 10022
(212) 758-2560
(also in San Francisco, Los Angeles, Atlanta, Houston, Chicago)

CULTURAL AGENCIES

For historic and tourist information and audiovisual materials relating to Austria, contact:

Austrian Cultural Institute
950 Third Avenue
New York, NY 10022
(212) 759-5165

Material on political matters is available from **Bundeszentrale für politische Bildung,** a German federal agency.

Bundeszentrale für politische Bildung
Berliner Freiheit 7
53111 Bonn, GERMANY
(0228) 5150

For free political, cultural, and statistical information, films, and videos, contact:

German Information Center
871 United Nations Plaza
New York, NY 10017
(212) 610-9800

For various materials and information about special events your classes might attend, contact the **Goethe Institut** nearest you. For regional locations, contact:

Goethe Haus, German Cultural Center
1014 Fifth Avenue
New York, NY 10028
(212) 439-8700

The **Institut für Auslandsbeziehungen** provides cultural information to foreigners. The institute offers books and periodicals on a limited basis as well as a variety of two- and three-week professional seminars which allow educators to learn about the people, education, history, and culture of German-speaking countries.

Institut für Auslandsbeziehungen
Charlottenplatz 17
70173 Stuttgart, GERMANY
(0711) 2225-147

Inter Nationes, a nonprofit German organization for promoting international relations, supplies material on all aspects of life in Germany (literature, posters, magazines, press releases, films, slides, audio and video tapes) to educational institutions and organizations abroad.

Inter Nationes
Kennedyallee 91-103
53175 Bonn, GERMANY
(0228) 8800

TOURIST BUREAUS

Write to the following tourist offices for travel information and brochures.

German National Tourist Office
122 East 42nd St. 52nd Floor
New York, NY 10168
(212) 661-7200
(also in Chicago and San Francisco)

Deutsche Zentrale für Tourismus e.V.
Beethovenstraße 69
60325 Frankfurt GERMANY
(609) 974840

Switzerland Tourism
608 Fifth Avenue
New York, NY 10020
(212) 757-5944

PROFESSIONAL ORGANIZATIONS

The two major organizations for German teachers at the secondary school level are:

American Council on the Teaching of Foreign Languages (ACTFL)
6 Executive Plaza
Yonkers, NY 10701
(914) 963-8830

American Association of Teachers of German (AATG)
112 Haddontowne Court
Suite 104
Cherry Hill, NJ 08034
(609) 795-5553

PERIODICALS

Following are some periodicals published in German. For the names of other German magazines and periodicals contact a subscription agency.

Deutschland Nachrichten, a weekly newsletter available in both German and English, is published by the German Information Center *(see address under Cultural Agencies).*

Goethe Haus *(see address under Cultural Agencies)* publishes **Treffpunkt Deutsch,** a magazine of information, bibliographies, and ideas for teachers.

Bundeszentrale für politische Bildung *(see address under Cultural Agencies)* publishes **Politische Zeitung (PZ),** a quarterly magazine covering issues of social interest.

The Austrian Press and Information Service publishes a monthly newsletter. Write to:

Austrian Information
3524 International Court N.W.
Washington, D.C. 20008

Juma classroom magazine is a free publication to which you can subscribe. You can order multiple copies by writing to:

Redaktion Juma
Frankfurter Straße 40
51065 Köln, GERMANY
(0221) 962513-0

SUBSCRIPTION SERVICES

German magazines can be obtained through subscription agencies in the United States. The following companies are among the many which can provide you with subscriptions:

EBSCO Subscription Services
P.O. Box 1943
Birmingham, AL 35201-1943
(205) 991-6600

Continental Book Company
8000 Cooper Ave. Bldg. 29
Glendale, NY 11385
(718) 326-0572

EXCHANGE PROGRAMS

German American Partnership Program (GAPP)
c/o Goethe-Institut New York
1014 Fifth Avenue
New York, NY 10028
(212) 439-8715

Experiment in International Living
World Learning
Kipling Road, P.O. Box 676
Brattleboro, VT 05302-0676
(802) 257-7751 or
(800) 345-2929

MISCELLANEOUS

(ADAC) Allgemeiner Deutscher Automobil Club
Am Westpark 8
81373 München, GERMANY
(089) 76760

For students who want to find a summer job in Germany, write to:

Zentralstelle für Arbeitsvermittlung (ZAV)
Dienststelle 08100
Postfach 170545
60079 Frankfurt, GERMANY
(069) 71110
(Applicants must have a good knowledge of German.)

For international student passes and other student services contact:

CIEE Student Travel Services
205 E. 42nd Street
New York, NY 10017-5706
(212) 822-2700
(has branch offices in several other large cities)

A Bibliography for the German Teacher

This bibliography is a compilation of several resources available for professional enrichment.

SELECTED AND ANNOTATED LIST OF READINGS

I. Methods and Approaches

Cohen, A. (1994). *Assessing language ability in the classroom* (2nd ed.). Boston: Heinle and Heinle.

- An introduction to assessing students' foreign language ability. Discussions of various assessment techniques including role-playing activities, portfolios, and oral interviews provide instructors with alternatives to more traditional testing techniques. Computer-based testing is also examined.

Lafayette, R. (Ed.). (1996). *National standards: A catalyst for reform.* Lincolnwood, IL: National Textbook Co.

- Provides an outline of the National Standards movement and its implications for the modern foreign language classroom. Issues such as technology, teacher training, materials development, and the changing learning environment are each addressed in terms of the national standards.

Lee, J., & VanPatten, B. (1995). *Making communicative language teaching happen.* New York: McGraw-Hill.

- Discussion of communicative language teaching centered on a task-based approach to second language education. The authors provide both a theoretical and a practical framework for teaching the four skills (reading, writing, listening, speaking). The book includes some two hundred activities as well as test sections to help instructors encourage communicative interaction in their classrooms.

Omaggio Hadley, A. (1993). *Teaching language in context* (2nd ed.). Boston: Heinle and Heinle Publishers.

- Overview of the proficiency movement as well as a survey of past foreign language teaching methods and approaches. The author briefly presents the theory and history of the proficiency movement and then applies these concepts to each of the five skills in foreign language education. Includes sample activities, teaching suggestions, summaries, and references for further reading.

II. Second-Language Theory

Brown, H. D. (1994). *Principles of language learning and teaching* (3rd ed.). Englewood Cliffs, NJ: Prentice Hall Regents

- Addresses the cognitive, psychological, and sociocultural factors influencing the language learning process. Also includes theories of learning, styles and strategies, motivation, and culture; as well as an introduction to assessment, error analysis, communicative competence, and theories of acquisition along with practical vignettes describing classroom applications.

Ellis, R. (1994). *The study of second language acquisition.* Oxford: Oxford University Press.

- Provides an overview of second language acquisition: error analysis, acquisition orders, social factors, affective variables, individual differences, and the advantages and disadvantages of classroom instruction.

Krashen, S. (1987). *Principles and practice in second language acquisition.* New York: Prentice-Hall.

- Summary and discussion of Krashen's Monitor Model and its implications for foreign language instruction. Krashen discusses each of his five hypotheses regarding second language acquisition and their implications for the foreign language classroom.

III. Technology Enhanced Language Learning

Bush, M., & Terry, R. (Eds.). (1997). *Technology enhanced language learning.* Lincolnwood, IL: National Textbook Co.

Muyskens, J. (Ed.). (1997). *New ways of learning and teaching: Focus on technology and foreign language education.* Boston: Heinle and Heinle.

- Both works include articles on application of technology in the modern foreign language classroom. Topics include: multimedia, electronic discussions and computer-mediated communication, the WWW, videos, hypermedia, and the Internet. The authors describe techniques for applying these tools to all aspects of foreign language learning including reading, writing, listening, speaking, and culture. Questions of implementation, teacher training, and language laboratories are also discussed.

IV. Professional Journals

Calico
(Published by the Computer Assisted Language Instruction Consortium)

- Emphasizes applications of technology to foreign language learning. Articles include research on computer assisted language learning, videos and television in the classroom, and the use of the Internet and the WWW for learning and instruction.

Foreign Language Annals
(Published by the American Council on the Teaching of Foreign Languages)

- Publishes both research-based and practical articles on foreign language instruction and learning. In addition to learning and teaching strategies and methods, the journal also features articles on curriculum development and recent trends in foreign language pedagogy.

The IALL Journal of Language Learning Technologies
(Published by the International Association for Learning Laboratories)

- Practical and theoretical articles on technology and language instruction with emphasis on the effective use of media centers for language teaching, learning, and research.

The Modern Language Journal

- Features articles on the most recent research in the fields of language learning and second language acquisition.

Die Unterrichtspraxis
(Published by the American Association of Teachers of German)

- Emphasizes practical reports of successful pedagogical methods and strategies. Ideas for the German language classroom can be found in every issue along with reports on the current state of German studies in the United States.

Komm mit!®

HOLT GERMAN

LEVEL 1

HOLT, RINEHART AND WINSTON

A Harcourt Classroom Education Company

Austin • New York • Orlando • Atlanta • San Francisco • Boston • Dallas • Toronto • London

EXECUTIVE EDITOR
George Winkler

SENIOR EDITOR
Konstanze Alex Brown

MANAGING EDITOR
Chris Hiltenbrand

EDITORIAL STAFF
Sara Anbari
Mark Eells,
 Editorial Coordinator
Augustine Agwuele,
 Department Intern
Sunday Ballew,
 Department Intern

EDITORIAL PERMISSIONS
Janet Harrington,
 Permissions Editor

ART, DESIGN, & PHOTO
BOOK DESIGN
Richard Metzger,
 Design Director
Marta L. Kimball,
 Design Manager
Virginia Hassell
Andrew Lankes
Jennifer Trost
Alicia Sullivan
Ruth Limon

IMAGE SERVICES
Joe London,
 Director
Tim Taylor,
 Photo Research Supervisor
Stephanie Friedman
Michelle Rumpf,
 Art Buyer Supervisor
Coco Weir

DESIGN NEW MEDIA
Susan Michael,
 Design Director
Amy Shank,
 Design Manager
Kimberly Cammerata,
 Design Manager
Czeslaw Sornat,
 Senior Designer
Grant Davidson

MEDIA DESIGN
Curtis Riker,
 Design Director
Richard Chavez

GRAPHIC SERVICES
Kristen Darby,
 Manager
Linda Wilbourn
Jane Dixon
Dean Hsieh

COVER DESIGN
Richard Metzger,
 Design Director
Candace Moore,
 Senior Designer

PRODUCTION
Amber McCormick,
 Production Supervisor
Diana Rodriguez,
 Production Coordinator

MANUFACTURING
Shirley Cantrell,
 Supervisor, Inventory &
 Manufacturing
Deborah Wisdom,
 Senior Inventory Analyst

NEW MEDIA
Jessica Bega,
 Senior Project Manager
Elizabeth Kline,
 Senior Project Manager

VIDEO PRODUCTION
Video materials produced by
Edge Productions, Inc.,
Aiken, S.C.

ACKNOWLEDGMENTS

Front Cover: house: Helga Lade/Peter Arnold, Inc

Front Cover: teens: Steve Ewert/HRW Photo

Back Cover: George Winkler/HRW Photo.

For permission to reprint copyrighted material, grateful acknowledgment is made to the following sources:

Baars Marketing GmbH: Advertisement, "Leerdammer Light: Das haben Sie jetzt davon," from *Stern*, no. 27, June 25, 1992.

Bauconcept: Advertisement, "Die Oase in der City!," from *Südwest Presse: Schwäbisches Tagblatt*, Tübingen, July 14, 1990.

KOMM MIT! is a trademark licensed to Holt, Rinehart and Winston, registered in the United States of America and/or other jurisdictions.

Printed in the United States of America

ISBN 0-03-056597-9

1 2 3 4 5 6 7   48   05 04 03 02 01

ACKNOWLEDGMENTS continued on page R58, which is an extension of the copyright page

AUTHOR

George Winkler
Austin, TX

Mr. Winkler developed the scope and sequence and framework for the chapters, created the basic material, selected realia, and wrote activities.

CONTRIBUTING WRITERS

Margrit Meinel Diehl
Syracuse, NY

Mrs. Diehl wrote activities to practice basic material, functions, grammar, and vocabulary.

Carolyn Roberts Thompson
Abilene Christian University
Abilene, TX

Mrs. Thompson was responsible for the selection of realia for readings and for developing reading activities.

CONSULTANTS

The consultants conferred on a regular basis with the editorial staff and reviewed all the chapters of the Level 1 textbook.

Maria L. Beck
University of North Texas
Denton, TX

Dorothea Bruschke, retired
Parkway School District
Chesterfield, MO

Ingeborg H. McCoy
Southwest Texas State University
San Marcos, TX

REVIEWERS

The following educators reviewed one or more chapters of the Pupil's Edition.

Inge Atkins
Arvada High School
Arvada, CO

Jerome R. Baker
Columbus East High School
Columbus, IN

Jerri Lynn Baxstrom
Smithville High School
Smithville, OH

Angela Breidenstein
Trinity University, previously at Robert Lee High School
San Antonio, TX

Nancy Butt
Washington and Lee High School
Arlington, VA

Kathleen Cooper
Burnsville High School
Burnsville, MN

Frank Dietz
University of Texas at Austin
Austin, TX

Donald R. Goetz
West High School
Davenport, IA

Jacqueline Hastay
Lyndon Baines Johns*on High School
Austin, TX

Gerlind Jenkner
Medina High School
Medina, OH

Leslie Kearney
Central High School
Little Rock, AR

LeRoy H. Larson
John Marshall High School
Rochester, MN

Diane E. Laumer
San Marcos High School
San Marcos, TX

Carol Masters
Edison High School
Tulsa, OK

Linnea Maulding
Fife High School
Tacoma, WA

Amy S. McMahon
Parkway Central High School
Chesterfield, MO

David A. Miller
Parkway South High School
Manchester, MO

Linda Miller
Craig High School
Janesville, WI

Douglas Mills
Greensburg Central Catholic High School
Greensburg, PA

Gisela Schubert
New Milford High School
New Milford, CT

Rolf M. Schwägermann
Stuyvesant High School
New York, NY

Esther Spease
Luverne High School
Luverne, MN

Margaret G. Thatcher
Newtown Junior High School
Newtown, PA

Mary Ann Verkamp
Hamilton Southeastern High School
Fishers, IN

Jim Witt
Grand Junction High School
Grand Junction, CO

FIELD TEST PARTICIPANTS

We express our appreciation to the teachers and students who participated in the field test. Their comments were instrumental in the development of this book.

Eva-Maria Adolphi
Indian Hills Middle School
Sandy, UT

Connie Allison
MacArthur High School
Lawton, OK

Dennis Bergren
West High School
Madison, WI

Margaret S. Draheim
Wilson Junior High School
Appleton, WI

Petra A. Hansen
Redmond High School
Redmond, WA

Christa Hary
Brien McMahon High School
Norwalk, CT

Ingrid S. Kinner
Weaver Education Center
Greensboro, NC

Diane E. Laumer
San Marcos High School
San Marcos, TX

Judith A. Lidicker
Central High School
West Allis, WI

Linnea Maulding
Fife High School
Tacoma, WA

Jane Reinkordt
Lincoln Southeast High School
Lincoln, NE

Elizabeth A. Smith
Plano Senior High School
Plano, TX

TO THE STUDENT

Some people have the opportunity to learn a new language by living in another country.
Most of us, however, begin learning another language and getting acquainted with a
foreign culture in a classroom with the help of a teacher, classmates, and a textbook.
To use your book effectively, you need to know how it works.

Komm mit! (*Come along*) is organized to help you learn German and become familiar with
the culture of the people who speak German. The Preliminary Chapter presents basic
concepts in German and strategies for learning a new language. This chapter is followed
by four Location Openers and twelve chapters.

Location Opener Four four-page
photo essays called Location
Openers introduce different
states or cities in Germany.

Chapter Opener The Chapter
Opener pages tell you the
chapter theme and goals.

Los geht's! (*Getting started*)
This illustrated story, which is
also on video, shows you German-
speaking people in real-life situations, using the language you'll
learn in the chapter.

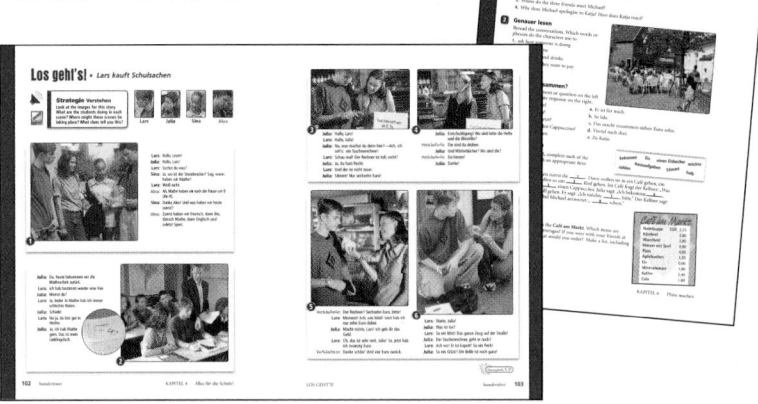

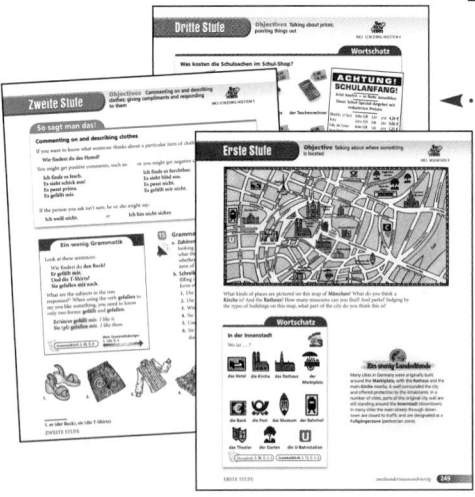

Erste, Zweite, and Dritte Stufe (*First, Second, and Third
Step*) After **Los geht's!**, the chapter is divided into three
sections called **Stufen**. Within the **Stufe** are **So sagt
man das!** (*Here's how you say it*) boxes that contain the
German expressions you'll need to communicate and
Wortschatz and **Grammatik / Ein wenig Grammatik**
boxes that give you the German words and grammar
structures you'll need to know. Activities in each **Stufe**
enable you to develop your skills in listening, speaking,
reading, and writing.

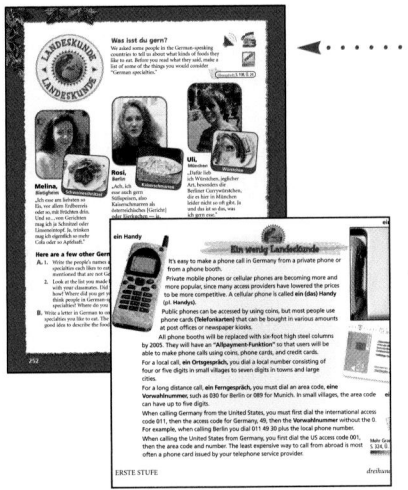

Landeskunde (*Culture*) On this page are interviews with German-speaking people. You can watch these interviews on video or listen to them on the CD-ROM Tutor, then check to see how well you understood by answering some questions about what the people say.

Ein wenig Landeskunde (*Culture Note*) In each chapter, there are notes with more information about the culture in German-speaking countries.

Zum Lesen (*For reading*) The reading section follows the three **Stufen**. The selections are related to the chapter themes and will help you develop your reading skills in German.

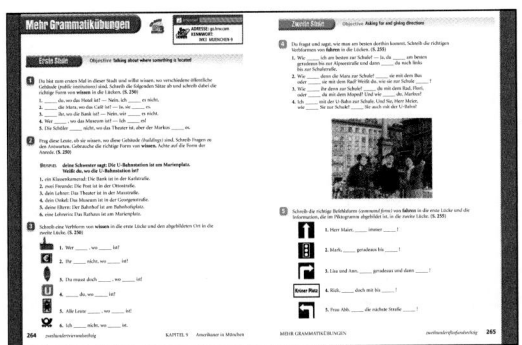

Mehr Grammatikübungen (*Additional grammar practice*) This section begins the chapter review. You will find four pages of activities that provide additional practice on the grammar concepts you learned in the chapter.

Anwendung (*Review*) The activities on these pages practice what you've learned in the chapter and help you improve your listening, reading, and comprehension skills. You'll also review what you've learned about culture. A section called **Zum Schreiben** (*Let's Write*) in chapters 3–12 will develop your writing skills.

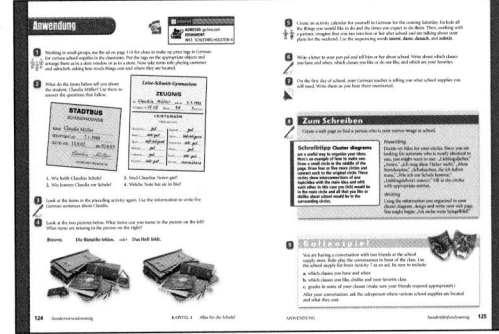

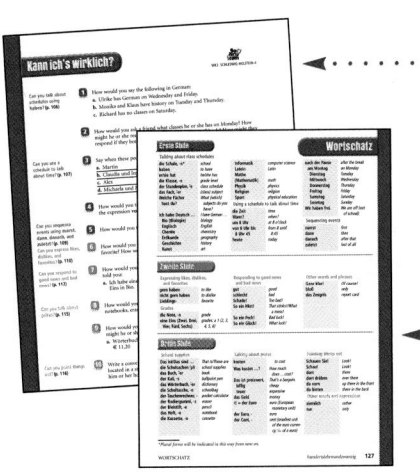

Kann ich's wirklich? (*Can I really do it?* . . .) This page at the end of each chapter contains a series of questions and short activities to help you see if you've achieved the chapter goals.

Wortschatz (*Vocabulary*) On the German-English vocabulary list on the last page of the chapter, the words are grouped by **Stufe**. These words and expressions will appear on quizzes and tests.

You'll also find special features in each chapter that provide extra tips and reminders.

Lerntrick (*Learning Hint*) offers study hints to help you succeed in the foreign language class.

Und dann noch . . . (*And then*) lists extra words you might find helpful. These words will not appear on quizzes and tests unless your teacher chooses to include them.

You'll also find German-English and English-German vocabulary lists at the end of the textbook. The words you'll need to know for the quizzes and tests are in boldface type.

At the end of your textbook, you'll find more helpful material, such as:
- a summary of the expressions you'll learn in the **So sagt man das!** boxes
- a summary of the grammar you'll study
- a section of additional activities to practice the grammar you'll learn
- additional vocabulary words that you might want to use
- a grammar index to help you find where grammar is presented

Komm mit! Come along on an exciting trip to a new culture and a new language!

Gute Reise!

Explanation of Icons in *Komm mit!*

Throughout **Komm mit!** *you'll see these symbols, or icons, next to activities. They'll tell you what you'll probably do with that activity. Here's a key to help you understand the icons.*

Video Whenever this icon appears, you'll know there is a related segment in the *Komm mit! Video Program*.

Listening Activities This icon indicates a listening activity.

Pair Work/Group Work Activities

Writing Activities

CD-ROM Activities Whenever this icon appears, you'll know there is a related activity on the *Komm mit! Interactive CD-ROM Tutor*.

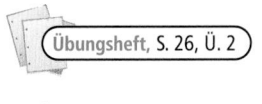
Übungsheft, S. 26, Ü. 2

Grammatikheft, S. 19, Ü. 1-2

Practice Activities These icons tell you which activities from the *Übungsheft* and the *Grammatikheft* practice the material presented.

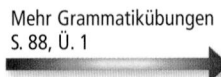
Mehr Grammatikübungen S. 88, Ü. 1

Mehr Grammatikübungen This reference tells you where you can find related additional grammar practice in the review section of the chapter.

go.hrw.com

Internet Activities This icon provides the keyword you'll need to access related online activities at **go.hrw.com**.

Komm mit! Contents

Come along—to a world of new experiences!

Komm mit! *offers you the opportunity to learn the language spoken by millions of people in several European countries and around the world. Let's find out about the countries, the people, and the German language.*

Vorschau

Teaching Suggestions T75–T81
Listening Scripts 15H

Komm mit! 1
- Map of Central Europe
- Getting acquainted with the German-speaking countries

Map of the Bundesrepublik Deutschland 2

Map of Liechtenstein, Schweiz, and Österreich 3

Schon einmal gesehen? 4
- Well-known images that come to mind

Bekannte Leute 5
- Famous men and women

Das Alphabet 6
- The German alphabet

Wie heisst du? 7
- Introducing yourself
- German names for boys and girls

Im Klassenzimmer 8
- Identifying classroom objects

Ausdrücke fürs Klassenzimmer 8
- Expressions for the classroom

Die Zahlen von 0 bis 20 9
- Numbers from 0 to 20

Warum Deutsch lernen? 10
- Reasons for learning German

Tipps fürs Deutschlernen 11
- Tips for studying German

KOMM MIT NACH

Brandenburg!

LOCATION • KAPITEL 1, 2, 3....12

LOCATION OPENER 11A–11B

KAPITEL 1

CHAPTER OVERVIEW 15A

CHAPTER RESOURCES 15B

PROJECTS & GAMES 15C

STORYTELLING & TRADITIONS 15D

TECHNOLOGY 15E–15F

LISTENING SCRIPTS 15G–15H

50 MINUTE LESSON PLAN 15I–15J

90 MINUTE LESSON PLAN 15K–15L

TEACHING SUGGESTIONS 15M–15X

Wer bist du? 16

LOS GEHT'S! 18
  Vor der Schule

Erste Stufe 21
  So sagt man das!
  • Saying hello and goodbye
  • Asking someone's name and giving yours
  • Asking who someone is
  Grammatik
  • Forming questions
  • The definite articles **der, die, das**

Zweite Stufe 25
  So sagt man das!
  • Asking someone's age and giving yours
  Wortschatz
  • The numbers 0 to 20
  Grammatik
  • Subject pronouns and the verb sein

Dritte Stufe 28
  So sagt man das!
  • Talking about where people are from
  • Talking about how someone gets to school
  Wortschatz
  • Means of transportation

LANDESKUNDE 31
  Wie kommst du zur Schule?

ZUM LESEN:
POSTKARTEN AUS DEN FERIEN 34
  Reading postcards written by German teenagers
  Reading Strategy: Using visual clues to determine meaning

MEHR GRAMMATIKÜBUNGEN 36

ANWENDUNG 38

KANN ICH'S WIRKLICH? 40

WORTSCHATZ 41

KAPITEL 2

CHAPTER OVERVIEW 41A
CHAPTER RESOURCES 41B
PROJECTS & GAMES 41C
STORYTELLING & TRADITIONS 41D

TECHNOLOGY 41E–41F
LISTENING SCRIPTS 41G–41H
50 MINUTE LESSON PLAN 41I–41J
90 MINUTE LESSON PLAN 41K–41L

TEACHING SUGGESTIONS 41M–41X

Spiel und Spaß 42

LOS GEHT'S! 44
Was machst du in deiner Freizeit?

Erste Stufe 47
So sagt man das!
• Talking about interests

Grammatik
• Present tense, singular verb forms

Zweite Stufe 50
So sagt man das!
• Expressing likes and dislikes

Wortschatz
• Sports and hobbies

Grammatik
• Present tense, plural subjects, and verb endings
• Present tense verb forms

LANDESKUNDE 54
Was machst du gern?

Dritte Stufe 55
So sagt man das!
• Saying when you do various activities
• Asking for an opinion and expressing yours
• Agreeing and disagreeing

Wortschatz
• The seasons
• Enthusiasm and boredom

Grammatik
• Word order: verb in second position
• Verbs with stem ending in **d, t,** or **n**

ZUM LESEN:
WAS MACHEN WIR AM WOCHENENDE? 60
Using ads and articles to plan free-time activities

Reading strategy: Scanning for specific information

MEHR GRAMMATIKÜBUNGEN 62

ANWENDUNG 64

KANN ICH'S WIRKLICH? 66

WORTSCHATZ 67

KAPITEL 3

CHAPTER OVERVIEW 67A
CHAPTER RESOURCES 67B
PROJECTS & GAMES 67C
STORYTELLING & TRADITIONS 67D

TECHNOLOGY 67E–67F
LISTENING SCRIPTS 67G–67H
50 MINUTE LESSON PLAN 67I–67J
90 MINUTE LESSON PLAN 67K–67L

TEACHING SUGGESTIONS 67M–67X

Komm mit nach Hause! 68

LOS GEHT'S! 70
Bei Jens zu Hause!

Erste Stufe 73
So sagt man das!
• Talking about where you and others live
• Offering something to eat or drink and responding to an offer
• Saying please, thank you, and you're welcome

Wortschatz
• Places to live   • Snacks

Grammatik
• The **möchte**-forms
• The indefinite articles **ein, eine**

LANDESKUNDE 77
Wo wohnst du?

Zweite Stufe 78
So sagt man das!
• Describing a room

Wortschatz
• Adjectives for describing furniture and appliances

Grammatik
• The pronouns **er, sie, es, sie** (*pl*)

Dritte Stufe 81
So sagt man das!
• Talking about family members
• Describing people

Wortschatz
• Family members
• Numbers 21 to 100
• Adjectives for describing people

Grammatik
• The possessive adjectives **mein, sein, dein, ihr**

ZUM LESEN: WO WOHNST DU DENN? 86
Analyzing advertisements for apartments and houses

Reading Strategy: Using root words to guess meaning

MEHR GRAMMATIKÜBUNGEN 88

ANWENDUNG 92
Zum Schreiben: Arranging ideas spatially
Creating a personal profile puzzle

KANN ICH'S WIRKLICH? 94

WORTSCHATZ 95

Schleswig-Holstein!

LOCATION • KAPITEL 4, 5, 6 96

LOCATION OPENER 93A–93B

KAPITEL 4

CHAPTER OVERVIEW 99A

CHAPTER RESOURCES 99B

PROJECTS & GAMES 99C

STORYTELLING & TRADITIONS 99D

TECHNOLOGY 99E–99F

LISTENING SCRIPTS 99G–99H

50 MINUTE LESSON PLAN 99I–99J

90 MINUTE LESSON PLAN 99K–99L

TEACHING SUGGESTIONS 99M–99X

Alles für die Schule! 100

LOS GEHT'S! 102
Lars kauft Schulsachen

Erste Stufe 105
So sagt man das!
• Talking about class schedules
• Using a schedule to talk about time
• Sequencing events
Wortschatz
• School subjects
Grammatik
• The verb **haben** *to have*, present tense

Zweite Stufe 110
So sagt man das!
• Expressing likes, dislikes, and favorites
• Responding to good news and bad news
Grammatik
• The prefix **Lieblings-**

LANDESKUNDE 113
Was sind deine Lieblingsfächer?

Dritte Stufe 114
So sagt man das!
• Talking about prices
• Pointing things out
Wortschatz
• School supplies
Grammatik
• Noun plurals

ZUM LESEN: LERNEN MACHT SPASS! 118
Analyzing advertisements for German schools and tutors
Reading Strategy: Using cognates to determine the meaning of compound words

MEHR GRAMMATIKÜBUNGEN 120

ANWENDUNG 124
Zum Schreiben: Cluster diagrams
Creating a Web page

KANN ICH'S WIRKLICH? 126

WORTSCHATZ 127

KAPITEL 5

CHAPTER OVERVIEW 127A
CHAPTER RESOURCES 127B
PROJECTS & GAMES 127C
STORYTELLING & TRADITIONS 127D

TECHNOLOGY 127E–127F
LISTENING SCRIPTS 127G–127H
50 MINUTE LESSON PLAN 127I–127J
90 MINUTE LESSON PLAN 127K–127L

TEACHING SUGGESTIONS 127M–127X

Klamotten kaufen 128

LOS GEHT'S! 130
Was ziehst du an?

Erste Stufe 133
So sagt man das!
• Expressing wishes when shopping
Wortschatz
• Clothes and accessories
• Colors
Grammatik
• Definite and indefinite articles, accusative case

Zweite Stufe 137
So sagt man das!
• Commenting on and describing clothes
• Giving compliments and responding to them
Wortschatz
• Words to describe the fit of clothes
Grammatik
• The verb **gefallen** to like, to be pleasing to
• Direct object pronouns

LANDESKUNDE 142
Welche Klamotten sind „in"?

Dritte Stufe 143
So sagt man das!
• Talking about trying on clothes
Grammatik
• Separable-prefix verbs
• The stem-changing verbs **nehmen** to get, to take and **aussehen** to look

ZUM LESEN: KLEIDER MACHEN LEUTE! 146
Using advertisements to buy clothing
Reading Strategy: Using what you already know

MEHR GRAMMATIKÜBUNGEN 148

ANWENDUNG 152
Zum Schreiben: Outlining
Writing a fashion show commentary

KANN ICH'S WIRKLICH? 154

WORTSCHATZ 155

KAPITEL 6

CHAPTER OVERVIEW 155A
CHAPTER RESOURCES 155B
PROJECTS & GAMES 155C
STORYTELLING & TRADITIONS 155D

TECHNOLOGY 155E–155F
LISTENING SCRIPTS 155G–155H
50 MINUTE LESSON PLAN 155I–155J
90 MINUTE LESSON PLAN 155K–155L

TEACHING SUGGESTIONS 155M–155X

Pläne machen 156

LOS GEHT'S! 158
Wollen wir ins Café gehen?

Erste Stufe 161
So sagt man das!
• Starting a conversation
• Telling time and talking about when you do things

Wortschatz
• Time of day expressions

Zweite Stufe 165
So sagt man das!
• Making plans

Wortschatz
• Places to go for fun

Grammatik
• The verb **wollen** *to want*

LANDESKUNDE 169
Was machst du in deiner Freizeit?

Dritte Stufe 170
So sagt man das!
• Ordering food and beverages
• Talking about how something tastes
• Paying the check

Wortschatz
• Restaurant food

Grammatik
• The stem-changing verb **essen** *to eat*

ZUM LESEN: WOHIN IN HAMBURG? 174
Using entertainment ads to plan an evening

Reading Strategy: Guessing the meaning of words from context

MEHR GRAMMATIKÜBUNGEN 176

ANWENDUNG 180
Zum Schreiben: Arranging ideas chronologically

Writing a descriptive letter

KANN ICH'S WIRKLICH? 182

WORTSCHATZ 183

T63

München!

LOCATION • KAPITEL 7, 8, 9....184
LOCATION OPENER 183A–183B

KAPITEL 7

CHAPTER OVERVIEW 187A

CHAPTER RESOURCES 187B

PROJECTS & GAMES 187C

STORYTELLING & TRADITIONS 187D

TECHNOLOGY 187E–187F

LISTENING SCRIPTS 187G–187H

50 MINUTE LESSON PLAN 187I–187J

90 MINUTE LESSON PLAN ...187K–187L

TEACHING SUGGESTIONS 187M–187X

Zu Hause helfen.....188

LOS GEHT'S! **190**

Was musst du machen?

Erste Stufe **193**

So sagt man das!
• Extending and responding to an invitation
• Expressing obligations

Wortschatz
• Household chores

Grammatik
• The verb **müssen** *to have to*

LANDESKUNDE **197**

Was tust du für die Umwelt?

Zweite Stufe **198**

So sagt man das!
• Talking about how often you have to do things
• Asking for and offering help and telling someone what to do

Wortschatz
• Time expressions

Grammatik
• The verb **können** *to be able to, can*
• The accusative pronouns **mich, dich, uns,** and **euch**

Dritte Stufe **202**

So sagt man das!
• Talking about the weather

Wortschatz
• Words to describe the weather
• Months

Grammatik
• Using present tense to express the future

ZUM LESEN: WEM HILFST DU? **206**

Reading articles from a German magazine about what teenagers do to help out

Reading Strategy: Finding relationships between ideas

MEHR GRAMMATIKÜBUNGEN **208**

ANWENDUNG **212**

Zum Schreiben: Making a writing plan
Writing a TV show script

KANN ICH'S WIRKLICH? **214**

WORTSCHATZ **215**

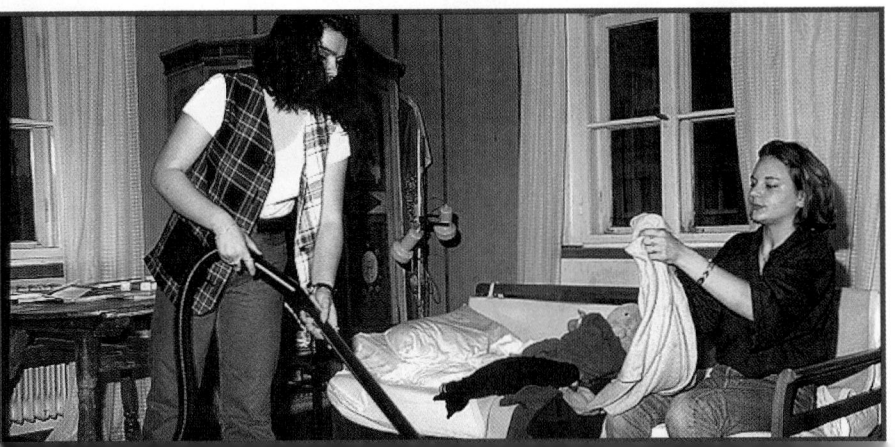

KAPITEL 8

CHAPTER OVERVIEW 215A
CHAPTER RESOURCES 215B
PROJECTS & GAMES 215C
STORYTELLING & TRADITIONS 215D

TECHNOLOGY 215E–215F
LISTENING SCRIPTS 215G–215H
50 MINUTE LESSON PLAN 215I–215J
90 MINUTE LESSON PLAN 215K–215L

TEACHING SUGGESTIONS 215M–215X

Einkaufen gehen 216

LOS GEHT'S! 218
Alles für die Oma!

Erste Stufe 221
So sagt man das!
• Asking what you should do
• Telling someone what to do

Wortschatz
• Groceries

Grammatik
• The verb **sollen** *should, supposed to*
• The **du**-command and **ihr**-command

LANDESKUNDE 225
Was machst du für andere Leute?

Zweite Stufe 226
So sagt man das!
• Talking about quantities
• Saying you want something else

Wortschatz
• Measurements

Dritte Stufe 229
So sagt man das!
• Giving reasons
• Saying where you were and what you bought

Wortschatz
• Time expressions

Grammatik
• The conjunctions **weil** and **denn**
• The past tense of **sein**

ZUM LESEN: RICHTIG ESSEN 234
Analyzing advertisements for food
Reading Strategy: Combining strategies

MEHR GRAMMATIKÜBUNGEN 236

ANWENDUNG 240
Zum Schreiben: Using the "5 W-How"
  Questions
Taking a nutrition survey

KANN ICH'S WIRKLICH? 242

WORTSCHATZ 243

KAPITEL 9

CHAPTER OVERVIEW 243A
CHAPTER RESOURCES 243B
PROJECTS & GAMES 243C
STORYTELLING & TRADITIONS 243D

TECHNOLOGY 243E–243F
LISTENING SCRIPTS 243G–243H
50 MINUTE LESSON PLAN 243I–243J
90 MINUTE LESSON PLAN ...243K–243L

TEACHING SUGGESTIONS 243M–243X

Amerikaner in München.....244

LOS GEHT'S! **246**
München besuchen

Erste Stufe **249**
So sagt man das!
• Talking about where something is located

Wortschatz
• Downtown places

Grammatik
• The verb **wissen** to know and dependent clauses with **wo**

LANDESKUNDE **252**
Was isst du gern?

Zweite Stufe **253**
So sagt man das!
• Asking for and giving directions

Wortschatz
• Phrases for giving directions

Grammatik
• The verbs **fahren** and **gehen**
• The formal commands with **Sie**

Dritte Stufe **257**
So sagt man das!
• Talking about what there is to eat and drink
• Saying you do or don't want more
• Expressing opinions

Grammatik
• The phrase **es gibt**
• Using **noch ein, kein**
• The conjunction **dass**

ZUM LESEN: EIN BUMMEL DURCH MÜNCHEN **262**
Reading excerpts from travel guides
Reading Strategy: Reading for a purpose

MEHR GRAMMATIKÜBUNGEN **264**

ANWENDUNG **268**
Zum Schreiben: Using drawings
Mapping and writing about your neighborhood

KANN ICH'S WIRKLICH? **270**

WORTSCHATZ **271**

Baden-Württemberg!

LOCATION • KAPITEL 10, 11, 12 272

LOCATION OPENER 271A–271B

KAPITEL 10

CHAPTER OVERVIEW 275A

CHAPTER RESOURCES 275B

PROJECTS & GAMES 275C

STORYTELLING & TRADITIONS 275D

TECHNOLOGY 275E–275F

LISTENING SCRIPTS 275G–275H

50 MINUTE LESSON PLAN 275I–275J

90 MINUTE LESSON PLAN ... 275K–275L

TEACHING SUGGESTIONS 275M–275X

Kino und Konzerte 276

LOS GEHT'S! 278

Wie verbringt ihr eure Freizeit?

Erste Stufe 281

So sagt man das!
• Expressing likes and dislikes
• Expressing familiarity

Wortschatz
• Movie genres
• Music

Grammatik
• The verb **mögen**
• The verb **kennen**

Zweite Stufe 285

So sagt man das!
• Expressing preferences and favorites

Wortschatz
• Adjectives for describing movies

Grammatik
• Using **lieber** and **am liebsten**
• The verb **sehen**

LANDESKUNDE 289

Welche kulturellen Veranstaltungen
besuchst du?

Dritte Stufe 290

So sagt man das!
• Talking about what you did in
your free time

Wortschatz
• Book genres

Grammatik
• The stem-changing verbs **lesen**
and **sprechen**

**ZUM LESEN: WAS SAGEN
DIE KRITIKER?** 294

Reading advertisements and reviews
for books, movies, and concerts

Reading Strategy: Recognizing false
cognates

MEHR GRAMMATIKÜBUNGEN 296

ANWENDUNG 300

Zum Schreiben: Using topic and
summary sentences

Writing publicity for a rock group

KANN ICH'S WIRKLICH? 302

WORTSCHATZ 303

KAPITEL 11

CHAPTER OVERVIEW 303A
CHAPTER RESOURCES 303B
PROJECTS & GAMES 303C
STORYTELLING & TRADITIONS 303D

TECHNOLOGY 303E–303F
LISTENING SCRIPTS 303G–303H
50 MINUTE LESSON PLAN 303I–303J
90 MINUTE LESSON PLAN ...303K–303L

TEACHING SUGGESTIONS 303M–303X

Der Geburtstag.....304

LOS GEHT'S! **306**
    Geschenke aussuchen

Erste Stufe **309**
    So sagt man das!
    • Using the telephone in Germany
    Wortschatz
    • Telephone vocabulary

Zweite Stufe **313**
    So sagt man das!
    • Inviting someone to a party and
      accepting or declining
    • Talking about birthdays and expressing
      good wishes
    Wortschatz
    • Ordinal numbers
    • Holidays

LANDESKUNDE **316**
    Was schenkst du zum Geburtstag?

Dritte Stufe **317**
    So sagt man das!
    • Discussing gift ideas
    Wortschatz
    • Popular gifts
    Grammatik
    • Introduction to the dative case

ZUM LESEN:
BILLIG EINKAUFEN GEHEN **322**
    Reading Strategy: Reading to
    understand ideas

MEHR GRAMMATIKÜBUNGEN **324**

ANWENDUNG **328**
    Zum Schreiben: Following logical order
    Writing a dialogue

KANN ICH'S WIRKLICH? **330**

WORTSCHATZ **331**

CHAPTER OVERVIEW 331A
CHAPTER RESOURCES 331B
PROJECTS & GAMES 331C
STORYTELLING & TRADITIONS 331D

TECHNOLOGY 331E–331F
LISTENING SCRIPTS 331G–331H
50 MINUTE LESSON PLAN 331I–331J
90 MINUTE LESSON PLAN 331K–331L

TEACHING SUGGESTIONS 331M–331X

Die Fete 332

LOS GEHT'S! 334
Die Geburtstagsfete

Erste Stufe 337
So sagt man das! (review)
• Offering help and explaining what to do
• Asking where something is located and giving directions
Wortschatz
• Ingredients
Grammatik (review)
• Personal pronouns, accusative case
• **können,** present tense
• **du/ihr**-commands
• **wissen,** present tense

LANDESKUNDE 341
Musst du zu Hause helfen?

Zweite Stufe 342
So sagt man das! (review)
• Making plans and inviting someone to come along
• Talking about clothing
• Discussing gift ideas
Wortschatz
• Places to go / things to do
• Words for describing clothes
Grammatik (review)
• The verbs **wollen** and **müssen,** present tense
• Definite and indefinite articles, nominative and accusative cases
• Personal pronouns, dative case

Dritte Stufe 346
So sagt man das! (review)
• Describing people and places
• Saying what you would like and whether you do or don't want more
• Talking about what you did
Wortschatz
• Furniture and kitchen appliances
Grammatik (review)
• Personal pronouns and possessives
• The **möchte**-forms
• **noch ein** and **kein**

ZUM LESEN: MAHLZEIT! 374
Reading German recipes
Reading Strategy: Using the main idea and context to determine meaning

MEHR GRAMMATIKÜBUNGEN 376

ANWENDUNG 380
Zum Schreiben: Combining sentences
Writing a descriptive letter

KANN ICH'S WIRKLICH? 382

WORTSCHATZ 383

REFERENCE SECTION
SUMMARY OF FUNCTIONS R3
ADDITIONAL VOCABULARY R9
GRAMMAR SUMMARY R15
GUIDE TO PRONUNCIATION FEATURES R27
VOCABULARY: GERMAN — ENGLISH R29
VOCABULARY: ENGLISH — GERMAN R47
GRAMMAR INDEX R55
ACKNOWLEDGMENTS AND CREDITS R59

Cultural References

Page numbers referring to material in the Pupil's Edition *appear in regular type.
When the material referenced is located in the* Teacher's Edition, *page numbers
appear in boldface type.*

ADDRESSING PEOPLE

Addressing parents **67T**
Definite articles with proper names 24
Formal address 52
Greetings: formal vs. informal 21

ADVERTISEMENTS

Realia: **Bäcker** 221
Realia: Clothing ads 133, 146, 344
Realia: Concert ads 174, 290
Realia: Daily specials board 240
Realia: Food ads 234
Realia: Furniture ads 347
Realia: Grocery ads 229
Realia: Housing ads 86
Realia: **Metzger** 221
Realia: Movie ads 287
Realia: Night spot ads 174
Realia: **Obst- und Gemüseladen** 221
Realia: Private schools and tutors 118
Realia: Restaurant ads 174
Realia: School supplies 114
Realia: **Supermarkt** 221

ARCHITECTURE

Bedrooms **67S**
Numbering of floors **67P**
Roofs made of reeds **95B**
Size of homes **67W**

BIRTHDAYS

Importance of birthdays 315
Interviews: **Was schenkst du zum
    Geburtstag?** 316
Realia: Invitation 313
Saints' Days 315

CASTLES AND PALACES

Altes Schloss in Meersburg, Baden-
    Württemberg 273, **271A**
Branitz Palace, Cottbus 14, **11B**
Cecilienhof Palace, Potsdam 15, **11B**
Sanssouci Palace, Potsdam 12, 14, **11A, 11B**
Wartburg, Thüringen 1, **T76**

CHURCHES

Frauenkirche, Munich 186, 256, **183B**
Realia: **Peterskirche,** Munich 263
Pfarrkirche Heiliger Geist **183A**
Theatinerkirche, Munich 256, **183A**

CINEMA

see also Advertisements

Admission prices 283
Dubbing and subtitles 283
Realia: Movie listings 283
Realia: Movie reviews 294
Rating system 283

CLOTHING

see also Advertisements

Realia: European-U.S. size chart 138
Realia: Fashion review 152
Gamsbart **183B**
Realia: Magazine excerpts 146
Regional clothing **127M, 183B**
Sizes 138
Stores *(see Shopping)*
Interview: **Welche Klamotten sind „in"?** 142

COATS OF ARMS

Baden-Württemberg **271A**
Bayern **183A**
Brandenburg **11A**
Schleswig-Holstein **95A**

ENTERTAINMENT

see also Advertisements, Cinema, Music, Sports and Activities

Realia: **Bestsellers** 290

Realia: **Book reviews** 294

Postal office role in broadcasting **267I**

Realia: **Video-Hits** 290

Interview: **Was machst du in deiner Freizeit?** . . . 169

Interview: **Welche kulturellen Veranstaltungen
besuchst du?** 289

ENVIRONMENT

Education **303W**

Recycling 197

Interview: **Was tust du für die Umwelt?** 197

FOOD

see also Advertisements and Recipes

Aale 96

Almonds **331W**

Bowle **331N**

Buttermilchsuppe 96

Gefüllte Eier **331V, 331W**

Hühnerfrikassee 13, **11A**

Kaiserschmarren **215N**

Krabben 96

Leberkäse 184, 257

Linseneintopf 12, **11A**

Matjes 96, **95A**

Maultaschen **243P**, 272, **271B**, **303D**

Quark **215S**

Räucherspeck 96

Rote Grütze 96, **95A**

Schinken 272

Schwarzwälder Kirschtorte 272, **271B**

Schweinshaxe 184

Spätzle 272, **271B**

Torte vs. **Kuchen** **215O**

Interview: **Was isst du gern?** 252

Weights and measures 226, 227

Weißwürste 184, **183A**

GERMAN INFLUENCE IN AMERICA

Family Names 10

Foods 10

Germantown, PA 10

Immigration 10, **T74**

Industry and technology 10

Town Names 10

Traditions 10

Words and Phrases 10

GIFTS

Realia: **Hilfe per Telefon** 318

Saints' Days **303R**

Sending cards **303P**

Typical gift ideas 317, 345

HISTORY

*see also Castles, Churches, Coats of Arms, German
Influence in America, People, Points of Interest, Statues*

Foreign workers in Germany **67Q**

Potsdam Agreement **11B**

Use of Latin **95A**

HOLIDAYS

Realia: **Fasching** 262

Realia: **Greeting cards** 315

Maibaum **183B**

HOME AND FAMILY LIFE

Addresses 93

Chores 193

Family members 81

Living in same building as your business **95B**

Interview: **Musst du zu Hause helfen?** 341

Pets 201

Preference for small refrigerators 222

Privacy **67M**

Interview: **Was machst du für andere Leute?** . . . 225

Realia: **Wem hilfst du?** 206

Interview: **Wo wohnst du?** 77

LEGENDS

Lorelei **271B**

Küchenhexe **271B**

MAPS

Central Europe 1

Federal Republic of Germany 2

German **Bundesländer** and **Hauptstädte** 27

Liechtenstein, Switzerland, and Austria 3

Mittersendling 253
Munich. 249
Stuttgart 356
Weather map 202, 213

MONEY

Currency 115
Euro. 115, **99U**
Postal savings account. **243O**
Prices.. 115
Realia: **Umrechnungstabelle**. 134
Wages.. . . . . **155V**

MUSEUMS

Alte Pinakothek, Munich. **183A**
Bezirksmuseum **11B**
Deutsches Museum, Munich. **183A**
Glyptothek, Munich. **183A**
Neue Pinakothek, Munich. **183A**

MUSIC

see also Advertisements
Realia: Eninger Jazz Festival.. 60
Falco.. . . . . **303M**
Realia: Music reviews.. 294
Popular music 283
Realia: Pop music chart 283
Realia: **Uni Sommerfest** 61

NAMES

First names.. 7
Last names. 10

NUMBERS

Counting on the fingers 9
Use of comma and period in numbers. **67W**
Written numbers 9, **67U**

PARKS

Englischer Garten, Munich 262
Hofgarten, Munich. 256

PEOPLE

Fürst Hans Adam II **T77**
Ludwig van Beethoven 5
Annette von Droste-Hülshoff. 5, **271A**

Albert Einstein. 5
Dwight D. Eisenhower **T80**
G.D. Fahrenheit. **187T**
Anna Freud 5
Sigmund Freud 5
Friedrich II (Friedrich der Große) . . . **11A, 11B, 67D**
Steffi Graf. 5
Günther Grass 5
Heinrich von Kleist. **11A**
George Wenzeslaus von Knobelsdorff **11A**
Herzog Heinrich der Löwe **183A**
Freiherr Joseph von Laßberg **271A**
John "Blackjack" Pershing. **T80**
Joseph Uphues **11B**
Wilhelm I **67N**

POINTS OF INTEREST

see also Castles, Churches, Museums, Parks,
Statues, and Theaters
Altes Rathaus, Munich 187
Austria **15S**
Babelsberg. **67N**
Baden-Württemberg. **271A**
Berlin Wall, Berlin 10
Besigheim an der Enz, Baden-Württemberg. . . . 274
Black Forest. **271A**
Brandenburg. **11A**
Brandenburg Gate, Berlin 4, **T77**
Cottbus **11A**
Englischer Garten, Munich **243M**
Fischmarkt, Hamburg. 166, 280
Frankfurt an der Oder **11A**
Heidelberg. **271B**
Hexenloch Mühle, Baden-Württemberg 274
Hexenwegle in Bietigheim,
    Baden–Württemberg. 275
Holstentor, Lübeck. 96, **95A**
Innsbruck, Austria. 1, **T76**
Realia: **Isar-Floßfahrt** 263
Isar, Munich **183A**
Karlsruhe **271B**
Kiel **95B**
Kieler Woche 98, **91B, 99D**
Königstraße, Stuttgart 356

Liechtenstein **T77**

Lübeck **95A**

Marienplatz, Munich **234M,** 187, **183B**

Matterhorn 1, 4, **T76, T78**

Maximilianeum, Munich **183A**

Maypole 186

Munich **183A**

Nordfriesland **95B**

North Frisian house 98

Oder-Havel-Kanal **11B**

Old City Hall, Munich **183B**

Realia: **Olympiapark,** Munich 263

Potsdam **67O**

Rathaus, Bietigheim 275

Reepschlägerhaus, Wedel 99

Salzspeicher, Lübeck **95A**

Ship hoist at Niederfinow, Brandenburg 15, **11B**

St. Märgen **271B**

Stuttgart **271A**

Switzerland **15S**

Unter den Linden, Berlin **T76**

Vaduz, Liechtenstein 4

Viktualienmarkt, Munich 187

Village in the Black Forest 274

Wedel **95B**

Westerhaver Leuchtturm 98

RECIPES

Bayerischer Wurstsalat **187D**

Dittmarscher Mehlbeutel **155D**

Holsteiner Buchweizenklöße **99D**

Kaiserschmarrn **215D**

Kartoffelpuffer **67D**

Kartoffelsuppe **15D**

Königsberger Klopse **41D**

Kopfsalat in Sahnesoße **127D**

Maultaschen **303D**

Schwäbischer Zwiebelkuchen **331D**

Schweinsbraten **243D**

Spätzle **275D**

Realia: **Apfelküchle** 338

Realia: **Gefüllte Eier** 350

Realia: **Käsespätzle** 338

Realia: **Kartoffelsalat mit Speck** 350

Realia: **Mandelkuchen** 351

Realia: **Obstsalat** 241

Realia: **Pikanter Quark** 228

Realia: **Salami-Riesenpizza** 228

RESTAURANTS AND CAFES

see also Advertisements

Realia: **Café am Markt** menu 160

Realia: **Café Freizeit Imbisskarte** 170

How food is served **155T**

Imbissstube **243S**

Realia: **Imbissstand** menu 181

Realia: **Milchbar** 175

Mineral water vs. tap water 75

Realia: Restaurant check 172

Realia: **Speisekarte** 348

Teestuben **155M**

Tipping 173

RHYMES AND SAYINGS

**Der April macht die Blumen und der
Mai hat den Dank dafür** **187U**

Erst die Arbeit, dann das Vergnügen **187P**

Höflichkeit ist Trumpf **15O**

Ohne Fleiß, kein Preis **187P**

**Wenn der Hahn kräht auf dem Mist, ändert sich das
Wetter, oder es bleibt wie es ist!** **187U**

SCHOOL LIFE

see also Sports and Activities

Au pair **187W**

Breaks **99Q**

Foreign students **15N**

Grading system 111, **99S**

Klassenlehrer **99O**

Lockers **99M**

Nachhilfestunden **187W**

Parallelklassen **99O**

Religion **99O**

School day 106

Realia: **Schülerausweis** 38

Realia: **Stundenplan** 105

Interviews: **Was sind deine Lieblingsfächer?** 113

Realia: **Zeugnis** 111, 124

SHOPPING

see also Advertisements

Baking powder packaging. **331W**
Realia: **Billig einkaufen gehen** 322
Egg packaging. **215O**
Realia: **Einkaufszettel** 227
Realia: **Kaufhäuser** 263
Ladenschlussgesetz **215V**
Realia: **Lebensmittel** 262
Realia: **Medizinische Versorgung** 263
Sales **127W**
Schaufensterbummeln **215U**
Schreibwarenladen **99U**
Store hours 136, **127Q**
Supermarkets vs. small specialty stores. 222
Viktualien **183B**

SOCIAL CUSTOMS

Informal names. **67T**

SPORTS AND ACTIVITIES

After-school. **155S**
Realia: **Badminton** 61
Realia: Ballooning 60
Realia: **Jugendzentrum** 343
Realia: **Polo mit Eskimorolle** 343
Realia: **Rollschuh laufen** 260
Soccer. **41M**
Realia: **Schach** 61
Realia: **Skat** 60
Sports and hobbies 51
Interviews: **Was machst du in
deiner Freizeit?** 169

STATUES

Frederick the Great, Potsdam 14, **11B**
Roland, Wedel 99, **95B**

TELEPHONE

Telephone advertisement **303P**
Answering the phone **303N**
Calling Germany 311

Cost of calling **303M**
Realia: **Gesprächs-Notiz** 312
Realia: Making a phone call in Germany 309

TEMPERATURE

Celsius vs. Fahrenheit. 204
Realia: **Durchschnittstemperaturen** 262

THEATERS

Movie theaters **275M**
State Opera, Vienna. 4, **T78**

TIME

Realia: Calendar page for **März**. 212
Clocks 163, **155P**
Informal time 162
Twenty-four hour time 107
Realia: Weekly planner page 56, 167

TRADITIONS

Friedrich der Große **67D**
Kaiser Wilhelm II. *(his favorite food)* **15D**
Kaiserschmarrn *(its origin)* **215D**
Kieler Woche **99D**
Literatur und Essen **331D**
Die Mönche von Maulbronn **303D**
Nudelwochen **15D**
Schleswig-Holsteins Küche **99D**
Schwaben in der Literatur **275D**
Wattwandern **127D**

TRANSPORTATION

Getting a driver's license **15M**
Intercity-Express train 4, **T77**
Realia: **Stadtbus Schülerausweis** 124
Realia: Train schedule 107
Interview: **Wie kommst du zur Schule?** 31

Preliminary Chapter: Vorschau
Chapter Overview

CONTENTS

MAP OF CENTRAL EUROPE **T82**

MAP OF THE FEDERAL REPUBLIC OF GERMANY **2**

MAP OF LIECHTENSTEIN, SWITZERLAND, AND AUSTRIA **3**

SCHON EINMAL GESEHEN? **4**

BEKANNTE LEUTE **5**

DAS ALPHABET **6**

WIE HEISST DU? **7**

IM KLASSENZIMMER **8**

DIE ZAHLEN VON 0 BIS 20 . . . . **9**

WARUM DEUTSCH LERNEN? **10**

TIPPS FÜRS DEUTSCHLERNEN **11**

Teaching Resources
pp. T76–11

PRINT
▶ Lesson Planner, pp. x–1
▶ Übungsheft, pp. 1–2
▶ Listening Activities, p. 2

MEDIA
▶ One-Stop Planner
▶ Teaching Transparencies
  Maps 1 and 2
▶ Audio Compact Discs, CD 1, Trs. 1–8

Matterhorn, southwest of Zermatt

VORSCHAU

Teacher Notes

- The **Vorschau** is meant to be an introduction to the study of German. Students should not be expected to fully master the material. We recommend spending no more than three class periods on the **Vorschau.**
- The script for Activity 1 can be found on p. 15H.

▶ PAGE 1

THE PHOTOGRAPHS AND MAPS

Building Context

Ask students to brainstorm and write down their ideas about the following question: "What comes to mind when you think of the German-speaking countries or the German language?" (Examples: German cars, foods, tennis players)

Background Information

1 This photograph depicts the Matterhorn.

2 This photograph depicts the city of Innsbruck. It was the site of the 1964 and 1976 Winter Olympics.

3 This photograph depicts the castle Wartburg in Eisenach, Germany. The Wartburg was commissioned in 1067 by Ludwig der Springer. According to legend, he is said to have exclaimed, **"Wart Berg, du sollst mir eine Burg werden!"**, hence the name Wartburg. The castle is situated 400 meters high on a rocky slope, and in its 900-year history, it has never been besieged, conquered, or destroyed. Martin Luther went into hiding at the Wartburg in 1521 under the alias "Junker Jörg." During the time he was at the Wartburg, Luther translated the Bible. This interior section of the Wartburg was built in the **Fachwerk** style. **Fachwerk** is a building style consisting of a framework of straight and crossed beams in which the area between the beams is filled in with clay or bricks. This style of architecture reached its high point in the 16th and 17th centuries.

Cultures and Communities

Teaching Suggestion

1 Before students listen to the recording, ask them to locate the countries where German is spoken. Then ask them also to point out the capital of each country.

Background Information

1 After students have done Activity 1, you might want to tell them about the following landmark.

Unter den Linden: a boulevard starting at the Brandenburg Gate which becomes Karl Liebknecht Straße at the Schloßplatz and was considered for the past 250 years to be the most beautiful street in Berlin.

Connections and Comparisons

Music Connection

1 Ask students if they know of a very famous composer who lived in Salzburg. (Mozart) Ask them if they can mention some of his works. (Examples: *Eine kleine Nachtmusik* and operas such as *Die Zauberflöte* and *Don Giovanni*)

Teaching Suggestion

1 Have students scan the map facing p. 1 and identify two geographical features (lakes, rivers, mountains, islands, coastlines) that also occur in the students' own geographic region. Next, ask them to identify two features that are unfamiliar.

▶ PAGES 2–3

Connections and Comparisons

Geography Connection

Ask students to locate the rivers that were mentioned in Activity 1: **der Rhein, die Donau, die Elbe,** and **die Oder.** Ask them why these rivers play such an enormous role in the country's economy. (Examples: transportation, commerce) Can they think of rivers in the United States of similar importance? (Examples: Mississippi, Missouri, Saint Lawrence, Ohio)

Connections and Comparisons

Geography Connection

The activity on p. 1 gave students examples of well-known ski resorts. Give students examples such as **St. Moritz** and **Zermatt** and have students find them on a map.

Multicultural Connection

Point out to students that Liechtenstein is a monarchy led by **Fürst Hans Adam II.** Ask students what other countries have a monarch. (Examples: Japan, Morocco, England, Sweden, Monaco, Belgium, The Netherlands, Denmark) Ask students if they know what type of government the other German-speaking countries have. (parliamentary democracies)

> **PAGE 4**

THE PHOTOGRAPHS
Background Information

1 Germany's highways are choking with automobiles, and the sky is crowded with air traffic during the day. (Many cities do not permit flights in or out of their airports between 10 P.M. and 6 A.M.) Therefore, trains are a vital part of Germany's transportation system. The ICE, or Intercity-Express, which is considerably faster than the automobile and therefore competitive with the airlines, began service in 1991. It runs between Europe's largest cities. In order to accommodate speeds of up to 406 km/h or 250 mph and to make the rails as straight as possible, new railroad beds had to be built, along with new bridges and tunnels. Since reunification, under *Verkehrsprojekte Deutsche Einheit,* Germany has invested more than 68 billion marks, (about 34 billion euros) to rebuild the infrastructure in the states in the east and to reconnect them to the states in the west. Over 50 percent of this amount was spent on railway infrastructure. Five thousand kilometers of railways were renewed. As an example of how fast travelling has become, it now takes only 2 hours and 15 minutes to go from Hamburg to Berlin-Zoo Mitte Station.

Cultures and Communities

Culture Note

Tell students that the railway system is the largest transportation enterprise in Germany. It is currently owned and operated by the federal government but will soon be privatized.

2 The **Brandenburger Tor** was built between 1788 and 1791 by architect Carl Gotthard Langhans and first named **Friedenstor.** It was modeled after the Propylaea of the Acropolis in Athens, Greece. It is the only one remaining of 18 original gates in Berlin.

Cultures and Communities

City walls originated in medieval times when many cities in Europe erected them as a defense against invaders. Gates became important because they were the only ways to enter and leave the towns. As cities expanded beyond the confines of the original walls, the walls were often torn down, but many of the gates survived.

Connections and Comparisons

Multicultural Connection

Have students compare the Brandenburg Gate to similar structures in other parts of the world. Examples might be the Great Wall of China and the fortifications of Zimbabwe in Africa. The Great Wall of China is a 30-ft. high fortification that runs for 1,500 miles from the Yellow Sea westward deep into central Asia. In the 3rd century B.C., Shih Huang Ti, the first emperor of united China, connected a number of existing walls into a single system to keep out barbarian tribes. The Great Wall remains the largest structure ever built. Zimbabwe (Bantu for "stone dwelling") was a large fortified city, now in ruins, located southeast of Nyanda in the modern African country of Zimbabwe. Between the 11th and the 15th centuries, Zimbabwe, with its impressive fortifications, was the center of a large empire.

3 Liechtenstein's history dates back as far as 800 B.C., but the principality was not officially founded until 1719. The country's government is headed by a male-line monarch. The present head, Prince Hans Adam II, shares the governmental power with the Liechtenstein parliament, which is elected directly by the public. Despite its small size (comparable to Washington, D.C.), Liechtenstein is one of the most highly industrialized countries. It has a population of 30,000. The capital, Vaduz, with a population of approximately 5,000, is the seat of government and the residence of the monarch and his family. The largest number of visitors to Liechtenstein come from Switzerland, Germany, and the United States, primarily for the alpine sports.

4 The Matterhorn (14,691 ft/4,478 m) is a mountain located along the border between Switzerland and Italy. It owes its German name (it is called *Mont Cervin* in French and *Monte Cervino* in Italian) to the Swiss village of Zermatt (Zer**matt**/**Matt**erhorn) located 6 mi/10 km from the mountain.

5 The State Opera in Vienna (**Wiener Oper**) was built in the 1860s and was faithfully reconstructed after it was destroyed in World War II. Performance season is September through June with performances daily.

Connections and Comparisons

Geography Connection

Have students look up the height of the Matterhorn in an encyclopedia or an atlas. (14,691 ft/4,478 m) Ask them to compare this peak to some American mountains. (Examples: Pikes Peak in Colorado 14,110 ft/4,301 m; Mount Shasta in California 14,162 ft/4,316 m; Mount McKinley in Alaska 20,320 ft/6,194 m, the highest in the United States and in North America)

Multicultural Connection

Like the Matterhorn, other mountains across the world have become identified with a particular culture or country. Mount Fuji in Japan, for example, is often used as a symbol of the Japanese people and culture. Your students may be able to suggest other mountains that are closely identified with a particular country or culture. (Examples: Olympus in Greece; Kilimanjaro in Tanzania; Popocatépetl in Mexico; Everest in Nepal; Etna in Italy)

PAGE 5

Teaching Suggestion

Have students look at the pictures on p. 5. Ask them which people they recognize. What can they tell you about them? Which areas of "culture" do these people represent? (science, music, literature, sports, psychology, and so on) Ask students if they know of any other famous German-speaking people.

Communication for All Students

Challenge

Have students choose a famous German-speaking person and write a short report explaining this person's contribution. Students may also give an oral presentation about that person.

PAGE 6

DAS ALPHABET
Teaching Suggestion

2 After students have listened to the rhyme, let them practice spelling their names. (Later when students have chosen their German names, you could ask them to spell those out as well.) As students get more comfortable with the sounds, they can then play the following game for auditory learners.

Game

Divide the class into two teams. One person from each team comes up to the board. As you spell a word in German, the contestants write each letter on the board. Each student who spells the word correctly wins a point for his or her team. At the conclusion of each round, have students spell the words aloud.

Language Note

3 The abbreviations in Activity 3 stand for the following: VW=Volkswagen; BMW=Bayerische Motorenwerke; BRD=Bundesrepublik Deutschland; ADAC=Allgemeiner Deutscher Automobil Club; BASF=Badische Anilin- und Soda-Fabrik. Here are some other frequently used abbreviations: Kfz=Kraftfahrzeug *(motor vehicle)*; LKW=Lastkraftwagen *(semitrailer)*; DSB=Deutscher Sportbund *(German athletic association)*.

PAGE 7

WIE HEIßT DU?
Teaching Suggestion

4 After the listening activity, distribute index cards to be used as name tags by the students. Before students choose a German name, address the girls in class and read them the list of female names. While the girls are choosing their names, address the boys in the class and read all the male names to them. Then go around the class and repeat any names that students have problems with as they decide on their names.

IM KLASSENZIMMER

Teaching Suggestion

7 Have signs with the corresponding German words on them taped to key objects in the classroom. Point to the signs as you pronounce the names of the objects. Repeat them several times. Remove signs shortly before doing Activity 7b.

Communication for All Students

Kinesthetic Learners

8 Explain to students the expressions **Bitte zeig auf …!** and **Bitte zeigt auf …!** to prepare for the following TPR activity. Model the appropriate action by repeating the command and carrying it out. Then motion for the class to imitate the action. Repeat commands several times. (Examples: **Zeig …/ Zeigt …/ auf die Tafel/ auf den Schreibtisch/ auf Kelly/ auf Steve!**)

TPR **Total Physical Response**
A simple way to introduce the **Ausdrücke fürs Klassenzimmer** is to teach them through TPR. Model the commands for the students and then have them follow your commands.

DIE ZAHLEN VON 0–20

Motivating Activity

Write the following numbers on the board: **24.8.88** (birthday given in order of date, month, and year); **24109 Kiel** (a ZIP code of Kiel); **0431/ 322370** (area code and phone number). Then ask students what they think the numbers correspond to. Students don't need to know how to say the numbers in German. This should only show them that numbers can be used in different ways in different countries.

Teaching Suggestion

9 Ask students to look at the handwritten numbers on the page and to compare the way Germans write numbers with the way people do in the United States.

Communication for All Students

Kinesthetic Learners

Bring a ball (soccer ball, tennis ball) to class. Throw the ball to individual students and ask them to bounce the ball as many times as the number between 0 and 20 that you call out in German. (If you call out **dreizehn**, the student bounces the ball 13 times.) You could also ask the student or the whole class to count aloud in German while the ball is being bounced. As a variation to this game, students could pass or throw the ball from person to person—the person catching the ball says the next number in the sequence.

Auditory Learners

10 After students have completed Activity 10c, ask them to stand up. Read off a list of your students' phone numbers, which you might have recorded on the first day of class. (If you don't have a list, ask your students to write their phone numbers on a slip of paper before beginning this activity.) When a student hears his or her number, he or she can sit down.

Teacher Note

When giving assignments that entail the disclosure of personal information, keep in mind that some students and their families may consider family matters private.

Reteaching: Numbers and Letters

Write the following German license plates on the board and have students read them aloud. This will help students review numbers, letters, and abbreviations. You might want to go over the abbreviations quickly first and point out that license plates in Germany always indicate the city where the car was registered.

KI – AM 199	(Kiel)
M – FB 345	(München)
K – NM 028	(Köln)
NMS – CG 607	(Neumünster)

VORSCHAU

WARUM DEUTSCH LERNEN?

Cultures and Communities

Culture Note

• Between 1830 and 1890, more than one-fourth of all immigrants to the United States were German. The peak years for German immigration were 1881–90, when 1,452,970 Germans came to America. In America, most Germans settled in the "German triangle," an area bounded by the three cities of Saint Louis, Cincinnati, and Milwaukee; however, German settlers could also be found across the country in places as distant as Anaheim, California, and areas around San Antonio, Texas. At one point, there were seventy-four daily and nearly four hundred weekly German newspapers published in America.

• In addition to such institutions of American life as kindergartens and delicatessens, the immigrants from Germany made other significant contributions ranging from the Kentucky rifle, a mainstay of colonial frontiersmen, to the Conestoga wagons in which pioneers moved west.

• Ironically, two of the most famous German-Americans, John "Blackjack" Pershing and Dwight D. Eisenhower, rose to national prominence because of their military leadership in World Wars I and II—against German forces. For additional information on German immigration, you may wish to consult *Coming to America: A History of Immigration and Ethnicity in American Life,* by Roger Daniels. © 1991 by Harper Perennial.

Thinking Critically

Drawing Inferences Ask students why they think some Germans decided to leave Germany and immigrate to the United States. Ask them when most Germans came to the United States. (Examples: overcrowding in Germany and availability of land in the United States; religious and political persecution; large influx of German immigrants from mid-19th century to World War I)

Connections and Comparisons

Geography Connection

Have students look at a map of the United States and look for other cities with German names.

Connections and Comparisons

Language Note

Ask students if they can think of any other German words that have been incorporated into the English language. (Examples: **Holstein, Gesundheit, Muesli, Sauerkraut, kaputt**)

Teaching Suggestion

You might want to give students extra credit for doing the following assignment. Have the whole class make a bulletin board display of famous German-Americans. Here are a few suggestions: Levi Strauss, Wernher von Braun, John Jacob Astor, Friedrich Wilhelm von Steuben, Maximilian Berlitz, Henry Kissinger, and Arnold Schwarzenegger, who is of Austrian descent. Students could group these famous people according to categories, for example, sports, politics, or science.

COMMUNITY LINK

If possible you might ask some guest speakers to come to your class and talk about the importance of German in their careers.

Group Work

Ask students to look through the classified ad section of a major newspaper and find advertised jobs that require another language. This should be done at home. Or you may want to collect the ads yourself and make them available to the class. Next put students in groups of three or four and give each group three or four ads. Each student in the group looks at every ad, and students as a group collect the following data: job title, job description, qualifications needed, and name of business or organization offering the job. Next you might have students brainstorm additional careers in which German or any other language would be necessary or be a valuable asset. Have every group present its list of jobs to the class, and the whole class can vote on the job for which they would most like to apply.

Teacher Note

There are many German-owned companies throughout the United States, with a large number of them located in New York, California, Illinois, Georgia, Texas, and New Jersey. Thus the demand for German language proficiency is high.

VORSCHAU

Cultures and Communities

Teaching Suggestion

Tell students that part of learning a language is also learning about the people who speak it. Knowledge of current events is therefore an asset. Ask students always to be on the lookout for news from any of the German-speaking countries, whether it is from TV or the newspaper. If they see or hear of news, they should report it briefly in class the next day. Students can also be encouraged to bring in newspaper clippings or short summaries of news reports. You can display these on a special bulletin board in your classroom labeled **Nachrichten aus deutschsprachigen Ländern.** Give extra credit for student participation in this ongoing project.

Connections and Comparisons

History Connection

• Ask students what the abbreviation UN stands for. Ask them what the purpose of the United Nations is.

• Ask students if they know when the Berlin Wall came down. (Nov. 9, 1989) Ask them what this symbolizes and what the historical significance of this event is.

Thinking Critically

Drawing Inferences Ask students to talk about the implications of other late twentieth-century events in Germany and the rest of Europe. (Examples: the spelling reform and downsizing of government-run systems in Germany, the lowering of trade barriers within Europe and the introduction of the euro, the expansion of NATO to Eastern Europe, the introduction of a UN peacekeeping force to the Balkans) Discuss with students some of the ways in which they may be directly affected by these events. (Examples: German textbooks have changed; a greater degree of European economic unity may affect prices on goods sold in this country.)

▶ PAGE 11

TIPPS FÜRS DEUTSCHLERNEN

Teaching Suggestions

• After introducing students to the paragraph on speaking, suggest that students always greet you and the other German students in German, even outside the classroom.

• For additional authentic listening, provide students occasionally with popular German songs and accompanying lyrics.

• Tell students that an excellent way to "connect" is in the oral and written portfolios they will soon start developing, the **Notizbuch** they will keep throughout the year, and the Process Writing activities (**Zum Schreiben**) they will start working on in Chapter 3. These will provide opportunities to experiment with the language. For more information on portfolios, please refer to the essay on pp. T40–T41 and the *Alternative Assessment Guide.* The **Notizbuch** is a personal diary in which students will be asked to write in German. There will be at least one **Notizbuch** activity per chapter. In the Process Writing activities, students are given a writing topic and a series of tasks that progress through the steps of prewriting, writing, and revising. Each topic has been carefully chosen to relate to the theme and the functions of each chapter. The tasks chosen encourage students to write about aspects of the topic that inspire or interest them personally. In addition, each **Zum Schreiben** activity focuses on one **Schreibtipp,** or writing strategy, that will help students develop their writing skills.

• If you have access to magazines, newspapers, or any other realia from German-speaking countries, make them available to your students. This will provide students with additional authentic input. Look on pp. T48–T49 for useful addresses where you can obtain such information.

VORSCHAU

1 **Matterhorn, Schweiz**

2 **Innsbruck, Österreich**

3 **Wartburg, Deutschland**

Komm mit!

German is the native language of nearly 100 million people in Austria, Germany, Switzerland, Liechtenstein, and parts of France and Italy. It is an official language of Luxembourg and is used as a second language by many other people in central Europe.

1 **Komm mit!** *Come along!*

CD1
Tr. 1

You are now going to take a trip to the German-speaking countries of **Deutschland**, **Österreich**, **Schweiz**, and **Liechtenstein**. As you listen to a description of these countries, try to locate on the map the places mentioned. When you have finished, do the following activities.

1. Find and identify: Possible answers: Frankreich, Niederlande, Belgien
   a. a non-German-speaking country west of Germany
   b. a river that runs through Germany, Austria, and Hungary Donau (Danube)

   Possible answers Hamburg, Bremen, Kiel; Wien, Salzburg; Vaduz

   c. a city in northern Germany; in Austria; in Liechtenstein

2. a. Look at the map on page 2. What three German cities have the status of city-states? Hamburg, Bremen, Berlin
   b. Look at the map on page 3. What is the name of the mountain peak southwest of Zermatt, Switzerland? Matterhorn

Bundesrepublik Deutschland
The Federal Republic of Germany

DÄNEMARK

Ostsee

N

Nordsee

0 50 100 Kilometer
0 50 100 Meilen

Kiel

SCHLESWIG-HOLSTEIN

Rostock

Lübeck

MECKLENBURG-VORPOMMERN

HAMBURG

Schwerin

Neubrandenburg

Elbe

BREMEN

Havel

POLEN

NIEDERSACHSEN

Weser

BUNDESREPUBLIK

BRANDENBURG

Oder

Ems

Teutoburger Wald

Hannover

BERLIN

Braunschweig

Potsdam

Frankfurt a.d. Oder

NIEDERLANDE

Magdeburg

Oder

Rhein

Münster

SACHSEN-ANHALT

Spree

NORDRHEIN-WESTFALEN

Harz

Elbe

Cottbus

Essen Dortmund

DEUTSCHLAND

Halle

Neiße

Ruhrgebiet

Kassel

Saale

Leipzig

Neuss Düsseldorf

Erfurt

SACHSEN

Dresden

Köln

Gera

Chemnitz

Aachen

Thüringer Wald

THÜRINGEN

Erzgebirge

Bonn

HESSEN

BELGIEN

Eifel *Westerwald*

Suhl

Rhein

Taunus

Koblenz

Oberpfälzer Wald

RHEINLAND-PFALZ

Frankfurt a. M.

Mosel

Wiesbaden

TSCHECHISCHE REPUBLIK

LUX.

Mainz

Main

Würzburg

Böhmerwald

Mannheim

SAARLAND

Nürnberg

Bayerischer Wald

Saarbrücken

Heidelberg

BADEN-WÜRTTEMBERG

BAYERN

Karlsruhe

Regensburg

Stuttgart

Schwäbische Alb

Donau

Rhein

Neckar

Ulm

Isar

FRANKREICH

Schwarzwald

Augsburg

Freiburg

München

Rhein

Salzburger Alpen

Bodensee

Bayerische Alpen

Zugspitze

SCHWEIZ

Rhein

ÖSTERREICH

Liechtenstein, Schweiz und Österreich
Liechtenstein, Switzerland, and Austria

Map of Austria and Switzerland

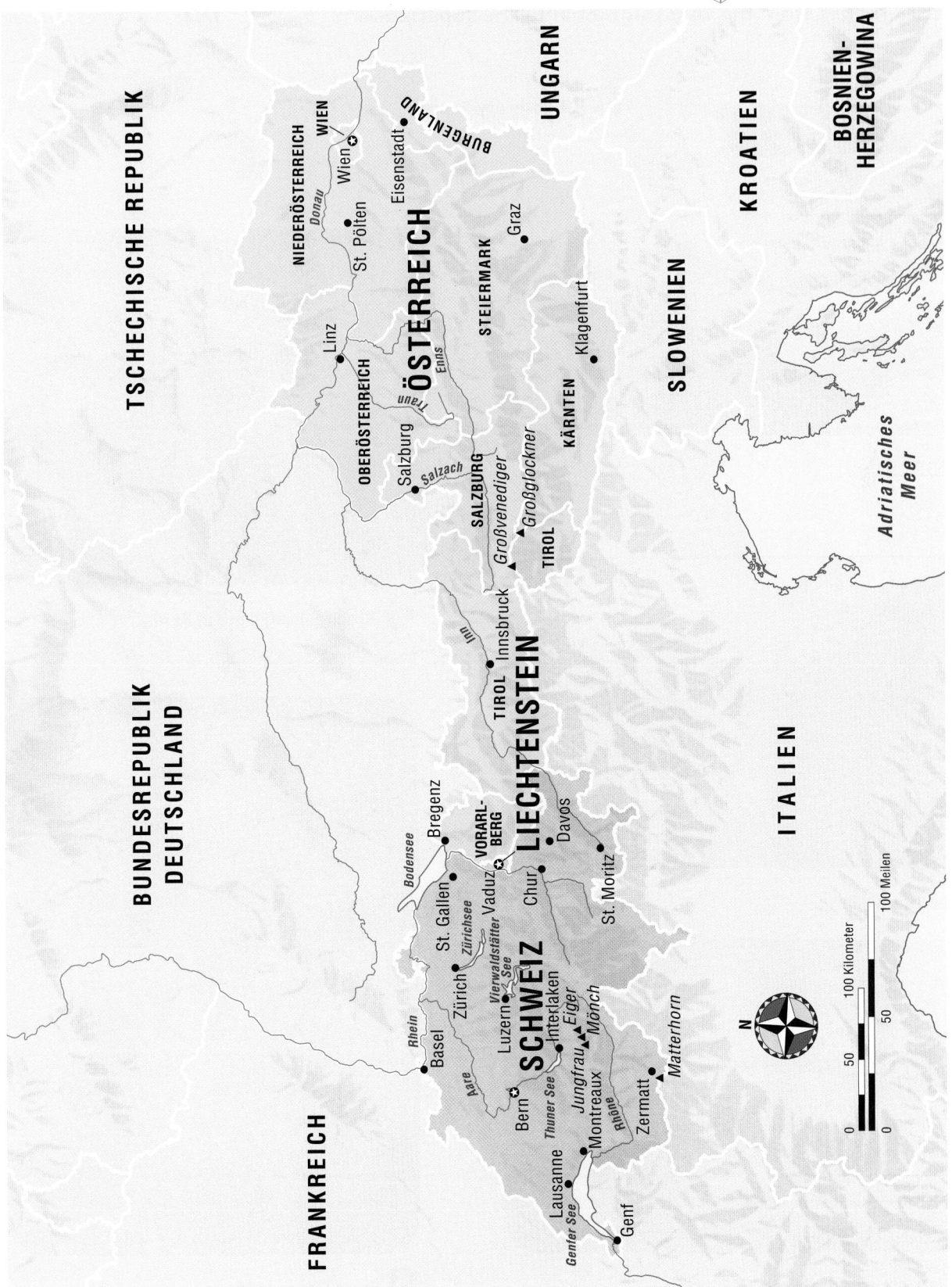

TSCHECHISCHE REPUBLIK

BUNDESREPUBLIK DEUTSCHLAND

FRANKREICH

WIEN

NIEDERÖSTERREICH

Donau

Wien

St. Pölten

Eisenstadt

BURGENLAND

ÖSTERREICH

UNGARN

Linz

Enns

OBERÖSTERREICH

STEIERMARK

Graz

Traun

Salzburg

Salzach

SALZBURG

Großvenediger

Großglockner

TIROL

KÄRNTEN

Klagenfurt

SLOWENIEN

KROATIEN

BOSNIEN-
HERZEGOWINA

Inn

Innsbruck

TIROL

LIECHTENSTEIN

ITALIEN

Adriatisches Meer

Bregenz

Bodensee

VORARL-
BERG

Vaduz

Davos

Chur

St. Moritz

Rhein

St. Gallen

Zürich

Zürichsee

Vierwaldstätter See

Luzern

Interlaken

Thuner See

Bern

SCHWEIZ

Eiger

Mönch

Jungfrau

Matterhorn

Basel

Aare

Montreux

Rhône

Zermatt

Lausanne

Genter See

Genf

N

100 Kilometer

100 Meilen

50

50

50

0

0

Schon einmal gesehen? ▪ *Seen before?*

There are many things that may come to mind when you hear of places like Germany, Switzerland, Austria, and Liechtenstein. As you can see from these photos, life in these countries ranges from the very traditional to the supermodern.

1 ICE, Intercity-Express

2 Brandenburg Gate in Berlin

3 Liechtenstein

4 Matterhorn, southwest of Zermatt

5 State Opera in Vienna

STANDARDS: 2.2

VORSCHAU

Bekannte Leute ▪ *Famous people*

Through the centuries, in areas as diverse as science and sports, literature and psychology, German-speaking women and men have made invaluable contributions, both in their own countries and abroad.

1 Albert Einstein (1879-1955) revolutionized physics with his theory of relativity. In 1933 he emigrated to the United States and began a lifetime teaching career at the Institute for Advanced Study in Princeton, New Jersey. He received the Nobel Prize for Physics in 1921.

2 Ludwig van Beethoven (1770-1827) is perhaps the best-known composer of classical music. Though his hearing became increasingly impaired, he composed his greatest masterpieces during the last years of his life.

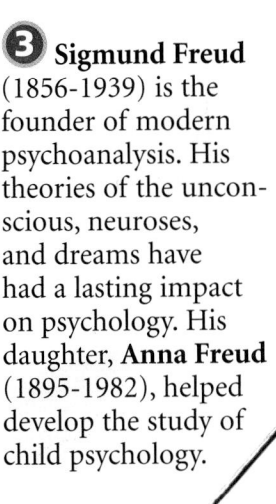

3 Sigmund Freud (1856-1939) is the founder of modern psychoanalysis. His theories of the unconscious, neuroses, and dreams have had a lasting impact on psychology. His daughter, **Anna Freud** (1895-1982), helped develop the study of child psychology.

4 Steffi Graf (1969-), one of the world's greatest tennis players, has won over one thousand career titles, including 7 victories at Wimbledon, 5 French Opens, 5 U.S. Opens, 4 Australian Opens, 21 Grand Slams, and Olympic Gold in 1988.

5 Annette von Droste-Hülshoff (1797-1848) was one of the leading writers of nineteenth-century Germany. She is remembered for both her poetry and her prose, her best-known work being the novella **Die Judenbuche**.

6 Günter Grass (1927-) is a major figure in contemporary German literature. Many of his works are controversial and deal with such issues as Germany's struggle with its Nazi past. Two well-known works are **Die Blechtrommel** and **Katz und Maus**. In 1998, Grass won the Nobel Prize for Literature for his lifetime achievement in German literature.

Das Alphabet · *The alphabet*

2 **Richtig aussprechen** *Pronounce correctly*

The letters of the German alphabet are almost the same as those in English, but the pronunciation is different. Listen to the rhyme and learn the alphabet the way many children in German-speaking countries learn it. Then pronounce each letter after your teacher or after the recording.

CD 1 Tr. 2

a b c d e,

der Kopf tut mir weh,

f g h i j k,

der Doktor ist da,

l m n o,

jetzt bin ich froh,

p q r s t,

es ist wieder gut, juchhe!

u v w x,

jetzt fehlt mir nix,

y z,

jetzt geh ich ins Bett.

There are a few more things you should remember about German spelling and pronunciation.

a. The letter **ß** (Eszett) is often used in place of the "double s" (ss) in German spelling. However, the **ß** cannot always be substituted for the "double s", so it is important that as you build your German vocabulary you remember which words are spelled with **ß**.

b. Many German words are spelled and pronounced with an umlaut (¨) over the a, o, or u (**ä, ö, ü**). The umlaut changes the sound of the vowels, as in **Käse**, **Österreich**, and **grün**. You will learn more about the use of the umlaut in the **Aussprache** sections of the book.

3 **Deutsche Abkürzungen** *German abbreviations*

Listen to how these common abbreviations are pronounced in German.

VW   BMW   USA   BRD   ADAC   BASF

CD 1 Tr. 3

6 *sechs*   STANDARDS: 4.1   VORSCHAU

Wie heißt du? ▪ *What's your name?*

4 **Hör gut zu!** *Listen carefully*   4. Two students are greeting each other and asking for each other's names.

a. Listen and try to figure out what these students are saying.

CD 1
Tr. 4

Mädchen:	Hallo! Wie heißt du?
Junge:	Ich heiße Holger. Und du? Wie heißt du?
Mädchen:	Ich heiße Handan.

b. Below are some popular first names of German girls and boys. Listen to how they are pronounced.

CD 1
Trs. 5–6

CD1 Tr. 5

Vornamen für Mädchen	
Daniela	**Julia**
Marina	**Inge**
Michaela	**Christiane**
Nicole	**Claudia**
Ute	**Gisela**
Silke	**Antje**
Ulrike	**Kristin**
Karin	**Katja**
Birgit	**Sara**
Christine	

CD1 Tr. 6

Vornamen für Jungen	
Mark	**Jens**
Sven	**Peter**
Jörg	**Daniel**
Holger	**Andreas**
Stefan	**Manfred**
Jochen	**Uwe**
Christof	**Christian**
Michael	**Alexander**
Benjamin	**Sebastian**

c. Pick a German name for yourself and practice pronouncing it.

5 **Namenkette** *Name chain*

One student begins the "name chain" by asking the name of the person next to him or her. That student answers and then asks the next person until everyone has had a turn. Students who wish to do so may use the German name they chose in Activity 4c above.

BEISPIEL   **Ich heiße Antje. Wie heißt du?**

6 **Wie heißt mein Partner?** *What's my partner's name?*

In this book you will be asked many times to work with a partner to find out new information and to practice the new things you are learning. Find a partner who sits near you and ask that person his or her name. Then he or she will ask you.   Model: Wie heißt du? Ich heiße ...

Im Klassenzimmer ▪ *In the classroom*

Übungsheft, S. 2, Ü. 2

7 **Was ist das?** *What's that?*

CD 1
Tr. 7

a. As you look at the picture to the right, listen to the way the names of the classroom objects are pronounced.

b. Pick one of the objects in the illustration and write the German word for it on an index card. When your teacher calls out that object, place your card next to the correct object in your classroom.

c. Take turns asking a partner what the different objects in the classroom are called. As you point to something, you will ask: **Was ist das?** and your partner will answer in German.

das Fenster · die Tür · die Tafel · der Tisch · der Stuhl · das Buch · der Bleistift · ein Stück Papier · der Kuli

Ausdrücke fürs Klassenzimmer
Expressions for the classroom

Here are some common expressions your teacher might use in the classroom:

Öffnet eure Bücher auf Seite …!	*Open your books to page …*
Nehmt ein Stück Papier!	*Take out a piece of paper.*
einen Bleistift!	*a pencil.*
einen Kuli!	*a pen.*
Steht auf!	*Stand up.*
Setzt euch!	*Sit down.*
Hört zu!	*Listen.*
Schreibt euren Namen!	*Write down your names.*
Passt auf!	*Pay attention.*
Geht an die Tafel!	*Go to the chalkboard.*

Here are some phrases you might want to use when talking to your teacher.

Wie sagt man …auf Deutsch?	*How do you say …in German?*
Was bedeutet …?	*What does …mean?*
Wie bitte?	*Excuse me?*

8 **Simon sagt …** *Simon says …*

Look over the classroom expressions for a few minutes. Now your teacher will give everyone in the class instructions in German, but you should do only what your teacher says if he or she first says **Simon sagt …**

BEISPIEL	LEHRER(IN)	**Simon sagt, steht auf!**
		Everyone in the class stands up.

STANDARDS: 1.2    VORSCHAU

Die Zahlen von 0 bis 20 ▪ *The numbers from 0 to 20*

9 **Hör gut zu!** *Listen carefully!*

Listen to how the numbers below are pronounced. Then read each number.

CD 1 Tr. 8

Wortschatz

0	*1*	*2*	*3*	*4*	*5*	*6*	*7*	*8*	*9*	*10*
null	eins	zwei	drei	vier	fünf	sechs	sieben	acht	neun	zehn

11	*12*	*13*	*14*	*15*	*16*	*17*	*18*	*19*	*20*
elf	zwölf	dreizehn	vierzehn	fünfzehn	sechzehn	siebzehn	achtzehn	neunzehn	zwanzig

Ein wenig Landeskunde

Look again at how the numbers are written in German. Pay particular attention to the numbers *1* and *7*. When using hand signals to indicate numbers or when counting on their fingers, Germans use the thumb to indicate one, the thumb and the index finger to indicate two, and so on. How do you indicate numbers with your fingers?

10 **Wir üben mit Zahlen!** *Practicing with numbers*

Übungsheft, S. 2, Ü. 3

   a. Each person in the class will count off in sequence: first student **eins**, second student **zwei**, etc. When you reach 20, start again with number one.

   b. With a partner, count aloud the girls, then the boys in your class.

   c. Tell your partner your phone number one digit at a time. Your partner will write it down, say it back to you, and then tell you his or her telephone number.

11 **Zahlenlotto** *Number Game*

Draw a rectangle and divide it into sixteen squares as shown. Number the squares randomly, using numbers between 0 and 20. Use each number only once. Your teacher will call numbers in random order. As you hear each number, mark the corresponding square. The winner is the first person to mark off four numbers in a vertical, horizontal, or diagonal row.

8	2	5	13
7	1	6	4
9	10	3	19
18	11	16	12

Warum Deutsch lernen? ▪ *Why learn German?*

Americans of German-speaking descent

Can you guess how many Americans trace all or part of their ethnic background to Germany, Austria, or Switzerland? — 10 million? 30 million? 50 million? If you guessed 50 million, you were close! Forty-nine million people, or about 20% of the population, reported that they were at least partly of German, Swiss, or Austrian descent.

The early settlers

Germans were among the earliest settlers in the United States. In 1683, the first group arrived from Krefeld and founded Germantown, Pennsylvania. Since 1683 more than seven million German-speaking immigrants have come to this country.

German towns and German words

Reminders of German settlers are everywhere in the United States. Town names such as Hannover in North Dakota, Berlin in Wisconsin, and Potsdam in New York are common, as are German family names like Klein, Meyer, and Schneider. Traditions such as Christmas trees and the Easter bunny, words like pumpernickel, noodle, wurst, dachshund, and kindergarten, and even "typically American" foods such as hamburgers, pretzels, and frankfurters were brought over by German-speaking immigrants and have become part of our everyday culture.

German and your career

German might play an important role in your future. Many employers consider knowledge of German to be an asset. You could use German in many professions — as a teacher, professor, librarian, travel agent, lawyer, buyer, economist, publisher, journalist, translator, flight attendant, engineer, doctor — and, of course, tour guide. Many high-tech companies name German as the language they prefer prospective employees to study. More than 1200 American companies have offices in German-speaking countries, and over 140,000 Americans live and work there.

November, 1989: The fall of the Berlin Wall

Berlin today: new buildings on Potsdamer Platz, again the hub of the city

Modern Germany

Above all, NOW is a great time to discover German. With the disappearance of the "iron curtain," you can travel freely in the former German Democratic Republic (East Germany), where travel was restricted for over 40 years. History-making events like the fall of the Berlin Wall and the unification of Germany in 1991 make this an interesting time to study German. Germany, together with most other European countries, has adopted the euro as its currency, opening up new opportunities for commerce and trade. To find out more about German-speaking countries and the language, **Komm mit!** (*Come along*), and learn German.

Tipps fürs Deutschlernen
Tips for studying German

Listen

It's important to listen carefully and take notes in class. Ask questions if you don't understand, even if you think your question is silly. Other people are probably wondering the same thing! You won't be able to understand everything you hear, but don't get frustrated. You're actually absorbing the language even when you don't realize it.

Speak

Practice speaking German every day. Talking with your teachers and classmates is an easy and fun way to learn. Don't be afraid to take risks when speaking! Your mistakes will help you identify problems and will show you important differences between the structure of German and English.

Practice

Learning a new language is like learning to play a sport or an instrument. You can't spend one night practicing and then expect to play perfectly the next morning. You didn't learn English that way either! Short, daily study sessions are more effective than once-a-week cramming sessions. Also, try to practice with a friend or a classmate, since language is all about communication.

Expand

Increase your contact with German outside of class in every way you can. Look for German programs such as **Deutsche Welle** on TV, or rent German-language videos and DVDs. Magazines and newspapers in German are available at libraries and bookstores in the United States. The Internet is another source for German-language material, including German websites with video or radio broadcasts. You won't understand every word, but you can get a lot out of a story or an article by concentrating on words you recognize and doing a little guesswork.

Organize

It's important to be organized and efficient when learning. Throughout the textbook you'll see tips for learning, speaking, reading, and writing (**Lerntrick, Sprachtipp, Lesestrategie, Schreibtipp**) that will help you study smart. For starters, try looking for cognates. Cognates are words that look similar and have the same meaning in German and English, such as **Musik** and *music*. By recognizing which words are cognates, you can then spend your time studying the words that look completely unfamiliar.

Connect

Because English is a Germanic language, your knowledge of English can give you clues about the meanings of German words such as **Bäckerei** (*bakery*) and **schwimmen** (*to swim*). Some German and English words have roots in Latin or Greek, such as **Atmosphäre** and *atmosphere* or **Ökonomie** and *economy*. You may find that learning German will help you in English class!

Have fun!

Above all, remember to have fun! The more you try, the more you'll learn. **Viel Glück!** (*Good luck!*), and **Komm mit!** (*Come along!*)

Brandenburg

Teaching Resources
pp. 12–15

PRINT
▸ Lesson Planner, p. 2
▸ Video Guide, pp. 1–2

MEDIA
▸ One-Stop Planner
▸ Video Program
   Videocassette 1, 00:56–04:19
▸ Interactive CD-ROM Tutor, Disc 1
▸ Map Transparency

go.hrw.com
WK3 BRANDENBURG

> **PAGES 12–13**

THE PHOTOGRAPH
Background Information

Sanssouci Palace was built between 1745 and 1747 by the famous German architect Georg Wenzeslaus von Knobelsdorff as a summer residence for the Prussian king Friedrich II (Friedrich der Große). Located at the foot of a hill with a view of Potsdam, it is considered one of the finest examples of German rococo architecture. On either side of the base of the six-terraced entrance to the palace are statues of Venus and Mercury. In the Marmorsaal (marble hall), statues of Venus, Urania, and Apollo represent the arts and sciences. French was the language used at the court of King Friedrich II. The name he chose for his palace comes from the French **sans souci,** which means *worry free.*

THE ALMANAC AND MAP

A coat of arms was originally painted on a knight's shield or armor so that his allies could distinguish him in battle. Over time, the study of coats of arms (called heraldry) became a complicated field, as coats of arms became more elaborate and formalized. The crest of the state of Brandenburg

shows a red eagle on a white background. This links the state to the medieval territory **Mark Brandenburg.** When Brandenburg was a part of Prussia, the eagle was black.

Terms in the Almanac

- **Cottbus** (129,000 inhabitants): an important center of chemical and power production

- **Brandenburg** (95,000 inhabitants): city dating back to the 6th century when it was called Brennabor. It is the home of the impressive St. Peter and Paul Cathedral, which was built between 1165 and 1240.

- **Frankfurt an der Oder** (88,000 inhabitants): an old trading and university city. Heinrich von Kleist (1777-1811), one of the greatest German dramatists, studied here.

- **Linseneintopf:** lentil stew made with bacon, leeks, carrots, potatoes, and pork sausage

- **Hühnerfrikassee:** chicken dish made with white asparagus, mushrooms, capers, and calf's tongue, and served on rice

Map Activities

- Have students use the map on p. 2 to identify the German states that border on Brandenburg. (Mecklenburg-Vorpommern, Sachsen-Anhalt, Sachsen) Then have them identify the country that shares a border with Brandenburg (Poland), and locate the Oder, the Havel, the Spree rivers as well as the cities of Potsdam, Cottbus, and Frankfurt an der Oder. You may also want to use *Map Transparency 1.*

- Ask students if they have ever heard of Frankfurt. Ask them why the city of Frankfurt in Brandenburg adds the words **an der Oder** to its name. Students should infer that the name of the river the city is built on has been added to the name of Frankfurt. One reason for doing this is to distinguish **Frankfurt am Main** from **Frankfurt an der Oder.**

- Have students locate the city of **Frankfurt am Main** and compare its location to that of **Frankfurt an der Oder.**

History Connection

In July and August of 1945, at the end of World War II, the world centered its attention on Potsdam, when Churchill (later, Atlee) of Great Britain, Stalin of the Soviet Union, and U.S. President Truman negotiated the Potsdam Agreement in the Cecilienhof Palace. Under the Potsdam agreement Germany was divided into four **Besatzungszonen** (occupation zones), one of which was controlled and overseen by U.S. forces.

Geography Connection

Have students look up Germany in an atlas and compare its size to that of the United States. Then ask students to locate the state of Maryland, which is approximately the same size as Brandenburg, and compare its size to the rest of the United States and to the students' own state.

▶ **PAGES 14–15**

THE PHOTO ESSAY

1 **Schloss Branitz** is located 2 km east of Cottbus. This two-story baroque building, dating back to 1772, was renovated around 1850 by architect Gottfried Semper for Hermann, Fürst von Pückler Muskau (1785-1871), who used it as his residence. Today it serves as the **Bezirksmuseum** *(district museum).*

2 **Friedrich der Große** was born in 1712 in Berlin and died in 1786 in Potsdam. He became king of Prussia after the death of his father, **Friedrich Wilhelm I.**, in 1740. Friedrich considered himself a servant to the state (**erster Diener meines Staates**). He loved the arts and encouraged science, philosophy, and free thinking, though only to the extent that it would not overstep his own interests. He led the Prussian army in several wars, including the Seven Years' War. During his reign Prussia became a major European power. The marble statue pictured here stands in front of the **Östliches Gärtnerhaus** on the grounds of Sanssouci Palace. It was sculpted by Joseph Uphues in 1899.

3 The wing of the Sanssouci Palace known as the **Neue Kammern** is a later addition to the palace. It was built by the original architect of Sanssouci, Knobelsdorff, in 1747. It was later rebuilt from 1771 to 1775 to become a guest house with separate apartments.

4 **Schloss Cecilienhof** was completed in 1917 and was occupied by the Hohenzollern royal family until 1945. At the end of World War II, the family fled from Stalin's Red Army but managed to take all the furnishings. In the summer of 1945 this site was chosen for the negotiations of the Potsdam Agreement. The palace had to be refurnished quickly to enable the delegation to live and work there. The **Tagesraum** with the famous **Runder Tisch** (the round table at which the delegates worked), as well as the studies that Churchill, Truman, and Stalin each occupied, are in their original condition and are open to the public.

5 The **Schiffshebewerk** in Niederfinow is an important ship hoist, or lock, that was built to connect the two rivers Oder and Havel by way of the **Oder-Havel-Kanal.** This hoist enables ships to travel despite elevation differences during the course of a waterway. The hoist operates much like an elevator. It lifts the ship in a huge water-filled trough from one level to the other.

Drawing Inferences Ask students why they think countries spend so much money and energy building locks and hoists. Ask them how commerce benefits from locks and hoists. (Locks and hoists facilitate ship travel by cutting time. Centers of trade are often located near waterways, and the hoists and locks provide ships with easy access for loading and transporting goods within a country or between countries.)

6 The students here attend the **Dreilinden Gymnasium** in Potsdam. Five of them were born in the Berlin area: Jens (top right), Tara (middle row left), Holger (middle row right), Steffi (bottom right), and Handan (bottom left). Ahmet (top left) was born in Turkey but has spent almost all his life in Germany. His parents are of Italian and Turkish descent. Jens, Holger, and Steffi have native German parents. Handan's parents are Turkish, and Tara has an Iranian father and a German mother.

Komm mit nach
Brandenburg!

Population: 2.64 million

Area: 29,056 square kilometers (11,216 square miles), approximately as large as the state of Maryland

Capital: Potsdam (176,000 inhabitants)

Cities: Cottbus, Brandenburg, Frankfurt an der Oder

Rivers: Oder, Havel, Spree

Canals: Oder-Spree-Kanal, Rhinkanal, Oder-Havel-Kanal

Lakes: Ruppiner See, Werbellinsee, Schwielochsee, Plauer See

Industries: Textiles, machinery, cement, porcelain, farming, forestry, petroleum, coal

Favorite local dishes: Lentil soup, chicken fricassee

Map of Germany

go.
hrw
.com
WK3 BRANDENBURG

VIDEO

CD-ROM
DISC 1

STANDARDS: 2.2, 3.1

Die Terrassen von Schloss Sanssouci ▶
in Potsdam

Brandenburg

Brandenburg, the heartland of former Prussia, is a state characterized by vast flat sandy lands, hundreds of beautiful lakes, and large wooded areas consisting mostly of fir trees. A trip through the towns in Brandenburg reveals stately buildings and churches in characteristic red brick, waiting to be restored to their former beauty.

internet

ADRESSE: go.hrw.com
KENNWORT:
WK3 BRANDENBURG

1 Schloss Branitz in Cottbus
Built in 1772, this castle, now a museum, is located in a beautiful nineteenth-century park.

2 Eine Marmorstatue Friedrichs des Großen
Sculpted by Joseph Uphues

3 Neue Kammern und Historische Mühle
This new wing of Sanssouci Palace was built in 1747. The Historic Windmill was renovated in 1992.

4 Schloss Cecilienhof

This palace was built for the last German emperor Wilhelm II. between 1913 and 1917. Here the Allied powers signed the Potsdam Agreement in 1945.

5 Schiffshebewerk am Oder-Havel-Kanal in Neufinow

This ship hoist makes it possible for barges to transport bulk goods such as coal, sand, or gravel through a network of canals.

Kapitel 1, 2, 3

The students in the following three chapters live in the Potsdam area. Potsdam is the capital of Brandenburg. In 1993, Potsdam celebrated its 1000th birthday. The city became famous when Frederick the Great decided to establish his summer residence there and built Sanssouci Palace.

6 Ahmet, Jens, Handan, Tara, Holger, and Steffi invite you to Potsdam.

Kapitel 1: Wer bist du?
Chapter Overview

Los geht's! pp. 18–20	*Vor der Schule, p. 18*		

	FUNCTIONS	GRAMMAR	VOCABULARY	RE-ENTRY
Erste Stufe pp. 21–24	• Saying hello and goodbye, p. 21 • Asking someone's name and giving yours, p. 22 • Asking who someone is, p. 23	• Forming questions, p. 23 • Definite articles **der, die, das,** p. 24	• **Ein wenig Landeskunde:** Greetings, p. 21	• Asking someone's name, p. 22 (from **Vorschau**)
Zweite Stufe pp. 25–27	• Asking someone's age and giving yours, p. 25	• Subject pronouns and the verb **sein,** p. 26	• Numbers 0–20, p. 25	• Numbers 0–20, p. 25 (from **Vorschau**) • Geography of German-speaking countries, p. 27 (from **Vorschau**)
Dritte Stufe pp. 28–33	• Talking about where people are from, p. 28 • Talking about how someone gets to school, p. 30		• How you get to school, p. 30	

Aussprache p. 33	The long vowels **e, ä, ü, ö,** the letter **w,** the letter **v:** Audio CD 1, Track 24	**Diktat:** Audio CD 1, Tracks 25–26
Zum Lesen pp. 34–35	**Postkarten aus den Ferien**	**Reading Strategy** Using visual clues
Mehr Grammatik-übungen	**pp. 36-37** **Erste Stufe,** p. 36	**Zweite Stufe,** pp. 36–37 — **Dritte Stufe,** p. 37
Review pp. 38–41	**Anwendung,** pp. 38–39	**Kann ich's wirklich?,** p. 40 — **Wortschatz,** p. 41

CULTURE

- **Ein wenig Landeskunde:** Greetings, p. 21
- **Ein wenig Landeskunde:** Using **der** and **die** in front of people's names, p. 24
- Map of German states, p. 27
- **Landeskunde: Wie kommst du zur Schule?,** p. 31

Kapitel 1: Wer bist du?
Chapter Resources

PRINT

Lesson Planning

One-Stop Planner

Lesson Planner with Substitute Teacher Lesson Plans, pp. 12–16, 65

Student Make-Up Assignments
- Make-Up Assignment Copying Masters, Chapter 1

Listening and Speaking

TPR Storytelling Book, pp. 1–4

Listening Activities
- Student Response Forms for Listening Activities, pp. 3–6
- Additional Listening Activities 1-1 to 1-6, pp. 7–10
- Additional Listening Activities (song), p. 6
- Scripts and Answers, pp. 101–106

Video Guide
- Teaching Suggestions, pp. 4–5
- Activity Masters, pp. 6–8
- Scripts and Answers, pp. 81–83, 111

Activities for Communication
- Communicative Activities, pp. 1–6
- Realia and Teaching Suggestions, pp. 74–77
- Situation Cards, pp. 123–124

Reading and Writing

Reading Strategies and Skills Handbook, Chapter 1

Lies mit mir! 1, Chapter 1

Übungsheft, pp. 3–12

Grammar

Grammatikheft, pp. 1–9

Grammar Tutor for Students of German, Chapter 1

Assessment

Testing Program
- Grammar and Vocabulary Quizzes, **Stufe** Quizzes, and Chapter Test, pp. 1–18
- Score Sheet, Scripts, and Answers, pp. 19–26

Alternative Assessment Guide
- Portfolio Assessment, p. 18
- Performance Assessment, p. 32
- CD-ROM Assessment, p. 46

Student Make-Up Assignments
- Alternative Quizzes, Chapter 1

MEDIA

 Online Activities
- Interaktive Spiele
- Internet Aktivitäten

 Video Program
- Videocassette 1
- Videocassette 5 (captioned version)

 Audio Compact Discs
- Textbook Listening Activities, CD 1, Tracks 9–27
- Additional Listening Activities, CD 1, Tracks 35–42
- Assessment Items, CD 1, Tracks 28–34

 Interactive CD-ROM Tutor, Disc 1

 Teaching Transparencies
- Situations 1-1 to 1-2
- Vocabulary 1-A to 1-C
- **Los geht's!**
- **Mehr Grammatikübungen** Answers
- **Grammatikheft** Answers

 **One-Stop Planner CD-ROM**

Use the **One-Stop Planner CD-ROM with Test Generator** to aid in lesson planning and pacing.

For each chapter, the **One-Stop Planner** includes:
- Editable lesson plans with direct links to teaching resources
- Printable worksheets from resource books
- Direct launches to the HRW Internet activities
- Video and audio segments
- Test Generator
- Clip Art for vocabulary items

Kapitel 1: Wer bist du?
Projects ·····················

Eine Reisebroschüre

In this activity students will create a travel brochure (or a poster) for a German city. It will be written and presented in English.

Tell students to imagine that the German Club's itinerary for the upcoming trip to Germany has all been planned except for the last day. The task for the club members is to choose their favorite city and convince the other members that this is where they should spend their last day in Germany. Have students prepare and present a travel brochure for this city. The brochure should be a persuasive presentation of things to see and do in the selected city. This project can be done individually or in small groups.

MATERIALS
✂ **Students may need**
- posterboard   • scissors
- glue   • tape
- pictures and other available realia

SUGGESTED TOPICS

Students must provide the following information for their visual and oral presentation:

Location: Bundesland; geographic location

Statistics: population, size; commercial interests

History: brief synopsis of city's history

Points of Interest: What is there to see? Why do people want to go to this city? What will this group of teenagers be able to do there?

Unusual/interesting facts

SUGGESTED SEQUENCE

1. Ask students to do research by looking up information in the school library or the local library, using almanacs, world reference books, or travel magazines. They can also visit local travel agencies that always have a variety of brochures and guides on Germany.

   Visit the HRW Web site at <u>go.hrw.com</u> for online resources. See p. 15F for more information.

2. Have students compile all their information and materials (including pictures) and begin to organize it.

3. Have students make a brief written outline of how they plan to present their city. Provide general feedback and suggestions if necessary.

4. Have students complete their project.

5. Have the students make a 2-3 minute presentation to the rest of the class.

6. Display all projects and have all students vote on the city they would like to visit on this imaginary trip to Germany.

GRADING THE PROJECT

Suggested point distribution (**total = 100 points**)
Content/Subject Matter 40
Presentation 40
Creativity 20

Games ·····················

Um die Welt

Here you will find suggestions for games in which students practice some of the functions, structures, vocabulary, and cultural features studied in Chapter 1.

This is a fast vocabulary review game that is easy to set up and fun for the students.

Materials You will need flashcards with pictures of vocabulary items.

Note Before the start of the game, let the class know that all students will be asked to write down as many vocabulary words as they can remember after the game.

Procedure Students sit in rows. The first student in the first row stands beside the desk of the second student in the row. They will compete. The teacher holds up a flashcard with a picture of a vocabulary item. The first one of the two competing students to name correctly the item on the flashcard wins. The student who named the word first continues down the row to compete with the next student. The other student sits down. A round is complete after each person has had a turn. Play as many rounds as you and your students would like. The winner is the student who has passed the most desks in the course of the game. As you play, make sure you show the flashcard to the whole class. All students should clearly see the picture on the flashcard so they can be thinking about the words.

Storytelling

Mini-Geschichte

*This story accompanies Teaching Transparency 1-C. The **Mini-Geschichte** can be told and retold in different formats, acted out, written down, and read aloud, to give students additional opportunities to practice all four skills.*

Wer ist das Mädchen?

USCHI	**Hallo, Holger!**
HOLGER	**Tag!**
USCHI	**Wer ist das?**
HOLGER	**Das Mädchen heißt Melina Kiritsis.**
USCHI	**Wie alt ist sie?**
HOLGER	**Sie ist 18 Jahre alt.**
USCHI	**Woher kommt sie?**
HOLGER	**Sie kommt aus Stuttgart.**
USCHI	**Stuttgart ist die Hauptstadt von Baden-Württemberg.**
HOLGER	**Ja, klar!**
USCHI	**Wie kommt sie zur Schule?**
HOLGER	**Ihre Mutter bringt sie mit dem Auto zur Schule.**
USCHI	**Oh, ich komme mit dem Rad zur Schule.**
HOLGER	**Ja, ich auch. Bis dann!**
USCHI	**Tschüs!**

Traditions

Nudelwochen

Hier geht es rund um die Kartoffel, denn in Brandenburg wird die Kartoffel 'Nudel' genannt. Friedrich der Große hatte mit seinem Kartoffelbefehl 1756 die Bauern zum Anbau der Kartoffel gezwungen. Zuvor war die Knolle nur als Zierpflanze oder allenfalls für die Viehfütterung angebaut worden. Allmählich begannen aber auch die Bauern die Kartoffel zu essen, und bald wurde sie zum wichtigsten Nahrungsmittel in Brandenburg. In Prenzlau wird alljährlich Anfang Oktober die Nudelwoche gefeiert. Da geht es rund um die Kartoffel. In den Gasthäusern werden die Pellnudeln auf den Tisch geschüttet und dazu gibt es Kräuterquark, Butter, Leberwurst oder Gänseschmalz.

Lob der Kartoffel

*Schön rötlich die Kartoffeln sind
und weiß wie Alabaster.
Sie däu'n sich lieblich und
geschwind
und sind für Mann und Frau und
Kind
ein rechtes Magenpflaster.*
(Matthias Claudius)

Rezept

Kartoffelsuppe Kaiser Wilhelm II. liebte Kartoffelsuppe, wenn sie auf Schinkenknochen serviert und mit einer Einlage aus fein geschnittener gekochter Rinderbrust serviert wurde. In den normalen Berliner Haushalten gab es stattdessen Würstchen oder Bockwurst dazu und hinterher einen „Eierkuchen". Das war dann das Standardgericht für den Samstag.

Kartoffelsuppe
Für 2 Personen

Zutaten

g=Gramm, l=Liter

400 g	Kartoffeln
1	Zwiebel
1	Bund Suppengrün
20 g	Butter
3/4 l	Gemüsebrühe
500 g	Crème fraîche
	Salz
	schwarzer Pfeffer
	Muskat

Einlage: Würstchen (Bockwurst) oder geröstete Speckwürfel

Zubereitung

Kartoffeln und Zwiebel in Würfel schneiden, Suppengrün zerkleinern. Butter erhitzen, Kartoffeln und Gemüse darin andünsten. Mit Brühe ablöschen, aufkochen und 20 Minuten kochen. Suppe pürieren, Crème fraîche dazugeben, erhitzen und mit Salz, Pfeffer und Muskat abschmecken.

Technology

Video

Videocassette 1, 5 (captioned version)
See Video Guide, pages 3–8

Los geht's! • Vor der Schule

Jens, Tara, Holger, and Ahmet are in the school yard on the first day after vacation when they meet a new student, Holger. They want to know where Holger is from, and when Holger wants to know Ahmet's last name, Tara offers to spell it for him.

Landeskunde

Wie kommst du zur Schule?

Students from different cities in Germany tell us who they are and how they get to school.

Fortsetzung

German class is first, and the students meet their new German teacher. He asks about the students' names and where they are from. Holger is from Walburg, but Ahmet? Ahmet is from a small town in Turkey on the Black Sea, which the teacher finds on the map.

Videoclips

- **WHK Wiener Handelskammer**® (Chamber of Commerce)
- **Scout Schultaschen**® (school bags)
- **Time Life Bücher**® (Time-Life Books)

Interactive CD-ROM Tutor

The **Interactive CD-ROM Tutor** contains videos, interactive games, and activities that provide students an opportunity to practice and review the material covered in Chapter 1.

Activity	Activity Type	Pupil's Edition Reference
1. So sagt man das!	Wozu gehört's?	pp. 21, 22
2. Grammatik	Was fehlt?	pp. 23, 24
3. Wortschatz	Was ist richtig?	p. 25
4. Grammatik	Was fehlt?	p. 26
5. So sagt man das!	Merkspiel	p. 28
6. Wortschatz	Wort und Bild Erfahren/Wählen	p. 30
Landeskunde	Wie kommst du zur Schule? Was ist richtig?	p. 31
Zum Sprechen	*Guided recording*	pp. 38–39
Zum Schreiben	*Guided writing*	pp. 38–39

Teacher Management System

Logging In

Logging into the *Komm mit!* TMS is easy. Upon launching the program, simply type "admin" in the password area of the log-in screen and press RETURN. Log on to **www.hrw.com/CDROMTUTOR** for a detailed explanation of the Teacher Management System.

One-Stop Planner CD-ROM

To preview all resources available for this chapter, use the **One-Stop Planner CD-ROM**, Disc 1.

Internet Connection ....

internet

ADRESSE: go.hrw.com
KENNWORT:
WK3 BRANDENBURG-1

*Have students explore the **go.hrw.com** Web site for many online resources covering all chapters. All Chapter 1 resources are available under the keyword WK3 Brandenburg-1. Interactive games practice the material and provide students with immediate feedback. You will also find a printable worksheet that provides Internet activities that lead to a comprehensive online research project.*

Interaktive Spiele

You can use the interactive activities in this chapter

- to practice grammar, vocabulary, and chapter functions
- as homework
- as an assessment option
- as a self-test
- to prepare for the Chapter Test

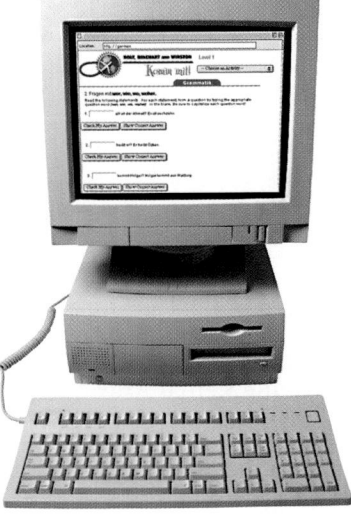

Internet Aktivitäten

Students will look at an administrative map of Germany and read about the inhabitants of a fictitious town in Germany.

- To prepare students for the **Arbeitsblatt,** you might want to have them study the map on p. 27.
- After completing the **Arbeitsblatt,** have students compare a map of Germany with a map of the United States. Consider asking them the following:

  What are the American equivalents of the **Bundesländer?**

  The river Main separates the northern part of Germany from the southern part. Can you think of a river in the US that separates the east from the west?

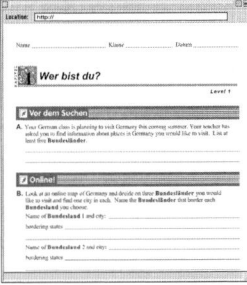

Webprojekt

Have students visit a German city, preferably the capital of a **Bundesland.** They should find the name of its mayor and the names of one or two famous people who live or have lived there. The information could then be displayed on or next to a map of Germany on the classroom wall. Encourage students to exchange useful Web sites with their classmates. Have students document their sources by referencing the names and URLs of all the sites they consulted.

Erste Stufe

6 p. 21

1. — Hallo! Bist du neu hier?
— Ja, ich heiße Ilse. Grüß dich.

2. — Guten Morgen! Bitte setzt euch!
— Guten Morgen, Herr Gerber!

3. — Ich muss jetzt los.
— Na, bis dann, Salmun.
— Tschüs, Martin!

4. — Da kommt die Leyla. Morgen, Leyla!
— Hallo! Wie geht's?

5. — Morgen ist Training.
— Ja. Ich komm auch. Tschüs!
— Tschau!

9 p. 23

1. — Heißt du Antje?
— Ja, ich heiße Antje.

2. — Wie heißt der Junge?
— Er heißt Kemal. Er ist neu hier.

3. — Heißt das Mädchen da Ute?
— Nein, sie heißt Sabine.

4. — Wie heißt du denn?
— Ich heiße Hans.

11 p. 24

1. — Wer ist das da?
— Das ist die Katrin.

2. — Und wer ist das?
— Das ist Frau Möller.

3. — Wer ist denn das?
— Das ist die Deutschlehrerin.

4. — Wer ist das?
— Das ist der Mathelehrer, Herr Scholz.

5. — Wer ist das?
— Das ist Frau Bach, die Deutschlehrerin.

6. — Wer ist das?
— Das ist doch die Silke.

7. — Wer ist das?
— Er heißt Christian Hansen.

8. — Und wer ist das?
— Hm, das ist der Jens.

Zweite Stufe

15 p. 25

HOLGER	Wie alt ist Handan? Ist sie 15?
AHMET	Ja. Ich glaube, sie ist schon 15.
HOLGER	Und sag mal, Ahmet, wie alt bist du eigentlich?
AHMET	Ich bin 16.
HOLGER	16? Bin ich auch. Und wie alt sind denn die Renate und der Jens?
AHMET	Renate ist erst 14, aber der Jens ist schon 16 Jahre alt.

17 p. 26

1. — Tag! Ich heiß Ulrike, und ich bin vierzehn.

2. — Wer ist der Junge da drüben?

3. — Wer ist denn das? Stefan?

4. — Sind Helmut und Jens auch schon hier?

5. — Ist Frau Bach die neue Sportlehrerin?

Dritte Stufe

22 p. 28

JÖRG	Ja also, ich heiß Jörg Schulze, und ich komm aus Berlin.
KEMAL	Ich heiße Kemal Acar und ich bin ziemlich neu hier in Düsseldorf.
WIEBKE	Ich bin die Wiebke Jansen und wohne in Hamburg.
BRIGITTE	Ja, und ich bin Brigitte Dennhöffer und komm halt aus München.
MELINA	Grüß Gott! Ich bin die Melina Kiritsis und komm aus Stuttgart.

27 p. 30

Die Heike kommt meistens mit dem Moped, und der Philipp kommt eigentlich immer mit der U-Bahn. Die Annette dagegen kommt mit dem Bus, und die Sara kommt auch mit dem Bus. Der Michael fährt mit dem Rad. Und ich …na ja, meine Mutter bringt mich oft mit dem Auto.

One-Stop Planner CD-ROM

For resource information, see the **One-Stop Planner CD-ROM**, Disc 1.

AUSSPRACHE, p. 33

Diktat, p. 33

You will hear two students, Jochen and Stefan, talking about another student. First, listen to what they are saying, then write down their conversation. Who are they talking about?

JOCHEN   Hallo, grüß dich, Stefan! Wer ist das Mädchen da?

STEFAN   Das ist die Erika.

JOCHEN   Wie alt ist sie denn?

STEFAN   Vierzehn.

JOCHEN   Und woher kommt sie?

STEFAN   Aus Österreich. Ich glaube Wien.

Anwendung

 1 **p. 38**

MARIA   Hallo, ich heiße Maria, bin 16 Jahre alt und komme aus Wien.

MARTIN   Ich bin der Martin. Ich bin 14 und komm aus Berlin.

FRAU BACH   Ich bin die Frau Bach. Ich bin eine Deutschlehrerin hier. Ich bin 29 Jahre alt und komme aus Brandenburg.

TARA   Also, ich heiße Tara. Ich bin 14 und komme aus der Stadt Potsdam.

Vorschau

 1 **p.1**

The Federal Republic of Germany, **die Bundesrepublik Deutschland,** is a land of contrasts and striking diversity. A divided country for almost 50 years, Germany was reunited in 1990 under one government. This relatively small country has something for everyone. In the east is cosmopolitan **Berlin,** the capital of Germany once again. A highly industrial region known as the **Ruhrgebiet** is in the west, and in the south lie the foothills of the **Alpen,** where rural traditions are still strong.

When visiting **Berlin** you can see the famous **Brandenburger Tor** and what's left of the **Mauer.** You can also visit the

Alexanderplatz, the hub of former **Ost-Berlin,** or take a stroll down **Unter den Linden,** a famous boulevard. The **Freistadt** of **Hamburg,** home of Germany's largest port, is in the north. In southwestern Germany you will find the spectacular **Schwarzwald.** East of the **Schwarzwald,** tucked away in the foothills of the Alps along Germany's southern border, is another great attraction, **Neuschwanstein,** Ludwig the Second's most famous castle. Directly on the border between Germany and Austria towers the **Zugspitze,** the tallest mountain in the German Alps.

Germany's rivers play an important role in its economy. If you travel to the western part of the country, you will see the famous **Rhein** river. In the south flows the **Donau,** and to the east are the **Elbe** and the **Oder.** To the north lie the **Nordsee** and the **Ostsee,** two major seas critical to Germany's economy and industry. Germany is surrounded by nine countries in all: **Polen, die Tschechische Republik, Österreich, die Schweiz, Frankreich, Luxemburg, Belgien, die Niederlande,** and **Dänemark.**

Southeast of Germany you will see **Österreich.** Two Austrian cities that you have probably heard about, **Salzburg** and **Wien,** host well-known music festivals every year. Other Austrian attractions are the **Großglockner** and the **Großvenediger,** the highest mountains in the Austrian Alps. Austria is also known for its many magnificent palaces and castles, such as the **Schönbrunn** near **Wien,** as well as its picturesque villages and colorful traditions. Although most Austrians live in the countryside, fully one-fifth of the population resides in **Wien,** the capital. **Wien** lies on the **Donau,** one of the most important and beautiful rivers in Europe. Other important Austrian cities are **Innsbruck, Salzburg,** and **Graz.**

Die Schweiz, which lies southwest of Germany across the **Rhein** river, is the land of the **Alpen.** Switzerland is famous for its breathtaking scenery and towering peaks, like the **Eiger** or **Matterhorn.** It is also known for its luxurious ski resorts, like **St. Moritz** or **Zermatt**—and of course, Swiss cheese, fine chocolates, and quality watches. The capital of Switzerland is **Bern.** Other important cities are **Zürich, Luzern,** and **Basel.** Switzerland has four official languages, German, French, Italian, and Romansch. Sixty percent of the population speaks German.

The principality of **Liechtenstein** is one of the smallest countries in the world. It is smaller in area than Washington, DC. In the west, the **Rhein** river forms **Liechtenstein**'s border with Switzerland, with which it has very close cultural and economic ties. **Vaduz** is the capital of **Liechtenstein.**

As you can see from this brief trip through **Deutschland, Österreich, die Schweiz,** and **Liechtenstein,** the German-speaking countries are rich in natural beauty, and have fascinating traditions and exciting cultures. You are probably eager to learn more about these countries and the language spoken there. So **Komm mit!** Let's learn German!

Kapitel 1: Wer bist du?
Suggested Lesson Plans 50-Minute Schedule

Day 1

LOCATION OPENER 15 min.
- Present **Location Opener**, pp. 12–15
- Show **Brandenburg** Video
- Do Viewing and Post-viewing Activities, Video Guide, p. 2

CHAPTER OPENER 10 min.
- Culture Notes, ATE, p. 15M

LOS GEHT'S! 20 min.
- Preteaching Vocabulary, ATE, p. 15N
- Have students read **Los geht's!**, pp. 18–19
- Teaching Suggestions, Video Guide, p. 4
- Culture Notes, ATE, p. 15N
- Show **Los geht's!** Video

Wrap-up 5 min.
- Students respond to **Los geht's!** questions

Homework Options
Pupil's Edition, p. 20, Comprehension Acts.

Day 2

ERSTE STUFE
Quick Review 10 min.
- Check homework, p. 20, Comprehension Acts.
- Bell Work, ATE, p. 15O

So sagt man das!, p. 21 10 min.
- Presenting **So sagt man das!**, ATE, p. 15O
- Play Audio CD for Activity 6, p. 21

Ein wenig Landeskunde, p. 21 15 min.
- Teacher Note (1), ATE, p. 15O
- Do Activities 7 and 8, p. 22

So sagt man das!, p. 22 10 min.
- Presenting **So sagt man das!**, ATE, p. 15P
- Play Audio CD for Activity 9, p. 23

Wrap-Up 5 min.
- Students say hello and good-bye to each other and to the teacher

Homework Options
Grammatikheft, p. 1, Acts. 1–2
Übungsheft, pp. 3–4, Acts. 1–3

Day 3

ERSTE STUFE
Quick Review 10 min.
- Check homework, Grammatikheft, p. 1, Acts. 1–2

Grammatik, p. 23 10 min.
- Presenting **Grammatik**, ATE, p. 15P
- Do Activity 10, p. 23

So sagt man das!, p. 23 15 min.
- Presenting **So sagt man das!**, ATE, p. 15P
- Game, **Um die Welt**, ATE, p. 15C

Grammatik, p. 24 10 min.
- Presenting **Grammatik**, ATE, p. 15P
- Play Audio CD for Activity 11, p. 24
- Do Activity 12, p. 24

Wrap-Up 5 min.
- Students respond to questions about their names and names of others

Homework Options
Grammatikheft, pp. 2–3, Acts. 3–6
Übungsheft, p. 5, Acts. 4–6

Day 4

ERSTE STUFE
Quick Review 10 min.
- Check homework, Übungsheft, p. 5, Acts. 4–6

Ein wenig Landeskunde, p. 24 10 min.
- Present **Ein wenig Landeskunde**, p. 24
- Present **Lerntrick**, p. 24
- Do Activities 13 and 14, p. 24

Quiz Review 10 min.
- Do **Mehr Grammatikübungen, Erste Stufe**

Quiz 20 min.
- Quiz 1-1A or 1-1B

Homework Options
Activities for Communication, p. 74, Realia 1-1, circle cognates

Day 5

ZWEITE STUFE
Quick Review 10 min.
- Return and review Quiz 1-1
- Bell Work, ATE, p. 15R

So sagt man das!, p. 25 10 min.
- Presenting **So sagt man das!**, ATE, p. 15R
- TPR Activity, ATE, p. 15R
- Do Activity 7, p. 4, Grammatikheft

Wortschatz, p. 25 10 min.
- Play Audio CD for Activity 15, p. 25
- Communication for all Students, ATE, p. 15R
- Do Activity 16, p. 25

Grammatik, p. 26 15 min.
- Presenting **Grammatik**, ATE, p. 15R
- Play Audio CD for Activity 17, p. 26
- Do Activities 18, 19, and 20, p. 26

Wrap-Up 5 min.
- Students respond to questions about how old they are

Homework Options
Übungsheft, pp. 6–7, Acts. 7–11
Grammatikheft, pp. 4–5, Acts. 8–10

Day 6

ZWEITE STUFE
Quick Review 15 min.
- Check homework, Grammatikheft, pp. 4–5, Acts. 8–10
- Do Activity 21, p. 27

Quiz Review 15 min.
- Do **Mehr Grammatikübungen, Zweite Stufe**
- Use Teaching Transparency 1-B to review numbers

Quiz 20 min.
- Quiz 1-2A or 1-2B

Homework Options
Activities for Communication, pp. 3–4, make notes and practice for Communicative Activity 1-2

One-Stop Planner CD-ROM

For alternative lesson plans by chapter section, to create your own customized plans, or to preview all resources available for this chapter, use the **One-Stop Planner CD-ROM**, Disc 1.

 For additional homework suggestions, see activities accompanied by this symbol throughout the chapter.

Day 7

DRITTE STUFE

Quick Review 15 min.
- Return and review Quiz 1-2
- Bell Work, ATE, p. 15T

So sagt man das!, p. 28 20 min.
- Presenting **So sagt man das!**, ATE, p. 15T
- Play Audio CD for Activity 22, p. 28
- Do Activity 23, p. 28
- Do Activities 24 and 25, p. 29

Sprachtipp, p. 29 10 min.
- Language Note, ATE, 15T
- Present **Sprachtipp**, p. 29
- Do Activity 26a, p. 29

Wrap-Up 5 min.
- Students respond to questions about where they are from

Homework Options
Übungsheft, pp. 8–9, Acts. 12–15
Grammatikheft, pp. 6–7, Acts. 11–13

Day 8

DRITTE STUFE

Quick Review 10 min.
- Check homework, Übungsheft, p. 9, Acts. 14–15
- Do Activities 26b and 26c, p. 29

Wortschatz, p. 30 10 min.
- Presenting **Wortschatz**, ATE, p. 15U
- Teaching Transparencies 1-A and 1-2
- Play Audio CD for Activity 27, p. 30

So sagt man das!, p. 30 10 min.
- Presenting **So sagt man das!**, ATE, p. 15U
- Do Additional Listening Activities 1–4, 1–5, and 1–6, pp. 8–10

LANDESKUNDE 15 min.
- Pre-viewing Suggestion, Video Guide, p. 5
- Background Information, ATE, p. 15U
- Show **Landeskunde** Video
- Do Activities A and B, p. 31
- Do Activity 28, p. 32

Wrap-Up 5 min.
- Students respond to questions about getting to school

Homework Options
Grammatikheft, pp. 8–9, Activities 14–19

Day 9

DRITTE STUFE

Quick Review 15 min.
- Check homework, Grammatikheft, pp. 8–9, Acts. 14–19
- Do Activity 29, p. 32

Quiz Review 30 min.
- Show **Fortsetzung** Video
- Do Activity 30, p. 32
- Do Activities 31 and 32, p. 33
- Begin **Mehr Grammatikübungen, Dritte Stufe**

Wrap-Up 5 min.
- Students respond to questions about their names, ages, how they get to school and where they are from

Homework Options
Complete **Mehr Grammatikübungen, Dritte Stufe**

Day 10

DRITTE STUFE

Quick Review 10 min.
- Check homework, **Mehr Grammatikübungen, Dritte Stufe**

Quiz 20 min.
- Quiz 1-3A or 1-3B

Aussprache, p. 33 15 min.
- Presenting Aussprache, ATE, p. 15V
- Do **Richtig aussprechen/Richtig lesen**
- Do **Richtig schreiben/Diktat**, p. 33

Wrap-Up 5 min.
- Students respond to pronunciation questions

Homework Options
Übungsheft, pp. 11–12, Acts. 18–19
Interaktive Spiele, see ATE, p. 15F

Day 11

DRITTE STUFE

Quick Review 10 min.
- Check homework, Übungsheft, pp. 11–12, Acts. 18–19
- Return and review Quiz 1-3

ZUM LESEN 30 min.
- Present **Lesestrategie**, p. 34
- Do Activities 1–11, pp. 34–35, in writing

Wrap-Up 10 min.
- Students respond to questions about greeting and saying good-bye, giving their name and asking someone else's, and asking and saying who someone is

Homework Options
Pupil's Edition, p. 40, **Kann ich's wirklich?**

Day 12

ANWENDUNG

Quick Review 30 min.
- Check homework, **Kann ich's wirklich?**, p. 40
- Career Path, ATE, p. 15X
- Do Activities 1–8, pp. 38–39

Chapter Review 20 min.
- Review chapter functions, vocabulary, and grammar; choose from **Mehr Grammatikübungen**, Grammar Tutor for Students of German, Activities for Communication, Listening Activities, Interactive CD-ROM Tutor, or **Interaktive Spiele**
- Review test format and provide sample test items for students

Homework Options
Study for Chapter Test

Assessment

Test, Chapter 1 45 min.
- Administer Chapter 1 Test. Select from Testing Program, Alternative Assessment Guide or Test Generator.

Kapitel 1: Wer bist du?
Suggested Lesson Plans *90-Minute Schedule*

LOCATION OPENER 30 min.
- Present **Location Opener**, pp. 12–15
- Background Information, ATE, p. 11A
- Show **Brandenburg** Video
- Do Viewing and Post-viewing Activities, Video Guide, p. 2
- Map Activities, ATE, p. 11A
- The Photo Essay, ATE, p. 11B

CHAPTER OPENER 5 min.
- Culture Notes, ATE, p. 15M

LOS GEHT'S! 30 min.
- Preteaching Vocabulary, ATE, p. 15N
- Play Audio CD, **Los geht's!**
- Have students read **Los geht's!**, pp. 18–19
- Teaching Suggestions, Video Guide, p. 4
- Culture Notes, ATE, p. 15N
- Show **Los geht's!** Video
- See **Fortsetzung**, ATE, p.15N

ERSTE STUFE
So sagt man das!, p. 21 10 min.
- Presenting **So sagt man das!**, ATE, p. 15O
- Language Notes, ATE, p. 15O
- Play Audio CD for Activity 6, p. 21

Ein wenig Landeskunde, p. 21 10 min.
- Teacher Note (1), p. 15O
- Do Activities 7 and 8, p. 22

Wrap-Up 5 min.
- Students respond to questions about saying hello and good-bye

Homework Options
Pupil's Edition, p. 20, Comprehension Acts.
Grammatikheft, pp. 1–3, Acts. 1–6
Übungsheft, pp. 3–5, Acts. 1–6

ERSTE STUFE
Quick Review 5 min.
- Check homework, Grammatikheft, pp. 1–3, Acts. 1–6

So sagt man das!, p. 22 10 min.
- Presenting **So sagt man das!**, ATE, p. 15P
- Play Audio CD for Activity 9, p. 23

Grammatik, p. 23 10 min.
- Presenting **Grammatik**, ATE, p. 15P
- Do Activity 10, p. 23

So sagt man das!, p. 23 10 min.
- Presenting **So sagt man das!**, ATE, p. 15P
- Repeat Activity 10 using **Wer ist das?/Das ist …**

Grammatik, p. 24 10 min.
- Presenting **Grammatik**, ATE, p. 15P
- Play Audio CD for Activity 11, p. 24
- Do Activity 12, p. 24

Ein wenig Landeskunde, p. 24 10 min.
- Present **Ein wenig Landeskunde**, p. 24
- Present **Lerntrick**, p. 24
- Do Activities 13 and 14, p. 24

Quiz Review 15 min.
- Do **Mehr Grammatikübungen, Erste Stufe**
- Do Additional Listening Activity 1-1, p. 7

Quiz 20 min.
- Quiz 1-1A or 1-1B

Homework Options
Activities for Communication, p. 74, Realia 1-1, circle cognates

ZWEITE STUFE
Quick Review 10 min.
- Return and review Quiz 1-1
- Bell Work, ATE, p. 15R

So sagt man das!, p. 25 15 min.
- Presenting **So sagt man das!**, ATE, p. 15R
- TPR Activity, ATE, p. 15R
- Do Activity 7, p. 4, Grammatikheft

Wortschatz, p. 25 25 min.
- Play Audio CD for Activity 15, p. 25
- Communication for all Students, ATE, p. 15R
- Do Activity 16, p. 25
- Game, **Um die Welt**, ATE, p. 15C
- Do Activity 8, p. 4, Grammatikheft

Grammatik, p. 26 35 min.
- Presenting **Grammatik**, ATE, p. 15R
- Play Audio CD for Activity 17, p. 26
- Do Activities 18, 19, and 20, p. 26
- Do Activity 21, p. 27
- Do Activities 9 and 10, p. 5, Grammatikheft
- Do **Mehr Grammatikübungen, Zweite Stufe**

Wrap-Up 5 min.
- Students respond to questions about how old they are

Homework Options
Übungsheft, pp. 6–7, Acts. 7–11

One-Stop Planner CD-ROM

For alternative lesson plans by chapter section, to create your own customized plans, or to preview all resources available for this chapter, use the **One-Stop Planner CD-ROM**, Disc 1.

 For additional homework suggestions, see activities accompanied by this symbol throughout the chapter.

Block 4

ZWEITE STUFE

Quick Review 10 min.
- Check homework, Übungsheft, pp. 6–7, Acts. 7–11

Quiz Review 15 min.
- Do Additional Listening Activities 1–2 and 1–3, pp. 7–8
- Use Teaching Transparency 1-B to review numbers

Quiz 20 min.
- Quiz 1-2A or 1-2B

DRITTE STUFE

So sagt man das!, p. 28 40 min.
- Presenting **So sagt man das!**, ATE, p. 15T
- Play Audio CD for Activity 22, p. 28
- Do Activity 23, p. 28
- Do Activities 24 and 25, p. 29
- Teaching Suggestions for **Fortsetzung** and **Videoclips** Videos, Video Guide, pp. 4–5
- Show **Fortsetzung** and **Videoclips** Videos
- Do **Fortsetzung** and **Videoclips** Activities, Video Guide, pp. 7–8

Wrap-Up 5 min.
- Students respond to questions about where they are from

Homework Options
Übungsheft, p. 9, Acts. 14–15
Grammatikheft, pp. 6–8, Acts. 11–16

Block 5

DRITTE STUFE

Quick Review 15 min.
- Check homework, Grammatikheft, pp. 6–8, Acts. 11–16
- Return and review Quiz 1-2

Sprachtipp, p. 29 10 min.
- Present **Sprachtipp**, p. 29
- Do Activity 26, p. 29

Wortschatz, p. 30 10 min.
- Presenting **Wortschatz**, ATE, p. 15U
- Teaching Transparencies 1-A and 1-2
- Play Audio CD for Activity 27, p. 30

So sagt man das!, p. 30 10 min.
- Presenting **So sagt man das!**, ATE, p. 15U
- Do Activities 12–13, p. 8, Übungsheft

LANDESKUNDE 20 min.
- Pre-viewing Suggestion, Video Guide, p. 5
- Background Information, ATE, p. 15U
- Show **Landeskunde** Video
- Do Activities A and B, p. 31
- Do Activity 28, p. 32

Aussprache, p. 33 15 min.
- Presenting **Aussprache**, ATE, p. 15V
- Do **Richtig aussprechen / Richtig lesen**, p. 33
- Do **Richtig schreiben / Diktat**, p. 33

Wrap-Up 5 min.
- Students respond to pronunciation questions

Homework Options
Mehr Grammatikübungen, Dritte Stufe
Interaktive Spiele, see ATE, p. 15F

Block 6

DRITTE STUFE

Quick Review 10 min.
- Check homework, **Mehr Grammatikübungen, Dritte Stufe**

Quiz Review 25 min.
- Do Activity 30, p. 32
- Do Activities 31 and 32, p. 33
- Do Additional Listening Activities 1–4, 1–5, and 1–6, pp. 8–10

Quiz 20 min.
- Quiz 1-3A or 1-3B

ZUM LESEN 25 min.
- Present **Lesestrategie**, p. 34
- Do Activities 1–11, pp. 34–35

Kann ich's wirklich, p. 40 5 min.

Wrap-Up 5 min.
- Students respond to questions about greeting and saying good-bye, giving their name and asking someone else's and asking and saying who someone is.

Homework Options
Pupil's Edition, p. 40, **Kann ich's wirklich?**, complete Acts. 3–9
Study for Chapter Test

Block 7

ANWENDUNG

Quick Review 10 min.
- Check homework, **Kann ich's wirklich?** p. 40, Acts. 3–9
- Return and review Quiz 1-3

Chapter Review 30 min.
- Review chapter functions, vocabulary, and grammar; choose from **Mehr Grammatikübungen**, Grammar Tutor for Students of German, Activities for Communication, Listening Activities, Interactive CD-ROM Tutor, or **Interaktive Spiele**
- Review test format and provide sample test items for students

Test, Chapter 1 45 min.
- Administer Chapter 1 Test. Select from Testing Program, Alternative Assessment Guide or Test Generator.

Kapitel 1: Wer bist du?
Teaching Suggestions, pages 16–41

Teacher Notes

- Some activities suggested in the *Teacher's Edition* ask students to contact various people, businesses, and organizations in the community. Before assigning these activities, it is advisable to request parental permission.
- Students will encounter both the traditional and the new spellings in the *Komm mit!* series. This reflects the reality of the German-speaking countries until the year 2005. In *Komm mit!* Level 1, most pieces that reflect the traditional spelling are *Zum Lesen* selections and pieces of realia. These are permissioned documents that cannot be altered.

PAGES 16–17

CHAPTER OPENER

Pacing Tips

In the **Erste Stufe** question formation and gender treatment are introduced. Additionally, the functions of 'saying hello', 'asking someone's name', and 'asking who someone is' are being taught. In the **Zweite Stufe** the complex verb **sein** is introduced. You might want to plan your lesson to accommodate slightly more time for the **Erste** and **Zweite Stufe** than for the **Dritte Stufe.** For Lesson Plans and timing suggestions, see pages 15I–15L.

Meeting the Standards

Communication
- Saying hello and goodbye, p. 21
- Asking someone's name and giving yours, p. 22
- Asking who someone is, p. 23
- Asking someone's age and giving yours, p. 25
- Talking about places of origin, p. 28
- Talking about how someone gets to school, p. 30

Cultures
- Ein wenig Landeskunde, p. 21
- Ein wenig Landeskunde, p. 24
- Landeskunde, p. 31
- Culture Notes, p. 15M
- Geography Connection, p. 15S
- Culture Note, p. 15S
- Language Note, p. 15T
- Culture Note, p. 15U

Connections
- Teacher Note, p. 15O
- Language Note, p. 15P
- Music Connection, p.15R

For resource information, see the **One-Stop Planner CD-ROM,** Disc 1.

Comparisons
- Language-to-Language, p. 15O
- Language Note, p. 15O
- Language Note, p. 15P
- Language-to-Language, p. 15P
- Background Information, p. 15V
- Thinking Critically, p. 15U
- Language Note, p. 15V
- Culture Note, p. 15V

Communities
- Culture Notes, p. 15N
- Career Path, p. 15X

Cultures and Communities

Culture Notes

- Most German students ride their bikes while others walk or take public transportation. Some older students ride a moped or drive a car. German teenagers must be 16 to get an operator's license for a moped and 18 to get a license to drive a car.

- Summer vacation is much shorter in Germany (maximum 6 weeks) than in the United States. However, students do get fall (**Herbstferien**), Christmas (**Weihnachtsferien**), and spring breaks which last about one or two weeks each (**Osterferien** and **Pfingstferien**). The dates for the summer vacation will differ from **Bundesland** to **Bundesland.**

Chapter Sequence

Los geht's! . . . . .p. 18

Erste Stufe . . . . .p. 21

Zweite Stufe . . . . .p. 25

Dritte Stufe . . . . .p. 28

Landeskunde . . . . .p. 31

Zum Lesen . . . . .p. 34

Mehr Grammatikübungen .p. 36

Anwendung . . . . .p. 38

Kann ich's wirklich? . . . . .p. 40

Wortschatz . . . . .p. 41

LOS GEHT'S!

Teaching Resources
pp. 18–20

PRINT
▶ Lesson Planner, p. 2
▶ Video Guide, pp. 3–4, 6
▶ Übungsheft, p. 3

MEDIA
▶ One-Stop Planner
▶ Video Program
  Los geht's!
  Videocassette 1, 04:56–06:40
  Videocassette 5 (captioned version),
  01:00–02:47
  Fortsetzung
  Videocassette 1, 06:42–08:50
  Videocassette 5 (captioned version),
  02:49–04:54
▶ Audio Compact Discs, CD1, Trs. 9–10
▶ **Los geht's!** Transparencies

PAGES 18–19

Los geht's! Transparencies

Preteaching Vocabulary

Recognizing Cognates

Los geht's! contains several words that students will be able to recognize as cognates. Have students find these cognates, then, have them guess what is happening in the story.

1 Hallo!, Moped, Super!, zur Schule
2 hier
4 Training
5 Türkei
6 der beste Mann im Team, Nummer

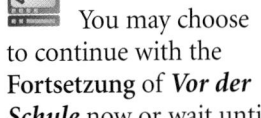
Fortsetzung
You may choose
to continue with the
Fortsetzung of *Vor der
Schule* now or wait until
later in the chapter. For a synopsis of the **Los geht's!**
and **Fortsetzung** episodes, see p. 15E.

Using the Captioned Video

 German captions for every **Los geht's!** and **Fortsetzung** are available on Videocassette 5. Target-language captions give students another opportunity to comprehend the language in the story and offer teachers further possibilities for presenting the new material in class.

Teaching Suggestions

• Have students listen to the text while looking at the photos, or have them watch this segment of the video. Remind them that they do not need to understand every word. They should try to get the gist of what is happening in the story. Have them match visual clues with words or phrases that they hear.

• After students have listened to or read the text, have them tell you one fact about each person.

Cultures and Communities

Culture Notes

• It is typical for schools in the large cities of Germany to have many students from foreign countries enrolled, especially students from Turkey, Greece, and Italy. The parents or grandparents of these young people went to Germany to find work, and many have settled there permanently.

• There are no drivers' education classes offered in German schools. Instead, teenagers must enroll in a **Fahrschule**. Fees for an automobile license course are usually over 1,000€.

PAGE 20

Comprehension Check

Teaching Suggestion
5 Pair students and let them fill in the blanks together. Next, let them role-play the dialogue to give them a chance to practice pronunciation.

Teaching Suggestion
Have students introduce themselves in German by telling their name, their age, and saying where they are from or where they live.

ERSTE STUFE

Teaching Resources
pp. 21–24

PRINT
▸ Lesson Planner, p. 3
▸ TPR Storytelling Book, pp. 1, 4
▸ Listening Activities, pp. 3–4, 7
▸ Activities for Communication, pp. 1–2, 74, 77, 123–124
▸ Grammatikheft, pp. 1–3
▸ Grammar Tutor for Students of German, Chapter 1
▸ Übungsheft, pp. 4–5
▸ Testing Program, pp. 1–4
▸ Alternative Assessment Guide, p. 32
▸ Student Make-Up Assignments, Chapter 1

MEDIA
▸ One-Stop Planner
▸ Audio Compact Discs, CD1, Trs. 11–13, 28, 35
▸ Teaching Transparencies
  Situation 1-1
  Mehr Grammatikübungen Answers
  Grammatikheft Answers
▸ Interactive CD-ROM Tutor, Disc 1

> PAGE 21

Bell Work

Before starting the **Erste Stufe,** let students list all the ways we greet and say goodbye to one another in English. Remind them to think of formal and informal expressions and also long and short forms. Put all the expressions on the board or a transparency. Ask students to give an example for when and how each expression may be used. Tell students that the German language also has many different ways to greet and say goodbye to people.

PRESENTING: So sagt man das!

The German saying "Höflichkeit ist Trumpf" (*courtesy is power*) is often practiced by Germans. Greetings and farewells are therefore a very important part of German culture. With this in mind, introduce the phrases of this function box by walking up to several students and greeting each in a different way and also using the farewell expressions.

Connections and Comparisons

Language-to-Language

You may want to point out to your students that while in English the pronoun "I" is always capitalized, in German, French, and Spanish "I" is capitalized only if it is the first word of a sentence.

Language Notes

• Tell students that **bis dann** literally means *until then* and that it is generally used as a parting phrase when a specific time has been mentioned for people to see each other again. It may also simply have the general meaning of *see you later.*

• The initial consonant cluster in **Tschau** or **Tschüs** can be compared to the English initial phoneme in words such as *chi*na or *cho*colate.

Teacher Note

Many German teenagers have adopted the American greeting "Hi" instead of **Guten Tag. Tschüs** is more typical for northern Germany and **Tschau** for southern Germany. There are other greetings and farewells not mentioned here which you might want to point out to your students. These greetings are typical of southern Germany: **Grüß dich! Grüß Gott! Servus!** and **Ade!**

Teaching Suggestions

After introducing **Ein wenig Landeskunde** to students, point out the difference between **Morgen** as a greeting and **morgen** meaning *tomorrow* as in **Ist morgen Training?**

Teacher Note

The listening activities in ***Komm mit!*** are designed to help students improve their ability to understand authentic spoken German. They will learn more from the listening tasks throughout the book if they are given at least two opportunities to listen. The first time you play the recorded activity, have students put down their pencils and listen carefully. They should write down their answers during the second listening.

Communication for All Students

A Slower Pace

Make up (or have students make up) index cards with greetings and goodbyes, especially the longer, more formal ones. Allow students to refer to the cards when they want to use a different greeting.

PRESENTING: So sagt man das!

Introduce the phrases from the **So sagt man das!** function box briefly. Have students use their name tags from Activity 8 and have them work in groups of 2 or 3 using functions and phrases such as introducing themselves and asking questions.
Example:

Student A: **Wie heißt du?**
Student B: **Ich heiße _____. Und du?**
Student A: **Ich heiße_____.**
            (points to another student in class)
            Wie heißt sie?
Student B: **Sie heißt _____.**

Connections and Comparisons

Language Note

The /ch/ sound in **Mädchen** can be compared to the English /h/ in words such as *humid* or *huge*.

PRESENTING: Grammatik

Open-ended and yes/no questions Before introducing the **Grammatik** box, ask students to list as many interrogative pronouns in English as they can, and write them on the left side of the board or on a transparency. Then, ask students what type of question starts with these pronouns. (open-ended question) Ask students what other type of question there is. (yes/no question) Ask them for an example of a yes/no question, and write it opposite the interrogative pronouns. Then present the **Grammatik** box. Students should realize that the concepts of open-ended and yes/no questions also exist in German.

Game

10 Divide the class into two teams. The first student on Team A identifies himself or herself saying **Ich heiße …** and then points to a student on the same team asking **Wer ist das?** The first student on Team B must give the correct name. If the answer is correct, the student stays in the game. If it is incorrect, the student is out. Continue in this way, alternating teams.

PRESENTING: So sagt man das!

Introduce the four pictures with their captions to your students. Then, point to one of the students in your class, and ask the rest of the class **Wer ist das?** The class should follow the model and respond in a chorus **Das ist der/die _____.**

PRESENTING: Grammatik

Articles Before explaining the **Grammatik** to students, point out that the grammatical definition of an article doesn't always correspond to the natural gender of a given noun; therefore, we speak in terms of grammatical gender. **Der, die, das** have one equivalent in English, *the.*

- The word **Mädchen** is neuter because of the diminutive suffix -**chen.** It comes from the Middle High German word **maget,** which means *unmarried, young.*

Connections and Comparisons

Language-to-Language

- Tell students that German has three definite articles (**der/die/das**) which correspond to the gender of the noun. French and Spanish have two definite articles (**le/la** and **el/la,** respectively) which also correspond to the gender of the noun. Ask students if they can think of any English words that have retained a gender designation. (Example: A ship is often referred to as *she.)*

- Your students may be interested to know that German, like Spanish and French, has masculine and feminine forms for professions. These forms correspond to the gender of the person. Examples:
English: the teacher - the teacher
German: der Lehrer - die Lehrer**in**
French: l'instituteur - l'institut**rice**
Spanish: el profesor - la profesor**a.**
Have students brainstorm a list of English words that retain this feature. (Examples: actor/actress, aviator/aviatrix) You may also want to mention that the plural for mixed groups is masculine in the above-mentioned languages.

Communication for All Students

A Slower Pace

Some students might have trouble with the grammatical term *definite article*. Try explaining that the definite article points out and refers to one or more "definite" or particular members of a group or class. Contrast the English definite and indefinite articles and usage, for example: "This is the president" and "This is a president."

Challenge

12 After students have completed the conversation, ask them to rewrite it, changing all names of people and places.

Tactile Learners

13 Have students make a blank seating chart of the class or have copies of one available. Have students work in pairs to fill in the names of their classmates. Each of the partners points to different students, asking **Wer ist das Mädchen?** or **Wie heißt der Junge?** Have students keep this chart for future activities.

Teaching Suggestion

14 Ask each student to bring two or three different pictures of famous people. Have a student stand in front of the class or at his or her desk and hold up a picture. It should be visible to everybody. The student asks the class **Wer ist das?** or **Wie heißt er/sie?** The student who correctly answers the question first gets to show his or her picture to the class and ask the class to identify the person in that picture. Continue until everyone has shown at least one picture.

Performance Assessment

At the end of each **Stufe,** you will find a reference to the Alternative Assessment Guide. There you will find an activity designed to assess the content of the **Stufe.**

The activity below is very similar to the one designed for the **Erste Stufe** in the Alternative Assessment Guide.

Write the following statements on a transparency or on the board. Have students form the question that would elicit each statement as an answer. This can be done orally or in writing.

1. Ich heiße Sabine. (Wie heißt du?)

2. Er heißt Robert. (Wie heißt er/der Junge/der Mann?)

3. Das ist die Karin. (Wer ist das?)

4. Sie heißt Frau Mayer. (Wie heißt sie/die Frau?)

Assess

▶ Testing Program, pp. 1–4
  Quiz 1-1A, Quiz 1-1B
  Audio CD1, Tr. 28

▶ Student Make-Up Assignments
  Chapter 1, Alternative Quiz

▶ Alternative Assessment Guide, p. 32

ZWEITE STUFE

Teaching Resources
pp. 25–27

PRINT

▸ Lesson Planner, p. 4
▸ TPR Storytelling Book, pp. 2, 4
▸ Listening Activities, pp. 4, 7–8
▸ Activities for Communication, pp. 3–4, 75, 77, 123–124
▸ Grammatikheft, pp. 4–5
▸ Grammar Tutor for Students of German, Chapter 1
▸ Übungsheft, pp. 6–7
▸ Testing Program, pp. 5–8
▸ Alternative Assessment Guide, p. 32
▸ Student Make-Up Assignments, Chapter 1

MEDIA

▸ One-Stop Planner
▸ Audio Compact Discs, CD1, Trs. 14–15, 29–30, 36–37
▸ Teaching Transparencies
Situation 1-1
Vocabulary 1-B, 1-C
Mehr Grammatikübungen Answers
Grammatikheft Answers
▸ Interactive CD-ROM Tutor, Disc 1

PAGE 25

Bell Work

Students were first introduced to the numbers 0–20 on p. 9 of the **Vorschau.** Quickly review the numbers in the **Wortschatz** box by having the whole class count to 20, and then backwards from 20 to 0. Repeat until the class seems warmed up.

(TPR) Total Physical Response

Practice the numbers using some of the expressions presented in the **Vorschau.** Give students the following commands.

Juan und Sam, schreibt die Nummer 13 an die Tafel!

Carol und Felicia, nehmt 2 Bücher!

Reggie und Bob, öffnet eure Bücher auf Seite 19!

Leticia und Suzy, nehmt 3 Kulis!

PRESENTING: So sagt man das!

After introducing the new phrases, walk around the classroom and ask individual students questions from this function box. Have them reply using the appropriate answer from the box.

Communication for All Students

Challenge

Ask students to create and write elementary math problems between the numbers 0 and 20 using the following kinds of expressions: **Was ist eins plus drei?** or **Wie viel ist sieben minus drei?** Have individual students call out their math problems, and the rest of the class give the correct answer in German.

PAGE 26

PRESENTING: Grammatik

Subject pronouns Before introducing the **Grammatik,** tell students that subject pronouns are words used only to replace nouns and noun phrases, often to avoid repetitiveness (pronoun = "for the noun"). Walk around the classroom addressing the students using the verb **sein.** (Example: Ich bin die Deutschlehrerin. Wer bist du?)

Connections and Comparisons

Music Connection

Give students a copy of the song *O du lieber Augustin,* Level 2 *Listening Activities,* p. 6, for additional reading. What form of the verb **sein** can they find? (**ist**) Which words do they think could be the subjects that go with this verb? (**alles, Geld, Mäd'l;** they may suggest **Augustin**) Which word cannot be the subject of this verb? (**du**) You might also want to play the song, Level 2 CD 1, Tr. 28.

Communication for All Students

Challenge

19 Have students first say how old the people in the pictures are, and then add a negative. (Examples: Steffi ist fünfzehn, nicht vierzehn. Melanie und Katja sind sechzehn, nicht siebzehn.)

A Slower Pace

20 On the board or transparency provide students with a sample of an introduction and then have them proceed with the activity.

ZWEITE STUFE

Writing Assessment

20 As a diagnostic you may choose to evaluate this short written assignment using the following rubric.

Writing Rubric	Points			
	4	3	2	1
Content (Complete – Incomplete)				
Comprehensibility (Comprehensible – Seldom comprehensible)				
Accuracy (Accurate – Seldom accurate)				
Organization (Well-organized – Poorly organized)				
Effort (Excellent – Minimal)				

18–20: A   16–17: B   14–15: C   12–13: D   Under 12: F

PAGE 27

Communication for All Students

Tactile Learners

Have students draw a map of Germany with labels on all the German states and the bordering countries, using heavy stock paper. Have students cut out the different states as well as Austria and Switzerland. Using the map like a puzzle, have students practice in pairs or small groups, naming the state or country and putting it in the right place.

Cultures and Communities

Geography Connection

Have students bring in maps of Europe and ask them to write down the names of all the countries that border Germany. Have them also name the waters that border the country and finally have them list three major German rivers.

 Culture Note
Switzerland is made up of 26 **Kantone** and Austria of 9 **Bundesländer**.

Teaching Suggestion

Have students take out the seating chart they made in the **Erste Stufe** when they filled in the names of their classmates. Let them go around the class again. They should ask the question **Wie alt bist du?** and add the answer under the correct name. Afterwards, call on several students and ask them the age of some of the students they questioned.

Performance Assessment

On a transparency show the following sentence fragments and call on students to form complete sentences. You might also have students write several answers in full sentences on the chalkboard. Then correct sentences on the board if there are any mistakes. Please see the *Alternative Assessment Guide*, p. 32, for a more comprehensive assessment suggestion.

ich	ist	15
du	bin	14
er	bist	16

Assess

▶ Testing Program, pp. 5–8
  Quiz 1-2A, Quiz 1-2B
  Audio CD1, Tr. 29–30

▶ Student Make-Up Assignments
  Chapter 1, Alternative Quiz

▶ Alternative Assessment Guide, p. 32

Answers to Activity 21

a. There are 16 **Bundesländer**: Schleswig-Holstein, Niedersachsen, Nordrhein-Westfalen, Rheinland-Pfalz, Hessen, Saarland, Baden-Württemberg, Bayern, Thüringen, Sachsen, Sachsen-Anhalt, Brandenburg, Mecklenburg-Vorpommern, Hamburg, Berlin, and Bremen.

b. Schleswig-Holstein: Kiel; Niedersachsen: Hannover; Nordrhein-Westfalen: Düsseldorf; Rheinland-Pfalz: Mainz; Hessen: Wiesbaden; Saarland: Saarbrücken; Baden-Württemberg: Stuttgart; Bayern: München; Thüringen: Erfurt; Sachsen: Dresden; Sachsen–Anhalt: Magdeburg; Brandenburg: Potsdam; Mecklenburg-Vorpommern: Schwerin; Hamburg: Hamburg; Berlin: Berlin; Bremen: Bremen

c. Baden-Württemberg borders on Switzerland. Bayern borders on Austria.

d. Bern; Wien

DRITTE STUFE

Teaching Resources
pp. 28–33

PRINT

- ▸ Lesson Planner, p. 5
- ▸ TPR Storytelling Book, pp. 3, 4
- ▸ Listening Activities, pp. 5, 8–10
- ▸ Activities for Communication, pp. 5–6, 76, 77, 123–124
- ▸ Grammatikheft, pp. 6–9
- ▸ Grammar Tutor for Students of German, Chapter 1
- ▸ Übungsheft, pp. 8–10
- ▸ Testing Program, pp. 9–12
- ▸ Alternative Assessment, p. 32
- ▸ Student Make-Up Assignments, Chapter 1

MEDIA

- ▸ One-Stop Planner
- ▸ Audio Compact Discs, CD1, Trs. 16–17, 31, 38–40
- ▸ Teaching Transparencies
  Situation 1-2
  Vocabulary 1-A
  Mehr Grammatikübungen Answers
  Grammatikheft Answers
- ▸ Interactive CD-ROM Tutor, Disc 1

> ### PAGE 28

Bell Work

Pair students and provide each group with a copy of a map of Germany. Have the names of at least 15 cities blanked out on the map but numbered, and put those 15 cities on the board or on a transparency in random order. Pairs must correctly fill the blanks on their copy of the map in a given amount of time. To review the results, call out the number and have students give you the name of the corresponding city.

PRESENTING: So sagt man das!

Introduce the new phrases of the **So sagt man das!** box by asking either/or questions or yes/no questions such as **Woher kommt der amerikanische Präsident? Aus _____ oder _____? Ist Arnold Schwarzenegger aus Österreich?** Students should be able to infer the meaning of the questions through contextual guessing, especially if many cognates are used.

Teaching Suggestion

23 On the overhead projector, list the key questions that students will need for their pair work. **Wer ist**

das? or Wie heißt er/sie? Wie alt ist er/sie? Woher ist er/sie? or Woher kommt er/sie?

Speaking Assessment

23a Have pairs of students peer-evaluate their dialogues, then ask pairs to come to you for assessment. You may wish to evaluate their dialogues using the following rubric.

Speaking Rubric	Points			
	4	3	2	1
Content (Complete – Incomplete)				
Comprehension (Total – Little)				
Comprehensibility (Comprehensible – Incomprehensible)				
Accuracy (Accurate – Seldom accurate)				
Fluency (Fluent – Not fluent)				

18–20: A   16–17: B   14–15: C   12–13: D   Under 12: F

> ### PAGE 29

Teaching Suggestions

24 Practice with students the pronunciation of all the city names before playing the game with partners. Note that the stress in these names is always on the first syllable except for Berlin and Schwerin. Then, practice the three-syllable names where the stress varies. In Magdeburg, Düsseldorf, and Wiesbaden, the stress is on the first syllable; in Hannover and Saarbrücken, it is on the second syllable.

- After introducing the **Sprachtipp,** have students make and keep a list of connectors. Connectors will be helpful for the students' **Notizbuch** entries, their oral and written portfolios, and their process writing assignments.

Cultures and Communities

Language Note

Words such as **ach ja, ja klar,** and **denn** are also called "flavoring words." They help the language sound more natural and flowing. Students should also keep a list of these words.

Connections and Comparisons

Thinking Critically

Comparing and Contrasting Before introducing the **Wortschatz**, ask students the following questions: How do American students typically get to school? Can you think of a reason why the U.S. public schools provide school bus transportation for most students? How do you think German students get to school every day? Why aren't there school buses in Germany? (Germany has a public transportation network that already accommodates students, thus eliminating the need for a separate system.)

PRESENTING: Wortschatz

Use flashcards with pictures and ask either/or and yes/no questions. (Example: While holding up a picture of a bus ask students: **Ist das ein Bus?** or **Ist das ein Bus oder ein Auto?**) Then practice with students the phrases denoting means of transportation by grouping all phrases with **mit dem …** together. Then practice **mit der U-Bahn** and **zu Fuß**.

Cultures and Communities

 ### Culture Note
It is quite common for German students who use the public transportation system to obtain a weekly, monthly, or annual pass (**Wochen-, Monats,- or Jahreskarte**). These passes allow unlimited rides for a discounted fare.

Communication for All Students

A Slower Pace
27 Have students make a list of the students' names from the **Wortschatz** box before listening to this activity.

PRESENTING: So sagt man das!

To help students with the pronunciation of the expressions of the **So sagt man das!** function box have students practice in pairs. Have one student ask the question and the other student give the answer. Monitor students and make corrections if needed.

 # LANDESKUNDE

 **Teaching Resources**
p. 31

PRINT
▸ Video Guide, pp. 3, 5–7
▸ Übungsheft, p. 12

MEDIA
▸ One-Stop Planner
▸ Video Program
  Videocassette 1, 09:27–12:15
▸ Audio Compact Discs, CD1, Trs. 18–23
▸ Interactive CD-ROM Tutor, Disc 1

Connections and Comparisons

Thinking Critically

• **Drawing Inferences** Ask students to compare the way the students interviewed get to school. How does the size of the town affect the way students travel to school? (Students in a large city such as Berlin must rely on the subway and buses because their schools are often far away from where they live.)

• **Drawing Inferences** Ask students if they can infer the age of Tim and Sandra by the way they get to school. What types of transportation do they use that would be an indication of their age? (Tim is at least 16 years old because he rides a moped, and Sandra must be at least 18 years old because she sometimes drives to school.)

Thinking Critically

Comparing and Contrasting Ask students to name the steps involved in getting a driver's license in the United States. What is the cost? How long is the license valid?

Teaching Suggestion

If possible, obtain a poster or booklet featuring road signs by writing to the German Automobile Club (ADAC). For addresses, see pp. T48–T49 or visit the HRW Web site at <u>www.hrw.com</u>.

DRITTE STUFE

Teacher to Teacher

Hildegard Becker-Lipp
Shawnee Heights High School
Tecumseh, Kansas

❝To practice the names of the **Hauptstädte**, make a copy master of all capital city names divided up by syllables. The syllables should be printed randomly. For example, **Düsseldorf = Dü/ssel/dorf, Schwerin =Schwe/rin, Wiesbaden = Wies/ba/den** etc. Individual students could work on finding capital city names as a worksheet activity, or each syllable could be cut out and the capital city names could be put together as a puzzle in a cooperative learning activity. To make it more difficult, don't capitalize the first letter of each capital.❞

Cultures and Communities

Background Information

Germans must be at least 18 years old in order to obtain a driver's license. Since the mandatory drivers' education courses are extremely expensive, many young people must wait even longer. When they have completed their course work, they must then pass a written exam and a road test. Once a license has been issued, it is good for life.

Culture Note

American students often want to know if they can drive in Germany if they are 16. The answer is no. Most rental car agencies require drivers to be at least 21 and ask foreign drivers for a valid driver's license and often an International Driving Permit.

 PAGE 32

Teacher Note

Versteckte Sätze activities will be recurring activities throughout the chapters of the book. There are many possible sentences that can be made. It is up to the teacher to set limits on the number and type of sentences.

Connections and Comparisons

Language Note

Point out to students that a **Gymnasium** is a school and not a *gymnasium*. It's a false cognate.

Communication for All Students

Visual Learners

28 Have each student come up with at least 3 sets of sentences (questions and answers) and write them on a sheet of paper. If time permits let some students put their sentences on the board.

Group Work

29 Have students form groups of three. Ask each group to prepare a 10- to 12-line conversation between two young people, one of them a new student in school. Give each group of students an overhead transparency and have them write the conversation on it. They should leave a blank line for each question in their dialogue, but supply the appropriate responses as cues. The other groups should then try to complete the conversation orally. Each conversation has to make sense. All people in the group must be able to supply the missing question if asked to do so.

 PAGE 33

Von der Schule zum Beruf

33 Von der Schule zum Beruf

There is a **Von der Schule zum Beruf** activity at the end of each chapter. Students are asked to put themselves into a job-like situation and apply and practice their language skills while exploring potential job interests through writing.

• Ask students about survey totals: **Wie viele Männer und Frauen kommen mit dem Bus? mit dem Rad?** and so on.

PRESENTING: Aussprache

Remind students that German vowels are pronounced with more muscular tension. Many English and German vowel sounds are similar, but not exactly the same.

• **ä/e:** There is no glide with this sound. The short vowels **ä/e** will be introduced in Chapter 5.

• **ü:** Remind students that an umlaut over a letter indicates a change in sound. You may want to point out that the **ü** sound can also be represented by a **y** in such words as **Lyrik** and **Mythos**. Students will learn the short **ü** in Chapter 8.

• **ö:** This sound can also be represented by **oe** in such words as **Goethe**. Students will learn the short **ö** in Chapter 8.

Game

Play the game **Um die Welt.** See p. 15C for the procedure.

Performance Assessment

Please refer to the *Alternative Assessment Guide,* p. 32, for an assessment suggestion of the **Dritte Stufe.**

Assess

▶ Testing Program, pp. 9–12
  Quiz 1-3A, Quiz 1-3B
  Audio CD1, Tr. 31

▶ Student Make-Up Assignments
  Chapter 1, Alternative Quiz

▶ Alternative Assessment Guide, p. 32

PAGES 34–35

ZUM LESEN

Teaching Resources
pp. 34–35

PRINT
▶ Lesson Planner, p. 6
▶ Übungsheft, p. 11
▶ Reading Strategies and Skills, Chapter 1
▶ Lies mit mir! 1, Chapter 1

MEDIA
▶ One-Stop Planner

Prereading

Connections and Comparisons

Thinking Critically
Drawing inferences Looking at the map of Germany on p. 2, can students think of which places could be popular vacation spots and why? (Examples: oceans, mountains, historical places)

Teacher Note

Questions 1–4 are prereading activities.

Reading
Skimming and Scanning

Remind students that most of the time when they read postcards like these, they are looking either for the global picture (skimming) to get an idea about the entertainment possibilities, or for specific information (scanning) such as the words that are used for greetings or the names of the cities the people are writing from. When students do Activities 5 and 6, they will be using the strategies of skimming and scanning. In Activities 7–10, students are reading for comprehension.

Cooperative Learning

Put students in groups of four. Ask them to choose a discussion leader, a recorder, a proofreader, and an announcer. Give students a specific amount of time in which to complete Activities 5–10. Monitor group work as you walk around, helping students if necessary. At the end of the activity, call on each group announcer to read his or her group's results. You can decide whether or not to collect their work for a grade at the end of the activity.

Post-Reading
Teacher Note

Activities 11a. and b. are post-reading tasks that will show whether students can apply what they have learned.

PAGES 36–37

MEHR GRAMMATIKÜBUNGEN

The **Mehr Grammatikübungen** activities are designed as supplemental activities for the grammatical concepts presented in the chapter. You might use them as additional practice, for review, or for assessment.

For more grammar presentations, review, and practice refer to the following:
• Grammatikheft
• Grammar Tutor for Students of German
• Grammar Summary on pp. R15–R25
• Übungsheft
• Grammar and Vocabulary quizzes
  (Testing Program)
• Test Generator
• Interactive CD-ROM Tutor
• **Interaktive Spiele** at go.hrw.com

ZUM LESEN

ANWENDUNG

Video Wrap-up

Videocassette 1, 04:56–14:50

Videocassette 5 (captioned version), 01:00–04:54

At this time, you might want to use the video resources for additional review and enrichment. See *Video Guide* for suggestions regarding:

• the **Los geht's!** episode
• the **Fortsetzung** episode
• the **Landeskunde** interviews
• the **Videoclips**

Apply and Assess

A Slower Pace

1 Write the names of the people in random order on the board or on a transparency. Students will then have only two pieces of information to listen for.

Portfolio

2 You might want to use Activity 2 as an oral portfolio item for your students. See *Alternative Assessment Guide*, p. 18.

Teaching Suggestions

• Have all students get out their seating chart one final time and ask each student to introduce one person in class, giving all the information collected about him or her.

• **4** Hand out index cards and have students use them as their own **Schülerausweise.** Students can add their picture to make them look more authentic. If possible, laminate all cards and either display them on the class bulletin board or have students keep them in their folders.

Career Path

Have students think of reasons why it could be useful for tour guides to know German. (Suggestions: Imagine you are a tour guide in the Grand Canyon leading a group of Austrian tourists down the trail on mules; imagine you are taking a group of American tourists to Vienna.)

KANN ICH'S WIRKLICH?

This page is intended to prepare students for the test. It is a brief checklist of the major points covered in the chapter. The students should be reminded that it is a checklist only and not necessarily everything that will appear on the test.

For additional self check options, refer students to the *Grammar Tutor*, the *Interactive CD-ROM Tutor*, and the Online self-test for this chapter.

WORTSCHATZ

Review and Assess

Game

Preparation The day before the game, have students write each word or expression from the **Wortschatz** on pieces of paper, cutting each word into its letter components. Then have students put the fragments of each word or phrase into a numbered envelope. Go around to each student and write the corresponding expression on a separate sheet of paper beside the number. Collect all envelopes. All this should be done a day ahead of this game, as making the envelopes and recording the expressions will take up time. Make as many envelopes as there are students in the class. To help you prepare for this game, you can ask students of one class to help you prepare the envelopes for the other class.

Procedure Pair students with one sheet of paper between them, and then distribute envelopes to each group. Students mark the number of the envelope they receive on their paper. Give the signal to open the envelope and set a specific time, such as 20 seconds per envelope, to unscramble the content and write the word or expression beside its number. When the teacher says "stop," students must immediately return the letters to the envelope and pass it on to the next group who will try to unscramble it. You may want to have each group receive 10 envelopes. The group with the most correct words or expressions wins.

Teacher Note

Give the **Kapitel 1** Chapter Test: *Testing Program*, pp. 13–18 Audio CD 1, Trs. 32–34.

REVIEW

1
Wer bist du?

Objectives

In this chapter you will learn to

Erste Stufe

- say hello and goodbye
- ask someone's name and give yours
- ask who someone is

Zweite Stufe

- ask someone's age and give yours

Dritte Stufe

- talk about where people are from
- talk about how someone gets to school

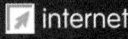 internet

 ADRESSE: go.hrw.com
KENNWORT:
  WK3 BRANDENBURG-1

◄ **Ich bin Holger. Wer bist du?**

Los geht's! · *Vor der Schule*

CD 1 Trs. 9–10

Strategie Verstehen

Look at the photos for this story. Where and when do you think these scenes are taking place? What clues tell you this?

Jens

Tara

Holger

Ahmet

Los geht's! is an abridged version of the video episode.

1

Tara: Hallo, Jens!
Jens: Hallo!
Tara: Ist das dein Moped?
Jens: Ja.
Tara: Super! Klasse!
Jens: Ich komme jetzt immer mit dem Moped zur Schule.
Tara: Ach ja! Du bist jetzt sechzehn!

2

Jens: Hallo! Wer bist du denn? Bist du neu hier?
Holger: Ja, ich bin neu hier.
Jens: Und wie heißt du?
Holger: Ich heiße Holger.
Jens: Ich bin Jens.

3

Jens: Das ist Tara.
Holger: Morgen, Tara!
Tara: Guten Morgen, Holger! Woher kommst du denn?

Holger: Aus Walburg.
Jens: Walburg? Walburg? Wo liegt denn Walburg?
Holger: In Hessen.

Tara: Schau mal! Da kommt der Ahmet. Hallo, Ahmet!

Ahmet: Hallo, Tara! Hallo, Jens! Was gibt's?

Jens: Sag mal, Ahmet, ist morgen Training?

Ahmet: Ja, klar! Um 3 Uhr.

Holger: Ich bin Holger. Wie heißt du?

Ahmet: Ahmet. Ahmet Özkan.

Holger: Wie bitte? Öz …

Tara: Ich buchstabier's für dich. Ö-Z-K-A-N. Stimmt doch, oder?

Ahmet: Ja, das stimmt!

Holger: Also, einfach! Und woher bist du?

Ahmet: Aus der Türkei.

Jens: Ahmet ist der beste Mann bei uns im Team. Die Nummer „Eins"!

Holger: Ja, prima!

Ahmet: Schon gut, tschüs!

Tara: Tschüs!

Holger: Tschüs!

Übungsheft, S. 3

1 **Was passiert hier?** *What's happening here?*

These activities check for global comprehension only. Students should not yet be expected to produce language modeled in **Los geht's!**

Do you understand what is happening in **Los geht's!**? Check your comprehension by answering these questions. Don't be afraid to guess.

1. What happens at the beginning of the story?
2. Why is Jens' age important?
3. What do you learn about the new student?
4. What information does Ahmet have for Jens? What "team" do you think they are talking about?

1. Students greet each other, Tara sees that Jens has a new moped.
2. Sixteen is the minimum required age to drive a moped.
3. Holger is from Walburg in Hessen.

4. Ahmet and Jens have practice tomorrow at 3 pm. A soccer team

2 **Genauer lesen** *Reading for detail*

Reread the conversations. Which words or phrases do the characters in **Los geht's!** use to

1. greet each other   1. Guten Morgen, Hallo, Morgen
2. ask someone's name   2. Wie heißt du?
3. ask where someone is from   3. Woher kommst du denn?
4. ask where a place is   4. Wo liegt denn ...?
5. say goodbye   5. Tschüs.

3 **Stimmt oder stimmt nicht?** *Right or wrong?*

Are these statements right or wrong? Answer each one with either **stimmt** or **stimmt nicht**. If a statement is wrong, try to state it correctly.

1. Jens ist jetzt sechzehn und kommt mit dem Moped zur Schule.
2. Ahmet ist neu in der Schule.
3. Walburg ist in Bayern.
4. Tara und Holger haben morgen Training.
5. Ahmet kommt aus der Türkei.

1. Stimmt.
2. Stimmt nicht. Holger ist neu.
3. Stimmt nicht. Walburg ist in Hessen.
4. Stimmt nicht. Jens und Ahmet haben morgen Training.
5. Stimmt.

4 **Wer macht was?** *Who is doing what?*

What have you learned about each of these students? Match the descriptions on the right with the names on the left, then read each completed sentence.

1. Holger   d
2. Tara   c
3. Jens   a
4. Ahmet   b

a. ...ist jetzt sechzehn und kommt mit dem Moped zur Schule.
b. ...ist der beste Mann im Team.
c. ...buchstabiert den Namen von Ahmet.
d. ...ist neu in der Schule.

5 **Wer bist du denn?** *Who are you?*

Using words from the box, complete this conversation between two new students.

ULRIKE   Hallo! Ich ___1___ (heiße) Ulrike. Wer bist ___2___ (du) denn? Bist du ___3___ hier? (neu)

GUPSE   Ja, ich heiße Gupse. Ich ___4___ aus der (komme) Türkei. ___5___ kommst du? (Woher)

ULRIKE   ___6___ Hessen. (Aus)

GUPSE   Schau mal! ___7___ ist das? (Wer)

ULRIKE   Das ist die Birgit. Sie ___8___ ist (ist) sechzehn und kommt ___9___ mit (mit) dem Moped zur Schule. Toll, was?

mit	Woher		Aus
	du	Wer	heiße
komme		ist	neu

Erste Stufe

Objectives Saying hello and goodbye; asking someone's name and giving yours; asking who someone is

WK3 BRANDENBURG-1

So sagt man das! *Here's how you say it!*

Saying hello and goodbye

Saying hello:

> **Guten Morgen!** *Good morning!*
> **Morgen!** *Morning!*
> **Guten Tag!** *Hello!*
> **Tag!**
> **Hallo!** } *Hi!*
> **Grüß dich!**

Saying goodbye:

> **Auf Wiedersehen!** *Goodbye!*
> **Wiedersehen!** *Bye!*
>
> **Tschüs!** }
> **Tschau!** } *Bye!*
> **Bis dann!** *See you later!*

1–1

Übungsheft, S. 4, Ü. 2–3

Grammatikheft, S. 1, Ü. 1–2

---

6 **Hallo! oder Tschüs!** Script on p. 15G

Zuhören Listen to the following people greet each other or say goodbye. For each exchange you hear, write whether it is a **hello** or a **goodbye**.

CD 1 Tr. 11

1. Hello
2. Hello
3. Goodbye
4. Hello
5. Goodbye

Ein wenig Landeskunde

(About the country and the people)

Guten Morgen! and **Guten Tag!** are standard greetings and can be used in almost any social situation. With whom do you think you might use the abbreviated forms **Morgen!** and **Tag!**? The phrases **Hallo!** and **Grüß dich!** are casual and are generally used with friends and family. **Grüß dich!** is heard more in southern Germany and Austria. **Auf Wiedersehen!, Wiedersehen!,** and **Tschüs!** are all ways of saying goodbye. Which of the three do you think would be the most formal? If you were going to greet a fellow student and good friend, and then say goodbye, which phrases would you use?

Grüß dich, Klaus!

Guten Tag, Frau Müller!

Auf Wiedersehen, Herr Kießling!

Tschau, Silvia!

7 Hallo!

Lesen Here you see some friends greeting each other and saying goodbye. Match the exchanges with the appropriate pictures.

a.

b.

c.

d.

1. —Tschüs, Lisa! c.
　　—Tschau, Christian!

2. —Wiedersehen, Frau Weber! a.
　　—Auf Wiedersehen, Peter!

3. —Tag, Alexander! Sebastian! d.
　　—Tag, Julia!

4. —Guten Morgen, Herr Koschizki! b.
　　—Morgen, Elisabeth!

8 Freunde begrüßen *Greeting friends*

Sprechen Make a name tag for yourself, using your own name or one chosen from the list in the **Vorschau.** Get together with a few of your classmates. For more German first names, turn to page R14 in the back of your book. Greet and say goodbye to each other, using the names on the tags. Don't forget to greet and say goodbye to your teacher.

Was sagt Anna zum Monster mit den drei Köpfen?

So sagt man das! *Here's how you say it!*

Asking someone's name and giving yours

When you meet a new student you'll want to find out his or her name.

You ask:

Wie heißt du? *What's your name?*

You might also ask:

Heißt du Holger? *Is your name Holger?*

To ask a boy's name:

Wie heißt der Junge?
Heißt der Junge Ahmet?
　Is that boy's name Ahmet?

To ask a girl's name:

Wie heißt das Mädchen?
Heißt das Mädchen Ulrike?

The student responds:

Ich heiße Holger.

Ja, ich heiße Holger.

Der Junge heißt Ahmet.
Ja, er heißt Ahmet.

Das Mädchen heißt Steffi.
Nein, sie heißt Steffi.

Grammatikheft,
S. 2, Ü. 3–4

9 **Was sagen sie?** Script on p. 15G

Zuhören To complete these conversations, match each exchange you hear with the correct illustration.

CD 1
Tr. 12

a.

b.

c.

d.

Grammatik

Forming questions

There are several ways of asking questions in German. One way is to begin with a question word (interrogative) such as **wie** (*how*). Some other question words are: **wer** (*who*), **wo** (*where*), and **woher** (*from where*).

Look at the questions below. How are they different from questions such as **Wie heißt der Junge?**[1] What is the position of the verb in these questions?[2]

Heißt du Holger?
Heißt das Mädchen Kristin?

Ja, ich heiße Holger.
Nein, sie heißt Antje.

Mehr Grammatikübungen
S. 36, Ü. 1–2

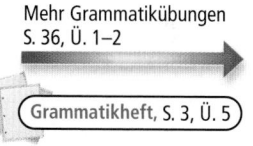
Grammatikheft, S. 3, Ü. 5

10 **Wie heißt er? Wie heißt sie?**

Sprechen How well do you remember the names of your classmates? When someone asks you: **Wie heißt das Mädchen?** or **Wie heißt der Junge?**, give the name of the person referred to. For practice, use complete sentences.

So sagt man das!

Asking who someone is

Grammatikheft, S. 3, Ü. 6

To find out someone else's name you ask: **Wer ist das?**

The response might be:

Das ist die Moni.

Das ist der Stefan.

Das ist Herr Gärtner,
der Deutschlehrer.

Das ist Frau Weigel,
die Biologielehrerin.

---

1. These questions anticipate *yes* or *no* as a response.
2. The verb is always at the beginning of a *yes/no* question.

The definite articles der, die, and das

German has three words for *the*: **der, die,** and **das,** called *definite articles*. These words tell us to which class or group a German noun belongs. Words that have **der** as the article, such as **der Junge** (*the boy*), are masculine nouns. Words that have the article **die,** such as **die Lehrerin** (*the female teacher*), are feminine nouns. The third group of nouns has the article **das,** as in **das Mädchen** (*the girl*), and are neuter nouns. You will learn more about this in **Kapitel 3.**

der-words *(masculine)*	**die**-words *(feminine)*	**das**-words *(neuter)*
		das Mädchen
der Junge		
der Lehrer	die Lehrerin	
der Deutschlehrer	die Deutschlehrerin	

Mehr Grammatikübungen
S. 36, Ü. 3

Übungsheft, S. 5, Ü. 4–6

 11 Grammatik im Kontext Script on p. 15G

Zuhören Holger is asking Jens and Tara about various people in the class. Listen and decide whether the person they are talking about is male or female.   1. Female 2. Female 3. Female 4. Male
CD 1 Tr. 13   5. Female 6. Female 7. Male 8. Male

12 Grammatik im Kontext

Lesen/Schreiben Holger is trying to learn the names of everyone in his class. He asks Tara for help. Rewrite the conversation, filling in the missing definite articles **der, die,** or **das.**

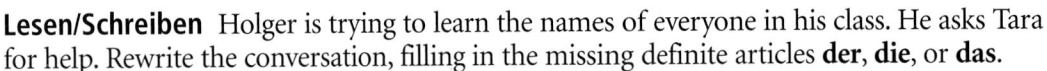

HOLGER   Wie heißt der Junge?

Der TARA   ____1____ Junge heißt Uwe.
          ____2____ Uwe kommt aus Der
          München.

HOLGER   Und ____3____ Mädchen? das

Das TARA   ____4____ Mädchen heißt
          Katja. ____5____ Katja Die
          kommt aus Hamburg.

HOLGER   Und wie heißt ____6____ die
          Lehrerin?

TARA   ____7____ Lehrerin heißt Die
          Frau Möller.

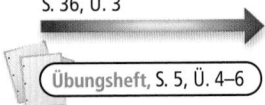

Ein wenig Landeskunde

In casual speech, the definite articles **der** and **die** are often used with first names (**Das ist die Tara. Das ist der Jens.**). This practice occurs more often in southern Germany, Austria, and Switzerland than in northern Germany. **Der** and **die** are also often used with the last names of celebrities and other well-known people. How would you refer to **Steffi Graf**?

 13 Wer sind meine Mitschüler?

Who are my classmates?

Sprechen Now team up with a classmate and ask each other the names of other students in the class. Be sure to use all of the ways of asking you have learned.

14 Ratespiel *Guessing Game*

Sprechen Bring in pictures of well-known people and ask your classmates to identify them.

LERNTRICK

In English, we know that the word "the" signals a noun. In German, we use **der, die,** and **das** in much the same way. Remember that in German, every time you learn a new noun, you must also learn the definite article (**der, die,** or **das**) that goes with it.

Zweite Stufe

Objectives Asking someone's age and giving yours

WK3 BRANDENBURG-1

So sagt man das!

Asking someone's age and giving yours

To find out how old someone is,
you might ask:

You might get responses like these:

1–B

Wie alt bist du?

{ **Ich bin vierzehn Jahre alt.**
   I am 14 years old.
Ich bin vierzehn.
Vierzehn.

Bist du schon fünfzehn?
Are you already 15?

Nein, ich bin vierzehn.

Wie alt ist der Peter?
Und die Monika? Ist sie auch fünfzehn?

Er ist fünfzehn.
Ja, sie ist auch fünfzehn.

Can you identify the verbs in the different examples?[1]
Why do you think the verbs change?[2]

Grammatikheft,
S. 4, Ü. 7

Wortschatz

Do you remember the numbers you learned in the Vorschau?

CD-ROM
DISC 1

0 null	1 eins	2 zwei	3 drei	4 vier	5 fünf
6 sechs	7 sieben	8 acht	9 neun	10 zehn	11 elf
12 zwölf	13 dreizehn	14 vierzehn	15 fünfzehn	16 sechzehn	17 siebzehn
18 achtzehn	19 neunzehn	20 zwanzig			

1–B

Übungsheft, S. 6, Ü. 7   Grammatikheft, S. 4, Ü. 8

15 **Wie alt?** Script on p.15G

Zuhören Holger wants to get to know his new classmates, so he asks Ahmet how old
everyone is. Listen to their conversation and write down the ages of the students below.

CD 1 Tr. 14

Handan: _____   Ahmet: _____   Renate: _____   Jens: _____
          ist 15   ist 16   ist 14   ist 16

16 **Wir stellen vor** *Introducing*

Sprechen Ask your partner's name and age and then introduce him or her to the rest of
the class.

---

1. The verbs are **bist, bin, ist.** 2. The verbs change because the subjects of the sentences change.

Subject pronouns and the verb **sein** (*to be*)

The phrases **ich bin, du bist, er ist, sie ist,** and **sie sind** each contain a subject pronoun corresponding to the English *I, you, he, she,* and *they,* and a form of the verb **sein** (*to be*): *I am, you are, he is, she is, they are.* **Sein** is one of the most frequently used verbs in German.*

Ich	**bin**	dreizehn.
Du	**bist**	auch dreizehn.
Karola Sie }	**ist**	vierzehn.
Jens Er }	**ist**	sechzehn.
Ahmet und Holger Sie }	**sind**	sechzehn.

Mehr Grammatikübungen
S. 36–37, Ü. 4–5

Übungsheft, S. 6–7, Ü. 8–11

Grammatikheft, S. 5, Ü. 9–10

CD-ROM
DISC 1

---

17 **Grammatik im Kontext** Script on p.15G

CD 1
Tr. 15

Zuhören Listen to the following sentences and determine if Ulrike is talking about herself, about one other person, or about more than one person. 1. self 2. one person 3. one person 4. more than one 5. one person

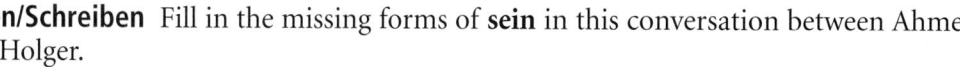

	about self	about one person	about more than one person
1			
2			

18 **Grammatik im Kontext**

Lesen/Schreiben Fill in the missing forms of **sein** in this conversation between Ahmet and Holger.

HOLGER Sag mal, wie alt ___1___ du? bist

AHMET Ich ___2___ 16. bin

HOLGER Du ___3___ 16? Ich auch. Und wie alt ___4___ Tara und Jens? bist; sind

AHMET Tara ___5___ 14, und Jens ___6___ 16. ist; ist

19 **Wie alt sind die Jungen und Mädchen?**

Sprechen Say who these people are and how old they are.

Steffi, 15
Steffi ist fünfzehn.

Melanie und Katja, 16
Melanie und Katja sind sechzehn.

Björn, 16
Björn ist sechzehn.

Karola, 14
Karola ist vierzehn.

20 **Zum Schreiben**

Schreiben You are preparing for a conversation with an exchange student from Germany. Write in German the questions you want to ask in order to find out the student's name and age. Then write how you would answer those questions yourself.

---

*There are three other forms of **sein** you will learn about and practice later: **wir sind** (*we are*), **ihr seid** (*you are, plural*) and **Sie sind** (*you are, formal*).

21 **Lesen/Schreiben** The **Bundesrepublik Deutschland** (*Federal Republic of Germany*) is made up of **Bundesländer** (*federal states*). Each **Bundesland** has a **Hauptstadt** (*capital*) and its own regional government. The **Bundesrepublik Deutschland** is abbreviated **BRD**.

1–C

a. How many **Bundesländer** are there? Make a list of them.

b. Write the **Hauptstadt** beside the name of each **Bundesland.**

c. Which **Bundesland** borders Switzerland? Austria?

d. What are the **Hauptstädte** of Switzerland and Austria?

For answers, see TE Interleaf, p. 15S

Kiel

SCHLESWIG-HOLSTEIN

MECKLENBURG-VORPOMMERN

Schwerin

HAMBURG

BREMEN

BRANDENBURG

NIEDERSACHSEN

Wiebke Jansen, 16

Potsdam   BERLIN

Hannover   Magdeburg

SACHSEN-ANHALT

Jörg Schulze, 19

NORDRHEIN-WESTFALEN

Düsseldorf

Dresden

Erfurt

SACHSEN

HESSEN   THÜRINGEN

Kemal Acar, 15

Wiesbaden

RHEINLAND-PFALZ

Brigitte Dennhöffer, 19

Mainz

SAAR-LAND   Saar-brücken

Stuttgart   BAYERN

Wien ✪

München

BADEN-WÜRTTEMBERG

Melina Kiritsis, 18

Zürich

Bern ✪   SCHWEIZ   LIECHTENSTEIN

ÖSTERREICH

✪—Vaduz

Dritte Stufe

Objectives Talking about where people are from; talking about how someone gets to school

WK3 BRANDENBURG-1

So sagt man das!

Talking about where people are from

To find out where someone is from you might ask:

> **Woher kommst du?** *or*
> **Woher bist du?**
> **Bist du aus Deutschland?**

The other person might respond:

> **Ich komme aus Texas.**
> **Ich bin aus Texas.**
> **Nein, ich bin aus Wisconsin.**

To find out where someone else is from you ask:

> **Und Herr Gärtner, der Deutschlehrer, woher ist er?**
> **Kommt die Inge auch aus Österreich?**

> **Er ist aus Österreich.**
>
> **Nein, sie kommt aus Thüringen.**

Übungsheft,
S. 9, Ü. 14–15

Grammatikheft,
S. 6–7, Ü. 11–13

What do you think the question word **woher** is equivalent to in English?[1]

Schülerausweis I | POTSDAM

gültig bis: **31. 7. 00**

00

gültig bis: **31. 7. 01**

01

gültig bis: **31. 7. 02**

02

Schulstempel/Unterschrift

POTSDAM

Schul II 285-1 – Schülerausweis (2. 92)
● ☏ Mat. 325. 0 9 8 7 6 5 4 3 2

---

22 **Woher kommen sie?** Script on p. 15G

Zuhören Look at the map on page 27 as you listen to the five students introducing themselves. For each introduction, write the name of the student who is speaking and where he or she is from.

CD 1 Tr. 16

1. Jörg Schulze - Berlin 2. Kemal Acar - Düsseldorf
3. Wiebke Jansen - Hamburg 4. Brigitte Dennhöffer - München
5. Melina Kiritsis - Stuttgart

23 **Woher sind sie?**

a. **Sprechen** Look at the photos of the people on page 27. Take turns asking and telling your partner about each person pictured, mentioning name, age, and where that person is from.

b. **Sprechen** Ask your partner where he or she is from, and your partner will ask you. Be prepared to share your partner's answer with the class.

c. **Sprechen** One student begins by calling on a classmate. That person says his or her name, age, and where he or she is from, then calls on someone else.

---

1. **Woher?** asks the question *From where?*

24 Rate mal

Sprechen/Schreiben Choose one of the **Landeshauptstädte** from the box below and write it down. The city you choose is your imaginary hometown. Your partner will try to guess where you are from. If he or she guesses incorrectly, you can say **Nein, ich komme nicht aus …** After your partner guesses correctly, switch roles and guess where your partner is from.

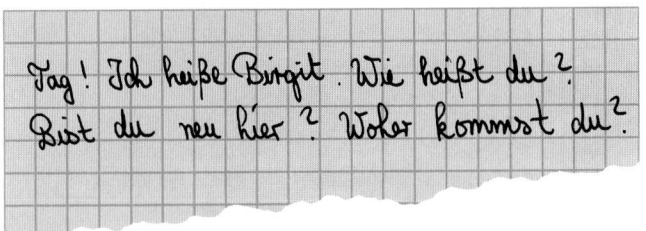

Erfurt	Magdeburg	Mainz	Dresden	Berlin	Wiesbaden
Düsseldorf	Saarbrücken	Hamburg	Hannover	Bremen	München
Kiel	Stuttgart	Potsdam	Schwerin		

25 Woher kommst du?

Lesen/Schreiben A classmate, Birgit, slips Holger the following note in class.

> Tag! Ich heiße Birgit. Wie heißt du? Bist du neu hier? Woher kommst du?

What does Holger write back to her?
Write his note. Possible answers include: **Ich heiße Holger. Ich bin neu hier. Ich komme aus Walburg.**

SPRACHTIPP

There are many short words in German that you can use to connect your ideas and to make your German sound more natural. Some of these words are: **und** (*and*), **auch** (*also*), **jetzt** (*now*), and **schon** (*already*).

The teenagers in the **Los geht's!** section also used some other expressions: **Ach so!** (*Yeah, I see!*), **Ach ja!** (*Oh, yeah!*), **Ja, klar!** (*Of course!*), and **Prima!** (*Great!*). Look back at the conversations in **Los geht's!** and see how these words are used.

26 Zum Schreiben

a. **Schreiben** Choose three of the students shown on the map on page 27 as possible pen pals and write three sentences about each of them, telling their names, ages, and where they are from.

b. **Lesen/Schreiben** Exchange papers with a partner and read your partner's sentences. Is everything written correctly? Make corrections on your partner's paper and he or she will do the same on your paper.

c. **Schreiben** Now write a few sentences about yourself that you might use in a letter to one of these people, giving the same information.

Wie kommen die Mädchen und Jungen zur Schule?

1–A, 1–2

CD-ROM DISC 1

Annette kommt mit dem Bus.

Michael kommt mit der U-Bahn.

Philipp kommt mit dem Rad.

Sara kommt zu Fuß.

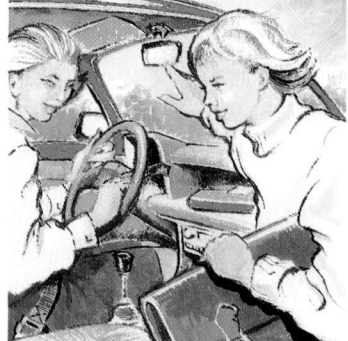

Meine Mutter bringt mich mit dem Auto.

Und Heike kommt mit dem Moped.

27 **Stimmt! oder Stimmt nicht!** Script on p. 15G

CD 1
Tr. 17

Zuhören Based on the information given in the **Wortschatz**, determine whether the statements you hear are right or not. List the names you hear and write beside the name **stimmt** if the information is correct or **stimmt nicht** if it is incorrect.

Heike: **stimmt**   Philipp: **stimmt nicht**
Annette: **stimmt**   Sara: **stimmt nicht**
Michael: **stimmt nicht**   ich: **stimmt**

So sagt man das!

Talking about how someone gets to school

To find out how someone gets to school you ask:

> **Wie kommst du zur Schule?**
> **Kommt Ahmet zu Fuß zur Schule?**
>
> **Wie kommt Ayla zur Schule?**
> **Und wie kommt der Wolfgang zur Schule?**

The responses might be:

> **Ich komme mit dem Rad.**
> **Nein, er kommt auch mit dem Rad.**
> **Sie kommt mit dem Bus.**
> **Er kommt mit der U-Bahn oder mit dem Bus.**

Mehr Grammatikübungen
S. 37, Ü. 6–7

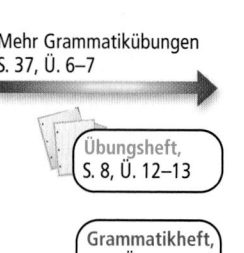

Übungsheft,
S. 8, Ü. 12–13

Grammatikheft,
S. 8, Ü. 14–16

Wie kommst du zur Schule?

CD1
Trs. 18-23

Übungsheft,
S. 12, Ü. 19

In Germany, many people of all ages ride bicycles—to school, to work, even to do their shopping. Why do you think this might be so? In addition to bicycles, there are a number of other possibilities available to German students for getting to and from school. Students who are at least 16 can drive a **Moped,** 14-year-olds can ride **Mofas,** and students 18 or over can get a driver's license for a car. We asked several students around Germany about how they get to school; here are their responses. CD1 Tr. 18

Christina, Bietigheim

„Ich heiße Christina, bin 17 Jahre alt und komme mit dem Leichtkraftrad zur Schule."
CD1 Tr. 19

Johannes, Bietigheim

„Also, ich heiße Johannes Hennicke, bin 12 Jahre alt und fahre jeden Morgen mit dem Fahrrad zur Schule." CD1 Tr. 22

Sonja, Berlin

„Ich heiße Sonja Wegener. Ich bin 17 Jahre alt. Ich fahre meistens mit der U-Bahn zur Schule, aber im Sommer fahr ich auch mit dem Fahrrad."
CD1 Tr. 20

Tim, Berlin

„Mein Name ist Tim Wiesbach. Ich bin 18 Jahre alt und komme mit meinem Moped jeden Tag, wenn das Wetter mitspielt, zur Schule." CD1 Tr. 23

Sandra, Berlin

„Also, ich heiße Sandra Krabbel, und ich bin achtzehn Jahre alt, und meistens also, ich geh auf die Max-Beckmann-Oberschule, und meistens fahr ich mit dem Bus. Aber ja manchmal ganz selten auch mit dem Fahrrad, und jetzt neuerdings auch manchmal mit dem Auto, aber nur sehr selten." CD1 Tr. 21

1. Christina-motorbike Johannes- bicycle Sonja-subway/bicycle
Tim-moped Sandra-bus/bicycle/ car

A. 1. How do these students get to school? List the names of the students that were interviewed, then beside each name write the way that each student gets to school.

   2. Look at the list you made, and try to determine where these students might live: in a large city? in a suburb? etc. First discuss this question with a partner, then together explain to the rest of the class how you came to the conclusions that you did.

   3. The photo above is fairly typical for a German city. What do you notice about it? Is the German city in the photo similar to or different from a city in the United States? What conclusions can you draw about possible differences in transportation in Germany and in the United States?

B. Ask several of your classmates how they get to school, and decide together if there are differences between the way American students get to school and the way German students get to school. Write a brief essay discussing this question.

STANDARDS: 2.2, 3.2, 4.2

Grammatik im Kontext

Sprechen/Schreiben How many questions and answers can you form?

Possible answers include:
Wie kommst du zur Schule?
Wie kommt der Jens zur Schule?
Wie kommen Ahmet und Holger zur Schule?

a. Viele Fragen *A lot of questions*

Wie	kommst kommen kommt	die Sonja der Jens du Ahmet und Holger	zur Schule?

b. Viele Antworten *A lot of answers*

Der Johannes Der Tim Ich Ahmet und Holger	komme kommen kommt	mit dem Rad. mit dem Bus. zu Fuß. mit dem Moped. mit dem Auto. mit der U-Bahn.

Der Tim kommt mit dem Rad.
Ich komme zu Fuß.
Ahmet und Holger kommen mit der U-Bahn.

29 **Grammatik im Kontext**

Lesen/Sprechen Can you complete this conversation between Susanne and Manfred, two students at Tara's school? (More than one question may be possible!)

SUSANNE Tag! 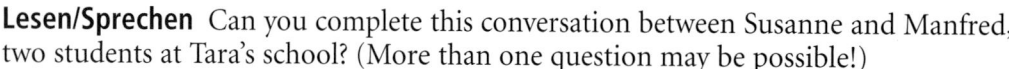? **Bist du neu hier?**

MANFRED Ja, ich bin neu hier.

SUSANNE ══════? **Wie heißt du?**

MANFRED Ich heiße Manfred.

SUSANNE Und ══════? **woher kommst du?**

MANFRED Aus Saarbrücken.

Inge kommt mit dem Moped.

MANFRED ══════? **Wie heißt das Mädchen?**

SUSANNE Das ist Inge.

MANFRED ══════? **Ist die Inge sechzehn?**

SUSANNE Ja, Inge ist sechzehn und kommt immer mit dem Moped zur Schule.
══════? **Kommst du mit dem Moped zur Schule?**

MANFRED Nein, ich komme mit dem Rad zur Schule.

Which one is the new student? How does he or she get to school? Manfred; by bicycle **(mit dem Rad)**

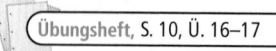
Übungsheft, S. 10, Ü. 16–17   Grammatikheft, S. 9, Ü. 17–19

30 **Interview**

Sprechen Write eight questions like the ones you came up with in Activity 29. Be sure to use questions beginning with question words, as well as yes/no questions. Then, working with a partner, use the questions you wrote to interview each other.

 **Eine Umfrage** *A survey*

a. Sprechen Form small groups. Each of you will take a turn asking the person to your right how he or she gets to school.

b. Sprechen/Schreiben Now take turns reporting to the whole class on how the classmate you asked gets to school. As everyone reports, one person will make a chart on the board. Discuss the survey results with the class.

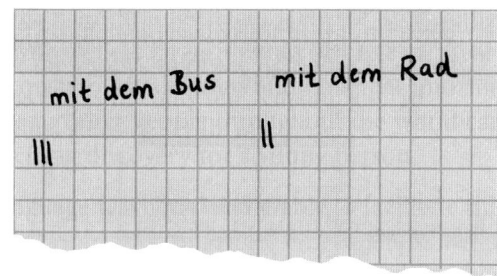

 **Für mein Notizbuch** *For my notebook*

Schreiben As your first entry in your **Notizbuch**, write something about yourself. Include your name (or your German name), your age, where you are from, and how you get to school.

 **Von der Schule zum Beruf**

Schreiben As part of a summer job for your local newspaper, you are asked to visit two businesses to find out how their employees get to work. Prepare a report.

AUSSPRACHE

Richtig aussprechen / Richtig lesen
Pronounce correctly / Read correctly

CD 1
Trs. 24–26

CD1 Tr. 24

A. To practice the following sounds, say the words and sentences below after your teacher or after the recording.

1. The letters **ä** and **e**: The long **ä** and **e** are pronounced much like the long *a* in the English word *gate*.
   Mädchen, dem, zehn / Das Mädchen kommt mit dem Bus.

2. The letter **ü**: To pronounce the long **ü**, round your lips as if you were going to whistle. Without moving your lips from this position, try to say the vowel sound in the English word *bee*.
   Grüß, begrüßen, Tschüs / Grüß dich, Klaus! Tschüs, Ahmet!

3. The letter **ö**: To pronounce the long **ö**, round your lips, then without moving your lips from this position, try to say the vowel sound in the English word *bay*.
   Hör, Österreich / Inge kommt aus Österreich.

4. The letter **w**: The letter **w** is pronounced like the *v* in the English word *viper*.
   wer, wo, woher, wie / Woher kommt Uwe? Aus Walburg?

5. The letter **v**: The letter **v** is usually pronounced like the *f* in the English word *fish*.
   vier, vor, von, viele / Er ist vierzehn, und Volker ist fünfzehn.

Richtig schreiben / Diktat *Write correctly / Dictation*

B. Write down the sentences that you hear.
Script on p. 15H

CD1 Tr. 25
CD1 Tr. 26 (with pauses)

Zum Lesen

Postkarten aus den Ferien

Lesestrategie

When you read the German texts in this book, you do not need to understand every word. As you progress, you will learn to pay attention to certain things—and you'll be amazed at how much you understand.

Using Visual Clues Certain clues will help you determine in advance what the reading might be about. Before you try to read a text, look at the title and at any visual clues, such as photos or illustrations, as well as at the format of the text. Very often these clues provide you with enough information to figure out what the text is about.

1. Look at the pictures as well as the format of these texts. What kinds of texts are they? informal notes/ postcards

2. What do you think **Postkarten aus den Ferien** means? The format of the texts should help you guess what the word **Postkarten** means. Once you know that, ask yourself: When do people usually write texts like this? How does the answer to this question help you understand what the words **aus den Ferien** mean?

3. Have you ever written to someone while you were on vacation? What did you write about?

4. With a friend, write down some phrases you use when you write to friends on vacation.

5. Which **Postkarte** mentions a lot of activities? 5. The card from the Schwarzwald

Schwarzwald

Hallo Rita!
Herzliche Grüße aus
dem Schwarzwald!
Das Wetter ist
prima – warm und
sonnig. Wir
schwimmen, wandern,
und spielen Tennis,
Volleyball, Minigolf!
Bis bald!

Monika

Rita Meyer
Gartenstraße 21
14482 Potsdam

London

Liebe Frau Polgert!
How do you do? Ich bin
in London und finde die
Stadt und die Engländer
ganz phantastisch! Ich
lerne viel Englisch.
Herzliche Grüße!
Ihre Claudia Bach

Fr. Anja Polgert
Vogelsangstr. 39
14478 Potsdam
Germany

Berliner Rathaus

Liebe Omi! Lieber Opi!

Ich bin mit meiner
Schulklasse in Berlin
– eine tolle Stadt, echt
super!
Wir kommen am Freitag
wieder zurück.
Liebe Grüße
        Euer Bernhard

Gottard u. Friede Schnitzler
Eichenstr. 7
14489 Potsdam

London Tower Bridge

ZUM LESEN

6. Hallo, herzliche Grüße, Bis bald!, Liebe Grüße.

6. Which words in these texts are types of greetings or farewells?

7. The one from London: to a teacher; from the **Schwarzwald:** to a friend; the one from Berlin: to relatives.

7. To whom are these texts written? What clues tell you how well the writers know the people to whom they are writing? Which **Postkarte** is probably written to a teacher? How can you tell?

8. Where is each person writing from? Why are they there? If they do not state the reason directly, what phrases help you infer why they are there?

8. London-vacation, **Schwarzwald**-vacation, Berlin-school trip

9. What is the weather like where Monika is? 9. warm and sunny.

10. Why does Claudia use an English expression in her **Postkarte**? Do you think she is enjoying herself? How do you know? 10. She is writing to her English teacher.

11. Write a postcard in German based on one of the following activities:

a. You and a friend have stayed with a German family while on vacation. After you leave, write a postcard to your host family, telling them where you are and how you like it.

b. Assume you are in Germany for the first time. Write a postcard to a friend who knows some German.

Liebe(r) …

Ich bin in _____.

Hier _____ es sehr

schön. _____ ist eine

interessante Stadt.

    Herzliche _____

Übungsheft, S. 11, Ü. 18

Mehr Grammatikübungen

Erste Stufe   **Objectives** Asking someone's name and giving yours; asking who someone is

1 You are asking someone's name and you get an answer. Complete each of the following exchanges by filling in the blanks with a form of the verb **heißen**. (**S. 23**)

1. A: Wie _____ du?   B: Ich _____ Mark.   heißt; heiße
2. A: _____ du Michael?   B: Nein, ich _____ John.   Heißt; heiße
3. A: Wie _____ das Mädchen? B: Das Mädchen _____ Steffi. heißt; heißt
4. A: Wie_____ der Junge?   B: Der Junge _____ Kurt.   heißt; heißt
5. A: _____ das Mädchen Brit? B: Nein, das Mädchen _____ Anja. Heißt; heißt
6. A: Und du _____ Stefan?   B: Ja, ich _____ Stefan.   heißt; heiße

2 You want to know the names of various boys and girls. Write questions, using the English questions as cues. (**S. 23**)

1. (Is your name Jack?)   _____   Heißt du Jack?
2. (Is his name Mark?)   _____   Heißt er Mark?
3. (What's the boy's name?) _____   Wie heißt der Junge?
4. (His name is Steven.)   _____   Er heißt Steven.
5. (What's the girl's name?) _____   Wie heißt das Mädchen?
6. (Her name is Jackie.)   _____   Sie heißt Jackie.

3 You want to know the names of various people or at least who they are. Write questions and statements by filling in each blank with the correct form of the definite article. (**S. 24**)

1. Wie heißt _____ Junge? Und _____ Mädchen?   der; das
2. Wie heißt _____ Deutschlehrer? Und _____ Biologielehrerin? der; die
3. Ist das Herr Gärtner, _____ Deutschlehrer?   der
4. Ist das _____ Steffi? Und das ist _____ Kristin, ja?   die; die

Zweite Stufe   **Objective** Asking someone's age and giving yours

4 You and your friends want to know the ages of various new classmates. Complete the following questions and statements by filling in the blanks with the appropriate form of the verb **sein**. (**S. 26**)

1. Wie alt _____ der Ahmet? _____ er schon fünfzehn?   ist; Ist
2. Der Ahmet und die Karola _____ schon sechzehn.   sind
3. Ich _____ dreizehn. Und wie alt _____ du?   bin; bist
4. Wie alt _____ der Deutschlehrer? _____ er schon 40? ist; Ist
5. Wie alt _____ du? _____ du schon fünfzehn?   bist; Bist
6. Ich _____ vierzehn, und du _____ schon sechzehn.   bin; bist

5 One of the new students in class wants to know how old certain people are, and you tell him or her. Complete the following answers by filling in each blank with the appropriate personal pronoun and the appropriate form of the verb **sein**. (S. 26)

1. Wie alt ist die Tara? _____ 14 Jahre alt. *Sie ist*
2. Wie alt bist du denn? _____ schon 16 Jahre alt. *Ich bin*
3. Wie alt ist der Deutschlehrer? _____ 35 Jahre alt. *Er ist*
4. Und die Biologielehrerin? _____ schon 47 Jahre alt. *Sie ist*
5. Wie alt sind Stefan und Moni? _____ 19 Jahre alt. *Sie sind*
6. Und wie alt _____ , Michaela? *bist du*

Dritte Stufe   **Objective** Talking about how someone gets to school

6 You seem to know how everyone gets to school. Complete the following statements by filling in each blank with the correct form of the verb **kommen** and the means of transportation given in parentheses. (S. 30)

1. Wie kommt die Steffi zur Schule? (by bike)   Sie _____ . *kommt mit dem Rad*
2. Wie kommt der Ahmet zur Schule? (he walks)   Er _____ . *kommt zu Fuß*
3. Wie kommt der Lehrer zur Schule? (by car)   Er _____ . *kommt mit dem Auto*
4. Wie kommt die Annette zur Schule? (by bus)   Sie _____ . *kommt mit dem Bus*
5. Wie kommt der Mark zur Schule? (by subway)   Er _____ . *kommt mit der U-Bahn*
6. Wie kommt die Heike zur Schule? (by moped)   Sie _____ . *kommt mit dem Moped*

7 At the beginning of the school year, someone reports to the teacher how everyone gets to school. Complete each of the following statements by filling in each blank with the appropriate means of transportation. (S. 30)

1. (by bus)   Sandra kommt _____ zur Schule.   *mit dem Bus*
2. (on his moped)   Tim kommt _____ zur Schule.   *mit dem Moped*
3. (by subway)   Michael kommt _____ zur Schule.   *mit der U-Bahn*
4. (by car)   Sandra kommt _____ zur Schule.   *mit dem Auto*
5. (by bike)   Philipp kommt _____ zur Schule.   *mit dem Rad*
6. (on foot)   Ich komme _____ zur Schule.   *zu Fuß*

Anwendung

internet

go.hrw.com
ADRESSE: go.hrw.com
KENNWORT:
WK3 BRANDENBURG-1

Script on p. 15H

The CD-ROM Tutor offers guided recording and writing activities to accompany the **Anwendung.** These activities are designed to practice students' oral and written communication skills and to review material from each chapter.

 Listen to four people talking about themselves. Write their names on a piece of paper, then beside each name write the person's age and where he or she is from.

CD1 Tr. 27

Maria, 16, Wien   Frau Bach, 29, Brandenburg

Martin, 14, Berlin   Tara, 14, Potsdam

a. Say hello to a classmate. Ask his or her name, age, and where he or she is from.

b. Introduce yourself to the class, giving your name, age, and where you are from. Then introduce the classmate you just met.

 Read the letter below and complete the activities that follow.

> Eisenach, den 10. Februar 2002
>
> Lieber Ralph!
>
> Ich heiße Mandy Gerber. Ich bin aus Eisenach. Das ist in Thüringen. Ich bin vierzehn Jahre alt. Wie alt bist du? Bist du auch vierzehn? Bitte, schreib mir und schick auch ein Foto von dir! Viele Grüße
>
>   Mandy

a. Make a list of things Mandy tells about herself.

a. Name, hometown (Eisenach), age (14)

b. Wie alt bist du? Bist du schon vierzehn?

b. What does Mandy want to know? Make a list of her questions.

Inhaber/in des Ausweises

Name: Özkan
Vorname: Ahmet
geboren am: 29. 12. 87
Straße: Eichenweg 17
Wohnort: 14882 Potsdam

Ahmet Özkan
Unterschrift

Verwendungszweck des Ausweises
Nachweis der Schülereigenschaft beim Kauf

● von Monatsmarken für Schülertickets, Ermäßigungssammelkarten und Ermäßigungsfahrscheinen der BVG/BVB
● verbilligter Eintrittskarten u. a. für

Aquarium   Botanischer Garten   Theater
Ausstellungen   Konzerte   Urania
Bäder   Museen   Zoo/Tierpark
Veranstaltungen der Volkshochschulen

Maßgebend sind die Bestimmungen der jeweiligen Träger
Altersnachweis für Filmvorführungen

4 Look at the **Schülerausweis** (*school identification card*) to the right and answer the questions that follow.

a. To whom does this **Schülerausweis** belong?

b. When was this person born?

c. Where does this person live?

4. a. Ahmet Özkan
   b. December 29, 1987
   c. Eichenweg 17, 14882 Potsdam

5 If you were an exchange student in one of the German-speaking countries, you would receive a **Schülerausweis**. Using the example to the right as a model, create a **Schülerausweis** for yourself, filling in all the required information.

6 Look at the picture below with a partner and take turns with your classmates telling how the people in the illustration get to school.

 **7** Write a letter to a pen pal in Germany like the one Mandy wrote to Ralph on page 38. Use the information you wrote about yourself from Activity 26c to help you.

8 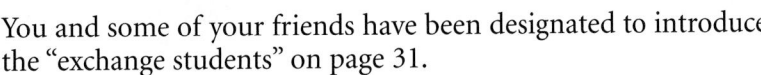 **Rollenspiel**

You and some of your friends have been designated to introduce the "exchange students" on page 31.

a. Working as a group, prepare statements that you can use in your introductions. Remember to give as much information as possible about each student, including name, age, where he or she is from, and how he or she gets to school. Include anything else that might be of interest to the class.

b. Using the pictures, present the visiting exchange students to the class.

Kann ich's wirklich?

Can you greet people and say goodbye? (p. 21)

Can you give your name and ask someone else's? (p. 22)

Can you ask and say who someone is? (p. 23)

1 How would you say hello and goodbye to the following people?

a. a classmate
a. Hallo! Tschau! Tschüs!

b. your principal
b. Guten Tag! Auf Wiedersehen! Guten Morgen!

2 How would you introduce yourself to a new student and ask his or her name?
Ich heiße ... Wie heißt du?

3 **a.** How would you ask who someone is? Say who these students are.
Wer ist das?

Das ist (die) ... **Tara**

Das ist (der) ... **Jens**

Das ist (der) ... **Holger**

Das ist (der) ... **Ahmet**

Can you supply the correct definite articles (der, die, das) for the nouns you have learned in this chapter? (p. 24)

4 Complete Birgit's explanation to Holger about who everyone is, using the articles **der, die,** and **das.**

Der Junge da? Er heißt Helmut. Und _das_ Mädchen heißt Monika. _Der_ Lehrer heißt Herr Becker. Und _die_ Deutschlehrerin heißt Frau Hörster.

Can you ask someone's age and tell yours? (p. 25)

5 **a.** How would you ask a classmate his or her age and say how old you are?
b. Say how old the following students are.
Wie alt bist du? Ich bin [vierzehn].

Silke, 15   Dirk, 13   Marina und Susi, 14
Silke ist fünfzehn. Dirk ist dreizehn.
Marina und Susi sind vierzehn.

Can you ask where someone is from and tell where you are from? (p. 28)

6 How would you ask a classmate where he or she is from?   Woher kommst du?

7 Say where the following students are from. Make statements with both **kommen** and **sein.**

a. Nicole, Brandenburg
b. Britte und Andreas, Sachsen-Anhalt
c. Mark, Niedersachsen

Nicole kommt aus Brandenburg. Mark ist aus Niedersachsen. Britte und Andreas kommen aus Sachsen-Anhalt.

8 How would you tell someone where you are from?
Ich komme aus ...

Can you say how someone gets to school? (p. 30)

9 How would you ask a classmate how he or she gets to school? How might he or she respond?   Wie kommst du zur Schule? Ich komme mit...

Say how these people get to school:

a. Steffi, bicycle
a. Steffi kommt mit dem Rad zur Schule.

b. Petra and Ali, moped
b. Petra und Ali kommen mit dem Moped zur Schule.

c. Anna, subway
c. Anna kommt mit der U-Bahn zur Schule.

Erste Stufe

Saying hello and goodbye

Guten Morgen!	*Good morning!*
Morgen!	*Morning!*
Guten Tag!	*Hello!*
Tag!	
Hallo!	*Hi!*
Grüß dich!	
Auf Wiedersehen!	*Goodbye!*
Wiedersehen!	*Bye!*
Tschüs!	*Bye!*
Tschau!	
Bis dann!	*See you later!*

Asking someone's name and giving yours

heißen	*to be called*
Wie heißt du?	*What's your name?*
Ich heiße …	*My name is…*
Wie heißt das Mädchen?	*What's the girl's name?*

Sie heißt …	*Her name is …*
Wie heißt der Junge?	*What's the boy's name?*
Er heißt …	*His name is …*
Heißt sie …?	*Is her name …?*
ja	*yes*
nein	*no*

Asking who someone is

Wer ist das?	*Who is that?*
Das ist …	*That's …*
Herr …	*Mr …*
Frau …	*Mrs …*
der Lehrer	*teacher (male)*
die Lehrerin	*teacher (female)*
der Deutschlehrer	*German teacher (male)*
die Deutschlehrerin	*German teacher (female)*

die Biologielehrerin	*biology teacher (female)*
der Junge	*boy*
das Mädchen	*girl*

Definite Articles

der	
die	*the*
das	

Other Useful Words

und	*and*
Also, einfach!	*That's easy!*
Ach ja!	*Oh, yeah!*
Ja, klar!	*Of course!*
Prima!	*Great!*

Zweite Stufe

Asking someone's age and giving yours

sein	*to be*
Wie alt bist du?	*How old are you?*
Ich bin 14 Jahre alt.	*I am 14 years old.*
Du bist …	*you are (sing)*
Er ist …	*He is …*

Sie ist …	*She is …*
Sie sind …	*They are …*

Die Zahlen von 0 bis 20

See page 25.

Other Useful Words

Bundesland, ¨er	*federal state (German)*
Hauptstadt, ¨e	*capital*
jetzt	*now*
auch	*also*
schon	*already*

Dritte Stufe

Talking about where people are from

kommen	*to come*
Woher bist (kommst) du?	*Where are you from?*
Ich bin (komme) aus …	*I'm from …*
Sie ist (kommt) aus …	*She's from …*
Er ist (kommt) aus …	*He's from …*
Sie sind (kommen) aus …	*They're from …*
Deutschland	*Germany*
Österreich	*Austria*

Talking about how someone gets to school

Wie kommst du zur Schule?	*How do you get to school?*
Ich komme …	*I come …*
mit dem Bus	*by bus*
mit dem Rad	*by bike*
mit dem Auto	*by car*
mit dem Moped	*by moped*
mit der U-Bahn	*by subway*
zu Fuß	*on foot (I walk)*
oder	*or*

Asking Questions

Wer?	*Who?*
Wie?	*How?*
Wo?	*Where?*
Woher?	*From where?*

Kapitel 2: Spiel und Spaß
Chapter Overview

Los geht's! pp. 44–46	*Was machst du in deiner Freizeit? p. 44*

	FUNCTIONS	GRAMMAR	VOCABULARY	RE-ENTRY
Erste Stufe pp. 47–49	• Talking about interests, p. 48	• The singular subject pronouns and present tense verb endings, p. 48	• Sports, instruments, and games you play, p. 47	• Question formation, pp. 47–49 (**Kap. 1**)
Zweite Stufe pp. 50–53	• Expressing likes and dislikes, p. 50	• The plural subject pronouns and verb endings, p. 50 • The present tense of verbs, p. 52	• Hobbies and leisure activities, p. 51	• Greetings, p. 53 (**Kap. 1**)
Dritte Stufe pp. 55–59	• Saying when you do various activities, p. 55 • Asking for an opinion and expressing yours, p. 57 • Agreeing and disagreeing, p. 58	• Inversion of time elements, p. 56 • Verbs with stems ending in **d**, **t**, or **n**, p. 57 • Verbs that end in **-eln**, p. 58	• Seasons of the year, p. 55	• Expressions **stimmt** and **stimmt nicht** used in a new context, p. 58 (**Kap. 1**)

Aussprache p. 59	The vowel combination **ie**, the vowel combination **ei**, the letter **j**, the letter **z**: Audio CD 2, Track 15	**Diktat:** Audio CD 2, Tracks 16–17
Zum Lesen pp. 60–61	Was machen wir am Wochenende?	**Reading Strategy** Scanning for specific information
Mehr Grammatik-übungen	**pp. 62–63** Erste Stufe, p. 62	Zweite Stufe, p. 62 Dritte Stufe, p. 63
Review pp. 64–67	Anwendung, pp. 64–65	Kann ich's wirklich?, p. 66 Wortschatz, p. 67

CULTURE

• **Ein wenig Landeskunde:** Formal and informal address, p. 52

• **Landeskunde: Was machst du gern?**, p. 54

• German weekly planner, p. 56

Kapitel 2: Spiel und Spaß
Chapter Resources

PRINT

Lesson Planning

One-Stop Planner

Lesson Planner with Substitute Teacher Lesson Plans, pp. 7–11, 66

Student Make-Up Assignments
- Make-Up Assignment Copying Masters, Chapter 2

Listening and Speaking

TPR Storytelling Book, pp. 5–8

Listening Activities
- Student Response Forms for Listening Activities, pp. 11–14
- Additional Listening Activities 2-1 to 2-6, pp. 15–18
- Additional Listening Activities (song), p. 14
- Scripts and Answers, pp. 107–112

Video Guide
- Teaching Suggestions, pp. 10–11
- Activity Masters, pp. 12–14
- Scripts and Answers, pp. 83–85, 111–112

Activities for Communication
- Communicative Activities, pp. 7–12
- Realia and Teaching Suggestions, pp. 78–81
- Situation Cards, pp. 125–126

Reading and Writing

Reading Strategies and Skills Handbook, Chapter 2

Lies mit mir! 1, Chapter 2

Übungsheft, pp. 13–24

Grammar

Grammatikheft, pp. 10–18

Grammar Tutor for Students of German, Chapter 2

Assessment

Testing Program
- Grammar and Vocabulary Quizzes, **Stufe** Quizzes, and Chapter Test, pp. 27–46
- Score Sheet, Scripts, and Answers, pp. 47–52

Alternative Assessment Guide
- Portfolio Assessment, p. 19
- Performance Assessment, p. 33
- CD-ROM Assessment, p. 47

Student Make-Up Assignments
- Alternative Quizzes, Chapter 2

MEDIA

 Online Activities
- Interaktive Spiele
- Internet Aktivitäten

 Video Program
- Videocassette 1
- Videocassette 5 (captioned version)

 Audio Compact Discs
- Textbook Listening Activities, CD 2, Tracks 1–19
- Additional Listening Activities, CD 2, Tracks 26–33
- Assessment Items, CD 2, Tracks 20–25

 Interactive CD-ROM Tutor, Disc 1

 Teaching Transparencies
- Situations 2-1 to 2-2
- Vocabulary 2-A to 2-B
- **Los geht's!**
- **Mehr Grammatikübungen** Answers
- **Grammatikheft** Answers

 **One-Stop Planner CD-ROM**

Use the **One-Stop Planner CD-ROM with Test Generator** to aid in lesson planning and pacing.

For each chapter, the **One-Stop Planner** includes:
- Editable lesson plans with direct links to teaching resources
- Printable worksheets from resource books
- Direct launches to the HRW Internet activities
- Video and audio segments
- Test Generator
- Clip Art for vocabulary items

Kapitel 2: Spiel und Spaß

Projects

Ein Schulplakat

In this activity students will prepare posters for homecoming at their school and decorate the hallway in the Foreign Language area with sports posters in German. It is a great way to advertise the big game and promote school spirit. Since this project will take several days to complete, you may want to break it up into smaller components.

MATERIALS

✄ **Students may need**
- posterboard
- photographs
- pictures from magazines
- tape
- markers
- scissors
- glue

SUGGESTED SEQUENCE

1. Working in groups of two or three, students choose a theme for their poster and decide on a title for it.

2. Students make a list of the German words to be used on their posters. Since students still have a very limited vocabulary, you can refer them to the vocabulary section at the end of the book and help them with difficult words.

3. Students work on their posters by putting on the title and arranging all their materials.

4. Students share their posters with the class in short oral presentations.

GRADING THE PROJECT

Suggested point distribution (**total = 100 points**)
Content 30
Appearance 15
Correct language usage 20
Originality...10
Presentation 25

Games

Wörterbau

This game is especially good for tactile learners. The objective is for students to be able to construct at least five German words from scrambled letters.

Materials   You will need 10 small squares of paper for each student.

Procedure   Divide the class into two teams. Each person looks up a German word from the **Wortschatz** on p. 67. Limit the number of letters in each word to 10. The students then write each letter that makes up that word on one of the pieces of paper. After everybody has finished, team members exchange their letters with a person on the other team. Students immediately try to arrange the letters in the correct order. Students who unscramble a word before their counterparts can each win a point for their team.

Kettenspiel

This game, which helps students review vocabulary and practice third person conjugations, is good for auditory learners.

Procedure   Begin by saying: **Am Wochenende besuche ich Freunde.** The first student then says: **Am Wochenende besucht sie Freunde, und ich spiele Fußball.** The second student repeats what has already been said in the third person and adds his or her own comment to the sentence. This "chain" continues until the last student has finished his or her sentence. This game focuses not only on vocabulary but also on verb conjugation and word order.

Was passt?

This game, in which students try to match German vocabulary words with their English definitions, is good for visual learners.

Materials You will need large index cards numbered 1–50, markers, and tape.

Procedure Tape 50 numbered index cards in rows of five on the chalkboard so that you can lift them up and write words underneath. Write 25 words from the **Wortschatz** on p. 67 under 25 randomly chosen cards. Write the English definitions under the other 25 cards. Divide the class into two teams. The first student calls out a number in German, and the teacher raises the index card and says the word for everybody to hear. Then the student must call out one more number to try to find the definition in the opposing language. If the student finds it, his or her team gets a point and gets another turn. Otherwise the opposing team has its turn. Each student must remember which words are under which number without any help from team members.

Storytelling ··········

Mini-Geschichte

*This story accompanies Teaching Transparency 2-1. The **Mini-Geschichte** can be told and retold in different formats, acted out, written down, and read aloud, to give students additional opportunities to practice all four skills.*

Was macht Heike in ihrer Freizeit?

Heike ist 15 Jahre alt. Sie kommt aus München. Sie hat viele Interessen. Nach der Schule macht sie Sport. Im Herbst wandert sie gern. Im Winter bastelt sie. Ski fahren findet sie auch toll. Im Frühling spielt sie Fußball und Volleyball. Tennis spielt sie nicht so gern. Golf findet sie sehr langweilig. Im Sommer geht sie oft schwimmen. Am Wochenende macht sie auch gern ein Picknick (*picnic*).

Traditions ··············

Rezept

Königsberger Klopse Die Königsberger Klopse werden mit mehligen Salzkartoffeln und einem Salat gereicht. Wer's mag, kann den Fleischteig zusätzlich mit klein geschnittenen Sardellenfilets würzen.

Königsberger Klopse
Für 4 Personen

Zutaten
g=Gramm, EL=Esslöffel, TL=Teelöffel, l=Liter

Für die Klopse		**Zum Garen**	
1	Brötchen	1 1/2 l	Wasser
1/4 l	Wasser		Salz
500 g	Hackfleisch	1	Lorbeerblatt
50 g	fetter Speck	1	Zwiebel
1	Zwiebel (40 g)	3	Pfefferkörner
1	Ei	3	Gewürzkörner
	Salz, weisser Pfeffer		

Für die Soße
30 g Margarine, 30 g Mehl, 2 EL Kapern, Saft einer halben Zitrone, 1/2 TL Senf, 1 Eigelb, 1 Prise Zucker, Salz, weißer Pfeffer

Zubereitung
Brötchen 10 Minuten in kaltem Wasser einweichen. Ausdrücken, zerpflücken und mit dem Hackfleisch in eine Schüssel geben. Speck und die geschälte Zwiebel fein hacken. Zum Hackfleisch geben. Ei zugeben. Gut mischen. Mit Salz und Pfeffer würzen.
Wasser mit Salz, Lorbeerblatt, der geschälten halbierten Zwiebel, Pfeffer und Gewürzkörnern in einem Topf aufkochen.
Aus dem Fleischteig Klopse von ca. 4 cm Durchmesser formen und in der Flüssigkeit in 20 Minuten gar ziehen lassen und warm stellen. Brühe durch ein Sieb gießen, auch warm stellen.
Für die Soße Margarine in einem Topf erhitzen. Mehl zugeben und 3 Minuten unter Rühren ablöschen. Kapern, Zitronensaft und Senf zugeben. 5 Minuten kochen lassen. Eigelb in einem Becher mit etwas Soße verquirlen. Wieder in die Soße rühren. Mit Zucker, Salz und Pfeffer würzen.

Kapitel 2: Spiel und Spaß
Technology

Video

Videocassette 1, 5 (captioned version)
See Video Guide, pages 9–14

Los geht's! • Was machst du in deiner Freizeit?

Holger finds his new friends Tara, Jens, and Ahmet playing a card game in the schoolyard. He wants to know which game they're playing, and they tell him. Then his new friends want to know about Holger's hobbies and interests and discover that they share many, but not all.

Fortsetzung

Holger has decided to take tennis lessons, and he works hard at learning to play. The next time Tara and Steffi go to play tennis, he joins them. They are impressed that he has learned so much so fast!

Landeskunde

Was machst du gern?

Students of various ages talk about what they like to do in their free time.

Videoclips

- **Nesfit** ® (sports drink)
- **Isostar** ® (sports drink)
- **Cebion Plus Magnesium** ® (magnesium tablets)
- **Wasserpark Alpamare** (water park)
- **Fremdenverkehrsverein Tirol** (tourism)

Interactive CD-ROM Tutor

The **Interactive CD-ROM Tutor** contains videos, interactive games, and activities that provide students an opportunity to practice and review the material covered in Chapter 2.

Activity	Activity Type	Pupil's Edition Reference
1. Wortschatz	Merkspiel	p. 47
2. Wortschatz	Wort und Bild Erfahren/Wählen	p. 51
3. Grammatik	Was fehlt?	p. 52
4. So sagt man das!	Was ist richtig?	p. 55
5. So sagt man das!	Was kommt dann?	pp. 48, 50, 55, 57
6. So sagt man das!	Wozu gehört's?	pp. 57, 58
Landeskunde	Was machst du gern? Was ist richtig?	p. 54
Zum Sprechen	*Guided recording*	pp. 64–65
Zum Schreiben	*Guided writing*	pp. 64–65

Teacher Management System

Logging In

Logging in to the *Komm mit!* TMS is easy. Upon launching the program, simply type "admin" in the password area of the log-in screen and press RETURN. Log on to **www.hrw.com/CDROMTUTOR** for a detailed explanation of the Teacher Management System.

One-Stop Planner CD-ROM

To preview all resources available for this chapter, use the **One-Stop Planner CD-ROM**, Disc 1.

Internet Connection

internet

ADRESSE: go.hrw.com
KENNWORT:
WK3 BRANDENBURG-2

*Have students explore the **go.hrw.com** Web site for many online resources covering all chapters. All Chapter 2 resources are available under the keyword **WK3 Brandenburg-2**. Interactive games practice the material and provide students with immediate feedback. You will also find a printable worksheet that provides Internet activities that lead to a comprehensive online research project.*

Interaktive Spiele

You can use the interactive activities in this chapter

- to practice grammar, vocabulary, and chapter functions
- as homework
- as an assessment option
- as a self-test
- to prepare for the Chapter Test

Internet Aktivitäten

Students will look at headlines of German sports sites and read about the leisure activities and hobbies of Germans.

- To prepare students for the **Arbeitsblatt,** you might want to ask them to give examples of headlines topping sports pages in American newspapers. Ask students to write down in German what they think German teens do in their leisure time.

- After completing the **Arbeitsblatt,** have students compare the hobbies and interests of German teens to those of American teens. For this activity, you might want to pair up students. One student should play a German teen and the other an American teen. They should tell each other what they do in their leisure time and why they like or dislike certain activities.

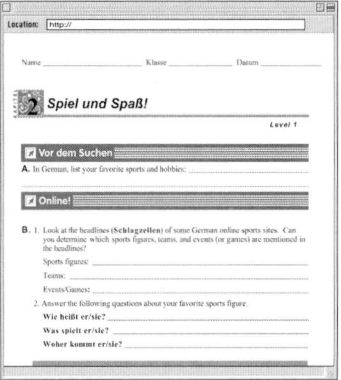

Webprojekt

Have students do a Web search for cultural activities offered in Potsdam or Cottbus. Have students write down the name of the activity, the date and time it takes place, and any other information they can find. Encourage students to exchange useful Web sites with their classmates. Have students document their sources by referencing the names and URLs of all the sites they consulted.

Kapitel 2: Spiel und Spaß
Textbook Listening Activities Scripts

Erste Stufe

6   **p. 47**

HOLGER   Du Stefan, was machst du denn in deiner Freizeit?

STEFAN   Ich? Also, ich spiele eigentlich sehr oft Klavier.

HOLGER   Und die Anne, was macht sie so?

STEFAN   Ich glaub, sie spielt sehr viel Basketball.

HOLGER   Und Helena? Was macht sie gern in ihrer Freizeit?

STEFAN   Helena spielt oft Golf. Sie spielt gar nicht schlecht.

HOLGER   Und was macht der Jörg?

STEFAN   Der Jörg? Der spielt fast immer nur Fußball. Er spielt in demselben Team wie der Ahmet und der Jens.

Zweite Stufe

12   **p. 50**

1.   GABI   Tag Karin, Tag Ute! Was macht ihr beiden denn?

  UTE   Ach, wir spielen Karten. Spielst du mit?

2.   GABI   Mensch, Ralf! Spielst du auch mit den anderen Karten?

  RALF   Nein, ich geh jetzt Volleyball spielen. Karten spiele ich ja nicht so gern.

3.   GABI   Du, Susanne, ich möchte gern Schach spielen. Spielst du mit mir?

  SUSANNE   Tut mir Leid, Gabi. Schach spiele ich wirklich nicht gern.

4.   GABI   He, Jochen und Sabine! Ihr seid ja noch hier! Was macht ihr denn?

  JOCHEN   Wir hören uns gleich die neueste Kassette von Ina Deter an.

5.   GABI   Und du, Ahmet? Du spielst doch gerne Schach. Spielst du vielleicht Schach mit mir?

  AHMET   Natürlich, gern!

15   **p. 52**

MICHAEL   Was machen wir denn, Claudia? Was machst du gern?

CLAUDIA   Ich zeichne eigentlich sehr gern. Und du?

MICHAEL   Nö, ich zeichne nicht so gern. Ich sammle lieber Briefmarken — aber ich schwimm gern und oft. Schwimmst du?

CLAUDIA   Nein, nicht so gern. Ich finde Schwimmen langweilig. Ich höre aber sehr gern Musik und finde Fernsehenschauen auch ganz interessant. Und du? Hörst du gern Musik? Oder schaust du gern Fernsehen?

MICHAEL   Musik höre ich schon gern — aber Fernsehen finde ich langweilig.

CLAUDIA   Dann hören wir eben Musik!

MICHAEL   Gut! Gehen wir zu Birgit? Sie hat immer die neuesten CDs!

16   **p. 53**

1.   MONIKA   Guten Tag, Herr Weber! Was machen Sie?

  H. WEBER   Guten Tag, Monika! Das Wetter ist so schön, da geh ich jetzt ein bisschen wandern.

  MONIKA   Wie schön! Ich wandere auch sehr gern.

2.   ANNE   Grüß dich, Andreas! Stefan, Antje und ich gehen jetzt tanzen. Kommst du mit?

  ANDREAS   Nee, Tanzen mag ich nicht so gern.

  FR. SCHILLING   Guten Tag, Ayla!

  AYLA   Guten Tag, Frau Schilling! Spielen Sie heute wieder Tennis?

  FR. SCHILLING   Ja, natürlich! Tennis spiel ich ja jeden Tag.

The following scripts are for the listening activities found in the *Pupil's Edition.* For Student Response Forms, see *Listening Activities,* pages 11–14. To provide students with additional listening practice, see *Listening Activities,* pages 15–18.

One-Stop Planner CD-ROM

For resource information, see the **One-Stop Planner CD-ROM**, Disc 1.

Dritte Stufe

22   p. 56

USCHI   Was ich am Wochenende so mache? Hmm—ich besuche oft Freunde. Und dann während der Woche, so nach der Schule, spiel ich oft Basketball mit meinen Freunden. Basteln tu ich viel am Nachmittag, besonders wenn das Wetter schlecht ist. Am Abend höre ich dann manchmal Musik, Kassetten und CDs. Im Frühling spiele ich gern Volleyball mit Freunden und so. Und im Sommer schwimme ich sehr gern, wenn ich Zeit habe. Aber am liebsten wandere ich, das mache ich besonders gern im Herbst.

30   p. 58

1. YASMIN   Ich finde Wandern toll.

AHMET   Ich auch, Yasmin. Besonders im Frühling.

2. YASMIN   Aber Basteln ist so langweilig.

AHMET   Das finde ich gar nicht.

3. YASMIN   Schwimmen finde ich auch langweilig, und du?

AHMET   Das finde ich gar nicht. Schwimmen macht viel Spaß!

4. YASMIN   Aber am liebsten gehe ich in die Disko tanzen.

AHMET   Ich nicht. Tanzen ist blöd.

5. YASMIN   He! Diese Musik ist super! Einfach stark!

AHMET   Ja, das finde ich auch.

AUSSPRACHE, p. 59

Diktat, p. 59

Silvia and Julia are talking about what they like to do in their free time. First listen to what they are saying, then write down their conversation in the pauses provided.

SILVIA   Du, Julia, was machst du gern am Wochenende?

JULIA   Ach, ich wandere gern. Und du, Silvia, was machst du so am Wochenende?

SILVIA   Ich zeichne gern und ah …ich spiele Volleyball.

JULIA   Volleyball spiele ich auch gern. Aber ich spiel nicht sehr gut.

SILVIA   Wirklich? Wie findest du Fußball? Ich find's toll.

JULIA   Ja, ich auch.

Anwendung

1   p. 64

1. *(Telefon klingelt)*

— Ahmet Özkan.

— Hallo Ahmet! Hier ist Tara! Willst du mit mir nach der Schule Tennis spielen?

— Ja, klar — um 4 Uhr, geht das?

2. — Du Steffi! Was machst du heute Nachmittag?

— Ich spiel Volleyball — unser Team spielt heute um 2.

3. — Tag, Katja! Was machst du am Wochenende?

— Also, Steffi, Holger und ich gehen wandern. Kommst du mit?

2   p. 64

Also, der Sporti hat wirklich viele Interessen. Er spielt Baseball, Volleyball und Eishockey. Er ist auch ziemlich musikalisch und spielt seit fünf Jahren Gitarre. Er kann auch ein bisschen Klavier spielen. Tanzen macht dem Sporti natürlich Spaß. Tennis spielt er immer im Frühling, und im Sommer schwimmt er gern. Er zeichnet auch gern. Fernsehenschauen findet er blöd, da spielt er schon lieber Karten mit Freunden.

Die Sporti ist auch sehr aktiv. Sie spielt in einem Volleyballteam, einem Basketball- und einem Fußballteam. Ihre Familie wandert immer gern im Sommer. Sie lernt gerade Golf spielen, das findet sie ganz einfach. Sie geht oft mit Freunden in die Disko zum Tanzen. Sie findet die Musik zu laut. Aber zu Hause Fernsehenschauen macht Spaß. Sie mag auch Schach spielen, Freunde besuchen und basteln.

Kapitel 2: Spiel und Spaß
Suggested Lesson Plans 50-Minute Schedule

Day 1

CHAPTER OPENER 15 min.
- Multicultural Connections, ATE, p. 41M
- Thinking Critically, ATE, p. 41M

LOS GEHT'S! 20 min.
- Preteaching Vocabulary, ATE, p. 41N
- Play Audio CD, **Los geht's!**, pp. 44–45
- Have students read **Los geht's!**, pp. 44–45
- Teaching Suggestions, Video Guide, p. 10
- Teacher Note, ATE, p. 41N
- Show **Los geht's!** Video
- Do Comprehension Activities, p. 46

ERSTE STUFE
- Bell Work, ATE, p. 41O

Wortschatz, p. 47 10 min.
- Presenting **Wortschatz**, ATE, p. 41O
- Teaching Transparency 2-A
- Present **Lerntrick,** p. 47
- Play Audio CD for Activity 6, p. 47
- Do Activity 7, p. 48

Wrap-Up 5 min.
- Student responses to questions about activities

Homework Options
Grammatikheft, p. 10, Acts. 1–2

Day 2

ERSTE STUFE
Quick Review 15 min.
- Check homework, Grammatikheft, p. 10, Acts. 1–2

So sagt man das!, p. 48 15 min.
- Presenting **So sagt man das!**, ATE, p. 41P
- Do Activity 8, p. 48
- Do Situation 2-1, pp. 125–126
- Do Act. 1, p. 62, **Mehr Grammatikübungen**

Ein wenig Grammatik, p. 48 15 min.
- Presenting **Ein wenig Grammatik**, ATE, p. 41P
- Do Activities 9 and 10, p. 49
- Do Activities 4–5, p. 15, Übungsheft

Wrap-Up 5 min.
- Student responses to questions about activities

Homework Options
Grammatikheft, pp. 10–11, Acts. 3–7

Day 3

ERSTE STUFE
Quick Review 15 min.
- Check homework, Grammatikheft, pp. 10–11, Acts. 3–7
- Review forms of **spielen** by doing Activity 11, p. 49

Quiz Review 15 min.
- Do Additional Listening Activities 2-1 and 2-2, p. 15
- Do Activities 6–8, pp. 15–16, Übungsheft

Quiz 20 min.
- Quiz 2-1A or 2-1B

Homework Options
Activities for Communication, p. 78, Realia 2-1: make a list of the three most important facts the ad contains

Day 4

ZWEITE STUFE
Quick Review 15 min.
- Return and review Quiz 2-1
- Bell work, ATE, p. 41Q
- Check homework, Realia 2-1, p. 78

So sagt man das!, p. 50 10 min.
- Presenting **So sagt man das!**, ATE, p. 41R
- Play Audio CD for Activity 12, p. 50

Ein wenig Grammatik, p. 50 10 min.
- Presenting **Ein wenig Grammatik**, ATE, p. 41R
- Do Activity 2, p. 62, **Mehr Grammatikübungen**

Wortschatz, p. 51 10 min.
- Presenting **Wortschatz**, ATE, p. 41R
- Teaching Transparencies 2-B, 2-2
- Do Activity 14, p. 52
- Play Audio CD for Activity 15, p. 52

Wrap-Up 5 min.
- Music Connection, ATE, p. 41R

Homework Options
Pupil's Edition, p. 50, Act. 13
Grammatikheft, pp. 12–13, Acts. 8–13
Übungsheft, p. 17, Acts. 9–10

Day 5

ZWEITE STUFE
Quick Review 10 min.
- Check homework, Grammatikheft, pp. 12–13, Acts. 8–13

Grammatik, p. 52 20 min.
- Presenting **Grammatik**, ATE, p. 41R
- Do Activity 14, p. 14, Grammatikheft
- Do Activity 3, Interactive CD-ROM
- Present **Ein wenig Landeskunde**, p. 52
- Play Audio CD for Activity 16, p. 53
- Do Activities 17, 18, and 19, p. 53

LANDESKUNDE 15 min.
- Background Information, ATE, p. 41S
- Multicultural Connection, ATE, p. 41S
- Pre-viewing Suggestion, Video Guide, p. 11
- Show **Landeskunde** Video
- Do Activities A and B, p. 54

Wrap-Up 5 min.
- Student responses to questions about playing sports and musical instruments

Homework Options
Grammatikheft, p. 14, Act. 15
Übungsheft, pp. 18–19, Acts. 11–15; p. 24, Act. 24

Day 6

ZWEITE STUFE
Quick Review 10 min.
- Check homework, Übungsheft, pp. 18–19, Acts. 11–15

Quiz Review 20 min.
- Do Activity 21, p. 53
- Do **Mehr Grammatikübungen, Zweite Stufe**
- Do **Interaktive Spiele**, at WK 3 BRANDENBURG-2

Quiz 20 min.
- Quiz 2-2A or 2-2B

Homework Options
Pupil's Edition, p. 53, Act. 20
Übungsheft, p. 24, Act. 24
Activities for Communication, pp. 9–10, Communicative Activity 2-2, make notes and practice

One-Stop Planner CD-ROM

For alternative lesson plans by chapter section, to create your own customized plans, or to preview all resources available for this chapter, use the **One-Stop Planner CD-ROM**, Disc 1.

 For additional homework suggestions, see activities accompanied by this symbol throughout the chapter.

Day 7

DRITTE STUFE

Quick Review 15 min.
- Return and review Quiz 2-2
- Bell Work, ATE, p. 41T
- Do Communicative Activity 2-2, pp. 9–10

So sagt man das!/Wortschatz, p. 55 20 min.
- Presenting **So sagt man das!**, ATE, pp. 41T–41U
- Presenting **Wortschatz**, ATE, p. 41U
- Teaching Transparency 2-1
- Play Audio CD for Activity 22, p. 56
- Do Activities 23, 24 and 25, p. 56

Grammatik, p. 56 10 min.
- Presenting **Grammatik**, ATE, p. 41U
- Do Activity 26, p. 56
- Do Activity 27, p. 57

Wrap-Up 5 min.
- Play **Kettenspiel**, ATE, p. 41C

Homework Options
Grammatikheft, p. 15, Acts. 16–17
Übungsheft, pp. 20–22, Acts. 16–22

Day 8

DRITTE STUFE

Quick Review 10 min.
- Check homework, Übungsheft, pp. 20–22, Acts. 16–22

So sagt man das!, p. 57 10 min.
- Presenting **So sagt man das!**, ATE, p. 41U
- Do Activity 28, p. 57

Grammatik, p. 57 10 min.
- Presenting **Grammatik**, ATE, p. 41U
- Do Activity 29, p. 58
- Do Communicative Activity 2-3, pp. 11–12

So sagt man das!, p. 58 15 min.
- Presenting **So sagt man das!**, ATE, p. 41V
- Do Activity 6, Interactive CD-ROM

Wrap-Up 5 min.
- Student responses to questions about when they do activities and how they like them

Homework Options
Grammatikheft, pp. 16–18, Acts. 18–25

Day 9

DRITTE STUFE

Quick Review 15 min.
- Check homework, Grammatikheft, pp. 16–18, Acts. 18–25

Ein wenig Grammatik, p. 58 15 min.
- Presenting **Ein wenig Grammatik**, ATE, p. 41V
- Play Audio CD for Activity 30, p. 58
- Do Activity 31, p. 58
- Do Activities 32 and 33, p. 59

Aussprache, p. 59 15 min.
- Presenting **Aussprache**, ATE, p. 41V
- Do **Richtig aussprechen/Richtig lesen**, p. 59
- Do **Richtig schreiben, Diktat**, p. 59

Wrap-Up 5 min.
- Student responses to questions about free time activities

Homework Options
Mehr Grammatikübungen, Dritte Stufe

Day 10

DRITTE STUFE

Quick Review 10 min.
- Check homework, **Mehr Grammatikübungen, Dritte Stufe**

Quiz Review 20 min.
- Do Additional Listening Activities 2-5 and 2-6, pp. 17–18
- Play **Was passt?**, ATE, p. 41D

Quiz 20 min.
- Quiz 2-3A or 2-3B

Homework Options
Activities for Communication, pp. 125–126, Situation 2-3, make notes and practice
Internet Aktivitäten, see ATE, p. 41F

Day 11

DRITTE STUFE

Quick Review 15 min.
- Return and review Quiz 2-3
- Do Situation 2-3, pp. 125–126

ZUM LESEN 30 min.
- Read **Lesestrategie**, p. 60
- Do Activities 1-7, pp. 60–61
- Do Activity 23, p. 23, Übungsheft

Wrap-Up 5 min.
- Student responses to **Kann ich's wirklich?** questions, p. 66

Homework Options
Pupil's Edition, p. 66, **Kann ich's wirklich?**

Day 12

ANWENDUNG

Quick Review 30 min.
- Check homework, p. 66, **Kann ich's wirklich?**
- Play **Wörterbau**, ATE, p. 41C
- Play Audio CD for Activities 1–2, p. 64
- Do Activities 3-8

Chapter Review 20 min.
- Review chapter functions, vocabulary, and grammar; choose from **Mehr Grammatikübungen,** Grammar Tutor for Students of German, Activities for Communication, Listening Activities, Interactive CD-ROM Tutor, or **Interaktive Spiele**
- Review test format and provide sample test items for students

Homework Options
Study for Chapter Test

Assessment

Test, Chapter 2 45 min.
- Administer Chapter 2 Test. Select from Testing Program, Alternative Assessment Guide, or Test Generator

Kapitel 2: Spiel und Spaß
Suggested Lesson Plans 90-Minute Schedule

Block 1

CHAPTER OPENER 20 min.
- Multicultural Connection, ATE, p. 41M
- Thinking Critically, ATE, p. 41M

LOS GEHT'S 25 min.
- Preteaching Vocabulary, ATE, p. 41N
- Play Audio CD, **Los geht's!**, pp. 44–45
- Have students read **Los geht's!**, pp. 44–45
- Teaching Suggestions, Video Guide, p. 10
- Teacher Note, ATE, p. 41N
- Show **Los geht's!** Video
- Do Comprehension Activities, p. 46

ERSTE STUFE
Wortschatz, p. 47 15 min.
- Presenting **Wortschatz**, ATE, p. 41O
- Teaching Transparency 2-A
- Present **Lerntrick**, p. 47
- Play Audio CD for Activity 6, p. 47
- Do Activity 7, p. 48

So sagt man das!, p. 48 10 min.
- Presenting **So sagt man das!**, ATE, p. 41P
- Do Activity 8, p. 48

Ein wenig Grammatik, p. 48 10 min.
- Presenting **Ein wenig Grammatik**, ATE, p. 41P
- Do Activities 9 and 10, p. 49

Wrap-up 10 min.
- Student responses to questions about activities and hobbies

Homework Options
Grammatikheft, pp. 10–11, Acts. 1–7
Übungsheft, pp. 13–16, Acts. 1–8

Block 2

ERSTE STUFE
Quick Review 15 min.
- Check homework, Grammatikheft, pp. 10–11, Acts. 1–7
- Review forms of **spielen** by doing Activity 11, p. 49

Quiz Review 15 min.
- Do Additional Listening Activities 2-1 and 2-2, p. 15
- Do **Mehr Grammatikübungen, Erste Stufe**

Quiz 20 min.
- Quiz 2-1A or 2-1B

ZWEITE STUFE
So sagt man das!, p. 50 10 min.
- Presenting **So sagt man das!**, ATE, p. 41R
- Play Audio CD for Activity 12, p. 50

Ein wenig Grammatik, p. 50 10 min.
- Presenting **Ein wenig Grammatik**, ATE, p. 41R
- Do Activity 2, p. 62, **Mehr Grammatikübungen**

Wortschatz, p. 51 10 min.
- Presenting **Wortschatz**, ATE, p. 41R
- Teaching Transparencies 2-B, 2-2
- Do Activity 14, p. 52
- Play Audio CD for Activity 15, p. 52

Wrap-Up 10 min.
- Music Connection, ATE, p. 41R

Homework Options
Pupil's Edition, p. 50, Act. 13
Grammatikheft, p. 12–13, Acts. 8–13
Übungsheft, pp. 17–19, Acts. 9–15
Interactive CD-ROM, Act. 3

Block 3

ZWEITE STUFE
Quick Review 20 min.
- Return and review Quiz 2-2
- Check homework, Grammatikheft, pp. 12–13, Acts. 8–13

Grammatik, p. 52 20 min.
- Presenting **Grammatik**, ATE, p. 41R
- Language-to-Language, ATE, p. 41R
- Do Activity 14, p. 14, Grammatikheft
- Do Activity 3, Interactive CD-ROM
- Present **Ein wenig Landeskunde**, p. 52
- Play Audio CD for Activity 16, p. 53
- Do Activities 17–20, p. 53

LANDESKUNDE 15 min.
- Background Information, ATE, p. 41S
- Multicultural Connection, ATE, p. 41S
- Pre-viewing Suggestion, Video Guide, p. 11
- Show **Landeskunde** Video
- Do Activities A and B, p. 54

Quiz Review 15 min.
- Do Activity 21, p. 53
- Do Activity 3, p. 62, **Mehr Grammatikübungen**
- Do Additional Listening Activities 2-3 and 2-4, pp. 15–16

Quiz 20 min.
- Quiz 2-2A or 2-2B

Homework Options
Übungsheft, p. 24, Act. 24
Activities for Communication, pp. 9–10, Communicative Activity 2-2, make notes and practice

One-Stop Planner CD-ROM

For alternative lesson plans by chapter section, to create your own customized plans, or to preview all resources available for this chapter, use the **One-Stop Planner CD-ROM**, Disc 1.

For additional homework suggestions, see activities accompanied by this symbol throughout the chapter.

Block 4

DRITTE STUFE

Quick Review 15 min.
- Bell work, ATE, p. 41T
- Return and review quizzes
- Review vocabulary cards

So sagt man das!/Wortschatz, p. 55 25 min.
- Presenting **So sagt man das!**, ATE, pp. 41T–41U
- Presenting **Wortschatz**, ATE, p. 41U
- Teaching Transparency 2-1
- Play Audio CD for Activity 22, p. 56
- Do Activities 23, 24 and 25, p. 56

Grammatik, p. 56 15 min.
- Presenting **Grammatik**, ATE, p. 41U
- Do Activity 26, p. 56
- Do Activity 27, p. 57
- Play **Kettenspiel**, ATE, p. 41C

So sagt man das!, p. 57 10 min.
- Presenting **So sagt man das!**, ATE, p. 41U
- Do Activity 28, p. 57

Grammatik, p. 57 15 min.
- Presenting **Grammatik**, ATE, p. 41U
- Do Activity 18, p. 16, Grammatikheft
- Do Activity 29, p. 58
- Do Communicative Activity 2-3, pp. 11–12

Wrap-Up 10 min.
- Students respond to questions about when they do activities and how they like them

Homework Options
Grammatikheft, pp. 15–18, Acts. 16–25
Übungsheft, pp. 20–22, Acts. 16–22

Block 5

DRITTE STUFE

Quick Review 20 min.
- Check homework, Übungsheft, pp. 20–22, Acts. 16–22
- Do Activity 5, Interactive CD-ROM

So sagt man das!, p. 58 15 min.
- Presenting **So sagt man das!**, ATE, p. 41V
- Do Activity 6, Interactive CD-ROM

Ein wenig Grammatik, p. 58 20 min.
- Presenting **Ein wenig Grammatik**, ATE, p. 41V
- Play Audio CD for Activity 30, p. 58
- Do Activity 31, p. 58
- Do Activities 32 and 33, p. 59

Quiz Review 15 min.
- Do Additional Listening Activities 2-5 and 2-6, pp. 17–18
- Do **Mehr Grammatikübungen, Dritte Stufe**
- Play **Was passt?**, ATE, p. 41D

Quiz 20 min.
- Quiz 2-3A or 2-3B

Homework Options
Activities for Communication, pp. 125–126, Situation 2-3, make notes and practice

Block 6

DRITTE STUFE

Quick Review 15 min.
- Return and review Quiz 2-3
- Do Situation 2-3, pp. 125–126

Aussprache, p. 59 15 min.
- Presenting **Aussprache**, ATE, p. 41V
- Do **Richtig aussprechen/Richtig lesen**, p. 59
- Do **Richtig schreiben, Diktat**, p. 59

ZUM LESEN 25 min.
- Present **Lesestrategie**, p. 60
- Do Activities 1-7, pp. 60–61
- Do Activity 23, p. 23, Übungsheft

ANWENDUNG 25 min.
- Teaching Suggestion, ATE, p. 41X
- Play Audio CD for Activities 1-2, p. 64
- Do Activities 3-8
- Show **Fortsetzung** Video

Wrap-Up 10 min.
- Student responses to **Kann ich's wirklich?** questions, p. 66

Homework Options
Pupil's Edition, p. 66, **Kann ich's wirklich?**
Internet Aktivitäten, see ATE, p. 41F

Block 7

ANWENDUNG

Quick Review 15 min.
- Check homework, p. 66, **Kann ich's wirklich?**
- Play **Wörterbau**, ATE, p. 41C

Chapter Review 25 min.
- Review chapter functions, vocabulary, and grammar; choose from **Mehr Grammatikübungen**, Grammar Tutor for Students of German, Activities for Communication, Listening Activities, Interactive CD-ROM Tutor, or **Interaktive Spiele**
- Review test format and provide sample test items for students

Test, Chapter 2 45 min.
- Administer Chapter 2 Test. Select from Testing Program, Alternative Assessment Guide or Test Generator.

Kapitel 2: Spiel und Spaß
Teaching Suggestions, *pages 42–67*

PAGES 42–43

CHAPTER OPENER

Pacing Tips
In the **Erste Stufe** the verb **spielen** is introduced, along with singular subject pronouns and present-tense verb endings. The concept of question formation is reintroduced. Plural subject pronouns and verb endings occur in the **Zweite Stufe**, where an overview of present-tense verb conjugation is given on p. 52. Also included is the function of 'expressing likes and dislikes.' Concepts introduced in the **Dritte Stufe** center around time elements and opinions. Present-tense verb conjugation is expanded for stems ending in **d, t,** or **n,** and **-eln** verbs. You may want to spend more time on the **Dritte Stufe** to allow for a little extra time to cover the three **So sagt man das!** boxes. For Lesson Plans and timing suggestions, see pages 41I–41L.

Meeting the Standards
Communication
• Talking about interests, p. 48
• Expressing likes and dislikes, p. 50
• Saying when you do various activities, p. 55
• Asking for an opinion and expressing yours, p. 57
• Agreeing and disagreeing, p. 58

Cultures
• **Ein wenig Landeskunde,** p. 52
• **Landeskunde,** p. 54
• Teacher Note, p. 41N
• Background Information, p. 41S
• Culture Note, p. 41V

Connections
• Multicultural Connection, p. 41M
• Thinking Critically, p. 41M
• Multicultural Connection, p. 41M
• Music Connection, p. 41R
• Multicultural Connection, p. 41S
• Career Path, p. 41X

Comparisons
• Language-to-Language, p. 41O
• Language-to-Language, p. 41R
• Language Note, p. 41U

Communities
• Information Gathering, p. 41W

One-Stop Planner CD-ROM
For resource information, see the **One-Stop Planner CD-ROM**, Disc 1.

Connections and Comparisons

Multicultural Connection
Ask students whether they can name typical sports and recreational activities of other countries that might not be as typical or as popular in the United States. (Examples: England: rugby, field hockey; Canada: broomball, curling; Nigeria: cricket; Germany: soccer, tennis; Norway: cross-country skiing)

Thinking Critically
Comparing and Contrasting Ask if any students play tennis. If they do, or know someone who does, ask them what they wear to play. Do they wear the same types of outfits as the students in the picture?

Multicultural Connection
Soccer is the most popular team sport in many countries around the world, including the German-speaking countries. Like American children, German children play on soccer teams, but large numbers of teenagers and adults also enjoy playing for fun and competition.

Chapter Sequence

Los geht's! . . . . .p. 44
Erste Stufe . . . . .p. 47
Zweite Stufe . . . . .p. 50
Landeskunde . . . . .p. 54
Dritte Stufe . . . . .p. 55
Zum Lesen . . . . .p. 60
Mehr Grammatikübungen . . . . .p. 62
Anwendung . . . . .p. 64
Kann ich's wirklich? . . . . .p. 66
Wortschatz . . . . .p. 67

LOS GEHT'S!

Teaching Resources
pp. 44–46

PRINT
▶ Lesson Planner, p. 7
▶ Video Guide, pp. 9–10, 12
▶ Übungsheft, p. 13

MEDIA
▶ One-Stop Planner
▶ Video Program
  Los geht's!
  Videocassette 1, 15:39–17:18
  Videocassette 5 (captioned version),
  05:34–07:15
  Fortsetzung
  Videocassette 1, 17:20–19:26
  Videocassette 5 (captioned version),
  07:16–09:22
▶ Audio Compact Discs, CD2, Trs. 1–2
▶ **Los geht's!** Transparencies

PAGES 44–45

Los geht's! Transparencies

Preteaching Vocabulary

Recognizing Cognates

Los geht's! contains several words that students will be able to recognize as cognates. Have students find these cognates, then have them guess what is happening in the story.

1 Karten, gewinnt, und

2 oft

3 Fußball, schwimmen, im Winter, Ski

4 Interessen, Musik, ein Instrument, Gitarre

5 Tennis, find

Fortsetzung

You may choose to continue with the **Fortsetzung** now or wait until later in the chapter. For a synopsis of the **Los geht's!** and **Fortsetzung** episodes, see p. 41E.

Cultures and Communities

Teacher Note

Mau-Mau is played with 32 cards. From a deck of 52, players take out the 2s, 3s, 4s, 5s, and 6s and make sure the deck has no jokers. Each player usually receives four cards. The winner is the one who first disposes of all his or her cards.

To get started, the dealer draws the top card of the pile and lays it face up on the table. The player to the left of the dealer has then a chance to discard any one of his or her cards that matches the dealer's card in suit (diamond on diamond, spade on spade) or kind (ten on ten, queen on queen). If a player is not able to discard, he or she has to draw a card from the pile. This card can be played immediately if it matches. Otherwise, the player must keep it. As soon as a player has only one card left, he or she has to say **mau.** When playing the last card, the player must say **mau mau.**

- If a player discards a seven, the next player has to take two cards from the pile unless he or she also has a seven to discard.

- If a player discards an eight, the next player loses his or her turn.

- A jack can be played on any card, except sevens and eights.

PAGE 46

Using the Captioned Video

 2 As an alternative to reading the conversations in the book, you might want to show the captioned version of *Was machst du in deiner Freizeit?* available on Videocassette 5.

Comprehension Check

Teaching Suggestion

Have students listen to the text while looking at the photos, or have them watch this segment of the video. Remind students that they do not need to understand every word. They should try to get the gist of what is happening in the story. Have them match visual clues with words or phrases that they hear.

A Slower Pace

3 Rather than having students look back at the conversation, have this activity prepared on a transparency. Then, have students look at the pictures in the story on pp. 44–45.

ERSTE STUFE

Teaching Resources
pp. 47–49

PRINT
- Lesson Planner, p. 8
- TPR Storytelling Book, pp. 5, 8
- Listening Activities, pp. 11, 15
- Activities for Communication, pp. 7–8, 78, 125–126
- Grammatikheft, pp. 10–11
- Grammar Tutor for Students of German, Chapter 2
- Übungsheft, pp. 14–16
- Testing Program, pp. 27–30
- Alternative Assessment Guide, p. 33
- Student Make-Up Assignments, Chapter 2

MEDIA
- One-Stop Planner
- Audio Compact Discs, CD2, Trs. 3, 20, 26–27
- Teaching Transparencies
  Situation 2-2
  Vocabulary 2-A
  Mehr Grammatikübungen Answers
  Grammatikheft Answers
- Interactive CD-ROM Tutor, Disc 1

PAGE 47

Bell Work

To help students prepare for the content and functions modeled in the **Erste Stufe,** put the following chart headings on the board or on a transparency.

SPORTS   HOBBIES   INSTRUMENTS

Ask students to name their interests from these categories and use the information they give you to fill in the chart.

PRESENTING: Wortschatz

To introduce the vocabulary and the activities presented in the illustrations, you'll need pictures of the vocabulary items (basketball, tennis ball, etc.) or the actual objects if you have them available. Present the vocabulary as follows: hold up a soccer ball and say: **Das ist ein Fußball.** Hold up a basketball and say: **Das ist ein Basketball.** Continue with all vocabulary items. In the next step hold up a tennis ball and ask: **Ist das ein Golfball?** to elicit a student response of **Ja** or **Nein.** If you want students to produce the new vocabulary, proceed one level further by asking either/or questions such as **Ist das eine Gitarre oder ein Klavier?**

Teacher Note

Und dann noch… boxes contain optional vocabulary, which is meant to help students personalize their conversations and writing. Students will not be expected to produce these words on tests or quizzes. Additional vocabulary arranged by topic is presented on pp. R9–R14 of the *Pupil's Edition.*

Connections and Comparisons

Language-to-Language

You may want to tell your students that German, like English, French, and Spanish, belongs to the Indo-European language group. This group includes most of the languages spoken in Europe and many of those spoken in southwestern Asia and India. This language group shows many cognitive similarities, especially for basic vocabulary. Have students compare the following words for "mother."

English: **mother**
German: **Mutter**
Latin: **mater**
Spanish: **madre**
French: **mère**
Russian: **mat'**
Persian: **madar**
Hindi: **maata**

Cognates are unusual across language groups. For example, in Arabic, which belongs to the Semitic language group (Arabic, Hebrew), "mother" is **"umm."** In Turkish, which belongs to the Turkic language group, "mother" is **"anne."** Discuss with the class possible historical reasons for the wide geographical distribution of the Indo-European language group. (Examples: migration patterns determined in part by climate changes and competition from other societies; cultural intermingling made necessary by trade may also have played a role, and so on.)

Communication for All Students

Visual Learners

7 Prepare several cutout pictures from magazines (large enough for students to see) of other activities with cognate names such as golf, yoga, or ballet. After reading the **Lerntrick** on p. 47 with students, hold up the pictures and have students say and write down the name of the activity.

PRESENTING: So sagt man das!

In German, tell students what sports, interests, or hobbies you enjoy. (Example: **Ich spiele gern Volleyball. Ich spiele Basketball.**) Next, ask several students yes/no questions: **Maria, spielst du Klavier?** and so on. Finally, ask the class either/or questions such as **Spielt Maria Klavier oder Gitarre?**

PRESENTING: Ein wenig Grammatik

Subject pronouns

1. Have students list the subject pronouns they learned in Chapter 1 (**ich, du, er, sie, sie** *pl).* Write the pronouns on the board or a transparency as students call them out to you.

2. For each subject pronoun, add the verb **spielen** in its correct form. Ask students to try to differentiate between the stems and the endings for each form of **spielen.** You could also have one student come to the front and underline the verb endings.

For Additional Practice

10 Have students name the activities associated with famous international or national sports celebrities or musicians. Have them include local people and schoolmates as well.

Examples: Shaquille O'Neal spielt Basketball.
Ken Griffey, Jr. spielt Baseball.
Steffi Graf spielt Tennis.
Kenny G spielt Saxophon.

Communication for All Students

Slower Pace

11 Rather than having students write an article, have them write two or three sentences about the activities of each person they interviewed.

Kinesthetic Learners

11 Divide the class into two teams to play this game practicing the **du**-form of the verbs students have learned. Have each team make a list of at least ten sentences using **du,** and write them on separate sheets of paper. (Examples: **Du spielst Karten. Du spielst Gitarre.**) Then, alternating between teams, a member of one team draws a sentence from the pile written by the other team and acts it out in front of his or her group. If the members of his or her team can guess the activity they get a point; if not, the team forfeits a point, and it is the other team's turn. Two points can be earned: one for naming the correct activity and one for using the correct verb ending in their answer. (Example: **Du spielst Karten.** or **Sie spielt Karten.**)

Visual Learners

Collect several pictures of various activities from calendars, postcards, or magazines. Distribute one picture to each student and have each student show and tell his or her activity to the class. Example: **Der Mann hier spielt Golf.**
Das ist Fechten.

Writing Assessment

11 You may wish to evaluate Activity 11 using the following rubric.

Writing Rubric	Points			
	4	3	2	1
Content (Complete – Incomplete)				
Comprehensibility (Comprehensible – Seldom comprehensible)				
Accuracy (Accurate – Seldom accurate)				
Organization (Well-organized – Poorly organized)				
Effort (Excellent – Minimal)				

18–20: A   16–17: B   14–15: C   12–13: D   Under 12: F

ERSTE STUFE

Performance Assessment

Give each student a piece of paper with the name of a well-known athlete or musician on it. Call on individual students and ask them to tell the rest of the class who their person is and what he or she does. (Example: **Andre Agassi spielt Tennis.**) Please see the *Alternative Assessment Guide*, p. 33, for an expanded assessment suggestion.

Assess

▸ Testing Program, pp. 27–30
Quiz 2-1A, Quiz 2-1B
Audio CD2, Tr. 20

▸ Student Make-Up Assignments
Chapter 2, Alternative Quiz

▸ Alternative Assessment Guide, p. 33

Teaching Resources
pp. 50–54

PRINT

▸ Lesson Planner, p. 9
▸ TPR Storytelling Book, pp. 6, 8
▸ Listening Activities, pp. 11–12, 15–16
▸ Activities for Communication, pp. 9–10, 79, 81, 125–126
▸ Grammatikheft, pp. 12–14
▸ Grammar Tutor for Students of German, Chapter 2
▸ Übungsheft, pp. 17–19
▸ Testing Program, pp. 31–34
▸ Alternative Assessment Guide, p. 33
▸ Student Make-Up Assignments, Chapter 2

MEDIA

▸ One-Stop Planner
▸ Audio Compact Discs, CD2, Trs. 4–6, 21, 28–29
▸ Teaching Transparencies
Situation 2-2
Vocabulary 2-B
Mehr Grammatikübungen Answers
Grammatikheft Answers
▸ Interactive CD-ROM Program, Disc 1

▸ PAGE 50

Bell Work

Ask students if there are any activities in which they participate during the school year (in their PE class for example) that they like and look forward to, and if there are any they do not like. Have students write in English about the activities they like and dislike. Use students' notes for presenting **So sagt man das!**

ZWEITE STUFE

PRESENTING: So sagt man das!

Using the students' notes from the Bell Work, write their activities on the board and use them to model the expressions in the function box.

Example: Michael spielt nicht gern Fußball. Er spielt gern Golf.

PRESENTING: Ein wenig Grammatik

Subject pronouns Walk around the classroom and address two or more students at a time, asking questions related to sports or other interests. Use verbs such as **machen, schwimmen, spielen, hören,** and **tanzen.** (Examples: **Macht ihr gern Sport? Tanzt ihr gern?**) Students should answer using **wir.** (Example: **Ja, wir tanzen gern.**)

▶ PAGE 51

PRESENTING: Wortschatz

Demonstrate some of the activities pictured, mimicking someone reading a book or writing a letter. Then ask yes/no questions such as **Höre ich Musik?** Once you feel students understand the vocabulary, ask either/or questions such as **Höre ich Musik oder schaue ich Fernsehen?** To practice additional pronouns, ask students to volunteer to mimic one of the activities. Then, you can ask yes/no or either/or questions such as **Schwimmt er? Wandert sie oder tanzt sie?**

▶ PAGE 52

PRESENTING: Grammatik

The present tense of verbs Write a simple sentence such as **Er schwimmt.** on the board or on a transparency. Ask students how they would translate this sentence into English. Once students understand that three different English sentences can be expressed by one German sentence (*He swims. He is swimming. He does swim.*), ask them to review the verb endings of the present tense by giving examples for each subject pronoun with the verb **schwimmen.**

Connections and Comparisons

Music Connection

Refer students to the song *Bruder Jakob,* Level 2 *Listening Activities,* p. 6, for additional reading. Have them find the two verbs used in the song. (**Schläfst, Hörst**) What are the endings on these verbs? (**-st**) What must therefore be the subject of the sentences? (**du**) You may also want to play the song, Level 2 CD 1, Tr. 27. Students might be interested to know that *Bruder Jakob* is a translation of the French song *Frère Jacques.* It was translated by a Viennese writer.

Language-to-Language

- You may want to tell your students that there are basically two different verb forms in English, one for third person singular and another one for all other persons. (Examples: I speak, you speak, he/she/it speaks, we speak, you speak, they speak.) The conjugation patterns in German, Spanish, and French are more varied. On the board or a transparency, write the following examples along with their English equivalents, and ask students to compare the forms of the four languages.

  Ich spreche, du sprichst, er/sie/es spricht, wir sprechen, ihr sprecht, sie sprechen; je parle, tu parles, il/elle/on parle, nous parlons, vous parlez, ils/elles parlent; yo hablo, tú hablas, él/ella habla, nosotros hablamos, vosotros habláis, ellos/ellas hablan.

  You may want to point out that the English of Shakespeare's time also had more verb forms than modern English. (Example: I have, thou hast, he/she hath, we/you (pl.)/they have)

- Your students may want to know that like German, French and Spanish also have a formal "you": "**Sie**" in German, "**vous**" in French, and "**usted**" in Spanish. Tell students that the English "you" was once used mainly for formal address, and ask them if they can identify archaic English words that once indicated informal address. (thee/thou)

Teaching Suggestions

17 Make students aware of the addition of the *e* in the **du-, er/sie,-** and **ihr**-forms of **zeichnen**. To help students remember, have them try to say these forms without the *e*: **zeichnst, zeichnt**. This will show them that these words cannot easily be pronounced without the *e*. This will be covered in the **Dritte Stufe** of this chapter.

17 Have students create new sentences by moving each group of subjects one picture to the right.

PAGE 54

LANDESKUNDE

Teaching Resources
p. 54

PRINT
▸ Video Guide, pp. 9, 11, 12–13
▸ Übungsheft, p. 24

MEDIA
▸ One-Stop Planner
▸ Video Program
  Videocassette 1, 20:06–23:50
▸ Audio Compact Discs, CD 2, Trs. 7–12
▸ Interactive CD-ROM Tutor, Disc 1

Advance Organizer

As an advance organizer to the **Landeskunde** interviews, ask students if they are familiar with German sports. Do they know which are popular? (The three most popular sports are soccer, gymnastics, and tennis.)

Cultures and Communities

Thinking Critically

Drawing Inferences Have students look up the locations of Berlin and Hamburg in an atlas. Given the location and the geography of Berlin and Hamburg, ask students if they can think of some sports that might be popular in those areas. (Examples: bike riding because there are few hills; sailing and rowing because of the proximity of water) Ask students if they can think of sports that would not be possible in these areas. (Examples: skiing or mountain climbing)

Preteaching Vocabulary

Before having students read, listen to, or watch the interviews, you might want to introduce them to the following vocabulary: **angucken** (*to watch or to look at something or someone*) **fernsehen** (*to watch television — as alternative to* **Fernsehen schauen**) **Trimm-dich-Pfad** (*fitness trail with suggested activities marked along its path*).

Cultures and Communities

Background Information

Trimm dich means *get fit* or *get yourself into shape*. **Trimm-dich-Pfade** are well-marked fitness trails that can be found all across Germany. They encourage people of all ages to integrate activities such as pushups and situps into their walk or run. The length of the trails varies anywhere from 1 to 3 km, and each station has clearly marked signs to explain the activities.

Connections and Comparisons

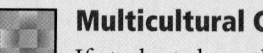

Multicultural Connection

If students have the opportunity, they should interview foreign exchange students and teachers from other countries to find out what activities are popular in those particular countries and cultures. Students should share their findings with the class.

Teacher Note

Mention to your class that the **Landeskunde** will also be included in Quiz 2-3B given at the end of the **Dritte Stufe**.

Expressing Likes and Dislikes

Tell students to imagine they are in Potsdam on an exchange and their host family is making suggestions about what to do and see around town. Using the activities mentioned, they should respond by telling their host what they like and do not like to do.

Schloss Sanssouci besuchen.
Im Bornstedter See schwimmen.
Ein Konzert in der Nikolaikirche hören.
In den Rehgarten mit dem Rad fahren.

Example: **Ich fahre nicht gern mit dem Rad.**

ZWEITE STUFE

Game

Divide the class into two groups and put a *Tic Tac Toe* game on the chalkboard or on a transparency. Have teams take turns creating complete sentences or questions using the verbs in their correct forms. If a team is able to make a correct statement or question with a particular verb, that team can mark an X or an O in that space. To use this game for performance assessment, see the *Alternative Assessment Guide*, p. 33.

Teacher to Teacher

Becky McQueen
Alexander Middle School
Nekoosa, Wisconsin

Becky's class plays "Dampfkochtopf" as a sponge activity.

"This activity is great for those extra three minutes at the end of class. Pick a student who must talk non-stop in German for one minute (or whatever time you choose). The topic could center on a theme or simply listing all the words he/she can that start with a certain letter. It can also be used for partners, who must carry on a conversation non-stop for one minute. Students often chime in and help the one in the pressure cooker."

Assess

▸ Testing Program, pp. 31–34
Quiz 2-2A, Quiz 2-2B
Audio CD2, Tr. 21

▸ Student Make-Up Assignments
Chapter 2, Alternative Quiz

▸ Alternative Assessment Guide, p. 33

DRITTE STUFE

Teaching Resources
pp. 55–59

PRINT
▸ Lesson Planner, p. 10
▸ TPR Storytelling Book, pp. 7, 8
▸ Listening Activities, pp. 13, 17–18
▸ Activities for Communication, pp. 11–12, 80, 125–126
▸ Grammatikheft, pp. 15–18
▸ Grammar Tutor for Students of German, Chapter 2
▸ Übungsheft, pp. 20–22
▸ Testing Program, pp. 35–38
▸ Alternative Assessment, p. 33
▸ Student Make-Up Assignments, Chapter 2

MEDIA
▸ One-Stop Planner
▸ Audio Compact Discs, CD2, Trs. 13–17, 22, 30–31
▸ Teaching Transparencies
Situation 2-1
Mehr Grammatikübungen Answers
Grammatikheft Answers
▸ Interactive CD-ROM Program, Disc 1

> **PAGE 55**

Bell Work
Ask students at what times during the week or weekend they are involved in their various activities. Is anybody involved in any activities outside of school? Take a quick survey in class to find out who participates in after-school activities and who belongs to a club that is not associated with school.

PRESENTING: So sagt man das!

Write the time expressions from this box on the board or on a transparency and write several verbs in their infinitive forms next to them. On the far right side, make a column of subject pronouns.

Example:

nach der Schule   schwimmen   ich

Go over the new vocabulary from the **So sagt man das!** function box and ask students to take out a sheet of paper and write three or four original sentences. Let students read them aloud in class.

PRESENTING: Wortschatz

To present this vocabulary use *Teaching Transparency 2-1* or other illustrations of the four seasons. Point to the pictures one at a time and introduce the new vocabulary in sentences, such as **Im Frühling spiele ich Tennis, aber im Winter spiele ich nicht Tennis.** Check comprehension by asking **Wann spiele ich Tennis?** and **Wann spiele ich nicht Tennis?** When you have presented all the seasons, you may want to ask students about their own habits, using questions like **Wann schwimmst du?**, **Wann spielst du Golf?** and **Wann spielst du nicht Golf?** For additional practice, you might want to read several sentences and have students judge whether each sentence is **logisch** or **unlogisch**.

Connections and Comparisons

Language Note

Herbst might look more familiar to students if they think of the English word *harvest.* The German word has its origin in its verb form **herbsten**, *to harvest grapes,* which refers to **Weinbau** (*wine-growing*).

PAGE 56

Communication for All Students

Challenge

24 Tell students to imagine that new neighbors have moved in across the street and are unfamiliar with the neighborhood. Have the students come up with as many suggestions as they can for activities and things to do in their town during the different seasons. Write the names of the seasons on the board and have students come up and write their ideas.

Example:

Winter	Frühling	Sommer	Herbst
Ski laufen	reiten	Baseball spielen	wandern

PRESENTING: Grammatik

Verb in second position Write several sentences in fragments on cardboard or construction paper. Hand out the pieces to students, who will go to the front of the class and hold their cards for the class to see. Have one other student manipulate the students into the correct positions to form a complete sentence with all pieces in the correct order. Then ask the student who is holding the time element to move to a different position and let the manipulator make all other necessary changes. Use a new set of students for the next sentence.

Example:
Im Winter	spielen	wir	oft	Eishockey.
1	2	3	4	5

Wir	spielen	im Winter	oft	Eishockey.
3	2	1	4	5

PAGE 57

PRESENTING: So sagt man das!

When introducing this vocabulary, begin by telling your students that you are going to express your opinions about some of the activities they have learned so far. Then make a series of statements such as **Briefmarkensammeln finde ich toll!**, using body language and facial expression to convey your opinion of the subject. Have students guess what the new word means, based on these visual cues. When they have guessed correctly, continue with the next word. Follow up by asking students for their own opinions: **Wie findest du Zeichnen?** You might also want to draw smiley and sad face images on the board and have students place each word in the appropriate category.

PRESENTING: Grammatik

Verbs with stem ending in d, t, or n Write the verb **finden** on the board and ask students to provide you with the present tense verb endings for each subject pronoun, leaving a space between the stem and the endings in the **du-**, **er/sie-**, and **ihr-** forms. Then have individual students or the class as a whole read the resulting verbs. Ask students what they would have to do to make sure that the stem ending **-d** and the personal endings are clearly pronounced. Then add an 'e' in the spaces between the stems and the endings. Go through the same process using the verb **zeichnen.** You may also want to preview the **möchte-**forms introduced in Chapter 3.

DRITTE STUFE

PRESENTING: **So sagt man das!**

Students may recognize the expressions **stimmt** and **stimmt nicht** from p. 20 in Chapter 1. Have students compare the meaning of **stimmt** and **stimmt nicht** in the context of Activity 3 on p. 20 and in the context of agreeing and disagreeing in the **So sagt man das!** function box on p. 58.

Communication for All Students

Challenge

29 Call on one student and ask him or her to express his or her opinion about an activity or interest. Have this student call on another student who must disagree with the opinion expressed. Then call on another student to start again.

Example:

Teacher:	Tom, wie findest du Briefmarkensammeln?
Tom:	Ich finde Briefmarkensammeln sehr langweilig. Und du, Lori?
Lori:	Aber ich finde Briefmarkensammeln interessant!

PRESENTING: **Ein wenig Grammatik**

Verbs ending in -eln As a follow-up to **So sagt man das!**, write the following statements on the board or on an overhead transparency:
Basteln ist blöd.
Ich finde Segeln langweilig.
Comics sammeln macht keinen Spaß.
Ask students to disagree with these statements and to say that they do these activities often. Guide them to responses like the following:
Stimmt nicht! Ich bastle oft.
Stimmt nicht! Ich segle oft.
Stimmt nicht! Ich sammle Comics gern.
Write these responses to the original statements and ask students to analyze the verb forms in relation to the infinitive **basteln**.

Teaching Suggestion

Have two students work together to plan weekend activities. For each activity one student suggests and is excited about, the other student should disagree and suggest something different. In the end they should both agree on five activities.

Cultures and Communities

 Culture Note
Brieffreundschaften among young people are very popular in Germany. There is usually a long list of ads in all the youth magazines. If any of your students are interested in finding a German-speaking pen pal, write to the *Student Letter Exchange* in New York. The address is on p. T48. There are fees involved, so be sure to write for information.

PRESENTING: **Aussprache**

• **ie** Remind students that like all German vowels, this sound is pronounced with more muscular tension in the mouth than English vowels. The English comparison is not an exact match. Also, students often confuse the pronunciation of the German vowels **ei** and **ie** with the English pronunciation. To help them "unlearn" this tendency, remind them to pronounce the second letter in each combination as if it were the English *i* as in *mine* and *e* as in *me*.

• **ei** Like German vowels, this diphthong is pronounced with more tension in the mouth than English vowels. This sound is sometimes written **ai**, **ay**, or **ey**.

Von der Schule zum Beruf

34 After finishing this activity, you might ask students to peer-edit another student's résumé.

Assess

▶ Testing Program, pp. 35–38
  Quiz 2-3A, Quiz 2-3B
  Audio CD2, Tr. 22

▶ Student Make-Up Assignments
  Chapter 2, Alternative Quiz

▶ Alternative Assessment Guide, p. 33

ZUM LESEN

Teaching Resources
pp. 60–61

PRINT
▸ Lesson Planner, p. 11
▸ Übungsheft, p. 23
▸ Reading Strategies and Skills, Chapter 2
▸ Lies mit mir! 1, Chapter 2

MEDIA
▸ One-Stop Planner

Prereading

Cultures and Communities

Information Gathering
Point out to students that Germans are very active and pursue many organized after-school and after-work activities. Have students bring the weekend newspaper section in which upcoming events are publicized. Ask them to make a list of various activities and any important information given for such events.

Teacher Note
There are prereading questions in the **Lesestrategie** box.

Reading
Cooperative Learning

Put students in groups of four. Ask them to choose a discussion leader, a recorder, a proofreader, and an announcer. Give students a specific amount of time in which to complete Activities 1–5. Monitor group work as you walk around, helping students if necessary. At the end of the activity, call on each group announcer to read his or her group's results.

Communication for All Students

A Slower Pace
Before working with all the ads on the page, group students to work with just one or two ads at a time. Each group should have three tasks: find the name of the activities, find the dates and times they take place, and make a list of the words they recognize. Students can report their findings to the class.

Post-Reading
Teacher Note

Questions 6–7 are post-reading tasks that will show whether students can apply what they have learned.

Teaching Suggestion

After completion of the **Zum Lesen** activities, have the students create an announcement for an upcoming event with the following German proverb as the jumping-off point: **Wer rastet, der rostet!** (*Use it or lose it!*)

Example: participate in the next 10k run

You may want to supply paper, scissors, and colored pens to help students get started. Have students display their ads in the classroom.

MEHR GRAMMATIKÜBUNGEN

The **Mehr Grammatikübungen** activities are designed as supplemental activities for the grammatical concepts presented in the chapter. You might use them as additional practice, for review, or for assessment.

For more grammar presentations, review, and practice refer to the following:
• Grammatikheft
• Grammar Tutor for Students of German
• Grammar Summary on pp. R15–R25
• Übungsheft
• Grammar and Vocabulary quizzes (Testing Program)
• Test Generator
• Interactive CD-ROM Tutor
• **Interaktive Spiele** at go.hrw.com

ZUM LESEN

ANWENDUNG

Video Wrap-up

Videocassette 1, 15:39–26:40
Videocassette 5 (captioned version), 05:34–9:22
At this time, you might want to use the video resources for additional review and enrichment. See *Video Guide* for suggestions regarding:

• the **Los geht's!** episode
• the **Fortsetzung** episode
• the **Landeskunde** interviews
• the **Videoclips.**

Apply and Assess

Teaching Suggestion

 Have one student describe another student in German class by talking about his or her interests and dislikes without naming or looking at that student. After the student has completed his or her description, the rest of the class can only ask yes/no questions to find out who is being described.

Portfolio

You might want to use the following activity as an oral portfolio item for your students. Have each student come up with at least three different questions for a survey about popular activities and interests. Each student will then interview a set number of people, other than German class students (parents, siblings, neighbors, librarian) for his or her survey. The student then records his or her questions and findings in German and reports them to the class.

Example: What is your favorite weekend activity?

See *Alternative Assessment Guide,* p. 19.

Career Path

Have students brainstorm situations in which it would be advantageous for Americans with careers in entertainment or sports to know German. (Suggestions: Imagine you are a basketball player who has been invited to play on a German team; imagine you are a guitarist who plays with a German rock band.)

KANN ICH'S WIRKLICH?

This page is intended to prepare students for the test. It is a brief checklist of the major points covered in the chapter. The students should be reminded that it is a checklist only and not necessarily everything that will appear on the test.

For additional self check options, refer students to the *Grammar Tutor,* the *Interactive CD-ROM Tutor,* and the Online self-test for this chapter

WORTSCHATZ

Review and Assess

Game

 Play the game **Kettenspiel** to review chapter 2 vocabulary and third person conjugations. See p. 41C for the procedure.

Play the game **Was passt?** to review Chapter 2 vocabulary. See p. 41D for the procedure.

Teacher Note

 Give the **Kapitel 2** Chapter Test: *Testing Program,* pp. 39–44 Audio CD 2, Trs. 23–25.

REVIEW

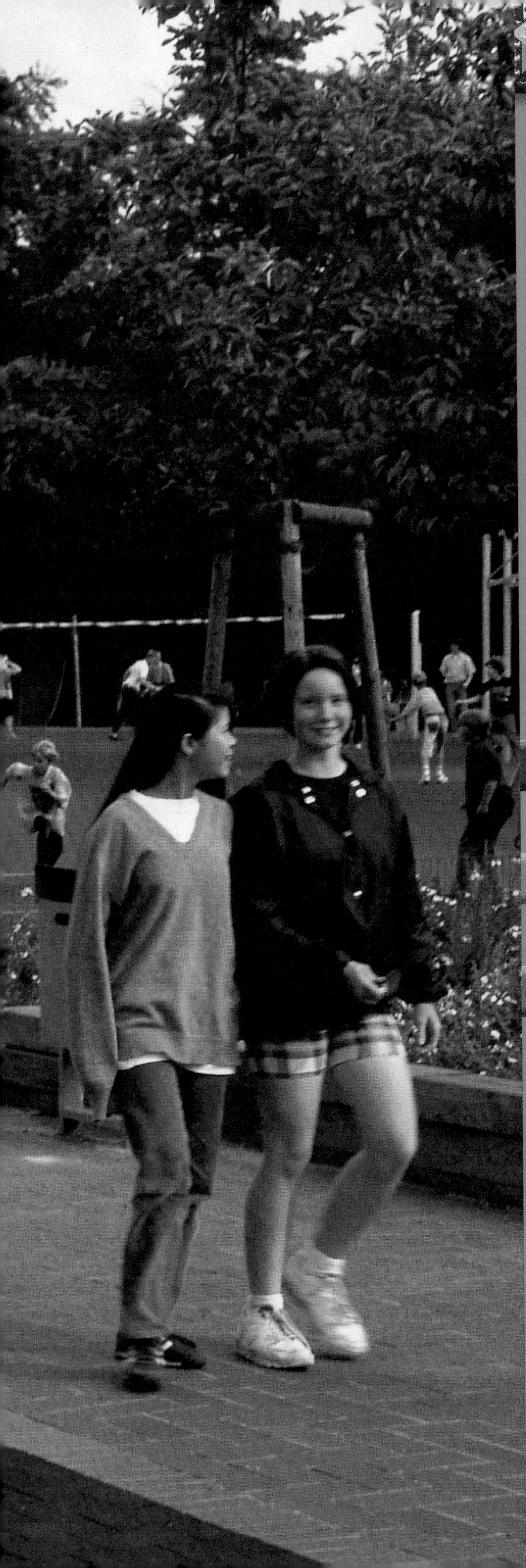

KAPITEL

2 Spiel und Spaß

Objectives

In this chapter you will learn to

Erste Stufe

- talk about interests

Zweite Stufe

- express likes and dislikes

Dritte Stufe

- say when you do various activities
- ask for an opinion and express yours
- agree and disagree

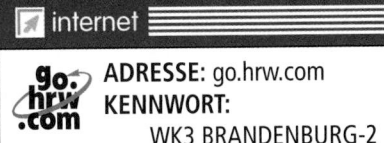

internet

go.hrw.com
ADRESSE: go.hrw.com
KENNWORT: WK3 BRANDENBURG-2

◀ **Was macht ihr jetzt?**

Los geht's! · *Was machst du in deiner Freizeit?*

Los geht's! is an abridged version of the video episode.

Los geht's!

CD 2 Trs. 1–2

Strategie Verstehen

Look at the images for this story. What are the students in each picture doing? What do you think Holger might be telling them about himself?

Jens   **Tara**   **Holger**   **Ahmet**   **Steffi**

1

Holger:	Hallo! Was spielt ihr denn da?
Ahmet:	Was fragst du?
Holger:	Ich frage, was ihr da spielt.
Ahmet:	Karten.
Holger:	Ja, das sehe ich. Aber was spielt ihr?
Tara:	Wir spielen Mau-Mau.
Holger:	Wer gewinnt?
Jens:	Tara und Ahmet, wie immer!

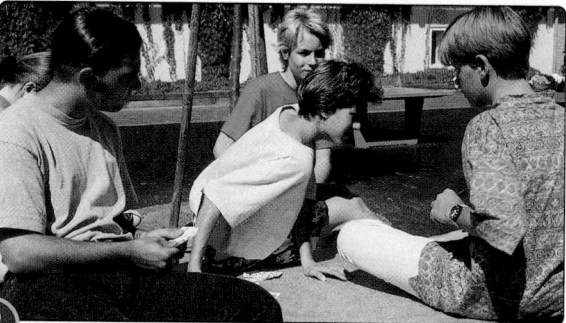

2

Ahmet:	Du gewinnst auch manchmal!
Jens:	Aber ihr mogelt oft.
Tara:	Was? Wir mogeln nicht.
Ahmet:	Du bist nur sauer, weil du verlierst.

3

Jens:	Spielst du auch Karten, Holger?
Holger:	Ja, aber nicht so gern.
Tara:	Was machst du denn sonst noch in deiner Freizeit?
Holger:	Tja, hm … Fußball, ich geh* gern schwimmen, ich …
Ahmet:	Was noch?
Holger:	Im Winter lauf ich Ski.

4

Jens:	Was noch? Hast du andere Interessen?
Holger:	Ich sammle Briefmarken. Und ich höre gern Musik.
Ahmet:	Spielst du auch ein Instrument?
Holger:	Ich spiele Gitarre.

** Frequently in spoken German, the **e**-ending on the **ich**-form of the verb is omitted.*

44   *vierundvierzig*   STANDARDS: 1.2   KAPITEL 2   Spiel und Spaß

5

Tara:	Und spielst du auch Tennis?
Holger:	Nein. Tennis find ich langweilig.
Tara:	Ach, das ist schade!
Holger:	Warum? Spielst du Tennis?
Tara:	Und wie! Mein Lieblingssport.
Holger:	Ich … ich hab …
Tara:	Macht nichts, Holger!

6

Steffi:	Ist Holger nett?
Tara:	Und wie! Und er läuft Ski, spielt Fußball, aber Tennis spielt er nicht gern.
Steffi:	Ach, schade!

Viel später

7

Tara:	Hallo, Holger! Wir gehen Tennis spielen. Aber schade, du spielst ja Tennis nicht gern! Tschüs!
Holger:	He! Ihr … Wartet doch! Ich … ich …

8

Holger:	So ein Mist!

Übungsheft, S. 13

1 Was passiert hier?

These activities check for global comprehension only. Students should not yet be expected to produce language modeled in **Los geht's!**

Do you understand what is happening in **Los geht's!**? Check your comprehension by answering these questions. Don't be afraid to guess!

1. What are Ahmet, Tara, and Jens doing at the beginning of the story? 1. playing cards
2. Which sports does Holger play? What other interests does Holger mention? 2. soccer, swimming, skiing; stamp collecting, listening to music, playing the guitar
3. Why is Tara teasing Holger? What does she say to him? 3. He thinks tennis is boring. „Aber schade, du findest Tennis langweilig
4. How does Holger feel at the end of the story? What does he say that lets you know how he feels? 4. He is annoyed. „So ein Mist!"

2 Genauer lesen

Reread the conversations. Which words or phrases do the characters use to

1. ask what someone likes to do in his or her free time 1. Was machst du denn in deiner Freizeit?
2. say they like to listen to music 2. Ich höre gern Musik.
3. ask if someone plays an instrument 3. Spielst du ein Instrument?
4. ask if someone has other interests 4. Hast du andere Interessen?
5. tell what their favorite sport is 5. Mein Lieblingssport ist…
6. say that they do something often 6. Ich gehe oft (schwimmen).
7. say that they find something boring 7. (Tennis) find ich langweilig.

3 Was passt zusammen? *What goes together?*

Jens and Tara ask Holger what he does in his free time. Match each question on the left with an appropriate response on the right.

1. Spielst du Karten? c.
2. Was machst du in deiner Freizeit? d.
3. Hast du auch andere Interessen? b.
4. Spielst du ein Instrument? e.
5. Spielst du auch Tennis? a.

a. Nein, Tennis finde ich langweilig.
b. Ja, ich sammle Briefmarken und höre gern Musik.
c. Ja, aber ich spiele Karten nicht so gern.
d. Ich spiele Fußball, ich geh schwimmen, und im Winter lauf ich Ski.
e. Ja, ich spiele Gitarre.

4 Welches Wort passt? *Which word fits?*

Based on the story you just read and heard, complete each of the sentences below with an appropriate word from the box.

Karten	Musik	sammelt
langweilig	spielen	Tennis

Tara, Ahmet und Jens spielen gern ___1___. Holger ___2___ lieber Briefmarken und hört auch gern ___3___. Holger findet Tennis ___4___, aber Tara findet den Sport super. ___5___ ist Taras Lieblingssport. Tara und Steffi ___6___ oft Tennis.

1. Karten 2. sammelt 3. Musik 4. langweilig 5. Tennis 6. spielen

5 Wer macht was?

What have you learned about these students? Match the statements with the people they describe.

1. Tara 1. c
2. Ahmet 2. e
3. Holger 3. b
4. Jens 4. a
5. Steffi 5. d

a. verliert oft beim Kartenspielen.
b. spielt Karten nicht gern.
c. findet Holger nett.
d. spielt oft mit Tara Tennis.
e. gewinnt oft beim Kartenspielen.

Erste Stufe

Objective Talking about interests

WK3 BRANDENBURG-2

Wortschatz

JENS   Was machst du in deiner Freizeit?

UTE   Ich mache viel Sport. Ich spiele …

2–A

Fußball

Basketball

Volleyball

Tennis

JENS   Spielst du auch Golf?

UTE   Nein, ich spiele nicht Golf.

JENS   Spielst du ein Instrument?

UTE   Ja klar! Ich spiele …

JENS   Hast du auch andere Interessen?

UTE   Ja, ich spiele auch …

Gitarre

Klavier

Karten

Schach

 Übungsheft, S. 14, Ü. 2–3    Grammatikheft, S. 10, Ü. 1–2

Und dann noch…

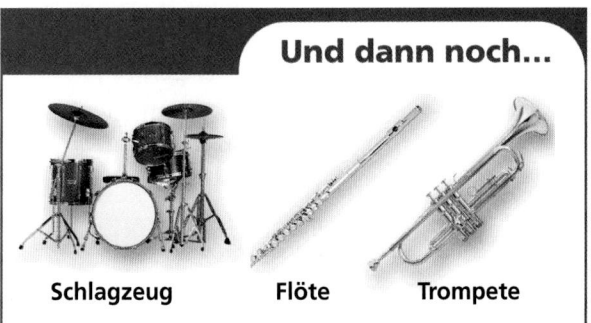

Schlagzeug   **Flöte**   **Trompete**

LERNTRICK

Look for cognates when you read. Cognates are words that look similar and have the same meaning in German and English. Some are identical, for example, *tennis* and **Tennis**. Others differ slightly in spelling, such as *trumpet* and **Trompete**. How many cognates can you find in the **Wortschatz**?

6 **Wer macht was?** Script on p. 41G

CD 2
Tr. 3

Zuhören Using the drawings above as a guide, listen as Holger asks what his classmates do in their free time. First write the name of any activity you hear mentioned. Then, listen again for the students' names. This time, write each student's name beside the activity he or she does.   Stefan spielt Klavier; Anne spielt Basketball; Helena spielt Golf; Jörg spielt Fußball.

7 **Bildertext** 1. Fußball 2. Karten 3. Schach 4. Gitarre 5. Klavier

Sprechen/Schreiben Complete the following description of Ahmet's free time activities, using the pictures as cues.

Ahmet spielt oft ____?____ . Mit Tara und Jens spielt er oft ____?____, aber

____?____ spielt er nicht so gern. Er spielt auch zwei Instrumente: er spielt

____?____, und er spielt auch ____?____ aber das spielt er nicht so gut.

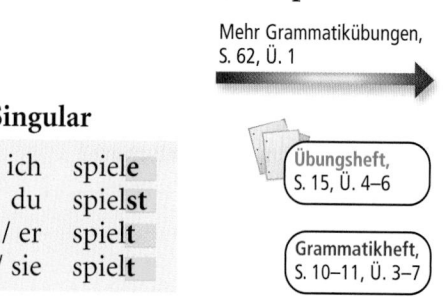

So sagt man das!

Talking about interests

If you want to know what a friend does in his or her free time, you might ask:

Was machst du in deiner Freizeit?
Spielst du Volleyball? *Do you play volleyball?*

Was macht Steffi?
Spielt sie auch Volleyball?
Toll! Und Jens? Spielt er auch Volleyball?

You might get these responses:

Ich spiele Gitarre.
Ja, ich spiele Volleyball. *or*
Nein, ich spiele nicht Volleyball.
Sie spielt Tennis und Basketball.
Ja, ich glaube, sie spielt oft Volleyball.
Nein, er spielt nicht Volleyball.

Ein wenig Grammatik

In the sentences above that use **spielen,** the subject pronouns change as different people are addressed or talked about. A question addressed to one person uses **du.** The response to such a question uses **ich.** What pronouns do you use in German when you talk about a female? a male?[1] As the subject pronoun changes, the forms of the verb also change: **ich spiele, du spielst, er/sie spielt.** The part of the verb that does not change is the *stem.* What is the stem of **spielen?**[2]

Mehr Grammatikübungen, S. 62, Ü. 1 →

Übungsheft, S. 15, Ü. 4–6

Grammatikheft, S. 10–11, Ü. 3–7

Singular

ich	spiel**e**
du	spiel**st**
Jens / er	spiel**t**
Tara / sie	spiel**t**

---

8 **Grammatik im Kontext**

Schreiben Holger wants to know what some of his classmates do in their free time. Supply the correct endings of the verbs.

1. HOLGER Mach ====== du oft Sport? -st
   HEIKE Ja, ich mach ====== viel Sport! -e
   HOLGER Was spiel ====== du denn alles? -st
   HEIKE Ich spiel ====== Fußball, -e Volleyball und auch Tennis.

2. HOLGER Und Werner? Was mach ====== er gern? -t
   HEIKE Er spiel ====== gern Klavier. -t
   HOLGER Spiel ====== Gabi auch -t Klavier?
   HEIKE Nein. Sie spiel ====== -t Gitarre.

3. Ich spiel ======, was du nicht e
   spiel ======; Tara spiel ====== Tennis, st; t
   Holger spiel ====== Gitarre, ich t
   spiel ====== Schach, und du e
   spiel ====== Karten! st

---

1. **sie, er** 2. **spiel-**

Übungsheft, S. 16, Ü. 7–8

9 Fragen und Antworten *Questions and answers*

Schreiben Steffi is trying to find people to play a game with her. Complete her conversation with Tara by filling in the missing lines with an appropriate question or answer from the boxes. Which game do they decide to play? Do all the girls like that game?

> Spielt die Elisabeth auch?

> Na klar! Basketball ist Klasse!

> Nein, aber sie spielt Volleyball.

> Spielst du auch Volleyball?

STEFFI   Hallo, Tara! Sag mal, spielst du Basketball?

TARA   ————— Na klar! Basketball ist Klasse!

STEFFI   ————— Spielt die Elisabeth auch?

TARA   Ja, Elisabeth spielt auch.

STEFFI   Und die Sybille?

TARA   ————— Nein, aber sie spielt Volleyball.

STEFFI   Und du? ————— Spielst du auch Volleyball?

TARA   Ja, ich spiele auch Volleyball. Und Elisabeth auch.

STEFFI   Prima! Also spielen wir heute Volleyball!

Volleyball; yes

10 In meiner Freizeit...

Schreiben Using the **Wortschatz** shown on page 47, write down three things you do in your free time. Tell these activities to your partner, and then ask if he or she does them, too.

BEISPIEL   **DU**   **Ich spiele …Und du?**

PARTNER   **Ja, ich spiele auch …** *or* **Nein, ich spiele nicht …**

11 Ein Interview

a. Sprechen You are a reporter for the school newspaper and are interviewing students about their interests. Get together with two other classmates and ask them questions in German to find out what they do in their free time. Then switch roles.

> ### Und dann noch...
>
> | | |
> |---|---|
> | Baseball | Tischtennis |
> | Handball | Brettspiele |
> | Videospiele | |

b. Schreiben After you talk to two classmates, write what you learned, so that your article can be ready for the next edition.

BEISPIEL   **DU**   **Was …?**

(JOHN)   **Ich spiele Fußball und Basketball, und …**

YOU WRITE   **John spielt Fußball und Basketball, und …**

Zweite Stufe

Objective Expressing likes and dislikes

So sagt man das!

Expressing likes and dislikes

To find out what someone likes
or doesn't like to do, you ask:

> **Was machst du gern, Ahmet?**
> **Schwimmst du gern?** *Do you like to swim?*
> **Steffi, Tara, was macht ihr gern?**

The responses might be:

> **Ich spiele gern Fußball.**
> **Nein, nicht so gern.**
> **Wir schwimmen sehr gern.**
> *We like to swim very much.*

To talk about what others like to do, you say:

> **Tara und Steffi schwimmen gern.** *or* **Sie schwimmen gern.**

Ein wenig Grammatik

In the question **Was macht ihr gern?** two
people are addressed directly; the subject
pronoun is **ihr**. The response to this question
is also plural and uses **wir: Wir schwimmen
gern.** The endings added to the verb stem
with **ihr** and **wir** are **-t** and **-en: Schwimmt
ihr? Ja, wir schwimmen gern.**

When you are talking *about* two or more
people, use the plural pronoun **sie**. What
ending is added to the verb stem when the
pronoun **sie** is used?[1]

Plural

wir	spiel**en**
ihr	spiel**t**
Jens und Tara/sie	spiel**en**

In the two boxes below, can you match the
verbs and pronouns correctly?[2]

| bist schwimmt machen | sie (pl) du |
| spielen komme | ich wir ihr |

Grammatikheft, S. 12, Ü. 8–10

Mehr Grammatikübungen,
S. 62, Ü. 2

---

1. -en **2.** Answers will vary. Possible answers:
**sie machen, du bist, ich komme, wir spielen,
ihr schwimmt**

---

12 **Grammatik im Kontext** Script on p. 41G

CD 2 Tr. 4

Gabi is trying to find someone to do
something with her. Listen as she talks
with her friends and determine if she is
speaking to one person or more than one.
Then figure out what game Gabi wants to
play and who finally plays it with her.

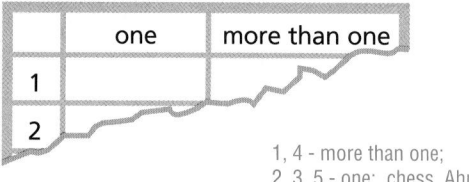

	one	more than one
1		
2		

1, 4 - more than one;
2, 3, 5 - one; chess, Ahmet

---

13 **Grammatik im Kontext**

Sprechen/Schreiben Complete the following conversation between Ahmet and
Holger with **ihr, wir,** or **sie** (pl).

HOLGER Tag Jens, Ahmet! Was macht
___1___ jetzt?

JENS UND ___2___ spielen jetzt
AHMET Fußball. Was machst du?

HOLGER Steffi, Uwe und ich hören
Musik. ___3___ hören
Country sehr gern. Ich glaube,
Tara und Stefan kommen
auch. ___4___ hören Country
auch gern. Und ___5___? Hört
___6___ das gern?

JENS UND Na klar!
AHMET 1. ihr 2. Wir 3. Wir 4. Sie 5. ihr 6. ihr

UWE   Sag mal, was machst du gern?

STEFAN   Oh, ich …

sammle Briefmarken und Comics   **zeichne**   **bastle viel**

UWE   Und ihr, Christiane und Ulrike?

CHRISTIANE   Tja, wir …

besuchen Freunde   **schauen Fernsehen**   **hören Musik**

UWE   Und deine Freunde, Katharina und Sven? Was machen sie?

CHRISTIANE   Sie …

schwimmen   **tanzen**   **wandern**

Übungsheft,
S. 17, Ü. 9–10

Grammatikheft,
S.13, Ü. 11–13

Und dann noch...

Wir ...

lesen   **malen**   **kochen**   **schreiben**   **joggen**

laufen Ski   **laufen Rollschuh**   **segeln**   **fahren Rad**   **reiten**

14 Mix-Match: Viele Interessen   *A lot of interests*

Sprechen Complete Jutta's description of her and her friends' free time activities by matching the following phrases to form complete sentences.

1. Ich besuche…   c.
2. Und ich spiele…   f.
3. Uwe und ich schauen…   b.
4. Christiane hört…   e.
5. Jörg sammelt…   a.
6. Und Peter und Uwe, sie…   d.

a. Briefmarken.
b. Fernsehen.
c. Freunde.
d. schwimmen sehr gern.
e. Musik gern.
f. Fußball gern.

15 Wer macht was?   Script on p. 41G

Zuhören Two of Tara's friends, Claudia and Michael, are trying to figure out what to do today. Listen to their conversation and write down which activities Claudia likes, which ones Michael likes, and what they finally decide to do together.   Musik hören

CD 2 Tr. 5   Claudia: Zeichnen, Musik hören, Fernsehen schauen; Michael: Briefmarken sammeln, schwimmen, Musik hören

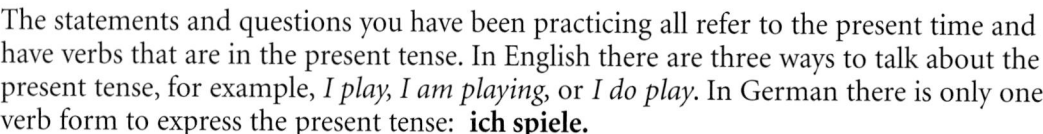

Grammatik

The present tense of verbs

The statements and questions you have been practicing all refer to the present time and have verbs that are in the present tense. In English there are three ways to talk about the present tense, for example, *I play, I am playing,* or *I do play.* In German there is only one verb form to express the present tense: **ich spiele.**

All verbs have a basic form, the form that appears in your word lists (**Wortschatz**) or in a dictionary. This form is called the *infinitive.* The infinitive of all verbs in German has the ending **-en** as in **spielen** or **-n,** as in **basteln.** When a verb is used in a sentence with a subject, the verb is conjugated. That means that the **-en** (or **-n**) of the infinitive is replaced with a specific ending. The ending that is used depends on the noun or pronoun that is the subject of the verb.

The following chart summarizes these different verb forms using **spielen** as a model.

ich	spiele		wir	spiel**en**
du	spiel**st**		ihr	spiel**t**
Holger / er	spiel**t**			
Tara / sie	spiel**t**	Holger und Tara /sie	spiel**en**	

Almost all German verbs follow this pattern. Two verbs that you already know—besides **spielen**—are **kommen** and **machen.**

When speaking to adults who are not family members or relatives, you must use the formal form of address, the pronoun **Sie,** together with the verb form that is used with **sie** plural.

Herr Meyer, spiel**en Sie** Tennis?
Herr und Frau Müller, spiel**en Sie** auch Tennis?

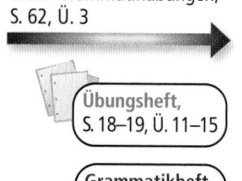

Mehr Grammatikübungen,
S. 62, Ü. 3

Übungsheft,
S. 18–19, Ü. 11–15

Grammatikheft,
S. 14, Ü. 14–15

Ein wenig Landeskunde

Germans tend to be more formal than Americans, and teenagers rarely call adults by their first names. While there are no hard and fast rules about using **du** and **Sie**, it is safer to err in the direction of being too formal. If people want you to call them **du**, they will tell you.

16 Grammatik im Kontext Script on p. 41G

Zuhören As you listen to these conversations, decide whether the speakers are talking to someone they know well, or someone they don't know so well.

CD 2 Tr. 6

1. not very well
2. very well
3. not very well

	very well	not very well
1		
2		

 17 Grammatik im Kontext

Sprechen/Schreiben Using the photos as cues, take turns with a partner saying what the following people do in their free time.

Wir … Wir hören Musik.
Du … Du hörst Musik.
Sie (*you*, formal) …
Sie hören Musik.

Klaus … Klaus zeichnet.
Du … Du zeichnest.
Ihr … Ihr zeichnet.

Ahmet und Holger …
Ich … Ahmet und Holger
Sie (pl) … sammeln Comics.
Ich sammle Comics.
Sie sammeln Comics.

Das Mädchen …
Der Junge …
Ihr … Das Mädchen spielt Gitarre.
Der Junge spielt Gitarre.
Ihr spielt Gitarre.

 **18 Frag mal deinen Lehrer!** *Ask your teacher!*

Schreiben Ask your teacher about his or her interests. Work with a partner and write down five questions to ask, for example, **Spielen Sie Tennis? Hören Sie gern Musik?**

> Ich surfe gern im Internet, besonders Sport.

 19 Was machst du gern?

Sprechen/Schreiben Look at the vocabulary on pages 47 and 51 again. Tell your partner five things you like to do and two that you do not like to do. Then your partner will do the same. Make a list of your partner's likes and dislikes and circle the items you both like and dislike.

 20 Für mein Notizbuch

Schreiben Write down some things you like to do in your **Notizbuch**. For the names of any activities not listed on pages 47 and 51, refer to the Additional Vocabulary section on page R9 in the back of your book. These are words and expressions you can use whenever you're asked about your own interests.

 21 Was macht ihr gern?

Sprechen Work with two or four other classmates. Students in your group should pair off, leaving one person to be IT (**ES**). Using German, each pair should decide on one activity they both like to do. The person who is IT has to find out what that activity is by asking questions: **Spielt ihr gern Volleyball? Besucht ihr gern Freunde?** Students should answer truthfully with **Nein, wir … nicht gern …** or, when IT guesses correctly, **Ja, wir … gern …** The person who is IT reports each pair's activity to the class. Take turns being IT.

Was machst du gern? CD 2 Tr. 7

What kinds of interests do you think German teenagers might enjoy? What sports do you play? What interests do you have? Make a list of the things you like to do in your free time. Then, read what these teenagers said about their free time activities.

CD 2 Trs. 7–12

Übungsheft, S. 24, Ü. 24

Michael, Hamburg CD 2 Tr. 8

„Also ich mach am liebsten in meiner Freizeit Basketball spielen oder ausgehen, so in Diskos oder so was mit Freunden und so und auch Fahrrad fahren."

CD 2 Tr. 9
Christina, Bietigheim

„Ich schwimm gern, ich les gern, ich hör gern Musik und ich fahr gern Moped."

Björn, Hamburg CD 2 Tr. 11

„Tja, ich sitze eigentlich ziemlich oft vor dem Computer. Ich seh auch gerne fern oder guck mir ein Video an. Dann fahr ich ganz gerne Rad und schwimme auch manchmal ganz gerne."

Elke, Berlin CD 2 Tr. 10

„Ich spiele jetzt gern Volleyball. Im Sommer surf ich, und im Winter geh ich mit meinen Eltern nach Österreich Ski laufen."

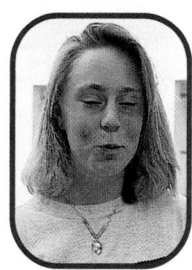

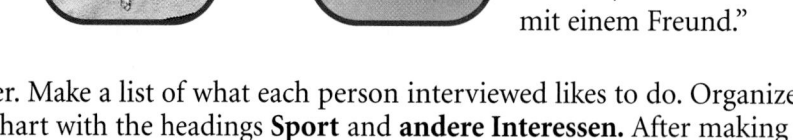
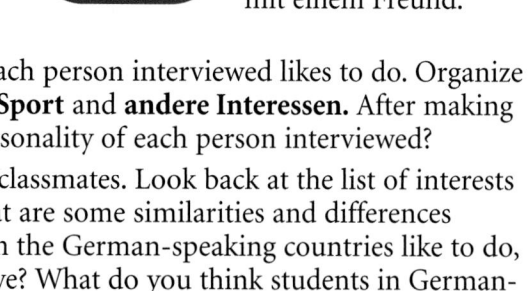

Heide, Berlin CD 2 Tr. 12

„Ich mach dreimal in der Woche Sport. Da jogg ich vier Kilometer mit Trimm-dich-Pfad, dann fahr ich auch noch Fahrrad, danach so eine Stunde mit einem Freund."

A. 1. Work with a partner. Make a list of what each person interviewed likes to do. Organize your answers in a chart with the headings **Sport** and **andere Interessen.** After making your chart, what can you say about the personality of each person interviewed?

2. Answer the following questions with your classmates. Look back at the list of interests you made for yourself before reading. What are some similarities and differences between the free time activities teenagers in the German-speaking countries like to do, and what teenagers like to do where you live? What do you think students in German-speaking countries imagine that teenagers in the United States like to do? Where do they probably get their ideas?

B. You and your partner are exchange students in Potsdam and have been asked to come up with a plan of activities for an afternoon at a local **Jugendzentrum** (youth center). There will also be some other exchange students there, so you will need to plan activities that most everyone will enjoy. Make your plan on a large piece of paper or poster board with a lot of color (you could even cut some pictures out of magazines). Then present your activity plans to the class.

STANDARDS: 1.2, 2.2, 3.2, 4.2

Dritte Stufe

Objectives Saying when you do various activities; asking for an opinion and expressing yours; agreeing and disagreeing

So sagt man das!

Saying when you do various activities

To find out when people do things, you might ask:

Was machst du nach der Schule?
What do you do after school?

They might tell you:

Am Nachmittag mache ich Sport.
In the afternoon I play sports.
Und am Abend mache ich die Hausaufgaben und schaue Fernsehen.
In the evening I do my homework and watch television.

Und am Wochenende? Was machst du am Wochenende?
Was machst du im Sommer?
What do you do in the summer?

Tja, am Wochenende besuche ich Freunde.

Im Sommer wandere ich gern.

What do you notice about the responses in this box? Do they all begin with the subject?[1] What do you observe about the position of the subject in these sentences? What is the position of the verb in all the sentences?[2]

Wortschatz

Wann machst du das?

im Frühling   im Sommer   im Herbst   im Winter

Übungsheft, S. 20, Ü. 16

Grammatikheft, S.15, Ü. 16

---

1. These sentences begin with a time expression, rather than with the subject.
2. The verb is in second position, followed by the subject.

22 Was? und Wann? Script on p. 41H

Zuhören You will hear one of Holger's new classmates, Uschi, talk about when she does various activities. First, write the activities as you hear them mentioned, then match the activities with the phrases that tell when Uschi does them.

CD 2 Tr. 13

a. im Frühling Volleyball   **c.** im Herbst wandern   **e.** im Sommer schwimmen

b. am Wochenende Freunde besuchen **d.** am Nachmittag basteln   **f.** am Abend Musik hören

 23 Wann ...?

Sprechen Based on the page from Tara's weekly planner, answer the following questions.

1. Was macht Tara nach der Schule? Sie spielt Basketball.
2. Wann wandert sie? Am Wochenende.
3. Wann besucht sie Steffis Familie? Am Abend.
4. Wann spielt sie Fußball? Am Samstag.

 24 Wann machst du das?

Schreiben List five activities you like to do and when you do them.

 **25 Zum Schreiben**

Schreiben Using complete sentences, write a description of what activities you like to do and when you like to do them. Use the list you made in Activity 24.

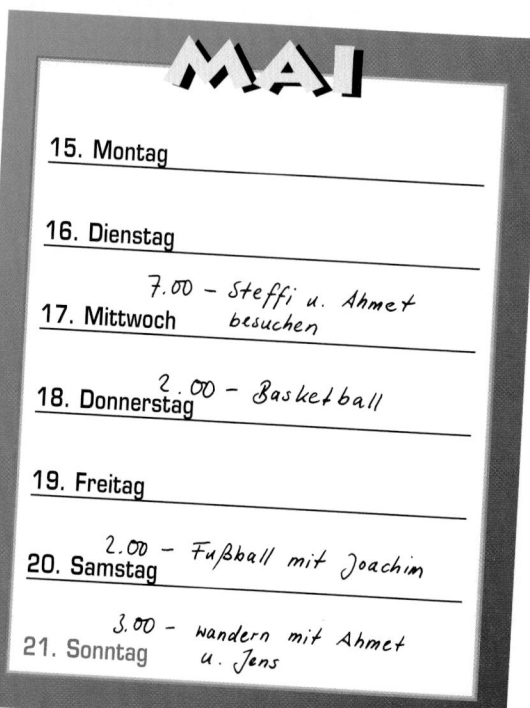

MAI

15. Montag

16. Dienstag

17. Mittwoch   7.00 – Steffi u. Ahmet besuchen

18. Donnerstag 2.00 – Basketball

19. Freitag

20. Samstag 2.00 – Fußball mit Joachim

21. Sonntag 3.00 – wandern mit Ahmet u. Jens

Grammatik

Word order: verb in second position

As you noticed on page 55, German sentences do not always begin with the subject. Often another word or expression (**nach der Schule, im Sommer**) is the first element. What happens to the verb in such cases?[1]

Wir	spielen	nach der Schule	Fußball.
Nach der Schule	spielen	**wir**	Fußball.
Tara und Steffi	besuchen	im Sommer	Freunde.
Im Sommer	besuchen	**Tara und Steffi**	Freunde.

Mehr Grammatikübungen, S. 63, Ü. 4–5

Übungsheft, S. 21–22, Ü. 18–22

Grammatikheft, S. 15, Ü. 17

 26 Für mein Notizbuch

Schreiben Exchange the sentences you wrote in Activity 25 with a partner. Check each other's sentences to make sure that the verbs are in second position and that all the verbs have the proper endings. Then trade papers back again, after you and your partner have made corrections or changes. You may want to modify some of your sentences, putting something else besides the subject at the beginning for a little variety. When you have finished, write your corrected sentences in your **Notizbuch**.

---

1. The verb is in second position, even when something other than the subject begins the sentence.

27 **Grammatik im Kontext**

Sprechen/Schreiben Ask your partner what he or she does at various times. Then switch roles. Use the phrases in the boxes below to help you answer your partner's questions. Be prepared to report your partner's answers to the class.

am Wochenende	im Herbst
am Nachmittag	im Sommer
am Abend	im Winter
nach der Schule	im Frühling

Hausaufgaben machen	Karten spielen
Freunde besuchen	Basketball spielen
Fernsehen schauen	Fußball spielen
Musik hören	schwimmen

So sagt man das!

Asking for an opinion and expressing yours

To find out what someone thinks about something, you might ask:

Some possible responses are:

Wie findest du Tanzen?

Ich finde Tanzen langweilig. *I think dancing is boring.*
Tanzen ist Spitze! *Dancing is great!*
Tanzen macht Spaß. *Dancing is fun.*

Und wie findet Georg Tanzen?

Er findet Tanzen langweilig.

Grammatik

Verbs with stems ending in **d**, **t** or **n**

Finden and other verbs with stems ending in **d**, **t** or **n** do not follow the regular pattern in the **du**- and **er/sie**-forms. These verbs add **-est** to the **du**-form (**du findest**) and **-et** to the **er/sie**- and **ihr**- forms (**er/sie findet, ihr findet**). Another verb that follows this pattern is **zeichnen** (**du zeichnest, er/sie zeichnet, ihr zeichnet**). Compare these verb forms:

	spielen	finden	zeichnen
du	spiel**st**	find**est**	zeich**nest**
er, sie	spiel**t**	find**et**	zeich**net**
ihr	spiel**t**	find**et**	zeich**net**

Mehr Grammatikübungen, S. 63, Ü. 6

28 **Blöd oder Spitze?**

Sprechen Express your opinion about the following activities. You may choose expressions from the list.

1. Ich finde Briefmarkensammeln …
2. Fernsehen ist …
3. Musik hören ist …
4. Basteln finde ich …
5. Wandern finde ich …
6. Volleyball …
7. Freunde besuchen …
8. Schach …

Some possible answers:
Musik hören ist toll!
Freunde besuchen macht Spaß!
Schach ist langweilig!
Basteln finde ich prima!

Wortschatz

Degrees of enthusiasm

Spitze!
super!
Klasse!
toll!
prima!
interessant!
macht Spaß!
langweilig!
blöd!
macht keinen Spaß!

Übungsheft, S. 20, Ü. 17

Grammatikheft, S. 17, Ü. 20–22

29 Wie findest du ...?

Sprechen Ask your partner his or her opinion of three activities. Then switch roles. Be prepared to report your partner's opinions to the class.

So sagt man das!

Agreeing and disagreeing

If someone expresses an opinion such as **Ich finde Volleyball langweilig,**
you might agree: Or you might disagree:

    Ich auch! *or*   **Ich nicht!** *or*
    Das finde ich auch.   **Das finde ich nicht.**

If someone makes a statement like **Basteln ist blöd!**
you might agree: or disagree:

    Stimmt!   **Stimmt nicht!**   Grammatikheft, S. 18, Ü. 23–24

Ein wenig Grammatik

Verbs that end in **-eln**, like the verb **basteln**, change in the **ich**-form: the **e** drops from the verb stem, and the verb becomes **ich bastle**. Can you guess what the **ich**-form of **segeln** is?

	seg**eln**	bast**eln**
ich	seg**le**	bast**le**

Mehr Grammatikübungen, S. 63, Ü. 7

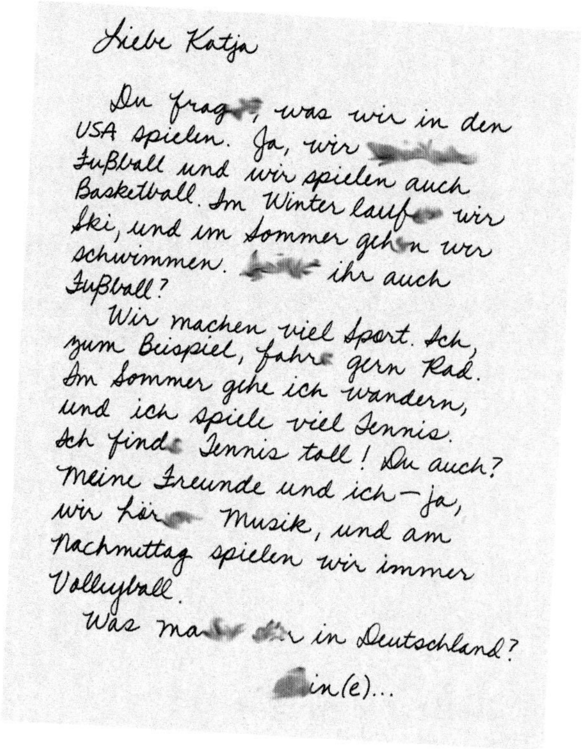

Grammatikheft, S. 18, Ü. 25

30 Stimmt! oder Stimmt nicht! Script on p. 41H

Zuhören Listen to the conversation between Ahmet and a friend as they discuss free time activities. Do they agree or disagree? About what?
CD 2 Tr. 14

1, 3, 5 agree
2, 4 disagree

Letter handwritten:

Liebe Katja

Du frag___, was wir in den USA spielen. Ja, wir Fußball und wir spielen auch Basketball. Im Winter lauf___ wir Ski, und im Sommer geh___ wir schwimmen. ___ ihr auch Fußball?

Wir machen viel Sport. Ich zum Beispiel, fahr___ gern Rad. Im Sommer gehe ich wandern, und ich spiele viel Tennis. Ich find___ Tennis toll! Du auch? Meine Freunde und ich — ja, wir hör___ Musik, und am Nachmittag spielen wir immer Volleyball.

Was ma___ ___ in Deutschland?

___in (e)...

31 Grammatik im Kontext

a. Sprechen/Schreiben Fill in the endings.

Wie find ===== Holger die Musik? – Er find ===== sie langweilig. Und du, wie find ===== du die Musik? Ich find===== sie prima! – Holger und Steffi, zeichn===== ihr? – Nein, aber der Jens zeichn===== , und die Steffi zeichn===== auch. Zeichn===== du? – Nein, ich zeichn===== nicht. Segel===== du? Nein, ich seg===== nicht, aber ich bast===== gern. – Bast===== du auch?

et; et; est; e; et; et; est; e; st; le; le; elst

b. Schreiben You have just written the letter above to your pen pal in Germany. Unfortunately, on the way to the post office it started to rain and your letter got a little smeared. Rewrite the letter, fixing all the smeared words.

Margin notes:
st
spielen

en
en
spielt

e

e

en

macht
Dein(e)

32 **Und deine Meinung?** *And your opinion?*

1. **Schreiben** List six activities and write your opinion of each one next to it.
2. **Sprechen** Work with a partner. Ask your partner what he or she thinks of each activity on your list. Agree or disagree with your partner's opinion. When you disagree, express your own opinion.
3. **Sprechen** Respond to your partner's list.
4. **Sprechen/Schreiben** Which activities do you and your partner agree on? Which ones don't you agree on? Make a list and be prepared to report to the class.

 33 **Zum Schreiben**

 Schreiben In this chapter you have learned a lot about how Germans spend their free time. Imagine you are Katja and respond to the letter on page 58. Refer to the **Landeskunde** for ideas.

 34  **Von der Schule zum Beruf**

Schreiben As part of a job application, you are asked to write a brief résumé giving your name, age, and your interests in sports or hobbies.

AUSSPRACHE

CD 2
Trs. 15–17

Richtig aussprechen / Richtig lesen CD 2 Tr. 15

A. To practice the following sounds, say the words and sentences below after your teacher or after the recording.

1. The letter combination **ie:** The vowel combination **ie** sounds much like the long *e* in the English word *me*.

   spielen, viel, vier / Sie und ihre sieben Brüder spielen Klavier.

2. The letter combination **ei:** The vowel combination **ei** is pronounced like the long *i* in the English words *mine* and *shine*.

   schreiben, deiner, Freizeit / Heike findet Zeichnen langweilig.

3. The letter **j:** The letter **j** is pronounced like the *y* in the English word *yes*. In words borrowed from other languages, such as **Jeans**, the **j** is pronounced as it is in English.

   Jens, Jürgen, Junge / Wer ist der Junge? Der Junge heißt Jens.

4. The letter **z:** The letter **z** is pronounced like the consonant combination *ts* as in the English word *hits*.

   zur, zehn, zwölf / Zwei und zehn sind zwölf.

Richtig Schreiben / Diktat
CD 2 Tr. 16
CD 2 Tr. 17 (with pauses)

B. Write down the sentences that you hear. Script on p. 41H

Was machen wir am Wochenende?

1. Scan the articles for the following information:

a. the day and time when you can hear a jazz concert in the **HAP-Grieshaber-Halle**   a) 30. Juni, 17-24 Uhr

b. the number of hot air balloon clubs in Hessen   b) 6

c. the three kinds of bands that will perform at the UNI summer festival

Did you have to read every word of the ad in order to find that information?   c) Big Band, jazz, dance

2. You live in Eningen and have friends visiting for the weekend. They are interested in jazz, so you want to take them to the jazz festival. Now you will need to get more specific information.

a. How many groups can you hear at the festival? Where are the groups from?   a) 5 groups, Reutlingen, Stuttgart, **Ungarn**

b. How much will the tickets cost if you buy them at the **Kreissparkasse** in Reutlingen? How much will they cost if you

Immer mehr machen mit

Immer mehr Leute unterschiedlichen Alters begeistern sich fürs Ballonfahren. Bei den sechs hessischen Ballon-Clubs, die die luftige Fahrt auch für Vereinsgäste anbieten, ist ein Jahr Wartezeit für die Aufnahme in den Club die Regel. Im März dieses Jahres war Stuttgart Ziel des 22. Deutschen Freiballonfahrertages.

Eninger HOT JAZZ Festival

Am 30. Juni 2002 von 17–24 Uhr in der HAP-Grieshaber-Halle

Mit   Tante Frieda's Jazz Kränzchen, Reutlingen
All Star Groove, Stuttgart
Royal Garden Ramblers, Stuttgart
Stuttgarter Dixieland All Stars
Budapest Ragtime Orchestra, Ungarn

Hallenbewirtschaftung mit Faßbier und kleineren Speisen.

Eintrittskarten sind zu € 10.– bei allen Zweigstellen der Kreissparkasse Reutlingen und »Sigi's Jazz House«, Im Bebenhäuser Hof, Reutlingen sowie an der Abendkasse zu € 12.– erhältlich.

Hallenöffnung: 16.00 Uhr

Skat

Die Karten in Mittelhand: Kreuz-Bube, Pik-Bube, Herz-Bube, Karo-Bube, Kreuz-As, Herz-As, Dame, Pik-König, Dame, 9 Vorhand paßt nach ausgereiztem Null ouvert Hand. Mittelhand spielt kurzentschlossen Pik Solo Hand, doch das Spiel endet, obwohl es kaum begonnen hat, mit 60:60 Augen. Die Gewinnchancen für einen Grand Hand waren sicher größer, doch käme es hierbei auch auf den Kartensitz bei der Gegenpartei an. Schließlich reizte Vorhand bis 59, und es war nicht auszuschließen, daß Vorhand im Besitz der restlichen Pikkarten sein konnte. Vorhand führt in zwei roten Farben (4+5 K.) 24 Augen, dazu eine schwarze Lusche. Hinterhand führt in zwei schwarzen Farben (1+6 K.) 17, dazu in einer roten Farbe 18 Augen.

Potsminton

BADMINTON-TURNIER

Sonntag, 23. Juni 2001, von 11.00 bis 16.00 Uhr

Vom Freizeitsportler bis zum Aktiven bieten wir für jeden etwas. Hobby-Sportler können alles Wichtige über Federball und Badminton erfahren. Aktiven Spielern verrät unser Fachtrainer **Volker Jürgens** Tricks und Kniffe oder gibt Tipps für das individuelle Training.

Natürlich können Sie auch unsere Courts einfach nur mal testen.

Leihschläger ligen für Sie bereit!

Potsminton/Potsdam Sport-Center
Brandenburger Str. 73
14467 Potsdam
Telefon (003733) 458317

Potsminton

UNI 19.00 Uhr

23. Juni

Sommerfest

-Eintritt frei - Bewirtung-
-Neue Aula-Geschwister-Scholl-Platz

Festsaal
- Workshop Orchester der Tübinger Musiktage
- Tanzband Die Piccolos
- Vorführgruppe Elementarer Tanz
- Die hüpfenden und tanzenden Tonnen
- Modern- und Jazz-Tanzgruppe des Sportinstituts

Neue Aula Foyer
- Big Band Such Over Sky

Geschwister-Scholl-Platz
- Neckartown-Jazzband

Bar
- Karl Springer - Piano

Schach

Nr. 2743 – Dr. Siegfried Brehmer
«Schachexpress» 1948

Matt in zwei Zügen
Weiß: Kb8, De7, Tb7, Ld6, Sd3 (5)
Schwarz: Kc6, De1, Ta5, Th4, Lh2, Lh3, Sc3, Sg3, Ba7, d5, d7, e5, h6 (13)

Liebe(Lieber) ‗‗‗‗ !

Morgen habe ich viel vor.
Am Vormittag ‗‗‗‗ .
Später ‗‗‗‗ . *Am Abend*
gehe ich zum Sommerfest.
Dort ‗‗‗‗ . *Bevor ich ins*
Bett gehe, ‗‗‗‗ .

Dein(e)

wait and buy them on the evening of the performance? How early can you enter the concert hall? b) € 10, € 12, 16 Uhr

3. What would you and your friends probably be interested in if you wanted to attend the **UNI Sommerfest**? Can you figure out who is sponsoring this event? When will the event take place (time and date) and where? How much will it cost to get into the festival?

3. Possible answers: Tanz, Musik. Die Uni. 23. Juni, 19 Uhr, Neue Aula, Geschwister-Scholl-Platz. Eintritt frei.

Weißt du noch? *Remember?* You will often be able to use visual clues to figure out the meaning of a text.

4. List any visual clues on this page that help you determine the meaning of the texts. Skat, chess, balloon, musical instrument

5. If your friends would like to learn badminton better, where should they go? What telephone number should they call?

5. Potsminton-Badminton. (003733) 458317

6. With a friend, make a list of places you want to go or activities you want to participate in. Use the ads on these two pages, but feel free to add activities that you particularly enjoy. Are there activities mentioned here that you would not want to do? Write those activities on a separate list.

6. Possible answers: ich spiele Tennis/ich gehe wandern Karten/Schach/ich höre Musik/ich schaue Fernsehen/ich spiele

7. Write a postcard to a friend about what you have planned for tomorrow. Use the partial sentences on the postcard as your guide, filling in the blanks with activities that you enjoy. Use words from the newspaper ads or other words you have learned.

Many *Zum Lesen* selections are permissioned documents that cannot be altered. They therefore do not reflect the changes enacted by the **Rechtschreibreform**.

Übungsheft, S. 23, Ü. 23

Mehr Grammatikübungen

CD-ROM
DISC 1

Answers

internet

go.hrw.com

ADRESSE: go.hrw.com
KENNWORT:
WK3 BRANDENBURG-2

Erste Stufe Objectives Talking about interests

1 You and your friends are talking about your interests and their interests. For each interchange, fill in each blank with an appropriate verb form. **(S. 46)**

1. A: Mark, _____ du Tennis? B: Ja, ich _____ Tennis. *spielst; spiele*
2. A: Was _____ die Steffi? B: Sie _____ Klavier. *spielt; spielt*
3. A: Was _____ der Mark? B: Er _____ Fußball. *spielt; spielt*
4. A: Was _____ du? Schach? B: Ja, ich _____ Schach. *spielst; spiele*
5. A: _____ du ein Instrument? B: Ja, ich _____ Gitarre. *Spielst; spiele*

Zweite Stufe Objectives Expressing likes and dislikes

2 You and your friends are discussing what you like to do and what you dislike. For each interchange, fill in each blank with the appropriate verb form. **(S. 48)**

1. A: Was _____ ihr gern, Heike und Ahmet? *macht/spielt*
2. B: Wir _____ gern Sport. Fußball, Tennis! *machen*
3. A: Tara und Steffi _____ gern Volleyball. *spielen*
4. B: Und was _____ ihr gern? Tennis? *spielt*
5. A: Wir _____ gern Klavier. Und was _____ ihr gern? *spielen; spielt*
6. B: Wir _____ gern Gitarre. *spielen*
7. A: Was _____ ihr nicht gern? *spielt/macht*
8. B: Wir _____ Golf nicht gern. *spielen*

3 Ask people about their interests, and they will tell you what they like and what they don't like. Complete each of the following statements and questions by filling in the blanks with the appropriate form of the verb given in parentheses. **(S. 50)**

1. Was (machen) _____ du gern, Ute? (zeichnen) _____ du gern? *machst; Zeichnest*
2. Ich (zeichnen) _____ gern, und ich (sammeln) _____ Briefmarken. *zeichne; sammle*
3. Was (machen) _____ ihr jetzt? (schauen) _____ ihr jetzt Fernsehen? *macht; Schaut*
4. Wir (hören) _____ jetzt Musik, und wir (spielen) _____ Karten. *hören; spielen*
5. Herr Meier, was (machen) _____ Sie? (spielen) _____ Sie Tennis? *machen; Spielen*
6. Ich (spielen) _____ heute Volleyball. *spiele*
7. Was (machen) _____ Tara und Stefan? (spielen) _____ sie Karten? *machen; Spielen*
8. Nein, sie (besuchen) _____ Freunde. *besuchen*

Objectives Saying when you do various activities; asking for an opinion and expressing yours

4 When are these students doing various activities? Write an answer to each of the following questions, beginning each answer with the underlined part of the question. **(S. 54)**

1. Was machst du <u>nach der Schule</u>? Freunde besuchen? — Ja, _____ .   … besuche ich Freunde
2. Was macht ihr <u>im Sommer</u>? Viel wandern? — Ja, _____ .   … wandern wir viel
3. Was machen Tara und Eva <u>am Nachmittag</u>? Tennis spielen? — Ja, _____ .   … spielen sie Tennis
4. Was machst du <u>am Abend</u>? Fernsehen schauen? — Ja, _____ .   … schaue ich Fernsehen
5. Was macht ihr <u>am Wochenende</u>? Musik hören? — Ja, _____ .   … hören wir Musik
6. Was machen Bob und Ed <u>am Abend</u>? Moped fahren? — Ja, _____ .   … fahren sie Moped

5 You are writing a note to a friend telling what you do after school. Complete the following paragraph by filling in each blank with the appropriate form of a verb. Suggested infinitives are given in the box. **(S. 56)**

besuchen	haben	gehen	hören
schauen		sammeln	spielen

Nach der Schule _____ ich Musik, oder ich _____ Freunde und wir   höre; besuche

_____ Karten. Am Nachmittag _____ ich schwimmen, und am Abend   spielen; gehe

_____ ich Fernsehen. Ich _____ auch andere Interessen: ich _____   schaue; habe; sammle

Briefmarken und Comics.

6 Ask your friends about their opinions regarding various activities. Then give your opinion. Complete the questions by filling in the blanks with the appropriate form of the verb used to ask for and to express an opinion. **(S. 57)**

1. Basteln macht Spaß. Und wie _____ du Basteln?   findest
2. Schach spielen ist langweilig. Und wie _____ ihr Schach?   findet
3. Volleyball ist Spitze. Und wie _____ Ahmet Volleyball?   findet
4. Wandern ist toll. Und wie _____ Tara und Steffi Wandern?   finden
5. Fußball ist super! Ich _____ Fußball auch super!   finde

7 Someone is expressing an opinion about various activities, and you agree. Complete your agreement by filling in each blank with the correct form of the verb that expresses the activity mentioned. **(S. 56)**

1. Ich finde Segeln Spitze! — Ja, ich _____ auch gern.   segle
2. Ich finde Wandern prima! — Ja, ich _____ auch sehr gern.   wandre / wandere
3. Ich finde Basteln toll! — Ja, ich _____ auch sehr gern.   bastle
4. Ich finde Zeichnen super! — Ja, ich _____ auch gern.   zeichne
5. Ich finde Schwimmen Spitze! — Ja, ich _____ auch gern.   schwimme
6. Ich finde Tanzen toll! — Ja, ich _____ auch gern.   tanze

Anwendung

The CD-ROM Tutor offers guided recording and writing activities to accompany the **Anwendung.** These activities are designed to practice students' oral and written communication skills and to review material from each chapter.

1 You will hear several people talk about their interests and activities. Take notes as you listen, then answer the questions **Wer? Was? Wann?** for each conversation.

1. **Ahmet und Tara/Tennis/vier Uhr**   2. **Steffi/Volleyball/zwei Uhr**   3. **Steffi, Holger, Katja/wandern/am Wochenende**

Script on p. 41H

CD 2 Tr. 18

2 **a.** Listen to the description of **der Sporti** and **die Sporti** pictured below. Write down any sports and activities that are mentioned but not pictured.   answers below

CD 2 Tr. 19   Script on p. 41H

b. Pick one of the **Sportis** below and tell your partner everything the **Sporti** does. Your partner will tell you about the other **Sporti**.

der Sporti

Baseball	wandern
Volleyball	Fernsehschauen
Klavier spielen	Eishockey
Tanzen	Schwimmen

die Sporti

Golf
Freunde besuchen
Tanzen
basteln
Fußball

3 Look at the drawings of **der Sporti** and **die Sporti** above and use them for clues to answer the following questions.

a. Was machst du in deiner Freizeit? Wann machst du das? Was machst du nicht?

b. Wie findest du das alles? Zum Beispiel, wie findest du Fußball, Tennis usw.?

4 Everyone in class will write on a slip of paper the German name for an activity presented in the chapter. Put all the slips of paper into a small box, then get into two teams. Two students, one from each team, together draw a slip of paper from the box. These two "mimes" will act out the activity, and the teams will take turns guessing what they are doing. The first person to guess right wins a point for his or her team. Guesses must be in this form: **Ihr spielt Tennis!**

5 Read the following student profiles. Working with a partner, take turns choosing one of the people pictured below and telling your partner about that person's name, age and interests.

Nicole König, 14
Hamburg
Tennis und Volleyball
spielen, zeichnen,
Freunde besuchen

Martin Braun, 16
Düsseldorf
Fußball und Gitarre
spielen, Briefmarken
sammeln, wandern

Julia Meier, 15
Ludwigsburg
schwimmen, Klavier
spielen, basteln, Schach
spielen, Musik hören

6 Working in groups of three, interview each member of your group and write descriptions like the ones above. First, decide together which questions you need to ask. Then, while one person interviews another, the third writes down the information on a separate piece of paper, leaving out the person's name. When the whole class is finished, put the descriptions in a box and take turns drawing them and telling the class about that person. Your classmates will guess who is being described.

7 One of the students pictured above is visiting your school, and you have to introduce him or her at a German club meeting. Write down what you are going to say in complete sentences.

8 ## R o l l e n s p i e l

Get together with two of your classmates and act out the following situation.

It's Friday after school. You and two of your friends are really bored, and you are trying to find something fun to do. Discuss the activities that each of you likes, then try to find several that you can do together. Make a plan that includes several different activities and discuss when you want to do them. Be prepared to report your plans to the class.

Kann ich's wirklich?

Can you ask about someone's interests, report them, and tell your own? (p. 48)

1 How would you ask a classmate about interests, using the verbs **spielen, machen, schwimmen,** and **sammeln?**
Some possible answers:
Spielst du…? Was machst du in deiner Freizeit? Schwimmst du? Sammelst du…?

2 How would you report someone else's interests?
a) Susanne tanzt/ wandert/ spielt Gitarre
b) Jörg spielt Golf/segelt/zeichnet
c) Johannes spielt Schach, besucht Freunde
d) Uschi schaut Fernsehen, hört Musik, spielt Karten

a. **Susanne: tanzen, wandern, Gitarre spielen**
b. **Jörg: Golf spielen, basteln, zeichnen**
c. **Johannes: Schach spielen, Freunde besuchen**
d. **Uschi: Fernsehen schauen, Musik hören, Karten spielen**

Can you ask what others like to do and don't like to do, report what they say, and tell what you and your friends like and don't like to do? (p. 50)

3 How would you tell some of the things you do?
a) Possible answers: **Ich spiele gern Fußball.** Ich schwimme nicht so gern. b) Was machst du gern? \ Possible answers: Sie spielt gern Klavier/schwimmt gern.

4
a. How would you say what activities you like and don't like to do?
b. How would you ask a classmate what he or she likes to do and report that information to someone else?
c. How would you ask these people what they like to do and then report what they say?
Katharina und Ute: schwimmen, Schach spielen, Musik hören
d. How would you ask your teacher if he or she plays basketball or chess, or if he or she collects stamps?

c) Katharina und Ute, was macht ihr gern? Sie schwimmen gern.   d) Spielen Sie Basketball? Spielen Sie
Sie spielen Schach gern. / Sie hören Musik gern.   Schach? Sammeln Sie Briefmarken?

Can you say when you do various activities? (p. 55)

5 How would you say that you
a. watch TV after school
b. play soccer in the afternoon
c. go hiking in the spring
d. swim in the summer
a) Nach der Schule schaue ich Fernsehen.   c) Im Frühling wandere ich.
b) Am Nachmittag spiele ich Fußball.   d) Im Sommer schwimme ich.

6 How would you ask a classmate what he or she thinks of
a. tennis   Wie findest du Tennis, Musik, Zeichnen, Wandern?
b. music
c. drawing
d. hiking

Answers will vary. Possible answers: a. Das finde ich auch.
b. Stimmt nicht. Basteln ist blöd.

Can you ask for an opinion, agree, disagree and express your own opinion? (pp. 57, 58)

7 Agree or disagree with the following statements. If you disagree, express your opinion.   c. Stimmt!   d. Das finde ich nicht. Tennis ist langweilig.
a. Schach ist langweilig.
b. Basteln macht Spaß.
c. Briefmarken sammeln ist interessant.
d. Tennis ist super!

Answers will vary. Possible answers:
8 How would you express your opinion of the following activities:
a. Fußball spielen   a. Fußballspielen ist Spitze.   c. wandern   c. Wandern ist prima.
b. Briefmarken sammeln   b. Briefmarkensammeln ist langweilig.   d. schwimmen   d. Schwimmen ist super.

Erste Stufe

Talking about interests

Was machst du in deiner Freizeit?	What do you do in your free time?
Machst du Sport?	Do you do sports?
machen	to do
spielen	to play
Ich spiele Fußball.	I play soccer.
Basketball	basketball
Volleyball	volleyball
Tennis	tennis

Golf	golf
Spielst du ein Instrument?	Do you play an instrument?
Ich spiele Klavier.	I play the piano.
Gitarre	guitar
Karten	cards
Schach	chess
Hast du andere Interessen?	Do you have other interests?

Other useful words and phrases

viel	a lot, much
nicht	not, don't
andere	other
Ich glaube …	I think …
oft	often

Zweite Stufe

Expressing likes and dislikes

gern (machen)	to like (to do)
nicht gern (machen)	to not like (to do)
nicht so gern	not to like very much

Activities

Briefmarken sammeln	to collect stamps
Comics sammeln	to collect comics
Freunde besuchen	to visit friends
Fernsehen schauen	to watch TV
Musik hören	to listen to music
zeichnen	to draw

basteln	to do crafts
schwimmen	to swim
tanzen	to dance
wandern	to hike
Spielen Sie Tennis, Herr Meyer?	Do you play tennis, Mr. Meyer?

Pronouns

ich	I
wir	we
du	you
ihr	you (pl)
er	he
sie	she

es	it
sie	they
Sie	you (formal)

Other useful words and phrases

so	so
sehr	very
Sag mal, …	Say, …
Tja …	Hm …
schreiben	to write
Ich gehe schwimmen.	I go swimming.

Dritte Stufe

Saying when you do various activities

die Hausaufgaben machen	to do homework
Wann?	When?
nach der Schule	after school
am Nachmittag	in the afternoon
am Abend	in the evening
am Wochenende	on the weekend
im Frühling	in the spring
im Sommer	in the summer
im Herbst	in the fall
im Winter	in the winter

Expressing opinions

Wie findest du (Tennis)?	What do you think of (tennis)?

Ich finde (Tennis) …	I think (tennis) is …
Spitze!	super!
super!	super!
Klasse!	great! terrific!
prima!	
toll!	
interessant	interesting
langweilig	boring
blöd	dumb
(Tanzen) macht Spaß.	(Dancing) is fun.
(Tennis) macht keinen Spaß.	(Tennis) is no fun.

Agreeing and disagreeing

Ich auch.	Me too.
Ich nicht.	I don't./Not me!
Stimmt!	That's right! True!
Stimmt nicht!	Not true!
Das finde ich auch.	I think so too.
Das finde ich nicht.	I disagree.

Other useful phrases

Ich surfe Sport im Internet.	I surf the 'Net for sports.
So ein Mist!	Darn it!

Kapitel 3: Komm mit nach Hause!
Chapter Overview

Los geht's! pp. 70–72	**Bei Jens zu Hause!, p. 70**

	FUNCTIONS	GRAMMAR	VOCABULARY	RE-ENTRY
Erste Stufe pp. 73–77	• Talking about where people live, p. 73 • Offering something and responding to an offer, p. 74 • Saying please, thank you, you're welcome, p. 76	• Indefinite articles **ein, eine**, p. 75 • The **möchte-forms**, p. 76	• Words to describe where you live, p. 73 • Food and drink items, p. 75	
Zweite Stufe pp. 78–80	• Describing a room, p. 79	• The pronouns **er, sie, es,** and **sie** *pl,* p. 79	• Words to describe a room, p. 78	
Dritte Stufe pp. 81–85	• Talking about family members, p. 82 • Describing people, p. 84	• The possessive adjectives **mein, dein, sein,** and **ihr**, pp. 82 and 83	• Members of the family, p. 81	• Asking someone's name and age, pp. 82 and 83; asking who someone is, p. 82 (**Kap. 1**); talking about interests, pp. 92 and 93 (**Kap. 2**)

Aussprache p. 85	The long vowel **o**, the long vowel **u**, the letters **s, ss,** and **ß**: Audio CD 3, Track 14	**Diktat:** Audio CD 3, Tracks 15–16

Zum Lesen pp. 86–87	Wo wohnst du denn?	**Reading Strategy** Using root words to form new words

Mehr Grammatik-übungen	**pp. 88–91**		
	Erste Stufe, p. 88	**Zweite Stufe**, pp. 89–90	**Dritte Stufe**, pp. 90–91

Review pp. 92–95	**Anwendung**, pp. 92–93	**Kann ich's wirklich?**, p. 94	**Wortschatz**, p. 95
	Zum Schreiben: Arranging ideas spatially (Drawing a personal profile puzzle)		

CULTURE

• **Landeskunde: Wo wohnst du?**, p. 77
• **Ein wenig Landeskunde:** Drinking water, p. 75

Kapitel 3: Komm mit nach Hause!
Chapter Resources

PRINT

Lesson Planning

One-Stop Planner

Lesson Planner with Substitute Teacher Lesson Plans, pp. 12–16, 67

Student Make-Up Assignments
- Make-Up Assignment Copying Masters, Chapter 3

Listening and Speaking

TPR Storytelling Book, pp. 9–12

Listening Activities
- Student Response Forms for Listening Activities, pp. 19–21
- Additional Listening Activities 3-1 to 3-6, pp. 23–26
- Additional Listening Activities (song), p. 22
- Scripts and Answers, pp. 113–118

Video Guide
- Teaching Suggestions, pp. 16–17
- Activity Masters, pp. 18–20
- Scripts and Answers, pp. 85–87, 112

Activities for Communication
- Communicative Activities, pp. 13–18
- Realia and Teaching Suggestions, pp. 82–85
- Situation Cards, pp. 127–128

Reading and Writing

Reading Strategies and Skills Handbook, Chapter 3

Lies mit mir! 1, Chapter 3

Übungsheft, pp. 25–36

Grammar

Grammatikheft, pp. 19–27

Grammar Tutor for Students of German, Chapter 3

Assessment

Testing Program
- Grammar and Vocabulary Quizzes, **Stufe** Quizzes, and Chapter Test, pp. 53–72
- Score Sheet, Scripts, and Answers, pp. 73–78

Alternative Assessment Guide
- Portfolio Assessment, p. 20
- Performance Assessment, p. 34
- CD-ROM Assessment, p. 48

Student Make-Up Assignments
- Alternative Quizzes, Chapter 3

MEDIA

 Online Activities
- Interaktive Spiele
- Internet Aktivitäten

 Video Program
- Videocassette 1
- Videocassette 5 (captioned version)

 Audio Compact Discs
- Textbook Listening Activities, CD 3, Tracks 1–18
- Additional Listening Activities, CD 3, Tracks 25–31
- Assessment Items, CD 3, Tracks 19–24

 Interactive CD-ROM Tutor, Disc 1

 Teaching Transparencies
- Situations 3-1 to 3-2
- Vocabulary 3-A to 3-C
- **Los geht's!**
- **Mehr Grammatikübungen** Answers
- **Grammatikheft** Answers

 **One-Stop Planner CD-ROM**

Use the **One-Stop Planner CD-ROM with Test Generator** to aid in lesson planning and pacing.

For each chapter, the **One-Stop Planner** includes:
- Editable lesson plans with direct links to teaching resources
- Printable worksheets from resource books
- Direct launches to the HRW Internet activities
- Video and audio segments
- Test Generator
- Clip Art for vocabulary items

Kapitel 3: Komm mit nach Hause!

Projects ·······························

Mein Traumhaus

In this activity students will design, furnish, label, and describe their dream house. You will probably want to begin this project after students have covered the vocabulary and functions introduced in the Zweite Stufe.

MATERIALS

✂ **Students may need**
- old magazines
- scissors
- catalogs
- posterboard
- glue
- markers
- weekend edition of newspapers

SUGGESTED SEQUENCE

1. Students plan the design of their dream house by gathering ideas from pictures from the home section of weekend newspapers, home magazines, furniture and decorating catalogs, etc.

2. Students paste the pictures they have chosen on posterboard.

3. Students make small German labels for each piece of furniture pasted on the posterboard. (Example: **die Stereoanlage**) You might want to provide additional vocabulary or make dictionaries available. Some additional vocabulary words are provided starting on p. R9 in the *Pupil's Edition.*

4. After students have designed, furnished, and labeled their dream house, ask them to write a paragraph describing their house. Where is it located? Supply necessary phrases such as **Ferienhaus am Meer** or **in den Bergen.** What are the colors of the different rooms?

5. Students present their project and read their written work to the class, a smaller group, or a partner.

6. Display the projects in your class or in the foreign language area.

GRADING THE PROJECT

Suggested point distribution (**total = 100 points**)
- Poster content and appearance..............30
- Written paragraph................................30
- Oral presentation..................................30
- Originality..10

You may wish to evaluate the written part of the project using the following rubric.

Writing Rubric	Points			
	4	3	2	1
Content (Complete – Incomplete)				
Comprehensibility (Comprehensible – Seldom comprehensible)				
Accuracy (Accurate – Seldom accurate)				
Organization (Well-organized – Poorly organized)				
Effort (Excellent – Minimal)				

18–20: A 16–17: B 14–15: C 12–13: D Under 12: F

FAMILY LINK

Ask students to share their project with their family. Students should teach the German words used for furniture to interested family members.

Games ·······························

Wortbilder

In this game, students practice the vocabulary from p. 95 by identifying words represented by Wortbilder.

Procedure Divide the class into two teams. Each team decides how to draw several pictures of words from the **Wortschatz** on p. 95 (**Wortbilder**). Have a student from Team 1 draw his or her **Wortbild** on the board. Team 2 has a set amount of time (determined by the teacher) to guess what the picture stands for. If Team 2 guesses the word correctly, that team scores, and it is that team's turn to draw another **Wortbild.** If a team gets five points in a row, it is automatically the other team's turn.

Example: HAUS + TIER = **Haustier**

 STANDARDS: 1.3, 5.1, 5.2

Das Subjekt fehlt!

*This game can be used at any time to review the vocabulary of the **Stufe** you are working on.*

Procedure Prepare strips of paper large enough to write one sentence on each. Write a German sentence on each strip of paper, omitting the subject. (Example: _____ **ist sehr unbequem.**) Use the vocabulary of the specific **Stufe** you're working on. Place all slips of paper into a hat. Divide the class into two groups. Alternating between groups, have each group member pull a sentence from the hat, read the incomplete sentence aloud, add an appropriate subject, and read the completed sentence aloud to the class. For the example above, the student could reply **Die Couch ist sehr unbequem.** If the subject fits and is grammatically correct, the student scores a point for his or her group. The game continues until each student has pulled a slip from the hat and made a complete sentence. The group with the most points wins.

Storytelling

Mini-Geschichte

*This story accompanies Teaching Transparency 3-A. The **Mini-Geschichte** can be told and retold in different formats, acted out, written down, and read aloud, to give students additional opportunities to practice all four skills.*

Bei Jens zu Hause

Holger fragt Jens: „Wo wohnst du?" Holger sagt: „Ganz in der Nähe. Komm doch mit mir nach Hause!" Holger und Jens gehen in Jens' Zimmer. Holger findet das Zimmer toll. Er findet das Sofa bequem und den Schrank sehr groß. Jens fragt: „Holger, möchtest du etwas trinken?" „Ja, eine Cola bitte." „Oh, ich habe nur Mineralwasser."

Traditions

Friedrich der Große

Friedrich wird am 24.1.1712 in Berlin als Sohn des Kronprinzen Friedrich Wilhelm I., des späteren Soldatenkönigs, und dessen Gemahlin Sophie Dorothea geboren. Der Vater fordert für Friedrich eine strenge militärische und religiös geprägte Erziehung. Die Konflikte zwischen dem tyrannischen, nur aufs Militärische und aufs Ökonomische fixierten Vater und dem Kronprinzen spitzen sich immer mehr zu. Brutale körperliche und seelische Züchtigungen sind an der Tagesordnung und veranlassen den Kronprinzen 1730 zu einem Fluchtversuch, der vereitelt wird. Das vom König eingesetzte Militärgericht verweigert ein Todesurteil für den Kronprinzen.

1738 komponiert Friedrich seine erste Sinfonie. Friedrich korrespondiert mit Voltaire, der später auch einige Zeit in Sansoucci lebt. Am 31.5.1740 wird Friedrich II. nach dem Tod seines Vaters preußischer König. Nach der Rückkehr aus dem 2. Schlesischen Krieg wird er erstmals „Friedrich der Große" genannt.

1770 bestätigt der König Immanuel Kant, den er ansonsten ignoriert, als Professor in Königsberg. Die letzten Jahre des Königs sind geprägt durch schriftstellerisch-historisch-philosophische Arbeiten, aber auch durch von Altersmüdigkeit geprägter Lyrik.

Am 17.8.1786 stirbt Friedrich II. in Sanssouci.

Rezept

Kartoffelpuffer

Für 2 Personen

Zutaten

g=Gramm, EL=Esslöffel

500 g Kartoffeln, ungekocht, geschält, gewaschen, grob geraspelt

Salz	2 Eier
4 EL Mehl	Schmalz oder Öl zum Braten

Zubereitung

Kartoffeln mit Salz, Eiern und Mehl verrühren. Schmalz oder Öl in der Pfanne erhitzen. Nacheinander bei mittlerer Hitze kleine Puffer goldbraun braten. Heiß servieren.

Beilage: Apfelmus

Technology

Video

Videocassette 1, 5 (captioned version)
See Video Guide, pages 15–20

Los geht's! • Bei Jens zu Hause!

Jens invites Holger to his house after school, where Holger meets Jens's mother. The boys have a snack and Jens shows Holger his room. Later, Jens's cousin comes to visit. Holger is surprised to find out that Jens's cousin is Tara.

Landeskunde

Wo wohnst du?

People from different cities talk about where they live.

Fortsetzung

Tara, Jens, and Holger go to Ahmet's house, where Tara is going to tutor Ahmet's cousin, Handan. As Tara and Handan go inside to study, Jens, Ahmet, and Holger leave to play soccer.

Videoclips

- **Apfel Botschaft Bodensee**® (growing apples)
- **Spezi**® (soda)
- **Apollinaris Mineralwasser**® (mineral water)
- **Pom-Bär**® (chips)
- **Gold Fischli**® (crackers)
- **BHW**® (bank)

Interactive CD-ROM Tutor

The **Interactive CD-ROM Tutor** contains videos, interactive games, and activities that provide students an opportunity to practice and review the material covered in Chapter 3.

Activity	Activity Type	Pupil's Edition Reference
1. Wortschatz	Merkspiel	p. 75
2. Grammatik	Was fehlt?	p. 75
3. Wortschatz	Was ist richtig?	p. 78
4. Grammatik	Was fehlt?	p. 79
5. Wortschatz	Wort und Bild Erfahren/Wählen	pp. 81, 82, 83
6. So sagt man das!	Wozu gehört's?	p. 84
Landeskunde	Wo wohnst du? Was ist richtig?	p. 77
Zum Sprechen	*Guided recording*	pp. 92-93
Zum Schreiben	*Guided writing*	pp. 92-93

Teacher Management System

Logging In

Logging in to the **Komm mit!** TMS is easy. Upon launching the program, simply type "admin" in the password area of the log-in screen and press RETURN. Log on to **www.hrw.com/CDROMTUTOR** for a detailed explanation of the Teacher Management System.

One-Stop Planner CD-ROM

To preview all resources available for this chapter, use the **One-Stop Planner CD-ROM**, Disc 1.

Internet Connection

ADRESSE: go.hrw.com
KENNWORT:
WK3 BRANDENBURG-3

*Have students explore the **go.hrw.com** Web site for many online resources covering all chapters. All Chapter 3 resources are available under the keyword **WK3 Brandenburg-3**. Interactive games practice the material and provide students with immediate feedback. You will find a printable worksheet that provides Internet activities that lead to a comprehensive online research project.*

Interaktive Spiele

You can use the interactive activities in this chapter

- to practice grammar, vocabulary, and chapter functions
- as homework
- as an assessment option
- as a self-test
- to prepare for the Chapter Test

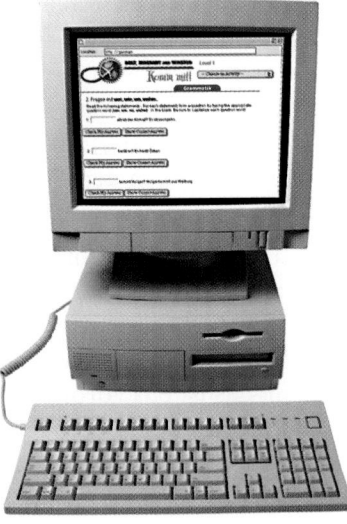

Internet Aktivitäten

Students will find out the name and address of a snack bar, a restaurant, and a movie theater in Potsdam.

- To prepare students for the **Arbeitsblatt,** you might want to have them review the ads in **Zum Lesen,** pp. 86–87. Here they will find examples of German addresses and phone numbers.

- After completing the **Arbeitsblatt,** have students list some snacks they could eat at the snack bar they found in Potsdam. You might want to have them review the **Erste Stufe** vocabulary.

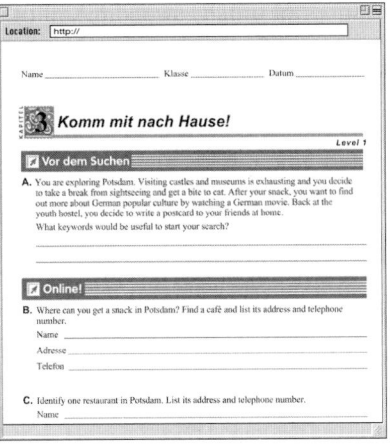

Webprojekt

Have students do a Web search for a German furniture store where they can choose furniture for their own room. Have students report on the name of the store and the items they chose. Encourage students to exchange useful Web sites with their classmates. Have students document their sources by referencing the names and URLs of all the sites they consulted.

Kapitel 3: Komm mit nach Hause!
Textbook Listening Activities Scripts

Erste Stufe

6 p. 74

1. Ich wohne in der Bahnhofstraße. Von der Schule ist das gar nicht weit. Also, ich komm immer zu Fuß zur Schule.

2. Ich wohne in der Stadt Berlin. Da gibt es zu viele Autos, da komm ich halt immer mit der U-Bahn zur Schule. Das ist einfacher.

3. Ich wohne auf dem Land. Wenn das Wetter gut ist, komme ich mit dem Rad zur Schule.

4. Ich wohne in einem Vorort von Potsdam. Die Schule ist nicht weit von hier, da komm ich also meistens mit dem Moped.

9 p. 75

JENS   Tag, Tara! Tag, Ahmet! Kommt 'rein. Der Holger ist auch grad hier.

TARA   Hallo, Holger!

JENS   Ja, ihr zwei! Möchtet ihr auch etwas zu essen und trinken?

AHMET   Ja klar! Zuerst möchte ich aber doch ein Mineralwasser.

JENS   Und du, Tara? Was kann ich dir holen?

TARA   Ja, also vielleicht ein Stück Kuchen und einen Orangensaft, bitte.

JENS   Und du, Ahmet? Was möchtest du essen? Auch ein Stück Kuchen?

AHMET   Nein, Danke. ich möchte lieber etwas Obst.

JENS   Gut. Ich bin gleich wieder da!

Zweite Stufe

13 p. 78

AHMET   Du, die Möbel sind aber schön, Steffi!

STEFFI   Meinst du? Die Stereoanlage ist neu, aber das Regal ist schon ziemlich alt. Und schau mal da! Der Schrank ist eigentlich auch ganz schön. Ich habe viel Platz darin.

AHMET   Der Schreibtisch ist aber groß! Das finde ich ganz praktisch.

STEFFI   Ja, ich auch. Nur der Stuhl ist etwas zu klein dafür. Und mein Bett, na ja, das ist ganz bequem. Es gefällt mir sehr.

Dritte Stufe

20 p. 82

1. Ich heiße Anja, und meine Mutter heißt Johanna. Meine Tante wohnt auch bei uns. Sie heißt Tante Lore. Ich hab auch einen Bruder. Das ist der Rolf und er ist elf. Mein Großvater, also der Opa, wohnt ganz in der Nähe, in der Holstenstraße.

2. Ich heiße Werner und wohne bei meinem Vater in Berlin. Mein Vater heißt Franz. Meine Großmutter und mein Großvater wohnen auch in Berlin, auch gar nicht weit von hier. Ich habe eine Schwester, die Ute. Sie studiert an der Uni hier. In Dahlem, das ist ein Vorort von Berlin, da wohnt mein Onkel. Er heißt Gerhard.

3. Ich heiße Christa. Meine Mutter heißt Christiane, und mein Vater heißt Frank. Wir wohnen alle in Potsdam. Meine Tante und mein Onkel wohnen auf dem Land, außerhalb von Potsdam. Ich habe auch einen Cousin, Karl, der ist zweiundzwanzig. Und mein Bruder Peter wohnt in Hamburg, wo er studiert.

22 p. 83

TARA   Du, Steffi, sag mal, wie alt ist eigentlich deine Kusine, die Anna?

STEFFI   Sie ist schon zweiundzwanzig.

TARA   Und wie alt sind denn deine Eltern?

STEFFI   Ja also, meine Mutter ist dreiundvierzig, und mein Vater, der ist fünfundvierzig. Hier ist ein Foto von Onkel Florian, hm … ich glaube, er ist schon fünfzig.

TARA   Und ist das dein Cousin?

STEFFI   Ja, das ist mein Cousin Bernhard. Er ist sechsundzwanzig. Seine Mutter, also meine Tante, ist schon einundfünfzig. Mein Großvater heißt Gerd. Er ist schon siebzig. Und meine Großmutter, die Oma Hannah, ist auch schon siebenundsechzig.

AUSSPRACHE, p. 85

Diktat, p. 85

You will hear Stefan and Uwe talking. First listen to what they are saying, then write down their conversation.

STEFAN   Hier ist mein Zimmer.

UWE   Die Couch ist aber bequem.

STEFAN   Wirklich? Sie ist schon sehr alt. Was möchtest du trinken?

UWE   Eine Cola oder Limo, bitte.

STEFAN   Und auch etwas zu essen?

UWE   Ja, ich möchte ein Stück Kuchen.

STEFAN   Also, hier ist deine Limo und der Apfelkuchen. Noch warm.

UWE   Danke.

Anwendung

4 p. 92

Das hier ist mein Zimmer. Die Couch ist ziemlich neu und wirklich sehr schön, nicht? Das Regal dagegen ist aber alt und einfach zu klein! Ich finde, es ist hässlich. Nun, das Bett ist relativ groß und sehr bequem. Leider ist der Schreibtisch ein bisschen zu klein und nicht sehr praktisch. Der Stuhl ist auch schon alt und etwas unbequem. Aber meine Stereoanlage ist neu und super! Eine tolle Anlage, nicht wahr? Ich finde mein Zimmer sehr modern, was meinst du?

7c p. 93

Das Mädchen heißt Sonja Schmidt. Sie ist 16 Jahre alt und wohnt in Wedel. Das ist ein Vorort von Hamburg. Sie wohnt in der Bachstraße 4. Sie hat wirklich viele Interessen. Sie malt gern, Landschaftszenen und so. Sie mag gern basteln am Abend. Am Wochenende geht sie auch gern Rad fahren mit Freunden, wenn das Wetter schön ist.

Kapitel 3: Komm mit nach Hause!
Suggested Lesson Plans *50-Minute Schedule*

Day 1

CHAPTER OPENER 10 min.
- Thinking Critically, ATE, p. 67M
- Culture Note, ATE, p. 67M

LOS GEHT'S! 25 min.
- Preteaching Vocabulary, ATE, p. 67N
- Play Audio CD for **Los geht's!**, pp. 70–71
- Have students read **Los geht's!**, pp. 70–71
- **Los geht's!** Transparencies
- Teaching Suggestions, Video Guide, p. 16
- Thinking Critically, ATE, p. 67N
- Show **Los geht's!** Video
- Do Comprehension Activities, p. 72

ERSTE STUFE
So sagt man das!/Wortschatz, p. 73 10 min.
- Presenting **So sagt man das!** and **Wortschatz**, ATE, p. 67P
- Play Audio CD for Activity 6, p. 74
- Do Activity 7, p. 74

Wrap-Up 5 min.
- Students respond to questions about where they live

Homework Options
Übungsheft, pp. 25–26, Acts. 1–2
Grammatikheft, p. 19, Acts. 1–2

Day 2

ERSTE STUFE
Quick Review 10 min.
- Check homework, Grammatikheft, p. 19, Acts. 1–2
- Bell Work, ATE, p. 67O

So sagt man das!, p. 74 10 min.
- Presenting **So sagt man das!**, ATE p. 67O
- Do Activity 8, p. 74

Wortschatz, p. 75 10 min.
- Presenting **Wortschatz**, ATE, p. 67P
- Do Activities 9 and 10, p. 75

Grammatik, p. 75 15 min.
- Present **möchte**-forms, p. 75
- Do Activities 11 and 12, p. 76
- Do Activity 3, p. 20, Grammatikheft

Wrap-Up 5 min.
- Students respond to questions about what they would like to eat or drink

Homework Options
Übungsheft, p. 26–28, Acts. 3–8
Grammatikheft, p. 20, Act. 4

Day 3

ERSTE STUFE
Quick Review 10 min.
- Check homework, Grammatikheft, p. 20, Act. 4
- Do Communicate Activity 3-1, pp. 13–14

So sagt man das!/Ein wenig Grammatik, p. 76 15 min.
- Presenting **So sagt man das!** and **Ein wenig Grammatik**, ATE p. 67P
- Do Activity 5, p. 21, Grammatikheft

LANDESKUNDE 20 min.
- Pre-viewing Suggestion, Video Guide, p. 16
- Background Information, ATE, p. 67Q
- Show **Landeskunde** Video
- Do Activities A and B, p. 77

Wrap-Up 5 min.
- Students practice saying thank you and you're welcome

Homework Options
Grammatikheft, p. 21, Acts. 6–7
Activities for Communication, pp. 127–128, Situation 3-1, make notes and practice

Day 4

ERSTE STUFE
Quick Review 15 min.
- Check homework, Grammatikheft, p. 21, Acts. 6–7
- Do Situtation 3-1, pp. 127–128

Quick Review 15 min.
- Do Additional Listening Activities 3-1 and 3-2, p. 23
- Do **Mehr Grammatikübungen, Erste Stufe**

Quiz 20 min.
- Quiz 3-1A or 3-1B

Homework Options
Activities for Communication, p. 82, Realia 3-1, circle cognates

Day 5

ZWEITE STUFE
Quick Review 10 min.
- Return and review Quiz 3-1
- Bell Work, ATE, p. 67R

Wortschatz, p. 78 10 min.
- Presenting **Wortschatz**, ATE, p. 67R
- Teaching Transparencies 3-1, 3-B

Ein wenig Grammatik, p. 78 10 min.
- Presenting **Ein wenig Grammatik**, ATE, p. 67R
- Play Audio CD for Activity 13, p. 78

So sagt man das!, p. 79 20 min.
- Presenting **So sagt man das!**, ATE, p. 67R
- Do Activities 10-12, pp. 29–30, Übungsheft

Homework Options
Übungsheft, p. 29, Act. 9; pp. 30–31, Acts. 13–15
Grammatikheft, pp. 22–23, Acts. 8–12
Pupil's Edition, p. 79, Activity 14

Day 6

ZWEITE STUFE
Quick Review 5 min.
- Check homework, Grammatikheft, pp. 22–23, Acts. 8–12

Grammatik, p. 79 10 min.
- Presenting **Grammatik**, ATE, p. 67R
- Do Activities 15, 16 and 17, p. 80

Quiz Review 15 min.
- Do Additional Listening Activities 3-3 and 3-4, pp. 24–25
- Do **Mehr Grammatikübungen, Zweite Stufe**

Quiz 20 min.
- Quiz 3-2A or 3-2B

Homework Options
Pupil's Edition, p. 80, Activity 18
Übungsheft, p. 35, Acts. 24–25

One-Stop Planner CD-ROM

For alternative lesson plans by chapter section, to create your own customized plans, or to preview all resources available for this chapter, use the **One-Stop Planner CD-ROM**, Disc 1.

For additional homework suggestions, see activities accompanied by this symbol throughout the chapter.

Day 7

DRITTE STUFE
Quick Review 5 min.
- Return and review Quiz 3-2
- Bell Work, ATE, p. 67T

Wortschatz, p. 81 20 min.
- Presenting **Wortschatz**, ATE, p. 67T
- Teaching Transparency 3-2
- Culture Note, ATE, p. 67T
- Do Activity 19, p. 81
- Do Communicate Activity 3-2, pp. 15–16
- Play Audio CD for Activity 20, p. 82

So sagt man das!, p. 82 10 min.
- Presenting **So sagt man das!**, ATE, p. 67T
- Do Activity 21, p. 82

Ein wenig Grammatik, p. 82 10 min.
- Presenting **Ein wenig Grammatik**, ATE, p. 67T
- Do Activity 14, p. 24, Grammatikheft

Wrap-Up 5 min.
- Students respond to questions about their parents and siblings.

Homework Options
Activities for Communication, p. 84, Realia 3-3, complete "Mein Stammbaum" Übungsheft, pp. 32–34, Acts 16–23

Day 8

DRITTE STUFE
Quick Review 10 min.
- Check homework, Übungsheft, pp. 32–34, Acts. 16–23

Wortschatz, p. 83 15 min.
- Presenting **Wortschatz**, ATE, p. 67U
- Language Note, ATE, p. 67U
- Do **Wortschatz** Activities a and b, p. 83
- Play Audio CD for Activity 22, p. 83

Ein wenig Grammatik, p. 83 10 min.
- Presenting **Ein wenig Grammatik**, ATE, p. 67U
- Do Activity 23, p. 83

Wortschatz, p. 84 10 min.
- Presenting **Wortschatz**, ATE, p. 67U
- Teaching Transparency 3-C
- Do Activity 25, p. 84

Wrap-Up 5 min.
- Students respond to questions about numbers

Homework Options
Pupil's Edition, p. 83, Activity 24
Grammatikheft, pp. 24–25, Acts. 13–16

Day 9

DRITTE STUFE
Quiz Review 15 min.
- Check homework, Grammatikheft, pp. 24–25, Acts. 13–16
- Do Situation 3-3, pp. 127–128

So sagt man das!, p. 84 20 min.
- Presenting **So sagt man das!**, ATE, p. 67V
- Do Activity 5, Interactive CD-ROM
- Do Activities 26, 27, 28, p. 85

Aussprache, p. 85 10 min.
- Do **Richtig aussprechen/Richtig lesen**, p. 85
- Do **Richtig schreiben, Diktat**, p. 85

Wrap-Up 5 min.
- Students describe other students

Homework Options
Grammatikheft, pp. 26–27, Acts. 17–20

Day 10

DRITTE STUFE
Quick Review 10 min.
- Check homework, Grammatikheft, pp. 26–27, Acts. 17–20

Quiz Review 20 min.
- Do Additional Listening Activities 3-5 and 3-6, pp. 25–26
- Do **Mehr Grammatikübungen, Dritte Stufe**

Quiz 20 min.
- Quiz 3-3A or 3-3B

Homework Options
Übungsheft, p. 36, Acts. 26–31

Day 11

DRITTE STUFE
Quick Review 15 min.
- Return and review Quiz 3-3
- Check homework, Übungsheft, p. 36, Acts. 26–31

ZUM LESEN 30 min.
- Teaching Suggestions, ATE, p. 67W
- Present **Lesestrategie**, p. 86
- Culture Notes, ATE, p. 67W
- Do Activities 1–7, pp. 86–87

Wrap-Up 5 min.
- Students introduce themselves to a partner

Homework Options
Pupil's Edition, p. 94, **Kann ich's wirklich?**

Day 12

ANWENDUNG 20 min.
Quick Review
- Check homework, p. 94, **Kann ich's wirklich?**
- Do **Anwendung** Activities, 1–7, pp. 92–93
- Video Wrap-up, ATE, p. 67X

Chapter Review 30 min.
- Review chapter functions, vocabulary, and grammar; choose from **Mehr Grammatikübungen**, Grammar Tutor for Students of German, Activities for Communication, Listening Activities, Interactive CD-ROM Tutor, or **Interaktive Spiele**
- Review test format and provide sample test items for students

Homework Options
Study for Chapter Test

Assessment

Test, Chapter 3 45 min.
- Administer Chapter 3 Test. Select from Testing Program, Alternative Assessment Guide or Test Generator.

Kapitel 3: Komm mit nach Hause!
Suggested Lesson Plans 90-Minute Block Schedule

Block 1

CHAPTER OPENER 10 min.
- Thinking Critically, ATE, p. 67M
- Culture Note, ATE, p. 67M

LOS GEHT'S! 25 min.
- Preteaching Vocabulary, ATE, P. 67N
- Play Audio CD for **Los geht's!**, pp. 70–71
- Have students read **Los geht's!**, pp. 70–71
- Teaching Suggestions, Video Guide, p. 16
- Thinking Critically, ATE, p. 67N
- Show **Los geht's!** Video
- Do Comprehension Activities, p. 72

ERSTE STUFE
So sagt man das!/Wortschatz, p. 73 15 min.
- Presenting **So sagt man das!** and **Wortschatz**, ATE, p. 67P
- Play Audio CD for Activity 6, p. 74
- Do Activities 7 and 8, p. 74

So sagt man das!, p. 74 10 min.
- Presenting **So sagt man das!**, ATE, p. 67O
- Do Activity 9, p. 75

Wortschatz, p. 75 10 min.
- Presenting **Wortschatz**, ATE, p. 67P
- Do Activity 10, p. 75

Grammatik, p. 75 10 min.
- Present **möchte**-forms, p. 75
- Do Activity 11, p. 76
- Do Activity 3, p. 20, Grammatikheft

Wrap-Up 10 min.
- Students respond to questions about what they would like to eat or drink

Homework Options
Übungsheft, pp. 25–28, Acts. 1–8
Grammatikheft, pp. 19–21, Acts. 1–7

Block 2

ERSTE STUFE
Quick Review 10 min.
- Check homework, Grammatikheft, pp. 19–21, Acts. 1–7
- Do Communicative Activity 3-1, pp. 13–14

So sagt man das!, p. 76 15 min.
- Presenting **So sagt man das!** and **Ein wenig Grammatik**, ATE, p. 67P
- Do Activity 12, p. 76

Quiz Review 15 min.
- Do Additional Listening Activities 3-1 and 3-2, p. 23
- Do **Mehr Grammatikübungen, Erste Stufe**

Quiz 20 min.
- Quiz 3-1A or 3-1B

LANDESKUNDE, p. 77 20 min.
- Pre-viewing Suggestion, Video Guide, p. 16
- Background Information, ATE, p. 67Q
- Show **Landeskunde** Video
- Do Activities A and B, p. 77

Wrap-Up 10 min.
- Students respond to questions about ethnic groups in Germany

Homework Options
Activities for Communication, pp. 127–128, Situation 3-1, make notes and practice; p. 82, Realia 3-1, circle cognates

Block 3

ZWEITE STUFE
Quick Review 10 min.
- Return and review Quiz 3-1
- Bell Work, ATE, p. 67R

Wortschatz, p. 78 10 min.
- Presenting **Wortschatz**, ATE, p. 67R
- Teaching Transparencies 3-1, 3-B

Ein wenig Grammatik, p. 78 10 min.
- Presenting **Ein wenig Grammatik**, ATE, p. 67R
- Play Audio CD for Activity 13, p. 78

So sagt man das!, p. 79 15 min.
- Presenting **So sagt man das!**, ATE, p. 67R
- Do Activity 14, p. 79

Grammatik, p. 79 15 min.
- Presenting **Grammatik**, ATE, p. 67R
- Do Activity 15, p. 79
- Do Activities 16 and 17, p. 80

Project, ATE, p. 67C 20 min.
- Culture Note, ATE, p. 67S
- Begin project: "Mein Traumhaus"

Wrap-Up 10 min.
- Several students present their partially completed projects

Homework Options
Complete "Mein Traumhaus" project begun in class
Übungsheft, pp. 29–31, Acts. 9–15
Grammatikheft, pp. 22–23, Acts. 8–12

One-Stop Planner CD-ROM

For alternative lesson plans by chapter section, to create your own customized plans, or to preview all resources available for this chapter, use the **One-Stop Planner CD-ROM**, Disc 1.

For additional homework suggestions, see activities accompanied by this symbol throughout the chapter.

Block 4

ZWEITE STUFE

Quick Review 10 min.
- Check homework, Grammatikheft, pp. 22–23, Acts. 8–12

Performance Assessment 20 min.
- Students present "Mein Traumhaus" projects

Quiz Review 10 min.
- Do Additional Listening Activities 3-3 and 3-4, pp. 24–25
- Do **Mehr Grammatikübungen, Zweite Stufe**

Quiz 20 min.
- Quiz 3-2A or 3-2B

DRITTE STUFE

Wortschatz, p. 81 20 min.
- Presenting **Wortschatz**, ATE, p.67T
- Teaching Transparency 3-2
- Culture Note, ATE, p. 67T
- Do Activity 19, p. 81
- Do Communicative Activity 3-2, pp. 15–16
- Play Audio CD for Activity 20, p. 82

Wrap-Up 10 min.
- Students respond to family questions

Homework Options
Pupil's Edition, p. 80, Activity 18
Grammatikheft, p. 24, Acts. 13–14
Activities for Communication, p. 84, Realia 3-3, complete "Mein Stammbaum"

Block 5

DRITTE STUFE

Quick Review 10 min.
- Check homework
- Review **Ein wenig Grammatik**
- Do Activity 15, Grammatikheft, p. 25

So sagt man das!, p. 82 15 min.
- Presenting **So sagt man das!** and **Ein wenig Grammatik**, ATE, p. 67T
- Do Activity 21, p. 82

Wortschatz, p. 83 20 min.
- Presenting **Wortschatz**, ATE, p. 67U
- Do **Wortschatz**, Activities **a** and **b**, p. 83
- Play Audio CD for Activity 22, p. 83
- Do Activity 5, Interactive CD-ROM

Ein wenig Grammatik, p. 83 15 min.
- Presenting **Ein wenig Grammatik**, ATE, p. 67U
- Do Activity 23, p. 83
- Do **Mehr Grammatikübungen, Dritte Stufe**

Wortschatz, p. 84 10 min.
- Presenting **Wortschatz**, ATE, p. 67U
- Teaching Transparency 3-C
- Do Activity 25, p. 84

Aussprache, p. 85 10 min.
- Do **Richtig aussprechen/Richtig lesen**, p. 85
- Do **Richtig schreiben, Diktat**, p. 85

Wrap-Up 10 min.
- Students describe other students

Homework Options
Pupil's Edition, Activity 21, p. 82; Activity 24, p. 83
Übungsheft, pp. 32–34, Acts. 16–23
Grammatikheft, pp. 25–27, Acts. 15–20

Block 6

DRITTE STUFE

Quick Review 10 min.
- Check homework, Pupil's Edition, Activity 21, p. 82
- Do Communicative Activity 3-3, pp. 17–18

So sagt man das!, p. 84 15 min.
- Presenting **So sagt man das!**, ATE, p. 67V
- Do Activities 26, 27, and 28, p. 85

Quiz Review 15 min.
- Do Additional Listening Activities 3-5 and 3-6, pp. 25–26
- Do **Mehr Grammatikübungen, Dritte Stufe**

Quiz 20 min.
- Quiz 3-3A or 3-3B

ZUM LESEN 20 min.
- Teaching Suggestions, ATE, p. 67W
- Present **Lesestrategie**, p. 86
- Culture Notes, ATE, p. 67W
- Do Activities 1–7, pp. 86–87

Wrap-Up 10 min.
- Students respond to **Kann ich's wirklich?** questions, p. 94

Homework Options
Übungsheft, p. 35, Acts. 24–25
Interaktive Spiele see ATE, p. 67F
Kann ich's wirklich? p. 94

Block 7

ANWENDUNG 20 min.
Quick Review
- Check homework. p. 94, **Kann ich's wirklich?**

Chapter Review 25 min.
- Do **Anwendung** Activities 1–7, pp. 92–93
- Video Wrap-up, ATE, p. 67X
- Review chapter functions, vocabulary, and grammar; choose from **Mehr Grammatikübungen**, Grammar Tutor for Students of German, Activities for Communication, Listening Activities, Interactive CD-ROM Tutor, or **Interaktive Spiele**
- Review test format and provide sample test items for students

Test, Chapter 3 45 min.
- Administer Chapter 3 Test. Select from Testing Program, Alternative Assessment Guide, or Test Generator

Kapitel 3: Komm mit nach Hause!
Teaching Suggestions, *pages 68–95*

 **PAGES 68–69**

CHAPTER OPENER

 Pacing Tips

The **Erste Stufe** begins with the function of 'talking about where you and others live' using the verb **wohnen.** The **möchte**-forms are then introduced along with snack vocabulary. The **Zweite Stufe** focuses on 'describing a room' using furniture vocabulary and adjectives describing furniture. Students also learn to use pronouns when refering to things. The **Dritte Stufe** centers around 'talking about family members' and 'describing people.' A family tree occurs on p. 81, followed by a presentation of numbers from 0 to 100 on p. 83. Because the **Dritte Stufe** contains extensive new vocabulary centering around the family, you may wish to spend a little more time on this section. For Lesson Plans and timing suggestions, see pages 67I–67L.

Meeting the Standards
Communication
- Talking about where you and others live, p. 73
- Offering something to eat and drink and responding, p. 74
- Saying please, thank you, and you're welcome, p. 76
- Describing a room, p. 79
- Talking about family members, p. 82
- Describing people, p. 84

Cultures
- Landeskunde, p. 77
- Culture Note, p. 67M
- Culture Note, p. 67O
- Culture Note, p. 67P
- Culture Notes, p. 67S
- Culture Notes, p. 67T

Connections
- Multicultural Connection, p. 67M
- History Connection, p. 67Q
- Culture Notes, p. 67S
- Language-to-Language, p. 67U

Comparisons
- Ein wenig Landeskunde, p. 75
- Language-to-Language, p. 67O
- Language-to-Language, p. 67P
- Language Note, p. 67U
- Culture Notes, p. 67W

Communities
- Jens und seine Familie, p. 81
- Career Path, p. 67V
- Reteaching: Family members, p. 67V

 **One-Stop** Planner CD-ROM

For resource information, see the **One-Stop Planner CD-ROM,** Disc 1.

Cultures and Communities

Culture Note
Privacy is very important to Germans. Homes are often protected by hedges, fences, or gates in front of the property as well as in the back.

Multicultural Connection
Germans like to make time for **Kaffeezeit** on a daily basis. Where else around the world is a routine break typical during the afternoon? (Example: Great Britain—afternoon tea)

Connections and Comparisons

Thinking Critically
Comparing and Contrasting Ask students what rooms they like to receive their friends in when they come to visit. Do the students serve food or soft drinks? If so, what do they typically serve? In German-speaking countries it is customary to serve guests cake if they arrive in the afternoon.

Inferring Can students guess the time of day in this picture? It is probably between 1 and 2 p.m., the time when most German students get off school.

Chapter Sequence

Los geht's! . . . . **p. 70**

Erste Stufe . . . . **p. 73**

Landeskunde . . . . **p. 77**

Zweite Stufe . . . . **p. 78**

Dritte Stufe . . . . **p. 81**

Zum Lesen . . . . **p. 86**

Mehr Grammatikübungen . . . . **p. 88**

Anwendung . . . . **p. 92**

Kann ich's wirklich? . . . . **p. 94**

Wortschatz . . . . **p. 95**

LOS GEHT'S!

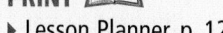

Teaching Resources
pp. 70–72

PRINT
▸ Lesson Planner, p. 12
▸ Video Guide, pp. 15–16
▸ Übungsheft, p. 25

MEDIA
▸ One-Stop Planner
▸ Video Program
  Los geht's!
  Videocassette 1, 27:32–30:28
  Videocassette 5 (captioned version),
  10:00–12:59
  Fortsetzung
  Videocassette 1, 30:30–32:07
  Videocassette 5 (captioned version),
  13:01–14:37
▸ Audio Compact Discs, CD3, Trs. 1–2
▸ **Los geht's!** Transparencies

PAGES 70–71

Los geht's! Transparencies

Preteaching Vocabulary

Recognizing Cognates

Los geht's! contains several words that students
will be able to recognize as cognates. Have
students find these cognates, then have them
guess what is happening in the story.

❸ ein Klassenkamerad
❹ trinken, eine Cola, ein Mineralwasser
❻ mein Bruder
❼ meine Kusine, braune Haare, charmant
❽ das Poster, phantastisch, das Bett

Background Information

In **Los geht's!**, Holger tells Jens that he lives in
Babelsberg. The suburb Babelsberg is known for its
park and castle (built 1834–1849). The prince and later
emperor, Wilhelm I, used this as his summer residence.

Thinking Critically

Drawing Inferences Ask students if they can think
of a reason why Germans have doors to every room
in a house and why the doors are usually kept closed.
(Doors are closed for privacy and heating efficiency,

which is very important, since space is limited and
energy is expensive.)

PAGE 72

Fortsetzung

You may choose to
continue with *Bei Jens zu
Hause!* now or wait until later in the chapter. For a
synopsis of **Los geht's!** and **Fortsetzung**, see p. 67E.

Using the Captioned Video

In random order, write short sentences
on the board describing what happens in
Bei Jens zu Hause! (Examples: Holger wohnt in
der Kopernikusstraße; Jens trinkt eine Cola.
Tara is Jens' Kusine.) Play the captioned version
of *Bei Jens zu Hause!* on Videocassette 5 and ask
students to raise their hands whenever they see a
sentence similar to one of those on the board.
Then, have students number the events in the
correct order according to the video.

Comprehension Check

Cooperative Learning

Put students in groups of four. Ask them to
choose a discussion leader, a recorder, a proofreader, and an announcer. Give students a
specific amount of time in which to complete
Activities 1-5. Monitor group work as you walk
around, helping students if necessary. At the end
of the activity, call on each group announcer to
read his or her group's results.

Challenge

❸ Have each student write down a statement
which would require a **stimmt** or **stimmt nicht**
response. Ask one or two students to read
their sentences to the class and ask the class to
respond. (Example: **Wir gehen am Abend in die
Schule. Stimmt nicht.**)

Visual Learners

❺ Before students do this activity, have them
match the sentences to the appropriate pictures.
Then proceed with Activity 5.

Teaching Suggestion

Ask students if they can name three similarities
and three differences between German homes
and American homes, based on the pictures on
pp. 70–71.

ERSTE STUFE

Teaching Resources
pp. 73–77

PRINT

- Lesson Planner, p. 13
- TPR Storytelling Book, pp. 9, 12
- Listening Activities, pp. 19, 23
- Activities for Communication, pp. 13-14, 82, 127-128
- Grammatikheft, pp. 19-21
- Grammar Tutor for Students of German, Chapter 3
- Übungsheft, pp. 26-28
- Testing Program, pp. 53-56
- Alternative Assessment Guide, p. 34
- Student Make-Up Assignments, Chapter 3

MEDIA

- One-Stop Planner
- Audio Compact Discs, CD3, Trs. 3-4, 19, 25-26
- Teaching Transparencies
  Vocabulary 3-A
  Mehr Grammatikübungen Answers
  Grammatikheft Answers
- Interactive CD-ROM Tutor, Disc 1

PAGE 73

Bell Work

On the board or a transparency write the following: **Wo wohnst du?** Have students respond in writing.

PRESENTING: So sagt man das!

To teach the verb **wohnen,** use the verb in context as you give examples of several famous people and the places where they live. (Examples: **Der amerikanische Präsident wohnt in Washington, D.C. Steffi Graf wohnt in Deutschland.**)

PRESENTING: Wortschatz

Have students infer the meaning of this vocabulary through contextual guessing. Give examples such as: **Los Angeles ist eine große Stadt. Beverly Hills ist ein Vorort von Los Angeles. Der Rodeo Drive ist eine Straße in Beverly Hills. Old MacDonald wohnt auf dem Land.** If necessary, draw a simple map on the board or on a transparency as you present your examples.

Connections and Comparisons

Language-to-Language

Tell your students that the English verb "to live" is expressed by two different verbs in German: **leben/wohnen.** French makes the same distinction: **vivre/habiter.** Ask students what English words correspond most closely to the German **leben/wohnen.** (live/reside)

Cultures and Communities

Culture Note

Potsdam (pop. 138,000) is located on the river Havel at the site of an early settlement near the **Alter Markt** that dates back as early as 993. The settlement didn't expand until the 16th century, when it became the second residence for Prussian kings such as King Friedrich I and Friedrich Wilhelm I.

PAGE 74

Communication for All Students

Challenge

7 Put the following words on the board for the students to refer to (in addition to the **Wortschatz** on p. 73) as they work in pairs on this activity: **wohnen; Vorort = Vorstadt; weit von hier; in der Nähe von; in der _____ Straße; Wohnung; Haus; Zweifamilienhaus.** Quickly explain these words so students will be able to use them for the activity.

Cultures and Communities

Culture Note
Germans have a different way of numbering the floors in buildings. If you live on the ground floor you live on the **Erdgeschoss,** the second floor is called **erster Stock,** the third floor is called **zweiter Stock,** and so on. (Example: **Ich wohne im ersten Stock.**)

PRESENTING: **So sagt man das!**

Ask individual students what they would like to eat or drink. Example: **Jill, was möchtest du trinken?** (You can add a drinking gesture to your question to help visual learners.) They can either point to the item they would like or try to use the food vocabulary in the **Wortschatz.**

> **PAGE 75**

PRESENTING: **Wortschatz**

Introduce the food vocabulary using the TPR method. You could check with the home economics teachers to see if they have plastic props or food posters to help with your presentation. First, tell students the name of each item as you point to it. Then, point to a student in the class and give the following command: **Kyle, eine Cola, bitte!** Your student should bring you the bottle of cola. Then, point to a second student and give another command: **Jenny, ein Glas Orangensaft, bitte!** Susan should bring you the glass of orange juice. Repeat your TPR commands until all the vocabulary items have been used. If you don't have access to props, use pictures.

Communication for All Students

Auditory Learners
After introducing the two parts of the **Wortschatz,** ask several students to respond to the following questions: **Was möchtest du gern essen? Was möchtest du gern trinken?**

PRESENTING: **Ein wenig Grammatik**

Ein/eine Review **der, die, das** with students. Then contrast the use of **the** and **an** or **a** in English and have students look again at the **Wortschatz** box on p. 75. How would they express those requests in English? What therefore must **ein** and **eine** mean?

Danke, nichts!

> **PAGE 76**

PRESENTING: **Grammatik**
The möchte-forms Ask students to look at **Los geht's!** on pp. 70-71. Point to the dialogue in which **möchte** is used. Then ask students if they can give an English translation for the phrases.

For Additional Practice

11 Tell students to imagine they have invited their partner to their house for the weekend. Students should find out what their partner would like to do, to eat, and to drink. Have students write down their partner's responses. Select one or two pairs to report to the class.

PRESENTING: **So sagt man das!**

Ask students to list typical expressions in English they would use to respond when someone serves them food or drink. How does the person serving the food or drink respond? Make a list on the board of the expressions the students come up with. Tell students that in German there are also several ways to thank somebody or say you're welcome. You might want to point out to students that the word **bitte** is also used in other contexts:
Bitte? (Pardon me?)
Bitte? (May I help you?)
Bitte! (Here you go!)

For Additional Practice

12 Have each group write a skit based on Activity 12 and present it to the class. Encourage students to use props.

Connections and Comparisons

Language-to-Language

Point out that like German, French and Spanish also express gender in the indefinite article. German uses **ein/eine/ein;** French, **un/une;** and Spanish, **un/una.**

▶ **PAGE 77**

LANDESKUNDE

Teaching Resources
p. 77

PRINT
▶ Video Guide, pp. 15, 17, 18–19
▶ Übungsheft, p. 36

MEDIA
▶ One-Stop Planner
▶ Video Program
  Videocassette 1, 32:45–34:22
▶ Audio Compact Discs, CD3, Trs. 5–10
▶ Interactive CD-ROM Tutor, Disc 1

Communication for All Students

Auditory Learners

After students have seen the video segment or listened to the recording, ask each of five students to read one of the interviews aloud for pronunciation practice.

Thinking Critically

- **Drawing Inferences** Ask students to observe how Jasmin and Thomas each state where they go to school. Have students compare the two expressions and find differences. (**Ich gehe in die** … versus **Ich bin an der** …)

- **Drawing Inferences** Ask students to review Dominick's statement about where he lives. What is Pinneberg (a suburb) and what does that say about the size of the city of Hamburg? (It's a large city. Its current population is 1,703,000.)

Connections and Comparisons

Background Information

In the 1960s, when Germany was in need of a larger labor force than it could supply from within, it opened its doors to foreign workers. These workers were invited to leave their own countries to work in Germany. They came mainly from countries such as Turkey, Italy, Greece, and Portugal, where recruiting offices had been set up initially. The foreign workers were formerly referred to as **Gastarbeiter** and are now called **Arbeitsemigranten.**

History Connection

Can students think of some reasons Germany was in need of a larger labor force at this time in history? (After World War II, Germany needed to rebuild its economy, but because of losses in World War II could not supply adequate manpower to handle the rapidly growing economy.)

Grammatik im Kontext: möchte

Have students tell you what they would like to eat and drink when they get home from school today, using the verb form **möchte.**

Assess

▶ Testing Program, pp. 53–56
  Quiz 3-1A, Quiz 3-1B
  Audio CD3, Tr. 19

▶ Student Make-Up Assignments
  Chapter 3, Alternative Quiz

▶ Alternative Assessment Guide, p. 34

ZWEITE STUFE

Teaching Resources
pp. 78–80

PRINT

▸ Lesson Planner, p. 14
▸ TPR Storytelling Book, pp. 10, 12
▸ Listening Activities, pp. 19, 24–25
▸ Activities for Communication, pp. 15–16, 83, 127–128
▸ Grammatikheft, pp. 22–23
▸ Grammar Tutor for Students of German, Chapter 3
▸ Übungsheft, pp. 29–31
▸ Testing Program, pp. 57–60
▸ Alternative Assessment Guide, p. 34
▸ Student Make-Up Assignments, Chapter 3

MEDIA

▸ One-Stop Planner
▸ Audio Compact Discs, CD3, Trs. 11, 20, 27–28
▸ Teaching Transparencies
  Situation 3-1
  Vocabulary 3-B
  Mehr Grammatikübungen Answers, Grammatikheft Answers
▸ Interactive CD-ROM Tutor, Disc 1

PAGE 78

Bell Work
Ask students to make a list of the furniture items in their room; they can add items they would like to have as well.

PRESENTING: Wortschatz

You might want to introduce the adjectives in this vocabulary box by describing specific objects in your classroom. Point to a small book and say: **Das Buch ist klein.** Point to a large book and say: **Das Buch ist groß.** Continue by asking yes/no questions such as **Ist der Tisch klein?** Then extend your questions by asking either/or questions. Example: **Ist die Tafel klein oder groß?**

Communication for All Students

A Slower Pace

13 Before students listen to the dialogue, review the vocabulary for this activity. Do this by showing pictures and asking yes/no and either/or questions.
Examples:
Ist das eine Stereoanlage? Nein.
Ist das ein Schrank oder ein Bett? Ein Bett.
Ist dieser Stuhl bequem oder unbequem?
Bequem.

PAGE 79

PRESENTING: So sagt man das!/Grammatik

Pronouns Use classroom objects to teach students how to replace nouns with pronouns. Example: Hold the small book you used in the presentation of the **Wortschatz** on p. 78 and say **Das Buch ist klein. Es ist klein.** Then write the sentence on the board or on a transparency. Give students an example of each gender and let them draw inferences as to what pronouns can replace certain nouns.

Teacher Note

You might want to point out to students that **die Möbel** (*furniture*) is plural in German, although it is singular in English. They should be aware that there are many nouns like this in German, as well as others that are singular in German and plural in English. Example: **die Hose** (*pants*)

Communication for All Students

A Slower Pace

15 Supply students with the vocabulary needed to do this task: **Stühle, Tische, Bücherregale,** and so on.

Game

Divide the class in half and call out an adjective. (Example: **alt**) The first person on team A responds with the opposite (**neu**). If the answer is wrong, the other team gets a turn. Call out a set number of adjectives. The team with the higher score wins.

Teaching Suggestion

18 At this point the project described on p. 67C should be introduced and explained.

Teaching Suggestion

Ask students about Jens's room in Babelsberg.
  Wie findest du sein Zimmer?
  Was findest du gut/nicht gut in Jens' Zimmer?

Cultures and Communities

 Culture Note
• Germans have a proverb which appropriately describes their feeling for their homes, no matter what size it might be: **Klein, aber mein!**

• German **Kinderzimmer** and **Schlafzimmer** seldom have built-in closets, unlike bedrooms in the United States. Therefore, you will usually find a **Kleiderschrank,** and perhaps also a **Kommode** (*dresser*) in a bedroom.

Teacher to Teacher

Jean Brooks
Livonia High School
Livonia, Michigan

Jean uses this technique to help students practice answering questions.

"I use this all the time! I have little plastic frogs named Johann and Gertrud who like to "spring" around the classroom. The student who catches Johann asks the question to be practiced (z.B. Wo wohnst du?) and the catcher of Gertrud must respond. They then get to make Johann and Gertrud "spring" (underhand, of course) to other students. I generally say the frogs must move more than 3 seats, minimum, to keep it lively. It seems too simple to be true, but my high schoolers love the frogs! They'll do anything to play with them.**"**

Assess

▸ Testing Program, pp. 57–60
  Quiz 3-2A, Quiz 3-2B
  Audio CD3, Tr. 20

▸ Student Make-Up Assignments
  Chapter 3, Alternative Quiz

▸ Alternative Assessment Guide, p. 34

ZWEITE STUFE

DRITTE STUFE

Teaching Resources
pp. 81–85

PRINT

- Lesson Planner, p. 15
- TPR Storytelling Book, pp. 11, 12
- Listening Activities, pp. 20–21, 25–26
- Activities for Communication, pp. 17–18, 84, 127–128
- Grammatikheft, pp. 24–27
- Grammar Tutor for Students of German, Chapter 3
- Übungsheft, pp. 32–34
- Testing Program, pp. 61–64
- Alternative Assessment Guide, p. 34
- Student Make-Up Assignments, Chapter 3

MEDIA

- One-Stop Planner
- Audio Compact Discs, CD3, Trs. 12–13, 21, 29–30
- Teaching Transparencies
  Situation 3-2
  Vocabulary 3-C
  Mehr Grammatikübungen Answers, Grammatikheft Answers
- Interactive CD-ROM Tutor, Disc 1

PAGE 81

Bell Work

Have students talk about their family, the people with whom they live, or the family members from a popular movie or TV show. List as many words as possible that show family relationships. (Examples: mother, father, cousin, aunt, uncle)

PRESENTING: Wortschatz

Before introducing the new vocabulary, give each student a generic family tree chart with blank lines. Put the vocabulary of the **Wortschatz** box in random order on the board. If they don't know the name of or have a relative for a particular blank, students should pick a likely name. Ask students to fill in the names of their family members or fantasy family members as best they can using the vocabulary on the board. (Example: **Die Tante: Shirley**) Then show the class a transparency with a sample family tree and introduce each of the family members in

German. (Example: **Das ist meine Mutter Cindy. Und das ist mein Vater Bill.**) Then, have students go back to their charts and correct whatever mistakes they might have made.

Cultures and Communities

Teaching Suggestion

The following vocabulary might be helpful for talking about **Jens und seine Familie: der Familienstammbaum** (family tree); **die Familienforschung** (genealogy); **der Vetter** (another word for male cousin); **der Vorfahre** (ancestor).

 Culture Note

- Just as in the United States, German children have informal names by which they call their parents. For example, the mother can be called **Mama, Mami,** or **Mutti,** and the father can be called **Papa, Papi,** or **Vati.**

- Point out to students the two words for male cousin (**Cousin, Vetter**). **Cousin** is pronounced as the French pronounce it [kuze~] and is used more frequently than **Vetter.** It is an example of the influence of the French language on German.

PAGE 82

PRESENTING: So sagt man das!

Ask students to take out the family tree they made at the beginning of the **Dritte Stufe.** Ask them questions about their family using the expressions in this function box.

PRESENTING: Ein wenig Grammatik

Possessives Use the transparency you made showing a family tree and reintroduce some of the members. Make sure that each of the statements you make is also written at the bottom of the transparency. Examples:

Das ist meine Tante Lucy.
Das ist mein Onkel Paul.
Das ist mein Cousin Gary.

Ask students why **mein(e)** has two different forms in the sentences you just pointed out. What conclusions can they draw?

Visual Learners

20 Make copies of the transcript on p. 67G–H available to students after they have listened to the three friends talking about their families. Let students use the transcript as they complete the chart.

PAGE 83

PRESENTING: Wortschatz

Use these additional activities to practice and review numbers.

Ask these questions:

1. Wie schnell darf man in der Stadt mit dem Auto fahren? or Wie schnell ist dein Auto?

2. Wie viele Sterne sind auf der amerikanischen Flagge?

3. Was ist deine Telefonnummer?

4. Wie viele Jungen und Mädchen sind in dieser Klasse?

5. Was ist die Notrufnummer? (Write the number 911 on the board.)

6. Welche Schuhgröße hast du?

Game

Draw a large tree on the board. At the end of each branch, draw a box containing the word for a number. (Example: **einundzwanzig**) The object is to see who can add the total of all the leaves (never higher than 100 for this **Stufe**) first and accurately. To prepare ahead of time, this can be drawn on a transparency.

Teaching Suggestion

Make conversion tables available on a handout or on a transparency. Include the metric system, temperature in Celsius, and clothing sizes. This will allow you to ask some more questions using numbers.

Language Note

Point out the fact that *one* and *seven* are written differently in German than they are in English.

	English	German
one	1	1
seven	7	7

Language-to-Language

Your students may want to know that numbers are formed the same in Arabic as they are in German, ones first, then tens.
Example:
Sixty-one (60+1) in German is **einundsechzig** (1+60) and in Arabic: **wâhid wa sittûn** (1+60). You may want to mention that this construction appears from time to time in older English writings, such as the following quote from Shakespeare's *Hamlet,* Act V, Scene I:"Here's a skull now; this skull has lain in the earth three and twenty years." Ask students if they can think of other examples of this structure in English. (Example:"Four and twenty blackbirds baked in a pie.")

PRESENTING: Ein wenig Grammatik

Possessive pronouns Write the singular subject pronouns on the board as headings and include phrases, such as **mein Bruder** and **meine Schwester** in the **ich** column. Then have students place each phrase in the column headed by the corresponding pronoun. Example:

ich	du	er	sie
mein Bruder	dein Bruder	sein Bruder	ihr Bruder
meine Schwester			

Next, have pairs ask and answer questions about their partners' family, such as **Wie heißen seine/ ihre Eltern? Wer ist sein/ ihr Onkel?** using the family trees they made at the beginning of the **Dritte Stufe.**

PAGE 84

PRESENTING: Wortschatz

To teach the expressions of this vocabulary box, begin by describing yourself. Then describe individual students to the rest of the class.

Teacher Note

You might want to point out to students the difference between **Er hat eine Glatze** and *He is bald.*

For Additional Practice

Tell students to imagine their family is having a big family reunion where not everybody knows everybody else. Therefore, attending members are asked to give a short personal introduction. Ask students to describe themselves to the rest of the family.

Cultures and Communities

Career Path

Have students work in pairs to brainstorm scenarios in law enforcement which would require knowledge of German. (Suggestions: Imagine you work for the NYPD, and the German **Kripo** [detective force] has asked you to help in its search for a convicted felon who has fled Germany and disappeared in New York; imagine you work for the customs service at the airport in Houston, and the German **Bundesgrenzschutz** [Federal Border Police] asks you to apprehend a smuggler, whom you will have to identify based on the description they faxed you.)

 **Game**

Divide the class into two groups and, alternating between groups, choose one person to come to the front. Show this person the name of a fellow classmate, teacher, or celebrity on an index card. Alternating between teams, students will try to guess the identity of the secret person by asking yes/no questions. If the answer to a question is yes, the team gets another turn; if the answer is no, the other team gets a turn. The team that guesses the correct name wins.
Example: Boris Becker
Ist es ein Mann? Ja.
Ist er alt? Nein.
Spielt er Musik? Nein.
Hat er rote Haare? Ja.

PRESENTING: So sagt man das!

Show Teaching Transparency 3-2 and have students describe Jutta's family members, using the expressions in the function box on p. 84. Then ask students questions about their own relatives. Finally, have pairs of students describe one of their relatives to a partner. The partner should draw the person based on the description.

Cultures and Communities

Reteaching: Family members

Put students in small groups and have them cut out magazine pictures of famous people to create a "unique" tree showing imaginary relationships among the celebrities. Students should write sentences about the relationships they have created. Ask one or two groups to read them aloud.

Teaching Suggestion

Show students pictures of famous people and ask them to describe the pictures.
or
Ask students to compare the characteristics of a young member of their family with an older member based on age, appearance, or any other relevant characteristics.

Von der Schule zum Beruf

 **28** Von der Schule zum Beruf

You could ask students to profile someone famous and have the rest of the class guess who it is. This activity could also be done on posterboard to be displayed in the classroom.

PRESENTING: Aussprache

Remind students that German vowels require more tension in the mouth than the English and do not glide. To illustrate this point, and as ongoing remedial work, contrast the German word **Boot** with the English *boat.*

Assess

▸ Testing Program, pp. 61–64
Quiz 3-3A, Quiz 3-3B
Audio CD3, Tr. 21

▸ Student Make-Up Assignments
Chapter 3, Alternative Quiz

▸ Alternative Assessment Guide, p. 34

ZUM LESEN

ZUM LESEN

Teaching Resources
pp. 86–87

PRINT
▸ Lesson Planner, p. 16
▸ Übungsheft, p. 35
▸ Reading Strategies and Skills, Chapter 3
▸ Lies mit mir! 1, Chapter 3

MEDIA
▸ One-Stop Planner

Prereading
Teacher Note
Activities 1 and 2 are prereading activities.

Scanning for Information
You will need several samples of ads from the classified section on rental properties and real estate. Ask students what kind of information is provided in the classified ad section for rental/real estate properties. Write students' responses on the board. What kinds of information would they want to know about a place when they decide to live on their own?

Teaching Suggestions
2 Help your students infer the meanings of these words by giving them clues. Example: adding **-ung** to the stem of a verb frequently makes a noun (**bilden: Bildung; erfahren: Erfahrung**)

• Ask students when they might need the information found in ads like these. Once they have told you that the ads have to do with places to live, ask them 1) where one might find ads like these; 2) what kinds of places are generally advertised in such ads (houses, apartments, and so on); and 3) what kinds of information might be important in such ads. (You are leading students to mention size, price, price per square foot, location, and so on.)

Connections and Comparisons

Thinking Critically
Comparing and Contrasting Have students scan the ad (**Wohnung**) and ask them to take a look at the address. How does the German way of writing an address differ from the American? (See the following Culture Note.)

Cultures and Communities

 Culture Note
In a German address, the name of the street comes before the street number, and the equivalent of a ZIP Code (**Postleitzahl**) comes before the name of the city.

Reading
Group Work
Assign groups of students an ad and have students make a list of all the words they recognize. Let them write their words on the board or on a transparency and tell the class what they found.

Cultures and Communities

 Culture Note
In Germany, the size of a home is determined by the number of rooms. If somebody is looking for a 3-bedroom house or apartment with a living room and dining room, he or she must look for a **5-Zimmer-Haus** or **Wohnung**. Bathrooms, kitchen, and hall areas are not included in the room count.

Culture Note
Germans use a space or a period to separate millions, thousands, and hundreds. The comma sets off the decimal fraction. Put the following examples on the board and point out the differences to students:
American way: $100,035,000.40
German way: €100.035.000,40
      or €100 035 000,40

Connections and Comparisons

Thinking Critically
Comparing and Contrasting In several ads the price is listed. How does the German way of writing prices differ from the American?

Teacher Note
None of the ads offer an apartment for rent. That's probably because there is a shortage of apartments, especially in university cities such as Tübingen.

Post-Reading
Teacher Note
Activities 7a and 7b are post-reading tasks.

Portfolio

7 You may want to use Activity 7a as a written portfolio item. See *Alternative Assessment Guide*, p. 20.

Zum Lesen Answers:
Answers to Activity 1 Ads describing houses and apartments; Ads looking for a place to live **Wohnen** (to live somewhere): **Wohnung** (apartment), **Eigentumswohnung** (condominium)
Answers to Activity 2 1. b 2. c 3. d 4. a
Answers to Activity 3 Ads describing houses and apartments: **Bauconcept, Gute Laune, Auf dem Lande, Tübingen-Lustnau;** Ads looking for a place to live: **Wohnung (Verlag J. C. B. Mohr), In/um Tübingen**
Answers to Activity 4 a. **Auf dem Lande** b. **Tübingen-Lustnau am Herrlesberg** c. **Immobilien-Kurcz**
Answers to Activity 5 a. 1-Fam. Haus in Remmingsheim, V 229 000,- b. 1-Zi-Apartment, Tü-Österberg, V 73 000.-1 c. Einfamilienhaus "Auf dem Lande" has 7 1/2 rooms d. 1-Fam.-Haus in Remmingsheim, 174m2 e. 1-Zi-Apartment, Tü-Österberg, 32 m2 f. 1-Zi-Apartment, Tü-Österberg, 31/2 -Zi-Wohnung (Bauconcept ad), Einfamilienhaus "Auf dem Lande", 2-Zi-Eigentumswohnung.

PAGES 88–91

MEHR GRAMMATIKÜBUNGEN

The **Mehr Grammatikübungen** activities are designed as supplemental activities for the grammatical concepts presented in the chapter. You might use them as additional practice, for review, or for assessment.

For more grammar presentations, review, and practice, refer to the following:
• Grammatikheft
• Grammar Tutor for Students of German
• Grammar Summary on pp. R15–R25.
• Übungsheft
• Grammar and Vocabulary quizzes (Testing Program)
• Test Generator
• Interactive CD-ROM Tutor
• **Interaktive Spiele** at <u>go.hrw.com</u>

Teacher to Teacher

Brenda Weimann Ludwig
West Milford High School
West Milford, New Jersey

"I found the following activity to be a great way to practice word order and sentence structure. Prepare 26 posters, each with a different phrase found on page 79, Activity 14. Example: | **die Couch** | | **ist neu** | | **aber sie ist unbequem** |. Each student is given one poster. Students then walk around and search for two other people with whom they can form a complete sentence. Each student will be part of a sentence.**"**

PAGES 92–93

ANWENDUNG

Video Wrap-up

Videocassette 1, 27:32–38:30
Videocassette 5 (captioned version), 10:00–14:37
At this time, you might want to use the video resources for additional review and enrichment. See the *Video Guide* for suggestions regarding:
• the **Los geht's!** episode • the **Landeskunde** interviews
• the **Fortsetzung** episode • the **Videoclips**

Apply and Assess

 Portfolio

1 You might want to use Activity 1 as an oral portfolio item for your students. See *Alternative Assessment Guide*, p. 20.

Process Writing

8 As students are finishing up their blueprints, have them number each puzzle piece. They should write a "1" in the piece containing the information they would present first when describing themselves, a "2" in the piece containing the topic they would address next, and so on.

PAGE 94

KANN ICH'S WIRKLICH?

This page is intended to prepare students for the test. It is a brief checklist of the major points covered in the chapter. The students should be reminded that it is a checklist only and not necessarily everything that will appear on the test.

For additional self check options, refer students to the *Grammar Tutor*, the *Interactive CD-ROM Tutor*, and the Online self-test for this chapter

PAGE 95

WORTSCHATZ

Review and Assess

 Game
Play **Das Subject fehlt!** to review numbers. See p. 67D.

 Teacher Note
Give the **Kapitel 3** Chapter Test: *Testing Program*, pp. 65–70
Audio CD 3, Trs. 22–24.

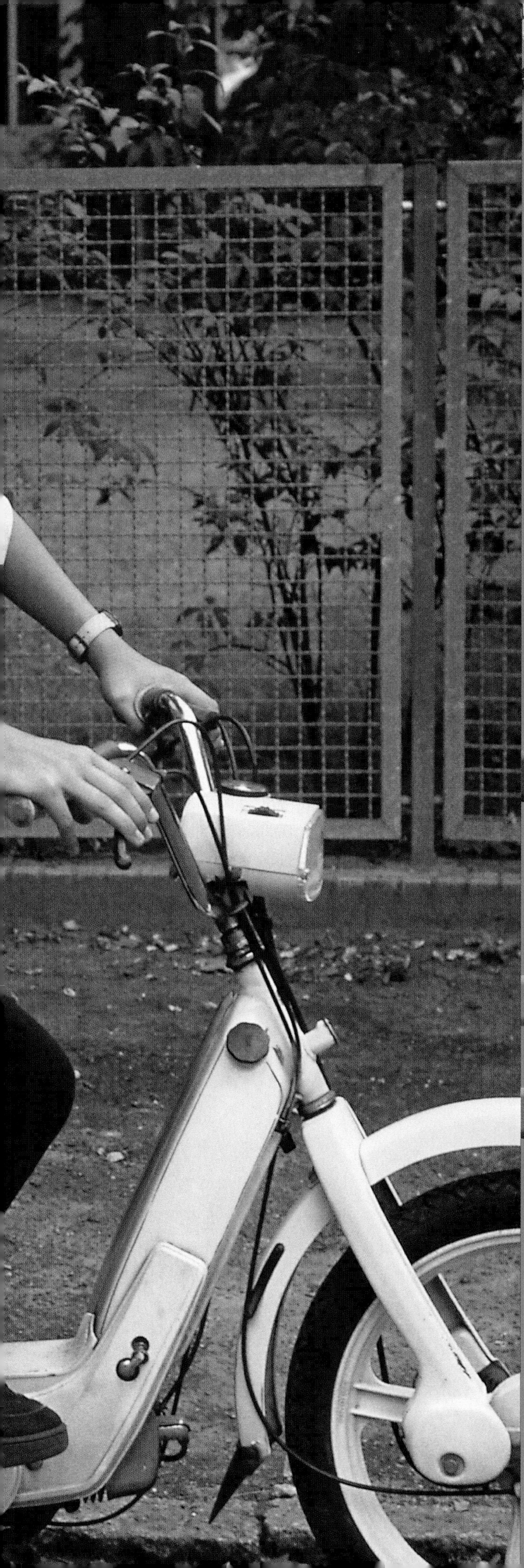

KAPITEL

3

Komm mit nach Hause!

Objectives

In this chapter you will learn to

Erste Stufe

- talk about where you live
- offer something to eat and drink and respond
- say please, thank you, and you're welcome

Zweite Stufe

- describe a room

Dritte Stufe

- talk about family members
- describe people

internet

go.hrw.com
ADRESSE: go.hrw.com
KENNWORT: WK3 BRANDENBURG-3

◀ **Fahr mit mir nach Hause!**

Los geht's! ▪ *Bei Jens zu Hause!*

CD 3 Trs. 1–2

VIDEO

Strategie Verstehen

Look at the photos on these two pages. Where and when do you think these scenes are taking place? What clues tell you this?

Jens   **Tara**   **Holger**   **Mutter**

Los geht's! is an abridged version of the video episode.

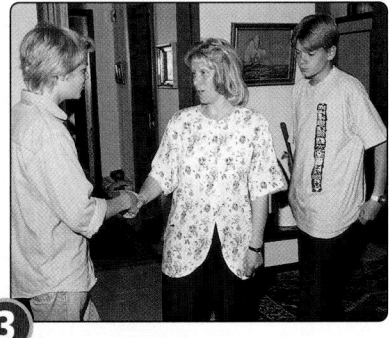

① Jens: Du gehst zu Fuß nach Hause?
Wo wohnst du denn?
Holger: In der Kopernikusstraße.
Jens: Wo ist die?
Holger: In Babelsberg.
Jens: Ich wohn auch dort in der Nähe. Möchtest du nicht mit mir nach Hause kommen?
Holger: Prima!

②

③ Jens: Hallo, Mutti! Wo bist du?
Mutter: Hier oben! Ich komme gleich runter.

Jens: Du, Mutti, das ist Holger, ein Klassenkamerad. Er ist neu.
Holger: Guten Tag, Frau Hartmann!
Mutter: Tag, Holger!

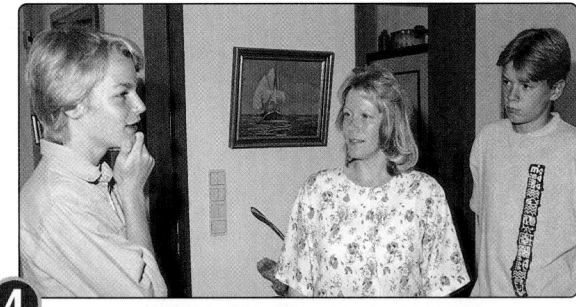

④ Mutter: Möchtet ihr etwas trinken? Oder was essen?
Jens: Ja, was möchtest du?
Holger: Ach, ich möchte ... ich trinke eine Cola.
Jens: Und ich ein Mineralwasser. Haben wir noch Kuchen?
Mutter: Ich glaube ja.

⑤ Jens: Hier, deine Cola und dein Kuchen.
Holger: Danke!
Jens: Bitte!

6

Holger: Sag mal, hast du Geschwister?

Jens: Ja, hier, schau! Mein Bruder und meine Schwester.

Holger: Hm, sie sieht nett aus. Wie alt ist sie?

Jens: Bine ist älter, sie ist neunzehn. Mein Bruder ist zwölf.

7

Jens: Ah, übrigens, meine Kusine kommt nachher.

Holger: Deine Kusine? Wie alt ist sie?

Jens: So alt wie ich. Auch sechzehn.

Holger: Ja, wirklich? Wie sieht sie aus?

Jens: Sie ist sehr hübsch. Sie hat braune Haare, braune Augen. Sie ist 1,65 groß und sehr charmant.

Holger: Genau mein Typ.

Jens: Ich weiß. Komm, ich zeig dir jetzt mein Zimmer.

8

Holger: He! Das Poster — Spitze! Wer ist das?

Jens: Na, rate mal!

Holger: Hm, ich weiß nicht.

Jens: Das ist Patricia Kaas!

Holger: Ach so! — Du hast es schön hier. Dein Zimmer ist phantastisch. Die Möbel sind toll! Neu, ja?

Jens: Ja, der Schrank ist neu ...das Regal, das Bett ... und ...

9

Jens: He, das ist bestimmt meine Kusine. — Komm mal mit, Holger!

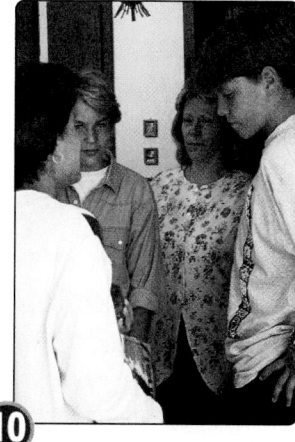

10

Holger: Was? Tara ist deine Kusine? Das glaub ich nicht.

Tara: Ja, sicher! Ich bin seine Kusine. — Hallo, Tante Monika!

Holger: Und ich denke, Tara ist deine Freundin!

Jens: Mensch, Holger! Du denkst zu viel!

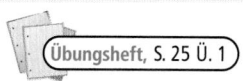

Übungsheft, S. 25 Ü. 1

1 Was passiert hier? These activities check for global comprehension only. Students should not yet be expected to produce language modeled in **Los geht's!**

Do you understand what is happening in the story „**Bei Jens zu Hause**"? Check your comprehension by answering these questions. Don't be afraid to guess.

1. Where do Jens and Holger go together after soccer practice? to Jens' house
2. What do the boys do first when they get home? greet Jens' mother, have a snack
3. What kinds of photos does Jens show Holger? family photos
4. How does Holger like Jens' room? very much
5. Who comes to visit? Why do you think Holger is surprised? Tara, Jens' cousin; he thought she was Jens' girlfriend

2 Genauer lesen

Reread the conversations. Which words or phrases do the characters use to

1. introduce someone else
   1. Das ist …
2. name foods or drinks
   2. Eine Cola; Mineralwasser; Kuchen
3. name family members
   3. Mutter („Mutti"), Bruder, Schwester, Kusine
4. describe people
   4. hübsch; braune Augen, braune Haare; charmant
5. name or describe furniture
   5. Der Schrank ist neu; das Regal; das Bett

3 Stimmt oder stimmt nicht?

Are these statements right or wrong? Answer each one with either **stimmt** or **stimmt nicht**. If a statement is wrong, try to state it correctly.

1. Holger geht mit Jens nach Hause. stimmt
2. Frau Hartmann ist Holgers Mutter. stimmt nicht; die Mutter von Jens
3. Holger trinkt eine Cola und isst ein Stück Kuchen. stimmt
4. Jens hat zwei Geschwister: einen Bruder und eine Schwester. stimmt
5. Der Bruder ist neunzehn, und die Schwester ist zwölf. stimmt nicht; Der Bruder ist zwölf, die Schwester ist neunzehn.
6. Holger hat auch eine Kusine. Sie heißt Tara. stimmt nicht; Tara ist die Kusine von Jens

4 Was passt zusammen?

Match each statement or question on the left with an appropriate response on the right.

1. Wo wohnst du? c
2. Mutti, das ist Holger. g
3. Möchtest du etwas trinken? e
4. Jens, hast du Geschwister? b
5. Wie sieht deine Kusine aus? f
6. Dein Zimmer ist schön! Sind die Möbel neu? a
7. Ich denke, Tara ist deine Freundin! d

a. Der Schrank ist neu.
b. Ja, das ist meine Schwester, und das ist mein Bruder.
c. In der Kopernikusstraße.
d. Nein, sie ist meine Kusine.
e. Ich möchte eine Cola, bitte!
f. Sie ist sehr hübsch.
g. Guten Tag, Holger!

5 Nacherzählen

Put the sentences in logical order to make a brief summary of the story.

1. Zuerst fährt Holger mit Jens nach Hause.

Und dann zeigt er Holger sein Zimmer. 5

Frau Hartmann sagt Holger „Guten Tag". 2

Und Jens gibt Holger eine Cola und ein Stück Kuchen. 3

Zuletzt kommt Tara, die Kusine von Jens. 6

Er zeigt Holger Fotos von der Familie. 4

Erste Stufe

Objectives Talking about where you live; offering something to eat and drink and responding; saying please, thank you, and you're welcome

So sagt man das!

Talking about where you live

To find out where someone lives, you ask:

Wo wohnst du?

Wo wohnt der Jens?

The responses might be:

Ich wohne in Los Angeles. *or*
In Los Angeles.

Er wohnt in Babelsberg. *or*
Ich denke, in Babelsberg.

Übungsheft,
S. 26, Ü. 2

How would you ask someone where Tara lives?[1]

Wortschatz

AHMET	Wo wohnt Dieter?
JENS	Er wohnt in (Babelsberg).

Michaela

in der Stadt

AHMET	Wohnt ihr **weit von hier?**
GÜNTHER	Nein, ich wohne **in der Nähe.**
ANDREA	Ja, ich wohne **weit von hier.**

Andrea

auf dem Land

Dieter

in Babelsberg, das ist ein Vorort von Potsdam

Günther

in der Brunnenstraße

Grammatikheft, S.19, Ü. 1–2

---

1. **Wo wohnt (die) Tara?**

6 Wo wohnen die Schüler? Script on p. 67G

Zuhören You will hear four students talk about where they live. Match each description with one of the pictures below. 1c 2b 3a 4d
CD 3 Tr. 3

a.

b.

c.

d.

7 Wo wohnen die Schüler?

Sprechen Ahmet wants to know where these students live. Answer his questions using the pictures as cues.

1. Wo wohnt die Sara?
auf dem Land

2. Wo wohnt der Georg?
in der Poststraße

3. Wo wohnen Jürgen und Simone? in der Stadt

4. Wo wohnt die Anja?
in einem Vorort

8 Wer wohnt wo?

Sprechen Ask your partner where he or she lives, then switch roles. Describe where you live in as much detail as you can, using the phrases you learned in the **Wortschatz** box. Be prepared to tell the class as much as you can about where your partner lives.

So sagt man das!

Offering something to eat and drink and responding

Often, when friends come over, you ask what they would like to eat and drink.
You might ask:

Was möchtest du trinken?
Was möchte Holger trinken?

The response might be:

Ich möchte ein Mineralwasser trinken.
Er möchte im Moment gar nichts.

To offer several friends something to eat,
you might ask:

Was möchtet ihr essen?

The response might be:

Wir möchten ein Stück Kuchen, bitte.

Can you figure out what **möchte** means?[1]

---

1. *would like to*

STANDARDS: 1.1, 1.2, 1.3, 5.1   KAPITEL 3   Komm mit nach Hause!

Grammatikheft, S. 20, Ü. 3

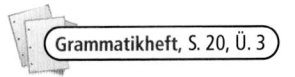

Wortschatz

Was möchtet ihr trinken?

Ein Glas Orangensaft.

Eine Cola, bitte!

Ein Mineralwasser.

Ein Glas Apfelsaft.

Und was möchtet ihr essen?

Ein Stück Kuchen, bitte!   **Ich möchte Obst.**

Ein paar Kekse.   **Danke, nichts!**

---

9 Bei Jens zu Hause   Script on p. 67G

Zuhören Ahmet and Tara come over to Jens' house. Listen to their conversation with Jens and write down what each one would like to eat and drink.

CD 3 Tr. 4   Tara: **Kuchen, Orangensaft** Ahmet: **Obst, Wasser**

Ein wenig Grammatik

Some of the names for the snack items pictured on this page are preceded by either **ein** or **eine**. What do you think these words mean?[1] Now look at the words below.

ein Junge   eine Limo   ein Stück (Kuchen)

Why are there different forms of **ein**?[2]

Und dann noch...

eine Tasse Kaffee   eine Orange

eine Tasse Tee   ein Stück Melone

eine Banane

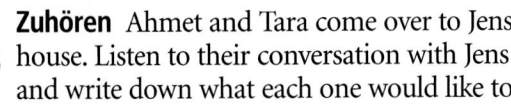

Ein wenig Landeskunde

If someone asks for **ein Glas Wasser, ein Glas Mineralwasser** will be served. Germans rarely drink tap water, considering it to be unhealthy. In addition, Germans very rarely use ice cubes in cold drinks, even in cafés and restaurants.

10 Grammatik im Kontext

a. Sprechen Look at the pictures in the **Wortschatz** box above and ask your partner what he or she would like to eat and drink.

BEISPIEL   DU   Möchtest du _____ Stück Kuchen?
          PARTNER   Ich möchte jetzt _____ paar Kekse.

b. Schreiben Copy these sentences and fill in the blanks with either **ein** or **eine**.

1. Ich möchte _____ Glas Saft.   ein
2. Wer möchte _____ Stück Kuchen?   ein
3. Holger möchte _____ Cola.   eine
4. Ich möchte _____ Mineralwasser.   ein
5. Wer möchte _____ Banane?   eine
6. Holger möchte _____ Orange.   eine

---

1. Both **ein** and **eine** mean *a, an.*   2. Masculine and neuter nouns are preceded by **ein**, feminine nouns by **eine**.

The *möchte*-forms

The **möchte**-forms express what you *would like* or *would like to do*. They are often used with another verb, but if the meaning is obvious, the second verb can be omitted.

> Ich **möchte** ein Glas Orangensaft **trinken**.
> Ich **möchte** Obst **essen**. *or* Ich **möchte** Obst.

Here are the forms of **möchte**:

ich	möchte	wir	möchten
du	möchtest	ihr	möchtet
er, sie, es	möchte	sie, Sie	möchten

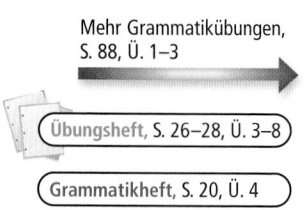

Mehr Grammatikübungen, S. 88, Ü. 1–3

Übungsheft, S. 26–28, Ü. 3–8

Grammatikheft, S. 20, Ü. 4

---

11 ## Grammatik im Kontext

a. Sprechen/Schreiben Say what everyone would like using the words and pictures as cues.

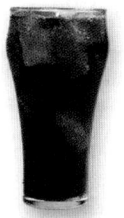

möchtet ein Glas Orangensaft.   möchte ein Glas Apfelsaft.

1. Wir ...   **2. Ihr ...**   **3. Er ...**   **4. Du ...**   **5. Ich ...**   **6. Jens und Holger ...**

möchten eine Cola.   möchte Obst.   möchtest ein paar Kekse.   möchten ein Stück Kuchen.

b. Schreiben Copy these sentences and fill in the blanks with the correct **möchte**-form.

1. Was ═══ du essen? *möchtest*   Ich ═══ ein Stück Kuchen. *möchte*
2. Was ═══ Holger trinken? *möchte*   Ich glaube, er ═══ ein Mineralwasser. *möchte*
3. Und ihr, Steffi und Jens, was ═══ ihr? *möchtet*   Wir ═══ Obst. *möchten*
4. Frau Weigel, was ═══ Sie trinken? *möchten*   Ach, ich ═══ jetzt ein Glas Apfelsaft. *möchte*

So sagt man das!

Saying please, thank you, and you're welcome

Grammatikheft, S. 21, Ü. 5

To say please, you can simply say **bitte**. You can also add **bitte** to a request:
Ich möchte eine Limo, bitte.

Here are several ways to say thank you: Here are several ways to say you're welcome:

> **Danke! Danke sehr! Danke schön!**   **Bitte! Bitte sehr! Bitte schön!**

---

12 ## Snacks für deine Freunde

Sprechen Role-play the following situation with three classmates. Use as many forms of **möchte** as possible. You have invited three friends home for a snack after school. One friend will help you get the snack ready by asking the other two "guests" what they would like to eat and drink. After they answer, your helper will tell you what everyone would like. When you have finished, switch roles until everyone has been the "host" and the "helper."

Wo wohnst du?

We asked several teenagers where they live. Before you read their interviews, write where you live, using as much detail as you can. Two of these teenagers were not born in Germany. Can you guess who they are?

CD 3 Tr. 5

CD 3 Trs. 5–10

Übungsheft, S. 36, Ü. 26-31

Dominick, Hamburg

„Ich heiß Dominick Klein. Ich bin zwölf Jahre alt und wohn in Hamburg, also Pinneberg." CD 3 Tr. 6

Jasmin, München

„Ich heiße Jasmin und bin fünfzehn. Ich geh in die Reichenau-Schule. Und ich wohne in München, und ich komme aus der Türkei." CD 3 Tr. 7

Thomas, München

„Ich heiße Thomas Schwangart. Ich wohne in München. Ich bin an der Reichenau-Schule und komme aus Italien." CD 3 Tr. 9

Johanna, Hamburg

„Ich heiß Johanna. Ich bin zwölf Jahre alt und ich wohn in Hamburg." CD 3 Tr. 8

Ingo, Hamburg

„Ich wohn hier in der Nähe, also in der Gustav-Falke-Straße. Das sind zehn Minuten von hier." CD 3 Tr. 10

A. 1. Write the name of each person interviewed and what each person says about where he or she lives.

  2. Now look at what you wrote earlier. Did any of these teenagers say where they live in the same way you did? If so, which ones? What seems to be the most natural response to the question **Wo wohnst du?** Is this also your first response?

  3. Discuss these questions with your classmates: Who are the two teenagers not born in Germany? Where are they from? Did you pick the right people before you read the interviews? What influenced your choice? Considering that two out of these five teenagers were not born in Germany, what can you infer about the ethnic makeup of German society in the large cities?

B. There are many ethnic groups represented in German society: Turks, Italians, Greeks, and many Eastern Europeans, just to name a few. Italian, Greek, Chinese, Indonesian and Thai foods have become very popular with native Germans. Why do you think some of these ethnic groups might be attracted to Germany? How does this compare with the situation in the United States? Discuss these questions with your classmates and then write a brief essay answering these questions.

STANDARDS: 1.2, 2.2, 3.2, 4.2

Zweite Stufe

Objective Describing a room

Wortschatz

Jens zeigt Holger sein Zimmer.

HOLGER   Deine Möbel sind schön!

JENS   Ja, wirklich? Schau!

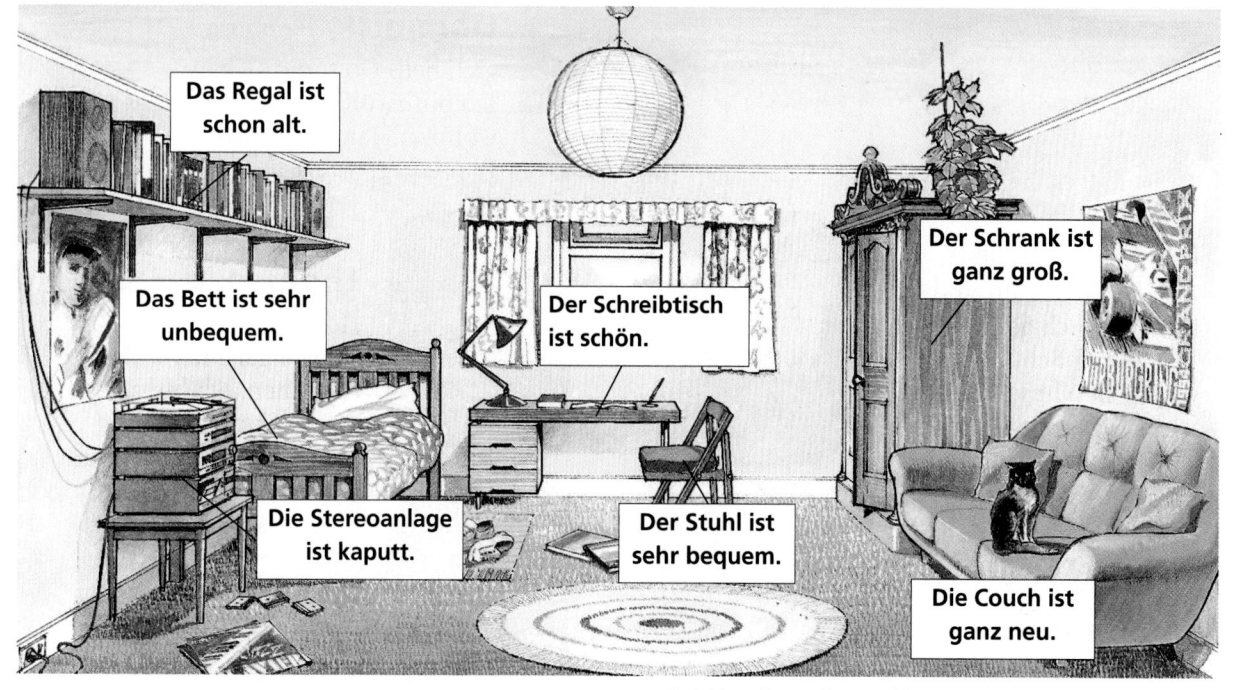

Das Regal ist schon alt.

Das Bett ist sehr unbequem.

Der Schreibtisch ist schön.

Der Schrank ist ganz groß.

Die Stereoanlage ist kaputt.

Der Stuhl ist sehr bequem.

Die Couch ist ganz neu.

uncomfortable; ugly; small; new; old

groß – klein
bequem – unbequem
alt – neu
schön – hässlich
kaputt

If **bequem** means *comfortable*, what does **unbequem** mean? What do you think the word **hässlich** means? **Groß** means *large*; what do you think **klein** means? The word **neu** looks like what word in English? What is its opposite?

(Übungsheft, S. 29, Ü. 9)   (Grammatikheft, S. 22, Ü. 8–10)

---

13 **Steffis Zimmer** Script on p. 67G

Zuhören Listen as Steffi describes her room to Ahmet, and match each piece of furniture on the left with the appropriate adjective on the right.

CD 3 Tr. 11

1. die Stereoanlage d   **a.** bequem

2. der Schrank b   **b.** schön

3. das Regal e   **c.** groß

4. der Schreibtisch c   **d.** neu

5. der Stuhl f   **e.** alt

6. das Bett a   **f.** klein

Describing a room

To describe your room, you might say:

Die Stereoanlage ist alt. Sie ist auch kaputt!
Das Bett ist klein aber ganz bequem. *or* **Das Bett ist klein, aber es ist ganz bequem.**

A friend might ask:

Ist der Computer neu?

You might respond:

Ja, er ist neu, aber er ist kaputt.

What do you think the words **er, sie,** and **es** refer to?[1] What is the English equivalent?[2] Why are there three different words that mean the same thing?[3]

> Übungsheft,
> S. 29–30, Ü. 10–12

---

14 **Versteckte Sätze**

Possible answers include:
Die Couch ist bequem, aber alt. Das Bett is neu, aber unbequem. Der Stuhl ist sehr groß, aber alt.

Sprechen/Schreiben How many sentences can you make using the words in the boxes? Use the picture of Jens' room on page 78 for clues.

BEISPIEL   **Die Couch ist neu, aber unbequem.**

| Die Couch
Der Schrank
Das Bett
Das Regal
Der Schreibtisch
Die Stereoanlage
Das Zimmer
Der Stuhl | ist | bequem
hässlich
klein
ganz unbequem
schon alt
schon kaputt
neu
ganz schön
sehr groß | aber | alt
neu
bequem
unbequem
schön
hässlich
groß
klein
kaputt |

Grammatik

Pronouns

Er, sie, and **es** are called pronouns. **Er** refers to a masculine noun, **sie** to a feminine noun, and **es** to a neuter noun.

masculine	**Der Schreibtisch** ist neu. *or* **Er** ist neu.	
feminine	**Die Stereoanlage** ist kaputt. *or* **Sie** ist kaputt.	
neuter	**Das Regal** ist hässlich. *or* **Es** ist hässlich.	

Mehr Grammatikübungen,
S. 89–90, Ü. 4–7

The pronoun **sie** is also used to refer to a plural noun.

plural   **Die Möbel** sind schön. *or* **Sie** sind schön.

> Übungsheft, S. 30–31, Ü. 13–15

> Grammatikheft, S. 23, Ü. 11–12

---

15 **Im Klassenzimmer**

Sprechen Describe your classroom and some of the furniture in it.

---

1. The nouns mentioned in the preceding sentences. 2. Here, **er, sie** and **es** are all equivalent to *it*.
3. The nouns they refer to belong to different noun classes, i.e., masculine, feminine, and neuter.

16 Grammatik im Kontext

Lesen/Sprechen Jens has seen Holger's new room and is talking to Steffi about it. Complete his description by filling in the correct article and pronoun.

___1___ Zimmer ist sehr groß, und ___2___ ist ganz schön. ___3___ Couch ist schön, und ___4___ ist auch neu. ___5___ Bett ist ziemlich klein, aber ___6___ ist sehr bequem. ___7___ Schrank ist wirklich alt, und ___8___ ist sehr groß. ___9___ Stereoanlage ist super! ___10___ ist ganz neu. ___11___ Schreibtisch ist groß, aber ___12___ ist leider hässlich. Und dann noch ___13___ Regal. ___14___ ist auch sehr groß. ___15___ Möbel sind wirklich toll. ___16___ sind Klasse!

1. Das 2. es 3. Die 4. sie 5. Das 6. es 7. Der 8. er 9. Die 10. Sie 11. Der 12. er 13. das 14. Es 15. Die 16. Sie

17 Wie findest du das Zimmer?

Sprechen Use one of these adjectives to describe the items below to your partner. Your partner may agree or disagree. Then switch roles.

DU **Der Schreibtisch ist sehr schön.**

PARTNER **Ja, stimmt! Er ist sehr schön.** *or* **Was? Er ist ganz hässlich!**

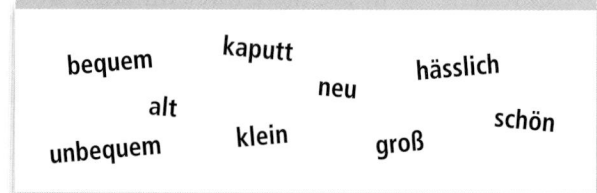

bequem   kaputt   neu   hässlich   alt   klein   groß   schön   unbequem

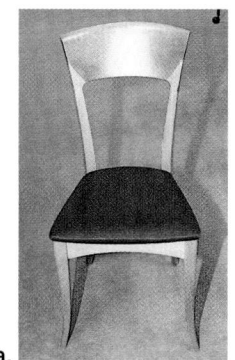

a.

b.

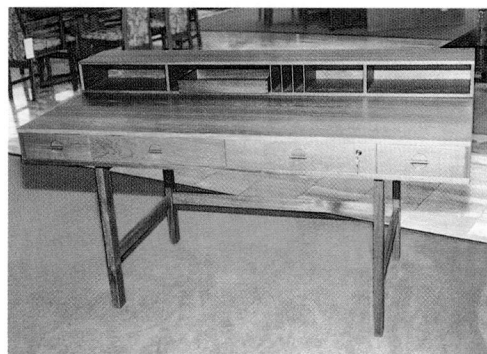

c.

d.

e.

f.

18 Mein Zimmer

Schreiben Draw a diagram of your room or a room you would like to have. Label the pieces of furniture. Then write a few sentences describing your room. If you need extra vocabulary, turn to page R9.

Dritte Stufe

Objectives Talking about family members; describing people

WK3 BRANDENBURG-3

Wortschatz

Jens und seine Familie

Grammatikheft, S. 24, Ü. 13

 3–2

die Großmutter (Oma)
Ella

der Großvater (Opa)
Georg

meine Großeltern

meine Eltern
die Mutter **der Vater**
Monika *Dieter*

die Tante **der Onkel**
Hannelore *Amir*

Jens

meine Geschwister
die Schwester **der Bruder**
Sabine *Andreas*

die Kusine **der Cousin**
Tara *Tawan*

die Katze
Fritzi

der Hund
Harras

meine Haustiere

Und dann noch...

Stiefmutter	*stepmother*
Stiefvater	*stepfather*
Stiefschwester	*stepsister*
Stiefbruder	*stepbrother*
Halbschwester	*half sister*
Halbbruder	*half brother*

19 **Familienquiz**

1. Monika und Dieter
2. Sabine und Andreas
3. Hannelore

Lesen/Sprechen Answer the following questions about Jens' family.

1. Wie heißen Sabines Mutter und Vater?
2. Wie heißen die Geschwister von Jens?
3. Wer ist die Schwester von Dieter?
4. Wie heißt Dieters Vater? Georg

5. Wer ist der Onkel von Sabines Bruder? Amir
6. Wer ist die Kusine von Tawan? Sabine
7. Wer ist der Bruder von Taras Mutter? Dieter
8. Wie heißen die Haustiere? Fritzi und Harras

20 Unsere Familien Script on p. 67G

CD 3 Tr. 12

1. Christa (6) 2. Werner 3. Anja
4. Werner 5. no

Zuhören Make a chart like the one below, listing all of the new vocabulary from Jens' family tree. Then listen as three friends of Jens' describe their families. Every time you hear a family member mentioned put a check next to the correct vocabulary word. After listening to the descriptions, try to answer these questions.

1. Who mentions the most family members?
2. Who does not mention the mother?
3. Who mentions an aunt but not an uncle?
4. Who mentions an uncle but not an aunt?
5. Do any of the three friends mention pets? If so, who mentions them?

	Anja	Werner	Christa
der Vater			
die Mutter			
der Bruder			

So sagt man das!

Talking about family members

To find out about someone's family you might ask:

Ist das deine Schwester?
Wie alt ist sie?
Und dein Bruder? Wie heißt er?
Wie alt ist er?
Und wer ist der Mann?
Und die Frau?
Wo wohnen deine Großeltern?

The responses might be:

Ja, das ist meine Schwester.
Sie ist einundzwanzig.
Mein Bruder heißt Robert.
Er ist schon dreiundzwanzig.
Das ist mein Opa.
Das ist meine Oma.
In Köln.

What is the difference between **dein** and **deine**? **Mein** and **meine**?
What do the words mean? When is each one used?

Übungsheft,
S. 32, Ü. 16–18

Ein wenig Grammatik

The words **dein** and **deine** (*your*) and **mein** and **meine** (*my*) are called *possessives*.

masculine **(der)**
neuter **(das)** } **mein, dein**

feminine **(die)**
plural **(die)** } **meine, deine**

These words are similar to **ein** and **eine**. Because of this similarity, **mein** and **dein** are often called **ein**-words.

Grammatikheft, S. 24, Ü. 14

Mehr Grammatikübungen,
S. 90–91, Ü. 8–9 →

21 Grammatik im Kontext

Lesen/Sprechen Steffi and Tara are looking at photos of their families. Complete their conversation by filling in the blanks with **mein/meine** or **dein/deine**.

TARA Ist das ___1___ Schwester? deine

STEFFI Ja, das ist Angelika.

TARA Wie alt ist ___2___ Schwester? deine

STEFFI ___3___ Schwester ist zwanzig. Meine
Und das ist ___4___ Bruder. Er ist mein
einundzwanzig.

TARA Und sind das ___5___ Großeltern? deine

STEFFI Ja, das ist ___6___ Oma, und das ist meine
___7___ Opa. Ist das ___8___ Vater? mein; dein

TARA Nein, das ist ___9___ Onkel Dieter. mein
Und das hier ist ___10___ Tante. meine

STEFFI Ist das ___11___ Kusine? deine

TARA Ja, das ist ___12___ Kusine, die Sabine. meine
Und das ist ___13___ Cousin, Jens. mein

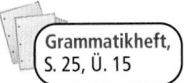
To talk about the ages of various family members, you need to review **die Zahlen von 0 bis 20** and learn **die Zahlen von 21 bis 100**.

Grammatikheft, S. 25, Ü. 15

21	einundzwanzig	26	sechsundzwanzig	30	dreißig	70	siebzig
22	zweiundzwanzig	27	siebenundzwanzig	40	vierzig	80	achtzig
23	dreiundzwanzig	28	achtundzwanzig	50	fünfzig	90	neunzig
24	vierundzwanzig	29	neunundzwanzig	60	sechzig	100	hundert
25	fünfundzwanzig				

a. With your classmates, count aloud to one hundred, first by tens, then by fives, then by twos. Students take turns leading the counting.

 b. Make up simple math problems with no results greater than 100. Working with a partner, ask each other the problems you each wrote down and see how fast you can solve them. Some words you may need are **und** (*plus*), **minus** (*minus*), **mal** (*times*), and **durch** (*divided by*).

---

22 Steffis Familie   Script on p. 67H

Zuhören Listen as Steffi tells Tara more about her family. First list the names of the family members in the order you hear them. Then listen a second time and write their ages beside their names.

CD 3 Tr. 13

die Kusine Anna, 22   der Vater, 45   der Cousin Bernhard, 26   der Großvater Gerd, 70
die Mutter, 43   der Onkel Florian, 50   die Tante, 51   die Großmutter Hannah, 67

die Kusine Anna   die Mutter   der Vater   der Cousin Bernhard

die Großmutter   der Onkel Florian   der Großvater   die Tante

---

Ein wenig Grammatik

The words **sein** (*his*) and **ihr** (*her*) are also possessives. They take the same endings as **mein** and **dein**.

masculine (**der**)
neuter (**das**) } **sein, ihr**

feminine (**die**)
plural (**die**) } **seine, ihre**

Grammatikheft, S. 25, Ü. 16

Mehr Grammatikübungen, S. 91, Ü. 10–11

23 Grammatik im Kontext

 Sprechen Bring some photos of family members to class, or if you like, bring in pictures from magazines and create a make-believe family. Show the photos to your partner, and he or she will ask you questions about them. Then switch roles. When you have finished, tell your classmates what you learned about one of your partner's relatives.

BEISPIEL   DU   **Das ist Bobs Vater. Sein … heißt …**   *or*

DU   **Das ist Kristins Kusine. Ihre … ist …**

24 Für mein Notizbuch

Schreiben Write four sentences in which you tell about two of your favorite family members or people who are close to you.

Steffi zeigt Tara ein Fotoalbum. Steffi:

3–C

Meine Mutter hat lange, rote Haare und grüne Augen. Sie spielt gern Schach.

Mein Vater hat braune Haare und blaue Augen. Er spielt sehr gut Klavier.

Und mein Bruder Ralf ist einundzwanzig. Er hat kurze, blonde Haare und hat eine Brille. Er schwimmt sehr gern.

Meine Großmutter Marie ist fünfundsechzig. Sie hat weiße Haare und blaue Augen. Sie hört gern Musik.

Und meine Kusine Anna ist zweiundzwanzig. Sie hat kurze, schwarze Haare und braune Augen. Sie geht oft wandern.

Mein Onkel Florian hat eine Glatze und grüne Augen. Er hat auch eine Brille. Er sammelt gern Briefmarken.

Grammatikheft, S. 26–27, Ü. 17–20

25 **Steffis Familie**

Sprechen Working with your partner, create a chart of the characteristics of Steffi's family. Write the names of the various family members across the top and their characteristics underneath using the categories **Alter, Haarfarbe, Augenfarbe,** and **Interessen.**

So sagt man das!

Describing people

Übungsheft, S. 33–34, Ü. 19–23

CD-ROM DISC 1

If you want to know what someone looks like, you might ask:

Wie sieht dein Bruder aus?

The response might be:

Er hat lange, blonde Haare und braune Augen.

If you are asking about more than one person, you say:

Wie sehen deine Großeltern aus?

Mein Opa hat weiße Haare und grüne Augen. Und meine Oma hat graue Haare und blaue Augen.

26 Wie sieht Steffis Familie aus?

Schreiben Referring to the chart you and your partner made for Activity 25, try to answer the following questions about Steffi's family.

1. Wer hat blaue Augen? 1. Vater, Großmutter Marie
2. Wie alt ist Steffis Bruder? Und ihre Kusine? 2. 21; 22
3. Wie sieht Onkel Florian aus? 3. Glatze, grüne Augen, Brille
4. Was macht die Mutter in der Freizeit? Der Vater? Anna? 4. spielt Schach; spielt Klavier; wandert

5. Mutter: lange, rote Haare, grüne Augen. Vater: braune Haare, blaue Augen

5. Wie sehen die Eltern aus?
6. Wer hat schwarze Haare? 6. Anna
7. Wer hat kurze Haare? Lange Haare?

7. Anna und Ralf, die Mutter (Großmutter, Vater, Onkel)

8. Wie alt ist die Großmutter? Wie sieht sie aus?
9. Wer hat eine Brille? 8. 65; weiße Haare, blaue Augen
9. Onkel Florian, Mutter, Ralf

27 Rate mal!

Sprechen Pick one person in the room and think about how you might describe him or her to someone else. Your partner will ask you questions and try to guess whom you have chosen. Then switch roles.

BEISPIEL   **PARTNER**   **Hat diese Person blonde Haare?**

28

Von der Schule zum Beruf

Schreiben You work as a police detective. You are trying to apprehend a wanted person. Write a profile of that person, giving name, age, residence, interests, and a physical description.

AUSSPRACHE

CD 3 Trs. 14–16

Richtig aussprechen / Richtig lesen CD 3 Tr. 14

A. To practice the following sounds, say the words and sentences below after your teacher or after the recording.

1. The letter **o**: The long **o** is pronounced much like the long *o* in the English word *oboe;* however, the lips are more rounded.

   Obst, Moped, schon / Wo wohnt deine Oma?

2. The letter **u**: The long **u** is similar to the vowel sound in the English word *do;* however, the lips are more rounded.

   Stuhl, super, Kuchen / Möchtest du ein Stück Kuchen?

3. The letters **s, ß, ss**: When the letter **s** begins a word or syllable and is followed by a vowel, it is pronounced like the *z* in the English word *zebra*. In the middle or final position of a syllable, the letter **s** sounds similar to the *s* in the English word *post*. The letters **ß** and **ss** are also pronounced this way.

   so, sieben, Sonja / Deine Kusine sieht sehr hübsch aus.
   aus, das, es / Die Couch ist zu groß und ganz hässlich.

Richtig schreiben / Diktat
CD 3 Tr. 15
CD 3 Tr. 16 (with pauses)

B. Write down the sentences that you hear.

Script on p. 67H

Note: You write **ß** after a long vowel (**groß**), diphthongs (**weiß**) and **ss** after a short vowel (**hässlich**). Exceptions are some short words, such as **das** and **was,** that are spelled with a single **s** after a short vowel.

Zum Lesen

Wo wohnst du denn?

Lesestrategie Using root words to form new words
German, like English, uses root words to form new words with related meanings. When you know the root word, you can often guess the meaning of words that are built on that word. An example is the word **wohnen**. A number of words related in meaning can be built on the stem of this word, such as **Wohnung**, **bewohnbar**, and **Eigentumswohnung**.

Answers to these activities in TE Interleaf, p. 67X

1. What do you think the classified ads are about? You know the word **wohnen**. Does knowing the meaning of **wohnen** help you understand the ads? Make a list of words built on the stem of **wohnen** (**wohn-/Wohn-**) and try to guess what they mean.

2. Working with a partner, match these German words with their English equivalents. Remember to look for the root words.

   1. **Wochenendheimfahrerin**
   2. **Eigentumswohnung**
   3. **Einfamilienhäuser**
   4. **Grundstück**

   a. *plot (of land)*
   b. *someone who goes home on the weekend*
   c. *condominium*
   d. *single-family homes*

3. There are two types of ads on this page: ads describing available houses and apartments, and ads placed by people looking for a place to live. Can you figure out which ads fit into each of these categories?

Bauvorhaben
Gösstraße – Tübingen

Die Oase in der City!

z. B. 1½ Zimmer-Wohnung, Südloggia, Garage, großzügiger Grundriß mit 34 m² Wohnfläche:
€ 95 000.–

z. B. 3½ Zimmer-Wohnung, großer Südbalkon, herrliche Aussicht. 62 m² Wohnfläche, Garage:
€ 143 500.–

BAUCONCEPT
Der leistungsstarke Immobilien-Spezialist.

Rufen Sie uns an: Mo – Fr 7.30 bis 20.00 , Sa. 8.00 bis 16.00
Telefon: (0 70 31) 87 70 91

KOMM MIT NACH HAUSE!

Go To: http://www.hause.de

Auf dem Lande

Großzügiges Einfamilienhaus mit Einliegerwohnung in Remmingsheim. Allerbeste Ausstattung mit wertvollen Einbauten und offenem Kamin. Insg. 174 m² Wfl. bei 7½ Zimmern, gepflegtes Grundstück mit 3,5 Ar, Garage und Autoabstellplätze, sofort beziehbar.

€ 229 000.–

2-Zi.-Eigentumswohnung

(Baujahr 1985) in Entringen, sofort beziehbar, 52 m² Wohnfläche, Einbauküche, Balkon, Keller, Stellplatz.

€ 95 000.–

4. Which ads would be most interesting to these people:
   a. a large family wanting to buy a house
   b. a couple in Tübingen-Lustnau looking for a condominium
   c. the owner of several rental properties, looking for prospective tenants

5. Working with a partner, try to find the following information.
   a. the most expensive house or apartment
   b. the least expensive house or apartment
   c. the house or apartment with the most rooms
   d. the house or apartment with the most square meters of living space
   e. the house or apartment with the least amount of living space
   f. the places that have either a garage or a space to park a car

6. If you were looking for a place to live, which of these ads would appeal to you the most? Be prepared to tell why you would choose one place over another.

7. a. Assume that you are going to Germany for a year and need a place to live. Write an ad in German that summarizes what you need.
   b. Many Americans and Europeans swap houses for several weeks at a time, so that they can live in a different culture without having to pay enormous hotel expenses. Imagine that you are going to take part in such an **Austausch** *(exchange)*. Using the format of these ads, write a classified ad for your home that you could place in a German newspaper.

Übungsheft, S. 35, Ü. 24–25

Mehr Grammatikübungen

CD-ROM DISC 1

internet
go.hrw.com
ADRESSE: go.hrw.com
KENNWORT:
WK3 BRANDENBURG-3

Answers

Erste Stufe

Objectives Offering something to eat and drink and responding to an offer

1 You have invited friends over, and you are offering food and beverages. Complete each of the following questions and statements by filling in each blank with the appropriate **möchte**-form. (S. 76)

1. Wer _____ ein paar Kekse essen? _____ du Kekse, Holger?   möchte; Möchtest

2. Die Tara _____ Obst. Und ihr, _____ ihr auch Obst?   möchte; möchtet

3. Wir _____ Apfelsaft. Und was _____ Tara und Steffi?   möchten; möchten

4. Der Holger _____ Kuchen, und ich _____ auch Kuchen.   möchte; möchte

5. Der Jens _____ nichts, aber die Steffi _____ Mineralwasser.   möchte; möchte

6. Sag, _____ du Kuchen, oder _____ du ein paar Kekse?   möchtest; möchtest

7. Was _____ ihr? _____ ihr ein Glas Apfelsaft?   möchtet; Möchtet

8. Wir _____ eine Cola, und die Tara _____ Orangensaft.   möchten; möchte

2 Your friends now want something else to eat or drink. Complete each of the following statements and questions by filling in the first blank with a **möchte**-form, and the second blank with the correct form of **ein**. (S. 76)

1. Der Holger _____ jetzt _____ Mineralwasser.   möchte; ein

2. Wir _____ jetzt _____ Stück Kuchen, bitte.   möchten; ein

3. Wer _____ jetzt _____ Limo trinken? Du, Holger?   möchte; eine

4. Der Holger und die Tara _____ jetzt _____ Glas Apfelsaft.   möchten; ein

5. Was _____ ihr jetzt? _____ paar Kekse?   möchtet; Ein

6. Was _____ du essen? _____ Stück Kuchen?   möchtest; Ein

7. Ich _____ gern _____ Cola trinken.   möchte; eine

3 Ask your friends what they would like to eat or drink. Complete each of the following statements and questions by filling in each blank with the correct form of the pronoun or the **möchte**-form. (S. 76)

1. Was _____ ihr essen? Danke, nichts! _____ möchten jetzt nichts essen.   möchtet; Wir

2. Was _____ du trinken? Ja, _____ möchte jetzt ein Glas Apfelsaft trinken.   möchtest; ich

3. Was _____ Tara trinken? Ja, _____ möchte Mineralwasser trinken.   möchte; sie

4. Was _____ Jens und Ahmet? _____ möchten eine Cola.   möchten; Sie

5. Ich _____ eine Cola trinken. Was möchtest _____ trinken, Jens?   möchte; du

6. Und ihr? Was _____ ihr trinken? Trinkt _____ Mineralwasser?   möchtet; ihr

4 You are describing to a friend of yours the various pieces of furniture in your room. Complete the following questions and statements by filling in the first blank with the correct form of the definite article, and the second blank with the correct pronoun. **(S. 79)**

1. Wo ist _____ Stereoanlage? Ist _____ kaputt?   *die; sie*
2. _____ Schreibtisch ist schön, und _____ ist so groß!   *Der; er*
3. Du, _____ Regal ist so alt, und _____ ist auch so hässlich.   *das; es*
4. Ja, _____ Schrank ist schön, und _____ ist sehr groß.   *der; er*
5. _____ Bett ist unbequem, und _____ ist so klein!   *Das; es*
6. Ja, _____ Couch ist schon alt, aber _____ ist ganz bequem.   *die; sie*
7. _____ Bett ist so klein, und _____ ist so unbequem!   *Das; es*
8. Und _____ Stuhl ist so alt, und _____ ist ganz kaputt.   *der; er*
9. Ja, _____ Zimmer ist toll, und _____ ist so groß!   *das; es*
10. _____ Möbel sind schön; _____ sind ganz neu.   *Die; sie*

5 Your friend is surprised at the condition of your furniture. Complete each of the following questions by filling in each blank with the correct form of the definite article. **(S. 79)**

1. Er ist kaputt. Wirklich? _____ Schreibtisch ist kaputt?   *Der*
2. Es ist kaputt. Wirklich? _____ Bett ist kaputt?   *Das*
3. Sie ist schon alt. Wirklich? _____ Couch ist alt?   *Die*
4. Er ist unbequem. Wirklich? _____ Stuhl ist unbequem?   *Der*
5. Sie sind ganz neu. Wirklich? _____ Möbel sind ganz neu?   *Die*
6. Es ist zu klein. Wirklich? _____ Regal ist zu klein?   *Das*
7. Es ist so groß! Wirklich? _____ Zimmer ist doch nicht groß!   *Das*
8. Er ist von meiner Oma. Wirklich? _____ Schrank von Oma Helen?   *Der*
9. Er ist neu. Wirklich? _____ Computer ist neu?   *Der*
10. Sie ist kaputt. Wirklich? _____ Stereoanlage ist kaputt?   *Die*

6 You are serving snacks to your friends. Complete the following statements and questions by filling in each blank with the correct pronoun. **(S. 79)**

1. Hier ist die Limo. Danke, _____ ist prima!   *sie*
2. Bitte, das Stück Kuchen. Hm, _____ ist so gut.   *es*
3. Das Obst ist sehr schön. Und _____ ist so gut für dich.   *es*
4. Ist das Glas kaputt? Nein, _____ ist nicht kaputt.   *es*
5. Hier ist die Cola. Ist _____ gut?   *sie*
6. Ja, der Kuchen ist so schön! Und _____ ist so gut!   *er*

Mehr Grammatikübungen

Answers

CD-ROM
DISC 1

go.
hrw.
com
WK3 BRANDENBURG-3

7 Your mother wants to know where all these misplaced items are. Fill in the first blank with the correct German noun and its definite article. Fill in the second blank with the pronoun that refers to that item. **(S. 79)**

1. (chair)   Wo ist _____ ? Ist _____ in Holgers Zimmer?   der Stuhl; er
2. (furniture) Wo sind _____ ? Sind _____ im Garten?   die Möbel; sie
3. (computer)   Wo ist _____ ? Ist _____ auch in Holgers Zimmer?   der Computer; er
4. (shelf)   Wo ist _____ ? Ist _____ kaputt?   das Regal; es
5. (desk)   Wo ist _____ ? Ist _____ in Taras Zimmer?   der Schreibtisch; er
6. (cabinet)   Wo ist _____ ? Ist _____ zu groß für das Zimmer?   der Schrank; er
7. (couch)   Wo ist _____ ? Ist _____ jetzt in Ahmets Zimmer?   die Couch; sie
8. (bed)   Wo ist _____ ? Ist _____ wirklich kaputt?   das Bett; es
9. (stereo)   Wo ist _____ ? Ist _____ kaputt?   die Stereoanlage; sie

Dritte Stufe

Objectives Talking about family members; describing people

8 You want to find out from a friend what the names of various members of his or her family are. Complete each of the following statements and questions by filling in each first blank with the correct form of the definite article, and each second blank with the correct form of the possessive **dein.** **(S. 82)**

1. _____ Vater von Andreas heißt Dieter. Wie heißt _____ Vater?   Der; dein
2. _____ Mutter von Andreas heißt Monika. Wie heißt _____ Mutter?   Die; deine
3. _____ Opa von Sabine heißt Georg. Wie heißt _____ Opa?   Der; dein
4. _____ Oma von Sabine heißt Ella. Wie heißt _____ Oma?   Die; deine
5. _____ Onkel von Jens heißt Amir. Und wie heißt _____ Onkel?   Der; dein
6. _____ Tante von Jens heißt Hannelore. Wie heißt _____ Tante?   Die; deine
7. _____ Kusine von Sabine heißt Tara. Wie heißt _____ Kusine?   Die; deine
8. _____ Cousin von Andreas heißt Tawan. Wie heißt _____ Cousin?   Der; dein
9. _____ Eltern von Tara heißen Tehrani. Wie heißen _____ Eltern?   Die; deine

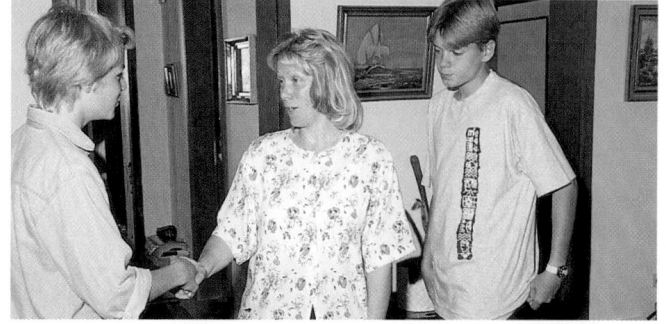

9 You want to find out from a friend how old various members of his or her family are or what they look like. You then tell your friend how old your relatives are and what they look like. Complete each of the following questions and statements by filling in each first blank with the correct form of **dein** and each second blank with the correct form of **mein.** (S. 82)

1. Wie alt ist _____ Opa? _____ Opa ist schon siebzig.   dein; Mein
2. Wie alt ist _____ Tante? _____ Tante ist vierzig Jahre alt.   deine; Meine
3. Ist _____ Cousin schon sechzehn? _____ Cousin ist schon zwanzig.   dein; Mein
4. Ist _____ Oma schon siebzig? _____ Oma ist schon achtzig.   deine; Meine
5. Hat _____ Onkel eine Brille? _____ Onkel hat auch eine Brille.   dein; Mein
6. Hat _____ Kusine blonde Haare? _____ Kusine hat rote Haare.   deine; Meine
7. Hat _____ Bruder blonde Haare? _____ Bruder hat schwarze Haare.   dein; Mein
8. Hat _____ Schwester blaue Augen? _____ Schwester hat grüne Augen.   deine; Meine

10 You want to find out the names of relatives of various classmates. Complete each question with the correct form of the appropriate possessive. (**sein** or **ihr**) (S. 83)

1. Tara hat eine Kusine. Wie heißt _____ Kusine?   ihre
2. Tara hat auch einen Cousin. Wie heißt _____ Cousin? ihr
3. Andreas hat eine Schwester. Wie heißt _____ Schwester? seine
4. Andreas hat auch einen Bruder. Wie heißt _____ Bruder? sein
5. Tara hat einen Bruder. Wie heißt _____ Bruder?   ihr
6. Tara hat auch eine Tante. Wie heißt _____ Tante?   ihre
7. Sabine hat einen Hund. Wie heißt _____ Hund?   ihr
8. Andreas hat auch einen Hund. Wie heißt _____ Hund?   sein
9. Andreas hat auch eine Katze. Wie heißt _____ Katze? seine

11 You are talking about members of your family. Complete each of the following sentences by filling in each first blank the German words for the English ones in parentheses, and by filling in each second blank with the correct pronoun. (S. 83)

1. (my mother)   _____ heißt Renate; _____ ist 39 Jahre alt.   Meine Mutter; sie
2. (my brother)   _____ heißt Mark; _____ ist 15 Jahre alt.   Mein Bruder; er
3. (my grandpa)   _____ heißt Herbert; _____ ist 68 Jahre alt.   Mein Opa; er
4. (my aunt)   _____ heißt Rosa; _____ ist 48 Jahre alt.   Meine Tante; sie
5. (my cousin)   _____ heißt Michael; _____ ist 19 Jahre alt.   Mein Cousin; er
6. (my sister)   _____ heißt Sarah; _____ ist 18 Jahre alt.   Meine Schwester; sie
7. (my grandma)   _____ heißt Maria; _____ ist 63 Jahre alt.   Meine Oma; sie
8. (my father)   _____ heißt Robert; _____ ist 44 Jahre alt.   Mein Vater; er

Anwendung

The CD-ROM Tutor offers guided recording and writing activities to accompany the **Anwendung**. These activities are designed to practice students' oral and written communication skills and to review material from each chapter.

1 You are at your partner's house in the afternoon. Your partner offers you something to eat and drink, and you say what you would like using **möchte**. Then ask your partner what he or she would like. Write the conversation and act it out together.

2 Write a brief physical description of your partner on a 3x5 card. Find out his or her age and where he or she lives and include that information as well. Everyone will put his or her description in a box. Students will take turns drawing cards and reading the information aloud while the other students take turns guessing who it is.

3 At a party last week you met someone you really like. You learned a lot about the person, but you don't know how to get in touch with him or her. Write a short paragraph describing him or her that you could pass along to your friends. Include the person's age, name, where he or she lives, his or her interests, and a physical description.

4 Listen to Tara's description of her room and indicate which of the drawings below matches the description you hear. Script on p. 67H

CD 3
Tr. 17

a.

b.

c.

5 Using the adjectives to the right, describe your room to your partner. He or she will draw a sketch based on your description. Then switch roles.

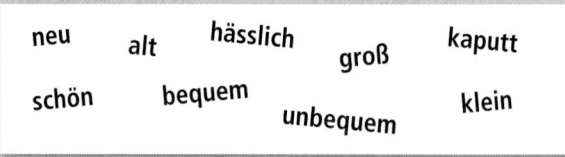

neu	alt	hässlich	groß	kaputt
schön	bequem		unbequem	klein

6 You would like to put a personal ad in a teen magazine.

a. Your partner is a reporter for the magazine and will interview you. Unfortunately, no photo can be found, so you must give a complete description of yourself. Your partner will ask questions and take down the information. Then switch roles. When you are the reporter, be prepared to share with the class the information you obtained.

b. Now write your partner's ad the way it will appear in the magazine. Your partner will write yours. Use the profiles on page 93 as models.

c. Write a short paragraph describing him or her that you could pass along to your friends.

7 **a.** Read each profile that appeared in a magazine for teenagers.

Bettina Schilling, 14 J.
Schulstraße 27
60594 Frankfurt a.M.
Interessen: Musik, Klavier,
Reiten, Schwimmen

Peter Fischer, 15 J.
Körtestraße 8
10967 Berlin
Interessen: Wandern,
Musik, Fußball

Helmut Heine, 16 J.
Königstraße 24
39116 Magdeburg
Interessen: Rad fahren,
Basteln, Comics sammeln

b. Describe one of the persons above using complete sentences.

c. Now listen to Holger's description of a girl named Sonja whom he read about in a magazine. Based on what he says, with which of the students above would Sonja have the most in common?   Script on p. 67H   Helmut Heine

CD 3 Tr. 18

---

8 # Zum Schreiben

You have just moved to a different city and attend a new school where you are required to introduce yourself at a newcomer orientation. Draw a personal profile puzzle to introduce yourself, your family, and your home to your new school mates.

> **Schreibtipp Arranging ideas spatially** is a useful way to organize information before you write. It's really a way of creating a type of blueprint of how your finished product will look. In this case, the puzzle pieces show different aspects of your life and different parts of your personality.

1. Decide on your categories, for instance: *Activities I enjoy; Me!* (Self-description); *My family; My ideal bedroom.* Jot down as many nouns and adjectives as you can for each category.

2. Now you are ready to create your blueprint. Draw four to six puzzle-shaped areas on a piece of poster board, and label each area with one of the categories you have chosen. Using one puzzle piece per category, complete the puzzle with the items and descriptions you have jotted down.

---

9 # Rollenspiel

Two friends whom you have not seen for a while come to your house after school. First, offer your friends something to eat and drink, then show them your room. You have recently made some changes, so the three of you talk about your furniture. Then your conversation turns to family. Take turns describing various family members, what they look like, and what their interests are. Write out the conversations and practice them. Then role-play them in front of the class.

Kann ich's wirklich?

Can you talk about where people live? (p. 73)

1 How would you ask a classmate where he or she lives and tell him or her where you live? *Wo wohnst du? Ich wohne in …*

2 Say where the following people live:

a. wohnt auf dem Land
b. wohnt in der Hegelstraße

  a. Thomas (Land)
  b. Britte (Hegelstraße)
  c. Marian und Karl (Brauhausberg, Vorort von Potsdam)
c. wohnen in Brauhausberg, das ist ein Vorort von Potsdam

  d. Renate (Köln)
  e. Sabine und Rolf (Stadt: Bismarckstr.)
d. wohnt in Köln
e. wohnen in der Stadt; in der Bismarckstraße

Can you offer something to eat and drink (using möchte) and respond to an offer? (p. 74)

3 How would you ask a classmate what he or she would like to eat and drink? How would you ask more than one classmate? How would you tell a classmate that you would like a lemon-flavored soda?
Was möchtest du essen/trinken? Was möchtet ihr essen/trinken? Ich möchte eine Limo.

4 If you and some of your classmates were at a friend's house, how would you help your friend by telling her or him what everyone was having for a snack?

  a. Anna, eine Cola
a. möchte
b. möchten
  b. Martin und Klaus, ein Stück Kuchen
c. möchten
d. möchte

  c. Nicole und Jörg, ein paar Kekse
  d. Ayla, Obst

Can you say please, thank you, and you're welcome? (p. 76)

5 How would you ask your friend politely for a few cookies? How would you thank him or her? How would he or she respond?
Ich möchte ein paar Kekse, bitte. Danke! Bitte schön!

Can you describe a room? (p. 77)

6 How would you describe these pieces of furniture? Make two sentences about each one using the correct pronoun **er, sie, es,** or **sie** (pl) in the second sentence. *a. Der Schrank ist alt und hässlich. Er ist groß.*
b. Das Bett ist klein und bequem. Es ist neu.

  a. der Schrank (*old, ugly, large*)
  b. das Bett (*small, comfortable, new*)
  c. die Möbel (*beautiful, new, large*)
  d. die Couch (*old, ugly, broken*)
c. Die Möbel sind schön und neu. Sie sind groß. d. Die Couch ist alt und hässlich. Sie ist kaputt.

Can you talk about family members? (p. 82)

7 How would you tell a classmate about five of your family members, giving their relationship to you, their names, and their ages?

Can you describe people? (p. 84)

8 How would you describe the people below?

 a.  b. c.  d.

9 How would you ask a classmate what his or her brother, sister, grandfather, parents, and cousins (male and female) look like?

Erste Stufe

Talking about where you live

nach Hause gehen	to go home
wohnen	to live
Wo wohnst du?	Where do you live?
in der Stadt	in the city
auf dem Land	in the country
ein Vorort von	a suburb of
weit von hier	far from here
in der Nähe	nearby
in der …Straße	on … Street
Wo wohnt Jens?	Where does Jens live?
Ich denke, in/auf …	I think in …

Things to eat and drink

möchten	would like (to)
essen	to eat
Was möchtest du essen?	What would you like to eat?
ein Stück Kuchen	a piece of cake
Obst	fruit
ein paar Kekse	a few cookies
trinken	to drink
Was möchtest du trinken?	What would you like to drink?
ein Glas Apfelsaft (Orangensaft)	a glass of apple juice (orange juice)
eine Cola	cola
eine Limo	a lemonade

ein Glas (Mineral) Wasser	a glass of (mineral) water
Nichts, danke!	Nothing, thank you!
Im Moment gar nichts.	Nothing at the moment (right now).

Saying please, thank you, and you're welcome

Bitte!	Please!
Danke!	Thank you!
Danke (sehr) (schön)!	Thank you (very much)!
Bitte (sehr) (schön)!	You're (very) welcome!

Zweite Stufe

Describing a room

das Zimmer, -	room
die Möbel (pl)	furniture
der Schrank, ¨e	cabinet
der Schreibtisch, -e	desk
die Stereoanlage, -n	stereo
die Couch, -en	couch
das Bett, -en	bed
das Regal, -e	bookcase, shelf
der Stuhl, ¨e	chair

neu	new
alt	old
klein	small
groß	big
bequem	comfortable
unbequem	uncomfortable
schön	pretty, beautiful
hässlich	ugly
kaputt	broken

Pronouns

er	he, it
sie	she, it
es	it
sie (pl)	they

Other Useful Words and Expressions

ganz	really, quite
aber	but
der Computer, -	computer

Dritte Stufe

Talking about the family

die Familie, -n	family
Das ist …	That's …
die Mutter, ¨	mother
der Vater, ¨	father
die Schwester, -n	sister
der Bruder, ¨	brother
die Großmutter, ¨ (Oma)	grandmother
der Großvater, ¨ (Opa)	grandfather
die Tante, -n	aunt
der Onkel, -	uncle
die Kusine, -n	cousin (female)
der Cousin, -s	cousin (male)
das Haustier, -e	pet
die Tante, -n	aunt

der Hund, -e	dog
die Katze, -n	cat
der Mann, ¨er	man
die Frau, -en	woman
Das sind …	These are …
die Eltern (pl)	parents
die Geschwister (pl)	brothers and sisters
die Großeltern (pl)	grandparents

Die Zahlen von 21 bis 100

siehe Seite 83	see page 83

Describing People

Wie sieht er aus?	What does he look like?

Wie sehen sie aus?	What do they look like?
lange (kurze) Haare	long (short) hair
rote (blonde, schwarze, weiße, graue, braune) Haare	red (blonde, black, white, gray, brown) hair
blaue (grüne, braune) Augen	blue (green, brown) eyes
eine Glatze haben	to be bald
eine Brille	a pair of glasses

Possessives

dein, deine	your
mein, meine	my
sein, seine	his
ihr, ihre	her

Schleswig-Holstein

LOCATION OPENER

Teaching Resources
pp. 96-99

PRINT
▸ Lesson Planner, p. 17
▸ Video Guide, pp. 21–22

MEDIA
▸ One-Stop Planner
▸ Video Program
   Videocassette 2, 01:17–04:44
▸ Interactive CD-ROM Tutor, Disc 1
▸ Map Transparency

go.hrw.com
WK3 SCHLESWIG-HOLSTEIN

PAGES 96–97

THE PHOTOGRAPH
Background Information

The **Holstentor** (Holsten Gate) was built in 1478 as part of a system of walls designed to protect the city of Lübeck from possible invaders. Near the gate are the original salt storehouses (**Salzspeicher,** 16th - 18th century). At its height, Lübeck was the trading center of the Hanseatic League and was one of the largest cities in Germany.

Thinking Critically

Drawing Inferences Lübeck was once a center of the very important salt trade. Ask students to brainstorm some reasons why salt was such an important commodity for the countries around the Baltic Sea. (Salt was not only used to preserve food products such as meats and fish, but was also necessary for the production of leather.)

Language Note

The saying above the gate is **Concordia domi foris pax.** Ask students what language that is (Latin), and whether they can translate the phrase or any part of it. (*Harmony at home and peace at the marketplace*) Point out that *marketplace* during this time period referred to commerce between cities. Ask students

why they think Latin would be used on a German structure such as this gate. (See the following Culture Note.)

Culture Note

Because of the enormous political and cultural importance of the Roman Empire, as well as the use of Latin by the Roman Catholic Church, Latin became the international language of Europe during the Middle Ages. Latin was also the language of higher learning, and most books during this time were written in Latin.

THE ALMANAC AND MAP

Schleswig-Holstein's vertically split coat of arms tells us about the two parts of this state, Schleswig and Holstein. Schleswig is represented by two lions on a gold background (related to the three lions on the coat of arms of Denmark). The symbol of Holstein is a silver nettle leaf on a red background.

Terms in the Almanac

• **Matjes:** salted fillets of young herring that are considered a great delicacy in northern Germany

• **Rote Grütze:** a very popular dessert in northern Germany made from a variety of berries and usually served with whipped cream

Map Activities

• Have students use the map on p. 2 to identify the German states and the country that border Schleswig-Holstein. You may also want to use *Map Transparency* 1. (**Hamburg, Niedersachsen, Mecklenburg-Vorpommern; Dänemark**)

• Have students compare the industries of Schleswig-Holstein with those of Brandenburg (see p. 13). Why are there differences? (Example: different geographical locations)

• Have students locate the Elbe and Eider rivers in an atlas. Then have them locate the **Inseln** mentioned in the almanac and identify the bodies of water in which they are located. (**Helgoland, Sylt,** and **Föhr** are in the **Nordsee;** Fehmarn is in the **Kieler Bucht.**)

PAGES 98–99

THE PHOTO ESSAY

1 Teaching Suggestion Have students locate the island Sylt on a map. Mention to students that this island is the largest of the North Frisian islands. In 1925 the island was connected to the mainland when the 11 km long **Hindenburgdamm** was built. Only trains can cross the dam, but cars can travel across on the trains.

• **Background Information** The traditional farm houses of northern Germany have roofs made of native reeds. This type of roof provides warmth but is often a fire hazard.

• **Drawing Inferences** Ask students why houses are built differently throughout the United States. (Example: Houses had to be built according to local climates and building materials that were available.) Have students give a few examples of different architectural styles in the United States. Ask them why they think reeds were a popular choice of roofing material for the coastal areas. (Example: a material readily available in that area)

• **Background Information** The beach chairs **Strandkörbe** shown in Photo 1 are large hooded wicker baskets that can seat two people comfortably. They can be found on many North Sea and Baltic Sea beaches. These chairs can be rented by the day, week, or month and provide both a sense of privacy on a crowded beach and some protection against the weather.

2 Kiel, named after the Old German word for *bay*, is the gateway to Scandinavia and known as *die Stadt der frischen Winde.* Kiel annually hosts the **Kieler Woche,** one of the world's greatest yachting events.

• **Comparing and Contrasting** Ask students what cities in the United States (also close to water) can be compared to Kiel. (Examples: Galveston, Texas; Norfolk, Virginia; Mobile, Alabama) Like Kiel, these cities are major ports and have attracted shipping and other industries.

3 Drawing Inferences Ask students where lighthouses are typically situated and how the need for them has changed over the years. (Lighthouses are usually located along coastlines to provide visual landmarks and safety for ship traffic. Today many lighthouses are no longer manned and are operated automatically. With the technological advances of navigation equipment, the need for lighthouses has decreased.)

4 Drawing Inferences A Reepschläger is a rope-maker. Given the location of Wedel, ask students to guess what the ropes that were originally manufactured in this house were used for. (For those working on the Elbe river, ropes were needed not only for fishing equipment, but also for tying down and pulling ships.)

Culture Note It is not unusual for business owners to live in the building where their business is located. The proprietor of the **Teestube** lives upstairs. The feather bed and pillow are put onto the windowsill in the morning to be aired out.

5 Almost every town and city in Germany has a certain day on which vendors set up their stands in a central location. It usually opens around 6:00 in the morning and lasts until the early afternoon. Florists, farmers, seafood vendors, and vendors of many other items sell their goods in the open-air market.

• **Background Information** The statue of the knight Roland is not unique to Wedel, but can be found on pillars in front of city halls and in market places all over Germany. Roland is always depicted with a shield and sword and symbolizes that a city fought for its independence and became a "free" city.

6 While northern Germans have the reputation of being cool and reserved, the five students from the **Johann-Rist-Gymnasium** do not fit this stereotype. They are outgoing young people with many interests, such as traveling to other countries to improve their language skills. Their school has active exchange programs with schools in France, England, and Russia.

LOCATION OPENER

Komm mit nach Schleswig-Holstein!

Map of Germany

Einwohner: 2,7 Millionen

Fläche: 16 000 Quadratkilometer (6 177 Quadratmeilen), ungefähr so groß wie Connecticut

Landeshauptstadt: Kiel (240 000 Einwohner)

Große Städte: Lübeck, Flensburg, Neumünster

Flüsse: Elbe, Eider

Inseln: Helgoland, Sylt, Föhr, Fehmarn

Kanäle: Nord-Ostsee-Kanal

Seen: über 300

Industrien: Schiffbau, Ackerbau, Viehzucht

Beliebte Gerichte: Matjes, Krabben, Aale, Räucherspeck, Buttermilchsuppe, Rote Grütze

Nordsee
DÄNEMARK   Ostsee
Kiel
Wedel
Hamburg
NIEDER-LANDE
Berlin
POLEN
BEL.
Frankfurt
LUX.
TSCHECHIEN
FRANK-REICH
München
SCHWEIZ
ÖSTERREICH

go.hrw.com

VIDEO

CD-ROM DISC 1

WK3 SCHLESWIG-HOLSTEIN

STANDARDS: 2.2, 3.1

Das Holstentor in Lübeck, Geburtsstadt ▶ von Thomas Mann (1875-1955)

CONCORDIA DOMI FORIS PAX

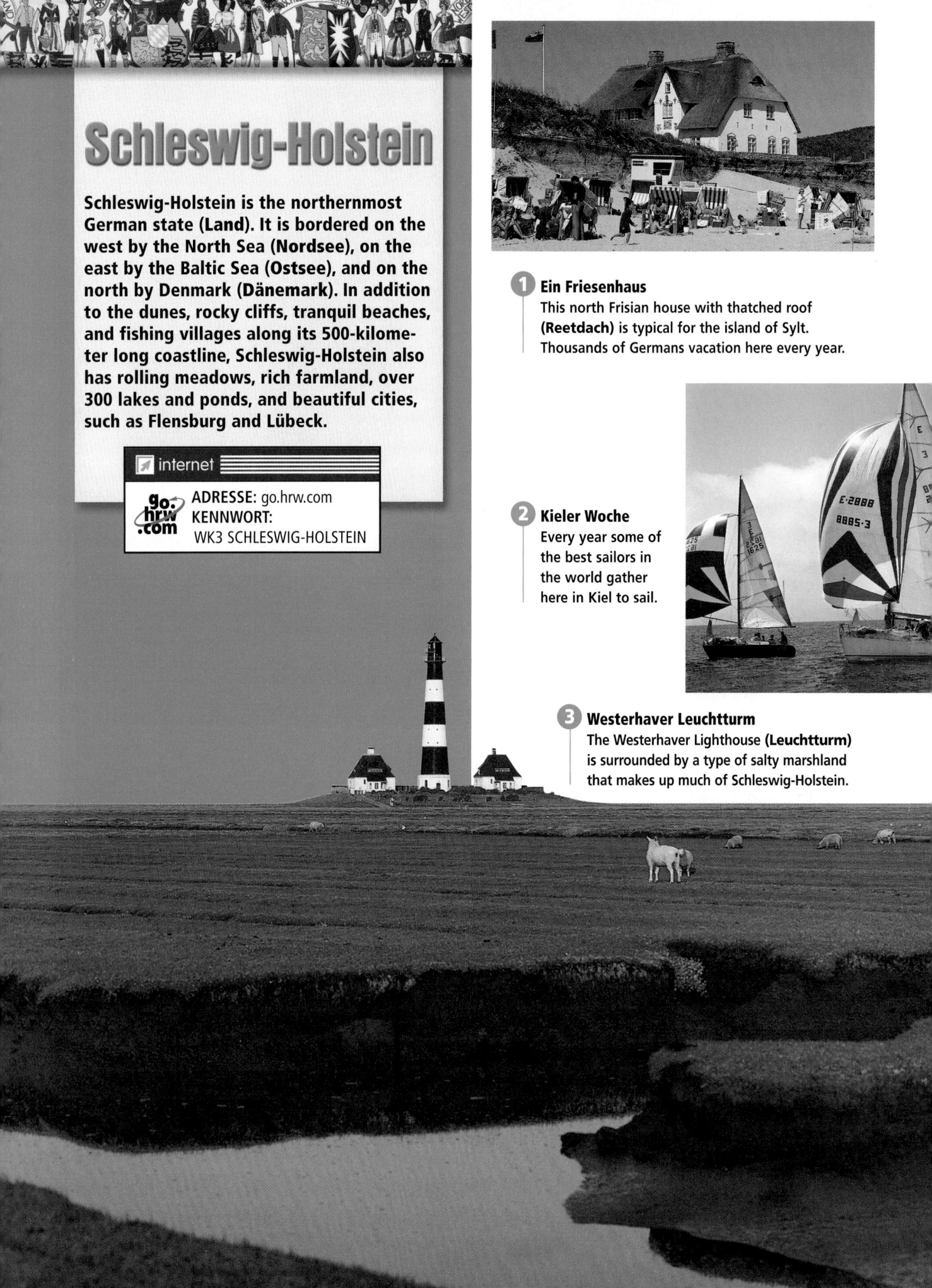

Schleswig-Holstein

Schleswig-Holstein is the northernmost German state (**Land**). It is bordered on the west by the North Sea (**Nordsee**), on the east by the Baltic Sea (**Ostsee**), and on the north by Denmark (**Dänemark**). In addition to the dunes, rocky cliffs, tranquil beaches, and fishing villages along its 500-kilometer long coastline, Schleswig-Holstein also has rolling meadows, rich farmland, over 300 lakes and ponds, and beautiful cities, such as Flensburg and Lübeck.

▸ internet

go.hrw.com
.com

ADRESSE: go.hrw.com
KENNWORT:
WK3 SCHLESWIG-HOLSTEIN

1 **Ein Friesenhaus**
This north Frisian house with thatched roof (**Reetdach**) is typical for the island of Sylt. Thousands of Germans vacation here every year.

2 **Kieler Woche**
Every year some of the best sailors in the world gather here in Kiel to sail.

3 **Westerhaver Leuchtturm**
The Westerhaver Lighthouse (**Leuchtturm**) is surrounded by a type of salty marshland that makes up much of Schleswig-Holstein.

Kapitel 4: Alles für die Schule!
Chapter Resources

PRINT

Lesson Planning

One-Stop Planner

Lesson Planner with Substitute Teacher Lesson Plans, pp. 17–21, 68

Student Make-Up Assignments
- Make-Up Assignment Copying Masters, Chapter 4

Listening and Speaking

TPR Storytelling Book, pp. 13–16

Listening Activities
- Student Response Forms for Listening Activities, pp. 27–29
- Additional Listening Activities 4-1 to 4-6, pp. 31–34
- Additional Listening Activities (song), p. 30
- Scripts and Answers, pp. 119–123

Video Guide
- Teaching Suggestions, pp. 24–25
- Activity Masters, pp. 26–28
- Scripts and Answers, pp. 87–90, 112

Activities for Communication
- Communicative Activities, pp. 19–24
- Realia and Teaching Suggestions, pp. 86–89
- Situation Cards, pp. 129–130

Reading and Writing

Reading Strategies and Skills Handbook, Chapter 4

Lies mit mir! 1, Chapter 4

Übungsheft, pp. 37–48

Grammar

Grammatikheft, pp. 28–36

Grammar Tutor for Students of German, Chapter 4

Assessment

Testing Program
- Grammar and Vocabulary Quizzes, **Stufe** Quizzes, and Chapter Test, pp. 79–96
- Score Sheet, Scripts, and Answers, pp. 97–104

Alternative Assessment Guide
- Portfolio Assessment, p. 21
- Performance Assessment, p. 35
- CD-ROM Assessment, p. 49

Student Make-Up Assignments
- Alternative Quizzes, Chapter 4

MEDIA

Online Activities
- Interaktive Spiele
- Internet Aktivitäten

Video Program
- Videocassette 2
- Videocassette 5 (captioned version)

Audio Compact Discs
- Textbook Listening Activities, CD 4, Tracks 1–17
- Additional Listening Activities, CD 4, Tracks 24–30
- Assessment Items, CD 4, Tracks 18–23

Interactive CD-ROM Tutor, Disc 1

Teaching Transparencies
- Situations 4-1 to 4-2
- Vocabulary 4-A to 4-B
- **Los geht's!**
- **Mehr Grammatikübungen** Answers
- **Grammatikheft** Answers

One-Stop Planner CD-ROM

Use the **One-Stop Planner CD-ROM with Test Generator** to aid in lesson planning and pacing.

For each chapter, the **One-Stop Planner** includes:
- Editable lesson plans with direct links to teaching resources
- Printable worksheets from resource books
- Direct launches to the HRW Internet activities
- Video and audio segments
- Test Generator
- Clip Art for vocabulary items

Kapitel 4: Alles für die Schule!

Projects ·············

Das Schulsystem

In this activity students will make a poster outlining some components of the public education systems of Austria, Germany, or Switzerland. This project is designed to be a cooperative learning activity, and students should be grouped accordingly. Each group should have a reader, a writer, a proofreader, and a presenter.

MATERIALS
✂ **Students may need**
- large sheets of paper or construction paper
- colored markers
- rulers
- tape

SUGGESTED OUTLINE

Posters should outline differences between the American school system and the school system chosen, such as

- structure (How do the grade levels work?)
- types of schools (**Realschule, Gymnasium,** and so on)
- compulsory age for attending schools
- grading system
- course requirements, end-of-year exams
- educational tracks chosen by students in secondary education

SUGGESTED SEQUENCE

1. Once students have been assigned or have chosen a country, each group will begin its research.
2. Students should be given a set time to look for information in their school library or on the Internet. You may also want to supply additional information and have it available for them on reserve.
3. Each member of a group should research one or two of the components of the topic.
4. Once all materials have been gathered, each group should make a draft of the information they will put on the poster.
5. The proofreader must check for correct spelling before the writer creates the final draft.
6. Encourage students to use charts and diagrams as visual aids for their presentation.

GRADING THE PROJECT
Suggested point distribution (**total = 100 points**)
Correct content information 25
Oral presentation 25
Appearance of project 25
Individual participation 25

Games ·············

Der Preis ist heiß

This game can be used to review numbers and to practice concrete vocabulary items from any chapter.

Materials You will need small pictures depicting the vocabulary you intend to practice (school supplies for this chapter), tape or glue, construction paper or cardboard, and index cards.

Preparation To prepare for the game, glue or tape pictures onto cardboard. Write an approximate German price for each item on the back of each card. On a separate index card write two prices for the same object, one of which matches the actual price on the back of the picture and another that is either lower or higher. Place each card face down in front of the corresponding picture.

Procedure The class is divided into two teams, and one student is the host. Each team sends one member at a time to the front, and the host asks "**Wie viel kostet …?**" as he or she holds up the item for the two players and the rest of the class to see. The players choose between the two prices on the index card. They then write down their answer. The host asks them to read their answers. If a team member gets the correct price, he or she wins a point for his or her team. After all items have been shown or the set time ends, all points are added up. The team with the most points wins.

Assoziationsfeld

*This game can be used to review the vocabulary of almost any topic. Suggestions for this chapter are **Schulfächer, Schreibwarenladen,** and hobbies (review topic).*

Procedure Depending on the class size, divide the class into two or more teams. Members of each team form a circle with their chairs and assign one student to be their designated recorder. Announce the topic to the groups and give the signal to start. The members of each team must come up with as many German words as possible that are associated with the topic. The recorder writes down all the suggested words, and each student must ensure that he or she knows the correct spelling. The team members continue to dictate words to their recorder until the teacher calls time. The recorder of each group copies his or her list on the board. After all lists are up, the teacher checks the words for appropriateness and correct spelling. The team with the most appropriate words correctly spelled wins.

Storytelling ·····················

*This story accompanies Teaching Transparency 4-2. The **Mini-Geschichte** can be told and retold in different formats, acted out, written down, and read aloud to give students additional opportunities to practice all four skills.*

Im Schul-Shop

Lars sagt zur Verkäuferin *(sales clerk)*: „Guten Morgen! Ich habe am Montag Mathe und mein Taschenrechner ist kaputt. Haben Sie Taschenrechner?" Die Verkäuferin sagt: „Ja, klar! Die Taschenrechner sind dort drüben." Lars schaut und schaut. Er findet die Taschenrechner nicht. Er fragt: „Wo sind die Taschenrechner? Ich finde sie nicht. So ein Mist!" Die Verkäuferin sagt: „Entschuldigung! *(Excuse me!)* Die Taschenrechner sind hier vorn. Sie kosten nur 10 Euro." Lars sagt: „Das ist preiswert. Ich habe am Montag auch Englisch. Ich finde mein Wörterbuch nicht." Die Verkäuferin sagt: „Ich habe auch Wörterbücher. Die sind sehr billig."

Traditions ·····················

Die Kieler Woche

Die Kieler Woche ist das größte und traditionsreichste Segelsportereignis der Welt. Die Veranstaltung kann auf eine über 100-jährige Tradition zurückblicken. Seit 1883 finden Segelregatten in der Kieler Förde statt. Über 5000 Segler aus über 50 Nationen nehmen heutzutage an den Segelregatten teil. Mehrere Millionen Besucher finden sich während der Tage der Kieler Woche in Kiel und Umgebung ein.

Rezept

Weil es so furchtbar stürmisch ist im Land zwischen den beiden Meeren, braucht der Schleswig-Holsteiner eine gewisse Menge Ballast. Darum ruht das Gebäude der schleswig-holsteinischen Küche auch auf zwei unendlich soliden Säulen: dem Mehl und dem Schwein. Die holsteiner Buchweizenklöße sind ein typisches Beispiel schleswig-holsteinischer Küche.

Holsteiner Buchweizenklöße
Für 4 Personen

Zutaten

g=Gramm, EL=Esslöffel, TL= Teelöffel

1 kg	Kartoffeln
100 g	Räucherspeck, durchwachsen
200 g	Buchweizenmehl
3	Eier
5 EL	Milch
2 TL	Salz

Zubereitung

Am Tag vorher die Kartoffeln ungeschält kochen, abgießen, abschrecken und pellen, dann auskühlen lassen. Kartoffeln zu feiner Masse stampfen, Speck fein würfeln, dann mit Kartoffeln, Buchweizenmehl, Eiern, Milch und Salz zu einem glatten Teig verrühren.

Am Tag des Essens reichlich Salzwasser in einem weiten Topf zum Kochen bringen. Aus dem Teig mit 2 Löffeln Klöße abstechen und glatt formen. Die Klöße ins kochende Wasser geben und im offenen Topf 10 Minuten ziehen lassen. Klöße herausnehmen und in eine Schüssel geben, in der auf dem Boden eine Untertasse verkehrt herum liegt. Sie hält das noch abtropfende Wasser von den Klößen fern und verhindert dadurch, daß diese matschig werden und zusammen kleben. Buchweizenklöße werden mit brauner Butter übergossen und zu frischem Salat gegessen.

Kapitel 4: Alles für die Schule!
Technology

Video
Videocassette 2, 5 (captioned version)
See Video Guide, pages 23–28

Los geht's! • Lars kauft Schulsachen

Lars, Julia, Sina, and Alex run into each other before class. They talk about their class schedule and the math test they later get back. Later on, Julia runs into Lars at the stationery store where Lars buys a calculator. On the way out, Lars drops all his things and discovers that his calculator does not work.

Fortsetzung

Lars and Julia return to the store to find out what's wrong with the calculator: it needs batteries, which he buys. Sina is also in the store paying for school supplies. All three leave the store together and decide to go home to study for another test.

Landeskunde
Was sind deine Lieblingsfächer?

Students from different cities talk about the school subjects they like, do well in, and don't like.

Videoclips

- **Herlitz Mickey Mouse Schultaschen**® (school bags)
- **Joker System Schultaschen**® (school bags)
- **Läufer Schreibunterlagen**® (writing pads)
- **Läufer Papierkörbe**® (wastebaskets)

Interactive CD-ROM Tutor

The **Interactive CD-ROM Tutor** contains videos, interactive games, and activities that provide students an opportunity to practice and review the material covered in Chapter 4.

Activity	Activity Type	Pupil's Edition Reference
1. Wortschatz	Merkspiel	p. 105
2. So sagt man das!	Was ist richtig?	pp. 106, 107, 109
3. Grammatik	Was fehlt?	p. 108
4. So sagt man das!	Wozu gehört's?	pp. 110, 112
5. Grammatik	Was fehlt?	p. 114
6. So sagt man das!	Wort und Bild Erfahren/Wählen	pp. 115, 116
Landeskunde	Was sind deine Lieblingsfächer? Was ist richtig?	p. 113
Zum Sprechen	*Guided recording*	pp. 124–125
Zum Schreiben	*Guided writing*	pp. 124–125

Teacher Management System
Logging In

Logging in to the *Komm mit!* TMS is easy. Upon launching the program, simply type "admin" in the password area of the log-in screen and press RETURN. Log on to **www.hrw.com/CDROMTUTOR** for a detailed explanation of the Teacher Management System.

One-Stop Planner CD-ROM

To preview all resources available for this chapter, use the **One-Stop Planner CD-ROM**, Disc 1.

Internet Connection

internet

go.hrw.com

ADRESSE: go.hrw.com
KENNWORT: WK3
SCHLESWIG-HOLSTEIN-4

*Have students explore the **go.hrw.com** Web site for many online resources covering all chapters. All Chapter 4 resources are available under the keyword **WK3 Schleswig-Holstein-4.** Interactive games practice the material and provide students with immediate feedback. You will also find a printable worksheet that provides Internet activities that lead to a comprehensive online research project.*

Interaktive Spiele

You can use the interactive activities in this chapter

- to practice grammar, vocabulary, and chapter functions
- as homework
- as an assessment option
- as a self-test
- to prepare for the Chapter Test

Internet Aktivitäten

Students will find information about schools in Schleswig-Holstein. They will visit an online shop for school supplies and look at online train schedules.

- To prepare students for the **Arbeitsblatt,** you might want to have them review the **Zeugnis** on p. 111 and the **Wortschatz** on p. 114.
- After completing the **Arbeitsblatt,** have students calculate the grade average of the report card in Activity A. Ask students what grade they would receive in the American system.

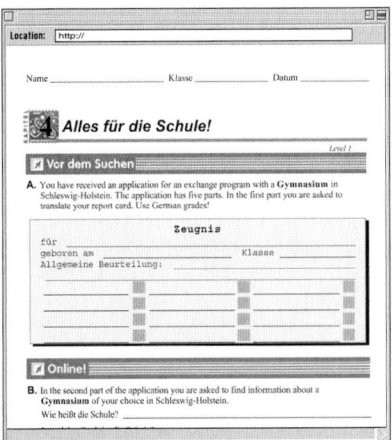

Webprojekt

Have students do a Web search for movie theaters in Germany. They should choose their favorite film from among the films showing in a particular theater. Have students report on the name and location of the theater. Have them provide the title of their favorite film and the day and time it is showing. Encourage students to exchange useful Web sites with their classmates.

Have students document their sources by referencing the names and URLs of all the sites they consulted.

Kapitel 4: Alles für die Schule!
Textbook Listening Activities Scripts

Erste Stufe

9   p. 107

MICHAEL   Sag mal, Peter, wann hast du denn Musik?

PETER   Am Dienstag um 9 Uhr 45, also gleich nach der Pause.

MICHAEL   Und wann hast du Erdkunde?

PETER   Hm … Erdkunde hab ich am Montag um acht — hab ich ja nicht so gern … das ist einfach zu früh. Dann hab ich auch noch Sport am Montag. Aber Sport ist ja mein Lieblingsfach.

MICHAEL   Und du, Katja? Wann hast du Geschichte?

KATJA   Sehr früh am Freitag — Freitag um 8 Uhr.

MICHAEL   Und Mathe?

KATJA   Oh … am Donnerstag um 9 Uhr 30. Das geht ja noch. Der Mathematiklehrer ist sehr sympathisch, und man lernt viel.

MICHAEL   Wie steht's mit Deutsch?

KATJA   Hm … Deutsch hab ich am Dienstag um 10 Uhr 45, direkt vor der Pause. Frau Bach ist die Lehrerin. Ich finde sie ganz nett.

MICHAEL   Du, Beate, wann hast du eigentlich Kunst?

BEATE   Am Mittwoch von 12 Uhr 20 bis 13 Uhr 10.

MICHAEL   Und wann hat Hannes Biologie?

BEATE   Ich glaube, am Freitag nach der Pause.

10   p. 108

SONJA   Du, Klaus, hast du mittwochs viel zu tun?

KLAUS   Um Gottes willen ja! Um 8 Uhr habe ich zuerst Mathe. Dann um 8 Uhr 45 hab ich Deutschstunde beim Herrn Rilke. Direkt nach der kleinen Pause, also um 9 Uhr 45, hab ich Englisch, und danach gleich um 10 Uhr 30 Latein.

Geschichtsunterricht ist um 11 Uhr 30. Erst in der letzten Stunde, von 12 Uhr 20 bis 13 Uhr 05, hab ich Erdkunde. Ich kann dir sagen, mittwochs hab ich den ganzen Tag viel zu tun. Am Ende bin ich ganz schön kaputt.

Zweite Stufe

17   p. 110

RAINER   Welche Fächer hast du denn gern, Katja?

KATJA   Ich? Tja — ich habe Musik und Latein eigentlich sehr gern. Latein macht viel Spaß und Musik ist Spitze!

RAINER   Und Englisch?

KATJA   Nein, Englisch habe ich nicht so gern, aber Deutsch finde ich nicht schlecht. Ja, ich hab Deutsch sehr gern.

RAINER   Und was meinst du ist dein Lieblingsfach?

KATJA   Ich habe so zwei Lieblingsfächer: Geschichte und Erdkunde. Geschichte habe ich am Montag, am Mittwoch und am Donnerstag. Und Erdkunde habe ich am Dienstag. Ich finde den Erdkundelehrer sehr nett. Hast du Erdkunde gern?

RAINER   Es geht. Nicht so sehr, aber Kunst macht Spaß.

KATJA   Wirklich? Das mag ich nicht. Ich finde Kunst langweilig. Na, und Mathe auch. Ich habe Mathe nicht gern, das ist oft schwer.

The following scripts are for the listening activities found in the *Pupil's Edition.* For Student Response Forms, see *Listening Activities,* pages 27–30. To provide students with additional listening practice, see *Listening Activities,* pages 31–34.

One-Stop Planner CD-ROM

For resource information, see the **One-Stop Planner CD-ROM**, Disc 1.

20 p. 111

Schau! Heute hab ich mein Zeugnis bekommen. Meine Schulnoten sind gar nicht mal schlecht! In Mathe habe ich sogar eine Eins! Das ist doch prima, oder? In Physik und Deutsch 'ne Zwei, in Erdkunde eine Drei. Klar, die Drei könnte besser sein! Nur Englisch ist ziemlich schlecht, eine Vier! So was Blödes! Die Note muss das nächste Mal besser werden! Englisch ist aber so langweilig!

Dritte Stufe

25 p. 115

JOHANNA	Hallo, Daniel!
DANIEL	Tag, Johanna!
JOHANNA	Was machst du denn hier?
DANIEL	Ach … Ich brauch ein paar Kulis für die Schule. Entschuldigen Sie? Was kostet dieser Kuli?
VERKÄUFERIN	Zwei Euro.
DANIEL	Und wo sind ihre Taschenrechner?
VERKÄUFERIN	Dort drüben. Auf dem Regal.
JOHANNA	Schau mal, Daniel! Die Taschenrechner sind doch toll, was?
DANIEL	Ja, so handlich und sehr preiswert. Also, ich glaube, das nehme ich dann.
VERKÄUFERIN	Ist das alles für heute?
DANIEL	Ja, danke.

AUSSPRACHE, p. 117

Diktat, p. 117

Martin and Anna are talking about Martin's moped and about their school subjects. First, listen to what they are saying, then write down their conversation.

ANNA	Martin, Tag!
MARTIN	Tag, Anna! Wie findest du mein Moped? Es ist neu.
ANNA	Spitze! Du bist jetzt sechzehn, nicht?
MARTIN	Ja, und jetzt komme ich gern mit dem Moped zur Schule.
ANNA	Welche Fächer hast du am Montag?
MARTIN	Hm, zuerst habe ich immer Deutsch, dann Mathe und Englisch. Nach der Pause habe ich Chemie. Das ist mein Lieblingsfach.
ANNA	Wirklich? In Chemie habe ich nur eine Drei. Mein Lieblingsfach ist Englisch. Da habe ich eine Eins.

Anwendung

7 p. 125

Also, es klingelt in zwei Minuten. Bevor ich es vergesse, hier sind einige Schulsachen, die ihr für die Deutschklasse braucht. Schreibt bitte die folgenden Sachen auf: Zuerst braucht ihr ein gutes Deutsch-Englisches Wörterbuch. Natürlich auch Bleistifte. Und ah, ja mindestens einen Kuli, der funktioniert, ja? Außerdem noch zwei Hefte und ach ja … eine neue, leere Kassette. Ja, ich glaub das ist alles. Also, bis morgen dann. Auf Wiedersehen!

Kapitel 4: Alles für die Schule!
Suggested Lesson Plans 50-Minute Schedule

Day 1

LOCATION OPENER 25 min.
- Background Information, ATE, p. 95A
- Show **Schleswig-Holstein** Video
- Do Viewing and Post-viewing Activities, Video Guide, p. 22
- Do **Schleswig-Holstein** Activity, Interactive CD-ROM

CHAPTER OPENER 20 min.
- Culture Note, ATE, p. 99M
- Thinking Critically, ATE, p. 99M

Wrap-Up 5 min.
- Students respond to questions about Schleswig-Holstein

Homework Options
Internet Aktivitäten, see ATE, p. 99F

Day 2

LOS GEHT'S! 30 min.
Quick Review
- Bell Work, ATE, p. 99O
- Preteaching Vocabulary, ATE, p. 99N
- Play Audio CD for **Los geht's!,** pp. 102–103
- Have students read **Los geht's!,** pp. 102–103
- Teaching Suggestions, Video Guide p. 24
- Teacher Note, ATE, p. 99N
- Show **Los geht's!** Video
- Do Comprehension Activities, p. 104

ERSTE STUFE
Wortschatz, p. 105 15 min.
- Presenting **Wortschatz,** ATE, p. 99O
- Teaching Transparencies 4-1, 4-A
- Do Activity 6, p. 105

Wrap-Up 5 min.
- Students respond to questions about school subjects

Homework Options
Grammatikheft, p. 28, Acts. 1–3
Übungsheft, pp. 37–38, Acts. 1–3

Day 3

ERSTE STUFE
Quick Review 10 min.
- Check homework, Grammatikheft, p. 28, Acts. 1–3

Ein wenig Landeskunde, p. 106 10 min.
- Presenting **Ein wenig Landeskunde,** p. 107
- Do Activity 7, p. 106

So sagt man das!, p. 106 15min.
- Presenting **So sagt man das!,** ATE, p. 99P
- Do Activity 8, p. 106
- Play Audio CD for Activity 9, p. 107

So sagt man das!, p. 107 10 min.
- Presenting **So sagt man das!,** ATE, p. 99P
- Do Activity 11, p. 108

Wrap-Up 5 min.
- Students respond to questions about class schedules

Homework Options
Grammatikheft, p. 29, Acts. 4–6
Übungsheft, p. 39, Acts. 4–5

Day 4

ERSTE STUFE
Quick Review 10 min.
- Check homework, Grammatikheft, p. 29, Acts. 4–6

Project 10 min.
- Have students make clocks to practice 24-hour clock times, ATE, p. 99P

Ein wenig Landeskunde, p. 107 15 min.
- Presenting **Ein wenig Landeskunde,** p. 107
- Play Audio CD for Activity 10, p. 108
- Using the student-made clocks, have students show the times of classes, sports activities, and movies

Grammatik, p. 108 10 min.
- Presenting **Grammatik,** ATE, p. 99Q
- Do Activity 12, p. 108
- Do Activity 13, p. 109

Wrap-Up 5 min.
- Students respond to questions about 24-hour time

Homework Options
Grammatikheft, p. 30, Acts. 7–11
Übungsheft, pp. 39–40, Acts. 6–8

Day 5

ERSTE STUFE
Quick Review 10 min.
- Check homework, Grammatikheft, p. 30, Acts. 7–11

So sagt man das!, p. 109 10 min.
- Presenting **So sagt man das!,** ATE, p. 99Q
- Do Activity 14, p. 109
- Do Activity 15, p. 109

Quiz Review 10 min.
- Do Communicative Activity 4-1, pp. 19–20
- Do **Mehr Grammatikübungen, Erste Stufe**

Quiz 20 min.
- Quiz 4-1A or 4-1B

Homework Options
Pupil's Edition, p. 109, Act.16
Activities for Communication, pp. 129–130, prepare Situation 4-1

Day 6

ZWEITE STUFE
Quick Review 10 min.
- Return and review Quiz 4-1
- Bell work, ATE, p. 99R
- Do Situation 4-1, pp. 129–130

So sagt man das!/ Ein wenig Grammatik, p. 110 15 min.
- Presenting **So sagt man das!,** ATE, p. 99R
- Presenting **Ein wenig Grammatik,** ATE, p. 99R
- Play Audio CD for Activity 17, p. 110
- Do Activities 18 and 19, p. 110

Ein wenig Landeskunde, p. 111 10 min.
- Presenting **Ein wenig Landeskunde,** ATE, p. 99S
- Play Audio CD for Activity 20, p. 111

So sagt man das!, p. 112 10 min.
- Presenting **So sagt man das!,** ATE, p. 99S
- Do Activity 21, p. 112

Wrap-Up 5 min.
- Students respond to questions about liking and disliking school subjects

Homework Options
Grammatikheft, p. 31, Acts. 12–13

One-Stop Planner CD-ROM

For alternative lesson plans by chapter section, to create your own customized plans, or to preview all resources available for this chapter, use the **One-Stop Planner CD-ROM**, Disc 1.

 For additional homework suggestions, see activities accompanied by this symbol throughout the chapter.

Day 7

ZWEITE STUFE

Quick Review 10 min.
- Check homework, Grammatikheft, p. 31, Acts. 12–13
- Do Activity 22, p. 112

Quiz Review 20 min.
- Do Activities 14–16, p. 32, **Grammatikheft**
- Do Activities 9–14, pp. 41–43, **Übungsheft**
- Do Additional Listening Activity 4–4, pp. 32–33

Quiz 20 min.
- Quiz 4-2A or 4-2B

Homework Options
Pupil's Edition, p. 112, Act. 23

Day 8

ZWEITE STUFE

Quick Review 15 min.
- Return and review Quiz 4-2
- Check homework, Pupil's Edition, p. 112, Act. 23

LANDESKUNDE 20 min.
- Pre-viewing Suggestion, Video Guide, p. 24
- Background Information, ATE, p. 99S
- Show **Landeskunde** Video
- Do Activities A and B, p. 113

DRITTE STUFE
- Bell work, ATE, p. 99T

Wortschatz, p. 114 10 min.
- Presenting **Wortschatz**, ATE, p. 99T
- Teaching Transparency 4-B
- Do Activity 24, p. 114

Wrap-Up 5 min.
- Students respond to questions about school supplies and what they cost

Homework Options
Übungsheft, p. 48, Acts. 24–25
Grammatikheft, p. 33, Act. 17

Day 9

DRITTE STUFE

Quick Review 5 min.
- Check homework, Grammatikheft, p. 33, Act. 17

Grammatik, p. 114 15 min.
- Presenting **Grammatik**, ATE, p. 99U
- Play Audio CD for Activity 25, p. 115
- Do Activity 5, Interactive CD-ROM (Disc 1)

So sagt man das!, p. 115 15 min.
- Presenting **So sagt man das!**, ATE, p. 99U
- Teaching Transparency 4-2
- Present **Ein wenig Grammatik**, p. 115
- Present **Ein wenig Landeskunde**, p. 115
- Do Activity 26, p. 116

So sagt man das!, p. 116 10 min.
- Presenting **So sagt man das!**, ATE, p. 99U
- Do Activities 27 and 28, pp. 116–117

Wrap-Up 5 min.
- Students respond to questions about buying school supplies

Homework Options
Pupil's Edition, p. 117, Acts. 29 and 30
Grammatikheft, p. 33–36, Acts. 18–25
Übungsheft, pp. 44–46, Acts. 15–22

Day 10

DRITTE STUFE

Quick Review 10 min.
- Check homework, Übungsheft, pp. 44–46, Acts. 15–22

Quiz Review 20 min.
- Do **Mehr Grammatikübungen, Dritte Stufe**
- Play **Der Preis ist heiß**, ATE, p. 99C

Quiz 20 min.
- Quiz 4-3A or 4-3B

Homework Options
Activities for Communication, p. 88, Realia 4-3: fill out form to sign up for dance classes
Interaktive Spiele, see ATE, p. 99F

Day 11

DRITTE STUFE

Quick Review 10 min.
- Return and review Quiz 4-3
- Check homework, Realia 4-3, p. 88

Aussprache, p. 117 15 min.
- Do **Richtig aussprechen/Richtig lesen**, p. 117
- Do **Richtig schreiben/Diktat**, p. 117

ZUM LESEN 20 min.
- Do Activities 1–7, pp. 118–119

Wrap-Up 5 min.
- Students respond to **Kann ich's wirklich?** questions, p. 126

Homework Options
Übungsheft, p. 47, Act. 23
Pupil's Edition, p. 126, **Kann ich's wirklich?**

Day 12

ANWENDUNG 30 min.

Quick Review
- Check homework, p. 126, **Kann ich's wirklich?**
- Do **Anwendung** Activities, pp. 124–125

Chapter Review 15 min.
- Review chapter functions, vocabulary, and grammar; choose from **Mehr Grammatikübungen**, Grammar Tutor for Students of German, Activities for Communication, Listening Activities, Interactive CD-ROM Tutor, or **Interaktive Spiele**

Wrap-Up 5 min.
- Students respond to questions about sequencing words

Homework Options
Study for Chapter Test

Assessment

Test, Chapter 4 45 min.
- Administer Chapter 4 Test. Select from Testing Program, Alternative Assessment Guide or Test Generator.

Kapitel 4: Alles für die Schule!
Suggested Lesson Plans *90-Minute Block Schedule*

Block 1

LOCATION OPENER 25 min.
- Background Information, ATE, p. 95A
- Show **Schleswig-Holstein** Video
- Do Viewing and Post-viewing Activities, Video Guide, p. 22
- Do **Schleswig-Holstein** Activity, Interactive CD-ROM
- Do **Internet Aktivitäten**, at WK3 Schleswig-Holstein

CHAPTER OPENER 20 min.
- Culture Note, ATE, p. 99M
- Thinking Critically, ATE, p. 99M

LOS GEHT'S! 30 min.
- Preteaching Vocabulary, ATE, p. 99N
- Play Audio CD for **Los geht's!**, pp. 102–103
- Have students read **Los geht's!**, pp. 102–103
- Teaching Suggestions, Video Guide, p. 24
- Teacher Note, ATE, p. 99N
- Show **Los geht's!** Video
- Do Comprehension Activities, p. 104

ERSTE STUFE
Wortschatz, p. 105 10 min.
- Presenting **Wortschatz**, ATE, p. 99O
- Teaching Transparencies 4-1, 4-A
- Do Activity 6, p. 105

Wrap-Up 5 min.
- Students respond to questions about school subjects

Homework Options
Grammatikheft, p. 28, Acts. 1–3
Übungsheft, p. 37–38, Acts. 1–3

Block 2

ERSTE STUFE
Quick Review 10 min.
- Check homework, Grammatikheft, p. 28, Acts. 1–3

Ein wenig Landeskunde, p. 106 10 min.
- Present **Ein wenig Landeskunde**, p. 106
- Do Activity 7, p. 106

So sagt man das!, p. 106 15 min.
- Presenting **So sagt man das!**, ATE, p. 99P
- Do Activity 8, p. 106
- Play Audio CD for Activity 9, p. 107

So sagt man das!, p. 107 10 min.
- Presenting **So sagt man das!**, ATE, p. 99P
- Do Activity 11, p. 108

Project 10 min.
- Have students make clocks to practice 24-hour clock times, ATE, p. 99P

Ein wenig Landeskunde, p. 107 20 min.
- Present **Ein wenig Landeskunde**, p. 107
- Play Audio CD for Activity 10, p. 108
- Using the student-made clocks, have students show the times of classes, sports activities, and movies

Grammatik, p. 108 10 min.
- Presenting **Grammatik**, ATE, p. 99Q
- Do Activity 12, p. 108
- Do Activity 13, p. 109

Wrap-Up 5 min.
- Students respond to questions about 24-hour time

Homework Options
Pupil's Edition, p. 109, Act. 16
Grammatikheft, pp. 29–30, Acts. 4–11
Übungsheft, pp. 39–40, Acts. 4–8

Block 3

ERSTE STUFE
Quick Review 10 min.
- Check homework, Grammatikheft, pp. 29–30, Acts. 4–11

So sagt man das!, p. 109 15 min.
- Presenting **So sagt man das!**, ATE, p. 99Q
- Do Activity 14, p. 109
- Do Activity 15, p. 109

Quiz Review 15 min.
- Do Communicative Activity 4–1, pp. 19–20
- Do **Mehr Grammatikübungen, Erste Stufe**

Quiz 20 min.
- Quiz 4-1A or 4-1B

ZWEITE STUFE
So sagt man das!/ Ein wenig Grammatik, p. 110 15 min.
- Presenting **So sagt man das!, / Ein wenig Grammatik**, ATE, p. 99R
- Play Audio CD for Activity 17, p. 110
- Do Activities 18 and 19, p. 110

Ein wenig Landeskunde, p. 111 10 min.
- Presenting **Ein wenig Landeskunde**, ATE, p. 99S
- Play Audio CD for Activity 20, p. 111

Wrap-Up 5 min.
- Students respond to questions about liking and disliking school subjects

Homework Options
Grammatikheft, pp. 31–32, Acts. 12–16
Mehr Grammatikübungen, Zweite Stufe

One-Stop Planner CD-ROM

For alternative lesson plans by chapter section, to create your own customized plans, or to preview all resources available for this chapter, use the **One-Stop Planner CD-ROM**, Disc 1.

 For additional homework suggestions, see activities accompanied by this symbol throughout the chapter.

Block 4

ZWEITE STUFE

Quick Review 15 min.
- Return and review Quiz 4-1
- Check homework, Grammatikheft, pp. 31–32, Acts. 12–16

So sagt man das!, p. 112 15 min.
- Presenting **So sagt man das!**, ATE, p. 99S
- Do Activity 21, p. 112
- Do Activity 22, p. 112

Quiz Review 20 min.
- Do Additional Listening Activity 4–4, pp. 32–33
- Do Activities 9–14, pp. 41–43, Übungsheft
- Do Activity 4, Interactive CD-ROM

Quiz 20 min.
- Quiz 4-2A or 4-2B

LANDESKUNDE 20 min.
- Pre-viewing Suggestion, Video Guide, p. 24
- Background Information, ATE, p. 99S
- Show **Landeskunde** Video
- Do Activities A and B, p. 113

Homework Options
Pupil's Edition, p. 112, Act. 23
Übungsheft, p. 48, Acts. 24–25
Activities for Communication, p. 88, Realia 4-3, fill out form to sign up for dance classes

Block 5

DRITTE STUFE

Quick Review 15 min.
- Return and review Quiz 4-2
- Bell work, ATE, p. 99T
- Check homework, Realia 4-3, p. 88

Wortschatz, p. 114 10 min.
- Presenting **Wortschatz**, ATE, p. 99T
- Teaching Transparency 4-B
- Do Activity 24, p. 114

Grammatik, p. 114 20 min.
- Presenting **Grammatik**, ATE, p. 99U
- Play Audio CD for Activity 25, p. 115
- Do Activity 5, Interactive CD-ROM

So sagt man das!, p. 115 20 min.
- Presenting **So sagt man das!**, ATE, p. 99U
- Teaching Transparency 4-2
- Do Activities 19 and 20, p. 34, Grammatikheft
- Present **Ein wenig Grammatik**, p. 115
- Present **Ein wenig Landeskunde**, p. 115
- Do Activity 26, p. 116

So sagt man das!, p. 116 20 min.
- Presenting **So sagt man das!**, ATE, p. 99U
- Do Activity 27, p. 116
- Do Activity 6, Interactive CD-ROM
- Do Activities 29 and 30, p. 117

Wrap-Up 5 min.
- Students respond to questions about buying school supplies

Homework Options
Pupil's Edition, p. 117, Act. 28
Grammatikheft, p. 33, Acts. 17–18; pp. 35–36, Acts. 21–25
Übungsheft, pp. 44–46, Acts. 15–22

Block 6

DRITTE STUFE

Quick Review 10 min.
- Check homework, Übungsheft, pp. 44–46, Acts. 15–22

Quiz Review 20 min.
- Do **Mehr Grammatikübungen, Dritte Stufe**
- Play **Der Preis ist heiß**, ATE, p. 99C

Quiz 20 min.
- Quiz 4-3A or 4-3B

Aussprache, p. 117 15 min.
- Do **Richtig aussprechen/ Richtig lesen**, p. 117
- Do **Richtig schreiben/Diktat**, p. 117

ZUM LESEN 20 min.
- Do Activities 1–7, pp. 118–119

Wrap-Up 5 min.
- Students respond to **Kann ich's wirklich?** questions, p. 126

Homework Options
Übungsheft, p. 47, Act. 23
Pupil's Edition, p. 126, **Kann ich's wirklich?**
Interaktive Spiele, see ATE, p. 99F

Block 7

ANWENDUNG 30 min.
Quick Review
- Return and review Quiz 4-3
- Check homework, p. 126, **Kann ich's wirklich?**
- Video Wrap-up, ATE, p. 99X
- Do **Anwendung** Activities, pp. 124–125

Chapter Review 15 min.
- Review chapter functions, vocabulary, and grammar; choose from **Mehr Grammatikübungen**, Grammar Tutor for Students of German, Activities for Communication, Listening Activities, Interactive CD-ROM Tutor, or **Interaktive Spiele**

Test, Chapter 4 45 min.
- Administer Chapter 4 Test. Select from Testing Program, Alternative Assessment Guide or Test Generator.

Kapitel 4: Alles für die Schule!
Teaching Suggestions, pages 100–127

PAGES 100–101

CHAPTER OPENER

Pacing Tips

In the **Erste Stufe** the verb **haben** is introduced. The German school day and 24-hour time are also discussed. The German grading system is introduced in the **Zweite Stufe,** along with the function of 'expressing likes, dislikes, and favorites' using the prefix **Lieblings-.** The **Dritte Stufe** focuses on prices, currency, and noun plurals. Since the **Erste Stufe** is five pages long and introduces the verb **haben,** you will probably want to spend more time on the **Erste Stufe** than on the **Zweite Stufe** or the **Dritte Stufe.** For Lesson Plans and timing suggestions, see pages 99I–99L.

Meeting the Standards
Communication
- Talking about class schedules, p. 106
- Using a schedule to talk about time, p. 107
- Sequencing events, p. 109
- Expressing likes, dislikes, and favorites, p. 110
- Responding to good news and bad news, p. 112
- Talking about prices, p. 115
- Pointing things out, p. 116

Cultures
- **Ein wenig Landeskunde,** p. 106
- **Ein wenig Landeskunde,** p. 107
- **Ein wenig Landeskunde,** p. 111
- **Landeskunde,** p. 113
- Teacher Note, p. 99N
- Culture Notes, p. 99O
- Culture Note, p. 99Q
- Culture Note, p. 99S
- Culture Notes, p. 99U

Connections
- Multicultural Connection, p. 99O
- Language Note, p. 99U
- Geography Connection, p. 99W
- Teacher Note, p. 99W

Comparisons
- Language-to-Language, p. 99Q
- Thinking Critically, p. 99S
- Language Note, p. 99U
- Language Note, p. 99V
- Thinking Critically, p. 99W

For resource information, see the **One-Stop Planner CD-ROM,** Disc 1.

Communities
- Thinking Critically, p. 99M
- Culture Note, p. 99M
- Teaching Suggestions, p. 99Q
- Background Information, p. 99T
- Career Path, p. 99T

Cultures and Communities

Thinking Critically

Drawing Inferences Ask students if they can think of some reasons why many German students ride their bikes to school. (Examples: shorter distances between home and school, few school buses, cost of public transportation, environmental awareness) Have the students think about what would happen if school were several miles from their homes and there were no school buses. How would they get to school? Could they use any public transportation? Discuss the students' responses with them.

Culture Note

Mention to your class that German students frequently ride their bikes to school. Books, folders, and other supplies have to be taken to and from school each day because German schools do not have lockers and students cannot leave any belongings in their classrooms.

Chapter Sequence

Los geht's! . . . . .p. 102

Erste Stufe . . . . .p. 105

Zweite Stufe . . . . .p. 110

Landeskunde . . . . .p. 113

Dritte Stufe . . . . .p. 114

Zum Lesen . . . . .p. 118

Mehr Grammatikübungen . . . . .p. 120

Anwendung . . . . .p. 124

Kann ich's wirklich? . . . . .p. 126

Wortschatz . . . . .p. 127

LOS GEHT'S!

Teaching Resources
pp. 102–104

PRINT
▸ Lesson Planner, p. 17
▸ Video Guide, pp. 23–24, 26
▸ Übungsheft, p. 37

MEDIA
▸ One-Stop Planner
▸ Video Program
  Los geht's!
  Videocassette 2, 05:20–09:22
  Videocassette 5 (captioned version),
  15:16–19:20
  Fortsetzung
  Videocassette 2, 09:24–12:10
  Videocassette 5 (captioned version),
  19:22–22:08
▸ Audio Compact Discs, CD4, Trs. 1–2
▸ **Los geht's!** Transparencies

PAGES 102–103

Los gehts! Transparencies

Preteaching Vocabulary

Identifying Keywords

Start by asking students to guess the context of
Los geht's! (being at school; shopping for school
supplies). Then have students use the German
they know and the context of the situation to
identify key words and phrases that tell what is
happening. Students should first look for words
that are related to school (**Mathe; Deutsch;
Pause;** etc.). Can students identify the phrase
that indicates who makes better grades in math?

2 (**Na ja, du bist gut in Mathe.**) Then have
students list keywords in the conversation that
occurs at the **Schreibwarenladen.** Which of the
keywords are cognates? Which of the keywords
do they already know?

Fortsetzung

You may choose
to continue with the
Fortsetzung of *Lars kauft
Schulsachen* now or wait
until later in the chapter. For a synopsis of the **Los
geht's!** and **Fortsetzung** episodes, see p. 99E.

STANDARDS: 4.2

Teaching Suggestions

- Ask students to list all the common school supplies
  that they need, especially at the beginning of a new
  school year. Where are they most likely to buy
  these supplies?

- To get students into the text, first do the prereading
  activity at the top of p. 102. Have students scan the
  dialogue of **Los geht's!** to look for cognates and any
  other words they might recognize. Write these
  words on the board as students call them out. What
  are they able to tell you from this brief glance about
  what might be happening in these scenes?

Cultures and Communities

Teacher Note

You may want to point out to students that the
sales tax is already included in the price in Germany. This is why the salesperson does not add
tax to the 16 euros Lars is paying for his calculator.

PAGE 104

Using the Captioned Video

 As an alternative to reading the conversations in the book, you might want to
show the captioned version of *Lars kauft
Schulsachen* available on Videocassette 5.

Comprehension Check

Cooperative Learning

Put students in groups of four. Ask them to
choose a discussion leader, a recorder, a
proofreader (proofreads group's answers before
they are turned in), and an announcer. Give students a specific amount of time in which to
complete Activities 1–5. Walk around the room
monitoring group work, and help students if
necessary. At the end of the activity, call on each
group announcer to read his or her group's
results. You can decide whether or not to collect
their work for a grade at the end of the activity.

Thinking Critically

Drawing Inferences Have students compare
what they know about the beginning of the
German school year with their own experiences
in the United States. Does it seem similar or different? Does the similarity surprise them?

ERSTE STUFE

Teaching Resources
pp. 105–109

PRINT

▸ Lesson Planner, p. 18
▸ TPR Storytelling Book, pp. 13, 16
▸ Listening Activities, pp. 27, 31–32
▸ Activities for Communication, pp. 19–20, 86, 89, 129–130
▸ Grammatikheft, pp. 28–30
▸ Grammar Tutor for Students of German, Chapter 4
▸ Übungsheft, pp. 38–40
▸ Testing Program, pp. 79–82
▸ Alternative Assessment Guide, p. 35
▸ Student Make-Up Assignments, Chapter 4

MEDIA

▸ One-Stop Planner
▸ Audio Compact Discs, CD4, Trs. 3–4, 18, 24–26
▸ Teaching Transparencies
  Situation 4-1
  Vocabulary 4-A
  Mehr Grammatikübungen Answers
  Grammatikheft Answers
▸ Interactive CD-ROM Tutor, Disc 1

PAGE 105

Bell Work
Make an overhead transparency of Sina's class schedule and show it at the beginning of class. Have students make a list of all the differences between Sina's schedule and their own.

6 Teaching Suggestion
Ask students what surprises them most about the schedule above Activity 6. (Examples: different classes each day, length of school days, two foreign languages) Have students make their own **Stundenplan** on 3 × 5 cards.

Connections and Comparisons

Multicultural Connection
The students in this chapter don't have school on Saturdays, but many students do in different parts of Germany. Ask students if they know of other countries where classes are sometimes held on Saturdays. (Examples: Japan, France)

Cultures and Communities

Thinking Critically
Drawing Inferences Tell students that they are looking at a typical **Stundenplan**. Ask them if they can determine which of the classes are considered **Hauptfächer** (*major subjects*) and which ones are **Nebenfächer** (*minor subjects*).

Culture Note
Religion is part of the public school curriculum in Germany; there is no separation between church and state. Students join the class that represents their denomination (mostly Protestant or Catholic). For any other denomination or religion, such as Islam, there are usually special classes. With parental consent or upon reaching the age of 14, students may instead choose to study ethics, which is taught similarly to Social Studies in the United States. Students learn about philosophy and the religions practiced around the world.

PAGE 106

Cultures and Communities

Culture Note
• Often, a grade level will be broken down into sections called **Parallelklassen**. For example, if there are 120 ninth-grade students, there might be 4 ninth-grade classes: 9a, 9b, 9c, and 9d. Each student is assigned to one of those classes, and each class has a **Klassenlehrer** (*homeroom teacher*). This teacher teaches at least one of the subjects, serves as liaison with parents, makes class announcements, and so on.

• Most classes are taught in the students' main classroom, and the teachers move from one class to the next. Only science classes, art, music, home economics, and physical education take place in specially equipped rooms.

• Students can usually expect homework, since their classes don't meet daily. After students get home from school, they usually spend the early afternoon doing their homework. Extracurricular activities generally start after 4:00 P.M. and can last until 8:00 or 9:00 P.M. depending on the types of activities in which students are involved.

Teaching Suggestion

7 Have students look back at the schedule they made for the motivating activity of this **Stufe** and use the back side for their schedule in German. Have one student write his or her schedule on the board. You can use this schedule to present "Talking about class schedules" in the **So sagt man das!** box.

PRESENTING: So sagt man das!

Personalize this function box by using the **Stundenplan** on the board and incorporating the expressions to be taught.

♞ Game

Create a **Kreuzworträtsel** (*crossword puzzle*) similar to the sample below using subjects in German.

1. Wir lesen *Tom Sawyer.*

2. Wir lernen a + b = c.

3. Wir lernen etwas über H2O und CO2.

4. Wir lernen etwas über Mozart und Beethoven.

5. Wir lernen etwas über Picasso und Ansel Adams.

6. Wir lernen etwas über England, Kanada, Deutschland und China.

```
        4.        1.        5.
    2. M A T H E M A T I K
       U         N         U
       S         G         N
       I         L         S
       K         I         T
                 S      6. E
              3. C H E M I E
                 H         R
                           D
                           K
                           U
                           N
                           D
                           E
```

For Additional Practice

9 As a second listening activity, let students add the names of the students that Michael is addressing.

Building on Previous Skills

Review the numbers 0–60 with simple math problems. Have a handout with at least 10 problems and let students work in pairs. Each student gets to read five math problems aloud, and then other students take turns answering the problems. This will prepare students for the **So sagt man das!** function "Using a schedule to talk about time."

PRESENTING: So sagt man das!

Make a transparency of the **Stundenplan** on p. 105. Using the expressions in the function box "Using a schedule to talk about time," talk about when Alex and Sina have their classes.

Teaching Suggestions

Have students make a clock to practice telling 24-hour time in German. They will each need two paper plates, brass fasteners, scissors, felt-tip markers, a pencil, a hole-puncher, and a ruler. After students receive supplies, have them draw a 24-hour clock on one paper plate. The *13* goes underneath the *1* but is just about half the size. To make the two hands of the clock, students use the second paper plate and cut two strips for the hour and second hands. Next, students punch a hole in the center of the clock and in the end of each hand of the clock and secure the hands with a brass fastener. The clocks will be used in activities to come.

Connections and Comparisons

Teaching Suggestion

- Have students practice telling time using the **Stundenplan** on p. 105, a TV program guide, and, if available, a German TV program guide or train schedule.

- Have students look at the **Bochum-München** train schedule and see if they can figure out the meaning of 1-2-3-4-5-6-7 under **Verkehrstage**. (days of the week)

Language-to-Language

Your students may want to know that Europeans often use a 24-hour system of telling time. Ask them what US organizations also use a 24-hour clock. (Example: the military)

PAGE 108

Communication for All Students

For Additional Practice

10 After completing the listening activity, have students work in pairs creating sentences that give times for different classes. One student reads the sentence he or she wrote down. (Example: **Um 8 Uhr hat er Mathe.**) The other student tries to show that time on his or her clock. Tell students to take turns reading their sentences from Activity 10 and showing time on the clocks.

Teacher Note

11 You can use the shortened form **um** (zehn) until noon. But you would say **um 13 Uhr**, not **um 13**.

PRESENTING: Grammatik

The verb haben Review the regular verb endings from previous chapters. (Example: **lernen**) Then introduce **haben** and its endings. Have students identify the two forms that do not conform to regular conjugation. (**hast, hat**)

Cultures and Communities

Culture Note

12 Unless bad weather prohibits it, students are asked to go outside during the breaks and use this time to socialize with others. Students must remain on the school grounds. Older students (grade varies by school) may leave the schoolyard during the breaks. At age 18 students may leave whenever they wish.

Teaching Suggestion

12 In pairs, have students read the four short conversations aloud.

PAGE 109

Portfolio Assessment

13 You might want to suggest this activity as an oral portfolio item for your students. See *Alternative Assessment Guide*, p. 21.

PRESENTING: So sagt man das!

Before introducing the new German words, ask students to name sequencing words they would typically use in English. Do they know what these words are called? (adverbs and prepositions) Tell students that German uses the same kinds of words to make the language flow more naturally. Using the schedule of one of the students in class, tell the rest the order of that student's schedule for a particular day using the sequencing words presented.

Teaching Suggestions

- Recommend that students keep a separate list of sequencing words. Tell them that the list will be useful for written and oral portfolio work as well as for the **Notizbuch** and process writing activities.

- If you feel your students can handle more expressions of time and frequency, you might want to introduce other adverbs such as **morgens, heute, nun** (expressions of time), **niemals, immer, oft, manchmal** (expressions of frequency).

Communication for All Students

Challenge

15 In pairs, have students create another conversation that deals with someone's schedule but uses a different arrangement of subjects and times. Have students cut their dialogues into sentence strips. Have groups exchange their strip stories and recreate the conversation.

Teaching Suggestion

16 Call on several students to read their short paragraphs aloud in class. This will give students extra speaking practice without the stress of having to speak spontaneously.

Reteaching
Talking about schedules

Ask students to look at the **Stundenplan** they made in Activity 7. Go around the classroom asking students questions using the expressions from the **Wortschatz** and **So sagt man das!** boxes of this **Stufe**.

Teaching Suggestion

Hand out the clocks that students made earlier in this **Stufe** and ask them to set the clocks as you call out different times. (Example: **11 Uhr 45, 23 Uhr 15**, and so on.)

Communication for All Students

Kinesthetic Learners

In pairs, have students look at the **Stundenplan** on p. 105. Have them choose three **Fächer** and invent gestures for them. Pairs should then present their gestures to the class, who will guess the **Fach**.

Assess

▸ Testing Program, pp. 79–82
  Quiz 4-1A, Quiz 4-1B
  Audio CD4, Tr. 18

▸ Student Make-Up Assignments, Chapter 4, Alternative Quiz

▸ Alternative Assessment Guide, p. 35

Deutsch	8.05
Geschichte	8.55
Latein	9.45
Sport	10.30

ZWEITE STUFE

Teaching Resources
pp. 110–113

PRINT
▸ Lesson Planner, p. 19
▸ TPR Storytelling Book, pp. 14, 16
▸ Listening Activities, pp. 28, 32–33
▸ Activities for Communication, pp. 21–22, 87, 129–130
▸ Grammatikheft, pp. 31–32
▸ Grammar Tutor for Students of German, Chapter 4
▸ Übungsheft, pp. 41–43
▸ Testing Program, pp. 83–86
▸ Alternative Assessment Guide, p. 35
▸ Student Make-Up Assignments, Chapter 4

MEDIA
▸ One-Stop Planner
▸ Audio Compact Discs, CD4, Trs. 5–6, 19, 27
▸ Teaching Transparencies
  Mehr Grammatikübungen Answers
  Grammatikheft Answers
▸ Interactive CD-ROM Tutor, Disc 1

PAGE 110

Bell Work

Ask the students to think about the grading system used in American schools. What do the grades A, B, C, D, and F stand for? Can they be expressed in alternate ways? How do students express feelings toward each grade? What do they say when they earn an A, B, C, and so on?

PRESENTING: So sagt man das!/Ein wenig Grammatik

- Before teaching the expressions in **So sagt man das!**, go around the class and ask students questions such as **Hast du Mathe gern? Welches Fach hast du nicht gern?**

- **Lieblings-** Tell your class about your own favorite activities and show them pictures if possible. Examples:
Ich habe Deutsch gern. Hier ist mein Lieblingsbuch. Ich spiele gern Tennis.

PAGE 111

PRESENTING: Ein wenig Landeskunde

On the chalkboard write the letter symbols used in the American grading system and the number symbols used in the German grading system. Ask students to compare the systems. Here is an approximation:

$1 = A^+$ $4 = D^+ \rightarrow C$

$2 = B^+ \rightarrow A$ $5 = D^- \rightarrow D$

$3 = C^+ \rightarrow B$ $6 = F$

Cultures and Communities

Culture Note   If students receive a 5 or 6 in a main subject (**Hauptfach**), they may have to repeat a grade. That is called **sitzen bleiben**. Therefore, school grades are very important. If students are held back more than once, they may be expelled from that school.

PAGE 112

PRESENTING: So sagt man das!

Ask two students, one girl and one boy, to read Sina's and Alex's lines. After each line, ask students what each response could mean and what it is similar to in English.

PAGE 113

LANDESKUNDE

Teaching Resources
p. 113

PRINT
▶ Video Guide, pp. 23–24, 26–27
▶ Übungsheft, p. 48

MEDIA
▶ One-Stop Planner
▶ Video Program
   Videocassette 2, 12:49–19:06
▶ Audio Compact Discs, CD4, Trs. 7–12
▶ Interactive CD-ROM Tutor, Disc 1

Teaching Suggestion

You might want to introduce these expressions before students watch this video segment or listen to the recording:

die Arbeitslehre	*vocational training*
zurechtkommen	*to manage, to do all right with*
mich basier	(colloquial) *I concentrate on something*
der Leistungskurs	*concentration on a specific subject in the* **Oberstufe** *of a* **Gymnasium**

Connections and Comparisons

Thinking Critically

Drawing Inferences Ask students to review Lugana's statement. After saying that she is Greek, why does she add "**wurde hier geboren**"? Remind students of what they learned about **Arbeitsemigranten** in the **Landeskunde** section of Chapter 3 to help them find an answer. (Lugana's family probably came to Germany in the 1960s as some of the many foreign workers who emigrated at that time. Her family and many other families decided not to return to their homeland and are still living in Germany.)

Comparing and Contrasting Ask students to review Björn's statement. He talks about his interest in his **Informatik** class. What would be the equivalent of this class in the American school system?(computer science class)

Cultures and Communities

Background Information

- Toward the end of the fourth year at the **Grundschule** *(elementary school)*, or in many states after the completion of the **Orientierungsstufe,** students, parents, and teachers come together to decide which of the three secondary schools the child should enter. This decision is based largely on academic performance. Although it is possible to change schools later, this is a very important decision in that it, to some extent, predetermines the future career path of the student.

- You might want to point out to your students that it is important for German **Gymnasiasten** planning to go to a university to get excellent grades in school. Most universities are overcrowded, which means that only a minimum number of students can be accepted, especially in majors such as medicine, dentistry, or pharmacy. Only the students with the best grades are accepted in overcrowded departments.

Career Path

Ask students to form small groups and brainstorm scenarios in which American teachers would need to know German. (Suggestion: Imagine you teach at an international school in Germany or at an American school for foreign students.)

Communication for All Students

Kinesthetic Learners

In pairs, have students give each other three easy tasks that can be done in the classroom. Students should use sequencing words to combine the tasks. (Example: **Zuerst gehst du zur Tafel, danach schreibst du deinen Namen, zuletzt setzt du dich.**)

Assess

▶ Testing Program, pp. 83–86
  Quiz 4–2A, Quiz 4–2B
  Audio CD4, Tr. 19

▶ Student Make-Up Assignments
  Chapter 4, Alternative Quiz

▶ Alternative Assessment Guide, p. 35

Teaching Resources
pp. 114–117

PRINT
▶ Lesson Planner, p. 20
▶ TPR Storytelling Book, pp. 15, 16
▶ Listening Activities, pp. 29, 33–34
▶ Activities for Communication, pp. 23–24, 88, 129–130
▶ Grammatikheft, pp. 33–36
▶ Grammar Tutor for Students of German, Chapter 4
▶ Übungsheft, pp. 44–46
▶ Testing Program, pp. 87–90
▶ Alternative Assessment Guide, p. 35
▶ Student Make-Up Assignments, Chapter 4

MEDIA
▶ One-Stop Planner
▶ Audio Compact Discs, CD4, Trs. 13–16, 20, 28–29
▶ Teaching Transparencies
  Situation 4-2
  Vocabulary 4-B
  Mehr Grammatikübungen Answers
  Grammatikheft Answers
▶ Interactive CD-ROM Tutor, Disc 1

PAGE 114

Teaching Suggestion

Bell Work
  Stand by the door and hand each student a strip of paper with one of the expressions from **Ein wenig Grammatik** on p. 110 (**Lieblingsfilm, Lieblings …**). Once the class is underway, ask each student what his or her "Lieblingsetwas" is. (Example: **Klaus, was ist dein Lieblingsetwas? Mein Lieblingsbuch ist …!**)

PRESENTING: Wortschatz

If possible, bring all eight items represented in the **Wortschatz** to class. Put them on a table in the front of the room. Make eight large index cards and write the name and price for each item on them. Go over the **Wortschatz** several times by pointing to each item and saying the appropriate German word. When you feel students are ready, ask questions such as: **Was kostet €20? Was kostet sehr viel? Was kostet nicht viel?**

PRESENTING: Grammatik

Noun plurals Ask students how plurals are formed in English. The formation of plurals in German often presents a problem for students, even among native Germans. Although there are always exceptions to the rule, there are several patterns students can use to decrease the time of memorization considerably. Refer students to the chart on p. R17 in the back of their books.

Communication for All Students

Visual Learners
Refer students to the German-English vocabulary pages at the end of the book (pp. R29–R45). Write 10 to 15 additional German nouns on the board and have students find the plural of each. Demonstrate the first noun. (Example: **das Wörterbuch, die Wörterbücher**)

Thinking Critically
Drawing Inferences Give these two sentences as samples and ask students how they might be able to tell whether they are looking at a singular or plural noun. **Der Vater spielt Fußball. Die Väter spielen Fußball.** Students should remember that **Vater** is masculine (**der**) and that -t is a singular verb ending, while -en is a plural verb ending. Ask students what changes occurred in the plural of **Vater.** (umlaut added; plural article **die**)

PAGE 115

PRESENTING: So sagt man das!

Use hand gestures (thumbs up/thumbs down) along with newspaper ads to teach **teuer, billig,** and **preiswert.** Use items such as school supplies that students are familiar with and would know the approximate prices of.

PRESENTING: Ein wenig Grammatik

Pronouns Read aloud simple sentences using the vocabulary introduced in the **Wortschatz** on p. 114. (Examples: **Das Heft kostet € 0,60** (read: **60 Cent**). **Die Schultasche ist teuer.**) Then ask questions about these statements (**Ist die Schultasche teuer?**), and have students answer using pronouns in place of the proper nouns (**Ja, sie ist teuer.**)

Cultures and Communities

 Culture Note
Euro bills increase in size according to the value of the bill. They are illustrated with architectural elements and bridges. As for euro coins, one side features a common European theme, and the other side contains a national symbol surrounded by the European Union's twelve stars. In 2002, all national currencies of participating countries were replaced by the euro.

Connections and Comparisons

Language Note
Ask students to suggest slang terms we use in English to refer to money. (Examples: dough, bucks) You might want to give them some terms used in the German-speaking world to refer to money.
Examples:
Ich hab keine **Kohle** mehr.
Meine **Piepen/Mäuse** sind alle.
Wie viel **Schotter/Kies** schaufelt er im Monat?
Diese Kutsche hat dich wohl 'nen Haufen **Knete** gekostet, was?
Das sind aber 'ne Menge **Moneten!**
Hast du drei **Groschen/Gulden** fürs Telefon?
Mensch, ich hab nicht so viel **Moos** dabei!
Die Welt dreht sich um die **Marie.**
Mensch, sag mal, wie viel Tonnen **Mehl** verdient der wohl im Jahr?

 **Game**

Play the game **Der Preis ist heiß.** See page 99C for the procedure.

PAGE 116

PRESENTING: So sagt man das!

Place a variety of school supplies around the room. Point them out to students using the expressions introduced in the **So sagt man das!** function box.

Cultures and Communities

 Culture Note
A **Schreibwarenladen** (*stationery shop*) is a small shop that carries mostly school supplies, some toys and games, wrapping paper, and cards. The owner of the store is the **Schreibwarenhändler** (-in).

Communication for All Students

For Additional Practice

- Have your students place various school supplies around the room as if they were being displayed in a store. Decide where the front and the back of the store will be. Set up a counter where the salesperson will give information. Have students take turns playing the role of salesperson and customer. The customer will ask where different items are, and the salesperson will say where they are depending on their location in the room.

- Have students "shop" in the **Schreibwarenladen.** They should each buy five different school items. Have them make a list of what they want beforehand. Working in pairs, have them make a map of the store and decide where various supplies are located and where the **Verkäufer(in)** will stand. One student asks the **Verkäufer(in)** where the various items can be found; then the **Verkäufer(in)** helps his or her partner find the items. Remind students to be polite. Have them switch roles.

PRESENTING: Aussprache

- **äu/eu** and **au**   You may want to use the following pairs of words to help students learn the **äu/eu** and **au** sounds: loiter/**Leute,** annoy/**Mäuse,** house/**Haus.**

- final **b, d,** and **g**   Tell students to put their hands in front of their mouths as they pronounce the sample words illustrating these sounds. If they pronounce them correctly, they should feel a small burst of air as the sound is released.

Connections and Comparisons

Language Note

In the word **Liebling** the final **b** in **Lieb-** is pronounced as /p/. The final **g** in **-ling,** however, is not pronounced as /k/ but sounds similar to the *-ing* ending in English.

Teaching Suggestion

Have students number each sentence of the **Diktat** as they write down what they hear. Once finished, call on students to write one sentence each on the board. Then call on those same students to read their sentences aloud. The class can make corrections together.

Game

Play the game **Assoziationsfeld.** See page 99C for the procedure.

Communication for All Students

Visual Learners

Collect examples of all the school supplies discussed in this chapter and place them around the room. In pairs, have students make up sentences that include one or more of the items. (Examples: **Wo ist der Kuli?; Das Heft kostet 1 Euro.**)

Assess

▸ Testing Program, pp. 87–90
  Quiz 4-3A, Quiz 4-3B
  Audio CD4, Tr. 20

▸ Student Make-Up Assignments
  Chapter 4, Alternative Quiz

▸ Alternative Assessment Guide, p. 35

ZUM LESEN

Teaching Resources
pp. 118–119

PRINT
▸ Lesson Planner, p. 21
▸ Übungsheft, p. 47
▸ Reading Strategies and Skills, Chapter 4
▸ Lies mit mir! 1, Chapter 4

MEDIA
▸ One-Stop Planner

Prereading
Finding Information

Ask students if they are having trouble in any of their classes or perhaps would like to get some help to catch up on a subject. How would they go about looking for help in their 'problem' subject?

Teacher Note

Activities 1 and 2 are prereading activities.

Teaching Suggestion

Before you begin the prereading activities, put the following compound words on the board and ask students for their meaning: **Brieffreund, Deutschbuch, Schreibwarenladen.** Tell students that compounds always take the article of the last noun. Using this information, ask students to tell you what article goes with each of the three nouns on the board.

Communication for All Students

Teacher Note

Compound nouns often give students the impression that German has many long words and, therefore, must be difficult. Show students that they can use skills such as recognizing cognates and drawing inferences to make compound words less intimidating. Use one of the compound words listed above to illustrate this point. (**Schreib/waren/laden** or **Brief/freund**)

Reading
Skimming and Scanning

Draw three columns with the following headings on the board: **Unterricht; Institut Rosenberg; Schulverbund Passau.** Ask students to skim the readings and come up to the board to write the cognates and other words they recognize under each column head. Quickly go over the three lists. Then proceed with Activities 3–5.

Communication for All Students

A Slower Pace

Ask students to look at each of the small ads and determine what type of tutoring is offered. Allow students to give the answers in English or German. (1. singing 2. math, physics, chemistry 3. piano, keyboard 4. German 5. English)

Teaching Suggestion

Before having students read the ad for the **Institut Rosenberg,** you might want to introduce the following additional vocabulary:

Internat *boarding school*
Abitur *school graduation examination that must be passed before students qualify for admission to a university*
vorbereiten *to prepare*
eidgenössisch *federal, referring to Switzerland*
Maturitätsprüfung *term used for* **Abitur** *in Switzerland and Austria*

gewährleistet *guaranteed*
überwacht *supervised*

Connections and Comparisons

Thinking Critically

Analyzing Can students differentiate among the eight schools listed in this reading? What grade levels are taught at each of the schools?

Analyzing What does the **Institut Rosenberg** offer that the Passau schools do not offer? (Swiss **Maturitätsprüfung,** Italian **Maturitätsprüfung,** preparation for universities in the United States and the United Kingdom)

Geography Connection

The **Institut Rosenberg** is in St. Gallen. Have students locate St. Gallen in an atlas. Given its location (near Lake Constance in Switzerland), what types of activities would students probably find there?

Teacher Note

The address of the **Institut Rosenberg** includes the country code **CH.** These letters stand for **Confoederatio Helvetica.** This code is used to designate Switzerland.

Post-Reading
Teacher Note

Activities 6 and 7 are post-reading tasks that will show whether students can apply what they have learned.

Applying Knowledge

Using the ads in the reading as a model, have students write a short advertisement for your school or an imaginary school.

▶ **PAGES 120–123**

MEHR GRAMMATIKÜBUNGEN

The **Mehr Grammatikübungen** activities are designed as supplemental activities for the grammatical concepts presented in the chapter. You might use them as additional practice, for review, or for assessment.

For more grammar presentations, review, and practice, refer to the following:
• Grammatikheft
• Grammar Tutor for Students of German
• Grammar Summary on pp. R15–R25
• Übungsheft

- Grammar and Vocabulary quizzes (Testing Program)
- Test Generator
- Interactive CD-ROM Tutor
- Interaktive Spiele at go.hrw.com

Teacher to Teacher

Elaine Bind
McDonogh School
Owings Mills, Maryland

Elaine suggests this activity for gender practice:

"Cut paper into 2.5 × 8.5 strips. On each strip print a noun from the current and previous chapters, but without the article. Make two or three teams. For each team label three columns on the board M, F, and N (or **der, die, das**). Each team receives four words per round and places each word in the appropriate column using magnets. Each team receives one point per correct placement. Announce how many they have correct, but not which ones. Teams able to correct another team's error receive an extra point."

PAGES 124–125

ANWENDUNG

 Video Wrap-up

Videocassette 2, 05:20–20:54
Videocassette 5 (captioned version), 15:16–22:08
At this time, you might want to use the video resources for additional review and enrichment. See *Video Guide* for suggestions regarding:

- the **Los geht's!** episode
- the **Fortsetzung** episode
- the **Landeskunde** interviews
- the **Videoclips.**

Apply and Assess

Teaching Suggestion

1 So as not to duplicate any items, assign five items to each group and let them make up prices accordingly.

Visual Learners

Make sure the items in your classroom are no longer labeled. As students walk into the classroom, hand each of the students one of the labels. Ask students to affix the labels to the appropriate objects.

Apply and Assess

Process Writing

8 Write the following sentences on the board as models for the students to use as they prepare their Web page:

Er / Sie hat (Biologie) gern.
Sein / Ihr Lieblingsfach ist (Deutsch).
Er / Sie hat (Chemie) nicht gern.

To add some variety to the activity, you may also want to allow students to write a description of someone who would be their exact opposite. (For example, if someone had math as a favorite subject, that student would say of his or her opposite Er / Sie hat Mathe nicht gern.)

PAGE 126

KANN ICH'S WIRKLICH?

This page is intended to prepare students for the test. It is a brief checklist of the major points covered in the chapter. The students should be reminded that it is a checklist only and not necessarily everything that will appear on the test.

For additional self check options, refer students to the *Grammar Tutor,* the *Interactive CD-ROM Tutor,* and the Online self-test for this chapter.

PAGE 127

WORTSCHATZ

Review and Assess

Teacher Note

As the students' vocabulary increases, you can add pairs of cards to the **Zieh eine Karte!** game from each **Wortschatz** studied. This will help students review vocabulary from previous chapters.

Tactile Learners

Use sentence strips to practice sentences that include sequencing words. Cut the strips into segments. Put the segments into numbered envelopes and have one envelope for each pair of students. Students work together trying to put the sentences back together. (Example: **Zuerst spielt Katja Tennis.**)

Teacher Note

Give the **Kapitel 4** Chapter Test:
Testing Program, pp. 91–96
Audio CD 4, Trs. 21–23.

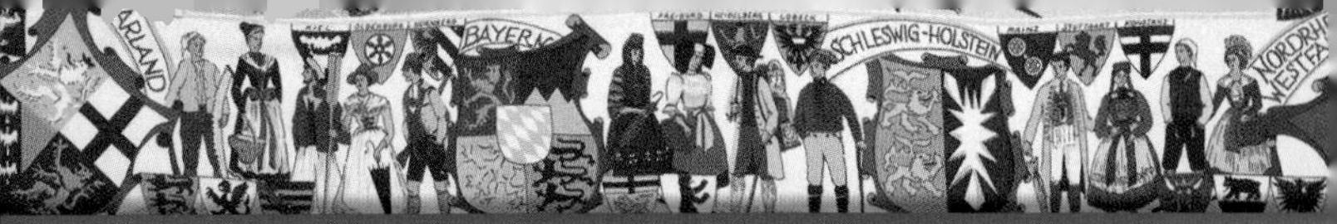

KAPITEL

4

Alles für die Schule!

Objectives

In this chapter you will learn to

Erste Stufe

- talk about class schedules
- use a schedule to talk about time
- sequence events

Zweite Stufe

- express likes, dislikes, and favorites
- respond to good and bad news

Dritte Stufe

- talk about prices
- point things out

internet

go.hrw.com

ADRESSE: go.hrw.com
KENNWORT:
WK3 SCHLESWIG-HOLSTEIN-4

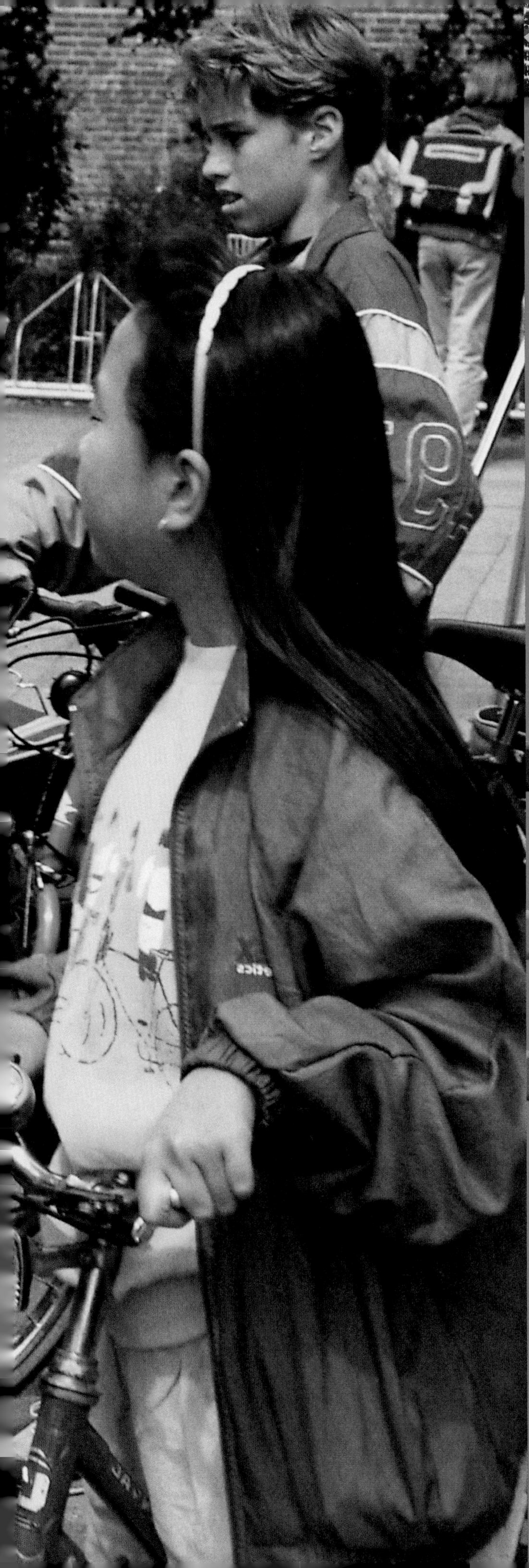

◀ **Vor der Schule**

Los geht's! · *Lars kauft Schulsachen*

CD 4 Trs. 1–2

Strategie Verstehen

Look at the images for this story. What are the students doing in each scene? Where might these scenes be taking place? What clues tell you this?

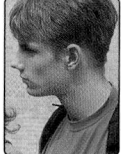   

Lars   **Julia**   **Sina**   **Alex**

Los geht's! is an abridged version of the video episode.

Lars: Hallo, Leute!

Julia: Hallo, Lars!

Lars: Suchst du was?

Sina: Ja, wo ist der Stundenplan? Sag, wann haben wir Mathe?

Lars: Weiß nicht.

Alex: Ah, Mathe haben wir nach der Pause um 9 Uhr 45.

Sina: Danke, Alex! Und was haben wir heute zuerst?

Alex: Zuerst haben wir Deutsch, dann Bio, danach Mathe, dann Englisch und zuletzt Sport.

❶

Julia: Du, heute bekommen wir die Mathearbeit zurück.

Lars: Ich hab bestimmt wieder eine Vier.

Julia: Meinst du?

Lars: Ja, leider. In Mathe hab ich immer schlechte Noten.

Julia: Schade!

Lars: Na ja, du bist gut in Mathe.

Julia: Ja, ich hab Mathe gern. Das ist mein Lieblingsfach.

❷

3

Julia: Hallo, Lars!

Lars: Hallo, Julia!

Julia: Na, was machst du denn hier?—Ach, ich seh's: ein Taschenrechner!

Lars: Schau mal! Der Rechner ist toll, nicht?

Julia: Ja, du hast Recht.

Lars: Und der ist nicht teuer.

Julia: Stimmt! Nur sechzehn Euro!

4

Julia: Entschuldigung! Wo sind bitte die Hefte und die Bleistifte?

Verkäuferin: Die sind da drüben.

Julia: Und Wörterbücher? Wo sind die?

Verkäuferin: Da hinten!

Julia: Danke!

5

Verkäuferin: Der Rechner? Sechzehn Euro, bitte!

Lars: Moment! Ach, wie blöd! Jetzt hab ich nur zehn Euro dabei.

Julia: Macht nichts, Lars! Ich geb dir das Geld.

Lars: Oh, das ist sehr nett, Julia! So, jetzt hab ich zwanzig Euro.

Verkäuferin: Danke schön! Und vier Euro zurück.

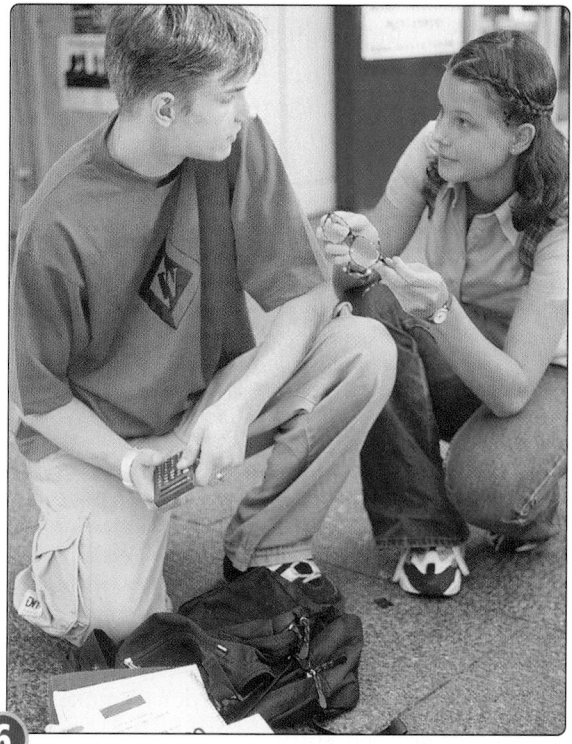

6

Lars: Warte, Julia!

Julia: Was ist los?

Lars: So ein Mist! Das ganze Zeug auf der Straße!

Julia: Der Taschenrechner, geht er noch?

Lars: Ach wo! Er ist kaputt! So ein Pech!

Julia: So ein Glück! Die Brille ist noch ganz!

 Übungsheft, S. 37

1 Was passiert hier?

These activities check for global comprehension only. Students should not yet be expected to produce language modeled in **Los geht's!**

Do you understand what is happening in the story? Check your comprehension by answering these questions. Don't be afraid to guess.

1. How is Julia in math? What about Lars?
2. Where do Julia and Lars meet again? What kinds of things are they looking for?
3. What does Lars want to buy? Why does he need it?
4. Lars has both bad luck and good luck on the way home. What happens to him?

1. good; Lars gets bad grades.
2. At the stationery store. School supplies.
3. A calculator for math.
4. His calculator breaks, but his glasses are still intact.

2 Genauer lesen

a. Reread the conversations. Which words or phrases do the characters use to

1. name school subjects
2. name school supplies
3. express annoyance
4. point out something
5. express regret
6. express bad luck; good luck

1. Mathe, Bio, Englisch, Sport
2. Taschenrechner, Hefte, Bleistifte, Wörterbücher
3. Ach, wie blöd, so ein Mist
4. Schau mal, da drüben, da hinten
5. Schade
6. So ein Pech! So ein Glück!

b. In what three ways are numbers used in the conversations? time, grades, prices

3 Stimmt oder stimmt nicht?

Are these statements right or wrong? Answer each one with either **stimmt** or **stimmt nicht**. If a statement is wrong, try to state it correctly.

1. Lars hat immer schlechte Noten in Mathe. 1. stimmt
2. Sina und Alex haben nach der Pause Deutsch. 2. stimmt nicht; Nach der Pause haben sie Mathe.
3. Julia hat Mathe nicht gern. 3. stimmt nicht; Mathe ist ihr Lieblingsfach.
4. Der Rechner ist sehr teuer. 4. stimmt nicht; Der Rechner kostet nur 16 Euro.
5. Julia gibt Lars das Geld. 5. stimmt
6. Die Brille ist kaputt. 6. stimmt nicht; Die Brille ist noch ganz.

4 Was passt zusammen?

Match each statement or question on the left with an appropriate response on the right.

1. Was haben wir zuerst? b
2. Und wann hast du Mathe? e
3. Dieser Taschenrechner ist toll — und nicht teuer. d
4. Ich habe nur 10 Euro dabei. a
5. Schau mal! Der Taschenrechner ist kaputt! c
6. Aber die Brille ist noch ganz. f

a. Macht nichts! Ich gebe dir das Geld.
b. Also, zuerst Deutsch, dann Bio.
c. So ein Pech!
d. Das stimmt! Er kostet nur 16 Euro.
e. Nach der Pause.
f. So ein Glück!

5 Nacherzählen

Put the sentences in logical order to make a brief summary of the story.

1. Sina sucht den Stundenplan.

Danach sprechen Julia und Lars über die Mathearbeit und Lars' Noten. 2

Später kommt Lars in einen Schreibwarenladen. Er möchte einen Taschenrechner. 3

Auf dem Weg nach Hause fällt Lars' Zeug auf die Straße. 6

Also gibt Julia Lars das Geld. 5

Aber er hat nur 10 Euro dabei. 4

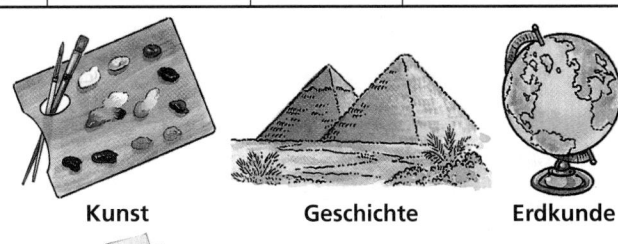

TPR Storytelling Book
pp. 13, 16

Erste Stufe

Objectives Talking about class schedules; using a schedule to talk about time; sequencing events

go.hrw.com

WK3 SCHLESWIG-HOLSTEIN-4

Wortschatz

Hier ist Alex' und Sinas Stundenplan *(class schedule)*:

4–1, 4–A

CD-ROM DISC 1

Stundenplan für

NAME ____Sina____   KLASSE ____9a____

ZEIT	MONTAG	DIENSTAG	MITTWOCH	DONNERSTAG	FREITAG	SAMSTAG
8:00 - 8:45	Deutsch	Deutsch	Mathe	—	Physik	frei
8:45 - 9:30	Deutsch	Bio	Deutsch	Physik	Mathe	
9:30 - 9:45	Pause	—	—	—	—	
9:45 - 10:30	Religion	Mathe	Englisch	Bio	Deutsch	
10:30 - 11:15	Bio	Englisch	Latein	Englisch	Latein	
11:15 - 11:30	Pause	—	—	—	—	
11:30 - 12:15	Latein	Sport	Geschichte	Englisch	Kunst	
12:20 - 13:05	Musik	Sport	Erdkunde	Latein	—	

What do you think the word **Zeit** in the schedule means? What do the other words next to **Zeit** (**Montag**, etc.) refer to? All but four of the class subjects are cognates. Which ones do you recognize?

Kunst   Geschichte   Erdkunde

Übungsheft, S. 38, Ü. 2–3   Grammatikheft, S. 28, Ü. 1–3

6 **Alex' und Sinas Stundenplan**

Sprechen Look at Alex's and Sina's class schedule and try to answer the following questions in German.

1. On what day(s) do Alex and Sina have religion? And biology? 1. Montag; Dienstag und Donnerstag

2. Which subjects do they have on Tuesday? On Wednesday? 2. Di: Deutsch, Bio. Mathe, Englisch, Sport. Mi: Mathe, Deutsch, Englisch, Latein, Geschichte, Erdkunde

3. On which day(s) do they have art? And history? 3. Freitag; Mittwoch

4. At what times do Alex and Sina have math?* On which day(s)? 4. Am Dienstag von 9:45 bis 10:30, am Mittwoch von 8:00 bis 8:45 und am Freitag von 8:45 bis 9:30.

5. At what time(s) do they have German?**

5. Am Montag von 8:00 bis 9:30, am Dienstag von 8:00 bis 8:45, am Mittwoch von 8:45 bis 9:30, am Freitag von 9:45 bis 10:30.

---

*To read times from a schedule simply read the numbers and insert **Uhr** between the hour and minutes: 10.30 reads **10 Uhr 30** (**zehn Uhr dreißig**); 8.45 reads **8 Uhr 45** (**acht Uhr fünfundvierzig**).

8:00–8:45 reads: **von acht **bis** acht Uhr fünfundvierzig

Look at the class schedule on page 105. How many different subjects do Alex and Sina have, and when do they have them? How does this compare to your class schedule?

German schools are also different in that Alex, Sina, and their classmates stay together for all their classes and, for the most part, in the same classroom. The teachers move from room to room. What do you think the word **Pause** means, judging by the time allotted for it? Where do you think German students eat lunch? Like you and your friends, students in German-speaking countries have some activities after school: school-sponsored sports, clubs, and social activities. There are, however, fewer such activities in Germany than in the United States.

7 Dein Stundenplan

Schreiben Now make your own class schedule in German. Here are some other subjects you may need to complete your schedule. Turn to page R9 for additional vocabulary.

Und dann noch…

Spanisch, Französisch, Chor, Algebra, Orchester, Werken, Sozialkunde, Technik, Hauswirtschaft

---

So sagt man das!

Talking about class schedules

If you want to discuss class schedules with your friends, you might ask:

> **Welche Fächer hast du?**
> **Was hast du am Donnerstag?**
> **Was hat die Sina am Donnerstag?**
>
> **Julia, Bernd, welche Fächer habt ihr heute nach der Pause?**
> **Und was habt ihr am Samstag?**

You might get the responses:

> **Ich habe Mathe, Bio, Kunst …**
> **Deutsch, Englisch und Sport.**
> **Sie hat Physik, Bio, Englisch und Latein.**
>
> **Wir haben Chemie und Musik.**
> **Wir haben frei!**

The word **Fächer** used above means *subjects*. What do you think the equivalent of **welche** is?[1] Could you use **welche** in the second, third and fifth questions? The word **am** always precedes the days of the week. What do you think this word means?[2] With what other time expressions have you already used **am**?[3]

8 Welche Fächer hast du?

Sprechen Using the schedule you created in Activity 7, tell your classmates which subjects you have and on what day you have them.

---

1. *which* 2. here: *on* 3. **am Wochenende, am Abend, am Nachmittag**

9 **Welche Fächer haben sie?** Script on p. 99G

Zuhören Listen carefully as Lars asks his classmates when they have various classes. Match the subjects below with the days of the week in the box to the right.

CD 4
Tr. 3

a. Bio
am Freitag

b. Musik
am Dienstag

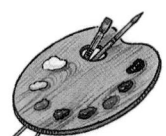

c. Kunst
am Mittwoch

√a̅ 9³

d. Mathe
am Donnerstag

e. Geschichte
am Freitag

f. Erdkunde
am Montag

g. Sport
am Montag

"GUTEN TAG"

h. Deutsch
am Dienstag

am Dienstag am Montag
am Mittwoch am Freitag
am Samstag am Donnerstag

So sagt man das!

Using a schedule to talk about time

It's the first day of school, and you are curious about when your friends have their classes.

You might ask:

Wann hast du Erdkunde?
Was hast du um 11 Uhr 20?
Was hast du von 8 Uhr 45 bis 9 Uhr 30?
Und wann hast du Kunst?

You might get the responses:

Um 11 Uhr 20.
Erdkunde.
Ich habe Informatik.
Um 10 Uhr 30, nach der Pause.

What do you think **wann** means?[1] How do you answer a question that starts with **wann**?[2] How is the answer to this question different from the answers to questions that begin with **was**? What is the English equivalent of **um**?[3]

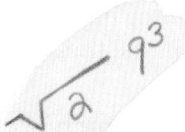

Ein wenig Landeskunde

Do any of the times in Alex's and Sina's schedule look unusual to you? When does their last class end? Schedules like this one, and other official schedules like the train schedule to the right, are based on the 24-hour system of telling time. This system starts immediately after midnight (**00.01 Uhr**) and ends at midnight (**24.00 Uhr**). What time would correspond to 2 P.M.? to 3 P.M.? to 8:30 P.M.? What time would you have to board the train in order to get to **Köln? Mannheim?**

13.05

14.00
15.00
20.30

14.49
15.49

Bochum ⟶ München
Hauptbahnhof   Hauptbahnhof

Preis pro Person in Euro. Einfache Fahrt.
* Bei Benutzung von EC/IC € 3,- Zuschlag.

| Mögliche Fahrpreisermäßigungen siehe Kapitel „So günstig fahren Sie Bahn". | | | | | | Fahrpreis 1. Kl. | ICE 293,- | Andere Züge* 263,- |
| | | | | | | Fahrpreis 2. Kl. | 188,- | 175,- |

ab	Zug	Umsteigen	an	Verkehrstage	Bemerkungen	ICE	Andere Züge*
14.49	IC 823	Köln IC Stuttgart EC	22.11	1234567			●
14.49	IC 823	Würzburg D	22.29	1234567			●
14.59	S	Duisburg IC Stuttgart EC	22.11	12345--	an Werktagen nicht 24., 31. 12.		●
15.23	IR 2553	Kassel-Wilh. ICE	22.06	1234567		●	
15.49	IC 523	Köln IC Mannheim ICE	22.17	1234567		●	
15.49	IC 523	Köln IC Karlsruhe IR	23.40	1234567			●
16.22	IC 517		23.11	12345-7	nicht 24, 12, -2. 1., 9,- 11.4.		●
16.49	IC 603	Mannheim ICE	23.17	------7	auch 12. 4.,	●	

―――――

1. *when* 2. with a time expression 3. here: *at*

10 **Welche Fächer hat Klaus?** Script on p. 99G

Zuhören Listen carefully as Klaus, a friend of Sonja's, talks about the busy schedule he has on Wednesdays. Copy the names of the following subjects onto a piece of paper, then complete his schedule by filling in the times as you hear them.

CD 4
Tr. 4

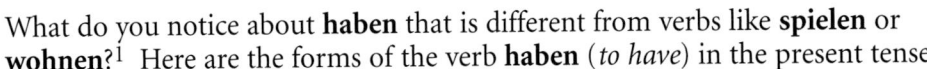

Mathe	Englisch	Latein
Deutsch	Erdkunde	Geschichte

Mathe 8:00; Deutsch 8:45; Englisch 9:45; Latein 10:30; Geschichte 11:30; Erdkunde 12:20–13:05

11 **Wann hast du Deutsch?**

Sprechen Working in small groups, take turns asking each other which subjects each of you has and at what times during the day. Remember, you do not need to answer in complete sentences. Sometimes just a phrase will do:

BEISPIEL   **PARTNER**   **Wann hast du Englisch?**
                     DU   **Um 10 Uhr.**   *oder*   **Um 10.**

Grammatik

The verb **haben**, present tense

Look at the conversation below:

JULIA   **Was hat Sina nach der Pause?**

BEATE   **Sie hat Bio. Und was hast du?**

JULIA   **Ich habe Deutsch.**

What do you notice about **haben** that is different from verbs like **spielen** or **wohnen?**[1] Here are the forms of the verb **haben** (*to have*) in the present tense:

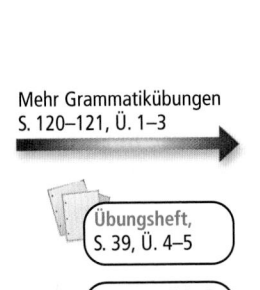

Mehr Grammatikübungen
S. 120–121, Ü. 1–3

Übungsheft,
S. 39, Ü. 4–5

Grammatikheft,
S. 29, Ü. 4–6

ich	**habe**		wir	**haben**
du	**hast**		ihr	**habt**
er/sie	**hat**	sie (plural)/Sie (formal)		**haben**

12 **Grammatik im Kontext**

Sprechen / Schreiben Several students in the **Schulhof** are talking about their schedules. First, fill in each blank with the missing form of the verb **haben,** and then match each conversation with one of the drawings.

1. – ═══ Monika und Bernd jetzt Englisch? / Nein, sie ═══ jetzt Musik.   Haben; haben; d

2. – Wann ═══ du Deutsch? / Nach der Pause ═══ ich Deutsch.   hast; habe; b

3. – Wann ═══ Sabine Kunst? / Um 12 Uhr ═══ sie Kunst.   hat; hat; c

4. – Wann ═══ ihr Physik? / Am Dienstag ═══ wir Physik.   habt; haben; a

a.

b.

c.

d.

---

1. haben is irregular in the **du-** and **er/sie-**forms: **du hast, er/sie hat**

13 Ein Interview

a. Schreiben Prepare a list of questions for your partner in order to find out exactly what his or her schedule is for the semester (which classes he or she has, the times of the classes).

b. Sprechen/Schreiben Now interview your partner using your list of questions and, as you interview, fill out his or her schedule on another piece of paper. Then your partner will interview you. Compare schedules to see if both of you understood everything correctly.

c. Lesen/Sprechen Be prepared to report the information you obtained back to the class.

So sagt man das!

Sequencing events

You might want to know the order in which your friends have their classes on a certain day.

(Übungsheft, S. 39-40, Ü. 6-8)

(Grammatikheft, S. 30, Ü. 7-11)

CD-ROM DISC 1

You might ask:

If your friend had the schedule on the right he or she would answer:

Welche Fächer hast du am Freitag?

Zuerst hab ich Deutsch, dann Geschichte, danach Latein, und zuletzt hab ich Sport.

Deutsch	8.05
Geschichte	8.55
Latein	9.45
Sport	10.30

What do the words **zuerst**, **dann**, **danach**, and **zuletzt** mean?[1]

---

14 Was hast du am Mittwoch?

Sprechen/Lesen Alex asks Julia which classes she has on Wednesday. Working with a partner, put these questions and answers in the appropriate order. Then, together with your partner, read the conversation out loud.

ALEX   Julia, was hast du zuerst am Mittwoch?

ALEX   Was hast du danach?
5

JULIA   Danach hab ich Deutsch um 10 und dann Kunst.
6

JULIA   Dann hab ich um 9 Uhr Musik.
4

JULIA   Zuletzt hab ich Informatik.
8

ALEX   Und zuletzt?
7

ALEX   Und dann?
3

JULIA   Zuerst habe ich Sport.
2

15 Was hast du zuerst? Und zuletzt?

Sprechen Using the sequencing words **zuerst**, **dann**, **danach**, and **zuletzt**, tell your classmates the order in which you have your classes on Monday. You can use **dann** and **danach** several times if you have more than four classes.

16 Typisch für einen Samstag!

Schreiben Write a short paragraph describing what you do on a typical Saturday, using some of the activities you learned in **Kapitel 2**, for example, **Tennis spielen**, **Freunde besuchen**, or **Hausaufgaben machen**. In your description, use the sequencing words you have learned (**zuerst**, **dann**, **danach**, and **zuletzt**).

---

1. *first, then, after that, last of all*

Zweite Stufe

Objectives Expressing likes, dislikes, and favorites; responding to good news and bad news

WK3 SCHLESWIG-HOLSTEIN-4

So sagt man das!

Expressing likes, dislikes, and favorites

In **Kapitel 2** you learned to say which activities you like and don't like to do using **gern** and **nicht gern**. You might also want to talk about which classes you like and don't like, and which is your favorite.

Your friend might ask you:

> **Welche Fächer hast du gern?**
> **Was hast du nicht so gern?**
> **Und was ist dein Lieblingsfach?**

You might respond:

> **Ich habe Kunst und Englisch gern.**
> **Chemie.**
> **Deutsch, ganz klar!**

Grammatikheft,
S. 31, Ü. 12–13

---

17 Katjas Fächer

Zuhören Listen as Katja describes to Rainer the subjects she is taking. Write down which subjects Katja likes, dislikes, and considers her favorite subjects. Script on p. 99G

CD 4
Tr. 5

gern	nicht gern	Lieblingsfächer

gern: Musik, Latein, Deutsch
nicht gern: Englisch, Kunst, Mathe
Lieblingsfächer: Geschichte, Erdkunde

Ein wenig Grammatik

Lieblings- is a prefix that can be used with many different nouns to indicate favorites. Can you guess what these words mean:

Lieblingsbuch, Lieblingsinstrument, and Lieblingsfilm?

Mehr Grammatikübungen
S. 121, Ü. 4-5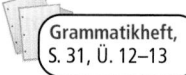

---

18 Und dein Lieblingsfach?

Schreiben/Sprechen Find out which subjects your partner likes and dislikes, and his or her favorite subject. Create a chart like the one you filled out for Activity 17. Using the chart, report the information about your partner back to the class. Remember to use **sein** or **ihr** when you are reporting about your partner's **Lieblingsfach**.

19 Trends: Eine Umfrage

Sprechen/Schreiben Working in small groups, conduct a survey about some of the things teenagers like best. Each member of the group asks two students at least three questions. Use topics from the box to prepare the questions. When you have finished the interviews, prepare a summary in chart form.

Lieblingsbuch	Lieblingsrockgruppe	
		Lieblingsauto	Lieblingssänger
Lieblingsmusik	Lieblingsfilm	Lieblingslehrer	Lieblingsfarbe

Zeugnis

für **Lars Lehmann**,

geboren am **7. 6. 1988**   Klasse **8 b**

Allgemeine Beurteilung: *Muss sich in Latein u. Mathe verbessern!*

Deutsch **3**	Mathematik **4**
mündlich ...... **1** schriftlich...... **4**	Physik **2**
Geschichte/Sozialkunde **2**	Chemie **2**
Geschichte ...... **2** Sozialkd **2**	Biologie **3**
Erdkunde **2**	Musik **1**
1. Fremdsprache: *Englisch* **1**	Bildende Kunst/Werken **2**
mündlich ...... **1** schriftlich...... **1**	Bildende Kunst... **2** Werken... **2**
2. Fremdsprache: *Latein* **5**	Sport **1**
mündlich .... schriftlich...... **5**	

Wahlpflichtfach

3. Fremdsprache: *Französisch* **2 +**

mündlich ...... **1** schriftlich...... **2**

Freiwillige Unterrichtsveranstaltungen

---

sehr gut *(excellent)*

gut *(good)*

befriedigend *(satisfactory)*

ungenügend *(failing)*

ausreichend *(just passing)*

mangelhaft *(unsatisfactory)*

Ein wenig Landeskunde

4, 2, 3, 5

Look at Lars's report card. What grades (the numbers) did he get in **Mathe, Erdkunde, Deutsch,** and **Latein**?

He was very happy about his geography grade, not too disappointed with the grade in German, very worried about his math grade, and didn't really want to show his Latin grade to his parents. With this information, can you figure out how the German grading system, which is based on the numbers 1-6 rather than on letters, works? Which numbers go with which descriptions?

20 **Sonjas Noten** Script on p. 99H

CD 4
Tr. 6

Zuhören Listen as Sonja talks about the grades she received on her last report card. First write down the subjects she mentions in the order you hear them. Then listen again and fill in the **Note** *(grade)* she got for each subject. In which subjects did Sonja do well? In which subjects did she not do so well? Then answer the following questions in German.

1. In which subject did she get the best grade? And the worst? Mathe; Englisch

2. In which subject did Sonja receive a "satisfactory" grade? Erdkunde

3. Judging by her grades, which subject do you think Sonja enjoys the most? Mathe

4. In which subject do you think Sonja needs to study more? Englisch

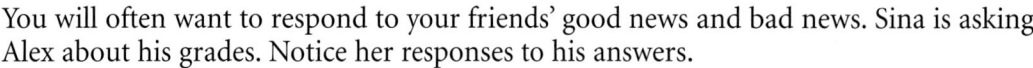

So sagt man das!

Responding to good news and bad news

You will often want to respond to your friends' good news and bad news. Sina is asking Alex about his grades. Notice her responses to his answers.

Sina asks:	Alex answers:	Sina responds:
Was hast du in Musik?	**Eine Eins.**	**Toll! Das ist prima!**
In Physik?	**Eine Drei.**	**Nicht schlecht.**
Und in Englisch?	**Ich habe bloß eine Vier.**	**Schade! So ein Pech!**
Und Mathe?	**Eine Fünf.**	**Schade!**
		Das ist sehr schlecht!

Alex was probably hoping for a better grade in English. What do you think he means by **bloß eine Vier**?[1]

(Übungsheft, S. 41–43, Ü. 9–14) (Grammatikheft, S. 32, Ü. 14–16)

21 Logisch oder unlogisch?

Lesen/Sprechen Read what these students say about their grades. Does the response in each case make sense? If so, answer **Das ist logisch**, if not, answer **Das ist unlogisch**, and try to think of a response that is more appropriate.

1. —Ich habe eine Fünf in Latein!
   —Toll! Das ist gut! unlogisch

2. —Du hast eine Vier in Informatik?
   —Ja, das ist blöd, nicht? logisch

3. —Englisch ist mein Lieblingsfach. Ich habe eine Zwei.
   —Super! Das ist wirklich gut! logisch

4. —In Erdkunde habe ich eine Drei.
   —Hm, nicht schlecht! logisch

5. —Und in Deutsch habe ich eine Eins!
   —Ach wie blöd! So ein Pech! unlogisch

Degrees of enthusiasm

Spitze!
Super!
Toll!
Prima!
Das ist gut!
Nicht schlecht!
Schade!
So ein Pech!
Das ist schlecht!
So ein Mist!

22 Dein Zeugnis

a. **Schreiben** Imagine that you are an exchange student in Wedel and have just received your report card for the semester. Design and fill out a German report card for yourself. Write all your subjects and give yourself a grade according to the German grading system.

b. **Lesen/Sprechen** With your report card in hand, have a conversation with a classmate, asking your partner which grades he or she has in various subjects, responding appropriately, and telling him or her about your classes and grades. Use the phrases above in your responses.

23 Für mein Notizbuch

Schreiben Schreib ein paar Sätze über dich und deine Schule! Welche Fächer hast du? Welche Fächer hast du gern? Welche Fächer hast du nicht gern? Was ist dein Lieblingsfach? In welchen Fächern sind deine Noten gut? In welchen sind die Noten nicht so gut?

---

1. *only a four* (**ausreichend**)

Was sind deine Lieblingsfächer?

We asked several teenagers in German-speaking countries what school subjects they have and which ones they like and don't like. Before you read the interviews, make a list of your classes and indicate which ones are your favorites and which ones you don't like very much. CD 4 Tr. 7

CD 4 Trs. 7–12

Übungsheft, S. 48, Ü. 24–25

Jasmin, München CD 4 Tr. 8

„Ich hab Arbeitslehre — als Lieblingsfach, und Kunst und Mathe mag ich gar nicht; Physik mag ich auch nicht so gerne. Und sonst Sport mag ich noch und dann Englisch, das mag ich auch — das ist auch mein Lieblingsfach, weil ich sehr gern Englisch lernen will."

Dirk, Hamburg CD 4 Tr. 10

„Ich bin eigentlich genau das Gegenteil von Michael, weil ich total auf Sprachen mich basier. Ich hab Englisch als Leistungskurs, Spanisch und Französisch hab ich gehabt. Ich will ja auch mit Sprachen mal was machen, Diplomatie oder so. Mal seh'n!"

Michael, Hamburg CD 4 Tr. 9

„Ich interessiere mich hauptsächlich für Mathe und Physik und Kunst, weil ich also ich Architekt werden will. Chemie mag ich überhaupt nicht. Also ich glaube, es ist auch wichtig. Sonst komm ich mit den meisten Fächern zurecht."

Lugana, Bietigheim

„Okay, ich heiße Lugana, bin Griechin, wurde hier geboren. Bin sechzehn Jahre alt, gehe aufs Ellental-Gymnasium, und Lieblingsfächer sind Englisch und Deutsch." CD 4 Tr. 11

Björn, Hamburg CD 4 Tr. 12

„In der Schule mag ich am liebsten Physik, Mathematik und Informatik — das ist mit Computern. Das kommt, weil …ich bin gut in Mathe. Ich arbeite gern an Computern, und ich mag Physik ganz gerne, weil mich die Themen einfach interessieren."

A. 1. What subjects do these teenagers like and dislike? Make a grid.

 2. Which of these teenagers likes the same subjects you do? What are these subjects?

 3. Several of these teenagers give reasons why they like certain subjects. Work with a partner and decide what these reasons are.

 4. Look at the list you made. Try to think of reasons why you like the subjects you indicated. What do your opinions have to do with your future career plans?

B. Do you think teenagers in German-speaking countries start thinking about their future careers earlier than teenagers in the United States do? What can you find in the interviews to support your answer? Discuss the topic with your classmates and then write a brief essay on this question.

STANDARDS: 2.2, 3.2, 4.2

Dritte Stufe

Objectives Talking about prices; pointing things out

Wortschatz

Was kosten die Schulsachen im Schul-Shop?

EUR 14,90	EUR 40,00	EUR 5,00	EUR 16,20
das Wörterbuch	die Schultasche	die Kassette	der Taschenrechner

EUR 1,20	EUR 0,95	EUR 0,70	EUR 2,50
das Heft	der Radiergummi	der Bleistift	der Kuli

ACHTUNG! SCHULANFANG!

Jetzt kaufen — in Ruhe auswählen

Unser Schul-Spezial-Angebot mit reduzierten Preisen

Bleistifte, 12 Stück	bisher EUR	5,40	jetzt	4,20 €
Hefte	bisher EUR	0,80	jetzt	0,60 €
Kulis, alle Farben	bisher EUR	1,60	jetzt	1,25 €
Jeans-Taschen	bisher EUR	24,50	jetzt	20,00 €
Taschenrechner	bisher EUR	9,75	jetzt	8,10 €
Stundenpläne	bisher EUR	0,85	jetzt	0,65 €
Kassetten, 3 Stück	bisher EUR	9,00	jetzt	7,50 €
Wörterbücher	bisher EUR	8,20	jetzt	7,45 €

Wo? Im Schul-Shop

KAUT-BULLING & Co. G M B H & CO KG

Rolandstr. 30 22880 Wedel - Telefon 04-10-5

Notice the prices that Germans pay for school supplies. How does this compare with the prices you would pay? How many of each of these supplies do you have with you right now in the classroom?

Grammatikheft, S. 33, Ü. 18

24 Im Schul-Shop

Schreiben/Lesen Compare the endings of the words in the school supplies ad with the words printed under each illustration. What do you observe? List the differences and compare your list with that of a classmate. Why do you think the words are written differently?

Grammatik

Noun plurals

As you discovered in Activity 24, there are many different plural endings for German nouns. There is no one rule that tells you which nouns take which endings.

Every German dictionary includes the plural ending of a noun next to the main entry, which is the singular form. In the **Vocabulary** in this book beginning on page R29, you will see entries like those above.

Look up the following words and write sentences using the plural forms of these words: **der Stuhl, der Keks, die Kassette.**

das **Wort,** ¨er *word,* 9*
das **Wörterbuch,** ¨er *dictionary,* 4
der **Wortschatz** *vocabulary,* 1
die **Wortschatzübung,** -en *vocabulary exercise, practice,* 1
wunderbar *wonderful,* 11

Mehr Grammatikübungen
S. 122, Ü. 6–7

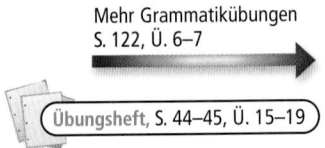

Übungsheft, S. 44–45, Ü. 15–19

---

* ¨**er** means that the plural form of **Wort** is **Wörter.**

25 Im Schul-Shop Script on p. 99H

Zuhören Listen to this conversation between Johanna and Daniel in the stationery store. As you listen, put the four pictures in the correct sequence. b-d-a-c

a.

b.

c.

d.

So sagt man das!

Talking about prices

 4–2

If you and your friend are in a store, you might ask one another about the prices of various items.

You might ask:

Was kostet der Taschenrechner?
Was kosten die Bleistifte?

Your friend might respond:

Er kostet nur 16 Euro.
Sie kosten 90 Cent.

After you hear the price you might comment to your friend:

Das ist (ziemlich) teuer!
Das ist (sehr) billig!
Das ist (sehr) preiswert!

That's (quite) expensive!
That's (very) cheap!
That's a (really) good deal!

Übungsheft, S. 46, Ü. 20–21
Grammatikheft, S. 34, Ü. 19–20

Ein wenig Landeskunde

As of January 1, 2002 the **Euro** (€) is the national currency in Germany as well as in most European countries. One **Euro** has **100 Cent**. € **1,00** reads **ein Euro**, € **0,90** reads **neunzig Cent**, € **2,30** reads **zwei Euro dreißig**. How would you read € **7,80**? € **1,70**? € **9,10**? € **24,35**?

There are seven euro bills with the following denominations: 5, 10, 20, 50, 100, 200 and 500 euros. And there are eight euro coins: 1, 2, 5, 10, 20 and 50 cents, and a 1 euro and a 2 euro coin. The tails of some coins show German symbols, such as the German Oak Leaf, the Brandenburg Gate, and the Federal Eagle, that are reminders of the beloved German mark.

Mehr Grammatikübungen
S. 123, Ü. 9

Ein wenig Grammatik

Schon bekannt

In **Kapitel 3** you learned that the pronouns **er, sie, es,** and **sie** (pl) can refer to objects: **Die Couch ist neu. Sie ist bequem.** When do you use each of these pronouns?[1]

Mehr Grammatikübungen
S. 122–123, Ü. 8

Grammatikheft, S. 35, Ü. 21–22

---

1. **er** refers to masculine nouns, **sie** to feminine nouns, **es** to neuter nouns, **sie** (pl) to plural nouns.

26 Was kostet ...?

Schreiben You are starting school and need to buy school supplies. You have 15 euros to spend. Make a list of the things you need to buy. Your partner is the **Verkäufer** (*salesclerk*) at the store and will create a price list, using the items and prices in the **Wortschatz** box as cues. Ask your partner how much the items on your list cost, then figure out how much you must spend. Be sure to be polite!

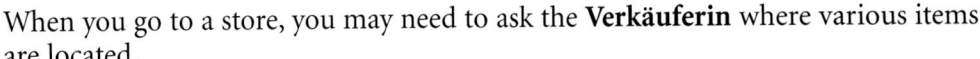 **So sagt man das!**

Pointing things out

When you go to a store, you may need to ask the **Verkäuferin** where various items are located.

You might ask:

> **Entschuldigung, wo sind die Schultaschen?**
> **Und Taschenrechner? Wo finde ich sie?**
> **Und die Kulis auch?**
> **Wo sind bitte die Kassetten?**
> **Und dann noch Hefte. Wo sind die, bitte?**

The responses might be:

> **Schauen Sie!* Dort drüben!**
> **Dort!**
> **Nein, sie sind dort drüben!**
> **Kassetten sind da hinten.**
> **Die sind hier vorn.**

How would the salesperson tell you that the pencils are in the front of the store if he or she were also in the front of the store?[1]

———

*This is the polite form of **Schau!** that is used among friends. In a store, a salesperson would use the polite form **Schauen Sie!**

Übungsheft, S. 46, Ü. 22

Grammatikheft, S. 36, Ü. 23–25

27 Im Schreibwarenladen

Schreiben Alex has asked the **Verkäuferin** where various school supplies are located and what they cost. Complete what the **Verkäuferin** says with the items pictured in the drawing. Be sure to use the correct endings for the plural (including umlauts). More than one answer may be possible.

Bitte, ___1___ sind hier vorn. Sie kosten nur € 1,30. ___2___ sind dort drüben und kosten € 14,00. Das ist sehr preiswert. Und ___3___ sind hier vorn. Sie sind im Sonderangebot für nur € 0,35. ___4___ sind auch hier vorn, und ___5___ sind da drüben, ___6___ sind aber weiter hinten. Oh, und ___7___ sind dort drüben. Sie kosten € 1,30.

Mehr Grammatikübungen
S. 123, Ü. 10 ➡

1. Hefte
2. Taschenrechner
3. Bleistifte
4. Schultaschen
5. Wörterbücher
6. Kassetten
7. Kulis

———

1. **Bleistifte sind hier vorn.**

28 **Eine Werbung** *Advertisement*

 Schreiben You are the owner of a store that sells school supplies and you are writing an advertisement to be read over the radio. Make up a name for your store, then pick five school supplies and write an ad describing them.

> **BEISPIEL** Wir haben Taschenrechner, sie kosten nur 10 Euro 95. Sehr preiswert, nicht? Und Bleistifte nur 45 Cent. Super! Die …

 29 **Wir brauchen Schulsachen** *We need school supplies*

a. Lesen Get together with three other classmates and take turns reading the advertisements you wrote in Activity 28. While one person reads, the others will be "listening to the radio" and will write down the various school supplies they hear mentioned and the price of each.

b. Sprechen/Schreiben Decide with your classmates which store your group will visit. The person whose store is chosen will play the **Verkäufer** and should set up his or her store (or draw a floorplan). The others will play the customers. The three customers will make a list of all the things they need from the store.

 30  **Von der Schule zum Beruf**

Schreiben You are an administrator at a German school. Lars's parents have called you to ask about his progress, since his last report card did not meet their high expectations (see his **Zeugnis** on p. 111). Write Lars's parents a letter on school letterhead describing how he is doing in his classes since the last report card.

AUSSPRACHE

CD 4 Trs. 14–16

Richtig aussprechen / Richtig lesen

A. To practice the following sounds, say the words and sentences below after your teacher or after the recording. CD 4 Tr. 14

1. The diphthongs **äu** and **eu:** The diphthongs **äu** and **eu** sound similiar to the *oy* sound in the English word *boy.*

   teuer, deutsch, Verkäufer / Der Verkäufer ist Deutscher.

2. The diphthong **au:** The diphthong **au** is pronounced much like the *ow* sound in the English word *cow.*

   Pause, schauen, bauen / Ich schaue Fernsehen nach der Pause.

3. The letters **b, d,** and **g:** At the end of a syllable or word, the consonants **b, d,** and **g** are pronounced as follows: the letter **b** sounds like the *p* in the English word *map;* the letter **d** is pronounced like the letter *t* in the English word *mat;* and the letter **g** is pronounced like the *k* sound in the English word *make.*

   Liebling, gelb, schreib / Schreib dein Lieblingsfach auf!
   Rad, Geld, blöd / Ich finde Radfahren blöd.
   Sag, Montag, Tag / Sag mal, hast du am Montag und Freitag Physik?

Richtig schreiben / Diktat
CD 4 Tr. 15
CD 4 Tr. 16 (with pauses)

B. Write down the sentences that you hear. Script on p. 99H

Lernen macht Spaß!

Lesestrategie

Understanding Compound Words German has many compound words. Often at least one part of a compound word is a cognate that you will recognize from English. Figuring out the meaning of individual words within a compound will often help you determine the meaning of the entire word.

1. Look at the following words and try to determine what they might mean by looking at the cognates within the compounds. You do not have to know the exact meaning of the compound word, but you can probably come close to figuring it out. For example, you can see that the word **Gesangunterricht** (abbreviated **Gesangunterr.** in the ad) has something to do with singing.

   a. **Keyboardschule** ══════

   b. **Deutschkurse** ══════

   c. **Privatunterricht** ══════

   d. **Volksschule** ══════

   e. **Schulverbund** ══════

2. Work with a partner. Write down the kinds of information you would be looking for if you were looking in the classified ads for a tutor in English.

3. Scan the ads for the following information:

   a. the telephone number you would call if you wanted singing lessons   3a. 0451-57328

   b. what the American wants to tutor   3b. English

Institut Rosenberg

Eine der führenden Schweizer Internatsschulen für Mädchen und Jungen seit 1889

Abitur

Deutsches Abitur im Hause
Vorbereitung für Eidgenössische Maturitätsprüfungen
Vorbereitung für das Studium in England und in den USA
Maturità Italiana

Privatunterricht gewährleistet • Überwachtes Studium
Internationale Atmosphäre

Sportarten:
Tennis • Wasserski • Reiten • Skifahren • Basketball • Volleyball etc.

Auskunft: O. Gademann
Institut Rosenberg • Höhenweg 60 • CH-9000 St. Gallen
Tel. 004171-277 92 91 Fax 004171-277 98 27

SCHULVERBUND PASSAU
Regensburger Straße 8, 94036 Passau, Tel. 0 851/23 26 71

—staatlich anerkannt—

DONAU-GYMNASIUM
Seit Sept. '93 zusätzlicher Schulzweig: SPORTGYMNASIUM

DONAU-REALSCHULE
Klassen 5-10 (Eintritt nach der 4. Klasse der Volksschule)

WIRTSCHAFTSSCHULE
Klassen 7-10 (berufsorientiert)

Passau

DONAU-VOLKSSCHULE
Teilhauptschule II, Klassen 7-9

Diese staatlich genehmigten Schulen bieten Schülern eine individuelle, differenzierte Beurteilung und Förderung.
Es gibt keinen Probeunterricht. Während der Probezeit wird die Eignung der Schüler individuell beurteilt.
Die in den letzten 25 Jahren erzielten überdurchschnittlichen Prüfungserfolge bestätigen unser Konzept.

MAYER-GYMNASIUM
MAYER-REALSCHULE
DONAU-VOLKSSCHULE
Klassen 1-4/Teilhauptschule I
Klassen 5+6 angeschl. Kindergarten

Einschreibung jederzeit möglich!

Ganztagsschulen mit Mittagstisch

Gesangunterr. u. Harmonielehre
☎ (0451) 57328

Dipl.-Physikerin für Mathe, Physik, Chemie
☎ (0451) 13566

Klavier- u. Keyboardschule Müller, Fachlehrer
☎ 89678

Deutschkurse für Ausländer Probestunde
kostenlos, kleine Gruppen, 68 Stunden,
☎ € 250,-
98105 u. 98287.

Amerikaner erteilt qualifizierten
Englischunterricht für Anfänger und
Fortgeschrittene. Auch Übersetzungen.
☎ 98120 ab 13 Uhr

---

c. the address of the **Schulverbund Passau**

> 3c. Regensburger Straße 8, 94036 Passau

4. Read the ads and answer the questions about each ad.

a. Who might be interested in the programs offered by the **Schulverbund**?

b. Can students eat at the schools in the **Schulverbund**? What tells you this information? Why would they need to?

c. What new branch of the **Donau-Gymnasium** has been operating since September 1993?

d. How much does the German course for foreigners cost? How much does a trial class period cost? How long is the course?

e. In what country is the **Institut Rosenberg** located? Is it a girls' school? What might it prepare you for?

> Switzerland; no-coed; university studies

5. Write some notes that you could use if you wanted to obtain more information from the school that offers German classes to foreigners. You might want to ask, for example, when and where the class meets.

6. With a partner write a short ad to offer tutoring in whatever you do best. It may be an academic class or a skills-oriented class. Use the classified ads on this page as your model.

7. You are going to be an exchange student in Germany. Which one of these schools would you like to attend? Why? Discuss this with a partner.

4a. students who want an individualized/ alternative program 4b. yes; "**Mittagstisch**"; school lasts all day: "**Ganztagsschulen**"
4c. Sportgymnasium 4d. € 250; free; 68 instruction hours

Übungsheft, S. 47, Ü. 23

Mehr Grammatikübungen

Erste Stufe

Objectives Talking about class schedules; using a schedule to talk about time

1 Sina, Alex, and Julia are talking about their class schedules. Complete the following dialogue by filling in each blank with the correct form of the verb **haben. (S. 108)**

SINA	Du, Alex, was _____ wir heute um 8 Uhr?	haben
ALEX	Um 8 Uhr _____ wir Mathe, glaube ich.	haben
SINA	Hm, die Julia _____ Informatik, sagt sie.	hat
ALEX	Sag, Sina, _____ du Informatik gern?	hast
SINA	Ich _____ Informatik sehr gern, das ist mein Lieblingsfach.	habe
JULIA	Hallo! Was _____ ihr denn morgen um 12 Uhr 20?	habt
ALEX	Um 12 Uhr 20 _____ wir Erdkunde.	haben
SINA	Und du _____ am Freitag frei. Ein Feiertag!	hast

2 Students are talking about class subjects, what they have on certain days, and when. Complete the following pairs of questions and statements by filling in each blank with the correct form of the verb **haben. (S. 108)**

1. Alex, _____ du heute Physik? — Du, ich _____ heute Physik und Chemie. — hast; habe
2. Was _____ ihr am Samstag? — Am Samstag _____ wir frei. — habt; haben
3. Was _____ Julia und Sina heute? — Sie _____ Deutsch, Latein und Sport. — haben; haben
4. Und was _____ der Alex heute? — Er _____ Physik, Bio und Englisch. — hat; hat
5. Wer _____ heute Kunst? — Ich _____ heute Kunst. — hat; habe
6. Wann _____ du Deutsch? — Deutsch _____ ich um zehn Uhr. — hast; habe
7. Wann _____ ihr denn frei? — Du, wir _____ am Samstag frei. — habt; haben
8. Wann _____ denn die Julia Bio? — Du, sie _____ am Freitag Bio. — hat; hat

3 Ask your classmates the following questions (when they have certain subjects, when they play certain sports, and what subjects they have) by filling in each blank with the correct verb form and pronoun. **(S. 108)**

Remember: When addressing one classmate, use the **du**-form of the verb.
When addressing several classmates *(you all)*, use the **ihr**-form.
When addressing your teacher or a stranger, use the **Sie**-form.
When addressing several teachers or strangers, use the same **Sie**-form.

1. Sag mal, Frank, wann _____ _____ Biologie? — hast du
2. Frank und Mary, wann _____ _____ heute Geschichte? — habt ihr
3. Frau Maier, wann _____ _____ heute frei? Nach der Pause? — haben Sie
4. Frau Meier und Herr Moser, wann _____ _____ heute frei? — haben Sie
5. Wann _____ _____ Tennis, Lisa? Nach der Schule? — spielst du
6. Wann _____ _____ Fußball, Leute? Heute oder morgen? — spielt ihr
7. Wann _____ _____ Golf, Frau Bruschke? Am Wochenende? — spielen Sie

8. Wann _____ _____ Volleyball, Herr Meier und Herr Wolff?   spielen Sie

9. Welche Fächer _____ _____ heute, Julia?   hast du

10. Welche Fächer _____ _____ am Freitag, Lars und Sina?   habt ihr

11. Welche Fächer _____ _____ gern, Herr Moser?   haben Sie

12. Und welche Fächer _____ _____ gern, Frau Maier und Frau Arndt?   haben Sie

Zweite Stufe

Objectives Expressing likes, dislikes, and favorites

4 Try to find out what your friends' favorite subjects in school are. For each response, fill in the first blank with the correct form of the possessive, and the second blank with the correct form of the verb **haben**. (S. 110)

1. Was ist Julias Lieblingsfach? — _____ Lieblingsfach ist Deutsch, aber sie _____ auch   Ihr; hat
Englisch und Biologie gern.

2. Was ist Alex' Lieblingsfach? — _____ Lieblingsfach ist Physik, aber er _____ auch   Sein; hat
Chemie und Geschichte gern.

3. Was ist dein Lieblingsfach? — _____ Lieblingsfach ist Englisch, aber ich _____ auch   Mein; habe
Erdkunde und Geschichte gern.

4. Was ist Sinas Lieblingsfach? — _____ Lieblingsfach ist Kunst, aber sie _____ auch   Ihr; hat
Geschichte und Erdkunde gern.

5. Was ist Ahmets Lieblingsfach? — _____ Lieblingsfach ist Sport, aber er _____ auch   Sein; hat
Latein und Englisch gern.

6. Und was ist dein Lieblingsfach? — _____ Lieblingsfach ist Geschichte, aber ich   Mein; habe
_____ auch Englisch und Französisch gern.

5 What school subjects don't these students like that much and what are their favorites? Complete each of the following statements by filling in the first blank with a correct form of the verb **haben** and the second blank with an appropriate possessive. (S. 110)

1. Mathe _____ ich nicht so gern, und _____ Lieblingsfach ist Biologie.   habe; mein

2. Alex _____ Bio nicht so gern, und _____ Lieblingsfach ist Physik.   hat; sein

3. Julia _____ Geschichte nicht so gern, und _____ Lieblingsfach ist Kunst.   hat; ihr

4. Ich _____ Latein nicht so gern, und _____ Lieblingsfach ist Chemie.   habe; mein

5. Sina _____ Physik nicht so gern, und _____ Lieblingsfach ist Sport.   hat; ihr

6. Jens _____ Erdkunde nicht so gern, und _____ Lieblingsfach ist Englisch.   hat; sein

 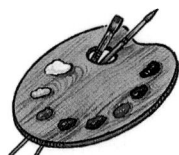 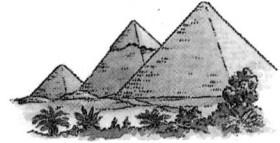

Dritte Stufe

Objectives Talking about prices; pointing things out

6 You are in the school supply store. You need a lot of supplies for school, but before you buy anything you inquire about the price of all the items on your list. Complete each of the following questions by writing the plural form of the noun in parentheses, together with the plural article. **(S. 114)**

1. (Schultasche)   Was kosten _____ ?   die Schultaschen
2. (Bleistift)   Was kosten _____ ?   die Bleistifte
3. (Kassette)   Was kosten _____ ?   die Kassetten
4. (Kuli)   Was kosten _____ ?   die Kulis
5. (Taschenrechner)   Was kosten _____ ?   die Taschenrechner
6. (Radiergummi)   Was kosten _____ ?   die Radiergummis
7. (Heft)   Was kosten _____ ?   die Hefte
8. (Wörterbuch)   Was kosten _____ ?   die Wörterbücher

Taschenrechner ab € 16,-

7 You are in a school supply store and want to know the prices of various school supplies. Complete each of the following questions by filling in each blank with the correct form of the verb **kosten** and the item given in parentheses (definite article and noun). **(S. 114)**

1. (notebook)   Was _____ bitte _____ _____ ?   kostet; das Heft
2. (pencils)   Was _____ bitte _____ _____ ?   kosten; die Bleistifte
3. (eraser)   Was _____ bitte _____ _____ ?   kostet; der Radiergummi
4. (dictionaries)   Was _____ bitte _____ _____ ?   kosten; die Wörterbücher
5. (school bag)   Was _____ bitte _____ _____ ?   kostet; die Schultasche
6. (ballpoint pen)   Was _____ bitte _____ _____ ?   kostet; der Kuli
7. (cassettes)   Was _____ bitte _____ _____ ?   kosten; die Kassetten
8. (calculator)   Was _____ bitte _____ _____ ?   kostet; der Taschenrechner

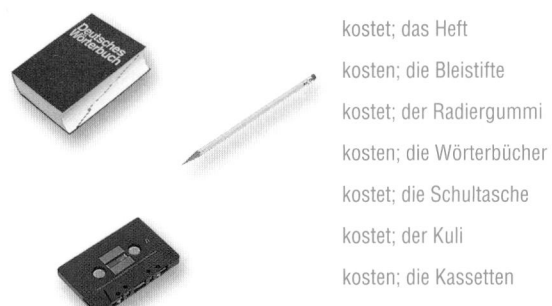

8 Still in the school supply store, you want to know how much one item is that you want to buy, and the salesperson tells you. Complete each question and statement by filling in the first blank with the correct form of the definite article, and the second blank with the correct form of the pronoun used to refer to the item. **(S. 115)**

1. Was kostet _____ Wörterbuch? — _____ kostet 10 Euro.   das; Es
2. Was kostet _____ Schultasche? — _____ kostet 15 Euro.   die; Sie
3. Was kostet _____ Heft? — _____ kostet zwei Euro.   das; Es
4. Was kostet _____ Taschenrechner? — _____ kostet 20 Euro.   der; Er
5. Was kostet _____ Kassette? — _____ kostet drei Euro.   die; Sie
6. Was kostet _____ Kuli? — _____ kostet vier Euro.   der; Er
7. Was kostet _____ Bleistift? — _____ kostet fünfzig Cent.   der; Er

8. Was kostet _____ Radiergummi? — _____ kostet zwanzig Cent. der; Er

9. Was kosten _____ Schulsachen? — _____ kosten 30 Euro. die; Sie

10. Was kosten _____ Bücher? — _____ kosten zwölf Euro. die; Sie

9 The new currency in most of Europe, the euro, necessitated adjustments in speaking and writing for hundreds of millions of people. Practice writing out some examples of prices, as shown in the model. Note that the words **Euro** and **Cent** are both singular and plural. **(S. 115)**

BEISPIEL   € 7,10   **sieben Euro und zehn Cent**   (spoken: sieben Euro zehn)

1. € 1,60
ein Euro und sechzig Cent
2. € 3,20
drei Euro und zwanzig Cent
3. €12,40
zwölf Euro und vierzig Cent
4. €16,30
sechzehn Euro und dreißig Cent

5. € 4,70
vier Euro und siebzig Cent
6. € 2,90
zwei Euro und neunzig Cent
7. € 7,80
sieben Euro und achtzig Cent
8. €14,50
vierzehn Euro und fünfzig Cent

10 Read the following conversation. Then fill in each blank with an appropriate word from the word box. **(S.116)**

Cent	der	die	du	er	Euro	Fächer
				Er	kostet	habe
habe	hast	kostet		kosten	kostet	
ich		Uhr			zuletzt	sie

– Sag mal, Peter, welche _____ hast _____ denn am Dienstag? Fächer; du

– Zuerst _____ ich Deutsch, dann Mathe und _____ habe _____ Bio. habe; zuletzt; ich

– Was _____ du nach der Pause um 10 _____ 20? hast; Uhr

– Informatik habe _____ , und danach _____ ich frei. ich; habe

– Sag, _____ Taschenrechner ist toll! Was _____ er? der; kostet

– Ich glaube, _____ kostet 14 _____ und 50 _____ . er; Euro; Cent

– Was _____ denn _____ Bleistifte? kosten; die

– Ja, _____ kosten nicht viel, ich glaube 80 _____ . sie; Cent

– Mein Taschenrechner _____ 30 Euro. _____ ist teuer. kostet; Er

Anwendung

The CD-ROM Tutor offers guided recording and writing activities to accompany the **Anwendung.** These activities are designed to practice students' oral and written communication skills and to review material from each chapter.

1 Working in small groups, use the ad on page 114 for clues to make up price tags in German for various school supplies in the classroom. Put the tags on the appropriate objects and arrange them as in a store window or as in a store. Now take turns role-playing customer and salesclerk, asking how much things cost and where they are located.

2 What do the items below tell you about the student, Claudia Müller? Use them to answer the questions that follow.

STADTBUS
SCHÜLERAUSWEIS

NAME Claudia Müller

GEBURTSDATUM 7.1.1988

GÜLTIG VON 15.9.02 BIS 30.6.03

Claudia Müller

UNTERSCHRIFT DES SCHÜLERS

Luise-Schmitt-Gymnasium

ZEUGNIS

für *Claudia Müller* geb am *7.1.1988*

Schuljahr 19 *01, 02* Klasse *9 B* *1* Halbjahr

LEISTUNGEN

Pflichtunterricht

Geschichte....	*gut*	Deutsch...........	*gut*
Mathe..........	*sehr gut*	Latein..........	*befriedigend*
Sport........	*befriedigend*	Französisch ...	*sehr gut*
Biologie..........	*gut*	Physik.............	*gut*
Erdkunde	*gut*	Kunst.............	*sehr gut*
Englisch..........	*sehr gut*	Chemie	*ausreichend*

1. Wie heißt Claudias Schule?
2. Wie kommt Claudia zur Schule?
3. Sind Claudias Noten gut?
4. Welche Note hat sie in Bio?

1. Luise-Schmitt-Gymnasium 2. mit dem Bus 3. ja 4. gut

3 Look at the items in the preceding activity again. Use the information to write five German sentences about Claudia.

4 Look at the two pictures below. What items can you name in the picture on the left? What items are missing in the picture on the right? Kassetten, Taschenrechner, Bleistifte

BEISPIEL **Die Bleistifte fehlen.** *oder* **Das Heft fehlt.**

5 Create an activity calendar for yourself in German for the coming Saturday. Include all the things you would like to do and the times you expect to do them. Then, working with a partner, imagine that you ran into him or her after school and are talking about your plans for the weekend. Use the sequencing words **zuerst**, **dann**, **danach**, and **zuletzt**.

6 Write a letter to your pen pal and tell him or her about school. Write about which classes you have and when, which classes you like or do not like, and which are your favorites.

7 On the first day of school, your German teacher is telling you what school supplies you will need. Write them as you hear them mentioned.　Script on p. 99H

Wörterbuch, Bleistifte, Kuli, Hefte, Kassette

CD 4
Tr. 17

8 ## Zum Schreiben

Create a web page to find a person who is your mirror image at school.

Schreibtipp Cluster diagrams
are a useful way to organize your ideas. Here's an example of how to make one. Draw a small circle in the middle of the page. Draw four or five more circles and connect each to the original circle. These circles show interconnections of one topic/idea with the main idea and with each other. In this case you (Ich) would be in the main circle and all that you like or dislike about school would be in the surrounding circles.

Prewriting
Decide on titles for your circles. Since you are looking for someone who is nearly identical to you, you might want to use: „Lieblingsfächer," „Noten," „Ich mag diese Fächer nicht," „Mein Stundenplan," „Schulsachen, die ich haben muss," „Wie ich zur Schule komme," „Lieblingslehrer(-innen)." Fill in the circles with appropriate entries.

Writing
Using the information you organized in your cluster diagram, design and write your web page. You might begin: „Ich suche mein Spiegelbild!"

9 ## Rollenspiel

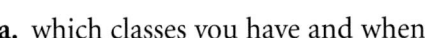

You are having a conversation with two friends at the school supply store. Role-play the conversation in front of the class. Use the school supply list from Activity 7 as an aid. Be sure to include:

a. which classes you have and when

b. which classes you like, dislike and your favorite class

c. grades in some of your classes (make sure your friends respond appropriately)

After your conversation, ask the salesperson where various school supplies are located and what they cost.

Kann ich's wirklich?

Can you talk about schedules using haben? (p. 106)

1 How would you say the following in German: a. Ulrike hat am Mittwoch und Freitag Deutsch.

a. Ulrike has German on Wednesday and Friday.

b. Monika and Klaus have history on Tuesday and Thursday.

c. Richard has no classes on Saturday.   b. Monika und Klaus haben am Dienstag und
c. Richard hat am Samstag frei.   Donnerstag Geschichte.

2 How would you ask a friend what classes he or she has on Monday? How might he or she respond? How would you ask two friends? How might they respond if they both have the same schedule?

Was hast du am Montag? Ich habe …Was habt ihr am Montag? Wir haben …

Can you use a schedule to talk about time? (p. 107)

3 Say when these people have these classes.

a. Martin	8.30	Mathe
b. Claudia und Ingrid	9.45	Latein
c. Alex	10.20	Musik
d. Michaela und Manfred	3.00	Kunst

a. Martin hat um 8 Uhr 30 Mathe.
b. Claudia und Ingrid haben um 9 Uhr 45 Latein.
c. Alex hat um 10 Uhr 20 Musik.
d. Michaela und Manfred haben um 3 Uhr Kunst.

4 How would you tell someone what time you have your German class, using the expression **von …bis …**?   Ich habe von 8 Uhr bis 8 Uhr 45 Deutsch.

Can you sequence events using zuerst, dann, danach, and zuletzt? (p. 109)

5 How would you tell a classmate the sequence of your classes on Thursday?

Am Donnerstag habe ich zuerst …dann …danach …zuletzt

Can you express likes, dislikes, and favorites? (p. 110)

6 How would you say which subjects you like, dislike, and which is your favorite? How would you ask your friend for the same information?

Welche Fächer hast du gern? / nicht gern? / Was ist dein Lieblingsfach?

Ich habe …gern. Ich habe …nicht gern.
…ist mein Lieblingsfach.

Can you respond to good news and bad news? (p. 112)

7 How would you respond if Ahmet, an exchange student at your school, told you:

a. Ich habe eine
Eins in Bio.
Toll!

b. Ich habe eine
Vier in Latein.
So ein Pech!

c. Ich habe eine
Zwei in Englisch.
Prima!

Can you talk about prices? (p. 115)

8 How would you ask a salesperson how much these items cost: calculators, notebooks, erasers, pencils, pens, school bags, dictionaries, and cassettes?

Was kosten die Taschenrechner/ Hefte/ Radiergummis/ Bleistifte/
Kulis/ Schultaschen/ Wörterbücher/ Kassetten?

9 How would you tell your friend what each of the following items costs? How might he or she comment on the prices?

a. Das
Wörterbuch
kostet 11
Euro 20. —Das
ist preiswert.

a. Wörterbuch
€ 11,20

b. Kuli
€ 2,10

c. Schultasche
€ 10,90

b. Der Kuli kostet 2 Euro 10. — Das ist teuer!   c. Die Schultasche kostet 10 Euro 90. — Das ist sehr billig!

Can you point things out? (p. 116)

10 Write a conversation in which your friend asks you where several things are located in a store. You point them out and give a general location. Then tell him or her how much they cost.

Talking about class schedules

die Schule, -n*	school
haben	to have
er/sie hat	he/she has
die Klasse, -n	grade level
der Stundenplan, ¨e	class schedule
das Fach, ¨er	(class) subject
Welche Fächer hast du?	What (which) subjects do you have?
Ich habe Deutsch …	I have German …
Bio (Biologie)	biology
Englisch	English
Chemie	chemistry
Erdkunde	geography
Geschichte	history
Kunst	art

Informatik	computer science
Latein	Latin
Mathe (Mathematik)	math
Physik	physics
Religion	religion
Sport	physical education

Using a schedule to talk about time

die Zeit	time
Wann?	when?
um 8 Uhr	at 8 o'clock
von 8 Uhr bis 8 Uhr 45	from 8 until 8:45
heute	today

nach der Pause	after the break
am Montag	on Monday
Dienstag	Tuesday
Mittwoch	Wednesday
Donnerstag	Thursday
Freitag	Friday
Samstag	Saturday
Sonntag	Sunday
Wir haben frei.	We are off (out of school).

Sequencing events

zuerst	first
dann	then
danach	after that
zuletzt	last of all

Zweite Stufe

Expressing likes, dislikes, and favorites

gern haben	to like
nicht gern haben	to dislike
Lieblings-	favorite

Grades

die Note, -n	grade
eine Eins (Zwei, Drei, Vier, Fünf, Sechs)	grades: a 1 (2, 3, 4, 5, 6)

Responding to good news and bad news

gut	good
schlecht	bad
Schade!	Too bad!
So ein Mist!	That stinks!/What a mess!
So ein Pech!	Bad luck!
So ein Glück!	What luck!

Other words and phrases

Ganz klar!	Of course!
bloß	only
das Zeugnis	report card

Dritte Stufe

School supplies

Das ist/Das sind …	That is/Those are
die Schulsachen (pl)	school supplies
das Buch, ¨er	book
der Kuli, -s	ballpoint pen
das Wörterbuch, ¨er	dictionary
die Schultasche, -n	schoolbag
der Taschenrechner, -	pocket calculator
der Radiergummi, -s	eraser
der Bleistift, -e	pencil
das Heft, -e	notebook
die Kassette, -n	cassette

Talking about prices

kosten	to cost
Was kostet …?	How much does …cost?
Das ist preiswert.	That's a bargain.
billig	cheap
teuer	expensive
das Geld	money
€ = der Euro	euro (European monetary unit)
der Euro, -	euro
der Cent, -	cent (smallest unit of the euro currency; $\frac{1}{100}$ of a euro)

Pointing things out

Schauen Sie!	Look!
Schau!	Look!
dort	there
dort drüben	over there
da vorn	up there in the front
da hinten	there in the back

Other words and expressions

ziemlich	rather
nur	only

*Plural forms will be indicated in this way from now on.

Kapitel 5: Klamotten kaufen
Chapter Overview

Los geht's! pp. 130–132	*Was ziehst du an? p. 130*

	FUNCTIONS	GRAMMAR	VOCABULARY	RE-ENTRY
Erste Stufe pp. 133–136	• Expressing wishes when shopping, p. 134	• Definite and indefinite articles in the accusative case, p. 135	• Clothing items, p. 133 • Colors, p. 136	• Numbers and prices, p. 135 (**Kap. 1, 3**, and **4**) • Colors, p. 136 (**Kap. 4**) • Pointing things out, p. 136 (**Kap. 4**)
Zweite Stufe pp. 137–142	• Commenting on and describing clothes, p. 137 • Giving compliments and responding to them, p. 139	• The verb **gefallen**, p. 137 • Direct object pronouns, p. 140	• Telling how clothes fit, p. 138	• Expressing likes and dislikes, p. 137 (**Kap. 2**) • Asking for and expressing opinions, p. 141 (**Kap. 2**)
Dritte Stufe pp. 143–145	• Talking about trying on clothes, p. 143	• Separable-prefix verbs, p. 143 • Stem-changing verbs **nehmen** and **aussehen**, p. 144		• The verb **aussehen**, p. 143 (**Kap. 3**)

Aussprache p. 145	The short vowels **i**, **ä**, and **e**, the vowel **a**, and the letter combinations **sch**, **st**, **sp**: Audio CD 5, Track 13	**Diktat:** Audio CD 5, Tracks 14–15

Zum Lesen pp. 146–147	**Kleider machen Leute!**	**Reading Strategy** Using what you already know

Mehr Grammatik-übungen	**pp. 148–151** Erste Stufe, pp. 148–149	Zweite Stufe, pp. 149–150	Dritte Stufe, p. 151

Review pp. 152–155	**Anwendung**, pp. 152–153 **Zum Schreiben:** Outlining (Writing a fashion show commentary)	**Kann ich's wirklich?**, p. 154	**Wortschatz**, p. 155

CULTURE

• **Ein wenig Landeskunde:** Exchange rates, p. 134
• **Ein wenig Landeskunde:** German store hours, p. 136
• **Ein wenig Landeskunde:** German clothing sizes, p. 138
• **Landeskunde:** Welche Klamotten sind „in"?, p. 142

Kapitel 5: Klamotten kaufen
Chapter Resources

 **PRINT**

Lesson Planning
One-Stop Planner
Lesson Planner with Substitute Teacher Lesson Plans, pp. 22–26, 69
Student Make-Up Assignments
- Make-Up Assignment Copying Masters, Chapter 5

Listening and Speaking
TPR Storytelling Book, pp. 17–20
Listening Activities
- Student Response Forms for Listening Activities, pp. 35–37
- Additional Listening Activities 5-1 to 5-6, pp. 39–42
- Additional Listening Activities (song), p. 38
- Scripts and Answers, pp. 124–128

Video Guide
- Teaching Suggestions, pp. 30–31
- Activity Masters, pp. 32–34
- Scripts and Answers, pp. 90–92, 113

Activities for Communication
- Communicative Activities, pp. 25–30
- Realia and Teaching Suggestions, pp. 90–93
- Situation Cards, pp. 131–132

Reading and Writing
Reading Strategies and Skills Handbook, Chapter 5
Lies mit mir! 1, Chapter 5
Übungsheft, pp. 49–60

Grammar
Grammatikheft, pp. 37–45
Grammar Tutor for Students of German, Chapter 5

Assessment
Testing Program
- Grammar and Vocabulary Quizzes, **Stufe** Quizzes, and Chapter Test, pp. 105–122
- Score Sheet, Scripts and Answers, pp. 123–130

Alternative Assessment Guide
- Portfolio Assessment, p. 22
- Performance Assessment, p. 36
- CD-ROM Assessment, p. 50

Student Make-Up Assignments
- Alternative Quizzes, Chapter 5

 **MEDIA**

 Online Activities
- Interaktive Spiele
- Internet Aktivitäten

 Video Program
- Videocassette 2
- Videocassette 5 (captioned version)

 Audio Compact Discs
- Textbook Listening Activities, CD 5, Tracks 1–16
- Additional Listening Activities, CD 5, Tracks 23–31
- Assessment Items, CD 5, Tracks 17–22

 Interactive CD-ROM Tutor, Disc 2

 Teaching Transparencies
- Situations 5-1 to 5-2
- Vocabulary 5-A to 5-C
- **Los geht's!**
- **Mehr Grammatikübungen** Answers
- **Grammatikheft** Answers

 **One-Stop** Planner CD-ROM

Use the **One-Stop Planner CD-ROM with Test Generator** to aid in lesson planning and pacing.

For each chapter, the **One-Stop Planner** includes:
- Editable lesson plans with direct links to teaching resources
- Printable worksheets from resource books
- Direct launches to the HRW Internet activities
- Video and audio segments
- Test Generator
- Clip Art for vocabulary items

Kapitel 5: Klamotten kaufen

Projects ··········· Games ···········

Junge Mode

*In this activity the class will create a German mail-order clothing catalog featuring clothing for teenagers. This project should be started after completion of the **Zum Lesen** part of this chapter. This project is designed to be carried out with the class divided into eight groups and each group working on one part of the catalog.*

MATERIALS

✂ **Each group may need**
- 1 sheet of colored construction paper size 16″ × 20″
- glue
- old catalogs and magazines
- scissors
- colored markers

SUGGESTED CATALOG SECTIONS

Front cover   Formal wear for girls/boys
Sportswear for boys/girls Shoes, accessories

SUGGESTED SEQUENCE

1. Assign a different topic to each group.

2. Have each group gather materials from old catalogs and magazine ads.

3. Once they have gathered items, the groups should decide what they want to include in their two-page section of the catalog and make an outline.

4. Prepare a short written description in German for each item in their section of the catalog, including fabric, colors, and sizes available. Each student is responsible for writing at least one of the descriptions.

5. Proofread each other's descriptions for accuracy and complete final layout of each group's pages.

6. Assemble all pages to resemble an actual catalog. Name the catalog.

GRADING THE PROJECT

Suggested point distribution (**total = 100 points**)
Appearance of pages..............................25
Accurate descriptions/
    correct language usage 50
Originality 25

Zeichne bitte . . .

This is a good game to help students practice clothing vocabulary.

Procedure   Divide the class into two teams. The first person from Team A asks a student from the other team to go to the board and draw the clothing item he or she names. (Example: **Peter, zeichne bitte einen Gürtel!**) The student at the board has a set time limit in which to draw the item. If his or her picture is the correct item, he or she scores a point for the team. If the student draws the wrong item, the team does not receive a point. In either case, players alternate drawing between teams. The team with the higher score at the end of the game wins.

FAMILY LINK

Students might want to play this game with their younger brothers and sisters. It would give students an opportunity to review the clothing vocabulary while introducing their siblings to the German language.

Wortbögen

This game, in which students test their knowledge of vocabulary by identifying "hidden" words, can be played by individuals or in pairs.

Preparation   Make several **Wortbögen** (such as the one shown on the following page) using the vocabulary from the **Wortschatz** that you intend to review. Put four or five **Wortbögen** on one sheet of paper and make a copy for each student or pair.

Procedure   Give students a time limit for this game depending on how many words are in your **Bögen**. As soon as you give the signal, students try to find as many words as possible within a specific topic. (Examples: clothing, adjectives, and separable-prefix verbs) Tell students that words must be made up of consecutive letters, and some letters may be used in more than one word. The person or team that finds the most words wins.

WEIT   HÜBSCH   SCHICK

starken Strömungen, können ungeübten Wanderern leicht zum Verhängnis werden.

Storytelling

Mini-Geschichte

*This story accompanies Teaching Transparency 5-2. The **Mini-Geschichte** can be told and retold in different formats, acted out, written down, and read aloud to give students additional opportunities to practice all four skills.*

Wer bin ich?

Ich heiße Freddie. Meine Lieblingsfarbe ist Rot. Mein Hemd ist rot. Es passt prima! Mein Gürtel ist rot. Er ist zu eng. Meine Schuhe sind rot. Sie sind ein bisschen groß. Meine Nase ist auch rot. Sie ist viel zu groß. Gelb gefällt mir auch. Meine Jacke ist gelb. Sie sieht echt lässig aus. Meine Hose ist zu kurz. Mein Freund heißt Fescher Eddie. Er ist ein Gangster. Er sieht scheußlich aus. Seine Lieblingsfarbe ist Schwarz. Ich finde seine Klamotten echt langweilig.

Traditions

Wattwandern

Das Wandern auf dem Watt ist ein wahres Naturerlebnis. Bei Ebbe liegt das flache Meer vor Schleswig-Holsteins Nordseeküste stundenweise trocken und erlaubt es Wanderern den Meeresgrund zu erforschen und sogar Inseln trockenen Fußes zu erreichen. Eine Fähre bringt die Wanderer dann wieder an das Festland. Ebbe und Flut leeren und füllen das Wattenmeer täglich zweimal. Jede Wanderung sollte unbedingt von einem kundigen Wattführer, der Pfade und Gezeiten kennt, geleitet werden. Priele, tiefere Wasserströme mit erstaunlich

Rezept

✺✺✺   ✺✺✺   ✺✺✺

Kopfsalat in Sahnesauce

4 Personen

Zutaten

l=Liter, EL=Eßlöffel

1/4 l	süße Sahne
	Salz
Saft	von 1 Zitrone
2 EL	Zucker
2	Kopfsalate

Zubereitung

Sahne mit Salz, Zitronensaft und Zucker verrühren, mindestens 10 Minuten stehen lassen und dick werden lassen. Salatköpfe putzen, waschen, abtropfen lassen und in mundgerechte Stücke zupfen. Unmittelbar vor dem Servieren mit der Salatsauce mischen.

Kapitel 5: Klamotten kaufen
Technology

Video

Videocassette 2, 5 (captioned version)
See Video Guide, pages 29–34

Los geht's! • Was ziehst du an?

Katja and Julia are talking about clothes they want to wear to Sonja's party and decide to go to a clothing store. Katja tries on some things and finally buys a T-shirt.

Fortsetzung

Michael had just bought a T-shirt in the same store, and Katja and Julia disliked it. Michael and Heiko go back to the store to find out what the girls bought. As a practical joke, the boys buy a number of T-shirts like Katja's.

Landeskunde
Welche Klamotten sind „in"?
People from different cities talk about clothes they like to wear on various occasions.

Videoclips
- **Quelle® Katalog** (clothing catalog)
- **Otto® Katalog** (clothing catalog)
- **Persil®** (laundry detergent)
- **Hypercolor Kleidung** (sports clothes)
- **Perwoll®** (laundry detergent)

Interactive CD-ROM Tutor

The **Interactive CD-ROM Tutor** contains videos, interactive games, and activities that provide students an opportunity to practice and review the material covered in Chapter 5.

Activity	Activity Type	Pupil's Edition Reference
1. Grammatik	Was fehlt?	p. 135
2. Wortschatz	Merkspiel	pp. 133, 136
3. So sagt man das!	Wort und Bild Erfahren/Wählen	pp. 137, 139
4. So sagt man das!	Was ist richtig?	pp. 137-140
5. So sagt man das!	Wozu gehört's?	pp. 134, 137, 139, 143
6. Grammatik	Was fehlt?	pp. 143, 144
Landeskunde	Welche Klamotten sind „in"? Was ist richtig?	p. 142
Zum Sprechen	*Guided recording*	pp. 152-153
Zum Schreiben	*Guided writing*	pp. 152-153

Teacher Management System
Logging In
Logging in to the *Komm mit!* TMS is easy. Upon launching the program, simply type "admin" in the password area of the log-in screen and press RETURN. Log on to **www.hrw.com/CDROMTUTOR** for a detailed explanation of the Teacher Management System.

One-Stop Planner CD-ROM

To preview all resources available for this chapter, use the **One-Stop Planner CD-ROM**, Disc 2.

Internet Connection

ADRESSE: go.hrw.com
KENNWORT: WK3
SCHLESWIG-HOLSTEIN-5

*Have students explore the **go.hrw.com** Web site for many online resources covering all chapters. All Chapter 5 resources are available under the keyword **WK3 Schleswig-Holstein-5.** Interactive games practice the material and provide students with immediate feedback. You will also find a printable worksheet that provides Internet activities that lead to a comprehensive online research project.*

Interaktive Spiele

You can use the interactive activities in this chapter

- to practice grammar, vocabulary, and chapter functions
- as homework
- as an assessment option
- as a self-test
- to prepare for the Chapter Test

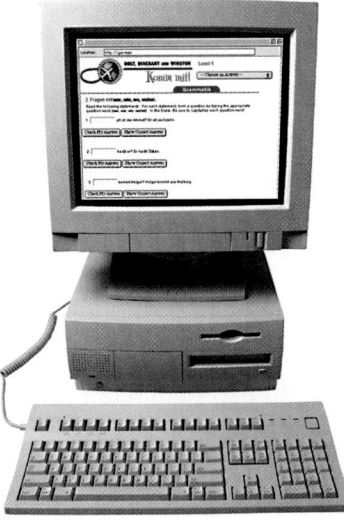

Internet Aktivitäten

Students will visit online department stores and learn how to use a currency converter.

- To prepare students for the **Arbeitsblatt,** you might want to have them look at the conversion table on p. 134. Have students review the catalog ads in **Zum Lesen,** pp. 146–147. Here they find descriptions and prices of different items of clothing.

- After completing the **Arbeitsblatt,** have students visit an online American department store and compare prices. Do German teens pay more or less for their clothes?

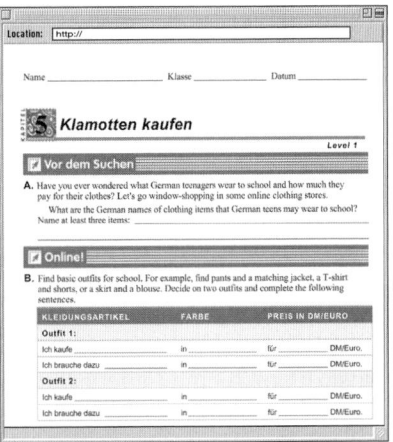

Webprojekt

Have students do a Web search for a German boutique or department store that sells their favorite kinds of clothes. Have them choose an outfit and price it. Students should report on the name of the boutique or store, the items they chose, and the price of each item. Encourage students to exchange useful Web sites with their classmates.

Have students document their sources by referencing the names and URLs of all the sites they consulted.

Kapitel 5: Klamotten kaufen
Textbook Listening Activities Scripts

Erste Stufe

6 p. 133

Ob flott oder elegant, es ist immer preiswert bei uns, Mode-Mania! Hier finden Sie wirklich alles! Für die Damen haben wir eine große Auswahl an Kleidern und Röcken. Und für den sportlichen Typ: flotte Jogging–Anzüge! Die Blusen aus Leinen und Baumwolle sind gerade im Sonderangebot. Und für ihn haben wir diese Woche auch tolle Sachen, sehr preiswert: schicke Gürtel, zum Beispiel, und bequeme Hemden und Hosen in allen Größen und Farben. Bei Mode-Mania gibt's fesche Sachen für die ganze Familie! Wir sind Montag bis Freitag immer von 10 bis 18 Uhr geöffnet und am Samstag von 10 bis 14 Uhr. Kommen Sie doch mal vorbei!

9 p. 135

1. — Was kostet denn der Gürtel, da?
   — Ja also der kostet nur 10 Euro. Sehr preiswert.
2. — Ich möchte den Pulli dort, aber lieber in Rot.
   — So einen Pulli möchte ich auch.
3. — Das T-Shirt kostet nur acht Euro, nicht?
   — Ja, das T-Shirt ist billig, was?
4. — Du, schau mal! Die Boutique hat die Bluse in Blau.
   — Ehrlich? Die Bluse hat Gaby doch auch, oder nicht?
5. — Du, Sabine, wie findest du den Jogging–Anzug in Grau?
   — Ich finde den einfach toll!
6. — Brauchst du auch eine neue Jacke für den Winter?
   — Ja, eine neue Jacke, vielleicht in Blau, brauch ich schon.
7. — Die Stiefel in Schwarz da kosten 100 Euro!
   — Wirklich? Die Stiefel sind zu teuer.
8. — Ich suche ein neues Hemd in Grau für meinen Vater, und du?
   — Ich suche ein Hemd in Grün für meinen Bruder.

Zweite Stufe

15 p. 137

1. Die Schuhe sehen echt blöd aus! Die sind total altmodisch!
2. Die Shorts finde ich ganz fesch! Sie passen gut zu meinem neuen T-Shirt.
3. Die Bluse sieht ja furchtbar aus. Sie gefällt mir wirklich nicht!
4. Hübscher Rock, nicht? So einen möchte ich auch gern haben.
5. Solche Jacken sind zur Zeit in Mode. Ich finde sie super!

19 p. 140

1. — Der Jogging-Anzug ist total schick, aber etwas zu teuer.
   — Probier ihn doch trotzdem mal an!
2. — Wie findest du den Rock, da?
   — Ich finde ihn schon schön, aber lieber in Blau!
3. — Ich möchte gern das T-Shirt in Hellgrün.
   — Ja, es ist schick!
4. — Das T-Shirt kostet nur acht Euro.
   — Wirklich? Es ist aber sehr preiswert.
5. — Die Turnschuhe hier sind toll!
   — Ja, die sind stark.
6. — Möchtest du den Pulli da in Schwarz?
   — Nein, ich möchte ihn wirklich nicht. Die Farbe mag ich einfach nicht.
7. — Wie findest du die Bluse da vorn?
   — Sie ist aber teuer!

The following scripts are for the listening activities found in the *Pupil's Edition*. For Student Response Forms, see *Listening Activities*, pages 35–38. To provide students with additional listening practice, see *Listening Activities*, pages 39–42.

For resource information, see the **One-Stop Planner CD-ROM**, Disc 2.

Dritte Stufe

23 p. 143

1. VERKÄUFER Ja, stimmt, ... sie ist zwar etwas teuer, aber die Qualität ist prima. Der Pulli ist aus Baumwolle. Er steht Ihnen wirklich ausgezeichnet!

JÜRGEN Finden Sie wirklich?

2. VERKÄUFER Wie passt denn der Schuh? Drückt er? Vorn haben Sie ja genug Platz.

JÜRGEN Ja, er passt eigentlich ganz gut. Welche Größe ist das?

VERKÄUFER Das hier ist 40. Gefällt Ihnen die Farbe?

3. JÜRGEN Ist die Jeans im Sonderangebot? Ich find die ja fesch. Gibt's die in meiner Größe?

VERKÄUFER Einen Moment. Da muss ich mal nachschauen ... Ja, wir haben noch Jeans in Ihrer Größe. Und auch im Angebot, nur 23 Euro.

4. VERKÄUFER Was darf es noch sein?

JÜRGEN Danke. Das ist alles. Ich möchte bitte zahlen.

VERKÄUFER Die Schuhe, die Jacke und die Jeans ... das macht 87 Euro 50.

JÜRGEN Bitte schön. Vielen Dank für Ihre Hilfe.

AUSSPRACHE, p. 145

Diktat, p. 145

First listen to what is said, then write the description.

Katja und Sonja gehen heute zu Mode–Mania. Sie brauchen neue Klamotten für die Fete bei Dieter am Samstag. Zuerst probiert Katja den Rock in Grün an. Er sieht aber scheußlich aus. Dann findet sie Jeans in Schwarz. Die sind wirklich fesch. Und Sonja? Sie findet eine Hose in Dunkelblau und einen Pulli in Weiß. Das passt alles prima!

Anwendung

5 p. 153

1. Schade! Die Bluse gefällt mir so gut, aber sie ist einfach viel zu groß für mich!

2. Die Jacke gefällt mir schon, aber nicht in der Farbe. Haben Sie die Jacke vielleicht in Braun?

3. Was, 100 Euro? Die Jeans ist ja toll, aber sie ist ja viel zu teuer! So viel kann ich nicht für Jeans bezahlen.

4. Die Hose ist zu lang und auch ein bisschen zu weit. Die sitzt einfach nicht so gut. Haben Sie eine Größe kleiner?

5. Der Pulli in Dunkelgrün ist schick, nur ist das nicht meine Farbe. Meine Lieblingsfarbe ist Blau.

Kapitel 5: Klamotten kaufen
Suggested Lesson Plans *50-Minute Schedule*

Day 1

CHAPTER OPENER 10 min.
- Teaching Suggestion, ATE, p. 127M
- Thinking Critically, ATE, p. 127M

LOS GEHT'S! 20 min.
- Preteaching Vocabulary, ATE, p. 127N
- Play Audio CD for **Los geht's!**, pp. 130–131
- Have students read **Los geht's!**, pp. 130–131
- Teaching Suggestions, Video Guide, p. 30
- Language Note, ATE, p. 127N
- Show **Los geht's!** Video
- Do Comprehension Activities, p. 132

ERSTE STUFE
Wortschatz, p. 133 15 min.
- Play Game, ATE, p. 127O
- Presenting **Wortschatz**, ATE, p. 127O
- Teaching Transparencies 5-A, 5-B
- Play Audio CD for Activity 6, p. 133

Wrap-Up 5 min.
- Students supply definite articles for various pieces of clothing

Homework Options
Grammatikheft, p. 37, Acts. 1–2
Übungsheft, pp. 49–50, Acts. 1–2

Day 2

ERSTE STUFE
Quick Review 10 min.
- Check homework, Grammatikheft, p. 37, Acts. 1–2

Ein wenig Landeskunde, p. 134 10 min.
- Presenting **Ein wenig Landeskunde**, ATE, p. 127O
- Do Activity 7, p. 134

So sagt man das!, p. 134 10 min.
- Presenting **So sagt man das!**, ATE, p. 127P
- Do Activity 8, p. 134

Grammatik, p. 135 15 min.
- Presenting **Grammatik**, ATE, p. 127P
- Play Audio CD for Activity 9, p. 135
- Do Activities 10 and 11, p. 135
- Play game, **Ich packe meinen Koffer…**, ATE, p. 127Q

Wrap-Up 5 min.
- Students respond to questions about clothing needs

Homework Options
Grammatikheft, p. 38, Acts. 3–4
Übungsheft, pp. 50–52, Acts. 3–7
Interactive CD-ROM, Acts. 1–2

Day 3

ERSTE STUFE
Quick Review 15 min.
- Check homework, Grammatikheft, p. 38, Acts. 3–4
- Do Activity 12, p. 136

Wortschatz, p. 136 15 min.
- Presenting **Wortschatz**, ATE, p. 127Q
- Do Activity 13, p. 136

Ein wenig Landeskunde, p. 136 15 min.
- Present **Ein wenig Landeskunde**, p. 136
- Thinking Critically, ATE, p. 127Q
- Do Activity 14, p. 136

Wrap-Up 5 min.
- Students respond to questions about clothing in various colors

Homework Options
Grammatikheft, p. 39, Acts. 5–6
Übungsheft, p. 52, Act. 8

Day 4

ERSTE STUFE
Quick Review 10 min.
- Check homework, Grammatikheft, p. 39, Acts. 5–6

Quiz Review 20 min.
- Do **Mehr Grammatikübungen, Erste Stufe**
- Do Additional Listening Activities 5-1 and 5-2, pp. 39–40

Quiz
- Quiz 5-1A or 5-1B 20 min.

Homework Options
Activities for Communication, p. 90, Realia 5-1, circle cognates

Day 5

ZWEITE STUFE
Quick Review 10 min.
- Return and review Quiz 5-1
- Bell Work, ATE, p. 127R

So sagt man das!, p. 137 10 min.
- Presenting **So sagt man das!**, ATE, p. 127R
- Teaching Transparency 5-1
- Play Audio CD for Activity 15, p. 137

Ein wenig Grammatik, p. 137 10 min.
- Presenting **Ein wenig Grammatik**, ATE, p. 127R
- Do Activity 16, p. 138

Wortschatz/Ein wenig Landeskunde, p. 138 15 min.
- Presenting **Wortschatz**, p. 127R
- Teaching Transparency 5-C
- Present **Ein wenig Landeskunde**, p. 138
- Do Activity 17, p. 139

Wrap-Up 5 min.
- Students describe how various articles of clothing fit

Homework Options
Grammatikheft, pp. 40–41, Acts. 7–10
Übungsheft, pp. 53–54, Acts. 9–11

Day 6

ZWEITE STUFE
Quick Review 10 min.
- Check homework, Grammatikheft, pp. 40–41, Acts. 7–10

So sagt man das!, p. 139 15 min.
- Presenting **So sagt man das!**, ATE, p. 127S
- Teaching Transparencies 5-1, 5-2
- Do Activity 18, p. 139

Grammatik, p. 140 20 min.
- Presenting **Grammatik**, ATE, p.127S
- Play Audio CD for Activity 19, p. 140
- Do Activities 20 and 21, p. 141
- Present **Minigeschichte, Zweite Stufe**, TPR Storytelling Book, p. 18

Wrap-Up 5 min.
- Students respond to questions about clothing likes and dislikes

Homework Options
Grammatikheft, pp. 42–43, Acts. 11–12
Mehr Grammatikübungen, Zweite Stufe

One-Stop Planner CD-ROM

For alternative lesson plans by chapter section, to create your own customized plans, or to preview all resources available for this chapter, use the **One-Stop Planner CD-ROM**, Disc 2.

For additional homework suggestions, see activities accompanied by this symbol throughout the chapter.

Day 7

ZWEITE STUFE

Quick Review 15 min.
- Check homework, Grammatikheft, pp. 42–43, Acts. 11–12
- Do Activity 22, p. 141

LANDESKUNDE 30 min.
- Pre-viewing Suggestion, Video Guide, p. 30
- Show **Landeskunde** Video
- Do Viewing and Post-viewing Activities, Video Guide, p. 33
- Do Activities A and B, p. 142
- Do Activities 1–4, p. 60, Übungsheft

Wrap-Up 5 min.
- Students answer questions about what kinds of clothes are "in" in Germany

Homework Options
Übungsheft, pp. 54–55, Acts. 12–15
Activities for Communication, pp. 27–28, prepare Communicative Activity 5-2

Day 8

ZWEITE STUFE

Quick Review 10 min.
- Check homework, Übungsheft, pp. 54–55, Acts. 12–15

Quiz Review 20 min.
- Do Communicative Activity 5-2, pp. 27–28
- Do Additional Listening Activities 5-3 and 5-4, pp. 40–41
- Do **Interaktive Spiele**, see ATE, p. 127F

Quiz 20 min.
- Quiz 5-2A or 5-2B

Homework Options
Activities for Communication, pp. 131–132, prepare Situation 5-2

Day 9

DRITTE STUFE

Quick Review 10 min.
- Return and review Quiz 5-2
- Bell work, ATE, p. 127T
- Do Situation 5-2, pp. 131–132

So sagt man das!, p. 143 10 min.
- Presenting **So sagt man das!**, ATE, p. 127T
- Play Audio CD for Activity 23, p. 143

Grammatik, p. 143 10 min.
- Presenting **Grammatik**, ATE, p. 127U
- Do Activity 24, p. 144

Ein wenig Grammatik/ Lerntrick, p. 144 15 min.
- Presenting **Ein wenig Grammatik**, ATE, p. 127U
- Present **Lerntrick**, p. 144
- Teacher Note, ATE, p. 127U
- Do Activities 25 and 26, p. 144

Wrap-Up 5 min.
- Students respond to clothing questions using verbs with separable prefixes

Homework Options
Pupil's Edition, p. 145, Activity 27
Grammatikheft, pp. 44–45, Acts. 13–16
Übungsheft, pp. 56–58, Acts. 16–22

Day 10

DRITTE STUFE

Quick Review 10 min.
- Check homework, Grammatikheft, pp. 44–45, Acts. 13–16

Quiz Review 20 min.
- Do **Mehr Grammatikübungen, Dritte Stufe**
- Play **Wortbögen**, ATE, p. 127D

Quiz 20 min.
- Quiz 5-3A or 5-3B

Homework Options
Pupil's Edition, p. 145, Activity 28
Übungsheft, p. 59, Act. 23
Activities for Communication, p. 92, Realia 5-3, have students make a list of things they want to buy, then write where they can find the items

Day 11

DRITTE STUFE

Quick Review 10 min.
- Return and review Quiz 5-3
- Check homework, Realia 5-3, p. 92

Aussprache, p. 145 10 min.
- Do **Richtig aussprechen/Richtig lesen**, p. 145
- Do **Richtig schreiben/Diktat**, p. 145

ZUM LESEN 20 min.
- Culture Note, ATE, p. 127W
- Do Activities 1–12, pp. 146–147

Kann ich's wirklich?, p. 154 5 min.
- Begin questions 1–10 in writing

Wrap-Up 5 min.
- Students respond orally to **Kann ich's wirklich?** questions, p. 154

Homework Options
- Pupil's Edition, p. 154, complete **Kann ich's wirklich?** questions
- **Internet Aktivitäten**, see ATE, p. 127F

Day 12

ANWENDUNG 30 min.

Quick Review
- Check homework, **Kann ich's wirklich?**, p. 154
- Teaching Suggestions, ATE, p. 127X
- Do **Anwendung Activities**, pp. 152–153

Chapter Review 15 min.
- Review chapter functions, vocabulary, and grammar; choose from **Mehr Grammatikübungen**, Grammar Tutor for Students of German, Activities for Communication, Listening Activities, Interactive CD-ROM Tutor, or **Interaktive Spiele**

Wrap-Up 5 min.
- Students respond to questions about choosing and buying clothing

Homework Options
Study for Chapter Test

Assessment

Test, Chapter 5 45 min.
- Administer Chapter 5 Test. Select from Testing Program, Alternative Assessment Guide or Test Generator.

Kapitel 5: Klamotten kaufen
Suggested Lesson Plans *90-Minute Schedule*

Block 1

CHAPTER OPENER 10 min.
- Teaching Suggestion, ATE, p. 127M
- Thinking Critically, ATE, p. 127M

LOS GEHT'S! 25 min.
- Preteaching Vocabulary, ATE, p. 127N
- Play Audio CD for **Los geht's!**, pp. 130–131
- Have students read **Los geht's!**, pp. 130–131
- Teaching Suggestions, Video Guide, p. 30
- Language Note, ATE, p. 127N
- Show **Los geht's!** Video
- Do Comprehension Activities, p. 132

ERSTE STUFE
Wortschatz, p. 133 15 min.
- Play Game, ATE, p. 127O
- Presenting **Wortschatz**, ATE, p. 127O
- Teaching Transparencies 5-A, 5-B
- Play Audio CD for Activity 6, p. 133

Ein wenig Landeskunde, p. 134 10 min.
- Presenting **Ein wenig Landeskunde**, ATE, p. 127O
- Do Activity 7, p. 134

So sagt man das!, p. 134 10 min.
- Presenting **So sagt man das!**, ATE, p. 127P
- Do Activity 8, p. 134

Grammatik, p. 135 15 min.
- Presenting **Grammatik**, ATE, p. 127P
- Play Audio CD for Activity 9, p. 135
- Do Activities 10 and 11, p. 135
- Play game, **Ich packe meinen Koffer…**, ATE, p. 127Q

Wrap-Up 5 min.
- Students respond to questions about clothing needs

Homework Options
Grammatikheft, pp. 37–39, Acts. 1–6
Übungsheft, pp. 49–52, Acts. 1–8

Block 2

ERSTE STUFE
Quick Review 15 min.
- Check homework, Grammatikheft, pp. 37–39, Acts. 1–6
- Do Activity 12, p. 136

Wortschatz, p. 136 15 min.
- Presenting **Wortschatz**, ATE, p. 127Q
- Do Activity 13, p. 136

Ein wenig Landeskunde, p. 136 15 min.
- Present **Ein wenig Landeskunde**, p. 136
- Thinking Critically, ATE, p. 127Q
- Do Activity 14, p. 136

Quiz Review 25 min.
- Do **Mehr Grammatikübungen, Erste Stufe**
- Do Additional Listening Activities 5-1 and 5-2, pp. 39–40

Quiz
- Quiz 5-1A or 5-1B **20 min.**

Homework Options
Activities for Communication, p. 90, Realia 5-1, circle cognates

Block 3

ZWEITE STUFE
Quick Review 15 min.
- Return and review Quiz 5-1
- Bell Work, ATE, p. 127R

So sagt man das!, p. 137 15 min.
- Presenting **So sagt man das!**, ATE, p. 127R
- Teaching Transparency 5-1
- Play Audio CD for Activity 15, p. 137

Ein wenig Grammatik, p. 137 10 min.
- Presenting **Ein wenig Grammatik**, ATE, p. 127R
- Do Activity 16, p. 138

Wortschatz/Ein wenig Landeskunde, p. 138 20 min.
- Presenting **Wortschatz**, p. 127R
- Teaching Transparency 5-C
- Present **Ein wenig Landeskunde**, p. 138
- Do Activity 17, p. 139

So sagt man das!, p. 139 10 min.
- Presenting **So sagt man das!**, ATE, p. 127S
- Teaching Transparencies 5-1, 5-2
- Do Activity 18, p. 139

Grammatik, p. 140 15 min.
- Presenting **Grammatik**, ATE, p.127S
- Play Audio CD for Activity 19, p. 140
- Do Activities 20 and 21, p. 141

Wrap-Up 5 min.
- Students respond to questions about clothing likes and dislikes

Homework Options
Grammatikheft, pp. 40–43, Acts. 7–12
Mehr Grammatikübungen, Zweite Stufe

One-Stop Planner CD-ROM

For alternative lesson plans by chapter section, to create your own customized plans, or to preview all resources available for this chapter, use the **One-Stop Planner CD-ROM**, Disc 2.

 For additional homework suggestions, see activities accompanied by this symbol throughout the chapter.

Block 4

ZWEITE STUFE
Quick Review 15 min.
- Check homework, Grammatikheft, pp. 40–43, Acts. 7–12
- Do Activity 22, p. 141

LANDESKUNDE 30 min.
- Pre-viewing Suggestion, Video Guide, p. 30
- Show **Landeskunde** Video
- Do Viewing and Post-viewing Activities, Video Guide, p. 33
- Do Activities A and B, p. 142
- Do Activities 1–4, p. 60, Übungsheft

Quiz Review 25 min.
- Do Communicative Activity 5-2, pp. 27–28
- Do Activities 9–15, pp. 53–55, Übungsheft
- Do **Interaktive Spiele**, see ATE, p. 127F

Quiz 20 min.
- Quiz 5-2A or 5-2B

Homework Options
Activities for Communication, pp. 131–132, prepare Situation 5-2

Block 5

DRITTE STUFE
Quick Review 15 min.
- Return and review Quiz 5-2
- Bell work, ATE, p. 127T
- Do Situation 5-2, pp. 131–132

So sagt man das!, p. 143 20 min.
- Presenting **So sagt man das!**, ATE, p. 127T
- Play Audio CD for Activity 23, p. 143
- Do Activities 5 and 6, Interactive CD-ROM

Grammatik, p. 143 10 min.
- Presenting **Grammatik**, ATE, p. 127U
- Do Activity 24, p. 144

Ein wenig Grammatik/Lerntrick p. 144 25 min.
- Presenting **Ein wenig Grammatik**, ATE, p. 127U
- Present **Lerntrick**, p. 144
- Teacher Note, ATE, p. 127U
- Do Activities 25 and 26, p. 144
- Do Activity 28, p. 145

Aussprache, p. 145 15 min.
- Do **Richtig aussprechen/Richtig lesen**, p. 145
- Do **Richtig schreiben/Diktat**, p. 145

Wrap-Up 5 min.
- Students respond to clothing questions using verbs with separable prefixes

Homework Options
Pupil's Edition, p. 145, Act. 27
Grammatikheft, pp. 44–45, Acts. 13–16
Übungsheft, pp. 56–59, Acts. 16–23

Block 6

DRITTE STUFE
Quick Review 15 min.
- Check homework, Grammatikheft, pp. 44–45, Acts. 13–16

Quiz Review 20 min.
- Do **Mehr Grammatikübungen, Dritte Stufe**
- Play **Wortbögen**, ATE, p. 127D

Quiz 20 min.
- Quiz 5-3A or 5-3B

ZUM LESEN 20 min.
- Culture Note, ATE, p. 127W
- Present **Lesestrategie**, p. 146
- Do Activities 1–12, pp. 146–147

Kann ich's wirklich?, p. 154 10 min.
- Begin questions 1–10 in writing

Wrap-Up 5 min.
- Students respond orally to **Kann ich's wirklich?** questions, p. 154

Homework Options
Pupil's Edition, p. 154, complete **Kann ich's wirklich?**
Internet Aktivitäten, see ATE, p. 127F

Block 7

ANWENDUNG 30 min.
Quick Review
- Return and review Quiz 5-3
- Teaching Suggestions, ATE, p. 127X
- Do **Anwendung** Activities, pp. 152–153

Chapter Review 15 min.
- Review chapter functions, vocabulary, and grammar; choose from **Mehr Grammatikübungen**, Grammar Tutor for Students of German, Activities for Communication, Listening Activities, Interactive CD-ROM Tutor, or **Interaktive Spiele**
- Review test format and provide sample test items for students

Test, Chapter 5 45 min.
- Administer Chapter 5 Test. Select from Testing Program, Alternative Assessment Guide or Test Generator.

Kapitel 5: Klamotten kaufen
Teaching Suggestions, *pages 128–155*

PAGES 128–129

CHAPTER OPENER

Pacing Tips

In the **Erste Stufe** the definite and indefinite articles in the accusative case are introduced. The function of 'expressing wishes when shopping' is presented, reintroducing the verb **möchten** from Chapter 3. In the **Zweite Stufe** accusative case is expanded to include the direct object pronouns. The verb **gefallen** is presented along with the functions of 'commenting on and describing clothes' and 'giving compliments and responding to them.' In the **Dritte Stufe**, students learn about separable-prefix verbs and the stem-changing verbs **nehmen** and **aussehen**. Because the **Dritte Stufe** has fewer pages and a much shorter **Wortschatz** than the **Erste Stufe** or the **Zweite Stufe**, you will probably use a bit less time to teach the **Dritte Stufe**. For Lesson Plans and timing suggestions, see pages 127I–127L.

Meeting the Standards
Communication
- Expressing wishes when shopping, p. 134
- Commenting on and describing clothes, p. 137
- Giving compliments and responding to them, p. 139
- Talking about trying on clothes, p. 143

Cultures
- **Ein wenig Landeskunde,** p. 134
- **Ein wenig Landeskunde,** p. 136
- **Ein wenig Landeskunde,** p. 138
- **Landeskunde,** p. 142
- Culture Note, p. 127Q
- Culture Note, p. 127W

Connections
- Multicultural Connection, p. 127S
- Thinking Critically, p. 127V
- Geography Connection, p. 127W
- Multicultural Connection, p. 127W

Comparisons
- Thinking Critically, p. 127M
- Language Note, p. 127N
- Language-to-Language, p. 127P
- Language Note, p. 127U
- Teaching Suggestion, p. 127W

Communities
- Thinking Critically, p. 127M
- Teaching Suggestion, p. 127M
- Thinking Critically, p. 127Q
- Career Path, p. 127Q

One-Stop Planner CD-ROM

For resource information, see the **One-Stop Planner CD-ROM**, Disc 2.

Cultures and Communities

Teaching Suggestion
Take a survey of students' attitudes toward clothing. Ask students how important clothes are to them on a scale of 1-10. How much time do they spend on average deciding what to wear in the morning? Find out who in the music or entertainment industry dresses in a style they admire and who, in their opinion, dresses the worst.

Thinking Critically
Drawing Inferences Certain careers require a traditional outfit. Can students think of any reasons for this? (Examples: clergy, judges, physicians)

Connections and Comparisons

Thinking Critically
- **Comparing and Contrasting** Ask students if they would find the types of clothing items in this picture in American stores. If so, which ones? Also, get students to look for other similarities or differences in the picture.

- **Analyzing** Germans have a saying: **Kleider machen Leute.** *(Clothes make the person.)* Discuss this phrase with students. Do they agree or disagree?

Chapter Sequence

Los geht's! . . . . .p. 130
Erste Stufe . . . . .p. 133
Zweite Stufe . . . . .p. 137
Landeskunde . . . . .p. 142
Dritte Stufe . . . . .p. 143
Zum Lesen . . . . .p. 146
Mehr Grammatikübungen . . . . .p. 148
Anwendung . . . . .p. 152
Kann ich's wirklich? . . . . .p. 154
Wortschatz . . . . .p. 155

LOS GEHT'S!

Teaching Resources
pp. 130–132

PRINT
▶ Lesson Planner, p. 22
▶ Video Guide, pp. 29–30, 32
▶ Übungsheft, p. 49

MEDIA
▶ One-Stop Planner
▶ Video Program
  Los geht's!
  Videocassette 2, 21:47–25:33
  Videocassette 5 (captioned version),
  22:47–26:35
  Fortsetzung
  Videocassette 2, 25:35–27:12
  Videocassette 5 (captioned version),
  26:36–28:12
▶ Audio Compact Discs, CD5, Trs. 1–2
▶ **Los geht's!** Transparencies

PAGES 130–131

Los geht's! Transparencies

Preteaching Vocabulary

Recognizing Cognates

Los geht's! contains several words that students will be able to recognize as cognates. Have students find these cognates, then have them guess what is happening in the story.

1 Fete, Jogging-Anzug, meine Shorts, eine Bluse, ein T-Shirt, meine Haare

3 allen, in Blau, Natürlich!

4 sportlich, gut

5 schick, ein Texas-Motiv

6 medium, hundert Prozent

8 kostet

Fortsetzung

You may choose to continue with the **Fortsetzung** of *Was ziehst du an?* now or wait until later in the chapter. For a synopsis of the **Los geht's!** and **Fortsetzung** episodes, see p. 127E.

Advance Organizer

As an advance organizer for **Los geht's!**, ask students how they dress when they are invited to a party.

Connections and Comparisons

Language Note

The word **Fete** comes from the French word *fête* (*party*). The word **Klamotten** is a very casual word used to refer to one's belongings. It is mostly used for items of clothing.

 Total Physical Response

For students who might have trouble understanding the scenes, bring to class the clothing items that are part of **Los geht's!**. Teach the vocabulary to the class in a short TPR lesson. Ask some students to come to the front of the class, and give each of them commands such as **Zieh den Pulli an!** or **Zieh das T-Shirt an!** To help visual learners, you might want to show the vocabulary words on cards while students are trying on the articles of clothing.

PAGE 132

Using the Captioned Video

 As an alternative to reading the conversations in the book, you might want to show the captioned version of *Was ziehst du an?* available on Videocassette 5.

Comprehension Check

1 After answering the questions, have students write one brief statement for each picture. Assemble several suggestions on the board and have students agree on one representative statement for each frame. Then proceed to the following activity.

3 Have each student write one true and one false statement. Have several students read their sentences for the class to decide whether the answer should be **Stimmt** or **Stimmt nicht.**

ERSTE STUFE

Teaching Resources
pp. 133–136

PRINT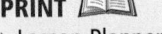
▸ Lesson Planner, p. 23
▸ TPR Storytelling Book, pp. 17, 20
▸ Listening Activities, pp. 35, 39–40
▸ Activities for Communication, pp. 25–26, 90, 93, 131–132
▸ Grammatikheft, pp. 37–39
▸ Grammar Tutor for Students of German, Chapter 5
▸ Übungsheft, pp. 50–52
▸ Testing Program, pp. 105–108
▸ Alternative Assessment Guide, p. 36
▸ Student Make-Up Assignments, Chapter 5

MEDIA
▸ One-Stop Planner
▸ Audio Compact Discs, CD5, Trs. 3–4, 17, 23–24
▸ Teaching Transparencies
   Situation 5-1
   Vocabulary 5-A, 5-B
   Mehr Grammatikübungen Answers
   Grammatikheft Answers
▸ Interactive CD-ROM Tutor, Disc 2

> **PAGE 133**

Bell Work
Show students the **Los geht's!** transparencies and have them write a list of all the items of clothing they can identify in German.

Game

Have all students stand up by giving the command **Steht auf!** Begin with the first student in the front and ask him or her to name any German noun he or she can think of, including its article. If the student says the word and article correctly, he or she remains standing. The next student says another noun (students can't use nouns that have already been named). If a student cannot think of a new noun, repeats a noun already used, or names a word that is not a noun, he or she must sit down. (Give the command **Setz dich!**) The last student standing wins the game.

PRESENTING: Wortschatz

Have a bag or a suitcase full of clothes and accessories that are part of the **Wortschatz**. Begin by naming the objects and showing them simultaneously. Then ask **ja/nein** questions followed by either/or questions, and finally, short response questions such as **Was ist das?**

Communication for All Students

Tactile Learners
6 As students listen to the recording for the first time, ask them to sketch each article of clothing instead of writing the word. When they have finished drawing all seven items of clothing, ask students to name the items.

> **PAGE 134**

PRESENTING: Ein wenig Landeskunde

• Ask for a volunteer to check the business section of the newspaper for three to five consecutive days. Have this student bring the exchange tables to class each day. Keep a record of the date and the daily exchange rate for the euro and the U.S. dollar.

• **Synthesizing** Ask students if they know why the rates change daily. (Rates fluctuate as interest rates change in any given country. Interest rates are tied to everyday events that take place in the country or the world.)

• **Drawing Inferences** As students monitor the changing rates, ask them if they know of any significant events that are currently taking place in Germany, Europe, or the United States that might be relevant to the fluctuation of the exchange rate.

PRESENTING: So sagt man das!

• With a collection of clothing in a bag or suitcase, approach a student, tell him or her to imagine that you are a salesperson, and ask: **Was möchten Sie? Einen Gürtel oder Jeans?** The student responds: **Ich möchte …** and takes the appropriate item. Continue the activity, varying the expressions by using those listed in **So sagt man das!**

• Now ask students to tell you in English what you asked them in the previous activity. Write down the different expressions students give you. (Examples: *What would you like?* and *How can I help you?*) Tell students that there are different ways of expressing wishes in German, just as there are in English. Point these out in **So sagt man das!**

Connections and Comparisons

Language-to-Language

Mention to your students that in German, as in many other languages (for example, Latin, Slavic languages, and Semitic languages), nouns and adjectives have a system of inflection to show case and convey meaning while English, French, and Spanish rely mostly on word order and prepositions. You may want to tell students that English still retains a form of the genitive case to express possession. Have them come up with examples of genitive inflection in English. (Examples: *the girl's coat, the boy's book, students' bicycles*)

PRESENTING: Grammatik

Articles and accusative case Since the concept of case is unfamiliar to many students, you might want to begin by putting some sentences on the board. Help students identify each part of the sentence. (Examples: **Die Frau kauft die Bluse. Er möchte das T-Shirt.**) Explain to students that the term *case* applies to nouns as well as pronouns. It categorizes their function within the sentence. In order to explain this function of sentence parts, grammar notes will traditionally refer to them as the four cases. The case of the subject is also referred to as the nominative case. A noun or pronoun used as a direct object is in the accusative case. Write the following sentences on the board: **Der Pulli ist rot. Ich kaufe den Pulli.** Ask students to label the parts of the sentence. What can they conclude about direct objects and masculine articles? (**der** changes to **den**)

Communication for All Students

A Slower Pace

9 If students were not able to follow the entire listening activity, write the eight exchanges on a transparency and let students determine the answers.

Visual Learners

For additional practice after the game, have a pile of clothing in front of the class. As students repeat items, one student packs the named items in the suitcase, and another student writes the name of each item on the board.

Point out to students that the forms they should use are modeled in the **Grammatik** on p. 135, or you may want to write on the board: **der/den, die/die, das/das, ein/einen, eine/eine, ein/ein.**

Teaching Suggestion

10 Assign this activity as pair work. Each pair begins by reading the conversation and answering questions 1-3 on a sheet of paper. They then practice reading the conversation aloud. As a final task, have students try to identify the subject and direct object in each sentence. Have them underline the two different sentence parts in two different colors.

Speaking Assessment

11 Have individual students come to your desk for assessment. You may wish to evaluate their monologue using the following rubric.

Speaking Rubric	Points			
	4	3	2	1
Content (Complete – Incomplete)				
Comprehension (Total – Little)				
Comprehensibility (Comprehensible – Incomprehensible)				
Accuracy (Accurate – Seldom accurate)				
Fluency (Fluent – Not fluent)				

18–20: A   16–17: B   14–15: C   12–13: D   Under 12: F

Game

Bring a suitcase and several items of clothing to class. Using the clothing vocabulary from the chapter, have one student start the game by saying the phrase **Ich packe meinen Koffer und nehme … mit.**, as he or she puts that item of clothing in the suitcase. The following student repeats the sentence, including the first student's addition, and adds his or her own item to the list. The third student adds a third, and so on. How many pieces of clothing and accessories can students remember?

Communication for All Students

For Additional Practice

13 Assign this to be prepared as a short skit with a set time limit of 1-2 minutes, in which students are encouraged to use props. Students should begin by making a draft of their skit. Offer to check drafts and make suggestions and corrections. Students finalize their skit by making a copy for each player. The performers set up in the front of the class and perform their skit. Use a video camera or tape recorder to record the skits, if possible.

PRESENTING: Wortschatz

First, teach the colors by showing objects in the colors to be taught. (Examples: flags, crayons, and clothing) Use sentences such as **Der Rock ist grün. Die Flagge ist rot, weiß und blau.** Then, using clothing items, have students ask you for each item in a different color than you are showing. (Example: **Haben Sie das auch in Blau?**)

Cultures and Communities

 Culture Note

Shopping hours are regulated all across Germany by federal law. If people need something after hours, they often go into train stations, gas stations, or even airports where small vendors provide a limited selection of essential food items.

Thinking Critically

Synthesizing Ask students to think about some reasons business hours are so strictly regulated. (This is done mainly to protect the interests of small business owners and their personnel, who might be forced to keep long hours to compete with other businesses. Furthermore, the strong influence of labor unions insures tolerable working hours.)

Reteaching: Colors

Students can make color associations as you ask questions such as **Welche Farbe hat die Sonne? Welche Farbe hat das Gras? Welche Farbe hat das Buch von Rebecca? … die Hose von …**

Reteaching: Nominative and accusative cases

Prepare a chart with the following columns on a transparency.

Subject/ Pronoun	Verb	Object
Ich	kaufen	das Buch
Susanne	haben	der Pulli
Der Junge	nehmen	der Kuli

Have students use the cues to form complete sentences. Remind students that the masculine article changes in the accusative case.

Connections and Comparisons

Career Path

Ask your students to think of careers in the fashion industry in which a solid knowledge of German would be to their advantage. (Suggestions: Imagine you are a buyer for a big fashion house and have been asked to attend a fashion show in Munich; imagine you are a fashion photographer in charge of the fall catalog of a Swiss fashion house.)

Assess

▸ Testing Program, pp. 105–108
Quiz 5-1A, Quiz 5-1B
Audio CD5, Tr. 17

▸ Student Make-Up Assignments
Chapter 5, Alternative Quiz

▸ Alternative Assessment Guide, p. 36

ZWEITE STUFE

Teaching Resources
pp. 137–142

PRINT

▸ Lesson Planner, p. 24
▸ TPR Storytelling Book, pp. 18, 20
▸ Listening Activities, pp. 36, 40–41
▸ Activities for Communication, pp. 27–28, 91, 93, 131–132
▸ Grammatikheft, pp. 40–43
▸ Grammar Tutor for Students of German, Chapter 5
▸ Übungsheft, pp. 53–55
▸ Testing Program, pp. 109–112
▸ Alternative Assessment Guide, p. 36
▸ Student Make-Up Assignments, Chapter 5

MEDIA

▸ One-Stop Planner
▸ Audio Compact Discs, CD5, Trs. 5–6, 18, 25–26
▸ Teaching Transparencies
  Situations 5-1, 5-2
  Vocabulary 5-C
  Mehr Grammatikübungen Answers
  Grammatikheft Answers
▸ Interactive CD-ROM Tutor, Disc 2

PAGE 137

Bell Work

Ask students to make a list of phrases they would use to compliment a friend's outfit. What expressions do their parents use to compliment other adults on their clothes?

PRESENTING: So sagt man das!

Ask students to look back at **Los geht's!** on pp. 130–131 and remind them of the functions that are targeted in the **Zweite Stufe** (commenting on and describing clothes, giving compliments and responding to them). Where do students see these functions modeled in **Los geht's!**? Have students make a list of the expressions they find.

For Additional Practice

In order to practice all the new expressions, have students react to you and express their opinions as you put on different pieces of clothing. Try to bring some fashionable items as well as some out-of-fashion pieces to get different reactions.

PRESENTING: Ein wenig Grammatik

Gefallen Suggest that students keep a list of idiomatic expressions for their portfolios, **Notizbücher,** and process writing assignments.

PAGE 138

PRESENTING: Wortschatz

Introduce this new vocabulary by emphasizing opposites. Incorporate other examples using pictures, classroom objects, and so on. (Example: short pencil *versus* long pencil)

PAGE 139

Communication for All Students

A Slower Pace
17 After doing this activity orally in class, assign it as written homework and have students include their opinions about the clothing pictured.

PRESENTING: So sagt man das!

Remind students of the motivating activity they did at the beginning of this **Stufe.** See if any of their suggestions are similar to the German expressions introduced in this function box. Explain that intonation plays a big role in how compliments are given and received. Give an example: **Peter, deine Jacke gefällt mir! Wirklich? Wirklich!** As in English, questions and responses have a much different intonation. The speaker's voice goes up at the end of a question, and it remains fairly flat for a response.

PRESENTING: Grammatik

Direct object pronouns Review personal pronouns by giving several examples in which students repeat sentences by replacing nouns with pronouns. Have the sentences of this grammar box on the board or on a transparency with the subject and direct objects underlined. Ask students what changes occur when a feminine, neuter, or masculine direct object is replaced by a pronoun. Make a chart of the changes as students name them.

Examples: Ich finde <u>den Gürtel</u> schick.
  Ich finde <u>ihn</u> schick.
  Ich finde <u>die Bluse</u> scheußlich.
  Ich finde <u>sie</u> scheußlich.
  Ich finde <u>das Hemd</u> furchtbar.
  Ich finde <u>es</u> furchtbar.

den	→	ihn
die	→	sie
das	→	es

Communication for All Students

Challenge

19 After students have successfully matched the articles of clothing with the appropriate adjectives, have them write the seven sentences as accurately as they can recall them. Have students read their sentences aloud.

Portfolio

22 You might want to use this activity as a written portfolio item for your students. See *Alternative Assessment Guide*, p. 22.

Reteaching: Direct object pronouns

Make a chart of sentence fragments as in the example below and have students replace nouns with pronouns.

Sabine	kauft	das Kleid	**(das Kleid = es)**
Sie kauft es.			
Rolf	möchte	den Kuli	_____
Er möchte ihn.			
Christian	nimmt	die Stiefel	_____
Er nimmt sie.			

LANDESKUNDE

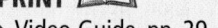

Teaching Resources
p. 142

PRINT
▶ Video Guide, pp. 29–30, 32–33
▶ Übungsheft, p. 60

MEDIA
▶ One-Stop Planner
▶ Video Program
  Videocassette 2, 27:52–33:02
▶ Audio Compact Discs, CD5, Trs. 7–11
▶ Interactive CD-ROM Tutor, Disc 2

• Ask students to give a short description of the clothing the four German students are wearing.

• Introduce the following vocabulary to your students before watching the video segment:
  der Body *bodysuit*
  locker *loose fitting*
  dadrüber *over, on top of*

• After students have seen the video segment or listened to the recording, ask each of four students to read one of the interviews aloud for pronunciation practice.

Connections and Comparisons

 Multicultural Connection

If possible, have students interview foreign exchange students or people they know from other countries. They should try to find out how clothing and clothing styles differ from country to country. Students should share the information they collect with the class.

ZWEITE STUFE

Teacher Note

Mention to your students that the **Landeskunde** will also be included in Quiz 5–2B given at the end of the **Zweite Stufe**.

Divide the class into two teams. Each person will need a piece of paper and a pen or pencil. The first student from Team A writes down an object that is in the classroom (Example: item of clothing or classroom object) and says the game phrase: **Ich sehe was, was du nicht siehst, und es ist ...**, inserting a color in the blank. One member from Team B has three guesses to figure out what object the student from Team A is referring to. If the student from Team B guesses correctly, that team gets a point and another turn to guess. If the opposing team does not guess correctly, then that team must ask the question to the other team. The team with the most points at the end of the game wins.

Assess

▶ Testing Program, pp. 109–112
  Quiz 5-2A, Quiz 5-2B
  Audio CD5, Tr. 18

▶ Student Make-Up Assignments
  Chapter 5, Alternative Quiz

▶ Alternative Assessment Guide, p. 36

DRITTE STUFE

Teaching Resources
pp. 143–145

PRINT

▶ Lesson Planner, p. 25
▶ TPR Storytelling Book, pp. 19, 20
▶ Listening Activities, pp. 37, 41–42
▶ Activities for Communication, pp. 29–30, 92, 93, 131–132
▶ Grammatikheft, pp. 44–45
▶ Grammar Tutor for Students of German, Chapter 5
▶ Übungsheft, pp. 56–58
▶ Testing Program, pp. 113–116
▶ Alternative Assessment Guide, p. 36
▶ Student Make-Up Assignments, Chapter 5

MEDIA

▶ One-Stop Planner
▶ Audio Compact Discs, CD5, Trs. 12–15, 19, 27–28
▶ Teaching Transparencies
  Mehr Grammatikübungen Answers
  Grammatikheft Answers
▶ Interactive CD-ROM Tutor, Disc 2

> **PAGE 143**

Bell Work

In pairs, have students compliment each other on three clothing items they are wearing. Have them also respond appropriately. They should use the expressions on p. 139.

TPR Total Physical Response

Prepare a suitcase or bag of clothing for this activity. First pull out each item and review the vocabulary by giving such commands as: **Zeigt auf die Jacke!** Then display all of the items and proceed with other commands using verbs such as **nehmen, geben,** and **bringen.**

PRESENTING: So sagt man das!

Use the suitcase of clothes from the TPR activity above to teach the new expressions in **So sagt man das!** Model the phrases first, telling students what you are doing. Then ask students to try on some clothes via TPR: **Probier das T-Shirt an!** Repeat the expressions using several clothing items and involve as many students as possible.

PRESENTING: Grammatik

Separable-prefix verbs Ask students if they can tell you what the word *prefix* means. (one or more syllables added to the beginning of a word to change its meaning) Ask students to give you some examples in English. (Example: social—*anti*social) Tell students that German has many separable-prefix verbs, and ask them to name the verb and the prefix in this example:

anziehen   Was ziehe ich heute an?

Continue with the **Grammatik** for more examples.

PAGE 144

Communication for All Students

Challenge
24 Ask students what they would wear to a school dance or a party. Have them respond in German. (Example: **Ich ziehe ein Kleid an.**)

Teacher Note

After presenting the **Lerntrick** to students, you may want to have them begin a list of possible prefixes in German. Students can later expand the list as they come across more prefixes in subsequent chapters. Students can start their list with **aus-** and **an-**. You may choose to introduce the following new prefixes immediately: **ab, bei, ein, her, hin, mit, nach, vor.**

PRESENTING: Ein wenig Grammatik

Stem changes Tell students that German has verbs that undergo changes. Usually, the stem of the second and third person singular changes. These verbs and changes must be memorized.

Teaching Suggestion

26 For this activity, students should bring several articles of clothing to class.

Communication for All Students

Challenge
26 One partner provides the context by telling the other partner where he or she will be going. (Examples: **ins Kino, ins Theater mit den Eltern, ins Café mit Freunden, zum Tennisspiel**) The student then selects the outfit appropriate for the occasion.

PAGE 145

Portfolio

28 You might want to use this activity as an oral portfolio item for your students. See *Alternative Assessment Guide,* p. 22.

PRESENTING: Aussprache

The letter **i** in instances such as **ihr, ihm, mir, dir** can also sound much like the /i/ sound in the English word *mean*. Remind students of the other way of pronouncing **ä** and **e**, as in the words **spät** and **sehen**. To help students hear the difference between the short and long **a**, contrast the sounds by using word pairs: **Stadt/Staat.**

Connections and Comparisons

Language Note

After presenting the **Aussprache** section to your students, you may want to tell them about a localized dialectal pronunciation of the letter combinations **sp, spr,** and **str,** which can be heard around Hamburg and Hannover. There, those initial sounds are pronounced similar to the initial sound of the English word *spit*. A person from Hamburg would pronounce **spucken** as "spucken" not "schpucken."

Reteaching: Separable-prefix verbs

Prepare strips of paper large enough to write one sentence on each. Write the sentences from the **Grammatik** on p. 143 on the strips. Cut each strip into its sentence components (subject, verb, object, and so on). Divide the class into 6 groups. Each group gets a sentence that it has to put together correctly without using the book. One member of each group puts the group's sentence on the board. Students check other groups' sentences for correct word order.

Von der Schule zum Beruf

29

For this activity you might consider having students collect a few health store flyers and bring them to class. Students could also research German health store Web sites. Helpful keywords for their search would be: **Reformhaus, Gesundheit, Bioladen, Bioanbau.**

Game

This game is much like *Tic Tac Toe*. Place a German adjective in each square. Divide the class into two teams. Every time a team member creates a correct sentence using the adjective in one of the squares, an X or O is added to that square. Students must use different subjects and verbs for each sentence.

 Total Physical Response

In pairs, have students negate each others' statements while acting them out simultaneously.

Example: Student A: **Ich kaufe das Hemd.** *Outlines shirt, points to self.*

Student B: **Ich kaufe das Hemd nicht.** *Outlines shirt, points to self, shakes index finger from left to right.*

Assess

▸ Testing Program, pp. 113–116
Quiz 5-3A, Quiz 5-3B
Audio CD5, Tr. 19

▸ Student Make-Up Assignments
Chapter 5, Alternative Quiz

▸ Alternative Assessment Guide, p. 36

ZUM LESEN

Teaching Resources
pp. 146–147

PRINT

▸ Lesson Planner, p. 26
▸ Übungsheft, p. 59
▸ Reading Strategies and Skills, Chapter 5
▸ Lies mit mir! 1, Chapter 5

MEDIA
▸ One-Stop Planner

Prereading
Building Context

Ask students about their favorite stores for buying clothes. What kinds of clothes do these stores sell? Why do students prefer these particular stores?

Reviewing

Before doing the prereading activities, you might want to review sizes, abbreviations, and the expressions found on labels affixed to clothing items.

Teacher Note

Activities 1 and 2 are prereading activities.

Reading
Skimming and Scanning

Have students briefly look at all the ads and descriptions and identify words that are also used to describe fashion in English ads. Make a list on the board or a transparency.

Connections and Comparisons

Thinking Critically
Drawing Inferences Ask students to think of some reasons there are so many English descriptions used in the ads. (Example: Clothing labels and designer names in English influence the fashion language all over the world.)

Communication for All Students

Cooperative Learning

Put students in groups of four. Ask them to choose a discussion leader, a recorder, a proofreader, and an announcer. Give students a specific amount of time in which to complete Activities 1–10. Monitor group work as you walk around, helping students if necessary. At the end of the activity, call on each group announcer to read his or her group's results. You can decide whether or not to collect their work for a grade.

Connections and Comparisons

Geography Connection

K+L Ruppert lists several cities at the bottom of the ad for women's wear to show where stores can be found. Have students locate some of the cities on a map.

Thinking Critically

Comparing and Contrasting The surveys in the reading were taken from *JUMA* magazine, which stands for **Jugendmagazin**. Surveys such as these are quite popular among German-speaking teenagers. Ask students to name a few American youth magazines where they would typically find similar surveys. (Examples: *Teen* and *Seventeen*)

Cultures and Communities

Culture Note

German stores do not have sales as frequently as stores in the United States do. The government enforces strict laws, and there are generally only two major sales per year, the **Sommerschlussverkauf** at the end of summer and the **Winterschlussverkauf** at the end of winter. At other times of the year, you might see signs that advertise **Sonderangebote** (*specials*), but you'd rarely see signs that advertise merchandise as 25% or 50% off.

Post-Reading
Teacher Note

Activities 11 and 12 are post-reading tasks that will show whether students can apply what they have learned.

Connections and Comparisons

Multicultural Connection

Ask teachers of other foreign languages to lend you realia similar to the clothing ads in this reading section. Let your students compare those ads to the German ones. Can they point out similarities and differences in the way clothing is advertised in those countries?

Teaching Suggestion

Ask students which of the advertised items in this reading section they would purchase as a present for their brother, sister, mother, or father if they had 50 euros to spend. Then, have students compare the prices of the items they chose with prices for similar items in the United States.

Zum Lesen Answers

Answers to Activity 4	reduced prices—**stark reduziert**
Answers to Activity 5	interviews/teenager magazine
Answers to Activity 6	sixteen/casual clothing/**Jeans, Sportschuhe**
Answers to Activity 7	**12 Monate Garantie**
Answers to Activity 8	Jeans, athletic shoes, hooded T-shirt/At Kriegbaum's for 12, 90 or 19, 90/Because of the hood
Answers to Activity 9	You can express something through fashion without speaking.
Answers to Activity 10	Manu is interested in brand-name fashion.

> **PAGES 148–151**

MEHR GRAMMATIKÜBUNGEN

The **Mehr Grammatikübungen** activities are designed as supplemental activities for the grammatical concepts presented in the chapter. You might use them as additional practice, for review, or for assessment.

For more grammar presentations, review, and practice, refer to the following:
- Grammatikheft
- Grammar Tutor for Students of German
- Grammar Summary on pp. R15–R25
- Übungsheft
- Grammar and Vocabulary quizzes (Testing Program)
- Test Generator
- Interactive CD-ROM Tutor
- Interaktive Spiele at go.hrw.com

ANWENDUNG

Video Wrap-up

Videocassette 2, 21:47–36:12
Videocassette 5 (captioned version), 22:47–28:12
At this time, you might want to use the video resources for additional review and enrichment. See *Video Guide* for suggestions regarding:

- the **Los geht's!** episode
- the **Fortsetzung** episode
- the **Landeskunde** interviews
- the **Videoclips.**

Apply and Assess

Teaching Suggestions

1 Have students make notes on index cards as they record the patterns and trends for their article. Students can then use these notecards as they write. These should be turned in along with the assignment.

3 Read the fashion review **Das weiße Hemd** to the class as you would hear it in a fashion review on TV or the radio. Ask students to make a list of all the expressions used in the article to describe the clothing.

Process Writing

6 You may want to make German-language magazines available to your students for use as inspiration or visual support when writing their show commentaries. You might also remind them that what they are writing is meant to be delivered orally when finished. Suggest that the students read their work aloud (or in an undertone) as they go, in order to get a better idea of how the language flows.

Using the Captioned Video

As a chapter review, write the conversation for a section of the **Los geht's!** episode and leave out targeted expressions students have learned in the chapter. Play the video for *Was ziehst du an?* on Videocassette 2 and have students fill in the cloze passage. Then play the captioned version of *Was ziehst du an?* on Videocassette 5 and have students check their answers.

KANN ICH'S WIRKLICH?

This page is intended to prepare students for the test. It is a brief checklist of the major points covered in the chapter. The students should be reminded that it is a checklist only and not necessarily everything that will appear on the test.

For additional self check options, refer students to the *Grammar Tutor,* the *Interactive CD-ROM Tutor,* and the Online self-test for this chapter.

WORTSCHATZ

Review and Assess

Visual Learners

Show pictures of actual pieces of clothing, and ask students to name them, including the German articles that accompany the nouns. Point to items in the classroom and ask students what color they are. Give an adjective such as **lang** and ask students for its opposite by asking: **Was ist das Gegenteil von lang?**

Game

Play the game **Wortbögen** using as many words from the **Wortschatz** as possible. See p. 127D for the procedure.

Teacher Note

Give the **Kapitel 5** Chapter Test: *Testing Program,* pp. 117–122 Audio CD 5, Trs. 20–22.

WEIT   **HÜBSCH**   **SCHICK**

REVIEW

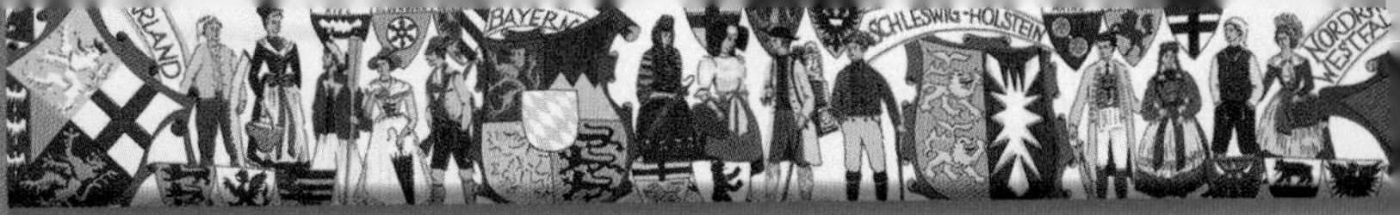

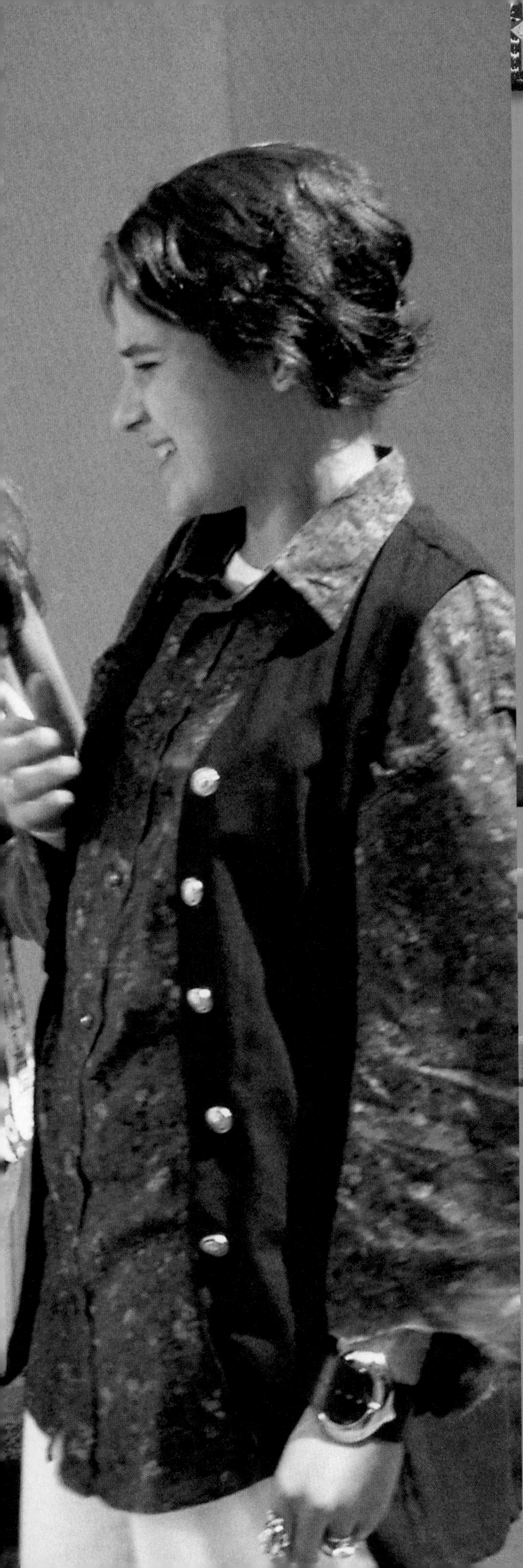

5

Klamotten kaufen

Objectives

In this chapter you will learn to

Erste Stufe

- express wishes when shopping

Zweite Stufe

- comment on and describe clothes
- give compliments and respond to them

Dritte Stufe

- talk about trying on clothes

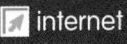 internet

 ADRESSE: go.hrw.com
KENNWORT:
  WK3 SCHLESWIG-HOLSTEIN-5

◀ **Wie findet ihr mein T-Shirt?**

Los geht's! · *Was ziehst du an?*

CD 5 Trs. 1–2

VIDEO

Strategie Verstehen
Look at the images for this story. Who are the people pictured? Where and when do you think these scenes are taking place? What clues tell you this?

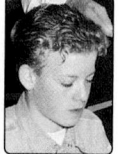

Michael

Katja

Julia

Los geht's! is an abridged version of the video episode.

① Katja: Was ziehst du denn zu Sonjas Fete an? Rock? Pulli?

Julia: Ach was! Ich zieh meinen Jogging-Anzug an.

Katja: Und ich meine Shorts. Ich brauche aber etwas, eine Bluse oder ein T-Shirt. Das ist zu alt und gefällt mir nicht.

Julia: Und ich brauche ein Stirnband für meine Haare. Komm, gehen wir zum Sport-Kerner!

② Katja: Schau, der Michael!

Michael: Hallo, ihr beiden!

Katja: Was hast du denn da in der Tüte?

Michael: Na, wie gefällt euch mein T-Shirt?

Katja: Mensch, scheußlich!

Michael: Wirklich? — Also, ich finde es stark!

③ Verkäuferin: Haben Sie einen Wunsch?

Katja: Ich suche eine Bluse.

Verkäuferin: Blusen haben wir in allen Größen und allen Farben. — Hier haben wir etwas für Sie. Toll, nicht?

Katja: Haben Sie auch Blusen in Blau?

Verkäuferin: Natürlich! Hier, in Blau. Größe 40. Passt bestimmt.

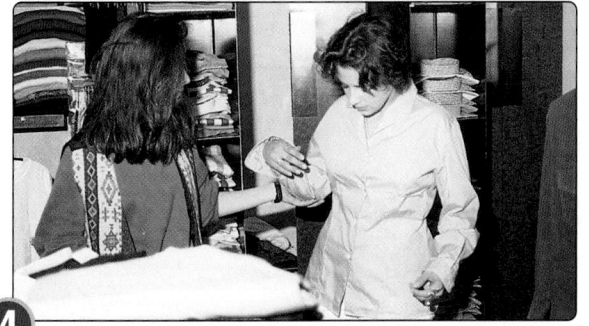

Julia: Sehr sportlich. Und sie passt dir gut.

Katja: Meinst du? — Ach, weißt du…Nein, die Bluse gefällt mir nicht. Die nehm ich nicht.

Katja: Haben Sie T-Shirts? In Blau oder lieber in Weiß.

Verkäuferin: Hier habe ich T-Shirts. Sehr sportlich, sehr schick.

Julia: Schau mal, Katja! Ein T-Shirt mit Aufdruck: ein Texas-Motiv! Sieht toll aus!

Verkäuferin: Das ist aber zu groß für Sie. Sie brauchen M, medium.

Katja: Ist das aus Baumwolle?

Verkäuferin: Hundert Prozent Baumwolle.

Katja: Prima! Das probier ich mal an.

Julia: Phantastisch, Katja! Das finde ich echt toll! Lässig. Weiß ist eine gute Farbe für dich.

Katja: Tja, du weißt, Weiß ist meine Lieblingsfarbe.

Katja: Was kostet das T-Shirt?

Verkäuferin: 21 Euro 50.

Katja: Was? So viel? Das ist teuer.

Verkäuferin: Das hat halt nicht jeder. Ein Spitze T-Shirt!

Julia: Na ja, wer schön sein will, muss zahlen, nicht?

Katja: Das ist toll für die Fete. Gut, ich nehme es.

Übungsheft, S. 49

1 Was passiert hier?

These activities check for global comprehension only. Students should not yet be expected to produce language modeled in **Los geht's!**

Do you understand what is happening in **Los geht's!**? Check your comprehension by answering these questions. Don't be afraid to guess.

1. What does the word **Fete** mean? Who is having one? 1. **Fete** means party. Sonja is having a party.
2. What do Katja and Julia still need to do before the **Fete**? 2. go shopping for clothes
3. What does Michael think about his purchase? What do Julia and Katja think of it?
4. Does Katja like the first thing she tries on? What does she say? 3. Michael likes his T-shirt but Julia and Katja think it's terrible.
5. What does Katja finally buy? Why does she hesitate at first? 4. She doesn't like it and says, „**Nein, die Bluse gefällt mir nicht.**"
6. What do you think about her purchase?

5. She buys a T-shirt but hesitates because it is rather expensive.
6. Answers may vary.

2 Genauer lesen

Reread the conversations. Which words or phrases do the characters use to

1. name articles of clothing
2. describe or comment on clothing
3. name colors
4. state a price

1. Rock, Pulli, Jogging-Anzug, Shorts, Bluse, Stirnband, T-Shirt.
2. Mensch, scheußlich; ich finde es stark; sehr sportlich; sieht toll aus; hundert Prozent Baumwolle; echt toll; lässig.
3. Blau; Weiß.
4. 6 Euro, 21 Euro 50.

3 Stimmt oder stimmt nicht?

Are these statements right or wrong? Answer each one with either **stimmt** or **stimmt nicht**. If a statement is wrong, try to state it correctly.

1. Julia hat eine Fete.
2. Katja hat Shorts, aber sie braucht eine Bluse.
3. Michael findet sein T-Shirt stark.
4. Katja sucht einen Pulli.
5. Katja möchte die Bluse in Blau haben.
6. Blau ist Katjas Lieblingsfarbe.

1. **Sonja hat eine Fete.**
2. stimmt
3. stimmt
4. **Sie sucht eine Bluse.**
5. stimmt
6. **Weiß**

4 Was passt zusammen?

Match each statement or question on the left with an appropriate response on the right.

1. Was ziehst du zu Sonjas Fete an? e
2. Wie gefällt euch mein T-Shirt? a
3. Haben Sie einen Wunsch? d
4. Wir haben Blusen in allen Farben. c
5. Das T-Shirt kostet 21 Euro 50. f
6. Das ist eine gute Farbe für dich. b

a. Mensch, scheußlich!
b. Weiß ist meine Lieblingsfarbe.
c. Gut! Ich möchte eine Bluse in Blau.
d. Ja, ich suche eine Bluse.
e. Meinen Jogging-Anzug.
f. Das ist teuer!

5 Welches Wort passt?

Based on **Los geht's!**, rewrite the following narrative by supplying the missing words.

Katja ___1___ eine Bluse für Sonjas Fete und geht mit Julia zum Sport-Kerner. Dort sehen die zwei ___2___ den Michael. Er zeigt ihnen sein neues T-Shirt. Katja ___3___ das T-Shirt scheußlich, aber Michael findet es ___4___. Im Sport-Kerner möchte Katja eine Bluse in ___5___ sehen, und sie probiert eine Bluse an. Die Bluse gefällt ihr aber nicht. Die T-Shirts sind aber ___6___ sportlich und fesch. Julia findet das T-Shirt mit dem Texas-Motiv ganz toll. Katja ___7___ das weiße T-Shirt an, denn Weiß ist Katjas ___8___. Sie möchte es nehmen, aber es ist ___9___. Am Ende kauft Katja das T-Shirt doch.

1. sucht
2. Mädchen
3. findet
4. stark
5. Blau
6. sehr
7. probiert
8. Lieblingsfarbe
9. teuer

| Blau | | Lieblingsfarbe | sehr | sucht | probiert | | stark | |
| findet | | | | | | teuer | | Mädchen |

Erste Stufe

Objective Expressing wishes when shopping

WK3 SCHLESWIG-HOLSTEIN-5

Wortschatz

Mir gefallen alle Klamotten. Mir gefällt/gefallen ...

 5A, 5B

der Rock   **das Hemd**   **die Stiefel**

das Kleid   **die Hose**   **der Gürtel**

die Bluse
die Jacke
die Jeans
die Socke
die Shorts
das T-Shirt
der Pulli (Pullover)
der Jogging-Anzug

die Turnschuhe

FÜR DAMEN

Hosen, Leinenstruktur	38.-
Damenhafte Röcke in Leinenoptik	27.-
T-Shirts, bedruckt, mit Perlen und Pailletten	19.-
Coloured Jeans mit Gürtel	30.-
Bedruckte Blusen mit modischen Details	27.-
T-Shirts mit Applikationen	18.-
<u>YOUNG COLLECTIONS</u> Strickkleider in verschiedenen Formen und Farben	14.-

FÜR HERREN

Jacken	42.-
Blouson oder Polo-Shirts, 1/2 Ärmel	25.-
Uni-Socken, Superstretch, 5 Paar	9.-
Seiden-Hemden, sandwashed bedruckt, 1/2 Ärmel	23.-
Streifen-Polo-Shirts, 1/2 Ärmel	24.-
Gymnastik-Shorts	15.-

Many clothing items in this ad are cognates. Which ones do you recognize? Which items are for women, which for men? Which words are used to describe shirts and T-shirts? What do they mean?

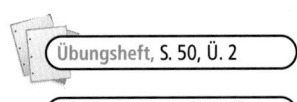

Übungsheft, S. 50, Ü. 2

Grammatikheft, S. 37, Ü. 1–2

---

6 **Was ist für Männer? Was ist für Frauen?** Script on p. 127G

 Zuhören A certain **Modegeschäft** (*clothing store*) has been doing a lot of advertising lately. As you listen to one of their radio ads, first write down the items in the order you hear them mentioned. Then figure out which items are for men, and which for women.

CD 5 Tr. 3 What does this store have for "**die ganze Familie**"? **Kleider** (women); **Röcke** (women); **Jogging-Anzug** (women); **Blusen** (women); **Gürtel** (men); **Hemden** (men); **Hosen** (men); The store has „**fesche Sachen für die ganze Familie**".

Ein wenig Landeskunde

When traveling to most countries in Europe, you need to convert dollars (USD) to euros (EUR), since almost all European countries have adopted this new currency. The conversion table (**Umrechnungstabelle**) on the right shows you how many euros you will receive for a certain amount of dollars and vice versa. The rates will vary, and you may want to look up the current rate of exchange in a newspaper or on a web site.

Looking at the clothing ad and using the conversion chart, compare the prices for clothing in Germany to what you pay in the United States. In general, in which country do you think clothes are more expensive? What types of clothes would you expect to be more expensive in Germany than in the United States?

Umrechnungstabelle Stand: Juni 2001

USA

EUR	USD	USD	EUR
0,10	0,08	0,10	0,11
0,20	0,17	0,20	0,22
0,50	0,44	0,50	0,56
1,00	0,88	1,00	1,13
5,00	4,42	5,00	5,65
10,00	8,84	10,00	11,31
20,00	44,20	20,00	22,62
50,00	77,68	50,00	56,55
100,00	88,41	100,00	113,10
200,00	176,83	200,00	226,20
500,00	442,08	500,00	565,50
1000,00	884,17	1000,00	1131,00

1 Dollar (USD) = 100 Cents

Diese errechneten Beträge schwanken täglich, da die Kurse für An-und Verkauf von Schecks, Noten und Münzen verschieden sind. Für die Tageskurse siehe Zeitungen und Web Sites.

COMMERZBANK
Die Bank an Ihrer Seite

---

7 ## Wie sind die Preise?

Sprechen/Schreiben Using the **Umrechnungstabelle** for clues, create a price list for the following items listed in the **Wortschatz** but not in the ad: **Gürtel**, **Jogging-Anzug**, **Turnschuhe**, **Pulli**, and **Stiefel**. Your partner will ask you how much these items cost, and you will answer, using your price list and the ad on page 133. Then switch roles. Be polite!

8 ## Was gibt es im Modegeschäft?

Lesen/Sprechen You want to buy something new to wear to your friend's party, but you can't decide what to buy. You have 100€ to spend. Using the ad on page 133 and your price list, put together three different outfits that would be within your budget. With which outfit would you have the most money left over?

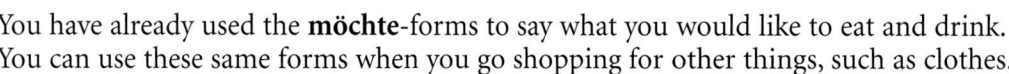

So sagt man das!

Expressing wishes when shopping

Übungsheft,
S. 50–51, Ü. 3–4

You have already used the **möchte**-forms to say what you would like to eat and drink. You can use these same forms when you go shopping for other things, such as clothes.

The salesclerk might ask:

Bitte? *or*
Was möchten Sie?
or
Was bekommen Sie?
or
Haben Sie einen Wunsch?

You can respond:

Ich möchte eine Jacke, bitte!
Ich brauche ein T-Shirt.
I need a T-shirt.
Einen Pulli in Grau, bitte!
A sweater in gray, please!
Ich suche eine Bluse.
I'm looking for a blouse.

What is the subject of the sentence in each of the salesclerk's questions? Look at the sentence **Einen Pulli in Grau, bitte!** Is there a subject or verb? What do you think is intended?

Definite and indefinite articles, accusative case

Look at the following sentences:

Der Pulli kostet 15 Euro.
Ein Pulli kostet 15 Euro.

Möchten Sie **den Pulli**?
Möchten Sie **einen Pulli**?

Mehr Grammatikübungen
S. 148–149, Ü. 1–3

Übungsheft,
S. 51–52, Ü. 5–6

Grammatikheft,
S. 38, Ü. 3–4

CD-ROM
DISC 2

What is the difference between the noun phrases **der Pulli/ein Pulli** on the left and the noun phrases **den Pulli/einen Pulli** on the right?

The noun phrases **der Pulli/ein Pulli** on the left are the *subjects* (nominative case) of the sentences. The noun phrases **den Pulli/einen Pulli** on the right are *direct objects* (accusative case) of the sentences. Only articles for masculine nouns change when they are used as direct objects. The articles for feminine, neuter, and plural nouns stay the same.

	Nominative	**Accusative**
Masculine	der / ein Pulli	de**n** / eine**n** Pulli
Feminine	die / eine Jacke	die / eine Jacke
Neuter	das / ein T-Shirt	das / ein T-Shirt
Plural	die / — Turnschuhe	die / — Turnschuhe

9 ### Grammatik im Kontext   Script on p. 127G

Zuhören Listen carefully to these students commenting on different clothes, and decide whether the item of clothing in each exchange is the subject or direct object of the sentences.
1. subject 2. direct object 3. subject 4. direct object 5. direct object 6. direct object 7. subject 8. direct object

CD 5 Tr. 4

10 ### Grammatik im Kontext

Lesen/Sprechen Read this conversation between Julia and the salesclerk at **Sport-Kerner**. Look carefully at the conversation and determine what the subject and/or direct object is in each sentence. Then answer the questions that follow.

VERKÄUFERIN	Guten Tag! Haben Sie einen Wunsch? direct object
JULIA	Ich suche einen Rock in Blau. Was kostet der Rock hier? direct object/subject
VERKÄUFERIN	Er kostet nur 30 Euro.
JULIA	Und haben Sie vielleicht auch eine Bluse in Weiß? direct object
VERKÄUFERIN	Ja, die Bluse hier kostet 23 Euro. Wir haben auch das weiße T-Shirt hier im Sonderangebot (*a special offer*). Nur 10 Euro. Passt auch schön zu Röcken. subject/direct object
JULIA	Das T-Shirt ist schön, aber ich brauche ein T-Shirt in Schwarz. Also ich nehme nur den Rock und die Bluse. Danke! subject/direct object direct objects

1. What is Julia looking for?   1. She is looking for a blue skirt and a white blouse.
2. Why doesn't she want the T-shirt?
3. How much is her final purchase?

2. She needs a black T-shirt.   3. 53 euros.

11 ### Grammatik im Kontext

Possible answers: **Ich brauche eine Jacke, … Socken, …**

a. **Sprechen** Tell some of your classmates what clothes you need, using the indefinite article when appropriate.

b. **Sprechen** Now point to various articles of clothing that your classmates are wearing and say that you would like to have them, using the definite article.   Answers may include the following:
Ich möchte den Pulli. Ich möchte die Hose. Ich möchte das Hemd.

Ich	brauche möchte	Pulli	Turnschuhe
		Rock	Bluse
		Jeans	Kleid
		Hemd	Hose
		T-Shirt	Socken
		Stiefel	Jacke
		Gürtel	

12 Grammatik im Kontext

Schreiben/Sprechen You are in a department store that has many items on sale (**im Sonderangebot**). Make a list of the clothes you would like to buy. Your partner will play the salesperson and ask you what you want and tell you where everything is. In the boxes to the right are some words and phrases you might need.

dort	der/ein
da drüben	den/einen
hier vorn	die/eine
da hinten	das/ein

13 Haben Sie das auch in ...?

Sprechen You didn't find the colors you like at the last store. Ask the salesperson at the new store on the right if he or she has the items you want in certain colors. Also ask about prices. Then switch roles.

Wortschatz

Farben!

Haben Sie das auch…?

CD-ROM
DISC **2**

| in Blau | in Grün | in Weiß | in Hellblau |

| in Rot | in Dunkelblau | in Braun | in Gelb |

| in Grau | in Schwarz |

Übungsheft,
S. 52, Ü. 8

Grammatikheft,
S. 39, Ü. 5–6

Ein wenig Landeskunde

The store hours listed below are typical for small stores in Germany. What are the hours for the different days of the week? Is this different from stores where you live?

In cities stores are allowed to stay open from 6 a.m. until 8 p.m. Stores in smaller communities close at 7 p.m. On Saturdays stores close at 4 p.m.

Guten Tag!
Wir haben geöffnet

Montag–Freitag
von 9⁰⁰ bis 12⁰⁰ Uhr

von 13⁰⁰ bis 20⁰⁰ Uhr

Samstag
von 9⁰⁰ bis 16⁰⁰ Uhr

Mittwoch Nachmittag
geschlossen

14 Alles ist im Sonderangebot!

Schreiben Design your own newspaper ad based on four items in the ad on page 133 or cut out pictures from a magazine. Remember, everything is on sale at your store. Be sure to mention prices and colors in stock. Be prepared to share your ads with the class.

Zweite Stufe

Objectives Commenting on and describing clothes; giving compliments and responding to them

WK3 SCHLESWIG-HOLSTEIN-5

So sagt man das!

Commenting on and describing clothes

5–1

If you want to know what someone thinks about a particular item of clothing, you might ask:

Wie findest du das Hemd?

You might get positive comments, such as: or you might get negative comments, such as:

Ich finde es fesch.	**Ich finde es furchtbar.**
Es sieht schick aus!	**Es sieht blöd aus.**
Es passt prima.	**Es passt nicht.**
Es gefällt mir.	**Es gefällt mir nicht.**

If the person you ask isn't sure, he or she might say:

Ich weiß nicht.   *or*   **Ich bin nicht sicher.**

Grammatikheft, S. 40, Ü. 7

Ein wenig Grammatik

Look at these sentences:

> **Wie findest du den Rock?**
> **Er gefällt mir.**
> **Und die T-Shirts?**
> **Sie gefallen mir auch.**

What are the subjects in the two responses?[1] When using the verb **gefallen** to say you like something, you need to know only two forms: **gefällt** and **gefallen**.

> **Er/sie/es gefällt mir.** *I like it.*
> **Sie (pl) gefallen mir.** *I like them.*

Grammatikheft, S. 40, Ü. 8

Mehr Grammatikübungen
S. 149, Ü. 4

---

15  **Grammatik im Kontext**   Script on p. 127G

CD 5
Tr. 5

a. Zuhören Several students are in a store looking at clothes and talking about what they like and don't like. Determine whether the person speaking likes the item of clothing or not. 1. **Nein** 2. **Ja** 3. **Nein** 4. **Ja** 5. **Ja**

b. Schreiben Copy these sentences by filling in the blank with the appropriate form of **gefallen**.

1. Die Bluse ======= mir sehr gut.   gefällt
2. Die Schuhe ======= mir auch.   gefallen
3. Wie ======= dir die Hose?   gefällt
4. Sie ======= mir; sie sieht toll aus.   gefällt
5. Und wie ======= dir die Jacke?   gefällt
6. Sie ======= mir, aber Jacken wie   gefällt
   die hier ======= mir besser.   gefallen

1.

2.

3.

4.

5.

---

1. er (der Rock), sie (die T-Shirts)

16 **Wie findest du das?**

Sprechen Look at the items pictured in Activity 15 and ask your partner if he or she likes each item. Then switch roles.

5–C

Nichts passt!

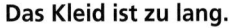

Das Kleid ist zu lang.

Der Pulli ist viel zu weit.

Die Jacke ist zu groß.

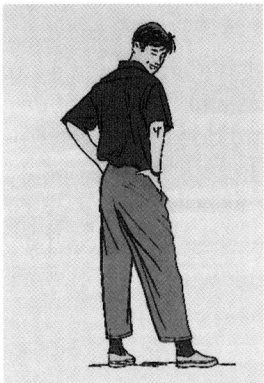

Die Hose ist zu kurz.

Das Hemd ist zu eng.

Die Schuhe sind ein bisschen zu klein.

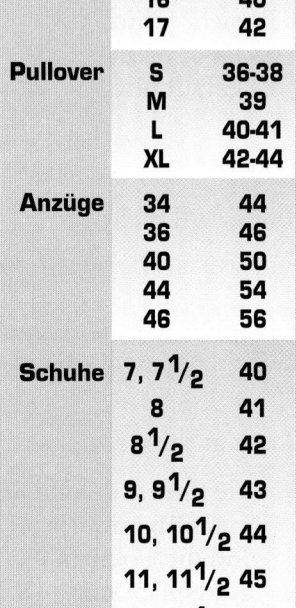

HERRENGRÖSSEN		
	USA	BRD
Hemden	13	36
	15	38
	16	40
	17	42
Pullover	S	36-38
	M	39
	L	40-41
	XL	42-44
Anzüge	34	44
	36	46
	40	50
	44	54
	46	56
Schuhe	7, 7$\frac{1}{2}$	40
	8	41
	8$\frac{1}{2}$	42
	9, 9$\frac{1}{2}$	43
	10, 10$\frac{1}{2}$	44
	11, 11$\frac{1}{2}$	45
	12, 12$\frac{1}{2}$	46

DAMENGRÖSSEN		
	USA	BRD
Blusen, Pullover	8	36
	10	38
	12	40
	14	42
Kleider, Mäntel	8	38
	10	40
	12	42
	14	44
Schuhe	5	36
	6	37
	7	38
	8	39
	9	40
	10	41

Ein wenig Landeskunde

German sizes are different from American sizes. However, clothes manufactured in the United States and imported to Germany carry U.S. sizes. For example, jeans are often measured in inches, and T-shirts have the designations **S, M, L, XL**, and **XXL**. Look at the size charts on the right. What size would you take if you were buying German clothes or shoes in Germany?

Grammatikheft, S. 41, Ü. 9

17 **Was ist los?**

Sprechen You and a friend are spending the afternoon **in der Innenstadt** (*downtown*).
You encounter the people pictured below and discuss their clothing. Take turns
describing the clothing pictured to each other. Answers may vary. Examples:
Der Pulli ist zu lang. Die Schuhe sind zu groß.

So sagt man das!

Giving compliments and responding to them

5–1, 5–2
CD-ROM
DISC **2**

On numerous occasions you'll want to be able to compliment
your friends on their clothes.

You could say:

> **Die Jacke sieht lässig aus!** *or* **Ich finde den Pulli echt stark.** *or* **Die Jacke gefällt mir!**

The other person might respond: You could answer:

Ehrlich? *or*	**Ehrlich!**
Wirklich? *or*	**Wirklich!**
Meinst du?	**Ja, bestimmt!**
Nicht zu lang (kurz, groß)?	**Nein, überhaupt nicht!**

Übungsheft, S. 53–54, Ü. 9–11

Grammatikheft, S. 41, Ü. 10

---

18 **Was meinst du?**

 a. Schreiben Find five pictures of clothing items in your favorite magazine. Write at
least two sentences to describe each item and one sentence to express your opinion
about each picture.

 b. Sprechen Show your partner the pictures you
cut out and ask what he or she thinks of your
clothing choices. If your partner compliments
you on your choices, respond appropriately.

fesch	schick	blöd	furchtbar	prima
Spitze	toll	scheußlich	stark	lässig

Direct object pronouns

In **Kapitel 3** you learned that the pronouns **er**, **sie**, **es**, and **sie** (pl) can refer to both people and objects. Look at the following sentences:

Der Pulli ist sehr preiswert.
Ja, **er** ist nicht teuer.

Ich finde **den Pulli** toll.
Ich finde **ihn** auch toll.

Mehr Grammatikübungen,
S. 149–150, Ü. 5–7

What are the pronouns in these sentences? What do you think **er** and **ihn** refer to? **Er**, the pronoun on the left, is the *subject* (nominative case) of the sentence and refers to **der Pulli**. The pronoun **ihn** on the right is the *direct object* (accusative case) of the sentence and refers to **den Pulli**. Only the masculine pronoun changes when it is used as a direct object. The feminine **sie**, neuter **es**, and plural pronoun **sie** stay the same:

	Subject: Nominative		Direct Object: Accusative	
	Noun Phrase	Pronoun	Noun Phrase	Pronoun
Masculine	der Pulli	er	den Pulli	**ihn**
Feminine	die Jacke	sie	die Jacke	sie
Neuter	das T-Shirt	es	das T-Shirt	es
Plural	die Turnschuhe	sie	die Turnschuhe	sie

Übungsheft,
S. 54–55,
Ü. 12–15

Grammatikheft,
S. 42–43,
Ü. 11–12

---

19 ### **Grammatik im Kontext**   Script on p. 127G

CD 5
Tr. 6

a. Zuhören Listen to this conversation between two students who are talking about clothes they want to buy. The first time you hear the conversation, figure out whether the pronouns they mention are subjects or direct objects. Then listen again and match the article of clothing with the words used to describe it.

Subject	Direct object	adjective
0	X	hübsch
1		
2		

1. subject; **Jogging-Anzug; schick**
2. direct object; **Rock; schön**
3. direct object; **T-Shirt; hellgrün**
4. subject; **T-Shirt; preiswert**
5. subject; **Turnschuhe; stark**
6. direct object; **Pulli; schwarz**
7. direct object; **Bluse; teuer**

BEISPIEL —Ich finde die blaue Bluse sehr schön. Und du?
—Ja, ich finde sie hübsch.

b. Schreiben Copy these sentences by filling in each blank with the correct form of the article and the pronoun.

1. Wie findest du ═══ Rock? Ich finde ═══ toll!   den / ihn

2. Ich finde ═══ Bluse schick. Ja, ═══ ist stark!   die / sie

3. Ich finde ═══ T-Shirt prima. Wie findest du ═══?   das / es

4. Ich finde ═══ Pulli stark. Wie findest du ═══?   den / ihn

5. Wie findest du ═══ Schuhe? Ich finde ═══ teuer.   die / sie

6. Wie findest du ═══ Hemd? Ich finde ═══ zu eng!   das / es

7. Wie findest du ═══ Hose? Ich finde ═══ zu klein!   die / sie

8. Wie findest du ═══ Gürtel? Ich finde ═══ zu lang!   den / ihn

Ich finde diese Klamotten echt toll!

20 **Welcher Satz passt?**

Lesen/Sprechen Katja and Sonja are in a store trying on clothes. Choose the appropriate responses to complete their conversation. Then read the conversation aloud with your partner.

a Ich finde ihn toll, aber er ist viel zu lang für dich.

b Hm, ich finde sie schön, aber sie passt nicht.

c Bist du sicher? Sie sind sehr teuer.

d Ja, es sieht super aus!

SONJA   Wie findest du die Bluse in Rot?

KATJA   ========. b

SONJA   Meinst du? Wie findest du den Rock hier in Schwarz?

KATJA   ========. a

SONJA   Ehrlich? So ein Mist! Vielleicht kaufe ich das T-Shirt in Blau.

KATJA   ========. d

SONJA   Dann kaufe ich das T-Shirt und die Schuhe.

KATJA   ========. c

SONJA   Ich weiß, aber sie gefallen mir sehr.

 21 **Wie findest du ...?**

Sprechen Find out what your partner thinks about the clothes that Georg and Beate are wearing to Sonja's party. One of you comments on Georg's clothing, and the other on Beate's. When you have finished, switch roles.

  **22** **Bildbeschreibung**

Schreiben With your partner, write a conversation that could go with the picture below. Practice your conversation and be prepared to share it with the class.

Georg   **Beate**

Welche Klamotten sind „in"?

What do you think German students usually like to wear when they go to a party? We asked many students, and here is what some of them said. Listen first, then read the text. CD 5 Tr. 7

CD 5
Trs. 7–11

Übungsheft,
S. 60, Ü. 1–4

Sandra, Stuttgart CD 5 Tr. 8

„Also, wenn ich zu einer Party gehe, dann ziehe ich am liebsten Jeans an und vielleicht einen Body …und einen weiten Pulli darüber; meistens dann etwas in Blau oder einen weißen Pulli, jetzt, wie grad' eben, denn meine Lieblingsfarben sind doch Blau und Weiß."

Melina, Bietigheim CD 5 Tr. 10

„Am liebsten mag ich Jeans, vor allem helle, oder ja so lockere Blusen, kurze halt, und jetzt vor allem T-Shirts, einfarbige; und sie sollen halt schön lang sein und ein bisschen locker. Und ja, meine Lieblingsfarben sind Blau, Apricot oder Rot, Lila auch noch."

Alexandra, Bietigheim

„Ja, ich zieh am liebsten Jeans an, und Lieblingsfarben sind dann so Blau oder Pastellfarben, und auf Partys oder so eigentlich immer in Jeans und mal etwas Schöneres oben, in Diskos dann auch, und ab und zu hab ich mal gern einen Rock." CD 5 Tr. 9

Iwan, Bietigheim CD 5 Tr. 11

„Also, wenn ich auf eine Party gehe, zieh ich am liebsten ein T-Shirt an und eine kurze Hose. Am liebsten trag ich Schwarz, so einfach, weil es halt schön aussieht und weil es bequem ist."

A. 1. What items of clothing are mentioned most by these students? Make a list of the clothing each student prefers and list the colors he or she seems to like best.

2. Which of these students would you like to meet and why? Do you and the student you selected have similar tastes in clothes? Explain. What do you generally wear and what are your favorite colors? What do you usually wear to a party?

B. What is your overall impression of the way these German teenagers dress? Compare it with the typical dress for teenagers in the United States. Do you think students in the United States are more or less formal than students in Germany? Why do you think so? Write a brief essay explaining your answer.

STANDARDS: 1.2, 2.2, 3.2, 4.2

Dritte Stufe

Objective Talking about trying on clothes

go.hrw.com
WK3 SCHLESWIG-HOLSTEIN-5

23 Was kommt zuerst? Script on p. 127H

CD 5
Tr. 12

Zuhören Jürgen goes to a clothing store to find something to wear to Sonja's party. You will hear four short pieces of his conversation with the salesman. On a separate sheet of paper, put the photos in order according to their conversation. c. a. b. d.

a.

b.

c.

d.

So sagt man das!

Talking about trying on clothes

When you go shopping for clothes, you will want to try them on.

You might say to the salesperson:

Ich probiere das T-Shirt an. *or*   **Ich ziehe das T-Shirt an.**

If you decide to buy it: If not:

Ich nehme es. *or*   **Ich nehme es nicht.** *or*
Ich kaufe es.   **Ich kaufe es nicht.**

CD-ROM
DISC 2

Grammatik

Separable-prefix verbs

The verbs **anziehen** (*to put on, wear*), **anprobieren** (*to try on*), and **aussehen** (*to look, appear*) belong to a group of verbs that have a separable prefix. The prefix is at the beginning of the verb: **anziehen**, **anprobieren**, **aussehen**. In the present tense, the prefix is separated from the verb and is at the end of the clause or sentence.

anziehen
Was **ziehe** ich **an**?
Ich **ziehe** Shorts **an**.
Ich **ziehe** Shorts und ein T-Shirt **an**.
Ich **ziehe** heute Shorts und ein T-Shirt **an**.
Ich **ziehe** heute zu Sonjas Fete Shorts und ein T-Shirt **an**.
Ja, zu Sonjas Fete **ziehe** ich ganz bestimmt Shorts und ein T-Shirt **an**!

Mehr Grammatikübungen
S. 151, Ü. 8

Übungsheft, S. 56–57, Ü. 16–19

Grammatikheft, S. 44, Ü. 13–14

24 **Grammatik im Kontext**

Sprechen/Schreiben Build as many sentences as you can. Be sure to use the correct articles.

LERNTRICK

Ich
Er
Bluse
Schuhe
Sie
Jogging-Anzug
Jeans
Gürtel

anziehen
aussehen
anprobieren

Hemd
gut
blöd
scheußlich
Pulli
Jacke
Jeans

A number of German verbs have prefixes but not all of them are separable (for example, **gefallen** and **bekommen**). You can usually recognize separable prefixes if they are words that can also stand alone (such as **mit**, **auf**, and **aus**) and if they carry the main stress of the compound verb. Compare **ánziehen** and **bekómmen**.

Ein wenig Grammatik

The verbs **nehmen** (*to take*) and **aussehen** (*to appear, look*) are called *stem-changing verbs*. In these verbs, the stem vowel changes in the **du**- and **er/sie**-forms. These verbs do not follow the regular patterns of verbs like **spielen.**

Du **nimmst** den Rock.   Du **siehst** gut **aus**!
Er **nimmt** die Jacke.   Sie **sieht** gut **aus**!

CD-ROM
DISC **2**

Mehr Grammatikübungen
S. 151, Ü. 9

You will learn more about these verbs later.

Übungsheft, S. 57–58, Ü. 20–22   Grammatikheft, S. 45, Ü. 15–16

25 **Grammatik im Kontext**

a. Sprechen Look at the pictures of clothing below and ask your partner what Julia, Katja, Michael, and Heiko will wear to Sonja's party. Your partner's responses will be based on the illustrations. Switch roles and vary your responses.

b. Sprechen You and your partner have been invited to Sonja's party. Ask your partner what he or she would wear based on the pictures of clothing. Then switch roles.

26 **Was nimmst du?**

Sprechen You have picked out five items of clothing that you like. Your partner asks you which items you will try on and which ones you would like to buy. Answer, then switch roles.

27 Für mein Notizbuch

Schreiben For your **Notizbuch** entry, write a paragraph describing what you and your friends usually wear to a party. Describe the kinds of clothes you like and some that you do not like. Describe some of the latest fashions for teens and write what you think about them.

Bei Sport-Kerner haben wir alles! T-Shirts ab 15 Euro in Gelb, Grün und Weiß—sehr schön, perfekt für den Sommer. Wie passt das T-Shirt?

Oh phantastisch! Es gefällt mir sehr! Und so preiswert. Ich kaufe T-Shirts immer bei Sport-Kerner!

28 Im Fernsehen

You work for an ad agency. Get together with two other classmates and write a TV commercial that will convince your audience to shop at a certain clothing store. Be sure to mention prices, colors, and how well the clothes fit and look.

29

 Von der Schule zum Beruf

Schreiben You are employed at an advertising agency. One of your jobs is to write copy for TV commercials. You are to convince your viewers to shop at a certain clothing store. Give your store a name, and be sure to mention in your ad the prices, colors, look, and fit of the items being advertised.

AUSSPRACHE

Richtig aussprechen / Richtig lesen CD 5 Trs. 13–15

A. To practice the following sounds, say the words and sentences below after your teacher or after the recording. CD 5 Trs. 13

1. The letter **i**: When the letter **i** is followed by two consonants, it sounds like the short *i* in the English word *pit*.
   schick, bestimmt, bisschen / Ich finde das Kleid schick. Ehrlich.

2. The letters **ä** and **e**: The letters **ä** and **e** are pronounced as short vowels when followed by two consonants. They sound similar to the short *e* in the English word *net*.
   lässig, hell, gefällt / Das fesche Hemd gefällt mir.

3. The letter **a**: The letter **a** is roughly equivalent to the *a* sound in the English word *father*.
   haben, lang, Jacke / Wir haben Jacken in allen Farben.

4. The letter combinations **sch, st,** and **sp:** The consonant combination **sch** is pronounced like the *sh* in the English word *ship*. When the letter **s** is followed by **p** or **t** at the beginning of a syllable, it is also pronounced in this way.
   schwarz, Turnschuh, Stiefel / Die schwarzen Stiefel sind Spitze!

Richtig schreiben / Diktat CD 5 Tr. 14
CD 5 Tr. 15 (with pauses)

B. Write down the sentences that you hear. Script on p. 127H

Zum Lesen

KLEIDER MACHEN LEUTE!

Lesestrategie **Using what you already know** When you are faced with an unknown text, use what you already know to anticipate the kind of information you might expect to find in the text. It is obvious that these texts are about clothing. Though you may see many words that you do not know, you have read clothing ads in English, and you know that they contain information about prices, styles, sizes, types of material, etc. Watch for this kind of information as you read.

1. Look at a clothing ad from a magazine written in English and make a list of some of the words and expressions that you find in the ad.

2. When you look in a newspaper or magazine for some good buys in clothing, what are some words or phrases that tell you that you would be getting a bargain? Write down some of these English words and phrases.

3. Scan these two pages and write any German words or phrases you find that correspond to the words and phrases you listed in Activities 1 and 2 above. Group the words you find in categories (prices, colors, etc.) and list as many words in each category as you can.

4. Look at the prices of the clothing being advertised. Judging from the photos, are these prices reasonable? Are there prices you could afford? Do you think they are the original prices in all cases? What phrase gives you the information to answer that question?

For answers to these questions, see TE interleaf, p. 127W.

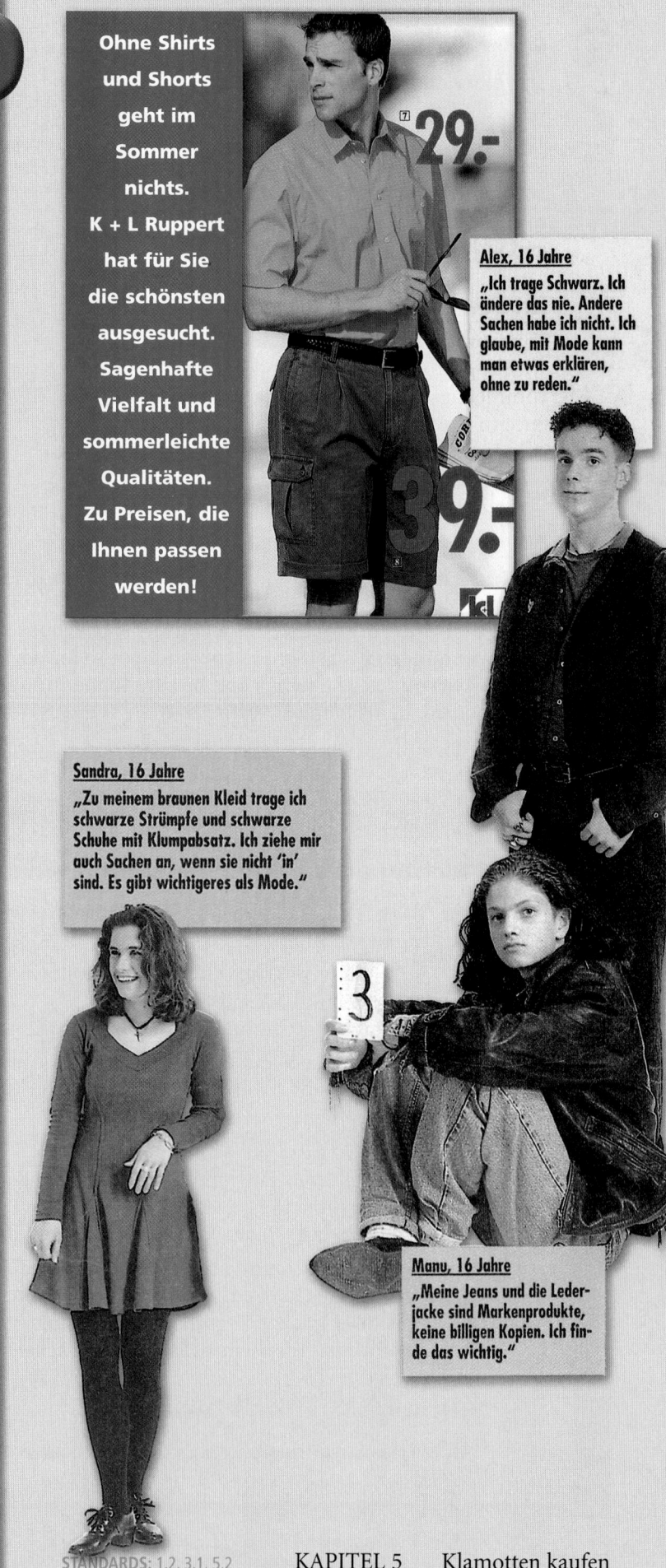

Ohne Shirts und Shorts geht im Sommer nichts. K + L Ruppert hat für Sie die schönsten ausgesucht. Sagenhafte Vielfalt und sommerleichte Qualitäten. Zu Preisen, die Ihnen passen werden!

29.-

39.5

Alex, 16 Jahre
„Ich trage Schwarz. Ich ändere das nie. Andere Sachen habe ich nicht. Ich glaube, mit Mode kann man etwas erklären, ohne zu reden."

Sandra, 16 Jahre
„Zu meinem braunen Kleid trage ich schwarze Strümpfe und schwarze Schuhe mit Klumpabsatz. Ich ziehe mir auch Sachen an, wenn sie nicht 'in' sind. Es gibt wichtigeres als Mode."

Manu, 16 Jahre
„Meine Jeans und die Lederjacke sind Markenprodukte, keine billigen Kopien. Ich finde das wichtig."

STANDARDS: 1.2, 3.1, 5.2   KAPITEL 5   Klamotten kaufen

KRIEGBAUM AKTUELL

Stark Reduziert!

19.90 (3)

12.90 (2)

2) Kapuzen-T-Shirts
100% reine Baumwolle, in vielen Farben sortiert, Größe M–XXL **12.90**
3) Kapuzen-T-Shirts
100% reine Baumwolle, top Farben, bedruckt **19.90**

Volker, 16 Jahre
„Das sind meine Sachen: Jeans, Sportschuhe, Kapuzen-Shirt. Ich trage sie, weil sie mir gefallen. Mode interessiert mich nicht."

29.-

29.-

QUALITÄTS-GARANTIE
Wenn Sie bei K + L Ruppert einkaufen, stimmt nicht nur der Preis, sondern auch die Qualität. Dafür geben wir Ihnen auf unsere Ware 12 Monate Garantie. Sicher ist sicher.

Amberg, Augsburg, Bayreuth, Deggendorf, Erlangen, Freilassing, Freising, Friedrichshafen, Ingolstadt, Kempten, Kaufbeuren, 2 x in Landshut, Memmingen, Mühldorf/Inn, München/Kaufingerstr. 15, Neumarkt/OpL, Nürnberg, Passau, Ravensburg, Regensburg, Rosenheim, Straubing, Weiden, Weilheim.

k+l ruppert

---

5. Not all the texts on these pages are ads. What other type of text can you identify? What type of magazine would you expect texts like these to come from?

6. What is the age of the students who are describing their clothing? What generalizations can you make about the clothing of these students? Find words in the text that support your answer.

7. In the ad to the left, what kind of guarantee does **K&L Ruppert** offer for its merchandise?

8. What does Volker wear? Where could he buy a shirt like the one he says he likes to wear? How much would it cost? Do you know why it has that name?

9. What does Alex mean when he says **„Ich glaube, mit Mode kann man etwas erklären, ohne zu reden."**? (ohne zu reden– *without speaking*) Work with a partner and come up with some examples that illustrate this statement.

10. How does Manu differ from Sandra and Volker?

11. You are planning a trip to Germany. Your hosts will meet you at the airport, but they have never seen you. Write them a postcard with a short description of what you look like and what you will be wearing (**Ich trage ...**).

12. Your club at school is planning a garage sale. Write an ad for the school or local newspaper in which you describe the kinds of clothing you will sell.

Übungsheft, S. 59, Ü. 23

Mehr Grammatikübungen

CD-ROM DISC 2

Answers

internet

ADRESSE: go.hrw.com
KENNWORT:
WK3 SCHLESWIG-HOLSTEIN-5

Erste Stufe   Objective Expressing wishes when shopping

1 You and your friend are in a clothing store talking about prices, color, and fit of various items of clothing. Complete your questions and statements by supplying the correct forms of the definite article. (S. 135)

1. Was kostet _____ T-Shirt, bitte? Und _____ Jacke da?   das; die
2. Ich nehme _____ T-Shirt, ___ Pulli und _____ Jacke da, aber in Grün.   das; den; die
3. Ja, _____ Hose ist preiswert und _____ Gürtel auch.   die; der
4. Möchten Sie _____ Hose, und nehmen Sie _____ Gürtel?   die; den
5. Du, _____ Rock gefällt mir gut. Ich glaube, ich kaufe ___ Rock.   der; den
6. Ich bekomme _____ Hemd, _____ Turnschuhe und _____ Socken.   das; die; die
7. Ich möchte _____ Jeans da und _____ Stiefel.   die; die
8. Ich nehme _____ Kleid, und was kostet _____ Bluse da?   das; die
9. Möchten Sie _____ Hemd oder _____ Pulli?   das; den
10. Ja, _____ Jogging-Anzug ist preiswert, aber _____ Farbe ist nicht schön.   der; die

2 You are still in the clothing store, telling the salespersons what you are looking for and asking about the availability of various items of clothing in the colors you want. Complete these questions and statements by supplying the correct form of the indefinite article. (S. 135)

1. Ich suche _____ T-Shirt und _____ Pulli. _____ Pulli in Blau, bitte.   ein; einen; Einen
2. Dann brauche ich _____ Jeans und _____ Gürtel.   eine; einen
3. Ich möchte _____ Rock in Weiß, bitte, und _____ T-Shirt in Blau.   einen; ein
4. Ich brauche _____ Jogging-Anzug und _____ Shorts.   einen; eine
5. Haben Sie _____ Wunsch? Suchen Sie _____ Kleid oder _____ Bluse?   einen; ein; eine
6. Möchtest du _____ Jeans, _____ Rock oder _____ Kleid?   eine; einen; ein
7. Ich suche _____ Shorts und _____ Jacke, beide in Blau.   eine; eine
8. Ich brauche _____ Hemd, _____ Hose und _____ Gürtel für die Party.   ein; eine; einen

3 You seem to like everything in the clothing store, and you're telling your friend that you need each item. Complete each of the following statements by filling in the first blank with the correct form of the definite article, and the second blank with the correct form of the indefinite article. (S. 135)

1. _____ T-Shirt gefällt mir. Ich brauche _____ T-Shirt. Das; ein
2. _____ Rock gefällt mir. Ich brauche _____ Rock. Der; einen
3. _____ Bluse gefällt mir. Ich brauche _____ Bluse. Die; eine
4. _____ Pulli gefällt mir. Ich brauche _____ Pulli. Der; einen
5. _____ Hemd gefällt mir. Ich brauche _____ Hemd. Das; ein
6. _____ Gürtel gefällt mir. Ich brauche _____ Gürtel. Der; einen
7. _____ Kleid gefällt mir. Ich brauche _____ Kleid. Das; ein
8. _____ Jacke gefällt mir. Ich brauche _____ Jacke. Die; eine
9. _____ Jogging-Anzug gefällt mir. Ich brauche _____ Jogging-Anzug. Der; einen
10. _____ Hose gefällt mir gut. Ich brauche _____ Hose. Die; eine

Zweite Stufe

Objectives Commenting on and describing clothes; giving compliments

4 You are still in the clothing store. You are asking a friend for comments on the looks and the fit of various items of clothing. Complete each of the following questions and statements, using the correct forms of the definite articles and the verb **gefallen**. (S. 137)

1. Wie findest du _____ Rock? — Prima! Er _____ mir gut. den; gefällt
2. Wie findet Sonja _____ Turnschuhe? — Sie _____ ihr sehr gut. die; gefallen
3. Also, ich finde _____ T-Shirt Spitze. Und _____ Farbe _____ mir sehr gut. das; die; gefällt
4. Ja, _____ Stiefel _____ mir. Und _____ passen prima. die; gefallen; sie
5. Du, _____ Pulli _____ mir überhaupt nicht. Mir _____ die T-Shirts da! der; gefällt; gefallen

5 You continue asking for comments on the looks and the fit of various items of clothing. Complete each of the following statements by supplying the correct definite article and pronoun. (S. 140)

1. Ja, du, _____ Rock sieht schick aus, und _____ passt prima! der; er
2. Ich finde _____ Pulli toll; _____ gefällt mir gut. den; er
3. Ja, _____ Pulli sieht gut aus, aber _____ passt dir nicht; _____ ist zu eng. der; er; er
4. Du, _____ Turnschuhe passen gut, aber _____ sind ein bisschen zu teuer. die; sie
5. Ich finde _____ Hemd sehr schick; _____ gefällt mir prima. das; es
6. _____ Stiefel sind toll, aber sind _____ nicht ein bisschen zu groß? Die; sie
7. Wie findest du _____ T-Shirt? Ist _____ nicht zu weit? das; es
8. Du möchtest _____ Gürtel? Ist _____ nicht zu kurz? den; er
9. Du, _____ Jogging-Anzug passt prima. _____ gefällt mir. der; Er
10. Ich finde _____ Jogging-Anzug echt stark, und _____ passt prima. den; er

6 You and your friend are disagreeing about various items of clothing. Your friend finds everything great while you think those items are ugly. Complete each of the following statements by filling in the first blank with the correct form of the definite article, and the second blank with the correct form of the pronoun. **(S. 140)**

1. Ich finde _____ Pulli toll. – Und ich finde _____ scheußlich!   den; ihn
2. Ich finde _____ Hemd super. – Und ich finde _____ furchtbar!   das; es
3. Ich finde _____ Jacke fesch. – Und ich finde _____ scheußlich!   die; sie
4. Ich finde _____ Stiefel prima. – Und ich finde _____ ganz hässlich!   die; sie
5. Ich finde _____ Gürtel schick. – Und ich finde _____ scheußlich!   den; ihn
6. Ich finde _____ Bluse prima. – Und ich finde _____ furchtbar!   die; sie
7. Ich finde _____ Kleid toll. – Und ich finde _____ scheußlich!   das; es
8. Ich finde _____ Rock zu lang. – Und ich finde _____ zu kurz!   den; ihn
9. Ich finde _____ T-Shirt zu weit. – Und ich finde _____ zu eng.   das; es
10. Ich finde _____ Klamotten zu teuer. – Und ich finde _____ billig!   die; sie

7 You have decided to buy new clothes and are telling your friend about your decisions. Complete each of the following statements by filling in the first blank with the correct form of the definite article, and the second and third blanks with the correct forms of the pronoun. **(S. 140)**

BEISPIEL   Ich nehme _____ Bluse. _____ gefällt mir. Ich kaufe _____ .
Ich nehme <u>die</u> Bluse. <u>Sie</u> gefällt mir. Ich kaufe <u>sie</u>.

1. Ich nehme _____ Rock. _____ gefällt mir. Ich kaufe _____ .   den; Er; ihn
2. Ich nehme _____ T-Shirt. _____ gefällt mir. Ich kaufe _____ .   das; Es; es
3. Ich nehme _____ Pulli. _____ gefällt mir. Ich kaufe _____ .   den; Er; ihn
4. Ich nehme _____ Hose. _____ gefällt mir. Ich kaufe _____ .   die; Sie; sie
5. Ich nehme _____ Gürtel. _____ gefällt mir. Ich kaufe _____ .   den; Er; ihn
6. Ich nehme _____ T-Shirt. _____ gefällt mir. Ich kaufe _____ .   das; Es; es
7. Ich nehme _____ Turnschuhe. _____ gefallen mir. Ich kaufe _____ .   die; Sie; sie
8. Ich nehme _____ Kleid. _____ gefällt mir. Ich nehme _____ .   das; Es; es
9. Ich nehme _____ Jacke. _____ gefällt mir. Ich kaufe _____ .   die; Sie; sie
10. Ich nehme _____ Klamotten. _____ gefallen mir. Ich kaufe _____ .   die; Sie; sie

8 You are asking a friend what to wear and what he or she is going to wear to a party. Complete each of the following statements by filling in the blanks with the correct form of the separable-prefix verb given in parentheses. **(S. 143)**

1. Sag, was _____ du denn zur Fete _____? (anziehen)   ziehst; an
2. Die Sonja und die Katja _____ heute sehr schick _____. (aussehen)   sehen; aus
3. Warum _____ du den Pulli nicht mal _____? (anprobieren)   probierst; an
4. Der Michael _____ das T-Shirt mit dem Texas-Motiv _____. (anziehen)   zieht; an
5. Wie _____ ihr denn heute _____! Fesch! (aussehen)   seht; aus
6. Du sagst, sie sind zu groß? Ich _____ mal die Stiefel _____. (anprobieren)   probiere; an
7. Was _____ die Katja zur Party _____? Jeans und T-Shirt? (anziehen)   zieht; an
8. Wie _____ wir heute nur _____? Scheußlich! (aussehen)   sehen; aus
9. Wer _____ den Jogging-Anzug _____? (anprobieren)   probiert; an

9 You are asking your friends why they are taking or not taking various items of clothing by commenting on their looks. Complete each of the statements by using the correct forms of the verbs **nehmen** and **aussehen**. **(S. 144)**

1. Warum _____ du den Rock nicht? Er _____ doch sehr fesch _____.   nimmst; sieht; aus
2. Wer _____ die Jacke? Du, Sonja? Sie _____ toll _____!   nimmt; sieht; aus
3. Du _____ heute so fesch _____! Warum _____ du nur dieses T-Shirt?   siehst; aus; nimmst
4. Die Sonja _____ den Pulli; er _____ einfach toll _____!   nimmt; sieht; aus
5. Ihr _____ die Stiefel, ja? Sie _____ doch gut _____.   nehmt; sehen; aus
6. Wer _____ die Klamotten? Sie _____ furchtbar _____.   nimmt; sehen; aus
7. Ich _____ den Pulli; er _____ doch fesch _____!   nehme; sieht; aus
8. Der Michael _____ das T-Shirt, und es _____ so scheußlich _____!   nimmt; sieht; aus

Anwendung

The CD-ROM Tutor offers guided recording and writing activities to accompany the **Anwendung**. These activities are designed to practice students' oral and written communication skills and to review material from each chapter.

1 You have been hired to write for a German fashion magazine on trends among teens today. Interview your partner about his or her taste in clothes. When you have finished, switch roles and then interview one other person. Find out what clothes they like to wear, what they wear to a party, their favorite color, and their favorite article of clothing. Take notes and write an article in German based on your interviews.

2 Look at the two display windows for **Mode-Welt.** With a partner compare the two windows and take turns telling each other which items are missing (**fehlen**) from the second window.

3 Read the fashion review to the right, then answer these questions.

1. What clothing item is the fashion editor talking about?
2. Is he or she enthusiastic or skeptical about the item?
3. What does he or she say about the clothing being reviewed?

3. It is elegant, yet casual—a basic fashion element. Designers are using it in many ways.

DAS WEISSE HEMD

Ein weißes Hemd ist das, was Modekenner einen „all time classic" nennen: schick, aber trotzdem leger—ein Basisstück für jede Garderobe. In dieser Saison ist das weiße Hemd das Lieblingskind der Designer, die sich in ihren Variationen gegenseitig übertreffen. Asymmetrisch, geknotet oder aus Leinen, lang oder kurz—zu Jeans, Shorts oder Röcken: alles geht.

4 You are in a store looking for some new clothes and your partner, a pushy salesperson, tries to convince you to try on and get clothes that are the wrong color and don't fit. You try them on, and he or she tells you how good they look and how well they fit. You're not so sure. Express your uncertainty and hesitancy. Will you succumb to the pressure in the end and buy the clothes? Develop a conversation based on this scenario and practice it with your partner.

 5 You will hear some conversations in a clothing store. In each case the customer has decided not to buy the item. Determine the reason. Is it the price, the color, or the fit?

Script on p. 127H   1. **passt nicht** 2. **Farbe** 3. **Preis** 4. **passt nicht** 5. **Farbe**

CD 5 Tr. 16

 6

Zum Schreiben

Plan, write (and videotape) a German Club fashion show spotlighting appropriate party wear. The show is being sponsored by a local clothing store.

> **Schreibtipp** Arrange your thoughts logically by using an outline form. To make an outline, first put your ideas in related groups. Then put these groups in the order you want to write about them. Within each group, you might add subgroups to develop your ideas in more detail.

Prewriting

Draw up your outline: in this case the introduction could be used for information about the store. Then, beginning with the most casual party possible, continue on to dress for more formal occasions (a formal wedding, etc.), and end with a fancy-dress party (Roman numerals I, II, etc.).

Writing

Now you are ready to begin your show commentary. Give a brief description of the clothing store, including the store's name, where it is located, and what a great bargain everything is. After placing each ensemble in the correct category, use some of the many descriptive words you've learned to talk about each ensemble. Be sure to give prices. Descriptions can be inserted beneath the name of the outfit in your outline.

 7 ## Rollenspiel

You and two friends are at home trying to find something to wear to a party.

a. One of you is trying on clothes, but you can't find anything that fits or is the right color. Your friends comment on the clothes you try on.

b. Unsuccessful, in the end you all decide to go to the store. Look at the display windows in Activity 2 on page 152 again. Choose one window on which to base your conversation. This time one of you is the salesperson. The other two will be the customers. Ask for items in specific colors. The salesperson will tell you what's available. Will you try the clothes on? How do they look? Will you buy them? Role-play your scene in front of the class using props.

Kann ich's wirklich?

Can you express wishes when shopping? (p. 134)

1 How would a salesperson in a clothing store ask what you would like?
1. Bitte? *or* Was möchten Sie? *or* Was bekommen Sie? *or* Haben Sie einen Wunsch?

2 How would you answer, saying that you were looking for the following? (Be Ich brauch sure to practice using the articles correctly, and watch out for direct objects.) suche/mö

a. a sweater   **c.** pants in red   **e.** a jacket in light gray
b. boots in black   **d.** a shirt in brown   **f.** a dress in blue
a. einen Pulli, bitte.   c. eine Hose in Rot.   e. eine Jacke in Hellgrau.
b. Stiefel in Schwarz.   d. ein Hemd in Braun.   f. ein Kleid in Blau.

Can you comment on and describe clothing? (p. 137)

3 How would you ask a friend what he or she thinks of these clothes:

a. Wie findest du Jacke?
b. Wie findest du Schuhe?
c. Wie findest du Jogging-Anzug?
d. Wie findest du Hemd?

a.   **b.**   **c.**   **d.**

4 How might your friend respond positively? Negatively? With uncertainty?
Er/Sie/Es gefällt mir. Ich finde ihn/sie/es furchtbar. Ich weiß nicht.

5 How would you disagree with the following statements by saying the opposite? Use the correct pronoun.   Answers may vary.

a. The jacket is too short.   **e.** I think the belt is terrible.
b. The shoes are too tight.   **f.** I like the tennis shoes.
c. The jogging suit is too small.   **g.** I think the dress is too long.
d. The shirt fits just right.   **h.** The skirt looks stylish.
a. Sie ist zu lang.   c. Er ist zu groß.   e. Er ist Spitze.   g. Es ist zu kurz.
b. Sie sind zu groß.   d. Es passt nicht.   f. Sie gefallen mir nicht.   h. Er ist furchtbar.

Can you compliment someone's clothing and respond to compliments? (p. 139)

6 How would you compliment Katja, using the cues below?   Answers may vary.

a. blouse   **b.** sweater   **c.** T-shirt   **d.** skirt
a. Die Bluse gefällt mir!   b. Der Pulli sieht lässig aus!   c. Das T-Shirt ist fesch!   d. Der Rock ist schick!

7 **a.** How might Katja respond to your compliments?
b. What would you say next?   a. Ehrlich? *or* Wirklich? *or* Meinst du?
b. Ehrlich! *or* Wirklich! *or* Ja, bestimmt!

8 How would you tell a friend what the following people are wearing to Sonja's party? (Remember to use **anziehen!**)

| Jeans | Bluse | T-Shirt | Jogging-Anzug |
| Shorts | Turnschuhe | Gürtel | |

a. Julia   **b.** Katja   **c.** Heiko
Answers may vary.   a. **Julia zieht Jeans und eine Bluse an.**   b. **Katja zieht Shorts und ein T-Shirt an.**
c. **Heiko zieht einen Jogging-Anzug an.**

Can you talk about trying on clothes? (p. 143)

9 How would you tell the salesperson that you would like to try on a shirt in red, pants in white, a sweater in yellow, and a jacket in brown?
Ich möchte ein Hemd in Rot anprobieren./eine Hose in Weiß/einen Pulli in Gelb/eine Jacke in Braun

10 How would you tell your friend that you will get the shirt, the sweater, and the jacket? (Use **nehmen** or **kaufen**.)   Ich nehme (kaufe) das Hemd, den Pulli und die Jacke.

Erste Stufe

Expressing wishes when shopping

Bitte?	Yes? Can I help you?
Was bekommen Sie?	What would you like?
Haben Sie einen Wunsch?	May I help you?
Ich möchte …	I would like …
Ich brauche …	I need …
Ich suche …	I'm looking for …
Einen Pulli in Grau, bitte.	A sweater in gray, please.
Haben Sie das auch in Rot?	Do you also have that in red?
die Farbe, -n	color
in Rot	in red
in Blau	in blue

in Grün	in green
in Gelb	in yellow
in Braun	in brown
in Grau	in gray
in Schwarz	in black
in Weiß	in white
in Dunkelblau	in dark blue
in Hellblau	in light blue
die Klamotten (pl)	casual term for clothes
die Bluse, -n	blouse
der Rock, ¨e	skirt
das Kleid, -er	dress
das Hemd, -en	shirt
die Jeans, -	jeans
der Gürtel, -	belt

die Hose, -n	pants
die Jacke, -n	jacket
der Pulli, -s (Pullover,-)	sweater
der Jogging-Anzug, ¨e	jogging suit
das T-Shirt, -s	T-shirt
der Turnschuh, -e	sneaker, athletic shoe
der Stiefel, -	boot
die Socke, -n	sock
die Shorts, -	shorts

Masculine articles: accusative case

den	the
einen	a, an

Zweite Stufe

Commenting on and describing clothes

Er/Sie/Es gefällt mir.	I like it.
Sie gefallen mir.	I like them.
Der Rock sieht … aus.	The skirt looks …
hübsch	pretty
lässig	casual
schick	chic, smart
fesch	stylish, smart
scheußlich	hideous
furchtbar	terrible, awful
Der Rock passt prima!	The skirt fits great!

Ich finde den Pulli echt stark!	I think the sweater is really awesome!
Ich bin nicht sicher.	I'm not sure.
Ich weiß nicht.	I don't know.
die Größe, -n	the size
zu	too
viel zu	much too
ein bisschen	a little
weit	wide
eng	tight
lang	long
kurz	short

Giving and responding to compliments

Meinst du?	Do you think so?
ehrlich	honestly
wirklich	really
überhaupt nicht	not at all
bestimmt	definitely
Nicht zu lang?	Not too long?

Masculine Pronoun: accusative case

ihn	it; him

Dritte Stufe

Talking about trying on clothes

aussehen (sep)*	to look (like), appear
er/sie sieht aus**	he/she looks
anprobieren (sep)	to try on

anziehen (sep)	to put on, wear
nehmen	to take
er/sie nimmt	he/she takes
kaufen	to buy

---

*Verbs with separable prefixes will be indicated with (sep) **For verbs with stem-vowel changes, the third person singular form will be listed to show you the vowel change that occurs.

Kapitel 6: Pläne machen
Chapter Overview

| Los geht's! pp. 158–160 | *Wollen wir ins Café gehen? p. 158* |

	FUNCTIONS	GRAMMAR	VOCABULARY	RE-ENTRY
Erste Stufe pp. 161–164	• Starting a conversation, p. 161 • Telling time and talking about when you do things, p. 162		• Telling time, p. 162	• Expressing time when referring to schedules, p. 162 (**Kap. 4**) • School and free time activity vocabulary, p. 164 (**Kap. 2** and **Kap. 4**)
Zweite Stufe pp. 165–169	• Making plans, p. 166	• The verb **wollen**, p. 166	• Making plans for free time activities, p. 165	• Inversion of time elements, p. 167 (**Kap. 2**) • Sequencing events, p. 168 (**Kap. 4**)
Dritte Stufe pp. 170–173	• Ordering food and beverages, p. 170 • Talking about how something tastes, p. 172 • Paying the check, p. 172	• The stem-changing verb **essen**, p. 171	• Food items on a **Café** menu, p. 171	• Accusative case, p. 171 (**Kap. 5**) • The verb **nehmen**, p. 171 • The **möchte**-forms, p. 171 (**Kap. 3**) used in a new context, ordering food

Aussprache p. 173	The letter combination **ch**, the letter **r**, and the final **er**: Audio CD 6, Track 13	**Diktat:** Audio CD 6, Tracks 14–15

Zum Lesen pp. 174–175	**Wohin in Hamburg?**	**Reading Strategy** Using context to guess meaning

Mehr Grammatik-übungen	**pp. 176–179**		
	Erste Stufe, p. 176	**Zweite Stufe**, pp. 177–178	**Dritte Stufe**, p. 179

Review pp. 180–183	**Anwendung**, pp. 180–181	**Kann ich's wirklich?**, p. 182	**Wortschatz**, p. 183
	Zum Schreiben: Arranging ideas chronologically (Writing a descriptive letter)		

CULTURE

• Pictures of clocks located outside of public buildings, p. 163

• **Landeskunde: Was machst du in deiner Freizeit?** p. 169

• **Ein wenig Landeskunde:** Tipping in Germany, p. 173

Kapitel 6: Pläne machen
Chapter Resources

 **PRINT**

Lesson Planning

One-Stop Planner

Lesson Planner with Substitute Teacher Lesson Plans, pp. 27–31, 70

Student Make-Up Assignments
- Make-Up Assignment Copying Masters, Chapter 6

Listening and Speaking

TPR Storytelling Book, pp. 21–24

Listening Activities
- Student Response Forms for Listening Activities, pp. 43–46
- Additional Listening Activities 6-1 to 6-6, pp. 47–50
- Additional Listening Activities (song), p. 46
- Scripts and Answers, pp. 129–135

Video Guide
- Teaching Suggestions, pp. 36–37
- Activity Masters, pp. 38–40
- Scripts and Answers, pp. 93–95, 113–114

Activities for Communication
- Communicative Activities, pp. 31–36
- Realia and Teaching Suggestions, pp. 94–97
- Situation Cards, pp. 133–134

Reading and Writing

Reading Strategies and Skills Handbook, Chapter 6

Lies mit mir! 1, Chapter 6

Übungsheft, pp. 61–72

Grammar

Grammatikheft, pp. 46–54

Grammar Tutor for Students of German, Chapter 6

Assessment

Testing Program
- Grammar and Vocabulary Quizzes, **Stufe** Quizzes, and Chapter Test, pp. 131–148
- Score Sheet, Scripts and Answers, pp. 149–156

- Midterm Exam, pp. 157–164
- Midterm Exam Score Sheet, Scripts and Answers, pp. 165–170

Alternative Assessment Guide
- Portfolio Assessment, p. 23
- Performance Assessment, p. 37
- CD-ROM Assessment, p. 51

Student Make-Up Assignments
- Alternative Quizzes, Chapter 6

 **MEDIA**

 Online Activities
- Interaktive Spiele
- Internet Aktivitäten

 Video Program
- Videocassette 2
- Videocassette 5 (captioned version)

 Audio Compact Discs
- Textbook Listening Activities, CD 6, Tracks 1–16
- Additional Listening Activities, CD 6, Tracks 29–35
- Assessment Items, CD 6, Tracks 17–28

 Interactive CD-ROM Tutor, Disc 2

 Teaching Transparencies
- Situations 6-1 to 6-2
- Vocabulary 6-A to 6-C
- **Los geht's!**
- **Mehr Grammatikübungen** Answers
- **Grammatikheft** Answers

 **One-Stop Planner CD-ROM**

Use the **One-Stop Planner CD-ROM with Test Generator** to aid in lesson planning and pacing.

For each chapter, the **One-Stop Planner** includes:
- Editable lesson plans with direct links to teaching resources
- Printable worksheets from resource books
- Direct launches to the HRW Internet activities
- Video and audio segments
- Test Generator
- Clip Art for vocabulary items

Kapitel 6: Pläne machen

Projects

Eine Informationsbroschüre

*In this activity students will create an information guide to **Schleswig-Holstein**, the location of Chapters 4, 5, and 6. This activity will take several days, so you may want to consider breaking it into smaller assignments and having it count as a major grade.*

This project is designed for students to do individually or in groups. Assign each group of students a topic or let them choose one.

MATERIALS

✂ Students may need
- posterboard
- glue
- scissors
- masking tape

SUGGESTED TOPICS

Economy
Natural resources; manufactured goods; important crops; importance of agriculture and industry

Geography
a. a map of Schleswig-Holstein showing rivers, lakes, canals, important cities (with special attention to the **Landeshauptstadt**), and borders with other **Bundesländer** and countries

b. population: pictures depicting types of housing; dialects

Culture
a. art, dances, folk music, **Trachten** for men and women

b. literature: biography and brief summaries of important works of Thomas Mann and Theodor Storm (special attention should be paid to Storm's novel *Der Schimmelreiter*)

c. history: poster illustrating the history of Schleswig-Holstein

SUGGESTED SEQUENCE

1. Students do research at a library (school, public, or university library) and look for information in atlases, almanacs, periodicals, world reference books, encyclopedias, and the Internet.

2. Students begin their project by giving it a title and compiling and organizing their materials into categories.

3. Students hand in a rough draft of their projects to get suggestions on improving them. Or have students exchange rough drafts for peer editing.

4. Students finish their projects with an oral presentation and then turn in their final project.

GRADING THE PROJECT

Suggested point distribution (**total = 100 points**)
Content 40
Oral presentation...............................20
Appearance 10
Correct language usage 10
Originality...10
Individual participation 10

Games

Das treffende Wort suchen

This game will help your students develop the skill of circumlocution, the linguistic art of communicating when a person doesn't know the precise word he or she needs. Explain to students that they will learn to paraphrase, use synonyms, describe essential elements, and utilize key phrases to communicate when they find themselves at a loss for the exact word they need.

Preparation   Create a list of words in English related to the vocabulary presented in the chapter/**Stufe.** On an index card, write one vocabulary word from the list you created. Arrange four desks at the front of the room in such a way so that two partners from each team can face each other. Place the cards face down where they can easily be reached by the players from any of the desks. On the board or on a transparency, write the following key phrases:

Aussehen	**Es ist ein Ding / eine Person / ein Tier …**
	Das Ding ist aus Metall / Glas / Kunststoff / Papier.
	Es ist … klein / groß / alt / neu. Es hat …
	Es sieht aus wie …
Funktion	**Man benutzt / braucht das Ding für … Das Gegenteil ist …**
	Man kann es … essen, trinken …
	Man sieht (hört) es …
Ort	**Man kann dort … Man findet es …**
	Es lebt (wohnt) im … Wald, Meer …

STANDARDS: 1.3, 2.2, 3.1, 3.2

Procedure Divide the class into two teams. Have two players from each team sit at the four desks. A player from Team A selects a card and shows it to one of the players from Team B. Using circumlocution phrases, the Team A player attempts to describe the vocabulary word to his or her partner without saying the word itself. (For example, one could say about an elephant: **Das ist ein Tier. Es ist groß und grau.**) If the partner in Team A guesses the word, Team A receives five points. If not, the Team B player in turn gives a clue to his or her partner. If the partner guesses correctly, Team B receives four points. Rotate players after four players.

Weltatlas

Playing this game will help students develop a better knowledge of the geography of the German-speaking countries.

Procedure Use a large map of German-speaking countries or use the overhead projector to project a map onto the wall. Divide the class into two teams and have one member from each team come to the front of the class. Call out a place, and the first student to point out the location correctly wins a point. This student then challenges another student. The winner is the team that has scored the most points.

Storytelling

Mini-Geschichte

*This story accompanies Teaching Transparency 6-2. The **Mini-Geschichte** can be told and retold in different formats, acted out, written down, and read aloud to give students additional opportunities to practice all four skills.*

Ein Nachmittag in der Stadt

Um Viertel nach drei gehen Silke und Monika in die Stadt. Silke sagt: „Wollen wir bei Mario essen? Ich möchte eine Pizza." Monika sagt: „Ja, klar! Ich möchte ein Stück Apfelkuchen." Es ist Viertel nach vier. Monika sagt: „Die Pizza ist nicht besonders gut. Wie schmeckt der Apfelkuchen?" „Der Apfelkuchen schmeckt lecker. Was machen wir nun?" Monika sagt: „Gehen wir ins Kino! Ich will *Gladiator* sehen. Das ist ein prima Film!" „Super! Der Film beginnt (*to begin*) um siebzehn Uhr. Wir haben noch Zeit."

Traditions

Rezept

Der Dithmarscher Mehlbeutel, der in Schleswig-Holstein auch unter dem Namen „Großer Hans" bekannt ist, kommt in zwei Arten auf den Tisch: Einmal gibt es die Standardausführung für den täglichen Mittagstisch. Das ist der sogenannte „weiße Mehlbeutel". Dann gibt es für Geburtstage und andere Feste noch eine Luxusausführung, den „bunten Mehlbeutel". In den Teig dafür kommen mehr Eier und außerdem Rosinen und Korinthen.

Dithmarscher Mehlbeutel
Für 4-6 Personen

Zutaten
g=Gramm, EL=Esslöffel, TL=Teelöffel, l=Liter

1/2 l	Milch
1 TL	Salz
8	Eier
500g	Mehl
1 EL	Zitronenschale, feingerieben
375g	Schweinebacke (Speck), geräuchert
50g	Zucker
150g	Butter

Zubereitung

Milch mit Salz, Eiern, Mehl und Zitronenschale zu einem glatten Teig verrühren und eine Stunde ruhen lassen. Ein großes Tuch heiß ausspülen, gut auswringen und in eine Schüssel legen. Den Teig hineinlegen und die Tuchzipfel darüber zusammenbinden. Einen möglichst großen Topf mit viel Wasser bei starker Hitze aufsetzen, den Speck hineingeben und aufkochen. Den Mehlbeutel an einem Holzlöffelstiel hineinhängen, so daß er den Boden des Topfes nicht berührt. Halb mit dem Topfdeckel zugedeckt 2 Stunden kochen lassen. Dabei immer wieder heißes Wasser auffüllen. Das Wasser muss immer kochen. Nach dem Kochen, den Mehlbeutel 10 Minuten ausdampfen lassen, das Tuch wegnehmen und auf einen Teller geben. Der Mehlbeutel wird dann wie eine Torte aufgeschnitten und jeder nimmt sich ein Stück und bestreut es dick mit Zucker. Dazu gießt man dann noch flüßige Butter darüber.

Technology

Video

Videocassette 2, 5 (captioned version)
See Video Guide, pages 35–40

Los geht's! • Wollen wir ins Café gehen?

Heiko runs into Julia. She tells him that she is going to Katja's and that they are going to have a bite to eat at a café. Heiko agrees to join them. At the café they meet Michael and everybody orders something. Michael accidentally spills his drink on Katja's new T-shirt.

Fortsetzung

Heiko orders something to eat and the two girls keep him company. All of a sudden, Michael returns with flowers for Katja and an apology for staining her T-shirt.

Landeskunde

Was machst du in deiner Freizeit?

People of various ages from different cities talk about what they do in their free time.

Videoclips

- **Junghans**® (watches)
- **Wagner-Pizza** ® (pizza)
- **Sacher Eis**® (ice cream)
- **Überkinger Mineralwasser**® (mineral water)

Interactive CD-ROM Tutor

The **Interactive CD-ROM Tutor** contains videos, interactive games, and activities that provide students an opportunity to practice and review the material covered in Chapter 6.

Activity	Activity Type	Pupil's Edition Reference
1. So sagt man das!	Wozu gehört's?	p. 161
2. Wortschatz	Merkspiel	p. 162
3. Wortschatz	Wort und Bild Erfahren/Wählen	p. 165
4. Wortschatz	Merkspiel	p. 171
5. Grammatik	Was fehlt?	pp. 166, 171
6. So sagt man das!	Was ist richtig?	pp. 162, 170, 172
Landeskunde	Was machst du in deiner Freizeit? Was ist richtig?	p. 169
Zum Sprechen	*Guided recording*	pp. 180–181
Zum Schreiben	*Guided writing*	pp. 180–181

Teacher Management System

Logging In

Logging in to the **Komm mit!** TMS is easy. Upon launching the program, simply type "admin" in the password area of the log-in screen and press RETURN. Log on to **www.hrw.com/CDROMTUTOR** for a detailed explanation of the Teacher Management System.

Internet Connection

One-Stop Planner CD-ROM

To preview all resources available for this chapter, use the **One-Stop Planner CD-ROM**, Disc 2.

internet

ADRESSE: go.hrw.com
KENNWORT:
WK3 SCHLESWIG-HOLSTEIN-6

*Have students explore the **go.hrw.com** Web site for many online resources covering all chapters. All Chapter 6 resources are available under the keyword **WK3 Schleswig-Holstein-6**. Interactive games practice the material and provide students with immediate feedback. You will also find a printable worksheet that provides Internet activities that lead to a comprehensive online research project.*

Interaktive Spiele

Use the interactive activities in this chapter

- to practice grammar, vocabulary, and chapter functions
- as homework
- as an assessment option
- as a self-test
- to prepare for the Chapter Test

Internet Aktivitäten

Students will calculate the time difference between their city and any other city in a German-speaking country. They will learn to read German menus and navigate the sites of German movie theaters.

- To prepare students for the **Arbeitsblatt,** you might want to have them scan the menus on pp. 170 and 181. Ask them to review the vocabulary of the **Dritte Stufe,** p. 183.

- After completing the **Arbeitsblatt,** have students write a dialogue between Mario and Max in which they decide on a leisure-time activity for the afternoon. Have them review **So sagt man das!** on p. 166 and the **Wortschatz** on p. 165 before they embark on this activity.

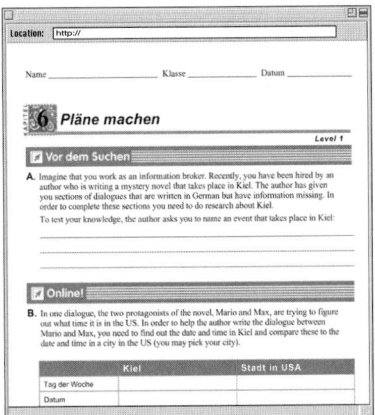

Webprojekt

Have students do a Web search for a concert that takes place in any city in Schleswig-Holstein. Have students report on the nature of the concert and where and when it takes place. Encourage students to exchange useful Web sites with their classmates.

Have students document their sources by referencing the names and URLs of all the sites they consulted.

Kapitel 6: Pläne machen
Textbook Listening Activities Scripts

6 p. 161

1. — Wie geht's denn?

— Ach, nicht so besonders gut.

— Wieso denn?

— Ich kann mein Geld nicht finden.

— Na, das tut mir Leid. Kann ich dir beim Suchen helfen?

2. — Wie geht's dir denn?

— Echt schlecht.

— Darf ich fragen warum?

— Ich habe 'ne Vier in Englisch.

— Ja, das ist wirklich nicht so gut! Der Herr Meier ist aber auch ganz schön schwer, nicht?

3. — Hallo!

— Grüß dich! Wie geht's denn?

— Oh, danke, ganz gut! Ich gehe am Wochenende in ein Rockkonzert. Darauf freue ich mich schon!

4. — Grüß dich!

— Hallo!

— Wie geht's denn so?

— Hm, nicht schlecht, ich bin nur müde.

5. — Hallo! Wie geht's denn?

— Danke, sehr gut!

— Um 3 Uhr gehen Sabine, Dieter und ich ins Kino. Kommst du mit?

— Na klar, danke!

13 p. 164

1. — Du, Gudrun, willst du heute Abend mit uns ins Kino gehen?

— Mensch, schade. Danke für die Einladung, aber um Viertel nach sieben will ich Fernseh schauen. Da kommt eine Sendung über Elefanten in Afrika. Das brauch ich halt für meine Erdkundeklasse am Mittwoch.

2. — Du Susanne, was machst du heute nachmittag?

— Ja, um zwanzig nach drei … hm … ja, hab ich meine Tennisstunde.

3. — Ich gehe jetzt ins Café Freizeit. Kommst du mit?

— Nein, ich möcht ja schon, aber ich kann nicht. Ich muss für Mathe lernen. Morgen um Viertel nach neun ist unsere Matheprüfung.

4. — Morgen, wie geht's? Du kommst ja heute schon so früh!

— Ja, meine erste Stunde ist heute schon um Viertel vor acht. Deutsch bei Frau Stegel. Da muss man pünktlich sein.

5. — Du, die Eva und ich wollen am Samstag um neun bei Karstadt Klamotten anschauen. Willst du mitkommen?

— Ich möchte schon mit, aber ich treffe um Viertel vor zwei Udo und Erika im Schwimmbad.

6. — Renate! Magda! Was macht ihr denn hier noch so spät? Es ist schon halb elf! Und morgen früh ist Schule.

— Tut uns Leid, Vati. Ist es zu laut? Diese Musik ist einfach Spitze!

— Nein, nein. Zu laut ist es nicht … aber es ist jetzt schon zu spät, Musik zu hören. Geht bitte ins Bett, hört ihr?

16 p. 165

BEATE Du, ich freue mich schon aufs Wochenende. Hast du heute auch Taschengeld bekommen?

SABINE Ja, ein Glück, da können wir endlich mal wieder in die Stadt gehen. Was meinst du dazu?

BEATE Ja klar doch, zuerst lass uns ins Café gehen. Da können wir uns gut unterhalten und …

SABINE Du, ich weiß was, danach gehen wir ins Kino …

BEATE Gibt's denn gute Filme?

SABINE Natürlich … und ach ja, ich will ja noch zu Karstadt. Ich brauch ein paar neue Klamotten für die Schule. Hast du Lust dazu?

BEATE Okay! Wenn wir Zeit haben, können wir ja anschließend baden gehen. Das neue Schwimmbad soll ganz toll sein!

SABINE Prima! Ich freue mich schon aufs Wochenende!

One-Stop Planner CD-ROM

For resource information, see the **One-Stop Planner CD-ROM**, Disc 2.

Dritte Stufe

27 p. 170

KATJA	Julia, was nimmst du?
JULIA	Ach, ich bestelle wie immer. Ich esse gern ein Stück Apfelkuchen und trinke einen Cappuccino dazu.
MICHAEL	Und du, Heiko? Was willst du? Auch Apfelkuchen?
HEIKO	Nein, keinen Kuchen für mich. Das ist zu süß. Ich möchte zuerst etwas trinken, ein Mineralwasser. Und dann esse ich lieber ein Wurstbrot. Vielleicht trinke ich einen Cappuccino zum Schluss.
JULIA	Und du, Katja?
KATJA	Hm! Ich hab einen Hunger, kann ich dir sagen! Ich glaube, ich nehme eine Nudelsuppe, dann zwei Paar Wiener mit Senf. Ich trinke eine Limonade, ein großes Glas.
HEIKO	Und du, Michael? Was willst du nehmen?
MICHAEL	Ich habe Hunger auf Pizza, und dazu trinke ich dann eine Cola. Danach gibt's natürlich wie immer einen Eisbecher. Eis esse ich immer hier.

31 p. 172

HEIKO	Hallo! Wir möchten zahlen!
MICHAEL	Ja schaut, es ist schon 4 Uhr. Wir müssen bald los!
KELLNER	Also für Sie … ein Mineralwasser, ein Euro 75; ein Käsebrot, zwei Euro 55; eine Tasse Kaffee, zwei Euro 15. Das macht zusammen sechs Euro 45.
HEIKO	Sieben Euro. Stimmt schon.
KELLNER	Danke. Und sie … einen Moment bitte … ja, eine Nudelsuppe mit Brot, zwei Euro 25; dann zwei Paar Wiener mit Senf, zwei Euro 90; und eine Limonade, ein Euro 80. Zusammen: sechs Euro 95.
KATJA	Sieben Euro. Stimmt so.
KELLNER	Ein Stück Apfelkuchen, ein Euro 40; ein Cappuccino, zwei Euro 60. Das macht zusammen genau vier Euro.
JULIA	Ja dann … vier fünfzig, bitte.
KELLNER	Vielen Dank! Und Sie, eine Pizza, drei Euro; eine Cola, ein Euro 50 und der Eisbecher, drei Euro 40. Alles zusammen: sieben Euro 90.

MICHAEL	Acht Euro 50.
KELLNER	Vielen Dank. Auf Wiedersehen!

AUSSPRACHE, p. 173

Diktat, p. 173

You will hear Angelika talking to Thomas about his plans for the weekend. First listen to what they are saying, then write down their conversation.

ANGELIKA	Und, was machst du denn am Wochenende, Thomas?
THOMAS	Ich bin noch nicht ganz sicher. Ach, vielleicht gehe ich Rad fahren. Und du?
ANGELIKA	Ich möchte gern ins Kino. Willst du am Samstagnachmittag mitkommen? So um 4 Uhr?
THOMAS	Ja, das heißt … nein, das geht leider nicht. Wir besuchen meine Großeltern.
ANGELIKA	Schade.
THOMAS	Du, um 20 Uhr spielt Udo Lindenberg, und es gibt noch Karten. Willst du ihn hören?
ANGELIKA	Ja prima. Also, bis später dann!

Anwendung

2 p. 180

1. Im Sommer reist Familie Bonsen gern an die Nordsee. Jedes Jahr bleiben sie für zwei Wochen im Hotel Hanseatik. Das hat sogar ein großes Schwimmbad. Die Familie isst dort auch gern im Restaurant. Das Essen ist immer gut und auch preiswert.

2. Susanne und Michaela spielen gern Tennis und hören gern Musik. Sie haben beide viele Kassetten und CDs, aber am liebsten gehen sie doch in Konzerte. Im Juni gehen sie in ein Rockkonzert. Susanne geht auch manchmal mit ihren Eltern in die Symphonie.

3. Dieter und Lutz sind bei Lutz zu Hause. Sie spielen Karten, und Dieter gewinnt — wie immer!

4. Ute geht nicht gern in die Stadt. Das findet sie langweilig. Sie bleibt lieber zu Hause und übt auf ihrer Gitarre. Sie spielt schon seit drei Jahren und ist ziemlich gut.

5. Anja und Martina gehen am Samstag in die Stadt. Sie brauchen ein paar neue Klamotten für die Schule.

Kapitel 6: Pläne machen
Suggested Lesson Plans *50-Minute Schedule*

Day 1

CHAPTER OPENER 10 min.
- Culture Note, ATE, p. 155M
- Background Information, ATE, p. 155M
- Teaching Suggestion, ATE, p. 155M

LOS GEHT'S! 20 min.
- Preteaching Vocabulary, ATE, p. 155N
- Play Audio CD for **Los geht's!**, pp. 158–159
- Have students read **Los geht's!**, pp. 158–159
- Teaching Suggestions, Video Guide, p. 36
- Culture Note, ATE, p. 155N
- Show **Los geht's!** Video
- Do Comprehension Activities, p. 160

ERSTE STUFE
So sagt man das!, p. 161 15 min.
- Presenting **So sagt man das!**, ATE, p. 155O
- Play Audio CD for Activity 6, p. 161
- Play *Tic Tac Toe*, ATE, p. 155O
- Do Activities 7 and 8, p. 161

Wrap-Up 5 min.
- Students respond to questions about how they are doing

Homework Options
Grammatikheft, p. 46, Act. 1

Day 2

ERSTE STUFE
Quick Review 5 min.
- Check homework, Grammatikheft, p. 46, Act. 1

Wortschatz, p. 162 10 min.
- Presenting **Wortschatz**, ATE, p. 155O
- Culture Note, ATE, p. 155P
- Teaching Transparencies 6-A, 6-1
- Do Activity 9, p. 162

So sagt man das!, p. 162 20 min.
- Presenting **So sagt man das!**, ATE p. 155P
- Do Activity 10, p. 162
- Do Activities 11 and 12, p. 163
- Play Audio CD for Activity 13, p. 164
- Do Activity 14, p. 164

Sprachtipp, p. 164 10 min.
- Present Sprachtipp, p. 164
- Do Activity 15, p. 164

Wrap-Up 5 min.
- Students respond to questions about time

Homework Options
Grammatikheft, pp. 46–47, Acts. 2–5
Übungsheft, pp. 62–64, Acts. 3–8

Day 3

ERSTE STUFE
Quick Review 10 min.
- Check homework, Grammatikheft, pp. 46–47, Acts. 2–5
Quiz Review 20 min.
- Do Additional Listening Activities 6-1 and 6-2, p. 47
- Do **Mehr Grammatikübungen, Erste Stufe**
Quiz 20 min.
- Quiz 6-1A or 6-1B

Homework Options
Activities for Communication, pp. 31–32, prepare Communicative Activity 6-1

Day 4

ZWEITE STUFE
Quick Review 15 min.
- Return and review Quiz 6-1
- Bell Work, ATE, 155Q
- Do Communicative Activity 6-1, pp. 31–32

Wortschatz, p. 165 10 min.
- Presenting **Wortschatz**, ATE, p. 155Q
- Teaching Transparency 6-B
- Play Audio CD for Activity 16, p. 165

So sagt man das!/Grammatik, p. 166 20 min.
- Presenting **So sagt man das!**, ATE, p. 155R
- Presenting **Grammatik**, ATE, p. 155R
- Do Activity 19, p. 166
- Do Activities 20, 21, and 22, p. 167

Wrap-Up 5min.
- Students respond to questions about making plans

Homework Options
Pupil's Edition, p. 165, Acts. 17 and 18
Grammatikheft, pp. 48–49, Acts. 6–10
Übungsheft, pp. 65–66, Acts. 9–14

Day 5

ZWEITE STUFE
Quick Review 10 min.
- Check homework, Übungsheft, pp. 65–66, Acts. 9–14
Ein wenig Grammatik, p. 167 15 min.
- Present **Ein wenig Grammatik**, p. 167
- Do Activities 23, 24, and 25, p. 168

LANDESKUNDE 20 min.
- Pre-viewing Suggestion, Video Guide, p. 36
- Culture Notes, ATE, p. 155S
- Show **Landeskunde** Video
- Do Activities A and B, p. 169

Wrap-Up 5 min.
- Students respond to questions about making plans using the verb **wollen**

Homework Options
Grammatikheft, p. 50, Acts. 11–12
Übungsheft, p. 67, Acts. 15–16

Day 6

ZWEITE STUFE
Quick Review 10 min.
- Check homework, Grammatikheft, p. 50, Acts. 11–12
Quiz Review 20 min.
- Do Communicative Activity 6-2, pp. 33–34
- Do **Mehr Grammatikübungen, Zweite Stufe**
- Do **Interaktive Spiele** at WK3 SCHLESWIG-HOLSTEIN-6
Quiz 20 min.
- Quiz 6-2A or 6-2B

Homework Options
Übungsheft, p. 72, Act. 26

One-Stop Planner CD-ROM

For alternative lesson plans by chapter section, to create your own customized plans, or to preview all resources available for this chapter, use the **One-Stop Planner CD-ROM**, Disc 2.

 For additional homework suggestions, see activities accompanied by this symbol throughout the chapter.

Day 7

DRITTE STUFE

Quick Review 10 min.
- Return and review Quiz 6-2
- Bell Work, ATE p. 155T

So sagt man das!, p. 170 20 min.
- Presenting **So sagt man das!**, ATE, p. 155T
- Teaching Transparency 6-2
- Do Activity 26, p. 170
- Play Audio CD for Activity 27, p. 170

Wortschatz, p. 171 15 min.
- Presenting **Wortschatz**, ATE, p. 155T
- Teaching Transparency 6-C
- Do Activity 28, p. 171

Wrap-Up 5 min.
- Students respond to questions about what they would like to eat or drink

Homework Options
Grammatikheft, p. 51, Acts. 13–15
Übungsheft, p. 68, Acts. 17–19

Day 8

DRITTE STUFE

Quick Review 15 min.
- Check homework, Übungsheft, p. 68, Acts. 17–19
- Play Circumlocution Game, ATE, p. 155C

Grammatik, p. 171 20 min.
- Presenting **Grammatik**, ATE, p. 155T
- Language to Language, ATE, p. 155U
- Present **Lerntrick**, p. 171
- Do Activity 29, p. 171
- Do Activities 4, 5, and 6, Interactive CD-ROM

So sagt man das!, p. 172 10 min.
- Presenting **So sagt man das!**, ATE, p. 155U
- Do Activity 30, p. 172

Wrap-Up 5 min.
- Students answer questions about what they would like to eat and drink

Homework Options
Grammatikheft, pp. 52–53, Acts. 16–20
Übungsheft, pp. 69–70, Acts. 20–24

Day 9

DRITTE STUFE

Quick Review 15 min.
- Check homework, Übungsheft, pp. 69–70, Acts. 20–24

So sagt man das!, p. 172 15 min.
- Presenting **So sagt man das!**, ATE, p. 155U
- Play Audio CD for Activity 31, p. 172
- Do Activity 32, p. 172

Ein wenig Landeskunde, p. 173 15 min.
- Present **Ein wenig Landeskunde**, p. 173
- Do Activity 33, p. 173

Wrap-Up 5 min.
- Students order various food and drink items in response to a waiter's questions

Homework Options
Pupil's Edition, p. 173, Act. 34
Grammatikheft, p. 54, Acts. 21–22

Day 10

DRITTE STUFE

Quick Review 10 min.
- Check homework, Grammatikheft, p. 54, Acts. 21–22

Quiz Review 20 min.
- Do Additional Listening Activities 6-5 and 6-6, pp. 49–50
- Do Mehr **Grammatikübungen, Dritte Stufe**

Quiz 20 min.
- Quiz 6-3A or 6-3B

Homework Options
Pupil's Edition, p. 181, Act. 5, **Zum Schreiben**
Übungsheft, p. 71, Act. 25

Day 11

DRITTE STUFE

Quick Review 10 min.
- Return and review Quiz 6-3
- Check homework, Übungsheft, p. 71, Act. 25

Aussprache, p. 173 15 min.
- Do **Richtig aussprechen/Richtig lesen**, p. 173
- Do **Richtig schreiben/Diktat**, p. 173

ZUM LESEN 20 min.
- Skimming and Scanning, ATE, p. 155W
- Do Activities 1–6, pp. 174–175

Wrap-Up 5 min.
- Students answer questions about ordering and paying for food

Homework Options
Pupil's Edition, p. 182, **Kann ich's wirklich?**
Quick Review 15 min.

Day 12

ANWENDUNG 30 min.
Quick Review
- Check homework, p. 182, **Kann ich's wirklich?**
- Do **Anwendung** Activities 1–6, pp. 180–181

Chapter Review 15 min.
- Review chapter functions, vocabulary, and grammar; choose from **Mehr Grammatikübungen**, Grammar Tutor for Students of German, Activities for Communication, Listening Activities, Interactive CD-ROM Tutor, or **Interaktive Spiele**

Wrap-Up 5 min.
- Students answer questions about paying for food

Homework Options
Study for Chapter Test

Assessment

Test, Chapter 6 45 min.
- Administer Chapter 6 Test. Select from Testing Program, Alternative Assessment Guide or Test Generator.

Kapitel 6: Pläne machen
Suggested Lesson Plans *90-Minute Schedule*

Block 1

CHAPTER OPENER 10 min.
- Culture Note, ATE, p. 155M
- Background Information, ATE, p. 155M

LOS GEHT'S! 25 min.
- Pre-teaching Vocabulary, ATE, p. 155N
- Play Audio CD for **Los geht's!**, pp. 158–159
- Have students read **Los geht's!**, pp. 158–159
- Teaching Suggestions, Video Guide, p. 36
- Culture Note, ATE, p. 155N
- Show **Los geht's!** Video
- Do Comprehension Activities, p. 160

ERSTE STUFE
So sagt man das!, p. 161 15 min.
- Presenting **So sagt man das!**, ATE, p. 155O
- Play Audio CD for Activity 6, p. 161
- Play *Tic Tac Toe,* ATE, p. 155O
- Do Activities 7 and 8, p. 161
- Do Activity 1, Interactive CD-ROM

Wortschatz, p. 162 15 min.
- Presenting **Wortschatz**, ATE, p. 155O
- Teaching Transparencies 6-A, 6-1
- Do Activity 9, p. 162
- Do Activity 2, Interactive CD-ROM

So sagt man das!, p. 162 20 min.
- Presenting **So sagt man das!**, ATE, p. 155P
- Do Activitiy 10, p. 162
- Do Activities 11 and 12, p. 163
- Play Audio CD for Activity 13, p. 164
- Do Activity 14, p. 164

Wrap-Up 5 min.
- Students respond to questions about time

Homework Options
Grammatikheft, pp. 46–47, Acts. 1–5
Übungsheft, pp. 61–64, Acts. 1–8

Block 2

ERSTE STUFE
Quick Review 15 min.
- Check homework, Grammatikheft, pp. 46–47, Acts. 1–5

Sprachtipp, p. 164 10 min.
- Present **Sprachtipp**, p. 164
- Do Activity 15, p. 164

Quiz Review 25 min.
- Do Additional Listening Activities 6-1 and 6-2, p. 47
- Do **Mehr Grammatikübungen, Erste Stufe**

Quiz 20 min.
- Quiz 6-1A or 6-1B

ZWEITE STUFE
Wortschatz, p. 165 15 min.
- Presenting **Wortschatz**, ATE, p. 155Q
- Teaching Transparency 6-B
- Play Audio CD for Activity 16, p. 165

Wrap-Up 5min.
- Students respond to questions about making plans

Homework Options
Pupil's Edition, p. 165, Acts. 17 and 18
Grammatikheft, p. 48, Acts. 6–8
Übungsheft, p. 65, Acts. 9–11

Block 3

ZWEITE STUFE
Quick Review 15 min.
- Return and review Quiz 6-1
- Check homework, Übungsheft, p. 65, Acts. 9–11

So sagt man das!/Grammatik, p. 166 30 min.
- Presenting **So sagt man das!**, ATE, p. 155R
- Presenting **Grammatik**, ATE, p. 155R
- Do Activity 19, p. 166
- Do Activities 20, 21, and 22, p. 167
- Do Activities 12–13, p. 66, Übungsheft

Ein wenig Grammatik, p. 167 15 min.
- Present **Ein wenig Grammatik**, p. 167
- Do Activities 23, 24, and 25, p. 168

LANDESKUNDE 25 min.
- Pre-viewing Suggestion, Video Guide, p. 36
- Culture Notes, ATE, p. 155S
- Show **Landeskunde** Video
- Do Viewing and Post-viewing Activities, Video Guide, p. 39
- Do Activities A and B, p. 169

Wrap-Up 5 min.
- Students respond to questions about making plans using the verb **wollen**

Homework Options
Grammatikheft, pp. 49–50, Acts. 9–12
Übungsheft, pp. 66–67, Acts. 14–16

One-Stop Planner CD-ROM

For alternative lesson plans by chapter section, to create your own customized plans, or to preview all resources available for this chapter, use the **One-Stop Planner CD-ROM**, Disc 2.

For additional homework suggestions, see activities accompanied by this symbol throughout the chapter.

Block 4

ZWEITE STUFE
Quick Review 20 min.
- Check homework, Grammatikheft, pp. 49–50, Acts. 9–12
- Do **Minigeschichte, Zweite Stufe,** TPR Storytelling Book, p. 22

Quiz Review 25 min.
- Do Communicative Activity 6-2, pp. 33–34
- Do **Mehr Grammatikübungen, Zweite Stufe**
- Do **Interaktive Spiele,** see ATE, p. 155F

Quiz 20 min.
Quiz 6-2A or 6-2B

DRITTE STUFE
So sagt man das!, p. 170 25 min.
- Presenting **So sagt man das!,** ATE, p. 155T
- Teaching Transparency 6-2
- Do Activity 26, p. 170
- Play Audio CD for Activity 27, p. 170

Homework Options
Übungsheft, pp. 71–72, Acts. 25–26

Block 5

DRITTE STUFE
Quick Review 10 min.
- Return and review Quiz 6-2
- Check homework, Übungsheft, pp. 71–72, Acts. 25–26

Wortschatz, p. 171 15 min.
- Presenting **Wortschatz,** ATE, p. 155T
- Teaching Transparency 6-C
- Do Activity 28, p. 171

Grammatik, p. 171 15 min.
- Presenting **Grammatik,** ATE, p. 155T
- Language to Language, ATE, p. 155U
- Present **Lerntrick,** p. 171
- Do Activity 29, p. 171

So sagt man das!, p. 172 10 min.
- Presenting **So sagt man das!,** ATE, p. 155U
- Do Activity 30, p. 172

So sagt man das!, p. 172 10 min.
- Presenting **So sagt man das!,** ATE, p. 155U
- Play Audio CD for Activity 31, p. 172
- Do Activity 32, p. 172

Ein wenig Landeskunde p. 173 10 min.
- Present **Ein wenig Landeskunde,** p. 173
- Do Activity 33, p. 173

Aussprache, p. 173 15 min.
- Do **Richtig aussprechen/Richtig lesen,** p. 173
- Do **Richtig schreiben/Diktat,** p. 173

Wrap-Up 5 min.
- Students order various food and drink items in response to a waiter's questions

Homework Options
Pupil's Edition, p. 173, Act. 34
Grammatikheft, pp. 51–54, Acts. 13–22
Übungsheft, pp. 68–70, Acts. 17–24

Block 6

DRITTE STUFE
Quick Review 15 min.
- Check homework, Grammatikheft, pp. 51–54, Acts. 13–22

Quiz Review 20 min.
- Do Additional Listening Activities 6-5 and 6-6, pp. 49–50
- Do **Mehr Grammatikübungen, Dritte Stufe**

Quiz 20 min.
- Quiz 6-3A or 6-3B

ZUM LESEN 30 min.
- Skimming and Scanning, ATE, p. 55W
- Present **Lesestrategie,** p. 174
- Do Activities 1–6, pp. 174–175

Wrap-Up 5 min.
- Students respond to **Kann ich's wirklich?** questions, p. 182

Homework Options
Pupil's Edition, p. 181, Act. 5, **Zum Schreiben**
Pupil's Edition, p. 182, **Kann ich's wirklich?**
Interaktive Spiele, see ATE, p. 155F

Block 7

ANWENDUNG 30 min.
Quick Review
- Return and review Quiz 6-3
- Check homework, p. 182, **Kann ich's wirklich?**
- Do **Anwendung** Activities 1–4 and 6, pp. 180–181
- Students present **Zum Schreiben** paragraphs

Chapter Review 15 min.
- Review chapter functions, vocabulary, and grammar; choose from **Mehr Grammatikübungen,** Grammar Tutor for Students of German, Activities for Communication, Listening Activities, Interactive CD-ROM Tutor, or **Interaktive Spiele**

Test, Chapter 6 45 min.
- Administer Chapter 6 Test. Select from Testing Program, Alternative Assessment Guide or Test Generator.

Kapitel 6: Pläne machen
Teaching Suggestions, *pages 156–183*

CHAPTER OPENER

Pacing Tips

The **Erste Stufe** covers the functions of 'starting a conversation' and 'telling time and talking about when you do things.' In the **Zweite Stufe**, the modal verb **wollen** is presented, along with the function of 'making plans.' The concepts of sequencing events and inversion of time elements are reintroduced. The **Dritte Stufe** focuses on restaurant functions: 'ordering food and beverages,' 'talking about how something tastes,' and 'paying the check.' The stem-changing verb **essen** is presented, as well as a reintroduction of the **möchte**-forms and the verb **nehmen**. You may want to spend more time on the **Dritte Stufe** than on the **Erste Stufe** or the **Zweite Stufe**, as the **Dritte Stufe** includes numerous verbs and functions, and also because of the importance (and fun!) of learning restaurant conduct. For Lesson Plans and timing suggestions, see pages 155I–155L.

Meeting the Standards
Communication
- Starting a conversation, p. 161
- Telling time and talking about when you do things, p. 162
- Making plans, p. 166
- Ordering food and beverages, p. 170
- Talking about how something tastes, p. 172
- Paying the check, p. 172

Cultures
- **Ein wenig Landeskunde,** p. 169
- **Landeskunde,** p. 173
- Culture Note, p. 155M
- Background Information, p. 155M
- Culture Note, p. 155P
- Culture Notes, p. 155S
- Culture Note, p. 155T
- Language Notes, p. 155W

Connections
- Language Note, p. 155N
- Multicultural Connection, p. 155P
- Music Connection, p. 155R
- Math Connection, p. 155T
- Language-to-Language, p. 155U

Comparisons
- Language Note, p. 155P

For resource information, see the **One-Stop Planner CD-ROM,** Disc 2.

- Thinking Critically, p. 155P
- Language Notes, p. 155S
- Thinking Critically, p. 155T
- Thinking Critically, p. 155U

Communities
- Group Work, p. 155S
- Culture Note, p. 155V
- Career Path, p. 155V

Teaching Suggestion

Ask students what they do with their friends when they go out. Where do they go out to eat? Have them look at the picture of the German students and the food the German teenagers are eating. Is it different from what Americans of the same age would eat?

Cultures and Communities

Culture Note
The students in the photo are at a local **Teestube. Teestuben** are quaint and comfortable teahouses where people like to meet. Coffee, tea, soft drinks, pastries, ice cream, and other popular snacks are served there.

Background Information
In German-speaking countries (and most other European countries) young people on a date usually each pay for themselves.

Chapter Sequence

Los geht's! . . . . .p. 158
Erste Stufe . . . . .p. 161
Zweite Stufe . . . . .p. 165
Landeskunde . . . . .p. 169
Dritte Stufe . . . . .p. 170
Zum Lesen . . . . .p. 174
Mehr Grammatikübungen . . . . .p. 176
Anwendung . . . . .p. 180
Kann ich's wirklich? . . . . .p. 182
Wortschatz . . . . .p. 183

LOS GEHT'S!

Teaching Resources
pp. 158–160

PRINT
▸ Lesson Planner, p. 27
▸ Video Guide, pp. 35–36, 38
▸ Übungsheft, p. 61

MEDIA
▸ One-Stop Planner
▸ Video Program
  Los geht's!
  Videocassette 2, 37:05–40:42
  Videocassette 5 (captioned version), 28:53–32:31
  Fortsetzung
  Videocassette 2, 40:45–42:42
  Videocassette 5 (captioned version), 32:34–34:30
▸ Audio Compact Discs, CD6, Trs. 1–2
▸ **Los geht's!** Transparencies

PAGES 158–159

Los geht's! Transparencies

Preteaching Vocabulary

Guessing Words from Context

Ask students what types of functions they would expect in a restaurant conversation between a waitperson and a patron (taking an order; ordering food; ordering drink; etc.). Then have students list some English phrases that express each function (Hello! What would you like? …I would like …) Students should then be able to scan **Los geht's!** for German phrases that match the functions they listed. Finally, have students look at several expressions used to order food and drink. Which are used for food, drink, or both? Compare these expressions to the phrases used to request snacks in **Kapitel 3.**

Fortsetzung

You may choose to continue with the **Fortsetzung** of *Wollen wir ins Café gehen?* now or wait until later in the chapter. For a synopsis of the **Los geht's!** and **Fortsetzung** episodes, see p. 155E.

Teaching Suggestion

To lead the students into the text, do the prelistening/prereading activity with them. Have students look for any visual clues that might help them figure out what the scene is about.

(TPR) Total Physical Response

Bring pictures of the various items on the menu (**Suppe, Käsebrot, Wurstbrot, Pizza,** and so on) and give students commands such as **Gib Mary die Nudelsuppe! Stell bitte die Pizza auf den Tisch!**

Cultures and Communities

Language Note

Point out that **Wie geht's?** is not used by Germans when they have just met someone for the first time. When asking **Wie geht's?** you can expect a detailed answer concerning the person's well-being.

PAGE 160

Using the Captioned Video

 2 An alternate way to complete Activity 2 would be to play the captioned version of *Wollen wir ins Café gehen?* on Videocassette 5.

Comprehension Check

Visual Learners

You might want students to watch the video with the sound turned off to help them focus on the actions and the storyline before they have to focus on the language. Since it helps visual learners to see written text, you may want to have students read **Los geht's!** before playing the video with the sound on.

Challenge

If you think your students are ready for it, ask some questions about **Los geht's!** in German, such as **Wohin geht Julia? Was machen Julia und Katja? Wer sind die Freunde von Julia? Wer ist schon im Café? Wer hat Hunger und isst viel? Wie viel muss Michael bezahlen? Wofür? Was hat er alles gegessen? Warum sagt Michael: „Es tut mir Leid."? Was hat er gemacht?** Some students will be able to answer the questions in German, but a correct answer in English is also an indication that students have understood the text.

Teaching Resources
pp. 161–164

PRINT

▸ Lesson Planner, p. 28
▸ TPR Storytelling Book, pp. 21, 24
▸ Listening Activities, pp. 43, 47
▸ Activities for Communication, pp. 31–32, 94, 97, 133–134
▸ Grammatikheft, pp. 46–47
▸ Grammar Tutor for Students of German, Chapter 6
▸ Übungsheft, pp. 62–64
▸ Testing Program, pp. 131–134
▸ Alternative Assessment Guide, p. 37
▸ Student Make-Up Assignments, Chapter 6

MEDIA

▸ One-Stop Planner
▸ Audio Compact Discs, CD6, Trs. 3–4, 17, 29–30
▸ Teaching Transparencies
  Situation 6-1
  Vocabulary 6-A
  Mehr Grammatikübungen Answers
  Grammatikheft Answers
▸ Interactive CD-ROM Tutor, Disc 2

▸ PAGE 161

Bell Work

Ask students to think of some ways to start a conversation in English. Have pairs of students make a list of a few of their ideas and share them with the class.

PRESENTING: So sagt man das!

Have students look at the pictures in this function box. Ask them to identify who is responding positively and who negatively to the question **Wie geht's?** If you want to introduce the complete phrase **Wie geht es dir?/Wie geht es Ihnen?,** do it without going into an explanation of the dative case. Treat these phrases as lexical items.

Building on Previous Skills

Before doing Activity 8, review numbers with the following game. Divide the class into teams of ten students. Give each team member a card with a number from 0 to 9. (Students may have more than one card

if you have an odd number of students.) Call out a number, for example, **zweiunddreißig.** The students from each team holding cards 3 and 2 run to the front of the room and arrange themselves in the correct order. The first team to have a pair arranged correctly wins a point.

Communication for All Students

For Additional Practice

Play *Tic Tac Toe* to review 24-hour time before beginning Activity 8. Put a *Tic Tac Toe* grid on the chalkboard or on a transparency. Write a time in each square. Divide the class into two teams. The game is played like traditional *Tic Tac Toe*, but in order to place an X or an O in a specific box, a team member must say the time written in that box. The team that gets three in a row wins the round. Draw additional grids if desired.

21.15	18.50	9.45
17.09	8.14	18.30
00.03	1.16	17.47

▸ PAGE 162

PRESENTING: Wortschatz

Use clocks with moveable hands to present the **Wortschatz.** Place the hands on, before, and after the hour and tell students what time the clock says. Or have students bring or make their own clocks (see Teaching Suggestion, Chapter 4, p. 99P) and demonstrate to you that they understand times as you say them aloud.

PRESENTING: So sagt man das!

Using a transparency, write each question from the **So sagt man das!** box. Write the question words and phrases **wann, wie spät, wie viel Uhr,** and **um wie viel Uhr** in a different color or underline them in red. Ask students which question words they recognize. Have them use the words they recognize to try to infer the meaning of the whole question. **Wie viel Uhr** might be more difficult to guess, but using their knowledge of **wie** from **Wie alt bist du?** and **viel** from **Ich habe viel zu tun,** students might be able to understand **wie viel Uhr.** Cover up the answers to the questions and ask students to provide answers themselves using the **Wortschatz** on p. 162.

Connections and Comparisons

Language Note

Remind students that there are often similarities between English and German that will help them. Point out to them that **vor** sounds similar to *before*.

Teaching Suggestion

Have three students draw clocks on the board that depict time on the hour, after the hour, and before the hour as a reference for coming activities.

> **PAGE 163**

Connections and Comparisons

Thinking Critically

11 Analyzing Ask students where one might see clocks like these. (See the following Culture Note.)

Multicultural Connection

Have students interview speakers of other languages to compare the German way of telling time with that of other cultures. Do other cultures (such as Spanish, French, Japanese) use both a 12-hour and a 24-hour time system? Have students try to find out how different cultures view time.

Cultures and Communities

Culture Note

Clocks like some of those pictured can be found on churches, towers, and town halls in European countries. You might want to tell students that the first mechanical clocks in Europe were invented by clergymen for the purpose of performing their religious duties promptly and regularly. The first mechanical clocks were not designed to show the time, but rather to sound it. (The Middle English *clock* came from the Middle Dutch word for *bell* and is a cognate of the German **Glocke,** which means *bell.*) Jacopo de Dondi of Chioggi, Italy, is said to have invented the clock dial in 1344.

Teaching Suggestion

11 Monitor pair work on this page by asking individual pairs to model one of the items for you as you move around the room.

Communication for All Students

Tactile Learners

Have students use the clocks they created in Chapter 4 to practice the times in pairs. (See Teaching Suggestion, p. 99P.) One student can say a time, the other student has to place the hands correctly.

A Slower Pace

12 Write each individual word in a sentence on large cards. Have eight students each hold up a card. A ninth student tells them where to stand to put the sentences in the correct order.

Reteaching: Telling time

- Show different times on your demonstration clock, and have students tell you what time you are showing.

- Show times on your clock and have students tell you what time it would be in 15 minutes, in half an hour, and so on.

▶ PAGE 164

Teaching Suggestion

15 After completing Activity 15, ask questions based on the pictures in Activity 13. Examples: **Wann (um wie viel Uhr) geht Heiko zur Schule? Was macht Heiko um Viertel vor acht?**

Assess

- ▶ Testing Program, pp. 131–134
  Quiz 6-1A, Quiz 6-1B
  Audio CD6, Tr. 17

- ▶ Student Make-Up Assignments, Chapter 6, Alternative Quiz

- ▶ Alternative Assessment Guide, p. 37

LIBERTY IM MOTORAMA 21.00-3.00
Liberty
DISKOTHEK CAFÉ
Oldie Disco
Hits der 60er u. 70er Jahre

ZWEITE STUFE

Teaching Resources
pp. 165–169

PRINT

- ▶ Lesson Planner, p. 29
- ▶ TPR Storytelling Book, pp. 22, 24
- ▶ Listening Activities, pp. 44, 48
- ▶ Activities for Communication, pp. 33–34, 95, 97, 133–134
- ▶ Grammatikheft, pp. 48–50
- ▶ Grammar Tutor for Students of German, Chapter 6
- ▶ Übungsheft, pp. 65–67
- ▶ Testing Program, pp. 135–138
- ▶ Alternative Assessment Guide, p. 37
- ▶ Student Make-Up Assignments, Chapter 6

MEDIA

- ▶ One-Stop Planner
- ▶ Audio Compact Discs, CD6, Trs. 5, 18, 31–32
- ▶ Teaching Transparencies
  Situation 6-1
  Vocabulary 6-B
  Mehr Grammatikübungen Answers
  Grammatikheft Answers
- ▶ Interactive CD-ROM Tutor, Disc 2

▶ PAGE 165

Bell Work

In pairs, have students ask each other in German about their favorite thing to do on a weekend. Suggest making use of expressions such as **Lieblings-, gern machen,** and sequencing words.

PRESENTING: Wortschatz

Present this vocabulary with transparency 6-B. Number each picture. Write the captions in random order at the bottom of the transparency and assign each caption a letter. Ask students to read the captions silently and match each letter to its corresponding picture. The captions have many cognates and phrases that students will be able to recognize. Once students have matched the captions and the pictures correctly, read the six captions to the class.

Teaching Suggestion

17 Ask students to do this activity in writing. They should create six sentences using the word **und** to connect the sentence parts. Upon completion call on six students to read their sentences aloud.

PAGE 166

PRESENTING: So sagt man das!

Ask students to look at the sentences from Activity 17 and have them restate each of the six sentences using **möchte** instead of **wollen**. Then introduce **So sagt man das!** and tell students that although **möchte** and **wollen** can be used interchangeably, **wollen** is somewhat more forceful and not quite as polite as **möchte**. Remind students not to confuse the German **will** with the English *will*. **Ich will** means *I want to*. It does not correspond to *I will,* which expresses the future in English.

PRESENTING: Grammatik

The verb wollen Introduce modal auxiliary verbs, or helping verbs. These verbs express ideas such as wish, obligation, ability, and permission. Can students name some of these verbs in English? (want, may, should, must, can)

Connections and Comparisons

Music Connection

For additional reading, refer students to the folk song *Es, es, es und es* (written around 1780), Level 2 *Listening Activities,* p. 22, and ask them if they can find a form of **wollen** and its corresponding infinitive(s). (**will … probieren, marschieren**) You might also want to play the song, Level 2 CD 3, Tr. 26.

Teaching Suggestion

19 Have students work in pairs reading the roles of Julia and Sonja as they complete this conversation. Monitor students' work and then ask a pair to read the dialogue aloud for additional pronunciation practice.

PAGE 167

Group Work

20 Divide the class into small groups of 3–4 students. Assign one student in each group to be the writer. Each group tries to create as many correct sentences as possible in a set time. (Example: three

minutes) Once the time is up, the writer comes to the board and lists the sentences his or her group created. As members of each group take turns reading their group's sentences, members of the other groups check for mistakes.

PRESENTING: Ein wenig Grammatik

Word order Write the words from the two sentences in random order on the board. Ask students to rewrite the two sentences using correct word order. Then write out the possible sentences underneath the scrambled words as students read theirs aloud.

PAGE 168

Communication for All Students

Cooperative Learning

23 **24** Activities 23 and 24 can be completed as a cooperative learning activity. Divide the class into several groups of 3–4 students each. Each group should have a leader, a recorder, a reporter, and a checker. Within a given time, ask each group to read Monika's letter and then answer the questions that follow.

Group Work

25 Divide the class into groups of three students. Ask them to create a short skit in which they discuss their busy schedules and finally reach an agreement on what to plan for the weekend.

Speaking Assessment

25 Ask groups to come to your desk for assessment. You may wish to evaluate their conversation using the following rubric.

Speaking Rubric	Points			
	4	3	2	1
Content (Complete – Incomplete)				
Comprehension (Total – Little)				
Comprehensibility (Comprehensible – Incomprehensible)				
Accuracy (Accurate – Seldom accurate)				
Fluency (Fluent – Not fluent)				

18–20: A   16–17: B   14–15: C   12–13: D   Under 12: F

LANDESKUNDE

Teaching Resources
p. 169

PRINT
▸ Video Guide, pp. 35–36, 38–39
▸ Übungsheft, p. 72

MEDIA
▸ One-Stop Planner
▸ Video Program
  Videocassette 2, 43:20–48:48
▸ Audio Compact Discs, CD6, Trs. 6-10
▸ Interactive CD-ROM Tutor, Disc 2

Teaching Suggestion

Recycle vocabulary by asking questions such as **Woher kommt Sandra?** and **Wo ist Hamburg?** Have students read the four paragraphs and make a list of what each person does in his or her free time.

Connections and Comparisons

 Culture Note
Annika says that she is a **Pfadfinder.** **Pfadfinder** are the German equivalent of Boy Scouts and Girl Scouts.

Language Notes

• Annika and Karsten, who are from Hamburg, might be familiar with **Plattdeutsch,** a dialect many northern Germans are trying to preserve. Here are some words in **Plattdeutsch** that students might recognize: **Grotvadder** (*grandfather*) and **Bookweeten-Pannkoken** (*buckwheat pancakes*). Ask students what other languages **Plattdeutsch** resembles. (English and Dutch)

• Sandra and Annika use the word **halt** in their interviews. This flavoring word is used frequently in casual conversation, especially in southern Germany.

Culture Note
Germans have a variety of after-school activities that are organized differently from those in the United States. Students often pay monthly dues to belong to private clubs, such as photo or sewing clubs, because these non-academic subjects are not offered at school.

Cultures and Communities

Group Work

Have students research and write reports about the cities mentioned in the **Landeskunde.** You may want to request brochures from the sources listed on pp. T48 and T49 of the *Teacher's Edition.* Reports could include information about the region where each city is located and how the location affects recreational activities. Additional reports could be done on other cities. The reports should be in English. Give each group a section of the bulletin board or an area of the classroom to display pictures and materials about their city.

Teacher Note

Mention to your students that the **Landeskunde** will also be included in Quiz 6-2B given at the end of the **Zweite Stufe.**

Reteaching: Making plans

Put the sequencing words on the board in a column (**zuerst, dann, danach, zuletzt**). In a second column, write **will ich.** In a third column, make a list of activities learned in this and earlier chapters. Ask the class to create sentences to plan for a busy weekend.

Teaching Suggestion

Have students tell you at least two things they want to do this weekend using at least one sequencing word.

Assess
▸ Testing Program, pp. 135–138
  Quiz 6-2A, Quiz 6-2B
  Audio CD6, Tr. 18

▸ Student Make-Up Assignments
  Chapter 6, Alternative Quiz

▸ Alternative Assessment Guide, p. 37

ZWEITE STUFE

DRITTE STUFE

Teaching Resources
pp. 170–173

PRINT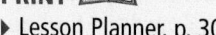

▶ Lesson Planner, p. 30
▶ TPR Storytelling Book, pp. 23, 24
▶ Listening Activities, pp. 44–45, 49–50
▶ Activities for Communication, pp. 35–36, 96, 97, 133–134
▶ Grammatikheft, pp. 51–54
▶ Grammar Tutor for Students of German, Chapter 6
▶ Übungsheft, pp. 68–70
▶ Testing Program, pp. 139–142
▶ Alternative Assessment Guide, p. 37
▶ Student Make-Up Assignments, Chapter 6

MEDIA

▶ One-Stop Planner
▶ Audio Compact Discs, CD6, Trs. 11–15, 19, 33–34
▶ Teaching Transparencies
  Situation 6-2
  Vocabulary 6-C
  Mehr Grammatikübungen Answers
  Grammatikheft Answers
▶ Interactive CD-ROM Tutor, Disc 2

PAGE 170

Bell Work
Have students write about their favorite place to eat and what they like to order. What common expressions do they use in English when ordering food?

Connections and Comparisons

Math Connection
Provide students with the current exchange rate and have them give you the approximate prices of several menu items in U.S. dollars.

Thinking Critically
Comparing and Contrasting Have students look at the menu again. Which items would they probably find on an American menu? Which ones would not likely appear?

Cultures and Communities

Culture Note
Sandwiches (**Käsebrot, Wurstbrot**) are served open-faced. **Käsekuchen,** made with **Quark** (a soft, fresh cheese), is not as dense or quite as sweet as American cheesecake. In German cafés and restaurants you can order a cup of coffee or a little pot which contains about two cups. Tea is served in a heat-proof glass with a handle. There are no free refills on coffee or tea.

Teaching Suggestion
27 Ask students to write the students' names on a piece of paper after the first listening (Katja, Julia, Michael, Heiko). As students listen a second time, they should write down what each of the four students is ordering. Let students listen a third time to check their answers.

PRESENTING: So sagt man das!
Model the functional expressions in **So sagt man das!** by addressing individual students using the questions the waiter would ask. Have students respond by reading the answers on the right side.

PAGE 171

PRESENTING: Wortschatz
Direct the question **Was nimmst du?** to a student who then answers with one of the expressions given in the **Wortschatz.** The same student can then ask a classmate, **Und du Frank, was nimmst du?** Frank answers, and so on.

PRESENTING: Grammatik
Stem-changing verbs Review with students the forms of the irregular verb **nehmen,** placing particular emphasis on the stem-vowel change that occurs in the **du-** and **er/sie-**forms. Then tell them that **essen** is also an irregular verb, conjugated in a similar manner with the 'e' changing to 'i' in second and third person singular. As you introduce the forms of **essen,** ask students if they can anticipate how the **du-** and **er/sie-**forms will look. Then have students practice the verb **essen** with the **Wortschatz** on p. 171. (Example: **Sie isst ein Käsebrot.**)

Connections and Comparisons

Language-to-Language

You may want to explain to your students that, as in German, some verbs undergo a stem change in the present tense in Spanish and French. For example, in German "brechen" changes to "er bricht," "du brichst," and "sie brechen"; in French, "venir" changes to "je viens," "nous venons," and "ils viennent"; and in Spanish, "tener" changes to "tengo," "tienes," and "tienen."

Game

29 Divide the class into two teams and have one member of Team A come to the board. Show the student the name of a food item. The student has to draw this item for his or her own group to guess. Set a time limit for the drawing. If students guess correctly, the team gets a point. If they cannot guess the word, the other team may guess and win the point if they guess correctly. Teams take turns. The team with the most points at the end of the game wins.

► **PAGE 172**

PRESENTING: So sagt man das!

Using large index cards, write the expressions **Gut!, Lecker!, nicht so gut,** and so on from this function box on one side of the index cards and put tape on the other side. List items from the **Imbisskarte** on p. 170 on the chalkboard or a transparency. Ask students to rate the taste of each of the items from 1 to 5. Depending on the general opinion, you then attach an index card with an appropriate expression to the chalkboard next to each item. For example, you could ask, **Wie schmeckt das Eis?** If students respond with a 5, you might tape the index card with the expression **Sagenhaft!** next to the **Eisbecher.** After all food items have been labeled, go over the expressions and have students make up sentences. (Example: **Der Eisbecher schmeckt sagenhaft!**)

PRESENTING: So sagt man das!

Divide your students into groups of three or four, and give each student a card on which you have written a type of food and/or drink (and the prices) from the menu on p. 170. Introduce the expressions from this function box, and then play the role of a waitperson with several students from different groups. (Consult the students' cards to find out what they ordered and how much they owe.) Add up their bills, and have them pretend to pay you for their meal. They should specify how much they have handed you before ending with **Stimmt schon!** Afterward, have students play the roles of waitpersons and customers within their groups, continuing until all students have had a chance to go through the process of paying a check.

Communication for All Students

A Slower Pace

31 To prepare students for the listening activity, have the class write down the students' names as they appear in order of the conversation: Heiko, Michael, Katja, Julia. During the first listening, have students write down the items the waiter lists for each teenager. As students listen a second time, have them write the prices for each food item, the total price, and the amount given to the waiter. Call on students to read out what they have written down.

► **PAGE 173**

Portfolio

33 You might want to use this activity as an oral portfolio item for your students. See *Alternative Assessment Guide,* p. 23.

Teacher Note

33 You might want to tell students that *to treat someone* or *to pay someone's way* is **jemanden einladen** in German.

Connections and Comparisons

Thinking Critically

Drawing Inferences After reading **Ein wenig Landeskunde,** ask students why tipping is more important in America than in Germany. Why do they think Germans do not tip as much? (See the following Culture Note.)

Culture Note

In the United States the minimum wage for waiters and waitresses is less than the minimum wage for other occupations. It is understood that they rely on tips to make up the difference. In German-speaking countries, waiters and waitresses are paid standard full salaries, so the tip is more a way to show appreciation for good service than a way of paying the waiter's or waitress's salary. The gratuity as well as a **Mehrwertsteuer** *(value-added tax)* are already included in the price of the meal.

Von der Schule zum Beruf

34

To expand on this activity, students could put together a 'restaurant guide' including every student's work in an abbreviated version. This could be displayed in the classroom.

PRESENTING: Aussprache

To help students distinguish between the two **ch** sounds, emphasize the differences between them. For the **ch** sound following i or e, tell students to exaggerate the pronunciation of the initial sound in the English word *huge*. For the **ch** sound following **a, o,** or **u,** have students imagine they are gargling without water. Then practice the different sounds using minimal pairs; **ich/ach, dich/doch, nicht/Nacht.**

Communication for All Students

Reteaching: Ordering from a menu

On the day before you plan to do this activity, ask students to make menus for a restaurant they have just opened. On the day of the activity, set up the classroom as a café, using butcher paper tablecloths. Have students bring food, utensils, and their menus. Review essential words and phrases using props. A group of students can then play the roles of the waitstaff and the rest will be patrons. Have students act out likely scenarios. Do not allow students to write out their conversations beforehand. The goal of this activity is to have students react as naturally and spontaneously as possible within the classroom setting.

Career Path

Ask your students to think of careers in hotel and restaurant management that would require a knowledge of German. (Suggestions: Imagine you are an apprentice in a Swiss hotel learning about hotel management; imagine you are an internationally renowned chef working in a hotel in Berlin.)

Teaching Suggestion

Distribute a copy of the school menu and ask students for the names of items offered on given days. Supply the names of foods not learned in this unit. Ask students about their favorite foods and ask them to rate the foods by using the expressions they learned for describing tastes on p. 172.

Teacher to Teacher

Petronella Gaal
International School of Prague
Czech Republic

Petronella uses this idea to practice word order.

❝To practice building correct German sentences, I write about twenty or so sentences on colored paper strips, cut them, and put the words into four envelopes. Each envelope contains five sentences. The class, split up into groups, has to organize the words into complete and correct sentences. I usually set a time limit for this activity. The group that has all sentences put together correctly wins.❞

Assess

▸ Testing Program, pp. 139–142
   Quiz 6-3A, Quiz 6-3B
   Audio CD6, Tr. 19

▸ Student Make-Up Assignments
   Chapter 6, Alternative Quiz

▸ Alternative Assessment Guide, p. 37

DRITTE STUFE

ZUM LESEN

Teaching Resources
pp. 174–175

PRINT
▸ Lesson Planner, p. 31
▸ Übungsheft, p. 71
▸ Reading Strategies and Skills, Chapter 6
▸ Lies mit mir! 1, Chapter 6

MEDIA
▸ One-Stop Planner

Prereading
Building Context

Have students bring in the arts and entertainment section of the Sunday edition of a local newspaper. Looking at it together and discussing what information is found in this part of the paper will prepare students for the German entertainment ads in **Zum Lesen.**

Teaching Suggestion

Have students look only at the bold print of the ads and tell you what activities come to mind. With whom would they go to the **Bahrenfelder Forsthaus**? To the **Nachteule** disco?

Teacher Note

Activity 1 is a prereading activity.

Reading
Group Work

Divide students into groups. Have each group perform three tasks for each ad: find the name of the establishment(s), find the address(es), and make a list of the words students recognize. They can report their findings to the whole class.

Skimming and Scanning

Remind students that most of the time when they read ads like these, they are looking either for the global picture (skimming) to get an idea about entertainment possibilities, or looking for specific information (scanning) such as the time a movie starts or the price of concert tickets. When students do activities 2b through 5, they will be using the strategies skimming and scanning.

Communication for All Students

Challenge

Ask students what the attraction of a **Tag und Nacht** restaurant is. What is the specialty of this particular restaurant?

Cultures and Communities

Language Notes

• Students may be curious about the abbreviations on the Lynyrd Skynyrd concert poster. **Vvk** = **Vorverkauf** (*advance ticket sales*); **Ak** = **Abendkasse** (*box office*); **Geb.** = **Gebühr** (*fee*)

• In the classical music ad, **Es** indicates the key of E-flat, **h** is the key of B, and **B** is the key of B-flat. The key name is capitalized when the piece is in major (**Dur**), while lower case letters are used when the piece is in minor (**Moll**).

Post-Reading
Teacher Note

Activities 6a, 6b, and 6c are post-reading tasks that will show whether students can apply what they have learned.

Portfolio

6c You might want to suggest this activity as a written portfolio item for your students. See *Alternative Assessment Guide,* p. 23.

MEHR GRAMMATIKÜBUNGEN

The **Mehr Grammatikübungen** activities are designed as supplemental activities for the grammatical concepts presented in the chapter. You might use them as additional practice, for review, or for assessment.

For more grammar presentations, review, and practice, refer to the following:
• Grammatikheft
• Grammar Tutor for Students of German
• *Grammar Summary* on pp. R15–R25
• Übungsheft
• Grammar and Vocabulary quizzes (Testing Program)
• Test Generator
• Interactive CD-ROM Tutor
• **Interaktive Spiele** at go.hrw.com

ANWENDUNG

 Video Wrap-up

Videocassette 2, 37:05–51:02
Videocassette 5 (captioned version), 28:53–34:30
At this time, you might want to use the video resources for additional review and enrichment. See *Video Guide* for suggestions regarding:

- the **Los geht's!** episode
- the **Landeskunde** interviews
- the **Fortsetzung** episode
- the **Videoclips.**

Apply and Assess

Teaching Suggestion

1 As a whole class activity, use your clock to review time expressions from the **Wortschatz** on p. 183 before beginning Activity 1.

A Slower Pace

2 Make the listening script available to students as they listen to the activity a second time.

Visual Learners

3 Write four sentences describing the pictured activities in fragments on large cards. (Example: **Wir/ spielen/ Schach.**) Give each sentence to a group of students. Have them arrange themselves in individual sentences across the room. Then give four sequencing words (**zuerst, dann, danach, zuletzt**) to four other students. Each goes to one of the original groups. They should rearrange their word order to accommodate the sequencing words. Continue with the other sentences.

Process Writing

6 Have students get together in pairs or groups to brainstorm a list of activities in which they could engage during spring break. If necessary, prompt them to use some of the vocabulary introduced earlier in the book. (Examples: **wandern, Fernsehen schauen**)

KANN ICH'S WIRKLICH?

This page is intended to prepare students for the test. It is a brief checklist of the major points covered in the chapter. The students should be reminded that it is a checklist only and not necessarily everything that will appear on the test.

For additional self check options, refer students to the *Grammar Tutor*, the *Interactive CD-ROM Tutor*, and the Online self-test for this chapter.

WORTSCHATZ

Review and Assess

 Circumlocution

To practice food and beverage vocabulary, play **Das treffende Wort suchen** using the items found on the **Café am Markt** and **Café Freizeit** menus (pp. 160 and 170). Introduce the phrases **etwas zum Essen / Trinken** to your students for use during the game. Example: **Es ist etwas zum Essen. Es ist kalt und süß. Es ist / schmeckt lecker. Was ist es?** (Eis) See p. 155C for procedures.

Teaching Suggestion

Take a few minutes to have students quiz each other in pairs on the vocabulary words.

Teacher Notes

- Give the **Kapitel 6** Chapter Test:
  Testing Program, pp. 143–148
Audio CD 6, Trs. 20–22.

- Give the Midterm Exam:
  Testing Program, pp. 157–164
Audio CD 6, Trs. 23–28.

REVIEW

6
Pläne machen

Objectives

In this chapter you will learn to

Erste Stufe

- start a conversation
- tell time
- talk about when you are doing things

Zweite Stufe

- make plans

Dritte Stufe

- order food and beverages
- talk about how something tastes
- pay the check

◢ internet

go.hrw.com	ADRESSE: go.hrw.com
	KENNWORT:
	WK3 SCHLESWIG-HOLSTEIN-6

◀ Was bekommst du?

Los geht's! · *Wollen wir ins Café gehen?*

CD 6 Trs. 1–2

Strategie Verstehen

Look at the images for this story. Where and when do you think these scenes are taking place? What clues tell you this? What do you think will happen in this story?

Heiko

Julia

Katja

Michael

Los geht's! is an abridged version of the video episode.

①

Julia: Hallo, Heiko! Wie geht's denn so?

Heiko: Hm ...So lala. Was machst du jetzt so hier? Wohin gehst du?

Julia: Zu Katja. Wir machen zuerst Hausaufgaben, und dann wollen wir ins Café Freizeit gehen, ein Eis essen. Willst du mitkommen?

Heiko: Gern! Wann wollt ihr gehen?

②

Julia: Wie spät ist es jetzt?

Heiko: Viertel nach drei.

Julia: Ja, so um halb fünf?

Heiko: Okay!

Julia: Bis dann, tschüs!

Heiko: Tschüs!

③

Kellner: Guten Tag! Was bekommt ihr?

Julia: Ich bekomme einen Eisbecher. Fruchteis.

Katja: Ich möchte einen Cappuccino, bitte.

Heiko: Hm ...Ich will im Moment gar nichts. Ich esse später etwas.

Michael: Und ich esse jetzt eine Pizza. Nummer eins, bitte!

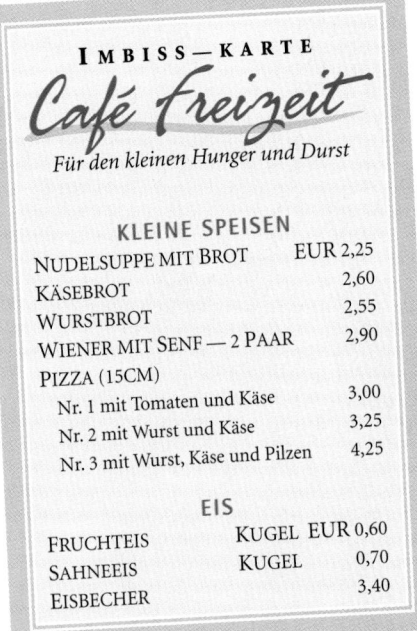

IMBISS—KARTE

Café Freizeit
Für den kleinen Hunger und Durst

KLEINE SPEISEN

NUDELSUPPE MIT BROT	EUR 2,25
KÄSEBROT	2,60
WURSTBROT	2,55
WIENER MIT SENF — 2 PAAR	2,90
PIZZA (15CM)	
Nr. 1 mit Tomaten und Käse	3,00
Nr. 2 mit Wurst und Käse	3,25
Nr. 3 mit Wurst, Käse und Pilzen	4,25

EIS

FRUCHTEIS	KUGEL EUR	0,60
SAHNEEIS	KUGEL	0,70
EISBECHER		3,40

4

Kellner:	Cappuccino?
Katja:	Ich bekomme den. Er ist für mich. Danke!
Kellner:	Eisbecher?
Julia:	Den Eisbecher bekomme ich.
Kellner:	Bitte sehr!
Julia:	Danke!
Kellner:	Die Pizza kommt gleich.
Michael:	Schon gut!

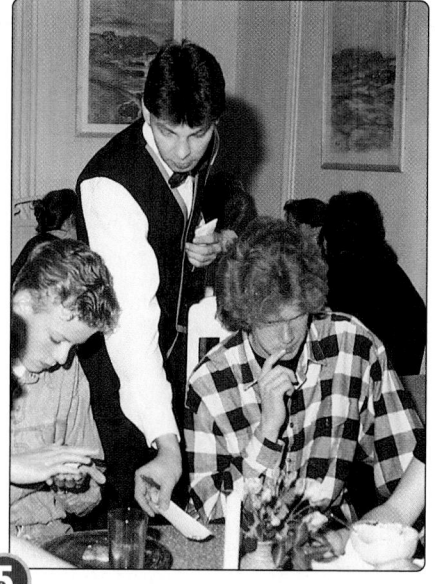

5

Michael:	Ich möchte zahlen, bitte.
Kellner:	Eine Pizza, drei Euro; ein Wurstbrot, zwei Euro sechzig; eine Cola, ein Euro fünfzig. Macht zusammen sieben Euro zehn.
Michael:	Stimmt schon!
Kellner:	Danke!

6

Michael:	Und nun trinke ich meine Cola aus und gehe.
Katja:	Du, pass auf! Pass doch auf!

7

Michael:	Oje! Katja, es tut mir Leid!
Katja:	Macht ja nichts! Es ist ja nur mein T-Shirt!

Übungsheft, S. 61

1 Was passiert hier?

These activities check for global comprehension only. Students should not yet be expected to produce language modeled in **Los geht's!**

Do you understand what is happening in **Los geht's!**? Check your comprehension by answering these questions. Don't be afraid to guess.

1. What plans have Julia and Katja made for the afternoon? **1.** do their homework, then go out for ice cream
2. What is Heiko going to do? **2.** join them
3. Where do the three friends meet Michael? **3.** Café Freizeit
4. Why does Michael apologize to Katja? How does Katja react? **4.** He spills soda on her T-Shirt. She says, **"Macht nichts. Es ist ja nur mein T-Shirt!"**

2 Genauer lesen

Reread the conversations. Which words or phrases do the characters use to

1. ask how someone is doing **1.** **Wie geht's denn?**
2. talk about time **2.** **Wie spät ist es?, Viertel nach drei, um halb fünf**
3. name foods and drinks **3.** **Eis, Eisbecher, Pizza, Wurstbrot, Cappuccino, Cola**
4. tell a waiter they want to pay **4.** **Ich möchte zahlen.**
5. apologize **5.** **Es tut mir Leid.**

3 Was passt zusammen?

Match each statement or question on the left with an appropriate response on the right.

1. Wie geht's denn? b
2. Wohin gehst du? e
3. Wie spät ist es jetzt? d
4. Wer bekommt den Cappuccino? a
5. Ich möchte zahlen. c

a. Er ist für mich.
b. So lala.
c. Das macht zusammen sieben Euro zehn.
d. Viertel nach drei.
e. Zu Katja.

4 Was fehlt hier?

Based on **Los geht's!,** complete each of the sentences below with an appropriate item from the list.

> bekommt   *Eis*   einen Eisbecher   möchte
> zahlen   Hausaufgaben   Stimmt   halb

Katja und Julia machen zuerst die ___1___. Dann wollen sie in ein Café gehen, ein ___2___ essen. Sie wollen so um ___3___ fünf gehen. Im Café fragt der Kellner: „Was ___4___ ihr?" Katja ___5___ einen Cappuccino. Julia sagt: „Ich bekomme ___6___, Fruchteis." Michael will gehen. Er sagt: „Ich möchte ___7___, bitte." Der Kellner sagt: „Sieben Euro zehn." Und Michael antwortet: „ ___8___ schon."

1. Hausaufgaben **2.** Eis **3.** halb **4.** bekommt **5.** möchte
6. einen Eisbecher **7.** zahlen **8.** Stimmt

5 Und du?

Look at the menu from the **Café am Markt**. Which items are foods, and which are beverages? If you were with your friends at the **Café am Markt**, what would you order? Make a list, including the prices.

foods: **Nudelsuppe, Käsebrot, Wurstbrot, Wiener mit Senf, Pizza, Apfelkuchen, Eis**
drinks: **Mineralwasser, Kaffee, Cola**

Café am Markt

Nudelsuppe	EUR 2,25
Käsebrot	2,60
Wurstbrot	2,80
Wiener mit Senf	2,90
Pizza	4,00
Apfelkuchen	1,20
Eis	0,60
Mineralwasser	1,80
Kaffee	2,40
Cola	1,60

Erste Stufe

Objectives Starting a conversation; telling time and talking about when you do things

go.
hrw
.com

WK3 SCHLESWIG-HOLSTEIN-6

So sagt man das!

Starting a conversation

CD-ROM
DISC **2**

If you want to find out how someone is doing, you ask:

Wie geht's?   *or*   **Wie geht's denn?**

The person might respond in one of these ways, depending on how he or she is doing.

| **Sehr gut! Prima!** | **Danke, gut! Gut!** | **Danke, es geht. So lala. Nicht schlecht.** | **Nicht so gut. Schlecht.** | **Sehr schlecht. Miserabel!** |

| **Sven** | **Silke** | **Nadja** | **Kemal** | **Jörg** |

Übungsheft, S. 62, Ü. 2   Grammatikheft, S. 46, Ü. 1

---

6 **Wie geht's?** Script on p. 155G

1. Kemal 2. Jörg 3. Silke 4. Nadja 5. Sven

Zuhören You will hear several students respond to the question **Wie geht's?** As you listen, look at the faces in the box above and determine who is speaking.
CD 6 Tr. 3

7 **Hallo! Wie geht's?**

Sprechen Greet several students around you and ask them how they are doing.

8 **Was hast du um …?**

Sprechen Get together with your partner, greet him or her, and ask how he or she is doing. Then take turns asking each other what classes you have at the times shown below.

BEISPIEL   Du   Was hast du um …?

| neun Uhr dreißig | acht Uhr | zehn Uhr zwanzig | elf Uhr dreißig |

a.

b.

c.

d.

Die Uhrzeit

You already know how to express time when referring to schedules: **um acht Uhr dreißig, um acht Uhr fünfundvierzig.** Now you will learn a more informal way of telling time.

6–A, 6–1

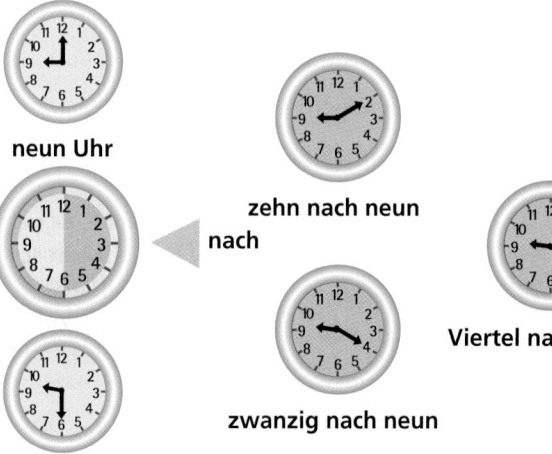

Viertel vor zehn

zehn vor zehn

vor

neun Uhr

zehn nach neun

nach

Viertel nach neun

zwanzig vor zehn

halb zehn

zwanzig nach neun

Grammatikheft, S. 46–47, Ü. 2–5

So sagt man das!

Telling time and talking about when you do things

You might ask your friend:

> **Wann gehst du ins Café?**
> **Und um wie viel Uhr gehst du schwimmen?**
> **Wie spät ist es?**
> **Wie viel Uhr ist es?** ⎰

The responses might be:

> **Um halb fünf.**
> **Um Viertel nach drei.**
>
> **Es ist Viertel vor zwei.**

Mehr Grammatikübungen
S. 176–177, Ü. 1–3

What specific information does each question ask for?

Übungsheft, S. 62–64, Ü. 3–8

---

9 ### Wie viel Uhr ist es, bitte?

Sprechen Using the clocks in the **Wortschatz** box, take turns asking and telling your partner what time it is.

10 ### Was fehlt hier?

Sprechen Katja is trying to find Heiko. His mom explains where he will be this afternoon. Complete what she says by filling in the blanks according to the times given. Use the words and phrases in the box to the right.

> fünf Uhr   nach vier   sechs
> Viertel   zwanzig nach sieben   halb

Um ════ drei (2.30) geht er ins Einkaufszentrum. Dann hat er um Viertel ════ (4.15) Fußballtraining. Danach geht er mit Michael um ════ (5.00) ins Schwimmbad. Um ════ vor ════ (5.45) gehen die zwei Jungen ins Café Freizeit. Und dann kommt Heiko um ════ (7.20) nach Hause.   halb; nach vier; fünf Uhr; Viertel ... sechs; zwanzig nach sieben

11 Wie spät ist es?

Sprechen You are making plans to meet friends. Ask your partner what time it is. Take turns.

1.

1. fünf vor sieben

2.

2. halb drei

3.

3. fünfundzwanzig nach zwei/vierzehn Uhr fünfundzwanzig

4.

4. fünfundzwanzig nach acht/acht Uhr fünfundzwanzig

5.

5. halb zehn

6.

6. halb zwölf

12 Wann macht Ulrike alles?

Sprechen/Schreiben Work with a partner to reorder these statements into a chronological description of how Ulrike spends a typical Monday.

1. Jeden Montag um acht Uhr gehe ich zur Schule.

Und am Abend schaue ich Fernsehen.
8

Dann um halb elf, direkt nach der Pause, habe ich Bio.
3

Um Viertel nach neun habe ich Mathe.
2

Um drei Uhr oder um halb vier esse ich Kuchen oder vielleicht etwas Obst.
5

Und jeden Montag um vier Uhr gehe ich schwimmen.
6

Danach mache ich so um fünf Hausaufgaben.
7

Nach der Schule gehe ich nach Hause.
4

13 **Was machen sie zu dieser Zeit?** Script on p. 155G

Zuhören Match what these students say with the illustrations below. 1. e 2. d 3. b 4. a 5. c 6. f

CD 6 Tr. 4

a. a. um 7.45: in die Schule gehen **b.** b. um 9.15: Matheprüfung **c.** c. um 1.45: schwimmen

d. d. um 3.20: Tennis spielen **e.** e. um 7.15: Fernsehen schauen **f.** f. um 10.30: Musik hören

 14 **Wann? Wer? Was?**

Schau die Zeichnungen an!

1. **Schreiben** Make a list of the times and corresponding activities shown in Activity 13.

2. **Schreiben** Choosing your own activities, write six sentences stating what you do at the times shown above.

 15 **Um wie viel Uhr ...?**

 Sprechen Ask your partner at what time he or she does various activities or has certain classes.

 LERNTRICK

Denn, mal, halt, and **doch** are words that you've seen a lot throughout this book. None of these words has a direct translation, but they are often used in everyday conversations to give emphasis to a question, command, or statement. For example, **Wie sieht er denn aus? Sag mal, wann gehst du? Das hat halt nicht jeder.** and **Wir gehen doch um vier.** Using these words in your conversations will help your German sound more natural.

Zweite Stufe

Objective Making plans

WK3 SCHLESWIG-HOLSTEIN-6

Wortschatz

Wohin gehen? Was machen?

Lies, was Katja und Julia planen! Julia sagt: „Katja und ich, wir wollen …"

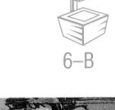 6–B   CD-ROM DISC 2

in ein Café gehen,
ein Eis essen

ins Schwimmbad gehen,
baden gehen

ins Kino gehen,
einen Film sehen

in eine Disko gehen,
tanzen und Musik hören

in die Stadt gehen,
Klamotten kaufen

ins Rockkonzert gehen,
Musik hören

Übungsheft, S. 65, Ü. 9–11   Grammatikheft, S.48, Ü. 6–8

---

16  **Wohin geht ihr?** Script and answers on p. 155G

Zuhören You will hear two students talk about their plans for the weekend. List all of the places they want to go in the order you hear them mentioned.
CD 6 Tr. 5

17 **Was wollen wir machen?**

Wir wollen … ins Schwimmbad / ins Kino / in ein Café / in die Stadt / in eine Disko / ins Rockkonzert gehen und … tanzen / Klamotten kaufen / Musik hören / schwimmen / einen Film sehen / ein Eis essen

18 **Für mein Notizbuch**

 Schreiben In your **Notizbuch** write some of the places you go and some of the things you do after school and on weekends. Look on page R9 for additional words you might want to use.

Making plans

You have been using the **möchte**-forms (*would like to*) to express your intentions:
Er möchte Musik hören. You can also use **wollen** (*to want to*).

Talking to someone: Talking about yourself:

Heiko, was willst du machen?   **Ich will in ein Café gehen.**

Talking about someone:

Wohin will Birte gehen?   **Sie will ins Schwimmbad gehen.**

Grammatik

The verb **wollen**

Wollen means *to want* or *to want to do.* The forms of this verb — and of other modal
verbs — are different from those of regular verbs. Here are the forms:

ich	will	wir	wollen
du	willst	ihr	wollt
er, sie, es	will	sie (pl), Sie	wollen

What do you notice about the **ich** and **er/sie** forms?[1] Like the **möchte**-forms
you learned in **Kapitel 3**, **wollen** is also a modal auxiliary verb. It is often used
with another verb, although the second verb can be omitted if the meaning
is obvious:

Mehr Grammatikübungen,
S. 177, Ü. 4–6

Ich will ins Schwimmbad gehen.
Ich will ins Schwimmbad.

Übungsheft, S. 66, Ü. 12–14

Note the position of the verb **wollen** and the second verb, the infinitive.

Grammatikheft, S. 49, Ü. 9–10

---

19 **Grammatik im Kontext**

Lesen/Schreiben Julia and her friend Sonja are talking about
their plans for the day. Complete their conversation with the
correct forms of **wollen**.

Julia   Was ___**1**___ du heute machen? willst

Sonja   Ich ___**2**___ nach Hamburg fahren. will
         Die Katja ___**3**___ mitkommen. will

Julia   Und Michael? ___**4**___ er auch mitkommen? will

Sonja   Ich glaube, ja. Katja, Heiko und Michael
         ___**5**___ alle mitkommen. wollen

Julia   Um wie viel Uhr ___**6**___ ihr fahren? wollt

Sonja   So um drei. Wir ___**7**___ um sieben wollen
         wieder zu Hause sein.

Fischmarkt in Hamburg

---

1. Though the pronouns are different, the verb forms are alike.
   They have no endings.

20 Grammatik im Kontext

Schreiben/Sprechen Wie viele Sätze kannst du bauen?

BEISPIEL **Katja will um vier Uhr ins Kino gehen.** *oder*
Um vier Uhr will Katja ins Kino gehen.

ich Katja du wir ihr die Jungen	wollen willst will wollt	am Nachmittag nach der Schule um vier Uhr von 3 bis 5 Uhr am Abend	in ein Café gehen ins Kino gehen tanzen gehen in die Stadt gehen ins Konzert gehen Musik hören

21 Heikos Pläne für nächste Woche

1. Sprechen Look at Heiko's plans for next week. Take turns saying what Heiko plans to do each day.

BEISPIEL **Am Dienstag will er ins Kino gehen.**

2. Sprechen Take turns asking each other when Heiko plans to do each of his activities.

22 Grammatik im Kontext

1. Schreiben Write your own plans for the coming week on a calendar page. For each day write what you want to do and at what time you plan to do it.

2. Sprechen Your partner will ask you about your plans. Tell him or her what you want to do and at what time. Then switch roles. Be prepared to share your partner's plans with the class.

3. Schreiben/Sprechen Restate each of the following sentences, beginning each one with a time expression.

  a. Ich habe am Samstag Klavierstunde.

  b. Ich gehe um 19 Uhr 30 in die Disko.

  c. Wir gehen am Montag ins Kino.

  d. Der Film beginnt um 14 Uhr 45.

  e. Wir gehen am Sonntag ins Konzert.

  f. Es beginnt um 8 Uhr 30.

  g. Julia will um 3 Uhr ins Café gehen.

  h. Sie will am Abend Hausaufgaben machen.

  a. Am Samstag habe ich Klavierstunde.
  b. Um 19 Uhr 30 gehe ich in die Disko.
  c. Am Montag gehen wir ins Kino.
  d. Um 14 Uhr 45 beginnt der Film.
  e. Am Sonntag gehen wir ins Konzert.
  f. Um 8 Uhr 30 beginnt es.
  g. Um 3 Uhr will Julia ins Café gehen.
  h. Am Abend will sie Hausaufgaben machen.

_____

1. The conjugated verb is in second position.

Calendar:

26 Montag	*Fußball 16³⁰* *Schach mit Sven 19⁰⁰* *Arbeitsgruppe Umwelt 20³⁰*
27 Dienstag	*Kino 14⁴⁵*
28 Mittwoch	*?*
29 Donnerstag	*schwimmen mit Michael 17⁴⁵*
30 Freitag	*16⁰⁰ - 18⁰⁰ zu Hause helfen*
31 Samstag	*13⁰⁰ Klavierstunde* *Disko 19³⁰*
1 Sonntag	*13¹⁵ segeln*

Ein wenig Grammatik

Schon bekannt

Monika could say of Katja:

  Katja will am Freitag in die Stadt gehen.
  or
  Am Freitag will Katja in die Stadt gehen.

You saw this type of word order before in **Kapitel 2**, when you learned about German word order:

  Wir spielen um 2 Uhr Fußball.
  Um 2 Uhr spielen wir Fußball.

What is the position of the conjugated verbs in the above sentences[1]?

Mehr Grammatikübungen, S. 178, Ü. 7

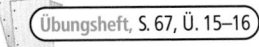

Übungsheft, S. 67, Ü. 15–16   Grammatikheft, S. 50, Ü. 11–12

23 Monikas Pläne fürs Wochenende

Lesen/Sprechen Read the letter that Monika has written to Katja, then answer the questions that follow.

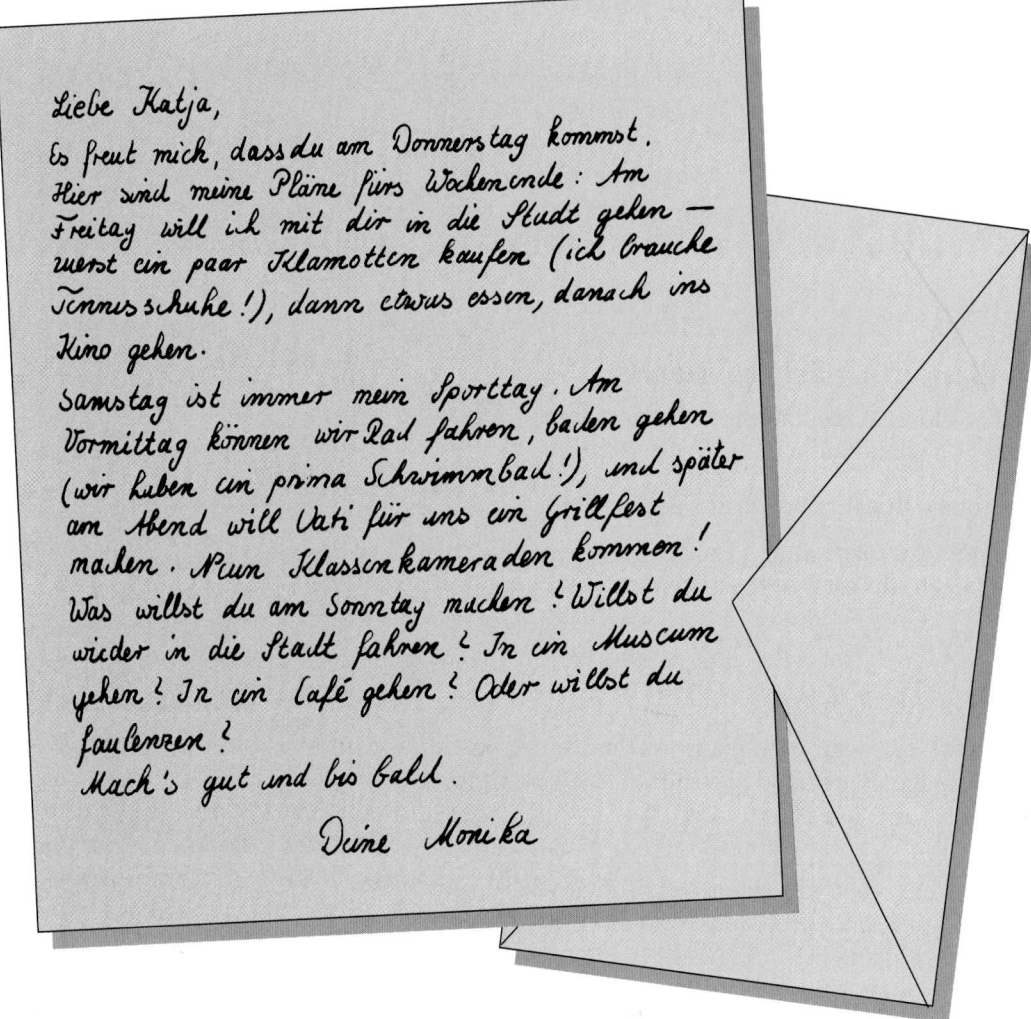

Liebe Katja,

Es freut mich, dass du am Donnerstag kommst. Hier sind meine Pläne fürs Wochenende: Am Freitag will ich mit dir in die Stadt gehen — zuerst ein paar Klamotten kaufen (ich brauche Tennisschuhe!), dann etwas essen, danach ins Kino gehen.

Samstag ist immer mein Sporttag. Am Vormittag können wir Rad fahren, baden gehen (wir haben ein prima Schwimmbad!), und später am Abend will Vati für uns ein Grillfest machen. Neun Klassenkameraden kommen! Was willst du am Sonntag machen? Willst du wieder in die Stadt fahren? In ein Museum gehen? In ein Café gehen? Oder willst du faulenzen?

Mach's gut und bis bald.

Deine Monika

1. Why is Monika writing to Katja? How do you know?
2. When will Katja visit Monika?
3. How long will she stay? How do you know?

1. to tell her the weekend plans: **Hier sind meine Pläne fürs Wochenende.**
2. Thursday through Sunday
3. She arrives on Thursday and stays through Sunday: Monika mentions those days.

24 Monikas Pläne

Schreiben List Monika's plans for Friday and Saturday and her suggestions for Sunday. Include all the words that indicate the sequence of the plans.

Am Freitag:	**in die Stadt gehen**	Klamotten kaufen	am Samstag:	Rad fahren
	Zuerst …	etwas essen		schwimmen
	Dann …	ins Kino gehen		ein Grillfest machen
			am Sonntag:	in die Stadt gehen
				in ein Museum gehen
				in ein Café gehen

25 Ihr macht Pläne

Sprechen You and two of your friends are discussing your plans for the weekend. All of you are very busy, but you want to get together. Decide on several things you could do and places you could go together, then create a conversation discussing your plans.

Was machst du in deiner Freizeit?

What do you think students in Germany like to do when they have time to spend with their friends? We have asked a number of students from different places this question, but before you read their responses, write down what you think they will say. Then read these interviews and compare your ideas with what they say. CD 6 Tr. 6

CD-ROM DISC 2

CD 6 Trs. 6-10

VIDEO

Übungsheft, S. 72, Ü. 26

Sandra, Stuttgart

„Also, meine Freizeit verbringe ich am liebsten mit ein paar Freundinnen oder Freunden. Dann gehen wir abends in die Stadt Eis essen, oder wir gehen tanzen, oder wir setzen uns einfach in ein Café rein und reden. Aber am liebsten gehen wir halt tanzen."
CD 6 Tr. 7

Annika, Hamburg

„Ich bin bei den Pfadfindern; da fährt man halt am Wochenende auf Fahrt, und ja, mit denen mach ich auch hauptsächlich ziemlich viel, auch mal außerhalb, ins Kino gehen und so —und sonst spiel ich noch Klavier." CD 6 Tr. 8

Marga, Bietigheim

„Ja, das ist sehr unterschiedlich. Wenn ich heimkomme, mach ich eigentlich erst einmal meine Hausaufgaben, dann gehe ich noch mit Freunden weg oder spiel Tennis und Gitarre, ja und ich mach auch Ballet und tänzerisch sehr viel. Ja, da ist meine Freizeit schon ausgebucht."
CD 6 Tr. 9

Karsten, Hamburg

„Also, ich mach als Erstes natürlich Hausaufgaben notgedrungen und dann irgendetwas mit Sport, oder ich geh in die Stadt einkaufen, oder meistens treff ich mich mit meiner Freundin." CD 6 Tr. 10

A. 1. Working with a partner, write beside each student's name where he or she likes to go and what he or she likes to do.

    2. Compare the lists you have prepared for the four German students. Which activities do they have in common?

    3. Discuss with your classmates which activities you and your friends like to do that are similar to those done by the students in Germany. Which are different?

B. Look at the list you made before you read the interviews. Does what you wrote match what the students say? If it is different, how? Where do your ideas about German students come from? How do you think students in Germany might describe a "typical" American student? Where might they get their ideas? Write a brief essay discussing these questions.

STANDARDS: 1.2, 2.2, 3.2, 4.2

Dritte Stufe

Objectives Ordering food and beverages; talking about how something tastes; paying the check

26 Im Café Freizeit

 Lesen/Schreiben Read the menu of **Café Freizeit**, then list what you would order for yourself. Add up the cost of your snack. With a partner, compare your order and the amount each of you would spend.

IMBISS-KARTE

Café Freizeit

Für den kleinen Hunger und Durst

KLEINE SPEISEN

NUDELSUPPE MIT BROT	€	2,25
KÄSEBROT		2,55
WURSTBROT		2,60
WIENER MIT SENF — 2 PAAR		2,90
PIZZA (15 CM)		
Nr. 1 mit Tomaten und Käse		3,00
Nr. 2 mit Wurst und Käse		3,25
Nr. 3 mit Wurst, Käse und Pilzen		4,25

EIS

FRUCHTEIS KUGEL	€	0,60
SAHNEEIS KUGEL		0,70
EISBECHER		3,40

GETRÄNKE

1 TASSE KAFFEE	€	2,15
1 KÄNNCHEN KAFFEE		3,80
1 TASSE CAPPUCCINO		2,60
1 GLAS TEE MIT ZITRONE		1,60

ALKOHOLFREIE GETRÄNKE

MINERALWASSER	0,5 l	€	1,75
LIMONADE, FANTA	0,5 l		1,80
APFELSAFT	0,2 l		1,25
COLA	0,2 l		1,50

KUCHEN

APFELKUCHEN	STÜCK	€	1,40
KÄSEKUCHEN	STÜCK		3,00

27 Was essen und trinken sie?   Script on p. 155G

 Zuhören You will hear four students saying what they want to eat and drink. Listen and decide what each one is ordering.   Julia: Apfelkuchen, Cappuccino; Heiko: Mineralwasser, Wurstbrot, Cappuccino; Katja: eine Nudelsuppe, zwei Paar Wiener mit Senf, eine Limonade; Michael: eine Pizza, eine Cola, einen Eisbecher

CD 6 Tr. 11

So sagt man das!

Ordering food and beverages

6–2

Here are some expressions you can use when you order something in a café or restaurant.

The waiter asks for your order:

Was bekommen Sie?
Ja, bitte?
Was essen Sie?
Was möchten Sie?
Was trinken Sie?

You order:

Ich möchte ein Wurstbrot.
Ich möchte ein Stück Kuchen, bitte.
Einen Eisbecher, bitte!
Ich trinke eine Limonade.
Ich bekomme einen Kaffee.

You might ask your friend:

Was nimmst du?
Was isst du?

Your friend might respond:

Ich nehme ein Käsebrot.
Ich esse ein Eis.

HEIKO: **Was nimmst du?**

MICHAEL: **Ich nehme …**

p. 155X 6–C

eine Nudelsuppe   ein Wurstbrot   ein Käsebrot   eine Pizza

Übungsheft,
S. 68, Ü. 17–19

ein Eis/einen Eisbecher   ein Stück Apfelkuchen   eine Tasse Kaffee   ein Glas Tee

Grammatikheft,
S. 51, Ü. 13–15

---

28 **Du hast Hunger!**

Sprechen Imagine that you are in **Café Freizeit**. You are very hungry and order a lot of food. Your partner plays the waiter, writing down everything you order, then tells the class what you have ordered. Switch roles.

BEISPIEL   **Was bekommen Sie?**
         DU   **Ich esse … dann … und danach …**

Grammatik

Stem-changing verbs

Remember the verb **nehmen** that you used in **Kapitel 5**? **Nehmen** has a change in the stem vowel of the **du-** and **er/sie** forms: **du nimmst, er/sie nimmt.** Another verb in this group is **essen** (*to eat*). Here are the forms of **essen**:

Mehr Grammatikübungen,
S. 178–179, Ü. 8–10

ich	esse	wir	essen
du	**isst**	ihr	esst
er, sie, es	**isst**	sie, Sie	essen

Übungsheft, S. 69–70, Ü. 20–24

Grammatikheft, S. 53, Ü. 19

---

29 **Grammatik im Kontext**

a. Sprechen Du hast großen Hunger! Schau auf die Speisekarte von Café Freizeit auf Seite 170.

   1. Was isst du?

   2. Was isst dein Partner? Frag ihn!

b. Schreiben Schreib die Sätze ab und setz die richtige Form von **essen** ein.

   1. Was ═══ du? – Ich ═══ ein   *isst / esse*
   Wurstbrot.

   2. Was ═══ denn die Julia? – Sie ═══
   nichts.   *isst / isst*

   3. Was ═══ der Michael? – Er ═══
   Kuchen.   *isst / isst*

   4. Was ═══ ihr? – Wir ═══ Eis.
              esst / essen

 **LERNTRICK**

Listening for gender cues. It is important to listen not only for meaning, but also for other cues that may be helpful. If someone asks: **Nimmst du einen Apfelsaft?** the **einen** tells you that **Apfelsaft** is a masculine noun. You can have your response ready immediately: Ja, **einen Apfelsaft**, bitte. *or* Ja, bitte! **Der Apfelsaft** ist wirklich gut.

So sagt man das!

Talking about how something tastes

If you want to ask how something tastes, you ask:

Some possible responses are:

Wie schmeckt's?

{ **Gut! Prima! Sagenhaft!**
Die Pizza schmeckt lecker! (*tasty, delicious*)
Die Pizza schmeckt nicht.

Schmeckt's?

{ **Ja, gut!**
Nein, nicht so gut.
Nicht besonders. *Not especially.*

Mehr Grammatikübungen, S. 179, Ü. 11

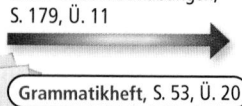

Grammatikheft, S. 53, Ü. 20

---

30 **Wie schmeckt's?**

1. **Sprechen** Your partner was really hungry and ordered a lot to eat. Everything looks great! Ask him or her how the different dishes taste. (React to the foods ordered in Activity 29.)

2. **Sprechen** The food doesn't taste very good. Ask your partner about different dishes that she or he has ordered. Then switch roles.

So sagt man das!

Paying the check

Calling the waiter's attention	**Hallo!**
Asking for the check	**Hallo! Ich will/möchte zahlen.**
Totaling up the check	**Das macht (zusammen)…**
Telling the waiter to keep the change	**Stimmt schon!**

Grammatikheft, S. 54, Ü. 21–22

Heiko: 2,30 EUR; 2,60 EUR; 2, 60 EUR / 7,50 EUR; 8 EUR
Katja: 2,30 EUR; 3,20 EUR; 2,40 EUR / 7, 90 EUR; 8 EUR

31 **Zahlen, bitte!** Script on p. 155H

Zuhören After Heiko and his friends eat, the waiter brings them the check. Listen as he adds up the bill, then write down each individual price you hear, the total, and what they round it off to as a tip.

CD 6 Tr. 12 Julia: 1,50 EUR; 2,60 EUR / 4,10 EUR; 5 EUR
Michael: 3,80 EUR; 1,50 EUR 3,50 EUR / 8,80 EUR; 9 EUR

32 **Du willst zahlen**

Sprechen You have finished your meal. Tell the waiter you want to pay. Before you pay the check, the waiter mentions every item you ordered and adds up the total. Role-play this situation with a partner, using the orders below and the menu on page 170. Be polite!

1. Nudelsuppe mit Brot, Mineralwasser

2. Tasse Cappuccino, Käsekuchen, Sahneeis

3. Wurstbrot, Cola, Tee mit Zitrone

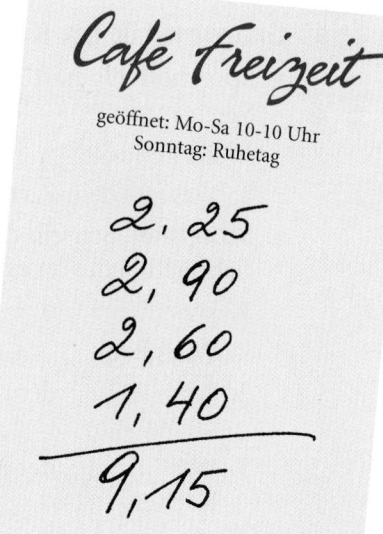

Café Freizeit

geöffnet: Mo-Sa 10-10 Uhr
Sonntag: Ruhetag

2, 25
2, 90
2, 60
1, 40
_____
9, 15

33 Kommst du mit?

Sprechen Get together with two other class-mates and role-play the following situations.

1. Your German pen pal is visiting you while you are in Wedel. Treat him or her to dinner at **Café Freizeit**. Talk about what both of you want to eat and drink. Order for the two of you. A waiter will take the order.

2. The waiter brings the order but can't remember who ordered what. Help him out.

3. While you are eating, you comment to each other about how the food tastes.

4. Your friend wants to order something else. Call the waiter over and tell him what else you want.

5. It is time to pay. Call the waiter and ask for the check. The waiter will name everything you ordered and add up the bill. You pay and leave a tip.

 **Ein wenig Landeskunde**

The prices on German menus include the tip. However, most people will round the check up to the next euro or to the next round sum, depending on the total of the bill.

Stimmt schon!

 34 **Von der Schule zum Beruf**

Schreiben You are the new owner of a small restaurant. Wanting to attract customers, you decide to design an unusual menu, listing items your chef can prepare. You also price the items. Give your restaurant a name, an address, a telephone number, and any other information that you consider appropriate.

AUSSPRACHE

 Richtig aussprechen / Richtig lesen CD 6 Trs. 13–15

A. To practice these sounds pronounce after your teacher or after the recording the words and sentences in bold. CD 6 Tr. 13

1. The letter combination **ch:** The consonant combination **ch** can be pronounced two different ways. When preceded by the vowels **i** and **e,** it sounds similar to the *h* in the English word *huge.* When preceded by the vowels **a, o** or **u,** it is produced farther back in the throat.

   ich, Pech, dich / So ein Pech! Ich habe es nicht.
   ach, doch, Buch / Was macht Heiko am Wochenende? Spielt er Schach?

2. The letter **r:** The German **r** sound does not exist in English. To produce this sound, put the tip of your tongue behind your lower front teeth. Then tip your head back and pretend that you are gargling.

   rund, recht, Freizeit / Rolf, Rudi, und Rita gehen ins Café Freizeit.

3. The letter combination **er:** At the end of a word the letter combination **er** sounds almost like a vowel. It is similar to the *u* in the English word *but.*

   super, Lehrer, Bruder / Wo ist meine Schwester?

Richtig schreiben / Diktat CD 6 Tr. 14
CD 6 Tr. 15 (with pauses)

B. Write down the sentences that you hear. Script on p. 155H

Wohin in Hamburg?

People who live in Wedel often go into Hamburg for a day of entertainment.

1. What are the two main types of ads on these pages? food, music

2. **a.** Use context clues to guess the meaning of these German words. Match each word with its English equivalent.

   1) **lädt** d   **a)** enjoy

   2) **genießen** a   **b)** meeting place

   3) **Treffpunkt** b   **c)** a dish of ice cream

   4) **Bratkartof-** d   **d)** invites
      felgerichte e

   5) **Eisbecher**   **e)** fried potato
      c   dishes

   b. What kinds of foods are advertised here? Which restaurant ad interests you the most? b. **Mexican, seafood, potato dishes, milk and ice cream**

HAMBURG
Kulinarische Highlights

Jeden **Dienstag** lädt Don Diego Gonzales zur **Fiesta Mexicana**: Ein buntes Spezialitäten-Buffet und feurige Gitarrenklänge sorgen für einen stimmungsvollen mexikanischen Abend.

Donnerstags und **freitags** entführt Sie Neptun in sein Reich der sieben Meere: Genießen Sie sein lukullisches **Seafood-Buffet**!

LIBERTY IM MOTORAMA 21.00-3.00

Liberty
DISKOTHEK · CAFÉ

Oldie Disco
Hits der 60er u. 70er Jahre

NACHTEULE
DISCOTEK

FREITAG:
OLDIES bis 3 Uhr

Täglich ab 20 Uhr   Montag Ruhetag

Dienstag, 26. Januar
Martha Argerich, Klavier
Guy Tourvton, Trompete
Württembergisches Kammerorchester Heilbronn
Dirigent: Jörg Faerber
Haydn: Konzert für Klavier und Orchester D-Dur
Janácek: Suite für Streichorchester
Hindemith: Fünf Stücke für Streichorchester op. 44
Schostakowitsch: Konzert für Klavier, Trompete und Streichorchester op. 35

Dienstag, 25. Mai
Murray Perahia, Klavier
Mozart: Sonate F-Dur KV 332
Brahms: Rhapsodie h-Moll op. 79, Intermezzo es-Moll op. 118
Capriccio h-Moll op. 76, Rhapsodie Es-Dur op. 119
Beethoven: Sonate B-Dur op. 106 (Hammerklavier)

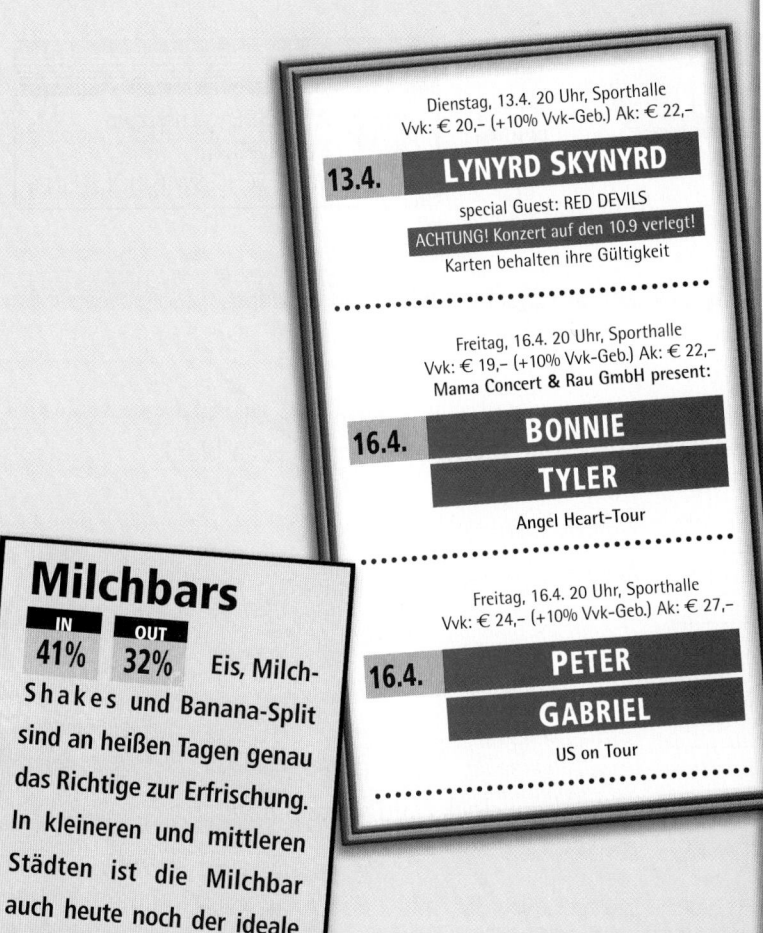

Milchbars

IN	OUT
41%	32%

Eis, Milch-Shakes und Banana-Split sind an heißen Tagen genau das Richtige zur Erfrischung. In kleineren und mittleren Städten ist die Milchbar auch heute noch der ideale Treffpunkt für die jungen Leute.

Dienstag, 13.4. 20 Uhr, Sporthalle
Vvk: € 20,– (+10% Vvk-Geb.) Ak: € 22,–

13.4.   LYNYRD SKYNYRD

special Guest: RED DEVILS

ACHTUNG! Konzert auf den 10.9 verlegt!

Karten behalten ihre Gültigkeit

Freitag, 16.4. 20 Uhr, Sporthalle
Vvk: € 19,– (+10% Vvk-Geb.) Ak: € 22,–
Mama Concert & Rau GmbH present:

16.4.   BONNIE
TYLER

Angel Heart-Tour

Freitag, 16.4. 20 Uhr, Sporthalle
Vvk: € 24,– (+10% Vvk-Geb.) Ak: € 27,–

16.4.   PETER
GABRIEL

US on Tour

Tag u. Nacht

deftige Bratkartoffelgerichte

Tag und Nacht warme Küche,
Frühstück zu jeder Zeit,
saftige Steaks,
das ganze Jahr Eisbergsalat,
tolle Eisbecher

gestern & heute treff
Kaiser-Wilhelm-Straße 55

Bahrenfelder Forsthaus

Hamburger Küche und feine Spezialitäten
Besondere Sonntagsmenüs
Restaurant, Romantischer Wintergarten, Café und Café-Terrasse
Von-Hutten-Str. 45 · Hamburg 22761 · Telefon (0 40) 89 40 21

---

c. Where can you eat Mexican food? On what day? *c. Don Diego Gonzales; Tuesday*

d. Where can you get "**tolle Eisbecher**"? Where is this place located? *d. Tag und Nacht gestern & heute treff, Kaiser-Wilhelm-Straße 55*

3. a. Where can you hear music? What kinds of music can you hear? *3a. Sporthalle (concerts) Discos (oldies)*

b. What are the names of the discos? How long is the **Liberty** open? *b. Liberty, 9 pm - 3 am (6 hours) Nachteule, (7 hours)*

c. When (day and time) can you see Bonnie Tyler? Peter Gabriel? Will Lynyrd Skynyrd fans get to hear them on 13.4.? If not, why not? *c. Friday, April 16, 8 pm Friday, April 16, 8 pm no; concert postponed until September 10*

4. What is the social purpose of the **Milchbar**? What word supports your opinion? *meeting place for young people: Treffpunkt*

5. Remembering the word you learned for "juice," find the word that means "juicy." *saftig*

6. Assume you and your family are in Wedel. You want to go to Hamburg for two or three days.

   a. To which places would you more likely go with your parents?

   b. To which places would you more likely go with your friends?

   c. Write a postcard to a friend telling of your plans for your weekend in Hamburg. Be sure to use sequencing words appropriately.

Übungsheft, S. 71, Ü. 25

Mehr Grammatikübungen

CD-ROM DISC 2

Answers

internet

go.hrw.com

ADRESSE: go.hrw.com
KENNWORT:
WK3 SCHLESWIG-HOLSTEIN-6

Erste Stufe

Objective Telling time and talking about when you do things

1 You and your friends are at the mall. You seem to be the only person with a watch, and a lot of people ask you what time it is. Rewrite the time statements by filling in each blank with the time given in parentheses. (S. 162)

1. Wie spät ist es, bitte?   Es ist (3:15) _____ .   Viertel nach drei
2. Wie viel Uhr ist es?   Es ist (3:30) _____ .   halb vier
3. Wie spät ist es jetzt?   Es ist (3:45) _____ .   Viertel vor vier
4. Wie viel Uhr ist es?   Es ist (4:55) _____ .   fünf vor fünf
5. Wie spät ist es, bitte?   Es ist (7:10) _____ .   zehn nach sieben
6. Wie viel Uhr ist es?   Es ist (8:20) _____ .   zwanzig nach acht

2 You are in Munich, Stuttgart, and Besigheim. Look at these clocks and write out what time it is. (S. 162)

Auf dieser Bahnhofsuhr ist es _____ .   halb zehn

Die Uhr an einer Münchner Apotheke zeigt _____ .   elf Uhr dreißig

Diese schöne Uhr am Turm des Stuttgarter Rathauses zeigt _____ .

zwei Uhr fünfundzwanzig

Auf dieser Rathausuhr in Besigheim ist es

_____ .

acht Uhr fünfundzwanzig

3 You are telling your parents when you and your friends are going to do various activities. Complete the following statements by filling in the blanks with the time given in parentheses. (S. 162)

1. (9:45) Um _____ spielen wir Fußball.　　　　　　　　　Viertel vor zehn
2. (12:10) Um _____ wollen wir mit dem Bus in die Stadt fahren.　zehn nach zwölf
3. (4:15) Wir kommen um _____ nach Hause.　　　　　　　Viertel nach vier
4. (4:30) Heute um _____ möchten wir Volleyball spielen.　　halb fünf
5. (5:50) Um _____ möchten wir Fernsehen schauen.　　　　zehn vor sechs
6. (6:00) Und um _____ kommt ein Fußballspiel!　　　　　　sechs Uhr

Zweite Stufe　　　Objective **Making plans**

4 During recess, you and your friends are planning activities for the afternoon. Complete each question or statement by filling in each blank with the correct form of the verb **wollen**. (S. 166)

1. Wer _____ heute Tennis spielen?　　　　　　　　　　will
2. Heiko und Julia _____ ins Café Freizeit gehen.　　　　wollen
3. Wohin _____ du gehen, Katja? _____ du ins Café gehen?　willst; Willst
4. Ich _____ Musik hören. Und du, was _____ du machen?　will; willst
5. _____ ihr ein Eis essen, Heiko und Julia?　　　　　　Wollt
6. Julia _____ ins Kino gehen, und Katja _____ ins Konzert.　will; will
7. Und was _____ wir jetzt machen? Was meinst du?　　　wollen

5 You are trying to find out from your friends when they want to do certain activities. Complete the following questions by filling in the first blank with the correct form of the verb **wollen** and the second one with an appropriate infinitive. (S. 166)

1. Um wie viel Uhr _____ ihr ins Kino _____?　　　wollt; gehen
2. Warum _____ du heute nicht Musik _____?　　　willst; hören
3. Wer _____ jetzt ein Eis _____?　　　　　　　　will; essen
4. Warum _____ du nicht mit Michael baden _____?　willst; gehen
5. Wir _____ heute mal einen Film _____.　　　　　wollen; sehen
6. Warum _____ ihr nicht die Klamotten _____?　　wollt; kaufen
7. Katja und Sonja _____ jetzt Tennis _____.　　　wollen; spielen

6 Rephrase these sentences using a form of **wollen**. (S. 166)

1. Ich gehe heute ins Kino.　　　　　　　Ich will heute ins Kino gehen.
2. Wer spielt heute Tennis?　　　　　　　Wer will heute Tennis spielen?
3. Warum hörst du nicht Musik?　　　　　Warum willst du nicht Musik hören?
4. Michael zieht den Pulli nicht an.　　　Michael will den Pulli nicht anziehen.
5. Probierst du die Jacke an?　　　　　　Willst du die Jacke anprobieren?
6. Wir fahren heute in die Stadt.　　　　Wir wollen heute in die Stadt fahren.

7 Begin each sentence with the underlined part. **(S. 167)**

1. Wir gehen <u>um drei Uhr</u> ins Café.
2. Ich höre <u>jetzt</u> Musik aus Deutschland.
3. Sonja spielt <u>nach der Schule</u> Tennis.
4. Ich will <u>am Abend</u> ins Kino gehen.
5. Julia will <u>am Freitag</u> in die Stadt fahren.
6. Der Michael will <u>im Moment</u> gar nichts.
7. Tom und Julia möchten <u>heute</u> ein Eis essen.
8. Wir möchten <u>am Nachmittag</u> ins Café gehen.
9. Ich möchte <u>danach</u> in die Disko gehen.

Um drei Uhr gehen wir ins Café.

Jetzt höre ich Musik aus Deutschland.

Nach der Schule spielt Sonja Tennis.

Am Abend will ich ins Kino gehen.

Am Freitag will Julia in die Stadt fahren.

Im Moment will der Michael gar nichts.

Heute möchten Tom und Julia ein Eis essen.

Am Nachmittag möchten wir ins Café gehen.

Danach möchte ich in die Disko gehen.

Dritte Stufe

Objectives Ordering food and beverages; talking about how something tastes; paying the check

8 You and your friends are in a snack bar ordering food and beverages. What does everyone want? Complete the sentences and questions by supplying the correct indefinite articles. **(S. 171)**

1. Ich bekomme _____ Eisbecher. Und du? Nimmst du _____ Käsebrot?

2. Wir möchten _____ Pizza, _____ Apfelsaft und _____ Glas Tee.

3. Michael nimmt _____ Käsebrot, und er trinkt _____ Cola.

4. Ich esse _____ Stück Kuchen und trinke _____ Tasse Kaffee.

5. Michael isst _____ Nudelsuppe und trinkt _____ Limo.

6. Sonja nimmt _____ Wurstbrot und _____ Mineralwasser.

einen; ein

eine; einen; ein

ein; eine

ein; eine

eine; eine

ein; ein

9 You are in a restaurant, talking about food and what you want to order. Complete each of the following questions and statements with the correct form of the verb **essen.** **(S. 171)**

1. Ja, was _____ du denn? Du _____ ein Käsebrot?

2. Ich _____ ein Eis, und die Julia _____ einen Eisbecher.

3. Und was _____ ihr? Auch was wir _____, Pizza?

4. Heiko und Michael _____ Nudelsuppe.

5. Wer _____ ein Stück Apfelkuchen?

6. Heiko, du _____ doch gern Apfelkuchen, nicht?

isst; isst

esse; isst

esst; essen

essen

isst

isst

10 You are offering your friend different items of food and telling how good everything tastes. Complete each of the following questions and statements by filling in the first blank with the correct form of the indefinite article, and the second blank with the correct form of the pronoun. Note: If no indefinite article is required, write 0 in the space provided. (**S. 171**)

1. Möchtest du _____ Eis? _____ schmeckt prima!   ein or 0; Es

2. Willst du _____ Pizza? _____ schmeckt prima!   eine or 0; Sie

3. Möchtest du _____ Eisbecher? _____ schmeckt gut!   einen; Er

4. Isst du _____ Nudelsuppe? _____ schmeckt sehr gut!   eine; Sie

5. Nimmst du _____ Käsebrot? _____ schmeckt bestimmt gut!   ein; Es

6. Trinkst du _____ Limo? _____ schmeckt prima!   eine; Sie

7. Oder trinkst du _____ Apfelsaft? _____ schmeckt auch gut!   einen; Er

8. Isst du _____ Obst? _____ ist so gut!   0; Es

11 You and your friend are ordering a meal in a restaurant. Complete the following dialogue by filling in each blank with the correct verb form. The verb to be used is indicated in parentheses. (**S. 172**)

Kellner	(to get)	Was _____ Sie, bitte? bekommen
Michael	(to take)	Ich _____ eine Suppe, die Nudelsuppe. nehme
Julia	(to eat)	Und ich _____ eine Pizza, die Nummer 2. esse
Kellner	(to drink)	Was _____ Sie? trinken
Julia	(to drink)	Ich _____ eine Limo. trinke
Michael	(would like)	Und ich _____ ein Glas Mineralwasser. möchte
(*später*)		
Kellner	(to taste)	Wie _____ die Suppe? schmeckt
Michael	(to be)	Sie _____ wirklich gut. ist
Julia	(to taste)	Meine Pizza _____ phantastisch! schmeckt
(*später*)		
Michael	(to pay)	Wir möchten _____ , bitte. Zusammen! zahlen
Kellner	(to make)	Das _____ zusammen 6 Euro 40. macht

Anwendung

The CD-ROM Tutor offers guided recording and writing activities to accompany the **Anwendung.** These activities are designed to practice students' oral and written communication skills and to review material from each chapter.

1 Express the times shown in as many different ways as you can.

1. sieben Uhr zwanzig, zwanzig nach sieben
2. zwei Uhr dreißig, halb drei
3. drei Uhr fünfundvierzig, Viertel vor vier
4. zehn Uhr fünfzehn, Viertel nach zehn
5. elf Uhr fünfundfünfzig, fünf vor zwölf

2 In each of the following reports, an activity is mentioned. If the activity mentioned is shown in the photos below, match the activity with the appropriate photo.

1. c, f   2. e, b   3. Karten spielen: not pictured   4. a   5 h   Script on p. 155H

CD 6
Tr. 16

a.

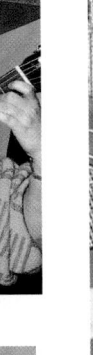
b.

c.

d.

e.

g.

f.

h.

3 Look at the photos. Your partner will ask you what you want to do. Choose three activities from above and tell your partner which ones you want to do and at what time you want to do them. Then switch roles.

4 Write in German a conversation you might have had when you last ate a meal or a snack in a restaurant. Include ordering your food, some comments on how it tasted, and paying for it.

5

Zum Schreiben

Write a letter to a friend describing your plans for the week. This letter should be so intriguing that it will convince your friend to come for a visit during spring break.

> **Schreibtipp Arranging your ideas chronologically** is helpful when planning activities for a week.

Prewriting

To arrange items chronologically, take a sheet of paper, turn it sideways, and divide it into seven columns. Write one day of the week at the top of each column, and *morning, after-noon,* and *evening* down the left side. Next, decide on activities you would like to do and at which times. Place this information in the appropriate column. (One of your activities might be to go to an **Imbissstand** where they have the best **Wurst** in town!)

Writing

Now, using the information you have organized on your chart, write a letter convincing your friend that the activities you have planned are so great that he or she absolutely has to come for a visit during spring break.

6

Rollenspiel

Du bist mit einem Freund in Hamburg. Ihr habt Hunger und möchtet etwas essen.

Verkauf am Fenster

Sensationell

1/2 Hähnchen	2,20
	1,50
Käsebrot	1,45
Wurstbrot	3,30
La Flute m. Schinken & Ananas	
Gr. Fladenbrot (Giros/Kochschinken/ Schinken/Spießbraten)	4,20
	4,75
Giros mit Krautsalat	gr. 2,00
Currywurst, kl. 1,85	0,95
Rostbratwurst	0,95
Bockwurst	1,35
Schokoladeneis	1,35
Vanilleeis	1,40
Fruchteis	

	Becher 0,3		0,4	
Cola	0,3	0,75	0,4	0,85
Milchshake	0,3	0,90	0,4	1,10
Apfelsaft	0,3	0,90	0,4	1,20
Orangensaft	0,3	0,90	0,4	1,20
Mineralwasser				1,00
Fanta	0,3	0,65	0,4	0,90

You are in a hurry for the Peter Gabriel concert, so you decide to put dinner off until later and just grab a snack at an **Imbissstand.** You also don't want to spend very much money—each of you is limited to six euros.

a. Create a conversation in which you discuss the possibilities that are available, decide what each of you wants, and figure out how much it will cost.

b. One partner can then play the role of ven-dor, and you can order the food and drink that each of you decided upon. After you receive your food, pay for it.

Kann ich's wirklich?

1 Answers will vary. Guten Tag!/Tag! Wie geht's? How would you greet a friend and ask how he or she is doing? If someone asks how you are doing, what could you say? Gut, danke!/Nicht schlecht!

Can you start a conversation? (p. 161)

Can you tell time? (p. 162)

2 How would you ask what time it is? Say the times shown below, using expressions you learned in this chapter.

1. 1.00 **2.** 11.30 **3.** 9.50 **4.** 2.15 **5.** 7.55
ein Uhr   halb zwölf   zehn vor zehn   Viertel nach zwei   fünf vor acht

Can you talk about when you do things? (p. 162)

3 Wir wollen um … Uhr … gehen.
Using the time expressions above, say when you and your friends intend to

a. go to the movies   ins Kino   **c.** go to the swimming pool   ins Schwimmbad

b. go to a café   ins Café

4 How would you ask a friend when he intends to do the activities in Activity 3?   Wann willst du …?

Can you make plans using wollen? (p. 166)

5 Say you intend to go to the following places and tell what you plan to do there. Establish a sequence: *first …, then …*

a. café   a. Erst gehe ich ins Café, dann esse ich ein Eis.   **d.** department store   d. ins Kaufhaus/Klamotten kaufen

b. swimming pool   b. Erst… ins Schwimmbad, dann schwimmen.   **e.** disco   e. in eine Disko/tanzen

c. movies   c. Erst… ins Kino, dann einen Film sehen.

6 How would you say that the following people want to go to a concert?

1. Michael   will   **3.** ihr   wollt   **5.** Peter und Monika   wollen

2. Silke   will   **4.** wir   wollen

Can you order food and beverages? (p. 170)

7 You are with some friends in a café. Order the following things for yourself.

a. (noodle) soup   Nudelsuppe   **c.** a cheese sandwich   ein Käsebrot

b. a glass of tea with lemon   ein Glas Tee mit Zitrone

8 Say that these people are going to eat the foods listed. Then say what you are going to eat (using **ich**). How would you ask your best friend what he or she is going to eat (using **du**)?

a. Michael - Käsekuchen   isst   **d.** Ahmet und ich -   essen   Wiener mit Senf

b. Holger und Julia -   essen   Apfelkuchen   **e.** Ich …   esse

c. Monika - Käsebrot   isst   **f.** Und du? Was …?   isst

Ich esse …   Was isst du?

Can you talk about how something tastes? (p. 172)

9 How would you ask a friend if his or her food tastes good? How might he or she respond?   Schmeckt's? Lecker, danke!

Can you pay the check? (p. 172)

10 Ask the waiter for the check, then tell him to keep the change.   Ich möchte zahlen, bitte./Stimmt schon!

Erste Stufe

Starting a conversation

Wie geht's (denn)?	How are you?
Sehr gut!	Very well!
Prima!	Great!
Gut!	Good/Well!
Es geht.	Okay.
So lala.	So-so.
Schlecht.	Bad(ly).
Miserabel.	Miserable.

Telling time

Wie spät ist es?	What time is it?
Wie viel Uhr ist es?	What time is it?
Um wie viel Uhr ...?	At what time ...?
Viertel nach halb (eins, zwei, usw.)	a quarter after half past (one, two, etc.)

Viertel vor ...	a quarter to ...
(zehn) vor ...	(ten) till ...
um (ein) Uhr ...	at (one) o'clock
um Viertel nach ...	at a quarter past ...

Zweite Stufe

Making plans

Wohin?	Where (to)?
in ein Café/ins Café	to a café
ein Eis essen	to eat ice cream
in die Stadt gehen	to go downtown
ins Schwimmbad gehen	to go to the (swimming) pool
baden gehen	to go swimming

ins Kino gehen	to go to the movies
einen Film sehen	to see a movie
in eine Disko gehen	to go to a disco
tanzen gehen	to go dancing
ins Konzert gehen	to go to the concert

in ein Konzert gehen	to go to a concert
wollen	to want (to)
er/sie will	he/she wants (to)

Dritte Stufe

p. 155X

Ordering food and beverages

Was bekommen Sie?	What will you have?
Ich bekomme ...	I'll have ...
eine Tasse Kaffee	a cup of coffee
ein Glas Tee mit Zitrone	a (glass) cup of tea with lemon
eine Limonade	a lemon-flavored soda
eine Limo	short for **Limonade**
eine Nudelsuppe mit Brot	noodle soup with bread
ein Käsebrot	cheese sandwich
einen Eisbecher	a dish of ice cream

ein Wurstbrot	sandwich with cold cuts
eine Pizza	pizza
Apfelkuchen	apple cake
ein Eis	ice cream
essen	to eat
er/sie isst	he/she eats

Talking about how food tastes

Wie schmeckt's?	How does it taste?
Schmeckt's?	Does it taste good?
Sagenhaft!	Great!
Lecker!	Tasty! Delicious!

Nicht besonders.	Not really.

Paying the check

Hallo! Ich möchte/ will zahlen!	The check please!
Das macht (zusammen) ...	That comes to ...
Stimmt (schon)!	Keep the change.

Other words and phrases

Pass auf!	Watch out!
nun	now

Note: Both **jetzt** and **nun** mean *now*. While **jetzt** can be used in all situations indicating a point in time, **nun** is used more to indicate a point in sequence. On p. 159, Michael says: **Und nun trinke ich meine Cola aus und gehe**, indicating that he has been doing other things before, such as ordering various dishes, and now he's ready to leave.

München

Teaching Resources
pp. 184–187

PRINT
▶ Lesson Planner, p. 32
▶ Video Guide, pp. 41–42

MEDIA
▶ One-Stop Planner
▶ Video Program
  Videocassette 3, 01:14–05:08
▶ Map Transparency
▶ Interactive CD-ROM Tutor, Disc 2

go.hrw.com
WK3 MUENCHEN

PAGES 184–185

THE PHOTOGRAPH
Background Information

With over one million inhabitants, Munich is the third largest city in Germany (after Berlin and Hamburg). It is a magnet to Germans and foreigners alike and is by far the most popular German city because of its many attractive features. Munich owes its origins to **Herzog Heinrich der Löwe,** Duke Henry the Lion, who built a bridge over the Isar river and established a customs station there in 1158. Munich draws business people to its fairs and trade shows, visitors to the annual **Oktoberfest,** athletes to its Olympic sport facilities, and tourists to its architecture as well as picturesque location at the foot of the Alps and the Alpine lakes.

Shown in the foreground of the picture is the **Pfarrkirche Heiliger Geist,** originally called **Spitalkirche.** Built between 1208 and 1397, the church was severely damaged during World War II and rebuilt shortly afterwards. It was remodeled in 1991.

THE ALMANAC AND MAP

The coat of arms of Bavaria shows the blue and white diamonds of the Wittelsbach dynasty that ruled the state from the Middle Ages until 1918.

Teaching Suggestion

Ask students to research the name of the city **München** to determine its origin. (It comes from a small ninth century village that was close to a Benedictine monastery; **Mönche** *(monks)* → **München.**)

Terms in the Almanac

• **Isar:** a tributary of the Danube that is 295 km (177 miles) long. The Isar generates enough energy to run several hydroelectric plants.

• **Maximilianeum:** built between 1857 and 1874, it is now the seat of the Bavarian **Landtag** and **Senat.**

• **Theatinerkirche:** a church famous for its baroque style. It dates back to 1663 when it was built to honor the birth of prince Max Emanuel, whose mother was of Italian descent.

• **Alte Pinakothek:** famous art gallery housing European paintings from the 14th to 18th centuries. It is considered one of the most impressive galleries in the world, with works by artists such as Dürer, Rembrandt, and Rubens.

• **Neue Pinakothek:** an art gallery holding 400 paintings and sculptures representing European art from the 18th to 20th centuries.

• **Deutsches Museum:** the largest museum of science and technology in the world. It offers more than 18,000 exhibits.

• **Glyptothek:** gallery housing Greek and Roman antique marble sculptures.

• **Schweinshaxe:** cured knuckle of pork cooked with junipers, bay leaves, greens, and pork drippings. It is served with steamed sauerkraut.

• **Leberkäs:** made from liver, pork, egg, milk, flour, and spices. It is served warm or cold on bread, often topped with mustard.

• **Weißwürste:** sausages made of veal, bacon, onions, lemon rind, parsley, herbs, and spices.

Map Activities

Have students look at the map of Germany on p. 2 and name the countries and the **Bundesländer** that border Bavaria. (Czech Republic, Austria, and Switzerland; Baden-Württemberg, Hessen, Thüringen, Sachsen) You may also want to use *Map Transparency 1.*

> **PAGES 186–187**

THE PHOTO ESSAY

1 **Lederhosen** originated in western Austria (Tyrol) and were introduced in Bavaria in 1800. As can be seen in the picture, the pants have suspenders with ornamental breastbands. Men usually wear a light-colored shirt with the **Lederhosen** as well as knee-high socks. A longer version of the **Lederhosen** comes below the knee and is worn on cool days.

Observing Ask students if they can tell by looking at the picture or the word **Leder** what the **Lederhosen** are made of. (leather)

Drawing Inferences Ask students when men might wear their **Lederhosen.** (Examples: **Oktoberfest,** dances, church festivals, holidays)

The **Gamsbart** is from the long back mane of the chamois. The display of the **Gamsbart** on the hat is considered to be a trophy which once indicated that the man had killed a chamois.

2 The **Frauenkirche** *(church of our Lady)* in the background is the most distinguishing landmark of the Munich skyline. It was built between 1468 and 1488 in the late Gothic style by Jörg v. Polling. Its onion-shaped towers stand 99 and 100 meters tall.

Teaching Suggestion

The many cafés in the foreground are part of the city's **Fußgängerzone.** Ask students if they can understand the meaning of the compound word **Fußgängerzone.** *(pedestrian zone)*

Comparing and Contrasting

Can students think of any pedestrian zones in U.S. cities? Why are they more common in the German-speaking countries than in the United States? (Designed to preserve older parts of towns where streets were very narrow and to encourage use of public transportation, **Fußgängerzonen** are very common in the German-speaking countries.

Stores and restaurants can be found in the center of a city rather than in big malls, which are more of an American concept. Since parking is difficult, pedestrians have to leave their cars at parking garages or use public transportation for easier access to the city.)

Building on Previous Skills

Can students tell from the sign what is being served at the outdoor restaurant in Photo 3? (Kaffee und Kuchen)

Culture Note

3 Traditionally, the first of May was celebrated with the **Maibaum** to signify the arrival of spring. It is a pole with a big wreath of green branches on the top. Long, colorful ribbons hang down from the wreath. Dances are performed around the pole. Each part of the pictured maypole depicts some historical or cultural aspect of life in Munich. The coat of arms of Munich at the bottom right of the pole bears the figure of a small, blue-clad monk, called **Münchner Kindl,** who symbolizes the city's origin as a village alongside a medieval monastery. The casks on the wagon represent the different local breweries, such as **Spatenbräu, Löwenbräu, Augustiner, Münchner Kindl, Paulaner, Hofbräu,** and **Franziskaner.** Next, two scenes from the famous **Oktoberfest** are shown. The scenes above depict barrel makers, **Schäffler,** performing their traditional dance. The dancing couple at the top wears the traditional costumes of Bavaria.

4 The old city hall was built from 1470 to 1475 by J. v. Halspach. The tower was completely destroyed during World War II and faithfully reconstructed in 1972.

The **Mariensäule** (built in 1638) is a focal point of the **Marienplatz,** which is the center of the city. It is surrounded by numerous outdoor cafés and restaurants.

5 **Viktualien** is an old-fashioned word for groceries. The original market dates back as early as 1365 when a city ordinance allowed the butchers to sell their goods only at this location. Today the market vendors offer many specialties besides fresh produce and meats.

6 Flori, Markus, and Claudia are originally from Munich, but Flori's mother is American. Mara is from Croatia. She has been living in Munich for a number of years.

Komm mit nach München

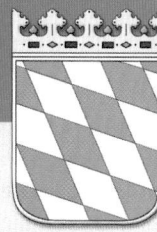

Map of Germany

Landeshauptstadt von Bayern

Einwohner: 1,3 Millionen

Fluss: München liegt an der Isar

Berühmte Gebäude: Frauenkirche, Rathaus, Maximilianeum, Theatinerkirche

Museen: Alte und Neue Pinakothek, Deutsches Museum, Glyptothek

Industrien: Elektrotechnik und Elektronik, Automobilindustrie, Brauereien, Verlage, Filmindustrie

Bedeutende Münchner: Josef von Fraunhofer (1787-1826, Physiker); Moritz von Schwind (1804-1871, Maler); Karl Valentin (1882-1948, Komiker); Annette Kolb (1870-1967, Schriftstellerin)

Typische Gerichte: Schweinshaxe, Leberkäs, Weißwürste

STANDARDS: 2.2, 3.1

WK3 MUENCHEN

Nordsee · DÄNEMARK · Ostsee

NIEDER-LANDE

Kiel

Hamburg

Berlin

POLEN

BEL.

Frankfurt

B A Y E R N

TSCHECHIEN

LUX.

FRANK-REICH

München

SCHWEIZ

ÖSTERREICH

Ein Blick über die Dächer von München ▶

München

München ist die Hauptstadt Bayerns. Die Stadt ist bekannt für ihre vielen Museen, Theater, Musikstätten und Sportanlagen. Hier haben 1972 die Olympischen Spiele stattgefunden. München ist auch ein Zentrum der Autoindustrie (BMW, MAN), Computer-Industrie (Siemens), High-Tech-Industrie, Raumfahrtindustrie, Medienindustrie und auch der Sitz von vielen anderen, sogenannten „sauberen" Firmen.

🖅 internet

go.hrw.com **ADRESSE:** go.hrw.com
KENNWORT:
WK3 MUENCHEN

1 **Bayrische Tracht**
Die Lederhose und der Gamsbart auf dem Hut gehören zur bayrischen Männertracht. Auch heute sieht man noch Tracht in Dörfern und Städten und besonders zu festlichen Anlässen.

2 **In der Neuhauserstraße**
Die Neuhauserstraße ist eine Fußgängerzone mit vielen Geschäften und Straßenlokalen, wo sich die Einkäufer und Touristen vom Einkaufen und Bummeln ausruhen können.

3 **Ein Maibaum**
Maibäume sieht man überall in Bayern. Dieser Maibaum auf dem Viktualienmarkt zeigt das bayrische Wappen, das weiß-blaue Rautenmuster, sowie Münchens Wahrzeichen, das Münchner Kindl, und zwei schwarz-gelbe Stadtfahnen.

5 **Auf dem Viktualienmarkt**
Drei Minuten vom Marienplatz entfernt ist der Viktualienmarkt, wo viele Münchner täglich ihre Lebensmittel und Obst und Gemüse einkaufen.

4 **Auf dem Marienplatz**
Der Marienplatz im Herzen Münchens ist ein Treffpunkt für Jung und Alt. Links ist die Mariensäule, im Hintergrund das Alte Rathaus mit dem Rathausturm.

Kapitel 7, 8, 9

Kapitel 7, 8 und 9 finden in München statt. Die Schüler in diesen Kapiteln gehen auf verschiedene Schulen. Flori besucht das Einstein-Gymnasium, Markus und Claudia gehen aufs Theodolinden-Gymnasium und Mara besucht die Rudolf-Diesel Realschule.

6 Mara, Flori, Markus und Claudia heißen euch in München willkommen.

Kapitel 7: Zu Hause helfen
Chapter Overview

| Los geht's!
pp. 190–192 | *Was musst du machen?* p. 190 |

	FUNCTIONS	GRAMMAR	VOCABULARY	RE-ENTRY
Erste Stufe pp. 193–197	• Extending and responding to an invitation, p. 194 • Expressing obligations, p. 194	• The verb **müssen**, p. 195 • The separable-prefix verb **abräumen**, p. 196	• Household chores, p. 193	• The verb **wollen**, p. 194 (**Kap. 6**) • Vocabulary for free-time activities, p. 195 (**Kap. 2** and **Kap. 6**) • Separable-prefix verbs, p. 196 (**Kap. 5**)
Zweite Stufe pp. 198–201	• Talking about how often you have to do things, p. 198 • Asking for and offering help and telling someone what to do, p. 199	• The verb **können**, p. 199 • The accusative pronouns, p. 200	• Words describing how often you have to do things, p. 198	• Time expressions, p. 198 (**Kap. 6**) • Vocabulary for free-time activities, p. 198 (**Kap. 2** and **Kap. 6**) • Vocabulary for school supplies, p. 201 (**Kap. 4**)
Dritte Stufe pp. 202–205	• Talking about the weather, p. 203	• Using **morgen** to refer to the future, p. 203	• Words to describe the weather, p. 202 • Months, p. 204	• Using numbers in a new context, temperature, p. 202 (**Kap. 1** and **Kap. 3**)

Aussprache p. 205	The short vowel **o**, the short vowel **u**, the letter **I**, the letter combination **th**, the letter combination **pf**: Audio CD 7, Track 11	**Diktat:** Audio CD 7, Tracks 11–13

Zum Lesen pp. 206–207	Wem hilfst du?	**Reading Strategy** Finding relationships between ideas

Mehr Grammatik-übungen	**pp. 208–211** **Erste Stufe**, pp. 208–209	**Zweite Stufe**, pp. 209–210	**Dritte Stufe**, p. 211

Review pp. 212–215	**Anwendung**, pp. 212–213	**Kann ich's wirklich?**, p. 214	**Wortschatz**, p. 215
	Zum Schreiben: Making a writing plan/Brainstorming (Writing a script for a TV show)		

CULTURE

- **Landeskunde: Was tust du für die Umwelt?** p. 197
- Weather map and weather report, p. 202
- **Ein wenig Landeskunde:** Weather in German-speaking countries, p. 204

Kapitel 7: Zu Hause helfen
Chapter Resources

 PRINT

Lesson Planning

 **One-Stop Planner**

Lesson Planner with Substitute Teacher Lesson Plans, pp. 32–36, 71

Student Make-Up Assignments
- Make-Up Assignment Copying Masters, Chapter 7

Listening and Speaking

TPR Storytelling Book, pp. 25–28

Listening Activities
- Student Response Forms for Listening Activities, pp. 51–53
- Additional Listening Activities 7-1 to 7-6, pp. 55–58
- Additional Listening Activities (songs), p. 54
- Scripts and Answers, pp. 136–140

Video Guide
- Teaching Suggestions, pp. 44–45
- Activity Masters, pp. 46–48
- Scripts and Answers, pp. 96–98, 114

Activities for Communication
- Communicative Activities, pp. 37–42
- Realia and Teaching Suggestions, pp. 98–101
- Situation Cards, pp. 135–136

Reading and Writing

Reading Strategies and Skills Handbook, Chapter 7

Lies mit mir! 1, Chapter 7

Übungsheft, pp. 73–84

Grammar

Grammatikheft, pp. 55–63

Grammar Tutor for Students of German, Chapter 7

Assessment

Testing Program
- Grammar and Vocabulary Quizzes, **Stufe** Quizzes, and Chapter Test, pp. 171–188
- Score Sheet, Scripts, and Answers, pp. 189–196

Alternative Assessment Guide
- Portfolio Assessment, p. 24
- Performance Assessment, p. 38
- CD-ROM Assessment, p. 52

Student Make-Up Assignments
- Alternative Quizzes, Chapter 7

 **MEDIA**

 Online Activities
- Interaktive Spiele
- Internet Aktivitäten

 Video Program
- Videocassette 3
- Videocassette 5 (captioned version)

 Audio Compact Discs
- Textbook Listening Activities, CD 7, Tracks 1–14
- Additional Listening Activities, CD 7, Tracks 21–26
- Assessment Items, CD 7, Tracks 15–20

 Interactive CD-ROM Tutor, Disc 2

 Teaching Transparencies
- Situations 7-1 to 7-2
- Vocabulary 7-A to 7-C
- **Los geht's!**
- **Mehr Grammatikübungen** Answers
- **Grammatikheft** Answers

 **One-Stop Planner CD-ROM**

Use the **One-Stop Planner CD-ROM with Test Generator** to aid in lesson planning and pacing.

For each chapter, the **One-Stop Planner** includes:
- Editable lesson plans with direct links to teaching resources
- Printable worksheets from resource books
- Direct launches to the HRW Internet activities
- Video and audio segments
- Test Generator
- Clip Art for vocabulary items

Kapitel 7: Zu Hause helfen

Projects ···········

Ein Wetterbericht

*In this activity, students will create a worldwide weather map. After completing the **Dritte Stufe** of this chapter, each student can be assigned a city in a different part of the world for which he or she will prepare an oral and written weather report.*

MATERIALS

✂ **Students may need**
- large pieces of light-colored construction paper, posterboard, or butcher paper
- markers

SUGGESTED CITIES

Berlin, Munich, Frankfurt, Vienna, Rome, Paris, Madrid, Moscow, Stockholm, New York City, Miami, Mexico City, Vancouver, Anchorage, Amsterdam, Athens, Auckland, Cairo, Dublin, Geneva, Hong Kong, London, Nairobi, Seoul, Toronto, Seattle, New Orleans, Beijing, Belgrade, Lima, New Dehli, Lagos, Istanbul

SUGGESTED SEQUENCE

1. Begin by asking several students to draw a large world map on construction paper.

2. Hang the completed map up on the wall.

3. Assign a city to each student and have the students label their cities on the map. Students should verify the location of the city in an atlas if necessary.

4. Have students check the weather section of a major newspaper for the weather conditions and forecasts of their assigned cities. Research can also be done online.

5. Have the class agree on symbols that reflect certain weather conditions. (Example: raindrops for rain)

6. Ask each student to prepare an oral and a written portion of the project. As the oral component, students should present the local weather conditions as a TV weather forecaster would do. Suggest that students begin their weather reports with **Guten Abend, liebe Zuschauer!** For a written exercise, students should write a complete weather report and forecast for their city.

Suggestion: Set a time limit of 1 to 2 minutes for the oral presentations.

GRADING THE PROJECT

Suggested point distribution (**total = 100 points**)
Oral presentation....................................50
Written report...50

COMMUNITY LINK

You might want to encourage your students to present their projects to geography classes in their school or other schools in the area.

Games ···········

Zeichenspiel

This game will help tactile learners review the vocabulary listed on p. 215.

Materials You will need small index cards with the vocabulary from this chapter (chores, weather, months), a timer or stopwatch, scorecard, pencils, and paper.

Procedure Divide the class into groups of four and have each group arrange their chairs together. Two students make up a team competing against the other two students in their group. Hand each group several index cards that must be turned face down. Partners take turns as "artists" and "guessers." The artists in each pair pick up the top card and look at the vocabulary item. All artists begin to draw when you give the signal. The guessers try to guess the word or phrase their partners are drawing as quickly as possible. The partner who guesses correctly first wins a point for the pair. If time runs out before the word is identified by the partner, no point is scored. Players take turns drawing and guessing.

Nenn die Hausarbeit!

This adaptation of a familiar party game is especially useful for helping kinesthetic learners review the vocabulary of household chores.

Materials You will need a set of index cards with a German phrase for a household chore written on each card. (Example: **den Tisch abräumen**)

Procedure Divide the class into two teams. Have a member of Team A come to the front of the class. Show that student a chore that you have written on an index card. This student must then try to act out the chore to his or her team in 30 seconds. Members of the student's team may only ask **ja/nein** questions as they try to guess the chore. If the team cannot guess the chore within the set time, no point is given. Then Team B sends a member to the front to act out the next chore. The team with the most points wins.

Storytelling ·····················

Mini-Geschichte

*This story accompanies Teaching Transparency 7-A. The **Mini-Geschichte** can be told and retold in different formats, acted out, written down, and read aloud to give students additional opportunities to practice all four skills.*

Richtig planen

Claudia sagt zu Flori: „Komm mit ins Kino!" Flori sagt: „Ich kann leider nicht. Ich muss Geschirr spülen. Danach muss ich mein Zimmer aufräumen, dann muss ich Staub saugen. Zuletzt muss ich noch den Müll sortieren." Claudia sagt: „Du planst nicht richtig! Ich mähe den Rasen am Montag. Am Dienstag räume ich meine Klamotten auf. Am Mittwoch putze ich die Fenster. Ich sortiere den Müll am Donnerstag und am Freitag gieße ich die Blumen." Flori sagt: „Prima Idee! So mach ich es auch. Ich komme mit ins Kino!"

Traditions ··························

Rezept

Der Bayerische Wurstsalat ist in ganz Deutschland bekannt und beliebt. Man findet hauseigene Variationen in fast allen bayrischen Wirtshäusern. Besonders beliebt ist der Wurstsalat auch bei Wanderern, die die deftige Mahlzeit gern auf einer Berghütte genießen.

Bayerischer Wurstsalat

Für 3 bis 4 Personen

Zutaten

g=Gramm, EL=Esslöffel

3	mittelgroße Möhren
300g	Fleischwurst
2-3	Zwiebeln
1	Gewürzgurke
1	großer Apfel
3EL	Essig
4EL	Öl
	Salz
	Pfeffer
1	Bund Schnittlauch

Zubereitung

Möhren putzen und in wenig Wasser 10 Minuten kochen. Inzwischen die Fleischwurst in 2 bis 3 cm lange Streifen oder Scheiben schneiden, die Zwiebeln pellen und in Ringe schneiden, die Gewürzgurke in dünne Streifen schneiden. Den Apfel schälen und vierteln, das Kerngehäuse herausschneiden. Die Apfelviertel in kleinere Stücke schneiden und mit den vorbereiteten Zutaten in eine Salatschüssel geben. Aus Essig, Öl, Salz und Pfeffer eine Salatsauce rühren und darüber gießen. Die gekochten Möhren grob würfeln und mit den anderen Zutaten unter die Apfelstücke mischen. Den Schnittlauch klein schneiden und vor dem Servieren über den Salat streuen.

Kapitel 7: Zu Hause helfen
Technology

Video

Videocassette 3, 5 (captioned version)
See Video Guide, pages 43–48

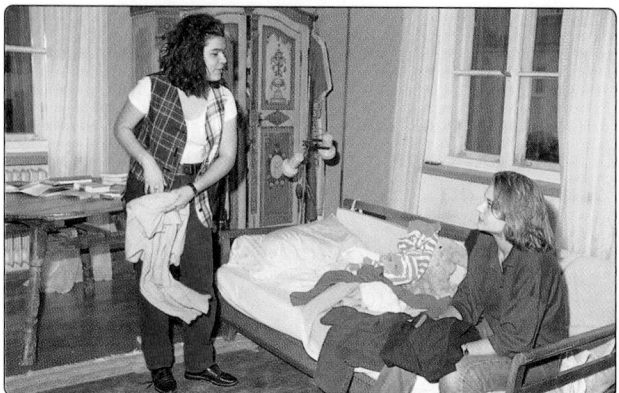

Los geht's! • Was musst du machen?

Mara, Flori, and Markus invite Claudia to go bike riding with them. Claudia declines their invitation because she has to do some chores at home. Her friends decide to help her with her chores. When they are finished they wonder where Micki the cat is.

Fortsetzung

Flori has found the cat and is feeding it in Claudia's kitchen when his mother calls to remind him that today is the day when he has to do chores around the house. All his friends decide to help Flori now. When they are done, Flori's mother sends them off to the park with a picnic basket full of goodies.

Landeskunde

Was tust du für die Umwelt?

People from different cities talk about what they and their communities do for the environment.

Videoclips

- **HK Selbstbausystem**® (do-it-yourself remodeling)
- **Der General**® (kitchen cleaner)
- **Dixan**® (laundry detergent)
- **AL-KO Ökostar**® (laundry detergent)

Interactive CD-ROM Tutor

The **Interactive CD-ROM Tutor** contains videos, interactive games, and activities that provide students an opportunity to practice and review the material covered in Chapter 7.

Activity	Activity Type	Pupil's Edition Reference
1. Wortschatz	Merkspiel	p. 193
2. Grammatik	Was fehlt?	p. 195
3. So sagt man das!	Was ist richtig?	pp. 194, 198, 199
4. Grammatik	Was fehlt?	pp. 199, 200
5. So sagt man das!	Wort und Bild Erfahren/Wählen	pp. 202, 203
6. So sagt man das!	Was kommt dann?	pp. 194, 198, 199, 203
Landeskunde	Was tust du für die Umwelt? Was ist richtig?	p. 197
Zum Sprechen	*Guided recording*	pp. 212–213
Zum Schreiben	*Guided writing*	pp. 212–213

Teacher Management System

Logging In

Logging in to the *Komm mit!* TMS is easy. Upon launching the program, simply type "admin" in the password area of the log-in screen and press RETURN. Log on to **www.hrw.com/CDROMTUTOR** for a detailed explanation of the Teacher Management System.

One-Stop Planner CD-ROM

To preview all resources available for this chapter, use the **One-Stop Planner CD-ROM**, Disc 2.

Internet Connection

internet

ADRESSE: go.hrw.com
KENNWORT:
WK3 MUENCHEN-7

*Have students explore the **go.hrw.com** Web site for many online resources covering all chapters. All Chapter 7 resources are available under the keyword **WK3 Muenchen-7**. Interactive games practice the material and provide students with immediate feedback. You will also find a printable worksheet that provides Internet activities that lead to a comprehensive online research project.*

Interaktive Spiele

You can use the interactive activities in this chapter

- to practice grammar, vocabulary, and chapter functions
- as homework
- as an assessment option
- as a self-test
- to prepare for the Chapter Test

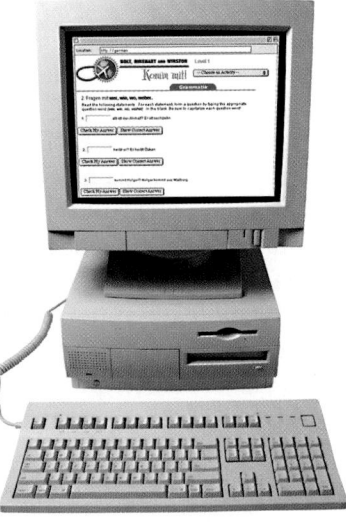

Internet Aktivitäten

Students will read the German weather forecast and visit pet stores and drugstores.

- To prepare students for the **Arbeitsblatt,** you might want to have them look closely at the weather map on p. 202 and review the **Wortschatz** on p. 202.

- After completing the **Arbeitsblatt,** have students convert the temperature they entered in Activity B from Celsius to Fahrenheit. (The formula for converting a Celsius temperature to Fahrenheit is $F = 9/5 \ C + 32$.) You might want to ask students to look at the thermometer on p. 204 and find the freezing and boiling points of water in both systems.

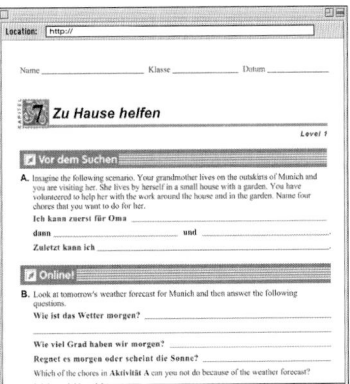

Webprojekt

Have students do a Web search for the weather forecast for any place in Austria or Switzerland. Have students report on the temperature, the amount of precipitation, and the hours of sunlight. Encourage students to exchange useful Web sites with their classmates. Have students document their sources by referencing the names and URLs of all the sites they consulted.

Kapitel 7: Zu Hause helfen
Textbook Listening Activities Scripts

Erste Stufe

7 p. 194

PETER — Du, Jürgen, der Kinofilm fängt um 15 Uhr an. Gehen wir jetzt!

JÜRGEN — Spitze! Du, aber bevor wir gehen, muss ich noch meine Hausarbeit machen.

PETER — Kann ich dir dabei helfen?

JÜRGEN — Prima! Danke. Zuerst muss ich die Wohnzimmerfenster putzen. Das geht ganz schnell.

PETER — Und jetzt?

JÜRGEN — Gehen wir in mein Zimmer! Ich muss noch meine Klamotten aufräumen.

PETER — Was noch?

JÜRGEN — Ja, … jetzt decken wir den Tisch fürs Abendbrot.

PETER — Wo sind denn die Teller?

JÜRGEN — Da oben im Schrank. Mensch, vielen Dank für deine Hilfe. Gehen wir!

PETER — Musst du später auch noch helfen?

JÜRGEN — Ja, normalerweise räum ich dann den Tisch auch abends ab. Und du?

PETER — Ja, ich helf auch oft zu Hause.

JÜRGEN — Nach dem Abendbrot muss ich dann das Geschirr spülen. Machst du das auch?

PETER — Nee, wir haben eine Geschirrspülmaschine. Gott sei Dank!

8 p. 194

1. — Hallo Mara! Wir wollen jetzt in die Eisdiele Rücker. Wir wollen mal wieder ein Eis essen gehen. Kommst du mit?

— Ja, gern doch! Ich hol schnell meine Tasche.

2. — Grüßt euch! Was habt ihr heute vor?

— Ja eigentlich wollen wir ins Kino. Der neue Film mit Kevin Costner spielt in der Holtenauerstraße. Möchtest du ihn auch sehen?

— Ja klar! Wann sollen wir uns denn treffen?

3. — Du, Claudia, ich brauche einen neuen Pulli für Monikas Fete am Samstag. Willst du mit ins Einkaufszentrum?

— Nee, kann leider nicht. Donnerstags helf ich immer meiner Oma zu Hause.

4. — Du, Robert, wir gehen jetzt Tennis spielen. Komm doch mit!

— Schade, ich kann nicht. Ich hab heute Nachmittag meine Klavierstunde.

— Na ja, vielleicht kannst du ja das nächste Mal mitspielen.

5. — He, willst du mit ins Café? Wir treffen da Lars und Frauke.

— Hm … ich weiß nicht. Ja doch! Ich muss nur später mit meiner Mutter einkaufen gehen.

Zweite Stufe

18 p. 199

Ja, also helfen muss ich ja schon zu Hause. Meine Schwester und ich teilen uns da halt die Arbeit. Am Samstag habe ich immer viel zu tun, denn da muss ich immer den Rasen mähen. Danach helf ich meinem Vater, das Auto waschen. Aber das macht eigentlich Spaß. Ja und dann muss ich auch noch den Müll sortieren. Das ist ja auch irgendwie wichtig, find ich. Na ja, Fenster putzen soll ich am Mittwoch, aber das tu ich manchmal auch am Donnerstag. Es kommt ganz darauf an. Und in der Küche helf ich nicht so gerne, meine Schwester räumt immer den Tisch ab, und ich spül dann das Geschirr. Das geht ja noch. Ja und mein Zimmer räum ich nicht so gern auf, aber meine Mutter besteht dadrauf. Also das mache ich ein- oder zweimal in der Woche.

Answers to Activity 18
Samstag: Rasen mähen, Auto waschen, Müll sortieren; Mittwoch/Donnerstag: Fenster putzen; immer: Geschirr spülen; ein- oder zweimal in der Woche: Zimmer aufräumen

One-Stop Planner CD-ROM

For resource information, see the **One-Stop Planner CD-ROM**, Disc 2.

Dritte Stufe

26   p. 203

1. — Und nun die Wettervorhersage für Donnerstag, den 6. Januar. Das Wetter ist unverändert schlecht. Es wird bewölkt sein mit zeitweisen Regenschauern und Temperaturen um 10 Grad.

2. — Und hier die weiteren Wetteraussichten. Heute sehr heiß und schwül. Die Höchsttemperaturen werden bei 38 Grad liegen.

3. — Und jetzt das Wetter für morgen, den 28. Dezember. Die Tieftemperaturen der Nacht bringen einen leichten Schneefall und kaum Änderungen im Wetter. Es bleibt weiterhin kalt. Wir erwarten sonniges Wetter mit leichtem Wind aus dem Südwesten.

4. — Und nun zum Wetter: sonnig und warm. Am Nachmittag teilweise bewölkt mit Temperaturen um 20 Grad.

AUSSPRACHE, p. 205

Diktat, p. 205

You will hear about the chores that Ulli and Peter have to do before they can go to the concert tonight. First listen to what is said, then write down the text you hear.

Ulli und Peter gehen heute Abend ins Rockkonzert. Zuerst müssen sie aber zu Hause etwas helfen. In der Küche gibt es viel zu tun. Ulli räumt den Tisch ab, und Peter spült das Geschirr auch gleich. Das Zimmer von Ulli ist wieder ziemlich schmutzig. Da hilft Peter schnell. Er räumt die Klamotten auf und macht das Bett. Zum Schluss saugt Ulli Staub im Haus, und der Peter sortiert den Müll. Jetzt ist es schon 19 Uhr, und das Konzert beginnt in einer Stunde.

Anwendung

1   p. 212

1. — Du, Silvia! Wir wollen ins Kino. Komm doch mit!

— Hm, ja gern. Was gibt's denn zu sehen?

— Den Film mit Wolf Schmidt, *Terror in den Alpen.*

2. — Sybille, kommst du mit zum Café Schulz, ein Eis essen?

— Schade, ich kann leider nicht. Ich muss Hausaufgaben machen. Ich hab zu viel zu tun. Und morgen hab ich auch noch Klavierstunde. Ich muss noch üben. Aber bestimmt das nächste Mal.

3. — Du, Claudia! Das Wetter ist toll. Gehen wir doch Tennis spielen!

— Nee, das geht nicht. Ich habe meiner Oma versprochen, den Rasen bei ihr zu mähen. Aber hab vielen Dank für die Einladung.

4. — Kommst du heute Abend zur Fete bei Markus? Das soll ganz stark werden. Mit gutem Essen und toller Musik.

— Ja, klar! Um 7 Uhr, ja? Was ziehst du denn dazu an?

— Nur Shorts und ein T-Shirt. Das ist schon fesch.

5. — Annette und ich wollen ins Einkaufszentrum gehen, weil ich eine neue Bluse für die Fete brauch. Willst du mitkommen?

— Ich brauch eigentlich ja auch neue Klamotten, aber heute kann ich wirklich nicht. Ich geh nämlich um 3 Uhr schwimmen.

Kapitel 7: Zu Hause helfen
Suggested Lesson Plans 50-Minute Schedule

Day 1

LOCATION OPENER 20 min.
- Present **Location Opener**, pp. 184–187
- Background Information, ATE, p. 183A
- Show **München** Video
- Do Viewing and Post-viewing Activities, Video Guide, p. 42
- Map Activities, ATE, p. 183A
- Photo Essay, ATE, p. 183B

CHAPTER OPENER 5 min.
- Thinking Critically, ATE, p. 187M

LOS GEHT'S! 20 min.
- Preteaching Vocabulary, ATE, p. 187N
- Play Audio CD for **Los geht's!**,
- Have students read **Los geht's!**, pp. 190–191
- Teaching Suggestions, Video Guide, p. 44
- Show **Los geht's!** Video
- Do Viewing and Post-viewing Activities, Video Guide, p. 46

Wrap-Up 5 min.
- Students respond to questions about the city of Munich

Homework Options
Übungsheft, p. 73, Act. 1
Pupil's Edition, p. 192, Comprehension Activities

Day 2

ERSTE STUFE
Quick Review 10 min.
- Check homework, Übungsheft, p. 73, Act. 1
- Bell Work, ATE, p. 187O

Wortschatz, p. 193 15 min.
- Presenting **Wortschatz**, ATE, p. 187O
- Teaching Transparencies 7-A, 7-B
- Do Activities 6 and 7, p. 193
- Play Circumlocution Game, ATE, p. 187X

So sagt man das!, p. 194 10 min.
- Presenting **So sagt man das!**, ATE, p. 187O
- Play Audio CD for Activity 8, p. 194

So sagt man das!, p. 194 10 min.
- Presenting **So sagt man das!**, ATE, p. 187O
- Do Activities 9, 10, and 11, p. 195

Wrap-Up 5 min.
- Students respond to questions about doing household chores

Homework Options
Grammatikheft, p. 55, Acts. 1–2
Übungsheft, p. 74, Acts. 2–3

Day 3

ERSTE STUFE
Quick Review 5 min.
- Check homework, Übungsheft, p. 74, Acts. 2–3

Grammatik, p. 195 25 min.
- Presenting **Grammatik**, ATE, p. 187O
- Teaching Transparency 7-1
- Do Activity 12, p. 195
- Do Activity 13, p. 196
- Do Acts. 3–4, p. 56, Grammatikheft
- Do Acts. 4–8, pp. 75–76, Übungsheft

Ein wenig Grammatik, p. 196 15 min.
- Presenting **Ein wenig Grammatik**, ATE, p. 187O
- Do Activities 14, 15, and 16, p. 196
- Do Acts. 5–6, p. 57, Grammatikheft

Wrap-Up 5 min.
- Students answer questions about what they do to help at home

Homework Options
Mehr Grammatikübungen, Erste Stufe

Day 4

ERSTE STUFE
Quick Review 10 min.
- Check homework, **Mehr Grammatikübungen, Erste Stufe**

Quiz Review 20 min.
- Do Additional Listening Activities 7-1 and 7-2, pp. 55–56
- Do Activities 1–2, Interactive CD-ROM

Quiz 20 min.
- Quiz 7-1A or 7-1B

Homework Options
Internet Aktivitäten, see ATE, p. 187F

Day 5

ZWEITE STUFE
Quick Review 10 min.
- Return and review Quiz 7-1
- Bell Work, ATE, p. 187Q

So sagt man das!/Wortschatz, p. 198 15 min.
- Presenting **So sagt man das!**, ATE, p. 187Q
- Presenting **Wortschatz**, ATE, p. 187Q
- Do Activity 17, p. 198
- Play Audio CD for Activity 18, p. 199

So sagt man das!/Ein wenig Grammatik, p. 199 20 min.
- Presenting **So sagt man das!**, ATE, p. 187R
- Present **Sprachtipp**, p. 199
- Presenting **Ein wenig Grammatik**, ATE, p. 187R
- Do Activity 19, p. 199
- Do Activity 20, p. 200

Wrap-Up 5 min.
- Students respond to questions about how often they do certain chores

Homework Options
Grammatikheft, pp. 58–59, Acts. 7–10
Übungsheft, p. 77, Acts. 9–11

Day 6

ZWEITE STUFE
Quick Review 10 min.
- Check homework, Grammatikheft, pp. 58–59, Acts. 7–10

Grammatik, p. 200 20 min.
- Presenting **Grammatik**, ATE, p. 187R
- Teaching Transparency 7-1
- Do Activities 21 and 22, p. 201
- Presenting **Und dann noch …**, ATE, p. 187S
- Do Additional Listening Activities 7-3 and 7-4, pp. 56–57

LANDESKUNDE 15 min.
- Pre-viewing Suggestion, Video Guide, p. 44
- Culture Note, ATE, p. 187P
- Show **Landeskunde** Video
- Do Activities A and B, p. 197

Wrap-Up 5 min.
- Students respond to questions about what they can do for others using the verb **können**

Homework Options
Pupil's Edition, p. 201, Acts. 23–24
Grammatikheft, p. 60, Acts. 11–12
Übungsheft, pp. 78–79, Acts. 12–14

One-Stop Planner CD-ROM

For alternative lesson plans by chapter section, to create your own customized plans, or to preview all resources available for this chapter, use the **One-Stop Planner CD-ROM**, Disc 2.

 For additional homework suggestions, see activities accompanied by this symbol throughout the chapter.

Day 7

ZWEITE STUFE

Quick Review 10 min.
- Check homework, Grammatikheft, p. 60, Acts. 11–12

Quiz Review 20 min.
- Do **Mehr Grammatikübungen, Zweite Stufe**
- **Interaktive Spiele**, see ATE, p. 187F

Quiz 20 min.
Quiz 7-2A or 7-2B

Homework Options
Activities for Communication, pp. 39–40, prepare Communicative Activity 7-2

Day 8

DRITTE STUFE

Quick Review 15 min.
- Return and review Quiz 7-2
- Bell Work, ATE, p. 187T
- Do Communicative Activity 7-2, pp. 39–40

Wortschatz, p. 202 15 min.
- Background Information, ATE, p. 187T
- Teaching Suggestion, ATE, p. 187U
- Language Note, ATE, p. 187U
- Do Activity 25, p. 202

So sagt man das!/Ein wenig Grammatik, p. 203 15 min.
- Presenting **So sagt man das!**, ATE, p. 187U
- Teaching Transparency 7-2
- Presenting **Ein wenig Grammatik**, ATE, p. 187U
- Play Audio CD for Activity 26, p. 203
- Do Activity 27, p. 203

Wrap-Up 5 min.
- Students respond to questions about weather during different seasons of the year

Homework Options
Grammatikheft, pp. 61–63, Acts. 13–18
Übungsheft, p. 80–82, Acts. 15–21; p. 84, Acts. 1–2

Day 9

DRITTE STUFE

Quick Review 10 min.
- Check homework, Grammatikheft, pp. 61–63, Acts. 13–18

Ein wenig Landeskunde/Wortschatz, p. 204 15 min.
- Present **Ein wenig Landeskunde**, p. 204
- Presenting **Wortschatz**, ATE, p. 187U
- Do Activity 28, p. 204
- Do Activities 29 and 30, p. 205

ZUM LESEN 20 min.
- Teaching Suggestion, ATE, p. 187V
- Present **Lesestrategie**, p. 206
- Do Activities 1–9, pp. 206–207

Wrap-Up 5 min.
- Students respond to questions about the weather during different months of the year

Homework Options
Pupil's Edition, p. 205, Act. 31
Mehr Grammatikübungen, Dritte Stufe

Day 10

DRITTE STUFE

Quick Review 10 min.
- Check homework, **Mehr Grammatikübungen, Dritte Stufe**

Quiz Review 20 min.
- Do Additional Listening Activities 7-5 and 7-6, pp. 57–58
- Play **Zeichenspiel**, ATE, p. 187C

Quiz 20 min.
- Quiz 7-3A or 7-3B

Homework Options
Interaktive Spiele, see ATE, p. 187F

Day 11

DRITTE STUFE

Quick Review 5 min.
- Return and review Quiz 7-3

Aussprache, p. 205 15 min.
- Do **Richtig aussprechen/Richtig lesen**, p. 205
- Do **Richtig schreiben/Diktat**, p. 205

ANWENDUNG 25 min.
- Teaching Suggestion, ATE, p. 187X
- Teaching Suggestions for **Fortsetzung** and **Videoclips** Videos, Video Guide, pp. 44–45
- Show **Fortsetzung** and **Videoclips** Videos
- Do **Anwendung** Activities, pp. 212–213

Wrap-Up 5 min.
- Students respond to **Kann ich's wirklich?** questions, p. 214

Homework Options
Pupil's Edition, p. 213, complete Act. 5, **Zum Schreiben**

Day 12

ANWENDUNG

Quick Review 15 min.
- Students present **Zum Schreiben** scripts

Kann ich's wirklich?, p. 214 15 min.
- Have students write answers to questions 1–10

Chapter Review 15 min.
- Review chapter functions, vocabulary, and grammar; choose from **Mehr Grammatikübungen**, Grammar Tutor for Students of German, Activities for Communication, Listening Activities, Interactive CD-ROM Tutor, or **Interaktive Spiele**

Wrap-Up 5 min.
- Students respond to questions about the day's weather

Homework Options
Study for Chapter Test

Assessment

Test, Chapter 7 45 min.
- Administer Chapter 7 Test. Select from Testing Program, Alternative Assessment Guide, or Test Generator

Kapitel 7: Zu Hause helfen
Suggested Lesson Plans 90-Minute Block Schedule

Block 1

LOCATION OPENER 30 min.
- **Present** Location Opener, pp. 184–187
- Background Information, ATE, p. 183A
- Show **München** Video
- Do Viewing and Post-viewing Activities, Video Guide, p. 42
- Map Activities, ATE, p. 183A
- Photo Essay, ATE, p. 183B
- Do **München** Activities, Interactive CD-ROM

CHAPTER OPENER 5 min.
- Thinking Critically, ATE, p. 187M

LOS GEHT'S! 20 min.
- Preteaching Vocabulary, ATE, p. 187N
- Play Audio CD for **Los geht's!**, pp. 190–191
- Have students read **Los geht's!**, pp. 190–191
- Teaching Suggestions, Video Guide, p. 44
- Show **Los geht's!** Video
- Do Comprehension Activities, p. 192

ERSTE STUFE
Wortschatz, p. 193 15 min.
- Presenting **Wortschatz**, ATE, p. 187O
- Teaching Transparencies 7-A, 7-B
- Do Activities 6 and 7, p. 193
- Play Circumlocution Game, ATE, p. 187X

So sagt man das!, p. 194 15 min.
- Presenting **So sagt man das!**, ATE, p. 187O
- Play Audio CD for Activity 8, p. 194

Wrap-Up 5 min.
- Students respond to questions about doing household chores

Homework Options
Grammatikheft, p. 55, Acts. 1–2
Übungsheft, pp. 73–74, Acts. 1–3

Block 2

ERSTE STUFE
Quick Review 10 min.
- Check homework, Übungsheft, pp. 73–74, Acts. 1–3

So sagt man das!, p. 194 10 min.
- Presenting **So sagt man das!**, ATE, p. 187O
- Do Activities 9, 10, and 11, p. 195

Grammatik, p. 195 15 min.
- Presenting **Grammatik**, ATE, p. 187O
- Teaching Transparency 7-1
- Do Activity 12, p. 195
- Do Activity 13, p. 196

Ein wenig Grammatik, p. 196 15 min.
- Presenting **Ein wenig Grammatik**, ATE, p. 187O
- Do Activities 14, 15, and 16, p. 196

Quiz Review 20 min.
- Do Activities 1–2, Interactive CD-ROM
- Do Acts. 3–6, pp. 56–57, Grammatikheft
- Do Acts. 4–8, pp. 75–76, Übungsheft
- Do **Mehr Grammatikübungen, Erste Stufe**

Quiz 20 min.
- Quiz 7-1A or 7-1B

Homework Options
Internet Aktivitäten, see ATE, p. 187F

Block 3

ERSTE STUFE
Quick Review 10 min.
- Return and review Quiz 6-1
- Bell Work, ATE, p. 187Q

LANDESKUNDE 15 min.
- Pre-viewing Suggestion, Video Guide, p. 44
- Culture Note, ATE, p. 187P
- Show **Landeskunde** Video
- Do Activities A and B, p. 197

ZWEITE STUFE
So sagt man das!/Wortschatz, p. 198 20 min.
- Presenting **So sagt man das!**, ATE, p. 187Q
- Presenting **Wortschatz**, ATE, p. 187Q
- Do Activity 17, p. 198
- Play Audio CD for Activity 18, p. 199

So sagt man das!/Ein wenig Grammatik, p. 199 25 min.
- Presenting **So sagt man das!**, ATE, p. 187R
- Present **Sprachtipp**, p. 199
- Presenting **Ein wenig Grammatik**, ATE, p. 187R
- Do Activity 19, p. 199
- Do Activity 20, p. 200

Grammatik, p. 200 15 min.
- Presenting **Grammatik**, ATE, p. 187R
- Teaching Transparency 7-1
- Do Activities 21 and 22, p. 201
- Presenting **Und dann noch …**, ATE, p. 187S

Wrap-Up 5 min.
- Students respond to questions about what they can do for others using the verb **können**

Homework Options
Pupil's Edition, p. 201, Acts. 23–24
Grammatikheft, pp. 58–60, Acts. 7–12
Übungsheft, pp. 77–79, Acts. 9–14

One-Stop Planner CD-ROM

For alternative lesson plans by chapter section, to create your own customized plans, or to preview all resources available for this chapter, use the **One-Stop Planner CD-ROM**, Disc 2.

 For additional homework suggestions, see activities accompanied by this symbol throughout the chapter.

Block 4

ZWEITE STUFE
Quick Review 20 min.
- Check homework, Grammatikheft, pp. 58–60, Acts. 7–12
- Do **Minigeschichte, Zweite Stufe,** TPR Storytelling Book, p. 26

Quiz Review 25 min.
- Do Additional Listening Activities 7-3 and 7-4, pp. 56–57
- Do **Mehr Grammatikübungen, Zweite Stufe**

Quiz 20 min.
- Quiz 7-2A or 7-2B

DRITTE STUFE
Wortschatz, p. 202 20 min.
- Background Information, ATE, p. 187T
- Teaching Suggestion, ATE, p. 187U
- Language Note, ATE, p. 187U
- Do Activity 25, p. 202

Wrap-Up 5 min.
- Students respond to questions about weather during different seasons of the year

Homework Options
Activities for Communication, pp. 39–40, prepare Communicative Activity 7-2

Block 5

DRITTE STUFE
Quick Review 15 min.
- Return and review Quiz 7-2
- Bell Work, ATE, p. 187T
- Do Communicative Activity 7-2, pp. 39–40

So sagt man das!/Ein wenig Grammatik, p. 203 15 min.
- Presenting **So sagt man das!,** ATE, p. 187U
- Teaching Transparency 7-2
- Presenting **Ein wenig Grammatik,** ATE, p. 187U
- Play Audio CD for Activity 26, p. 203
- Do Activity 27, p. 203

Ein wenig Landeskunde/Wortschatz, p. 204 15 min.
- Present **Ein wenig Landeskunde,** p. 204
- Presenting **Wortschatz,** ATE, p. 187U
- Do Activity 28, p. 204
- Do Activities 29 and 30, p. 205
- Do Activities 17–18, Grammatikheft

Aussprache, p. 205 15 min.
- Do **Richtig aussprechen/Richtig lesen,** p. 205
- Do **Richtig schreiben/Diktat,** p. 205

ZUM LESEN 25 min.
- Teaching Suggestion, ATE, p. 187V
- Present **Lesestrategie,** p. 206
- Do Activities 1–9, pp. 206–207

Wrap-Up 5 min.
- Students respond to questions about the weather during different months of the year

Homework Options
Pupil's Edition, p. 205, Act. 31
Grammatikheft, pp. 61–62, Acts. 13–16
Übungsheft, p. 80–82, Acts. 15–21; p. 84, Acts. 1–2

Block 6

DRITTE STUFE
Quick Review 15 min.
- Check homework, Grammatikheft, pp. 61–62, Acts. 13–16

Quiz Review 20 min.
- Do **Mehr Grammatikübungen, Dritte Stufe**
- Play **Zeichenspiel,** ATE, p. 187C

Quiz 20 min.
- Quiz 7-3A or 7-3B

ANWENDUNG 30 min.
- Teaching Suggestion, ATE, p. 187X
- Teaching Suggestions for **Fortsetzung** and **Videoclips** Videos, Video Guide, pp. 44–45
- Show **Fortsetzung** and **Videoclips** Videos
- Do **Anwendung** Activities, pp. 212–213

Wrap-Up 5 min.
- Students respond to **Kann ich's wirklich?** questions, p. 214

Homework Options
- Pupil's Edition, p. 213, complete Act. 5, **Zum Schreiben**
- **Interaktive Spiele,** see ATE, p. 187F

Block 7

ANWENDUNG
Quick Review 15 min.
- Return and review Quiz 7-3
- Students read **Zum Schreiben** scripts

Kann ich's wirklich?, p. 214 15 min.
- Students write out answers to questions 1–10

Chapter Review 15 min.
- Review chapter functions, vocabulary, and grammar; choose from **Mehr Grammatikübungen,** Grammar Tutor for Students of German, Activities for Communication, Listening Activities, Interactive CD-ROM Tutor, or **Interaktive Spiele**
- Review test format and provide sample test items for students

Test, Chapter 7 45 min.
- Administer Chapter 7 Test. Select from Testing Program, Alternative Assessment Guide or Test Generator

Kapitel 7: Zu Hause helfen
Teaching Suggestions, *pages 188-215*

PAGES 188–189

CHAPTER OPENER

Pacing Tips

In the **Erste Stufe** the modal verb **müssen** is introduced alongside chore vocabulary and the function of 'expressing obligations.' The modal verb **wollen** is reused for the function of 'extending and responding to an invitation.' Another modal verb, **können**, is presented in the **Zweite Stufe**. The function of 'asking for and offering help and telling someone what to do' utilizes the accusative pronouns, which occur on p. 200. The **Dritte Stufe** centers around talking about the weather in German-speaking countries, with weather-related vocabulary and the months of the year. You might want to spend about the same amount of time teaching each **Stufe**. For Lesson Plans and timing suggestions, see pages 187I–187L.

Meeting the Standards

Communication
• Extending and responding to an invitation, p. 194
• Expressing obligations, p. 194
• Talking about how often you have to do things, p. 198
• Asking for and offering help and telling someone what to do, p. 199
• Talking about the weather, p. 203

Cultures
• **Landeskunde**, p. 197
• **Ein wenig Landeskunde**, p. 204
• Language Note, p. 187P
• Culture Note, p. 187P
• Background Information, p. 187T

Connections
• Teaching Suggestion, p. 187N
• Language Note, p. 187N
• Math Connection, p. 187U
• Language Note, p. 187U
• Thinking Critically, p. 187U
• Thinking Critically, p. 187W
• Culture Note, p. 187W

Comparisons
• Thinking Critically, p. 187M
• Teacher Note, p. 187M
• Multicultural Connection, p. 187P
• Language-to-Language, p. 187R
• Multicultural Connection, p. 187S

For resource information, see the **One-Stop Planner CD-ROM**, Disc 2.

• Language Note, p. 187V
• Thinking Critically, p. 187W

Communities
• Career Path, p. 187P
• Culture Note, p. 187W

Connections and Comparisons

Thinking Critically
Comparing and Contrasting Begin by asking students what kinds of chores the girl still needs to do in her room. (make bed, pick up books, put up clothes) Then have students tell you what kinds of chores they most often have to do in their own rooms.

Teacher Note
You might want to point out to students that in Germany, cannister-type vacuum cleaners are more common than upright vacuum cleaners.

Building on Previous Skills
Ask students to name and describe in German all the objects they recognize in the room, using vocabulary from previous chapters. (Examples: clothing, furniture)

Chapter Sequence

Los geht's! . . . . .p. 190
Erste Stufe . . . . .p. 193
Landeskunde . . . . .p. 197
Zweite Stufe . . . . .p. 198
Dritte Stufe . . . . .p. 202
Zum Lesen . . . . .p. 206
Mehr Grammatikübungen . . . . .p. 208
Anwendung . . . . .p. 212
Kann ich's wirklich? . . . . .p. 214
Wortschatz . . . . .p. 215

LOS GEHT'S!

Teaching Resources
pp. 190–192

PRINT
▸ Lesson Planner, p. 32
▸ Video Guide, pp. 43–44, 46
▸ Übungsheft, p. 73

MEDIA
▸ One-Stop Planner
▸ Video Program
  Los geht's!
  Videocassette 3, 05:45–08:34
  Videocassette 5 (captioned version),
  35:10–37:37
  Fortsetzung
  Videocassette 3, 08:36–12:38
  Videocassette 5 (captioned version),
  37:39–42:03
▸ Audio Compact Discs, CD7, Trs. 1–2
▸ **Los geht's!** Transparencies

PAGES 190–191

 Los geht's! Transparencies

Preteaching Vocabulary

Recognizing Cognates

Los geht's! contains several words that students will be able to recognize as cognates. Have students find these cognates, then have them guess what is happening in the story.

❶ in den Englischen Garten, zu Hause helfen, Wetter, musst, sortieren

❷ Ein Moment!, eine Idee

❺ die Sonne scheint, die Katze

❻ ins Haus

Fortsetzung

You may choose to continue with the **Fortsetzung** of *Was musst du machen?* now or wait until later in the chapter. For a synopsis of the **Los geht's!** and **Fortsetzung** episodes, see p. 187E.

Advance Organizer

As an advance organizer for the storyline of **Los geht's!**, ask students how they help out around the house. Do they have any chores they have to do today?

Building on Previous Skills

Ask students to scan each picture and name the items they have learned in preceding units. (Examples: clothing items, furniture) Ask students to try to come up with at least two familiar words per picture.

Connections and Comparisons

Teaching Suggestion

Point out the word **radeln** in the first picture and ask if students know the meaning of that verb. Tell them to use the pictures as a clue.

Language Note

The word **radeln** is a dialect form for **Rad fahren** commonly used in southern Germany.

PAGE 192

Using the Captioned Video

 As an alternative to reading the conversations in the book, you might want to show the captioned version of *Was musst du machen?* available on Videocassette 5.

Comprehension Check

Teaching Suggestion

❶ Ask students to work in pairs as they answer Questions 1–5 in writing. Once the students have finished, go over their responses in class.

Visual Learners

❷ Write the four phrases on the board and ask students to write the phrases they think belong underneath.

A Slower Pace

❺ Begin by asking students to read the sentences quietly and to number them. Then have pairs of students read the sentences to each other, practicing pronunciation and intonation. Have a few volunteers read the whole sequence.

ERSTE STUFE

Teaching Resources
pp. 193–197

PRINT
- Lesson Planner, p. 33
- TPR Storytelling Book, pp. 25, 28
- Listening Activities, pp. 51, 55–56
- Activities for Communication, pp. 37–38, 98, 101, 135–136
- Grammatikheft, pp. 55–57
- Grammar Tutor for Students of German, Chapter 7
- Übungsheft, pp. 74–76
- Testing Program, pp. 171–174
- Alternative Assessment Guide, p. 38
- Student Make-Up Assignments, Chapter 7

MEDIA
- One-Stop Planner
- Audio Compact Discs, CD7, Trs. 3–4, 15, 21–22
- Teaching Transparencies
  Situation 7-1
  Vocabulary 7-A
  Mehr Grammatikübungen Answers
  Grammatikheft Answers
- Interactive CD-ROM Tutor, Disc 2

PAGE 193

Bell Work
Have students list at least three activities in German that they would like to do with a friend.

Thinking Critically

Drawing Inferences Ask students why the definite article in several picture captions is **den**. What can they infer about the noun in the phrase? (masculine)

PRESENTING: Wortschatz

Divide your class into two teams, and give six volunteers from each team a card with a particular chore written on it. Have the volunteers come to the front of the class and either act out the task in question or draw a picture of it on the board. The first team that can name the chore in a complete sentence (**Ich muss das Geschirr spülen.**) wins a point. The team with the most points at the end of the game wins. You may want to use **Hausaufgaben machen** as a tie breaker.

PAGE 194

PRESENTING: So sagt man das!

Ask students if they can think of ways to extend an invitation to an event such as a concert using previously learned vocabulary. (Examples: **möchte,** time expressions) Can they think of ways to respond to an invitation? Make a list as students name expressions such as **Nein, danke! Ja, gern!** or **Ja, bitte!** Then, go over the new expressions introduced in **So sagt man das!**

PRESENTING: So sagt man das!

As you introduce the expressions in the second function box, have your students come up with variations on the example presented here, such as **Ich muss zuerst den Tisch abräumen** or **Ich muss Schulsachen kaufen.** Then, go around the room, asking students if they want to do something they really don't enjoy doing. (Example: **Willst du das Geschirr spülen?**) They should respond by telling you about their prior obligations.

PAGE 195

PRESENTING: Grammatik

Modals Before introducing the verb **müssen,** ask students about the function of modal auxiliaries. Which one have they learned so far? (**wollen**)

Communication for All Students

Challenge
12 Ask four students to each describe one of the chores in the pictures.

PAGE 196

PRESENTING: Ein wenig Grammatik

Separable-prefix verbs After reading the grammar note with the class, give students some statements and questions containing separable-prefix verbs. (Example: **Räumst du dein Zimmer auf?**) Students should respond using one of the modals learned so far: **möchten, wollen,** or **müssen.** (Example: **Ja, ich muss mein Zimmer aufräumen.**)

Language Note

Here are some German **Sprichwörter** that are appropriate for this **Stufe.**

- **Erst die Arbeit, dann das Vergnügen!** (*First work, then play!*)

- **Ohne Fleiß, kein Preis!** (*No pain, no gain!*)

> PAGE 197

LANDESKUNDE

Teaching Resources
p. 197

PRINT
▶ Video Guide, pp. 43–44, 46–47
▶ Übungsheft, p. 84

MEDIA
▶ One-Stop Planner
▶ Video Program
  Videocassette 3, 13:16–19:49
▶ Audio Compact Discs, CD7, Trs. 5–8
▶ Interactive CD-ROM Tutor, Disc 2

Teaching Suggestions

- You might want to introduce the following phrases to help students better understand the video segment or listening script.

  streng einhalten *to adhere to*
  den Müll vermeiden *to avoid generating trash*
  wiederverwerten *to recycle*
  die Mehrwegflasche *recyclable glass bottle*
  das Putzmittel *cleaning solution*

- After students have read the introductory paragraph above the pictures, ask them to close their books. While students watch the video segment or listen to the recording, ask them to take notes of the expressions or phrases they are able to understand from each of the three interviews. Play the interviews several times. Then divide the board into three sections with the name of one of the three German teenagers written on the top of each section. Ask students to tell you the expressions they were able to understand and write them in each column. Then read the three interviews in the book and have students compare the phrases on the board with the actual readings.

STANDARDS: 2.2, 4.2

Culture Note

In Germany, almost all glass bottles are returned to stores for deposit. They are called **Pfandflaschen,** and consumers get a deposit refund. To reduce excessive packaging, consumers also have the right to refuse the packaging materials of purchased items at the check-out. The retailers must accept it and either reuse the packing or sort it for recycling.

Career Path

Ask your students to brainstorm careers in international environmental organizations or aid agencies that would require a knowledge of German. (Suggestions: Imagine you are an employee of USAID stationed in a German-speaking country; imagine you are an environmental engineer studying in Germany.)

Connections and Comparisons

Multicultural Connection

If possible, have students find information about other countries and how they deal with environmental issues such as the protection of water and soil, as well as the reduction of garbage, noise, and air pollution.

(TPR) Total Physical Response

Ask all students to stand. Direct commands to individual students, asking them to perform imaginary chores around the classroom. Once the student has correctly completed the chore, he or she may be seated. Give commands such as **Gieß die Blumen!** or **Mach das Bett!**

Assess

▶ Testing Program, pp. 171–174
  Quiz 7-2A, Quiz 7-2B
  Audio CD7, Tr. 15

▶ Student Make-Up Assignments, Chapter 7, Alternative Quiz

▶ Alternative Assessment Guide, p. 38

ERSTE STUFE

KAPITEL 7   ERSTE STUFE   **187P**

ZWEITE STUFE

Teaching Resources
pp. 198–201

PRINT

- Lesson Planner, p. 34
- TPR Storytelling Book, pp. 26, 28
- Listening Activities, pp. 52, 56–57
- Activities for Communication, pp. 39–40, 99, 101, 135–136
- Grammatikheft, pp. 58–60
- Grammar Tutor for Students of German, Chapter 7
- Übungsheft, pp. 77–79
- Testing Program, pp. 175–178
- Alternative Assessment Guide, p. 38
- Student Make-Up Assignments, Chapter 7

MEDIA

- One-Stop Planner
- Audio Compact Discs, CD7, Trs. 9, 16, 23–24
- Teaching Transparencies
  Situation 7-1
  Vocabulary 7-B
  Mehr Grammatikübungen Answers
  Grammatikheft Answers
- Interactive CD-ROM Tutor, Disc 2

PAGE 198

Bell Work

In pairs, have students interview each other about house chores they do after school. Have them make a list of the each others' chores with times (**Wann …**) and frequency (**Wie oft …**).

Game

Play the game **Nenn die Hausarbeit!** See p. 187D for the procedure.

Communication for All Students

Kinesthetic Learners

Before introducing the expressions in **So sagt man das!**, give a series of rapid commands that you have prepared ahead of time. Students are to carry out any command that applies to them. (Example: **Wenn du am Montag Müll sortierst, steh auf!**) To extend this activity and introduce **einmal, zweimal,** and so on, model the action first and then ask students to follow your command. (Example: **Schreib deinen Namen zweimal auf das Papier! Dreh dich einmal um!**)

PRESENTING: **So sagt man das!**

Have students make a chart showing how many times they do certain chores in one month; one week. Then ask questions using the vocabulary the students learned in the **Erste Stufe.** (Example: **Wer spült oft das Geschirr?**)

PRESENTING: **Wortschatz**

Prepare a transparency of a calendar page showing all the activities in which a German teenager might engage in a month's time. Then ask individual students or the class as a whole **Wie oft … ?** questions related to the activities shown. For further practice, you may want to go around the room asking students **Was machst du in deiner Freizeit?** and then following up on their responses with questions, such as **Und wie oft (spielst) du (Tennis)?**

Teaching Suggestion

17 After having done this activity orally in class, you can assign it as homework and ask students to come up with a minimum of ten written sentences.

PAGE 199

Teaching Suggestion

18 Provide each student with a blank copy of a page from a German calendar.

PRESENTING: So sagt man das!

Ask students how they would offer somebody help in English and how they would express their willingness to help. Make a list of the expressions students come up with. After introducing the German expressions, ask the class to compare the two.

PRESENTING: Ein wenig Grammatik

Können On the board or on a transparency, write out six sentences that are identical except for changes in the subject. (Example: **Ich/du/er/sie/wir/ihr/ sie/Sie _____ die Katze füttern.**) Fill in the blanks in these sentences by reviewing with students the forms of **wollen** and **müssen**. Then introduce the modal **können**, letting students know it is a cognate and asking them if they can infer its meaning. Using the same sentences as above, introduce the forms of **können**.

Group Work

19 Have students work in groups of three and write appropriate exchanges for the pictures. Set a time limit for this activity. When students have finished, call on several groups to read their conversations to the class.

Speaking Assessment

19 As an alternative to having students read their dialogues to the class, you may choose to ask groups to come to your desk and evaluate their spoken conversation using the following rubric.

Speaking Rubric	Points			
	4	3	2	1
Content (Complete – Incomplete)				
Comprehension (Total – Little)				
Comprehensibility (Comprehensible – Incomprehensible)				
Accuracy (Accurate – Seldom accurate)				
Fluency (Fluent – Not fluent)				

18–20: A   16–17: B   14–15: C   12–13: D   Under 12: F

> **PAGE 200**

Teaching Suggestion

20 Ask students to look at the title of this activity, **Peter macht ein Geschäft.** What do they think this conversation might be about? Put students in groups of three. Have the groups read the conversation aloud with a lot of expression. After they have practiced, have one or two groups read for the class.

Building on Previous Skills

20 After students have answered Questions 1-3, have them recall the accusative pronouns they have already learned. Provide sentences on a transparency in which students must replace the direct object with an accusative pronoun. Examples: **Ich sauge für meine Mutter Staub. (sie); Sie kauft ein Buch für Michael. (ihn); Angela und Hermann besuchen Markus und Detlev. (sie)** Then proceed with Questions 4-6.

PRESENTING: Grammatik

The accusative pronouns Review the accusative pronouns introduced in **Kapitel 5** (**ihn, sie, es**) by using them in sentences written on the board. Have students provide additional sentences orally. Next, introduce the four new accusative pronouns by using them in similar sentences written on the board. Help students infer the meaning of the new pronouns through demonstration and context. (Example: **Hier ist dein Kuli. Der Kuli ist für dich.**)

Connections and Comparisons

Language-to-Language

Explain to your students that English, French, and Spanish all have accusative pronouns just as German does. Before introducing these in German, give an example in English and have the class brainstorm the rest of the accusative pronouns. Once you have a thorough list, ask your students if they can explain the use and function of the accusative case.
Example:
I see **him**:   Ich sehe **ihn**.
                Je **le** vois.
                (Yo) **lo** veo.

ZWEITE STUFE

Communication for All Students

For Additional Practice

21 Ask students to think of additional items that could be purchased at the **Schreibwarenladen** and create additional exchanges.

Group Work

22 This activity could be performed as a skit. Ask students to work in groups of three to prepare an outline for their skit. Encourage students to use props. They should bring these items the day you plan for them to act out their skit. If possible videotape the groups' performances.

PRESENTING: Und dann noch …

Teach the pet vocabulary by holding up pictures (use children's books for pictures). Progress from **ja/nein** to either/or and finally to short-answer questions. (Examples: **Ist das ein Vogel? Ist das eine Maus? Ist das ein Vogel oder eine Maus?**)

Teaching Suggestion

Animals make different sounds all over the world. The German dog, for example, says **wau, wau,** the bird says **piep, piep,** the rooster says **kikeriki,** and the frog says **quak.** Ask students to give examples of animal sounds they learned when they were younger.

Connections and Comparisons

Multicultural Connection

Have students ask friends from other countries about the sounds that animals make. You could also ask other foreign language teachers to help with the list. Then compare all the different sounds an animal can make around the world.

Reteaching: Accusative pronouns

To prepare for this activity, make sentence strips which include a direct object that can be replaced by an accusative pronoun. (Examples: **Daniel kauft ein Buch für Brigitte. Hier ist die Pizza für Jens und dich.**) Make one envelope per student and number each envelope. Each student receives a numbered envelope and begins by putting the sentence strips in the correct order. Then the student must rewrite the sentence on a sheet of paper, replacing the direct object with the appropriate accusative pronoun. When students have finished with their sentences, they put the strips back in the envelope and pass it to the next person. Remind students to number each sentence with the number that appears on the envelope. Have the sentences written on a transparency so that students can check their work at the end of this activity.

Teacher to Teacher

Lilo Townsend
Notre Dame High School
Batavia, New York

Lilo suggests the following activity for the Zweite Stufe.

❝After students are familiar with the phrase **Kann ich etwas für dich tun?**, I work on making them familiar with the formal form: **Kann ich etwas für Sie tun?** Students ask me **Kann ich etwas für Sie tun?** and I have a list of classroom chores ready for them, such as a) **Du kannst das Datum für mich an die Tafel schreiben.** b) **Du kannst für mich das Wetter an die Tafel schreiben (z.B. Es ist kalt und sonnig heute.)** c) **Du kannst die Tür aufmachen** or **zumachen.** d) **Du kannst die Schüler für mich zählen.** The students answer with **Gut! Mach' ich!** and then do the task.❞

Total Physical Response

Ask each student to perform a chore in the classroom before allowing him or her to leave the classroom. (Example: **John, kannst du für mich bitte das Fenster zumachen? Robin, kannst du für mich die Tafel sauber machen? Sylvia, kannst du für mich die Bücher einsammeln?**)

Teaching Suggestions

Have students conduct a survey addressing the functions introduced in the **Zweite Stufe.** Have them ask questions related to chores around the house. (Examples: **Musst du ein Haustier füttern? Wie oft musst du Staub saugen? Was machst du nicht gern zu Hause? Wann mähst du den Rasen?**)

Assess

▸ Testing Program, pp. 175–178
   Quiz 7-2A, Quiz 7-2B
   Audio CD7, Tr. 16

▸ Student Make-Up Assignments,
   Chapter 7, Alternative Quiz

▸ Alternative Assessment Guide, p. 38

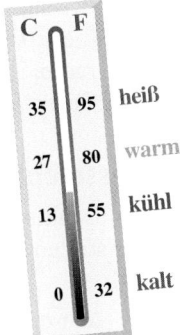

DRITTE STUFE

Teaching Resources
pp. 202–205

PRINT
▸ Lesson Planner, p. 35
▸ TPR Storytelling Book, pp. 27, 28
▸ Listening Activities, pp. 53, 57–58
▸ Activities for Communication, pp. 41–42, 100, 101, 135–136
▸ Grammatikheft, pp. 61–63
▸ Grammar Tutor for Students of German, Chapter 7
▸ Übungsheft, pp. 80–82
▸ Testing Program, pp. 179–182
▸ Alternative Assessment Guide, p. 38
▸ Student Make-Up Assignments, Chapter 7

MEDIA
▸ One-Stop Planner
▸ Audio Compact Discs, CD7, Trs. 10–13, 17, 25–26
▸ Teaching Transparencies
   Situation 7-2
   Vocabulary 7-C
   Mehr Grammatikübungen Answers
   Grammatikheft Answers
▸ Interactive CD-ROM Tutor, Disc 2

PAGE 202

Bell Work

Ask students in English about their favorite time of the year. What is the weather like during that time? What is their least favorite season and why? Have them think about the ways in which weather influences their activities.

Cultures and Communities

Background Information

The German physicist G.D. Fahrenheit (1686–1736) invented the Fahrenheit measurement of temperature, which is used in the United States and in England. The other measurement, Celsius, is named after the Swedish astronomer and physicist Anders Celsius (1701–1744) and is used in most European countries.

Connections and Comparisons

Math Connection

Give students examples of temperatures reported from around the country. You could make a transparency from the weather report in a local newspaper. Ask students to convert Fahrenheit degrees into Celsius. (To convert Fahrenheit to Celsius, subtract 32, multiply by 5, and divide by 9. To convert Celsius into Fahrenheit, multiply by 9, divide by 5, and add 32.)

Language Note

The German language has several proverbs related to weather. Here are some examples you can share with your class:

- **Wenn der Hahn kräht auf dem Mist, ändert sich das Wetter, oder es bleibt wie es ist!** *When the rooster crows on the dunghill, the weather changes, or it stays the same!*

- **Der April macht die Blumen, und der Mai hat den Dank dafür.** *April showers bring May flowers.*

Thinking Critically

Comparing and Contrasting Ask students if they know of any English proverbs, sayings, or expressions about the weather. (Example: *It's raining cats and dogs.*)

Additional Weather Vocabulary

You may want to give your students some additional weather vocabulary: **das Barometer; das Hoch; das Tief; das Thermometer; die Luftmasse** *(air mass);* **die Kaltfront/Warmfront; Wetter in Übersee; zeitweise** *(occasionally);* **wechselhaft** *(changing);* **unbeständig** *(unstable)*

PAGE 203

PRESENTING: **So sagt man das!**

Teach the weather expressions using gestures (Examples: shivering, fanning), or simple drawings or photos. Describe the weather in such places as Alaska and Hawaii, or make general statements about typical weather during the four seasons.

PRESENTING: **Ein wenig Grammatik**

Time expressions Ask students to name other time expressions they have learned that could refer to the near future. (Example: **am Montag, am Wochenende, im Frühling**)

Communication for All Students

For Additional Practice

Have the class keep a local weather chart for a week, with one person in charge of recording the weather conditions each day. After the data has been recorded each day, ask the students about the weather.

PAGE 204

PRESENTING: **Wortschatz**

To teach this vocabulary in context, ask students such questions as: **Wann ist Frühling?, St. Patrickstag?, Vatertag?, Muttertag?, Valentinstag?, Kolumbustag?**

Group Work

28 Ask students to work with a partner to put the sentences in order, and then practice reading the dialogue together. Monitor students' activity and make suggestions if necessary.

PAGE 205

Teaching Suggestion

29 Have students write the report as if they were going to read it over the radio. Suggest that students begin their reports with **Guten Abend, liebe Zuhörer!**

Portfolio Assessment

29 You might want to use this activity as an oral portfolio item for your students. See *Alternative Assessment Guide,* p. 24.

Connections and Comparisons

Language Note

Many northern Germans pronounce the letter combination **pf** as a simple **f.** For example, they pronounce the words **Pflaume** and **Pforte** as "flaume" and "forte."

Teaching Suggestion

After students have written the sentences of the **Diktat,** ask them to exchange their papers with other students. Put up the script on the overhead projector, one sentence at a time. Have individual students read the sentences aloud and check the paper in front of them for errors. They should mark the errors and make corrections if necessary.

Take a soft, light ball and throw it to a student who must then say the first word of a series determined by you. For example, if the series is **Monate,** the student says **Januar.** He or she then throws the ball to another student who must say the next word in that series, **Februar.** For an added twist, have any student who drops the ball stand up and repeat all the words that have been said up to that point. This is a great way to review seasons, months, numbers, or days of the week.

Von der Schule zum Beruf

You may want to tape the weather segment of a **Deutsche Welle** news report and show to students before assigning this activity.

PRESENTING: Aussprache

To help students hear the difference between short and long **o,** contrast the sounds by using the word pair: **Sohn/Sonne.** To help students hear the difference between long and short **u,** contrast the sounds by using the word pair: **Du/dumm.** You might also want to point out to students that the letter combination **th** in German is always pronounced like the letter **t.**

ZUM LESEN

Prereading
Building Context

Go around the classroom and ask students whom they have helped this past week and in what way.

Making Connections

Ask students what *conjunction* means (joining together), and how this part of speech can be used in a sentence. Can they give examples? Do students know what the word *subordinate* means? (not equal; a part that cannot stand by itself and depends on the rest of the sentence)

Teacher Note

Activities 1–2 are prereading tasks.

Reading
Skimming/Scanning

• Ask students to compare the written bold print of the three surveys. Do they notice anything? (repeated questions)

• Ask students to scan for expressions they recognize that refer to chores.

Thinking Critically

Observing Have students look at the title of the article and the questions that are listed with the title. Can they point out the yes/no questions and also the questions that require a short answer? Ask students to make a list of the verbs in the questions. (**helfen, verdienen, anbieten, haben, sich umhören**)

Teaching Suggestions

• As students orally list questions for Activity 4, write the interrogative pronouns they use on the board.

• Before reading Heiko's interview, you may want to introduce this additional vocabulary: **schimpfen** *to scold;* **aufdringlich** *pushy;* **Last abnehmen** *to remove a burden.*

Connections and Comparisons

Thinking Critically

Analyzing Ask students if they can understand from his last statement why Heiko likes to help others. What words were clues that helped them find the answer?

Culture Note

Sven talks about giving **Nachhilfestunden.** Tutorials are often advertised on the bulletin board (**Anschlagbrett, schwarzes Brett, Pinnwand**) in the school lobby, on which students are allowed to put up notes. If a school has its own paper, **Nachhilfestunden** ads are also printed there.

Communication for All Students

Challenge

Ask students to write an ad advertising their offer to tutor in their best subject(s). They should list the subjects they can tutor, their hourly rate, and how they can be contacted. Students can also refer to the **Zum Lesen** section of Chapter 4 for examples.

Post-Reading
Teacher Note

Activities 8 and 9 are post-reading tasks that will show whether students can apply what they have learned.

 Portfolio Assessment

9 You might want to suggest this activity as a written portfolio item for your students. See *Alternative Assessment Guide,* p. 24.

Connections and Comparisons

Thinking Critically

Comparing and Contrasting Ask students to work with a partner and go back over the three surveys. Have them make a list of all the chores that Heiko, Sven, and Tina mentioned. Then have students number each chore by order of importance. Do American students seem to have attitudes toward helping similar to their German counterparts?

Cultures and Communities

 Culture Note

Being an *au pair* is a very popular way for German students to study a foreign language after graduating from school. Being an *au pair* usually requires doing chores at the house in which you stay. Popular countries for *au pairs* are the United States, England, France, and Monaco.

Answers to Activity 7
a. Heiko: mother; housework
   Tina: family and friends; caring for children, helping sister with homework, housework
   Sven: friends; helping with schoolwork
b. when he spends a long period of time not helping; yes; because of the phrase **sie haben Recht;** it's an important thing to do.
c. helping her sister with her homework; day care center; to help others
d. He's good at these subjects; all nice people

▶ *PAGES 208–211*

MEHR GRAMMATIKÜBUNGEN

The **Mehr Grammatikübungen** activities are designed as supplemental activities for the grammatical concepts presented in the chapter. You might use them as additional practice, for review, or for assessment.

For more grammar presentations, review, and practice, refer to the following:
• Grammatikheft
• Grammar Tutor for Students of German
• Grammar Summary on pp. R15–R25
• Übungsheft
• Grammar and Vocabulary quizzes (Testing Program)
• Test Generator
• Interactive CD-ROM Tutor
• **Interaktive Spiele** at **go.hrw.com**

ANWENDUNG

 Video Wrap-up

Videocassette 3, 05:45–24:00
Videocassette 5 (captioned version), 35:10–42:03
At this time, you might want to use the video resources for additional review and enrichment. See *Video Guide* for suggestions regarding:

- the **Los geht's!** episode
- the **Landeskunde** interviews
- the **Fortsetzung** episode
- the **Videoclips.**

Apply and Assess

Teaching Suggestion

1 As an advance organizer to the listening activity, ask students to list expressions they have learned for accepting and declining invitations. Tell them to listen for these in the activity.

Process Writing

5 You may want to guide your students through this writing activity by writing the following chart on the board as an example for them to follow:

Was?	Wann?	Wie oft?	bei schlechtem Wetter
Fußball spielen	im Mai	zweimal	Basketball spielen

If necessary, expand the activity to include German Club events held earlier in the year.

KANN ICH'S WIRKLICH?

This page is intended to prepare students for the test. It is a brief checklist of the major points covered in the chapter. The students should be reminded that it is a checklist only and not necessarily everything that will appear on the test.

For additional self check options, refer students to the *Grammar Tutor*, the *Interactive CD-ROM Tutor*, and the Online self-test for this chapter

WORTSCHATZ

Review and Assess

Game

Play the game **Zeichenspiel** to review the Chapter 7 vocabulary. See p. 187C for the procedure.

Circumlocution

Have your students utilize their circumlocution skills to describe the items one uses when doing household chores. Bring in pictures of objects related to this vocabulary, such as a vacuum cleaner, a garbage can, or a lawn mower. Split the class into groups and divide the pictures among them. Then allow them time to brainstorm German words they can use to describe the physical appearance and function of each item, and play **Das treffende Wort suchen.** For **Staubsauger,** one might say: **Er ist groß und laut. Er macht das Zimmer sauber.**

Teaching Suggestion

Create scrambled versions of the vocabulary to be reviewed. For example, you could make a list of scrambled words using weather expressions or months. Each student gets a copy of the list and students then try to unscramble all the words. (Example: NESNO → SONNE)

Teacher Note

Give the **Kapitel 7** Chapter Test: *Testing Program,* pp. 183–188
Audio CD 7, Trs. 18–20.

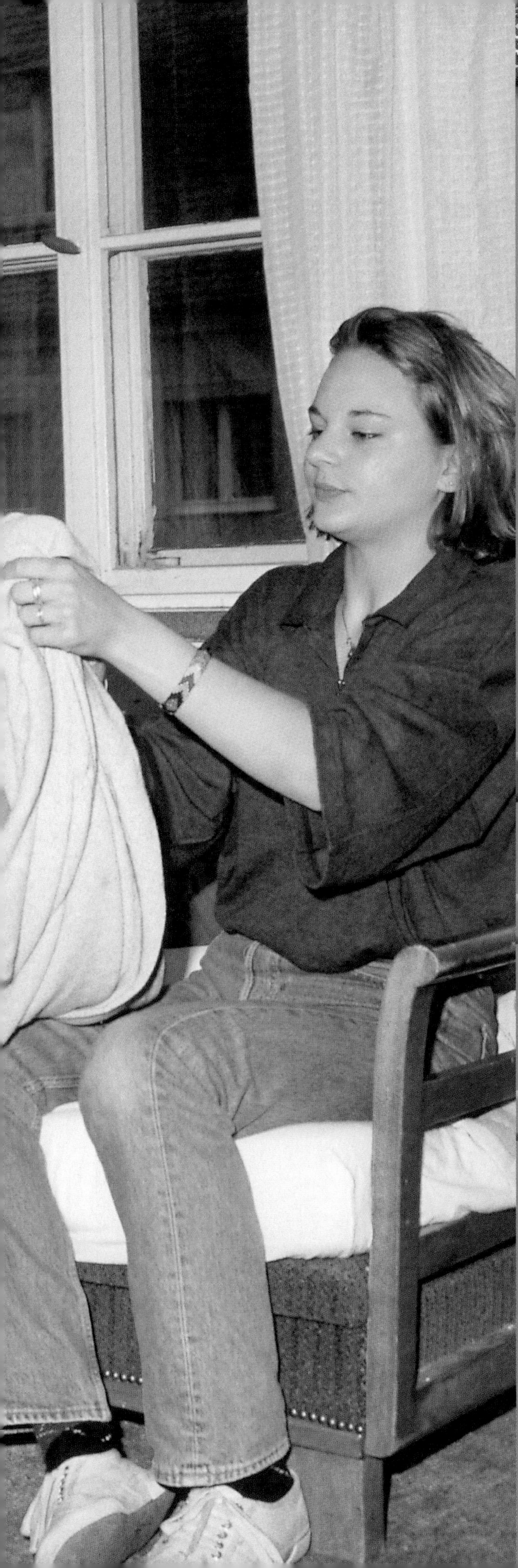

7

Zu Hause helfen

Objectives

In this chapter you will learn to

Erste Stufe

- extend and respond to an invitation
- express obligations

Zweite Stufe

- talk about how often you have to do things
- ask for and offer help and tell someone what to do

Dritte Stufe

- talk about the weather

 internet

 ADRESSE: go.hrw.com
KENNWORT:
  WK3 MUENCHEN-7

◀ **Mara hilft beim Aufräumen.**

Los geht's! · *Was musst du machen?*

Strategie Verstehen

Look at the images for this story. Who are these students? What are they doing? Where and when do you think these scenes are taking place? What clues tell you this?

CD 7 Trs. 1–2

Claudia **Flori** **Markus** **Mara**

Los geht's! is an abridged version of the video episode.

1

Mara: Claudia, hallo!

Claudia: Wohin geht's?

Mara: In den Englischen Garten. Komm doch mit!

Claudia: Das geht heute nicht. Ich muss zu Hause helfen.

Flori: Schade, dass du nicht mitkommen kannst! Es ist heute so schönes Wetter zum Radeln.

Markus: Was musst du denn tun, Claudia?

Claudia: Ich muss mein Zimmer aufräumen, Müll sortieren, das …

Flori: Einen Moment! Ich hab eine Idee. Fahren wir alle zur Claudia und helfen ihr.

Mara: Prima Idee! — Ja, dann ist sie schnell fertig und kann mitkommen.

Claudia: Das ist lieb von euch.

Bei Claudia

2

Claudia: Markus, du und der Flori, ihr könnt den Müll sortieren. Die Flaschen kommen hier rein, die Dosen kommen da rein.

Markus: Und die Zeitungen?

Claudia: Die Zeitungen kommen in den Korb da.

Miau!

3

Mara: Deine Klamotten musst
du selber aufräumen.
Claudia: Mach ich schon! —
Willst du für mich
Staub saugen?
Mara: Das muss ich auch immer
zu Hause machen.

4

Flori: So, wir sind fertig!
Mara: Wir auch.
Markus: Also, gehen wir! Die Sonne scheint noch
immer.
Claudia: Ich muss nur noch die Katze füttern.

Flori: Wer weiß denn, wie morgen das Wetter wird?
Mara: Morgen regnet es.
Flori: Ach, Quatsch! Es bleibt schön.
Mara: Was sagt denn der Wetterbericht?
Markus: Ich weiß nicht. Der stimmt aber sowieso nie!

5

Claudia: Micki! Micki! Wo bist du?
Flori: Ist die Katze schon wieder weg?
Claudia: Ja. Und sie muss ins Haus!
Markus: Also los, Kinder! Wir müssen die Katze suchen.

Übungsheft, S. 73

1 Was passiert hier?

These activities check for global comprehension only. Students should not yet be expected to produce language modeled in **Los geht's!**

Do you understand what is happening in **Los geht's!**? Check your comprehension by answering these questions. Don't be afraid to guess.

1. Where do Claudia's three friends (Mara, Markus, and Flori) invite Claudia to go?
2. Does Claudia go along? Why or why not?
3. What does Flori suggest?
4. What are some things the friends do at Claudia's house?
5. Is the weather good enough for an outing in the park? What about tomorrow's weather?
6. At the end of the story, there is still a problem. What is it?

1. in den Englischen Garten
2. No, she has chores at home.
3. that they all help her
4. clean her room, sort garbage for recycling, vacuum
5. Yes, but it might rain tomorrow.
6. They have to search for Claudia's cat.

2 Genauer lesen

Reread the conversations. Which words or phrases do the characters use to

1. invite someone
Komm doch mit!

2. express obligation
wir müssen, ich muss

3. name chores
zu Hause helfen:
das Zimmer aufräumen,
den Müll sortieren, die
Klamotten aufräumen, Staub saugen.

4. describe the weather
Die Sonne scheint.
Es bleibt schön.
Morgen regnet es.

3 Was ist richtig?

Was ist die beste Antwort, a., b. oder c.?

1. Claudia muss ═══. b
   a. in den Englischen Garten gehen   b. zu Hause helfen   c. radeln
2. Claudias Freunde wollen helfen. Das findet Claudia ═══. c
   a. furchtbar   b. nicht schlecht   c. lieb
3. Mara will ═══. c
   a. die Katze füttern   b. den Müll sortieren   c. Claudias Klamotten nicht aufräumen
4. Die Katze ist ═══. b
   a. schon im Haus   b. nicht zu Hause   c. im Englischen Garten

4 Was passt zusammen?

Match each statement or question on the left with an appropriate response on the right.

1. Wohin geht's? c
2. Komm doch mit! a
3. Was musst du tun? d
4. Du kannst den Müll sortieren. b
5. Was sagt der Wetterbericht? f
6. Ist die Katze wieder weg? e

a. Das geht nicht.
b. Gut! Mach ich!
c. In den Englischen Garten.
d. Ich muss zu Hause helfen.
e. Ja. Wir müssen sie suchen.
f. Morgen regnet es.

5 Nacherzählen

Put the sentences in a logical order to make a brief summary of **Los geht's!**.

1. Mara, Markus und Flori wollen in den Englischen Garten gehen.

Dann wollen sie gehen, aber Micki ist weg.
5

Sie müssen zuerst die Katze suchen.
6

Sie müssen den Müll sortieren, das Zimmer aufräumen, Staub saugen und die Katze füttern.
4

Aber Claudia kommt nicht mit, denn sie muss zu Hause helfen.
2

Claudias Freunde wollen helfen.
3

Erste Stufe

Objectives Extending and responding to an invitation; expressing obligations

WK3 MUENCHEN-7

Wortschatz

Was musst du zu Hause tun? — Ich muss ...

7–A, 7–B

CD-ROM DISC 2

mein Zimmer aufräumen

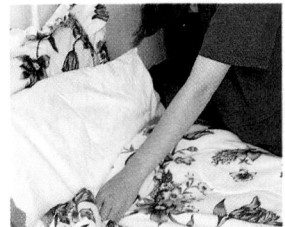

das Bett machen

meine Klamotten aufräumen

die Katze füttern

den Tisch decken

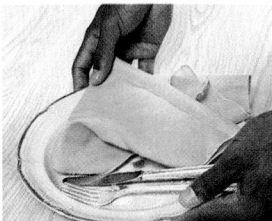

den Tisch abräumen

das Geschirr spülen

die Blumen gießen

den Müll sortieren

den Rasen mähen

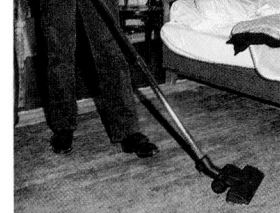

Staub saugen

die Fenster putzen

Übungsheft, S. 74, Ü. 2–3   Grammatikheft, S. 55, Ü. 1–2

---

6 **Was muss Claudia tun?**  p. 187X

Schreiben Claudia muss eine Liste machen und alles aufschreiben, was sie zu Hause tun muss. Du kannst ihr dabei helfen: Schreib das passende Verb hinter jeden nummerierten Ausdruck.

spülen	füttern	aufräumen
machen		mähen
decken	gießen	sortieren

1. das Zimmer
2. das Bett
3. den Rasen
4. die Katze

5. den Tisch
6. das Geschirr
7. den Müll
8. die Blumen

1. aufräumen
2. machen
3. mähen
4. füttern

5. decken
6. spülen
7. sortieren
8. gießen

7 **Was kommt zuerst?** Script on p. 187G

Zuhören Jürgen has a few chores to do before he and Peter can go to the movies. Listen to their conversation and put the illustrations below in the correct order. b e a c d

CD 7 Tr. 3

a.   b.   c.   d.   e.

So sagt man das!

Extending and responding to an invitation

In **Kapitel 6** you learned to make plans. How would you invite someone to come along with you?

You might ask:

> **Willst du in den Englischen Garten?** *or*
> **Wir wollen in den Englischen Garten. Komm doch mit!** *or* **Möchtest du mitkommen?**

Your friend might accept: Or decline:

> **Ja, gern!** *or*
> **Toll! Ich komme gern mit.**

> **Das geht nicht.** *or*
> **Ich kann leider nicht.**

8 **Kommst du oder kommst du nicht?** Script on p. 187G

Zuhören Listen to the following conversations and decide if the person being invited is accepting or declining the invitation. What is each person being invited to do? 1. **ein Eis essen** - accepts
2. **ins Kino** - accepts
3. **ins Einkaufszentrum** - declines
4. **Tennis spielen** - declines
5. **ins Café** - accepts

CD 7 Tr. 4

So sagt man das!

Expressing obligations

If you decline an invitation, you might want to explain your prior obligations.

You might say:

> **Ich habe keine Zeit. Ich muss zu Hause helfen.**

Your friend might ask: You might respond:

> **Was musst du denn tun?**   **Ich muss den Rasen mähen.**

What do you think the phrase **keine Zeit** means?[1]

---

1. *no time*

9 Kommst du mit?

Sprechen Du lädst deine Freunde zu verschiedenen Aktivitäten ein. Was sagen die Freunde, die mitgehen, und was sagen die Freunde, die nicht mitgehen können?

> ins Kino gehen
>
> in ein Konzert gehen
>
> Tennis spielen
>
> ein Eis essen
>
> in die Disko gehen
>
> schwimmen gehen

10 Was ist los?

Sprechen Der kleine Junge tut etwas, was er nicht tun soll! Was sagst du zu ihm? **(Du musst ...)**

Answers may vary. Examples: **Du musst**

a.
die Blumen gießen!

b.
die Katze füttern!

c.
den Rasen mähen!

d.
den Tisch decken!

e.
das Bett machen!

11 Ich muss zu Hause ...

Schreiben/Sprechen Mach eine Liste und schreib darauf alles, was du zu Hause machen musst. Frag danach deine Klassenkameraden, was sie zu Hause tun müssen, und berichte, was du tun musst.

Grammatik

The verb müssen

7–1 CD-ROM DISC 2

The verb **müssen** expresses obligation and means that you *have to* or *must* do something. Here are the forms of **müssen**:

ich	muss	wir	müssen
du	musst	ihr	müsst
er, sie, es	muss	sie, Sie	müssen

Müssen is usually used with a second verb (an infinitive), although the second verb can be omitted if the meaning is obvious. Ich **muss** nicht (**helfen**).

Mehr Grammatikübungen, S. 208, Ü. 1–2

Übungsheft, S. 75–76, Ü. 4–8

Grammatikheft, S. 56, Ü. 3–4

12 Grammatik im Kontext

Sprechen/Schreiben Einige Klassenkameraden sind zu Thomas gekommen, um ihm zu helfen. Was muss jeder tun? Was sagt Thomas? Schreibe die Sätze zu Ende.

1. Zuerst muss ich ...
mein Zimmer/meine Klamotten aufräumen.

2. Mara und ich, wir ...
müssen den Müll sortieren.

3. Du ...
musst Staub saugen.

4. Und die Nikki ...
muss die Fenster putzen.

ERSTE STUFE

STANDARDS: 1.1, 4.1, 5.1

hundertfünfundneunzig **195**

13 **Grammatik im Kontext**

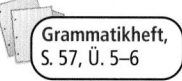 **Sprechen/Schreiben** Nimm die Liste von Übung 11 zur Hand und such dir einen Partner. Frag ihn, was er zu Hause tun muss und schreib es auf. Danach fragt dein Partner dich und schreibt auf, was du tun musst. Tauscht (*exchange*) dann eure Listen. Stimmt alles?

Ein wenig Grammatik

Schon bekannt

In **Kapitel 5** you learned the separable prefix verbs **anziehen**, **anprobieren**, and **aussehen**. Note that **aufräumen**, **abräumen**, and **mitkommen** are also verbs with separable prefixes. Compare the sentences below:

> **Ich räume den Tisch ab.**
> **Ich muss den Tisch abräumen.**

In the first sentence, the prefix **ab** is in last position. Now look at the second sentence. As with other verbs, when a separable prefix is used with a modal, like **müssen**, the conjugated form is in second position, and the second verb is in infinitive form in final position.

Grammatikheft, S. 57, Ü. 5–6

Mehr Grammatikübungen, S. 208–209, Ü. 3–4 →

---

14 **Und meine Familie ...**

Sprechen Wer muss in deiner Familie zu Hause helfen? Wer muss was tun? Sag das deinen Klassenkameraden.

15 **Grammatik im Kontext**

 a. **Schreiben** Was möchtest du heute Nachmittag tun und wann? Mach eine Liste.

 b. **Sprechen** Frag dann deine Partnerin, ob sie mitkommen möchte. Sie akzeptiert oder sagt dir, warum sie nicht mitgehen kann. Tauscht dann die Rollen. Schreibt danach auf eine Liste, was ihr zusammen tun möchtet und teilt das euren Klassenkameraden mit.

---

16 **Ein Brief**

a. **Lesen/Sprechen** Lies Markus' Brief an Roland. Beantworte dann die Fragen.

  1. Wer kommt am Wochenende nach München?

      a. 1. **Roland**

  2. Was wollen Markus und Flori am Freitag machen?

      2. **ins Konzert**

  3. Was muss Markus am Samstag machen?

  4. Gefällt es Markus, dass er zu Hause helfen muss? Woher weißt du das?

b. **Schreiben** Schreib Markus einen Brief und lade ihn für das Wochenende ein. Schreib ihm, was du für ihn planst. Schreib ihm auch, dass du dieses Wochenende zu Hause helfen musst. Du hoffst, dass ihr trotzdem viel Zeit für eure Pläne habt.

    3. zu Hause helfen: den Rasen mähen, sein Zimmer aufräumen, die Blumen gießen, Staub saugen
    4. Nein, er sagt: „Das ist zu viel" und „Wie blöd!".

---

4. März 2001

Lieber Roland!

Mensch, das freut mich, dass du am Wochenende hier in München bist!

Flori und ich wollen am Freitag ins Konzert. Die „Jungen Katzen" spielen! Toll, nicht! Willst du auch mitkommen?

Am Samstag muss ich wie immer zu Hause helfen. Wie blöd! Ich muss den Rasen mähen, mein Zimmer aufräumen, die Blumen gießen und auch Staub saugen. Ach, das ist zu viel, nicht? Musst du auch zu Hause so viel tun?

Na ja, macht nichts. Am Sonntag hab ich frei. Du, Flori und ich machen alles, was wir wollen.

Bis dann!
Dein Markus

Was tust du für die Umwelt?

CD 7 Trs. 5–8

In both the old and new states, Germans today are very aware of the need to protect the environment. Young people all over Germany are involved in projects that range from recycling to cleaning up rivers and forests. We asked several students what they do for the environment, and here is what they told us.

CD 7 Tr. 5

Marga, Bietigheim

„Also bei uns zu Hause wird jeder Müll sortiert, eben in Plastik, Aluminium, Papier und so weiter. Das halten wir also ziemlich streng ein. Ja, und wenn schönes Wetter ist und es sich vermeiden lässt, mit dem Auto zu fahren, nehme ich lieber das Fahrrad."

CD 7 Tr. 6

Fabian, Hamburg

„Wir tun für die Umwelt, dass wir einmal Müll vermeiden, dass wir unser Altpapier wegbringen, Glas sammeln und möglichst auch Glas, was wiederverwertet werden kann, kaufen, also sprich Mehrwegflaschen, und dass wir halt möglichst wenig Putzmittel oder so sparsam brauchen." CD 7 Tr. 7

Elke, Berlin

„Ich habe mit meinen Eltern angefangen, Flaschen zu sortieren und regelmäßig zum Container zu bringen. Der Müll wird meistens auch separat sortiert und dann, ja, einzeln weggebracht. Jetzt zähl ich dazu, dass man mit dem Bus zur Schule fährt und nicht mit dem Auto.

CD 7 Tr. 8

A. 1. Write the names of the students interviewed, and beside each name, write what that student does for the environment. What things do they have in common?

2. Think about what you have learned about Germany. Do you think the environmental concerns of the Germans are the same as those of Americans? Why or why not?

3. Compare what you and your friends do for the environment with what these German students do. Is there anything you do that was not mentioned in these interviews?

B. a. Discuss with your classmates what you think the biggest environmental concerns in Germany and in the United States are.

b. Write in German your answer to the question **Was tust du für die Umwelt?**

STANDARDS: 1.2, 2.2, 3.2, 4.2

Zweite Stufe

Objectives Talking about how often you have to do things; asking for and offering help and telling someone what to do

WK3 MUENCHEN-7

So sagt man das!

Talking about how often you have to do things

You might want to ask a friend how often he or she has to do certain things, such as chores.

You might ask:

Wie oft musst du Staub saugen?
Und wie oft musst du den Tisch decken?
Und wie oft musst du den Rasen mähen?

Your friend might respond:

Einmal in der Woche.
Jeden Tag.
Ungefähr zweimal im Monat.

Look at the words **einmal** and **zweimal**. What words do you recognize within each of these words?[1] What do you think the phrases **einmal in der Woche** and **zweimal im Monat** mean?[2] How would you say "three times a week"?[3] "Four times a month"?[4] What does the expression **jeden Tag** mean?[5] (*Hint: Look at the chore the speaker above does* **jeden Tag**. *How often would you do that task?*)

Übungsheft, S. 77, Ü. 9–10

Wortschatz

Wie oft ... ?

einmal, zweimal, dreimal
...in der Woche
...im Monat

    immer *always*   **oft** *often*   **manchmal** *sometimes*   **nie** *never*

 Grammatikheft, S. 58, Ü. 7–8

17 **Grammatik im Kontext**   Example: Im Herbst spiele ich einmal in der Woche Fußball.

Sprechen/Schreiben Wie viele Sätze kannst du bauen? Wann und wie oft machst du das alles?

Im Herbst			Karten
Im Frühling			Gitarre
Im Winter	spiele	(ein)mal in der Woche	Klavier
Im Sommer	spüle	(zwei)mal im Monat	Geschirr
Am Montag	putze	nie	die Fenster
Am Wochenende	gehe	ich oft	ins Konzert
Nach der Schule	decke	manchmal	den Tisch
Am Nachmittag	räume...auf	immer	Fußball
Am Abend			Basketball
			in eine Disko
			mein Zimmer

---

1. ein(s), zwei **2.** *once a week, twice a month* **3. dreimal in der Woche** **4. viermal im Monat**
5. *every day*

18 Wie oft tut Markus das? Script and answers on p. 187G

CD 7 Tr. 9

Zuhören Listen as Markus describes when and how often he does things. First make a calendar page for one month and then fill in a possible schedule for his activities.

 SPRACHTIPP

Often, other elements besides the subject are placed at the beginning of a sentence to give them special emphasis. For example, if someone asks you: **Kannst du heute Volleyball spielen?**, you might respond: **Nein, heute muss ich zu Hause helfen, aber morgen kann ich sicher spielen.** The time expressions are placed first, because time is the most important issue in this conversation. By putting something other than the subject in first position, you not only add variety to your conversations, but also express yourself more exactly.

So sagt man das!

Asking for and offering help and telling someone what to do

 CD-ROM DISC 2

If your friend has a lot to do, you might offer to help. Then he or she could explain what to do.

You might ask:

Was kann ich für dich tun? *or*
Kann ich etwas für dich tun?

Your friend might answer:

Ja, du kannst den Müll sortieren. *or*
Willst du für mich Staub saugen?

You agree:

Gut! Mach ich!

What are the English equivalents of the phrases **für dich** and **für mich**?[1]

Ein wenig Grammatik

The words **kann** and **kannst** are forms of the verb **können**, a modal auxiliary verb. **Kann** is a cognate. What does it mean?[2] Here are the forms of **können**:

ich	kann	wir	können
du	kannst	ihr	könnt
er, sie, es	kann	sie, Sie	können

Übungsheft, S. 77, Ü. 11

Grammatikheft, S. 59, Ü. 9–10

Mehr Grammatikübungen, S. 209, Ü. 5–7

19 Grammatik im Kontext

Schreiben Deine Freunde wollen dir zu Hause helfen. Schreib Gespräche, die zu den Zeichnungen *(sketches)* passen.

BEISPIEL Können wir etwas für dich tun? Ja, ihr könnt den Rasen mähen. Danke!

Kann ich etwas für dich tun? Ja, du kannst den Tisch abräumen.
Können wir etwas für dich tun? Ja, ihr könnt die Blumen gießen.
Können wir etwas für dich tun? Ja, ihr könnt den Müll sortieren.

---

1. *for me/for you;* **2.** *can*

20 **Peter macht ein Geschäft**

Lesen/Sprechen Katrin und ihr Bruder Peter haben am Wochenende viel zu tun. Lies die folgenden Gespräche und beantworte die Fragen.

KATRIN Ach, ich hab heute viel zu tun. He, du Peter! Kannst du etwas für mich tun?

PETER Vielleicht.

KATRIN Kannst du die Blumen gießen?

PETER Ja, gern. Was kann ich noch für dich tun?

KATRIN Müll sortieren?

PETER Okay, aber das kostet drei Euro. Danke!

Ayla und Mario kommen vorbei.

MARIO Na, Katrin und Peter, was macht ihr? Können wir etwas für euch tun?

PETER Sicher! Ihr könnt für uns die Blumen gießen und dann den Müll sortieren. Geht das?

MARIO Klar. Wir helfen gern!

1. Katrin; Katrin and Peter

1. Compare the following sentences from the conversations above: **Was kann ich noch für dich tun?** and **Können wir etwas für euch tun?** To whom do the pronouns **dich** and **euch** refer in the conversations?

2. Now compare these sentences: **Kannst du etwas für mich tun?** and **Du kannst für uns die Blumen gießen.** To whom do the pronouns **mich** and **uns** refer? 2. Katrin; Katrin and Peter

3. Which of these pronouns are used for talking to others? Which ones are used to talk about yourself? 3. dich, euch; mich, uns

4. What is the English equivalent for each of these pronouns? 4. you, you, me, us

Grammatik

The accusative pronouns

7–1

CD-ROM
DISC 2

In **Kapitel 5** you learned the accusative forms of the third person pronouns **er**, **sie**, **es**, and **sie** (pl). They are **ihn**, **sie**, **es**, and **sie**. The first and second person pronouns are in boldface in the summary chart below.

Person	Nominative	Accusative	Nominative	Accusative
	Singular		Plural	
First	ich	**mich**	wir	**uns**
Second	du	**dich**	ihr	**euch**
Third	er	ihn		
	sie	sie	sie	sie
	es	es		
Formal	Sie	**Sie**	Sie	**Sie**

Mehr Grammatikübungen
S. 210, Ü. 8–9

The accusative forms are used as direct objects, as in **Ich besuche dich morgen,** or as objects of prepositions such as **für,** as in **Du kannst für mich den Müll sortieren.** To ask for whom someone is doing something, use **für wen: Für wen machst du das?**

Übungsheft,
S. 78–79, Ü. 12–14

Grammatikheft,
S. 60, Ü. 11–12

21 Grammatik im Kontext

Sprechen/Schreiben Mara is going to the **Schreibwarenladen** to buy a few things for herself. Before she leaves she asks some friends if she can buy anything for them. Create an exchange for each picture, telling what Mara would ask, and how the person or people pictured would respond.

BEISPIEL MARA **Kann ich etwas für dich kaufen?**
MARKUS **Ja, bitte. Du kannst für mich einen Bleistift kaufen.**

1.
für euch/für uns ein Heft kaufen

2.
für dich/für mich einen Kuli kaufen

3.
für euch/für uns ein Wörterbuch kaufen

4.
für dich/für mich eine Kassette kaufen

22 Zu Hause helfen

Schreiben/Sprechen Two of your friends are coming over to help you with your chores so that you can go swimming together. Before they arrive, make a list of six chores you have to do today. Then, with your partners, develop a conversation in which your friends offer to help and you discuss together who will do each of the chores. Be creative!

23 Arbeit suchen

Schreiben Du brauchst Geld und willst dir einen Job suchen. Schreib auf einen Zettel, was du alles tun kannst und wann und wie oft du arbeiten kannst. Wie viel Geld möchtest du verdienen? Vergiss deine Telefonnummer nicht!

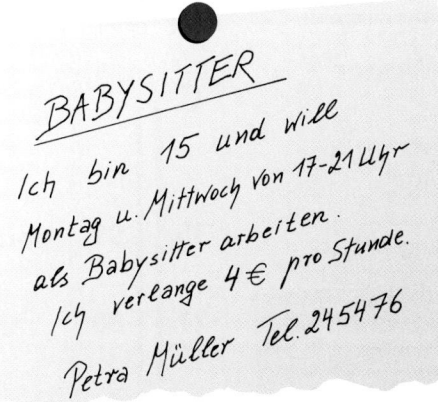

BABYSITTER

Ich bin 15 und will Montag u. Mittwoch von 17-21 Uhr als Babysitter arbeiten. Ich verlange 4 € pro Stunde.

Petra Müller Tel. 245476

24 Für mein Notizbuch

Schreiben Schreib, was du zu Hause alles machen musst! Wann und wie oft machst du das? Was machst du gern? Was machst du nicht gern? Hast du ein Haustier? Wie heißt es? Wer füttert das Tier?

Und dann noch...

der Vogel

die Maus

das Meerschweinchen

der Fisch

das Kaninchen

der Hamster

Dritte Stufe

Objective Talking about the weather

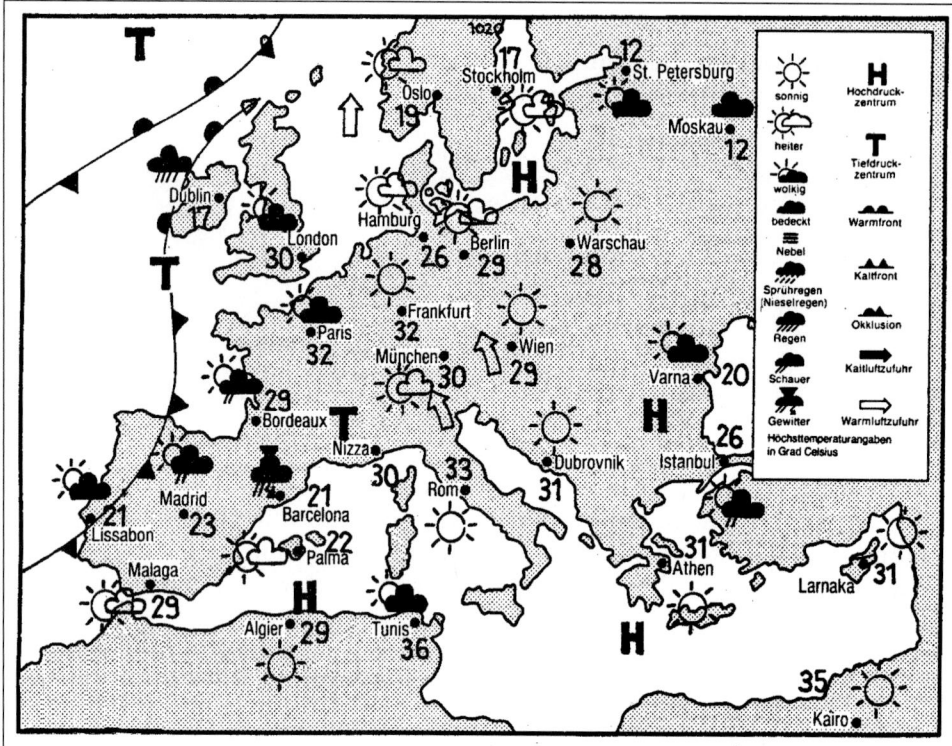

Wettervorhersagekarte für Europa
13. Juni 2001

Lage: Deutschland liegt am Rande eines umfangreichen Hochs über dem östlichen Mitteleuropa. Dabei ist es teils sonnig und warm.

Vorhersage: Am Montag überwiegend sonnig, nur vereinzelt auch wolkig. Höchsttemperaturen 28 bis 32 Grad. In der Nacht auf Dienstag Abkühlung auf 20 Grad. Schwacher bis mäßiger Wind aus Nordwest.

Aussichten: Am Dienstag sonnig und heiter mit Temperaturen von 26 bis 32 Grad. Tiefstwerte um 15 Grad. Schwacher, örtlich auch mäßiger Wind aus dem Norden.

1. Europe
2. Temperatures, air pressure, wind, cloudiness, rain
3. **sonnig**=sunny; **heiter**=clear; **wolkig**=cloudy; **bedeckt**=overcast; **Nebel**=fog; **Sprühregen**=drizzle; **Regen**=rain; **Schnee**=snow; **Schauer**=shower; **Gewitter**=thunderstorm

4. St. Petersburg and Moscow; farther north
5. Barcelona, Madrid, Dublin
6. Frankfurt, Dubrovnik, Kairo
7. Monday: **sonnig, sehr warm, wolkig**
   Tuesday: **sonnig; heiter; schwacher Wind**

25 ## Was sagt der Wetterbericht?

Sprechen Beantworte die folgenden Fragen zu der Wetterkarte.

1. What area of the world is this weather map for?
2. What kinds of information can you get from the map?
3. Look at the table of symbols and the words that go with them. Can you figure out what each word means?
4. Which cities are the coldest? What do you think the reason for this is?
5. Name three cities where you might need an umbrella.
6. Name three cities where you might do outdoor activities.
7. List the words in the weather forecast that describe the weather for Monday and Tuesday.

Wortschatz

Das Wetter

Regen
Gewitter
nass
wolkig

Schnee
Eis

sonnig
trocken

C	F	
35	95	heiß
27	80	warm
13	55	kühl
0	32	kalt

Talking about the weather

For some plans you make with your friends, you might first need to know about the weather.

You could ask:

Wie ist das Wetter heute?

Or you might want to ask about tomorrow:

Wie ist das Wetter morgen?

Or you might want to ask for specific information:

Regnet es heute?
Schneit es heute Abend?
Wie viel Grad haben wir heute?

Some possible responses are:

Heute regnet es.
Wolkig und kühl.

Sonnig, aber kalt.

Ich glaube schon.
Nein, es schneit nicht.
Ungefähr 10 Grad.

Übungsheft,
S. 80–82, Ü. 15–21

Grammatikheft,
S. 61, Ü. 13–14

What do you think the word **Grad** means?[1] Look at the response for a clue. When you tell someone the temperature, you might not know exactly what it is, so you say **ungefähr …** What do you think **ungefähr** means?[2]

---

26 Was machst du bei diesem Wetter? Script on p. 187H

CD 7 Tr. 10

Listen to the following weather reports from German radio. For each report determine which activity fits best with the weather described.
1. d 3. c
2. a 4. b

a.

b.

c.

d.

Ein wenig Grammatik

What do you notice about the verb that is used to ask and tell about the weather for tomorrow? The present tense is often used when referring to the near future. The meaning is made clear with words such as **morgen.** How would you invite a German friend to go to the movies tomorrow?[3]

Mehr Grammatikübungen,
S. 211, Ü. 10–11

Grammatikheft, S. 62, Ü. 15-16

27 Grammatik im Kontext

Sprechen Sprich mit einer Partnerin über das Wetter in eurer Stadt. Sprecht über folgende Themen. Zusätzliche (additional) Wörter findet ihr auf Seite R9.

1. Wie ist das Wetter heute?
2. Wie viel Grad haben wir heute?
3. Und was sagt der Wetterbericht für morgen?
4. Wie ist das Wetter im Januar? Und im Juli?
5. Und im April? Und im Oktober?

1. *degree* 2. *approximately* 3. **Ich gehe morgen ins Kino. Kommst du mit?**

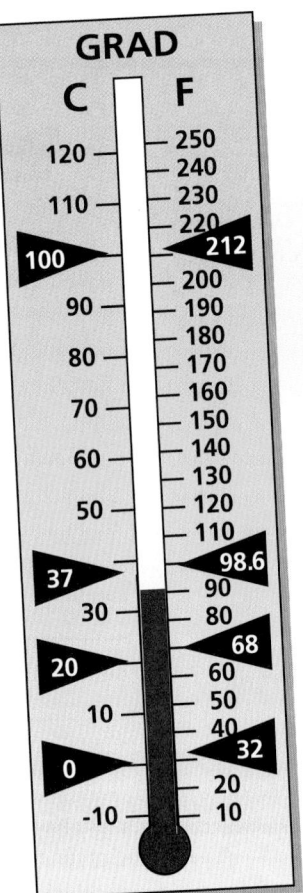

GRAD

C	F
120	250
	240
110	230
	220
100	**212**
	200
90	190
	180
80	170
70	160
	150
60	140
	130
50	120
	110
37	**98.6**
	90
30	80
20	**68**
	60
10	50
	40
	32
0	
	20
-10	10

Ein wenig Landeskunde

Weather in the German-speaking countries is extremely variable, depending on the latitude and seasons. These countries usually get a lot of rainfall. Summers are often rainy, and winters can be cold, especially in the Alps. As in other European countries, German-speaking countries use the Celsius system of measuring temperature, rather than the Fahrenheit system. Look at the thermometer. If it were 35°C would you need a jacket? If the temperature fell below 0°C would you expect rain or snow? What is a comfortable room temperature in Celsius? Look at the weather map on p. 202. If you were in Moscow, what kinds of clothes would you be wearing? In Athens?

Übungsheft, S. 84, Ü. 1–2

Wortschatz

Wie ist das Wetter im ...?　7–C

Januar	Juni	November
Februar	Juli	Dezember
März	August	
April	September	
Mai	Oktober	

Grammatikheft, S. 63, Ü. 17–18

28 Gespräche

Lesen/Sprechen Ordne die Sätze für jede Zeichnung.

1. BRITTE Hallo, Gupse! Gehen wir morgen schwimmen?

> Toll! Also, bis morgen! 5

> Ja, klar. Aber was sagt der Wetterbericht? 2

> Gut! Dann gehen wir schwimmen. 4

> Morgen ist es sonnig und warm. 3

1. HANNES Tag, Jörg! Ich geh ins Kino. Kommst du mit?

> Nein, ich kann nicht. Ich muss den Rasen mähen. 2

> Gut! Mach ich! Aber schau mal, Hannes! Es regnet jetzt! 5

> Gern! Du kannst für mich die Blumen gießen. 4

> Ach, dann gehen wir doch ins Kino! 6

> Brauchst du Hilfe, Jörg? 3

29 **Ein Wetterbericht für …**

Schreiben Schau auf die Wetterkarte auf Seite 202. Wähle eine Stadt aus und schreib einen Wetterbericht für diese Stadt.

 30 **Pläne machen**

Sprechen With a partner, pretend that you are meeting tomorrow in the city that you chose for Activity 29. You would like to invite your friend to do something special that is appropriate for the expected weather. Create a conversation in which you invite your partner to do something. He or she will ask about the weather, and you say what you know about it. Your partner can either accept or decline the invitation. Then switch roles and create another conversation, using your partner's city.

31  **Von der Schule zum Beruf**

Schreiben You have been hired by a local radio station to be the weather reporter. Your job is to write the weather report for today and tomorrow. Give the conditions, temperature, and forecast for your area.

AUSSPRACHE

 Richtig aussprechen / Richtig lesen CD 7 Trs. 11–13

A. To practice the following sounds, say the words and sentences below after your teacher or after the recording. CD 7 Tr. 11

1. The letter **o**: In **Kapitel 3** you learned how to pronounce the letter **o** as a long vowel, as in **Oma**. However, when the letter **o** is followed by two or more consonants, it is pronounced as a short vowel, like the *o* in the English word *cot*.

   wolkig, Sonne, Woche / Im Oktober ist es sonnig und trocken.

2. The letter **u**: In **Kapitel 3** you learned how to pronounce the letter **u** as a long vowel, as in **super**. However, when the letter **u** is followed by two or more consonants, it is pronounced as a short vowel, like the *u* in the English word *put*.

   uns, muss, putzen / Mutti, ich muss die Fenster putzen.

3. The letter **l**: The letter **l** is pronounced like the *l* in the English word *million*. It is much more tense than the *l* sound in the English word *bill*.

   Müll, kühl, April / Der Lehrer kann im Juli mit dem Müll helfen.

4. The consonant combination **th**: The combination **th** within the same syllable is pronounced the same as the letter **t** in German.

   Theater, Mathe, Theatinerkirche / Wie komme ich zur Theatinerkirche und zum Theater?

5. The letter combination **pf**: The consonant combination **pf** sounds similiar to the *pf* combination in English, as in the word *cupful*. However, in German this letter combination often occurs at the beginning of a word and is pronounced as one sound.

   Pfennig, Pfund, Kopfsalat / Zwei Pfund Pflaumen kosten neunundneunzig Pfennig.

Richtig schreiben / Diktat CD 7 Tr. 12
CD 7 Tr. 13 (with pauses)

B. Write down the words and sentences that you hear. Script on p. 187H

Wem hilfst du?

Weißt du noch? Using visual clues, such as illustrations or photos, will give you advance information about a text before you try to read it.

1. Before you try to read these three interviews, look at the title and at the photos. What do you expect the articles to be about? Answers will vary.

2. What do these three texts have in common? What kind of texts do you think they are? Teenagers helping people interviews

3. You probably figured out that these articles have to do with young people helping others. Working in groups of three or four students, write as many German phrases as you can that have to do with offering to help people. Whom do you help? And how do you help? Do you receive anything for your help? Are there

4. Read the interview questions. people or special Even though you may not know organizations all the words in each question, that you you can probably figure out would like to what is being asked. With a help? Why partner, write what you think is do you help being asked in each question. other people?

WEM
Helfen Jugendliche ihren Eltern und Freunden? Verdienen sie dabei Taschengeld?

HILFST
Oder bieten sie Hilfe freiwillig an? JUMA— Reporter Bernd hat sich umgehört.

DU?

Hallo Heiko!

Wem hilfst du? Ich helfe meiner Mutter.

Und wobei hilfst du? Ab und zu bei der Hausarbeit. Zum Beispiel helfe ich meiner Mutter beim Staubsaugen oder beim Wäscheaufhängen. Mein Zimmer räume ich allerdings seltener auf. Dazu habe ich meistens keine Lust. Und das Auto wäscht mein Vater lieber selbst. Dann wird es sauberer als bei mir.

Bekommst du etwas für deine Hilfe? Nein. Aber <u>wenn</u> ich längere Zeit nichts mache, schimpfen meine Eltern. Natürlich haben sie damit recht, <u>wenn</u> ich faul bin.

Gibt es Menschen oder besondere Organisationen, denen du gerne helfen würdest? Ich weiß jetzt nichts Spezielles. Aber ich weiß, wem ich nicht gerne helfen würde: aufdringlichen Freunden.

Warum hilfst du anderen Menschen? Ich finde es wichtig, <u>daß</u> man anderen eine Last abnimmt. Außerdem ist Mithilfe eine nette Geste, über die sich wahrscheinlich jeder freut.

Hallo Tina!

Wem hilfst Du? Meiner Familie, meinen Freunden und meinen Bekannten.

Und wobei hilfst Du? Ich passe auf Kinder auf oder helfe meiner Schwester bei den Hausaufgaben. Im Haushalt mache ich eigentlich alles: Spülen, Bügeln oder Putzen.

Bekommst Du etwas für Deine Hilfe? Ich helfe freiwillig, <u>obwohl</u> ich meiner Schwester die Hausaufgaben nicht so gerne erkläre. Meinen Eltern und Bekannten biete ich auch schon mal Hilfe an.

Gibt es Menschen oder besondere Organisationen, denen Du gerne helfen würdest? Ja. Ich möchte gerne einmal in einem Kinderhort mitarbeiten. Das ist bestimmt anstrengend, aber interessant.

Warum hilfst du anderen Menschen? Wichtig für mich ist es, Pflichten zu erfüllen. Anderen zu helfen, ist eine Pflicht.

Hallo Sven!

Wem hilfst du? Ich helfe meistens meinen Freunden.

Und wobei hilfst du? Eigentlich bei allem, was mit Schule zu tun hat. Meistens aber bei Hausaufgaben und Prüfungsvorbereitungen. Nachhilfestunden in Biologie oder Chemie gebe ich ziemlich regelmäßig, <u>weil</u> ich in diesen Fächern ganz gut bin.

Bekommst du etwas für Deine Hilfe? Ja, manchmal. Ich bessere mein Taschengeld mit Nachhilfe auf.

Gibt es Menschen oder besondere Organisationen, denen du gerne helfen würdest? Allen netten Leuten helfe ich gerne.

Warum hilfst du anderen Menschen? Es ist schön, <u>wenn</u> sie sich über Mithilfe freuen.

ZUM LESEN

STANDARDS: 1.2, 3.1, 5.2

---

5. Scan the articles and list any subordinating conjunctions that you find. Using the information in the **Lesestrategie**, determine what you expect each of the clauses introduced by these conjunctions to contain: a condition, a reason, a concession, an opinion, or a statement of fact. Write your guess beside the corresponding conjunction.

6. Read each clause that begins with a subordinating conjunction. Can you determine what the clause means? Now read the entire sentence. What does each sentence mean?

7. Now read the articles for the following information:

   a. Whom do these young people help? What are some of the things they do to help?

   b. When do Heiko's parents complain? Does Heiko think they have a right to complain? How do you know? What does Heiko say about "taking a burden from others"?

   c. What does Tina not like to do? Where does she want to work someday? What does she say is a "duty"?

   d. Why does Sven tutor other students in biology and chemistry? Whom does he like to help?

8. If you had been asked these questions by *JUMA*, how would you have answered them?

9. Imagine that you will spend the next year as an exchange student with a German family. Write a letter to your host family and include an explanation of some of the chores you regularly do at home. Offer to do them for your German family while you are there.

5. **wenn** (condition)
   dass (statement of opinion)
   weil (reason)
   obwohl (concession)
7. Annos for rest of
   Zum Lesen, p. 187W

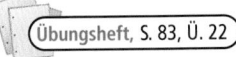

Übungsheft, S. 83, Ü. 22

Erste Stufe

Objective Expressing obligations

1 Du und deine Freunde, ihr habt heute viel zu tun. Setze die richtigen Formen von **müssen** ein *(insert)*. (S. 195)

1. Was _____ du jetzt tun? — Ich _____ jetzt die Katze füttern.   musst; muss
2. Was _____ die Mara tun? — Sie _____ Staub saugen.   muss; muss
3. Was _____ ihr heute tun? — Wir _____ heute den Müll sortieren.   müsst; müssen
4. Was _____ die Jungen tun? — Sie _____ den Rasen mähen.   müssen; müssen
5. Was _____ der Flori tun? — Er _____ sein Zimmer aufräumen.   muss; muss
6. Was _____ wir jetzt tun? — Ihr _____ jetzt den Tisch abräumen.   müssen; müsst

2 Alle müssen heute etwas tun. Vervollständige *(complete)* die folgenden Aussagen *(statements)* und benutze dabei die richtige Form von **müssen** und die Ausdrücke in Klammern *(parentheses)*. (S. 195)

1. (das Geschirr spülen)   Der Flori _____ .   muss das Geschirr spülen
2. (die Fenster putzen)   Der Markus _____ .   muss die Fenster putzen
3. (den Tisch decken)   Ich _____ .   muss den Tisch decken
4. (Staub saugen)   Du _____ .   musst Staub saugen
5. (den Müll sortieren)   Ihr _____ .   müsst den Müll sortieren
6. (den Rasen mähen)   Wir _____ .   müssen den Rasen mähen
7. (die Blumen gießen)   Mara und Claudia _____ .   müssen die Blumen gießen

3 Wer macht was? Beantworte die folgenden Fragen und setze dabei die richtige Form von **müssen** in die erste Lücke *(blank)* und eine passende Infinitivform in die zweite Lücke. (S. 196)

1. Wer räumt den Tisch ab? — Der Markus _____ den Tisch _____ .   muss; abräumen
2. Wer räumt die Klamotten auf? — Die Mara _____ die Klamotten _____ .   muss; aufräumen
3. Wer kommt mit? — Du _____ _____ .   musst; mitkommen
4. Wer probiert die Stiefel an? — Ihr _____ die Stiefel _____ .   müsst; anprobieren
5. Wer zieht Turnschuhe an? — Die Mara _____ Turnschuhe _____ .   muss; anziehen

4 Dein Freund hat viele Fragen. Schreib die folgenden Sätze ab *(copy)* und schreib dabei die richtige Verbform und das richtige Präfix in die Lücken. **(S. 196)**

1. (abräumen)   Wer _____ heute Abend den Tisch _____ ?   räumt; ab
2. (aufräumen)   Wer _____ heute das Wohnzimmer _____ ?   räumt; auf
3. (mitkommen)   Wer _____ in die Stadt _____ ?   kommt; mit
4. (anprobieren) Wer _____ die Klamotten _____ ?   probiert; an
5. (anziehen)   Wer _____ die alten Klamotten _____ ?   zieht; an
6. (aussehen)   Wer _____ in den Klamotten gut _____ ?   sieht; aus

---

Zweite Stufe

Objective Asking for and offering help and telling someone what to do

5 Ihr helft euren Freunden. Was könnt ihr für sie tun? Schreib die richtige Form von **können** in die Lücken. **(S. 199)**

1. Was _____ ich tun? — Du _____ den Rasen mähen.   kann; kannst
2. Was _____ Mara tun? — Sie _____ die Katze füttern.   kann; kann
3. Was _____ wir tun? — Ihr _____ den Müll sortieren.   können; könnt
4. Was _____ die Jungen tun? — Die Jungen _____ die Blumen gießen.   können; können
5. Was _____ der Flori tun? — Der Flori _____ den Tisch decken.   kann; kann
6. Was _____ ich tun? — Du _____ zu Hause helfen.   kann; kannst
7. Was _____ ich tun? — Herr Meier, Sie _____ die Katzen füttern.   kann; können
8. Und was _____ die Mädchen tun? — Sie _____ Mutti helfen.   können; können

6 Alle müssen helfen. Schreib die richtige Form von **können** und den Ausdruck in Klammern in die Lücken. **(S. 199)**

1. (das Geschirr spülen)   Mara, du _____ .   kannst das Geschirr spülen
2. (das Zimmer aufräumen)   Der Flori _____ .   kann das Zimmer aufräumen
3. (den Tisch abräumen)   Wir _____ .   können den Tisch abräumen
4. (den Müll sortieren)   Ihr _____ .   könnt den Müll sortieren
5. (die Fenster putzen)   Die Claudia _____ .   kann die Fenster putzen
6. (Staub saugen)   Und ich _____ .   kann Staub saugen

7 Deine Freunde wollen dir helfen, und du sagst ihnen, was sie für dich tun können. Schreib die folgenden Sätze ab *(copy)* und schreib die richtige Verbform von **können** in die erste Lücke, die richtige Verbform von **müssen** in die zweite Lücke und die richtige Verbform von **wollen** in die dritte Lücke. **(S. 199)**

1. Was _____ ich für dich tun? – Ich _____ einkaufen gehen. _____ du mitkommen?   kann; muss; Willst
2. Was _____ wir für euch tun? – Mein Bruder _____ den Rasen mähen. _____ ihr ihm helfen?   können; muss; Wollt
3. Was _____ Flori für uns tun? – Wir _____ den Müll sortieren, und vielleicht _____ er uns helfen.   kann; müssen; will
4. Du _____ etwas für uns tun. – Ich _____ die Fenster putzen, und du _____ bestimmt die Garage aufräumen.   kannst; muss; willst
5. Ihr _____ uns helfen. Die Claudia _____ in der Küche helfen, und ich _____ heute ins Kino gehen.   könnt; muss; will

Mehr Grammatikübungen

Answers

CD-ROM
DISC 2

go.
hrw
.com
WK3 MUENCHEN-7

8 Alle wollen helfen. Was können sie tun? Vervollständige *(complete)* die folgenden Sätze und schreib dabei das richtige Pronomen (**mich, dich, uns, euch**) in die Lücken. (S. 200)

1. Mara, was kann ich für _____ tun? — Du kannst für _____ den Müll sortieren.   dich; mich
2. Flori und Jens, was kann ich für _____ tun? — Du kannst für _____ Staub saugen.   euch; uns
3. Markus, was können wir für _____ tun? — Ihr könnt für _____ den Rasen mähen.   dich; mich
4. Mara und Jens, was können wir für _____ tun? — Ihr könnt nichts für _____ tun.   euch; uns

9 Du willst deinen Freunden helfen und fragst sie, was du für sie tun kannst. Deine Freunde geben dir zwei Aufgaben *(tasks)*. Schreib die Antworten ab und schreib dabei die richtige Form von **können** in die erste Lücke, das richtige Pronomen in die zweite Lücke und ein passendes Verb aus dem Kasten *(box)* in die dritte und vierte Lücke. (S. 200)

füttern	abräumen	gießen	mähen
putzen	saugen	sortieren	spielen

1. Was kann ich jetzt für euch tun? Die Blumen gießen? — Ja, du _____ jetzt   kannst
   für _____ die Blumen _____ und den Rasen _____ .   uns; gießen; mähen
2. Was kann ich jetzt für dich tun? Den Tisch abräumen? — Ja, du _____ jetzt   kannst
   für _____ den Tisch _____ und das Geschirr _____ .   mich; abräumen; spülen
3. Was können wir jetzt für euch tun? Staub saugen? — Ja, ihr _____ jetzt   könnt
   für _____ Staub _____ und die Katze und den Hund _____ .   uns; saugen; füttern
4. Was können wir jetzt für dich tun? Den Müll sortieren? — Ja, ihr _____ jetzt   könnt
   für _____ den Müll _____ und die Fenster _____ .   mich; sortieren; putzen

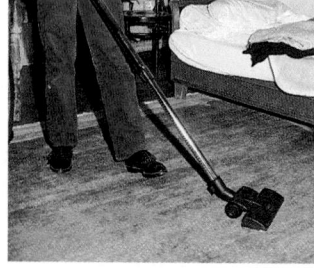

10 Du willst wissen, wie das Wetter heute, morgen, und heute Abend ist. Schreib Fragen und benutze dabei die gegebene Information. **(S. 203)**

BEISPIEL   **You want to know whether it is going to snow today.**
Schneit es heute? *or* **Wird es heute schneien?**

You want to know whether it is going to:

1. rain tomorrow.   Regnet es morgen? / Wird es morgen regnen?

2. snow tonight.   Schneit es heute Abend? / Wird es heute Abend schneien?

3. be cloudy today.   Ist es heute bewölkt? / Wird es morgen bewölkt sein?

4. be cool tonight.   Ist es heute Abend kühl? / Wird es heute Abend kühl sein?

5. be dry tomorrow.   Ist es morgen trocken? / Wird es morgen trocken sein?

11 Sieh dir die Wetterkarte an, und beantworte die folgenden Fragen. **(S. 203)**

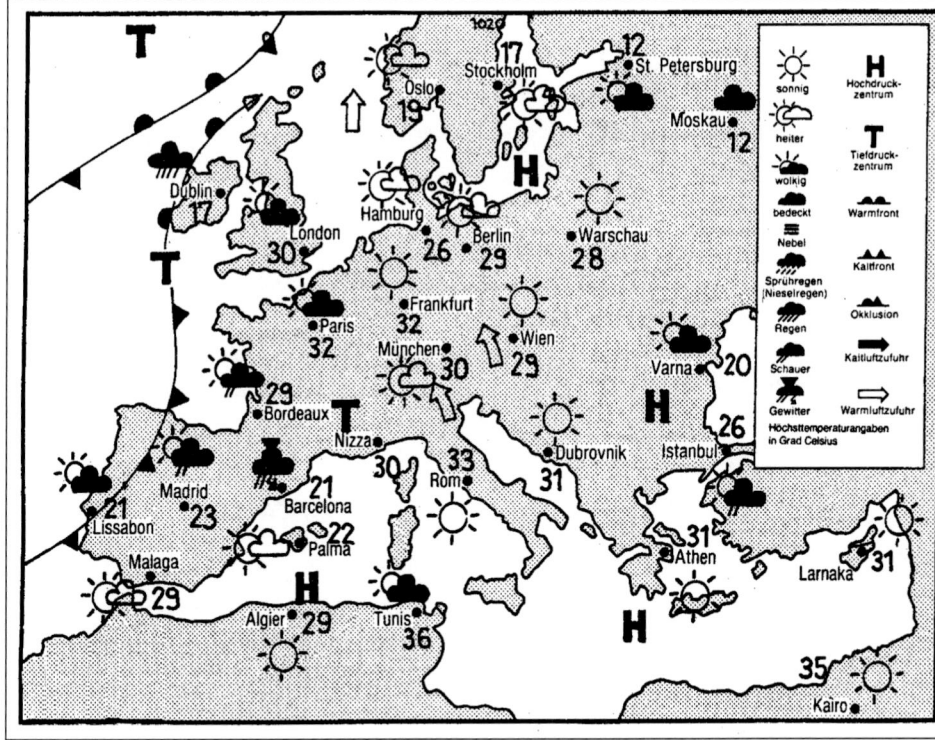

Wettervorhersagekarte für Europa 13. Juni 2001

Lage: Deutschland liegt am Rande eines umfangreichen Hochs über dem östlichen Mitteleuropa. Dabei ist es teils sonnig und warm.

Vorhersage: Am Montag überwiegend sonnig, nur vereinzelt auch wolkig. Höchsttemperaturen 28 bis 32 Grad. In der Nacht auf Dienstag Abkühlung auf 20 Grad. Schwacher bis mäßiger Wind aus Nordwest.

Aussichten: Am Dienstag sonnig und heiter mit Temperaturen von 26 bis 32 Grad. Tiefstwerte um 15 Grad. Schwacher, örtlich auch mäßiger Wind aus dem Norden.

1. Wo regnet es? _____   in Dublin

2. Wie ist das Wetter in Rom und in Wien? _____   Es ist sonnig.

3. Wie hoch ist die Temperatur in Paris? _____   32 Grad

4. Wie ist das Wetter in Moskau? _____   Es ist bedeckt; die Temperatur ist 12 Grad.

5. Wie ist das Wetter in Lissabon? _____   Es ist wolkig; die Temperatur ist 21 Grad.

Anwendung

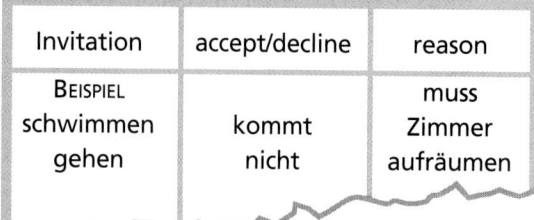
Script on p. 187H

The CD-ROM Tutor offers guided recording and writing activities to accompany the **Anwendung.** These activities are designed to practice students' oral and written communication skills and to review material from each chapter.

CD 7
Tr. 14

1 You will hear five students invite their friends to do something. Sometimes their friends accept, and sometimes they decline and give a reason. Listen to the exchanges and write the information you hear. Compare your notes with those of a classmate. The chart to the right will help you organize your information.

Invitation	accept/decline	reason
BEISPIEL schwimmen gehen	kommt nicht	muss Zimmer aufräumen

1. Ins Kino gehen / kommt
2. Ins Café gehen / kommt nicht / muss Hausaufgaben machen
3. Tennis spielen / kommt nicht / muss Rasen mähen
4. Fete bei Markus / kommt
5. ins Einkaufszentrum gehen / kommt nicht / geht schwimmen

2 Below is a page from Flori's calendar for the month of **März**. Take turns asking and telling your partner when and how often Flori does the activities. Now make your own calendar page. Fill in all the activities you do in a typical month. Describe to your partner the things you wrote on your calendar, and he or she will try to find out when and how often you do them. Then switch roles.

März

Mo	Di	Mi	Do	Fr	Sa	So
	1 Staub saugen	2	3	4 Müll sortieren	5 Fenster putzen 4:00 Fußball spielen	6
7 9:30 mit Michael ins Konzert	8 Staub saugen	9 3:30 Klavier= unterricht 7:00 Volleyball	10	11 9:00 Disko	12 Rasen mähen 4:00 Fußball spielen	13
14 8:30 Kino mit Sabine	15 Staub saugen	16 3:30 Klavier= unterricht	17	18 Müll sortieren	19 Fenster putzen 4:00 Fußball spielen	20
21 4:00 Schwimmen	22 Staub saugen	23 3:30 Klavier= unterricht	24	25 9:00 Disko	26 Rasen mähen 4:00 Fußball spielen	27
28	29 Staub saugen	30 3:30 Klavier= unterricht	31			

3 Ask your partner when and how often he or she does the activities shown in the photos below. Does he or she enjoy each activity? Then your partner will ask you the same questions.

a.

b.

c.

d.

e.

4 Look at the weather map and answer the following questions in German.

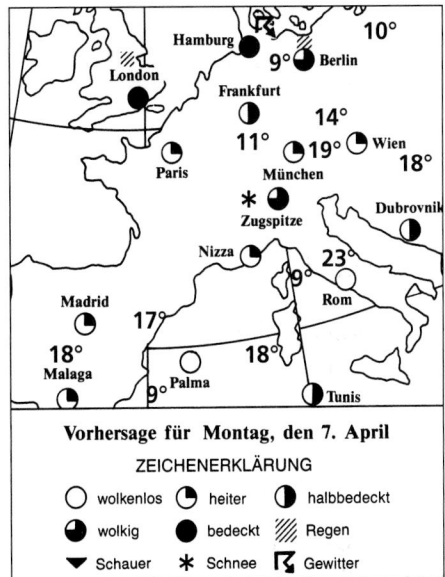

1. Which cities are expecting rain?

2. In which cities could you probably go swimming?

3. Which city will be the warmest?

4. What kinds of activities might you plan in **Berlin** for Monday, April 7?

5. Where might you go skiing?

6. Claudia is planning to drive to the **Zugspitze,** and then to have a picnic in the **Englischer Garten.** What would she say if she wanted to invite you? Would you accept or decline?

5 ## Zum Schreiben

Write a TV script for your portion of the school "Teen Show," a program that reports on planned school activities. You represent the German club and give a summary of all the activities this club has planned for the semester.

Schreibtipp Making a writing plan before you begin is important. Think about your topic carefully. Do you know all the vocabulary you'll need? If not, use a bilingual dictionary or ask your teacher for help. Will your topic require you to use certain grammatical structures frequently? If you are not sure you can use them correctly, consult your textbook or your teacher.

1. Brainstorm types of activities and types of weather expressions with your group. Activities might include helping out with chores some afternoon at the local home for the elderly (**Altersheim**) or a French Club/German Club soccer match. Activities, however, are dependent on the weather, so you need to give alternatives for some of the outdoor activities in case of rain or other bad weather. How many creative activities can your "club" sponsor?

Remember also the expression, „**Guten Tag, liebe Zuschauer!**" which is used at the beginning of many weather reports and other information shows.

2. Using your list of activities and weather expressions, write your script. Videotape your program and show it to the class.

6 ## Rollenspiel

It's raining today, so you are at home doing your chores. Your friends show up and offer to help. As you and your friends work around the house, you decide to invite your friends to go somewhere tomorrow. Great crashes of thunder turn your conversation to the weather for tomorrow. What will you do? Create a conversation with two other classmates. Be prepared to act it out in front of the class with props that will convey the idea of doing chores around the house.

Kann ich's wirklich?

Can you extend and respond to an invitation? (p. 194)

1 How would you invite a friend to go   Willst du … / möchtest du …

a. to a movie   **b.** to a café   **c.** shopping   **d.** swimming
ins Kino gehen?   ins Café gehen?   einkaufen gehen?   schwimmen gehen?

2 Accept or decline the following invitations. If you decline, give a reason why you can't go.   Answers may vary. Some possible answers:

a. Wir gehen jetzt in eine Disko. Komm doch mit!

b. Ich muss in die Stadt gehen. Möchtest du mitkommen?

c. Wir spielen jetzt Tennis. Kannst du mitkommen?

a. Das geht nicht. Ich muss zu Hause helfen.
b. Ja, gern!
c. Ich kann leider nicht. Ich muss Hausaufgaben machen.

Can you express obligation using müssen? (p. 194)

Bernd muss den Rasen mähen.
Leyla muss die Blumen gießen.
Pedro und Felipe müssen den Tisch decken.
Karin muss ihr Zimmer aufräumen.

3 Say that the people below have to do the things indicated.

Bernd   **Leyla**   **Pedro und Felipe**   **Karin**

Can you talk about how often you have to do things? (p. 198)

4 How would you ask a classmate how often he or she has to

a. wash the windows   **c.** clear the table
b. vacuum

Wie oft musst du …
a. die Fenster putzen?
b. Staub saugen?

c. den Tisch abräumen?
d. das Geschirr spülen?

d. do the dishes

5 How would you tell a classmate how often you have to do each of the things above?   Answers may vary: zweimal in der Woche, dreimal in der Woche, jeden Tag

Can you offer help and tell someone what to do using expressions with für? (p. 199)

6 How would you ask a classmate if you could help him or her? How would you ask two classmates?   Kann ich etwas für dich/für euch tun?

7 Using **können**, explain to each of these people what they can do to help you:

a. Sara: das Geschirr spülen

b. Silke und Peter: das Zimmer aufräumen

c. Markus: das Bett machen

d. Claudia und Daniel: den Tisch decken

a. Sara, du kannst das Geschirr spülen.
b. Silke und Peter, ihr könnt das Zimmer aufräumen.
c. Markus, du kannst das Bett machen.
d. Claudia und Daniel, ihr könnt den Tisch decken.

8 How might a friend respond if he or she agreed to do some chores for you?
Answers will vary: **Ja, gern!** or **Gut, mach ich!**

Can you talk about the weather? (p. 203)

9 How would you tell a classmate what the weather is like today? How would you tell him or her the weather forecast for tomorrow?
Answers will vary: **Heute ist es schön. Morgen regnet es/schneit es/wird es kühl.**

10 How would you tell someone new to your area what the weather is like in

a. January   **c.** June   **e.** December
b. March   **d.** October

Answers will vary. Possible answers:
Im Januar ist es kalt. Im März ist es kühl und windig.

Erste Stufe

 p. 187X

Extending and responding to invitations

mitkommen (sep)	to come along
Komm doch mit!	Why don't you come along!
Ich kann leider nicht.	Sorry, I can't.
Das geht nicht.	That won't work.

Expressing obligation

tun	to do
helfen	to help
zu Hause helfen	to help at home
müssen	to have to

ich muss …	I have to …
mein Zimmer aufräumen (sep)	clean up my room
Staub saugen	vacuum
den Müll sortieren	sort the trash
den Rasen mähen	mow the lawn
die Katze füttern	feed the cat
den Tisch decken	set the table
den Tisch abräumen (sep)	clear the table
das Geschirr spülen	wash the dishes

die Blumen gießen	water the flowers
das Bett machen	make the bed
meine Klamotten aufräumen	pick up my clothes
die Fenster putzen	clean the windows
Ich habe keine Zeit.	I don't have time.

Zweite Stufe

Saying how often you have to do things

Wie oft?	How often?
nie	never
manchmal	sometimes
immer	always
einmal, zweimal, dreimal …	once, twice, three times …
in der Woche	a week
im Monat	a month
jeden Tag	every day

Asking for and offering help and telling someone what to do

können	can, to be able to
Was kann ich für dich tun?	What can I do for you?
Kann ich etwas für dich tun?	Can I do something for you?
Du kannst …	You can …
Gut! Mach ich!	Okay! I'll do that!
für	for
Für wen?	For whom?

mich	me
dich	you
uns	us
euch	you (pl)

Other useful words and expressions

ungefähr	about, approximately

Dritte Stufe

Talking about the weather

Was sagt der Wetterbericht?	What does the weather report say?
Wie ist das Wetter?	How's the weather?
Es ist …	It is …
heiß	hot
warm	warm
kühl	cool
kalt	cold
trocken	dry
nass	wet
sonnig	sunny
wolkig	cloudy

der Schnee	snow
Es schneit.	It's snowing.
der Regen	rain
Es regnet.	It's raining.
das Eis	ice
das Gewitter	thunderstorm
Die Sonne scheint.	The sun is shining.
heute	today
morgen	tomorrow
heute Abend	this evening
Wie viel Grad haben wir?	What's the temperature?
der Grad	degree(s)
zwei Grad	two degrees

der Monat, -e	month
der Januar	January
im Januar	in January
Februar	February
März	March
April	April
Mai	May
Juni	June
Juli	July
August	August
September	September
Oktober	October
November	November
Dezember	December

Kapitel 8: Einkaufen gehen
Chapter Overview

Los geht's! pp. 218–220	*Alles für die Oma! p. 218*

	FUNCTIONS	GRAMMAR	VOCABULARY	RE-ENTRY
Erste Stufe pp. 221–225	• Asking what you should do, p. 222 • Telling someone what to do, p. 223	• The modal **sollen,** p. 223 • The **du**-command and the **ihr**-command, p. 224	• Groceries, p. 221	• The **möchte**-forms, p. 222 (**Kap. 3**) • The modal **können,** p. 222 (**Kap. 7**) • Household chores vocabulary, p. 224 (**Kap. 7**)
Zweite Stufe pp. 226–228	• Talking about quantities, p. 226 • Saying that you want something else, p. 227		• Weights, p. 226	• Numbers, p. 226 (**Kap. 1** and **Kap. 3**) used in a new context, weights and measures • Expressing wishes when shopping, p. 227 (**Kap. 5**)
Dritte Stufe pp. 229–233	• Giving reasons, p. 230 • Saying where you were and what you bought, p. 231	• The conjunctions **weil** and **denn**, p. 230 • The past tense of **sein,** p. 231	• Time expressions, p. 231	• Responding to invitations, p. 230 (**Kap. 7**) • Activity vocabulary, p. 230 (**Kap. 2** and **Kap. 6**) • Household chores vocabulary, p. 232 (**Kap. 7**) • Sequencing words, p. 232 (**Kap. 4**) • Clothing vocabulary, p. 233 (**Kap.5**)

Aussprache p. 233	The short vowel **ü**, the short vowel **ö**, review diphthong **ei**, review vowel combination **ie**, review letter **z**: Audio CD 8, Track 14	**Diktat:** Audio CD 8, Tracks 15–16

Zum Lesen pp. 234–235	Richtig essen!	**Reading Strategy** Combining the strategies that you have learned

Mehr Grammatik- übungen	**pp. 236–239** Erste Stufe, pp. 236–237	Zweite Stufe, pp. 237–238	Dritte Stufe, pp. 238–239

Review pp. 240–243	Anwendung, pp. 240–241 **Kann ich's wirklich?**, p. 242 Wortschatz, p. 243 **Zum Schreiben:** Using the "Five-W How?" questions (Taking a nutrition survey)

CULTURE

- **Ein wenig Landeskunde:** Preference for small shops, p. 222
- **Landeskunde: Was machst du für andere Leute?** p. 225
- **Ein wenig Landeskunde:** Weights and measures, p. 227
- German advertisements, p. 229

Kapitel 8: Einkaufen gehen
Chapter Resources

 **PRINT**

Lesson Planning

One-Stop Planner

Lesson Planner with Substitute Teacher Lesson Plans, pp. 37–41, 72

Student Make-Up Assignments
- Make-Up Assignment Copying Masters, Chapter 8

Listening and Speaking

TPR Storytelling Book, pp. 29–32

Listening Activities
- Student Response Forms for Listening Activities, pp. 59–61
- Additional Listening Activities 8-1 to 8-6, pp. 63–66
- Additional Listening Activities (song), p. 62
- Scripts and Answers, pp. 141–147

Video Guide
- Teaching Suggestions, pp. 50–51
- Activity Masters, pp. 52–54
- Scripts and Answers, pp. 98–100, 114–115

Activities for Communication
- Communicative Activities, pp. 43–48
- Realia and Teaching Suggestions, pp. 102–105
- Situation Cards, pp. 137–138

Reading and Writing

Reading Strategies and Skills Handbook, Chapter 8

Lies mit mir! 1, Chapter 8

Übungsheft, pp. 85–96

Grammar

Grammatikheft, pp. 64–72

Grammar Tutor for Students of German, Chapter 8

Assessment

Testing Program
- Grammar and Vocabulary Quizzes, **Stufe** Quizzes, and Chapter Test, pp. 197–214
- Score Sheet, Scripts, and Answers, pp. 215–222

Alternative Assessment Guide
- Portfolio Assessment, p. 25
- Performance Assessment, p. 39
- CD-ROM Assessment, p. 53

Student Make-Up Assignments
- Alternative Quizzes, Chapter 8

 **MEDIA**

 Online Activities
- Interaktive Spiele
- Internet Aktivitäten

 Video Program
- Videocassette 3
- Videocassette 5 (captioned version)

 Audio Compact Discs
- Textbook Listening Activities, CD 8, Tracks 1–17
- Additional Listening Activities, CD 8, Tracks 24–29
- Assessment Items, CD 8, Tracks 18–23

 Interactive CD-ROM Tutor, Disc 2

 Teaching Transparencies
- Situations 8-1 to 8-2
- Vocabulary 8-A to 8-B
- **Los geht's!**
- **Mehr Grammatikübungen** Answers
- **Grammatikheft** Answers

 **One-Stop** Planner CD-ROM

Use the **One-Stop Planner CD-ROM** with **Test Generator** to aid in lesson planning and pacing.

For each chapter, the **One-Stop Planner** includes:
- Editable lesson plans with direct links to teaching resources
- Printable worksheets from resource books
- Direct launches to the HRW Internet activities
- Video and audio segments
- Test Generator
- Clip Art for vocabulary items

Kapitel 8: Einkaufen gehen

Projects

Gesund essen

*In this activity students will prepare a poster promoting a balanced diet. This project should be started after students have completed the **Zum Lesen** section of this chapter. This project can be done individually or in groups of three students, in which case each student would be responsible for featuring one of the meals—breakfast, lunch, or dinner.*

MATERIALS

✂ **Students may need**
- 1 posterboard per group
- health and food magazines
- scissors
- glue
- mail-order catalogs that feature food
- pens and markers
- grocery advertisements

SUGGESTED SEQUENCE

1. Decide whether to do this project as individual or group work, depending on your class size and time allotment for this activity.

2. Have students look for pictures to illustrate a nutritious meal. If students are not able to find a picture of a certain food item but would like to include it in their project, encourage them to draw the item.

3. Once a selection of items has been gathered, students should make an outline of the information and materials they will include on their poster.

4. Students must label each food with its German name and indicate quantity per serving. (Example: **100 Gramm Kartoffeln**)

5. Suggest that students review the quantity expressions from the **Zweite Stufe**. They could also ask the health teacher or check their health textbook for guidelines for appropriate serving sizes and daily totals of the different food groups.

6. Students in each group must proofread each other's features before putting the final descriptions on the poster.

7. Each group presents its poster.

GRADING THE PROJECT

Suggested point distribution (**total = 100 points**)
Appearance and neatness......................25
Accurate descriptions/
   correct language usage 50
Oral presentation..............................25

Games

Ausreden finden

*This game will help students review giving excuses and reasons using **weil** clauses.*

Materials Each student needs a sheet of paper and a pen.

Procedure Before the game gets underway, each student writes a question that begins with the interrogative pronoun **Warum**. Students should write this question close to the top of the paper. (Example: **Warum gehst du heute nicht ins Kino?**) Once all students have written their sentences, they should fold the paper so that the question is covered up. Then each student passes his or her paper to the next person. Each student should write a statement below the fold without looking at the question. This statement should begin with the conjunction **weil**. (Example: **Weil ich kein Geld habe.**) At this point, each paper should have two phrases—one question and one statement. Ask students to pass all papers to the front and shuffle them. Next, divide the class into two teams and redistribute the papers so that each team member has a piece of paper. Members of each team then take turns reading the questions and responses, which tend to be quite humorous. As each student reads the phrases on his or her sheet of paper, he or she must also translate the sentences. If the translation is correct, that student scores a point for his or her team.

Was ist hier falsch?

With this game, students can review vocabulary and parts of speech.

Materials You will need one index card for each student and the **Wortschatz** to be reviewed.

Procedure Begin by asking each student to write down four words on his or her index card. Three of the four words should belong to a group, one of the words should not belong. (Example: **Milch, Brot, Schuhe, Apfel**) The groups can be based on meaning or part of speech. When students have finished, collect all the cards and shuffle them. Divide the class into two teams and give each person on both teams one index card. The first person on team A asks the first person on team B: **Was ist hier falsch?** and reads the four words on his or her index card. If the person on team B answers correctly by pointing out the wrong word, he or she scores a point for the team. Teams alternate asking the questions until all cards have been read, giving every student a chance to talk. The team with the most points at the end of the game wins.

Storytelling ....

Mini-Geschichte

*This story accompanies Teaching Transparency 8-2. The **Mini-Geschichte** can be told and retold in different formats, acted out, written down, and read aloud to give students additional opportunities to practice all four skills.*

Alles für die Fete *(party)*

Sandra fragt Iwan: „Wo warst du gestern?" „Ich war einkaufen, für die Fete." Sandra fragt: „Was hast du gekauft?" „Viel zu viel! Zuerst war ich beim Bäcker und habe Brot und Semmeln gekauft. Dann war ich beim Metzger und habe Wurst und Aufschnitt gekauft. Danach war ich im Obst- und Gemüseladen und habe ein Kilo Tomaten gekauft, und zuletzt war ich im Klamotten-Express und hab mir eine neue Jeans gekauft." Sandra fragt: „Hast du sonst noch etwas gekauft?" „Nein, denn danach war ich total pleite *(broke)*."

Traditions ....

Rezept

Der Kaiserschmarrn verdankt seinen Namen einer kaiserlichen Verirrung. Franz Joseph, österreichischer Kaiser von 1848–1916, hatte sich bei der Jagt verirrt und traf spät abends auf ein Bauernhaus. Die Bäuerin, verlegen um der hochherrschaftlichen Gesellschaft, bereitete ein Mahl aus all den Zutaten, die sie im Haus hatte. Der Kaiser lobt ihre Kochkunst sehr, worauf sie antwortete: „Ach, es war doch nur ein Schmarrn *(österreichisch oder bayerisch für Unsinn, Abfall).*" Darauf erwiderte der Kaiser: „Na, aber dann war es ein Kaiserschmarrn!"

Kaiserschmarrn
Für 2 Personen

Zutaten
g=Gramm, EL=Esslöffel, ml=Milliliter

2 El	Butter
2 El	Zucker
2	Eier
	Salz
80g	Mehl
250ml	Milch oder Rahm
	Butter oder Schmalz
	Zucker
1TL	Zimt
60g	Rosinen oder Obst

(z.B. Apfel, Kirsche, oder Pfirsich)

Zubereitung
Die Butter schaumig rühren und nach und nach Zucker, Eigelb, Salz, Mehl und Milch zugeben. Den Eierschnee unterziehen. In einer Pfanne Butter oder Schmalz erhitzen, 1 Schöpflöffel Teig darin zerlaufen lassen und goldgelb backen. Wenden und mit zwei Gabeln in kleine Vierecke teilen. Auf einer heißen Platte mit Zucker und Zimt bestreut und mit in Butter gedünsteten Apfelscheiben, Kirschen, Pfirsichstückchen oder eingeweichten Rosinen vermengt anrichten.

Kapitel 8: Einkaufen gehen
Technology

Video

Videocassette 3, 5 (captioned version)
See Video Guide, pages 49–54

Los geht's! • Alles für die Oma!

Flori visits his grandmother, who has prepared his favorite dish, **Kaiserschmarrn.** After lunch, his grandmother gives him a shopping list and money to go run errands for her. Flori goes to different stores, and when he comes back to his grandmother's, he discovers that the wallet is missing.

Landeskunde
Was machst du für andere Leute?

Young people from different cities talk about what they do to help other people.

Fortsetzung

Flori returns to his last stop, a flower shop, but no wallet. He then bumps into his friends Mara and Claudia, and they invite him to come along. Flori calls his grandmother to tell her about his change of plans, and she tells him that she found the wallet. The three end up at an open-air market where Claudia buys produce.

Videoclips
- **Nuss-Nougat Brötchen** (rolls)
- **Weihenstephan®** (dairy products)
- **Milram Fruchtquark®** (quark)
- **Gerolsteiner Stille Quelle®** (mineral water)
- **Sonnen-Bassermann®** (canned stew)
- **Gutfried Wurst®** (cold cuts)
- **CMA Gütezeichen®** (quality control symbol)

Interactive CD-ROM Tutor

The **Interactive CD-ROM Tutor** contains videos, interactive games, and activities that provide students an opportunity to practice and review the material covered in Chapter 8.

Activity	Activity Type	Pupil's Edition Reference
1. Wortschatz	Wort und Bild Erfahren/Wählen	p. 221
2. Grammatik	Was fehlt?	pp. 223, 224
3. So sagt man das!	Wozu gehört's?	pp. 222, 223, 226, 227
4. Grammatik	Was kommt dann?	p. 230
5. Grammatik	Was fehlt?	p. 231
6. So sagt man das!	Was ist richtig?	pp. 226, 227, 231
Landeskunde	Was tust du für die Umwelt? Was ist richtig?	p. 225
Zum Sprechen	*Guided recording*	pp. 240–241
Zum Schreiben	*Guided writing*	pp. 240–241

Teacher Management System
Logging In

Logging in to the *Komm mit!* TMS is easy. Upon launching the program, simply type "admin" in the password area of the log-in screen and press RETURN. Log on to **www.hrw.com/CDROMTUTOR** for a detailed explanation of the Teacher Management System.

One-Stop Planner CD-ROM

To preview all resources available for this chapter, use the **One-Stop Planner CD-ROM**, Disc 2.

Internet Connection

internet

ADRESSE: go.hrw.com
KENNWORT: WK3 MUENCHEN-8

*Have students explore the **go.hrw.com** Web site for many online resources covering all chapters. All Chapter 8 resources are available under the keyword **WK3 Muenchen-8**. Interactive games practice the material and provide students with immediate feedback. You will also find a printable worksheet that provides Internet activities that lead to a comprehensive online research project.*

Interaktive Spiele

You can use the interactive activities in this chapter

- to practice grammar, vocabulary, and chapter functions
- as homework
- as an assessment option
- as a self-test
- to prepare for the Chapter Test

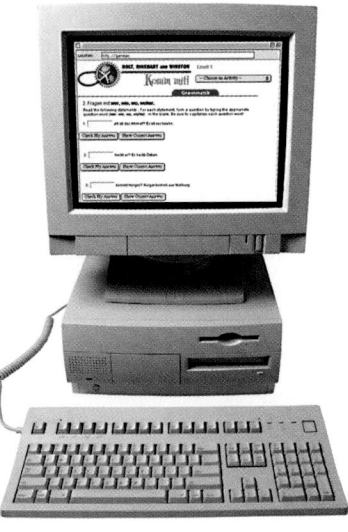

Internet Aktivitäten

Students will shop for basic food items in German grocery stores. They will learn how to price and specify amounts of certain food items.

- To prepare students for the **Arbeitsblatt,** you might want to have them review the **Wortschatz** on pp. 221 and 226.
- After completing the **Arbeitsblatt,** have students visit a local grocery store and write down the prices of basic food items. How do the prices they noted compare to the prices of basic food items in German supermarkets?

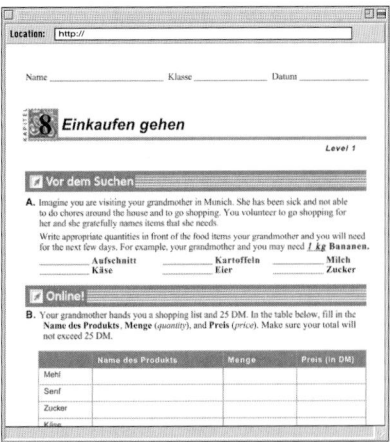

Webprojekt

Have students do a Web search for a recipe for **Obsttorte** or **Obstsalat**. They should list all ingredients and the amounts required of each ingredient. Encourage students to exchange useful Web sites with their classmates. Have students document their sources by referencing the names and URLs of all the sites they consulted.

Kapitel 8: Einkaufen gehen
Textbook Listening Activities Scripts

Erste Stufe

6 **p. 222**

CLAUDIA	So Flori, was brauchen wir denn für heute Abend? Wann kommen Sabine und Udo?
FLORI	Sie kommen gegen 6 Uhr. Erst essen wir zusammen Abendbrot, dann schauen wir uns die zwei Videos an. Wohin gehen wir zuerst?
CLAUDIA	Ja also, fangen wir doch beim Metzger an. Der ist gleich um die Ecke.
FLORI	Was brauchen wir denn da?
CLAUDIA	Hm, etwas Hackfleisch und auch Aufschnitt.
FLORI	Und Udo isst gern Wurst. Also auch Wurst kaufen für ihn und für mich, ja … ich esse Bratwurst sehr gern.
CLAUDIA	Na und dazu brauchen wir ja frisches Brot. Danach gehen wir zur Bäckerei und holen Brot. Was meinst du?
FLORI	Klar und meine Mutter braucht noch Semmeln. Die hole ich dann auch gleich.
CLAUDIA	Die neue Bäckerei hat immer frische Brezeln. Da will ich eine für mich kaufen.
FLORI	Nee, Brezeln mag ich nicht. Die sind mir zu salzig.
CLAUDIA	Wirklich? … Du, wir dürfen nicht vergessen, zum Supermarkt zu gehen.
FLORI	Wieso? Was brauchen wir denn da?
CLAUDIA	Butter fürs Brot und … na Milch zum Trinken.
FLORI	Oh ja, natürlich. Und zum Schluss müssen wir dann noch beim Obst- und Gemüseladen vorbei.
CLAUDIA	Wieso?
FLORI	Äpfel kaufen, damit wir Bratäpfel backen können als Nachtisch. Das schmeckt so lecker!
CLAUDIA	Also, dann los! Wir haben viel zu tun.

11 **p. 224**

OMI	Na, ist ja schön, dass ihr alle hier seid. Flori, kannst du bitte zuerst den Tisch decken?
FLORI	Okay Omi! Wie können wir dir sonst noch helfen?
OMI	Na, da lass mal sehen. Ja, bitte Flori, hol doch danach etwas Limo und Mineralwasser aus dem Keller!
FLORI	Klar doch, mach ich schon.
MARKUS	Mara und ich können auch helfen.
OMI	Das ist ja nett. Hm, Moment. Also, Markus, geh bitte zum Supermarkt und hol zwei Pfund Tomaten! Hier sind 5 Euro. Das soll reichen. Und du, Mara, vielleicht kannst du zum Bäcker gehen und ein Dutzend Semmeln holen. Hier sind 3 Euro für dich!
MARA	Soll ich sonst noch etwas beim Bäcker kaufen?
OMI	Tja, zum Kaffeetrinken brauchen wir ja noch etwas. Dann kauf mal einen kleinen Kuchen! Hier sind noch mal 5 Euro.

MARA	Oh nein, ich brauche das Geld nicht. Das bezahl ich schon.
OMI	Doch, doch! Nimm das Geld! Es ist schon gut so. Beeilt euch! Bis später!

Zweite Stufe

14 **p. 226**

VERKÄUFER	Was darf es sein, bitte?
KUNDE	Ja, ich hätte gern Tomaten.
VERKÄUFER	Wie viel denn?
KUNDE	Hm, … lassen Sie mal sehen. Also, ein Pfund bitte. Das soll reichen.
VERKÄUFER	Sonst noch etwas?
KUNDE	Ja bitte zwei Pfund Äpfel, die dort. Und das ist dann alles.
VERKÄUFER	Also, ein halbes Kilo Tomaten, zwei Pfund Äpfel. Vielen Dank. Wer ist der Nächste, bitte?
KUNDIN	Ja, bitte, ein Kilo Kartoffeln, und haben Sie auch frische Trauben?
VERKÄUFER	Ja, unsere Trauben kommen täglich frisch. Hier, probieren Sie mal!
KUNDIN	Oh, sehr lecker, dann nehme ich ein viertel Pfund, nein, lieber ein halbes Pfund.
VERKÄUFER	So, ein Kilo Kartoffeln, ein halbes Pfund Trauben. Sonst nocht etwas?

16 **p. 227**

1. — Was darf's heute denn sein?
   — Ich möchte bitte 500 g Hackfleisch.
   — 500 g Hackfleisch. Sonst noch etwas?
   — Ja, noch 200 g Aufschnitt. Das ist alles.

2. — Guten Tag, Frau Motz!
   — Guten Tag, Frau Schmidt!
   — Und was bekommen Sie denn heute?
   — Es ist fast Viertel vor sieben.

3. — Und wie kann ich Ihnen helfen, bitte?
   — Ja, bitte einen Liter Milch. Hier ist meine Flasche.
   — Haben Sie sonst noch einen Wunsch?
   — Ja, dann auch noch zehn Eier, aber braune, bitte.

4. — Was brauchen Sie heute?
   — Ich brauche heute Äpfel. Zwei Pfund, bitte.
   — Sonst noch etwas? Unsere Tomaten sind heute sehr frisch, gerade gekommen.
   — Na ja, gut. Dann geben sie mir mal das Brot. Wie viel macht das zusammen?

5. — Ein Liter Milch, 250 g Butter, 100 g Käse. Ist das alles heute?
   — Ja, das soll's sein. Danke schön.

The following scripts are for the listening activities found in the *Pupil's Edition*. For Student Response Forms, see *Listening Activities*, pages 59–62. To provide students with additional listening practice, see *Listening Activities*, pages 63–66.

For resource information, see the **One-Stop Planner CD-ROM**, Disc 2.

Dritte Stufe

21   p. 230

1. MARA   Hallo! Hier ist die Mara. Ich bin jetzt leider nicht zu Hause. Bitte, hinterlassen Sie mir eine kurze Nachricht, und ich rufe so bald wie möglich zurück. Danke!

(Beep of answering machine)

MARKUS   Hallo Mara! Hier ist der Markus. Tut mir Leid, aber ich kann zu deiner Fete nicht kommen, weil ich am Samstagabend mit Heiko ins Kino gehe. Wir haben die Karten schon gekauft. Also, bis bald!

CLAUDIA   Du, Mara. Ich bin's … Claudia. Hab Dank für die Einladung. Leider kann ich nicht kommen, denn ich habe viele Hausaufgaben. Tschüs!

FLORI   Ja, hier ist Flori. Mara, klar komm ich. Kann ich den Udo mitbringen? Lass mich's wissen. Du kennst ja meine Nummer.

CHRISTIAN   Christian hier. Ja, Mara, danke für die Einladung. Ich würde ja gern kommen, aber ich muss da zu Hause helfen. Nächstes Mal komme ich aber bestimmt.

STEFAN   Servus, Mara. Ich bin's, Stefan. Ja, wann fängt denn die Fete an, und soll ich etwas mitbringen? Sag Bescheid! Bis dann!

BARBARA   Hallo Mara, hier Barbara. Super! Find ich ja toll, dass du 'ne Fete am Wochenende hast. Ich komme so gegen sieben und bring ein paar neue CDs. Bis dann!

BRIGITTE   Grüß dich Mara! Habe gerade deine Einladung bekommen. Leider habe ich eine Chemieprüfung am Montag und muss noch jede Menge lernen. Schade! Ach ja, ich bin's... Brigitte. Tschau!

24   p. 232

1. CLAUDIA   Du, Mara, was machst du denn heute?

MARA   Hm, zuerst geh ich ins Einkaufszentrum, so ein paar Klamotten kaufen. Danach geht's nach Hause, um Hausaufgaben zu machen.

2. CLAUDIA   Mensch du, Flori! Wo warst du denn heute Morgen? Ich hab versucht, dich anzurufen.

FLORI   Ich war beim Bäcker. Da hab ich Brot für meine Oma gekauft. Und im Musikhaus Walter war ich auch kurz. Hab die neue CD von Peter Maffay gekauft. Total stark!

3. CLAUDIA   He, Markus, ich geh jetzt ins Eiscafé, ein Spaghettieis essen. Komm doch mit!

MARKUS   Kann leider nicht. Um 3 Uhr kommt Stefan. Wir lernen Chemie.

4. CLAUDIA   Grüß dich, Heike, Tag, Marianne! Ich bin gestern vorbeigekommen, aber ihr wart ja nicht zu Hause. Wo wart ihr denn?

HEIKE   Gestern? Was haben wir denn gestern gemacht? Ach ja, wir waren im Kino. Wir haben den neuen Film aus Italien gesehen. Der war aber blöd.

5. CLAUDIA   Und du, Ahmet, wo warst du gestern, so um vier? Ich bin vorbeigekommen, und keiner war da.

AHMET   Tja, ich war im Supermarkt. Meine Mutter hat mir die Einkaufsliste für die ganze Woche gegeben. Das hat vielleicht lange gedauert. Nächste Woche ist meine Schwester aber dran.

6. CLAUDIA   Hi, Andreas! Ich geh am Nachmittag in den Schreibwarenladen. Brauchst du etwas, das ich dir mitbringen kann?

ANDREAS   Oh ja! Morgen ist die Mathearbeit! Da brauche ich noch ein paar Bleistifte. Du, vielen Dank, Claudia!

AUSSPRACHE, p. 233

Diktat, p. 233

You will hear about the different foods and drinks Mara's friends plan to bring to her party. First listen to what is said, then write down what you hear.

Am Samstag hat Mara eine Fete, und sie hat viele Freunde eingeladen. Alle Freunde bringen etwas zu essen mit. Die Sabine geht zum Bäcker und kauft frischen Kuchen, und der Stefan holt beim Metzger drei Hähnchen für den Grill. Brigitte geht zum Supermarkt und kauft Gemüse und auch etwas Obst. Und der Ahmet will wieder die Getränke mitbringen. Wenn jeder etwas hilft, hat Mara nicht so viel Arbeit.

Anwendung

1   p. 240

MUTTER   Du, Flori, kannst du bitte für mich einkaufen gehen? Die Omi kommt gleich. Und ich habe keine Zeit dafür.

FLORI   Ja klar, Mutti. Mach ich schon. Hast du den Einkaufszettel fertig?

MUTTER   Noch nicht ganz, Moment mal! Was brauche ich denn da alles? Tomaten … Also, ein Kilo, das soll wohl reichen. Und zwei Pfund Kartoffeln. Was noch? Ich will später noch einen Apfelkuchen backen, dazu brauche ich zwei Kilo Äpfel, ein Pfund Butter und, hmm, haben wir noch Eier? Ach, nein, Eier haben wir nicht. Also, auch zehn Eier.

FLORI   Ist das denn alles, Mutti?

MUTTER   Moment, ich glaub nicht. Morgen ist Sonntag. Hm, dann brauchen wir ja auch einen Liter Orangensaft, ein bisschen Käse, ja, 200 g Emmentaler am liebsten. Aber nur wenn er im Sonderangebot ist. Klar?

FLORI   Ja, ich werd schon sehen. Ist das alles Mutti?

MUTTER   Oh ja, ich hab fast vergessen. Ich hab keinen Kaffee mehr, und Brot haben wir auch nicht genug. Kauf bitte noch ein Pfund Kaffee, den milden und ein Brot. Das ist jetzt aber wirklich alles. Hier ist das Geld. Das soll ausreichen.

FLORI   Tschüs, Mutti! Bis später!

Kapitel 8: Einkaufen gehen
Suggested Lesson Plans 50-Minute Schedule

Day 1

CHAPTER OPENER 5 min.
- Multicultural Connection, ATE, p. 215M
- Culture Note, ATE, p. 215M

LOS GEHT'S! 20 min.
- Preteaching Vocabulary, ATE, p. 215N
- Play Audio CD for **Los geht's!**, pp. 218–219
- Have students read **Los geht's!**, pp. 218–219
- Show **Los geht's!** Video
- Do Comprehension Activities, p. 220

ERSTE STUFE
Wortschatz/Ein wenig Landeskunde, p. 221–222 20 min.
- Presenting **Wortschatz**, ATE, p. 215O
- Present **Ein wenig Landeskunde**, p. 222
- Play Audio CD for Activity 6, p. 222
- Do Activities 7 and 8, p. 222
- Play Circumlocution Game, ATE, p. 215X

Wrap-Up 5 min.
- Students answer questions about what kinds of items they could buy

Homework Options
Grammatikheft, p. 64, Acts. 1–2
Übungsheft, pp. 85–87, Acts. 1–4

Day 2

ERSTE STUFE
Quick Review 10 min.
- Check homework, Grammatikheft, p. 64, Acts. 1–2

So sagt man das!/Grammatik, pp. 222–223 20 min.
- Presenting **So sagt man das!**, ATE, p. 215O
- Presenting **Grammatik**, ATE, p. 215P
- Teaching Transparency 8-2
- Do Activities 9 and 10, p. 223
- Do Activities 3–4, p. 65, Grammatikheft

So sagt man das!/Grammatik, p. 223–224 15 min.
- Presenting **So sagt man das!**, ATE, p. 215P
- Presenting **Grammatik**, ATE, p. 215P
- Play Audio CD for Activity 11, p. 224
- Do Activities 12 and 13, p. 224

Wrap-Up 5 min.
- Students respond to questions about shopping for food

Homework Options
Grammatikheft, p. 66, Acts. 5–6
Übungsheft, pp. 87–88, Acts. 5–8

Day 3

ERSTE STUFE
Quick Review 10 min.
- Check homework, Übungsheft, pp. 87–88, Acts. 5–8

Quiz Review 20 min.
- Do Activities 1–2, Interactive CD-ROM
- Play game, **Was ist hier falsch?**, ATE, p. 215D
- Do **Mehr Grammatikübungen, Erste Stufe**

Quiz 20 min.
- Quiz 8-1A or 8-1B

Homework Options
Activities for Communication, pp. 137–138, prepare Situation 8-1

Day 4

ERSTE STUFE
Quick Review 10 min.
- Return and review Quiz 8-1
- Do Situation 8-1, pp. 137–138

LANDESKUNDE 20 min.
- Pre-viewing Suggestion, Video Guide, p. 50
- Culture Note, ATE, p. 215P
- Show **Landeskunde** Video
- Do Activities A and B, p. 225
- Do **Landeskunde** Activity, Interactive CD-ROM

ZWEITE STUFE
Wortschatz/ So sagt man das!, p. 226 15 min.
- Presenting **Wortschatz**, ATE, p. 215R
- Presenting **So sagt man das!**, ATE, p. 215R
- Play Audio CD for Activity 14, p. 226

Wrap-Up 5 min
- Students answer question about liters, grams, and kilos

Homework Options
Grammatikheft, p. 67, Acts. 7–8
Übungsheft, p. 89–90, Acts. 9–10

Day 5

ZWEITE STUFE
Quick Review 10 min.
- Check homework, Übungsheft, p. 89–90, Acts. 9–10

Ein wenig Landeskunde, p. 227 10 min.
- Present **Ein wenig Landeskunde**, p. 227
- Do Activity 15, p. 227

So sagt man das!, p. 227 25 min.
- Presenting **So sagt man das!**, ATE, p. 215R
- Play Audio CD for Activity 16, p. 227
- Do Activities 17 and 18, p. 228
- Present **Lerntrick**, p. 228
- Present **Und dann noch…**, p. 228
- Do Activity 19, p. 228

Wrap-Up 5 min.
- Students answer questions about wanting something else

Homework Options
Grammatikheft, p. 68, Acts. 9–11
Übungsheft, pp. 90–91, Acts. 11–14

Day 6

ZWEITE STUFE
Quick Review 10 min.
- Check homework, Übungsheft, pp. 90–91, Acts. 11–14

Quiz Review 20 min.
- Do **Mehr Grammatikübungen, Zweite Stufe**
- Do **Minigeschichte, Zweite Stufe**, TPR Storytelling Book, p. 30

Quiz 20 min.
- Quiz 8-2A or 8-2B

Homework Options
Übungsheft, p. 96, Act. 24

 **One-Stop** Planner CD-ROM

For alternative lesson plans by chapter section, to create your own customized plans, or to preview all resources available for this chapter, use the **One-Stop Planner CD-ROM**, Disc 2.

 For additional homework suggestions, see activities accompanied by this symbol throughout the chapter.

Day 7

DRITTE STUFE

Quick Review 10 min.
- Return and review Quiz 8-2
- Bell Work, ATE, p. 215T
- Check homework, Übungsheft, p. 96, Act. 24

So sagt man das!/Ein wenig Grammatik, p. 230 20 min.
- Presenting **So sagt man das!**, ATE, p. 215T
- Do Activity 20, p. 229
- Presenting **Ein wenig Grammatik**, ATE, p. 215T
- Play Audio CD for Activity 21, p. 230
- Music Connection, ATE, p. 215T
- Do Activity 22, p. 230
- Do Activity 23, p. 231

So sagt man das!, p. 231 15 min.
- Presenting **So sagt man das!**, ATE, p. 215U
- Do Activities 14–15, p. 70, Grammatikheft

Wrap-Up 5 min.
- Students use the conjunction **weil**

Homework Options
Grammatikheft, p. 69, Acts. 12–13
Übungsheft, pp. 92–93, Acts. 15–19

Day 8

DRITTE STUFE

Quick Review 10 min.
- Check homework, Übungsheft, pp. 92–93, Acts. 15–19

Wortschatz/Grammatik, p. 231 20 min.
- Presenting **Wortschatz**, ATE, p. 215U
- Presenting **Grammatik**, ATE, p. 215U
- Play Audio CD for Activity 24, p. 232
- Do Activities 25 and 26, p. 232
- Present **Sprachtipp**, p. 233
- Do Activity 27, p. 233

Aussprache, p. 233 15 min.
- Do **Richtig aussprechen/Richtig lesen**, p. 233
- Do **Richtig schreiben/Diktat**, p. 233

Wrap-Up 5 min.
- Students answer questions about where they were and what they did

Homework Options
Pupil's Edition, p. 233, Act. 28
Grammatikheft, pp. 71–72, Acts. 16–18
Übungsheft, p. 94, Acts. 20–22

Day 9

DRITTE STUFE

Quick Review 10 min.
- Check homework, Grammatikheft, pp. 71–72, Acts. 16–18

Quiz Review 20 min.
- Do **Mehr Grammatikübungen, Dritte Stufe**
- Play game, **Ausreden finden**, ATE, p. 215C

Quiz 20 min.
Quiz 8-3A or 8-3B

Homework Options
Activities for Communication, pp. 137–138, prepare Situation 8-3

Day 10

DRITTE STUFE

Quick Review 10 min.
- Return and review Quiz 8-3
- Do Situation 8-3, pp. 137–138

ZUM LESEN 15 min.
- Thinking Critically, p. 215V
- Present **Lesestrategie**, p. 234
- Do Activities 1–10, pp. 234–235

Project 20 min
- Start **Gesund essen** project, ATE, p. 215C

Wrap-Up 5 min.
- Students answer questions about nutritious foods

Homework Options
Complete **Gesund essen** project

Day 11

ANWENDUNG 15 min.
- Students present **Gesund essen** projects

Quick Review 30 min.
- Thinking Critically, ATE, p. 215W
- Teaching Suggestions for **Fortsetzung** and **Videoclips** Videos, Video Guide, pp. 50–51
- Show **Fortsetzung** and **Videoclips** Videos
- Do **Anwendung** Activities 1–4, pp. 236–237

Wrap-Up 5 min.
- Students respond to questions about where they bought certain grocery items

Homework Options
Übungsheft, p. 95, Act. 23
Interaktive Spiele, see ATE, p. 215F

Day 12

ANWENDUNG

Quick Review 15 min.
- Check homework, Übungsheft, p. 95, Act. 23

Kann ich's wirklich?, p. 242 15 min.
- Students write out answers to questions 1–8

Chapter Review 20 min.
- Review chapter functions, vocabulary, and grammar; choose from **Mehr Grammatikübungen**, Grammar Tutor for Students of German, Activities for Communication, Listening Activities, Interactive CD-ROM Tutor, or **Interaktive Spiele**
- Review test format and provide sample test items for students

Homework Options
Study for Chapter Test

Assessment

Test, Chapter 8 45 min.
- Administer Chapter 8 Test. Select from Testing Program, Alternative Assessment Guide, or Test Generator.

Kapitel 8: Einkaufen gehen
Suggested Lesson Plans 90-Minute Block Schedule

Block 1

CHAPTER OPENER 10 min.
- Multicultural Connection, ATE, p. 215M
- Culture Note, ATE, p. 215M

LOS GEHT'S! 20 min.
- Preteaching Vocabulary, ATE, p. 215N
- Play Audio CD for **Los geht's!**, pp. 218–219
- Have students read **Los geht's!**, pp. 218–219
- Teaching Suggestions, Video Guide, p. 50
- Show **Los geht's!** Video
- Do Comprehension Activities, p. 220

ERSTE STUFE

Wortschatz/Ein wenig Landeskunde, pp. 221–222 25 min.
- Presenting **Wortschatz**, ATE, p. 215O
- Teaching Transparencies 8-A, 8-B
- Present **Ein wenig Landeskunde**, p. 222
- Play Audio CD for Activity 6, p. 222
- Do Activities 7 and 8, p. 222
- Play Circumlocution Game, ATE, p. 215X

So sagt man das!/Grammatik, pp. 222–223 15 min.
- Presenting **So sagt man das!**, ATE, p. 215O
- Presenting **Grammatik**, ATE, p. 215P
- Teaching Transparency 8-2
- Do Activities 9 and 10, p. 223

So sagt man das!/Grammatik, pp. 223–224 15 min.
- Presenting **So sagt man das!**, ATE, p. 215P
- Presenting **Grammatik**, ATE, p. 215P
- Play Audio CD for Activity 11, p. 224
- Do Activities 12 and 13, p. 224

Wrap-Up 5 min.
- Students respond to questions about shopping for food

Homework Options
Grammatikheft, pp. 64–66, Acts. 1–6
Übungsheft, pp. 85–88, Acts. 1–8

Block 2

ERSTE STUFE

Quick Review 10 min.
- Check homework, Grammatikheft, pp. 64–66, Acts. 1–6

LANDESKUNDE 20 min.
- Pre-viewing Suggestion, Video Guide, p. 50
- Culture Note, ATE, p. 215P
- Show **Landeskunde** Video
- Do Activities A and B, p. 225
- Do **Landeskunde** Activity, Interactive CD-ROM

Quiz Review 15 min.
- Do Activities 1–2, Interactive CD-ROM
- Do **Mehr Grammatikübungen, Erste Stufe**

Quiz 20 min.
- Quiz 8-1A or 8-1B

ZWEITE STUFE

Wortschatz/ So sagt man das!, p. 226 20 min.
- Presenting **Wortschatz**, ATE, p. 215R
- Presenting **So sagt man das!**, ATE, p. 215R
- Play Audio CD for Activity 14, p. 226

Wrap-Up 5 min
- Students answer question about liters, grams, and kilos

Homework Options
Grammatikheft, p. 67, Acts. 7–8
Übungsheft, pp. 89–90, Acts. 9–10

Block 3

ZWEITE STUFE

Quick Review 15 min.
- Return and review Quiz 8-1
- Check homework, Übungsheft, pp. 89–90, Acts. 9–10

Ein wenig Landeskunde, p. 227 10 min.
- Present **Ein wenig Landeskunde**, p. 227
- Do Activity 15, p. 227

So sagt man das!, p. 227 20 min.
- Presenting **So sagt man das!**, ATE, p. 215R
- Play Audio CD for Activity 16, p. 227
- Do Activities 17 and 18, p. 228
- Present **Lerntrick**, p. 228
- Present **Und dann noch…**, p. 228
- Do Activity 19, p. 228

Quiz Review 25 min.
- Do Acts. 9–11, p. 68, Grammatikheft
- Do Acts. 11–14, pp. 90–91, Übungsheft
- Do **Mehr Grammatikübungen, Zweite Stufe**
- Do **Minigeschichte, Zweite Stufe**, TPR Storytelling Book, p. 30

Quiz 20 min.
- Quiz 8-2A or 8-2B

Homework Options
Übungsheft, p. 96, Act. 24

 **One-Stop** Planner CD-ROM

For alternative lesson plans by chapter section, to create your own customized plans, or to preview all resources available for this chapter, use the **One-Stop Planner CD-ROM**, Disc 2.

 For additional homework suggestions, see activities accompanied by this symbol throughout the chapter.

Block 4

DRITTE STUFE

Quick Review 15 min.
- Return and review Quiz 8-2
- Bell Work, ATE, p. 215T
- Check homework, Übungsheft, p. 96, Act. 24

So sagt man das!/ Ein wenig Grammatik, p. 230 25 min.
- Presenting **So sagt man das!**, ATE, p. 215T
- Do Activity 20, p. 229
- Presenting **Ein wenig Grammatik**, ATE, p. 215T
- Play Audio CD for Activity 21, p. 230
- Music Connection, ATE, p. 215T
- Do Activity 22, p. 230
- Do Activity 23, p. 231

So sagt man das!, p. 231 20 min.
- Presenting **So sagt man das!**, ATE, p. 215U
- Do Activities 14–15, p. 70, Grammatikheft

Wortschatz/Grammatik, p. 231 25 min.
- Presenting **Wortschatz**, ATE, p. 215U
- Presenting **Grammatik**, ATE, p. 215U
- Play Audio CD for Activity 24, p. 232
- Do Activities 25 and 26, p. 232
- Present **Sprachtipp**, p. 233
- Do Activity 27, p. 233

Wrap-Up 5 min.
- Students respond to questions about where they were and what they bought

Homework Options
Pupil's Edition, p.233, Act. 28
Grammatikheft, p. 69, Acts. 12–13; pp. 71–72, Acts. 16–18
Übungsheft, pp. 92–94, Acts. 15–22

Block 5

DRITTE STUFE

Quick Review 15 min.
- Check homework, Übungsheft, pp. 92–94, Acts. 15–22

Aussprache, p. 233 20 min.
- Do **Richtig aussprechen/Richtig lesen**, p. 233
- Do **Richtig schreiben/Diktat**, p. 233

Quiz Review 35 min.
- Do **Mehr Grammatikübungen, Dritte Stufe**
- Do Situation 8-3, pp. 137–138
- Play game, **Ausreden finden**, ATE, p. 215C

Quiz 20 min.
Quiz 8-3A or 8-3B

Homework Options
Übungsheft, p. 95, Act. 23
Activities for Communication, pp. 47–48, prepare Communicative Activity 8-3

Block 6

DRITTE STUFE

Quick Review 15 min.
- Return and review Quiz 8-3
- Do Communicative Activity 8-3

ZUM LESEN 20 min.
- Thinking Critically, p. 215V
- Present **Lesestrategie**, p. 234
- Do Activities 1–10, pp. 234–235

ANWENDUNG 30 min.
- Thinking Critically, ATE, p. 215W
- Teaching Suggestions for **Fortsetzung** and **Videoclips** Videos, Video Guide, pp. 50–51
- Show **Fortsetzung** and **Videoclips** Videos
- Do **Anwendung** Activities 1–4, pp. 236–237

Project 20 min.
- Start **Gesund essen** project, ATE, p. 215C

Wrap-Up 5 min.
- Students respond to questions about where they bought certain grocery items

Homework Options
Complete **Gesund essen** project
Interaktive Spiele, see ATE , p. 215F

Block 7

ANWENDUNG

Quick Review 15 min.
- Students present **Gesund essen** projects

Kann ich's wirklich?, p. 242 15 min.
- Students write out answers to questions 1–8

Chapter Review 15 min.
- Review chapter functions, vocabulary, and grammar; choose from **Mehr Grammatikübungen**, Grammar Tutor for Students of German, Activities for Communication, Listening Activities, Interactive CD-ROM Tutor, or **Interaktive Spiele**
- Review test format and provide sample test items for students

Test, Chapter 8 45 min.
- Administer Chapter 8 Test. Select from Testing Program, Alternative Assessment Guide or Test Generator.

Kapitel 8: Einkaufen gehen
Teaching Suggestions, *pages 216–243*

PAGES 216–217

CHAPTER OPENER

Pacing Tips

In the **Erste Stufe** the modal **sollen** is introduced, as well as the **du**- and **ihr**-commands. The vocabulary deals with groceries and where to buy them. In the **Zweite Stufe** students learn the functions of 'talking about quantities' and 'saying that you want something else.' Conversions of German quantities are presented in the **Wortschatz** box on p. 226. The **Dritte Stufe** centers around the functions of 'giving reasons' and 'saying where you were and what you bought.' The conjunctions **weil** and **denn** are introduced, along with the past tense of **sein** and time expressions. You may want to spend more time on the grammar-intense **Erste Stufe** and **Dritte Stufe** than on the **Zweite Stufe**. For Lesson Plans and timing suggestions, see pages 215I–215L.

Meeting the Standards
Communication
- Asking what you should do, p. 222
- Telling someone what to do, p. 223
- Talking about quantities, p. 226
- Saying that you want something else, p. 227
- Giving reasons, p. 230
- Saying where you were and what you bought, p. 231

Cultures
- Ein wenig Landeskunde, p. 222
- Landeskunde, p. 225
- Ein wenig Landeskunde, p. 227
- Culture Notes, p. 215O
- Culture Notes, p. 215S
- Culture Note, p. 215V
- Language Note, p. 215V

Connections
- Multicultural Connection, p. 215M
- Music Connection, p. 215P
- Math Connection, p. 215S
- Music Connection, p. 215T
- Health Connection, p. 215W

Comparisons
- Language-to-Language, p. 215R
- Language Note, p. 215U
- Language-to-Language, p. 215U
- Language Note, p. 215V
- Multicultural Connection, p. 215W

One-Stop Planner CD-ROM

For resource information, see the **One-Stop Planner CD-ROM**, Disc 2.

Communities
- Culture Note, p. 215M
- Culture Note, p. 215P
- Career Path, p. 215Q

Connections and Comparisons

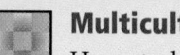 **Multicultural Connection**

Have students try to guess where the pictured tomatoes could come from. (Italy, warmer climate) Can students think of produce items that are imported to the United States? Ask them to name some examples (Avocados, Mexico).

Building on Previous Skills

Do students recall two open-air markets from preceding units? (the **Marktplatz** in Wedel and the **Viktualienmarkt** in Munich)

Cultures and Communities

 Culture Note

German parents routinely send their older children shopping for them. The children know what their parents usually buy, and the local merchants often do, too. Much shopping is done in specialty stores and open-air markets.

Chapter Sequence

Los geht's! . . . . .p. 218
Erste Stufe . . . . .p. 221
Landeskunde . . . . .p. 225
Zweite Stufe . . . . .p. 226
Dritte Stufe . . . . .p. 229
Zum Lesen . . . . .p. 234
Mehr Grammatikübungen . . . . .p. 236
Anwendung . . . . .p. 240
Kann ich's wirklich? . . . . .p. 242
Wortschatz . . . . .p. 243

LOS GEHT'S!

Fortsetzung

You may choose to continue with the Fortsetzung of *Alles für die Oma!* now or wait until later in the chapter. For a synopsis of the **Los geht's!** and **Fortsetzung** episodes, see p. 215E.

Advance Organizer

To help students prepare for the content and functions modeled in the pictures, ask them to imagine that they will be in charge of getting the groceries for the next two to three days at their home. What would they need to get, and where would they go? Have them make a list and tell them to be as specific as possible.

Teaching Resources
pp. 218–220

PRINT
▸ Lesson Planner, p. 37
▸ Video Guide, pp. 49–50, 52
▸ Übungsheft, p. 85

MEDIA
▸ One-Stop Planner
▸ Video Program
  Los geht's!
  Videocassette 3, 24:49–28:30
  Videocassette 5 (captioned version), 42:43–46:27
  Fortsetzung
  Videocassette 3, 28:35–31:12
  Videocassette 5 (captioned version), 46:28–49:06
▸ Audio Compact Discs, CD8, Trs. 1–2
▸ **Los geht's!** Transparencies

PAGES 218–219

Los geht's! Transparencies

Preteaching Vocabulary

Identifying Keywords

Start by asking students to guess the context of the **Los geht's!** episode (shopping for food). Then have students use the German they know and the context of the situation to identify keywords and phrases that tell what is happening. Students should first list the sequence of functions that occur in a conversation between a salesperson and a customer. Here are some of the words and phrases they might identify as keywords: **Tomaten; Supermarkt; Brot; Euro; Verkäuferin; Gramm; Das ist alles.; bitte; Alles, dann?.** Can they identify the three phrases that the salespeople use to ask Flori if he wants something else? (**Hast du noch einen Wunsch, bitte?; Sonst noch einen Wunsch?;** and **Sonst noch etwas?**) Using the list of functions between a salesperson and a customer, have students scan **Los geht's!** for phrases that are used to indicate those functions.

PAGE 220

Using the Captioned Video

As an alternative to reading the conversations in the book, you might want to show the captioned version of *Alles für die Oma!* available on Videocassette 5.

Comprehension Check

2 Challenge After students have completed Activity 2, ask them to find all the phrases in which the speaker has abbreviated a sentence and implied part of it.
Examples: (**Du machst**)**Kaiserschmarren?**
(**Das ist**) **super!**
(**Haben Sie**) **sonst noch einen Wunsch?**

3 Challenge Have students use vocabulary from preceding chapters to try to name one additional item that can also be purchased at each of the four stores.

4 Challenge After students have completed Activity 4, ask them to replace one part of each of the sentences on the left (not the subject) in such a way that the reason given on the right still fits. (Example: **Omi gibt Flori Geld, denn er geht für sie einkaufen.**)

5 Visual Learners Have the eight sentences written on sentence strips before starting this activity. Have students work with a partner to figure out the correct sequence of the sentences in Activity 5. Then give one sentence strip to each of eight pairs of students and have them arrange themselves in the correct order. Have one student help oversee the activity. Ask students to read the sentences aloud.

LOS GEHT'S!

STANDARDS: 1.2

KAPITEL 8 LOS GEHT'S! 215N

ERSTE STUFE

Teaching Resources
pp. 221–225

PRINT
▶ Lesson Planner, p. 38
▶ TPR Storytelling Book, pp. 29, 32
▶ Listening Activities, pp. 59, 63–64
▶ Activities for Communication, pp. 43–44, 102, 105, 137–138
▶ Grammatikheft, pp. 64–66
▶ Grammar Tutor for Students of German, Chapter 8
▶ Übungsheft, pp. 86–88
▶ Testing Program, pp. 197–200
▶ Alternative Assessment Guide, p. 39
▶ Student Make-Up Assignments, Chapter 8

MEDIA
▶ One-Stop Planner
▶ Audio Compact Discs, CD8, Trs. 3–4, 18, 24–25
▶ Teaching Transparencies
 Situations, 8-1, 8-2
 Vocabulary 8-A, 8-B
 Mehr Grammatikübungen Answers
 Grammatikheft Answers
▶ Interactive CD-ROM Tutor, Disc 2

PAGE 221

Bell Work
Ask students to brainstorm a list of some popular foods in America they believe to be of German origin. Here are some examples: hamburger, strudel, muesli (Swiss), pretzel, sauerkraut, selzer, zwieback, frankfurter, marzipan (from Lübeck), wiener.

PRESENTING: Wortschatz

Look through your local grocery ads and cut out items representative of the vocabulary in the **Wortschatz.** Tape the pictures on construction paper (you might want to laminate these for future activities). Using these as visual aids, introduce the vocabulary by naming the items, then using **ja/nein** questions, continuing with either/or questions, and finally building up to short-answer questions.

For Additional Practice

- Have students identify all the compound nouns in the ads. (Examples: **Hackfleisch, Bratwurst**)

- Have students identify the cognates in the ads and practice the pronunciation of these words. (Examples: **Sal<u>a</u>t, <u>Ä</u>pfel, Tom<u>a</u>ten**)

Cultures and Communities

Culture Notes
- In Germany, eggs are typically sold in cartons of ten, rather than twelve as in the United States.

- You might want to point out to students the difference between a **Torte** and a **Kuchen. Torte** and **Kuchen** are both cakes. However, the word **Torte** is used for more elaborate cakes with several layers, creamy icing, and decorations. **Kuchen** tend to be less fancy than **Torten** and often look like coffeecake or even fruit pies (Example: **Apfelkuchen**).

PAGE 222

Connections and Comparisons

Teaching Suggestion
7 Provide students with the current exchange rate and ask them to compare prices using the information on how to use the exchange rate from Chapter 5.

PRESENTING: So sagt man das!

Prepare a three-column chart on the board, a transparency, or a handout for students. In the left-hand column write the following questions: **Was soll ich für dich tun? Wo soll ich … kaufen? Wo soll ich … holen?**
In the second column write the "was" answers: **einkaufen gehen, Brot kaufen, Brot holen, Fleisch holen, Tomaten kaufen.**
In the third column write the "wo" answers: **beim Bäcker, beim Metzger, im Supermarkt, im Gemüseladen.**
Ask the questions and have students answer using one of the entries in columns 2 or 3:
Was soll ich für dich tun?
Du kannst für mich Brot holen.
After students have practiced with you, have them practice in pairs. Then have them answer the questions in **So sagt man das!**

PAGE 223

PRESENTING: Grammatik

The verb sollen Review with students the verbs **wollen, müssen,** and **können,** and the verb form **möchte.** Then practice the forms of **sollen** by asking questions and having students answer them. Write on the board the three questions: **Was soll ich …? Was soll er …? Was sollen wir …?** Have students quickly answer, using the expressions in the **Grammatik** as a guide: **Du sollst …, Er soll …, Ihr sollt …** After they have practiced the forms in this way, have them answer the discovery questions in the **Grammatik.**

Teaching Suggestion

9 This activity could be done first as an oral exercise in class and then, for additional practice, assigned as written homework.

PRESENTING: So sagt man das!

Begin by having each student ask you the question: **Was soll ich für Sie tun?** Using the vocabulary of the **Erste Stufe** (**Wortschatz** and verbs such as **einkaufen, holen, gehen**), address commands to several students in response to their questions.

PAGE 224

PRESENTING: Grammatik

The du- and ihr-commands Write several command forms on the board (Examples: **geh, zeig, gib, such, lauf, iss, nimm**). Then call on individual students to use one of the verbs on the board to command another student in class to do something. When all listed verbs have been used, ask the students what the infinitive of each verb is and which form of address they used to form the commands. (**du**-form) Ask students if they see how the **du**-command form differs from the regular **du**-form of a verb. (minus **st**) Repeat the same process, this time asking individual students to command two or more classmates using the **ihr**-command.

(TPR) Total Physical Response

To review the **du**- and **ihr**-command forms, have students prepare a list of three to five commands that can be carried out in class. Each student will then give his or her commands to individual students or small groups of students. (Examples: **Mary, nimm mein Buch! Gary und Debra, kommt zu mir!**)

Connections and Comparisons

Music Connections

• Refer students to the folksong *Der Jäger aus Kurpfalz,* Level 2 *Listening Activities,* p. 86, for additional reading. Which of the three stanzas contains **ihr**-command forms? (the second) Have students underline these commands. (**sattelt, legt**) You may also want to play the song, Level 2 CD 11, Tr. 25.

• For additional reading, refer students to the text of *Das Lied der Deutschen,* Level 1 *Listening Activities,* p. 78, and ask them if they can find the **du**-command forms. (**Blüh/ Blühe**) You might also want to play the song, Level 1 CD 10, Tr. 33.

PAGE 225

 # LANDESKUNDE

Teaching Resources
p. 225

PRINT
▶ Video Guide, pp. 49–50, 52–53
▶ Übungsheft, p. 96

MEDIA
▶ One-Stop Planner
▶ Video Program
  Videocassette 3, 31:51–33:22
▶ Audio Compact Discs, CD8, Trs. 5–9
▶ Interactive CD-ROM Tutor, Disc 2

Cultures and Communities

Teaching Suggestions

• Take a survey of your students in which you have them list the things they do most often to help other people. Write the small jobs and chores on the board and determine what things the class does most often to help others.

• You may want to introduce the following vocabulary to help students with the video segment and the readings.

  die Rechtschreibung *spelling and punctuation*
  die Kinderkirche *Sunday school*
  unregelmäßig *irregular*

Cultures and Communities

Culture Note

In the German-speaking countries, high school students like Silvana often offer tutorials (**Nachhilfe**) in their strongest subjects. Tutoring younger students is a good way for teenagers to earn extra spending money.

Teaching Suggestion

Ask students to read Sandra's interview and point out the word **grad'**. Can students guess its meaning within the context of the sentences? Is the word necessary to understand the sentence in which it is being used?

Reteaching: Stores and grocery items

Make a list of stores and all the items that can be found in each store. List the items in random order on one side of the board and list the names of the stores on the other side. Ask students to come to the board and draw lines correctly matching each store with its merchandise.

 **Game**

Play the game **Was passt?** to review the food vocabulary introduced in the **Erste Stufe.** See Chapter 2, p. 41C for the procedure.

Cultures and Communities

Career Path

Have students think of reasons why it would be useful for employees of American soft drink and food companies to know German. (Suggestion: Imagine you are an employee of one of those firms working in an affiliate in Vienna, Austria, or Zurich, Switzerland.)

Teaching Suggestion

Have the following information listed on a transparency you have prepared ahead of time. List ten items that can be bought in different specialty shops. For each item, students have to determine the specialty shop where it can be purchased.

Wurst (Metzger)
Bananen (Obst- und Gemüseladen)
Kuchen (Bäcker)
Papier (Schreibwarenladen)
…

Teacher to Teacher

Kristine Conlon
Muscatine High School
Muscatine, Iowa

Kristine introduces sound shifts in this chapter.

"We use sound shifts to decode vocabulary words, and the vocabulary in Chapter 8 provides excellent examples."

German [ ] often becomes English [ ]	Example
[t] > [d]	Teig > dough, Salat > salad, Brot > bread, Tag > day
[z] > [t]	Salz > salt,
[pf] > [p]	Pfund > pound, Pfeffer > pepper, Apfel > apple
[g] > [y]	gestern > yesterday, Tag > day sag > say
[b] > [v]	haben > have, geben > give
[f] > [p]	Streifen > stripe, Pfeffer > pepper

Assess

▸ Testing Program, pp. 197–200
  Quiz 8-1A, Quiz 8-1B
  Audio CD8, Tr. 18

▸ Student Make-Up Assignments
  Chapter 8, Alternative Quiz

▸ Alternative Assessment Guide, p. 39

ZWEITE STUFE

Teaching Resources
pp. 226–228

PRINT
▸ Lesson Planner, p. 39
▸ TPR Storytelling Book, pp. 30, 32
▸ Listening Activities, pp. 60, 64–65
▸ Activities for Communication, pp. 45–46, 103, 105, 137–138
▸ Grammatikheft, pp. 67–68
▸ Grammar Tutor for Students of German, Chapter 8
▸ Übungsheft, pp. 89–91
▸ Testing Program, pp. 201–204
▸ Alternative Assessment Guide, p. 39
▸ Student Make-Up Assignments, Chapter 8

MEDIA
▸ One-Stop Planner
▸ Audio Compact Discs, CD8, Trs. 10–11, 19, 26–27
▸ Teaching Transparencies
  Situation 8-1
  Vocabulary 8-A
  Mehr Grammatikübungen Answers
  Grammatikheft Answers
▸ Interactive CD-ROM Tutor, Disc 2

> **PAGE 226**

Bell Work
Bring empty cereal boxes, flour bags, cans of food, and so on, and ask students to look at the labels. Have them write the quantities on the chalkboard.

PRESENTING: Wortschatz

Try to get a scale with grams on it from the science department and have students bring different foods in different amounts. Ask them to guess how much each food item weighs using German (metric) measurements. Then measure each item and state the weight in German.

Connections and Comparisons

Language-to-Language
You may want to explain to your students that Europeans and most other peoples use the metric system for length, weight, and volume, and measure temperature in Celsius. Ask students what units of measure the United States has in common with the rest of the world. (For example, units of measure relating to time: seconds, minutes, hours)

Background Information
Here are some additional conversions students might want to use as they try to compare the weights of different foods.

1 **Gramm (g)** = 0.035 ounces
1 **Pfund (pfd)** =1.1 pounds
1 **Kilogramm (kg)** = 2.2 pounds
1 **Liter (l)** = 2.11 pints; 1.06 quarts
3,78 **Liter** = 1 gallon

PRESENTING: So sagt man das!

Pass out to each student a card on which has been written a specific quantity of a type of food or beverage. (**500 g Käse, 3 l Milch**) Then introduce the expressions in **So sagt man das!** Be sure to emphasize the fact that in German, unlike English, the word specifying the unit of measurement remains singular in form. (Example: **drei Pfund Tomaten**/ *three pounds of tomatoes*) Go down the rows asking students what item and how much of it they need; they should base their replies on the information on their cards. (**Was bekommen Sie? — Kaffee, bitte.; Wie viel Kaffee? — 300 Gramm.**) You may want to point out to your students that in spoken German, the word **Kilo** is used much more frequently than **Kilogramm.**

Teaching Suggestion

Have students look back at frame 5 of **Los geht's!** on p. 219 (where Flori is at the butcher shop). Ask students how and what Flori orders. Then have students turn to p. 221 and, with a partner, read the names and quantities of the items pictured. (Example: **1 Kilo Hackfleisch**)

> **PAGE 227**

PRESENTING: So sagt man das!

Ask students to look at frames 5 and 6 of **Los geht's!** on p. 219. Can students infer the meaning of the vendor's lines (**Sonst noch einen Wunsch? Sonst noch etwas?**) from Flori's responses?

Communication for All Students

A Slower Pace

16 Have students listen a second time and determine in which stores the conversations take place. (1. **Metzger** 2. can't be determined 3. **Supermarkt** 4. **Obst- und Gemüseladen** 5. **Supermarkt**)

▶ PAGE 228

Connections and Comparisons

Math Connection

17 Have students find out the conversion ratio of centimeters to inches, and then determine how big the pizza crust for this recipe should be. (1 inch = 2.54 centimeters; the pizza crust should be about 12.5 inches in diameter.)

Teacher Note

17 Point out to students that the abbreviation **cm** in the pizza recipe stands for **Zentimeter.** Students might also want to know that **gitterförmig** means *criss-crossed* in this context.

Building on Previous Skills

17 The pizza needs to be baked at **250 Grad.** Using the conversion formula for Celsius to Fahrenheit degrees given in the Math Connection on p. 187U of Chapter 7, have students determine how much **250 Grad** would be in Fahrenheit degrees. (482° F)

Cultures and Communities

Culture Notes

17 • **Quark** is a soft, fresh cheese often used in the preparation of **Käsekuchen**, dips, or eaten as a spread as is the case of the **Pikanter Quark** in the recipe. Since **Quark** might not be readily available in the United States, tell students that they can substitute ricotta cheese or smooth cottage cheese.

• **Joule** is a unit used to indicate the amount of energy in food. The term was introduced because it is more precise than the word **Kalorien.** It is named after the English physicist James Prescott Joule (1818–1889). This term is often used in German recipes along with the word **Kalorien,** although most Germans use "**Kalorien**" in everyday speech.

Reteaching: Vocabulary and word order

Write out various sentences from the activities of the **Zweite Stufe** and **Los geht's!** on sentence strips. Cut the sentences apart and put them into numbered envelopes. Have students practice word order by putting the words into the correct order. Have students work individually or in pairs. When students have finished, call on several volunteers to read their sentences aloud to the class.

Teaching Suggestion

Have students working in pairs come up with as many food items as possible for a given topic in 30-45 seconds. (Examples: **Frühstück, Fete, Abendessen, Mittagessen, Oktoberfest**) Students should write all their words down. Monitor work, and ask students to read the food items they have listed when you call time.

Communication for All Students

Challenge

Have students find recipes for a German three-course meal (appetizer, entrée, dessert) on the Internet. Helpful keywords for their search might be: **Vorspeisen, Hauptgerichte,** and **Nachspeisen.**

You can follow this assignment up with the performance assessment activity in the *Alternative Assessment Guide,* p. 39.

Assess

▶ Testing Program, pp. 201–204
  Quiz 8-2A, Quiz 8-2B
  Audio CD8, Tr. 19

▶ Student Make-Up Assignments, Chapter 8, Alternative Quiz

▶ Alternative Assessment Guide, p. 39

DRITTE STUFE

Teaching Resources
pp. 229–233

PRINT
- Lesson Planner, p. 40
- TPR Storytelling Book, pp. 31, 32
- Listening Activities, pp. 60–61, 65–66
- Activities for Communication, pp. 47–48, 104, 105, 137–138
- Grammatikheft, pp. 69–72
- Grammar Tutor for Students of German, Chapter 8
- Übungsheft, pp. 92–94
- Testing Program, pp. 205–208
- Alternative Assessment Guide, p. 39
- Student Make-Up Assignments, Chapter 8

MEDIA
- One-Stop Planner
- Audio Compact Discs, CD8, Trs. 12–16, 20, 28–29
- Teaching Transparencies
  Situation 8-2
  Vocabulary 8-B
  Mehr Grammatikübungen Answers
  Grammatikheft Answers
- Interactive CD-ROM Tutor, Disc 2

PAGE 229

Bell Work

In pairs, ask students to find out what their partner had for breakfast or lunch that day. Students should be able to report what they found out to the class.

Communication for All Students

A Slower Pace

20 Ask students to scan each ad for words or expressions they recognize. On the board write down what students recognize in each ad. Paraphrase the words or parts of sentences that students do not understand.

PAGE 230

PRESENTING: So sagt man das!

Ask students to come up with an excuse for not doing their homework. (Example: Ich höre jetzt Musik.) Write some of the students' answers on the board, underlining the verbs in each sentence. Then write the sentence Ich kann meine Hausaufgaben nicht machen and connect it with the students' sentences, using weil or denn. (Example: Ich kann meine Hausaufgaben nicht machen, weil ich jetzt Musik höre.)

PRESENTING: Ein wenig Grammatik

Conjunctions Introduce **denn** and **weil** by telling your students that both words are equivalent to the English *because*. Then tell them that there is an important difference in the way these words are used in a sentence, and read off several statements in which **denn** and **weil** are used. Ask students what difference they noticed in sentence construction. For further practice, write the first part of a sentence on the board (**Ich kann nicht mitkommen, …**), and ask each student to complete the statement by explaining that there is a chore or other activity he or she has to do instead. Specify which conjunction each student is to use.

Connections and Comparisons

Music Connection

Refer students to the folksong *Es, es, es und es* (written around 1780), Level 2 *Listening Activities*, p. 22, for additional reading. Can they find the **weil**-clause? (**weil ich aus Frankfurt muss**) What infinitives could go together here with the modal **muss**? You may also want to play the song, Level 2 CD 3, Tr. 26.

Thinking Critically

Drawing Inferences Ask students what type of function the words **denn** and **weil** fulfill in a sentence. (They join clauses.) What can students tell from the examples about the word order in the following subordinate clause? (**weil ich keine Zeit habe**)

	Subject	Direct object	Conjugated verb
weil	ich	keine Zeit	habe

Language Note

Mention to students that in German a comma must be used between a main clause and a subordinate clause.

Teaching Suggestion

22 Ask students to do this activity orally with a partner and later assign it as written homework. Have students come up with at least five pairs of sentences.

Writing Assessment

22 You may wish to evaluate students' written homework using the following rubric.

Writing Rubric	Points			
	4	3	2	1
Content (Complete – Incomplete)				
Comprehensibility (Comprehensible – Seldom comprehensible)				
Accuracy (Accurate – Seldom accurate)				
Organization (Well-organized – Poorly organized)				
Effort (Excellent – Minimal)				

18–20: A   16–17: B   14–15: C   12–13: D   Under 12: F

> *PAGE 231*

PRESENTING: So sagt man das!

Ask students how they would ask a friend in English about his or her activities during the past weekend. Record the different forms students would use. Underline the verbs in these sentences. (Examples: What did you do last weekend? What were you doing last weekend?) Tell students that the German language also has several ways of expressing the past tense.

Teacher Note

The conversational past tense of **kaufen** in **So sagt man das!** is introduced here as a lexical item only. As few grammar explanations as possible should be given at this stage. The conversational past tense is introduced as a grammar item in Chapter 3 of Level 2.

Language-to-Language

Mention to your students that the German "**bei**" is used similarly to the French "**chez.**"
Example:
Ich wohne bei meiner Tante.
J'habite chez ma tante.

PRESENTING: Wortschatz

Use a current calendar to introduce the **Wortschatz** by giving examples of each new expression as you point to the day. (Example: **Vorgestern war Montag. Gestern war Dienstag.**)

PRESENTING: Grammatik

The verb sein In Chapter 1 students learned the present tense forms of **sein**. Review these forms with students before introducing the past tense of **sein**.

> *PAGE 232*

Communication for All Students

A Slower Pace

24 Before students listen to the recording, ask them what types of markers they need to listen for in order to distinguish between present/future and past tenses. (verbs and adverbs) Note some of their examples on the board.

For Additional Practice

25 Ask students to go over Flori's and Mara's lists again and have them tell you what the two teenagers did at certain times using 24-hour time.

Teaching Suggestion

26 For reading practice, ask students to read the brief dialogues in pairs. Students should switch roles for additional practice.

> *PAGE 233*

Von der Schule zum Beruf

28

You might want to bring to class several grocery store ads from the newspaper to illustrate various approaches to this activity.

Cultures and Communities

 Culture Note
According to the **Ladenschlussgesetz** of November 1, 1996, stores may stay open from 6:00 A.M. until 8 P.M. on weekdays, and until 4:00 P.M on Saturdays. Many stores, however, keep shorter hours. Stores are generally not allowed to open on Sundays and holidays.

Language Note
Schaufensterbummeln (from **bummeln**—*to stroll*) is very popular in all of the German-speaking countries. People often go window shopping on Sunday afternoons, when stores are closed.

Reteaching: Past tense of *sein*

Prepare a transparency or handout with four columns listing the following expressions from the **Dritte Stufe.**

vorgestern	warst	ich	im Kino
gestern	war	du	im Café
Abend	wart	Michael	im Englischen
heute	waren	ihr	Garten
Morgen		wir	auf dem Land
letztes			bei meinen
Wochenende			Freunden

Ask four students to create as many sentences as possible using expressions from all four columns.

Teaching Suggestions

• Provide students with the following **Lückensatz** which each one of them should try to complete in a creative or interesting way.

Vorgestern war ich nicht in der Schule, denn ...
Point out that students should use the past tense of sein.

PRESENTING: Aussprache

Point out to students that the short vowels ö and ü are articulated with less muscular exertion than the long ö and ü. Have students compare the following words.
Wörter vs. **Größe**; **hübsch** vs. **Gemüse**

Assess
▸ Testing Program, pp. 205–208
  Quiz 8-3A, Quiz 8-3B
  Audio CD8, Tr. 20

▸ Student Make-Up Assignments
  Chapter 8, Alternative Quiz

▸ Alternative Assessment Guide, p. 39

PAGES 234–235

ZUM LESEN

Teaching Resources
pp. 234–235

PRINT
▸ Lesson Planner, p. 41
▸ Übungsheft, p. 95
▸ Reading Strategies and Skills, Chapter 8
▸ Lies mit mir! 1, Chapter 8

MEDIA
▸ One-Stop Planner

Prereading
Building Context

Ask students to list foods that they consider to be healthful from all major food groups. This should be done in German. Then take a survey asking students which of these foods they like and dislike.

Teacher Note

Activities 1 and 2 are prereading tasks.

Reading
Teaching Suggestion

5 Before students scan the texts for the German words, ask them to look for parts of words they recognize from preceding units. (Example: **Tag** in the word **alltäglich**)

Connections and Comparisons

Language Note
Man ist, was man isst. is the original German saying that is used in one of the **Müller Brot** ads. It can be compared to the English saying *You are what you eat.*

Thinking Critically

• **Comparing and Contrasting** Can students think of American proverbs or sayings that involve foods? See if they can guess the English equivalent of this German saying: **Liebe geht durch den Magen.** (*The best way to a man's heart is through his stomach.*)

• **Analyzing** Ask students if they can tell by looking at the ads what product names are mentioned. (**Almenrausch, Leerdammer**) What company name appears? (**Müller**)

Communication for All Students

A Slower Pace

Ask students to look at the **Müller Brot** ad and make a list of words that they already know or believe might be cognates. (Examples: Fitness, Marathon, Vitamine, Mineralstoffe, Tag, Mahlzeit, Fett) Then, ask them what varieties of bread **Müller Brot** has to offer. (Isartaler, Zwergerl, Sonne, 4 Korn plus)

Connections and Comparisons

Health Connection

Ask students to name the major food groups of a balanced diet. How does the ad "**Der Mensch ist, wie er ißt**" (*old spelling*) tie into those requirements? From a nutritional point of view, how important are the products featured in the readings?

Thinking Critically

Drawing Inferences Before reading the **Müller Brot Hotline** ad, ask students why there might be such hotlines. Who would call for information? (Example: people concerned about what they eat and the nutritional value of products) After reading the ad with students, have them think of one question they might ask if they called the **Müller Brot Hotline.**

Comparing and Contrasting After looking at the cheese ads, ask students to think of similar products in the United States that advertise their low fat content. Why is it so important to consumers that cheeses be light?

Post-Reading

Teacher Note

Activity 10 is a post-reading task that will show whether students can transfer what they have learned.

 Portfolio

10 You might want to use this activity as a written portfolio item for your students. See *Alternative Assessment Guide*, p. 25.

MEHR GRAMMATIKÜBUNGEN

The **Mehr Grammatikübungen** activities are designed as supplemental activities for the grammatical concepts presented in the chapter. You might use them as additional practice, for review, or for assessment.

For more grammar presentations, review and practice, refer to the following:
- Grammatikheft
- Grammar Tutor for Students of German
- Grammar Summary on pp. R15–R25
- Übungsheft
- Grammar and Vocabulary quizzes (Testing Program)
- Test Generator
- Interactive CD-ROM Tutor
- Interaktive Spiele at <u>go.hrw.com</u>

USING ANWENDUNG

Video Wrap-up

Videocassette 3, 24:49–36:40
Videocassette 5 (captioned version), 42:43–49:06
At this time, you might want to use the video resources for additional review and enrichment. See *Video Guide* for suggestions regarding:
- the **Los geht's!** episode
- the **Landeskunde** interviews
- the **Fortsetzung** episode
- the **Videoclips.**

Apply and Assess

Teaching Suggestion

1 Have students listen to the activity twice. During the first listening, students should write down only what Flori is supposed to get. During the second listening, have students add the needed quantities next to each item.

Portfolio Assessment

3 You might want to use this activity as an oral portfolio item for your students. See *Alternative Assessment Guide*, p. 25.

Connections and Comparisons

Thinking Critically

Comparing and Contrasting Ask students to contrast the meals typically prepared in the United States with those in Germany. Also ask them to compare the times of day the meals are served. (Example: The main meal in Germany is served at noon as **Mittagessen,** whereas the main meal in the United States is usually served around 6 P.M. for dinner.)

Multicultural Connection

Foods and food preferences differ among nationalities and cultures. Have students conduct a survey of students of other nationalities to determine their eating habits. What do typical meals consist of? Include other foreign language teachers in the survey to tell about meals of other countries. Have students share their findings with the class.

Apply and Assess

Process Writing

5 Have students get together in groups of three or four to assist each other in writing their surveys. When they have finished, they should ask the other members of the group their questions and keep track of the results. Have them then write a summary of their findings to include with their surveys.

Teaching Suggestion

6 Ask students to bring to class the actual ingredients for the recipe. At the end of the role-playing activity, ask students to prepare their **Obstsalat** and serve it to the class. Students should be responsible for bringing plates, napkins, and plastic utensils to prepare and serve their dishes.

Using the Captioned Video

As a chapter review, write the conversation for a section of the **Los geht's!** episode and leave out targeted expressions students have learned in the chapter. Play the video for *Alles für die Oma!* on Videocassette 3 and have students fill in the cloze passage. Then, play the captioned version of *Alles für die Oma!* on Videocassette 5 and have students check their answers.

PAGE 242

KANN ICH'S WIRKLICH?

This page is intended to prepare students for the test. It is a brief checklist of the major points covered in the chapter. The students should be reminded that it is a checklist only and not necessarily everything that will appear on the test.

For additional self check options, refer students to the *Grammar Tutor*, the *Interactive CD-ROM Tutor*, and the Online self-test for this chapter.

PAGE 243

WORTSCHATZ

Review and Assess

Teaching Suggestion

Practice giving vocabulary definitions in German. Describe an item without saying the word. For example, you could say **Banane: es ist Obst; lang und gelb** or **Pfund: es hat 500 Gramm.** Have students try to guess the word you describe. This activity will prepare students for the following Circumlocution game.

Circumlocution

Play **Das treffende Wort suchen** with the new food vocabulary. (See p. 155C for procedures.) Assign each student or group of students a word from the **Erste Stufe,** and allow them time to find German vocabulary they can use to describe the food. Then ask them to read aloud the clues they've come up with, and have the rest of the class try to guess the food item in question. For **Kartoffel,** one might say: **Sie ist oft klein und braun. Sie ist auch gesund. Du isst sie mit Butter.**

Games

• Play the game **Ausreden finden** with the vocabulary of this chapter. See p. 215C for the procedure.

• Play the game **Was ist hier falsch?** See p. 215D for the procedure.

Teacher Note

Give the **Kapitel 8** Chapter Test: *Testing Program,* pp. 209–214 Audio CD 8, Trs. 21–23

8
Einkaufen gehen

Objectives

In this chapter you will learn to

Erste Stufe

- ask what you should do
- tell someone what to do

Zweite Stufe

- talk about quantities
- say that you want something else

Dritte Stufe

- give reasons
- say where you were and what you bought

☑ internet

go.
hrw
.com
ADRESSE: go.hrw.com
KENNWORT:
WK3 MUENCHEN-8

◀ **Ich war beim Gemüsehändler.**

Los geht's! · *Alles für die Oma!*

Los geht's! is an abridged version of the video episode.

CD 8 Trs. 1–2

Strategie Verstehen

Look at the images for this story. Who are the people pictured? What are they doing? Where and when do you think these scenes are taking place? What clues tell you this?

Flori   **Omi**

1

Flori:	Hallo, Omi!
Omi:	Hallo, Flori!
Flori:	Hm, Omi, was kochst du denn? Es riecht so gut! Kaiserschmarren? Super!
Omi:	Den isst du doch so gern!
Flori:	Und wie!

2

Flori: Hm, Omi, der Kaiserschmarren war gut! Wie immer!

Omi: Wirklich? Nicht zu süß?

Flori: Nein, überhaupt nicht. Er war gerade richtig!

Omi: Na, das freut mich!

3

Flori: Und was soll ich heute für dich einkaufen?

Omi: Hier ist der Einkaufszettel.

Flori: Wo soll ich denn die Tomaten kaufen?

Omi: Die kaufst du im Supermarkt. Dort sind sie nicht so teuer.

Flori: Und das Brot? Kann ich es auch gleich da kaufen?

Omi: Hol das Brot lieber beim Bäcker! Dort ist es immer frisch und schmeckt besser.

④

Omi: Hier sind hundert Euro. Verlier das Geld nicht!

Flori: Keine Sorge, Omi! Ich pass schon auf!

⑤

Flori: Hm…ein Pfund Hackfleisch, bitte!

Verkäuferin: Hast du noch einen Wunsch, bitte?

Flori: Dann noch hundert Gramm Aufschnitt.

Verkäuferin: Sonst noch einen Wunsch?

Flori: Nein, danke! Das ist alles.

⑥

Verkäuferin: Bitte schön?

Flori: So ein Brot, bitte!

Verkäuferin: Dieses hier?

Flori: Ja, genau das.

Verkäuferin: Sonst noch etwas?

Flori: Und dann noch zwei Semmeln.

Verkäuferin: Alles dann?

Flori: Danke, das ist alles.

Verkäuferin: Macht zwei Euro neunzig, bitte!

Flori: Einen Moment! Dann noch bitte so eine Brezenstange für mich. Nein, die brauchen Sie nicht einpacken, die ess ich gleich.

Verkäuferin: Alles dann? Drei Euro vierzig dann, bitte!

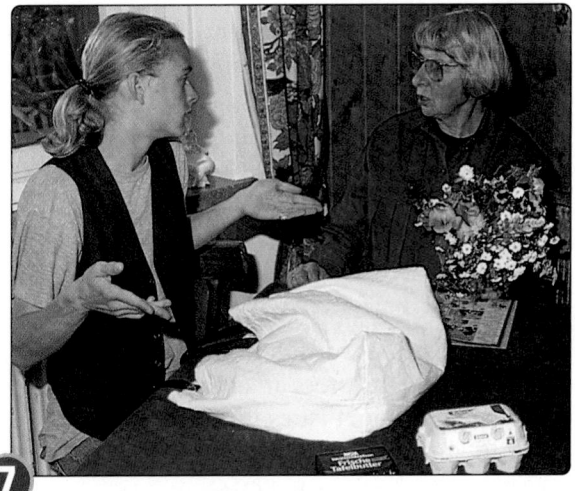

⑦

Flori: So, Omi, hier bin ich wieder. Hier sind noch ein paar Blumen für dich!

Omi: Das ist aber nett!

Flori: So, jetzt packen wir erst mal aus! Die Eier, die Butter …Tja, wo ist denn das Portemonnaie?

Omi: Wo warst du denn zuletzt?

Flori: Einen Moment, Omi, ich bin gleich wieder da! Tschau!

Übungsheft, S. 85

1 Was passiert hier?

These activities check for global comprehension only. Students should not yet be expected to produce language modeled in **Los geht's!**

Do you understand what is happening in the story? Check your comprehension by answering these questions. Don't be afraid to guess.

1. What does Flori do when he first arrives at his grandmother's house?
2. What does Flori offer to do for his grandmother?
3. Why does she give him money? What else does she give him for his errand?
4. What types of stores does Flori go to?
5. Why do you think Flori rushes out of his grandmother's house at the end of the story?

1. greets her, asks what she is cooking, eats **Kaiserschmarren**
2. go shopping
3. so that he can go shopping; a shopping list
4. supermarket, butcher, bakery.
5. He can't find his wallet.

2 Genauer lesen

Reread the conversations. Which words or phrases do the characters use to

1. express satisfaction or praise
2. refer to different kinds of stores
3. name foods
4. express quantities in weight
5. ask if someone wants more

1. Super, freut mich
2. Supermarkt, Bäcker
3. Kaiserschmarren, Tomaten, Brot, Hackfleisch, Aufschnitt, Semmeln, Brezenstange, Butter, Eier
4. Ein Pfund, hundert Gramm
5. Sonst noch einen Wunsch? Sonst noch etwas?

3 Wo war Flori?

Flori went to several different stores when he was shopping for his grandmother. In which of the places listed might he have made these statements?

1. Ein Pfund Hackfleisch, bitte! b
2. Jetzt bekomme ich noch zwei Semmeln. a
3. Ein Kilo Tomaten, bitte! d
4. Ich möchte bitte ein paar Rosen. c

a. beim Bäcker
b. beim Metzger
c. im Blumengeschäft
d. im Supermarkt

4 Was passt zusammen?

You can use the word **denn** (*since, for, because*) to show the relationship between two sentences that express an action and the reason for that action: **Hol das Brot beim Bäcker, denn dort ist es immer frisch!** Connect the following pairs of sentences in this way to logically explain some of the actions in the story.

1. Es riecht sehr gut bei Omi, e
2. Flori kauft Tomaten im Supermarkt, c
3. Flori kauft Brot beim Bäcker, b
4. Omi gibt Flori einen Einkaufszettel, a
5. Flori geht schnell weg, d

a. er geht für sie einkaufen.
b. dort ist es immer frisch.
c. dort sind sie nicht so teuer.
d. er kann das Portemonnaie nicht finden.
e. sie kocht Kaiserschmarren.

5 Nacherzählen

Put the sentences in logical order to make a brief summary of the story.

1. Zuerst kocht die Großmutter Kaiserschmarren für den Flori.

Dann gibt sie Flori auch das Geld. 4

Dann fragt Flori die Großmutter, was er für sie einkaufen soll. 2

Zuletzt kauft er auch Blumen für die Großmutter. 6

Die Tomaten kauft er im Supermarkt, das Brot beim Bäcker und das Hackfleisch beim Metzger. 5

Sie gibt Flori den Einkaufszettel. 3

Nach dem Einkaufen kommt Flori wieder zurück. 7

Aber er kann das Portemonnaie nicht finden und geht es suchen. 8

Erste Stufe

Objectives Asking what you should do; telling someone what to do

WK3 MUENCHEN-8

Wortschatz

Einkaufen gehen

Schau dir die Werbung an. Welche Geschäfte werben hier? Was kannst du in diesen Geschäften kaufen?

 p. 215X 8–A, 8–B

Beim Bäcker Motz

Brot
1 kg 1,70

Semmel
Stück -,30

Brezeln
Stück -,55

Torte
Stück 1,40

BEIM METZGER SEIBT

Hackfleisch
1 kg
2,98

Hähnchen
4,20

Aufschnitt
100 g 1,19

Bratwurst
100 g 0,69

Im Obst- und Gemüseladen Frisch

Tomaten
1 kg 2,40

Kartoffeln
1 kg 0,98

Äpfel
1 kg 1,60

Salat
St. -,59

Trauben
1 kg 1,98

IM SUPERMARKT KRAUS

Kleefeld
H
fettarme
Milch
1,5 %
1 Liter

Milch
l 1,10

Eier
10 St.
1,10

IDEE KAFFEE

Kaffee
1 Pfd.
4,49

Comptit milch
Süßrahm-
Butter
Deutsche Markenbutter

Butter
250 g
1,19

Fisch 100 g 0,89

WARBURGER
ZUCKER
FEIN

Zucker
1 kg 2,10

Käse
100 g
0,99

Goldstaub
Mehl

Mehl
500 g
Beutel
0,79

LEBENSMITTEL • GANZ PREISWERT!

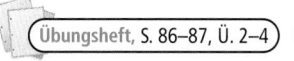
Übungsheft, S. 86–87, Ü. 2–4   Grammatikheft, S. 64, Ü. 1–2

Ein wenig Landeskunde

Although there are many large, modern supermarkets in Germany, many people still shop in small specialty stores or at the open-air markets in the center of town. Many Germans shop frequently, buying just what they need for one or two days. Refrigerators are generally much smaller than in the United States, and people prefer to buy things fresh.

Script on p. 215G

6 Flori und Claudia gehen einkaufen

CD 8 Tr. 3

Zuhören Flori and Claudia are at a café discussing their plans for the day. They decide to do their shopping together. Make a list of the things they are going to buy at each of the following kinds of stores.

im Supermarkt   beim Bäcker

beim Metzger   im Obst- und Gemüseladen

Milch	Kuchen	Wurst
Fisch	Hackfleisch	Aufschnitt
Butter	Bratwurst	Brot	Äpfel
	Semmeln	Brezeln

Im Supermarkt: Milch, Butter
Beim Metzger: Hackfleisch, Aufschnitt, Wurst, Bratwurst

Beim Bäcker: Semmeln, Brot, Brezeln
Im Obst- und Gemüseladen: Äpfel

7 Was möchtest du kaufen?

Schreiben Schau dir die Artikel auf Seite 221 an und schreib auf eine Einkaufsliste, was du in den verschiedenen Geschäften kaufen möchtest. Addiere die Preise. Gibst du zu Hause mehr aus? Weniger *(less)*?

8 Was möchte dein Partner?

Schreiben Gebrauche deinen Einkaufszettel von Übung 7 und frag deine Partnerin, was sie kaufen möchte. Mach dir Notizen. *(Take notes.)* Tauscht dann die Rollen. Sag dann der Klasse, was deine Partnerin kaufen möchte.

BEISPIEL Du Beim Bäcker möchte er/sie ...

So sagt man das!

Asking what you should do

If you were going to help a friend or relative run errands, you would first ask what you should do: The responses might be:

Was soll ich für dich tun?   **Du kannst für mich einkaufen gehen.**
Wo soll ich das Brot kaufen?   **Beim Bäcker.**
Soll ich das Fleisch im Supermarkt holen?   **Nein, du holst das besser beim Metzger.**
Und die Tomaten? Wo soll ich sie kaufen?   **Im Gemüseladen, bitte.**

What do you think the word **soll** means? In the sentences with **soll** and **kannst,** what happens to the word order? Where is the main verb?

The verb **sollen**

Sollen is used to express what you *should* or *are supposed to* do.

Du **sollst** das Brot beim Bäcker **kaufen.**

What verbs do you already know that are similar to **sollen?** In what ways are they similar? Here are the forms of **sollen.**

ich	soll	wir	soll**en**
du	soll**st**	ihr	soll**t**
er, sie, es	soll	sie, Sie	soll**en**

8–2

Mehr Grammatikübungen, S. 236, Ü. 1–3

Übungsheft, S. 87, Ü. 5–6   Grammatikheft, S. 65, Ü. 3–4

9 **Grammatik im Kontext**

Schreiben/Sprechen Wie viele Fragen kannst du bauen? (Be sure to match the food items with the correct store.)

Sollen	ich
Sollt	wir
Sollst	er
Soll	ihr
	du
	Flori und Claudia

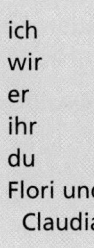

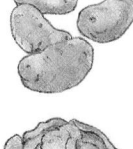

holen?
kaufen?

Examples: **Soll ich die Wurst beim Metzger holen? Soll er die Semmeln beim Bäcker kaufen?**

10 **Wo soll ich ... kaufen?**

Lesen/Sprechen Du bist Austauschschüler *(exchange student)* bei einer deutschen Familie. Deine Gastmutter gibt dir einen Einkaufszettel, und du sollst für sie einkaufen gehen. Gebrauche die Einkaufsliste auf der rechten Seite und frag deine Partnerin, wo du diese Lebensmittel kaufen sollst. Tauscht dann die Rollen.

Wurst
Käse
Brot
Äpfel
Semmeln
Salat
Mineralwasser
Zucker
Aufschnitt

So sagt man das!

Telling someone what to do

You have learned one way to tell someone what he or she can do to help you using **können.** Here are some other ways to express the same thing:

Someone might ask:

> **Was soll ich für dich tun?**
> **Was sollen wir für dich tun?**

The response might be:

> **Geh bitte einkaufen!**
> **Geht bitte einkaufen!**

What would be the English equivalent of the first response?[1] What would be the English equivalent of the second response?[2] What is the difference?[3]

---

1. *Go shopping, please.* **2.** *Go shopping, please.* **3.** The first is a singular command, the second is a plural command.

Grammatik

The **du**-command and the **ihr**-command

Look at the following commands:

du-command		**ihr**-command	
Kauf	Brot für die Oma!	**Kauft**	Brot für die Oma!
Komm	doch mit!	**Kommt**	doch mit!
Nimm	das Geld mit!	**Nehmt**	das Geld mit!

The above sentences are commands. These command forms are used to tell a person or persons you know well what to do. The **du**-command is formed by using the **du**-form of the verb without the **-st** ending. The **ihr**-command uses the **ihr**-form of the verb.

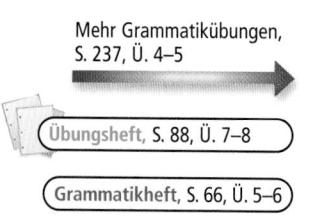

Mehr Grammatikübungen,
S. 237, Ü. 4–5

Übungsheft, S. 88, Ü. 7–8

Grammatikheft, S. 66, Ü. 5–6

---

11 **Grammatik im Kontext** Script on p. 215G

CD 8 Tr. 4

Zuhören Flori's grandmother is preparing lunch on Saturday for him and his friends, Markus and Mara. She needs help and tells everyone what to do. Listen and decide what each person is supposed to do. Under each of their names (Markus, Mara, Flori) list their tasks.

Markus: zum Supermarkt gehen und Tomaten holen
Mara: zum Bäcker gehen und Semmeln und einen Kuchen holen
Flori: den Tisch decken, Limo und Mineralwasser holen

12 **Grammatik im Kontext** Answers will vary. Examples: Putz die Fenster! Spül das Geschirr!

a. Sprechen/Schreiben Welche Verbformen sind richtig?

1. Flori, ═══ jetzt zum Bäcker und ═══ ein Brot! geh / kauf (hol)

2. Und Flori, ═══ das Geld mit und ═══ es nicht! nimm / verlier

3. Und ihr, Markus und Mara, ═══ bitte die Blumen für mich! gießt

4. Und, Markus und Mara, ═══ dann die Katze und ═══ das Geschirr! füttert / spült

b. Sprechen Frank hat zu Hause schon lange nicht mehr geholfen. Schau dir die Zeichnung mit einer Partnerin an und sagt, was Franks Eltern ihm wohl sagen werden.

13 **Eine Fete**

Sprechen You are having a party and two friends are helping you get ready. You've already gone shopping but have forgotten some of the things you need. Get together with two other classmates and, using your lists from Activity 7, each of you chooses six things you still need to buy. First you are the host, and your partners will ask what they can do to help. Tell each person to buy three items and where to buy them. Then switch roles so that each person plays the host once.

Was machst du für andere Leute?

How do you think students in German-speaking countries help others? We asked several students whom they help and in what ways they help them. Before you read, try to guess what they might say. CD 8 Tr. 5

CD 8 Tr. 5-9

Silvana, Berlin

„Zweimal in der Woche gebe ich Nachhilfe. Da hab ich einen kleinen Schüler. Der ist in der dritten Klasse, und dem geb ich Nachhilfe in Rechtschreibung und Lesen und Mathematik." CD 8 Trs. 6

Sandra, Stuttgart

„Bei uns in der Nachbarschaft gibt's grad' ältere Leute. Und unter uns wohnt eine Frau, die …für die mach ich manchmal kleine Einkäufe oder geh einfach nur hin und rede mit ihr, damit sie halt nicht grad' so allein ist, und besuch sie einfach oder bring ihr halt mal was rüber, wenn wir zum Beispiel Obst aus dem Garten haben." CD 8 Tr. 7

Brigitte, Bietigheim

„Also, ich hab mit Kindern zu tun. Ich hab mal Kinderkirche sonntags, und da beschäftigt man sich mit kleinen Kindern und spielt mit denen, und das mach ich aber unregelmäßig. Also ich habe das auch schon lange Zeit nicht mehr gemacht." CD 8 Tr. 8

Iwan, Bietigheim

„Also meistens da helf ich zum Beispiel meinem Bruder irgendwie, wenn er irgendwelche Probleme in der Schule hat. Und wenn ich bei meiner Oma bin, dann helf ich auch meiner Oma." CD 8 Tr. 9

A. 1. Write each student's name. Then write whom each student helps.   two groups; young children, older people

2. The people whom the students help fall into two groups. What are they? With a partner, make a chart for these two groups and list the ways in which the students help each one.

3. Now make a list of the people you help and how you help them. Ask your partner what he or she does to help others: **Was machst du für andere Leute?** Then switch roles.

B. With your classmates, discuss some of the ways you help other people. Do you do any of the same things the German students do? What is your impression: Do people help others more in Germany than in the United States? What are your reasons for deciding one way or the other? When you have finished your discussion, write a brief essay explaining your answers.

Zweite Stufe

Objectives Talking about quantities;
saying that you want something else

Wortschatz

Und wie viel?

8–1

wiegen ungefähr
1 Kilo (kg)
= 1000 Gramm (g)
= (*2.2 lb.*)

wiegen ungefähr
1/2 (ein halbes) Kilo
= 500 Gramm
= 1 (deutsches)
Pfund (Pfd.)

wiegt ungefähr
100 Gramm

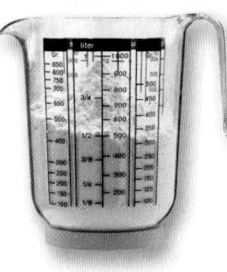

1 Liter (l) ist
ein bisschen mehr
als 1 *quart*
= (1.057 *quarts*)

2 Pfund = 1 Kilo = 1000 Gramm

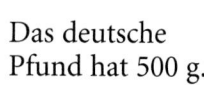

Das amerikanische
Pfund hat nur 453 g.

Das deutsche
Pfund hat 500 g.

Übungsheft,
S. 89–90, Ü. 9–10

Grammatikheft,
S. 67, Ü. 7–8

So sagt man das!

Talking about quantities

When shopping for groceries in Germany, you will need to know how much to ask for
using weights. For example, at the butcher's the salesperson
might ask you:

Was bekommen Sie?
Wie viel Hackfleisch?
Und wie viel Aufschnitt?

You might respond:

Aufschnitt und Hackfleisch, bitte.
500 Gramm Hackfleisch.
100 Gramm, bitte!

14 **Was kaufen sie und wie viel?** Script on p. 215G

Zuhören You are standing in line at the **Gemüseladen** and overhear other customers
asking the salesperson for specific amounts of certain items. First, listen to the conversations and write down what the customers are asking for. Then listen again and decide
how much of each item they want. Tomaten - ein Pfund Äpfel - zwei Pfund Kartoffeln - ein Kilo Trauben - 1/2 Pfund

CD 8
Tr. 10

Übungsheft, S. 96, Ü. 24

Look back at the ads on page 221 and find the abbreviations that are used to describe quantities. What do they stand for? How many different units of measurement are listed? How does this compare with measures in the United States? In German-speaking countries, the metric system is used for weights and measures. At the open-air markets and in many specialty stores, such as the bakery and the butcher shop, you will have to ask the salesperson for certain foods rather than serve yourself. You will need to be able to tell the vendor how much of each item you would like.

15 Was bekommen Sie?

Lesen/Sprechen Du bist mit deiner Einkaufsliste (siehe rechts) in einem Laden. Dein Partner, der Verkäufer, fragt dich, was du kaufen möchtest. Du nennst vier Dinge, die auf deiner Liste stehen und sagst, wie viel du brauchst. Tauscht dann die Rollen.

VERKÄUFER	**Was …?**
DU	**Ich brauche …**
VERKÄUFER	**Wie viel?**
DU	**…**

> 1 kg Tomaten
> 250 g Kaffee
> 350 g Butter
> 1 ℓ Milch
> 100 g Käse
> 200 g Aufschnitt
> 500 g Hackfleisch

So sagt man das!

Saying that you want something else

In **Kapitel 5** you learned how to tell a salesperson what you would like. You will also need to know how to tell him or her if you need something else.

The salesperson might ask:

Sonst noch etwas?
or
Was bekommen Sie noch?
or
Haben Sie noch einen Wunsch?
Ist das alles?

You might respond:

Ja, ich brauche noch ein Kilo Kartoffeln.
Ich bekomme noch sechs Semmeln.
Nein, danke. *or*
Danke, das ist alles.

Mehr Grammatikübungen, S. 237–238, Ü. 6–7

Übungsheft, S. 90–91, Ü. 11–14

Grammatikheft, S. 68, Ü. 9-11

In several of the questions and answers, the word **noch** appears. Can you guess what it means?

16 Logisch oder unlogisch? Script on p. 215G

Zuhören Listen to these conversations in various food stores and determine whether the response in each case is logical or not.

CD 8
Tr. 11

1. logisch
2. unlogisch
3. logisch
4. unlogisch
5. logisch

	logisch	unlogisch
1		
2		

17 Noch einen Wunsch?

Sprechen You are trying out new recipes tonight, and you still need to buy several things. Make shopping lists for the two recipes below. Then get together with two other classmates. One will play the salesperson at the supermarket, and the other will be another customer shopping for the second recipe. The salesperson will ask the customers what and how much they need and if they need something else.

Salami-Riesenpizza

Pizzateig (32 cm ⌀) für 2 Personen mit 4-6 Esslöffeln Tomatenstückchen belegen. 125 g Pizzakäse in Streifen schneiden, gitterförmig darüber legen.

10-12 Scheiben Salami und 6-8 blättrig geschnittene Champignons auf der Pizza verteilen.

Mit 1/2 Teelöffel Pizzagewürz bestreuen und bei 250 Grad 14 Minuten im Ofen backen.

Pikanter Quark

Zutaten:

250 g Quark
• etwa 4 Esslöffel Sahne
• etwa 4 Esslöffel Milch
• 1 Knoblauchzehe
• 1 Teelöffel Kümmel
• Salz

Insgesamt etwa 2370 Joule/565 Kalorien

 **18 Das Angebot der Woche**

Schreiben Pick a specific kind of food store and make your own ad. Either cut pictures from a newspaper or draw your own pictures. You may want to refer to page 221 for a model. Below are some additional grocery items you may want to include. Remember to include prices per unit (**Kilo, Gramm, Pfund,** or **Liter**).

Und dann noch...

Bananen	Apfelstrudel
Erdnussbutter	Joghurt
peanut butter	Ananas *pineapple*
Marmelade *jam, jelly*	Birnen *pears*
Erdbeeren	Melonen
strawberries	Müsli

 **LERNTRICK**

When you are learning a lot of new words, group them together in meaningful categories: group baked goods under **die Bäckerei**, meat items under **die Metzgerei**, etc. Putting the words in context will help you recall them more easily.

---

 19 Für mein Notizbuch

Schreiben Schreib in dein Notizbuch, wo du gern einkaufst! Was kaufst du? Was kaufst du gern? Was ist dein Lieblingsgericht (*favorite dish*)? Welches Essen schmeckt dir und welches Essen schmeckt dir nicht?

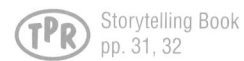

Dritte Stufe

Objectives Giving reasons; saying where you were and what you bought

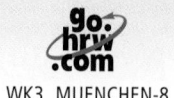

go.hrw.com
WK3 MUENCHEN-8

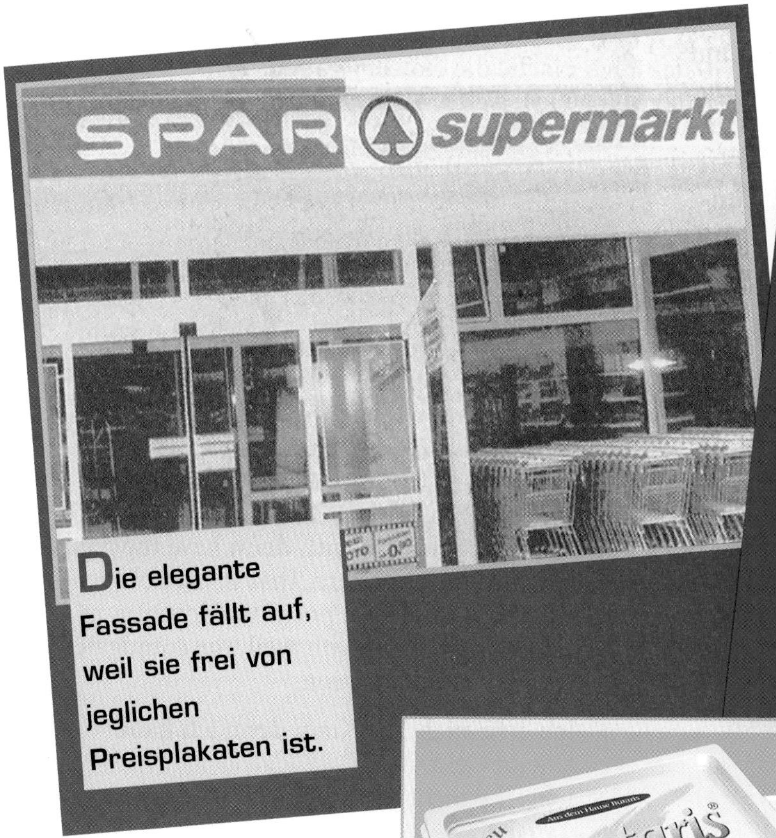
SPAR supermarkt
Die elegante Fassade fällt auf, weil sie frei von jeglichen Preisplakaten ist.

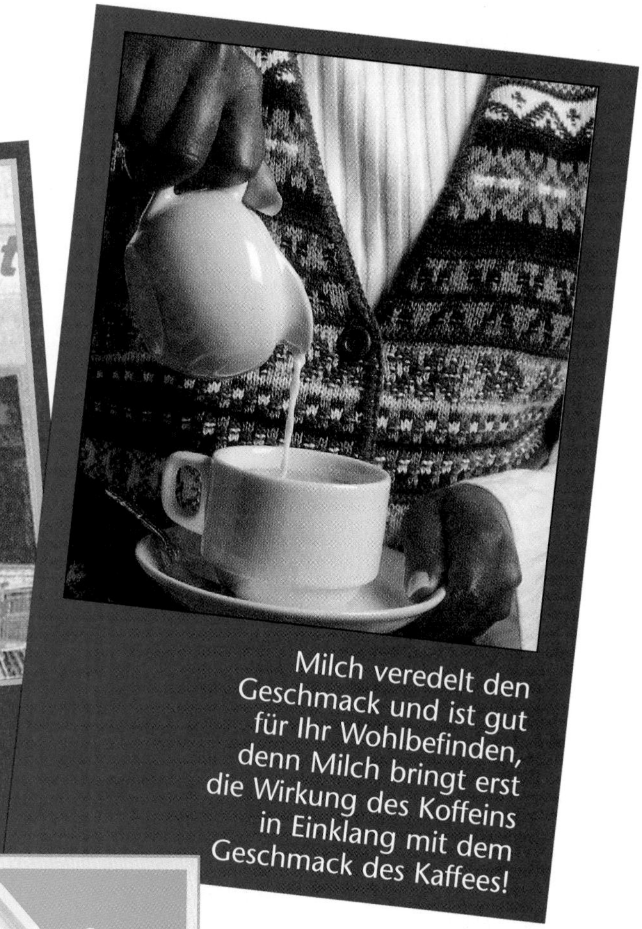
Milch veredelt den Geschmack und ist gut für Ihr Wohlbefinden, denn Milch bringt erst die Wirkung des Koffeins in Einklang mit dem Geschmack des Kaffees!

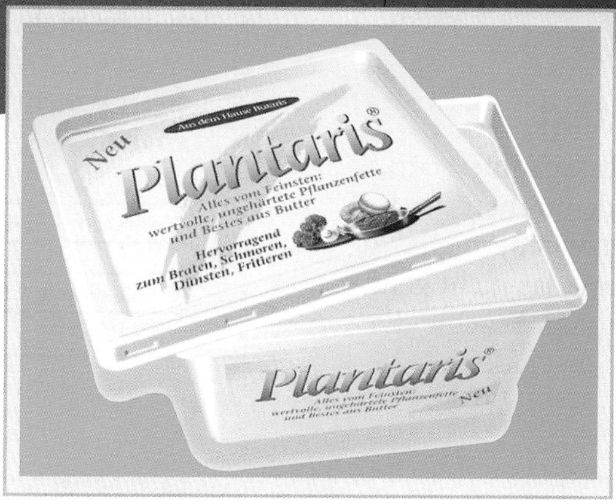
Neu
Plantaris
Alles vom Feinsten:
wertvolle, ungehärtete Pflanzenfette
und Bestes aus Butter
Hervorragend
zum Braten, Schmoren,
Dünsten, Fritieren

Note that in the Plantaris ad, the colon indicates that an explanation is following.

1. A supermarket, milk, shortening. Milk is supposed to improve the taste of coffee and harmonize the effect of caffeine. **Plantaris** contains unsaturated vegetable fat and the best of butter. It is excellent for roasting, braising, steaming and frying. SPAR Supermarket has an elegant look because the display window is not covered with price posters and signs.
2. **Weil** and **denn** mean "because." They express the reason for something.
3. In a **weil**-clause the verb is in final position, in a **denn**-clause it is in second position.

20 Warum?

Lesen/Sprechen Schau dir die drei Werbungen an und beantworte die Fragen.

1. Using the reading strategies you have learned so far, try to get the gist of each ad. What is each ad promoting? What reason does each ad give to persuade you to buy the product or to shop at a particular store?
2. Identify the words **weil** and **denn**. What do they mean? How do you know?
3. In the **SPAR Supermarkt** ad, what is the position of the verb in a clause that starts with **weil**? How does this compare with clauses starting with **denn**?

Giving reasons

In **Kapitel 7** you learned how to make an excuse and express obligation using **müssen**:
Claudia kommt nicht mit. Sie muss zu Hause helfen. You can also do this with
expressions beginning with **weil** or **denn**.

A friend might ask you:

**Kannst du für mich
einkaufen gehen?**

You might respond giving a reason:

Es geht nicht, denn ich mache die Hausaufgaben. *or*
Ich kann jetzt nicht (gehen), weil ich die Hausaufgaben mache.

---

21 **Wer kommt zur Party?** Script on p. 215H

Zuhören Mara is having a party on the
weekend. Listen to the messages left on her
answering machine and take down the following information: the name of the person who called, if that person is coming to
the party, and if not, the reason why not.

CD 8
Tr. 12

For answers, see bottom of page.

wer	ja oder nein?	warum (nicht)?
BEISPIEL Markus	nein	geht ins Kino

22 **Grammatik im Kontext**

Sprechen Sag deinen Klassenkameraden,
was du dieses Wochenende machen
kannst. Sag ihnen danach, was du nicht
machen kannst und warum das nicht geht.
Gebrauche das Beispiel unten. Beachte die
Wortstellung *(word order)* nach der
Konjunktion **weil**.

BEISPIEL

DU Am Wochenende kann ich
ins Kino gehen.
Am Wochenende kann ich
nicht ins Konzert gehen,
weil ich keine Zeit habe.

Answers will vary.
Examples: **Ich kann nicht Baseball
spielen, weil ich zu Hause helfe.**

Answers for Activity 21.
**Claudia/nein/macht Hausaufgaben/
Flori/ja/
Christian/nein/muss zu Hause helfen/
Stefan/ja/
Barbara/ja/
Brigitte/nein/lernt für die Prüfung**

Ein wenig Grammatik

The conjunctions denn and weil

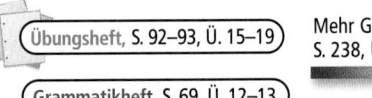

Denn and **weil** are called *conjunctions*.
Using them will help your German sound
more natural. Both words begin clauses that
give reasons for something (for example,
why you can or can't do something).
Clauses beginning with **denn** have the regular word order pattern, that is, the conjugated verb is in second position. However, in
clauses that begin with **weil**, the conjugated
verb is in final position.

Ich gehe nicht ins Kino, **denn** ich **habe**
kein Geld.
Ich gehe nicht ins Kino, **weil** ich kein Geld
habe.

 Übungsheft, S. 92–93, Ü. 15–19

Grammatikheft, S. 69, Ü. 12–13

Mehr Grammatikübungen,
S. 238, Ü. 8

BEISPIEL

Am Wochenende

Was?		Warum?
Baseball spielen		ich habe keine Zeit
ins Kino gehen		ich habe kein Geld
tanzen gehen		ich muss zu Hause helfen
Klamotten kaufen		ich mähe den Rasen
wandern		ich putze die Fenster
ins Café gehen		ich lerne für die
Freunde besuchen	**weil**	(Mathe)prüfung
Volleyball spielen		ich mache Hausaufgaben
Pizza essen		die Großeltern besuchen uns
?		?

23 Grammatik im Kontext

Schreiben/Sprechen Look at the following statements. Agree or disagree and give a reason why. First write your answers, then discuss your opinions with your classmates.

BEISPIEL   Ich bin damit einverstanden, weil/denn …
Ich bin nicht damit einverstanden, weil/denn …

1. Jugendliche sollen das ganze Jahr in die Schule gehen.
2. Jugendliche sollen nicht Auto fahren, bevor sie 18 sind.
3. Wir sollen mehr Geld für die Umwelt (*environment*) ausgeben.
4. Jugendliche müssen vor 10 Uhr abends zu Hause sein.

So sagt man das!

Saying where you were and what you bought

If a friend wants to find out where you were or what you bought, he or she might ask:

You might respond:

Wo warst du heute Morgen?

Zuerst war ich beim Bäcker und dann beim Metzger. Danach war ich im Supermarkt und zuletzt war ich im Kaufhaus.

Und was hast du beim Bäcker gekauft?
Wo warst du gestern?

Ich habe Brot gekauft.
Ich war zu Hause.

What do the phrases **ich war** and **du warst** mean? What are their English equivalents? What other words or expressions in these sentences indicate the past?

Grammatikheft, S. 70, Ü. 14–15

Wortschatz

gestern *yesterday*
vorgestern *day before yesterday*
gestern Abend *yesterday evening*

heute Morgen *this morning*
heute Nachmittag *this afternoon*
letztes Wochenende *last weekend*

Grammatik

The past tense of sein

War and **warst** are past tense forms of the verb **sein** (*to be*) and are used to talk about events in the past.

Wo **warst** du denn?   Ich **war** beim Bäcker.

Here are the past tense forms of **sein:**

ich	**war**	wir	**waren**
du	**warst**	ihr	**wart**
er, sie, es	**war**	sie, Sie	**waren**

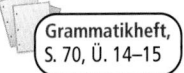

Mehr Grammatikübungen, S. 239, Ü. 9–10

Übungsheft, S. 94, Ü. 20–22

Grammatikheft, S. 71–72, Ü. 16–18

DRITTE STUFE   STANDARDS: 1.1, 4.1   *zweihunderteinunddreißig*   **231**

24 Grammatik im Kontext Script on p. 215H

Zuhören Listen to the following exchanges as Claudia talks with her friends. For each conversation, decide if the person Claudia is talking to has already done the activity mentioned or plans to do it in the future.

CD 8
Tr. 13

1. plans to do 2. already done 3. plans to do
4. already done 5. already done 6. plans to do

	already done	plans to do
1		
2		

25 Grammatik im Kontext

Sprechen Look at the pages out of Mara's and Flori's lists of things to do. Your partner will ask you where Flori was during the day. Use his schedule to answer your partner's questions. Then switch roles and ask your partner about Mara's day. Remember to use **zuerst**, **dann**, **danach**, and **zuletzt** to organize your answers.

Mara
10:00 Supermarkt für Mutti
12:00 mit Markus im Café essen
13:00 ins Einkaufszentrum gehen, Klamotten kaufen
14:30 Zimmer aufräumen

Flori
9:30 Brot und Äpfel für die Omi kaufen
13:00 zu Hause Mittag essen
13:30 Omis Fenster putzen
15:00 Kaufhaus, Fußball kaufen

26 Grammatik im Kontext

Schreiben Claudia hat viele Pläne. Aber sie kann ihre Freunde nicht erreichen *(contact)*.

a. Schreib die vier Dialoge ab und setze dabei die richtige Vergangenheitsform *(past tense form)* von **sein** in die Lücken.

b. Welches Bild passt zu welchem Dialog? 1. a 2. c 3. d 4. b

a.    b.    c.    d.

1. CLAUDIA   Sag mal, Petra, wo ════ du denn heute Morgen?   *warst*

PETRA   Ich ════ in der Stadt. Zuerst ════ ich beim Bäcker, dann im Obstladen. Heute Abend essen meine Tante und mein Onkel bei uns.   *war; war*

2. CLAUDIA   Und wo ════ denn die Michaela? Weißt du das? Sie ════ auch nicht zu Hause.   *war; war*

PETRA   Na, sie ════ im Eiscafé mit Gabi und Susanne. Die drei essen immer nur Joghurteis! Ingo hat sie später in der Disko gesehen.   *war*

3. CLAUDIA   Tag, Oma! Wo ════ du denn heute Morgen? Ich bin vorbeigekommen, und du ════ nicht da.   *warst*
warst

OMA   Die Tante Dorle ════ da, und wir haben im Café am Markt zu Mittag gegessen. Ach, Kind, das Essen ════ köstlich!   *war*
war

4. CLAUDIA   Hallo, ihr zwei! Wo ════ ihr am Samstagabend?   *wart*

HEIKE   Robert und ich, wir ════ im Kino — im neuen Cinedom. Mensch, das ════ echt toll! Wir haben den Film *Metro* gesehen. Unheimlich spannend!   *waren*
war

27 **Einkaufsbummel**

Sprechen Your partner just got back from shopping on a rainy Saturday. Your partner will decide on three items that he or she bought at each of the stores pictured. Ask your partner what he or she bought at each store. Switch roles, and be prepared to tell the class about your **Einkaufsbummel.**

LERNTRICK

Sometimes you don't know the exact word for something even in your own language. One way you can get your message across is by describing what you can't remember. Use a phrase like **Es ist etwas …** and then tell what it does, how it's used, or where it is. As practice, look around your classroom and pick three things you don't know how to say in German. How could you describe them so a German speaker would understand? Test your skills on a classmate! Look at these two drawings. Can you describe these items to a friend?

28 **Von der Schule zum Beruf**

Schreiben You have advanced to the position of store manager at a large food chain. Your job is to work with the marketing department, creating colorful and descriptive flyers that advertise the specials of the week for your various departments, such as produce, bakery, milk, cheese, etc.

AUSSPRACHE

 Richtig aussprechen / Richtig lesen CD 8 Trs. 14–16

A. To practice or review the following sounds, say the words and sentences below after your teacher or after the recording. CD 8 Tr. 14

1. The letters **ü** and **ö**: In **Kapitel 1** you learned how to pronounce the letters **ü** and **ö** as long vowels, as in **Grüß** and **Österreich**. However, when the letters **ü** and **ö** are followed by two or more consonants, they are pronounced as short vowels.

   müssen, Stück, Würste / Wir müssen fünf Stück Kuchen holen.
   können, köstlich, Wörterbuch / Könnt ihr für mich ein Wörterbuch kaufen?

2. The letter combinations **ei** and **ie**: The letter combination **ei** is pronounced like the *i* in the English word *mine*. The combination **ie** is pronounced like the *e* in the English word *me*.

   Bäckerei, Eier, Fleisch / Kauf das Fleisch in der Metzgerei!
   wieder, wie viel, lieber / Wie viel bekommen Sie? Vier Stück?

3. The letter **z**: In **Kapitel 2** you learned that the letter **z** is always pronounced like the *ts* sound in the English word *hits*, although in German, this sound often occurs at the beginning of a word.

   Zeit, zahlen, ziehen / Ich habe keine Zeit, in den Zoo zu gehen.

Richtig schreiben / Diktat CD 8 Tr. 15 / CD 8 Tr. 16 (with pauses)

B. Write down the sentences that you hear. Script on p. 215H

Zum Lesen

Richtig essen!

Lesestrategie Combine the strategies that you have learned As you learn to read German, keep in mind that you will use many different reading strategies at the same time. You will combine them in different ways, depending on the type of text you are trying to read. You will probably go through several steps every time you read new material: you may start by looking at visual clues, then skim to get the gist, scan for specific information, and finally read the text for comprehension.

1. Before you read these ads, think about what foods you like to eat. Which of the food items you eat on a regular basis are really good for you?

2. Compare your weekly diet to a partner's and try to figure out together what percentage of your diet is carbohydrate, fat, and protein.

3. Look at the illustrations in the ads, then try to figure out the meaning of the boldfaced titles and subtitles. Judging from what you learned from these two sources, what do you think these ads are about? b
   a. snack foods
   b. healthful foods
   c. ways to make sandwiches

4. You have figured out the general topic of these articles. Now skim the ads to get the gist. What information are these ads trying to get across to you? These foods taste good and are good for you.

MÜLLER BROT

HOTLINE
Armin Roßmeier
08165/79345

Das Thema im Juli:

Die herzhaften Fünf – Original Mühlbacher Bauernbrote

Nur wenige Brote verdienen den Namen Bauernbrot. Was darf rein, was nicht? Der bekannte Ernährungsexperte und Fernsehkoch Armin Roßmeier sagt Ihnen alles, was Sie schon immer über Brot wissen wollten: Rufen Sie ihn an. Jeden ersten Mittwoch im Monat: 7. Juli, 4. August, 1. September

Das haben Sie jetzt davon.

Alle wollen Leerdammer, nur:

Manche mögen's leicht. Na gut.

Dann nehmen manche jetzt eben den

Leerdammer Light. Und wer's nicht

leicht nimmt, läßt sich den

Leerdammer so schmecken wie bisher.

GOURMETS GENIESSEN PUR.

Der Leichte Almenrausch
WEICHKÄSE
NEU
150 g e · Fettstufe · Nur 20% Fett

SAHNIGER GESCHMACK
AUF DIE LEICHTE ART.

Der Leichte Almenrausch. Eine Weichkäse-Spezialität mit dem sahnig-milden Geschmack, den Gourmets noch pur zu genießen verstehen. Almenrausch gibt es auch extrasahnig als de Luxe und mit feinem Knoblauch.

GUTER GESCHMACK AUS TRADITION.

Der Mensch ist, wie er ißt.

Körperliche Fitness und Leistungsvermögen beruhen in erster Linie auf einer ausgewogenen Ernährung. Das gilt für den Spitzensport ebenso wie für den alltäglichen Lebens-„Marathon".

Wir alle benötigen bestimmte Mengen an Kohlehydraten, Proteinen, Vitaminen und Mineralstoffen, um gesund und in Form zu bleiben.

Wichtigste Voraussetzung für Leistungsvermögen und körperliche Fitness ist die richtige Kombination der drei Hauptnahrungsgruppen.

Als Faustregel für den Wochendurchschnitt gilt: 50% Kohlehydrate, 30% Fett und 20% Eiweiß sind ideal für 100%iges Wohlbefinden.

Auf das Frühstück kommt es an.

Besonders wichtig ist es, wie Sie den Tag beginnen: Das „richtige" Frühstück ist die wichtigste Mahlzeit des Tages. Dafür serviert Ihnen Müller-Brot auf den folgenden Seiten wertvolle Tips: Gesunden Appetit!

Beispielhafte Fitmacher für den Start in den Tag:

Die Vollkorn-Spezialitäten von Müller-Brot – Fitness, die man essen kann.

---

5. Based on your knowledge of German, match these compound words with the most logical English equivalent.

> **Weißt du noch?** Remember that knowing the meaning of root words can help you guess the meaning of many compound words.

1. Mahlzeit e   a. daily
2. Fernsehkoch d   b. soft cheese
3. alltäglich a   c. whole-grain bread
4. Ernährungs-experte f   d. television chef
5. Vollkornbrot c   e. meal
6. der Weichkäse b   f. nutrition expert

Wohlbefinden

6. Read the ad for **Vollkornbrot**. Which word in the ad means "well-being"? According to the ad, in order to have 100% physical well-being, what is the percentage of carbohydrates you should eat on the average in a week? What is the percentage of fat? And what is the percentage of protein?

50% 30% 20%

7. According to the ad, what is the most important meal of the day?

7. breakfast

8. What is the name of the person who has the hotline? When can you call him? What kind of information would he give you?

9. Scan the articles for the following information.

   a. Who can enjoy **Almenrausch** soft cheese? Gourmets

   b. What kind of **Leerdammer** do some people want to eat? light

   c. What company advertises itself as a whole-grain specialist? Müller-Brot

10. You are an exchange student in Germany. You and your friends are opening up a student-run snack stand at school, and you plan to have plenty of healthful snacks. Write an article for the school newspaper describing the foods you will offer at your stand.

8. **Armin Roßmeier;** first Wednesday of the month: July 7, August 4, September 1.

Übungsheft, S. 95, Ü. 23

Mehr Grammatikübungen

CD-ROM DISC 2

internet
ADRESSE: go.hrw.com
KENNWORT:
WK3 MUENCHEN-8
Answers

Erste Stufe   **Objectives** Asking what you should do; telling someone what to do

1 Du und deine Freunde, ihr wollt zu Hause helfen. Ihr fragt, was jeder *(everyone)* tun soll. Setze die richtige Form von **sollen** ein. **(S. 223)**

1. Omi, _____ ich für dich zum Supermarkt gehen?   soll

2. Was _____ wir für euch tun, Mara und Flori?   sollen

3. Wer _____ für die Mutti zum Metzger gehen?   soll

4. Du _____ nach der Schule nach Hause gehen.   sollst

5. Ich sage euch, ihr _____ mit dem Bus zur Schule fahren.   sollt

6. Was _____ die Schüler nach der Schule tun?   sollen

7. Wir _____ zum Bäcker gehen und Brot kaufen.   sollen

8. Was _____ der Flori für die Omi tun? Zum Supermarkt gehen?   soll

2 Jeder soll etwas tun. Setze die richtige Form von **sollen** in die erste Lücke und eine passende Verbform in die zweite und dritte Lücke. **(S. 223)**

1. Der Flori _____ für mich zum Metzger _____ und Wurst _____ .   soll; gehen; kaufen

2. Du _____ für die Omi zum Bäcker _____ und Brot _____ .   sollst; gehen; kaufen

3. Ihr _____ für Vati den Rasen _____ und den Müll _____ .   sollt; mähen; sortieren

4. Mara _____ für mich einkaufen _____ , etwas Obst _____ .   soll; gehen; kaufen

5. Wir _____ nach Hause _____ , die Hausaufgaben _____ .   sollen; gehen; machen

6. Wohin _____ ich _____ ? Was _____ ich für dich _____ ?   soll; gehen; soll; tun

3 Du und deine Freunde, ihr fragt deine Mutter, wo ihr die Lebensmittel kaufen sollt, die *(that)* sie braucht. Schreib die folgenden Sätze ab und schreib die richtige Verbform von **sollen** in die erste Lücke und die richtige Form des bestimmten Artikels *(definite article)* in die zweite und dritte Lücke. **(S. 223)**

BEISPIEL   Wo _____ wir denn _____ Limo und _____ Kuchen kaufen?
Wo **sollen** wir denn **die** Limo und **den** Kuchen kaufen?

1. Wo _____ ich denn _____ Aufschnitt und _____ Hähnchen kaufen?   soll; den; das / die *(pl)*

2. Wo _____ wir denn _____ Hackfleisch und _____ Wurst kaufen?   sollen; das; die

3. Wo _____ Flori denn _____ Salat und _____ Tomaten kaufen?   soll; den; die

4. Wo _____ du denn _____ Zucker und _____ Kaffee kaufen?   sollst; den; den

5. Wo _____ ihr denn _____ Milch und _____ Käse kaufen?   sollt; die; den

6. Wo _____ Claudia denn _____ Fisch und _____ Gemüse kaufen?   soll; den; das

7. Wo _____ Vati denn _____ Eier und _____ Mehl kaufen?   soll; die; das

8. Wo _____ ich denn _____ Obst und _____ Kartoffeln kaufen?   soll; das; die

4 Was sollst du tun? Was sollen deine Freunde tun? Beantworte die folgenden Fragen und gebrauche dabei den **du**-Imperativ. (S. 224)

1. Soll ich das Brot beim Bäcker kaufen? — Ja, _____ das Brot beim Bäcker!   kauf
2. Wo soll Flori die Milch holen? — Flori, _____ die Milch im Supermarkt!   hol
3. Soll ich zum Metzger gehen? — Klar, _____ zum Metzger!   geh
4. Soll ich jetzt den Tisch decken? — Ja, _____ jetzt den Tisch!   deck
5. Wann soll ich die Kartoffeln kochen? — Du, _____ sie heute Abend!   koch
6. Soll ich jetzt den Müll sortieren? — Ja, _____ jetzt den Müll!   sortier
7. Wann soll ich die Fenster putzen? — Ach, _____ die Fenster morgen!   putz

5 Flori und seine Freunde wollen für seine Mutter einkaufen gehen. Floris Mutter sagt ihnen, wo sie die Lebensmittel kaufen sollen. Beginn jede Antwort mit einem Imperativ. Benutze das richtige Pronomen in der Antwort. (S. 224)

BEISPIEL   **Wo soll ich die Butter kaufen? Im Supermarkt?**
Ja, kauf sie doch im Supermarkt!
Wo sollen wir das Eis kaufen? Im Eiscafé?
Ja, kauft es doch im Eiscafé!

1. Wo soll ich den Fisch kaufen? Im Fischladen?   Ja, kauf ihn doch im Fischladen!
2. Wo sollen wir das Obst kaufen? Im Obstladen?   Ja, kauft es doch im Obstladen!
3. Wo soll ich die Kartoffeln holen? Auf dem Markt?   Ja, hol sie doch auf dem Markt!
4. Wo sollen wir den Salat kaufen? Im Gemüseladen?   Ja, kauft ihn doch im Gemüseladen!
5. Wo soll ich das Brot kaufen? Beim Bäcker?   Ja, kauf es doch beim Bäcker!
6. Wo sollen wir den Käse kaufen? Im Supermarkt?   Ja, kauft ihn doch im Supermarkt!
7. Wo soll ich die Milch kaufen? Im Milchladen?   Ja, kauf sie doch im Milchladen!
8. Wo sollen wir das Fleisch kaufen? Beim Metzger?   Ja, kauft es doch beim Metzger!

Zweite Stufe

Objectives Talking about quantities; saying that you want something else

6 Was weißt du über Kilo, Pfund, Gramm und Liter? Beantworte die folgenden Fragen. Schreib einen ganzen Satz für Fragen 1 - 5. Achte darauf, dass Kilo, Pfund, Gramm und Liter in Sätzen wie diesen keine Pluralform haben. (S. 226)

1. Wie viel Gramm hat ein Kilo?
2. Wie viel Pfund hat ein Kilo?
3. Wie viel Gramm hat ein halbes Pfund?
4. Wie viel Gramm hat ein amerikanisches Pfund?
5. Was ist mehr Wasser, ein Liter oder ein Quart?
6. Was sind die Abkürzungen für:

   a. Kilogramm? _____   kg   **c.** Gramm?_____   g
   b. Pfund?_____   Pfd.   **d.** Liter?_____   l

1. Ein Kilo hat 1000 Gramm.

2. Ein Kilo hat zwei Pfund.

3. Ein halbes Pfund hat 250 Gramm.

4. Ein amerikanisches Pfund hat 453 Gramm.

5. Ein Liter ist mehr Wasser.

7 Du bist in einem Laden und kaufst ein. Schau auf die Einkaufsliste und schreib auf, was du kaufen willst. Vervollständige *(complete)* die Sätze und schreib dabei in die Lücke, was und wie viel du kaufen willst. **(S. 226)**

1. (2 lbs. of apples)   Ich bekomme _____ .
2. (500 grams of butter)   Ich möchte _____ .
3. (1 lb. of tomatoes)   Ich brauche _____ .
4. (100 grams of cheese)   Ich bekomme noch _____ .
5. (1 liter of milk)   Ich möchte _____ .
6. (2 liters of mineral water) Ich bekomme _____ .

1. zwei Pfund / ein Kilo Äpfel; 2. 500 Gramm / ein Pfund Butter; 3. ein Pfund Tomaten;
4. hundert Gramm Käse; 5. einen Liter Milch; 6. zwei Liter Mineralwasser

Dritte Stufe

Objectives Giving reasons; saying where you were and what you bought

8 Warum kannst du das nicht tun? Schreib die folgenden Sätze zweimal um. Der Nebensatz *(clause)* soll einmal mit **denn** beginnen und einmal mit **weil.** Achte auf die Stellung des Verbs. **(S. 230)**

BEISPIEL   **Ich esse das Eis nicht. Es ist zu kalt.**
  a. Ich esse das Eis nicht, *denn* es **ist** zu kalt.
  b. Ich esse das Eis nicht, *weil* es zu kalt **ist.**

1. Ich kann nicht ins Café gehen. Ich habe keine Zeit.   , denn ich habe ...; weil ich ... habe.
2. Ich kann nicht ins Kino gehen. Ich habe kein Geld.   , denn ich habe ...; weil ich ... habe.
3. Flori geht zum Bäcker. Er muss Brot kaufen.   , denn er muss...; weil er ... muss.
4. Mara geht zum Metzger. Sie muss Fleisch kaufen.   , denn sie muss ...; weil sie ... muss.
5. Jens möchte die Trauben. Sie sind so gut.   , denn sie sind ...; weil sie ... sind.
6. Wir essen viel Fisch. Er ist so lecker.   , denn er ist ...; weil er ... ist.

9 Du fragst deine Klassenkameraden, wo sie waren. Beantworte die folgenden Fragen mit der Antwort in Klammern. (S. 231)

1. Wo warst du heute Morgen? (in der Stadt)   Ich _____ .   war in der Stadt
2. Wo war Flori? (im Supermarkt)   Er _____ .   war im Supermarkt
3. Wo waren die Schüler? (in der Schule)   Sie _____ .   waren in der Schule
4. Wo war ich? (zu Hause)   Du _____ .   warst zu Hause
5. Wo waren wir gestern? (im Kino)   Ihr _____ .   wart im Kino
6. Wo wart ihr? (beim Bäcker)   Wir _____ .   waren beim Bäcker

10 Lies das folgende Telefongespräch. Schreib es ab und setze die Vergangenheit (*past tense*) von **sein** in die Lücken. (S. 231)

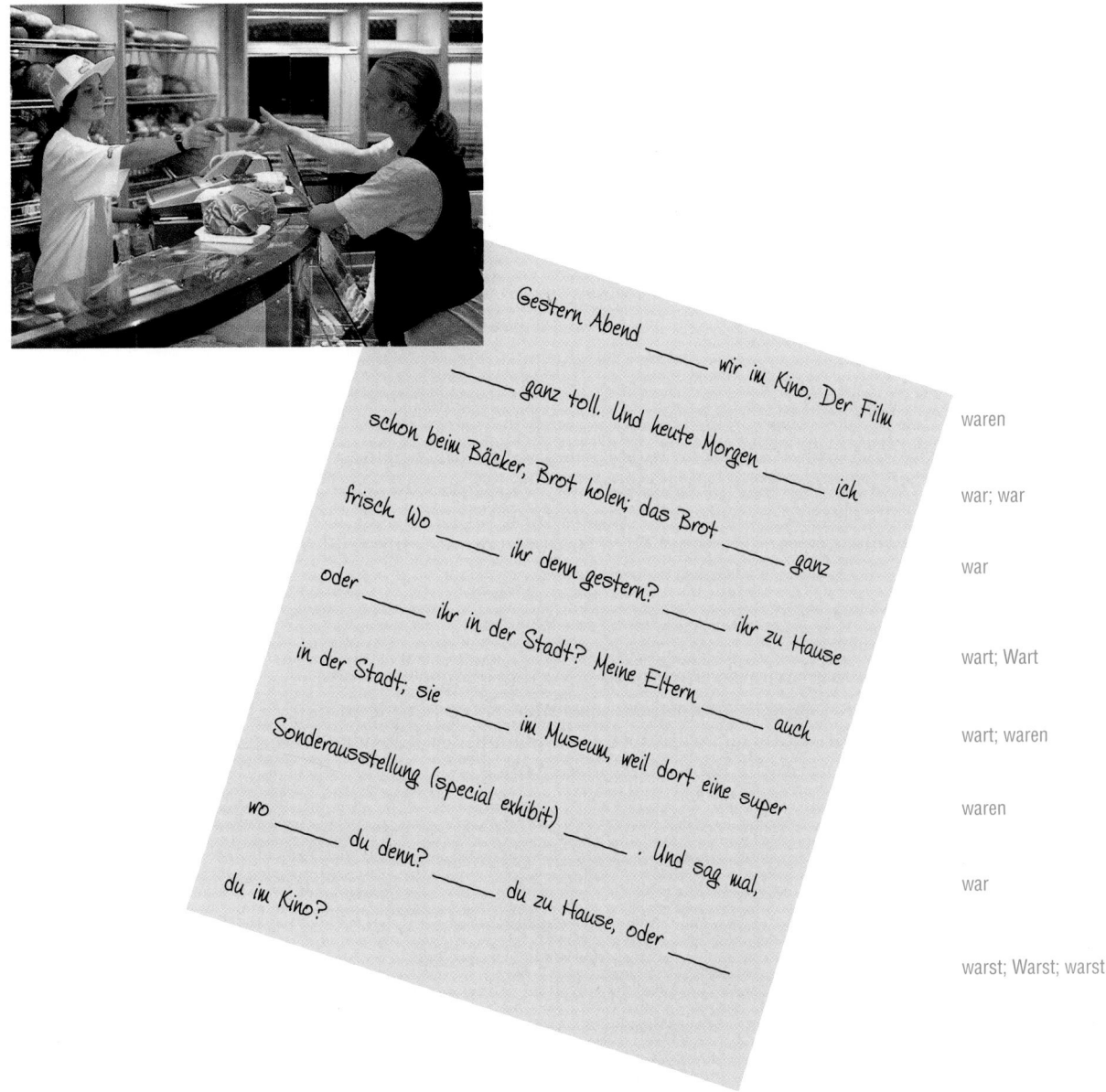

Gestern Abend _____ wir im Kino. Der Film _____ ganz toll. Und heute Morgen _____ ich schon beim Bäcker, Brot holen; das Brot _____ ganz frisch. Wo _____ ihr denn gestern? _____ ihr zu Hause oder _____ ihr in der Stadt? Meine Eltern _____ auch in der Stadt, sie _____ im Museum, weil dort eine super Sonderausstellung (*special exhibit*) _____ . Und sag mal, wo _____ du denn? _____ du zu Hause, oder _____ du im Kino?

waren

war; war

war

wart; Wart

wart; waren

waren

war

warst; Warst; warst

Anwendung

The CD-ROM Tutor offers guided recording and writing activities to accompany the **Anwendung.** These activities are designed to practice students' oral and written communication skills and to review material from each chapter.

1 Flori's mother would like him to go shopping for her. Listen as she tells him what to get, and make a shopping list for Flori. Be sure to include the amounts she needs. Script on p. 215H

1 Kilo Tomaten	2 Kilo Äpfel	10 Eier	200 g Käse	1 Liter Orangensaft
2 Pfd. Kartoffeln	1 Pfd. Butter	1 Brot	1 Pfd. Kaffee	

CD 8 Tr. 17

2 You and a friend are about to go grocery shopping. You have only 12 euros and want to get the most for your money. **Kaufmarkt** always has great daily specials. Look at the ads on the right and tell your partner eight things you want to buy and how much of each you are buying. Your partner will make a list and add up the cost for you. When finished, switch roles.

Fleisch

Schweine-Kotelett
zart 1kg **3,24**

Schweinebraten
ohne Knochen,
mit Kruste 1kg **2,49**

Schweine-Schulter
wie gewachsen 1kg **1,49**

Schweine-Halsgrat
saftig 1kg **3,74**

Schweine-Brustspitzen
frisch 1kg **2,98**

Hals-Steaks
vom Schwein 1kg **4,99**

Sur-Hax'n
mild gesalzen 1kg **1,98**

Holzfällersteak
gewürzt 1kg **2,98**

Konditorei

Erdbeerkuchen
mit frischen
Früchten Stück **1,25**

Gemischter
Obstkuchen
auf zartem
Wiener Biskuit Stück **1,10**

Himbeerkuchen
mit Mandeln nach
Hausfrauenart Stück **0,95**

Bamberger
Butterhörnchen
mit reiner Butter
gebacken Stück **0,45**

Schwäbischer
Käsekuchen
mit bestem Konditorquark
und mit Sahne verfeinert
Stück **0,95**

Fleisch

Schweinswürstel
frisch 100g **0,54**

Wollwurst 100g **0,49**
Kalbsbratwürstl
gebrüht 100g **0,59**

Kalbsbrust 1kg **4,98**

Kalbsrücken
(Lende ohne
Knochen) 1kg **16,45**

Frische
Putenschnitzel
1kg **4,98**

Neuseeland
Hirschkalb-Steak
frisch,
Spitzenqualität 1kg **14,98**

Lammsteak
gefr. 1kg **5,98**

3 Could you convince someone to buy a specific product? Bring in pictures of several food or clothing items from a magazine, or use props, and create a commercial to convince your classmates to buy one or more of the products. Use statements with **denn** and **weil** to persuade them. Then present your commercial to the class.

4 You and two of your friends work with a local organization that helps elderly people around the house. Your team has been assigned three people to help. The team leader goes over each list with each volunteer and tells him or her what to do. Switch roles, so that each person on the team is the leader once.

Frau Meyer:
Fenster putzen
Müll sortieren
½ Pfd. Kaffee kaufen
Staub saugen
5 Semmeln kaufen
375 g Wurst kaufen

Herr Schmidt:
Wohnzimmer aufräumen
500 g Aufschnitt kaufen
250 g Butter kaufen
Müll sortieren
400 g Hackfleisch
holen

Frau Heppner:
Blumen gießen
1 Kilo Kartoffeln kaufen
Staub saugen
Fisch holen
Rasen mähen
1 Pfd. Tomaten kaufen

5 Zum Schreiben

Do you and your classmates have good nutrition habits? Take a nutrition survey of your classmates using the **"Six-W questions"** - **"Wer? Was? Wann? Wo? Warum?** and **Wie?"** to find out.

Schreibtipp

Have you thought about how reporters collect information for their news stories? They often use the **"Five-W How?" questions:** Who? What? Where? When? Why? How? Remember though, not every question applies to every topic, and sometimes you can think of more than one good question for a question word. For example, you can ask: "What do you eat for breakfast?" or "What happens if you don't eat breakfast?"

Prewriting

First, decide which questions best fit the information you would like to gather about the food habits of the group with which you are working. You might choose to ask about buying food, about preparing food, or about food habits.

Writing

Write your survey questions in complete sentences. Choose a category of questions and ask 10 questions from this category. Ex: Where do you buy your food? when? how? (cash, credit card, check), or "Who shows up for dinner in your family? What meals does your family prefer?" Compile your answers (ex: six students eat dinner at 6 p.m.; 4 eat at 7 p.m.) and present to your group or class.

6 Rollenspiel

Get together with a classmate and role-play the following scenes.

OBSTSALAT

1 Apfel, 2 Bananen, 1 Birne,

1 Kiwi, 150 g Trauben (blau),

1 Orange, 2 EL Zitronensaft,

3 EL Honig, 2 EL Rosinen,

2 EL Walnusskerne, gehackt

Zubereitung: 20 Minuten

185 Kalorien

a. You and a friend are preparing lunch. Read the recipe for **Obstsalat** and tell your friend what you need, where to get it, and how much you need based on the recipe. Your friend will make a shopping list.

b. With your list in hand, go to the store to get what you need. Your partner plays the salesperson and will ask what you need, how much, and if you need anything else.

Can you ask someone what you should do using sollen? (p. 222)

1 How would you ask someone what you should do for him or her? How might he or she answer using the following items?

a. bread: at the baker's

b. ground meat: at the butcher's

c. milk: at the supermarket

d. apples: at the produce store

Was soll ich für dich tun?
a. Du kannst für mich Brot beim Bäcker kaufen.
b. Du kannst für mich Hackfleisch beim Metzger kaufen.
c. Du kannst für mich Milch im Supermarkt kaufen.
d. Du kannst für mich Äpfel im Obstladen kaufen.

Can you tell someone what to do using a du-command? (p. 223)

2 How would you tell someone where to buy the food items above?

a. Hol das Brot …
b. Kauf das Fleisch …
c. Kauf die Milch …
d. Kauf die Äpfel …

3 How would you tell a friend to

a. mow the lawn

b. buy 500 grams of tomatoes

c. clean the room

d. get 6 apples

a. Mäh den Rasen!
b. Kauf 500 g Tomaten!
c. Räum das Zimmer auf!
d. Kauf/Hol sechs Äpfel!

Can you ask for specific quantities? (p. 226)

4 How would you tell a salesperson you need the following things?

a. 500 Gramm Hackfleisch

b. Brot

c. 1 Liter Milch

d. 1 Pfd. Tomaten

e. 2 Kilo Kartoffeln

a. 500g Hackfleisch, bitte!
b. Ein Brot, bitte!
c. Einen Liter Milch, bitte!
d. Ein Pfund Tomaten, bitte.
e. Zwei Kilo Kartoffeln, bitte.

Can you say that you want something else? (p. 227)

5 How would a salesperson ask you if you wanted something else? How would you respond using the following items? 5. Sonst noch etwas? or Was bekommen Sie noch? or Noch einen Wunsch?

a. 10 Semmeln **b.** 100 Gramm Aufschnitt **c.** 200 Gramm Käse

a. Ich bekomme noch zehn Semmeln.
b. Ich brauche noch 100 Gramm Aufschnitt.
c. Ich bekomme noch 200 Gramm Käse.

Can you give reasons using denn and weil? (p. 230)

6 How would you say that you can't do each of the following and give a reason why not?

a. go to a movie **b.** go shopping **c.** go to a café

Answers will vary. Examples: Ich kann nicht ins Kino gehen, denn ich habe kein Geld …., weil ich zu Hause helfe.

Can you say where you were (using sein) and what you bought? (p. 231)

7 How would you ask someone where he or she was yesterday? How would you ask two friends? Can you say where you were using the following cues?

a. at the baker's in the morning

b. at the supermarket yesterday

c. at the butcher's yesterday morning

d. at home this afternoon

7. Wo warst du gestern?
   Wo wart ihr gestern?
a. Ich war am Morgen beim Bäcker.
b. Ich war gestern im Supermarkt.
c. Ich war gestern Morgen beim Metzger.
d. Ich war heute Nachmittag zu Hause.

8 How would you ask your friend what he or she bought? How would you say that you bought the following items?

a. bread **c.** a sweater **e.** pants

b. a shirt **d.** cheese

8. Was hast du gekauft?
a. Ich habe Brot gekauft.
b. Ich habe das (ein) Hemd gekauft.
c. … den (einen) Pulli
d. … den Käse
e. … die (eine) Hose

Erste Stufe

p. 215X

Asking what you should do; telling someone what to do

sollen	should, to be supposed to
einkaufen gehen	to go shopping
einkaufen (sep)	to shop
holen	to get, fetch
der Laden, ¨	store
die Lebensmittel (pl)	groceries
die Bäckerei, -en	bakery
beim Bäcker	at the baker's
das Brot, -e	bread
die Semmel, -n*	roll
die Brezel, -n	pretzel
die Torte, -n	layer cake
die Metzgerei, -en	butcher shop
beim Metzger	at the butcher's
das Fleisch	meat

das Hackfleisch	ground meat (mixture of beef and pork)
die Wurst, ¨e	sausage
der Aufschnitt	cold cuts
das Hähnchen, -	chicken
der Obst- und Gemüseladen, ¨	fresh produce store
im Obst- und Gemüseladen	at the produce store
das Obst	fruit
die Traube, -n	grape
der Apfel, ¨	apple
das Gemüse	vegetables
die Kartoffel, -n	potato
die Tomate, -n	tomato

der Salat, -e	lettuce
der Supermarkt, ¨e	supermarket
im Supermarkt	at the supermarket
die Milch	milk
die Butter	butter
der Käse	cheese
das Ei, -er	egg
der Kaffee	coffee
der Zucker	sugar
das Mehl	flour
der Fisch, -e	fish

Other Useful Words

besser	better
frisch	fresh

Zweite Stufe

Talking about quantities

Wie viel?	How much?
wiegen	to weigh
das Pfund	pound
das Gramm	gram
das Kilo	kilogram

der Liter	liter
ein bisschen mehr	a little more
ungefähr	approximately

Saying you want something else

Sonst noch etwas?	Anything else?
Haben Sie noch einen Wunsch?	Would you like anything else?
Ich brauche noch …	I also need …
Das ist alles.	That's all.

Dritte Stufe

Giving reasons

denn	because, for
weil	because

Saying where you were and what you bought

war	was (see p. 231)
Wo warst du?	Where were you?
Ich war beim Bäcker.	I was at the baker's. I went to the bakery.

Was hast du gekauft?	What did you buy?
Ich habe Brot gekauft.	I bought bread.

Time expressions

heute Morgen	this morning
heute Nachmittag	this afternoon
gestern	yesterday
gestern Abend	yesterday evening

vorgestern	day before yesterday
letztes Wochenende	last weekend
letzte Woche	last week

---

*In northern Germany these are called **Brötchen,** and in Baden-Württemberg and in other areas in southern Germany they are called **Wecken.**

Kapitel 9: Amerikaner in München
Chapter Overview

Los geht's!
pp. 246–248

München besuchen, p. 246

	FUNCTIONS	GRAMMAR	VOCABULARY	RE-ENTRY
Erste Stufe pp. 249–252	• Talking about where something is located, p. 250	• The verb **wissen**, and dependent clauses with **wo**, p. 250	• Places in a city, p. 249	• Places around town, p. 251 (**Kap. 8**)
Zweite Stufe pp. 253–256	• Asking for and giving directions, p. 254	• The verbs **fahren** and **gehen**, p. 255 • The formal commands with **Sie**, p. 255	• Words used to give directions, p. 253	• Types of stores, p. 254 (**Kap. 8**) • **Zu**, p. 254 (**Kap. 1**) • **Du**-commands, p. 255 (**Kap. 8**)
Dritte Stufe pp. 257–261	• Talking about what there is to eat and drink, p. 257 • Saying you do or don't want more, p. 258 • Expressing opinions, p. 260	• The phrase **es gibt**, p. 257 • Using **noch ein**, p. 258 • Using **kein**, p. 259 • The conjunction **dass**, p. 260	• Food and appetite, p. 257	• Food items, p. 258 (**Kap. 8**) • The accusative of indefinite articles, p. 258 (**Kap. 5**) • Saying you want something else, p. 258 (**Kap. 8**) • **Möchte**, p. 258, (**Kap. 3**) • Expressing opinions, p. 260 (**Kap. 2**) • Subordinate-clause word order, p. 260 (**Kap. 8**)

Aussprache p. 261	Review long vowels **ü** and **ö**, review letters **s**, **ss**, and **ß**: Audio CD 9, Track 12	**Diktat:** Audio CD 9, Tracks 13–14
Zum Lesen pp. 262–263	Ein Bummel durch München	**Reading Strategy** Reading for a purpose

Mehr Grammatik-übungen

pp. 264–267

Erste Stufe, p. 264	**Zweite Stufe**, pp. 265–266	**Dritte Stufe**, pp. 266–267

Review pp. 268–271

Anwendung, p. 268	**Kann ich's wirklich?**, p. 270	**Wortschatz**, p. 271

Zum Schreiben: Using Drawings
(Mapping and writing about your neighborhood)

CULTURE

• **Ein wenig Landeskunde:** The **Innenstadt**, p. 249
• **Landeskunde: Was isst du gern?**, p. 252
• Map of a German neighborhood, p. 253
• **Imbissstube** menu, p. 257
• **Ein wenig Landeskunde: Leberkäs**, p. 257

Kapitel 9: Amerikaner in München
Chapter Resources

Lesson Planning

One-Stop Planner

Lesson Planner with Substitute Teacher Lesson Plans, pp. 42–46, 73

Student Make-Up Assignments
- Make-Up Assignment Copying Masters, Chapter 9

Listening and Speaking

TPR Storytelling Book, pp. 33–36

Listening Activities
- Student Response Forms for Listening Activities, pp. 67–69
- Additional Listening Activities 9-1 to 9-6, pp. 71–74
- Additional Listening Activities (song), p. 70
- Scripts and Answers, pp. 148–154

Video Guide
- Teaching Suggestions, pp. 56–57
- Activity Masters, pp. 58–60
- Scripts and Answers, pp. 100–102, 115

Activities for Communication
- Communicative Activities, pp. 49–54
- Realia and Teaching Suggestions, pp. 106–109
- Situation Cards, pp. 139–140

Reading and Writing

Reading Strategies and Skills Handbook, Chapter 9

Lies mit mir! 1, Chapter 9

Übungsheft, pp. 97–108

Grammar

Grammatikheft, pp. 73–81

Grammar Tutor for Students of German, Chapter 9

Assessment

Testing Program
- Grammar and Vocabulary Quizzes, **Stufe** Quizzes, and Chapter Test, pp. 223–240
- Score Sheet, Scripts, and Answers, pp. 241–248

Alternative Assessment Guide
- Portfolio Assessment, p. 26
- Performance Assessment, p. 40
- CD-ROM Assessment, p. 54

Student Make-Up Assignments
- Alternative Quizzes, Chapter 9

Online Activities
- Interaktive Spiele
- Internet Aktivitäten

Video Program
- Videocassette 3
- Videocassette 5 (captioned version)

Audio Compact Discs
- Textbook Listening Activities, CD 9, Tracks 1–15
- Additional Listening Activities, CD 9, Tracks 22–27
- Assessment Items, CD 9, Tracks 16–21

Interactive CD-ROM Tutor, Disc 3

Teaching Transparencies
- Situations 9-1 to 9-2
- Vocabulary 9-A to 9-B
- **Los geht's!**
- **Mehr Grammatikübungen** Answers
- **Grammatikheft** Answers

One-Stop Planner CD-ROM

Use the **One-Stop Planner CD-ROM with Test Generator** to aid in lesson planning and pacing.

For each chapter, the **One-Stop Planner** includes:
- Editable lesson plans with direct links to teaching resources
- Printable worksheets from resource books
- Direct launches to the HRW Internet activities
- Video and audio segments
- Test Generator
- Clip Art for vocabulary items

Kapitel 9: Amerikaner in München

Projects

Unser Stadtführer

In this activity, students will compile and design an extended guide to their own town, city, or area written completely in German. It should be started after completion of the Zum Lesen section of this chapter. The project should be divided equally among students to facilitate completion of all parts of the guide. Divide students into 6 groups.

MATERIALS

✄ **Students may need**
- Large piece of construction paper or posterboard, which will display all 6 projects
- glue or masking tape
- scissors
- markers

SUGGESTED OUTLINE

The guide should include

- a detailed map of the area, including landmarks, labeled streets, and noteworthy sights;
- places of interest, including background information and descriptions (this can be completed by two groups, each describing a minimum of five places);
- food and drink, including popular restaurants and what is served there;
- lodging, including the types of accommodations available, location, and cost;
- other important information that would be useful to visitors.

SUGGESTED SEQUENCE

1. Assign students to groups, dividing them equally according to the number of project parts.

2. Once groups have been assigned, have students look over the possible topics. They might want to choose their topic depending on their strength in certain areas. For example, students with artistic abilities might want to work on designing a detailed map.

3. Groups begin gathering materials for their topics by making a list of possible resources. Make suggestions for such resources. (Examples: chamber of commerce, tourist information center, school or public library, local historical foundations, the Internet)

4. Once groups have compiled their information, they make an outline of their projects. This outline should be shown to you for suggestions and approval.

5. Students begin their final drafts using all gathered information and materials.

6. Allow class time for all groups to give a short presentation of their parts of the guide.

7. Upon completion of all parts of the guide, students attach and display their project on the construction paper or posterboard.

8. Display the guide on your bulletin board in your classroom, in the foreign language area, or a hallway in your school.

GRADING THE PROJECT

Suggested point distribution (**total = 100 points**)
Appearance/originality...........................25
Completion of assignment requirements...25
Correct language usage 25
Oral presentation...............................25

Games

Kettenspiel

This game is a good vocabulary review for auditory learners.

Begin the game by making the following statement: **Wenn ich in München bin, besuche ich das Deutsche Museum.** The next student repeats your sentence and adds another place or activity he or she would do when visiting Munich. The game continues with each student repeating all locations and/or activities that have been named up to his or her turn.

Was bedeutet dieses Zeichen?

Playing this game will help your students review the vocabulary of city buildings and landmarks.

Procedure In preparation for this game, have a set of ten large index cards that you have numbered and labeled with the symbols used in this chapter to represent buildings or landmarks in a city. Divide students into groups of two or three, depending on your class size. Give each group a sheet of paper that is numbered from 1 to 10. Begin by calling out the number of the first card, and then hold the card so that all students will be able to see it. Students will have ten seconds to decide what the symbol stands for. The writer of the group then records the word, including the article. You may want to give bonus points to students who can use the words correctly in a sentence. After you have shown all ten cards, put up a transparency with the correct words. The group with the most correct locations wins.

Storytelling ·······················

Mini-Geschichte

*This story accompanies Teaching Transparency 9-1. The **Mini-Geschichte** can be told and retold in different formats, acted out, written down, and read aloud to give students additional opportunities to practice all four skills.*

Wo ist Nicole?

Nicole will Briefmarken kaufen. Sie geht aus dem Haus in die Pfarrgasse. Dann geht sie rechts in die Gartenstraße und von dort bis zur nächsten Straße. Hier geht sie nach links. Dann geht sie nach rechts in die Wengertgasse und geradeaus bis zur Königsstraße. Jetzt geht sie in einen Laden. Sie sagt zur Verkäuferin *(sales clerk)*: „Ich möchte Briefmarken, bitte!" „Es tut mir Leid. Hier gibt es nur Brot und Semmeln. Sie müssen zur Post gehen. Dort können Sie Briefmarken kaufen." „Ach, Entschuldigung! Ich habe nicht aufgepasst *(paid attention)*."

Traditions ··················

Rezept

Der Schweinsbraten, ein wirklich deftiges Gericht, schmeckt besonders gut bei kaltem Wetter und wird dann gern mit Semmelknödeln und Kraut serviert.

Schweinsbraten

Für 4 bis 6 Personen

Zutaten

kg=Kilogramm, TL=Teelöffel, l=Liter

1 kg	Schweinefleish mit Schwarte (aus der Schulter)
2-3	Zwiebeln
1TL	Nelken
1	Bund Suppengrün
1	Zwiebel, geschnitten
1	Lorbeerblatt
4	Pfefferkörner
1	Knoblauchzehe, gequetscht
1TL	Speisestärke
	gekörnte Brühe
	Pfeffer

Zubereitung

Das Fleisch mit Salz einreiben und bei 225 Grad mit der Schwarte nach unten in eine Bratenpfanne im Backofen legen. Mit 1/4l heißem Wasser übergießen und kräftig durchbraten. Den Braten herausnehmen, die Schwarte mit einem scharfen Messser kreuzweise einritzen und an den Schnittpunkten mit Nelken spicken. Zurück in die Saftpfanne legen, diesmal mit der Schwarte nach oben, und weiterbraten. Das Fleisch häufig begießen. Nach 45 Minuten Suppengrün, Zwiebel, Lorbeerblatt, Pfefferkörner und Knoblauch zum Fleisch geben. Pro Kilo Fleisch wird die Bratzeit beim Schwein mit 60 bis 70 Minuten berechnet. Kurz vor Ende der Garzeit die Schwarte mit Salzwasser bestreichen. Das Fleisch herausnehmen und warm stellen. Es muss vor dem Aufschneiden mindestens 10 Minuten rasten, damit der Saft sich setzt und nicht herausläuft. Den Bratenfond durch ein Sieb streichen. Mit angerührter Speisestärke binden und mit etwas gekörnter Brühe, Salz und Pfeffer abschmecken.

Kapitel 9: Amerikaner in München
Technology

Video

Videocassette 3, 5 (captioned version)
See Video Guide, pages 55–60

Los geht's! • München besuchen

Mara and Markus are having some juice at a juice bar when some American students ask them for directions. Later on, they run into each other again at a snack stand. Mara and Markus talk the Americans into trying a Bavarian specialty, **Leberkäs,** and then decide to show them around Munich.

Fortsetzung

The Americans see different sights in Munich, and Mara explains what they are. When it is time for the Americans to return to Rosenheim, Markus and Mara give them directions to the **U-Bahn,** which will take them to the train station. Mara gives them an **U-Bahn** ticket and shows them how to validate it.

Landeskunde

Was isst du gern?

People of various ages from different cities tell us what they like to eat.

Videoclips

- **Siemens Museum** (science museum)
- **Nordsee**® (fast food)
- **Postbank**® (banking by mail)
- **Postbank**® (business by mail)

Interactive CD-ROM Tutor

The **Interactive CD-ROM Tutor** contains videos, interactive games, and activities that provide students an opportunity to practice and review the material covered in Chapter 9.

Activity	Activity Type	Pupil's Edition Reference
1. Wortschatz	Merkspiel	p. 249
2. Grammatik	Was fehlt?	p. 250
3. So sagt man das!	Wozu gehört's?	pp. 250, 254
4. So sagt man das!	Was ist richtig?	pp. 249, 253, 254, 255
5. Grammatik	Was fehlt?	p. 259
6. Grammatik	Was kommt dann?	p. 260
Landeskunde	Was isst du gern? Was ist richtig?	p. 252
Zum Sprechen	*Guided recording*	pp. 268–269
Zum Schreiben	*Guided writing*	pp. 268–269

Teacher Management System

Logging In

Logging in to the *Komm mit!* TMS is easy. Upon launching the program, simply type "admin" in the password area of the log-in screen and press RETURN. Log on to **www.hrw.com/CDROMTUTOR** for a detailed explanation of the Teacher Management System.

One-Stop Planner CD-ROM

To preview all resources available for this chapter, use the **One-Stop Planner CD-ROM**, Disc 3.

Internet Connection ....

ADRESSE: go.hrw.com
KENNWORT:
WK3 MUENCHEN-9

*Have students explore the **go.hrw.com** Web site for many online resources covering all chapters. All Chapter 9 resources are available under the keyword **WK3 Muenchen-9.** Interactive games practice the material and provide students with immediate feedback. You will also find a printable worksheet that provides Internet activities that lead to a comprehensive online research project.*

Interaktive Spiele

You can use the interactive activities in this chapter

- to practice grammar, vocabulary, and chapter functions
- as homework
- as an assessment option
- as a self-test
- to prepare for the Chapter Test

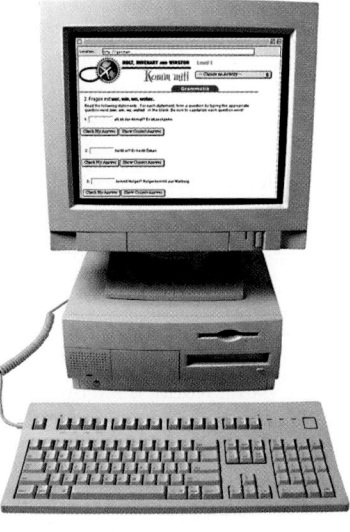

Internet Aktivitäten

Students will use a city map of Munich. They will follow directions and locate places on the map.

- To prepare students for the **Arbeitsblatt,** you might have them practice giving and following directions. Using the map of Munich on p. 249, have them role-play a conversation between a tourist and a resident of Munich.
- After completing the **Arbeitsblatt,** have students design the menu of a snack bar in Munich. They should give their snack bar a name and address and include snacks, drinks, and prices.

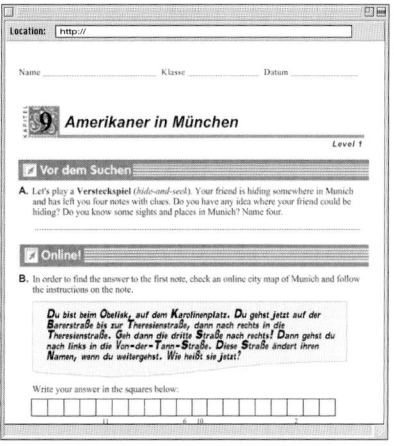

Webprojekt

Have students do a Web search for a sight in Munich. They should report on the nature of the sight and why they chose it. Encourage students to exchange useful Web sites with their classmates. Have students document their sources by referencing the names and URLs of all the sites they consulted.

Kapitel 9: Amerikaner in München
Textbook Listening Activities Scripts

Erste Stufe

6 p. 250

TOURIST   Entschuldigen Sie bitte … Hallo, können Sie mir helfen?

MÜNCHNER   Ich?… Ja, selbstverständlich.

TOURIST   Ich kenne München nicht so gut, und ich suche das Hotel International.

MÜNCHNER   Ja, da lassen Sie mich mal nachdenken. Ja also, das Hotel International … Ich glaube, das ist in der Brienner Straße.

TOURIST   Und wie finde ich eine Post? Ich brauche nämlich Briefmarken.

MÜNCHNER   Ja … mal sehen. Na, vom Hotel gehen Sie rechts in die Brienner Straße und dann fünf Straßen weiter, geradeaus bis Sie zur Schönfeldstraße kommen. Da ist die Post … in der Schönfeldstraße.

TOURIST   Und wo kann man hier Geld umtauschen?

MÜNCHNER   Ja, sicher in einer Bank.

TOURIST   Und wo find ich die?

MÜNCHNER   Ah, muss mal nachdenken. Ich glaube, es gibt eine Bank am Marienplatz neben dem Rathaus.

TOURIST   Und wo finde ich die U-Bahnstation?

MÜNCHNER   Ganz einfach. Die U-Bahnstation ist direkt am Karlstor, in der Schwanthalerstraße.

TOURIST   Ja, ich möchte auch gern das Stadtmuseum besuchen. Wie komm ich dahin?

MÜNCHNER   Ja, das finden Sie ganz leicht. Das ist nämlich gleich neben der Post in der Schönfeldstraße.

TOURIST   Ja, ich muss natürlich auch in den Englischen Garten. Wie komme ich denn dahin?

MÜNCHNER   Ja also, der Garten ist so 100 Meter südlich vom Odeonsplatz.

TOURIST   Und zum Schluss möchte ich noch schnell wissen, wo die Frauenkirche ist.

MÜNCHNER   Ja, die können Sie von hier sehen. Schauen Sie mal da drüben. Da ist sie, in der Neuhauser-Kaufingerstraße.

TOURIST   Haben Sie recht vielen Dank!

MÜNCHNER   Gern geschehen! Viel Spaß noch in München!

Zweite Stufe

12 p. 254

STUDENT   Entschuldigen Sie bitte! Könnten Sie mir bitte helfen?

FUSSGÄNGER   Selbstverständlich.

STUDENT   Wie komme ich am besten zum Obst- und Gemüseladen von hier?

FUSSGÄNGER   Da gehen Sie hier von der Guardinistraße, bis Sie in die Ehrwalder Straße kommen. An der Ehrwalder Straße sehen Sie rechts die Mittenwalder Straße. Da gehen Sie dann nach rechts und sehen den Obst- und Gemüseladen auf der linken Seite.

STUDENT   Und wo liegt bitte das große Einkaufszentrum?

FUSSGÄNGER   Ja, also ganz einfach. Hier vom Metzger gehen Sie in die Neufriedenheimer Straße, bis Sie zum Hans-Grässel-Weg kommen. Da gehen Sie nach rechts, und das Einkaufszentrum ist auf der rechten Seite, gleich nach der Rheinsteinstraße.

STUDENT   Die Bäckerei hier im Ort … wo kann ich sie finden?

FUSSGÄNGER   Ja, wie gesagt, von hier gehen Sie auf der Guardinistraße, bis Sie zur Werdenfelsstraße kommen. Da gehen Sie rechts. Die Bäckerei sehen Sie nach der zweiten Straße auf der rechten Seite.

STUDENT   Vielen Dank!

FUSSGÄNGER   Gern geschehen! Auf Wiedersehen!

15 p. 255

AUSKUNFT   Guten Tag! Wie kann ich Ihnen behilflich sein?

FREUND   Ja, hallo. Können Sie mir bitte sagen, wie ich am besten von hier aus zum Viktualienmarkt komme?

AUSKUNFT   Ja also, da schauen Sie mal hier auf den Stadtplan. Hier sind wir … und da ist der Viktualienmarkt. Da gehen Sie also die Bayerstraße entlang bis Sie zum Karlsplatz in der Neuhauserstraße kommen. An der linken Seite sehen Sie die Frauenkirche. Gehen Sie geradeaus zum Marienplatz und dann rechts in die Prälat-Zistl-Straße. Dann kurz geradeaus und nach der nächsten Kreuzung sehen Sie den Viktualienmarkt auf der linken Seite.

FREUND   Hoffentlich kann ich mir das alles merken. Vielen Dank!

AUSKUNFT   Gern geschehen! Auf Wiedersehen!

The following scripts are for the listening activities found in the *Pupil's Edition*. For Student Response Forms, see *Listening Activities*, pages 67–70. To provide students with additional listening practice, see *Listening Activities*, pages 71–74.

One-Stop Planner CD-ROM

For resource information, see the **One-Stop Planner CD-ROM**, Disc 3.

Dritte Stufe

21 p. 258

MARKUS So, Mara, möchtest du noch eine Semmel? Die schmecken gut, nicht?

MARA Stimmt! Nein, keine Semmel mehr für mich, aber ich möchte noch einen Saft. Ich habe Durst.

MARKUS Klar … bin gleich wieder da. Und du Silvia? Schmeckt das Hähnchen?

SILVIA Lecker!

MARKUS Und kann ich dir noch eine Limo holen?

SILVIA Nee, danke. Ich habe wirklich genug gegessen und getrunken.

MARKUS He, Thomas, tolle Fete, was? Kann ich dir noch eine Brezel holen und auch noch etwas Saft?

THOMAS Klar, 'ne Brezel mit Senf. He du, wo ist denn die Mara?

MARKUS Die steht da drüben, … mit Silvia. Du Flori, wie geht's, wie steht's? Noch 'nen Leberkäs?

FLORI Nee, danke. Ich habe schon genug.

MARKUS Aber kann ich dir das Glas mit Mineralwasser auffüllen?

FLORI Ja, danke dir!

MARKUS Na, Claudia, wie geht's dir? Bist du schon satt, oder möchtest du noch etwas?

CLAUDIA Du, die Weißwurst schmeckt lecker. Ich möchte noch eine und auch noch ein Glas Limo bitte. Danke, Markus. Das ist nett von dir.

FRANK Du, Markus … der Salat schmeckt echt gut.

MARKUS Ja, die Tomaten sind aus unserem Garten. Willst du noch mehr davon, Frank? Auch noch etwas mehr Apfelsaft?

FRANK Nee, nichts mehr, danke! Du, Markus, die Fete ist wirklich toll!

27 p. 261

1. Ja also, ich heiße Christoph Nolte. Ich bin 12. Unsere Katze heißt Jupp, so wie mein Vater. Ich mag Katzen am liebsten. Ich finde, dass sie nicht so viel Arbeit machen wie andere Tiere. Jupp hat manchmal sogar lebende Mäuse mit nach Hause gebracht. Die mussten wir dann natürlich schnell einfangen. Aber das passiert jetzt nur noch selten. Besonders toll ist es, wenn Jupp auf der Lauer liegt und Vögel im Garten beobachtet.

2. Ich heiße Birgit und wohne in Regensburg. Ich bin jetzt 14 Jahre alt. Mein Hobby ist Tanzen, und mein Lieblingstanz ist Rock 'n Roll. Meine Tanzpartnerin heißt Katarina. Ich finde es OK, dass in Deutschland zwei Mädchen miteinander tanzen dürfen. In einigen Ländern ist das ja nicht erlaubt. Darum dürfen wir nicht an Wettbewerben im Ausland teilnehmen. Das finde ich total blöd! Später möchte ich schon gern Tanzlehrerin werden.

3. Ich heiße Nils und bin 19. Ein guter Freund muss zu mir halten, mit mir durch dick und dünn gehen. Mit einem Mädchen geht das nicht so gut. Mit meinen Freunden kann ich meistens über alles reden, mit meiner Freundin nicht immer. Meine Freunde verstehen meine Probleme. Vielleicht liegt das auch nur daran, dass ich meine Freundin noch nicht so lange kenne. Kann sein. Ich glaube aber, dass es leichter ist, eine Freundin zu finden als einen guten Freund.

4. Ich heiße Alex, und ich bin 16 Jahre alt. Ich trage ausschließlich Schwarz. Ich find das total stark. Hosen, Hemden, Stiefel, alles ist bei mir schwarz. Ich ändere das nie. Und andere Sachen habe ich nicht viel. Ich glaube, dass die Mode, die man trägt, etwas über einen aussagt.

AUSSPRACHE, p. 261

Diktat, p. 261

You will hear Thomas and Silvie talking about what they did last weekend. First listen to what they are saying. Then write down their conversation.

THOMAS Grüß dich, Silvie!

SILVIE Tag, Thomas!

THOMAS Wo warst du denn am Wochenende?

SILVIE Ich war im Münchener Stadtzentrum und habe ein bisschen eingekauft.

THOMAS Hast du sonst was gemacht?

SILVIE Oh, ja. Ich war auch im Kino, und am Samstag habe ich das Deutsche Museum besucht. Das ist total interessant. Was hast du gemacht?

THOMAS Ich war zu Hause. Ich habe nur Fernsehen geschaut und auch gelesen. Das war langweilig.

SILVIE Du, ich muss jetzt weiter, Thomas. Also, bis später!

THOMAS Tschüs! Ich rufe dich diese Woche an, dann können wir ja etwas machen.

Anwendung

1 p. 268

Heute waren wir den ganzen Tag in München. Das war echt super! München ist eine tolle Stadt. Da gibt es so viel zu sehen und zu tun. Die Mara und der Markus sind mit uns einkaufen gegangen. Zuerst waren wir bei Dallmayr, da haben wir Weißwürste gekauft. Und ja, dann waren wir im Kaufhaus Ludwig Beck. Das ist ziemlich groß. Da haben wir ein paar CDs und etwas Schmuck gekauft. Das war gerade im Sonderangebot. Na, und zum Schluss waren wir dann noch in einem Fotogeschäft, denn die Mara wollte sich noch ein neues Fotoalbum kaufen. Danach sind wir mit der Straßenbahn nach Hause gefahren. Das war ein toller Tag!

Kapitel 9: Amerikaner in München
Suggested Lesson Plans 50-Minute Schedule

Day 1

CHAPTER OPENER 10 min.
- Culture Note, ATE, p. 243M

LOS GEHT'S! 20 min.
- Preteaching Vocabulary, ATE, p. 243N
- Play Audio CD for **Los geht's!**, pp. 246–247
- Have students read **Los geht's!**, pp. 246–247
- Show **Los geht's!** Video
- Do Comprehension Activities, p. 248

ERSTE STUFE
Wortschatz/Ein wenig Landeskunde, p. 249 15 min.
- Presenting **Wortschatz**, ATE, p. 243O
- Teaching Transparency 9-A
- Present **Ein wenig Landeskunde**, p. 249
- Do Map Activity, p. 249
- Play **Kettenspiel**, ATE, p. 243C

Wrap-Up 5 min.
- Students respond to questions about places to go in München

Homework Options
Grammatikheft, p. 73, Acts. 1–2
Übungsheft, pp. 97-98, Acts. 1–3

Day 2

ERSTE STUFE
Quick Review 10 min.
- Check homework, Grammatikheft, p. 73, Acts. 1–2

So sagt man das!, p. 250 15 min.
- Presenting **So sagt man das!**, ATE, p. 243O
- Play Audio CD for Activity 6, p. 250
- Do Activities 5–6, p. 75, Grammatikheft

Grammatik, p. 250 20 min.
- Presenting **Grammatik**, ATE, p. 243O
- Do Activities 7, 8, 9, and 10, p. 251
- Do Activities 5–7, pp. 99–100, Übungsheft

Wrap-Up 5 min.
- Students respond to questions about knowing the location of places in München

Homework Options
Grammatikheft, p. 74, Acts. 3–4
Übungsheft, pp. 99–100, Acts. 4 and 8

Day 3

ERSTE STUFE
Quick Review 15 min.
- Check homework, Grammatikheft, p. 74, Acts. 3–4
- Do Situation 9-1, pp. 139–140

Quiz Review 15 min.
- Do Activities 1–2, Interactive CD-ROM
- Do **Mehr Grammatikübungen, Erste Stufe**

Quiz 20 min.
- Quiz 9-1A or 9-1B

Homework Options
Activities for Communication, pp. 49–50, prepare Communicative Activity 9-1

Day 4

ERSTE STUFE
Quick Review 10 min.
- Return and review Quiz 9-1
- Bell Work, ATE, p. 243Q
- Do Communicative Activity 9-1, pp. 49–50

LANDESKUNDE 15 min.
- Pre-viewing Suggestion, Video Guide, p. 56
- Background Information, ATE, p. 243P
- Show **Landeskunde** Video
- Do Activities A and B, p. 252

ZWEITE STUFE
Wortschatz, p. 253 20 min.
- Presenting **Wortschatz**, ATE, p. 243Q
- Teaching Transparency 9-B
- Do Activity 11, p. 253
- Play Audio CD for Activity 12, p. 254
- Do Activity 13, p. 254

Wrap-Up 5 min.
- Students give directions from the school to the nearest grocery store

Homework Options
Grammatikheft, pp. 76–77, Acts. 7–10
Übungsheft, pp. 101–102, Acts. 9–11

Day 5

ZWEITE STUFE
Quick Review 10 min.
- Check homework, Grammatikheft, pp. 76–77, Acts. 7–10

So sagt man das!/Ein wenig Grammatik, pp. 254–255 15 min.
- Presenting **So sagt man das!**, ATE, p. 243Q
- Presenting **Ein wenig Grammatik**, ATE, p. 243R
- Do Activity 14, p. 255
- Do Activities 12–13, p. 102, Übungsheft

Grammatik, p. 255 20min.
- Presenting **Grammatik**, ATE, p. 243R
- Play Audio CD for Activity 15, p. 255
- Do Activity 16, p. 255
- Do Activities 17 and 18, p. 256

Wrap-Up 5 min.
- Students ask and respond to questions about how to get to different locations in their city

Homework Options
Pupil's Edition, p. 256, Activity 19
Grammatikheft, p. 78, Acts. 11–12
Übungsheft, p. 103, Acts. 14–15

Day 6

ZWEITE STUFE
Quick Review 10 min.
- Check homework, Übungsheft, p. 103, Acts. 14–15

Quiz Review 20 min.
- Do Additional Listening Activities 9-3 and 9-4, pp. 72–73
- Do **Mehr Grammatikübungen, Zweite Stufe**

Quiz 20 min.
Quiz 9-2A or 9-2B

Homework Options
Activities for Communication, pp. 51–52, prepare Communicative Activity 9-2

One-Stop Planner CD-ROM

For alternative lesson plans by chapter section, to create your own customized plans, or to preview all resources available for this chapter, use the **One-Stop Planner CD-ROM**, Disc 3.

 For additional homework suggestions, see activities accompanied by this symbol throughout the chapter.

Day 7

DRITTE STUFE

Quick Review 15 min.
- Return and review Quiz 9-2
- Bell Work, ATE, p. 243S
- Do Communicative Activity 9-2, pp. 51–52

So sagt man das!/ Ein wenig Grammatik, p. 257 20 min.
- Presenting **So sagt man das!**, ATE, p. 243S
- Teaching Transparency 9-2
- Do Activities 16–17, p. 104, Übungsheft
- Presenting **Ein wenig Grammatik**, ATE, p. 243T
- Present **Ein wenig Landeskunde**, p. 257
- Do Activity 20, p. 257

So sagt man das!, p. 258 10 min.
- Presenting **So sagt man das!**, ATE, p. 243T
- Play Audio CD for Activity 21, p. 258

Wrap-Up 5 min.
- Students respond to questions about what there is to eat and drink

Homework Options
Grammatikheft, pp. 79–80, Acts. 13–15
Übungsheft, p. 105, Act. 18

Day 8

DRITTE STUFE

Quick Review 10 min.
- Check homework, Grammatikheft, pp. 79–80, Acts. 13–15

Ein wenig Grammatik, p. 258 10 min.
- Presenting **Ein wenig Grammatik**, ATE, p. 243T
- Do Activity 22, p. 258

Grammatik, p. 259 25 min.
- Presenting **Grammatik**, ATE, p. 243T
- Do Activity 23, p. 259
- Do Communicative Activity 9-3, pp. 53–54
- Present **Lerntrick**, p. 259
- Do Activities 24 and 25, p. 259
- Do Activity 26, p. 260

Wrap-Up 5 min.
- Students respond to questions about wanting more/not wanting more of certain foods

Homework Options
Grammatikheft, p. 80, Acts. 16–17
Übungsheft, p. 105, Acts. 19–20

Day 9

DRITTE STUFE

Quick Review 10 min.
- Check homework, Übungsheft, p. 105, Acts. 19–20

So sagt man das!/Grammatik, p. 260 20 min.
- Presenting **So sagt man das!**, ATE, p. 243U
- Presenting **Grammatik**, ATE, p. 243U
- Play Audio CD for Activity 27, p. 261
- Do Activities 28 and 29, p. 261
- Do Activities 18–19, p. 81, Grammatikheft

Aussprache, p. 261 15 min.
- Do **Richtig aussprechen/Richtig lesen**, p. 261
- Do **Richtig schreiben/Diktat**, p. 261

Wrap-Up 5 min.
- Using the conjunction **dass**, students respond to questions about how they feel about certain things

Homework Options
Übungsheft, p. 106, Acts. 21–22

Day 10

DRITTE STUFE

Quick Review 10 min.
- Check homework, Übungsheft, p. 106, Acts. 21–22

Quiz Review 20 min.
- Do **Mehr Grammatikübungen, Dritte Stufe**
- Play Circumlocution Game, ATE, p. 243X

Quiz 20 min.
- Quiz 9-3A or 9-3B

Homework Options
Übungsheft, p. 108, Act. 24

Day 11

DRITTE STUFE

Quick Review 15 min.
- Return and review Quiz 9-3
- Check homework, Übungsheft, p. 108, Act. 24

ZUM LESEN 30 min.
- Culture Note, ATE, p. 243V
- Present **Lesestrategie**, p. 262
- Do Activities 1-9, pp. 262–263

Wrap-Up 5 min.
- Students ask and respond to questions about how to get to different locations in München

Homework Options
Pupil's Edition, **Kann ich's wirklich?**, p. 270
Übungsheft, p. 107, Act. 23
Interaktive Spiele, see ATE, p. 243F

Day 12

ANWENDUNG

Quick Review 35 min.
- Check homework, **Kann ich's wirklich?**, p. 270
- Video Wrap-up, ATE, p. 243W
- Teaching Suggestions, Video Guide, pp. 50–51
- Show **Fortsetzung** and **Videoclips** Videos
- Do **Anwendung** Activities 1–5, pp. 268–269

Chapter Review 15 min.
- Review chapter functions, vocabulary, and grammar; choose from **Mehr Grammatikübungen,** Grammar Tutor for Students of German, Activities for Communication, Listening Activities, Interactive CD-ROM Tutor, or **Interaktive Spiele**

Homework Options
Study for Chapter Test

Assessment

Test, Chapter 9 45 min.
- Administer Chapter 9 Test. Select from Testing Program, Alternative Assessment Guide or Test Generator.

Kapitel 9: Amerikaner in München
Suggested Lesson Plans *90-Minute Block Schedule*

Block 1

CHAPTER OPENER 10 min.
- Culture Note, ATE, p. 243M

LOS GEHT'S! 20 min.
- Preteaching Vocabulary, ATE, p. 243N
- Play Audio CD for **Los geht's!**, pp. 246–247
- Have students read **Los geht's!**, pp. 246–247
- Teaching Suggestions, Video Guide, p. 56
- Show **Los geht's!** Video
- Do Comprehension Activities, p. 248

ERSTE STUFE
Wortschatz/Ein wenig Landeskunde, p. 249 20 min.
- Presenting **Wortschatz**, ATE, p. 243O
- Teaching Transparency 9-A
- Present **Ein wenig Landeskunde**, p. 249
- Do Map Activity, p. 249
- Play **Kettenspiel**, ATE, p. 243C

So sagt man das!, p. 250 15 min.
- Presenting **So sagt man das!**, ATE, p. 243O
- Play Audio CD for Activity 6, p. 250
- Do Activities 5–6, p. 75, Grammatikheft

Grammatik, p. 250 20 min.
- Presenting **Grammatik**, ATE, p. 243O
- Do Activities 7, 8, 9, and 10, p. 251
- Do Activities 5–8, pp. 99–100, Übungsheft

Wrap-Up 5 min.
- Students respond to questions about places to go in München

Homework Options
Grammatikheft, pp. 73–74, Acts. 1–4
Übungsheft, pp. 99–100, Acts. 1–4

Block 2

ERSTE STUFE
Quick Review 20 min.
- Check homework, Grammatikheft, pp. 73–74, Acts. 1–4
- Do **Minigeschichte, Erste Stufe**, TPR Storytelling Book, p. 33

LANDESKUNDE 30 min.
- Pre-viewing Suggestion, Video Guide, p. 56
- Background Information, ATE, p. 243P
- Show **Landeskunde** Video
- Do Activities A and B, p. 252
- Do **Landeskunde** Activity, Interactive CD-ROM

Quiz Review 20 min.
- Do Activities 1–2, Interactive CD-ROM
- Do **Mehr Grammatikübungen, Erste Stufe**

Quiz 20 min.
- Quiz 9-1A or 9-1B

Homework Options
Activities for Communication, pp. 49–50, prepare Communicative Activity 9-1

Block 3

ZWEITE STUFE
Quick Review 15 min.
- Return and review Quiz 9-1
- Bell Work, ATE, p. 243Q
- Go over Communicative Activity 9-1, pp. 49–50

Wortschatz, p. 253 20 min.
- Presenting **Wortschatz**, ATE, p. 243Q
- Teaching Transparency 9-B
- Do Activity 11, p. 253
- Play Audio CD for Activity 12, p. 254
- Do Activity 13, p. 254
- Do Activities 7–9, pp. 76–77, Grammatikheft

So sagt man das!/Ein wenig Grammatik, pp. 254–255 20 min.
- Presenting **So sagt man das!**, ATE, p. 243Q
- Presenting **Ein wenig Grammatik**, ATE, p. 243R
- Do Activity 14, p. 255
- Do Activities 12–13, p. 102, Übungsheft

Grammatik, p. 255 30 min.
- Presenting **Grammatik**, ATE, p. 243R
- Play Audio CD for Activity 15, p. 255
- Do Activity 16, p. 255
- Do Activities 17 and 18, p. 256
- Do Activities 11–12, p. 78, Grammatikheft

Wrap-Up 5 min.
- Students ask and respond to questions about how to get to different locations in their city

Homework Options
Grammatikheft, p. 77, Act. 10
Übungsheft, p. 101–103, Acts. 9–11, 14–15

One-Stop Planner CD-ROM

For alternative lesson plans by chapter section, to create your own customized plans, or to preview all resources available for this chapter, use the **One-Stop Planner CD-ROM**, Disc 3.

 For additional homework suggestions, see activities accompanied by this symbol throughout the chapter.

Block 4

ZWEITE STUFE

Quick Review 10 min.
- Check homework, Übungsheft, p. 101–103, Acts. 9–11, 14–15

Quiz Review 20 min.
- Do Additional Listening Activities 9-3 and 9-4, pp. 72–73
- Do **Mehr Grammatikübungen, Zweite Stufe**

Quiz 20 min.
- Quiz 9-2A or 9-2B

DRITTE STUFE

So sagt man das!/ Ein wenig Grammatik, p. 257 25 min.
- Presenting **So sagt man das!**, ATE, p. 243S
- Teaching Transparency 9-2
- Do Activities 16–17, p. 104, Übungsheft
- Presenting **Ein wenig Grammatik**, ATE, p. 243T
- Present **Ein wenig Landeskunde**, p. 257
- Do Activity 20, p. 257

So sagt man das!, p. 258 10 min.
- Presenting **So sagt man das!**, ATE, p. 243T
- Play Audio CD for Activity 21, p. 258

Wrap-Up 5 min.
- Students respond to questions about what there is to eat and drink

Homework Options
Grammatikheft, pp. 79–80, Acts. 13–15
Übungsheft, p. 105, Act. 18; p. 108, Act. 24

Block 5

DRITTE STUFE

Quick Review 15 min.
- Return and review Quiz 9-2
- Check homework, Grammatikheft, pp. 79–80, Acts. 13–15

Ein wenig Grammatik, p. 258 15 min.
- Presenting **Ein wenig Grammatik**, ATE, p. 243T
- Do Activity 22, p. 258

Grammatik, p. 259 25 min.
- Presenting **Grammatik**, ATE, p. 243T
- Do Activity 23, p. 259
- Do Communicative Activity 9-3, pp. 53–54
- Present **Lerntrick**, p. 259
- Do Activities 24 and 25, p. 259
- Do Activity 26, p. 260
- Do Activities 18–19, p. 81, Grammatikheft

So sagt man das!/Grammatik, p. 260 30 min.
- Presenting **So sagt man das!**, ATE, p. 243U
- Presenting **Grammatik**, ATE, p. 243U
- Play Audio CD for Activity 27, p. 261
- Do Activities 28 and 29, p. 261
- Do Additional Listening Activities 9-5 and 9-6, pp. 73–74

Wrap-Up 5 min.
- Students respond to questions about wanting more/not wanting more of certain foods

Homework Options
Grammatikheft, p. 80, Acts. 16–17
Übungsheft, pp. 105–106, Act. 19–22

Block 6

DRITTE STUFE

Quick Review 10 min.
- Check homework, Übungsheft, pp. 105–106, Act. 19–22

Aussprache, p. 261 10 min.
- Do **Richtig aussprechen/Richtig lesen**, p. 261
- Do **Richtig schreiben/Diktat**, p. 261

Quiz Review 20 min.
- Do **Mehr Grammatikübungen, Dritte Stufe**
- Play Circumlocution Game, ATE, p. 243X

Quiz 20 min.
- Quiz 9-3A or 9-3B

ZUM LESEN 25 min.
- Culture Note, ATE, p. 243V
- Present **Lesestrategie**, p. 262
- Do Activities 1–9, pp. 262–263

Wrap-Up 5 min.
- Students ask and respond to questions about how to get to different locations in München

Homework Options
Pupil's Edition, **Kann ich's wirklich?**, p. 270
Übungsheft, p. 107, Act. 23
Interaktive Spiele, see ATE, p. 243F

Block 7

ANWENDUNG

Quick Review 35 min.
- Return and review Quiz 9-3
- Check homework, **Kann ich's wirklich?**, p. 270
- Teaching Suggestions, Video Guide, pp. 50–51
- Do **Anwendung** Activities 1–5, pp. 268–269

Chapter Review 10 min.
- Review chapter functions, vocabulary, and grammar; choose from **Mehr Grammatikübungen**, Grammar Tutor for Students of German, Activities for Communication, Listening Activities, Interactive CD-ROM Tutor, or **Interaktive Spiele**

Test, Chapter 9 45 min.
- Administer Chapter 9 Test. Select from Testing Program, Alternative Assessment Guide or Test Generator.

Kapitel 9: Amerikaner in München
Teaching Suggestions, pp. 244–271

PAGES 244–245

CHAPTER OPENER

Pacing Tips

The **Erste Stufe** begins with the function of 'talking about where something is located' utilizing **Innenstadt** vocabulary and a map of **Muenchen** on p. 249. The verb **wissen** and dependent clauses with **wo** are introduced. In the **Zweite Stufe,** students again use a map on p. 253 to learn the function of 'asking for and giving directions.' The verbs **fahren** and **gehen** are presented alongside the formal commands with **Sie.** Several grammar concepts occur in the **Dritte Stufe:** the phrase **es gibt;** using **noch ein** and **kein;** and the conjunction **dass.** Because the **Erste Stufe** is shorter in both page length and amount of material than the **Zweite Stufe** or the **Dritte Stufe,** you may want to spend slightly less time on the **Erste Stufe.** For Lesson Plans and timing suggestions, see pages 243I–243L.

Meeting the Standards

Communication
- Talking about where something is located, p. 250
- Asking for and giving directions, p. 254
- Talking about what there is to eat and drink, p. 257
- Saying you do or don't want more, p. 258
- Expressing opinions, p. 260

Cultures
- **Ein wenig Landeskunde,** p. 249
- **Landeskunde,** p. 252
- **Ein wenig Landeskunde,** p. 257
- Culture Note, p. 243M
- Background Information, p. 243O
- Background Information, p. 243P

Connections
- Language Note, p. 243N
- History Connection, p. 243P
- Multicultural Connection, p. 243P
- Multicultural Connection, p. 243T
- Music Connection, p. 243U

Comparisons
- Language-to-Language, p. 243Q
- Language Note, p. 243T
- Thinking Critically, p. 243T
- Language Note, p. 243U

Communities
- Career Path, p. 243U
- Culture Note, p. 243V

For resource information, see the **One-Stop Planner CD-ROM,** Disc 3.

Cultures and Communities

Culture Note

Munich's parks and gardens are a source of relaxation and calm for the city's residents. During the summer people take every chance they get to enjoy the parks, also called **Grüne Oasen** of Munich. Most famous is the **Englischer Garten,** originally conceived by an American, Benjamin Thompson, to serve as common ground for all social classes as well as for agricultural education. Other important parks and gardens in Munich are: **Alter Botanischer Garten, Hofgarten, Luitpold Park, Olympiapark, Maximilians Anlagen, Westpark, Finanzgarten,** and **Schlosspark Nymphenburg.**

Students can obtain more information on the city's Web site. Most German cities' Web sites can be found at <u>www. [city name].de</u>.

Building on Previous Skills

Munich is a very popular city for American tourists. Do students recall some of Munich's sights introduced in the Location Opener? (**Neuhauserstraße, Marienplatz, Viktualienmarkt**) You might encourage students to explore these and other sights in Munich further on the Internet at WK3 MUENCHEN on <u>go.hrw.com</u> or using a search engine with the name of the sight as the keyword.

Chapter Sequence

Los geht's! . . . . .p. 246

Erste Stufe . . . . .p. 249

Landeskunde . . . . .p. 252

Zweite Stufe . . . . .p. 253

Dritte Stufe . . . . .p. 257

Zum Lesen . . . . .p. 262

Mehr Grammatikübungen . . . . .p. 264

Anwendung . . . . .p. 268

Kann ich's wirklich? . . . . .p. 270

Wortschatz . . . . .p. 271

LOS GEHT'S!

PAGES 246–247

Los geht's! Transparencies

Preteaching Vocabulary

Recognizing Cognates

Los geht's! contains several words that students
will be able to recognize as cognates. Have
students find these cognates, then have them
guess what is happening in the story.

③ direkt
④ Amerikaner, München
⑦ Bratwurst, Spezialität
⑩ Gute Idee!

Fortsetzung

You may choose
to continue with the
Fortsetzung of *München*
besuchen now or wait until
later in the chapter. For a
synopsis of the **Los geht's!** and **Fortsetzung** episodes,
see p. 243E.

Advance Organizer

Ask students how they would prepare for a sightseeing tour in a city such as Munich. What items
might they want to bring along? Have students make
suggestions. (Examples: maps, dictionary, coins for
using public transportation)

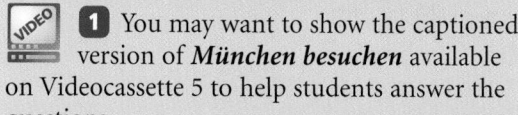

Connections and Comparisons

Language Note

The term **Pommes frites,** which means *French*
fries, was borrowed from the French language by
the Germans.

PAGE 248

Using the Captioned Video

① You may want to show the captioned
version of *München besuchen* available
on Videocassette 5 to help students answer the
questions.

Comprehension Check

A Slower Pace

② Begin this activity by having students work
in pairs, concentrating on pronunciation as they
reread the conversations on pp. 246–247.
Monitor their work and make pronunciation
corrections as appropriate. Then, while students
are working on Activity 2, write the numbers 1
through 5 on the board. Afterwards, have
students write their answers on the board. Go
over the phrases with the class.

Challenge

④ Have students think of a different response
to each of the questions and expressions given on
the left. (Example: **Was macht ihr hier? Wir sind**
aus Amerika und wollen München besuchen.)

Visual Learners

⑤ Make enlarged copies of the sentences from
this activity and cut them into sentence strips
ahead of time. Make one set per student or pair
of students, depending on your class size. Put
these strips into numbered envelopes. Ask
students to arrange the sentence strips in the
correct order on their desks. Once all students
have finished, ask several volunteers to read the
summary of the story.

ERSTE STUFE

ERSTE STUFE

Teaching Resources
pp. 249–252

PRINT

▸ Lesson Planner, p. 43
▸ TPR Storytelling Book, pp. 33, 36
▸ Listening Activities, pp. 67, 71
▸ Activities for Communication, pp. 49–50, 106, 109, 139–140
▸ Grammatikheft, pp. 73–75
▸ Grammar Tutor for Students of German, Chapter 9
▸ Übungsheft, pp. 98–100
▸ Testing Program, pp. 223–226
▸ Alternative Assessment Guide, p. 40
▸ Student Make-Up Assignments, Chapter 9

MEDIA

▸ One-Stop Planner
▸ Audio Compact Discs, CD9, Trs. 3, 16, 22–23
▸ Teaching Transparencies
  Situation 9-1
  Vocabulary 9-A
  Mehr Grammatikübungen Answers
  Grammatikheft Answers
▸ Interactive CD-ROM Tutor, Disc 3

PAGE 249

Bell Work

Ask students to brainstorm phrases they might need to know in order to ask for and understand directions in an unfamiliar city.

Teaching Suggestion

Have students familiarize themselves with the map of Munich while scanning for cognates. (Examples: **Nationaltheater, Englischer Garten**) Also have students go back to the Location Opener on pp. 184–187 and find some of the locations pictured on the map on p. 249.

PRESENTING: Wortschatz

Ask students to find each of the places listed in the **Wortschatz** on the map of Munich. Point out that many of these words for places do not appear by themselves on the map, but are part of proper names. (Examples: **Theatinerkirche, Viktualienmarkt**)

Thinking Critically

Drawing Inferences Ask students to think of symbols that could replace some of these places in town. Have them describe or draw them. Ask students for reasons symbols are helpful and to whom they are helpful. Might there be other places where signs without words might be helpful? (Examples: women's and men's restrooms, gas stations, banks that exchange currency)

Cultures and Communities

Background Information

German post offices also perform some banking functions that the U.S. Postal Service does not. Many Germans keep a postal savings account, which is convenient for travelers because it can be drawn on in different **Bundesländer** and countries.

PAGE 250

PRESENTING: So sagt man das!

Ask students what they usually say in English when they approach strangers to ask for information. (Excuse me.) What form of address would they expect to use in German when asking a stranger where something is located? (**Sie**-form)

PRESENTING: Grammatik

The verb wissen Review with students the word order changes that occur in phrases beginning with the conjunctions **denn** or **weil**. Do they recall the type of clause that the conjunctions introduce? (dependent, meaning that it cannot stand by itself without the main clause of the sentence.) Explain that **wissen** is often used to introduce a dependent clause that begins with an interrogative such as **wo**. In this case, the verb in the dependent clause is in the final position.

PAGE 251

Communication for All Students

A Slower Pace

7 Ask students to do this activity in writing. Students may refer back to the **Grammatik** on p. 250 to complete this task. Call on several students to read their statements aloud.

Group Work

8 Suggest that students expand this activity by performing a skit. Students should begin by making a brief outline and making note of any props that might be appropriate. They could perform this skit the following day or when time permits. This could also be done for extra credit.

Cooperative Learning

10 Divide the class into groups of three students each for this activity. Each group will need an "artist," a reader, and a demonstrator. Students will need construction paper, permanent markers, masking tape, and rulers. Set a time limit for this activity during which students should work together on the list of important places. The artist of the group draws the map as the other two students help to label the places. Finally, have students write out directions to at least three places that a visitor would enjoy seeing. Have each group come up to the front and tape its map to the board. The reader of the group reads the directions out loud as the demonstrator traces the directions with a ruler.

> **PAGE 252**

LANDESKUNDE

Teaching Resources
p. 252

PRINT
▸ Video Guide, pp. 55–56, 58–59
▸ Übungsheft, p. 108

MEDIA
▸ One-Stop Planner
▸ Video Program
  Videocassette 3, 43:27–49:13
▸ Audio Compact Discs, CD9, Trs. 4–7
▸ Interactive CD-ROM Tutor, Disc 3

Teaching Suggestion

Take a survey of the class asking students to list the German foods they have tried before. Which ones did they like or dislike?

Cultures and Communities

Background Information

Here are a few descriptions of some of the specialities mentioned by the interviewees: **Berliner Currywurst** is sausage that is browned and then cut lengthwise. Curry, pepper, and paprika are then sprinkled on top. **Scholle** is flounder. **Maultaschen** are triangular-shaped dough pockets filled with spinach, bacon, onion, egg, herbs, and spices and cooked in broth. See p. 303D for more background information and the recipe. **Schnitzel** is cutlet, either pork (**Schweineschnitzel**) or veal (**Kalbsschnitzel**).

Connections and Comparisons

History Connection

German immigrants in several different areas of the United States have tried to preserve their language and many culinary specialties. Ask students about such areas and have them research a few foods that are well known within those particular areas. (Example: The Pennsylvania Germans in eastern Pennsylvania—often referred to as the Pennsylvania Dutch—have a specialty called *shoofly pie*.)

Multicultural Connection

Ask students to interview foreign exchange students or people from other countries about their countries' culinary specialities. Have students report their findings to the class.

Game

Play the game **Was bedeutet dieses Zeichen?** See p. 243D for the procedure.

Assess
▸ Testing Program, pp. 223–226
  Quiz 9-1A, Quiz 9-1B
  Audio CD9, Tr. 16

▸ Student Make-Up Assignments
  Chapter 9, Alternative Quiz

▸ Alternative Assessment Guide, p. 40

ZWEITE STUFE

Teaching Resources
pp. 253–256

PRINT
▸ Lesson Planner, p. 44
▸ TPR Storytelling Book, pp. 34, 36
▸ Listening Activities, pp. 67–68, 72–73
▸ Activities for Communication, pp. 51–52, 107, 109, 139–140
▸ Grammatikheft, pp. 76–78
▸ Grammar Tutor for Students of German, Chapter 9
▸ Übungsheft, pp. 101–103
▸ Testing Program, pp. 227–230
▸ Alternative Assessment Guide, p. 40
▸ Student Make-Up Assignments, Chapter 9

MEDIA
▸ One-Stop Planner
▸ Audio Compact Discs, CD9, Trs. 8–9, 17, 24–25
▸ Teaching Transparencies
  Situation 9-1
  Vocabulary 9-B
  Mehr Grammatikübungen Answers
  Grammatikheft Answers
▸ Interactive CD-ROM Tutor, Disc 3

PAGE 253

Bell Work

In pairs, ask students to give each other the simplest directions possible from school to another place with which they are familiar. Have them be as specific as possible.

PRESENTING: Wortschatz

Teach the three basic directions first, using the appropriate symbols on the board or a transparency: **nach rechts, nach links, geradeaus.** Then teach **bis zum (zur) … dann …,** using the names of streets and symbols for landmarks. Finally, introduce **die nächste (erste, zweite) Straße nach (links, rechts),** using a simplified street map.

TPR Total Physical Response

Practice the expressions in the **Wortschatz** by first modeling and then asking individual students to follow your directions as they move around the classroom. Students could also perform certain tasks that

would be additional practice of some familiar vocabulary and expressions. (Example: directions to the door: Angela, steh auf und geh zwei Schritte geradeaus! Jetzt bitte einmal links, mach die Tür auf. Danke!)

PAGE 254

Communication for All Students

A Slower Pace

13 Make this activity into a guided oral production. Choose students randomly to give directions in stages. For example, you could have one student give the first directions, then call on another student to continue, then another until the destination is reached. Then begin again. Always have students start at the place where the previous student left off.

PRESENTING: So sagt man das!

Introduce **Wie komme ich …** as an alternate way of asking for directions. Prepare a transparency with several requests for directions written out both ways. (Example: **Verzeihung! Wissen Sie, wo das Rathaus ist? Verzeihung! Wie komme ich zum Rathaus?**) Be sure to vary the subject pronouns so all forms of **kommen** are practiced. Then, practice responses with **gehen** and **fahren** plus the specific directions introduced in the **Wortschatz.** Finally, using a simple street map, have students give you directions to certain key places indicated.

Connections and Comparisons

Language-to-Language

The German "**man**" and the French "**on**" are used similarly. Spanish expresses this concept with the impersonal **se** construction.
Example:
Man sagt, dass das Wetter in Miami schön ist.
On dit qu'il fait beau à Miami.
Se dice que hace buen tiempo en Miami.
What is the most common way of expressing this idea in English? ("They say …")

PRESENTING: Ein wenig Grammatik

The verb fahren Have students practice the use of fahren vs. gehen by providing cue cards with picture cues (a man walking, a bus, the **U-Bahn** symbol, and so on) or verbal cues (**mit dem Bus, zu Fuß,** and so on). Students should make up sentences based on the cues. (Examples: **Er geht zu Fuß. Sie fährt mit dem Bus.**)

PRESENTING: Grammatik

Sie-command Before introducing the Sie-commands, review the **du**-command forms by asking students to give random commands to each other using the vocabulary of this chapter. Then ask students to write the verb form of their commands on the board. Now use the same commands but address the students formally, using their last names. (Example: **Fräulein Osborn, gehen Sie bitte …!**) Then address two students formally and give them a series of commands. (Example: **Herr Walter und Herr Borau, stehen Sie bitte auf und gehen Sie …!**) Make sure students recognize the change in verb form and the addition of the personal pronoun.

Teaching Suggestion

16 Have students work with a partner as they take turns reading and following the directions. Monitor students' work and offer suggestions in pronunciation if needed.

Communication for All Students

For Additional Practice

18 To review the conjunctions **weil** and **denn** from Chapter 8, ask students to include a reason why they would like to see a certain landmark. Students can work this into the skit by asking: **Warum wollen Sie das sehen?**

Speaking Assessment

18 You may choose to ask groups to come to your desk and evaluate their skit using the following rubric.

Speaking Rubric	Points			
	4	3	2	1
Content (Complete – Incomplete)				
Comprehension (Total – Little)				
Comprehensibility (Comprehensible – Incomprehensible)				
Accuracy (Accurate – Seldom accurate)				
Fluency (Fluent – Not fluent)				

18–20: A   16–17: B   14–15: C   12–13: D   Under 12: F

Reteaching: Giving directions

Tell students that the new student in school is not sure how to get from German class to the office, the band hall, the school nurse, the math class, or the gymnasium. Ask students to write out directions in German to help the new student find his or her way around.

ZWEITE STUFE

Teaching Suggestion

Blindfold one student as the rest of the class (one student at a time) gives that student directions around the classroom. Students should be careful to word their directions so as not to endanger the blindfolded student. Have the blindfolded student guess where he or she is at the end.

Giving Directions

Make student copies of a section of your town's street map and hand one to each student. Each student picks a starting and an end point on the map and then draws a travel route connecting both points. Next, each student writes precise directions on a separate sheet beginning with the starting point. Students exchange directions and with a different color trace their partner's route on their map. Then, students compare routes and destination points and make corrections as necessary.

Assess

▸ Testing Program, pp. 227–230
  Quiz 9-2A, Quiz 9-2B
  Audio CD9, Tr. 17

▸ Student Make-Up Assignments,
  Chapter 9, Alternative Quiz

▸ Alternative Assessment Guide, p. 40

DRITTE STUFE

Teaching Resources
pp. 257–261

PRINT

▸ Lesson Planner, p. 45
▸ TPR Storytelling Book, pp. 35, 36
▸ Listening Activities, pp. 68-69, 73–74
▸ Activities for Communication, pp. 53–54, 108, 109, 139–140
▸ Grammatikheft, pp. 79–81
▸ Grammar Tutor for Students of German, Chapter 9
▸ Übungsheft, pp. 104–106
▸ Testing Program, pp. 231–234
▸ Alternative Assessment Guide, p. 40
▸ Student Make-Up Assignments, Chapter 9

MEDIA

▸ One-Stop Planner
▸ Audio Compact Discs, CD9, Trs. 10–14, 18, 26–27
▸ Teaching Transparencies
  Situation 9-2
  Mehr Grammatikübungen Answers
  Grammatikheft Answers
▸ Interactive CD-ROM Tutor, Disc 3

> **PAGE 257**

Bell Work

In pairs, ask students to recall some of the Bavarian food specialties from the Munich Location Opener on pp. 184–187 and the Chapter 9 **Los geht's!** on pp. 246–247. What seems different and unusual to them? Which of these regional specialities would they like to try? Have students tell each other.

PRESENTING: So sagt man das!

Ask students to look back at picture 7 of **Los geht's!** and name the expressions that the German teenagers use to show their American friends what they've ordered from the **Imbissstube.**

STANDARDS: 1.1

Connections and Comparisons

Language Note

Mention to students that Germans have several words to refer to rolls. For example, in southern Bavaria people use the word **Semmel**, in Baden-Württemberg they use the word **Wecken**, in the Berlin area, **Schrippe**, and in northern Germany, **Brötchen**. And there are often local terms for rolls and bread.

Thinking Critically

Comparing and Contrasting Can students think of foods or beverages that have different names in different parts of the United States? (Examples: soda, soda pop, pop, soft drink)

Comparing and Contrasting Ask students to name some specialties popular in their area. Do they know of foods that are associated with a city or region in the United States? (Examples: New York: bagels; New Orleans: Creole-style food; Philadelphia: cheesesteak sandwiches; Texas: chili)

Multicultural Connection

To expand this comparison beyond the United States, ask students whether they know of specialties of other countries. Have students make a list.

PRESENTING: Ein wenig Grammatik

Es gibt … Ask students a question such as **Haben wir hier in (Austin) einen Marktplatz?** and then tell them that another way of asking the same question involves the use of the phrase **es gibt: Gibt es in (Austin) einen Marktplatz?** Based on this information, see if they can guess the English equivalents of this phrase. *(there is, there are)* Using the **Wortschatz** terms from p. 249, ask students questions like the one above and have them answer in the affirmative. (**Ja, es gibt hier einen Marktplatz.**) What do they notice about the case of nouns that follow **es gibt?**

PAGE 258

PRESENTING: So sagt man das!

Ask students for the different ways they would respond to a friend when he or she offers more food or drink at his or her home. Can students make suggestions in German as to how to express these statements? Write the expressions on the board or on a transparency as students name them. Then introduce the responses from **So sagt man das!** Practice the dif-ferent yes-and-no responses by offering individual students something else to eat or drink and cueing a positive response with a nod and a negative response with a shake of the head.

Communication for All Students

Visual Learners

21 Make the transcript from this activity available to students after they have listened to it once. Students could use the script to complete the chart.

PRESENTING: Ein wenig Grammatik

Indefinite articles Begin this grammar review by preparing a transparency on which several partial sentences have been written, such as **Ich möchte bitte _____ haben.** and **_____ sieht gut aus!** Split the class into two teams and have representatives from each team go in turn to the board. Project these statements one at a time on a wall of the classroom, and provide the contestants with the English equivalent of the German words they are to use to complete the sentence. (Example: for the second sentence above, say 'your jacket'; students should write **Deine Jacke** on the board.) The team whose representative first answers correctly wins the point. Keep going until you have reviewed the various nominative and accusative forms of **ein, mein, dein, sein,** and **ihr.**

PAGE 259

PRESENTING: Grammatik

The word kein Begin by asking students to negate a sentence such as **Ich gehe morgen ins Kino. → Ich gehe morgen nicht ins Kino.** Then put the following sentences on a transparency, one in the affirmative and one in the negative: **Ich kaufe einen Taschenrechner. Ich kaufe keinen Taschenrechner.** Can students infer the difference between the two negated sentences? (**Nicht** negates a verb and means *not*, whereas **kein** negates a noun and means *no* or *none*.) Point out to students that **kein** used before a noun takes the same endings as other **ein**-words.

Teaching Suggestion

23 Start this activity by having students think of as many things as they can that they don't like to eat or drink. List them on the board with their articles. Then give students the following three phrases to complete:

Ich esse kein _____.
Ich esse keine _____.
Ich esse keinen _____.

Building on Previous Skills

24 In Chapter 8 students were introduced to the adverb **noch**. Ask students what **noch** refers to in sentences such as **Was bekommen Sie noch?** or **Ich brauche noch eine Semmel.** (refers to the items they buy) Tell students that in conjunction with **ein** (**noch ein**), **noch** means *one more* or *another*.

Cultures and Communities

Career Path

Have students brainstorm careers in writing in which a knowledge of German would be helpful. (Suggestions: Imagine you are a travel writer describing towns in the eastern part of Germany; imagine you are writing a book about the holiday traditions of the Austrian Tyrol.)

PAGE 260

Teaching Suggestion

26 You might ask students to report (in third person) what Eva says in her letter. (Example: **Sie kommt aus _____.**)

PRESENTING: So sagt man das!

Hand each student an index card with the name of a food item, a sport, or a leisure activity, accompanied by a verb in the infinitive. (Example: **Tennis spielen**) Then go around the class and ask several students to express their opinion about the phrase listed on their card. You might want to begin by expressing your own opinion about a sport you do or do not like. Next, use one of the opinions stated in **So sagt man das!** and write it on the board. (Example: **Ich finde Tennis toll.**) Then rewrite the statement using **dass.** (Example: **Ich finde, dass Tennis toll ist.**) Ask students to compare the two statements on the board, inferring the meaning of **dass.** Then you could ask some students to restate the opinion they already expressed about the phrase written on their index card, this time using **dass** in their statement.

PRESENTING: Grammatik

Dass Write these two sentences on a transparency: **Ich will essen, weil ich Hunger habe. Ich glaube, dass du auch Hunger hast.** Have students compare these two sentences, especially the word order in the dependent clauses.

Connections and Comparisons

Music Connection

For additional reading, refer students to the folksong **Doktor Eisenbart**, Level 2 *Listening Activities*, p. 38, and have them circle the two **dass**-clauses. (**dass die Blinden gehen; dass die Lahmen wieder sehen**) You may also want to play the song, Level 2 CD 5, Tr. 26.

Language Note

Dass-clauses, like all dependent clauses, are always separated from their preceding phrases by a comma.

PAGE 261

Communication for All Students

Challenge

27 As students listen a second time, have them make note of any additional information in each caller's topics or opinions.

Reteaching: Dass-clauses

Use sentence strips to write out various sentences which include the conjunction **dass**, as well as phrases that state opinions. Prepare enough envelopes so that each student or group has one. Give students a time limit in which to reconstruct each statement. Have students pass the envelope to the next student or group after they have finished with it.

Grammatik im Kontext

28 To expand on this activity, have pairs of students come up with five new statements to hand to another pair, who then have to form **dass**-clauses from those statements. Have each pair read one statement and **dass**-clause.

Von der Schule zum Beruf

You might want to request information from one of the agencies listed in the Professional References on pp. T48–T49 of the Teacher's Edition.

PRESENTING: Aussprache

An explanation of these sounds can be found in Chapters 1 and 3 of the *Pupil's Edition.*

Teaching Suggestion

As a closing activity, hand each student an index card with the name of a Munich landmark written on it. Have students tell the class where they are going and what they expect to see or do there based on the landmark written on their cards.

Assess

▸ Testing Program, pp. 231–234
  Quiz 9-3A, Quiz 9-3B
  Audio CD9, Tr. 18

▸ Student Make-Up Assignments
  Chapter 9, Alternative Quiz

▸ Alternative Assessment Guide, p. 40

ZUM LESEN

Teaching Resources
pp. 262–263

PRINT
▸ Lesson Planner, p. 46
▸ Übungsheft, p. 107
▸ Reading Strategies and Skills, Chapter 9
▸ Lies mit mir! 1, Chapter 9

MEDIA
▸ One-Stop Planner

Prereading
Building Context

Before doing Activity 1, ask students how they would plan a trip to a foreign country, such as Germany. What type of information would they look for? Where would they get information? What preparations would they make?

Teacher Note

Activities 1–3 are prereading activities.

Reading
Thinking Critically

Drawing Inferences Can students infer the meaning of abbreviations such as **S-Bahn** and **U-Bahn**? (**Schnellbahn/Untergrundbahn**) Why is the abbreviation **U-/S-Bahn** followed by the word **Marienplatz**? (to tell tourists the station at which they need to get on or off)

Cultures and Communities

 Culture Note

If tourists fall ill in Germany, they might find immediate help at an **Apotheke** *(pharmacy).* The local phone book will direct customers to the one or two pharmacies that are open all night. In pharmacies in major cities, the personnel also speak several languages. Flags posted on the door inform people of the languages spoken by the personnel.

Post-Reading
Teacher Note

Activity 9 is a post-reading task that will show whether students can apply what they have learned.

Zum Lesen Answers
Answers to Activity 1
c. a travel guide

Answers to Activity 2
skim to gather general information; scan to find specific information (For example, in the Dallmayr excerpt, students would be skimming to find out that food items are sold at Dallmayr, and they would be scanning to find the address of the store.)

Answers to Activity 3
Essen und Trinken: **Cafés, Restaurants, Stehimbisse, Konditoreien**; Einkaufen: **Sportmode, Geschenkwaren, Kaufhäuser, Fotogeschäfte**; Sehenswertes: **Deutsches Museum, Alte Pinakothek, Peterskirche, Englischer Garten**

Answers to Activity 4
Essen und Trinken: **Dallmayr**; Einkaufen: **Dallmayr, Ludwig Beck**; Sehenswertes: **Englischer Garten, Olympiapark, Peterskirche**

Answers to Activity 5
fine foods: **Dallmayr**; fashionable clothes: **Ludwig Beck**

Answers to Activity 6
a. **Faschingsball (Chrysanthemenball, Magnolienball, Madameball, Filmball, Presseball)**;
b. **Englischer Garten**; c. **Internationale Ludwigs-Apotheke** or **Von Mendel'sche Apotheke**; d. **Dallmayr**

Answers to Activity 7
take the **Isar-Floßfahrt**; you must plan ahead because the trips are booked well in advance; **Termine sind schon lange im Voraus gebucht.**

Answers to Activity 8 over nine hundred years old; the four bells and the city; 1972; 52 meters; ruins from World War II

PAGES 264–267

MEHR GRAMMATIKÜBUNGEN

The **Mehr Grammatikübungen** activities are designed as supplemental activities for the grammatical concepts presented in the chapter. You might use them as additional practice, for review, or for assessment.

For more grammar presentations, review, and practice, refer to the following:
• Grammatikheft
• Grammar Tutor for Students of German
• Grammar Summary on pp. R15–R25
• Übungsheft
• Grammar and Vocabulary quizzes
  (Testing Program)
• Test Generator
• Interactive CD-ROM Tutor
• **Interaktive Spiele** at go.hrw.com

PAGES 268–269

ANWENDUNG

 Video Wrap-up
Videocassette 3, 37:30-52:48
Videocassette 5 (captioned version), 49:47–55:05
At this time, you might want to use the video resources for additional review and enrichment. See *Video Guide* for suggestions regarding:
• the Los geht's! episode
• the **Landeskunde** interviews
• the **Fortsetzung** episode
• the **Videoclips.**

Apply and Assess

Challenge
1 Have students give a reason why they would like to see the local landmarks that the American students saw. Students should use **weil** or **denn** in their answers.

Thinking Critically
2 **Drawing Inferences** Can students think of other locations that a foreign visitor would need to know about? (Examples: **Jugendherberge, Pension, Flughafen, Polizei, Konsulat**)

Portfolio Assessment
4 You might want to use this activity as a written portfolio item for your students. See *Alternative Assessment Guide,* p. 26.

5 You might want to use this activity as an oral portfolio item for your students. See *Alternative Assessment Guide,* p. 26.

Apply and Assess

Process Writing

6 You may want to have your students pretend they are living in Munich, in order to enable them to use more of the vocabulary presented in this chapter. They should design a neighborhood in that city for the purpose of drawing their maps and describing their activities. Encourage students to use the sequencing words **zuerst, dann, danach,** and **zuletzt** when writing directions to the places on their maps.

Teaching Suggestion

7 Ask students to refer to **Los geht's!** on p. 247 for some foods typically found at an **Imbissstube** and the prices asked for such foods.

Using the Captioned Video

 Divide the class into two groups. As you play the captioned version of **München besuchen** on Videocassette 5, ask one group to compile a list of the expressions used for talking about where something is located and asking for and giving directions. The other group should write a list of the expressions that model talking about what there is to eat and drink, saying you do or don't want more, and expressing opinions. Then, collect the papers and randomly read aloud expressions from the lists. Ask students to identify which function is modeled by each expression you read.

▶ **PAGE 270**

KANN ICH'S WIRKLICH?

This page is intended to prepare students for the test. It is a brief checklist of the major points covered in the chapter. The students should be reminded that it is a checklist only and not necessarily everything that will appear on the test.

For additional self check options, refer students to the *Grammar Tutor,* the *Interactive CD-ROM Tutor,* and the Online self-test for this chapter

▶ **PAGE 271**

WORTSCHATZ

Teacher to Teacher

Carolyn Ostermann-Healey
Oakton High School
Vienna, Virginia

Carolyn uses this activity to review vocabulary.

❝Using Teaching Transparency Master 9-A, I prepare a Concentration® board on an overhead. The students have to match the picture to the word. I use small sticky notes to cover (and successfully re-cover) the squares. I split the class into two or three teams. The students may not help each other or take notes. The team with the most matches wins.❞

Review and Assess

♞ **Game**
Play the game **Kettenspiel.** See p. 243C for the procedure.

❓ **Circumlocution**
Play **Das treffende Wort suchen** with the **Erste Stufe** vocabulary. Your students are in a foreign city and want to visit some of the sights and public buildings, but have forgotten the necessary words. They must describe to the ticket seller the appearance of the place they want to go, and what one does at that location. Give the *tourists* index cards with pictures of locations. The *ticket sellers* should figure out where the tourists want to go. See p. 155C for procedures.

 Teacher Note
Give the **Kapitel 9** Chapter Test: *Testing Program,* pp. 235-240
Audio CD 9, Trs. 19-21

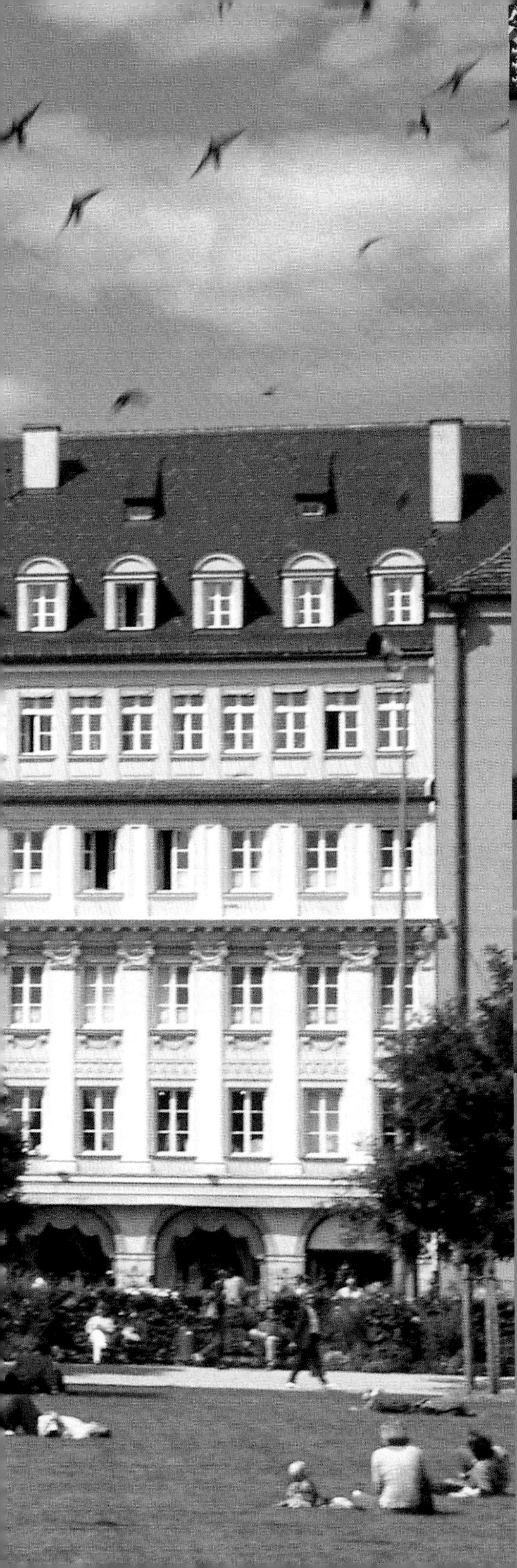

9

Amerikaner in München

Objectives

In this chapter you will learn to

Erste Stufe

* talk about where something is located

Zweite Stufe

* ask for and give directions

Dritte Stufe

* talk about what there is to eat and drink
* say you do or don't want more
* express opinions

internet

ADRESSE: go.hrw.com
KENNWORT:
WK3 MUENCHEN-9

◀ **Im Zentrum von München**

Los geht's! · *München besuchen*

CD 9 Trs. 1–2

Strategie Verstehen

Look at the images for this story. Who are the people? What are they doing? Where are they? What do you think they are talking about? What do you suppose will happen in the story?

Amerikaner

Markus

Mara

Los geht's! is an abridged version of the video episode.

①

Mara: Die Säfte hier sind doch wirklich Spitze!
Markus: Ja, und vor allem gesund!

②

Amerikaner: Entschuldigung!
Markus: Ja?
Amerikaner: Wie kommen wir zum Marienplatz?
Markus: Ganz einfach! Immer geradeaus bis zur Ampel und dann nach rechts.

③

Mara: Das stimmt doch gar nicht! An der Ampel nach links!
Markus: Klar, nach links! Dann kommt ihr direkt zum Marienplatz.
Amerikaner: Ah, vielen Dank!
Markus: Bitte, gern geschehen.

④

Mara: Ihr seid Amerikaner, nicht?
Amerikaner: Ja, wir sind aus Wisconsin.
Mara: Wirklich? Was macht ihr hier?
Amerikaner: Ja ...wir wohnen in Rosenheim, und heute besuchen wir München.

5 **Mara:** Prima! Na dann, viel Spaß!

6 **Markus:** Noch einen Saft?
Mara: Nein, danke! Keinen Saft mehr.

Später

7
Mara: Schau, da kommen die Amerikaner.
Markus: Hallo, Wisconsin! Wohin geht's?
Amerikaner: Was esst ihr hier?
Mara: Schau, hier gibt's Bratwurst, Weißwurst, Leberkäs …
Markus: Der Leberkäs ist hier echt gut.
Amerikaner: Was ist Leber …Leberkäs?
Markus: Eine bayrische Spezialität. Die musst du mal probieren!

8
Markus: So, schmeckt's?
Amerikaner: Wirklich gut.

9
Markus: Ich ess jetzt noch eine Bratwurst. Wer möchte auch noch etwas? Noch einen Leberkäs?
Amerikaner: Nein, danke! Ich habe genug.

10
Mara: Weißt du was, Markus? Wir zeigen den Amerikanern jetzt die Stadt. Was meint ihr?
Amerikaner: Gute Idee!

Übungsheft, S. 97

1 **Was passiert hier?**

These activities check for global comprehension only. Students should not yet be expected to produce language modeled in **Los geht's!**

Verstehst du die Gespräche in „München besuchen"? Versuche, die folgenden Fragen zu beantworten.

1. Where are Mara and Markus at the beginning of the story? What are they doing?

2. Who approaches Mara and Markus? What kind of information do these people need?

3. What does Markus recommend to eat? Why do you think he recommends this?

4. What do Markus and Mara decide to do at the end of the story?

1. at a snack bar, drinking juice   3. **Leberkäs**, because it is a typical Bavarian dish.
2. American students; how to get to **Marienplatz**   4. give the American students a tour of the city

2 **Genauer lesen**

Lies die Gespräche noch einmal. Welche Wörter gebraucht man, um:

1. to start conversations or get someone's attention

4. to ask for and give directions

2. to end conversations

5. to ask if someone would like more of

3. to name foods and drinks
1. Entschuldigung; Hallo.
2. Gern geschehen!; Na dann, viel Spaß.
something
3. Säfte, Bratwurst, Weißwurst, Leberkäs
4. Wie kommen wir zum…? geradeaus/ bis zur/nach rechts/nach links
5. Noch etwas?

3 **Stimmt oder stimmt nicht?**

Sind die folgenden Aussagen richtig oder falsch? Sag „stimmt", wenn sie richtig sind, sag „stimmt nicht", wenn sie falsch sind. Gib die richtige Antwort für jede falsche Aussage.

1. Zuerst trinken Markus und Mara Kaffee.

2. Der Amerikaner möchte zum Marienplatz gehen.

3. Mara und Markus besuchen Amerika.

1. Stimmt nicht. Sie trinken Säfte.
2. Stimmt.
3. Stimmt nicht. Sie sind in München.
4. Stimmt.
5. Stimmt nicht. Er isst Leberkäs gern.

4. Dann wollen der Amerikaner und seine Freunde etwas essen, denn sie haben Hunger.

5. Aber Markus isst Leberkäs nicht gern.

6. Stimmt.
7. Stimmt.

6. Leberkäs ist eine bayrische Spezialität.

7. Dann wollen Markus und Mara den Amerikanern die Stadt München zeigen.

4 **Was passt zusammen?**

Welche Aussagen in der rechten Spalte *(column)* passen zu den Fragen in der linken Spalte?

1. Wie kommen wir zum Marienplatz?

a. Wir besuchen die Stadt München.

2. Vielen Dank!

b. Gern geschehen!

1. c
2. b
3. a
4. e
5. f
6. d

3. Was macht ihr hier?

c. Ihr müsst an der Ampel nach links.

4. Was esst ihr hier?

d. Ja, wirklich gut!

5. Isst du noch eine Bratwurst?

e. Hier gibt's Leberkäs und Weißwurst.

6. Schmeckt's?

f. Nein, danke! Ich habe genug.

5 **Nacherzählen**

Put the sentences in a logical order to make a brief summary of **Los geht's!**

1. Am Saftstand trinken Mara und Markus einen Saft.

5 Dann probiert er den Leberkäs.

4 Später wollen der Junge und seine Freunde wissen, was Mara und Markus essen.

3 Er wohnt in Rosenheim und besucht heute München.

6 Danach zeigen Mara und Markus den Amerikanern München.

2 Ein Junge kommt vorbei und möchte wissen, wie er zum Marienplatz kommt.

Erste Stufe

Objective Talking about where something is located

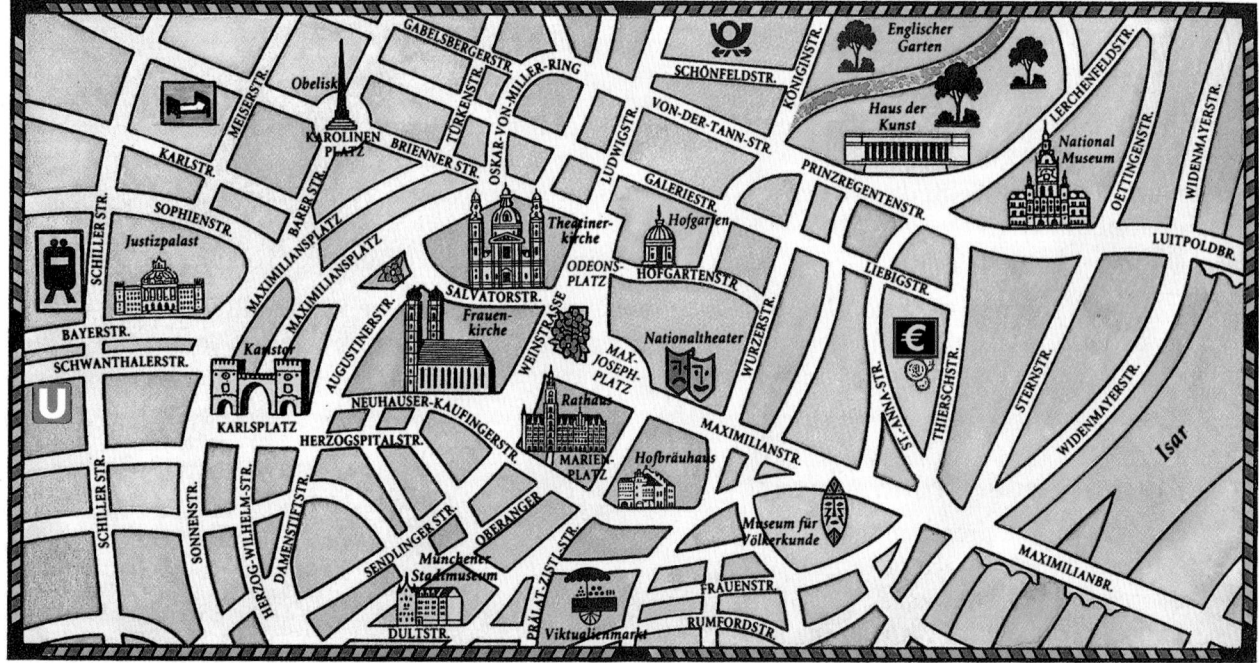

What kinds of places are pictured on this map of **München**? What do you think a **Kirche** is? And the **Rathaus**? How many museums can you find? And parks? Judging by the types of buildings on this map, what part of the city do you think this is?

Wortschatz

In der Innenstadt

Wo ist … ?

p. 243X   9–A   CD-ROM DISC 3

das Hotel   die Kirche   das Rathaus   der Marktplatz

die Bank   die Post   das Museum   der Bahnhof

das Theater   der Garten   die U-Bahnstation

Übungsheft, S. 98, Ü. 2–3   Grammatikheft, S. 73, Ü. 1–2

Ein wenig Landeskunde

Many cities in Germany were originally built around the **Marktplatz,** with the **Rathaus** and the main **Kirche** nearby. A wall surrounded the city and offered protection to the inhabitants. In a number of cities, parts of the original city wall are still standing around the **Innenstadt** (*downtown*). In many cities the main streets through downtown are closed to traffic and are designated as a **Fußgängerzone** (*pedestrian zone*).

Talking about where something is located

Grammatikheft, S. 75, Ü. 5–6

If you are in a new city, you might need to ask where things are located.
You might ask a passerby:

You might get the responses:

Verzeihung! Wissen Sie, wo das Rathaus ist?
Und wo ist das Karlstor?
Entschuldigung! Weißt du, wo der Bahnhof ist?
Und wo ist hier ein Café?

In der Innenstadt am Marienplatz.
In der Neuhauser Straße.
Es tut mir Leid. Das weiß ich nicht.

Keine Ahnung! Ich bin nicht von hier.

What is the position of the second verb in questions that begin with **wissen** and **weißt**? Which expression might you use to ask someone older than yourself? To ask a person your own age? Which responses were probably made by someone who does not live in Munich?

Script on p. 243G

6 Stimmt? oder Stimmt nicht?

CD 9 Tr. 3

Zuhören At the tourist information center in **München,** you overhear a conversation between an American tourist and someone who doesn't know the city very well. Using the map on page 249, decide whether the information the tourist is given for each of the places listed below is correct or incorrect.

1. ein Hotel — correct
2. die Post — correct
3. eine Bank — incorrect
4. eine U-Bahnstation — correct
5. das Stadtmuseum — incorrect
6. der Englische Garten — incorrect
7. die Frauenkirche — correct

Grammatik

The verb **wissen**

The verb **wissen** means *to know* (a fact, information, etc.). Here are the forms:

ich	**weiß**	wir	wissen
du	**weißt**	ihr	wisst
er, sie, es	**weiß**	sie, Sie	wissen

Mehr Grammatikübungen, S. 264, Ü. 1–3

Look at the sentences below.

Wo ist das Museum?
Weißt du, wo das Museum **ist**?

Ich weiß nicht.
Ich weiß nicht, wo das Museum **ist**.

Übungsheft, S. 99–100, Ü. 4–8

What is the position of the verbs in the clauses introduced by **wo**? Used in this way, **wo** introduces a dependent clause. The verb is in final position.

Grammatikheft, S. 74, Ü. 3–4

7 **Grammatik im Kontext**

a. **Sprechen** Mara und ihre Familie fahren heute in die Innenstadt. Sie möchten sich viel ansehen, und sie müssen auch viel einkaufen *(to shop)*. Wissen sie, wo alles ist? Ergänze Maras Aussagen mit der richtigen Form von **wissen**!

b. **Schreiben** Schreib die Antworten!

Ich weiß, wo das Rathaus ist. Vater und ich wissen, wo die Frauenkirche ist. Ali weiß, wo die Post ist. Du weißt, wo der Hofgarten ist. Ihr wisst, wo die Bank ist. Leyla und Jasmin wissen, wo das Theater ist.

BEISPIEL **Mutti weiß, wo das Theater ist.**

1. Ich … 2. Vater und ich … 3. Ali … 4. Du … 5. Ihr … 6. Leyla und Jasmin …

8 **Amerikaner treffen Engländer in München**

Sprechen Eine amerikanische Schülergruppe hat sich in München verlaufen. Die Schüler fragen eine Gruppe von Leuten, aber das sind Touristen aus England und sie wissen auch nicht, wo sie sind. Schreibe ein Gespräch und benutze dabei die richtigen Verbformen von „wissen". Answers will vary.

Wissen Sie, wo die Post ist? / Nein, es tut mir Leid.

Wisst ihr, wo der Bahnhof ist?/ Keine Ahnung.

Weißt du, wo der Marktplatz ist? Nein, ich weiß nicht.

Wissen Sie, wo die U-Bahnstation ist? / Nein …

9 **Entschuldigung! Wissen Sie, wo …?**

Sprechen Du hast deinen Stadtplan verloren. Wie kannst du jetzt diese Sehenswürdigkeiten *(sights)* in München finden? Schau auf die Stadtkarte auf Seite 249 und such dir fünf Sehenswürdigkeiten aus. Setz dich jetzt mit zwei Klassenkameraden zusammen. Ein Partner ist ein Fußgänger, ungefähr 50 Jahre alt, der andere Partner eine junge Person in deinem Alter. Frag jetzt beide Partner nach den Orten, die du sehen möchtest. Tauscht dann die Rollen.

10 **Wie sieht deine Stadt aus?**

Schreiben Ein deutscher Austauschschüler möchte wissen, wo die Sehenswürdigkeiten in deinem Ort sind. Zeichne mit einer Klassenkameradin einen Stadtplan, der alle Sehenswürdigkeiten in deinem Ort zeigt. Wo kann der Austauschschüler etwas zum Anziehen oder zum Essen kaufen? Beschrifte *(label)* alle Straßen und wichtigen Sehenswürdigkeiten. Mehr Wörter findest du auf Seite R9.

Was isst du gern?

We asked some people in the German-speaking countries to tell us about what kinds of foods they like to eat. Before you read what they said, make a list of some of the things you would consider "German specialties." CD 9 Tr. 4

CD 9
Trs. 4–7

Übungsheft, S. 108, Ü. 24

Schweineschnitzel

Kaiserschmarren

Würstchen

Melina,
Bietigheim

„Ich esse am liebsten so Eis, vor allem Erdbeereis oder so, mit Früchten drin. Und so…von Gerichten mag ich ja Schnitzel oder Linseneintopf. Ja, trinken mag ich eigentlich so mehr Cola oder so Apfelsaft."
CD 9 Tr. 5

Rosi,
Berlin

„Ach, ich esse auch gern Süßspeisen, also Kaiserschmarren als österreichisches [Gericht] oder Eierkuchen — ja, also eigentlich alles Mögliche!" CD 9 Tr. 6

Uli,
München

„Dafür lieb ich Würstchen, jeglicher Art, besonders die Berliner Currywürstchen, die es hier in München leider nicht so oft gibt. Ja und das ist so das, was ich gern esse." CD 9 Tr. 7

Here are a few other German specialties.

Scholle, Hamburg

Maultaschen, Baden-Württemberg

A. 1. Write the people's names and list the German specialties each likes to eat. Are there any foods mentioned that are not German specialties? 1. yes; ice cream

2. Look at the list you made before reading and discuss the following questions with your classmates. Did your guesses differ from what the people said? If so, how? Where did you get your ideas about German specialties? What do you think people in German-speaking countries would name as American specialties? Where do you think they get their ideas?

B. Write a letter in German to one of the people interviewed telling her about the local specialties you like to eat. The person may not know what they are, so it might be a good idea to describe the foods in as much detail as you can.

STANDARDS: 1.2, 2.2, 3.2, 4.2

Zweite Stufe

Objective Asking for and giving directions

11 Den Weg zeigen

Sprechen Hier ist ein Teil einer Karte von Mittersendling, einem Stadtteil in München. Beginne an der U-Bahnstation und folge den Richtungsangaben *(directions)* im Wortschatz. Wohin kommst du, wenn du diesen Richtungsangaben folgst? die Bäckerei

Wortschatz

Gehen Sie ...

9–B

nach rechts	bis zum Krüner Platz	dann geradeaus	bis zur Ampel, dann nach rechts	dann die erste (zweite, dritte) Straße nach rechts

die nächste Straße nach links	bis zur Herrschinger Str.	und wieder nach rechts	dann geradeaus. Da ist ...

Grammatikheft, S. 76–77, Ü. 7–10

12 **Stimmt die Richtung?** <small>Script on p. 243G</small>

An American exchange student is trying to find the produce store, shopping center, and the bakery in Mittersendling. He is standing in front of the butcher's asking a passerby for directions. Listen to their conversation several times and determine whether the directions given will take him where he wants to go or not. If not, where do they lead him? <small>1. Yes 2. No-**Jugendclub** 3. Yes</small>

<small>CD 9 Tr. 8</small>

13 **Du gehst nach links, dann nach ...**

Zeig den Weg zu den folgenden Orten (*places*) in Mittersendling! Fang beim Hotel an! Tausche die Rolle mit deinen Klassenkameraden aus!

a. vom Hotel bis zur Post

b. von der Post bis zum Supermarkt

c. von der Bank bis zum Hotel

So sagt man das!

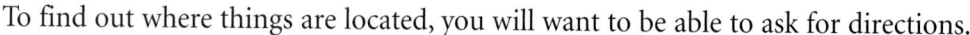

Asking for and giving directions

To find out where things are located, you will want to be able to ask for directions.

<small>9–1</small> CD-ROM DISC **3**

You might ask a passerby:

> **Verzeihung! Wie komme ich zum Hotel am Bahnhof?**
>
> **Und wie kommt man* zur Bäckerei? Entschuldigung! Wie kommen wir zum Einkaufszentrum?**
>
> **Und wie kommen wir zur U-Bahnstation?**

The responses might be:

> **Gehen Sie geradeaus bis zur Alpseestraße, dann nach links!**
>
> **Die nächste Straße nach rechts. Fahren Sie geradeaus bis zur Ampel, dann nach links!**
>
> **Sie fahren hier nach rechts, dann die zweite Straße wieder nach rechts.**

What do you think the words **zum** and **zur** mean?[1] Why is there a difference and what does it depend on?[2] In two of the responses, the verb is in first position. Can you figure out why?

Übungsheft, S. 101–102, Ü. 9–11

---

[1] *to the* [2] It depends on the noun that follows: masculine/neuter nouns > **zu dem (zum)**; feminine nouns > **zu der (zur)**.
*****man** means *one, you* (in general), *people*; it is used with the **er/sie**-form of the verb: **man geht, man fährt**.

14 Grammatik im Kontext

 Lesen/Sprechen Du stehst vor der Post in Mittersendling, und du musst heute noch viel erledigen. Du musst noch Semmeln kaufen, Geld umtauschen (du warst in den USA) und ein T-Shirt kaufen. Danach willst du deine Freunde im Jugendclub treffen. Schau dir den Stadtplan auf Seite 253 an, wähle zwei Orte aus und frag deinen Partner, wie du am besten dorthin kommst. Tauscht dann die Rollen.

zum Einkaufszentrum	**zur Bank**
zur Bäckerei	**zum Jugendclub**

Ein wenig Grammatik

In the **So sagt man das!** box on page 254, both **gehen** and **fahren** are used. How is **fahren** different in meaning from **gehen**? **Fahren** is used whenever someone is using a vehicle to go somewhere, such as **ein Auto, ein Bus,** or **ein Fahrrad. Fahren** has a stem-vowel change in the **du-** and **er/sie-** forms: **Du fährst mit dem Bus, und sie fährt mit dem Auto.** However, with **du-** commands, the umlaut is not used: **Fahr jetzt nach Hause!**

Übungsheft, S. 102, Ü. 12–13

Mehr Grammatikübungen, S. 265, Ü. 4

Grammatik

The formal commands with Sie

In **Kapitel 8** you learned how to use commands with people you know well: **Kauf ein Kilo Kartoffeln, bitte!** In this chapter you have seen how you would give a command to a person whom you do not know well and who is older than yourself. Look at the following sentences:

Fahren Sie nach links!   **Gehen Sie geradeaus!**

What do you notice about the word order in formal commands?[1] How would you give a command to someone your own age using **fahren** and **gehen**?[2] To two strangers older than yourself?[3]

Mehr Grammatikübungen, S. 265–266, Ü. 4–6

Übungsheft, S. 103, Ü. 14–15

Grammatikheft, S. 78, Ü. 11–12

 15 Grammatik im Kontext

 a. Zuhören At the information counter at the main train station in Munich, a friend of yours is asking how to get to the **Viktualienmarkt**. Listen to the directions given several times and jot down some notes as you listen. Script on p. 243G

CD 9 Tr. 9

b. Lesen Check your notes with the map on page 249. Did you understand the directions?

c. Sprechen Now use your notes to explain in your own words to another friend how he or she can get to the **Viktualienmarkt**. Answers will vary.

Formal: Warten Sie; Steigen Sie; ein; fahren Sie; Steigen Sie; aus; gehen Sie; gehen Sie; Gehen Sie; kommen Sie

 16 Grammatik im Kontext

Schreiben Your parents are having a party for you. You decided to e-mail an invitation to a classmate and to one of your teachers, giving directions to your home. Write the directions by filling in the command forms of the verbs given in parentheses.

Hallo: (warten) ===== am Bahnhof auf einen Bus. (einsteigen) ===== in die # 3 =====, und (fahren) ===== bis zur Meisestraße. (aussteigen) ===== ===== und (gehen) ===== immer geradeaus bis zur Ampel. An der Ampel (gehen) ===== rechts in die Drosselstraße. Unser Haus ist das dritte Haus rechts. (gehen) ===== nicht ins Haus, sondern (kommen) ===== gleich in den Garten. Hier ist die Party.

Warte; Steig
ein; fahr; Steig; aus
geh; geh
Geh;
komm

---

1. The verb is in first position and is followed by **Sie**. **2. Fahr/Geh …! 3. Fahren/Gehen Sie …!**

17 Wohin?

b. **Theatinerkirche**

Lesen Your friend wants you to see some famous places in Munich and has left behind a set of directions from the **Bahnhof** to somewhere in Munich. However, he forgot to tell you what you will see. Read his directions and use the map of Munich (page 249) to find out where they lead. Match the destination with one of the photos.

> Also, du kommst aus dem Bahnhof, gehst über die Straße und dann in Richtung Karlsplatz. Du gehst durchs Karlstor, und hier kommst du in die Neuhauser und Kaufingerstraße. Die führen zum Marienplatz. Am Marienplatz musst du links in die Weinstraße einbiegen. Geh jetzt immer geradeaus, bis du zum Odeonsplatz kommst. Auf der linken Seite ist ein großes Gebäude. Da bin ich!

a.

b.

c.

18 Also, fahren Sie …

Sprechen Role-play the following situation with two classmates. One of you will be a German student at the **Rathaus** where several people ask you for directions. Another will be an American high school teacher sightseeing in Munich by car, and the third classmate will be a young student from Los Angeles on a bike. Each tourist will think of two places he or she wants to see in downtown **München** and will ask you for directions. Use the map on page 249 to help them. Then switch roles.

BEISPIEL Wie komme ich …?

> zum Hofbräuhaus zum Haus der Kunst
> zum Münchner Stadtmuseum
> zum Karlstor zum Hofgarten
> zum Nationalmuseum
> zum Bahnhof zum Englischen Garten
> zur Theatinerkirche
> zum Nationaltheater zur Frauenkirche

19 Für mein Notizbuch

Schreiben Ein deutscher Austauschschüler möchte dich besuchen. Beschreib in deinem Notizbuch den Weg von deiner Schule bis zu deinem Haus! Fährst du mit dem Bus oder vielleicht mit der U-Bahn? Das kannst du auch beschreiben.

BEISPIEL Du gehst …   *oder*
Du fährst mit dem Bus/der U-Bahn
Nummer … bis …, dann …

Dritte Stufe

Objectives Talking about what there is to eat and drink; saying you do or don't want more; expressing opinions

WK3 MUENCHEN-9

So sagt man das!

Talking about what there is to eat and drink

9–2

If you go to a restaurant for the first time, you might ask your friend or a waiter what there is to eat or drink.

You might ask:

Was gibt es hier zu essen?

Und zu trinken?

The response might be:

Es gibt Leberkäs, Vollkornsemmeln, Weißwurst …

Cola, Apfelsaft und auch Mineralwasser.

What do you think the expressions **Was gibt es?** and **Es gibt** … mean?

Übungsheft, S. 104, Ü. 16–17

Ein wenig Grammatik

The phrase **es gibt** (*there is*, *there are*) is a fixed expression that stays the same despite the number of objects referred to. In the example **Gibt es hier in der Nähe einen Supermarkt?** is **Supermarkt** in the nominative or accusative case? How can you tell? What can you say about noun phrases following **es gibt**?[1]

Grammatikheft, S. 79, Ü. 13–14

Mehr Grammatikübungen, S. 266, Ü. 7

IMBIß STUBE
am Rathaus

Leberkäs mit Senf	4,00	Brezel	1,00
mit Semmel	4,50	Käsebrot	3,20
Hähnchen vom Grill	6,00	Milch	2,00
Gyros		Mineralwasser	1,00
mit Salat	4,50	Apfelsaft	2,40
Weißwurst	7,50 3,80	Tee, Glas	2,50
Volkornsemmel	-,50		

---

20 Grammatik im Kontext

a. Sprechen Du kannst dich nicht entscheiden (*to decide*), was du in der **Imbissstube am Rathaus** bestellen (*order*) möchtest. Frag deinen Partner, was es zu essen und zu trinken gibt! Sag deinem Partner, was du möchtest! Tauscht dann die Rollen aus!

b. Schreiben Was fehlt? Schreib es in die Lücken!

MARK   Was gibt ▬▬▬ hier zu essen?

SARA   Es ▬▬▬ …

MARK   Und was ▬▬▬ hier zu trinken?

SARA   ▬▬▬ Milch, Mineralwasser, und so.

Ein wenig Landeskunde

Leberkäs is a Bavarian specialty of ground beef or pork liver, pork, and spices. Most people eat it with a **Semmel** or **Brezel** and sweet mustard. How would you tell a German friend about specialties available in your area?

es

gibt (Gyros/Leberkäs)

gibt es

Es gibt

---

[1]. Noun phrases that follow **es gibt** are always in the accusative case.

Saying you do or don't want more

In **Kapitel 8** you learned how to ask if someone wants something else when shopping. When eating at a café or at your friend's house, you may also be asked what else you would like.

The host or your friend might ask:

Möchtest du noch etwas?

Möchtest du noch einen Saft?

Noch eine Semmel?

You might respond:

Ja, bitte, ich nehme noch eine Brezel. *or*
Nein, danke! Ich habe keinen Hunger mehr. *or*
Nein, danke! Ich habe genug. *or*
Danke, nichts mehr für mich.
Ja, bitte. Noch einen Saft. *or*
Nein, danke, keinen Saft mehr.
Ja, gern!

Übungsheft,
S. 105, Ü. 18

What do you think the phrases **noch einen Saft** and **keinen Saft mehr** mean?[1] What subject and verb might be understood in the question **Noch eine Semmel?**[2]

Grammatikheft,
S. 80, Ü. 15

Script on p. 243H

21 Wollt ihr noch etwas?

CD 9
Tr. 10

Zuhören Markus is having a **Grillfest**. His friends have just finished eating, and he asks them if they want more. Listen to the conversations and decide what each person had to eat or drink. Then listen again and determine whether each person wanted more or not.

	Mara	Silvia	Thomas	Flori	Claudia	Frank
zu essen	Semmel	Hähnchen	Brezel	Leber-käs	Weiß-wurst	Salat
zu trinken	Saft	Limo	Saft	Mineral-wasser	Limo	Apfel-saft
noch mehr?	ja	nein	ja	ja	ja	nein

22 Logisch oder unlogisch?

Lesen/Sprechen Sind die folgenden Aussagen logisch oder unlogisch? Wenn sie unlogisch sind, ändere die Aussagen, damit sie logisch sind!

1. Ja, bitte, ich möchte noch einen Leberkäs. Ich habe keinen Hunger.
2. Nein, danke! Nichts mehr für mich. Ich möchte noch eine Weißwurst.
3. Ja, ich habe Hunger. Ich möchte noch eine Semmel.
4. Ja, bitte, ich trinke noch einen Saft. Ich habe Apfelsaft gern.
5. Ich habe noch Hunger. Ich nehme noch ein Käsebrot.
6. Ja, bitte, noch eine Tasse Tee. Ich trinke Tee nicht gern.

1. Unlogisch. „Ich habe Hunger."
2. Unlogisch. „Ich möchte keine Weißwurst mehr." 3. Logisch
4. Logisch 5. Logisch 6. Unlogisch. „Ich trinke Tee gern."

Ein wenig Grammatik

Schon bekannt

In **Kapitel 5** you learned about the indefinite article **ein** (*a, an*). If the noun is a subject, **ein** is used with masculine and neuter nouns, and **eine** with feminine nouns. When the noun following **ein** is used as a direct object, the masculine form is **einen**. The possessive pronouns **mein, dein, sein,** and **ihr** also have these same endings.

When **noch** precedes the indefinite article **ein**, it has the meaning of *another*.

Übungsheft, S. 105, Ü. 19

Mehr Grammatikübungen,
S. 266, Ü. 8

---

1. *another juice, no more juice* 2. **Möchtest du**

Negation of indefinite articles with **kein**

You have already learned some expressions using **kein: Ich habe keinen Hunger. Ich habe keine Zeit.** What does **kein** mean?[1] What do you notice about the endings that **kein** takes?[2] **Kein** is used to negate a noun, rather than an entire statement. Often when people say that they want more, they say **Ja, noch ein** (Käsebrot). If they don't want more, they simply say: **Keinen** (Kaffee) **mehr, danke.**

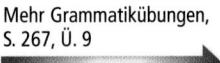

Mehr Grammatikübungen, S. 267, Ü. 9

Übungsheft, S. 105, Ü. 20

Grammatikheft, S. 80, Ü. 16–17

---

23 **Grammatik im Kontext**

Sprechen Are there some things that you refuse to eat or drink? Take turns asking and telling your classmates about these things, using **kein** in your answers, for example, **Ich trinke keine Limo.** Use the box for ideas or turn to page R9 for additional words. *Answers will vary. Examples:* **Ich esse keine Zwiebeln. Ich esse keinen Spinat.**

> (der) Blumenkohl (cauliflower)
> (der) Rosenkohl (Brussels sprouts)
> (die) Zwiebel (onion)
> (die) Milch
> (der) Spinat (spinach)
> (der) Haferbrei (oatmeal)
> (die) Wurst
> (die) Leber (liver)

24 **Grammatik im Kontext**

Schreiben Nach der Schule sind einige Freunde bei Mara zu Hause und essen etwas. Ergänze das Gespräch mit den Wörtern im Kasten und der richtigen Form von **kein** und **noch ein**!

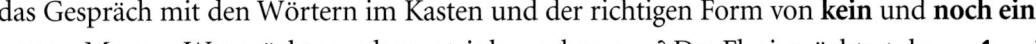

1. noch einen Apfel
2. Keinen Orangensaft
3. noch ein Stück Kuchen
4. keine Semmel
5. keinen Hunger
6. noch eine Brezel

MARA	Wer möchte noch was trinken oder essen? Du, Flori, möchtest du ___1___?
FLORI	Ja, gern, Äpfel esse ich sehr gern.
MARA	Und mehr Orangensaft?
FLORI	Nein, danke. ___2___ mehr.
MARA	Und du Claudia, du hast nur ein Stück Kuchen gegessen. Möchtest du noch etwas?
CLAUDIA	Ja, ___3___ bitte und auch ein Mineralwasser.
MARA	Und Markus? Willst du auch noch eine Semmel?
MARKUS	Nein, ___4___ mehr. Danke! Ich habe ___5___.
MARA	Und du, Rolf? Hast du noch Hunger?
ROLF	Ja, ein bisschen. Ich hab nur eine Brezel gegessen. Ich möchte ___6___. Brezeln esse ich immer gern!
CLAUDIA	Das weiß ich!

> (die) Semmel
> (der) Orangensaft
> (die) Brezel
> (der) Hunger
> (das) Stück Kuchen
> (der) Apfel

25 **Möchtest du noch ein ...?**

Sprechen Du machst jetzt ein Grillfest. Es gibt noch viel zu essen und zu trinken. Frag deinen Partner, ob er noch etwas haben möchte! („Dein Partner") sagt ja (mit **noch ein**) oder nein (mit **kein ...mehr**). Dann tauscht ihr die Rollen aus!

LERNTRICK

Take note of words that are similar and follow the same grammatical patterns. For example, **ein** and **kein** look and sound alike and have the same endings before nouns. Can you think of other words you have learned that look and sound like **ein** and **kein**?[3]

---

1. *not, not any, or no* **2. Kein** has the same endings as **ein**. **3. mein, dein,** and **sein.**

26 **Ein Leserbrief**

Lesen/Schreiben Lies diesen Brief an die Zeitschrift **Jugend** und beantworte die Fragen!

a. 1. Woher kommt Eva?

   2. Wann ist sie geboren?

   3. Welches Hobby hat Eva?

   4. Wie finden die Eltern Evas Hobby?

   5. Was hofft Eva? (**hoffen** *to hope*)

b. **Lesen** Find the two sentences in which the word **dass** is used. What is Eva trying to express in these sentences? What is the English equivalent of **dass**? What is the position of the verb in the clauses that begin with **dass**?

b.: **Dass** introduces clause that tells what her parents find good and what she (Eva) believes. **Dass**=*that*. verb-at end of clause

Hobby

Ich heiße Eva Hörster und bin am 17.10.88 in München geboren. Ich

laufe mit den Rollschuhen auf der Straße oder auf der Rollschuhbahn. Meine Eltern finden es gut, dass ich Sport treibe. Sie begleiten mich immer zum Training und Langlauf. Ich hoffe, dass Rollschuhlaufen eine olympische Sportart wird. Das Foto ist nach meinem ersten Pokalsieg aufgenommen worden.

Viele Grüße,
Eva Hörster, München

So sagt man das!

Expressing opinions

In **Kapitel 2** you learned to express opinions such as: **Ich finde Tennis super**! You can also use a **dass**-clause to elaborate on your opinions.

Your friend might ask:

Wie findest du München?

You might respond:

Super! Ich finde es toll, dass es hier so viele Parks und Museen gibt. Und ich glaube, dass die Leute sehr freundlich sind. Aber ich finde es schlecht, dass das Essen so teuer ist.

What are the different phrases that begin the sentences expressing opinions? What is the subject in each **dass**-clause? What opinion is being expressed in each sentence?

Grammatik

The conjunction dass

Look again at the responses in the **So sagt man das!** box. Name the verbs in the **dass**-clauses.[1] What is the position of these verbs?[2] The conjunction **dass** often begins clauses that express opinions: **Ich finde, dass … Ich glaube, dass …** In clauses that begin with **dass**, the conjugated verb is at the end of the clause.

München **ist** sehr schön.
Ich glaube, **dass** München sehr schön **ist**.

What other conjunction do you know that affects the word order in the same way?[3]

Mehr Grammatikübungen,
S. 267, Ü. 10

Übungsheft, S. 106, Ü. 21–22

Grammatikheft, S. 81, Ü. 18–19

CD-ROM
DISC 3

---

1. gibt, sind, ist 2. at the end of the clause **3. weil**

27 **Wer spricht im Radio?** Script on p. 243H

Zuhören You're listening to a radio talk show as several teenagers call in to give their opinion on different topics. Listen to the four call-ins and for each one write the name and the age of the person calling and the general topic on which he or she is expressing an opinion.

 CD 9 Tr. 11 Christoph-12-Katze; Birgit-14-Tanzen; Nils-19-Freunde; Alex-16-Mode

28 **Grammatik im Kontext**

 **Sprechen/Schreiben** Sag deinen Klassenkameraden, was du glaubst! Schreib danach deine Meinungen (*opinions*).

> **BEISPIEL** **Die Münchner sind sehr freundlich.**
> **DU** **Ich glaube, dass die Münchner sehr freundlich sind.** *oder*
> **Ich glaube nicht, dass die Münchner sehr freundlich sind.**

1. Kinokarten sind zu teuer.
2. Politik ist interessant.
3. Hausaufgaben machen macht Spaß.
4. Fernsehen macht klug (*smart*).
5. Schüler sind faul (*lazy*).
6. Pizza essen ist gesund (*healthy*).

29  **Von der Schule zum Beruf**

Schreiben You have been hired to work at your city's Chamber of Commerce. One of your first assignments is to design and describe an area of your city that is a family tourist attraction. As part of your assignment, you are to draw a plan of the area, place the buildings, and label them. Underneath your city plan, give a brief description of the various sights.

AUSSPRACHE

 Richtig aussprechen / Richtig lesen

 CD 9 Trs. 12–14

A. To practice the following sounds, say the words and sentences below after your teacher or after the recording.

1. The long vowels **ü** and **ö**: In **Kapitel 1** you learned how to pronounce the letters **ü** and **ö** as long vowels.
   CD 9 Tr. 12
   führen, für, spülen / Kannst du für mich das Geschirr spülen?
   blöd, hören, Österreich / Ich höre gern Rock, aber Disko finde ich blöd.

2. The letters **s, ss,** and **ß:** At the beginning of a syllable, the letter **s** is pronounced much like the *z* in the English word *zebra*. However, if it is followed by the letters **t** or **p,** it sounds like the *sh* combination in the English word *shine*. In the middle or at the end of a syllable, the letter **s** is pronounced the same as the *s* in the English word *post;* the letters **ß** and **ss** are always pronounced this way as well.

   Senf, super, Semmel / Sonja will eine Wurst mit Senf und eine Semmel.
   Straße, Innenstadt, Spaß / Wo ist die Spatzenstraße? In der Innenstadt?
   Wurst, besser, Imbiss / Die Wurst ist besser in der Imbissstube hier rechts.

Richtig schreiben / Diktat
CD 9 Tr. 13
CD 9 Tr. 14 (with pauses)

B. Write down the sentences that you hear. Script on p. 243H

Ein Bummel durch München

Lesestrategie Reading for a purpose When you read for information, it is a good idea to decide beforehand what kind of information you want. If you simply want an overview, a general reading will suffice. If you need specific information, a close reading will be required.

1. These articles are from a book called **Merian live! München.** What kind of book do you think it is?
   a. a history book
   b. a book about parks and gardens
   c. a travel guide

2. When you read a travel guide, you generally have one of two specific purposes: to gather general information about what is going on, or to find specific information about an event — cost, time, date, etc. In which case would you skim to get the gist, and in which case would you scan for specific information?

3. How is information in a travel guide organized? Group the places listed below under one of these three general headings: **Essen und Trinken, Einkaufen, Sehenswertes.**

   Sportmode, Deutsches Museum, Cafés, Restaurants, Geschenkwaren, Alte Pinakothek, Peterskirche, Stehimbisse, Kaufhäuser, Englischer Garten, Konditoreien, Fotogeschäfte

   Answers on p. 243W.

	Durchschnittstemperaturen in °C		Sonnenstunden	Regentage
	Tag	Nacht	pro Tag	
Januar	1,4	-5,6	1,8	11
Februar	3,4	-5,1	2,9	10
März	8,7	-1,5	3,9	9
April	13,5	2,8	5,4	10
Mai	18,0	6,6	6,0	12
Juni	21,3	10,0	7,5	14
Juli	23,2	12,1	7,8	13
August	22,7	11,4	6,7	12
September	19,6	8,4	6,0	10
Oktober	13,3	3,7	4,5	9
November	6,6	0,1	1,9	9
Dezember	2,3	-3,8	1,2	10

Quelle: Deutscher Wetterdienst, Offenbach

Lebensmittel

Dallmayr
In den heiligen Hallen der Gaumenfreuden wird sogar der Kauf einer banalen Kiwi zum gastronomischen Ereignis. Münchens ältestes Feinkosthaus ist nicht zuletzt seines aromatischen Kaffees wegen weit über die Grenzen der Stadt hinaus bekannt geworden.
2 Dienerstr. 14/15
U-/S-Bahn: Marienplatz

Englischer Garten
Münchens vielgeliebte »grüne Lunge« – etwa 5 km lang, bis zu 1 km breit und mit einer Gesamtausdehnung von nahezu 4 km². Entstanden ist der Englische Garten aus einer Anregung des unter Kurfürst Karl Theodor amtierenden Ministers Benjamin Thompson (später Graf Rumford), einen Volkspark in der Art der englischen Landschaftsgärten in den Isarauen anzulegen. 1789 begannen die Arbeiten am Park, die ab 1804 vom Gartenarchitekten Ludwig von Sckell geleitet wurden. Am auffälligsten unter den Bauten im Park sind der Chinesische Turm (1790), nach der Zerstörung im Krieg 1952 originalgetreu wiederaufgebaut, der Monopteros, ein klassizistischer Rundtempel nach einem Entwurf Leo von Klenzes im Auftrag Ludwigs I. (1837/38), das Japanische Teehaus, das Mitsuo Nomura 1972 anläßlich der Olympischen Spiele in München als Geschenk Japans an die Olympia-Stadt erbaut hat. Hinzu kommt der künstlich angelegte Kleinhesseloher See mit drei kleinen Inseln, einem Bootsverleih und dem Seehaus (Restaurant und Biergarten).
Zugänge zum Park gibt es am Haus der Kunst, an der Veterinärstraße (Nähe Universität), Gunezrhainerstraße (Nähe Münchner Freiheit), am Seehaus (Ausfahrt Mittlerer Ring) sowie an der Tivolistraße (Nähe Max-Joseph-Brücke). (→ Spaziergänge)

Januar
Fasching
Die »närrische Saison« beginnt in München mit dem 7. Januar und endet in der Nacht zwischen Faschingsdienstag und Aschermittwoch. In diesen Wochen quillt das städtische Veranstaltungsprogramm über von Faschingsbällen aller Art – exklusiven und volkstümlichen, intimen und massenhaften.
Als gesellschaftliche Höhepunkte der Faschingssaison gelten der Chrysanthemenball, Magnolienball, Madameball, Filmball und Presseball. Die phantasievollsten oder auch aufwendigsten Kostüme und Dekorationen sind beim Karneval in Rio im Bayerischen Hof, bei den Festen der Damischen Ritter, den Weißen Festen und der Vorstadthochzeit zu sehen.
Seiner Tradition nach findet der Münchner Fasching im Saal statt, nicht auf der Straße wie etwa der Rheinische Karneval. Nur während der drei letzten Faschingstage – von Sonntag bis Dienstag – tummelt sich das närrische Volk auch im Freien, vor allem in der Fußgängerzone, am Marienplatz und auf dem Viktualienmarkt, wo am Faschingsdienstag ab 6 Uhr in der Früh die Marktfrauen tanzen.

Olympiapark

Auf dem ehemaligen Oberwiesenfeld wurde für die XX. Olympischen Spiele 1972 von der Architektengemeinschaft Günter Behnisch und Partner dieser Park entworfen.

Der 52 m hohe Olympiaberg wurde auf zusammengetragenen Ruinentrümmern des Zweiten Weltkrieges angelegt und mit voralpiner Vegetation begrünt.

Als weitere Sportstätten gibt es das Eissportstadion, die Schwimmhalle (»Europas schönstes Garten-Hallenbad«) und das Radstadion. Die Olympiahalle selbst dient auch Kongressen, Ausstellungen und Konzerten.

Kaufhäuser

Ludwig Beck

Eine Münchner Institution. Auf vier Stockwerken gibt es vom Lodenmantel bis zum Gaultier-Jäckchen vor allem Mode zu kaufen; man findet aber auch den passenden Schmuck dazu, Tisch- und Bettwäsche, originelles Küchenzubehör, eine riesige Jazz-Auswahl auf CD – sowie Münchens netteste Verkäufer! Für das leibliche Wohl empfehlen sich drei Restaurants, darunter eine Sushi-Bar.
Marienplatz 11
U-/S-Bahn: Marienplatz

Medizinische Versorgung

Bitte wenden Sie sich an den Hotelportier.

Auskunft dienstbereiter Apotheken:
Tel. 59 44 75

Große Apotheken im Zentrum:
Internationale Ludwigs-Apotheke
Neuhauser Str. 8
Von Mendel'sche Apotheke
(große Abteilung für homöopathische Medikamente)
40 Leopoldstr. 58

Peterskirche, St. Peter

Erste und lange Zeit einzige Pfarrkirche der Stadt, deren erster Bau (erste Hälfte 11. Jh.) älter als die Stadt selbst ist. In der Folgezeit erlebte das Gotteshaus zahlreiche Erweiterungen und Modernisierungen in den Stilen der Gotik, der Renaissance und des Barock. Die Bombenzerstörungen der Jahre 1944/45 waren so schwer, daß man die Kirche beinahe gänzlich gesprengt hätte.

Der Turm »Alter Peter« ist – neben den Türmen der Frauenkirche – das Wahrzeichen der Stadt geblieben. 302 hölzerne Stufen führen an den vier Glocken vorbei zur Aussichtsgalerie.

Der Besondere Tip

Isar-Floßfahrt Floßfahrten auf der Isar zwischen Wolfratshausen und München sind eine bei Alt und Jung sehr beliebte »Gaudi«. Die Fahrt selbst dauert etwa sieben Stunden; eine Mittagspause wird an Land eingelegt. Zu einer Floßfahrt kann man sich freilich nicht spontan entschließen: Die meisten Termine sind (von Firmen, Vereinen, Freundeskreisen) schon lange im voraus gebucht. Einzelpassagiere wenden sich an das Amtliche Bayerische Reisebüro (ABR), das sich ein Kontingent für »Individualisten« zu sichern pflegt.

Feuchtfröhliche Gaudi ohnegleichen: Isarfloßfahrten

4. What general types of information appear in these texts? Which excerpts can you classify, using the categories you developed in Activity 3?

5. What are the names of some places to go shopping for fine foods? For fashionable clothes?

6. Where would you go in these situations?
   a. It's the middle of January and you want to go dancing.
   b. You want to go for a long relaxing walk.
   c. You have a sore throat and you need throat lozenges.
   d. You have been invited to someone's home and you want to buy a special coffee for them.

7. If you had a whole day free and wanted to do something out of the ordinary, what special tip does the guidebook give? Could you do it on the spur of the moment, or do you have to plan ahead? How do you know?

8. Read the excerpts **Peterskirche, St. Peter,** and **Olympiapark** and see if you can answer these questions. How old is the **Peterskirche**? What would you see if you climbed the steps of the **Alter Peter**? When was the **Olympiapark** built? How high is the mountain in the **Olympiapark**, and what is it made out of?

9. You are going to be in Munich for a day in June. Plan what you would do. How will the weather chart help you in making your plans? What can you do in June that you could not have done in January? What could you have done in January that you cannot do in June?

in January: **Fasching** parties;
in June: **Isar-Floßfahrt**

Übungsheft, S. 107, Ü. 23

Mehr Grammatikübungen

Answers

Erste Stufe

Objective Talking about where something is located

1 Du bist zum ersten Mal in dieser Stadt und willst wissen, wo verschiedene öffentliche Gebäude (*public institutions*) sind. Schreib die folgenden Sätze ab und schreib dabei die richtige Form von **wissen** in die Lücken. (**S. 250**)

1. _____ du, wo das Hotel ist? — Nein, ich _____ es nicht.   Weißt; weiß
2. _____ die Mara, wo das Café ist? — Ja, sie _____ es.   Weiß; weiß
3. _____ ihr, wo die Bank ist? — Nein, wir _____ es nicht.   Wisst; wissen
4. Wer _____ , wo das Museum ist? — Ich _____ es!   weiß; weiß
5. Die Schüler _____ nicht, wo das Theater ist, aber der Markus _____ es.   wissen; weiß

2 Frag diese Leute, ob sie wissen, wo diese Gebäude (*buildings*) sind. Schreib Fragen zu den Antworten. Gebrauche die richtige Form von **wissen.** Achte auf die Form der Anrede. (**S. 250**)

BEISPIEL   **deine Schwester sagt: Die U-Bahnstation ist am Marienplatz.**
                 Weißt du, wo die U-Bahnstation ist?

1. ein Klassenkamerad: Die Bank ist in der Karlstraße.   Weißt du, wo die Bank ist?
2. zwei Freunde: Die Post ist in der Ottostraße.   Wisst ihr, wo die Post ist?
3. dein Lehrer: Das Theater ist in der Maxstraße.   Wissen Sie, wo das Theater ist?
4. dein Onkel: Das Museum ist in der Georgenstraße.   Weißt du, wo das Museum ist?
5. deine Eltern: Der Bahnhof ist am Bahnhofsplatz.   Wisst ihr, wo der Bahnhof ist?
6. eine Lehrerin: Das Rathaus ist am Marienplatz.   Wissen Sie, wo das Rathaus ist?

3 Schreib eine Verbform von **wissen** in die erste Lücke und den abgebildeten Ort in die zweite Lücke. (**S. 250**)

1. Wer _____ , wo _____ ist?   weiß; das Rathaus

2. Ihr _____ nicht, wo _____ ist?   wisst; die Bank

3. Du musst doch _____ , wo _____ ist!   wissen; das Museum

4. _____ du, wo _____ ist?   Weißt; die U-Bahnstation

5. Alle Leute _____ , wo _____ ist!   wissen; der Bahnhof

6. Ich _____ nicht, wo _____ ist.   weiß; die Post

4 Du fragst und sagst, wie man am besten dorthin kommt. Schreib die richtigen
Verbformen von **fahren** in die Lücken. (**S. 255**)

1. Wie _____ ich am besten zur Schule? — Ja, du _____ am besten   fahre; fährst
   geradeaus bis zur Alpseestraße und dann _____ du nach links   fährst
   bis zur Schulstraße.

2. Wie _____ denn die Mara zur Schule? _____ sie mit dem Bus   fährt; Fährt;
   oder _____ sie mit dem Rad? Weißt du, wie sie zur Schule _____ ?   fährt; fährt

3. Wie _____ ihr denn zur Schule? _____ du mit dem Rad, Flori,   fahrt; Fährst;
   oder _____ du mit dem Moped? Und wie _____ du, Markus?   fährst; fährst

4. Ich _____ mit der U-Bahn zur Schule. Und Sie, Herr Meier,   fahre;
   wie _____ Sie zur Schule? _____ Sie auch mit der U-Bahn?   fahren; Fahren

5 Schreib die richtige Befehlsform *(command form)* von **fahren** in die erste Lücke und die
Information, die im Piktogramm abgebildet ist, in die zweite Lücke. (**S. 255**)

   1. Herr Maier, _____ immer _____ !   fahren Sie; geradeaus

   2. Mark, _____ geradeaus bis _____ !   fahr; zur Ampel

   3. Lisa und Ann, _____ geradeaus und dann _____ !   fahrt; nach rechts

   4. Rick, _____ doch mit bis _____ !   fahr; zum Krüner Platz

   5. Frau Abb, _____ die nächste Straße _____ !   fahren Sie; nach links

6 Du bist in der Stadt und gibst verschiedenen Erwachsenen *(adults)* Auskünfte und Ratschläge *(advice)*. Gebrauch die korrekte Befehlsform. **(S. 255)**

1. (fahren) _____ immer geradeaus bis zur Ampel!   Fahren Sie
2. (gehen) _____ die nächste Straße nach rechts!   Gehen Sie
3. (kaufen) _____ das Brot und die Semmeln beim Bäcker!   Kaufen Sie
4. (holen) _____ das Obst im Obst- und Gemüseladen!   Holen Sie
5. (vergessen) _____ nicht die grünen Bohnen!   Vergessen Sie
6. (probieren) _____ doch mal eine bayrische Spezialität!   Probieren Sie
7. (essen) _____ doch den Leberkäs! Er ist so gut!   Essen Sie
8. (trinken) _____ doch mal einen Apfelsaft!   Trinken Sie

Dritte Stufe   **Objectives** Talking about what there is to eat and drink; saying you do or don't want more; expressing opinions

7 Du bist mit einer Freundin in einer Imbissstube und sagst ihr, was es hier zu essen und zu trinken gibt. Schreib den Ausdruck *(expression)* **es gibt** *(there is, there are)* in die Lücken. **(S. 257)**

Ja, in dieser Imbissstube _____ so viele kleine Gerichte. _____ zum   gibt es; Es gibt

Beispiel Leberkäs und Hähnchen, und dann _____ Gyros, und _____   gibt es; es gibt

Semmeln, Brötchen, und _____ auch viel zum Trinken. Da _____   es gibt; gibt es

Mineralwasser, und _____ auch Milch.   es gibt

8 Du bist in einer Imbissstube und willst von allem noch etwas bestellen. Schreib die richtige Form von **noch ein** zusammen mit dem Ausdruck in Klammern in die Lücken. **(S. 258)**

BEISPIEL (ein Eis) Hallo! Ich möchte _____ , bitte.
Hallo! Ich möchte <u>noch ein Eis</u>, bitte.

1. (ein Leberkäs) Hallo! Ich möchte _____ .   noch einen Leberkäs
2. (eine Semmel) Hallo! Ich möchte _____ , bitte.   noch eine Semmel
3. (ein Brötchen) Hallo! Für mich _____ , bitte.   noch ein Brötchen
4. (ein Apfelsaft) Bitte, _____ für mich.   noch einen Apfelsaft
5. (eine Weißwurst) _____ , bitte!   Noch eine Weißwurst
6. (ein Mineralwasser) Ich möchte _____ , bitte.   noch ein Mineralwasser

9 Du bist zu Hause und hast Hunger und Durst. Du fragst deine Eltern, was es noch zu essen und zu trinken gibt. Aber es gibt nichts mehr! Schreib die richtige Form von **kein** in die Lücken. (S. 259)

1. Gibt es noch Semmeln? — Nein, es gibt _____ Semmeln mehr.   keine
2. Gibt es noch Kaffee? — Nein, es gibt _____ Kaffee mehr.   keinen
3. Gibt es noch Milch? — Nein, es gibt _____ Milch mehr.   keine
4. Gibt es noch Kuchen? — Nein, es gibt _____ Kuchen mehr.   keinen
5. Gibt es noch Obst? — Nein, es gibt _____ Obst mehr.   kein
6. Gibt es noch Weißwurst? — Nein, es gibt _____ Weißwurst mehr.   keine
7. Gibt es noch Leberkäs? — Nein, es gibt _____ Leberkäs mehr.   keinen
8. Gibt es noch Mineralwasser? — Nein, es gibt _____ Mineralwasser mehr.   kein

10 Jemand *(someone)* hat viele Fragen, und du gibst deine Meinung *(opinion)* dazu. Schreib in jede Lücke die Antwort zu jeder Frage. Beachte die Wortstellung *(word order)*! (S. 260)

1. Ist das Essen hier teuer? — Ich glaube, dass _____ .   das Essen hier teuer ist
2. Gibt es noch Leberkäs? — Ich glaube, dass _____ .   es noch Leberkäs gibt
3. Ist der Salat gut? — Ich finde, dass _____ .   der Salat gut ist
4. Ist das Brot frisch? — Ich glaube, dass _____ .   das Brot frisch ist
5. War die Mara beim Bäcker? — Ich glaube, dass _____ .   die Mara beim Bäcker war
6. Ist München sehr schön? — Ich finde, dass _____ .   München sehr schön ist

Anwendung

internet

ADRESSE: go.hrw.com
KENNWORT:
WK3 MUENCHEN-9

The CD-ROM Tutor offers guided recording and writing activities to accompany the **Anwendung.** These activities are designed to practice students' oral and written communication skills and to review material from each chapter.

1 Listen to some American students tell their friends back in Rosenheim about their day in **München** with Mara and Markus. Make a list of where they were and what they bought.

CD 9 Tr. 15
Script on p. 243H

Dallmayr-Weißwürste; Ludwig Beck-CDs, Schmuck; Fotogeschäft-Fotoalbum

2 You work at the information desk in the train station, and several people need your help. Take turns with your partner asking for and giving the requested information. Use the cues below to formulate your questions. Different people want to know:

where a bank is

where the post office is

where a restaurant is

if there is a hotel here

if there's a subway station here

where to buy flowers

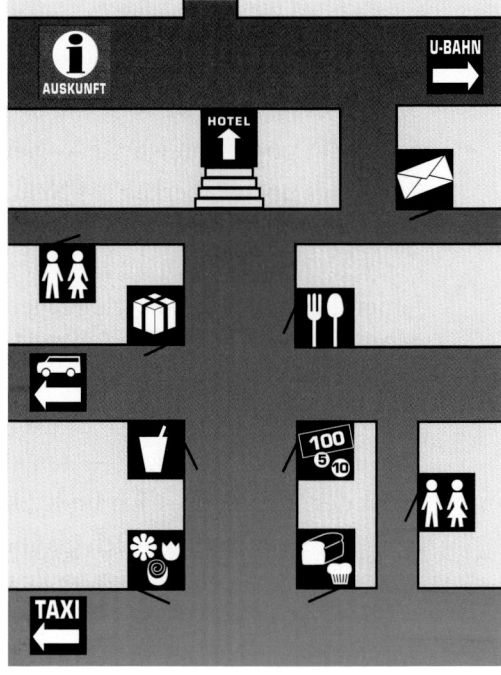

3 Lies die Postkarte unten und beantworte die folgenden Fragen!

a. Wie findet Jörg die Stadt München? Was sagt er?

a. **unheimlich stark**

b. Warum isst er soviel Leberkäs und so viele Weißwürste?

b. **weil sie sagenhaft gut sind**

c. Was besichtigt (besichtigen: *to sightsee*) Jörg in München?

c. **die Frauenkirche, das Rathaus**

4 In this chapter you have learned a lot about Munich. Write a postcard either to your parents or to a friend giving your opinions about the city or write a postcard about some other place you have visited. Use the postcard here as a model for your salutation and closing.

Hallo Bärbel!
Einen kurzen Gruß aus
München, wo ich kaum was
anderes als Leberkäs und
Weißwurst esse, weil sie hier
sagenhaft gut sind. Ich mache
aber auch hier einen echten
Kulturtrip mit Frauenkirche,
Rathaus usw. Ich finde, dass
München eine unheimlich starke
Stadt ist, weil es hier eine gute
Szene gibt, viele junge Leute,
viel zu tun.
Mehr wenn wir uns wieder
sehen. Bis dann, Alles Gute
Jörg

Bärbel Hörster
Eichenwegstr. 35
48161 Münster

STANDARDS: 1.1, 1.2, 1.3   KAPITEL 9   Amerikaner in München

5 You have learned your way around Mittersendling but your visiting American friend has not. Your friend will tell you three things he or she needs to do or buy. Tell your friend where he or she needs to go (bakery, butcher shop, etc.) and how to get there. Decide together on a starting point and use the map on page 253. Then switch roles.

Du **Ich brauche …** *oder* **Ich muss … kaufen.**

Partner **Also, du musst zum/zur … gehen!** *oder* **Geh …!**

6

Zum Schreiben

Your German pen pal wants to know about your after-school and weekend activities. He is especially interested in hearing about your neighborhood and about the places you go and what you do there. Write several paragraphs describing these activities.

> **Schreibtipp Drawing a map** and including on this map places you frequently go and activities you do at each of these places is a good way to organize your thoughts about where things are located in your neighborhood.

Prewriting

In order to organize your thoughts before you begin writing, draw a map of your area and indicate at least 5 places you frequently go. Then think of an activity you do in each place, list the activity under each location, and under each activity list some adjectives to describe these activities.

Writing

Use your drawing to help you write a paragraph describing where your favorite places are located in relation to where you live, and to describe what you like to do in each place. Be sure to include a restaurant or snack bar on your map. You might also include others' opinions of the restaurant, i.e. „**Mein Vater sagt, dass ….**"

7

Rollenspiel

Get together with two classmates and role-play the following scene.

Design a menu for an **Imbissstube** and write it on a piece of paper or poster board. Then, with three other classmates, develop a conversation at the snack stand that is based on this situation.

a. You are discussing with your friends what's available at the stand. Then each of you orders something. Ask what it costs and pay the person behind the counter. Be polite!

b. As you enjoy the food, discuss how the food tastes and if someone wants more or not. If so, order more. Discuss with your friends some of your opinions about the city of Munich, which you are visiting today.

Kann ich's wirklich?

Wissen Sie, wo … ist?
Weißt du, wo … ist?

Can you talk about where something is located? (p. 250)

1 How would you ask an older passerby where the following places are using **wissen**? How would you ask someone who is your own age? How would you answer?

in der
am
in der

a. Frauenkirche (… Straße)

b. Rathaus (Marienplatz)

c. Museum (Maximilianstraße)

Can you ask for and give directions? (p. 254)

2 How would you ask for directions from the **X**-mark to the following places?

a. Bahnhof

b. Theater

c. Marktplatz

d. Bank

a. Wie komme ich zum Bahnhof?
b. zum Theater?
c. zum Marktplatz?
d. zur Bank?

3 How would you tell an older person to get to the following places using the command forms? Someone your own age? Use the **X**-mark as the starting point. Answers will vary.

By vehicle:

a. to the train station

b. to the town hall

On foot:

a. to the supermarket

b. to the café

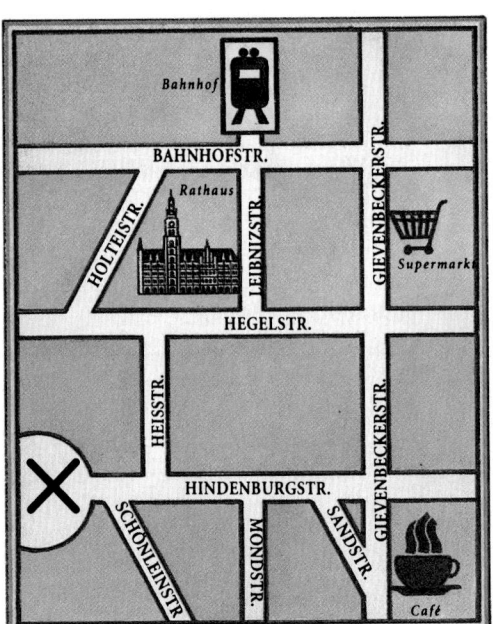

Can you talk about what there is to eat and drink? (p. 257)

4 How would you ask what there is to eat? And to drink? How would you tell someone what there is to eat or drink, using the items below?

a. Leberkäs   **c.** apple juice   **e.** salad

b. whole wheat rolls   **d.** tea   **f.** grilled chicken

4. Was gibt es zu essen? Zu trinken? Es gibt a. Leberkäs   b. Vollkornsemmeln   c. Apfelsaft   d. Tee   e. Salat
f. Hähnchen

Can you ask or tell someone that you do or don't want more? (p. 258)

5 How would you ask someone if he or she wants more? How would you tell someone that you want more of the items below or that you don't want more, using **noch ein** and **kein … mehr?**

Möchtest du noch etwas?
a. Ja bitte, noch ein Stück Kuchen
Nein danke, keinen Kuchen me
b. Ja bitte, noch eine Semmel. N
danke, keine Semmel mehr.

a. piece of cake   **c.** mineral water

b. roll   **d.** ice cream

c. Ja bitte, noch ein Mineralwasser. Nein danke, kein Mineralwasser mehr. d. Ja bitte, noch ein Eis. Nein danke,

Can you express opinions using dass-clauses? (p. 260)

6 **a.** How would you give your opinion about the following statement? How would you agree with it? And disagree?

kein Eis mehr

Autofahren ist gefährlich.

Answers will vary. Examples: Ich finde, dass Autofahren gefährlich ist. Ich finde nicht, dass Autofahren gefährlich ist.

b. State your opinions about school in general. Write at least two sentences using **dass**-clauses.

Erste Stufe

p. 243X

In der Innenstadt

die Stadt, ⁻e	city	das Museum, die Museen	museum
das Rathaus, ⁻er	city hall	das Theater, -	theater
der Marktplatz, ⁻e	market square	die U-Bahnstation, -en	subway station
die Post	post office		
der Bahnhof, ⁻e	railroad station		
die Bank, -en	bank		
die Kirche, -n	church		
das Hotel, -s	hotel		
der Garten, ⁻	garden, yard		

Talking about where something is located

in der Innenstadt	downtown

die Straße, -n	street
am … Platz	on …Square
wissen	to know (a fact, information, etc.)
Entschuldigung! Verzeihung!	} Excuse me!
Es tut mir Leid.	I'm sorry.
Keine Ahnung!	I have no idea!

Zweite Stufe

Asking for and giving directions

Wie komme ich zum (zur) …	How do I get to …
nach links	to the left
nach rechts	to the right
geradeaus	straight ahead
bis zur Ampel	until you get to the traffic light
bis zur … Straße	until you get to … Street

bis zum … Platz	until you get to … Square
die nächste Straße	the next street
die erste (zweite, dritte, vierte) Straße	the first (second, third, fourth) street
wieder	again

fahren	to go somewhere, ride, drive (using a vehicle)
er/sie fährt	he/she drives/is driving/is going
Vielen Dank!	Thank you very much!
Gern geschehen!	My pleasure!

Dritte Stufe

Talking about what there is to eat and drink

die Imbissstube, -n	snack bar
Was gibt's zu essen?	What's there to eat?
Es gibt …	There is/are …
der Leberkäs	Bavarian specialty (see p. 257)
mit Senf	with mustard
die Weißwurst, ⁻e	Southern German sausage specialty (see p. 257)
die Vollkornsemmel, -n	whole grain roll
das Gyros	gyros

Saying you do or don't want more

Möchtest du noch etwas?	Would you like anything else?
Ich möchte noch ein(e)(en) …	I'd like another …
Ich möchte kein(e) (en) … mehr.	I don't want another …/ anymore
noch ein(e) (en)	more, another one
genug	enough
kein	no, none, not any
kein (en) … mehr	no more …
Nichts mehr, danke!	No more, nothing else, …thanks!

Ich habe genug.	I've had enough.
Ich habe keinen Hunger mehr.	I'm not hungry anymore.

Expressing opinions

dass	that
Ich finde, dass …	I think that …
Ich finde es gut/ schlecht, dass …	I think it's good/ bad that …
die Leute (pl)	people

Other words and phrases

probieren	to try
mal	(short for einmal) once

Baden-Württemberg

Teaching Resources
pp. 272–275

PRINT
▸ Lesson Planner, p. 47
▸ Video Guide, pp. 61–62

MEDIA
▸ One-Stop Planner
▸ Video Program
  Videocassette 4, 01:14–04:00
▸ Map Transparency
▸ Interactive CD-ROM Tutor, Disc 3

go.hrw.com
WK3 BADEN-WUERTTEMBERG

PAGES 272–273

THE PHOTOGRAPH
Background Information

• The building pictured is **das Alte Schloss** in **Meersburg am Bodensee.** At the center of this elongated castle is the **Dagobert-Turm,** which was built at the end of the 12th century. In 1803, Freiherr Joseph von Laßberg bought the castle from the state, which had planned to tear it down. Von Laßberg kept his collection of art, sculptures, and antiques in this castle. His sister-in-law, the poet Annette von Droste-Hülshoff, lived here from 1841 until she died in 1848.

• Known as the **Schwäbisches Meer,** Lake Constance, or **Bodensee,** it is the largest inland body of water that Germany has any claim to. The lake encompasses 538 square kilometers (207.67 square miles) and is up to 252 meters deep in some places. The Romans established the first harbor and wharf in Lintavia, which is known today as Lindau. Until the 17th century, only military ships used the lake. Later, commercial ships transported goods across the lake. Today, one of the most modern fleets of ships in Europe travels this lake, and it is operated jointly by Germany, Switzerland, and Austria. In addition to such historic seaports as Lindau, Konstanz, and Friedrichshafen, the lake has two beautiful islands, Reichenau and Mainau, which are popular tourist spots.

Teaching Suggestion
Have students locate Lake Constance on a map. Ask them to name the two other countries with which Germany shares this lake. (Switzerland and Austria)

THE ALMANAC AND MAP

The three striding lions on the Baden-Württemberg shield date back to the 12th century, when the Swabian ruler Duke Philipp was crowned German king. Up until then (1198), Swabian kings had used a single standing lion as their crest. When a public referendum created the Federal State of Baden-Württemberg in 1951, crests were selected from the old Duchy of Swabia, which had once represented all of what is now southwest Germany. The symbol selected for the Swabian coat of arms was that of the ruling Staufer Family and shows three lions on a golden shield.

Background Information

Baden-Württemberg is the third largest **Bundesland** in Germany. In 1951 a public referendum created this **Bundesland** from the three smaller provinces of Baden, Württemberg-Hohenzollern, and Württemberg-Baden. Most people who have never heard of Baden-Württemberg are at least familiar with the **Schwarzwald** *(Black Forest),* which is located in the southwestern part of the state.

Culture Notes
• The Black Forest received its name because the density of the towering fir trees makes the forest appear almost black and very frightening. Even the Romans avoided it when possible. They rarely ventured into the gloomy forest unless drawn by the many refreshing springs.

• Stuttgart, the capital of Baden-Württemberg, is also called **Bäderstadt Stuttgart** *(City of Baths and Wells)* as it has, following Budapest, the most plentiful deposits of mineral water in Europe. It is home to a multitude of businesses including 138 publishing houses, two universities, several colleges, and Germany's largest wine-growing community. Some of the most important companies located in the city are DaimlerChrysler, Porsche, and Bosch.

Terms in the Almanac

- **Donau:** at 2,850 km, the second longest river in Europe. It originates in the Black Forest and ends in the Black Sea. In English, it is known as the Danube.

- **Rhein:** the third longest river in Europe at 1,320 km, 867 km of which run through Germany. It originates in the Swiss Alps and ends in the North Sea in Holland. The drive along the **Rhein** is known for its endless vineyards, fairy tale castles, and fortresses.

- **Karlsruhe:** the seat of the **Bundesverfassungsgericht** (*Federal Constitutional Court*) and the **Bundesgerichtshof** (*Federal Court of Justice*)

- **Heidelberg:** home of the oldest university in Germany. The university was founded in 1386.

- **Spätzle:** small dumplings made by dropping bits of dough into boiling salt water

- **Schwarzwälder Kirschtorte:** most famous product of Baden-Württemberg. It is a delicate chocolate cake layered with sour cherries, cherry liqueur, shavings of dark chocolate, red currant jelly, and whipped cream.

- **Maultaschen:** triangular-shaped dough pockets filled with spinach, ground meat, onion, egg, herbs, and spices cooked in broth

Using the Map

- Have students look at the map of Germany on p. 2 and name the countries and **Bundesländer** that border on Baden-Württemberg. (**Frankreich; Schweiz; Bayern; Hessen; Rheinland-Pfalz**) You may also want to use *Map Transparency* 1.

- Looking at the map on p. 2, ask students which two **Bundesländer** are larger than Baden-Württemberg. (**Bayern, Niedersachsen**)

Culture Note

According to the **Lorelei** legend, a beautiful blond mermaid sat on a cliff overlooking the **Rhein.** With her beauty and her song, she often distracted the crewmen of ships and caused many shipwrecks.

PAGES 274–275

THE PHOTO ESSAY

1. Small villages such as this arose in the 12th and 13th centuries. Farmers, charcoal burners, and woodcutters cleared the forest and used its natural resources for their livelihood.

2. St. Märgen is a popular vacation spot in the Black Forest. Mills like this one were used to crush or grind materials such as grains and wood.

   Drawing Inferences Ask students what natural resource was used to operate this particular mill. (water)

3. With a population of only 9,700, Besigheim is a typical Swabian town. It has an old bridge spanning the Enz river that dates back to 1581.

4. The witch on the broomstick is called a **Küchenhexe,** a good witch who brings good luck. She is believed to keep the fire in the stove burning, help dough rise, and protect the house in general.

5. Construction of this city hall dates back to 1507. It was completed in 1783. The **Rathaus** is used for official functions and festivities such as weddings. The detailed facade of the building reflects different aspects of the city's history.

6. These students all live in the Bietigheim-Bissingen area and attend the **Ellental Gymnasium** in Bietigheim. They are Andreas (top row), Martin (middle row left), Sabine (middle row center), Sandra (middle row right), Thomas (front row left), and Nicole (front row right).

LOCATION OPENER

Komm mit nach Baden-Württemberg!

Map of Germany

Einwohner: 10 000 000

Fläche: 36 000 Quadratkilometer (13 896 Quadratmeilen), etwa halb so groß wie Südkarolina

Landeshauptstadt: Stuttgart (570 000 Einwohner)

Große Städte: Mannheim, Karls-ruhe, Freiburg, Heilbronn, Heidelberg, Pforzheim

Flüsse: Donau, Rhein, Neckar, Jagst, Kocher

Seen: Bodensee

Berge: Feldberg (1493 Meter hoch), Belchen (1414 Meter hoch)

Industrien: Maschinenbau, Automobilindustrie, Elektrotechnik, Chemie, Feinmechanik, Optik

Beliebte Gerichte: Spätzle, Schwarzwälder Kirschtorte, Maultaschen, Schinken

STANDARDS: 2.2, 3.1

Nordsee · Ostsee · DÄNEMARK · Kiel · Hamburg · NIEDER-LANDE · Berlin · POLEN · BEL. · Frankfurt · TSCHECHIEN · LUX. · Karlsruhe · Stuttgart · Ulm · München · FRANK-REICH · Freiburg · ÖSTERREICH · SCHWEIZ

go.hrw.com

WK3 BADEN-WUERTTEMBERG

VIDEO

CD-ROM DISC 3

Das Alte Schloss in Meersburg am Bodensee

Baden-Württemberg

Baden-Württemberg ist bekannt für seine reizvolle Landschaft und für seine Hightechindustrie. Der Schwarzwald (Black Forest) mit seinen traditionsreichen Bauernhöfen und Häusern ist eine der beliebtesten Touristenattraktionen Deutschlands.

Im Umkreis von Stuttgart, der Hauptstadt Baden-Württembergs, findet man wichtige Automobil- und Elektronikkonzerne, sowie viele mittelgroße Unternehmen, die Textilien, Uhren und optische Geräte herstellen.

internet

go.hrw.com

ADRESSE: go.hrw.com
KENNWORT: WK3 BADEN-WUERTTEMBERG

1 Dorf im Schwarzwald
Ein typisches Schwarzwalddorf

2 Hexenloch Mühle
Diese alte Mühle in Märgen ist typisch für Schwarzwälder Holzbauten.

3 Besigheim
Das einzigartige Stadtbild von Besigheim an der Enz, mit dem Schloss im Hintergrund

4 **Am Hexenwegle**
Hexen dekorieren viele
Häuser am Hexenwegle.

5 **Bietigheimer Rathaus**
Das Bietigheimer Rathaus
stammt aus dem Jahre 1507.

6 Martin, Andreas, Thomas, Sabine,
Sandra und Nicole laden euch zu
einem Besuch in Bietigheim ein.

Kapitel 10, 11, 12

Die Szenen in diesen letzten drei Kapiteln
kommen aus Bietigheim-Bissingen, einer
historischen Stadt an der Enz, nördlich von
Stuttgart. Die Schüler in diesen Kapiteln
gehen aufs Ellental Gymnasium in Bietigheim.

Kapitel 10: Kino und Konzerte
Chapter Overview

Los geht's!
pp. 278–280

Wie verbringt ihr eure Freizeit? **p. 278**

	FUNCTIONS	GRAMMAR	VOCABULARY	RE-ENTRY
Erste Stufe pp. 281–284	• Expressing likes and dislikes, p. 282 • Expressing familiarity, p. 284	• The verb **mögen**, p. 282 • The verb **kennen**, p. 284	• Film genres, p. 281 • Words describing how much you do or don't like something, p. 282 • Types of music, p. 283 • Entertainers and forms of entertainment, p. 284	• Expressing likes and dislikes, p. 282 **(Kap. 2)** • **Wissen**, p. 284 **(Kap. 9)** • Talking about when you do things, p. 284 **(Kap. 2** and **Kap. 6)** • Talking about how often you do things, p. 284 **(Kap. 7)**
Zweite Stufe pp. 285–289	• Expressing preferences and favorites, p. 285	• Using **lieber** and **am liebsten** with **haben**, p. 285 • The stem-changing verb **sehen**, p. 285	• Words used to describe films, p. 288	• **Aussehen**, p. 285 **(Kap. 5)** • Activity vocabulary, p. 286 **(Kap. 2** and **Kap. 6)** • **Können**, p. 286 **(Kap. 7)** • Expressing opinions, p. 288 **(Kap. 2)** • Giving reasons, p. 288 **(Kap. 8)** • Describing people, p. 288 **(Kap. 3)**
Dritte Stufe pp. 290–293	• Talking about what you did in your free time, p. 292	• The phrase **sprechen über**, p. 291 • The stem-changing verbs **lesen** and **sprechen**, p. 291	• Book genres, p. 291	• **Nehmen** and **essen**, p. 291 **(Kap. 5** and **Kap. 6)** • Giving reasons, p. 291 **(Kap. 8)** • Talking about when you do things, p. 292 **(Kap. 2** and **Kap. 6)** • The verb **sein** (past tense), p. 292 **(Kap. 8)**

Aussprache p. 293	Review short vowel **o**, review long vowel **o**, review short vowel **u**, review long vowel **u**, review combination **ch**: Audio CD 10, Track 16	**Diktat:** Audio CD 10, Tracks 17–18
Zum Lesen pp. 294–295	Was sagen die Kritiker?	**Reading Strategy** Watching for false cognates
Mehr Grammatik-übungen	**pp. 296–299** Erste Stufe, pp. 296–297	Zweite Stufe, pp. 297–298 Dritte Stufe, pp. 298–299
Review pp. 300–303	Anwendung, pp. 300–301 **Kann ich's wirklich?,** p. 302 **Wortschatz,** p. 303 **Zum Schreiben:** Using a topic sentence (Writing and designing an ad)	

CULTURE

- **Ein wenig Landeskunde:** Movie-rating system, p. 283
- **Ein wenig Landeskunde:** A pop chart, p. 283
- Movie ads, p. 287
- **Landeskunde: Welche kulturellen Veranstaltungen besuchst du?,** p. 289
- Upcoming events poster, Best-seller and Video-hits lists, p. 290
- German reading materials, p. 291

Kapitel 10: Kino und Konzerte
Chapter Resources

Lesson Planning

One-Stop Planner

Lesson Planner with Substitute Teacher Lesson Plans, pp. 47–51, 74

Student Make-Up Assignments
- Make-Up Assignment Copying Masters, Chapter 10

Listening and Speaking

TPR Storytelling Book, pp. 37–40

Listening Activities
- Student Response Forms for Listening Activities, pp. 75–77
- Additional Listening Activities 10-1 to 10-6, pp. 79–82
- Additional Listening Activities (song), p. 78
- Scripts and Answers, pp. 155–161

Video Guide
- Teaching Suggestions, pp. 64–65
- Activity Masters, pp. 66–68
- Scripts and Answers, pp. 103–105, 115–116

Activities for Communication
- Communicative Activities, pp. 55–60
- Realia and Teaching Suggestions, pp. 110–113
- Situation Cards, pp. 141–142

Reading and Writing

Reading Strategies and Skills Handbook, Chapter 10

Lies mit mir! 1, Chapter 10

Übungsheft, pp. 109–120

Grammar

Grammatikheft, pp. 82–90

Grammar Tutor for Students of German, Chapter 10

Assessment

Testing Program
- Grammar and Vocabulary Quizzes, **Stufe** Quizzes, and Chapter Test, pp. 249–266
- Score Sheet, Scripts and Answers, pp. 267–274

Alternative Assessment Guide
- Portfolio Assessment, p. 27
- Performance Assessment, p. 41
- CD-ROM Assessment, p. 55

Student Make-Up Assignments
- Alternative Quizzes, Chapter 10

 Online Activities
- Interaktive Spiele
- Internet Aktivitäten

 Video Program
- Videocassette 4
- Videocassette 5 (captioned version)

 Audio Compact Discs
- Textbook Listening Activities, CD 10, Tracks 1–19
- Additional Listening Activities, CD 10, Tracks 26–31
- Assessment Items, CD 10, Tracks 20–25

Interactive CD-ROM Tutor, Disc 3

 Teaching Transparencies
- Situations 10-1 to 10-2
- Vocabulary 10-A
- **Los geht's!**
- **Mehr Grammatikübungen** Answers
- **Grammatikheft** Answers

Use the **One-Stop Planner CD-ROM** with **Test Generator** to aid in lesson planning and pacing.

For each chapter, the **One-Stop Planner** includes:
- Editable lesson plans with direct links to teaching resources
- Printable worksheets from resource books
- Direct launches to the HRW Internet activities
- Video and audio segments
- Test Generator
- Clip Art for vocabulary items

Kapitel 10: Kino und Konzerte

Projects

Unsere Litfaßsäule

*In this project, each student will create a **Flugblatt** (flyer) and an oral presentation reviewing a movie, book, or concert. These will be put up on a **Litfaßsäule** (kiosk) that students can make together. Start this project after completing the **Zum Lesen** activities.*

MATERIALS
✂ **Students may need**
- paper
- sources for written assignment
- pens
- sturdy cardboard paper that can be rolled into the shape of a **Litfaßsäule**

SUGGESTED TOPICS

Book Review

Title and author; brief summary; short review explaining why the student did or did not like the book and whether he or she would recommend it to others; where it can be purchased and for what approximate price

Movie Review

Title, director, and important actors and actresses; brief summary; short review explaining why the student did or did not like the film and whether he or she would recommend it to others; where it is showing

Music Review

Name of music group, group members, and concert; brief summary; review explaining why the student did or did not like the concert and whether he or she would recommend it to others; where tickets were available and ticket price

SUGGESTED SEQUENCE

1. Students choose a topic and make an outline showing how they plan to organize their flyer.

2. Students prepare the written assignment.

3. As an oral component, students should also prepare a brief (about 1 minute) statement about their flyer. Students should not read directly from the flyer; instead, they should use index cards on which a few phrases are written to give their oral report.

4. Students show their flyers and give their oral presentations.

5. Students display their flyers on the **Litfaßsäule** in the classroom or foreign language department.

GRADING THE PROJECT

Suggested point distribution (**total = 100 points**)

Originality and design...........................30
Written assignment 40
Oral presentation................................30

Cultures and Communities

Culture Note

Litfaßsäulen were named after Ernst Litfaß, a printer from Berlin who created this type of pillar in 1854.

Games

Was beginnt mit …?

This game will help students review the vocabulary they have learned so far in a fun, fast-paced way.

Procedure Begin by dividing the class into groups of three or four students, depending on the size of your class. Choose a word from the **Wortschatz** you want to review and write it on the chalkboard. (Example: A B E N T E U E R F I L M) Each group writes that word on a sheet of paper, spacing the letters across the page. Each group must come up with as many German words as they can that begin with each letter of the word. Emphasize before the game begins that each word can only be used once, and proper names are not allowed. The group with the most correct words at the end of a specified time limit wins. To make this game more challenging, you could specify a topic ahead of time and require that all words be related to that topic.

A P F E L	B A N A N E	E L T E R N	N E U	T A N T E	E S S E N	U N T E N	E I S	R O L L S C H U H	F A H R E N	I N N E N S T A D T	L E S E N	M U S I K

Könnt ihr mein Wort erraten?

In this game, students will be challenged to test their recall of previously learned vocabulary.

Procedure For this game you will need the letters from a Scrabble® game. Call one student to the front of the class and have him or her pull ten letters from a box or hat. He or she has 30 seconds to make a word using as many of the ten letters as possible. (Check for spelling). Then the student writes the ten letters randomly on the blackboard, and the rest of the class tries to guess the word that he or she has made.

Storytelling ·················

Mini-Geschichte

*This story accompanies Teaching Transparency 10-2. The **Mini-Geschichte** can be told and retold in different formats, acted out, written down, and read aloud to give students additional opportunities to practice all four skills.*

Ein langes Wochenende

„Hallo, Peter. Was hast du am Wochenende gemacht?" „Ach, Markus, das Wochenende war total langweilig. Es gab nur Mist im Fernsehen. Meine Eltern haben nur über Politik und Umwelt gesprochen. Und du weißt ja, meine Schwester hat nur Mode im Kopf. Was hast du gemacht?" „Am Samstag habe ich einen Gruselroman gelesen, dann habe ich Musik gehört. Danach habe ich dann Hausaufgaben gemacht. Am Sonntag war ich mit Freunden im Kino. Wir haben einen Sciencefictionfilm gesehen. Es war ein langes Wochenende."

Traditions ·················

Schwaben in der Literatur

Schon Johann Wolfgang von Goethe hatte Liebliches über die Speise und Landschaft des Schwabenlandes zu sagen.

„Lasst uns nach Schwaben entfliehen!

Wir halten uns nach des Landes Weise daselbst.

Hilf Himmel! Es findet süße Speise sich da und alles Gute in Fülle …

Und man bäckt im Lande das Brot mit Butter Und Eiern. Rein und klar ist das Wasser, Die Luft ist heiter und lieblich."

(Goethe: Reineke Fuchs)

Rezept

Das Spätzleschaben vom Brett ist eine Kunst, die früher von Schwäbin auf Schwäbin vererbt wurde. Dieser Brauch ist nun fast ausgestorben. Da man in Schwaben allerdings nicht auf Spätzle verzichten möchte, sind in Laufe der Jahre eine ganze Reihe von Spätzlemaschinen erfunden worden. Für die Schwaben sind nämlich selbst die mit der Maschine gemachten Spätzle weitaus besser als fertig gekaufte! Die Augsburger und Allgäuer Version der Spätzle heißt Knöpfle.

Spätzle

Für 4 Personen

Zutaten

g=Gramm, EL=Esslöffel, TL=Teelöffel

375g Mehl
2 Eier
 Salz
1EL Öl oder Butter

Zubereitung

Das Mehl, die Eier und etwas Salz zu einem Teig verarbeiten, 1/8 bis 1/4 Liter Wasser zugießen (je nach Größe der Eier) und den Teig weiterrühren und schlagen, bis er Blasen wirft, dann auch das Öl (oder die Butter) unterrühren. In einem großen Topf Salzwasser zum Kochen bringen. Ein kleines Brett mit kaltem Wasser anfeuchten. Eine kleine Portion Teig auf das Brett geben und mit einem nassen Messer schmale Teigstreifen ins kochende Salzwasser schaben. Das Messer zwischendurch immer wieder nass machen, damit der Teig nicht daran kleben bleibt. Die Spätzle sofort mit dem Schaumlöffel *(slotted spoon)* aus dem Wasser nehmen, wenn sie an die Oberfläche kommen. Die fertigen Spätzle unter heißem Wasser abbrausen und abtropfen lassen.

Kapitel 10: Kino und Konzerte
Technology

Video

Videocassette 4, 5 (captioned version)
See Video Guide, pages 63–68

Los geht's! • Wie verbringt ihr eure Freizeit?

Do young people have cultural interests? —Sabine loves reading, Martin enjoys classical music, and they meet their friends Thomas, Sandra, and Nicole at the movie theater. What movie do they want to see? They agree to see an action film.

Fortsetzung

After the movie, the five friends exchange opinions about it, agreeing in general that they didn't enjoy it very much. They go home to watch a music video by the famous German group **Die Prinzen.**

Landeskunde
Welche kulturellen Veranstaltungen besuchst du?

Students of various ages from different locations talk about the cultural events they attend.

Videoclips

- **Die unendliche Geschichte**® (video)
- **Gute Zeiten / Schlechte Zeiten**® (music CD)
- **Andreas Elzholz**® (CD single)
- **Howard Carpendale**® (album)
- **Bravo Hits 4**® (album)
- **NDR 2 Open Air Festival**® (concert)
- **Leibnitz Butterkeks**® (cookies)
- **Rätselhafte Phänomene**® (magazine)

Interactive CD-ROM Tutor

The **Interactive CD-ROM Tutor** contains videos, interactive games, and activities that provide students an opportunity to practice and review the material covered in Chapter 10.

Activity	Activity Type	Pupil's Edition Reference
1. Wortschatz	Merkspiel	p. 281
2. Grammatik	Was fehlt?	p. 282
3. So sagt man das!	Wozu gehört's?	pp. 282, 284, 285
4. Wortschatz	Wozu gehört's?	pp. 282, 283, 284, 285, 288
5. Wortschatz	Wort und Bild Erfahren/Wählen	p. 291
6. Grammatik	Was fehlt?	p. 292
Landeskunde	Welche kulturellen Veranstaltungen besuchst du? Was ist richtig?	p. 289
Zum Sprechen	*Guided recording*	pp. 300–301
Zum Schreiben	*Guided writing*	pp. 300–301

Teacher Management System

Logging In

Logging in to the *Komm mit!* TMS is easy. Upon launching the program, simply type "admin" in the password area of the log-in screen and press RETURN. Log on to **www.hrw.com/CDROMTUTOR** for a detailed explanation of the Teacher Management System.

One-Stop Planner CD-ROM

To preview all resources available for this chapter, use the **One-Stop Planner CD-ROM**, Disc 3.

Internet Connection ....

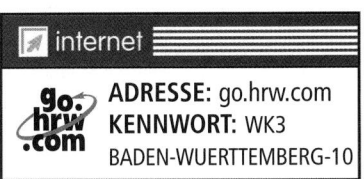

☑ internet

ADRESSE: go.hrw.com
KENNWORT: WK3
BADEN-WUERTTEMBERG-10

*Have students explore the **go.hrw.com** Web site for many online resources covering all chapters. All Chapter 10 resources are available under the keyword WK3 Baden-Wuerttemberg-10. Interactive games practice the material and provide students with immediate feedback. You will also find a printable worksheet that provides Internet activities that lead to a comprehensive online research project.*

Interaktive Spiele

You can use the interactive activities in this chapter

- to practice grammar, vocabulary, and chapter functions
- as homework
- as an assessment option
- as a self-test
- to prepare for the Chapter Test

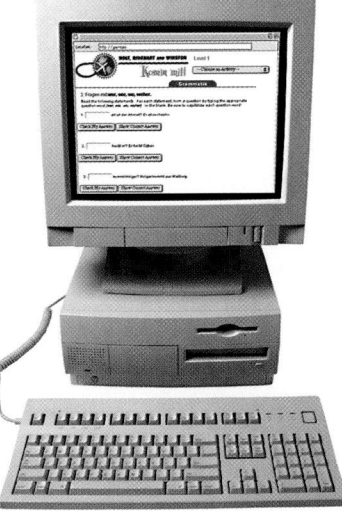

Internet Aktivitäten

Students will read German movie and theater schedules. They will also visit German bookstores.

- To prepare students for the **Arbeitsblatt,** have them review the movie ads on p. 287 and **Zum Lesen** on pp. 294–295.
- After completing the **Arbeitsblatt,** ask students to write in German the script for a play or the lyrics for a song. Have students do this activity as a class project or in groups. Students could perform the play. Alternatively, they could find a melody for the song they wrote and perform it.

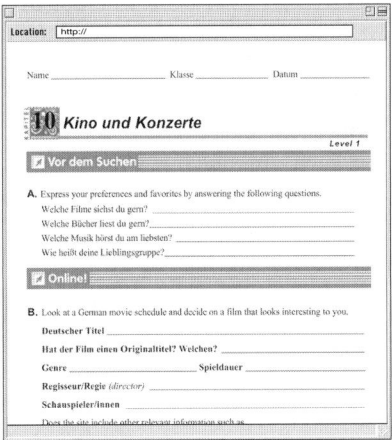

Webprojekt

Have students do a Web search for **Top Ten Filme** or **Top Ten Bücher**. They should list the titles and the directors or authors. You might want to ask students if any of the ten films or books has an original version. What is the title of the original version? Encourage students to exchange useful Web sites with their classmates. Have students document their sources by referencing the names and URLs of all the sites they consulted.

Kapitel 10: Kino und Konzerte
Textbook Listening Activities Scripts

Erste Stufe

7 p. 282

ERWIN Ja also, ich bin der Erwin, und ich geh schon gern mal ins Kino. Meistens ja mit meinem Freund Udo, denn wir mögen beide die gleichen Filme … besonders ja Komödien, die halt lustig sind und einen zum Lachen bringen. Die finden wir am besten. Dagegen aber mag ich Kriegsfilme überhaupt nicht. Zu brutal und deprimierend. Da kann man sich nicht entspannen.

DAVID Ich heiße David und ah … ich sehe Kinofilme unwahrscheinlich gern. Welche? Tja … eine ganze Reihe, aber doch am liebsten Fantasy-filme, so wie zum Beispiel *Die unendliche Geschichte*. Die finde ich Spitze. Ich mag auch andere Filme, aber ich sehe mir nie Western an, die finde ich nämlich langweilig und auch ein bisschen albern.

JUDITH Guten Tag! Ich bin Judith, und meine beste Freundin und ich gehen regelmäßig ins Kino, meistens am Wochenende. Welche Filme bevorzuge ich? Na, James-Bond-Filme zum Beispiel … also Abenteuerfilme. Die sind immer spannend und interessant. Was ich so gar nicht mag sind so Krimis. Die sind oft zu brutal. Ich finde sie furchtbar blöd.

AYSHA Hin und wieder geh ich auch ins Kino, aber meistens mit Freunden. Ach ja, ich heiße Aysha. Wenn ich ins Kino gehe, schau ich mir nur Liebesfilme an — so wie *Ghost*. Das ist so romantisch, nicht wahr? Solche Filme sehe ich mir oft mehrmals an. Was ich an Filmarten nicht besonders gern sehe, sind Science-fictionfilme. Das interessiert mich nämlich überhaupt nicht.

11 p. 284

1. — Kennst du schon den neuesten Film mit Arnold Schwarzenegger?
   — Meinst du den *Terminator 2*®?
   — Ja klar! Hast du den Film auch schon gesehen?
   — Ja, fand ich echt stark! Seine Filme sind immer spannend.
2. — Am Freitag war ich mit Rolf im Konzert. Die *Toten Hosen* haben gespielt. Kennst du die?
   — Welche Lieder haben sie gespielt?
   — Die von der neuen CD!

— Die sind total gut. Die CD habe ich gerade letzte Woche gekauft.
3. — Am liebsten höre ich eigentlich Disko. Kennst du das neue Lied *Hals über Kopf*?
   — Und wer singt das denn?
   — Na, die Nicki!
   — Noch nie von ihr gehört!
4. — Ich wollte heute Nachmittag mal wieder ins Kino. Da im Cinedom läuft gerade *Dead Again*. Schon davon gehört?
   — Ja, sicher doch! Ich hab ihn schon vor zwei Wochen mit Flori gesehen. Der war echt toll. Aber ich seh mir den gern noch mal mit dir an!

Zweite Stufe

13 p. 285

1. Grüß Gott! Ich heiße Marianne. Also Filme sehe ich gern, aber nicht alle Arten davon. Im Fernsehen seh ich abends gern Krimis. Die find ich doch schon gut … sind immer ganz interessant. Wenn ich aber ins Kino gehe, sehe ich lieber Western. Aber Horrorfilme, die mag ich überhaupt nicht … zu gruselig für mich. Und am liebsten sehe ich Abenteuerfilme, weil sie eben so spannend sind.
2. Ich bin der Stefan. Was ich gern sehe? Tja … Komödien mag ich gern, weil sie unterhaltend sind. Neulich war ich mit meiner Freundin im Kino und habe einen Liebesfilm gesehen. Schrecklich! Liebesfilme mag ich also wirklich nicht … zu schmalzig. Da sehe ich schon lieber Fantasyfilme, die sind wenigstens ganz phantasievoll. Am liebsten sehe ich natürlich Sciencefictionfilme. Die sind total stark. Wenn's die im Kino gibt, bin ich immer da.

Dritte Stufe

26 p. 292

1. — Ich war im Konzert. Das war echt toll!
   — So? Wer hat denn dieses Mal gespielt?
2. — Susanne und ich haben am Samstag einige Klamotten gekauft. Das hat Spaß gemacht!
   — Find ich toll! Wie war der Film denn?
3. — Hab mir drei neue Krimis in der Buchhandlung gekauft.
   — Und … wie hat dir die neue CD gefallen? Starke Musik, nicht?
4. — Ich habe heute das Buch *Jurassic Park*® gekauft. Hast du es schon gelesen?
   — Nein, aber ich habe den Film letzte Woche gesehen.
5. — Wir haben zuerst das Museum besucht, danach eine Schifffahrt auf dem Bodensee gemacht.

The following scripts are for the listening activities found in the *Pupil's Edition*. For Student Response Forms, see *Listening Activities*, pages 75–78. To provide students with additional listening practice, see *Listening Activities*, pages 79–82.

— Ja, das höre ich auch gern. Aber Rockmusik höre ich am liebsten.

AUSSPRACHE, p. 293

Diktat, p. 293

You will hear a description of what Thomas and his friends Martin and Sandra, and her friend Sabine, like to do in their free time. First listen to the description, then write down what you hear.

Am Wochenende haben Thomas und Martin viel gemacht. Zuerst haben sie gekegelt, und Thomas hat dabei gewonnen. Sie gehen auch gern ins Kino, und so haben sie einen Abenteuerfilm gesehen. Er war sehr spannend. Sandra und Sabine haben andere Interessen. Sie sind lieber zu Hause und hören neue Kassetten oder CDs. Natürlich diskutieren sie viel, über Musik, Filme, Stars und so. Und wenn das Wetter schlecht ist, spielen sie Brettspiele oder auch Karten.

Anwendung

1 p. 300

INTERVIEWER	Grüß dich! Wir schreiben einen Artikel über Freizeit, was Jugendliche so machen. Wie heißt du denn?
PETRA	Ich heiße Petra.
INTERVIEWER	So, Petra, wenn du mit deinen Freunden ausgehst, wohin geht ihr?
PETRA	Tja, wir gehen meistens in die Innenstadt.
INTERVIEWER	Und was macht ihr da?
PETRA	Wir gehen oft ins Kino und sehen uns einen Film an.
INTERVIEWER	Wann geht ihr denn gewöhnlich ins Kino?
PETRA	Jeden Montag nach dem Abendbrot.
INTERVIEWER	Soso. Also abends.
PETRA	Ja, wir haben immer Spaß dabei.
INTERVIEWER	Vielen Dank, Petra! Nun sag mal, wer ist der Junge da drüben?
PETRA	Das ist der Rudi. Soll ich ihn mal holen?
INTERVIEWER	Ja, bitte!
PETRA	Du, Rudi, komm mal her!
RUDI	Ja, was gibt's?
PETRA	Die Leute möchten dich auch mal fragen, wie du deine Freizeit verbringst. Geht das?
RUDI	Ja, gern. Was wollen Sie wissen?

INTERVIEWER	Wohin gehst du, wenn du ausgehst, und mit wem gehst du aus?
RUDI	Ich geh ja mit meinen Freunden aus, und tja … wir gehen gern ins Konzert, um gute Musik zu hören.
INTERVIEWER	Wann macht ihr das denn und wie oft?
RUDI	Wir machen das meistens sonntags. Und wenn wir genug Taschengeld haben, machen wir das sogar zweimal im Monat.
INTERVIEWER	Vielen Dank, Rudi!
RUDI	Klar doch! Gern geschehen.
INTERVIEWER	Grüß dich! Dürfte ich dir ein paar Fragen stellen?
MAX	Na sicher!
INTERVIEWER	Könntest du dich vorstellen und uns sagen, was du in deiner Freizeit machst?
MAX	Ja also, ich bin der Max, und ja … meine Freizeit verbringe ich gern mit meinem Freund, dem Otto. Wir sind dann meistens bei ihm zu Hause. Der hat nämlich eine total starke Stereoanlage. Da hören wir uns nachmittags seine CDs an.
INTERVIEWER	Macht ihr das jeden Tag?
MAX	Nee, das nicht. Aber mindestens einmal in der Woche.
INTERVIEWER	Dank dir, Max! Könntest du uns das Mädchen da drüben mal vorstellen?
MAX	Ja, das da ist die Renate. Einen Augenblick mal!
INTERVIEWER	Guten Tag! Renate?
RENATE	Ja, ich heiße Renate.
INTERVIEWER	Wir wollten dir auch einige Fragen stellen für unsere Umfrage. Geht das?
RENATE	Ja, warum nicht?
INTERVIEWER	Was machst du gern in deiner Freizeit, und wann und wie oft hast du Zeit dafür?
RENATE	Ich gehe nicht so gern aus, denn so viel freie Zeit habe ich nicht … Da bleib ich schon lieber mal zu Hause.
INTERVIEWER	Und was machst du da?
RENATE	Am liebsten lese ich ja Bücher und …
INTERVIEWER	Entschuldigung … und wann machst du das?
RENATE	Lesen? … Ja, manchmal abends, wenn ich mit den Hausaufgaben fertig bin. Ich wünschte, ich hätte mehr Zeit dafür.
INTERVIEWER	Ja, also hab recht vielen Dank, Renate.
RENATE	Ja, bitte. Tschüs!

Kapitel 10: Kino und Konzerte
Suggested Lesson Plans *50-Minute Schedule*

Day 1

LOCATION OPENER 15 min.
- Present Location Opener, pp. 272–275
- Show **Baden-Württemberg** Video
- Do Viewing and Post-viewing Activities, Video Guide, p. 62

CHAPTER OPENER 10 min.
- Background Information, ATE, p. 275M
- Building on Previous Skills, ATE, p. 275M

LOS GEHT'S! 20min.
- Preteaching Vocabulary, ATE, p. 275N
- Have students read **Los geht's!**, pp. 278–279
- Teaching Suggestions, Video Guide, p. 64
- Culture Note, ATE, p. 275N
- Show **Los geht's!** Video

Wrap-Up 5 min.
- Students respond to **Los geht's!** questions

Homework Options
- Pupil's Edition, p. 280, Comprehension Acts.
- Übungsheft, p. 109, Act. 1

Day 2

ERSTE STUFE
Quick Review 10 min.
- Check homework, p. 280, Comprehension Acts.

Wortschatz, p. 281 10 min.
- Presenting **Wortschatz**, ATE, p. 275O
- Teaching Transparency 10-A
- Do Activity 6, p. 282

So sagt man das!/Wortschatz, p. 282 15 min.
- Presenting **So sagt man das!**, ATE, p. 275O
- Teaching Transparency 10-1
- Play Audio CD for Activity 7, p. 282
- Presenting **Wortschatz**, ATE, p. 275O
- Do Activity 8, p. 282

Grammatik, p. 282 10 min.
- Presenting **Grammatik**, ATE, p. 275O
- Do Activity 3, p. 83, Grammatikheft
- Do Activity 5, p. 111, Übungsheft

Wrap-Up 5 min.
- Students respond to questions about how well they like different films

Homework Options
Grammatikheft, p. 82, Acts. 1–2
Übungsheft, pp. 110–111, Acts. 2–4

Day 3

ERSTE STUFE
Quick Review 15 min.
- Check homework, Übungsheft, pp. 110–111, Acts. 2–4

Ein wenig Landeskunde, p. 283 10 min.
- Presenting **Ein wenig Landeskunde**, ATE, p. 275O
- Do Activity 9, p. 283

Wortschatz/ Ein wenig Landeskunde, p. 283 10 min.
- Presenting **Wortschatz**, ATE, p. 275P
- Present **Ein wenig Landeskunde**, p. 283
- Do Activity 10, p. 284

Wortschatz/So sagt man das!, p. 284 10 min.
- Presenting **Wortschatz**, ATE, p. 275P
- Presenting **So sagt man das!**, ATE, p. 275P
- Play Audio CD for Activity 11, p. 284

Wrap-Up 5 min.
- Students respond to questions about how well they like various types of movies

Homework Options
- Übungsheft, p. 112, Acts. 7–8; p. 120, Act. 24

Day 4

ERSTE STUFE
Quick Review 10 min.
- Check homework, Übungsheft, p. 112, Acts. 7–8; p. 120, Act. 24

Ein wenig Grammatik, p. 284 10 min.
- Presenting **Ein wenig Grammatik**, ATE, p. 275P
- Do Activity 6, p. 112, Übungsheft
- Do Activity 12, p. 284

Quiz Review 10 min.
- Do **Mehr Grammatikübungen, Erste Stufe**

Quiz 20 min.
- Quiz 10-1A or 10-1B

Homework Options
Activities for Communication, p. 110, Realia 10-1, have students identify films by their classifications

Day 5

ZWEITE STUFE
Quick Review 10 min.
- Return and review Quiz 10-1
- Bell Work, ATE, p. 275Q

So sagt man das!/ Ein wenig Grammatik, p. 285 15 min.
- Presenting **So sagt man das!**, ATE, p. 275Q
- Presenting **Ein wenig Grammatik**, ATE, p. 275Q
- Play Audio CD for Activity 13, p. 285

Ein wenig Grammatik/Lerntrick, pp. 285, 287 20 min.
- Presenting **Ein wenig Grammatik**, ATE, p. 275Q
- Do Activities 14 and 15, p. 286
- Present **Lerntrick**, p. 287
- Do Activity 17, p. 287
- Do Activity 18, p. 288

Wrap-Up 5 min.
- Students discuss what they like, prefer, and like to do the most during leisure time

Homework Options
Pupil's Edition, p. 286, Act. 16
Grammatikheft, pp. 85–86, Acts. 7–9

Day 6

ZWEITE STUFE
Quick Review 10 min.
- Check homework, Grammatikheft, pp. 85–86, Acts. 7–9

Wortschatz, p. 288 10 min.
- Presenting **Wortschatz**, ATE, p. 275R
- Do Activity 19, p. 288

LANDESKUNDE 25 min.
- Pre-viewing Suggestion, Video Guide, p. 64
- Background Information, ATE, p. 275R
- Show **Landeskunde** Video
- Do Activities A and B, p. 289
- Do Activity 4, p. 66, Video Guide

Wrap-Up 5 min.
- Students respond to questions about what they think of various films and music

Homework Options
Pupil's Edition, p. 288, Act. 20
Grammatikheft, p. 87, Acts. 10–11
Übungsheft, pp. 113–115, Acts. 9–15

One-Stop Planner CD-ROM

For alternative lesson plans by chapter section, to create your own customized plans, or to preview all resources available for this chapter, use the **One-Stop Planner CD-ROM**, Disc 3.

 For additional homework suggestions, see activities accompanied by this symbol throughout the chapter.

Day 7

ZWEITE STUFE
Quick Review 15 min.
- Check homework, Übungsheft, pp. 113–115, Acts. 9–15

Quiz Review 15 min.
- **Mehr Grammatikübungen, Zweite Stufe**
- Do Activities 3 and 4, Interactive CD-ROM
- **Interaktive,** see ATE, p. 275F

Quiz 20 min.
- Quiz 10-2A or 10-2B

Homework Options
Activities for Communication, pp. 141–142, prepare Situation 10-2

Day 8

DRITTE STUFE
Quick Review 15 min.
- Return and review Quiz 10-2
- Bell work, ATE, p. 275T
- Do Situation 10-2, pp. 141–142

Wortschatz, p. 291 15 min.
- Presenting **Wortschatz**, ATE, p. 275T
- Teaching Transparency 10-2
- Do Activity 21, p. 290
- Do Activity 22, p. 291

Grammatik, p. 291 15 min.
- Presenting **Grammatik**, ATE, p. 275T
- Do Activities 23, 24, and 25, p. 292

Wrap-Up 5 min.
- Students respond to questions using the verbs **nehmen, lesen** and **sprechen**

Homework Options
Grammatikheft, pp. 88–89, Acts. 12–16
Übungsheft, pp. 116–117, Acts. 16–20
Activities for Communication, pp. 59–60, prepare Communicative Activity 10-3

Day 9

DRITTE STUFE
Quick Review 15 min.
- Check homework, Grammatikheft, pp. 88–89, Acts. 12–16
- Do Communicative Activity 10-3, pp. 59–60

So sagt man das!, p. 292 30 min.
- Presenting **So sagt man das!**, ATE, p. 275U
- Play Audio CD for Activity 26, p. 292
- Do Activities 27 and 28, p. 293
- Do Situation 10-3, pp. 141–142

Wrap-Up 5 min.
- Students respond to questions about what they did last weekend

Homework Options
Grammatikheft, p. 90, Acts. 17–19
Übungsheft, p. 118, Acts. 21–22

Day 10

DRITTE STUFE
Quick Review 15 min.
- Check homework, Grammatikheft, p. 90, Acts. 17–19
- Do Communicative Activity 10-3, pp. 59–60

Quiz Review 15 min.
- Do **Mehr Grammatikübungen, Dritte Stufe**
- Do Additional Listening Activities 10-5 and 10-6, pp. 81–82

Quiz 20 min.
- Quiz 10-3A or 10-3B

Homework Options
Pupil's Edition, p. 293, Acts. 29 and 30
Activities for Communication, p. 112, Realia 10-3, have students write a newspaper ad or design a poster for the Summer Jazz Concert Series at Waldwirtschaft

Day 11

DRITTE STUFE
Quick Review 10 min.
- Return and review Quiz 10-3
- Check homework, Realia 10-3, p. 112

Aussprache, p. 293 10 min.
- Do **Richtig aussprechen/Richtig lesen**, p. 293
- Do **Richtig schreiben/Diktat**, p. 293

ZUM LESEN 25 min.
- Present **Lesestrategie**, p. 294
- Do Activities 1–7, pp. 294–295

Wrap-Up 5 min.
- Students respond orally to **Kann ich's wirklich?** questions, p. 302

Homework Options
Pupil's Edition, p. 302, **Kann ich's wirklich?** questions
Übungsheft, p. 119, Act. 23
Internet Aktivitäten, see ATE, p. 275F

Day 12

ANWENDUNG
Quick Review 35 min.
- Check homework, **Kann ich's wirklich?**, p. 302
- Teaching Suggestion, ATE, p. 275X
- Video Wrap-Up, ATE, p. 275X
- Do **Anwendung** Activities, pp. 300–301

Chapter Review 15 min.
- Review chapter functions, vocabulary, and grammar; choose from **Mehr Grammatikübungen,** Grammar Tutor for Students of German, Activities for Communication, Listening Activities, Interactive CD-ROM Tutor, or **Interaktive Spiele**

Homework Options
Study for Chapter Test

Assessment

Test, Chapter 10 45 min.
- Administer Chapter 10 Test. Select from Testing Program, Alternative Assessment Guide or Test Generator.

Kapitel 10: Kino und Konzerte
Suggested Lesson Plans 90-Minute Schedule

Block 1

LOCATION OPENER 20 min.
- Present Location Opener, pp. 272–275
- Background Information, ATE, p. 271A
- Show **Baden-Württemberg** Video
- Do Viewing and Post-viewing Activities, Video Guide, p. 62
- Using the Almanac and Map, ATE, p. 271B
- Photo Essay, ATE, p. 271B

CHAPTER OPENER 10 min.
- Background Information, ATE, p. 275M
- Culture Note, p. 275M

LOS GEHT'S! 25 min.
- Preteaching Vocabulary, ATE, p. 275N
- Play Audio CD for **Los geht's!**, pp. 278–279
- Have students read **Los geht's!**, pp. 278–279
- Teaching Suggestions, Video Guide, p. 64
- Culture Note, ATE, p. 275N
- Show **Los geht's!** Video

ERSTE STUFE
Wortschatz, p. 281 15 min.
- Presenting **Wortschatz**, ATE, p. 275O
- Teaching Transparency 10-A
- Do Activity 6, p. 282
- Do Activity 1, p. 82, Grammatikheft

So sagt man das!, p. 282 15 min.
- Presenting **So sagt man das!**, ATE, p. 275O
- Teaching Transparency 10-1
- Play Audio CD for Activity 7, p. 282

Wrap-Up 5 min.
- Students respond to questions about how well they like different films and music

Homework Options
Pupil's Edition, p. 280, Comprehension Acts.
Grammatikheft, p. 82, Act. 2
Übungsheft, pp. 109–111, Acts. 1–4

Block 2

ERSTE STUFE
Quick Review 10 min.
- Check homework, p. 280, Comprehension Acts.

Wortschatz p. 282 10 min.
- Presenting **Wortschatz**, ATE, p. 275O
- Do Activity 8, p. 282

Grammatik, p. 282 10 min.
- Presenting **Grammatik**, ATE, p. 275O
- Do Activity 3, p. 83, Grammatikheft

Ein wenig Landeskunde, p. 283 20 min.
- Presenting **Ein wenig Landeskunde**, ATE, p. 275O
- Do Activity 9, p. 283
- Do Activity 24, p. 120, Übungsheft

Wortschatz/ Ein wenig Landeskunde, p. 283 10 min.
- Presenting **Wortschatz**, ATE, p. 275P
- Present **Ein wenig Landeskunde**, p. 283
- Do Activity 10, p. 284

Wortschatz/So sagt man das!, p. 284 15 min.
- Presenting **Wortschatz**, ATE, p. 275P
- Presenting **So sagt man das!**, ATE, p. 275P
- Play Audio CD for Activity 11, p. 284

Ein wenig Grammatik, p. 284 10 min.
- Presenting **Ein wenig Grammatik**, ATE, p. 275P
- Do Activity 6, p. 112, Übungsheft
- Do Activity 12, p. 284

Wrap-Up 5 min.
- Students respond to questions about how well they like various types of movies

Homework Options
Grammatikheft, p. 83–84, Acts. 4–6
Übungsheft, pp. 111–112, Acts. 5, 7–8
Interactive CD-ROM, Acts. 1–2

Block 3

ERSTE STUFE
Quick Review 10 min.
- Check homework, Grammatikheft, p. 83–84, Acts. 4–6

Quiz Review 15 min.
- Do **Mehr Grammatikübungen, Erste Stufe**
- Do Additional Listening Activities 10-1 and 10-2, pp. 79–80

Quiz 20 min.
- Quiz 10-1A or 10-1B

ZWEITE STUFE
So sagt man das!/ Ein wenig Grammatik, p. 285 15 min.
- Presenting **So sagt man das!**, ATE, p. 275Q
- Presenting **Ein wenig Grammatik**, ATE, p. 275Q
- Play Audio CD for Activity 13, p. 285

Ein wenig Grammatik/Lerntrick, pp. 285, 287 25 min.
- Presenting **Ein wenig Grammatik**, ATE, p. 275Q
- Do Activities 14, 15, and 16, p. 286
- Present **Lerntrick**, p. 287
- Do Activity 17, p. 287
- Do Activity 18, p. 288

Wrap-Up 5 min.
- Students discuss what they like, prefer and like to do the most during leisure time

Homework Options
Grammatikheft, pp. 85–86, Acts. 7–9
Übungsheft, pp. 113–115, Acts. 9–15

One-Stop Planner CD-ROM

For alternative lesson plans by chapter section, to create your own customized plans, or to preview all resources available for this chapter, use the **One-Stop Planner CD-ROM**, Disc 3.

 For additional homework suggestions, see activities accompanied by this symbol throughout the chapter.

Block 4

ZWEITE STUFE
Quick Review 15 min.
- Return and review Quiz 10-1
- Check homework, Übungsheft, pp. 113–115, Acts. 9–15

Wortschatz, p. 288 10 min.
- Presenting **Wortschatz**, ATE, p. 275R
- Do Activity 19, p. 288

Quiz Review 15 min.
- **Mehr Grammatikübungen, Zweite Stufe**
- Do Activities 3 and 4, Interactive CD-ROM
- **Interaktive Spiele** , see ATE, p. 275F

Quiz 20 min.
- Quiz 10-2A or 10-2B

LANDESKUNDE 30 min.
- Pre-viewing Suggestion, Video Guide, p. 64
- Background Information, ATE, p. 275R
- Show **Landeskunde** Video
- Do Activities A and B, p. 289
- Do Activity 4, p. 66, Video Guide

Homework Options
Pupil's Edition, p. 288, Act. 20
Activities for Communication, pp. 141–142, prepare Situation 10-2

Block 5

DRITTE STUFE
Quick Review 10 min.
- Return and review Quiz 10-2
- Bell work, ATE, p. 275T
- Do Situation 10-2, pp. 141–142

Wortschatz, p. 291 30 min.
- Presenting **Wortschatz**, ATE, p. 275T
- Teaching Transparency 10-2
- Do Activity 21, p. 290
- Do Activities 12–14, p. 88, Grammatikheft
- Do Activity 22, p. 291
- Do Activities 15–16, p. 89, Grammatikheft

Grammatik, p. 291 20 min.
- Presenting **Grammatik**, ATE, p. 275T
- Do Activities 23, 24, and 25, p. 292

So sagt man das!, p. 292 25 min.
- Presenting **So sagt man das!**, ATE, p. 275U
- Play Audio CD for Activity 26, p. 292
- Do Activities 27 and 28, p. 293
- Do Situation 10-3, pp. 141–142

Wrap-Up 5 min.
- Students respond to questions using the verbs nehmen, lesen and sprechen

Homework Options
Grammatikheft, pp. 89–90, Acts. 15–19
Übungsheft, pp. 116–118, Acts. 16–22

Block 6

DRITTE STUFE
Quick Review 15 min.
- Check homework, Übungsheft, pp. 116–118, Acts. 16–22

Quiz Review 10 min.
- Do **Mehr Grammatikübungen, Dritte Stufe**

Quiz 20 min.
- Quiz 10-3A or 10-3B

Aussprache, p. 293 10 min.
- Do **Richtig aussprechen/Richtig lesen**, p. 293
- Do **Richtig schreiben/Diktat**, p. 293

ZUM LESEN 25 min.
- Present **Lesestrategie**, p. 294
- Do Activities 1–7, pp. 294–295

Wrap-Up 5 min.
- Students respond to questions about which movies and music they know and which they like, prefer or like the best

Homework Options
Pupil's Edition, p. 302, **Kann ich's wirklich?** questions
Übungsheft, p. 119, Act. 23
Internet, see ATE, p. 275F

Block 7

ANWENDUNG
Quick Review 25 min.
- Return and review Quiz 10-3
- Check homework, p. 302, **Kann ich's wirklich?**
- Teaching Suggestion, ATE, p. 275X
- Do **Anwendung** Activities, pp. 300–301

Chapter Review 20 min.
- Review chapter functions, vocabulary, and grammar; choose from **Mehr Grammatikübungen,** Grammar Tutor for Students of German, Activities for Communication, Listening Activities, Interactive CD-ROM Tutor, or **Interaktive Spiele**

Test, Chapter 10, 45 min.
- Administer Chapter 10 Test. Select from Testing Program, Alternative Assessment Guide or Test Generator.

Kapitel 10: Kino und Konzerte
Teaching Suggestions, *pages 276–303*

CHAPTER OPENER

Pacing Tips

In the **Erste Stufe**, students learn the functions of 'expressing likes and dislikes' and 'expressing familiarity' using the verbs **mögen** and **kennen**. The vocabulary and culture deal with movie genres and music. The **Zweite Stufe** centers around 'expressing preferences and favorites' using **lieber** and **am liebsten** with **haben**. Several movie ads appear on p. 287. In the **Dritte Stufe**, the function of 'talking about what you did in your free time' occurs with the phrase **sprechen über** and the stem-changing verbs **lesen** and **sprechen**. Because the three **Stufen** are similar in length and amount of material presented, you will probably spend about the same amount of time on each. For Lesson Plans and timing suggestions, see pages 275I–275L.

Meeting the Standards
Communication
- Expressing likes and dislikes, p. 282
- Expressing familiarity, p. 284
- Expressing preferences and favorites, p. 285
- Talking about what you did in your free time, p. 292

Cultures
- **Ein wenig Landeskunde,** p. 283
- **Ein wenig Landeskunde,** p. 283
- **Landeskunde,** p. 289
- Background Information, p. 275M
- Culture Note, p. 275N
- Background Information, p. 275R

Connections
- Multicultural Connection, p. 275M
- Music and Theater Connection, p. 275R
- Thinking Critically, p. 275R
- Multicultural Connection, p. 275S

Comparisons
- Thinking Critically, p. 275M
- Language-to-Language, p. 275P

Communities
- Career Path, p. 275S

Background Information
The photo shows teenagers at the box office of a movie theater. German movie theaters operate differently than American theaters. Moviegoers can enter the theater up to 30 minutes before showtime to watch advertisements. Refreshments are generally not purchased at a concession stand. Vendors use the 30 minutes prior to showtime to walk through the aisles selling ice cream, candy, and drinks.

One-Stop Planner CD-ROM

For resource information, see the **One-Stop Planner CD-ROM**, Disc 3.

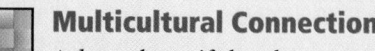

Connections and Comparisons

Thinking Critically
Observing Have students look at the advertisement between the boy and the girl in the picture. Can they tell what is being advertised? The brand name of the products? (ice cream; **Langnese; Cornetto Nuss**)

Multicultural Connection
Ask students if they have ever watched a movie with subtitles. If so, which movies, and what languages were spoken in them?

Teaching Suggestion
Ask students to look at the bulletin board and scan it for special announcements. (**Montag-Kinotag, Jugend bis 14 J(ahre) nur nachmittags …**)

Chapter Sequence
Los geht's! . . . . .p. 278
Erste Stufe . . . . .p. 281
Zweite Stufe . . . . .p. 285
Landeskunde . . . . .p. 289
Dritte Stufe . . . . .p. 290
Zum Lesen . . . . .p. 294
Mehr Grammatikübungen . . . . .p. 296
Anwendung . . . . .p. 300
Kann ich's wirklich? .p. 302
Wortschatz . . . . .p. 303

LOS GEHT'S!

Teaching Resources
pp. 278–280

PRINT
▶ Lesson Planner, p. 47
▶ Video Guide, pp. 63–64, 66
▶ Übungsheft, p. 109

MEDIA
▶ One-Stop Planner
▶ Video Program
  Los geht's!
  Videocassette 4, 04:36–08:07
  Videocassette 5 (captioned version),
  55:46–59:16
  Fortsetzung
  Videocassette 4, 08:10–11:15
  Videocassette 5 (captioned version),
  59:19–1:02:25
▶ Audio Compact Discs, CD10, Trs. 1–6
▶ **Los geht's!** Transparencies

PAGES 278–279

 Los geht's! Transparencies

Preteaching Vocabulary

Recognizing cognates

Los geht's! contains several words that students
will be able to recognize as cognates. Have
students find these cognates, then have them
guess what is happening in the story.

Thomas: eine Clique, Sport, joggen, Interessen,
Konzerte, Rockkonzerte, Country
Sandra: eine Kassette, eine CD
Martin: Sänger, klassische Musik, die Oper
Nicole: Fantasyfilme, Actionfilme, brutal
Sabine: Filme, Stars

Fortsetzung

You may choose
to continue with the
Fortsetzung of *Wie ver-*
bringt ihr eure Freizeit?
now or wait until later in the chapter. For a synopsis of
the **Los geht's!** and **Fortsetzung** episodes, see p. 275E.

Advance Organizer

Take a survey of class members. Ask students about
the last movie they saw. When did they go and what
did they see?

Teaching Suggestions

• Before reading *Wie verbringt ihr eure Freizeit?*
remind students of the many reading strategies they
have learned so far. (Using visual clues, scanning for
specific information, using root words, using what
you already know; using context to determine
meaning; finding relationships between ideas, reading for a purpose, understanding compound words)

Cultures and Communities

Culture Note
Remind students that German teenagers
get out of school early in the afternoon (around
1:00). That explains the many activities they
have time for in the afternoon after they've
completed their homework.

PAGE 280

Using the Captioned Video

4 As an alternative to reading the interviews
in the book, you might want to show the
captioned version of *Wie verbringt ihr eure*
Freizeit? available on Videocassette 5. For
synopses of both episodes, see p. 275E.

Comprehension Check

A Slower Pace
1 To ensure comprehension of the text, go
through the frames individually, eliciting responses
to each of the three questions from students.

Visual Learners
4 Write the six phrases on the chalkboard and
ask students to write appropriate expressions
under each phrase. Each category should have
several examples. Review all expressions with
the class.

Teaching Suggestion
5 This activity could be assigned for homework.
Students could begin in class by making an
outline and then complete the final draft at home.

Teaching Resources
pp. 281–284

PRINT
- Lesson Planner, p. 48
- TPR Storytelling Book, pp. 37, 40
- Listening Activities, pp. 75, 79–80
- Activities for Communication, pp. 55–56, 110, 113, 141–142
- Grammatikheft, pp. 82–84
- Grammar Tutor for Students of German, Chapter 10
- Übungsheft, pp. 110–112
- Testing Program, pp. 249–252
- Alternative Assessment Guide, p. 41
- Student Make-Up Assignments, Chapter 10

MEDIA
- One-Stop Planner
- Audio Compact Discs, CD10, Trs. 7–8, 20, 26–27
- Teaching Transparencies
  Situation 10-1
  Vocabulary 10-A
  Mehr Grammatikübungen Answers
  Grammatikheft Answers
- Interactive CD-ROM Tutor, Disc 3

PAGE 281

Bell Work
In pairs, have students ask each other for directions to the closest movie theater. Have them review **So sagt man das!**, p. 282.

Game

Ask one player to leave the classroom while the rest of the class chooses the name of a movie. Have the player from outside return and stand in front of the class. He or she begins by asking questions that will eventually lead him or her to identify the film. (Example: **Ist der Film alt oder neu? Wer spielt in dem Film?**) Have several students take turns guessing.

PRESENTING: Wortschatz

The items in the **Wortschatz** provide students with the vocabulary to talk about different kinds of movies. After introducing the vocabulary, have students name some current films and have others say what kinds of films they are.

PAGE 282

PRESENTING: So sagt man das!

Before presenting **So sagt man das!**, brainstorm with students the ways they have already learned to express likes and dislikes. Take some already familiar expressions with **gern haben** or **gefallen** and substitute **mögen** orally. Then have students look at the examples in **So sagt man das!** and ask them what they mean. Focus on **mag** and **magst**. Make up other examples.

(TPR) Total Physical Response
Have students stand up at their desks. Give a series of quick commands based on **So sagt man das!**, using verbs such as **heben, klatschen, applaudieren, buhen, hinsetzen.** (Examples: **Wenn du Rockmusik magst, applaudiere! Wenn du klassische Musik magst, heb die linke Hand!**)

PRESENTING: Grammatik

The verb mögen Ask students to point out changes they observed in the conjugation of the verb **mögen.** What other verbs have they learned that follow a similar pattern? (**können, sollen, wollen, müssen**) Have students read the sample sentences in the **Grammatik.** Then, have them make their own sentences using the **Wortschatz** on p. 282. Have one student call out a pronoun and another student finish the sentence.

PRESENTING: Wortschatz

Conduct a class survey using this vocabulary in connection with the titles of several popular movies. You might want to limit the categories.
Examples:
Hast du *(Titanic)* furchtbar gern, gern, nicht gern oder überhaupt nicht gern?
Hast du *(Les Misérables)* besonders gern, sehr gern, nicht gern oder gar nicht gern?

PAGE 283

PRESENTING: Ein wenig Landeskunde

Ask students why they think rating guidelines have been established in the United States. Have them compare the ratings systems in Germany and in the United States.

Teaching Suggestion

9 Have students take turns going to the front of the class and conducting a survey about the most popular kind of movie. Students would ask: **Was für Filme mag (Carlos) besonders gern?** Have them create an ongoing chart on the board.

(Cathy) mag … (Joe) mag …

PRESENTING: Wortschatz

Take a straw poll of class members using this vocabulary and the verb **mögen. (Wer mag Jazz?)** Have students summarize the results in writing.

> **PAGE 284**

PRESENTING: Wortschatz

Call out names of several popular groups, songs, singers, actors, and films and have students classify the names using this **Wortschatz.**

PRESENTING: So sagt man das!

Starting in a front corner of the room, ask a student **Kennst du (den Schauspieler Jürgen Prochnow)?** He or she should answer using an expression from **So sagt man das!** This student should then turn to the student behind him or her and ask a similar question; the second student should reply following the same model. Students should go down the rows asking and answering questions until everyone has had a chance to do both. As a challenge, you might want to ask students to answer in a complete sentence, substituting a pronoun for the proper noun. (Example: **Ja, ich kenne ihn.**)

PRESENTING: Ein wenig Grammatik

Kennen/wissen Prepare several sentences on a transparency illustrating the difference between **kennen** and **wissen.** (Examples: **Ich kenne den Film** *Dracula.* **Ich weiß, wo er jetzt spielt. Ich kenne München sehr gut. Ich weiß, wie man zum Marienplatz kommt.**) Ask students if they can see the difference in the way the two verbs are used. Next, give students several sentences for which they must supply the correct verb: **kennen** or **wissen.** (Examples: _____ du, wer die Schauspielerin ist? _____ du die Schauspielerin?)

Connections and Comparisons

Language-to-Language

You may want to tell your students that the English verb *to know* is expressed by two different verbs in French and Spanish just as it is in German. German uses the verbs **wissen/kennen,** French uses **savoir/connaître,** and Spanish **saber/conocer.** Ask your students if they can think of the rarely-used English word similar to **kennen.** Hint: It retains the meaning of **kennen.** (ken, as in *beyond one's ken* or *Do you ken?*)

Teaching Suggestion

To prepare for this activity, cut out several movie ads with large pictures from your local newspaper. Hold up one picture from a movie ad and ask students in German what kind of film it is. (Example: **Was für ein Film ist das?**) Students must reply in a complete German sentence. (Example: **Das ist ein Liebesfilm.**) To expand the activity, write the following adjectives on the board along with their accompanying numbers. Then, ask students to rate the film.

1. furchtbar!   4. sehr gut!

2. blöd!   5. Klasse!

3. ziemlich gut

Assess

▸ Testing Program, pp. 249–252
  Quiz 10-1A, Quiz 10-1B
  Audio CD10, Tr. 20

▸ Student Make-Up Assignments
  Chapter 10, Alternative Quiz

▸ Alternative Assessment Guide, p. 41

ZWEITE STUFE

Teaching Resources
pp. 285–289

PRINT
- Lesson Planner, p. 49
- TPR Storytelling Book, pp. 38, 40
- Listening Activities, pp. 76, 80–81
- Activities for Communication, pp. 57–58, 111, 113, 141–142
- Grammatikheft, pp. 85–87
- Grammar Tutor for Students of German, Chapter 10
- Übungsheft, pp. 113–115
- Testing Program, pp. 253–256
- Alternative Assessment Guide, p. 41
- Student Make-Up Assignments, Chapter 10

MEDIA
- One-Stop Planner
- Audio Compact Discs, CD10, Trs. 9, 21, 28–29
- Teaching Transparencies
  Situation 10-1
  Mehr Grammatikübungen Answers
  Grammatikheft Answers
- Interactive CD-ROM Tutor, Disc 3

PAGE 285

Bell Work

As a warm-up for the activities in this **Stufe,** put the following incomplete statement on the board and ask students to think about how they would complete it. (Example: **Ich sehe gern …**)

PRESENTING: So sagt man das!

Remind students that they learned to express preferences when they talked about sports and hobbies in Chapter 2. To refresh their memories, ask students several questions about their preferences. (Examples: **Was spielst du besonders gern? Was machst du nicht so gern? Was kaufst du lieber, Karten für Fußball oder Tennis? Was spielst du am liebsten?**) Then introduce the new functions, asking students what they like to see: **Was siehst du gern? Was siehst du lieber? Was siehst du am liebsten?**

PRESENTING: Ein wenig Grammatik

Gern, lieber, am liebsten Have students write on a piece of paper what they do **gern, lieber,** and **am liebsten,** following the model presented in this box.

Encourage them to be as original as possible and to use vocabulary from any chapter they wish. (They could say, for example, **Ich spiele Basketball gern, aber ich spiele Baseball lieber. Am liebsten spiele ich Tennis.**) When all students have finished, take up their papers and read them aloud, asking students to guess which of their classmates wrote which statements.

Communication for All Students

Challenge

13 Have students listen to the activity a third time. They should listen for one word or phrase that would justify Marianne's or Stefan's likes or dislikes. (Examples: **langweilig, schmalzig, lustig**) Then ask follow-up questions to elicit these from students. (Example: **Warum sieht Stefan nicht gern Liebesfilme?**)

PRESENTING: Ein wenig Grammatik

The verb sehen Review the forms of **sehen** by asking someone a question and then asking the class what that person said. (Example: **David, was für Filme siehst du gern? Was für Filme sieht David gern?**) Use this opportunity to review other verbs that have a stem-vowel change from e → i: **essen, geben,** and **nehmen.** Again, use question/answer practice and directed dialogue to elicit the critical forms.

PAGE 286

Communication for All Students

A Slower Pace

14 Before doing Activity 14, help students understand the idea of **lieber** with some structured practice. Hold up two cards at a time with words or pictures on them. (Examples: **Actionfilme; Horrorfilme**) Ask individual students: **Was siehst du lieber? Was spielst du lieber? Was isst du lieber?**

For Additional Practice

15 Ask students to use the same information, this time describing the likes and dislikes of their best friend, brother, or sister. This could be assigned for homework.

PAGE 287

PAGE 288

Speaking Assessment

18 You may wish to evaluate students' conversations using the following rubric.

Speaking Rubric	Points			
	4	3	2	1
Content (Complete – Incomplete)				
Comprehension (Total – Little)				
Comprehensibility (Comprehensible – Incomprehensible)				
Accuracy (Accurate – Seldom accurate)				
Fluency (Fluent – Not fluent)				

18–20: A   16–17: B   14–15: C   12–13: D   Under 12: F

PRESENTING: Wortschatz

Use these new adjectives in context and have students guess their meanings. (Examples: **James-Bond-Filme sind sehr spannend. Filme mit Robin Williams sind lustig. Filme mit Jean-Claude van Damme oder Schwarzenegger sind meistens brutal.**) Be sure to help students with the pronunciation of the new adjectives, concentrating especially on the cognates.

Teaching Suggestion

20 After students have completed their descriptive paragraphs, divide the class into two teams. Teams take turns asking yes/no questions to guess who the mystery person is.

PAGE 289

 # LANDESKUNDE

Teaching Resources
p. 289

PRINT
▸ Video Guide, pp. 63–64, 66–67
▸ Übungsheft, p. 120

MEDIA
▸ One-Stop Planner
▸ Video Program
  Videocassette 4, 11:53–15:23
▸ Audio Compact Discs, CD10, Trs. 10–14
▸ Interactive CD-ROM Tutor, Chapter 10

Teaching Suggestions

- Ask students to name the last cultural event they attended. When was it, where did it take place, and with whom did they go?

- You might want to introduce the following expressions to help students understand the interviews with the four German teenagers.
  die Ausstellung   *exhibition, display*
  witzig   *funny, comical*
  die Vergünstigung   *discount*
  verabreden   *to make plans to meet someone*
  dafür sein   *to be in favor of, to advocate*

Connections and Comparisons

Music and Theater Connection

Provide students with the Arts and Entertainment section of a local newspaper or that of a major city nearby. Ask students to categorize upcoming events (plays, shows, concerts, ballets, exhibitions, and so on) and to determine which event in each category they would most like to attend.

Thinking Critically

Comparing and Contrasting German students grow up learning about German-speaking composers such as Mozart, Beethoven, Bach, and Händel. Ask students if they know any American composers. (Examples: Ellen Zwilich, Aaron Copland, Leonard Bernstein, John Williams, John Phillip Sousa, George Gershwin, Amy Beach)

Multicultural Connection

Ask students to interview foreign exchange students, other foreign language teachers, or anybody else they know from a different country as to what cultural events teenagers there typically attend. Have students report their findings in class.

Teacher Note

Mention to your students that the **Landeskunde** will also be included in Quiz 10-2B given at the end of the **Zweite Stufe.**

Reteaching: Expressing preferences and favorites

Put the following groups of incomplete sentences on the board and let students complete the statements in a meaningful way.

Ich sehe _____ gern, aber _____ sehe ich lieber. Am liebsten sehe ich _____.

Ich höre _____ gern, aber ich höre _____ lieber. Am liebsten höre ich _____.

In der Schule habe ich _____ gern. _____ habe ich lieber. Am liebsten habe ich _____. Ja, mein Lieblingsfach ist _____.

Teaching Suggestion

Have students write down their favorite movie and list three reasons why a friend should see that movie.

Cultures and Communities

Career Path

Have students work in pairs to brainstorm careers in communications in which a knowledge of German would be helpful. (Suggestions: Imagine you are employed by Blue Danube Radio, the English-language radio station in Vienna, Austria; imagine you are a TV correspondent gathering news in German-speaking countries; imagine you are a translator composing subtitles for German films and videos.)

Game

Play the game **Was beginnt mit …?** See p. 275C for the procedure.

Assess

▸ Testing Program, pp. 253–256
Quiz 10-2A, Quiz 10-2B
Audio CD10, Tr. 21

▸ Student Make-Up Assignments
Chapter 10, Alternative Quiz

▸ Alternative Assessment Guide, p. 41

Hanns-Martin-Schleyer-Halle

Sonntag, 1. März
Peter Maffay

Montag, 2. März
Joe Cocker

Sonntag, 8. März
Musikantenstadl

Samstag, 14. März
Udo Jürgens

Sonntag, 15. März
**Placido Domingo und
Julia Migenes**

Samstag, 28. März
Schöller Oldie Night

Vor und nach der Vorstellung!

Der Treff • für Leute von heute!

**WÜRTTEMBERGER-STUBEN
- Dieter Franke -**

70174 Stuttgart 10, Schloßstraße 33 (bei der Liederhalle) 0711/29 03 14

Täglich von 11-24 Uhr geöffnet. | **Küche bis 24 Uhr.**

DRITTE STUFE

Teaching Resources
pp. 290–293

PRINT
▸ Lesson Planner, p. 50
▸ TPR Storytelling Book, pp. 39, 40
▸ Listening Activities, pp. 76, 81–82
▸ Activities for Communication, pp. 59–60, 112, 113, 141–142
▸ Grammatikheft, pp. 88–90
▸ Grammar Tutor for Students of German, Chapter 10
▸ Übungsheft, pp. 116–118
▸ Testing Program, pp. 257–260
▸ Alternative Assessment Guide, p. 41
▸ Student Make-Up Assignments, Chapter 10

MEDIA
▸ One-Stop Planner
▸ Audio Compact Discs, CD10, Trs. 15–18, 22, 30–31
▸ Teaching Transparencies Situation 10-2
  Mehr Grammatikübungen Answers
  Grammatikheft Answers
▸ Interactive CD-ROM Tutor, Disc 3

PAGE 290

Bell Work

Go around the class and ask students what they have recently read for pleasure. What was the name of the book, magazine, or article? Who was the author? Why did they choose that particular reading material?

Teaching Suggestion

21 Have students work with partners for this activity. After students have completed their assignments, have three or four of them write their answers to each of the five questions on the board. Go over the responses with the class.

PAGE 291

PRESENTING: Wortschatz

To introduce the new vocabulary, bring an example of each vocabulary item and teach the types of books by holding up each book for all students to see. Tell them what type of book it is, as well as its title and the author's name. In addition, you might want to ask students if they know the book, using **kennen,** and whether or not they like that kind of book.

Teaching Suggestion

After introducing **sprechen,** ask students if they can recall similar verbs they have previously learned. (**sagen**)

PRESENTING: Grammatik

Stem-changing verbs Read the examples from the **Grammatik** aloud to students. Have individual students repeat the sentences. Ask individual students questions using **lesen** and **sprechen.** (Example: **Liest du oft Sachbücher?**) Vary the subject form of the questions (**du, ihr, Sie, er, sie, sie** *pl*), and have students respond using the correct verb form. Then, have students take turns asking each other these questions.

Teacher to Teacher

Larry B. Tenbarge
Forest Park High School
Ferdinand, IN

Larry has students act out parts of their favorite movies.

❝I have students select a favorite movie, then work in groups of four or five to stage a scene from it in German. They translate the original scene and provide props and simple scenery for their 3 to 5 minute presentation. The scene is videotaped in class and then replayed for the whole class to view. The class critiques the video on style and use of the language.**❞**

DRITTE STUFE

📁 Portfolio

24 You might want to use this activity as an oral portfolio item for your students. See *Alternative Assessment Guide,* p. 27.

Writing Assessment

24 You may choose to assign this activity as a written task. Students should have at least five interchanges between the salesperson and the customer. For assessment you might wish to use the following rubric.

Writing Rubric	Points			
	4	3	2	1
Content (Complete – Incomplete)				
Comprehensibility (Comprehensible – Seldom comprehensible)				
Accuracy (Accurate – Seldom accurate)				
Organization (Well-organized – Poorly organized)				
Effort (Excellent – Minimal)				

18–20: A   16–17: B   14–15: C   12–13: D   Under 12: F

PRESENTING: So sagt man das!

In Chapter 8, students learned the simple past tense of the verb **sein.** Review the different forms by asking students personalized questions such as **Wo warst du gestern abend?** Then ask students to name some of the adverbs they have learned for expressing past time. (Examples: **gestern, vorgestern**) See Chapter 8, p. 231 for a complete list. Finally, ask students to recall the meaning of the sentence **Was hast du gestern beim Bäcker gekauft?** Then introduce the items from **So sagt man das!** on p. 292. Have students find the four new past tense verb forms (**gemacht, gelesen, gesehen, gesprochen**). Ask students to look at the word order in the sentences that use the conversational past. Where is the past participle? Students should see that the auxiliary **haben** is always in the second position (before or after the subject) while the past participle is in the last position.

Challenge

26 After students have completed the activity, play the recording again and ask students to listen for the word or phrase that did not make sense.

Teaching Suggestion

27 Ask several students to create a few sentences orally, then assign the activity as written homework.

Teaching Suggestion

28 This works well as a warm-up activity after a weekend. Put the activity on the board before the students enter the classroom. Have students work on the activity in pairs at the beginning of class.

Reteaching: The verb *lesen*

Using the verb **lesen,** ask students about their reading preferences. (Examples: **Was liest du gern? Was lest ihr gern?**) Have them tell you what they enjoyed reading last week, something interesting they are reading today, and what they have to read for tomorrow. (**Was hast du letzte Woche gelesen? Was liest du heute? Was liest du morgen?**)

DRITTE STUFE *(side tab)*

Game

Begin this **Kettenspiel** by making the following statement: **Letzten Sommer war ich in Hollywood und habe drei Fernsehstars gesehen.** Have the next student repeat your statement and add his or her own phrase, using one of the past tense phrases he or she has learned. See how many phrases students can remember.

Teaching Suggestion

29 After students have finished, you may want to have them peer-edit a partner's entry. Students should pay special attention to the use of the past tense.

Following this, students should write down any questions they have for their partner about the weekend described. (Example: **Warst du allein oder mit Freunden im Kino?**)

Von der Schule zum Beruf

30 Von der Schule zum Beruf

At this point you may wish to have your students look at the movie links provided in the **Internet Aktivitäten** for Chapter 10. For more information, see p. 275F.

PRESENTING: Aussprache

An explanation of these sounds can be found in Chapters 3, 6, and 7 of the *Pupil's Edition*.

Assess

▸ Testing Program, pp. 257–260
Quiz 10-3A, Quiz 10-3B
Audio CD10, Tr. 22

▸ Student Make-Up Assignments
Chapter 10, Alternative Quiz

▸ Alternative Assessment Guide, p. 41

DRITTE STUFE

ZUM LESEN

Prereading
Building Context

Go around the classroom and ask several students to tell the class about the last movie they saw in a theater or on video. Ask them to give a brief, simple summary in German.

Teaching Suggestion

Remind students that many of the words they have learned so far were easy to understand because they were similar to English. Tell students that words that appear similar across languages and have the same meaning are called cognates. False cognates, on the other hand, appear similar but have different meanings. Learning to use context clues to determine whether a word is a cognate or a false cognate will help students improve their reading ability.

Teacher Note

Activities 1–2 are prereading activities.

Reading
Teaching Suggestion

On the chalkboard or a transparency, make a chart divided into three parts: cognates, false cognates, familiar words and phrases. As students skim and scan for answers to activities 3 through 5, note their comments in the appropriate place on the chart.

Thinking Critically

Observing Ask students to scan the ads to find out which of the films will be shown in English. (*Groundhog Day*) How did they know? (The title is given in English first.) Some students may also be able to infer the meaning of **Englische**

Originalfassung at the bottom of the ad. This is addressed in activity 7a.

Thinking Critically

Drawing Inferences Can students think of reasons why *Groundhog Day* would be shown in English while *Jurassic Park®* is dubbed in German? (Cost-effectiveness, interest in the original version)

Portfolio
8 You might want to use this activity as a written portfolio item for your students. See *Alternative Assessment Guide*, p. 27.

Post-Reading
Teacher Note

Activity 8 is a post-reading activity that will show whether students can transfer what they have learned.

‚Pro und Contra'

Divide the class into two groups and ask each group to come up with the pros and cons of video rental. Divide the chalkboard in half and write students' arguments **für** or **gegen** on each side. Remind students to use conjunctions such as **denn, weil, und,** and **aber** in their discussion.

PAGES 296–299

MEHR GRAMMATIKÜBUNGEN

The **Mehr Grammatikübungen** activities are designed as supplemental activities for the grammatical concepts presented in the chapter. You might use them as additional practice, for review, or for assessment.

For more grammar presentations, review and practice, refer to the following:
• Grammatikheft
• Grammar Tutor for Students of German
• Grammar Summary on pp. R15–R25
• Übungsheft
• Grammar and Vocabulary quizzes (Testing Program)
• Test Generator
• Interactive CD-ROM Tutor
• Interaktive Spiele at go.hrw.com

PAGES 300–301

ANWENDUNG

Video Wrap-up

Videocassette 4, 04:40–19:50
Videocassette 5 (captioned version), 58:09–1:05:22
At this time, you might want to use the video resources for additional review and enrichment. See *Video Guide* for suggestions regarding:
• the **Los geht's!** episode
• the **Landeskunde** interviews
• the **Fortsetzung** episode
• the **Videoclips.**

Apply and Assess

Challenge

1 After students have completed the chart, ask them which of the students interviewed they would most like to spend their free time with and why. Questions and answers should be in German.

Process Writing

6 To help your students flesh out their ad, write the following chart on the board and ask them individually or in groups to fill in the blanks:

Mitglieder der Gruppe	Filme	Lieder
Sänger(in)		
Gitarrenspieler(in)		
Synthesizerspieler(in)		
Schlagzeugspieler(in)		

PAGE 302

KANN ICH'S WIRKLICH?

This page is intended to prepare students for the test. It is a brief checklist of the major points covered in the chapter. The students should be reminded that it is a checklist only and not necessarily everything that will appear on the test.

For additional self check options, refer students to the *Grammar Tutor,* the *Interactive CD-ROM Tutor,* and the Online self-test for this chapter.

PAGE 303

WORTSCHATZ

Review and Assess

Games
• Play the game **Was beginnt mit …?** See p. 275C for the procedure.

• Play the game **Könnt ihr mein Wort erraten?** See p. 275D for the procedure.

Circumlocution
Many of the German words for films, types of music, and singers and groups, as well as some adjectives in this chapter, are cognates of English words. Use the cognates to play **Das treffende Wort suchen.** See p. 155C for procedures.

Teacher Note
Give the **Kapitel 10** Chapter Test: *Testing Program,* pp. 261–266
Audio CD 10, Trs. 23–25.

10
Kino und Konzerte

Objectives

In this chapter you will learn to

Erste Stufe

- express likes and dislikes
- express familiarity

Zweite Stufe

- express preferences and favorites

Dritte Stufe

- talk about what you did in your free time

internet

ADRESSE: go.hrw.com
KENNWORT:
WK3 BADEN-WUERTTEMBERG-10

◀ **Wie war der Film?—Cool!**

zweihundertsiebenundsiebzig **277**

Los geht's! ▪ *Wie verbringt ihr eure Freizeit?*

CD 10 Trs. 1–6

Strategie Verstehen

Look at the images that accompany the interviews. What are the students doing and what clues help you determine what they might be talking about?

Thomas Sandra Martin Nicole Sabine

Los geht's! is an abridged version of the video episode.

1

Thomas: Wir sind eine Clique, drei Jungen und drei Mädchen, und—na ja—wir machen viel zusammen, besonders Sport. Wir joggen zusammen, wir fahren Rad, einmal im Monat gehen wir kegeln. Aber sonst hat jeder auch seine eigenen Interessen. Ich zum Beispiel gehe oft in Konzerte. Rockkonzerte höre ich am liebsten.

Sandra: Ab und zu gehe ich auch in ein Rockkonzert. Aber die Karten sind so furchtbar teuer und, ehrlich gesagt, höre ich lieber Country. Die Clique kommt manchmal zu mir, und jeder bringt eine Kassette oder eine CD. Wir hören dann Musik und spielen Karten oder Brettspiele.

2

Martin: Ich muss sagen, ich mag Rock überhaupt nicht. Ich mag auch die meisten Country Sänger nicht. Ich mag am liebsten klassische Musik, Brahms, Ravel und so. Ich gehe sehr gern ins Konzert und auch in die Oper.

3

Nicole: Was ich am liebsten mache? Ganz einfach! Ich geh am liebsten ins Kino. Fantasyfilme und Komödien sind meine Lieblingsfilme. Was ich nicht mag? Ich hasse Actionfilme. Die sind meistens so brutal. Mein Lieblingsfilm ist und bleibt *Kevin—Allein zu Haus*, und meine Lieblingsschauspieler sind Joe Pesci und Whoopi Goldberg.

Sabine: Ja, unsere Clique ist toll. Es stimmt, wir sind viel unterwegs, sehen viel. Wir kommen aber oft zusammen und diskutieren über Filme, Musik, Stars und so. Ich selbst bin auch gern zu Hause. Ich lese furchtbar gern. Ich habe viele Bücher.

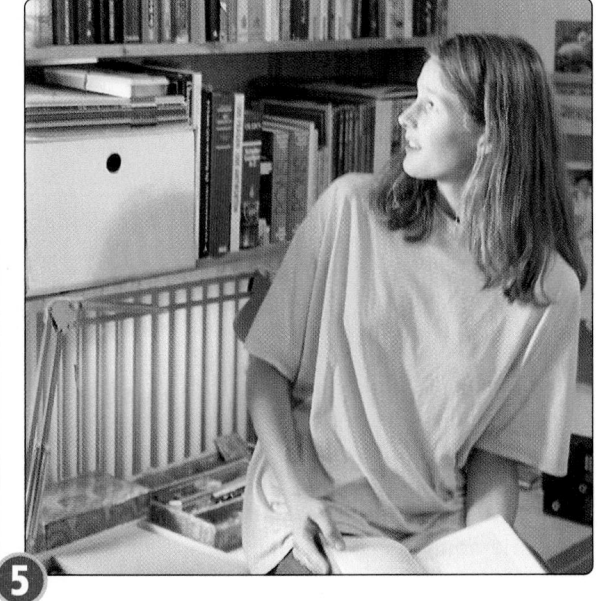

5

 Übungsheft, S. 109

1 Was passiert hier?

These activities check for global comprehension only. Students should not yet be expected to produce language modeled in **Los geht's!**

Verstehst du, worüber die fünf Schüler sprechen? Beantworte die folgenden Fragen so gut du kannst.

1. What is the main idea of each of the five interviews?
2. What is each student's main interest or interests?
3. Which of the students mention something they don't like? What do they mention?

1. The students' interests and how they spend their free time.
2. Thomas—sports; rock music; Sandra—Country and Western; games, especially cards or board games; Martin—classical music, concerts, opera; Nicole—movies; Sabine—books, talking with friends.
3. Martin—rock music, country music; Nicole—action films.

2 Mix und Match: Interessen

Welcher Schüler hat welche Interessen? Welche Aussage *(statement)* passt zu welchem Namen?

1. Thomas   b   **a.** klassische Musik hören und in Konzerte und in die Oper gehen
2. Sandra   d   **b.** joggen, Rad fahren, kegeln
3. Martin   a   **c.** über Filme, Musik, Stars usw. diskutieren, Bücher lesen
4. Nicole   e   **d.** Musik hören, Karten und Brettspiele spielen
5. Sabine   c   **e.** ins Kino gehen, besonders Fantasyfilme und Komödien sehen

3 Erzähl weiter!

Wer von den Schülern hat wahrscheinlich *(most likely)* die folgenden Aussagen gemacht?

1. Heute Abend, zum Beispiel, gehe ich ins Beethovenkonzert. Martin
2. Mein Lieblingsbuch ist *Die unendliche Geschichte.* Sabine
3. Und ich habe alle Filme mit Steve Martin gesehen. Nicole
4. Meine Freunde hören auch gern Country. Sandra
5. Ach ja! Wir segeln auch gern. Thomas

Frühkonzert in einer Halle auf dem Hamburger Fischmarkt

4 Genauer lesen

Reread the interviews. Which words or phrases do the students use to

1. name sports   1. joggen, fahren Rad, kegeln
2. name different kinds of music   2. Rock, Country, klassische Musik
3. name other free-time activities
4. name different kinds of films
5. express likes and dislikes
6. say that something is their favorite

3. Karten spielen, Brettspiele spielen, diskutieren, lesen   4. Actionfilme, Fantasyfilme, Komödien   5. lieber, mag…überhaupt nicht, hasse   6. Lieblings-…, am liebsten

5 Und du?

Now write your own interview. First choose the interview that most closely describes the free-time activities you like to do. Then rewrite the interview, replacing any information with your own particular interests.

Erste Stufe

Objectives Expressing likes and dislikes;
expressing familiarity

WK3 BADEN-WUERTTEMBERG-10

Wortschatz

SANDRA Wie verbringst du deine Freizeit?
MARTIN Ich gehe gern mit Freunden ins Kino und sehe …

 10–A

 CD-ROM DISC 3

Actionfilme
Der Terminator 2

Horrorfilme
Dracula

Krimis
Eine Frage der Ehre

Abenteuerfilme
Indiana Jones–und der letzte Kreuzzug

Liebesfilme
Entscheidung aus Liebe

Kriegsfilme
Das Boot

Komödien
Kevin - Allein in New York

Western
Zwölf Uhr mittags

Sciencefictionfilme
Star Trek 6 - Das unbekannte Land

Grammatikheft, S. 82, Ü. 1

6 **Welche Filme erkennst du?** *Which films do you recognize?*

Sprechen Welche Filme auf Seite 281 kennst du? Wie heißen sie auf Englisch? Was bedeuten Wörter wie, zum Beispiel, Horrorfilme oder Krimis? Wie heißen diese Filmarten auf Englisch?

So sagt man das!

Expressing likes and dislikes

You have learned several ways of expressing likes and dislikes, using **gern** and **nicht gern** with various verbs, and using the verb **gefallen**. Another way to express what you like or don't like is with the present tense of the verb **mögen**.

You might ask:	The responses might be:
Was für Musik magst du?	**Ich mag Rock und auch Jazz.**
Und Filme?	**Horrorfilme mag ich sehr gern.**
Magst du auch Abenteuerfilme?	**Ja, furchtbar gern!** *or* **Nein, überhaupt nicht.**
Magst du Kevin Costner?	**Ja, ich mag ihn besonders gern.**

What do you think the phrase **Was für …** means?[1]

Übungsheft, S. 110–111, Ü. 2–4

Grammatikheft, S. 82, Ü. 2

7 **Was seht ihr gern?** Script on p. 275G

Zuhören Listen to the following interviews about the kinds of movies these German teenagers enjoy seeing. For each interview, write the name of the person being interviewed. Then, beside each name, write the kinds of movies the person likes and does not like.

CD 10 Tr. 7

Erwin: mag Komödien, mag Kriegsfilme nicht
David: mag Fantasyfilme, mag Western nicht
Judith: mag Abenteuerfilme, mag Krimis nicht
Aysha: mag Liebesfilme, mag Sciencefictionfilme nicht

Grammatik

The verb **mögen**

The verb **mögen** (*to like, care for*) is used in sentences such as:

Magst du Krimis?   Nein, aber ich **mag** Horrorfilme.

Here are the forms of **mögen**:

ich	mag	wir	mögen
du	magst	ihr	mögt
er, sie, es	mag	sie/Sie	mögen

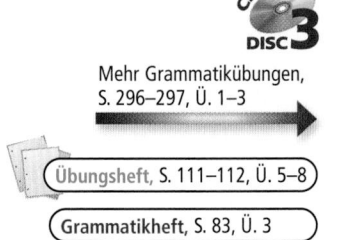

Mehr Grammatikübungen, S. 296–297, Ü. 1–3

Übungsheft, S. 111–112, Ü. 5–8

Grammatikheft, S. 83, Ü. 3

8 **Grammatik im Kontext**

Schreiben Schreib einem Freund die folgende E-Mail und setze dabei die richtige Form von **mögen** in jede Lücke.

Lieber Ralph: Viele Klassenkameraden und auch ich, wir ═══ Abenteuerfilme. Aber die Sara und die Amy ═══ Komödien lieber. Und der Rolf ═══ nur Sciencefiction. Was können wir zusammen sehen? Ich ═══ auch Kriegsfilme. Schreib mir, welche Filme du am liebsten ═══. Welche Filme ═══ ihr in eurer Familie am liebsten? Tschüs, John

mögen
mögen
mag
mag
magst
mögt

1. *what kind of …*

Wortschatz

You can use these expressions to talk about how much you like or don't like someone or something.

furchtbar gern
besonders gern
sehr gern
gern
───────────
nicht gern
gar nicht gern
überhaupt nicht gern

UTOPIA - KINO
053890
053890
Reihe 1-3
Spätvorstellung
2,50 €
Abriss
Aufbewahren und auf
Verlangen vorzeigen
Landgrabenstr. 9

	3/5/7/9	
Alba 252 25 45 Central	**BALTO—Ein Hund mit dem Herzen eines Helden** Als mitverantwortlicher Produzent für dieses Zeichentrickabenteuer bleibt Steven Spielberg seinem Stil treu—actionsgeladen, gefühlvoll und dramatisch.	
Capitol 2 251 37 00 beim Central	2.45/4.45/6.45/8.45 Fr/Sa 22.45 8. Woche **DER DUMMSCHWÄTZER** Ab 6 J. —eine ebenso intelligente, wie turbulente Familienkomödie. Jim Carrey spielt einen Anwalt, der es mit der Wahrheit nicht allzu genau nimmt, weder vor Gericht noch privat.	
Radium 251 18 07 Mühlengasse 7	3/5/7/9 **DAS ATTENTAT** Rob Reiners eloquent erzähltes und spannend inszeniertes Gerichtsdrama. Ab 12 Jahren	

Judging by the excerpt of movie listings from Germany to the left, from which country do you think most foreign films come? Think about how movies are rated in the U.S. Then scan the movie listing and see if you can find the rating system used in Germany. (*Hint: Look for something that has to do with age.*) How is it different from the one in the U.S.? How much does admission for one person cost in Germany? As you discovered, American movies are very popular in German-speaking countries. Most movies are dubbed into German; however, larger cities usually have at least one movie theater that shows foreign movies with the original sound track.

Übungsheft, S. 120, Ü. 24

9 **Eine Umfrage**

a. **Sprechen** Ask your partner what kinds of movies he or she likes and does not like. Then ask what kinds of movies he or she especially likes. Switch roles.

b. **Schreiben/Sprechen** Working with your classmates, conduct a survey about the most popular kinds of movies (**Abenteuerfilme, Krimis usw.**). Take turns going to the front of the room and asking someone **Was für Filme mag (Susan) besonders gern?** Write the answers you get in an ongoing chart on the chalkboard. When everyone has been asked, discuss together which types of movies are most popular.

BEISPIEL   (Cathy) mag …besonders gern.

Wortschatz

Rock and Roll	Jazz
Heavy Metal	Disko
klassische Musik	Oper
Country	

Grammatikheft, S. 83, Ü. 4

in DEUTSCHLAND
10 TOP
SINGLES

1 (3)	**Ms. Jackson** OutKast
2 (1)	**Stan** Eminem
3 (7)	**Overload** Suababes
4 (9)	**Operation Blade** Public Domain
5 (6)	**Gravel Pit** Wu-Tang Clan
6 (2)	**Ich Geh Nicht Ohne Dich** Walter
7 (10)	**What A Feeling** DJ Bobo & Irene Cara
8 (5)	**La Passiont** Gigi D' Agostino
9 (4)	**Who Let The Dogs Out** Baha Men
10 (8)	**Götterfunken** Tanzwut

Ein wenig Landeskunde

Looking at the pop chart from a well-known magazine for young people, what can you say about popular music among teenagers in Germany? Where does most of it come from? There are many well-known German singers, such as Herbert Grönemeyer, Marius Müller-Westernhagen, and Ina Deter.

Much of it comes from the United States.

Herbert Grönemeyer

10 Ein Interview

a. Sprechen/Schreiben Create a list of questions to ask your partner about his or her taste in music. Be sure to obtain the following information: name, age, what kind of music the person likes or dislikes, how much he or she likes or dislikes the music mentioned; if he or she goes to concerts, when, and how often. Take notes using a chart like the one below. Then switch roles.

wer?	wie alt?	was für Musik?	gern/ nicht gern?	Konzerte?	wie oft/ wann?

b. Schreiben Schreib einen Bericht über deinen Partner! Verwende dabei die Information aus dem Interview oben (*above*)!

So sagt man das!

Expressing familiarity

You may want to find out if your friend is familiar with the films, songs, and groups that you like. You might ask:

Kennst du den Film *Das Russlandhaus?*

Your friend might respond positively:

Ja, sicher! *or*
Ja, klar!

Or negatively:

Nein, den Film kenne ich nicht. *or*
Nein, überhaupt nicht.

11 Kennst du die Gruppe? Script on p. 275G

Zuhören Listen to some students talking about movies and music with their friends. For each exchange decide whether the person they are speaking to is or is not familiar with the groups, songs, or films mentioned.
1. familiar 2. familiar 3. not familiar 4. familiar

CD 10
Tr. 8

12 Kennst du die neuste Gruppe aus Amerika?

Sprechen List three lesser-known films, songs, or groups that you like (for example, local musicians). Ask your partner if he or she is familiar with them. If not, he or she will ask questions to find out what kind of movie/music you are talking about. Describe it to your partner. Then switch roles.

Ein wenig Grammatik

Schon bekannt

In **Kapitel 7** you learned the verb **wissen** (*to know a fact, information*). The verb **kennen** means *to know* as in *to be acquainted or familiar with* someone or something:

> **Ja, ich kenne Udo Lindenberg.**
> **Kennst du das Lied „Sonderzug nach Pankow"?**

The forms of **kennen** are regular in the present tense.

Mehr Grammatikübungen,
S. 297, Ü. 4

Grammatikheft, S. 84, Ü. 6

Zweite Stufe

Objective Expressing preferences
and favorites

So sagt man das!

Expressing preferences and favorites

When discussing music groups and movies, your friend might ask you about your preferences and favorites.

He or she might ask:

> **Siehst du gern Horrorfilme?**

> **Siehst du lieber Abenteuerfilme oder Sciencefictionfilme?**

> **Und du, Gabi? Was siehst du am liebsten?**

You might respond:

> **Ja, aber Krimis sehe ich lieber. Und am liebsten sehe ich Western.**

> **Lieber Sciencefictionfilme. Aber am liebsten sehe ich Liebesfilme.**

> **Am liebsten sehe ich Komödien.**

What is the idea expressed by **gern**, **lieber**, and **am liebsten**?[1] What other way can you express that something is your favorite?[2]

---

13 **Grammatik im Kontext** Script on p. 275G

a. Zuhören Listen to the following students tell you what they like and don't like, what they prefer, and what they like most of all. Make a chart like the one below and fill in the information.

CD 10
Tr. 9

	likes	doesn't like	prefers	likes most of all
Marianne	Krimis	Horror-filme	Western	Abenteuer-filme
Stefan	Komödien	Liebes-filme	Fantasy-filme	Science-fiction-filme

b. Sprechen Using the chart you've just completed, take turns with your classmates reporting back in your own words the information from Marianne's and Stefan's interviews.

Ein wenig Grammatik

The words **lieber** and **am liebsten** express preferences and favorites. They are used with **haben** and other verbs in the same way **gern** is used.

> **Ich sehe gern Actionfilme, aber ich sehe Komödien lieber.**
> **Am liebsten sehe ich Krimis.**

Mehr Grammatikübungen,
S. 297–298, Ü. 5–6  Grammatikheft, S. 85, Ü. 7

Ein wenig Grammatik

In **Kapitel 5** you learned that the verb **aussehen** (*to look, appear*) is irregular in the **du-** and **er/sie-**forms. The verb **sehen** (*to see*), of course, follows this same pattern:

> **Siehst du gern Horrorfilme?**
> **Er sieht Abenteuerfilme am liebsten.**

How would you answer the question **Siehst du gern Horrorfilme?**

Grammatikheft,
S. 86, Ü. 8–9

---

1. *like; prefer; like best of all* 2. **Lieblings-**

14 **Was wollen wir tun?**

Sprechen Du willst heute Abend mit deinem Partner etwas tun. Du wählst etwas von der linken Seite aus, dein Partner von der rechten. Er sagt dir, was er lieber tun möchte. Dann tauscht die Rollen aus!

DU **Wir können …**
PARTNER **Ich möchte lieber …**

Jerry Maguire
Vorstellungen um:
16.00
18.30
20.30

 15 **Grammatik im Kontext**

Sprechen Stell Fragen an einen Klassenkameraden! Dann beantworte die Fragen selbst (*yourself*)! Verwende die Wörter im Kasten (*in the box*) unten mit verschiedenen (*different*) Verben!

Frag deinen Partner:

a. Was hast du oder was machst du gern?

b. Was hast du oder was machst du nicht gern? Was hast du oder was machst du lieber?

c. Was hast du oder was machst du am liebsten?

Western	Country and Western	Kuchen	Pizza	Heavy Metal	Basketball
Rock'n'Roll	Fußball	Tennis		Mathe	Klavier Cola
Oper	Horrorfilme	Lied Kaffee	schwimmen		Schach
Technik	Gitarre	Apfelsaft	sammeln	Karten	Jazz
	kegeln		angeln		

 16 **Und du? Wie steht's mit dir?**

a. Schreiben/Sprechen Create a chart in German similar to the one you used in Activity 13 and fill in the following information about yourself: the music you like, prefer, or like the best, and the music you do not like at all. Then get together with your partner and ask him or her questions in order to find out the same information. Take notes using your chart. Then switch roles. Use the chart to help you organize your answers.

b. Lesen/Sprechen You must introduce your partner at the next German Club meeting, where the topic of the afternoon is music. Use the notes you took on your partner's preferences and favorites in music and write a paragraph introducing him or her and describing his or her interests in music.

17 Das Kinoprogramm

Lesen/Sprechen Schau dir die Werbung an und beantworte die Fragen.

Mittwoch, 7. 7.
20:00 Uhr
Olympia Bissingen

Absolute Power
mit Clint Eastwood und
Gene Hackman
Regie: Clint Eastwood

Donnerstag, 8. 7.
21:00 Uhr
Delta Bietigheim

IMAX

ALASKA
Ruf der Wildnis

deutsche Fassung

Mo: 12,18,21 Uhr   Fr: 14,17,20 Uhr
Di: 13,17,21 Uhr   Sa: 11,19,21 Uhr
Mi: 11,18,21 Uhr   So: 11,21 Uhr
Do: 10,16,21 Uhr
Schwanthalerstr. 3   Tel. 55 57 54 - ab 6 J.
14.45, 17.30, 20.15, Fr./Sa. a. 23.00

☎ **55 75 40**

16.00 **MICHAEL COLLINS**
mit Liam Neeson, Julia Roberts
12. Wo./ab 16 J.

18.00 **DER GEIST UND DIE**
20.15 **DUNKELHEIT**
mit Michael Douglas, Val Kilmer
26. Wo./ab 16 J.

22.30 **DIEBE DER NACHT**
mit Catherine Deneuve
10. Wo./ab 12 J.

EIN FILM VON
SIDNEY LUMET

NACHT über
MANHATTAN

ANDY GARCIA
RICHARD DREYFUSS
LENA OLIN

3. Woche

im Verleih der TOBIS Filmkunst
Internet: http://www.tobis.de
14.00/16.00/18.00/20.00 Fr./Sa. auch 22.00

DO
27.05.   21.30   Filmkritikers Liebling
FR
28.05.
SA   **Jerry Maguire—**
29.05.   **Spiel des Lebens**
SO
30.05.   von Cameron Crowe,
MO   mit Tom Cruise und Kelly
31.05.   Preston
DI
1.06.
MI
2.06.   USA 1996

„DIE LUSTIGSTE KOMÖDIE
AUS DEUTSCHLAND
SEIT ÜBER 10 JAHREN"

Hollywood Reporter

13. Wo.

GÖTZ GEORGE • UWE OCHSENKNECHT

▼ **SCHTONK!**
DER FILM ZUM BUCH VOM FÜHRER

RIO-PALAST
Rosenheimer Platz, Tel. 48 69 79
18.15, 20.30, Di./Mi. auch 16.00

NEUES REX
Agricolastraße 16, Tel. 56 25 00
Täglich 20.30 Uhr

Mittwoch, 7. 8.
20:00 Uhr
Olympia Bissingen

Jack
mit Robin Williams
und Diane Lane
Regie: Francis Ford
Coppola

Donnerstag, 8. 8.
21:00 Uhr
Delta Bietigheim

1. movie ads
2. [Answers will vary]
3. day and time of showing, names of actors, age rating, how many weeks the film has been showing, critics' comments
4. 14:00, 16:00, 18:00, 20:00, 22:00
5. 55 75 40; ten weeks
6. Yes: Rio-Palast, Rosenheimer Platz and Neues Rex, Agricolastr. 16.
7. director or directed by
8. [Answers will vary]

1. What kind of ads are these?

2. Which films do you recognize? Using the pictures and cognates as cues, try to guess what the English titles are for all the different movies listed.

3. What specific kinds of information can you find in these ads?

4. At what times on Friday can you see the movie *Nacht über Manhattan*?

5. What telephone number do you need to call to find out what day *Diebe der Nacht* is showing? Figure out how long *Diebe der Nacht* has been showing.

6. Is the movie *Schtonk* showing in more than one movie theater? If so, what are the addresses of the theaters?

7. Look at the listing for *Absolute Power*. What does **Regie** mean?

8. How would you describe these movies using the movie categories you learned on page 281 (for example, **Horrorfilme**)?

LERNTRICK

In the expression **am liebsten**, the part of the word that expresses the superlative (= most of all) is the suffix **-sten**. Watching for this suffix will frequently help you understand the meaning of new words. In the ad for *Schtonk* you see the phrase: **die lustigste Komödie.** *Lustig* means *funny*. What is the ad saying about the film *Schtonk*? What kind of film are you talking about if you say **der traurigste Film**? You will learn more about the superlative forms later.

18 Wie findest du ...?

Schreiben/Sprechen From the films listed on page 287, choose three that you've already seen or three other movies. Write them on a piece of paper and give it to your partner. He or she will do the same. Now ask your partner his or her opinion of the movies on the list. Then switch roles. Use **weil**-clauses and the adjectives below to express why you do or don't like the movie.

> BEISPIEL   PARTNER   Wie findest du den Film *Vater der Braut?*
> DU   Den Film mag ich gar nicht, weil er zu doof ist.

Wortschatz

Gut!
phantasievoll
lustig
spannend
sensationell
Schlecht!
grausam
zu brutal
zu schmalzig *(corny, mushy)*
dumm
zu traurig
doof *(stupid)*

Don't forget these words that you already know:

| Spitze | toll | langweilig |
| interessant | blöd | prima |

(Übungsheft, S. 113–115, Ü. 9–15)   (Grammatikheft, S. 87, Ü. 10–11)

CD-ROM
DISC **3**

Komödien sind lustig.

Horrorfilme sind grausam, aber Krimis sind spannend.

Liebesfilme können traurig oder oft sehr schmalzig sein.

 19 Welchen Film sehen wir heute Abend?

 Sprechen You and your partner are using the movie listings on page 287 to select a movie to see tonight. Discuss the types of movies each of you prefers, then make a suggestion and see if your partner agrees. Once you agree on a movie, decide on a time. Share your plans with your classmates.

 20 Rate mal!

 a. Schreiben Write a paragraph describing your favorite film or rock star using the new vocabulary and phrases you've learned in this chapter. Refer to your favorite star as **mein Lieblingsstar** or **mein(e) Lieblingssänger(in).** Here are some questions you will want to answer in your paragraph.

1. Woher kommt er/sie?

2. Wie sieht er/sie aus?

3. Was für Filme macht er/sie? (Was für Lieder singt er/sie?)

4. Was ist sein/ihr neuster Film? (Was ist sein/ihr neustes Lied?)

b. Lesen/Sprechen Now read your description to the class. Your classmates will take turns asking questions and guessing who the mystery person is.

Welche kulturellen Veranstaltungen besuchst du?

We asked several teenagers in the German-speaking countries what cultural events they usually go to for entertainment. What do you think they might have said? Before you read the interviews, make a list of the types of cultural events that you think German-speaking teenagers might find interesting. *CD 10 Tr.10*

Silvana, Berlin *CD 10 Tr. 11*

„Also, kulturelle Veranstaltungen …geh ich manchmal ins Ballett mit meiner Mutter, also uns interessiert das Ballett: *Schwanensee* war ich schon, *Nussknacker* von Tschaikowsky, und ab und zu gehen wir mit der Schule ins Museum oder zu irgendwelchen Ausstellungen, aber eigentlich nicht so oft."

Silke, Hamburg *CD 10 Tr. 13*

„Ich geh auch gern ins Theater, ich kuck mir auch mal Shakespeare an oder so und auch mal so witzige Theaterstücke, und ich geh auch sehr gern ins Museum. Und es gab da hier vor kurzem die Picasso-Ausstellung, und die war auch ganz gut."

Tim, Berlin *CD 10 Tr. 12*

„Also, ich versuch's so oft wie möglich—bei jeder Chance—in ein Theater oder in eine Oper zu gehen, sobald ich günstig Karten bekomme, das heißt über die Schule krieg ich Vergünstigung, oder dass meine Eltern mich halt einladen oder was sponsern, dass ich dann ins Theater gehe."

Rosi, Berlin *CD 10 Tr. 14*

„Ich geh nicht oft zu kulturellen Veranstaltungen, weil …meine Eltern wollen mich da immer mitnehmen, aber ich hab dann andere Sachen vor, dann bin ich verabredet und hab keine Lust. Aber meine Eltern sind schon dafür, dass ich dahin gehen würde."

A. 1. What events do these teenagers like to attend? Make a list of the events each one attends.

2. With your partner, write answers for the following questions. Are all of these teenagers interested in cultural events? If not, what reasons are given for not going to the events? What does the person say? Now look at Tim's interview. What do you think might keep Tim from attending a play or an opera?

3. Compare the list you made before reading the text with what the teenagers actually said. Do teenagers in the German-speaking countries like the same types of cultural events as teenagers where you live? What are some of the differences? Do you think teenagers in the German-speaking countries are more or less interested in cultural events than teenagers where you live? Why do you think this is so? Discuss these answers with your classmates and then write a brief essay in German about the topic.

B. What would you say if you were interviewed about the kinds of cultural events you like? Write your answer in German giving reasons for why you do or don't like particular events.

STANDARDS: 1.2, 2.2, 3.2, 4.2

Dritte Stufe

Objective Talking about what you did in your free time

Hanns-Martin-Schleyer-Halle

Sonntag, 1. März
Peter Maffay

Montag, 2. März
Joe Cocker

Sonntag, 8. März
Musikantenstadl

Samstag, 14. März
Udo Jürgens

Sonntag, 15. März
**Placido Domingo und
Julia Migenes**

Samstag, 28. März
Schöller Oldie Night

> Vor und nach der Vorstellung!
>
> *Der Treff • für Leute von heute!*
> WÜRTTEMBERGER-STUBEN
> - Dieter Franke -

70174 Stuttgart 10, Schloßstraße 33 (bei der Liederhalle) ☎ 0711/29 03 14

Täglich von 11-24 Uhr geöffnet. | **Küche bis 24 Uhr.**
Sonn - u. feiertags geschlossen.

TOP 10 Sachbücher

1 Haffner, Sebastian
Geschichte eines Deutschen
Deut. Verlgs. Anst. EUR 20,35

2 Schwanitz, Dietrich
Bildung
Eichborn Verlag EUR 25,45

3 Kohl, Helmut
Mein Tagebuch 1998-2000
Droemer Knaur EUR 23,00

4 The Beatles Anthology
Ullstein GMBH EUR 65,45

5 Illies, Florian
Generation Gold
Argon Verlag EUR 18,40

**6 Armstrong, Lance/
Jenkins, Sally**
Tour des Lebens
Luebbe EUR 18,40

7 Henkel, Hans-Olaf
Die Macht der Freiheit
Econ Verlag EUR 20,40

8 Schäuble, Wolfgang
Mitten im Leben
Bertelsmann EUR 21,50

9 Carnegie, Dale
Sorge dich nicht-lebe!
Scherz Verlag EUR 23,50

10 Reich-Ranicki, Marcel
Mein Leben
Deut. Verlagsanst. EUR 25,45

TOP 10 Belletristik

1 Rowling, Joanne K.
Harry Potter und der Stein
des Weisen
Carlsen Verlag EUR 14,35

2 Rowling, Joanne K.
Harry Potter und der Feuerkelch
Carlsen Verlag EUR 22,50

3 Rowling, Joanne K.
Harry Potter und die Kammer
des Schreckens
Carlsen Verlag EUR 14,35

4 Rowling, Joanne K.
Harry Potter und der
Gefangene von Askaban
Carlsen Verlag EUR 15,35

5 Pilcher, Rosamunde
Wintersonne
Wunderlich Verlag EUR 25,50

6 Link, Charlotte
Die Rosenzüchterin
Blanvalet Verlag EUR 24,50

7 Mankell, Henning
Mittsommermord
Zsolnay-Verlag EUR 23,00

8 Grisham, John
Das Testament
Heyne Wilhelm EUR 23,50

9 Leon, Donna
In Sachen Signora Brunetti
Diogenes Verlag EUR 20,40

10 Marai, Sandor
Die Glut
Piper Verlag EUR 18,40

TOP 10 Leihvideos

1 Nur noch 60 Sekunden	6 Haunted Hill
2 Gladiator	7 Crazy
3 Scream3	8 Mission to Mars
4 Der Sturm	9 Harte Jungs
5 Bats-Fliegende Teufel	10 Ein Herz und eine Kanone

21 Was machen die Jugendlichen in ihrer Freizeit?

Lesen/Sprechen Sieh dir die Anzeigen (*ads*) zur Freizeitplanung an!

1. Was für Anzeigen siehst du hier? 1. ads for concerts, videos, and books

2. Welche Bücher, Filme oder Stars kennst du schon? Mach eine Liste! 2. Answers will vary.

3. Lies die Buchtitel auf den Bestsellerlisten! Was bedeuten „Sachbuch" und „Belletristik"? 3. non-fiction, fiction

4. Wenn du Konzerte magst, welche Anzeige interessiert dich? Wann ist das Konzert von Udo Jürgens? Wo ist es? 4. the concert schedule on the left; Saturday, March 14 in the Hans-Martin-Schleyer-Halle

5. Welche Leihvideos kennst du schon? Was kannst du im Allgemeinen (*in general*) über den deutschen Videomarkt sagen? 5. Answers will vary. American movies are very popular.

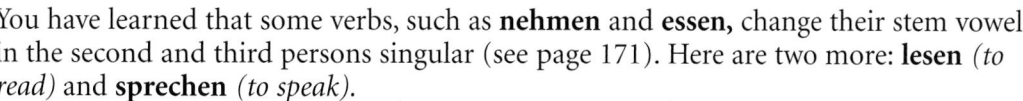

Wortschatz

JOACHIM   Was liest du?

UTE   Oh, ich lese viel, zum Beispiel …
   Romane
   Krimis
   Gruselromane
   Liebesromane
   Fantasyromane
   Sciencefictionromane
   Hobbybücher

JOACHIM   Und worüber sprichst du mit deinen Freunden?

UTE   Wir sprechen oft über …
   Politik, Mode, die Umwelt

Sachbücher

Zeitungen

Zeitschriften

Übungsheft, S. 116–117, Ü. 16–18

Grammatikheft, S. 88, Ü. 12–14

---

22   **Was liest du?**

Sprechen   Beantworte die folgenden Fragen mit deinen Klassenkameraden!

1. Liest du gern? Wenn nicht, warum nicht?
2. Was liest du am liebsten?
3. Was ist dein Lieblingsbuch? Was für ein Buch ist das?
4. Worüber sprichst du mit deinen Freunden?

Grammatik

Stem-changing verbs

You have learned that some verbs, such as **nehmen** and **essen,** change their stem vowel in the second and third persons singular (see page 171). Here are two more: **lesen** *(to read)* and **sprechen** *(to speak).*

	lesen	**sprechen**
ich	lese	spreche
du	li**e**st	spr**i**chst
er, sie, es	li**e**st	spr**i**cht

The verb phrase **sprechen über** means *to talk about* or *to discuss.* When you use **sprechen über,** the noun phrase or pronoun following the preposition **über** must be in the accusative case.

   Wir sprechen über **den Deutschlehrer.**—Wir sprechen auch über **ihn.**

When you want to find out what topic people are talking about, use **worüber** to begin your sentence.

   Worüber sprecht ihr?—Wir sprechen über **den Film.**

Mehr Grammatikübungen, S. 299, Ü. 7

Übungsheft, S. 117, Ü. 19–20

Grammatikheft, S. 89, Ü. 15–16

---

23 **Grammatik im Kontext**

a. Lesen/Sprechen Vervollständige das Gespräch von Nicole mit ihren Freunden und wähle dabei eins der gegebenen Wörter aus.

REPORTER Was für Bücher ____1____ du am liebsten? (lese, sprecht, liest)

NICOLE Tja, normalerweise ____2____ ich Fantasybücher oder Krimis. (lesen, lest, lese)

REPORTER ____3____ du auch die Zeitung? (Liest, Sprechen, Lesen)

NICOLE Na klar! Aber Zeitschriften ____4____ ich lieber. (lese, sprecht, spricht)

REPORTER Und worüber ____5____ du mit deinen Freunden? (spreche, lesen, sprichst)

NICOLE Hm…normalerweise ____6____ wir über Klamotten oder über einen Film, aber manchmal auch über Politik oder die Umwelt. (sprechen, lesen, spreche)

REPORTER Und ihr zwei, was ____7____ ihr am liebsten? (sprechen, lest, lesen)

MONIKA Ganz einfach! Wir beide haben Gruselromane furchtbar gern. Wir ____8____ sie immer! (sprechen, liest, lesen)

b. Schreiben Kopiere die Sätze und schreib die richtigen Formen von **lesen** oder **sprechen** in die Lücken.

1. Der Thomas ═══ über den Krimi. – Und worüber ═══ du? spricht; sprichst

2. Ich weiß, dass du gern Zeitschriften ═══. Mein Bruder ═══ sie auch gern. liest; liest

3. Meine Mutter ═══ Deutsch, und mein Vater ═══ Spanisch. Was ═══ du? spricht; spricht; sprichst

4. Ich ═══ hier, dass unser Präsident gern Krimis ═══. lese; liest

24 **In einer Buchhandlung**

Sprechen You are the salesperson in a bookstore and your partner is a customer. Using the cues below, ask questions to find out what type of book to recommend. Make your recommendation, then switch roles.

> Was für Bücher …? Was für Interessen …?
>
> Worüber sprechen Sie …? Lieblingsbuch?

25 **Was machst du heute Abend?**

Sprechen Diskutiere mit deinem Partner, was du heute machen willst! Was macht dein Partner? Wenn du Ideen brauchst, verwende die vier Anzeigen auf Seite 290.

So sagt man das!

Talking about what you did in your free time

To find out what someone did last weekend you ask:

Was hast du am Wochenende gemacht?

The response might be:

Am Samstag war ich im Herbert-Grönemeyer-Konzert. Und ich war am Sonntag zu Hause. Am Nachmittag habe ich gelesen, und am Abend habe ich mit Thomas und Martin das Video „Der mit dem Wolf tanzt" gesehen. Danach haben wir über den Film gesprochen.

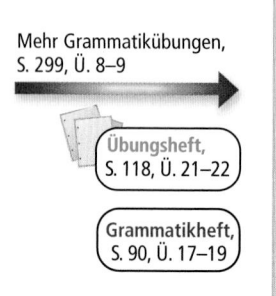

Mehr Grammatikübungen, S. 299, Ü. 8–9

Übungsheft, S. 118, Ü. 21–22

Grammatikheft, S. 90, Ü. 17–19

26 **Logisch oder unlogisch?** Script on p. 275G

Zuhören Schüler erzählen, was sie letztes Wochenende gemacht haben. Sind die Antworten zu jedem Gespräch logisch oder unlogisch? 1. logisch 2. unlogisch 3. unlogisch 4. logisch 5. unlogisch
CD 10 Tr. 15

27 **Sätze bauen**
Answers will vary. Possible answers:
Ich war zu Hause und habe das Video *Hamlet* gesehen.

Sprechen/Schreiben Was hast du letztes Wochenende gemacht? Wie viele Sätze kannst du bauen?

| Ich war … | im Konzert
im Kino
zu Hause
bei meinen Freunden | und ich/wir habe(n) … | den Film …
die Gruppe …
das Buch …
das Video …
über (die Hausaufgaben) | gemacht
gesprochen
gesehen
gelesen |

28 **Hat es Spaß gemacht?** *Was it fun?*

Schreiben/Sprechen Was hast du am Wochenende gemacht? Mach eine Liste! Dann frag deinen Partner, was er gemacht hat! Danach tauscht ihr die Rollen aus!

29 **Für mein Notizbuch**

Schreiben Beschreib in deinem Notizbuch dein Lieblingswochenende! Wo warst du? Was hast du alles gemacht? Was hast du gesehen, gelesen oder gekauft?

30  Von der Schule zum Beruf

Schreiben You have become the manager of a movie theater. As part of your duties, you send the local newspaper a listing of movies that will be shown at your theater in the coming week. In order to attract moviegoers, you have decided to describe the movies briefly, along with giving any other details useful to the viewer.

AUSSPRACHE

Richtig aussprechen / Richtig lesen CD 10 Trs. 16–18

A. To review the following sounds, say the sentences below after your teacher or after the recording. CD 10 Tr. 16

1. The long and short **o**: The long **o** sounds similar to the long *o* in the English word *toe*. When the letter **o** is followed by two or more consonants (except when followed directly by **h**), it is pronounced as a short vowel, as in the English word *on*.
   Wo wohnt die Monika? In der Bodenstraße?
   Mein Onkel Otto kommt oft in der Woche zu Besuch.

2. The long and short **u**: The long **u** is pronounced much like the vowel sound in the English word *do*. However, when the letter **u** is followed by two or more consonants, it is pronounced as a short vowel like the *u* in the English word *put*.
   Ich find die Musik super. Du auch, Uwe?
   Ulrike mag die Gruppe „Untergrund" furchtbar gern. Und ihr?

3. The letter combination **ch**: When the consonant combination **ch** follows the vowels **e, i, ä, ö,** and **ü**, it is pronounced like the *h* in the English word *huge*. Following the vowels **a, o,** and **u**, it is pronounced further back in the throat.
   So ein Pech! Ich möchte gern mit Michaela ins Kino, aber ich kann nicht.
   Jochen geht doch lieber nach Hause und liest ein Buch und macht Hausaufgaben.

Richtig schreiben / Diktat

B. Write down the sentences that you hear. CD 10 Tr. 17 CD 10 Tr. 18 (with pauses)
Script on p. 275H

Was sagen die Kritiker?

Lesestrategie **Watch for false cognates** Remember to look for cognates as individual words as well as in compound words to help you determine meanings. Occasionally, you will encounter false cognates (words that look alike in both languages but have totally different meanings). Context clues can sometimes help you recognize false cognates. (A good example of a false cognate is the English word *gift*. You will find the same word in German (**Gift**), but you would hardly want to give it to someone you care about: it means *poison*!)

1. Write the English equivalents for the following cognates:
   a. **exklusiv**   exclusive
   b. **militärisch**   military
   c. **desillusioniert**   disillusioned
   d. **Radio-Meteorologe**   meteorologist
   e. **zynisch**   cynical

2. You already know a couple of false cognates. Try to determine (from the choices given) what the false cognates in the following sentences might mean.

   a. Wenn du wissen möchtest, welche Themen in Deutschland **aktuell** sind, musst du eine deutsche Zeitung lesen.
   1. *actual*   2. *out of date*
   3. *current*

   b. Wer einmal diesen Krimi zu lesen begonnen hat, kann **die Lektüre** nicht unterbrechen, weil das Buch so spannend ist.
   1. *lecture* 2. *lesson* 3. *reading*

3. a. With a partner, write down all the cognates you can find in these selections. Include those cognates that are in compound words, even if part of the compound is not a cognate.

Groundhog Day
(UND TÄGLICH GRÜSST DAS MURMELTIER)

Phil ist ein Ekel. Doch eines Tages wird der zynische und oberflächliche Radio-Meteorologe verzaubert: Die Zeit steht still. Wieder und wieder muß er den von ihm so gehaßten GROUNDHOG DAY, ein Frühlingsfest, in den skurrilsten und wahnwitzigsten Situationen erleben, bis aus ihm endlich ein liebenswerter Mensch geworden ist.

GROUNDHOG DAY von Harold Ramis, mit Bill Murray, Andie MacDowell, Chris Elliott, Stephen Tobolowski u.a.
Englische Originalfassung   103 Min.

MEDIEN NEWS

- Jo Backe hat sich die Arbeit zu seinem neuen Video leicht gemacht. Er engagierte den Kamaramann von Regisseur Bertoli und überließ ihm die ganze Arbeit.

- Harry McBride macht seinen deutschen Fans ein ganz großes Kompliment: Sie unterstützen ihn mehr als die Irländer!

John Grisham
Die Firma

Etwas ist faul an der exklusiven Kanzlei, bei der Mitch McDeere arbeitet. Der hochbegabte junge Anwalt wird auf Schritt und Tritt beschattet, er ist umgeben von tödlichen Gefahren. Als er dann noch vom FBI unter Druck gesetzt wird, erweist sich der Traumjob endgültig als Alptraum…

Roman. 544 Seiten.
Gebunden mit Schutzumschlag.

Nr. 02001 6
Club-Preis   **17.45**

K-PUR TAGESTIP

The Romeos

Nicht aus dem New Yorker Italo-Distrikt, sondern aus Bremen und Oldenburg kommen die Mitglieder der Band. Weniger banal die Musik der Jungs. Bei einer großen Plattenfirma unter Vertrag gelten sie als vielleicht eines der größten Talente der deutschen Popszene.

29.4. Marquee, 21:00 Uhr

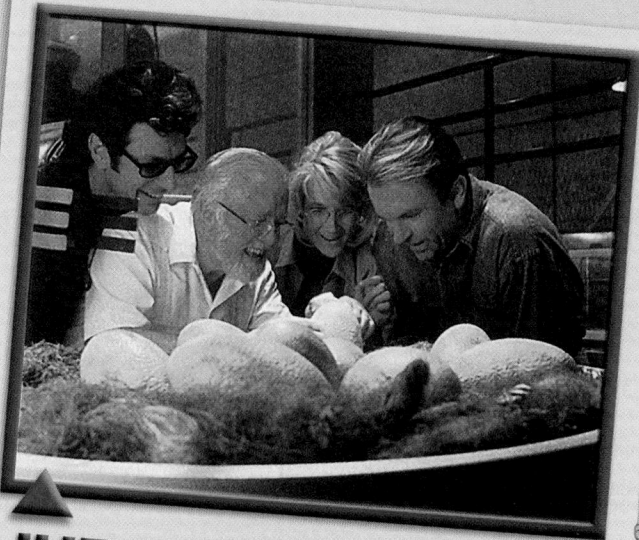

JURASSIC PARK™

Spielbergs spektakulärster Film seit Jahren. Gen-Ingenieure haben für einen Freizeitpark Dinosaurier zum Leben erweckt. Eines Tages wird aus dem Spiel mit der Vorzeit blutiger Ernst...

Mit: Sam Neill, Laura Dern, Richard Attenborough
Regie: Stephen Spielberg
Verleih: UIP

FREITAG, 9. JULI 1993

DER MIT DEM WOLF TANZT

USA 1990, 180 Minuten, CinemaScope, Dolby-Stereo;
Ein Film von Kevin Costner.
Mit Kevin Costner, Mary MacDowell und anderen.

𝒱om Bürgerkrieg und militärischem Drill desillusioniert, läßt sich Lieutenant John J. Dunbar, ein Offizier der Nordstaaten im äußersten Westen, am Rand der Zivilisation, im Sioux-Gebiet nieder. In einem abgelegenen Blockhaus

bezieht er Stellung und knüpft behutsamen Kontakt mit den Indianern, deren Kultur er langsam zu begreifen und zu schätzen lernt. Er nimmt ihre Sitten und Gebräuche an, und sie beginnen, ihn als einer der ihren zu akzeptieren. Sie geben ihm den Namen "der mit dem Wolf tanzt". Doch die scheinbare Idylle findet ein jähes Ende, als eine Einheit der US-Kavallerie anrückt, die den verschollen geglaubten Dunbar aufspüren soll.

b. List any false cognates that you find. Were you able to figure out the meaning? If so, how?

4. culture/entertainment; in the entertainment section of a newspaper or magazine

4. What do these reading selections have in common? Where do you think you might find them?

5. How many of the selections mention something or someone you are familiar with? How does being familiar with the topics help you read the selections? Answers will vary.

6. a. Hire Bertoli's camera operator and let him do the work
b. in Germany
c. The Romeos

6. Read the articles and see if you can figure out

a. what Jo Backe did to ease the difficulties in making his new video

b. where Harry McBride thinks he has more fans: in Germany or in Ireland

c. the name of the group regarded as one of the most talented on the German pop scene

7. a. original version; das Murmeltier
b. civil war
c. dream job/nightmare

7. In groups of two to four, read the articles about the movies and the book, then answer these questions. Be prepared to share your findings with the class.

a. What do you think **Originalfassung** means at the end of the article on *Groundhog Day*? What is the German word for groundhog?

b. What do you think the word **Bürgerkrieg** means in the article on *Der mit dem Wolf tanzt?*

c. What do you think **Traumjob** means in the article on *Die Firma*? Knowing the story, what do you think then that **Alptraum** means?

8. Your German pen pal wants to know what movies or books you have seen or read recently and would recommend. Write a two or three sentence response in German, recommending one movie or book that you like.

Übungsheft, S. 119, Ü. 23

Mehr Grammatikübungen

internet

go.
hrw
.com

ADRESSE: go.hrw.com
KENNWORT:
WK3 BADEN-WUERTTEMBERG-10

Answers

Erste Stufe

Objectives Expressing likes and dislikes

1 Welche Musik hast du gern, und welche Musik haben deine Freunde gern? Schreib die folgenden Sätze ab und schreib dabei die richtige Form von **mögen** in die Lücken. (S. 282)

1. Was für Musik _____ du gern? — Ich _____ Country gern.   magst; mag

2. Und was _____ dein Bruder? — Er _____ nur Rock.   mag; mag

3. Deine Eltern, was _____ sie? — Sie _____ klassische Musik.   mögen; mögen

4. Die Sabine, was _____ sie gern? — Sie _____ alles gern.   mag; mag

5. Was _____ ihr gern, Eva und Bob? — Wir _____ gern Jazz.   mögt; mögen

2 Welche Filme magst du nicht und welche Filme haben deine Freunde nicht gern? Schreib die folgenden Sätze und Fragen ab und schreib dabei die richtige Form von **mögen, kein** und die Art des Filmes in die Lücken. (S. 282)

BEISPIEL   (Sciencefictionfilme)   Wir _____ _____ _____ .
                Wir <u>mögen</u> <u>keine</u> <u>Sciencefictionfilme</u>.

1. (Horrorfilme)   Also, ich _____ .   mag keine Horrorfilme

2. (Western)   Und du _____ , nicht?   magst keine Western

3. (Kriegsfilme)   Wir _____ .   mögen keine Kriegsfilme

4. (Krimis)   Ihr _____ , nicht wahr?   mögt keine Krimis

5. (Liebesfilme)   Meine Freunde _____ .   mögen keine Liebesfilme

6. (Komödien)   Der Martin _____ .   mag keine Komödien

---

3 Ihr sprecht über Filme. Wer mag welchen Film am liebsten? Schreib Sätze und gebrauche dabei alle Wörter, wie im Beispiel. **(S. 282)**

BEISPIEL **wir / Horrorfilme / am liebsten / mögen**
Wir mögen Horrorfilme am liebsten.

1. ich / Western / am liebsten / mögen   Ich mag Western am liebsten.
2. Paul / Kriegsfilme / am liebsten / mögen   Paul mag Kriegsfilme am liebsten.
3. die Schüler / Krimis / am liebsten / mögen   Die Schüler mögen Krimis am liebsten.
4. ihr / Actionfilme / am liebsten / mögen   Ihr mögt Actionfilme am liebsten.
5. Mary / Komödien / am liebsten / mögen   Mary mag Komödien am liebsten.
6. die Kinder / Videos / am liebsten / mögen   Die Kinder mögen Videos am liebsten.

4 Für das englische Verb „*to know*" gibt es im Deutschen zwei Verben, **wissen,** *to know a fact* und **kennen,** *to know a person* oder *to be familiar with something*. Schreib die folgenden Sätze ab und schreib dabei die richtige Verbform in die Lücken. **(S. 284)**

1. Sag mal, _____ du, wann der Film „Das Boot" beginnt, und _____ du den Schauspieler? Ich möchte _____ , wie er heißt.   weißt; kennst   wissen
2. Ich _____ den Schauspieler nicht, aber ich _____ , wo er wohnt.   kenne; weiß
3. Martin und Sandra, _____ ihr, wo wir diese Rockgruppe hören können, und _____ ihr den Sänger der Gruppe? ___ ihr, wie er heißt?   wisst; kennt   Wisst
4. Sag, _____ der Martin dieses Lied, und _____ er, wo ich eine CD mit diesem Lied finden kann? — Du, ich frag meinen Bruder. Der _____ das!   kennt; weiß   weiß

Zweite Stufe   Objective **Expressing preferences and favorites**

5 Was hast du und was haben deine Freunde gern, lieber, am liebsten? Schreib die folgenden Sätze ab und schreib dabei die richtige Form von **sehen** und **gern, lieber,** oder **am liebsten** in die Lücken. **(S. 285)**

1. Ich _____ _____ Krimis, aber Kriegsfilme _____ ich _____ ; und _____ _____ ich Abenteuerfilme.   sehe gern; sehe ... lieber   am liebsten; sehe
2. Was _____ du _____ ? Krimis? Oder _____ du Komödien _____ ? Was _____ du denn _____ ?   siehst ... gern; siehst ... lieber   siehst ... am liebsten
3. Wir _____ Western _____ , aber der Martin _____ Krimis _____ . Ja, aber er _____ doch Komödien _____ .   sehen ... gern; sieht ... lieber   sieht ... am liebsten

6 Du sagst deinen Freunden, was du gern tust und was du am liebsten tust. Schreib Sätze mit einem Verb und „gern" und „am liebsten" und suche dir dabei passende Wortpaare aus dem Kasten aus. (S. 285)

BEISPIEL   **gern trinken [Kaffee / Cola]**
             <u>Ich trinke gern Kaffee, aber Cola trinke ich am liebsten.</u>

Cola	Deutsch	Fußball	Hamburger
Hemden			Krimis
		Horrorfilme	Jazz
Mathe			meine Tante
Limo	meine Oma		
Pizza			
Pullis		Rock	
			Volleyball

1. gern haben
2. gern sehen
3. gern hören
4. gern spielen
5. gern besuchen
6. gern anziehen
7. gern essen
8. gern trinken

"GUTEN TAG"

$\sqrt{a}$ q^3

1. Ich habe Mathe gern, aber Deutsch hab ich am liebsten.

2. Ich sehe Horrorfilme gern, aber Actionfilme sehe ich am liebsten.

3. Ich höre Rock gern, aber Jazz höre ich am liebsten.

4. Ich spiele Fußball gern, aber Volleyball spiele ich am liebsten.

5. Ich besuche meine Tante gern, aber meine Oma besuche ich am liebsten.

6. Ich ziehe gern Hemden an, aber Pullis ziehe ich am liebsten an.

7. Ich esse gern Hamburger, aber Pizza esse ich am liebsten.

8. Ich trinke gern Cola, aber Limo trinke ich am liebsten.

Dritte Stufe

Objectives Telling about what you do or did in your free time

7 Worüber lesen und sprechen deine Freunde in ihrer Freizeit? Schreib die folgenden Sätze ab und schreib dabei die richtige Verbform von **lesen** oder **sprechen** in die Lücken. (S. 291)

1. Also, ich _____ gern Romane. Und du, was _____ du gern?   lese; liest

2. Mein Bruder _____ gern Krimis, und mein Vater _____ sie auch gern.   liest; liest

3. Was _____ ihr denn gern, Sandra und Michael? _____ ihr auch Krimis?   lest; Lest

4. Worüber _____ ihr in der Deutschklasse? _____ ihr über Mode?   sprecht; Sprecht

5. Ich weiß, worüber du gern _____ . Politik. Ich _____ auch über Politik.   sprichst; spreche

6. Wir _____ gern über die Umwelt. _____ ihr auch über die Umwelt?   sprechen; Sprecht

8 Du sagst jemandem, was du in deiner Freizeit gemacht hast. Schreib die folgenden Sätze ab und schreib dabei ein passendes Partizip *(past participle)* in die Lücken. (**S. 292**)

1. Am Samstag _____ ich in einem super Konzert.   war
2. Am Sonntag habe ich einen prima Film _____ .   gesehen
3. Am Nachmittag habe ich ein Buch _____ .   gelesen
4. Danach habe ich mit meiner Freundin über Mode _____ .   gesprochen
5. Ja, und was hast du am Wochenende _____ ?   gemacht

9 Schreib, was du mit deinen Freunden letztes Wochenende gemacht hast. (**S. 292**)

BEISPIEL   Wir _____ im Kino, und wir _____ einen _____ _____ .
Wir <u>waren</u> im Kino und wir <u>haben</u> einen <u>Western</u> <u>gesehen</u>.

Actionfilm	Gruselroman	Politik
Hausaufgaben	Pandabär	Video

1. Ich _____ im Kino, und ich _____ einen _____ _____ .   war; habe; Actionfilm; gesehen
2. Peter _____ zu Hause. Er __ einen _____ _____ .   war; hat; Gruselroman; gelesen
3. Ich _____ mit Mark im Zoo. Wir _____ einen _____ _____ .   war; haben; Pandabär; gesehen
4. Wir _____ in der Schule und _____ über _____ _____ .   waren; haben; Politik; gesprochen
5. Ich _____ am Abend zu Hause und _____ _____ _____ .   war; habe; Hausaufgaben; gemacht
6. Ann _____ zu Hause, und sie _____ mit Monika ein _____ _____ .   war; hat; Video; gesehen

Anwendung

internet

ADRESSE: go.hrw.com
KENNWORT:
WK3 BADEN-WUERTTEMBERG-10

The CD-ROM Tutor offers guided recording and writing activities to accompany the **Anwendung.** These activities are designed to practice students' oral and written communication skills and to review material from each chapter.

1 You will hear four students talk about how they spend their free time. Make a chart like the one here and fill in the information for each student as you listen.

Script on p. 275H

CD 10
Tr. 19

2 Now interview two classmates, asking them where they go and what they do in their free time, and when and how often they do these things. Continue the above chart, filling in the appropriate information for your classmates. Then switch roles.

Name	wohin?	was?	wann?	wie oft?
1	Petra/ins Kino/einen Film sehen/abends/jeden Montag; Rudi/ins Konzert/Musik hören/sonntags/zweimal im Monat; Max/zu Otto/CDs hören/nachmittags/einmal in der Woche; Renate/zu Hause/Bücher lesen/abends/manchmal			
2				

3 Read the text of this movie ad and answer the following questions about it:

1. What is the name of the main character in the ad?

2. What is this character's profession?

3. Where does he settle?

4. What change is taking place in this man?

5. Is he being accepted by the Indians?

6. Why doesn't he stay with the Indians?

4 Working in pairs, write a review of a movie expressing your feelings about a specific movie that you have seen.

5 Write down the nine different kinds of films you learned on page 281, each on a separate slip of paper, and put them into a container. The class will divide up into two teams. Partners from each team will take turns drawing a movie type and acting that movie type out in front of the class. The two teams will take turns guessing what kind of movie it is. Answers will vary.

1. Lieutenant John J. Dunbar
2. **Offizier** (officer)
3. **im Sioux-Gebiet** (in Sioux territory)
4. **er begreift ihre Kultur** (he understands their culture)
5. **ja; sie akzeptieren ihn und geben ihm den Namen „Der mit dem Wolf tanzt."** (yes, they accept him and give him the name ...)
6. **die US-Kavallerie kommt** (the US cavalry is looking for him)

FREITAG, 9. JULI 1993

DER MIT DEM WOLF TANZT

USA 1990, 180 Minuten, CinemaScope, Dolby-Stereo;
Ein Film von Kevin Costner.
Mit Kevin Costner, Mary MacDowell und anderen.

Vom Bürgerkrieg und militärischem Drill desillusioniert , läßt sich Lieutenant John J. Dunbar, ein Offizier der Nordstaaten im äußersten Westen, am Rand der Zivilisation, im Sioux-Gebiet nieder. In einem abgelegenen Blockhaus bezieht er Stellung und knüpft behutsamen Kontakt mit den Indianern, deren Kultur er langsam zu begreifen und zu schützen lernt. Er nimmt ihre Sitten und Gebräuche an, und sie beginnen, ihn als einer der ihren zu akzeptieren. Sie geben ihm den Namen "der mit dem Wolf tanzt". Doch die scheinbare Idylle findet ein jähes Ende, als eine Einheit der US-Kavallerie anrückt, die den verschollen geglaubten Dunbar aufspüren soll.

6 Zum Schreiben

You are a famous talent agent with a hot new German rock group to publicize during the "Summer Rock" festival in your town. Write a publicity blurb for a local newspaper and design an eye-catching poster to publicize the group.

> **Schreibtipp** Using a topic sentence at the beginning of a paragraph lets the reader know what to expect in the rest of the paragraph. A topic sentence also helps focus your writing. The summary sentence at the end of the paragraph helps pull all the details in the paragraph together.

Prewriting

The rock group needs a name and a type of rock music. **Brainstorm** with your group/class for rock group names and other necessary information for your advertisement. Your publicity blurb should include (but not be limited to) the group's song titles, the places they have played, the movies they have made, and the stars with whom they made the movies. Also include any future movie plans, book rights the group may own, and the date and location the group will be featured at the festival. Include the movie houses/video rental stores which will feature their movies during the coming festival to help convince your audience that this is the group to see. Include this information on your poster.

Writing

Using this information, begin your writing with a **topic sentence** that will introduce your subject and focus your writing, then develop your publicity, and end with a **summarizing sentence.**

Revising

- After writing your paragraph, set it aside for a day and then reread it.
- Assess its strengths and weaknesses.
- Make changes, then read your paper aloud, listening for confusing statements and awkward wording. Have a peer evaluate strengths and weaknesses of your paragraph.
- Revise, proofread, and submit your paragraph to your teacher.

7 Rollenspiel

Get together with two or three other classmates and create an original scene for one of the following situations. Role-play your scene in front of the class.

a. You are in front of a movie theater and want to see a film. Talk about the different movies and say which ones you like, dislike, and strongly dislike, and which one(s) you have already seen. Then decide together which movie you will see.

b. You and your friends are at the video store to rent (**ausleihen**) a movie. Talk about what kinds of movies each of you likes and decide on a movie everyone will enjoy. Don't forget to mention any movies you have already seen.

Can you express likes and dislikes using mögen? (p. 282)

1 How would you ask a friend what type of movie he or she likes? How might he or she respond?   Was für Filme magst du? Ich mag …

2 How would you say that
   a. Thomas likes horror films a lot   a. Thomas mag Horrorfilme sehr gern.
   b. Julia really doesn't like rock music at all   b. Julia mag Rockmusik überhaupt nicht.
   c. Sabine and Nicole like fantasy films   c. Sabine und Nicole mögen Fantasyfilme.
   d. We don't care for romance movies   d. Wir mögen Liebesfilme nicht.

Can you express familiarity using kennen? (p. 284)

3 How would a friend ask if you are familiar with
   a. the movie *Air Force One*
   b. the singer Ina Deter   a. Kennst du den Film *Air Force One*?
   c. the group R.E.M.   b. Kennst du die Sängerin Ina Deter?
   d. the film star Clint Eastwood   c. Kennst du die Gruppe R.E.M.?
   d. Kennst du den Filmstar Clint Eastwood?

4 How would you respond to each of your friend's questions?
   Answers will vary.

Can you express preferences and favorites? (p. 285)

5 How would you tell a friend what type of movies you like to see, what type of movies you prefer, and what type of movies you like best of all?
   Ich sehe gern …   ich sehe lieber …   am liebsten sehe ich …

6 How would you say that   a. Martin mag Abenteuerfilme, aber Liebesfilme sieht er lieber.
   a. Martin likes adventure movies, but prefers movies about romance.
   b. Sandra likes horror films best of all.   b. Sandra sieht am liebsten Horrorfilme.
   c. Sabine doesn't like to read magazines and prefers to read newspapers.
      c. Sabine liest nicht gern Zeitschriften; sie liest lieber Zeitungen.

Can you talk about what you did in your free time? (p. 292)

7 How would you ask a friend what he or she did on the weekend? How would your friend respond if he or she   7. Was hast du am Wochenende gemacht?
      a. Am Samstagabend habe ich den Film *The*
   a. saw the movie *The Lost World* on Saturday evening   *Lost World* gesehen.
      b. Am Sonntag habe ich eine Zeitung gelesen.
   b. read a newspaper on Sunday   c. Am Freitagabend habe ich das Video *Michael*
   c. saw the movie *Michael Collins* on video on Friday evening   *Collins* gesehen.
   d. read the book *The Horse Whisperer* on Saturday
   e. was at the Billy Joel concert on Friday evening
   f. bought clothes and talked about fashion with his or her friends
   d. Am Samstag habe ich das Buch *The Horse Whisperer* gelesen.
   e. Am Freitagabend war ich im Billy Joel-Konzert.
   f. Ich habe Klamotten gekauft und mit meinen Freunden über Mode gesprochen.

8 Write a short paragraph describing what you saw, read, or talked about with your friends last weekend.   Answers will vary.

Erste Stufe

Expressing likes and dislikes

verbringen	to spend (time)	der Science-fictionfilm, -e	science fiction movie
mögen	to like, care for	der Western, -	western (movie)
Was für Filme magst du gern?	What kind of movies do you like?	Was für Musik hörst du gern?	What kind of music do you like?
der Film, -e	movie	klassische Musik	classical music
der Abenteuerfilm, -e	adventure movie	die Oper, -n	opera
der Actionfilm, -e	action movie		
der Horrorfilm, -e	horror movie		
die Komödie, -n	comedy		
der Kriegsfilm, -e	war movie		
der Krimi, -s	detective movie, crime drama		
der Liebesfilm, -e	romance		

Expressing familiarity

kennen	to know, be familiar or acquainted with
der Schauspieler, -	actor
die Schauspielerin, -nen	actress

der Sänger, -	singer (male)
die Sängerin, -nen	singer (female)
die Gruppe, -n	group
das Lied, -er	song

Degrees of liking and disliking

besonders gern	especially like
furchtbar gern	like a lot
gar nicht gern	not like at all
überhaupt nicht gern	strongly dislike
sehr gern	very much

Zweite Stufe

Expressing preferences and favorites

lieber (mögen)	prefer	spannend	exciting, thrilling	schmalzig	corny, mushy
am liebsten (mögen)	like most of all	sensationell	sensational	traurig	sad
sehen	to see	lustig	funny	doof	dumb
er/sie sieht	he/she sees	zu grausam	too cruel		
phantasievoll	imaginative	dumm	dumb, stupid		
		brutal	brutal, violent		

Dritte Stufe

 p. 275X

Talking about what you did in your free time

Was hast du am Wochenende gemacht?	What did you do on the weekend?	der Fantasyroman, -e	fantasy novel	er/sie spricht über …	he/she talks about …
lesen	to read	der Sciencefiction-roman, -e	science fiction novel	Worüber habt ihr gesprochen?	What did you (pl) talk about?
er/sie liest	he/she reads	der Krimi, -s	detective novel	die Politik	politics
Was hast du gelesen?	What did you read?	das Sachbuch, ̈-er	nonfiction book	die Mode	fashion
der Roman, -e	novel	die Zeitung, -en	newspaper	die Umwelt	environment
der Gruselroman, -e	horror novel	die Zeitschrift, -en	magazine	Was hast du gesehen?	What did you see?
der Liebesroman -e	love story	das Hobbybuch, ̈-er	hobby book	das Video, -s	video (cassette)
		sprechen über	to talk about		

Kapitel 11: Der Geburtstag
Chapter Overview

Los geht's! pp. 306–308	Geschenke aussuchen, p. 306

	FUNCTIONS	GRAMMAR	VOCABULARY	RE-ENTRY
Erste Stufe pp. 309–312	• Using the telephone in Germany, p. 310		• Telephone vocabulary, p. 309	• Numbers 0–20, p. 311 **(Vorschau, Kap. 1)** • Time and days of the week, p. 311 **(Kap. 6)**
Zweite Stufe pp. 313–316	• Inviting someone to a party and accepting or declining, p. 313 • Talking about birthdays and expressing good wishes, p. 314		• Dates of the year, p. 314 • Holidays and holiday greetings, p. 315	• Numbers, p. 314 **(Vorschau, Kap. 1, and Kap. 3)** • Months, p. 314 **(Kap. 7)**
Dritte Stufe pp. 317–321	• Discussing gift ideas, p. 318	• Introduction to the dative case, p. 319 • Word order in dative case, p. 320	• Gift ideas, p. 317	• Accusative case, p. 319 **(Kap. 5)** • Family members, p. 320 **(Kap. 3)**

Aussprache p. 321	Review the sounds **r** and **er**, review the vowel **a**, review the diphthongs **eu**, **äu**, and **au**: Audio CD 11, Track 14	**Diktat:** Audio CD 11, Tracks 15–16

Zum Lesen pp. 322–323	Billig einkaufen gehen	**Reading Strategy** Reading for comprehension

Mehr Grammatik-übungen	**pp. 324–327** **Erste Stufe,** p. 324	**Zweite Stufe,** p. 325	**Dritte Stufe,** pp. 325–327

Review pp. 328–331	**Anwendung,** pp. 328–329 **Zum Schreiben:** Following logical order (Writing a dialogue)	**Kann ich's wirklich?,** p. 330	**Wortschatz,** p. 331

CULTURE

- **Ein wenig Landeskunde:** Using the telephone, p. 309
- **Ein wenig Landeskunde:** Saints' days, p. 315
- Good luck symbols, p. 315
- **Was schenkst du zum Geburtstag?** p. 316
- German gift ideas, p. 317
- Magazine article, p. 318

Kapitel 11: Der Geburtstag
Chapter Resources

Lesson Planning

 **One-Stop Planner**

Lesson Planner with Substitute Teacher Lesson Plans, pp. 52–56, 75

Student Make-Up Assignments
- Make-Up Assignment Copying Masters, Chapter 11

Listening and Speaking

TPR Storytelling Book, pp. 41–44

Listening Activities
- Student Response Forms for Listening Activities, pp. 83–86
- Additional Listening Activities 11-1 to 11-6, pp. 87–90
- Additional Listening Activities (song), p. 86
- Scripts and Answers, pp. 162–169

Video Guide
- Teaching Suggestions, pp. 70–71
- Activity Masters, pp. 72–74
- Scripts and Answers, pp. 105–107, 116

Activities for Communication
- Communicative Activities, pp. 61–66
- Realia and Teaching Suggestions, pp. 114–117
- Situation Cards, pp. 143–144

Reading and Writing

Reading Strategies and Skills Handbook, Chapter 11

Lies mit mir! 1, Chapter 11

Übungsheft, pp. 121–132

Grammar

Grammatikheft, pp. 91–99

Grammar Tutor for Students of German, Chapter 11

Assessment

Testing Program
- Grammar and Vocabulary Quizzes, **Stufe** Quizzes, and Chapter Test, pp. 275–292
- Score Sheet, Scripts and Answers, pp. 293–300

Alternative Assessment Guide
- Portfolio Assessment, p. 28
- Performance Assessment, p. 42
- CD-ROM Assessment, p. 56

Student Make-Up Assignments
- Alternative Quizzes, Chapter 11

Online Activities
- Interaktive Spiele
- Internet Aktivitäten

Video Program
- Videocassette 4
- Videocassette 5 (captioned version)

Audio Compact Discs
- Textbook Listening Activities, CD 11, Tracks 1–18
- Additional Listening Activities, CD 11, Tracks 25–30
- Assessment Items, CD 11, Tracks 19–24

Interactive CD-ROM Tutor, Disc 3

Teaching Transparencies
- Situations 11-1 to 11-2
- Vocabulary 11-A to 11-B
- **Los geht's!**
- **Mehr Grammatikübungen** Answers
- **Grammatikheft** Answers

One-Stop Planner CD-ROM

Use the **One-Stop Planner CD-ROM with Test Generator** to aid in lesson planning and pacing.

For each chapter, the **One-Stop Planner** includes:
- Editable lesson plans with direct links to teaching resources
- Printable worksheets from resource books
- Direct launches to the HRW Internet activities
- Video and audio segments
- Test Generator
- Clip Art for vocabulary items

Kapitel 11: Der Geburtstag
Projects ....

Darf ich mich vorstellen?

In this activity students will design a personality collage describing themselves. The project could be called **Darf ich mich vorstellen?** *The project will help review previously learned vocabulary such as descriptive adjectives, leisure activities, hobbies, and dates. It should be written in and presented in German.*

MATERIALS

✂ **Students may need**
- personal pictures
- old magazines
- posterboard
- 5 × 7 index cards
- scissors
- glue
- markers

SITUATION

Have students imagine that a group of German-speaking students is visiting their school and attending a meeting of the German Club. As sponsor of the German Club, you have asked each of them to introduce themselves to the visitors by giving a presentation. They should describe themselves and tell a little about their interests and hobbies. When they make their presentations, you might want to designate some of the students to be the visitors and ask them to listen closely and find the American students whose interests and hobbies are most compatible with their own.

SUGGESTED ITEMS TO INCLUDE IN PRESENTATION

- pictures: from their childhood, of friends and family, of their home
- birth certificate or something showing important dates
- items that represent something they have done that is important to them (Examples: report cards, medals, certificates)
- pictures of themselves doing activities they are interested in (Examples: ice skating, playing football) or of others doing those activities
- objects or pictures of objects or pets that mean a lot to them (Examples: a car, a certain book, the family dog)

SUGGESTED SEQUENCE

1. Announce the title and content of the project and brainstorm with students to help develop ideas about what could be used as part of the collage. (See above list.)

2. After students have had the opportunity to gather materials, ask them to arrange and begin to paste the pictures they have chosen on the poster board.

3. Ask students to provide a brief label for each picture (Example: **Mein erster Geburtstag, 15. Mai 1987**)

4. After students make the labels, ask them to write a short description of each picture or illustration on a 5 × 7 index card.

5. After projects are completed, have students present their collages, show the pictures, and talk about themselves. **Note:** At this point students are encouraged not to read from the cards, but rather to present each illustration spontaneously.

6. Once each student has made his or her presentation, you may want to display the projects in the classroom until the end of the school year.

GRADING THE PROJECT

Suggested point distribution (**total = 100 points**)
Written work (labels and description) 50
Poster (originality and appearance).....25
Oral presentation................................25

Games ....

Schnell, das richtige Wort!

This game is especially good for helping visual learners acquire new vocabulary words.

Preparation Make a set of 4 × 6 inch index cards based on the **Wortschatz** for this chapter. On one side of each card write a German vocabulary item, and write its English equivalent on the other side. Make at least ten cards for every pair of students.

Procedure Have students sit facing each other in pairs. Give each pair an equal number of index cards. Then give students five to ten minutes to learn or review the vocabulary. One partner gives a word in English and the other responds with the German equivalent. After the review period, have the pairs go through their set of words in a specific amount of time. (Example: ten words in twenty seconds.) You can also vary this game by using German synonyms rather than English equivalents.

STANDARDS: 1.3

Storytelling

Mini-Geschichte

*This story accompanies Teaching Transparency 11-2. The **Mini-Geschichte** can be told and retold in different formats, acted out, written down, and read aloud to give students additional opportunities to practice all four skills.*

Omas Geburtstag

„Tag, Ute! Oma hat nächste Woche Geburtstag. Was schenkst du ihr?" „Grüß dich, Thomas! Ich schenke ihr wahrscheinlich einen Blumenstrauß. Oma mag auch gern Pralinen und Parfüm. Hast du eine Geschenkidee?" Thomas sagt: „Tja, vielleicht möchte sie ins Kino gehen. Und danach können wir sie ins Café Freizeit einladen." „Aber, Thomas, unsere Oma will doch nicht ins Kino gehen! Sie ist viel zu alt!" „Unsinn (*nonsense*)! Unsere Oma geht gern ins Kino. Sie findet Abenteuerfilme toll. Sie geht auch gern ins Café Freizeit."

Traditions

Die Mönche von Maulbronn

So alt wie die Maultaschen sind, so alt ist auch der Streit um die richtige Füllung. Jede schwäbische Hausfrau hat ihr eigenes Rezept, von dem sie steif und fest behauptet, ihres sei das einzige und richtige.

Im Gegensatz zur Füllung ist der Ursprung der Maultasche selber fast völlig geklärt. Sie sind eigentlich eine richtige Fastenspeise, wenn auch keine richtig fromme.

Denn: Als die Mönche des Klosters Maulbronn in den Hungerjahren des Dreißigjährigen Krieges (1618–1648, eine Reihe von Kriegen, ausgelöst durch konfessionelle Gegensätze nach der Reformation) durch einen glücklichen Zufall ausgerechnet in der Fastenzeit in den Besitz eines großes Stückes Fleisches gerieten, wollten sie diese seltene Gabe natürlich unter keinen Umständen (wie die Schwaben sagen) „umkommen" lassen. Listig mischten sie das Fleisch mit allerlei Grünzeug und versteckten es in Teigfladen – den Maultaschen.

Rezept

Maultaschen

Für 6 bis 8 Portionen

Zutaten

g=Gramm, EL=Esslöffel

400g	Mehl
4	Eier
250g	gemischtes Hackfleisch
200g	Kalbsbratwurstbrät
250g	frischer Spinat
1	Bund Petersilie
2	Eier
1	Eiweiß
	Salz, Pfeffer, Muskat, Fleischbrühe

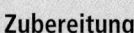

Zubereitung

Aus Mehl, Eiern, etwas Salz und etwa 8 EL Wasser einen Nudelteig kneten und dünn ausrollen. Das Hackfleisch mit dem Brät mischen. Spinat in Salzwasser blanchieren, mit einer Schaumkelle *(slotted spoon or ladle)* aus dem Topf nehmen, abtropfen lassen und grob hacken. Die Petersilie auch hacken und untermischen. Den Spinat unter die Hackmasse kneten, die Eier zugeben, mit Salz, Pfeffer und Muskat abschmecken.
Den Teig in knapp 15 cm große Quadrate schneiden, auf jedes Quadrat so viel wie möglich von der Füllung geben. Die Teigränder mit Eiweiß bepinseln. Die Quadrate über Eck zusammenklappen, die Ränder fest andrücken. Die Maultaschen in der heißen Fleischbrühe etwa 10 Minuten ziehen, aber nicht kochen lassen.

Kapitel 11: Der Geburtstag
Technology

Video

Videocassette 4, 5 (captioned version)
See Video Guide, pages 69–74

Los geht's! • Geschenke aussuchen

Nicole calls Sabine to invite her to the birthday party she is organizing for Martin. The girls go shopping and discuss what they should give Martin for his birthday. Nicole decides to get him a T-shirt and also finds a birthday card that she likes.

Fortsetzung

Sabine and Nicole talk about Thomas's birthday. When Nicole looks it up in her calendar, she discovers that Martin's birthday is not next Saturday, but in August! She doesn't know what to do because she has already planned his party for Saturday!

Landeskunde
Was schenkst du zum Geburtstag?

People of various ages and from different cities talk about what they give friends and relatives for their birthdays.

Videoclips

- **Milka**® (chocolates)
- **Merci**® (chocolates)
- **Brockhaus**® (encyclopedias)

Interactive CD-ROM Tutor

The **Interactive CD-ROM Tutor** contains videos, interactive games, and activities that provide students an opportunity to practice and review the material covered in Chapter 11.

Activity	Activity Type	Pupil's Edition Reference
1. Wortschatz	Was kommt dann?	p. 309
2. So sagt man das!	Wozu gehört's?	pp. 313, 314
3. Wortschatz	Was ist richtig?	pp. 314, 315
4. Wortschatz	Merkspiel	p. 317
5. Grammatik	Was fehlt?	p. 319
6. Grammatik	Was kommt dann?	p. 320
Landeskunde	Was schenkst du zum Geburtstag?	p. 316
	Was ist richtig?	
Zum Sprechen	*Guided recording*	pp. 328–329
Zum Schreiben	*Guided writing*	pp. 328–329

Teacher Management System
Logging In

Logging in to the *Komm mit!* TMS is easy. Upon launching the program, simply type "admin" in the password area of the log-in screen and press RETURN. Log on to **www.hrw.com/CDROMTUTOR** for a detailed explanation of the Teacher Management System.

To preview all resources available for this chapter, use the **One-Stop Planner CD-ROM**, Disc 3.

Internet Connection

ADRESSE: go.hrw.com
KENNWORT: WK3 BADEN-WUERTTEMBERG-11

*Have students explore the **go.hrw.com** Web site for many online resources covering all chapters. All Chapter 11 resources are available under the keyword **WK3 Baden-Wuerttemberg-11**. Interactive games practice the material and provide students with immediate feedback. You will also find a printable worksheet that provides Internet activities that lead to a comprehensive online research project.*

Interaktive Spiele

You can use the interactive activities in this chapter

- to practice grammar, vocabulary, and chapter functions
- as homework
- as an assessment option
- as a self-test
- to prepare for the Chapter Test

Internet Aktivitäten

Students will glean specific information from the Web sites of German online gift shops. They will also visit an online flower shop.

- To prepare students for the **Arbeitsblatt,** you might ask them to review the **Wortschatz** on p. 317 and the **Grammatik** on p. 319.
- After completing the **Arbeitsblatt,** have students create a birthday card for Mike in Activity B or the little sister in Activity C. The card should have a drawing or picture on the front page and a verse on the second or third page.

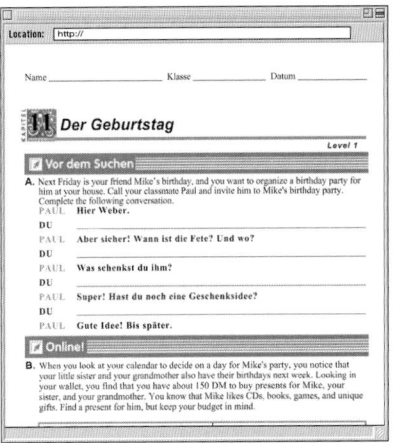

Webprojekt

Have students imagine that their grandfather has a birthday and that they want to give him a gift basket filled with specialty foods. Have students do a Web search for an online shop that sells **Feinkost.** Students should report on the items they would choose and on the prices of these items. Encourage students to exchange useful Web sites with their classmates. Have students document their sources by referencing the names and URLs of all the sites they consulted.

Kapitel 11: Der Geburtstag
Textbook Listening Activities Scripts

Erste Stufe

7　　p. 310

1. — Rezeption hier. Einen Moment bitte!… Wie kann ich Ihnen behilflich sein?

— Ja. Entschuldigung … ich bin in 319, und mein Fernseher scheint nicht richtig zu funktionieren.

— Das tut mir Leid. Ich werde sofort jemanden schicken. Sie sagten 319, nicht?

— Ja, stimmt. Wird das lange dauern?

— Nein, in den nächsten fünf Minuten kommt jemand bei Ihnen vorbei.

2. — … Ja, was meinst du? Was sollen wir denn alles mitnehmen?

— Vielleicht zwei Flaschen Limo, einige Wurstbrote und etwas Obst. Hast du darauf Hunger?

— Klar doch! Prima! Ich bringe die Decke.

— Also, bis später. Wir treffen uns so gegen 12 Uhr unter der alten Eiche.

— Ich freu mich schon. Tschüs!

3. — Ja, guten Tag! Ich möchte mich gern nach Ihren Reparaturpreisen erkundigen.

— Ja, das kommt natürlich auf die Reparatur an. Könnten Sie etwas genauer sein?

— Ja. Mein Fahrrad braucht unbedingt neue Speichen. Die jetzigen sind schon alle ziemlich verrostet.

— Ja, das ist einfach und dauert auch nicht lange.

— Ja. Könnte ich mein Rad morgen Vormittag abliefern?

— Sicher, und ihr Name bitte?

— Klaus … Klaus Schmidt.

4. — Guten Morgen! Unser Motto hier bei Autowinkel: Wir kommen schnell und fahren sicher. Womit kann ich Ihnen heute helfen?

— Ich möchte gern ein Taxi für 8 Uhr 30 bestellen.

— Und ihre Adresse, bitte?

— Holtenauerstraße 54.

— Und wohin darf es sein?

— Ja, zum Hauptbahnhof. Mein Zug fährt um 9 Uhr 12 ab. Kann man das schaffen?

— Aber natürlich, mein Herr … das Taxi ist schon auf dem Weg. Vielen Dank und nicht vergessen: Wir kommen schnell und fahren sicher. Auf Wiederhören!

12　　p. 312

— Hier bei Hansen.

— Ja, Ludwig Ottman hier. Könnt ich bitte mit Ditmar oder Ursel sprechen?

— Das tut mir Leid, aber die sind zur Zeit nicht zu Hause.

— Mensch, schade! Ich wollte dem Ditmar …, na macht nichts. Darf ich bitte eine Nachricht hinterlassen?

— Natürlich. Einen Moment, ich hole nur schnell einen Bleistift und das Gesprächs-Notizbuch … ja, so hier hab ich's. Ja bitte? Wie war noch gleich ihr Name?

— Ludwig … Ludwig Ottman. Ich bin ein Verwandter der Familie. Bin gerade umgezogen, am besten gebe ich gleich meine neue Adresse und Telefonnummer, ja? Also, ich wohne jetzt in der Neubaustraße 9, das ist in Marktbreit.

— Und was ist die Postleitzahl bitte?

— Na, da muss ich schnell mal nachdenken. Ach ja … Die ist 97413.

— Und die Telefonnummer?

— Ja, die Vorwahl hier ist, hm … 09331 und dann anschließend 1367.

— Das hab ich nicht ganz mitgekriegt. Könnten Sie das noch mal wiederholen?

— Also 09331 und dann 1367. Alles klar?

— Ja … danke.

— Ich rufe an, weil wir meinem Vater, also dem Onkel Michael, eine Geburtstagsparty geben, und dazu wollen wir ja den Ditmar und die Ursel einladen. Die Feier soll am 2. Juni stattfinden, in Nürnberg, wo er ja auch wohnt. Die Feier beginnt so um 17 Uhr im Hotel Löwe. Das ist leicht zu finden auf der Straßenkarte. Die Adresse ist Rosenthal 8. Alles mitbekommen?

— Ja, ich glaube schon. Danke.

— OK, dann noch vielen Dank. Also auf Wiederhören!

— Auf Wiederhören!

Zweite Stufe

19　　p. 314

ANJA　　Du, sag mal Bernd, wann hast du eigentlich Geburtstag?

BERND　　Wieso willst du das wissen?

ANJA　　Nur so, für mein Adressbuch.

BERND　　Mein Geburtstag ist am 22. Mai.

ANJA　　Und wie steht's mit dir, Maja?

MAJA　　Mein Geburtstag war im Winter, am 4. Februar.

ANJA　　Ach ja, stimmt. Wir sind ja alle an dem Tag ins Kino gegangen. Das war toll! He, du Benjamin! Wann ist denn dein Geburtstag? Ich kann mich daran nicht mehr erinnern.

BENJAMIN　　Im Frühling, so wie du.

ANJA　　Wann war das noch gleich?

BENJAMIN　　Am 28. März.

ANJA　　Katrin, dein Geburtstag war aber noch nicht. Das weiß ich bestimmt. Ist der nicht bald?

KATRIN   Ja, am 14. August. Ich ruf dich dann an und lad dich zu meiner Fete ein.

ANJA   Mensch, toll! Danke … Und den Mario muss ich auch noch fragen, denn seinen Geburtstag weiß ich auch nicht. Mario, wann hast du eigentlich Geburtstag?

MARIO   Im Winter, also am 29. Dezember … gleich nach Weihnachten.

ANJA   Prima, jetzt habe ich alle Geburtstage, die mir in meinem Buch fehlten.

21   p. 315

1. — Ich muss noch schnell zum Schreibwarengeschäft.

— Wieso denn?

— Ich habe ganz vergessen, für Sonntag eine Karte zu kaufen. Was machst du denn für deine Mutter?

— Ich mache immer selber eine Karte, und dann mache ich meistens Frühstück und kaufe ihr einen schönen Blumenstrauß.

— Gute Idee!

2. — Die haben hier ja eine große Auswahl an Karten.

— Prima! Ich will meiner Freundin und ihrer Familie eine Karte kaufen.

— Und wofür ist die Karte?

— Na, die feiern doch Chanukka im Dezember.

— Stimmt ja …

3. — Dieses Jahr haben wir viel Besuch über die Feiertage. Dann muss ich meiner Mutter immer viel helfen. Und wie ist das bei euch?

— Genauso, nur fahren wir dieses Jahr zu meiner Oma nach Bayern. Da trifft sich dann unsere ganze Familie. Da bleiben wir drei Tage, bis zum 27. Dezember.

4. — Der Rolf wird sich bestimmt freuen. Die CD wollte er immer schon haben.

— Die fand ich im Musikhaus Schlemmer. Hoffentlich kauft ihm nicht noch einer das gleiche Geschenk!

— Ach, bestimmt nicht. Du, wie alt wird Rolf eigentlich?

— Hm … 16.

Dritte Stufe

25   p. 318

— Interkulturelle Beratung und Information … Kaldenkirchen am Apparat. Wie kann ich Ihnen behilflich sein?

— Ja, also ich hoffe, dass Sie mir aushelfen können. Diesen Sommer besuche ich verschiedene Länder in Europa, und während meines Aufenthaltes übernachte ich bei Gastfamilien. Nur weiß ich eben nicht so ganz, was ich denn jeder Familie mitbringen soll … was da so üblich ist, wissen Sie das?

— Natürlich. Dazu sind wir da. Sagen sie mir doch, wohin ihre Reisen gehen, und ich kann Ihnen ja einige Ratschläge geben.

— Also, meine erste Gastfamilie besuche ich in Frankreich.

— Für Frankreich gibt es eine Anzahl von akzeptablen Geschenken, aber am sichersten sind Getränke.

— Oh, das ist eine gute Idee. Und anschließend besuche ich eine Familie in Italien. Was schlagen Sie dafür vor?

— Italien. Ja, es ist eigentlich allgemein bekannt, dass die Italiener gerne Blumen bei einem Besuch erhalten.

— Wirklich?

— Ja, aber sie müssen frisch sein.

— Klar, das kann ich machen … und dann reise ich auch für einen kurzen Aufenthalt nach Spanien. Was soll ich der Familie mitbringen?

— Ja, das kommt ganz darauf an. Ich würde da ebenfalls Getränke vorschlagen.

— Interessant. Zum Schluss besuche ich dann noch Österreich. Darauf freue ich mich schon sehr. Was kann ich der Gastfamilie mitbringen?

— Das ist einfach. Die Österreicher lieben Schokolade. Also, eine Schachtel Pralinen wäre da ein sehr passendes Geschenk.

— Ja, vielen Dank für Ihre Hilfe! Ich habe mir das alles aufgeschrieben.

— Kann ich Ihnen sonst noch behilflich sein?

— Nein, vielen Dank! Auf Wiederhören!

— Auf Wiederhören!

26   p. 319

Also, du kannst deinem Opa eine CD kaufen. Der hört doch gern klassische Musik, nicht wahr? Und deiner Oma kannst du ein gutes Buch schenken—die Verkäuferin da kann uns dabei helfen, ein passendes Buch zu finden. Deinem Vater—hmmm—vielleicht einen Kalender? So was finden wir bestimmt in einer Buchhandlung. Anschließend im Kaufhof kaufen wir deiner Mutter ein schönes Parfüm. So was mag meine Mutter immer gern als Geschenk. Sollen wir deinem Freund Otto ein Poster von den „Toten Hosen" geben? Das findet er bestimmt stark. Und der Martina können wir Schmuck schenken. Schmuck ist immer ein gutes Geschenk. Na, gehen wir los!

AUSSPRACHE, p. 321

Diktat, p. 321

You will hear about different items Gerd and Frauke would like to buy their mother for her birthday.

Gerd und Frauke wollen heute im Kaufhof einkaufen gehen, denn ihre Mutter hat am Donnerstag Geburtstag. Sie sehen verschiedene Sachen. Gerd findet eine schicke Armbanduhr, aber die kostet zu viel. Frauke sieht eine flotte Bluse, leider weiß sie die Größe von ihrer Mutter nicht genau. Schließlich finden sie eine Kette, die ihrer Mutter bestimmt gefallen wird. Schmuck passt ja zu vielen Sachen. Und zum Schluss gehen Gerd und Frauke noch beim Blumengeschäft vorbei und kaufen einen frischen Blumenstrauß.

For **Anwendung,** Activities 1 and 3 scripts, see *Listening Activities,* p. 165.

Kapitel 11: Der Geburtstag
Suggested Lesson Plans 50-Minute Schedule

Day 1

CHAPTER OPENER 10 min.
- Background Information, ATE, p. 303M
- Thinking Critically, ATE, p. 303M
- Culture Note, ATE, p. 303M

LOS GEHT'S! 20 min.
- Preteaching Vocabulary, ATE, p. 303N
- Have students read **Los geht's!**, pp. 306–307
- Teaching Suggestions, Video Guide, p. 70
- Culture Note, ATE, p. 303N
- Show **Los geht's!** Video

ERSTE STUFE
Wortschatz, p. 309 15 min.
- Present **Wortschatz**, p. 309
- Teaching Transparency 11-A
- Do Activity 6, p. 309

Wrap-Up 5 min.
- Students respond to questions about how to use the telephone in Germany

Homework Options
Pupil's Edition, p. 308, Comprehension Activities
Grammatikheft, pp. 91–92, Acts. 1–2
Übungsheft, p. 121, Act. 1

Day 2

ERSTE STUFE
Quick Review 10 min.
- Check homework, Grammatikheft, pp. 91–92, Acts. 1–2

So sagt man das!, p. 310 20 min.
- Presenting **So sagt man das!**, ATE, p. 303O
- Play Audio CD for Activity 7, p. 310
- Do Activity 8, p. 310
- Do Activities 9 and 10, p. 311

Ein wenig Landeskunde, p. 311 15 min.
- Present **Ein wenig Landeskunde**, p. 311
- Do Activity 11, p. 312
- Play Audio CD for Activity 12, p. 312
- Do Activities 13 and 14, p. 312

Wrap-Up 5 min.
- Students respond to questions about making telephone calls in Germany

Homework Options
Grammatikheft, p. 92, Act. 3
Übungsheft, pp. 122–125, Acts. 2–8; p. 132, Act. 24

Day 3

ERSTE STUFE
Quick Review 15 min.
- Check homework, Übungsheft, pp. 122–125, Acts. 2–8; p. 132, Act. 24

Quiz Review 15 min
- Do **Mehr Grammatikübungen, Erste Stufe**
- Do Communicative Activity 11-1, pp. 61–62

Quiz 20 min.
- Quiz 11-1A or 11-1B

Homework Options
Activities for Communication, Realia 11-1, p. 114, have students circle the name days of students in the class or of people they know

Day 4

ZWEITE STUFE
Quick Review 15 min.
- Return and review Quiz 11-1
- Check homework, Realia 11-1, p. 114
- Bell Work, ATE, p. 303Q

So sagt man das!, p. 313 15 min.
- Presenting **So sagt man das!**, ATE, p. 303Q
- Do Activities 15, 16, and 17, p. 313

So sagt man das!/ Wortschatz, p. 314 15 min.
- Presenting **So sagt man das!**, ATE, p. 303Q
- Presenting **Wortschatz**, ATE, p. 303Q
- Do Activity 18, p. 314
- Play Audio CD for Activity 19, p. 314

Wrap-Up 5 min.
- Students respond to questions about birthdays and name days

Homework Options
Pupil's Edition, p. 314, Act. 20
Grammatikheft, pp. 93–95, Acts. 4–8

Day 5

ZWEITE STUFE
Quick Review 10 min.
- Check homework, Grammatikheft, pp. 93–95, Acts. 4–8

Ein wenig Landeskunde/ Wortschatz, p. 315 35 min.
- Present **Ein wenig Landeskunde**, p. 315
- Presenting **Wortschatz**, ATE, p. 303R
- Teaching Transparency 11-1
- Play Audio CD for Activity 21, p. 315
- Do Activity 22, p. 315
- Present **Minigeschichte, Zweite Stufe**, TPR Storytelling Book, p. 42

Wrap-Up 5 min.
- Students respond to questions about good luck symbols and greetings for holidays

Homework Options
Übungsheft, pp. 126–127, Acts. 9–15

Day 6

ZWEITE STUFE
Quick Review 10 min.
- Check homework, Übungsheft, pp. 126–127, Acts. 9–15

Quiz Review 20 min.
- Do **Mehr Grammatikübungen, Zweite Stufe**
- Do Activities 2 and 3, Interactive CD-ROM
- **Interaktive Spiele**, see ATE, p. 303F

Quiz 20 min.
- Quiz 11-2A or 11-2B

Homework Options
Activities for Communication, p. 115, Realia 11-2, have students circle the cognates

One-Stop Planner CD-ROM

For alternative lesson plans by chapter section, to create your own customized plans, or to preview all resources available for this chapter, use the **One-Stop Planner CD-ROM**, Disc 3.

 For additional homework suggestions, see activities accompanied by this symbol throughout the chapter.

Day 7

ZWEITE STUFE

Quick Review 10 min.
- Return and review Quiz 11-2
- Check homework, Realia 11-2, p. 115

LANDESKUNDE 25 min.
- Pre-viewing Suggestion, Video Guide, p. 70
- Background Information, ATE, p. 303S
- Show **Landeskunde** Video
- Do Activities A and B, p. 316
  Do Activity 3, p. 72, Video Guide

DRITTE STUFE

Wortschatz, p. 317 10 min.
- Presenting **Wortschatz**, ATE, p. 303T
- Teaching Transparency 11-B
- Do Activity 23, p. 317

Wrap-Up 5 min.
- Students respond to questions about gifts to give on various occasions

Homework Options
Grammatikheft, p. 96, Act. 9
Übungsheft, p. 132, Act. 24

Day 8

DRITTE STUFE

Quick Review 10 min.
- Check homework, Grammatikheft, p. 96, Act. 9

So sagt man das!, p. 318 25 min.
- Presenting **So sagt man das!**, ATE, p. 303T
- Do Activity 24, p. 318
- Present **Geschenke**, p. 318
- Play Audio CD for Activity 25, p. 318
- Do Activities 16–18, pp. 128–129, Übungsheft

Grammatik, p. 319 10 min.
- Presenting **Grammatik**, ATE, p. 303T
- Teaching Transparency 11-2
- Play Audio CD for Activity 26, p. 319

Wrap-Up 5 min.
- Students answer questions about giving gifts to various people

Homework Options
Grammatikheft, pp. 96–98, Acts. 10–14

Day 9

DRITTE STUFE

Quick Review 10 min.
- Check homework, Grammatikheft, pp. 96–98, Acts. 10–14

Grammatik, p. 320 25 min.
- Presenting **Grammatik**, ATE, p. 303U
- Do Activities 27, 28, and 29, p. 320
- Do Activity 15, p. 99, Grammatikheft
- Present **Lerntrick**, p. 320
- Do Activity 30, p. 320
- Do Activity 31, p. 321

Aussprache, p. 321 10 min.
- Do **Richtig aussprechen/Richtig lesen**, p. 321
- Do **Richtig schreiben/Diktat**, p. 321

Wrap-Up 5 min.
- Students respond to questions about appropriate gifts for various people

Homework Options
Übungsheft, pp. 129–130, Acts. 19–22
Interactive CD-ROM, Acts. 4–6

Day 10

DRITTE STUFE

Quick Review 10 min.
- Check homework, Übungsheft, pp. 129–130, Acts. 19–22

Quiz Review 20 min.
- Do **Mehr Grammatikübungen, Dritte Stufe**
- Do Communicative Activity 11-3, pp. 65–66

Quiz 20 min.
- Quiz 11-3A or 11-3B

Homework Options
Pupil's Edition, p. 321, Acts. 32 and 33
Übungsheft, p. 131, Act. 23

Day 11

DRITTE STUFE

Quick Review 15 min.
- Return and review Quiz 11-3
- Check homework, Übungsheft, p. 131, Act. 23

ZUM LESEN 30 min.
- Background Information, ATE, p. 303V
- Present **Lesestrategie**, p. 322
- Do Activities 1–9, pp. 322–323

Wrap-Up 5 min.
- Students respond orally to **Kann ich's wirklich?** questions, p. 330

Homework Options
Pupil's Edition, p. 330, **Kann ich's wirklich?**
Internet Aktivitäten, see ATE, p. 303F

Day 12

ANWENDUNG

Quick Review 35 min.
- Check homework, p. 330, **Kann ich's wirklich?**
- Video Wrap-up, ATE, p. 303X
- Do **Anwendung** Activities, pp. 328–329

Chapter Review 15 min.
- Review chapter functions, vocabulary, and grammar; choose from **Mehr Grammatikübungen**, Grammar Tutor for Students of German, Activities for Communication, Listening Activities, Interactive CD-ROM Tutor, or **Interaktive Spiele**
- Review test format and provide sample test items for students

Homework Options
Study for Chapter Test

Assessment

Test, Chapter 11 45 min.
- Administer Chapter 11 Test. Select from Testing Program, Alternative Assessment Guide or Test Generator.

Kapitel 11: Der Geburtstag
Suggested Lesson Plans *90-Minute Schedule*

Block 1

CHAPTER OPENER 10 min.
- Background Information, ATE, p. 303M
- Thinking Critically, ATE, p. 303M
- Culture Note, ATE, p. 303M

LOS GEHT'S! 25 min.
- Preteaching Vocabulary, ATE, p. 303N
- Have students read **Los geht's!**
- Teaching Suggestions, Video Guide, p. 70
- Culture Note, ATE, p. 303N
- Show **Los geht's!** Video
- Do Comprehension Activities, p. 308

ERSTE STUFE
Wortschatz, p. 309 15 min.
- Present **Wortschatz**, p. 309
- Teaching Transparency 11-A
- Do Activity 6, p. 309

So sagt man das!, p. 310 20 min.
- Presenting **So sagt man das!**, ATE, p. 303O
- Play Audio CD for Activity 7, p. 310
- Do Activity 8, p. 310
- Do Activities 9 and 10, p. 311

Ein wenig Landeskunde, p. 311 15 min.
- Present **Ein wenig Landeskunde**, p. 311
- Do Activity 11, p. 312
- Play Audio CD for Activity 12, p. 312
- Do Activities 13 and 14, p. 312

Wrap-Up 5 min.
- Students respond to questions about how to use the telephone in Germany

Homework Options
Grammatikheft, pp. 91–92, Acts. 1–3
Übungsheft, pp. 121–125, Acts. 1–8; p. 132, Act. 24

Block 2

ERSTE STUFE
Quick Review 15 min.
- Check homework Übungsheft, pp. 121–125, Acts. 1–8; p. 132, Act. 24

Quiz Review 15 min
- Do **Mehr Grammatikübungen, Erste Stufe**
- Do Communicative Activity 11-1, pp. 61–62

Quiz 20 min.
- Quiz 11-1A or 11-1B

ZWEITE STUFE
So sagt man das!, p. 313 15 min.
- Presenting **So sagt man das!**, ATE, p. 303Q
- Do Activities 15, 16, and 17, p. 313

So sagt man das!/Wortschatz, p. 314 20 min.
- Presenting **So sagt man das!**, ATE, p. 303Q
- Presenting **Wortschatz**, ATE, p. 303Q
- Do Activity 18, p. 314
- Play Audio CD for Activity 19, p. 314

Wrap-Up 5 min.
- Students respond to questions about birthdays and name days

Homework Options
Pupil's Edition, p. 314, Act. 20
Grammatikheft, pp. 93–95, Acts. 4–8

Block 3

ZWEITE STUFE
Quick Review 15 min.
- Return and review Quiz 11-1
- Check homework, Grammatikheft, pp. 93–95, Acts. 4–8

Ein wenig Landeskunde/Wortschatz, p. 315 35 min.
- Present **Ein wenig Landeskunde**, p. 315
- Presenting **Wortschatz**, ATE, p. 303R
- Teaching Transparency 11-1
- Play Audio CD for Activity 21, p. 315
- Do Activity 22, p. 315
- Present **Minigeschichte, Zweite Stufe**, TPR Storytelling Book, p. 42

LANDESKUNDE 35 min.
- Pre-viewing Suggestion, Video Guide, p. 70
- Background Information, ATE, p. 303S
- Show **Landeskunde** Video
- Do Activity 3, p. 72, Video Guide
- Do Activities A and B, p. 316
- Do **Landeskunde** Activity, Interactive CD-ROM

Wrap-Up 5 min.
- Students respond to questions about good luck symbols and greetings for holidays

Homework Options
Übungsheft, pp. 126–127, Acts. 9–15
Activities for Communication, p. 115, Realia 11-2, have students circle the cognates

One-Stop Planner CD-ROM

For alternative lesson plans by chapter section, to create your own customized plans, or to preview all resources available for this chapter, use the **One-Stop Planner CD-ROM**, Disc 3.

For additional homework suggestions, see activities accompanied by this symbol throughout the chapter.

Block 4

ZWEITE STUFE

Quick Review 10 min.
- Check homework, Übungsheft, pp. 126–127, Acts. 9–15

Quiz Review 15 min.
- Do **Mehr Grammatikübungen, Zweite Stufe**
- Do Communicative Activity 11-2, pp. 63–64

Quiz 20 min.
- Quiz 11-2A or 11-2B

DRITTE STUFE

Wortschatz, p. 317 10 min.
- Presenting **Wortschatz**, p. 303T
- Teaching Transparency 11-B
- Do Activity 23, p. 317

So sagt man das!, p. 318 20 min.
- Presenting **So sagt man das!**, ATE, p. 303T
- Do Activity 24, p. 318
- Present **Geschenke**, p. 318
- Play Audio CD for Activity 25, p. 318
- Do Activity 10, p. 96, Grammatikheft

Grammatik, p. 319 10 min.
- Presenting **Grammatik**, ATE, p. 303T
- Teaching Transparency 11-2
- Play Audio CD for Activity 26, p. 319

Wrap-Up 5 min.
- Students respond to questions about gifts to give to various people

Homework Options
Grammatikheft, pp. 96–98, Acts. 9, 11–14
Übungsheft, pp. 128–130, Acts. 16–22

Block 5

DRITTE STUFE

Quick Review 15 min.
- Check homework, Grammatikheft, p. 96, Act. 9; pp. 97–98, Acts. 11–14

Grammatik, p. 320 25 min.
- Presenting **Grammatik**, ATE, p. 303U
- Do Activities 27, 28, and 29, p. 320
- Do Activity 15, p. 99, Grammatikheft
- Present **Lerntrick**, p. 320
- Do Activity 30, p. 320
- Do Activity 31, p. 321

Aussprache, p. 321 10 min.
- Do **Richtig aussprechen/Richtig lesen**, p. 321
- Do **Richtig schreiben/Diktat**, p. 321

Quiz Review 20 min.
- Do **Mehr Grammatikübungen, Dritte Stufe**
- Do Communicative Activity 11-3, pp. 65–66

Quiz 20 min.
- Quiz 11-3A or 11-3B

Homework Options
Pupil's Edition, p. 321, Acts. 32 and 33
Activities for Communication, pp. 143–144, prepare Situation 11-3
Interactive CD-ROM, Acts. 4–6

Block 6

DRITTE STUFE

Quick Review 10 min.
- Return and review Quiz 11-3
- Do Situation 11-3, pp. 143–144

ZUM LESEN 20 MIN.
- Background Information, ATE, p. 303V
- Present **Lesestrategie**, p. 322
- Do Activities 1–9, pp. 322–323

ANWENDUNG 25 min.
- Video Wrap-up, ATE, p. 303X
- Do **Anwendung** Activities, pp. 328–329

Project 30 min.
- Begin **Darf ich mich vorstellen?** Project, ATE, p. 303C

Wrap-Up 5 min.
- Students respond to questions about giving gifts for various occasions

Homework Options
Complete **Darf ich mich vorstellen?** Project
Internet Aktivitäten, see ATE, p. 303F

Block 7

ANWENDUNG

Quick Review 25 min.
- Students present projects

Chapter Review 20 min.
- Review chapter functions, vocabulary, and grammar; choose from **Mehr Grammatikübungen**, Grammar Tutor for Students of German, Activities for Communication, Listening Activities, Interactive CD-ROM Tutor, or **Interaktive Spiele**
- Review test format and provide sample test items for students

Test, Chapter 11 45 min.
- Administer Chapter 11 Test. Select from Testing Program, Alternative Assessment Guide or Test Generator.

Kapitel 11: Der Geburtstag
Teaching Suggestions, *pages 304–331*

One-Stop Planner CD-ROM

For resource information, see the **One-Stop Planner CD-ROM**, Disc 3.

PAGES 304–305

CHAPTER OPENER

Pacing Tips

In the **Erste Stufe** the function of 'using the telephone in Germany' occurs with telephone phrases and cultural information. In the **Zweite Stufe**, students practice 'inviting someone to a party and accepting or declining' and 'talking about birthdays and expressing good wishes.' Saints' days and good luck symbols are identified. The dative case is introduced in the **Dritte Stufe** alongside the function of 'discussing gift ideas.' You might spend more time teaching the **Dritte Stufe**, since it includes the dative case and is longer than the **Erste Stufe** or the **Zweite Stufe**. For Lesson Plans and timing suggestions, see pages 303I–303L.

Meeting the Standards
Communication
- Using the telephone in Germany, p. 310
- Inviting someone to a party and accepting or declining, p. 313
- Talking about birthdays and expressing good wishes, p. 314
- Discussing gift ideas, p. 318

Cultures
- **Ein wenig Landeskunde**, p. 311
- **Ein wenig Landeskunde**, p. 315
- **Landeskunde**, p. 316
- Background Information, p. 303M
- Culture Note, p. 303O
- Culture Note, p. 303P
- Background Information, p. 303S
- Background Information, p. 303V
- Culture Note, p. 303W

Connections
- Multicultural Connection, p. 303O
- Multicultural Connection, p. 303R
- Music Connection, p. 303T

Comparisons
- Culture Note, p. 303M
- Culture Note, p. 303N
- Language-to-Language, p. 303R
- Language-to-Language, p. 303T

Communities
- Career Path, p. 303P

Cultures and Communities

Background Information
Young people in German-speaking countries are very aware of birthdays, anniversaries, and other special occasions. They know this not only for immediate family members, but very often for extended family and close friends. Young people are usually expected to attend family celebrations. This is possible because, for the most part, families still live close to each other.

Thinking Critically
Drawing Inferences When German students shop for small gifts, the emphasis is on *small*. Ask students if they know the reason. (In general, German teenagers do not have part-time jobs to make extra money. The job market is so regulated that it is against the law to hire people who have not had training in the position they're about to enter.)

Connections and Comparisons

Culture Note
It is customary to send cards for special occasions in Germany, but not to the extent that it is in the United States. Children and young people are expected to sign birthday cards and letters sent to relatives.

Chapter Sequence

Los geht's! . . . . .p. 306
Erste Stufe . . . . .p. 309
Zweite Stufe . . . . .p. 313
Landeskunde . . . . .p. 316
Dritte Stufe . . . . .p. 317
Zum Lesen . . . . .p. 322
Mehr Grammatikübungen . . . . .p. 324
Anwendung . . . . .p. 328
Kann ich's wirklich? . . . . .p. 330
Wortschatz . . . . .p. 331

CHAPTER OPENER

LOS GEHT'S!

Teaching Resources
pp. 306–308

PRINT
- ▸ Lesson Planner, p. 52
- ▸ Video Guide, pp. 69–70, 72
- ▸ Übungsheft, p. 121

MEDIA
- ▸ One-Stop Planner
- ▸ Video Program
  Los geht's!
  Videocassette 4, 20:27–22:08
  Videocassette 5 (captioned version),
  1:03:04–1:04:45
  Fortsetzung
  Videocassette 4, 22:12–23:32
  Videocassette 5 (captioned version),
  1:04:46–1:05:37
- ▸ Audio Compact Discs, CD11, Trs. 1–2
- ▸ **Los geht's!** Transparencies

PAGES 306–307

Los geht's! Transparencies

Preteaching Vocabulary

Recognizing Cognates

Los geht's! contains several words that students will be able to recognize as cognates. Have students find these cognates, then have them guess what is happening in the story.

1. eine Fete organisieren
2. Kein Problem!, CD-Player
3. Eine Idee?, ein Buch
4. der Vers
5. im Sommer, im August

Fortsetzung

You may choose to continue with the **Fortsetzung** of *Geschenke aussuchen* now or wait  until later in the chapter. For a synopsis of the **Los geht's!** and **Fortsetzung** episodes, see p. 303E.

Advance Organizer

Ask students how they would divide the work of organizing a party in order to dispute the following

statement: **Eingeladen werden ist schön, aber einladen ist zu viel Arbeit.**

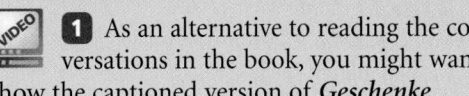
Connections and Comparisons

Thinking Critically

Analyzing After students have watched the video, ask them to look at the first frame of **Los geht's!**. What can students say about phone etiquette based on this frame? How do Germans identify themselves on the phone?

Culture Note

When Germans answer the phone, they normally state their family name. Children in the house usually give their first and last name. A caller usually identifies himself or herself immediately along with an appropriate greeting for the time of day.

PAGE 308

Using the Captioned Video

1 As an alternative to reading the conversations in the book, you might want to show the captioned version of *Geschenke aussuchen* available on Videocassette 5.

Comprehension Check

Group Work

2 Ask students to work with a partner as they read the conversations from pp. 306–307 aloud. Monitor students' pronunciation and intonation and make suggestions when needed. Next, put the five language functions on the board, elicit the appropriate words and phrases from students, and have them write them underneath.

A Slower Pace

3 Ask students to do this activity in writing as they refer to **Los geht's!** to complete the statements. When finished, call on several students to read their sentences.

Thinking Critically

4 Analyzing After students have completed this activity, ask them to read through it again and underline or make note of all the connectors, conjunctions, and adverbs that tie the summary together.

ERSTE STUFE

Teaching Resources
pp. 309–312

PRINT
- Lesson Planner, p. 53
- TPR Storytelling Book, pp. 41, 44
- Listening Activities, pp. 83, 87
- Activities for Communication, pp. 61–62, 114, 117, 143–144
- Grammatikheft, pp. 91–92
- Grammar Tutor for Students of German, Chapter 11
- Übungsheft, pp. 122–125
- Testing Program, pp. 275–278
- Alternative Assessment Guide, p. 42
- Student Make-Up Assignments, Chapter 11

MEDIA
- One-Stop Planner
- Audio Compact Discs, CD11, Trs. 3–4, 19, 25–26
- Teaching Transparencies
  Vocabulary 11-A
  Mehr Grammatikübungen Answers
  Grammatikheft Answers
- Interactive CD-ROM Tutor, Disc 3

> **PAGE 309**

Bell Work

Ask students to imagine that they are in a phone booth trying to call someone. In pairs, have them tell each other step-by-step how they make the call, up until the point when the person answers the phone. Tell students that at the end of the **Erste Stufe** they will be able to do this in German.

Thinking Critically

6 Observing Ask students if they can tell where this phone booth is located. (München, Kemptener-Allgäuer Str.)

(TPR) Total Physical Response
Demonstrate the expressions of the **Wortschatz** using a telephone as a prop. Act out each of the actions with the phone and model the appropriate expression. After going over the expressions several times, hand the phone to a student and give him or her instructions based on the expressions just introduced. (Example: **Jesse, nimm bitte den Hörer ab!** **Danke. Gib Robert das Telefon!**)

Cultures and Communities

Culture Note
Students have already learned that many Germans keep a savings account at their local post office. While the German Federal Post Office no longer administers the telephone network, it still offers services such as local and long distance calling, transferring of money into bank accounts, sending telegrams, and distribution of mail. Because of its satellite equipment, it also functions as a transmission facility for several television stations. Though the new telephone booths are gray and red, most postal vehicles and buildings are easily recognized by their trademark color: bright yellow.

Connections and Comparisons

Multicultural Connection
Have students ask students from other countries and students taking other foreign languages about the phone service in their country or the country (countries) they are studying. What is the trademark color? Have them describe public phone booths.

> **PAGE 310**

PRESENTING: So sagt man das!
Ask students to look back at **Los geht's!** and have them find some of the expressions introduced in **So sagt man das!** How were the expressions used in the context of **Los geht's!?** As an alternative to reading **Los geht's!**, you may want students to watch the captioned version of **Geschenke aussuchen.** See the following Captioned Video suggestion.

Using the Captioned Video

Divide the class into two groups. As you play the captioned version of the **Los geht's!** episode on Videocassette 5, ask one group to compile a list of the expressions used when calling someone and the other group a list of the expressions used when answering the telephone. Then, collect the papers and randomly read aloud expressions from the lists. Ask students to identify which function is modeled by each expression you read.

Connections and Comparisons

Thinking Critically

Comparing and Contrasting Ask students how they learned to say *goodbye* in Ch. 1. Why do they think **Auf Wiederhören!** is used instead of **Auf Wiedersehen!** when people talk on the phone?

Teaching Suggestion

Ask students to name some ways they might end a conversation in English. Put these expressions on the board. Then mention to students that Germans also have several different ways of ending a phone conversation depending on the situation (formal vs. informal) and time of day. However, you might want to point out that the expressions **Auf Wiederhören!** and **Wiederhören!** are acceptable regardless of formality or time of day.

PAGE 311

Portfolio

9 You might want to use this activity as an oral portfolio item for your students. See *Alternative Assessment Guide*, p. 28.

Speaking Assessment

10 You may choose to use this activity for speaking assessment. Have students come to your desk individually performing the role of the youth office worker while you play the person being called. For evaluation you may wish to use the following rubric.

Speaking Rubric	Points			
	4	3	2	1
Content (Complete – Incomplete)				
Comprehension (Total – Little)				
Comprehensibility (Comprehensible – Incomprehensible)				
Accuracy (Accurate – Seldom accurate)				
Fluency (Fluent – Not fluent)				

18–20: A   16–17: B   14–15: C   12–13: D   Under 12: F

 PAGE 312

Cultures and Communities

Culture Note

Germans have an advertisement similar to "Reach out and touch someone" to encourage the use of phones. In Germany, you will see stickers inside phone booths which say **Ruf doch mal an!** This can be translated loosely as *Go ahead and call!*

Career Path

Have students think of reasons a telephone operator or an employee of an American airline might need to know German. (Suggestions: Telephone operators sometimes have to connect with operators in German-speaking countries; flight attendants occasionally must communicate with passengers who speak German; American ticket agents and ground crew sometimes work in Germany, Austria, and Switzerland; ticket agents in America must occasionally communicate with German-speaking tourists.)

Reteaching: Using the telephone

Prepare a text in which you give step-by-step instructions on how to use the phone. Leave out key words and phrases. This can be done on a transparency, or you can provide a copy for each student. Also provide the students with a random-order list of the missing words and phrases. Ask students to read the directions and fill in the missing words from the list provided.

Teaching Suggestion

Hand every other student an index card that you have prepared ahead of time. Ask students with a card to find a partner who does not have one. Each pair of students will then make up a phone conversation that is based on the following situation. The student with the card is calling the other student around dinner time and is trying to sell him or her the item written on the card. The student answering the phone is annoyed by the timing of the call and is trying to get rid of the caller.

Assess

▸ Testing Program, pp. 275–278
  Quiz 11-1A, Quiz 11-1B
  Audio CD11, Tr. 19

▸ Student Make-Up Assignments
  Chapter 11, Alternative Quiz

▸ Alternative Assessment Guide, p. 42

ZWEITE STUFE

Teaching Resources
pp. 313–316

PRINT
- Lesson Planner, p. 54
- TPR Storytelling Book, pp. 42, 44
- Listening Activities, pp. 84, 88
- Activities for Communication, pp. 63–64, 115, 117, 143–144
- Grammatikheft, pp. 93–95
- Grammar Tutor for Students of German, Chapter 11
- Übungsheft, pp. 126–127
- Testing Program, pp. 279–282
- Alternative Assessment Guide, p. 42
- Student Make-Up Assignments, Chapter 11

MEDIA
- One-Stop Planner
- Audio Compact Discs, CD11, Trs. 5–6, 20, 27–28
- Teaching Transparencies
  Situation 11-1
  Mehr Grammatikübungen Answers
  Grammatikheft Answers
- Interactive CD-ROM Tutor, Disc 3

PAGE 313

Bell Work

Ask students how they are usually invited to a party. Do they get a written or oral invitation? What kind of information are they typically given when they are invited to a party?

PRESENTING: So sagt man das!

Brainstorm with students some different expressions they would use to invite someone to a party in German. Write students' ideas and suggestions on the board. Can they also think of ways to accept and decline? Compare the expressions in **So sagt man das!** to the expressions the students came up with.

Portfolio

16 You might want to use this activity as a written portfolio item for your students. See *Alternative Assessment Guide,* p. 28.

PAGE 314

Building on Previous Skills

Review the months by asking questions such as **In welchem Monat ist dein Geburtstag? Weihnachten? Muttertag? Schulanfang?**

PRESENTING: So sagt man das!

Write the question **Wann hast du Geburtstag?** on the board. (Make sure that all students understand the word **Geburtstag.**) Answer the question for yourself and write your answer on the board, writing out the number and all the endings: **Ich habe am dreiundzwanzigsten März Geburtstag.** Write two or three other birth dates on the board. Ask **Wann hast du Geburtstag?** and call on volunteers to answer. Then have students imagine that one or several of them have their birthday today. Walk around the room and say: **Ach, Carmelita! Du hast heute Geburtstag? Herzlichen Glückwunsch!** or **Alles Gute zum Geburtstag, Carmelita!** Now have students look at **So sagt man das!**

PRESENTING: Wortschatz

First introduce the ordinal numbers introduced in the **Wortschatz.** Then, holding up a calendar large enough for students to see, tell students about certain days using the expressions from **So sagt man das!** (Examples: **Heute ist Freitag, der erste Mai. Hier ist mein Geburtstag. Der ist am einundzwanzigsten Oktober.**)

Thinking Critically

Comparing and Contrasting Have students observe the endings of the ordinal numbers and the differences in spelling when compared to cardinal numbers.

Communication for All Students

Auditory Learners

19 After students have completed this activity, personalize it by using students' own birthdays. Using a list of students' birthdays, ask students to identify themselves when they hear their birthday called. (Example: **Wer hat am zweiten August Geburtstag?** Possible student replies: **Das ist mein Geburtstag.** or **Ich habe am zweiten August Geburtstag.**) Keep in mind that some students and their families may consider this type of information private.

Language-to-Language

Point out that dates are written as day/month/year in most of Europe and many other areas of the world.

PAGE 315

PRESENTING: Wortschatz

Teach the names of the holidays in the **Wortschatz** and tie the names in with your classroom calendar by pointing out the month and date of each of the holidays.

Language-to-Language

Your students may want to know that people in France and Spain also celebrate their Saint's Day (name-day). Show students a calendar that lists the **Namenstage**. If you don't have one, you might want to search for one on the Internet.

Thinking Critically

Analyzing Ask students if they can determine the meaning of the statement below the **Namenstage** in July. (**Gratulieren Sie mit Blumen!** = *Congratulate with flowers!*)

Multicultural Connection

Ask students from other countries to share holidays that might be different and unusual to American students. Students could get information about other countries' holidays from exchange students, other foreign language teachers, students taking other foreign languages, or the library.

Thinking Critically

22 **Comparing and Contrasting** Here students are introduced to some of the good luck symbols in German. Are they the same in the United States? Can students think of some symbols they know of for good luck? For those who do not believe in good luck symbols, Germans have a saying: **Jeder ist seines Glückes Schmied.**

Teaching Suggestion

22 Ask each student to make this card for the special occasion in the near future. You might want to provide students with colored paper, glue, scissors, and pens.

PAGE 316

LANDESKUNDE

Teaching Resources
p. 316

PRINT
▶ Video Guide, pp. 69–70, 72–73
▶ Übungsheft, p. 132

MEDIA
▶ One-Stop Planner
▶ Video Program
  Videocassette 4, 23:38–27:57
▶ Audio Compact Discs, CD11, Trs. 7–11
▶ Interactive CD-ROM Tutor, Chapter 11

Teaching Suggestions

• Ask students to name one gift they really liked that they have received as a birthday present from a friend or family member.

• You might want to introduce the following additional vocabulary to help students understand the four interviews:
  Ähnliches (colloq) *something similar*
  die Kleinigkeit *a little something*
  bemalt *painted*

• Begin **Landeskunde** by having students do the pre-reading activity. Then either play the Audio CD or have students watch the interviews on video. Divide the class into four groups and have each group work with one of the interviews and figure out 1. how that person celebrates birthdays, 2. to whom that person gives presents, and 3. what kinds of presents that person gives. Have each group share this information with the rest of the class, using as much German as possible. Do Questions 2, 3, and 4 together in class. Have students work in pairs on Question B, then discuss it together.

Thinking Critically

Synthesizing Books are popular gifts in German-speaking countries. However, the prices of hardbound and paperback books are generally much higher in Germany than they are in the United States. Can students think of a reason for this? (See the following Background Information.)

Teaching Suggestion

In pairs, have students ask each other for the date of their birthday. Then, have them ask for a friend's birthday.
Example:
Wann hast du Geburtstag?
Wann hat Tom Geburtstag?

Cultures and Communities

Background Information

In the United States publishers deal with a much larger market and can offer a lower price than can publishers in the smaller German market. In addition, the international market for English books is far greater than that for German books. Finally, the production cost of books is higher in Germany because of the higher cost of labor and raw materials.

Teaching Suggestion

A1 Ask students to review Eva's statement about giving **Gutscheine** (*gift certificates*). Why does she like giving them instead of gifts? Ask students to agree or disagree.

Reteaching: Expressing good wishes

Name several different holidays and occasions in German and ask students to give an appropriate expression of good wishes.

 Game

Play the game **Was beginnt mit …?** See p. 275C for the procedure.

Teacher to Teacher

Alice Harrill
Harding University High School
Charlotte, North Carolina

Alice concludes the chapter with a party.

"A great end-of-the-year activity is a birthday party for everyone. Each student writes a list of his/her interests and hobbies, and these are chosen at random by a secret pal. The secret pal must write his/her partner an invitation to the class party, and then bring a present which costs $5 or less."

Assess

▶ Testing Program, pp. 279–282
Quiz 11-2A, Quiz 11-2B
Audio CD11, Tr. 20

▶ Student Make-Up Assignments
Chapter 11, Alternative Quiz

▶ Alternative Assessment Guide, p. 42

DRITTE STUFE

Teaching Resources
pp. 317–321

PRINT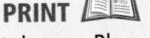
- Lesson Planner, p. 55
- TPR Storytelling Book, pp. 43, 44
- Listening Activities, pp. 84–85, 89–90
- Activities for Communication, pp. 65–66, 116, 117, 143–144
- Grammatikheft, pp. 96–99
- Grammar Tutor for Students of German, Chapter 11
- Übungsheft, pp. 128–130
- Testing Program, pp. 283–286
- Alternative Assessment Guide, p. 42
- Student Make-Up Assignments, Chapter 11

MEDIA
- One-Stop Planner
- Audio Compact Discs, CD11, Trs. 12–16, 21, 29–30
- Teaching Transparencies
  Situation 11-2
  Vocabulary 11-B
  Mehr Grammatikübungen Answers
  Grammatikheft Answers
- Interactive CD-ROM Tutor, Disc 3

▶ **PAGE 317**

Bell Work

In pairs, have students ask each other what kind of gifts they typically buy for a friend's birthday. Students should do this in German. For words they don't know, encourage them to give a description of the gift.

PRESENTING: Wortschatz

Have the items from the **Wortschatz** on hand, or bring pictures of the items you are not able to bring. Use the items to introduce the new words. Work especially with the pronunciation of the cognates in which the stress in the German word is on a different syllable than the stress in the English word. (For example, the stress in the following words falls on the second syllable: **Kalender, Pralinen, Parfüm.**)

▶ **PAGE 318**

PRESENTING: So sagt man das!

Ask students if they can think of a synonym for the verb **schenken** that they have learned in preceding units. (**geben**)

▶ **PAGE 319**

PRESENTING: Grammatik

The dative case Put several sentences on the board and ask students to come to the front and label the parts of the sentences. (Examples: **Michael gibt seinem Bruder das Geld. Tina schenkt ihrer Mutter einen Blumenstrauß.**) Help students recognize the indirect objects in the sentences. Remind students of the article changes that occur in the accusative, then let students discover the dative changes through further examples using nouns that clearly show a change. Examples:

Sein Vater hat Geburtstag.
Er schenkt seinem Vater ein Buch.
(sein → seinem)

Meine Kusine besucht uns jetzt.
Ich schenke meiner Kusine eine neue CD.
(meine → meiner)

Das Kind hat Geburtstag.
Ilse schenkt dem Kind ein Buch. (das → dem)

You might want to underline the articles in a different color to emphasize the difference between the nominative and the dative case.

Connections and Comparisons

Music Connection

Refer students to the text of the poem **Wem Gott will rechte Gunst erweisen,** Level 1 *Listening Activities,* p. 94, for additional reading. Ask them to look at the first stanza and find there the two examples of dative case use. Then translate the stanza for them and ask why the dative case was necessary in those instances. You may also want to play the song, Level 1 CD 12, Tr. 35.

Language-to-Language

In order to help explain the difference between the dative (indirect object) and accusative case (direct object) to your students, you may want to mention that the dative case is used in German if the student can add in English the prepositions *to* or *for* to the object. For example, the sentence "She gives me the book." could be rewritten as "She gives the book **to** me."

PAGE 320

PRESENTING: Grammatik

Dative case word order Prepare for this presentation by writing on a piece of paper five sentences that contain both direct and indirect objects. (Use either proper nouns or pronouns as indirect objects and nouns as direct objects.) Then cut up these sentences into their component parts (subject, verb, indirect object, direct object). Divide your class into groups of three or four, and provide each group with the mixed-up parts of all five sentences. The first group that can create five grammatically correct sentences from the mix wins the game.

Communication for All Students

A Slower Pace

27 To give students the opportunity to work individually on word order and dative case, assign this activity to be done in writing in class. Set a time limit, then ask several students to put their sentences on the board. Go over each sentence with the class and make necessary corrections.

For Additional Practice

28 Ask students to add a specific occasion to each statement. (Example: **Was schenkst du deinem Bruder zu Weihnachten?**)

30 Ask students who finish this activity early to change the occasion from birthday to another occasion and make another list.

PAGE 321

For Additional Practice

31 Ask students if they can think of at least two more souvenirs that would be typical for each of the five countries. Help students to name them in German.

Writing Assessment

32 This activity could be assigned as written homework. Remind students to use the conversational past in their letters to describe what they did on their trip.

You may wish to evaluate their homework using the following rubric.

Writing Rubric	Points			
	4	3	2	1
Content (Complete – Incomplete)				
Comprehensibility (Comprehensible – Seldom comprehensible)				
Accuracy (Accurate – Seldom accurate)				
Organization (Well-organized – Poorly organized)				
Effort (Excellent – Minimal)				

18–20: A   16–17: B   14–15: C   12–13: D   Under 12: F

PRESENTING: Aussprache

Have those students who feel comfortable doing so demonstrate the guttural **r** in class. Students have used all of these sounds a great deal by this time and should be able to find a number of words containing them. Divide students into pairs and assign each pair one of the three targeted sounds. Have them find as many words as they can that contain those sounds, then use those words in sentences. Their sentences should be in context and should, when read together, present either a coherent paragraph or a conversation. (Encourage humor and creativity.) Have as many pairs as time permits read their sentences to the class. After they have done the **Diktat,** have them exchange papers and make corrections.

Teaching Suggestion

Divide the class into two groups and have each group argue for and against **Geschenkegeben.** Each group should find several arguments (in German) to support its point of view. Divide the chalkboard in half and write down students' arguments.

Assess

▸ Testing Program, pp. 283–286
Quiz 11-3A, Quiz 11-3B
Audio CD11, Tr. 21

▸ Student Make-Up Assignments
Chapter 11, Alternative Quiz

▸ Alternative Assessment Guide, p. 42

ZUM LESEN

Teaching Resources
pp. 322–323

PRINT
▸ Lesson Planner, p. 56
▸ Übungsheft, p. 131
▸ Reading Strategies and Skills, Chapter 11
▸ Lies mit mir! 1, Chapter 11

MEDIA
▸ One-Stop Planner

Prereading
Building Context

Ask students if they have ever heard their grandparents or parents refer to the "good ol' days" when everything was cheaper and they could, for example, buy a soda for a nickel. What types of comparisons can students recall? Ask them to name a few.

Making Connections

Ask students how they choose to read a particular article or story when they pick up a magazine or newspaper. What makes them decide to read a certain text? Do they skim a newspaper for interesting headlines or look for eye-catching features in the table of contents of a magazine? People generally do not begin reading without having some idea of what they are about to read. Point out to students that whether they read for pleasure or information, they always have some expectation or ideas about the materials they are about to read.

Building on Previous Skills

1 Write the different gift items students come up with on the board. Then ask students to categorize them according to where these items could be purchased. (Examples: **Schreibwarenladen, Musikgeschäft, Kaufhaus, Supermarkt**)

Teacher Note

Activities 1–4 are prereading tasks.

Reading
Thinking Critically

Drawing Inferences Ask students where they might find a reading selection similar to this one in American magazines. Can they think of magazines where such texts could appear? (Examples: *Seventeen, US*)

Teaching Suggestions

• Ask students to name any words or phrases that stand out. Which ones are they familiar with and which ones are they curious about? Make two separate lists on the chalkboard and ask students to write down words or phrases in either category.

• Before reading Stefan's article, you may want to introduce this additional vocabulary: **zufrieden** *satisfied, content*; **nützlich** *useful*; **Filzschreiber** *felt-tipped pen*; **der Betrag** *the amount*; **auswandern** *emigrate.*

Cultures and Communities

Background Information

You might want to remind students that the price shown on an item for sale reflects the total purchase price. **Mehrwertsteuer** *(value added tax)* is always included in the labeled price.

Communication for All Students

A Slower Pace

Stefan's article is divided into three parts. Ask students to give the main idea for each of those parts.

Teaching Suggestion

Before reading Ben's article, you may want to introduce the following additional vocabulary: **vergleichen** *to compare*; **die Auswahl** *selection*; **der Unterschied** *difference*; **die Werbung** *advertisement*; **sparen** *to save*; **das Tauchen** *scuba diving.*

Communication for All Students

Visual Learners

Divide the board in half and put the name Stefan on one side, and Ben on the other. Ask students to list the items each boy purchased and how much each item cost. Then ask students where they would buy these same items in the United States. (Example: **Wo kaufst du … ? Wo kann man … billig kaufen?**)

Cultures and Communities

Thinking Critically

Drawing Inferences Ask students to compare Stefan's and Ben's thoughts about what they would do if they had a lot of money. (Stefan: **Tierschutz- und Umweltorganisationen;** Ben: **Schutz der Weltmeere** and **Schutz der Umwelt**) Can students make a general statement about German teenagers and their interests and concerns for the environment? (Remind students of the teenagers in Chapter 7 who sorted garbage to have it recycled.)

Culture Note

For highly industrialized countries, protecting the environment is extremely important. Many German children are introduced to environmental awareness activities as early as the seventh or the eighth grade. For example, they are taught in their **Erdkunde** classes how they can help recycle paper products, bottles, or aluminum cans.

Post-Reading
Teacher Note

Activity 9 is a post-reading task that will show whether students can apply what they have learned.

Connections and Comparisons

Thinking Critically

Comparing and Contrasting Ask students to work with a partner and make a list of possible gift ideas they feel are representative or typical of their town, area, or state.

Drawing Inferences Ask students what gifts they think are typical of German-speaking countries. If they were traveling to one of the German-speaking countries, what kinds of small gifts would they plan to bring back for friends and family members in the United States?

Answers to Activity 7 a. **Schreibwarengeschäft;** sketchpad, colored pencils, pencil sharpener, eraser, birthday card; **5,02 Euro** b. **25,00 Euro;** candy, CDs, small gifts; school supplies c. emigrate to Australia or the United States
Answers to Activity 8 a. supermarket; things for everyday use b. school supplies and clothes; CDs, small gifts c. scuba gear; protection of the oceans and the environment

▶ **PAGES 324–327**

MEHR GRAMMATIKÜBUNGEN

The **Mehr Grammatikübungen** activities are designed as supplemental activities for the grammatical concepts presented in the chapter. You might use them as additional practice, for review, or for assessment.

For more grammar presentations, review, and practice, refer to the following:
• Grammatikheft
• Grammar Tutor for Students of German
• Grammar Summary on pp. R15–R25
• Übungsheft
• Grammar and Vocabulary quizzes (Testing Program)
• Test Generator
• Interactive CD-ROM Tutor
• **Interaktive Spiele** at **go.hrw.com**

ANWENDUNG

 Video Wrap-up

Videocassette 4, 20:27–30:48
Videocassette 5 (captioned version), 1:03:04–1:05:37

At this time, you might want to use the video resources for additional review and enrichment. See *Video Guide* for suggestions regarding:

- the **Los geht's!** episode
- the **Landeskunde** interviews
- the **Fortsetzung** episode
- the **Videoclips.**

Apply and Assess

A Slower Pace

1 Tell students that they will hear the recording twice. As they listen the first time, they should try to listen only for the answer to **wer.** As they listen the second time, students should listen for the answers to **wem** and **was.**

Challenge

3 Once students have put the drawings in order, ask them to give specific details about what the teenagers need to do. What do they need to write on the invitations? What kind of presents should they buy, and where? What do they plan to serve at the party? What specific chores need to be done to have the house look nice?

Process Writing

5 Have students work in groups to brainstorm clothing vocabulary, as well as vocabulary from earlier chapters which could be used in the context of discussing gifts for a friend's birthday party (school supplies, for example, or even different foods or types of furniture). Encourage your students to use the functions introduced in this chapter which relate to German telephone etiquette.

Teaching Suggestion

6 Set a specific time limit for students to prepare the role-playing activity. Once all groups have their assignments, they should make an outline detailing the content and sequence of their commercial. They should also make note of the props they plan to use. Students may want to share their outline with you for suggestions and answers to questions they might have. On the day of the performances, plan to video- or audiotape the performances if possible.

KANN ICH'S WIRKLICH?

This page is intended to prepare students for the test. It is a brief checklist of the major points covered in the chapter. The students should be reminded that it is a checklist only and not necessarily everything that will appear on the test.

For additional self check options, refer students to the *Grammar Tutor*, the *Interactive CD-Rom Tutor*, and the Online self-test for this chapter.

WORTSCHATZ

Review and Assess

Teaching Suggestions

- Give vocabulary definitions in German and have students try to guess the word or expression.

- Divide students into small groups and assign each group a **Stufe.** Have them write short skits using the words in that **Stufe** and present their skits to the class.

 Games
Play the game **Schnell, das richtige Wort!** See p. 303C for the procedure.

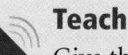 **Circumlocution**
Play **Das treffende Wort suchen** with the gift ideas from the **Dritte Stufe** vocabulary. Tell students that they are in a store and need to tell the person at the information desk what they are seeking, in order to find out the location of the department which carries the item. See p. 155C for procedures.

Teacher Note
Give the **Kapitel 11** Chapter Test:
Testing Program, pp. 287–292
Audio CD 11, Trs. 22–24.

Objectives

In this chapter you will learn to

Erste Stufe

- use the telephone in Germany

Zweite Stufe

- invite someone to a party and accept or decline
- talk about birthdays and express good wishes

Dritte Stufe

- discuss gift ideas

▸ internet

ADRESSE: go.hrw.com
KENNWORT:
WK3 BADEN-WUERTTEMBERG-11

◂ **Was schenkst du deiner Freundin?**

dreihundertfünf **305**

Los geht's! · *Geschenke aussuchen*

Los geht's! is an abridged version of the video episode.

CD 11 Trs. 1–2

VIDEO

> **Strategie** Verstehen
> Look at the images for the story.
> Where are the girls? What are they
> doing? What do you think they are
> talking about?

Sabine   **Nicole**

Frau Kroll: Kroll.
Nicole: Guten Tag, Frau Kroll! Hier ist die Nicole. Ist die Sabine da?
Frau Kroll: Nein, Sabine ist mit ihrem Vater weg. Kann ich ihr etwas sagen?
Nicole: Ja, hm …sagen Sie ihr bitte, dass der Martin am Samstag Geburtstag hat! Und ich möchte für ihn eine Fete organisieren.
Frau Kroll: Na, prima! Ich sag es Sabine. Tschüs!
Nicole: Wiederhören, Frau Kroll!

1

2

Sabine: Was schenkst du dem Martin?	**Nicole:** Na und?
Nicole: Kein Problem! Ich kaufe ihm eine Kassette.	**Sabine:** Warum kaufst du ihm keine CD?
Sabine: Aber er hat doch schon so viele Kassetten.	**Nicole:** Er hat doch noch keinen CD-Player.

③ **Sabine:** Was soll ich ihm bloß schenken? Was meinst du? Du kennst ihn besser. Eine Idee?

Nicole: Kauf ihm doch ein Buch! Er liest auch gerne.

Sabine: Bücher sind so teuer.

④ **Nicole:** Dann schenk ihm halt ein T-Shirt mit einem Komponisten drauf! Das mag er bestimmt auch.

Sabine: Eine prima Idee! — Schau mal, Nicole! Die Karte ist lustig, nicht?

Nicole: Wahnsinn! Und lies mal den Vers!

Sabine: Die schenk ich dem Martin!

Zu Hause bei Nicole

⑤ **Sabine:** Übrigens, weißt du, wann der Thomas Geburtstag hat?

Nicole: Irgendwann im Sommer. Ich glaub, im August.

Sabine: An welchem Tag?

Nicole: Warum fragst du? Willst du …?

Sabine: Nein, nein. Seinen Geburtstag feiern wir nie.

⑥ **Nicole:** Im August haben wir immer Ferien.

Sabine: Zeig her!

Nicole: Schau, hier: am elften August!

Sabine: Hier steht: „Martin am achtzehnten". Er hat also nicht diesen Samstag Geburtstag!

Nicole: Was? Das kann doch nicht wahr sein! Was soll ich jetzt machen? Die kommen alle diesen Samstag!

Übungsheft, S. 121

1 Was passiert hier?

These activities check for global comprehension only. Students should not yet be expected to produce language modeled in **Los geht's!**

Do you understand what is happening in **Los geht's!**? Check your comprehension by answering these questions. Don't be afraid to guess.

1. Why does Nicole call Sabine? She wants to organize a birthday party for Martin.

2. What do they discuss when they get together later? what gifts to give him

3. What suggestions does Nicole make to Sabine? Which one does Sabine like the best? book, T-shirt Sabine thinks Martin will like the T-shirt best.

4. What does Sabine discover when she looks up Thomas's birthday? What is Nicole's predicament? that Martin's birthday is also in the summer—and not Saturday. She has already invited people.

2 Genauer lesen

Reread the conversations. Which words or phrases do the characters use to

1. begin and end a phone conversation
   Hier …(name); Tag; Wiederhören

2. name gift ideas Kassetten, CD; Buch; T-Shirt

3. ask for advice and opinions
   Was meinst du? Eine Idee?

4. say when someone's birthday is …hat am 18. Geburtstag.
   …hat am Samstag …
   …hat im Sommer …

5. express disbelief Was!
   Das kann doch nicht wahr sein!

3 Was ist richtig?

Was ist die beste Antwort, a., b., oder c.?

1. Nicole ruft Sabine an. Sie will ihr sagen, ====. b
   a. dass sie eine Kassette gekauft hat
   b. dass sie für Martin eine Party geben will
   c. dass sie mit Martin ausgeht

2. Nicole kauft dem Martin keine CD, ====. b
   a. weil er so viele Kassetten hat
   b. weil er keinen CD-Player hat
   c. weil er gern liest

3. Sabine schenkt Martin auch ==== zum Geburtstag. c
   a. eine CD   b. ein Buch   c. eine Karte

4. Nicole und Sabine feiern nie den Geburtstag von Thomas, ====. b
   a. weil sie Martin eine Karte schenken möchten
   b. weil alle im August Ferien haben
   c. weil Martin am 18. Geburtstag hat

5. Am Ende weiß Nicole nicht, was sie tun soll, ====. a
   a. denn Martin hat am 18. Geburtstag, nicht diesen Samstag
   b. denn Thomas gibt Martin ein Buch
   c. denn sie hat Ferien

4 Nacherzählen

Put the sentences in logical order to make a brief summary of **Los geht's!**.

1. Nicole ruft Sabine an. Sie möchte über Martins Geburtstag sprechen.

5 Aber Sabine weiß nicht genau, was sie Martin kaufen soll.

7 Sabine findet, dass das T-Shirt die beste Idee ist.

Aber die Sabine ist nicht zu Hause. 2

Nicole will Martin eine Kassette kaufen. 4

Am Ende sieht Sabine in ihrem Adressbuch, dass Martin am 18. Geburtstag hat. 9

6 Dann hat Nicole eine Idee: vielleicht ein Buch oder ein T-Shirt.

Später sprechen die zwei Mädchen über Martins Geschenk. 3

Danach findet Sabine eine tolle Geburtstagskarte für Martin. 8

5 Und du?

Was möchtest du zum Geburtstag? Mach eine Liste! Dann frag deinen Partner, was er zum Geburtstag haben möchte!

Erste Stufe

Objective Using the telephone in Germany

den Hörer abheben   Münzen einstecken   die Nummer wählen   wieder auflegen

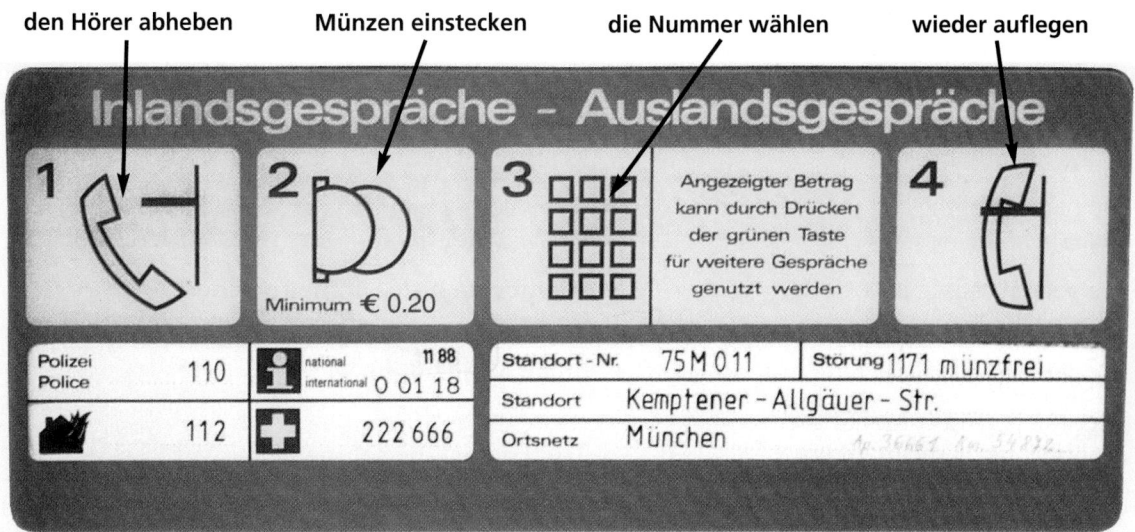

Inlandsgespräche – Auslandsgespräche

1   **2** Minimum € 0.20   **3** Angezeigter Betrag kann durch Drücken der grünen Taste für weitere Gespräche genutzt werden   **4**

Polizei Police	110	national 11 88 international 0 01 18		Standort - Nr.	75 M 0 11	Störung 1171 münzfrei
	112	+	222 666	Standort	Kemptener - Allgäuer - Str.	
				Ortsnetz	München	

6 In der Telefonzelle

Lesen/Sprechen Schau dir die obige Information an und beantworte die Fragen.

1. What kind of information is this? Where would you expect to find it? 1. directions on using a phone; in a phone booth
2. What number could you call to find out someone else's number in Germany? 3. 1188
3. Which emergency numbers are provided? 5. 110-police; 112-fire; 222-666-hospital
4. How would you tell a German exchange student (in German) how to use a phone booth in the United States? Use the four steps pictured above. Answers may vary.

Wortschatz

Telefonieren ist nicht schwer!

Grammatikheft, S. 91–92, Ü. 1–2

CD-ROM DISC **3**

11–A

der Apparat/ das Telefon

der Hörer

den Hörer abheben
die Münzen einstecken
die Telefonnummer wählen
den Hörer auflegen

telefonieren/anrufen   besetzt *(busy)*

die Telefonzelle

Using the telephone in Germany

Mehr Grammatikübungen
S. 324, Ü. 1

Übungsheft, S. 122–124, Ü. 2–7

Grammatikheft, S. 92, Ü. 3

Here are some phrases you will need to know in order to talk on the phone in German:

The person who answers says his or her name:	**Kroll.** *or* **Hier Kroll.**
The person calling says who he or she is:	**Hier ist die Nicole.**
The person calling asks to speak to someone:	**Ich möchte bitte Sabine sprechen.** *or* **Kann ich bitte Sabine sprechen?**
The person who answered says:	**Einen Moment, bitte.**
After the person comes to the phone, he or she might say:	**Tag! Hier ist die Sabine.**
The conversation may end with:	**Wiederhören!** *or* **Auf Wiederhören!** *or* **Tschüs!**

How are these phrases different from the ones you use when talking on the phone?

---

7 **Was passt?**   Script on p. 303G   1. c   2. b   3. d   4. a

Zuhören Listen to the four telephone conversations and match each one with an appropriate illustration.

CD 11
Tr. 3

a.

c.

b.

d.

8 **Tag! Hier ist ...**

Sprechen Get together with a classmate and practice "calling" a friend on the telephone. Your partner will be the parent of the friend you are calling. Use the expressions you have learned so far. Then practice saying good-bye. When you are finished, switch roles.

9 Willst du einen Film sehen?

Sprechen Ruf deinen Partner an und frag ihn, ob er heute Abend mit dir ins Kino gehen will. Besprich mit ihm, was ihr euch ansehen wollt. Gebraucht dabei die Wörter in den Kästen.

person answering

Was für Filme magst du?
Tschüs!
Ja, prima!   Hier ist …   Tag …!

person calling

Hier …   Tag …!   Ich mag Liebesfilme sehr gern.
Willst du einen Film sehen?   Wiederhören!

10 Ich möchte bitte … sprechen

Sprechen You worked in the office at the youth center today, and a lot of people called in and left messages for their friends. Work with a partner to create the telephone conversations you would have as you attempt to pass along the messages to the appropriate people. Take turns playing the role of the office worker.

1. Call Stefan (who is not at home; you reach his mother) and let him know that Petra wants to play tennis tomorrow at 4 P.M.
2. Call Ulrike and remind her that the biology class on Tuesday is at 9 A.M. instead of (**anstatt**) at 10 A.M.
3. Call Holger and tell him that soccer practice is at 3 P.M. on Tuesday.
4. Monika is not home yet, but you need to let her know that Ulla called and wants to go shopping with her on Saturday morning at 9 A.M.

ein Kartentelefon

ein Handy

Ein wenig Landeskunde

It's easy to make a phone call in Germany from a private phone or from a phone booth.

Private mobile phones or cellular phones are becoming more and more popular, since many access providers have lowered the prices to be more competitive. A cellular phone is called **ein (das) Handy** (pl. **Handys**).

Public phones can be accessed by using coins, but most people use phone cards (**Telefonkarten**) that can be bought in various amounts at post offices or newspaper kiosks.

All phone booths will be replaced with six-foot high steel columns by 2005. They will have an **"Allpayment-Funktion"** so that users will be able to make phone calls using coins, phone cards, and credit cards.

For a local call, **ein Ortsgespräch**, you dial a local number consisting of four or five digits in small villages to seven digits in towns and large cities.

For a long distance call, **ein Ferngespräch**, you must dial an area code, **eine Vorwahlnummer**, such as 030 for Berlin or 089 for Munich. In small villages, the area code can have up to five digits.

When calling Germany from the United States, you must first dial the international access code 011, then the access code for Germany, 49, then the **Vorwahlnummer** without the 0. For example, when calling Berlin you dial 011 49 30 plus the local phone number.

When calling the United States from Germany, you first dial the US access code 001, then the area code and number. The least expensive way to call from abroad is most often a phone card issued by your telephone service provider.

eine Telefonkarte

Übungsheft,
S. 132, Ü. 24

Mehr Grammatikübungen,
S. 324, Ü. 2

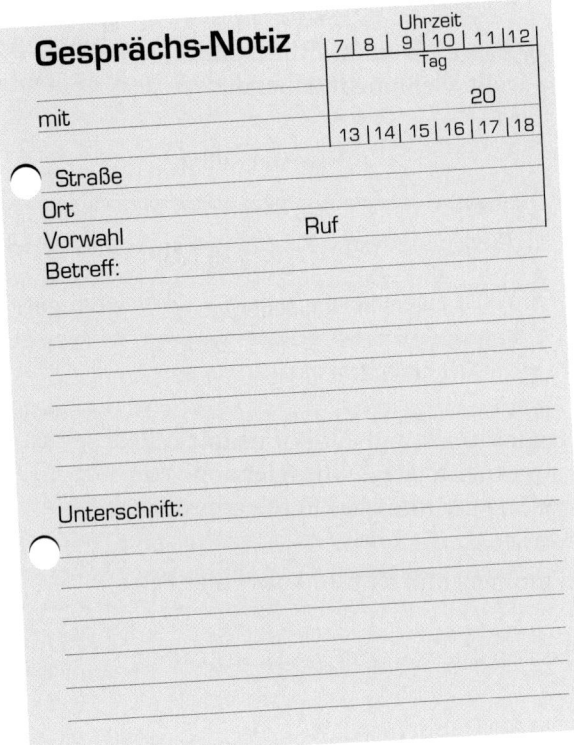

Gesprächs-Notiz

Uhrzeit 7 | 8 | 9 | 10 | 11 | 12
Tag
20
13 | 14 | 15 | 16 | 17 | 18

mit

○ Straße
Ort
Vorwahl   Ruf
Betreff:

Unterschrift:

○

---

11 **Gesprächs-Notiz**

Sprechen Beantworte die folgenden Fragen.

1. What do you think the page on the left is used for? Which words are the clues for your answer? To record phone messages; **Gespräch / Notiz**

2. Where would you record the date and time? **Tag/Uhrzeit**

3. Where would you record the information about the person who called? What specific information is asked for in this section?

4. Where would you write the message? **Betreff:**

5. Where would you sign the page if you took the call? **Unterschrift**

3. Beside **mit**, name of person who called. Other information: address **(Straße, Ort)**, area code **(Vorwahl)**, and telephone number **(Ruf)**.

Übungsheft, S. 125, Ü. 8

---

12 **Schreib auf, was du hörst!** Script on p. 303G

CD 11
Tr. 4

Zuhören/Schreiben At your host family's home in Germany, someone calls while one of the family members is out. Make a German phone message page like the one pictured above. Then take down all the information asked for on the **Gesprächs-Notiz.** For the actual message, just write down a few notes. What phrase did the person answering the phone use at the beginning of the conversation? What is its English equivalent? phrase: **Hier bei …**
Answers below.   means: **…residence**

13 **Deine Gesprächs-Notiz**

Schreiben Using your notes from Activity 12, rewrite the message in neat sentences so that it can be easily understood by the person receiving it. Then switch papers with a partner and check whether your partner wrote his or her message correctly.

14 **Ruf mal an!**

Sprechen Decide on a free time activity that you would like to do with your partner. Call your partner and invite him or her to come along. Then switch roles. Here are a few possibilities: Suggested answers:

Ich mache am Samstag eine Party. Kannst du kommen?

Ich möchte heute in die Stadt fahren. Kommst du mit?

12. Uhrzeit: **9**; Tag: **3.5.02** mit: **Ludwig Ottmann**; Straße: **Neubaustr. 9**; Ort: **97413 Marktbreit** Vorwahl: **09331**, Ruf: **1367** Betreff: **Geburtstagsparty für Onkel Michael-2. Juni, um 17 Uhr in Nürnberg, Hotel Löwe, Rosenthal 8**

Zweite Stufe

Objectives Inviting someone to a party and accepting or declining; talking about birthdays and expressing good wishes

 go.
hrw
.com

WK3-BADEN-WUERTTEMBERG-11

15 Eine Einladung

Lesen/Sprechen Schau die Einladung an und beantworte die folgenden Fragen!

1. Wer schickt die Einladung? 1. Nicole
2. Für wen ist die Fete? Warum? 2. Martin/ Geburtstag
3. Wann ist die Fete? An welchem Tag? Um wie viel Uhr? 3. Am Samstag, den 11. Juni, um 19 Uhr
4. Wo ist die Fete? 4. Martin-Luther-Str. 8
5. Welche Nummer kannst du anrufen, um Information zu bekommen? 5. 07142-6376
6. Was musst du tun, um zu sagen, ob (*whether*) du kommen kannst?
   6. Ruf Nicole an.

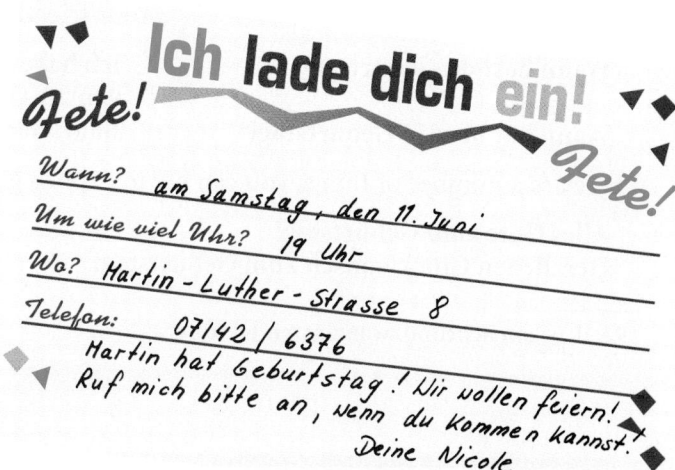

Fete! **Ich lade dich ein!** Fete!

Wann? am Samstag, den 11. Juni
Um wie viel Uhr? 19 Uhr
Wo? Martin-Luther-Strasse 8
Telefon: 07142 / 6376
Martin hat Geburtstag! Wir wollen feiern!
Ruf mich bitte an, wenn du kommen kannst!
Deine Nicole

So sagt man das!

Inviting someone to a party and accepting or declining

You invite a friend:

Ich habe am Samstag eine Party.
Ich lade dich ein.
Kannst du kommen?

Your friend might respond:

Ja, gern! *or*
Aber sicher! *or*
Natürlich! *or*
Leider kann ich nicht.

Which response would you use if you already had a previous engagement?[1]

 Grammatikheft, S. 93, Ü. 4

16 Eine Einladung

Schreiben Schreib eine Einladung! Was für eine Fete ist das? An welchem Tag ist die Fete? Um wie viel Uhr beginnt sie? Wo ist sie? Wenn man nicht kommen kann, soll man anrufen?

17 Ich möchte dich einladen!

 **Sprechen** You are having a party and want to invite several of your friends. "Call" two other classmates and invite each of them to the party. They will ask you for information about the party and then tell you whether they can come. If not, they should give you a reason. You should respond appropriately. End your conversation, then switch roles so that each person takes a turn extending the invitations.

---

1. **Leider kann ich nicht.**

Talking about birthdays and expressing good wishes

If you want to find out when a friend has his or her birthday, you ask:

Wann hast du Geburtstag?

Wann hat Martin Geburtstag?

Your friend might respond:

Ich habe am 28. Oktober* Geburtstag. *or*
Am 28. Oktober.
Bald. Nächste Woche.

There are a number of things you can say to express good wishes:

Alles Gute zum Geburtstag!
Herzlichen Glückwunsch zum Geburtstag!

*Read as: **am achtundzwanzigsten Oktober.**

Grammatikheft, S. 94, Ü. 5–6

Wortschatz

Wann hast du Geburtstag?

am 1. = am ersten (Juli)
am 2. = am zweiten
am 3. = am dritten
am 4. = am vierten
am 5. = am fünften
am 6. = am sechsten
am 7. = am siebten
am 8. = am achten
am 9. = am neunten
am 10. = am zehnten
am 11. = am elften
        usw.
am 20. = am zwanzigsten
am 21. = am einundzwanzigsten
        usw.

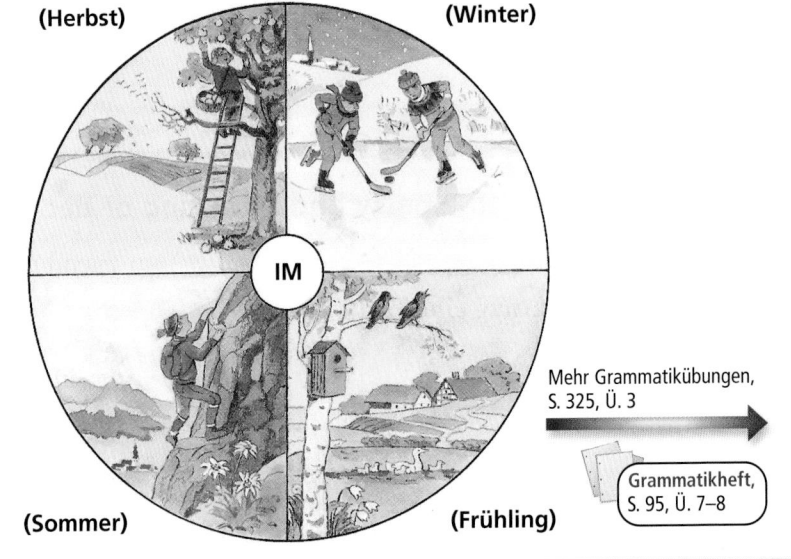

(Herbst)   (Winter)

IM

(Sommer)   (Frühling)

Mehr Grammatikübungen,
S. 325, Ü. 3

Grammatikheft,
S. 95, Ü. 7–8

18 Geburtstagskette

Sprechen One person in the class begins the chain by asking another: **Wann hast du Geburtstag**? That person answers and asks someone else. Continue until everyone has been asked.

19 Wann haben Anjas Freunde Geburtstag? Script on p. 303G

Zuhören Das Schuljahr ist bald zu Ende. Anja will wissen, wer im Sommer Geburtstag hat. Sie fragt ihre Klassenkameraden und schreibt dann die Geburtstage in ihr Adressbuch. Schreib, wann Anjas Freunde Geburtstag haben!

CD 11
Tr. 5

1. Bernd   **2.** Maja   **3.** Benjamin   **4.** Katrin   **5.** Mario
22. Mai   4. Februar   28. März   14. August   29. Dezember

20 Für mein Notizbuch

Schreiben Schreib, wann du Geburtstag hast! Welches Geschenk hast du am liebsten? Schreib auch, wann deine Eltern, deine Geschwister und deine Freunde Geburtstag haben!

Ein wenig Landeskunde

Birthdays are important occasions in German-speaking countries and are usually celebrated with family and friends. In some areas of Germany (primarily in the strongly Catholic areas) and in Austria, the **Namenstag,** or Saint's Day, is also celebrated. Children in these areas are named after certain saints, such as **Johannes, Josef,** and **Maria.** There is a saint's day for each day of the year. Anyone named for a saint also celebrates on the day that honors that saint. The **Namenstag** celebration is similar to a birthday celebration, with a party, gifts, and flowers for the honoree.

Namenstag im Juli

10. Erich/Erika
13. Margarete
15. Heinrich
24. Christine
25. Jakob
26. Anne Marie
29. Martha

Gratulieren Sie mit Blumen!

Wortschatz

Feiertage

Weihnachten:
Fröhliche Weihnachten!

Chanukka:
Frohes Chanukka-Fest!

Ostern:
Frohe Ostern!

CD-ROM DISC 3

Vatertag:
Alles Gute zum Vatertag!

 11–1

Muttertag:
Alles Gute zum Muttertag!

Mehr Grammatikübungen, S. 325, Ü. 4

Übungsheft, S. 126–127, Ü. 9–15

Script on p. 303G

21

Was passt?

CD 11
Tr. 6

Zuhören You will hear four conversations about four different holidays. Match each conversation to the most appropriate card.
1. Muttertag 2. Chanukka
3. Weihnachten 4. Geburtstag

22 ### Eine Geburtstagskarte

Schreiben Design a German birthday card or a card for another special occasion to send to a friend or family member. Below are some common German good luck symbols.

Schornsteinfeger

Glücksschwein

Glücksklee

Hufeisen

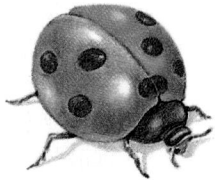

Marienkäfer

Was schenkst du zum Geburtstag?

We asked several teenagers what they usually give as birthday presents. Before you read the interviews, write what you give your friends and relatives for their birthdays.
CD 11 Tr. 7

CD 11
Trs. 7–11

Melanie, Hamburg CD 11 Tr. 8

„Ich geh mit Freunden essen oder lade sie zu mir ein. Und dann sitzen wir zusammen und unterhalten uns nett oder Ähnliches, … ansonsten gar nichts weiter. Bei Familienmitgliedern ist es ähnlich, da feiern wir auch in der Familie. Und schenken tu ich dann meiner Schwester zum Beispiel, die hört ziemlich gerne Musik, und der schenk ich dann <u>Kassetten</u> oder <u>CDs</u> oder Ähnliches. Und ansonsten eben schenk ich <u>Bücher</u> oder eben andere Kleinigkeiten, für die sich die Freunde oder Familienmitglieder interessieren."

Eva, Berlin CD 11 Tr. 9

„Eigentlich hass ich Geburtstage, weil ich nie weiß, was ich schenken soll. Es ist irgendwie immer dasselbe, <u>Bücher</u> oder <u>Kassetten</u> oder <u>CDs</u>. Und na ja, dann sucht man sich immer was aus. Meistens verschenkt man <u>Gutscheine</u>, weil … da kann man nichts falsch machen."
cassettes (sister, brother); CDs, books

Rosi, Berlin CD 11 Tr. 10

„Also wenn ich auf Geburtstage gehe von Freunden oder Freundinnen, die ich gut kenne, dann geb ich auch mal mehr Geld aus. Dann kriegen sie schon <u>persönliche Geschenke</u>, wo sie sich auch darüber freuen. Und wenn ich auf Geburtstage gehe von Leuten, die ich nicht so gut kenne, dann nehme ich nur <u>Kleinigkeiten</u> mit. Aber ich nehm eigentlich immer was mit, wenn ich auf Geburtstage gehe."

Jutta, Hamburg CD 11 Tr. 11

„Ich hab einen kleinen Bruder, und er ist elf, und der spielt unheimlich gern mit <u>Lego</u>,™ und dem schenk ich dann <u>was zum Spielen</u> oder eine <u>Musikkassette</u>. Und wenn ich bei Freunden eingeladen bin, meistens was <u>Selbstgemachtes</u>, ein bemaltes <u>T-Shirt</u>, ja auch <u>eine Musikkassette</u>, <u>ein Buch</u> oder ein <u>gemaltes Bild</u>."

A. 1. Make a list of the gifts these teenagers give as birthday presents and to whom they give them. What do you think **Gutscheine** might be? *Hint: they are available for many different things, such as cassettes, CDs, and books.* **Gutschein** (gift certificate)

2. Rosi has two categories of people she buys gifts for. What are they? What are some of the differences in the types of gifts she buys for each one? good friends/acquaintances; less money on acquaintances

3. Why does Eva not care much for birthdays? Do you agree or disagree with her?   hard to find right present

4. Of the four people interviewed, who do you think puts the most thought and time into giving just the right gift? What statements support your answer?   Answer will vary.

B. Use the list you made earlier to write an answer to the questions **Was schenkst du zum Geburtstag, und wem schenkst du das?** Share your answers with your classmates and decide which of the interviews above most closely resembles your own. Are there any differences in the things teenagers give as gifts in the German-speaking countries and in the United States? If so, what are they and why do you think this is so? If not, why not?

STANDARDS: 1.2, 2.2, 3.2, 4.2

Dritte Stufe

Objective Discussing gift ideas

Geschenkladen=gift shop

23 **Im Geschenkladen**

Lesen/Sprechen Here is an excerpt from an article in the teen magazine *JUMA.* Look at the photo and read the caption. Then answer the questions that follow.

1. Using the photo as a clue, what do you think a **Geschenkladen** is? What do you think the topic of this article is?

2. Reread the caption. Do you think Martina is finding a lot of things she could buy? Why or why not?

3. What gift does Martina decide to buy for her friend? Do you think she buys anything else? If so, what?

4. Was für Geschenke schenkst du Verwandten (*relatives*) und Freunden? Wo kaufst du gewöhnlich Geschenke? Fünf Euro sind ungefähr sechs Dollar. Was kannst du für sechs Dollar kaufen?

1.giving/finding present   2. no-too expensive
3. a candle; yes; candy   4. Answers will vary.

Martina, 14, will ihrer Freundin etwas zum Namenstag schenken. Im Geschenkladen sucht sie lange nach einer Kleinigkeit. Die meisten Sachen kosten mehr als fünf Euro. Martina entscheidet sich für eine Kerze. Dann geht sie in ein Süßwarengeschäft.

Wortschatz

Geschenkideen

Bärbel: Was schenkst du Jutta zum Geburtstag?
Berndt: Ich weiß noch nicht. Vielleicht …

 p. 303X   11–B   CD-ROM DISC 3

eine Armbanduhr

Pralinen

einen Blumenstrauß

einen Kalender

ein Poster

eine CD

Parfüm

Schmuck

Was schenkst du zu verschiedenen Feiertagen, z. B. zum Muttertag?

 Grammatikheft, S. 96, Ü. 9

So sagt man das!

Discussing gift ideas

When talking about birthdays and holidays with friends, you'll also want to be able to discuss gift ideas.

You might ask your friend:

> **Schenkst du deinem Vater einen Kalender zum Geburtstag?**

> **Und was schenkst du deiner Mutter zum Muttertag?**
> **Kauf ihr doch ein Buch!**
> **Wem schenkst du den Blumenstrauß?**

Your friend might respond:

> **Nein, ich schenke ihm wahrscheinlich eine CD, weil er doch Musik so gern hört.**
> **Ich weiß noch nicht. Hast du eine Idee?**
> **Prima Idee! Das mach ich!**
> **Der Nicole schenke ich den Strauß.**

Can you find the subject and the verb in each of these sentences? What is the item being given (the direct object) in the first question?[1] Who is the person receiving the gift (the indirect object)?[2] In the first response, you see the word **ihm**. To whom does it refer?[3] To whom does the word **ihr** refer in the sentence **Kauf ihr doch ein Buch!**? [4]

Übungsheft,
S. 128–129, Ü. 16–18

Grammatikheft,
S. 96, Ü. 10

---

1. Interkulturelle Beratung und Information;
Information über Gastgeschenke im Ausland

24 ## Was soll man schenken?

Lesen/Sprechen Mechtild Kaldenkirchen and Gothild Thomas of Essen offer a unique information service. Read the article on the right, then answer these questions.

1. Wie heißt der Informationsservice von Mechtild und Gothild? Was für Information können sie uns geben? Gib ein oder zwei Beispiele!

2. Was muss man machen, um die Information zu bekommen?   anrufen

3. Wie sagt man den letzten Satz auf Englisch?   Other countries, other customs (When in Rome …)

25 ## Welches Geschenk?   Script on p. 303H

CD 11
Tr. 12

Zuhören You call **Interkulturelle Beratung und Information** to find out the proper gift or gifts for families you'll visit on your trip to France, Italy, Spain, and Austria. On a separate piece of paper, write the gift(s) they advise you to give in each country: **Frankreich, Italien, Spanien,** and **Österreich.**

Frankreich: Getränke; Italien: Blumen;
Spanien: Getränke; Österreich: Pralinen

GESCHENKE
Hilfe per Telefon

Was bringt man als Gast einer Familie in Frankreich mit – Blumen, Pralinen oder Getränke? Wer viel reist, hat solche Probleme öfter. Helfen kann ein Bürgertelefon in Essen. Mechtild Kaldenkirchen und Gothild Thomas leiten die „Interkulturelle Beratung und Information": Sie informieren Anrufer aber nicht nur über Gastgeschenke im Ausland. Man kann nämlich auch erfahren, wie man sich im Ausland richtig benimmt. Denn eines ist ja allgemein bekannt: andere Länder, andere Sitten.

---

1. **einen Kalender** 2. **deinem Vater** 3. **ihm = Vater** 4. **ihr = Mutter**

Introduction to the dative case

You have learned that the subject of a sentence is in the nominative case and that the direct object is in the accusative case. A third case, the dative case, is used for indirect objects, which express the idea of "to someone" or "for someone." Look at the following sentences:

Robert, was schenkst du **deinem Opa**?
Und was schenkst du **deiner Oma**?

Ich schenke **ihm** einen Taschenrechner.
Ich schenke **ihr** ein Buch.

How would you say each of the above sentences in English?[1] Look at the photos for clues. You have already seen several examples of the dative case with definite articles after prepositions: **mit dem Bus, mit der U-Bahn.** Definite articles may also be used with proper names in the dative case:

Was kaufst du **dem Martin**?
Gibst du **der Sandra** das Geld?

Ich kaufe **ihm** ein T-Shirt.
Ja, ich gebe **ihr** morgen das Geld.

To ask the question "To whom …?" or "For whom …?" you use the dative form "**Wem** …?"

Wem schenkst du die Blumen?
Wem kaufst du das Buch?

To whom are you giving the flowers?
For whom do you buy the book?

Dative Case

masculine ⎫	**dem, ihm, deinem, meinem**
neuter ⎰	
feminine ⎱	**der, ihr, deiner, meiner**

What pattern do you notice in the formation of the dative case? Make a chart of the definite articles, pronouns for *he* and *she*, and the possessive **mein** for all the cases you have learned so far. What patterns do you notice?

Mehr Grammatikübungen,
S. 325–326, Ü. 5–7

Übungsheft, S. 129–130, Ü. 19–22   Grammatikheft, S. 97–98, Ü. 11–14

---

26 **Grammatik im Kontext**   Script on p. 303H

Zuhören You're visiting Germany during the holiday season and would like to send something to your friends and family members. You ask your German friend for gift ideas. Your friend makes suggestions for specific family members and friends. Write down which gift he suggests for each person.

CD 11
Tr. 13

Opa-eine CD; Oma-ein Buch; Vater-einen Kalender; Mutti-das Parfüm; Otto-ein Poster; Martina-Schmuck

1. *Robert, what are you giving your grandfather? I'm giving him a calculator. And what are you giving your grandmother? I'm giving her a book.*

27 **Grammatik im Kontext**

 Schreiben/Lesen Put the following sentence elements in the correct order to express what you and others are planning to give as presents at an upcoming party.

1. kaufe
eine Bluse
Ich
meiner Oma

2. eine CD
Peter
schenken
Wir

3. meiner Mutter
ein Handy
Mein Vater
kauft

4. Und ich
ihm
schenke
auch ein Buch

5. Sie
dem Opa
kauft
einen Kalender

6. schenken
ein Buch über Musik
Wir
meiner Mutter

7. eine Telefonkarte
schenke
meiner Freundin
Ich

Grammatik

Notice the word order when you use the dative case. The indirect object (dative case) comes before the direct object (accusative case):

Ich schenke meiner Mutter ein Buch.
Ich schenke ihr ein Buch.

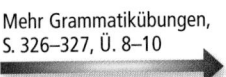 *Mehr Grammatikübungen,*
S. 326–327, Ü. 8–10
Grammatikheft, S. 99, Ü. 15

1. Ich kaufe meiner Oma eine Bluse. 2. Wir schenken Peter eine CD. 3. Mein Vater kauft meiner Mutter ein Handy. 4. Und ich schenke ihm auch ein Buch. 5. Sie kauft dem Opa einen Kalender. 6. Wir schenken meiner Mutter ein Buch über Musik. 7. Ich schenke meiner Freundin eine Telefonkarte.

28 **Grammatik im Kontext**

Sprechen/Schreiben Take turns with your classmates asking and telling who is getting which gift. Practice replacing the noun phrases with the appropriate pronoun in the response. Use the drawings below as cues.

BEISPIEL　DU　**Was schenkst du deinem Bruder?**
　　　　MITSCHÜLER　**Ich schenke ihm einen Kuli.**

dein Bruder　**dein Vater**　**deine Kusine**　**deine Oma**　**deine Lehrerin**　**dein Onkel**　**deine Schwester**

29 **Memory-Spiel**

Sprechen Wem schenkst du ein Buch?

BEISPIEL　DU　**Ich schenke meiner Mutter ein Buch.**

　　MITSCHÜLER　**Ich schenke meiner Mutter und meinem Freund ein Buch.**

When you use indirect objects in your conversations, they must be in the dative case. It helps to remember that the dative forms for masculine and neuter articles and pronouns always end in **-m: dem, ihm, meinem, deinem.** The dative forms for feminine articles and pronouns always end with **-r: der, ihr, meiner, deiner.**

30 **Eine Geschenkliste**

 Schreiben/Sprechen Make a list of what you would like to buy for three of your friends or family members for their birthdays. Give your partner a list with just the names of the people receiving gifts. Your partner will ask you what you plan to give them. Respond according to your list. Then switch roles. Jot down your partner's answers, then compare lists to see if you understood everything.

 **31 Deine Europareise**

Schreiben You're going to Europe! Decide which three countries you would like to visit. On a card write down the countries you choose, the souvenir you would buy from each, and the name of the person to whom you would like to give each souvenir.

Examples: **Deutschland-einen Pulli-Opa/Spanien-einen Fächer-Susanne/Italien-Schuhe-Mutter**

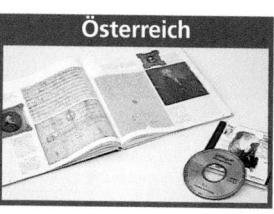
Österreich

ein Buch   eine CD von Mozart

Schweiz (in der Schweiz)

Pralinen   eine Armbanduhr

Spanien

einen Fächer Kastagnetten

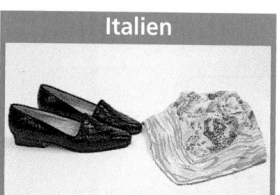
Italien

Schuhe   ein Halstuch

Deutschland

einen Pulli   eine Kerze

 32 Ein Brief aus Europa

 Schreiben Schreib einem Freund oder deiner Familie einen Brief über deine Europareise! Schreib, wo du warst, was du gekauft hast und wem du die Andenken (*souvenirs*) schenkst! Benutze deine Information von Übung 31!

 33  **Von der Schule zum Beruf**

Schreiben You are the advertising manager of a souvenir shop chain in Germany. Your glossy advertising brochure has to be revised because many new items have been added to your inventory. Describe these items and target them for a particular audience.

AUSSPRACHE

 Richtig aussprechen / Richtig lesen CD 11 Trs. 14–16

A. To review the following sounds, say the sentences below after your teacher or after the recording. CD 11 Tr. 14

1. **The letters r and er:** The letter **r** is pronounced by placing the tip of the tongue behind your lower front teeth and then tipping the head back and pretending to gargle. The combination **er** at the end of a syllable or word is pronounced like the *a* in the English word *sofa*.

   Ich schenke meinem Bruder Rolf und seiner Frau ein Radio.
   Und ich schenke meiner Mutter Bücher und einen Kalender.

2. **The letter a:** The letter **a** is pronounced much like the *a* sound in the word *father*.

   Kaufst du dem Vater eine Armbanduhr oder eine Jacke zum Vatertag?

3. **The diphthongs eu, äu, and au:** The vowel combinations **eu** and **äu** sound similar to the *oy* sound in the English word *toy*. The diphthong **au** is pronounced like the *ow* sound in the English word *how*.

   Heute war der Verkäufer am Telefon ganz unfreundlich.
   Ich kaufe der Claudia einen Blumenstrauß.

Richtig schreiben / Diktat   CD 11 Tr. 15 / CD 11 Tr. 16 (with pauses)

B. Write down the sentences that you hear. Script on p. 303H

Billig einkaufen gehen

Lesestrategie Reading for Comprehension

When you are reading something in your native language, you don't look up every word you don't know. The same is true for German. Remember to read for understanding of ideas, not of isolated words. Then make educated guesses about the relative importance of words you don't know.

1. You are invited to a party and need to bring a gift. What can you buy for $5.00?

2. A foreign exchange student is also invited to the party. Where would you suggest that person should go to buy a gift for $5.00? What would you suggest might be a good gift for the foreign exchange student to buy?

3. Look at the title, the pictures, and the captions. Without actually reading the texts, what would you say is the type of reading selection on these pages? Are they ads, postcards, poems, or articles? articles

4. Judging by the title, what kind of information do you expect to find in these selections? gifts you can buy for 5 euros or under

5. Read the article about Stefan through without stopping to ask about words you don't know. Then summarize the article in two or three sentences.

Was gibt's heute noch für 5 Euro?

Im Supermarkt läuft Ben durch die Regalreihen und vergleicht Preise. Viele Dinge nimmt er zuerst aus dem Regal und stellt sie wieder zurück, nachdem er den Preis gelesen hat. Er kauft Orangensaft und Cola.

▶ „Ich möchte etwas Sinnvolles kaufen. Etwas, das ich auch brauchen kann." Stefan lebt in der kleinen Stadt Schwalmtal nahe der niederländischen Grenze. Dort gibt es nicht viele Läden. Darum entscheidet er sich für ein kleines Schreibwarengeschäft am Marktplatz. Dort kauft er einen Zeichenblock, zwei Buntstifte, einen Anspitzer, ein Radiergummi und eine Geburtstagskarte. Die Geburtstagskarte ist das teuerste Teil seines Einkaufs: 1,75 Euro. Insgesamt hat er 5,02 Euro ausgegeben. Zwei Cent zu viel! „Es ist fast unmöglich, für genau 5 Euro einzukaufen."

Stefan ist mit seinem Einkauf zufrieden. „Nur die Geburtstagskarte fand ich ganz schön teuer. Aber insgesamt konnte ich doch einige nützliche Dinge kaufen. Einen dicken Filzschreiber für 1,40 Euro fand ich übertrieben teuer. Den habe ich nicht gekauft." Stefan bekommt 25 Euro Taschengeld im Monat. Den Betrag findet er „in Ordnung", obwohl das Geld selten reicht. In den Ferien verdient Stefan etwas dazu. „Dann räume ich in einem Lebensmittelgeschäft Ware in Regale ein." Von seinem Taschengeld kauft Stefan Süßigkeiten, Musik-CDs, kleine Geschenke wie Notizbücher oder Stifte und Pflanzen. Schulsachen muß er nicht kaufen. „Die bezahlen meine Eltern." Sein größter Wunsch: „Wenn ich Geld zu verschenken hätte, würden es Tierschutz- und Umweltorganisationen bekommen."

▶ Stefans Freund Ben wohnt in der Kleinstadt Brüggen. Er entscheidet sich für den Einkauf in einem Supermarkt. „Wenn man nur 5 Euro zur Verfügung hat, bekommt man in einem Supermarkt wahrscheinlich die meisten Dinge. Außerdem gibt es in Supermärkten viele nützliche Sachen, die man für das tägliche Leben braucht." Im Supermarkt geht Ben durch die Regalreihen und vergleicht Preise. Die Auswahl fällt ihm schwer. Manche Dinge stellt er wieder ins Regal zurück. Ben bekommt für 5,05 Euro eine Zahnbürste, eine Flasche Orangensaft, eine Dose Cola, einen Sportdrink und einen Lippenpflege-Stift. DerLippenpflege-Stift ist teuer. Er kostet 1,35 Euro. Ben glaubt, daß er gut eingekauft hat. „Ich habe mehr bekommen, als ich dachte. Einen Riesen-Unterschied gab es allerdings bei den Preisen für Getränkedosen. Das Marken-Getränk aus der Werbung kostete 99 Cent. Die Dose Cola war dagegen spottbillig: nur 25 Cent." Ben bekommt pro Woche 4 Euro Taschengeld. Ihm reicht der Betrag. „Ich kann sogar ein bißchen Geld sparen, denn Schulsachen oder Kleidung muß ich nicht bezahlen. Diese Dinge kaufen meine Eltern." Von seinem Taschengeld kauft Ben ab und zu eine Compact Disc für sich oder ein kleines Geschenk, zum Beispiel ein Taschenbuch, für seine Freunde. Was würde Ben mit viel Geld machen? „Ich würde sofort eine Taucherausrüstung kaufen. Tauchen ist mein Hobby. Und wenn ich Geld verschenken könnte, dann würde ich es zum Schutz der Weltmeere und zum Schutz der Umwelt einsetzen."

6. Read the article about Ben through without stopping to ask about words you don't know. Then summarize the article in two or three sentences. In both articles, notice how much you can understand without knowing every word!

7. Read the article about Stefan again and try to answer these questions.

   a. What kind of store did Stefan shop in? What did he buy? What was his total bill?

   b. How much is Stefan's allowance per month? What does he buy with that money? What do his parents buy for him?

   c. What would Stefan do if he had a lot of money?

8. Read the article about Ben again and try to answer these questions.

   a. Where does Ben think he can find the largest selection of useful items for 5 euros? How does he define "useful"?

   b. What do Ben's parents buy for him? For what does he use his own money?

   c. If Ben had a lot of money, what would he buy? To what cause would he give?

9. You are planning a trip to a German-speaking country in the summer and are going to stay with a family. Write a short note asking them what small items you might bring them.

Answers to these questions appear on page 303W of the TE Interleaf.

Stefan wird im Schreibwarengeschäft von der Verkäuferin beraten. Sie zeigt ihm verschiedene Dinge und nennt ihm die Preise. Stefan braucht einige Zeit, bis er möglichst viele Sachen für fünf Euro gekauft hat.

ZUM LESEN   STANDARDS: 1.2, 1.3, 3.1, 5.2

Übungsheft, S. 131, Ü. 23

Mehr Grammatikübungen

CD-ROM DISC 3

Answers

☑ internet

go.hrw.com
ADRESSE: go.hrw.com
KENNWORT:
WK3 BADEN-WUERTTEMBERG-11

Erste Stufe

Objective Using the telephone

1 Was machst du, wenn du telefonieren willst? Schreib den folgenden Absatz (*paragraph*) ab und schreib dabei die fehlenden Wörter in die Lücken. Benutze die Wörter im Kasten. **(S. 310)**

anrufen	Apparat	Handy	Hörer
Münzen	Nummer	Telefonkarte	Telefonzelle

Du bist in der Stadt beim Einkaufen. Du willst zu Hause _____ , aber   anrufen

du hast kein _____ . Was machst du? Du gehst in eine _____ . Du   Geld; Telefonzelle

nimmst den _____ ab und du schiebst eine _____ ein. Dann wählst   Hörer; Telefonkarte

du die _____ . Aber du hörst *tüt, tüt, tüt*: der _____ ist besetzt.   Nummer; Apparat

2 Es gibt noch immer Münztelefone in Deutschland, und hier sind einige Anweisungen (*instructions*) für den Gebrauch solcher Telefone. Schreib den folgenden Absatz ab und schreib dabei passende Verbformen und passende Wörter in die Lücken. **(S. 310)**

Also, zuerst _____ du in die Telefonzelle _____ . Du _____ den Hörer   musst; gehen; musst

_____ und die Münzen _____ . Dann _____ du die Nummer _____ .   abnehmen; einwerfen; musst; wählen

Wenn es besetzt ist, _____ du den Hörer wieder _____ . — Wenn aber   musst; auflegen

jemand an den Apparat kommt, dann sagst du: _____ ich bitte Sabine   Kann

_____ ? Oder du _____ auch sagen: Ich _____ Sabine _____ , bitte.   sprechen; kannst; möchte; sprechen

Ist sie zu Hause?

Wenn du aber von einem Telefon mit einer „Allpayment-Funktion"

anrufst, so kannst du auch eine_____ benutzen. Aber vielleicht   Telefonkarte

brauchst du kein öffentliches Telefon mehr, weil du ein _____ hast.   Handy

Das ist bequem!

3 An welchem Tag finden diese Geburtstage und Feiertage statt? Schreib die richtigen Daten in die Lücken. (**S. 314**)

BEISPIEL   **Mein Vater, 17. Mai**   Am ___ .
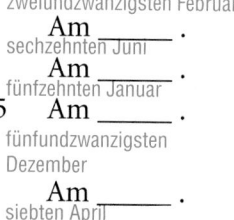
Am <u>siebzehnten Mai</u>.

1. Wer hat wann Geburtstag?
   a. George Washington, February 22   zweiundzwanzigsten Februar   Am _____ .
   b. Susan B. Anthony, June 16   sechzehnten Juni   Am _____ .
   c. Martin Luther King Jr., January 15   fünfzehnten Januar   Am _____ .

2. Wann sind diese Feiertage?
   a. Weihnachten, 25. Dezember   fünfundzwanzigsten Dezember   Am _____ .
   b. Ostern, 7. April   siebten April   Am _____ .
   c. Tag der Arbeit, 3. September   dritten September   Am _____ .

4 Schreib Grüße zu diesen Feiertagen! (**S. 315**)

Was schreibst du:

1. zu Weihnachten?   Fröhliche Weihnachten!
2. zum Muttertag?   Alles Gute zum Muttertag!
3. zu Ostern?   Frohe Ostern!
4. zu Chanukka?   Frohes Chanukka-Fest!
5. zum Namenstag?   Alles Gute / Herzlichen Glückwunsch zum Namenstag!
6. zum Geburtstag?   Herzlichen Glückwunsch / Alles Gute zum Geburtstag!

5 Du sprichst über Geschenke für verschiedene Familienmitglieder. Schreib die folgenden Fragen ab und schreib dabei die richtige Form des bestimmten Artikels (**der, die, das**) in die Lücken. (**S. 319**)

1. Was schenkst du _____ Opa zum Geburtstag?   dem
2. Was schenkst du _____ Tante Helene?   der
3. Was schenkst du _____ Mama zum Muttertag?   der
4. Was schenkst du _____ Papa zum Vatertag?   dem
5. Was schenkst du _____ Beatrice zum Namenstag?   der
6. Was schenkst du _____ Mark zu Weihnachten?   dem

6 Jetzt sprichst du über Geschenkideen für andere Leute. Schreib die folgenden Fragen und Antworten ab und schreib dabei die richtige Form des Possessivpronomens in die Lücken. **(S. 319)**

1. Was schenkst du _____ Mutter und _____ Vater zu Weihnachten?   deiner; deinem

2. Ich schenke _____ Vater und _____ Mutter zwei CDs.   meinem; meiner

3. Was schenkst du _____ Onkel und _____ Tante?   deinem; deiner

4. Ich schenke _____ Onkel ein Buch und _____ Tante Pralinen.   meinem; meiner

5. Was schenkst du _____ Oma und _____ Opa zum Hochzeitstag?   deiner; deinem

6. Ich schenke _____ Opa Blumen und _____ Oma Pralinen.   meinem; meiner

7 Jetzt sprichst du wieder über Geschenkideen für deine Familienmitglieder. Lies die Fragen und schreib das richtige Pronomen in die Lücken. **(S. 319)**

1. Was schenkst du dem Vati?—Ich schenke _____ ein Buch.   ihm

2. Was schenkst du der Mutti?—Ich schenke _____ eine CD.   ihr

3. Was schenkst du dem Opa?—Ich schenke _____ eine Armbanduhr.   ihm

4. Was schenkst du der Oma?—Ich schenke _____ Blumen.   ihr

5. Was schenkst du dem Bernd?—Ich schenke _____ ein Poster.   ihm

6. Was schenkst du der Erika?—Ich schenke _____ Parfüm.   ihr

8 Du sagst einem Freund, was du deinen Verwandten *(relatives)* schenken willst. Schreib die folgenden Sätze ab und schreib dabei das richtige Possessivpronomen in die erste Lücke und das richtige Pronomen in die zweite Lücke. **(S. 320)**

1. Ich schenke _____ Bruder ein Buch, und ich schenke _____ auch eine CD.   meinem; ihm

2. Ich schenke _____ Oma Blumen, und ich schenke _____ auch Pralinen.   meiner; ihr

3. Ich schenke _____ Mutter ein Poster, und ich schenke _____ auch Parfüm.   meiner; ihr

4. Ich schenke _____ Opa Pralinen, und ich schenke _____ auch eine CD.   meinem; ihm

5. Ich schenke _____ Onkel ein Poster, und ich schenke _____ auch ein Buch.   meinem; ihm

6. Ich schenke _____ Tante Pralinen, und ich schenke _____ auch ein Poster.   meiner; ihr

Du hast viele Geschenkideen. Sag, welche Ideen du hast. Schreib Sätze, die ein indirektes und ein direktes Satzobjekt enthalten. **(S. 320)**

BEISPIEL   **Was schenkst du deinem Bruder? (CD) Ich schenke _____ .**
   Ich schenke <u>meinem Bruder eine CD</u>.

1. Was schenkst du deiner Mutter? (Buch)   Ich schenke _____ .   *meiner Mutter ein Buch*
2. Was schenkst du deinem Opa? (CD)   Ich schenke _____ .   *meinem Opa eine CD*
3. Was schenkst du deiner Oma? (Blumen)   Ich schenke _____ .   *meiner Oma Blumen*
4. Was schenkst du deinem Vater? (Hemd)   Ich schenke _____ .   *meinem Vater ein Hemd*
5. Was schenkst du deinem Onkel? (Uhr)   Ich schenke _____ .   *meinem Onkel eine Uhr*
6. Was schenkst du deiner Tante? (Rock)   Ich schenke _____ .   *meiner Tante einen Rock*

10 Was gibst du den Leuten zum Geburtstag oder zum Namenstag? Schreib die folgenden Antworten ab und gebrauche dabei ein passendes Pronomen und den unbestimmten Artikel für jedes Hauptwort *(noun)*. **(S. 320)**

1. Was schenkst du deiner Freundin zum Namenstag?
   (Buch; Blumenstrauß) — Ja, ich schenke _____ .   *ihr ein Buch und einen Blumenstrauß*
2. Was schenkst du deinem Großvater zum Namenstag?
   (Hemd; Kalender) — Ja, ich schenke _____ .   *ihm ein Hemd und einen Kalender*
3. Was schenkst du deiner Mutter zum Namenstag?
   (Armbanduhr; Pralinen) — Ja, ich schenke _____ .   *ihr eine Armbanduhr und Pralinen*
4. Was schenkst du denn deiner Biolehrerin zum Namenstag?
   (Poster; Blumen) — Ja, ich schenke _____ .   *ihr ein Poster und Blumen*
5. Was schenkst du deinem Freund Kurt zu Weihnachten?
   (T-Shirt; Gürtel) — Ja, ich schenke _____ .   *ihm ein T-Shirt und einen Gürtel*
6. Was schenkst du deinem Bruder zum Geburtstag?
   (Hobbybuch; Roman) — Ja, ich schenke _____ .   *ihm ein Hobbybuch und einen Roman*

Anwendung

The *CD-ROM Tutor* offers guided recording and writing activities to accompany the **An-wendung.** These activities are designed to practice students' oral and written communication skills and to review material from each chapter.

1 Listen to Helene and Volker's conversation about what they are buying their friends as birthday presents. Write down who's giving what to whom as a present. CD 11 Tr. 17

1. Helene, dem Ulf, eine CD
2. Volker, der Sonja, einen Kalender
3. Helene, der Ute, ein Buch
4. Volker, dem Ralf, ein Videospiel

For script, see *Listening Activities*, p. 165.

2 Drei Schüler sprechen darüber, was sie am liebsten zum Geburtstag bekommen möchten und warum.

a. Read the interviews and decide what each of the three teenagers would like to have and why. Write down the information.

„Du fragst, was ich am liebsten zum Geburtstag haben möchte? — Ganz einfach! Du weißt doch, dass ich gern lese. Du kannst mir also ein Buch kaufen, vielleicht etwas über gefährdete Tiere in Afrika, oder — ich hab da noch eine Idee. Du kannst mir zum Geburtstag ein Karl-May-Buch schenken, denn seine Bücher sind wieder ganz populär. Und ich lese Karl May furchtbar gern."

ein Buch über gefährdete Tiere in Afrika oder von Karl May (Er liest gern.)

Ingo, 17

„Ja, am liebsten möchte ich irgendetwas, was mit Musik zu tun hat. Eine prima Kassette, Mathias Reim vielleicht, oder eine CD. Du weißt, ich höre auch klassische Musik gern. Und unter den Klassikern gibt es eine wirklich große Auswahl, zum Beispiel etwas von …nein, ich hab's: die schönsten Arien aus den populärsten Opern. Das ist etwas für mich!"

eine Kassette-Mathias Reim-oder eine CD (Sie mag Musik.)

Margot, 16

„Du kannst mir eine große Freude machen und mir eine Karte zum nächsten Rockkonzert schenken. Die „Toten Hosen" kommen nächsten Monat hierher, und die möchte ich unbedingt hören. Natürlich sind die Karten furchtbar teuer, ich weiß. Aber du kannst dich vielleicht mit zwei andern Leuten zusammentun, und ihr könnt mir gemeinsam eine Karte kaufen. Dann ist es für jeden nicht so teuer." **Karte für Rockkonzert (Sie möchte „Die Toten Hosen" hören.)**

Clarissa, 16

3 Gabriele und Philipp sprechen über Bernhards Geburtstag und machen Pläne. Was wollen sie zuerst machen? First look at the pictures and decide what Gabriele and Philipp are doing in each one. Then listen to their conversation and put the following drawings in the correct order. For script, see *Listening Activities*, p. 165.

b, d, a, c

CD 11 Tr. 18

a.

b.

c.

d.

4 Ihr möchtet der Lehrerin oder dem Lehrer etwas schenken. Macht eine Liste von Geschenkideen! Dann sprecht darüber, was ihr schenken möchtet. Fragt alle in der Gruppe, was sie schenken wollen. Wie sind ihre Ideen? Toll oder blöd?

5 # Zum Schreiben

Write a dialogue in which you call a friend to discuss a birthday party that will take place soon. Agree to buy a gift together.

> **Schreibtipp** Think about the **logical order** in which you will build the conversation. Be sure to make the conversation flow in a logical way, building from saying hello, asking questions in a logical order, and saying good-bye.

Prewriting

Make **lists** of gift ideas, clothing to wear to a party, and dates and times.

Writing

Create your **dialogue** using the following sentences: Say hello, and ask your friend's mother (who answers the phone) if you may talk to your friend. Greet the friend; ask if he/she is going to the party. Discuss what you both will wear. Ask if she/he wants to go in with you to buy a gift. After discussing several choices, decide on a gift. Decide on a day and time to go shopping. Say good-bye.

Revising

- Read the conversation aloud with a partner, looking for strengths and weaknesses. Are your questions and responses clear? Are the ideas well organized? Check over spelling and grammar and make changes. Set the conversation aside and go back to it later.

- Proofread your dialogue once more as a final check for spelling and grammar errors, making corrections as necessary.

- Revise and submit it to your teacher. You might ask two of your classmates to present this dialogue to the class.

6 # Rollenspiel

Role-play the following situation with two or three classmates:

Each group picks one type of store you have learned about (**Metzgerei, Modegeschäft, Schreibwarenladen …**). Write it on a card, and put the cards in a box. One person from each group draws a card from the box. Your group has just been hired by the store you drew to write some commercials to help boost sales for the holidays. Write a commercial to convince people to buy the items at your store as gifts. Suggest people in the family to give the gifts to. (You will have to be pretty persuasive in order to convince people to buy gifts at a **Metzgerei**!) Bring in props and perform your commercial in front of the class.

Kann ich's wirklich?

Can you use the telephone in Germany? (p. 310)

1 If you were calling someone in Germany, how would you
   a. say who you are   Tag, hier ist …
   b. ask to speak to someone   Kann ich bitte …sprechen?
   c. say hello to the person you want to speak with   Tag, …
   d. say goodbye   Auf Wiederhören!

2 If you were answering the phone in Germany, how would you
   a. identify yourself   **b.** ask the caller to wait a minute
   Hier ist …(last name)   Einen Moment, bitte.

3 How would you tell someone how to use a public telephone to make a call?
   (Use **zuerst, dann, danach,** and **zuletzt.**)   Zuerst hebst du den Hörer ab.
   Dann steckst du die Münzen ein. Danach wählst du die Nummer. Zuletzt legst du wieder auf.

Can you invite someone to a party and accept or decline? (p. 313)

4 How would a friend invite you to his or her birthday party on Saturday evening at 8:00?   Ich habe am Samstag um 8 Uhr eine Geburtstagsparty. Ich lade dich ein!

5 How would you respond if
   a. you can come   Ja, gern!
   b. you can't come because a relative is coming to visit   Leider kann ich nicht, (meine Kusine) kommt zu Besuch.
   c. you can't come because you are going to a concert   … weil ich ins Konzert gehe.
   d. you can't come because you have to do your homework
   … denn ich muss Hausaufgaben machen.

Can you talk about birthdays and express good wishes? (p. 314)

6 How would you ask a friend when he or she has a birthday?   Wann hast du Geburtstag?

7 How would your friend respond if he or she has a birthday on
   a. May 29   **b.** March 9   **c.** February 16   **d.** July 7
   am 29. Mai   am 9. März   am 16. Februar   am 7. Juli

8 How would you express good wishes for the following occasions?
   a. birthday   **b.** Christmas   **c.** Hanukkah
   Alles Gute zum Geburtstag!   Frohe/Fröhliche Weihnachten!   Frohes/Fröhliches Chanukka-Fest!

Can you discuss gift ideas? (p. 318)

9 How would you ask a friend what he or she is getting another friend for his or her birthday? How might your friend respond?   Was schenkst du
   Ich schenke ihm/ihr …   dem/der …zum Geburtstag?

10 How would you tell a friend that you are going to give these items to various relatives for their birthdays?   Answers will vary.

a.   **b.**   **c.**   **d.**
mein Vater   meine Tante   meine Oma   mein Bruder

Erste Stufe

Using the telephone in Germany

telefonieren	to call on the phone	abheben (sep)	to pick up (the phone)
anrufen (sep)	to call	auflegen (sep)	to hang up (the phone)
der Apparat, -e	telephone		
das Telefon, -e	telephone	die Nummer wählen	to dial the number
der Hörer, -	receiver		
die Telefonzelle -n	telephone booth	besetzt	busy
die Telefonnummer, -n	telephone number	Einen Moment, bitte!	Just a minute, please.
Münzen einstecken (sep)	to insert coins		

Hier (ist) …	This is …
Hier bei …	The …residence
Kann ich bitte … spechen?	Can I please speak to …?
Auf Wiederhören!	Goodbye!
Wiederhören!	Bye!

Other useful words

das Handy, -s	cell phone
die Telefonkarte, -n	phone card

Zweite Stufe

Inviting someone to a party

einladen (sep)	to invite
er/sie lädt …ein	he/she invites

Accepting or declining

Natürlich!	Certainly!
Ja, gern!	Sure!
Aber sicher!	Sure!

Talking about birthdays and expressing good wishes

der Geburtstag, -e	birthday
die Party, -s	party
Ich habe am … Geburtstag.	My birthday is on …

Wann hast du Geburtstag?	When is your birthday?
am ersten (1.), zweiten (2.), dritten (3.), usw.	on the first, second, third, etc …
bald	soon
nächste Woche	next week
Alles Gute zum Geburtstag!	Happy Birthday!
Herzlichen Glückwunsch zum Geburtstag!	Best wishes on your birthday!
der Feiertag, -e	holiday
Weihnachten	Christmas

Fröhliche Weihnachten!	Merry Christmas!
Chanukka	Hanukkah
Frohes Chanukka-Fest!	Happy Hanukkah!
Ostern	Easter
Frohe Ostern!	Happy Easter!
der Muttertag	Mother's Day
Alles Gute zum Muttertag!	Happy Mother's Day!
der Vatertag	Father's Day
Alles Gute zum Vatertag!	Happy Father's Day!

Dritte Stufe

p. 303X

Discussing gift ideas

schenken	to give (a gift)
geben	to give
er/sie gibt	he/she gives
die Geschenkidee, -n	gift idea
das Geschenk, -e	gift
die Praline, -n	fancy chocolate
die Armbanduhr, -en	(wrist)watch
der Kalender, -	calendar
der Blumenstrauß, ¨e	bouquet of flowers

das Poster, -	poster
die CD, -s	compact disc
das Parfüm, -e	perfume
der Schmuck	jewelry
deinem Vater	to/for your father
meinem Vater	to/for my father
deiner Mutter	to/for your mother
meiner Mutter	to/for my mother

Pronouns, dative case

ihm	to/for him
ihr	to/for her

wem?	whom? to whom? for whom?

Articles, dative case

dem	the (masc.)
der	the (fem.)

Other useful words

wahrscheinlich	probably
vielleicht	maybe
verschieden	different

Chapter Overview

Los geht's! pp. 334–336	*Die Geburtstagsfete, p. 334*

	FUNCTIONS	GRAMMAR	VOCABULARY	RE-ENTRY
Erste Stufe pp. 337–341	• Offering help and explaining what to do, p. 337 • Asking where something is located and giving directions, p. 339	• The verb **können**; the preposition **für**; accusative pronouns; **du**- and **ihr**-commands, p. 337 • The verb **wissen** and word order in clauses following **wissen**, p. 340	• Cooking ingredients, p. 338	• Chapter 12 is a global review of *Komm mit!* Level 1
Zweite Stufe pp. 342–345	• Making plans and inviting someone to come along, p. 342 • Talking about clothing, p. 344 • Discussing gift ideas, p. 345	• The verbs **wollen** and **müssen**; word order, p. 342 • Nominative and accusative pronouns; definite and indefinite articles, p. 345 • Dative endings, p. 345	• Freetime activities, p. 342 • Words used to describe clothing, p. 344	• Chapter 12 is a global review of *Komm mit!* Level 1
Dritte Stufe pp. 346–349	• Describing people and places, p. 346 • Saying what you would like and whether you do or don't want more, p. 348 • Talking about what you did, p. 349	• The nominative pronouns **er, sie, es,** and **sie** *pl;* possessive pronouns, p. 346 • The **möchte**-forms; **noch ein** and **kein … mehr,** p. 348	• Furniture and appliances, p. 347	• Chapter 12 is a global review of *Komm mit!* Level 1

Aussprache p. 349	Review letters **w** and **j**; review short vowels **ä** and **e**; review long vowels **ä** and **e**: Audio CD 12, Track 12	**Diktat:** Audio CD 12, Tracks 13–14

Zum Lesen pp. 350–351	**Mahlzeit**	**Reading Strategy** Combining reading strategies (Using visual clues, cognates, and context to determine meaning)

Mehr Grammatik-übungen	**pp. 352–355**		
	Erste Stufe, pp. 352–353	**Zweite Stufe**, pp. 353–354	**Dritte Stufe**, pp. 354–355

Review pp. 356–359	**Anwendung**, pp. 356–357	**Kann ich's wirklich?**, p. 358	**Wortschatz**, p. 359
	Zum Schreiben: Combining sentences (Writing a descriptive letter)		

CULTURE

- **Ein wenig Landeskunde: Spätzle/Apfelküchle**, p. 338
- **Landeskunde: Musst du zu Hause helfen?** p. 341
- **Polo mit Eskimorolle**, p. 343
- German gift ideas, p. 345
- Photos from furniture ads, p. 347
- Menu from an **Imbissstube**, p. 348

Kapitel 12: Die Fete
Chapter Resources

 **PRINT**

Lesson Planning

One-Stop Planner

Lesson Planner with Substitute Teacher Lesson Plans, pp. 57–61, 76

Student Make-Up Assignments
- Make-Up Assignment Copying Masters, Chapter 12

Listening and Speaking

TPR Storytelling Book, pp. 45–48

Listening Activities
- Student Response Forms for Listening Activities, pp. 91–93
- Additional Listening Activities 12-1 to 12-6, pp. 95–98
- Additional Listening Activities (song), p. 94
- Scripts and Answers, pp. 170–176

Video Guide
- Teaching Suggestions, pp. 76–77
- Activity Masters, pp. 78–80
- Scripts and Answers, pp. 107–110, 116

Activities for Communication
- Communicative Activities, pp. 67–72
- Realia and Teaching Suggestions, pp. 118–121
- Situation Cards, pp. 145–146

Reading and Writing

Reading Strategies and Skills Handbook, Chapter 12

Lies mit mir! 1, Chapter 12

Übungsheft, pp. 133–144

Grammar

Grammatikheft, pp. 100–108

Grammar Tutor for Students of German, Chapter 12

Assessment

Testing Program
- Grammar and Vocabulary Quizzes, **Stufe** Quizzes, and Chapter Test, pp. 301–318
- Score Sheet, Scripts and Answers, pp. 319–326

- Final Exam, pp. 327–334
- Final Exam Score Sheet, Scripts and Answers, pp. 335–340

Alternative Assessment Guide
- Portfolio Assessment, p. 29
- Performance Assessment, p. 43
- CD-ROM Assessment, p. 57

Student Make-Up Assignments
- Alternative Quizzes, Chapter 12

 **MEDIA**

 Online Activities
- Interaktive Spiele
- Internet Aktivitäten

 Video Program
- Videocassette 4
- Videocassette 5 (captioned version)

 Audio Compact Discs
- Textbook Listening Activities, CD 12, Tracks 1–15
- Additional Listening Activities, CD 12, Tracks 28–33
- Assessment Items, CD 12, Tracks 16–27

 Interactive CD-ROM Tutor, Disc 3

 Teaching Transparencies
- Situations 12-1 to 12-2
- Vocabulary 12-A to 12-B
- **Los geht's!**
- **Mehr Grammatikübungen** Answers
- **Grammatikheft** Answers

 **One-Stop Planner CD-ROM**

Use the **One-Stop Planner CD-ROM with Test Generator** to aid in lesson planning and pacing.

For each chapter, the **One-Stop Planner** includes:
- Editable lesson plans with direct links to teaching resources
- Printable worksheets from resource books
- Direct launches to the HRW Internet activities
- Video and audio segments
- Test Generator
- Clip Art for vocabulary items

Kapitel 12: Die Fete

Projects ·····················

Eine tolle Schulspeisekarte

In this project students will create a poster displaying a nutritious five-day menu they have planned for the school cafeteria.

MATERIALS

✄ **Students may need**
- large posterboard
- scissors
- grocery advertisement flyers
- glue or tape
- markers
- food magazines

ORGANIZATION

Students' menus should include the following:

Days of the week and corresponding dates

Prices for each item

Nutritional information

German Day (offering German specialties)

SUGGESTED SEQUENCE

1. Students get into groups of three or four students, depending on the class size.
2. All groups discuss and make outlines of what they plan to include on their menus. (pizza, hamburgers, and hot dogs are NOT allowed.) Caution students that each menu should be nutritionally balanced and include all food groups.
3. Students write a complete lunch menu for five days, including the information outlined above.
4. Students display their menu on posterboard.
5. Groups present their menus orally.
6. The class votes via secret ballot for the best menu.

GRADING THE PROJECT

Suggested point distribution (**total = 100 points**)

Appearance	20
Accuracy of written language	20
Creativity of ideas	20
Oral presentation	40

COMMUNITY LINK

If there are any German **Vereine** in your community or neighboring areas, you might want to suggest that students organize a **Kulturabend** or a **Fete** with them.

Games ·····························

Wortfamilien

This game will help students review vocabulary from the whole book.

Procedure For this activity, prepare a list of vocabulary items that are related to a particular category. (Examples: **eine Fete, die Stadt, zu Hause helfen, Schule**) Have students work with a partner or in a small group. Announce the first category to the class and give students two minutes to write down as many related words as they can think of. Then have each group write its words on the chalkboard. Go through each list and verify that the words belong to the right category and that they are spelled correctly. The group with the most correct words wins.

Heiss auf der Spur

*This game can be used to review vocabulary and culture notes that have been introduced throughout the book in the almanacs, location openers, chapter openers, and **Landeskunde** entries.*

Procedure Go through the chapters and compile a "Scavenger List" of questions and cues that you feel will help students review the material. Give a copy of the list to each group. The group that has the most correct answers within a set time wins.

Suggestions for Scavenger Cues

1. — heißt die Hauptstadt von Bayern.
2. — ist das deutsche Wort für *pedestrian zone.*
3. — sind zwei Getränke.
4. Die Familie sitzt am — und isst zu Mittag.
5. — ist ein Spezialgeschäft für Fleischwaren.

Storytelling ·············

*This story accompanies Teaching Transparency 12-A. The **Mini-Geschichte** can be told and retold in different formats, acted out, written down, and read aloud to give students additional opportunities to practice all four skills.*

Ein Sonntagnachmittag

„Du, Marika, was tun wir heute Nachmittag? Willst du basteln oder willst du lieber ein Brettspiel spielen?" „Ach, Jens, heute ist es so warm und sonnig. Ich will nicht im Haus sein. Willst du vielleicht in den Park gehen oder wandern?" „Wandern ist langweilig! Und wir waren letztes Wochenende im Park! Ich möchte lieber in den Zoo gehen. Ich sehe gern die Elefanten und die Affen *(monkeys)*." „Gute Idee! Gehen wir in den Zoo!"

Traditions ·············

Literatur und Essen

Zwiebelkuchen gibt es überall in Süddeutschland, wo man Wein anbaut: in Schwaben, in Baden, in der Pfalz und in Franken. Ein guter Zwiebelkuchen regte Eduard Mörike zu folgendem Gedicht an.

Zwiebelkuchen
Ganz richtig hört ich sagen
Daß wer in Zwiebeln schlief,
hinunter wird getragen
in Träume schwer und tief.
Dem Wachen selbst geblieben
Sei irren Wahnes Spur:
Die Nahen und die Lieben
Hielt er für Zwiebeln nur.
Und gegen dieses Übel,
Das gar nicht angenehm,
Hilft selber nur die Zwiebel
Nach Hahnemanns System.

Das lass uns gleich versuchen!
Gott gebe, daß es glückt!—
Und schafft mir Zwiebelkuchen!
Sonst werd ich noch verrückt!

(Eduard Mörike)

Schwäbischer Zwiebelkuchen

Zutaten für 4 bis 6 Portionen

Zutaten

g=Gramm, EL=Esslöffel, l=Liter

1/8 l	lauwarme Milch
8EL	Öl
250g	Mehl
Salz	
20g	Hefe
1,5kg	Zwiebeln
3	große Eier (oder 4 kleine)
1	Becher saure Sahne
	etwas Kümmel
	Öl für die Form
150g	durchwachsener Speck

Zubereitung

Die lauwarme Milch mit 6 EL Öl, Mehl und 1 guten Prise Salz in eine Rührschüssel geben und die Hefe darüber zerbröseln. Die Zutaten gut mischen und einen glatten, geschmeidigen Teig daraus kneten. Den Teig zugedeckt an einem warmen Platz 20 Minuten gehen lassen. Inzwischen die Zwiebeln schälen und in Würfel schneiden. 2 EL Öl in einem möglichst großen und weiten Topf erhitzen, die Zwiebelwürfel glasig braten. Den Topf vom Herd nehmen, die Zwiebelmasse etwas abkühlen lassen, dann die Eier und die saure Sahne unterrühren. Die Masse mit Salz und Kümmel nach Geschmack würzen. Den gegangenen Hefeteig noch einmal kurz durchkneten, dann dünn ausrollen. Eine Springform (26 cm Durchmesser) mit Öl ausfetten, den Teig hineinlegen und einen hohen Rand hochziehen. Die Zwiebelmasse einfüllen. Den durchwachsenen Speck in kleine Würfel schneiden und darüber streuen. Den Kuchen im vorgeheizten Ofen bei 220 Grad 1 Stunde backen, bis er an der Oberfläche goldbraun ist. Der Zwiebelkuchen muss unbedingt warm serviert werden.

Technology

Video

Videocassette 4, 5 (captioned version)
See Video Guide, pages 75–80

Los geht's! • Die Geburtstagsfete

Nicole and her friends prepare for a party to celebrate Martin's birthday. They do the shopping and cleaning, and they're helping around the kitchen.

Landeskunde

Musst du zu Hause helfen?

People of various ages and from different cities talk about how they help out at home.

Fortsetzung

The guests arrive for the party with birthday gifts for Martin. Nicole's father is grilling, and her mother is serving the food. After everyone has had something to eat and drink, they sing "Happy Birthday" to Martin in English.

Videoclips

- **Konditorei Coppenrath u. Wiese**® (frozen cakes)
- **Konditorei Coppenrath u. Wiese**® (frozen cakes)
- **Tengelmann und Kaisers**® (vegetables)
- **Frosta**® (frozen dinners)
- **Neudorff Bio-Fibel**® (environmental products)

Interactive CD-ROM Tutor

The **Interactive CD-ROM Tutor** contains videos, interactive games, and activities that provide students an opportunity to practice and review the material covered in Chapter 12.

Activity	Activity Type	Pupil's Edition Reference
1. So sagt man das!	Wozu gehört's?	pp. 337, 339
2. Wortschatz	Wort und Bild Erfahren/Wählen	p. 342
3. Grammatik	Was fehlt?	pp. 340, 342
4. Grammatik	Was fehlt?	pp. 345, 346
5. Wortschatz	Merkspiel	p. 347
6. So sagt man das!	Was ist richtig?	pp. 344, 345, 346, 348
Landeskunde	Musst du zu Hause helfen? Was ist richtig?	p. 341
Zum Sprechen	*Guided recording*	pp. 356–357
Zum Schreiben	*Guided writing*	pp. 356–357

Teacher Management System

Logging In

Logging in to the *Komm mit!* TMS is easy. Upon launching the program, simply type "admin" in the password area of the log-in screen and press RETURN. Log on to **www.hrw.com/CDROMTUTOR** for a detailed explanation of the Teacher Management System.

One-Stop Planner CD-ROM

To preview all resources available for this chapter, use the **One-Stop Planner CD-ROM**, Disc 3.

Internet Connection ....

📡 internet

go. hrw .com
ADRESSE: go.hrw.com
KENNWORT:
WK3 BADEN-WUERTTEMBERG-12

*Have students explore the **go.hrw.com** Web site for many online resources covering all chapters. All Chapter 12 resources are available under the keyword **WK3 Baden-Wuerttemberg-12**. Interactive games practice the material and provide students with immediate feedback. You will also find a printable worksheet that provides Internet activities that lead to a comprehensive online research project.*

Interaktive Spiele

You can use the interactive activities in this chapter

- to practice grammar, vocabulary, and chapter functions
- as homework
- as an assessment option
- as a self-test
- to prepare for the Chapter Test

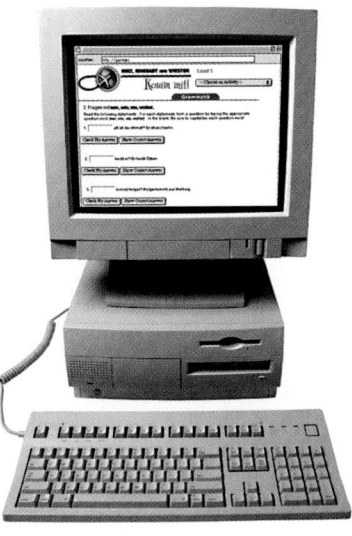

Internet Aktivitäten

Students will give directions using a city map of Stuttgart. They will visit an online bakery and music shop.

- To prepare students for the **Arbeitsblatt,** have them practice giving and following directions. You might want to use the map on p. 339 or on p. 356 for this activity.
- After completing the **Arbeitsblatt,** have students design an invitation for Mike's birthday party. The invitation should include the place and time of the party and other particulars, such as the food to be served or the music to be played.

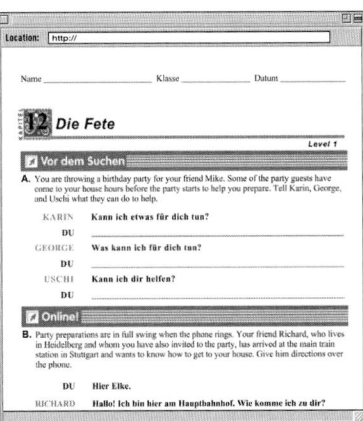

Webprojekt

Have students visit Stuttgart or any other city in Baden-Württemberg. Ask them to plan a sightseeing tour in the city they chose. They should make an itinerary of the places they want to see. Encourage students to exchange useful Web sites with their classmates. Have students document their sources by referencing the names and URLs of all the sites they consulted.

Erste Stufe

5 p. 337

THOMAS   Das wird ja eine dufte Fete, was, Nicole?

NICOLE   Bestimmt, aber ihr müsst mir wirklich ein wenig dabei helfen. Das kann ich alles gar nicht alleine schaffen.

THOMAS   Mensch, sicher … sag mal, wie ich helfen kann.

NICOLE   Thomas, am besten sortier erst mal den Müll. Da ist diesmal eine Menge. Die Tüten findest du in der Abstellkammer. Anschließend könntest du den Rasen mähen.

THOMAS   Und wo ist der Rasenmäher?

NICOLE   In der Garage. Und du, Andreas, sei nicht so faul! Zeitung lesen gibt es hier nicht. Hier sind saubere Tücher und Putzmittel.

ANDREAS   Und was soll ich damit?

NICOLE   Was wohl? Fenster putzen! Und wenn du damit fertig bist, sei so lieb und sauge Staub hier oben!

SABINE   Ich bin ja auch noch hier. Wie kann ich dir helfen, Nicole?

NICOLE   Ja, du kannst zuerst den Tisch decken, du weißt ja, wo das Geschirr und das Besteck bei uns sind.

SABINE   Sonst noch was? Soll ich in der Küche helfen?

NICOLE   Nee, Sabine, du kannst lieber das Geschirr spülen. Das ist wohl alles. Ach, Moment mal! Mir fehlen einige Sachen zum Essen. Anschließend kannst du ja diese Sachen im Supermarkt kaufen, geht das?

SABINE   Ja, sicher!

THOMAS   Bin fertig! Ah … jetzt ruh ich mich mal aus.

NICOLE   Ja, also wenn du so schnell fertig bist, Thomas, dann räum dieses Zimmer etwas auf. Dann ist alles getan.

THOMAS   So ein Pech!

9 p. 340

SABINE   Du wohnst gar nicht so weit von mir, Laubenweg 17, ja? Also von euch geht das am einfachsten, wenn du rechts auf dem Laubenweg bis zur Königstraße gehst. Bei der Kreuzung an der Königstraße gehst du dann nach rechts, und kurz danach gehst du in die erste Straße links. Auf der rechten Seite kannst du die Post sehen. Da bist du dann auf der Wengertgasse und bleibst darauf, bis du zur Pfarrgasse kommst. Geh nach links in die Pfarrgasse bis zur Gartenstraße. Dort wohne ich an der Ecke. Du brauchst nur zu klingeln. Vergiss nicht, Sonntag um 12 Uhr!

NICOLE   Ich hatte ganz vergessen, dass du ja noch nie bei mir warst. Also, ich glaub, von euerem Haus, … geh am besten links auf dem Laubenweg, bis du zur Ursulinergasse kommst. Da gehst du dann in die erste Straße rechts, also in die Ursulinergasse, und bleibst darauf, bis du das Schild von der Rosmaringasse siehst. Da gehst du in die erste Straße rechts, also in die Rosmaringasse, bis zur Herzog-Ernst-Straße. Du gehst links in die Herzog-Ernst-Straße und dann geradeaus bis zur Marktstraße. Da wohne ich. Wir wohnen im Erdgeschoss. Die Tür ist unten auf. Alles verstanden? Und die Fete fängt so um halb acht an. Bis dann!

Zweite Stufe

12 p. 343

PETER   Grüß Gott! Mein Name ist Peter Ludwig. Freizeit hab ich ja nicht sehr viel, mit Hausaufgaben nach der Schule, dann noch die ganze Hausarbeit, da will ich schon ausspannen. Meinem Freund Guido geht das genauso. Wir treffen uns meistens bei mir zu Hause und spielen Schach oder andere Brettspiele. Dabei hören wir immer Musik. Und der Guido hat eine tolle Stereoanlage. Da bringe ich auch mal meine CDs, wenn wir uns bei ihm zu Hause treffen.

SANDRA   Ich bin die Sandra. Ich komme aus München, aber jetzt wohne ich in Stuttgart. Das ist mir noch alles ein bisschen neu, aber es ist auch gleichzeitig sehr interessant. Wenn das Wetter gut ist, nehm ich meistens mein Rad und fahr in der Altstadt herum. Ja, und manchmal geh ich dann auch ins Kino, aber allein macht das ja nicht immer so viel Spaß. Neulich war ich auf dem Stuttgarter Fernsehturm. Der befindet sich auf dem Bopser. Von der oberen Aussichtsplattform konnte man die ganze Stadt sehen, das war echt toll.

FRANZ   Ich heiße Franz Stifter, und in meiner Freizeit bin ich oft mit meinen Freunden unterwegs. Was wir so tun? Tja … kommt ganz darauf an. Meistens treffen wir uns im Jugendzentrum. Die Leute da brauchen manchmal unsere Hilfe. Dann helfen wir halt mit Ausflügen für die Kinder. Die gehen dann in Parks oder im Winter Schlittschuh laufen. Einmal haben wir sogar den Tierpark besucht. Das hat natürlich Spaß gemacht.

JUDITH   Mein Name ist Judith Heinemann, und ich wohne auch hier in der Nähe. Ich interessier mich hauptsächlich für Sport, schon seit ich klein war. Zuerst habe ich Gymnastik gemacht, aber

One-Stop Planner CD-ROM

For resource information, see the **One-Stop Planner CD-ROM**, Disc 3.

das war irgendwie langweilig. Dann habe ich Tennisspielen angefangen. Und das mache ich am liebsten. Ich trainiere drei-, manchmal auch viermal in der Woche. Das mache ich immer nachmittags, wenn ich mit meinen Hausaufgaben fertig bin.

15   p. 344

1. — Bei Biedermeyers gibt es diese Woche wieder mal tolle Sonderangebote.

— Wirklich? Stand das in der Zeitung?

— Ja, gestern. Und ich brauche unbedingt neue Fußballschuhe. Eigentlich brauche ich auch ein paar Socken. Meine haben alle Löcher vorne.

— Wir können ja mal hingehen. Ich möchte sehen, ob sie eine Badehose in meiner Größe haben.

2. — Die jungen Leute sind ja wie wild in den Laden Lassofänger gestürmt.

— Ja, also deren Waren finde ich schrecklich, und du, Irma?

— Na, Jeans mag ich ja schon mal anziehen, aber diese Cowboystiefel, die sehen doch unmöglich aus, findest du nicht?

— Du hast Recht. Ich habe auch einen anderen Geschmack.

3. — Für die Fete am Samstag bei Rudi möchte ich mir bei Zimmermanns gern eine neue Bluse und vielleicht einen schwarzen Rock kaufen. Die haben fesche Sachen und gute Preise.

— Da habe ich mir neulich dieses Kleid gekauft. Wie findest du es?

— Es steht dir wirklich ausgezeichnet.

4. — Bist du schon in das neue Geschäft neben Neckermann gegangen? Wie heißt das noch gleich?

— Du meinst Walters. Die haben schicke Hosen … und ganz tolle Anzüge. Die sind aber auch ganz schön teuer. Die haben italienische Hemden und Schuhe. Also, für die Disko kannst du da eine Menge Sachen finden.

— Tja, dafür reicht mein Taschengeld nicht ganz aus.

Dritte Stufe

■ AUSSPRACHE, p. 349

Diktat, p. 349

You will hear about the clothes Bärbel would like to buy to go to Werner's party. First listen to what is said, then write down what you hear.

Für Werners Fete am 18. Juni will Bärbel sich einige neue Klamotten kaufen. Sie hat von dem neuen Modegeschäft Zimmermanns gehört und hofft, da vielleicht einen Rock und eine neue Bluse zu finden. Sie hat nämlich in der Zeitung gelesen, dass es in dem Geschäft zur Zeit gute Sonderangebote gibt. Ihre Freundinnen Julia und Bettina waren gerade gestern in dem Geschäft und haben schicke Hosen und T-Shirts für die Fete gefunden. Wenn Bärbel bei Zimmermanns nichts findet, will sie ins große Einkaufszentrum fahren, denn da gibt es noch andere Boutiquen.

Anwendung

1   p. 356

1. — Mensch, der Kartoffelsalat war ja ganz schön salzig, findest du nicht?

— Nee, mir hat der eigentlich ganz gut geschmeckt. Ich habe auch die belegten Brötchen gehabt. Die waren sehr schmackhaft. Vielleicht solltest du die auch mal probieren.

— Nein, danke! Jetzt bin ich zu voll.

2. — Bayern München liegt jetzt an der Tabellenspitze, nach dem Spiel am letzten Wochenende. Hast du das im Fernsehen gesehen?

— Ja, die haben wirklich ausgezeichnet gespielt, und der Kopfschuss von Matthäus war ja einmalig, was?

— Ja, klar! Wollen wir wetten, die gewinnen den Pokal diese Saison?

— Ganz sicher!

3. — Was, du hast noch Karten dafür bekommen?

— Ich dachte, die wären schon alle ausverkauft. Mit wem gehst du denn in das Konzert?

— Sandra und ich wollen gehen. Ihre Lieblingsgruppe spielt nämlich. Sie hat alle CDs von denen. Kannst du das glauben?

4. — … und wie hast du *Drei Männer und ein Baby* gefunden?

— Ach, das war doch blöd. Da seh ich schon lieber Abenteuerfilme. Das nächste Mal suche ich den Film aus.

— Wieso? Wer hat denn den Film ausgesucht?

— Na, die Ute, und die mag solche Filme unwahrscheinlich gern.

5. — Was hat der Scholz dir denn gestern gegeben?

— Eine Drei.

— Das geht ja noch.

— Wieso, was hast du bekommen?

— 'ne Vier. Das wird meinen Eltern nicht besonders gefallen. Da muss ich dieses Wochenende sicher zu Hause bleiben und Mathe lernen, damit meine Noten besser werden.

Kapitel 12: Die Fete

Review Chapter

Suggested Lesson Plans *50-Minute Schedule*

Day 1

CHAPTER OPENER 10 min.
- Thinking Critically, ATE, p. 331M

LOS GEHT'S! 20 min.
- Preteaching Vocabulary, ATE, p. 331N
- Have students read **Los geht's!**, pp. 334–335
- Teaching Suggestions, Video Guide, p. 76
- Show **Los geht's!** Video

ERSTE STUFE
So sagt man das!, p. 337 15 min.
- Present **So sagt man das!**, p. 337
- Teaching Transparency 12-1
- Play Audio CD for Activity 5, p. 337

Wrap-Up 5 min.
- Students respond to questions about things they can do for others

Homework Options
Pupil's Edition, p. 336, Comprehension Activities
Übungsheft, pp. 133–136, Acts. 1–8

Day 2

ERSTE STUFE
Quick Review 10 min.
- Check homework, Übungsheft, pp. 133–136, Acts. 1–8

Ein wenig Grammatik, p. 337 10 min.
- Presenting **Ein wenig Grammatik,** ATE, p. 331O
- Do Activity 6, p. 337

Ein wenig Landeskunde/Wortschatz, p. 338 15 min.
- Present **Ein wenig Landeskunde,** p. 338
- Presenting **Wortschatz,** ATE, p. 331P
- Do Activities 7 and 8, p. 338

So sagt man das!, p. 339 10 min.
- Presenting **So sagt man das!,** p. 339
- Do Activity 9, p. 340

Wrap-Up 5 min.
- Students respond to questions about doing chores for others

Homework Options
Grammatikheft, pp. 100–101, Acts.1–3

Day 3

ERSTE STUFE
Quick Review 10 min.
- Check homework, Grammatikheft, pp. 100–101, Acts.1–3

Ein wenig Grammatik, p. 340 15 min.
- Presenting Ein wenig Grammatik, ATE, p. 331Q
- Present **Lerntrick,** p. 340
- Do Activities 10 and 11, p. 340

LANDESKUNDE 25 min.
- Pre-viewing Suggestion, Video Guide, p. 76
- Background Information, ATE, p. 331Q
- Show **Landeskunde** Video
- Do Activities A and B, p. 341

Homework Options
Grammatikheft, p. 102, Acts. 4–5
Übungsheft, p. 144, Acts. 25–26

Day 4

ERSTE STUFE
Quick Review 10 min.
- Check homework, Grammatikheft, p. 102, Acts. 4–5

Quiz Review 20 min
- Do **Mehr Grammatikübungen, Erste Stufe**
- Do Additional Listening Activities 12-1 and 12-2, pp. 95–96
- Do Communicative Activity 12-1, pp. 67–68

Quiz 20 min.
- Quiz 12-1A or 12-1B

Homework Options
Activities for Communication, p. 118, Realia 12-1, have students circle the cognates

Day 5

ZWEITE STUFE
Quick Review 10 min.
- Return and review Quiz 12-1
- Bell Work, ATE, p. 331R
- Check homework, Realia 12-1, p. 118

So sagt man das!, p. 342 15 min.
- Presenting **So sagt man das!,** ATE, p. 331R
- Teaching Transparency 12-A
- Do Activity 7, p. 103, Grammatikheft

Wortschatz/Ein wenig Grammatik, p. 342 20 min.
- Presenting **Wortschatz,** ATE, p. 331S
- Presenting **Ein wenig Grammatik,** ATE, p. 331S
- Play Audio CD for Activity 12, p. 343
- Do Activities 13 and 14, p. 343

Wrap-Up 5 min.
- Students respond to questions about making plans with friends

Homework Options
Grammatikheft, p. 103, Act. 6
Übungsheft, pp. 137–138, Acts. 9–12

Day 6

ZWEITE STUFE
Quick Review 10 min.
- Check homework, Übungsheft, pp. 137–138, Acts. 9–12

So sagt man das!/Wortschatz, p. 344 20 min.
- Presenting **So sagt man das!,** ATE, p. 331S
- Presenting **Wortschatz,** ATE, p. 331S
- Play Audio CD for Activity 15, p. 344
- Do Activities 16 and 17, p. 345

Ein wenig Grammatik/So sagt man das!, p. 345 10 min.
- Presenting **Ein wenig Grammatik,** ATE, p. 331S
- Presenting **So sagt man das!,** ATE, p. 331S
- Do Activity 18, p. 345

Ein wenig Grammatik, p. 345 10 min.
- Present **Ein wenig Grammatik,** p. 345
- Do Activities 10–11, p. 105, Grammatikheft

Homework Options
Grammatikheft, p. 104, Acts. 8–9
Übungsheft, pp. 138–139, Acts. 13–15

One-Stop Planner CD-ROM

For alternative lesson plans by chapter section, to create your own customized plans, or to preview all resources available for this chapter, use the **One-Stop Planner CD-ROM**, Disc 3.

 For additional homework suggestions, see activities accompanied by this symbol throughout the chapter.

Day 7

ZWEITE STUFE

Quick Review 10 min.
- Check homework, Übungsheft, pp. 138–139, Acts. 13–15

Quiz Review 20 min.
- Do **Mehr Grammatikübungen, Dritte Stufe**
- Do Additional Listening Activities 12-3 and 12-4, pp. 96–97

Quiz 20 min.
- Quiz 12-2A or 12-2B

Homework Options
Activities for Communication, pp. 145–146, prepare Situation 12-3

Day 8

DRITTE STUFE

Quick Review 15 min.
- Return and review Quiz 12-2
- Bell Work, ATE, p. 331T
- Do Situation 12-3, pp. 145–146

So sagt man das!/Ein wenig Grammatik, p. 346 15 min.
- Presenting **So sagt man das!**, ATE, p. 331U
- Presenting **Ein wenig Grammatik**, ATE, p. 331U
- Do Activities 19 and 20, p. 346
- Do Activity 21, p. 347

Wortschatz, p. 347 15 min.
- Presenting **Wortschatz**, p. 331U
- Teaching Transparency 12-B
- Do Activities 22 and 23, p. 347
- Do Circumlocution Activity, ATE, p. 331X

Wrap-Up 5 min.
- Students answer questions about giving gifts to various people

Homework Options
Grammatikheft, pp. 106–107, Acts. 12–15
Übungsheft, pp. 140–141, Acts. 16–20

Day 9

DRITTE STUFE

Quick Review 10 min.
- Check homework, Grammatikheft, pp. 106–107, Acts. 12–15

So sagt man das!/Ein wenig Grammatik, p. 348 15 min.
- Presenting **So sagt man das!**, ATE, p. 331U
- Present **Ein wenig Grammatik**, p. 348
- Do Activities 24 and 25, p. 348

So sagt man das!, p. 349 10 min.
- Presenting **So sagt man das!**, ATE, p. 331U
- Do Activity 26, p. 349

Aussprache, p. 349 10 min.
- Do **Richtig aussprechen/Richtig lesen**, p. 349
- Do **Richtig schreiben/Diktat**, p. 349

Wrap-Up 5 min.
- Students respond to questions about where they were and what they did

Homework Options
Pupil's Edition, p. 349, Act. 27
Grammatikheft, p. 108, Acts. 16–18
Übungsheft, p. 142, Acts. 21–23
Interactive CD-ROM, Acts. 4–6

Day 10

DRITTE STUFE

Quick Review 10 min.
- Check homework, Übungsheft, p. 142, Acts. 21–23

Quiz Review 20 min.
- Do **Mehr Grammatikübungen, Dritte Stufe**
- Do Communicative Activity 12-3, pp. 71–72
- **Interaktive Spiele**, see ATE, p. 331F

Quiz 20 min.
- Quiz 12-3A or 12-3B

Homework Options
Activities for Communication, p. 120, Realia 12-3, have students fill out the questionnaire

Day 11

DRITTE STUFE

Quick Review 10 min.
- Return and review Quiz 12-3
- Check homework, Realia 12-3

ZUM LESEN 20 min.
- Home Economics Connection, ATE, p. 331V
- Culture Note, ATE, p. 331W
- Thinking Critically, ATE, p. 331W
- Present **Lesestrategie**, p. 350
- Do Activities 1–11, pp. 350–351

Kann ich's wirklich?, p. 358 15 min.
- Do questions 1–10 in writing

Wrap-Up 5 min.
- Students respond orally to **Kann ich's wirklich?** questions, p. 358

Homework Options
Übungsheft, p. 143, Act. 24
Pupil's Edition, p. 357, **Zum Schreiben**
Internet Aktivitäten, see ATE, p. 331F

Day 12

ANWENDUNG

Quick Review 35 min.
- Check homework, Übungsheft, p. 143, Act. 24
- Show **Fortsetzung** and **Videoclips** Videos
- Do **Anwendung** Activities 1–4, pp. 356–357

Chapter Review 15 min.
- Review chapter functions, vocabulary, and grammar; choose from **Mehr Grammatikübungen,** Grammar Tutor for Students of German, Activities for Communication, Listening Activities, Interactive CD-ROM Tutor, or **Interaktive Spiele**

Homework Options
Study for Chapter Test

Assessment

Test, Chapter 12 45 min.
- Administer Chapter 12 Test. Select from Testing Program, Alternative Assessment Guide or Test Generator.

Kapitel 12: Die Fete

Suggested Lesson Plans *90-Minute Schedule*

Block 1

CHAPTER OPENER 10 min.
- Thinking Critically, ATE, p. 331M

LOS GEHT'S! 25 min.
- Preteaching Vocabulary, ATE, p. 331N
- Have students read **Los geht's!**, pp. 334–335
- Teaching Suggestions, Video Guide, p. 76
- Show **Los geht's!** Video

ERSTE STUFE
So sagt man das!, p. 337 15 min.
- Present **So sagt man das!**, p. 337
- Teaching Transparency 12-1
- Play Audio CD for Activity 5, p. 337

Ein wenig Grammatik, p. 337 10 min.
- Presenting **Ein wenig Grammatik,** ATE, p. 331O
- Do Activity 6, p. 337

Ein wenig Landeskunde/Wortschatz, p. 338 15 min.
- Present **Ein wenig Landeskunde,** p. 338
- Presenting **Wortschatz,** ATE, p. 331P
- Do Activities 7 and 8, p. 338

So sagt man das!, p. 339 10 min.
- Presenting **So sagt man das!,** p. 339
- Do Activity 9, p. 340

Wrap-Up 5 min.
- Students respond to questions about doing chores for others

Homework Options
Pupil's Edition, p. 336, Comprehension Activities
Grammatikheft, pp. 100–102, Acts. 1–5
Übungsheft, pp. 133–136, Acts. 1–8

Block 2

ERSTE STUFE
Quick Review 10 min.
- Check homework, Grammatikheft, pp. 100–102, Acts. 1–5

Ein wenig Grammatik, p. 340 15 min.
- Presenting Ein wenig Grammatik, ATE, p. 331Q
- Present **Lerntrick,** p. 340
- Do Activities 10 and 11, p. 340

LANDESKUNDE 25 min.
- Pre-viewing Suggestion, Video Guide, p. 76
- Background Information, ATE, p. 331Q
- Show **Landeskunde** Video
- Do Activities A and B, p. 341

Quiz Review 20 min.
- Do **Mehr Grammatikübungen, Erste Stufe**
- Do Additional Listening Activites 12-1 and 12-2, pp. 95–96
- Do Communicative Activity 12-1, pp. 67–68

Quiz 20 min.
- Quiz 12-1A or 12-1B

Homework Options
Übungsheft, p. 144, Acts. 25–26
Activities for Communication, p. 118, Realia 12-1, have students circle the cognates

Block 3

ZWEITE STUFE
Quick Review 15 min.
- Return and review Quiz 12-1
- Check homework, Realia 12-1, p. 118
- Bell Work, ATE, p. 331R

So sagt man das!, p. 342 15 min.
- Presenting **So sagt man das!,** ATE, p. 331R
- Teaching Transparency 12-A
- Do Activity 7, p. 103, Grammatikheft

Wortschatz/Ein wenig Grammatik, p. 342 20 min.
- Presenting **Wortschatz,** ATE, p. 331S
- Presenting **Ein wenig Grammatik,** ATE, p. 331S
- Play Audio CD for Activity 12, p. 343
- Do Activities 13 and 14, p. 343

So sagt man das!/Wortschatz, p. 344 20 min.
- Presenting **So sagt man das!,** ATE, p. 331S
- Presenting **Wortschatz,** ATE, p. 331S
- Play Audio CD for Activity 15, p. 344
- Do Activities 16 and 17, p. 345

Ein wenig Grammatik/So sagt man das!, p. 345 15 min.
- Presenting **Ein wenig Grammatik,** ATE, p. 331S
- Presenting **So sagt man das!,** ATE, p. 331S
- Do Activity 18, p. 345

Wrap-Up 5 min.
- Students respond to questions about making plans with friends

Homework Options
Grammatikheft, pp. 103–104, Acts. 6, 8–9
Übungsheft, pp. 137–138, Acts. 9–13

One-Stop Planner CD-ROM

For alternative lesson plans by chapter section, to create your own customized plans, or to preview all resources available for this chapter, use the **One-Stop Planner CD-ROM**, Disc 3.

 For additional homework suggestions, see activities accompanied by this symbol throughout the chapter.

Block 4

ZWEITE STUFE

Quick Review 10 min.
- Check homework, Übungsheft, pp. 137–138, Acts. 9–13

Ein wenig Grammatik, p. 345 15 min.
- Present **Ein wenig Grammatik,** p. 345
- Do Activities 10–11, p. 105, Grammatikheft
- Do Activities 14–15, p. 139, Übungsheft

Quiz Review 20 min.
- Do **Mehr Grammatikübungen, Dritte Stufe**
- Do Additional Listening Activities 12-3 and 12-4, pp. 96–97

Quiz 20 min.
- Quiz 12-2A or 12-2B

DRITTE STUFE

So sagt man das!/Ein wenig Grammatik, p. 346 20 min.
- Presenting **So sagt man das!,** ATE, p. 331U
- Presenting **Ein wenig Grammatik,** ATE, p. 331U
- Do Activities 19 and 20, p. 346
- Do Activity 21, p. 347

Wrap-Up 5 min.
- Students answer questions about the members of their families and how they look

Homework Options
Grammatikheft, p. 106, Act. 12
Übungsheft, pp. 140–141, Acts. 16–20
Interactive CD-ROM, Acts. 4–6

Block 5

DRITTE STUFE

Quick Review 15 min.
- Return and review Quiz 12-2
- Check homework, Übungsheft, pp. 140–141, Acts. 16–20

Wortschatz, p. 347 20 min.
- Presenting **Wortschatz,** p. 331U
- Teaching Transparency 12-B
- Do Activities 22 and 23, p. 347
- Do Activities 13–15, p. 107, Grammatikheft

So sagt man das!/Ein wenig Grammatik, p. 348 30 min.
- Presenting **So sagt man das!,** ATE p. 331U
- Do Activities 21–23, p. 142, Übungsheft
- Present **Ein wenig Grammatik,** p. 348
- Do Activities 24 and 25, p. 348
- Do Activities 16–17, p. 108, Grammatikheft

So sagt man das!, p. 349 10 min.
- Presenting **So sagt man das!,** ATE, p. 331U
- Do Activity 26, p. 349

Aussprache, p. 349 10 min.
- Do **Richtig aussprechen/Richtig lesen,** p. 349
- Do **Richtig schreiben/Diktat,** p. 349

Wrap-Up 5 min.
- Students respond to questions about what kind of furniture they have

Homework Options
Pupil's Edition, p. 349, Act. 27
Mehr Grammatikübungen, Dritte Stufe
Grammatikheft, p. 108, Act. 18
Activities for Communication, p. 120, Realia 12-3, have students fill out the questionnaire

Block 6

DRITTE STUFE

Quick Review 10 min.
- Return and review Quiz 12-3
- Check homework, **Mehr Grammatikübungen, Dritte Stufe**

Quiz Review 10 min.
- Do Additional Listening Activities 12-5 and 12-6, pp. 97–98

Quiz 20 min.
- Quiz 12-3A or 12-3B

ZUM LESEN 25 min.
- Home Economics Connection, ATE, p. 331V
- Culture Note, ATE, p. 331W
- Thinking Critically, ATE, p. 331W
- Present **Lesestrategie,** p. 350
- Do Activities 1-11, pp. 350–351

ANWENDUNG 20 min.
- Teaching Suggestions, Video Guide, pp. 76–77
- Do **Anwendung** Activities 1–4, pp. 356–357

Wrap-Up 5 min.
- Students respond orally to **Kann ich's wirklich?** questions, p. 358

Homework Options
Übungsheft, p. 143, Act. 24
Interaktive Spiele , see ATE, p. 331F

Block 7

ANWENDUNG

Quick Review 10 min.
- Check homework, Übungsheft, p. 143, Act. 24

Kann ich's wirklich?, p. 358 20 min.
- Do questions 1–10 in writing

Chapter Review 15 min.
- Review chapter functions, vocabulary, and grammar; choose from **Mehr Grammatikübungen,** Grammar Tutor for Students of German, Activities for Communication, Listening Activities, Interactive CD-ROM Tutor, or **Interaktive Spiele**

Test, Chapter 12 45 min.
Administer Chapter 12 Test. Select from Testing Program, Alternative Assessment Guide or Test Generator.

Kapitel 12: Die Fete

Review Chapter

Teaching Suggestions, *pages 332–359*

CHAPTER OPENER

Pacing Tips

In the **Erste Stufe** the functions of 'offering help and explaining what to do' and 'asking where something is located and giving directions' are reviewed, along with the verbs **können** and **wissen, für** with accusative pronouns, and the **du-/ihr-**commands. The **Zweite Stufe** reintroduces the functions of 'making plans and inviting someone to come along,' 'talking about clothing,' and 'discussing gift ideas.' The verbs **wollen** and **müssen**, definite and indefinite articles, and dative endings also occur. The **Dritte Stufe** centers around the nominative and possessive pronouns, the **möchte-**forms, and **noch ein / kein ... mehr**. Because the three **Stufen** are similar in length and amount of material presented, you should spend more time on whichever **Stufe** your class needs to review the most in preparation for the Final Exam. For Lesson Plans and timing suggestions, see pages 331I–331L.

Meeting the Standards

Communication
• Offering help and explaining what to do, p. 337
• Asking for and giving directions, p. 339
• Making plans and inviting someone, p. 342
• Talking about clothing, p. 344
• Discussing gift ideas, p. 345
• Describing people and places, p. 346
• Saying what you would like and whether you do or don't want more, p. 348
• Talking about what you did, p. 349

Cultures
• **Ein wenig Landeskunde**, p. 338
• **Landeskunde**, p. 341
• Language Note, p. 331N
• Language Note, p. 331Q
• Culture Note, p. 331Q
• Culture Note, p. 331S
• Culture Note, p. 331W

Connections
• Math Connection, p. 331P
• Math Connection, p. 331S
• Home Economics Connection, p. 331V
• Geography Connection, p. 331W
• Teaching Suggestion, p. 331W

Comparisons
• Language Note, p. 331P
• Language-to-Language, p. 331P

One-Stop Planner CD-ROM

For resource information, see the **One-Stop Planner CD-ROM**, Disc 3.

Communities
• Language Note, p. 331P
• Thinking Critically, p. 331P
• Career Path, p. 331X

Building on Previous Skills
The students in this picture are being served **Bratwurst**. What other types of German sausage have students learned about in previous chapters? (**Frankfurter** and **Weißwurst**)

Connections and Comparisons

Thinking Critically
Comparing and Contrasting Ask students what they would wear if they were invited to a backyard barbecue during the summer. Would their clothes look different from the clothing students in the picture are wearing?

Comparing and Contrasting Ask students if they think American students in general eat as much salad and fruit as German students do.

Communication for All Students

Challenge
Can students give simple instructions in German for the preparation of their favorite salad? Remind students to use connectors in their directions.

Chapter Sequence

Los geht's! .... p. 334
Erste Stufe .... p. 337
Landeskunde .... p. 341
Zweite Stufe .... p. 342
Dritte Stufe .... p. 346
Zum Lesen .... p. 350
Mehr Grammatikübungen .... p. 352
Anwendung .... p. 356
Kann ich's wirklich? .... p. 358
Wortschatz .... p. 359

CHAPTER OPENER

LOS GEHT'S!

Teaching Resources
pp. 334–336

PRINT
▶ Lesson Planner, p. 57
▶ Video Guide, pp. 75–76, 78
▶ Übungsheft, p. 133

MEDIA
▶ One-Stop Planner
▶ Video Program
  Los geht's!
  Videocassette 4, 31:38–35:53
  Videocassette 5 (captioned version),
  1:06:16–1:10:32
  Fortsetzung
  Videocassette 4, 35:58–40:15
  Videocassette 5 (captioned version),
  1:10:36–1:14:54
▶ Audio Compact Discs, CD12, Trs. 1–2
▶ **Los geht's!** Transparencies

PAGES 334–335

Los geht's! Transparencies

Preteaching Vocabulary

Activating Prior Knowledge

Point out that the setting for this **Los geht's!** is a party and that the young people are helping to prepare food alongside the adults. As a review, have students list food and drinks mentioned in the photo spread. Can they find any new words in these categories? Then ask students to look for sentences that use modal verbs, listing the modals as they are found. Finally, ask students to identify the one sentence that is in the past tense. (**Was habt ihr mitgebracht?**)

Fortsetzung

You may choose to continue with the **Fortsetzung** of *Die Geburtstagsfete* now or wait until later in the chapter. For a synopsis of the **Los geht's!** and **Fortsetzung** episodes, see p. 331E.

Advance Organizer

As an advance organizer for the story line of **Los geht's!,** ask students how they would help a friend get ready for a party. What things need to get done before the guests arrive?

Using the Captioned Video

If students have trouble understanding, you may want to play the captioned version of *Die Geburtstagsfete* on Videocassette 5. Ask students to use vocabulary and expressions they know to write two or three sentences in German to describe some of the things the teenagers did in the video episode.

Cultures and Communities

Background Information

In southern Germany, **Bowle** is served at parties of all kinds. It is made with fresh, canned, or frozen fruit, such as apples, oranges, strawberries, raspberries, peaches, or cherries. Fruit juice is added to cover the fruit and then the mixture is refrigerated. Cloves are also added, but they are removed before the **Bowle** is served.

Language Note

What is known as **Bowle** in southern Germany is often referred to as **Punsch** in the northern parts of the country.

PAGE 336

Comprehension Check

1 Students should find one phrase or statement from **Los geht's!** that supports each of their answers.

Challenge

2 Ask students to find one additional description for each person that has not been mentioned before.

Thinking Critically

3 **Analyzing** Once students have put the sentences in order, ask them to point out the connectors (adverbs of time). You may want to write them in order on the chalkboard.

ERSTE STUFE

Teaching Resources
pp. 337–341

PRINT

▸ Lesson Planner, p. 58
▸ TPR Storytelling Book, pp. 45, 48
▸ Listening Activities, pp. 91, 95–96
▸ Activities for Communication, pp. 67–68, 118, 121, 145–146
▸ Grammatikheft, pp. 100–102
▸ Grammar Tutor for Students of German, Chapter 12
▸ Übungsheft, pp. 134–136
▸ Testing Program, pp. 301–304
▸ Alternative Assessment Guide, p. 43
▸ Student Make-Up Assignments, Chapter 12

MEDIA

▸ One-Stop Planner
▸ Audio Compact Discs, CD12, Trs. 3–4, 16, 28–29
▸ Teaching Transparencies
   Situation 12-1
   Mehr Grammatikübungen Answers
   Grammatikheft Answers
▸ Interactive CD-ROM Tutor, Disc 3

PAGE 337

Bell Work

Have the following skeletal script on the board or a transparency as students walk into the classroom. As a warm-up activity, ask students to copy the script and to complete it. Students can then read their short paragraphs aloud.

Die beste Party war _____. Sie war so gut, weil _____. Die _____ und _____ schmeckten einfach Klasse! Wir haben viel _____ und _____. Wir haben die Musik von _____ und _____ gehört und dazu getanzt.

PRESENTING: So sagt man das!

Ask students to work with a partner and imagine the following situation. One of them has won a bet, and now the other has to do all the chores around the house. The winner has to tell the loser of the bet what needs to be done. Students take turns using the expressions from **So sagt man das!** and those learned in preceding units (especially Chapter 7).

Communication for All Students

Challenge

5 After students have completed this activity, ask them if anyone at home has ever made them an **Arbeitsliste**. What are some typical things they get asked to do?

PRESENTING: Ein wenig Grammatik

The preposition für Have students come up with three or four creative answers to the question **Kann ich/ Können wir etwas für dich tun?** Let them know that all their responses must begin with **Du kannst/ Ihr könnt für mich …** or a **du-** or **ihr-**command, but make no further stipulations. After allowing the students several minutes to work, have them read aloud their favorite response.

Using the Captioned Video

You may wish to divide the class into two groups and have one group compile a list of the expressions used for offering help and the other group a list of those used to explain what to do, as they watch *Die Geburtstagsfete* on Videocassette 5.

PAGE 338

Building on Previous Skills

Ask students to look at the recipes and give definitions of the abbreviations **g, l,** and **EL.** (**Gramm, Liter, Esslöffel**)

Teacher to Teacher

> **Mary Ann R. Boyce**
> Linglestown Junior High
> and East Junior High
> Harrisburg, Pennsylvania

Mary Ann has students write a "Liebe(r) Deutschlehrer(in)" letter to conclude Level 1.

"At the end of the year, my students write a letter in German to their German teacher for next year. They introduce and tell about themselves. They are given an outline of topics to cover as well as a list of required grammatical usages. It's a great way to wrap up the year and provides the students with a huge sense of accomplishment! It also gives the German 2 teacher an overview of what the students understand from Level 1. If you will be their teacher again the next year, this letter provides a starting point for review and conversation in German 2."

Teaching Suggestion

7 You may want to introduce the following new vocabulary from the two recipes: **verdünnen** (*dilute*); **das Spatzenbrett** (*a board on which Spätzle are made and cut*); **der Emmentaler** (*a type of mild cheese*).

Connections and Comparisons

Math Connection

7 Have students make all possible conversions from metric to U.S. measurements. You may need to remind students that 1 **Gramm** equals 0.035 ounces and that 1 **Liter** equals 1.056 quarts.

Language Note

Ask students to look at the words **Spätzle** and **Apfelküchle**. Knowing that these are both words used in southern regional dialects, can students draw a general conclusion about regional language usage as they note the endings of both words? Have students guess how people in northern Germany would spell and say **Apfelküchle**. (Apfelkuchen)

PRESENTING: Wortschatz

Bring the items from this **Wortschatz** to class if possible. Introduce the vocabulary to the class.

Connections and Comparisons

Language-to-Language

• Review the meaning of the word 'cognate,' and ask students to find cognates for as many of the food words used on p. 338 as they can. Some English cognates are **Öl**/ *oil*, **Salz**/ *salt*, **Mehl**/ *meal*; some French possibilities are **Zitrone**/ *citron*, **Zucker**/ *sucre*, **Öl**/ *huile*; Spanish cognates include **Zucker**/ *azúcar* and **Salz**/ *sal*.

• You may want to point out to your students that many modern English and German words, even some that now look very different, are derived from the same original Germanic, Latin, or Greek root; the words **Zimt** and *cinnamon* provide a good example of this. Both come from the Latin **cinnamum**. Ask students why they think the two words may have evolved so differently. (The modern English *cinnamon* comes to us today through an old French form of the word; the German term evolved independently of this influence.)

 Total Physical Response

Give students commands using the objects you brought to class to introduce the new vocabulary. (Examples: Peter, gib Mary zwei Sachen, die in einen Salat gehören! Susy, gib Uwe bitte das Salz!)

Teaching Suggestion

8 Before students begin with this activity, review the vocabulary for rooms in a house and furniture using pictures or eliciting words by giving oral descriptions.

▶ **PAGE 339**

PRESENTING: So sagt man das!

Divide the class into several groups and give each group a piece of paper on which has been written one of the locations from the map on page 339. Then have students turn to that map and formulate a list of directions (using the **du**-command form) that would take someone from the **Rosmaringasse/ Gartenstraße** intersection to their location. When all groups have finished, ask a speaker from each group to read their directions aloud. The other students should follow along and try to figure out which destination is intended.

Cultures and Communities

Language Note

The ending **-gasse** means *alley* and **-weg** means *path* or *way*.

Thinking Critically

• **Drawing Inferences** Ask students to look up the following words in a German or bilingual dictionary: **Schuster, Pfarrer, Laube, Mühle**. Then ask students what type of businesses were or might still be found on streets with these words as part of their names. What does the street name reveal about the street? Example: **Laubenweg** (*covered arbor*)

• **Analyzing** Have students determine what the words **Rupp, Bischof, Vogt**, and **Schellmann** refer to. (the names of business owners)

Connections and Comparisons

Thinking Critically

9 Comparing and Contrasting After students have completed the listening portion of this activity, you might want to ask them what foods would probably be served at Nicole's party on Saturday evening and compare it to what would be served at Sabine's house on Sunday afternoon. Would students in the United States serve similar foods for both occasions if they had friends over? If not, what would they serve? This discussion should be done in the target language.

PRESENTING: Ein wenig Grammatik

The verb wissen Copy a local street map (or draw part of your town or city) onto a transparency. Specify your starting point and then call on individual students, asking questions such as **Weißt du/ Wisst ihr, wie ich (zum Park) komme?** They should respond with **Ja, ich weiß/ wir wissen, wie …**, and then give directions using formal commands. Follow their directions with a transparency marker. You may want to turn it into a contest in which the winner is the student who gives directions most quickly and with the fewest mistakes.

Cultures and Communities

Language Note

11 Ask students to take a closer look at the milk. How much of the carton inscription can they understand or guess? (Examples: <u>Kleefeld</u> = <u>clover</u> field; **fettarm** = *lowfat*; **1,5% fett** = 1.5% *fat*) Point out that in Germany, milk can be purchased in this type of carton, and it doesn't have to be refrigerated until after it is opened.

 LANDESKUNDE

Teaching Resources
p. 341

PRINT
▶ Video Guide, pp. 75–76, 78–79
▶ Übungsheft, p. 144

MEDIA
▶ One-Stop Planner
▶ Video Program
  Videocassette 4, 40:55–45:15
▶ Audio Compact Discs, CD12, Trs. 5–9
▶ Interactive CD-ROM Tutor, Chapter 12

Teaching Suggestions

• Begin by asking students to compare chores that need to be done in a house versus chores that need to be done in an apartment.

• Additional vocabulary:
Mülleimer *trash can*
zusammenlegen *to fold*
anfallen, here: *to come up*
teilweise *on and off, occasionally*

Cultures and Communities

Culture Note

In Silvana's interview, students heard that she hangs, takes down, and folds the laundry. In the German-speaking countries, **Wäscheleinen** (*clotheslines*) are a common sight on apartment balconies and in backyards. Not all German households have dryers; even if they do they are very compact, so hanging laundry is often necessary. Many people don't use dryers in an attempt to save energy, since oil, gas, and electricity costs are much higher in Germany than in the United States.

Background Information

In his interview, Gerd mentions that he often buys **Getränke**. German families tend to buy their **Limo** and **Brause** (*soft drinks*) at a **Getränkeladen** rather than at the grocery store because they can buy bottles by the case instead of individually. They pay a deposit for the bottles and the plastic case. This deposit is refunded upon return or applied toward the next purchase.

ERSTE STUFE

Game

Play the game **Wortfamilien.** See p. 331C for the procedure.

Teaching Suggestion

Ask students to look at the map on p. 339. Then choose a starting point and an end point and have students describe in writing how they would get from point to point.

You may wish to evaluate their work using the following rubric.

Writing Rubric	Points			
	4	3	2	1
Content (Complete – Incomplete)				
Comprehensibility (Comprehensible – Seldom comprehensible)				
Accuracy (Accurate – Seldom accurate)				
Organization (Well-organized – Poorly organized)				
Effort (Excellent – Minimal)				

18–20: A   16–17: B   14–15: C   12–13: D   Under 12: F

Assess

▸ Testing Program, pp. 301–304
  Quiz 12-1A, Quiz 12-1B
  Audio CD12, Tr. 16

▸ Student Make-Up Assignments
  Chapter 12, Alternative Quiz

▸ Alternative Assessment Guide, p. 43

ZWEITE STUFE

Teaching Resources
pp. 342–345

PRINT
▸ Lesson Planner, p. 59
▸ TPR Storytelling Book, pp. 46, 48
▸ Listening Activities, pp. 92, 96–97
▸ Activities for Communication, pp. 69–70, 119, 121, 145–146
▸ Grammatikheft, pp. 103–105
▸ Grammar Tutor for Students of German, Chapter 12
▸ Übungsheft, pp. 137–139
▸ Testing Program, pp. 305–308
▸ Alternative Assessment Guide, p. 43
▸ Student Make-Up Assignments, Chapter 12

MEDIA
▸ One-Stop Planner
▸ Audio Compact Discs, CD12, Trs. 10–11, 17, 30–31
▸ Teaching Transparencies
  Situation 12-2
  Vocabulary 12-A
  Mehr Grammatikübungen Answers
  Grammatikheft Answers
▸ Interactive CD-ROM Tutor, Disc 3

PAGE 342

Bell Work

Ask students to copy the following incomplete statement and complete it as they see fit. **Das Leben in** *(insert name of your town or city)* **ist** _____ **und auch** _____. **Man kann hier** _____. Then ask students to read what they have written.

PRESENTING: So sagt man das!

Ask students to imagine that they are calling a friend to invite him or her to come along on an errand. Have them practice the expressions from this **So sagt man das!** and from previous chapters (especially Chapter 11) to extend the invitation, and to accept or decline, giving a reason.

PRESENTING: Wortschatz

As you read through the new phrases, practice the difficult words: be-sich-ti-gen, Schlitt-schuh-lau-fen, Brett-spiel. Follow up with question and answer practice, providing students a context to guide their responses. (Examples: **Es ist Winter. Die Sonne scheint. Was willst du heute tun? Du bist neu in dieser Stadt. Was möchtest du tun?**)

Teaching Suggestion

After you have introduced the **Wortschatz,** ask students specifically why they would want to do each of these activities. Make a list of suggestions on the board.

PRESENTING: Ein wenig Grammatik

The verbs wollen and müssen Prepare a list of questions such as **Musst du oft zu Hause helfen?** and **Willst du morgen in den Zoo gehen?** Ask these questions of individual students, requiring that they respond in complete sentences. When they have done so, follow up on their answer: **Warum willst du nicht in den Zoo gehen?** You may want to allow students to write out a response to this second question, in which they give as creative a response as possible.

▶ PAGE 343

Communication for All Students

For Additional Practice

13 Ask students to indicate which of the activities listed on the **Anschlagbrett im Jugendzentrum** they absolutely would not do. Have them give a reason using **weil** or **denn.** Remind students of the word order in dependent clauses.

▶ PAGE 344

PRESENTING: So sagt man das!

Bring clothes of different sizes and styles to the classroom. Have two students come to the front. Ask the first student to put on clothes that you know are too long or too large. This student must ask his or her partner questions such as **Wie passt der Pulli?** The partner answers with phrases such as **Er passt überhaupt nicht.** or **Er ist zu lang.**

Communication for All Students

Challenge

15 After having completed the listening portion of this activity, ask several students in which of the four stores they would like to shop and what they would buy there.

PRESENTING: Wortschatz

Bring articles of clothing that feature the characteristics of the **Wortschatz.** Show these items as you introduce the new vocabulary.

Connections and Comparisons

Culture Note

C & A is a large clothing department store chain in Germany. Other popular stores for clothing are **Karstadt, Kaufhof,** and **Hertie.**

Math Connection

Provide students with the current exchange rate and ask them to convert the prices of the items in the **C & A** ad to U.S. dollars. Then ask students to comment on the prices using expressions such as **preiswert, günstig, billig,** and **teuer.**

▶ PAGE 345

Teaching Suggestion

16 Since this activity involves extra time, you could assign it as homework for extra credit.

PRESENTING: So sagt man das!/Ein wenig Grammatik

Cases Put the four German sentences from **So sagt man das!** on the chalkboard. Call four students to the board and have each label the sentence parts to review the nominative, accusative, and dative cases. Use different colored chalk for each case.

Reteaching: Sentence building

Compile a list of sentences from the **Zweite Stufe,** write them on paper, and cut them into sentence strips. Place each of the sentence strips in an envelope and number them. Distribute the envelopes to pairs of students, who then try to put their sentence in correct order. Pairs should write down their sentence twice, once exactly as it appears on the paper, and a second time, substituting appropriate pronouns for each noun. Students then pass their envelopes to the next group and continue with the activity until each pair has solved each sentence puzzle, or until time is up. Go over all the sentences with the class. This activity is good for tactile and visual learners.

 **Game**

Write the different activities from the **Tafel** on p. 343 on small pieces of paper and put them into a bag. Have a student come to the front of the class and pull a piece of paper from the bag. He or she then acts out the activity as the rest of the class tries to guess the activity. The student who guesses the activity first gets to act out the next one.

Speaking Assessment

17 You may choose to use this activity for assessment. The following rubric may aide you in evaluating the spoken dialogue.

Speaking Rubric	Points			
	4	3	2	1
Content (Complete – Incomplete)				
Comprehension (Total – Little)				
Comprehensibility (Comprehensible – Incomprehensible)				
Accuracy (Accurate – Seldom accurate)				
Fluency (Fluent – Not fluent)				

18–20: A   16–17: B   14–15: C   12–13: D   Under 12: F

Assess
▸ Testing Program, pp. 305–308
  Quiz 12-2A, Quiz 12-2B
  Audio CD12, Tr. 17
▸ Student Make-Up Assignments
  Chapter 12, Alternative Quiz
▸ Alternative Assessment Guide, p. 43

DRITTE STUFE

Teaching Resources
pp. 346–349

PRINT
▸ Lesson Planner, p. 60
▸ TPR Storytelling Book, pp. 47, 48
▸ Listening Activities, pp. 97–98
▸ Activities for Communication, pp. 71–72, 120, 121, 145–146
▸ Grammatikheft, pp. 106–108
▸ Grammar Tutor for Students of German, Chapter 12
▸ Übungsheft, pp. 140–142
▸ Testing Program, pp. 309–312
▸ Alternative Assessment Guide, p. 43
▸ Student Make-Up Assignments, Chapter 12

MEDIA
▸ One-Stop Planner
▸ Audio Compact Discs, CD12, Trs. 12–14, 18, 32–33
▸ Teaching Transparencies
  Situation 12-2
  Vocabulary 12-A, 12-B
  Mehr Grammatikübungen Answers
  Grammatikheft Answers
▸ Interactive CD-ROM Tutor, Disc 3

PAGE 346

 **Bell Work**

In pairs, have students ask each other for the birthdays of two friends (**deine Freundin Anne**) or family members (**deine Tante Judy**). The answer should include day and month of the birthday. Then, have students switch roles.

 **Game**

Divide the class into two groups to play *Tic Tac Toe*. Fill the nine squares of the *Tic Tac Toe* grid with nine infinitives of irregular verbs, such as **lesen, sehen, haben, sprechen, sein, fahren, nehmen,** and **essen.** Alternating between teams, have team members form sentences in the present tense using the verbs indicated in order to get an X or an O in a square. The first team to get three in a row wins. Encourage students to change pronouns or proper nouns frequently so that different verb forms must be used.

PRESENTING: So sagt man das!

Prepare a description of a room to read out loud to the class. The room should have typical furniture and other items reflecting the vocabulary learned in earlier chapters. Ask students to take out a blank sheet of paper. As you read the description, students should try to visualize it and make a rough sketch of the room on their paper, indicating the items mentioned.

PRESENTING: Ein wenig Grammatik

Nominative pronouns Bring to class props representing some of the vocabulary students have learned this year. (Examples: types of clothes, school supplies, pictures of furniture) Give each student one or more props. Go around the class asking students questions about their own props or about those in the possession of other students. (Examples: **Wie sehen deine Stiefel aus?**, **Welche Farbe ist sein/ ihr Regal?**) During the first round of questions, require that students answer using proper nouns; the second time around, have them substitute pronouns for these nouns.

Teaching Suggestion

19 Remind students to include physical attributes as well as personality features in their descriptions.

PAGE 347

PRESENTING: Wortschatz

Use pictures from decorating magazines, catalogs, and newspapers to introduce the items in this **Wortschatz.**

Connections and Comparisons

Thinking Critically

Comparing and Contrasting From what students have learned so far, what are their impressions of how Germans furnish their homes? What similarities and differences between the United States and Germany can they think of?

Communication for All Students

Challenge

To reinforce the new vocabulary, write a definition or description for each word. Ask students to guess the object or adjective that is defined or described.

PAGE 348

PRESENTING: So sagt man das!

Ask students to work with a partner as they use the expressions from **So sagt man das!** to role-play the following situation: two students are going to Student A's house after school. They are hungry and thirsty and ready to raid the refrigerator. They should create a brief dialogue talking about what they want to eat.

PRESENTING: Ein wenig Grammatik

Kein … mehr Make a long list of foods and beverages the students know in German. Try to bring the actual items, props, or pictures of each to class. Offer each student a second helping of one of the items and have them respond with **Ja, bitte, noch ein(e, en) …** or **Nein, danke, kein(e, en) … mehr.**

PAGE 349

PRESENTING: So sagt man das!

Ask students to recall some adverbs which can express events that have already taken place. (Examples: **gestern, vorgestern, letzte Woche, letzten Monat**) Then ask students to use one of those adverbs and tell about something they have done in the recent past.

Reteaching: Talking about what you did

Ask students to review the Baden-Württemberg Location Opener on pp. 272–275 and write a fictional postcard detailing what they saw and did on an imaginary trip there.

Teaching Suggestion

Show a picture that students can describe. For example, show a picture of some teenagers sitting in a living room, watching TV, and munching on snacks. Have students describe the people, the room, and the snacks.

Von der Schule zum Beruf

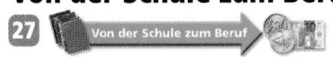

You may want to use a final draft of this written assignment for assessment using the following rubric.

Writing Rubric

	Points			
	4	3	2	1
Content (Complete – Incomplete)				
Comprehensibility (Comprehensible – Seldom comprehensible)				
Accuracy (Accurate – Seldom accurate)				
Organization (Well-organized – Poorly organized)				
Effort (Excellent – Minimal)				

18–20: A   16–17: B   14–15: C   12–13: D   Under 12: F

PRESENTING: Aussprache

After students have listened to the recording of these sounds and sentences, have them do the dictation. Have them exchange papers and correct each other's sentences. Then ask students, working in pairs, to find as many words as they can that contain these sounds. Using the words they find, have them try to think of funny sentences, such as tongue twisters, using the words. Ask for volunteers to read the sentences to the class.

Assess

▶ Testing Program, pp. 309–312
   Quiz 12-3A, Quiz 12-3B
   Audio CD12, Tr. 18

▶ Student Make-Up Assignments
   Chapter 12, Alternative Quiz

▶ Alternative Assessment Guide, p. 43

ZUM LESEN

Teaching Resources
pp. 350–351

PRINT
▶ Lesson Planner, p. 61
▶ Übungsheft, p. 143
▶ Reading Strategies and Skills, Chapter 12
▶ Lies mit mir! 1, Chapter 12

MEDIA
▶ One-Stop Planner

Prereading
Building Context

Ask students when they last prepared or helped prepare a dish. What was it and what were some of the ingredients?

Teaching Suggestion

Bring pictures of recipes from magazines and show them to your class. Ask students to guess what ingredients go into each dish based only on the picture.

Connections and Comparisons

Home Economics Connection

Ask students to list measurements that are commonly used in the directions of a recipe, first in English and then in German.

Teacher Note

Activities 1, 2, and 3 are prereading tasks.

Reading
Skimming and Scanning

Ask students to look at the names of the recipes and have them guess at what meal they might be served in Germany. (**Kartoffelsalat:** supper—Germans generally have a cold meal at night; **gefüllte Eier:** appetizer; **Mandelkuchen:** afternoon coffee break)

Building on Previous Skills

Ask students to make a list of the measurement abbreviations that are used in the recipes and what they stand for. (**Pfd.: Pfund; g: Gramm**) You may want to remind students that solids are measured by weight and liquids by volume, in contrast to recipes in the United States, where most ingredients are measured by volume only.

Cultures and Communities

Culture Note
In the German-speaking countries, baking powder is mostly sold in individual packages. Although the recipe for **Mandelkuchen** printed here calls for a teaspoon of baking powder, it is more common for recipes to call for **ein Päckchen Backpulver.**

Connections and Comparisons

Geography Connection

The recipe for **Mandelkuchen** calls for almonds. Almonds are grown in two areas of Germany, Westphalia and the Upper Rhine region. Ask students to locate those two areas on a map.

Thinking Critically

6 **Comparing and Contrasting** Provide students with a copy of a recipe for a typical American potato salad. Ask students to compare the American recipe to the German recipe. How do they differ? (Germans generally do not make **Kartoffelsalat** with mayonnaise.)

Teaching Suggestion

9 Remind students that temperatures in Celsius can be converted to Fahrenheit by multiplying the number (here 175) by 9, dividing by 5, and adding 32 (= 347). Emphasize to students that learning the conversion formula is a way to help them learn to relate Celsius temperatures to their own experiences. Their goal should be *not* to convert, but rather to "feel" the differences and make accurate approximations.

Communication for All Students

Tactile Learners

Bring the ingredients mentioned in the recipes to class. Ask several students to group or arrange the ingredients according to each recipe.

Cultures and Communities

Background Information

10 **Gefüllte Eier** are eaten as an appetizer throughout Germany, but the filling may vary, depending on the region. In northern Germany, for example, diced crabmeat and dill make a popular filling.

Communication for All Students

Cooperative Learning

Put students in groups of four. Ask them to choose a discussion leader, a recorder, a proofreader, and an announcer. Give students a specific amount of time in which to complete Activities 4–10. Monitor group work as you walk around, helping students if necessary. At the end of the activity, call on each group announcer to read his or her group's results. You can decide whether or not to collect their work for a grade at the end of the activity.

Post-Reading
Teacher Note

Activity 11 is a post-reading task that will show whether students can apply what they have learned.

Teaching Suggestion

11 Ask students to act out this situation with a partner. Encourage students to use props and not to read from a prepared script.

Cooking Time

If you have not had a food party earlier, you might consider it now. Ask students to prepare one of the three recipes and bring them to class for a food day. You may also include any of the other recipes found in the Traditions feature on the D page of the chapter interleaf. Make sure students take the size of the class into account and prepare enough for everyone to try.

PAGES 352–355

MEHR GRAMMATIKÜBUNGEN

The **Mehr Grammatikübungen** activities are designed as supplemental activities for the grammatical concepts presented in the chapter. You might use them as additional practice, for review, or for assessment.

For more grammar presentations, review, and practice, refer to the following:
• Grammatikheft

- Grammar Tutor for Students of German
- Grammar Summary on pp. R15–R25
- Übungsheft
- Grammar and Vocabulary quizzes (Testing Program)
- Test Generator
- Interactive CD-ROM Tutor
- **Interaktive Spiele** at go.hrw.com

PAGES 356–357

ANWENDUNG

 Video Wrap-up

Videocassette 4, 31:38–49:30
Videocassette 5 (captioned version), 1:08:40–1:17:52
At this time, you might want to use the video resources for additional review and enrichment. See *Video Guide* for suggestions regarding:

- the **Los geht's!** episode • the **Landeskunde** interviews
- the **Fortsetzung** episode • the **Videoclips.**

Apply and Assess

Teaching Suggestions

1 As an advance organizer for the listening activity, ask students to list at least three vocabulary words or phrases that are associated with each of the five topics.

2 If students want to keep the identity of their favorite person anonymous, they can use a fictitious name.

Portfolio

2 You might want to use this activity as a written portfolio item for your students. See *Alternative Assessment Guide*, p. 29.

Process Writing

5 Supply your students with a list of the coordinating and subordinating conjunctions they have learned this year (**und, aber, denn, weil, ob,** and **dass**), and encourage them to use as many of these as they can while composing their letter. You may also want to suggest that they include various 'flavoring words' (such as **schon, ganz, eigentlich, bloß, ziemlich, wirklich, bestimmt, mal,** and **vielleicht**) to make their work sound more like something a native German-speaker would write.

Career Path

Have students imagine they are translators working for a publishing company and brainstorm what types of books they might be translating. (Suggestions: cookbooks, travel books, novels, bulletins from international conferences, medical books)

PAGE 358

KANN ICH'S WIRKLICH?

This page is intended to prepare students for the test. It is a brief checklist of the major points covered in the chapter. The students should be reminded that it is a checklist only and not necessarily everything that will appear on the test.

For additional self check options, refer students to the *Grammar Tutor*, the *Interactive CD-Rom Tutor*, and the Online self-test for this chapter.

PAGE 359

WORTSCHATZ

Review and Assess

Teaching Suggestions

- Ask students to make a list of ingredients for a typical salad.

- Show students some photos or ads from furniture catalogs or magazines featuring the vocabulary of the **Dritte Stufe.** Ask students to work with a partner to write down as many of the items in the pictures as they can recall. Students then read their lists aloud in class.

Games
Play the game **Heiss auf der Spur.** See p. 331D for the procedure.

Circumlocution
Play **Das treffende Wort suchen** with the **Dritte Stufe** vocabulary. Ask your students to explain in German the function of the items. (**Wofür benutzt man das?**) They may also describe the object, explain what it is made of, where in the house it is located or, in the case of rooms such as **die Küche** and **das Wohnzimmer,** what one does or what is located there. See p. 155C for procedures.

Teacher Note
- Give the **Kapitel 12** Chapter Test: *Testing Program*, pp. 313–318 Audio CD 12, Trs. 19–21.

- Give the Final Exam: *Testing Program*, pp. 327–334 Audio CD 12, Trs. 22–27.

REVIEW

STANDARDS: 1.1, 5.1

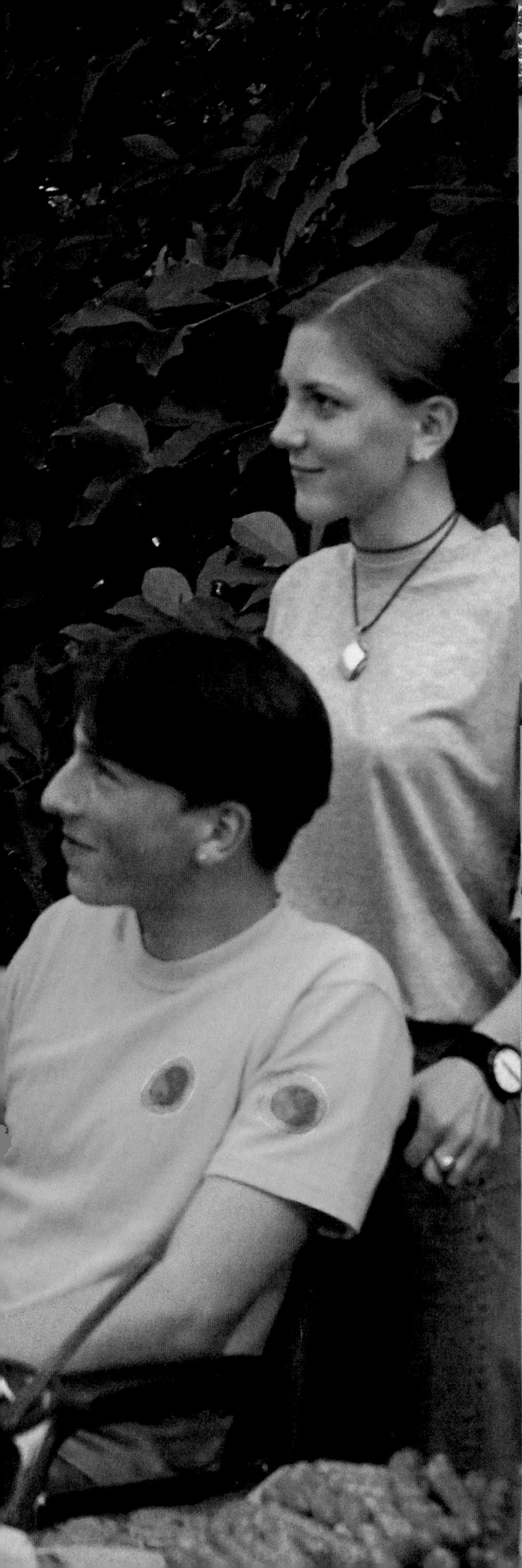

12
Die Fete

Objectives

In this chapter you will review and practice how to

Erste Stufe

- offer help and explain what to do
- ask where something is located and give directions

Zweite Stufe

- make plans and invite someone to come along
- talk about clothing
- discuss gift ideas

Dritte Stufe

- describe people and places
- say what you would like and whether you do or don't want more
- talk about what you did

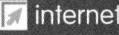 internet

 ADRESSE: go.hrw.com
KENNWORT:
WK3 BADEN-WUERTTEMBERG–12

◀ **Was möchtet ihr essen?**

Los geht's! · *Die Geburtstagsfete*

CD 12 Trs. 1–2

VIDEO

Strategie **Verstehen**

Look at the images for this story. What big event is taking place? What preparations are being made? Who is helping? What is everyone doing?

Los geht's! is an abridged version of the video episode.

Nicole   **Andreas**   **Thomas**   Sabine   **Mutter**   **Vater**   Martin

Nicoles Freunde sind da. Sie wollen ihr helfen.

Andreas: So, Nicole, was können wir für dich tun?

Nicole: Zuerst müssen wir einkaufen gehen. Wer will mitkommen? Ich muss zum Supermarkt.

Andreas: Wir können ja beide mit den Rädern fahren.

Nicole: Lieb von dir! Aber wir müssen so viel einkaufen. Die Mutti fährt uns mit dem Auto hin. — Aber du kannst mitkommen, wenn du willst.

Andreas: Klar!

①

②

Thomas: Und was mache ich?

Nicole: Thomas, du kannst dem Vati im Garten helfen, und dann müssen wir noch das Gemüse waschen.

Andreas: Okay! Wir können das ja machen, wenn wir zurückkommen.

Nicole und Andreas kommen vom Einkaufen zurück.

 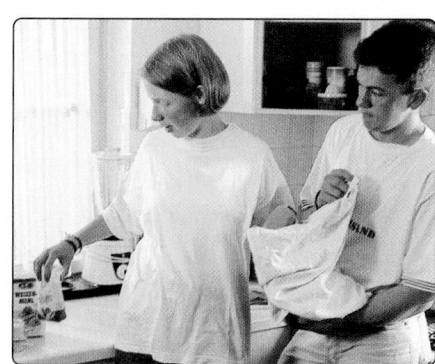

③

Vater: Was habt ihr mitgebracht? Oh, die Bratwurst sieht gut aus! Hm …ganz frisch. Und, was habt ihr sonst noch?

Nicole: Wir haben noch Eier, Mehl, Zucker …Andreas und ich, wir backen dann einen Kuchen.

Vater: Schön!

Die Fete beginnt. Martin kommt.

Nicole: Vati! Das ist Martin!

Vater: Hallo Martin! Herzlich willkommen bei uns!

Martin: Guten Tag! Vielen Dank für die Einladung!

Vater: Schon gut! Wir freuen uns, wenn wir einmal im Jahr Nicoles Freunde zu uns einladen können. — Was willst du trinken? — Andreas, willst du Martin etwas zu trinken geben? Ich muss zum Grill.

Andreas: Okay, Martin, was möchtest du denn haben?

Nicole: Die Bowle schmeckt gut.

Martin: Gut, dann probier ich die Bowle.

Andreas: Prost!

Martin: — Hm, die ist wirklich gut!

Mutter: So, wer möchte was? Es gibt Kartoffelsalat, Krautsalat, Gurkensalat, Tomatensalat … Thomas? Möchtest du Kartoffelsalat?

Thomas: Ja, bitte! — Die Wurstbrote sehen auch ganz lecker aus!

Mutter: Nimm doch gleich zwei! — Und eine Brezel!

Thomas: Okay. — Wo ist denn der Kuchen?

Mutter: Pst! Der Kuchen kommt erst nachher.

Thomas: Ach so!

Birthday to you...

Martin: Was für eine Überraschung! Vielen, vielen Dank!

Übungsheft, S. 133

1 Was passiert hier?

These activities check for global comprehension only. Students should not yet be expected to produce language modeled in **Los geht's!**

Do you understand what is happening in the story? Check your comprehension by answering these questions. Don't be afraid to guess. 1. helping with preparations for a birthday party / help with shopping and in the kitchen; help father in the garden.

1. Why are Nicole's friends at her house? What does Nicole tell them they can do to help?
2. Why does Nicole need **Eier, Mehl,** and **Zucker**? 2. to bake a cake.
3. Why does Nicole's mother tell Thomas to keep his voice down? 3. It is supposed to be a surprise.
4. What do you think might happen next in the story? 4. Answers may vary.

2 Welche Beschreibung passt zu welcher Person?

Match each person from the story with the most appropriate description.

1. Martin c
2. Thomas b
3. Nicole d
4. Andreas a
5. Nicoles Vater e

a. geht mit Nicole einkaufen.
b. hilft Nicoles Vater im Garten und fragt Nicoles Mutter, wo der Kuchen ist.
c. bekommt heute einen Geburtstagskuchen.
d. lädt ihre Freunde zur Fete ein, geht einkaufen und bäckt den Kuchen.
e. findet es super, dass Nicoles Freunde kommen, steht am Grill und grillt die Bratwurst.

3 Nacherzählen

Put the sentences in logical order to make a brief summary of the story.

1. Andreas, Sabine und Thomas kommen vorbei, um Nicole zu helfen.

Als letzter kommt der Martin. 4

Zuerst gehen Andreas und Nicole zum Supermarkt, und Thomas hilft Nicoles Vater im Garten. 2

Später am Nachmittag kommen die Gäste. 3

Andreas gibt Martin etwas zu trinken. 5

Es gibt Bowle zu trinken, und es gibt viel zu essen: Kartoffelsalat, Tomatensalat, Krautsalat, Gurkensalat und Bratwurst. 6

Nach dem Essen bringen Nicole und Thomas den Geburtstagskuchen, und die Freunde singen „Happy Birthday!" 7

4 Und ihr?

Du und dein Partner habt heute Abend eine Fete. Was gibt's zu essen? Und zu trinken? Macht eine Liste! Schreibt alles auf, was ihr braucht! Dein Partner sagt dir, was er bringt, dann sagst du ihm, was du bringst. Dann besprich mit deinem Partner, wen ihr eingeladen habt und wer kommt!

BEISPIEL **PARTNER** Ich bringe …mit. Was bringst du?
 DU Ich bringe …
 PARTNER Und wen hast du eingeladen?
 DU Ich habe …eingeladen.

Erste Stufe

Objectives Offering help and explaining what to do; asking where something is located and giving directions

WK3 BADEN-WUERTTEMBERG-12

So sagt man das!

Offering help and explaining what to do

12–1 Schon bekannt

You are having a party! Your friends come over to help you get things ready.

A friend might ask:

> **Kann ich etwas für dich tun?**
> *or*
> **Was kann ich für dich tun?**
>
> **Was kann ich für euch tun?**

You could respond:

> **Du kannst für mich das Geschirr spülen.**
>
> **Geh bitte einkaufen! Hol ein Pfund Bratwurst und 10 Semmeln!**
> **Holt die Bratwurst beim Metzger und kauft das Brot beim Bäcker!**

Übungsheft, S. 134–136, Ü. 2–7

Thomas: **Müll sortieren, Rasen mähen, Zimmer aufräumen**
Andreas: **Staub saugen, Fenster putzen**
Sabine: **Tisch decken, Geschirr spülen, Einkaufen gehen**

5 Die Fete Script on p. 331G

CD 12 Tr. 3

Zuhören Nicole hat viel zu tun, denn sie muss alles für die Fete vorbereiten. Schau ihre Arbeitsliste an! Hör dir das Gespräch gut an und schreib auf, was jede Person macht, um Nicole zu helfen!

Ein wenig Grammatik

Schon bekannt

The preposition **für** is always followed by an accusative case form: **Kannst du für mich 200 Gramm Aufschnitt kaufen?** See page R18 to review the accusative pronouns. To review **du/ihr**-commands, see page R22. If you need to review the forms of **können,** see page R21.

Grammatikheft, S. 100–101, Ü. 1–3

Mehr Grammatikübungen, S. 352–353, Ü. 1–3 ➡

Arbeitsliste für die Fete
Müll sortieren
Rasen mähen
Staub saugen
Fenster putzen
Zimmer aufräumen
Tisch decken
Geschirr spülen
Einkaufen gehen – Tomaten,
Brot, Semmeln, Bratwurst,
Hackfleisch, Eier, Mehl,
Zucker, Äpfel, Orangen,
Kartoffeln, Mineralwasser, Cola
kaufen

6 Grammatik im Kontext

a. **Schreiben** Heute Abend hast du eine Fete für eine Freundin. Schreib einen Einkaufszettel und eine Arbeitsliste!

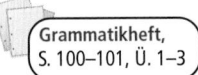

b. **Sprechen** Dein Partner fragt dich, wie er dir helfen kann. Sag ihm, was er für dich kaufen und machen kann! Sag deinem Partner auch, wo er die Lebensmittel kaufen soll! Dann tauscht ihr die Rollen aus!

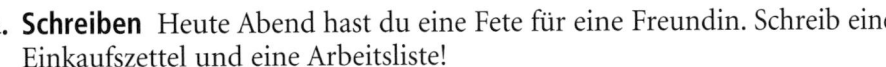

Ein wenig Landeskunde

Spätzle and **Apfelküchle** are specialties of Baden-Württemberg. **Spätzle** ("little sparrow" in the local dialect) are thick, round noodles made by spreading dough onto a board, then cutting it into small strips or pieces, and dropping them into boiling water.

Apfelküchle is a dessert made of apple slices dipped in a pancake batter and fried. The apples are then sprinkled with sugar and cinnamon. **Apfelküchle** is often served with vanilla sauce or vanilla ice cream.

7 ## Soll ich backen oder kochen?

Lesen/Sprechen Some friends are coming over for dinner. You and your partner are planning to make **Apfelküchle** and **Spätzle,** two popular southern German dishes. Each of you picks one recipe. Tell your partner what to buy for your recipe and how much. Then switch roles.

Käsespätzle
Für 4 Personen

400 g Mehl
2 Eier
etwas Salz
1/8 - 1/4 l Wasser
(oder Milch verdünnt)
1 EL Öl
200 g Emmentaler
4 Zwiebeln
50 g Butter
1 Spatzenbrett

Apfelküchle
Für 4 Portionen

200 g Mehl
3 Eier
1/4 l Milch
1 Prise Salz
4 möglichst säuerliche
   Äpfel (groß)
1 Zitrone
1 EL Zucker
1 EL Zimt
Butterschmalz zum Ausbacken

Wortschatz

das Salz
der Zimt *cinnamon*
das Butterschmalz *shortening*

(die) Zwiebel   **(die) Zitrone**   **(das) Öl**

Answers may vary. Some examples **Du kannst den Müll sortieren. Du kannst Staub saugen.**

8 ## Am nächsten Tag

Sprechen What a party! You and your friends had a great time last night, but now it's time to clean up the mess. You also promised your parents that you would do some other things around the house. Look at the picture of the house on the right and tell your partner what he or she can do to help. Then switch roles.

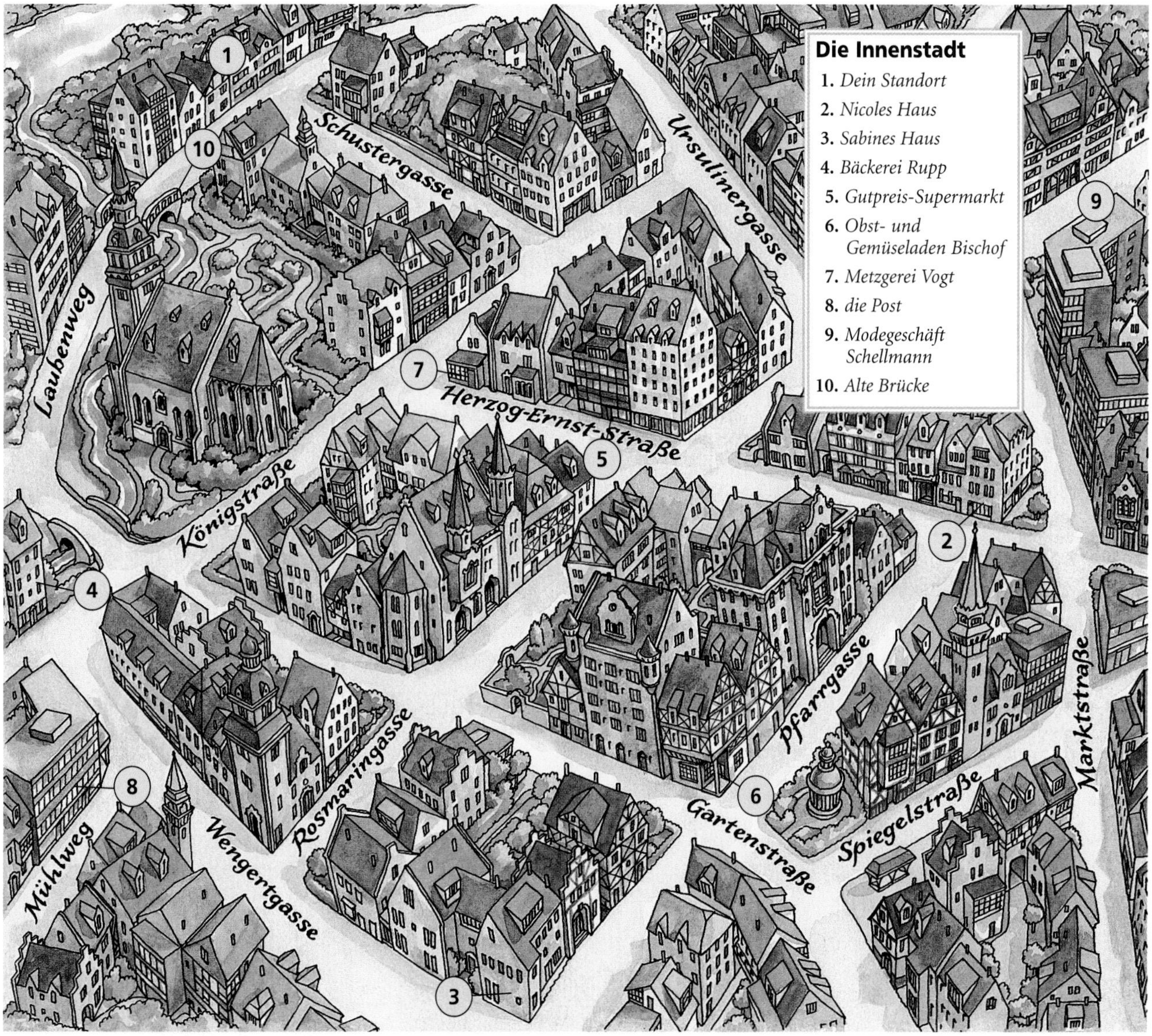
Die Innenstadt
1. Dein Standort
2. Nicoles Haus
3. Sabines Haus
4. Bäckerei Rupp
5. Gutpreis-Supermarkt
6. Obst- und Gemüseladen Bischof
7. Metzgerei Vogt
8. die Post
9. Modegeschäft Schellmann
10. Alte Brücke
Schustergasse
Ursulinergasse
Laubenweg
Herzog-Ernst-Straße
Königstraße
Pfarrgasse
Marktstraße
Rosmaringasse
Gartenstraße
Spiegelstraße
Mühlweg
Wengertgasse

So sagt man das!

Asking where something is located and giving directions *Schon bekannt*

CD-ROM DISC 3

If your friend asks you to pick up a few things at the butcher shop, you might first have to ask someone:

Weißt du, wo die Metzgerei ist?

The response might be:

In der Herzog-Ernst-Straße.

After you leave the house, you realize that you don't know how to get to **Herzog-Ernst-Straße.**

You ask a passerby:

Entschuldigung! Wie komme ich zur Metzgerei?

The response might be:

Gehen Sie geradeaus bis zur Schustergasse, dann nach rechts, dann die nächste Straße nach links.

Sabine: nach rechts in den Laubenweg bis zur Königstr., dann nach rechts und die erste Straße links. Geh bis zur Gartenstr. Dort ist mein Haus.

9 **Grammatik im Kontext** Script on p. 331G

CD 12
Tr. 4

Zuhören Following Nicole's party on Saturday, Sabine has invited everyone over on Sunday afternoon for a little get-together. Listen as both Sabine and Nicole give directions over the phone from where you are (**dein Standort**) to their houses. Write each set of instructions so that you know how to get to both parties. Check your directions on the map to see if you got them right. Nicole: Nach links und die erste Straße rechts bis zur Rosmaringasse. Dann rechts und die erste Straße links (Herzog-Ernst-Str.) bis zur Marktstraße. Da wohne ich.

10 **Grammatik im Kontext**

Sprechen You are at the **Bäckerei Rupp** and your partner is at Nicole's house. Tell your partner how to get to the bakery. Then switch roles: Now you're at Sabine's house, and your partner will give you directions to the **Modegeschäft Schellman.**

1. Nach rechts in die Herzog-Ernst.-Str. bis zur Königstr. Dann links und die erste Straße rechts.
2. Nach links in die Pfarrgasse. Die zweite Straße rechts. Dann links und die erste Straße rechts.

11 **Ihr habt Hunger**

Lesen/Sprechen Du und deine Partnerin, ihr seid bei Sabine. Ihr habt Hunger. Wähl zwei von den folgenden Lebensmitteln aus und erzähl deiner Partnerin, wo sie die kaufen kann und wie sie dahin kommt. Schau auf den Stadtplan auf Seite 339!

---

die nächste Straße nach … nach links
nach rechts an der Ampel nach …
bis zum …platz geradeaus bis zur …straße
die (erste, zweite …) Straße nach …

Ein wenig Grammatik

Schon bekannt

See pages R24 and R19 to review the forms of **wissen** and word order following **wissen.** To review formal commands, see page R22.

Übungsheft, S. 136, Ü. 8

Grammatikheft, S. 102, Ü. 4–5

Mehr Grammatikübungen,
S. 353, Ü. 4–5 →

LERNTRICK

When you are learning or reviewing vocabulary, remember to use the word or phrase in a sentence or conversation that gives it meaning. For example, when trying to learn the phrase **zur Bäckerei**, use it in an imaginary conversation:

— **Wie komme ich zur Bäckerei? Ich muss Brot kaufen.**
— **Die nächste Straße nach links.**

Musst du zu Hause helfen? CD 12 Tr. 5

You've already discovered how German students like to spend their free time, and you know that they enjoy planning and going to parties. However, life isn't all fun! Often before they go out or meet with their friends, they have to help around the house. What chores do you think German students have to do? Make a list of chores that the following German students might mention. Then read the interviews.

Übungsheft,
S. 144, Ü. 25–26

Heide, Berlin CD 12 Tr. 6

„Ich muss zweimal in der Woche die Toilette sauber machen, und dann ab und zu halt den Geschirrspüler ausräumen oder die Küche wischen und halt mein Zimmer aufräumen."

Silvana, Berlin CD 12 Tr. 7

„Zu Hause helf ich meistens so beim Abwaschen, Spülmaschine ausräumen, oder die Wäsche aufhängen oder abnehmen, zusammen-legen, immer so, was anfällt."

Monika, Berlin CD 12 Tr. 8

„Also, ich muss fast jeden Tag den Mülleimer runterbringen und ab und zu mal Waschmaschine an, Waschmaschine aus, Wäsche aufhängen …Dann ab und zu Staub saugen, wischen — also wir haben in der Küche so Fliesen (*tiles*) und — aber meistens, wenn meine Eltern keine Zeit dazu haben. Abwaschen muss ich nicht, also, wir haben einen Geschirrspüler."

Gerd, Bietigheim CD 12 Tr. 9

„Ich saug halt ab und zu Staub, räum die Spülmaschine aus, bring Müll raus, hol halt teilweise Getränke und so, mäh manchmal den Rasen — kommt ganz darauf an."

Some chores in common: **Wäsche aufhängen; Spülmaschine ausräumen; Staub saugen; Müll raustragen**

A. **1.** Make a list of the chores that are mentioned by each of the students. Do they have chores in common? How do the chores they mention compare to those you listed before reading the interviews?

   2. Which of these students do the same kinds of things that you do at home? Answers will vary.

   3. Which of the chores mentioned do you like or dislike? Give a reason in English.

B. You and your friends probably have chores to do at home. Make a list in German, indicating what you have to do and for whom, and report it to your class. Keep track of which chores your classmates do. How do the chores that American students do at home compare to those of German students? Write a brief essay in which you discuss this question, pointing out the differences and similarities.

STANDARDS: 1.2, 2.2, 3.2, 4.2

Zweite Stufe

Objectives Making plans and inviting someone to come along; talking about clothing; discussing gift ideas

go.hrw.com

WK3 BADEN-WUERTTEMBERG-12

So sagt man das!

Making plans and inviting someone to come along

Schon bekannt

There are many times when you will want to make plans with your friends and invite them to go places with you. You could say:

> **Ich will um halb drei ins Einkaufszentrum gehen, Klamotten kaufen.**
> **Willst du mitkommen?** *or* **Kommst du mit?**

Your friend might accept:

> **Ja gern!** *or*
> **Super! Ich komme gern mit!**

Or decline and give a reason:

> **Das geht leider nicht, denn ich muss am**
> **Nachmittag die Hausaufgaben machen.**

Übungsheft,
S. 137, Ü. 9–11

Wortschatz

THOMAS **Wohin willst du gehen? Was willst du tun?**
SABINE **Ich will …**

12–A
CD-ROM DISC 3

die Stadt besichtigen

in den Park gehen

in den Zoo gehen

Schlittschuh laufen

joggen

ein Brettspiel spielen

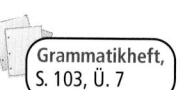
Grammatikheft,
S. 103, Ü. 7

Ein wenig Grammatik

Schon bekannt

See page R21 to review the forms of **wollen** and **müssen**. In German the conjugated verb in a main clause of a statement is always in second position. If there is a second verb, it is at the end of the sentence or clause and is in the infinitive. To review German word order, see page R19.

CD-ROM DISC 3

Übungsheft, S. 138, Ü. 12

Grammatikheft, S. 103, Ü. 6

Mehr Grammatikübungen,
S. 353, Ü. 6

STANDARDS: 4.1
KAPITEL 12 Die Fete

12 Grammatik im Kontext

Script on p. 331G

CD 12
Tr. 10

Zuhören A youth magazine recently interviewed four teens in the German-speaking countries about what they like to do in their free time. Match each person interviewed with the activity below that best fits that person's interests.

1. …in den Zoo gehen
2. …jeden Tag joggen
3. …Brettspiele spielen, z. B., Monopoly®
4. …die Altstadt besichtigen

Peter-3; Sandra-4; Franz-1; Judith-2

13 Grammatik im Kontext

Lesen/Sprechen Du und dein Partner, ihr seid Austauschschüler in der Stadt Bietigheim. Heute besucht ihr das Jugendzentrum. Schaut auf die Tafel, dann wählt vier Tätigkeiten, die ihr zwei gern macht, und sagt, wann ihr diese Tätigkeiten machen könnt.

Tennis spielen	14⁰⁰–15³⁰
joggen	12¹⁵–13¹⁵
Schach spielen	13⁰⁰–17⁰⁰
Tanzunterricht	16⁰⁰–17⁰⁰
schwimmen	14⁰⁰–16³⁰
Film: "Der mit dem Wolf tanzt"	12⁰⁰–14¹⁵
basteln	15⁴⁵–17⁴⁵
Karten spielen (Skat)	13⁴⁵–15³⁰
Gitarrenunterricht	14³⁰–15³⁰
Zeichenunterricht	17⁰⁰–18⁰⁰
Basketballturnier	13⁰⁰–14³⁰

14 Willst du mitkommen? Answers may vary.

a. Lesen/Sprechen Schau die Fotos an und lies den Text! Dann beantworte die Fragen!

1. Was spielen die Jungen hier? Polo
2. Wo spielen sie? im Wasser
3. Warum nennt (to name) man den Sport „Polo mit Eskimorolle"? Weil sie oft eine Eskimorolle machen.
4. Glaubst du, dass dieser Sport Spaß macht? Answers may vary.
5. Möchtest du „Polo mit Eskimorolle" spielen? Warum oder warum nicht?

b. Schreiben/Sprechen Hast du Freizeitinteressen, die so ungewöhnlich sind, wie „Polo mit Eskimorolle"? Mach eine Liste mit drei Aktivitäten, die du gern machst, und lad dazu deinen Partner ein! Tauscht dann die Rollen aus!

Kein Sport für Wasserscheue: Manchmal muss man mit dem Kopf ins Wasser. In der Fachsprache heißt das „Eskimorolle".

Wo ist der Ball? Besonders geschickte Spieler führen ihn mit ihrem Paddel unter Wasser.

Wo ist das Tor? Der Ball muss zwei Meter über dem Wasser in einen Korb.

Talking about clothing

Schon bekannt

You might have the following conversation with the salesperson in a clothing store:

VERKÄUFERIN:	**Haben Sie einen Wunsch?**
DU:	**Ich brauche einen Pulli, in Gelb, bitte! Oh, und ich suche auch ein T-Shirt. Der Pulli dort drüben sieht sehr fesch aus. Ich probiere ihn mal an.**
VERKÄUFERIN:	**Wie passt er? Nicht zu lang oder zu eng?**
DU:	**Nein, überhaupt nicht. Er passt prima, und er gefällt mir.**
VERKÄUFERIN:	**Ja, er sieht phantastisch aus.**
DU:	**Wirklich?**
VERKÄUFERIN:	**Wirklich!**
DU:	**Ja, das finde ich auch. Ich nehme ihn.**

Grammatikheft, S. 104, Ü. 8–9

---

15 **In welchem Geschäft kaufst du deine Klamotten?** Script on p. 331H   1 d.   2 a.   3 c.   4 b.

Zuhören Heute gibt es viele neue Modegeschäfte in Bietigheim. Leute in einem Eiscafé sprechen über diese Geschäfte. Welches Gespräch passt zu welchem Schaufenster?

CD 12 Tr. 11

a.

b.

c.

d.

Wortschatz

aus Seide	*made of silk*
aus Baumwolle	*made of cotton*
aus Leder	*made of leather*
gestreift	*striped*
gepunktet	*polka-dotted*

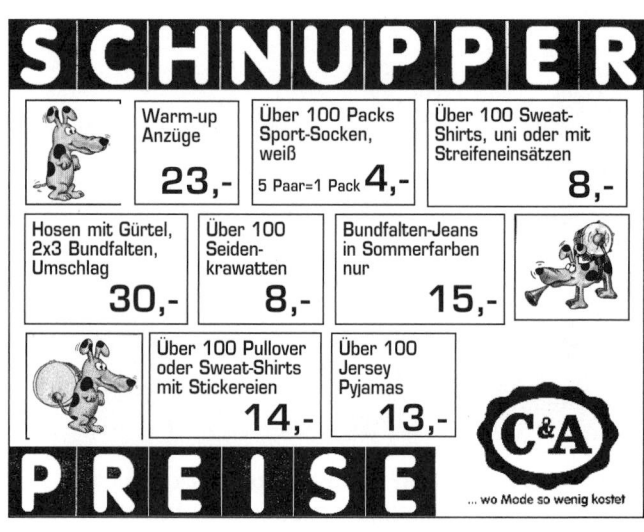

SCHNUPPER

Warm-up Anzüge **23,-**	Über 100 Packs Sport-Socken, weiß 5 Paar=1 Pack **4,-**	Über 100 Sweat-Shirts, uni oder mit Streifeneinsätzen **8,-**
Hosen mit Gürtel, 2x3 Bundfalten, Umschlag **30,-**	Über 100 Seiden-krawatten **8,-**	Bundfalten-Jeans in Sommerfarben nur **15,-**
	Über 100 Pullover oder Sweat-Shirts mit Stickereien **14,-**	Über 100 Jersey Pyjamas **13,-**

C&A
... wo Mode so wenig kostet

PREISE

16 Grammatik im Kontext

Schreiben Make a window display for a clothing store. Either draw the items of clothing or cut pictures out of magazines and newspapers, then add price tags to your items. Name your store and write an advertisement for it. Look at the **C & A** ad on page 344 for ideas.

17 Grammatik im Kontext

Sprechen You are looking for one of the items to the right in a clothing store. Your partner is the salesclerk. Find out if his or her store has the exact item you want. Find out the cost and where the item is located in the store. Then switch roles.

> ### Ein wenig Grammatik
>
> *Schon bekannt*
> To review the nominative and accusative pronouns, see page R18. To review the definite and indefinite articles in the nominative and accusative cases, see pages R15–R16.
>
> (Übungsheft, S. 138, Ü. 13)

So sagt man das!

Discussing gift ideas

Schon bekannt
12–2

In **Kapitel 11** you learned to talk about giving gifts on special occasions.

A friend might ask:

> **Was schenkst du deinem Bruder zum Geburtstag?**
> **Und was schenkst du deiner Kusine zu Weihnachten?**

You might respond:

> **Ich schenke ihm eine Armbanduhr.**
>
> **Ich schenke ihr ein Buch.**

---

18 Grammatik im Kontext

Sprechen Unten sind ein paar typische Geschenke aus Deutschland und der Schweiz. Schau dir die Geschenke an. Dann erzähl deinem Partner, wem du sie schenkst (z.B. dem Vater, der Mutter). Dann erzählt dir dein Partner, wem er was schenkt.

die Kuckucksuhr   **der Krug**

das Poster   **ein Stück von der Berliner Mauer**   **die Armbanduhr**

> ### Ein wenig Grammatik
>
> *Schon bekannt*
> Do you remember the dative pronouns **ihm** (*to him*) and **ihr** (*to her*) and the definite articles **dem** and **der**? Don't forget the dative endings for **dein** and **mein**.
>
> | *masculine* | | *feminine* | |
> |---|---|---|---|
> | dein- | } em | dein- | } er |
> | mein- | | mein- | |
>
> (Übungsheft, S. 139, Ü. 14–15)
> (Grammatikheft, S. 105, Ü. 10–11)
>
> Mehr Grammatikübungen, S. 354, Ü. 7–8 →

Dritte Stufe

Objectives Describing people and places; saying what you would like and whether you do or don't want more; talking about what you did

go.hrw.com

WK3-BADEN-WUERTTEMBERG-12

So sagt man das!

Describing people and places

12–2 *Schon bekannt*

You will probably meet people at parties who will ask you about yourself, your friends, and your family.

Someone might ask:

Woher kommst du, Lisa?
Und wo wohnst du jetzt?

Ist das deine Schwester?

Und was machst du in deiner Freizeit?
Wer ist denn Michael?
Wie sieht er aus?

You might respond:

Aus Kalifornien.
Ich wohne jetzt in Berlin, in der Schönleinstraße.
Ja, das ist meine Schwester. Sie heißt Jennifer.
Ich spiele oft Schach mit Michael.
Mein Freund.
Er hat lange, braune Haare und grüne Augen und er hat eine Brille.

You'll also want to be able to describe places, like your own room:

Mein Zimmer, das ist wirklich toll! Die Möbel sind echt schön, das Bett sogar ganz neu, ja und auch der Schreibtisch. Dann habe ich auch eine Couch. Die Farbe, na ja, das Grün ist nicht sehr schön, aber sonst ist die Couch wirklich sehr bequem.

> Übungsheft, S. 140–141, Ü. 16–20

> Grammatikheft, S.106, Ü. 12

Ein wenig Grammatik

Schon bekannt

When you refer to people and places, you will use the nominative pronouns **er, sie, es,** and **sie** (pl), for example, **Das ist mein Vater. Er heißt Gerd.** To review these pronouns, look at page R18. To review possessives like **mein** and **dein,** see page R16.

CD-ROM DISC 3

Mehr Grammatikübungen,
S. 354, Ü. 9 ➡️

19 ## Grammatik im Kontext

Sprechen Cut out magazine photos of two famous people and bring them to class. Place the photos in a container. Each student will take out a photo. Describe the person in the photo you picked with as much detail as possible so that your partner can guess who it is. Switch roles.

20 ## Grammatik im Kontext

Schreiben/Sprechen Dein Freund hat eine Fete, und du bist eingeladen. Du möchtest auf der Fete andere Leute kennen lernen (*meet*). Mach eine Liste mit acht Fragen, z.B. **Wo wohnst du? Was machst du in deiner Freizeit?** Frag deine Partnerin, und schreib ihre Antworten auf! Dann tauscht ihr die Rollen aus.

Deine Partnerin vorstellen *Introducing your partner*

Sprechen Heute tagt (*meets*) der Deutsch-Club. Du musst deine Partnerin vorstellen. Erzähl der Klasse alles, was du über deine Partnerin weißt! (Verwende Information von Übung 20.)

Wortschatz

Welche Möbel habt ihr im Wohnzimmer?

Wir haben …

ein Sofa
einen Tisch
  aus Holz
  aus Kunststoff
eine Lampe

einen Teppich   **einen Sessel**

rund
eckig (*with corners*)
modern

Und in der Küche gibt es … einen Esstisch

CD-ROM DISC **3**

einen Kühlschrank   **einen Herd**

 12–B

 p. 331X

einen Ofen   **ein Spülbecken**

 Grammatikheft, S. 107, Ü. 13–15

22

Beschreib den Raum!

Sprechen/Schreiben Beschreib deinem Partner die Möbel im Wohnzimmer! Frag ihn, wie er die Möbel findet! Sag ihm, wie du die Möbel findest! Jetzt beschreibt dein Partner die Möbel in der Küche.

allmilmö®

23

Für mein Notizbuch

Schreiben Beschreib dein Wohnzimmer und deine Küche! Was für Möbel gibt es da? Wie sehen diese Möbel aus? Du kannst auch eine Skizze machen.

Saying what you would like and whether you do or don't want more

Schon bekannt

When eating at a friend's house,
you may be asked by your host:

You could respond:

Was möchtest du trinken?

Ich möchte eine Limo, bitte!

Later your host might ask if you want more of something:

Möchtest du noch etwas?

Ja, bitte! Noch einen Saft.

Und noch eine Semmel?

Nein, danke! Keine Semmel mehr.

Übungsheft,
S. 142, Ü. 21–23

Ein wenig Grammatik

Schon bekannt

To review the **möchte** forms, see page R21. To review the use of **kein ... mehr**, see page R16.

Mehr Grammatikübungen,
S. 355, Ü. 10–11

Grammatikheft,
S. 108, Ü. 16–17

---

24 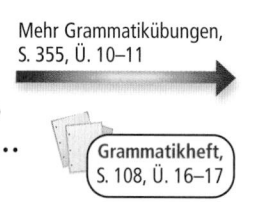 **Grammatik im Kontext**

Sprechen Spiel mit zwei oder drei Klassenkameraden die folgende Szene vor der Klasse: Ihr seid auf einer Geburtstagsfete. Ein Schüler spielt den Gastgeber *(host).* Er fragt die Gäste, was sie essen und trinken möchten. Später sagen die Gäste, wie das Essen schmeckt. Dann fragt der Gastgeber, wer noch etwas möchte.

25 **Eine Imbissstube in Bietigheim**

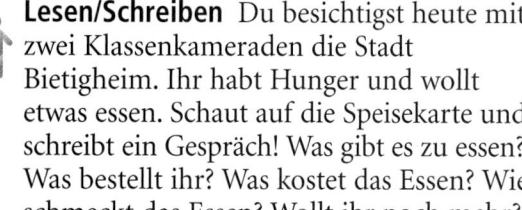

Lesen/Schreiben Du besichtigst heute mit zwei Klassenkameraden die Stadt Bietigheim. Ihr habt Hunger und wollt etwas essen. Schaut auf die Speisekarte und schreibt ein Gespräch! Was gibt es zu essen? Was bestellt ihr? Was kostet das Essen? Wie schmeckt das Essen? Wollt ihr noch mehr?

Unser Vollwertbuffett:

Bärlauchsuppe 4,90
Szegediner Sojagulasch
mit Vollkornknödel 7,40
Weizen-Obstsalat
Dessert 3,35
Salatteller groß 8,40
klein 6,40
Frühlingsrolle
mit Rohkostsalat 4,80
Brotzeitteller 5,90
Millirahmstrudel
mit Vanillesoße 5,90

Talking about what you did

Schon bekannt

You will often want to describe to friends or family what you did in the past, for example, last week or over the weekend.

A friend might ask: **Was hast du am Wochenende gemacht?**

Your response might be:

> **Am Samstag war ich in der Innenstadt. Zuerst habe ich Klamotten gekauft, dann war ich im Supermarkt, danach im Eiscafé mit Andreas und zuletzt bei Andreas zu Hause. Am Sonntag war ich die ganze Zeit zu Hause. Am Nachmittag habe ich gelesen, und am Abend habe ich ein Video gesehen. Danach haben Antje, Jörg und ich über Filme und Musik gesprochen.**

Grammatikheft, S. 108, Ü. 18

26

Hast du ein schönes Wochenende gehabt?

Sprechen Frag deine Partnerin, was sie am Wochenende gemacht hat! Dann fragt dich deine Partnerin. Verwende die Vorschläge (*suggestions*) hier rechts.

> Wo warst du am Wochenende?
> im Kaufhaus
> beim Bäcker
> zu Hause
> bei Freunden
> in der Stadt
> im Konzert
>
> Was hast du gemacht?
> gekauft?
> gelesen?
> gesehen?
> Worüber habt ihr gesprochen?

---

27  Von der Schule zum Beruf

Schreiben You have been hired as copy writer for your local newspaper. Your boss wants to print a special insert for newcomers to your town, an insert familiarizing them with the local attractions, theaters, stores, etc. Your boss lets you choose which topic you want to cover.

AUSSPRACHE

CD 12
Trs. 12–14

Richtig aussprechen / Richtig lesen

A. To review the following sounds, say the sentences below after your teacher or after the recording.   CD 12 Tr. 12

1. The letter **w:** The letter **w** is always pronounced like the *v* in the English word *vent*.
   Weißt du, wann Werners Geburtstag ist? Am Mittwoch?

2. The letter **j:** The letter **j** is pronounced the same as the *y* in the English word *you*.
   Die Julia besucht Jens im Juli, nicht Juni.

3. The letters **ä** and **e:** The letters **ä** and **e** are pronounced as short vowels when followed by two consonants. When followed by one consonant or the letter **h** the **ä** and **e** are usually pronounced as long vowels.
   Ich finde den Sessel hässlich. Er gefällt mir nicht.
   Peter kauft Käse. Das Mädchen mäht den Rasen.

Richtig schreiben / Diktat
CD 12 Tr. 13
CD 12 Tr. 14 (with pauses)

B. Write down the sentences that you hear.   Script on p. 331H

Mahlzeit!

Lesestrategie Combining reading strategies You can often derive the main idea of a text by looking at visual clues and format, and then searching for cognates and words you already know. In trying to figure out the meaning of unknown words, look at the context in which they occur. Often the surrounding text will give you clues about the meaning of the unknown word.

recipes

1. Judging by their form, what kinds of texts are these? What kinds of expressions do you expect to find in them? List in English the words and expressions you would find in typical recipes at home.

2. Recalling what you know about cognates and compound words, what do the following words mean in English?
   gefüllte Eier deviled eggs
   Kartoffelsalat potato salad
   Mandelkuchen almond cake
   (**Mandeln**=*almonds*)

3. Since German recipes often use infinitives in the directions, you need to look at the end of the sentences to determine what to do with the ingredients. Make an educated guess about the meaning of the verbs in these phrases.

1. mit Salz und Pfeffer **abschmecken** b
2. die Eier **halbieren** d
3. die Dotter **herausnehmen** a
4. Essig **dazugeben** f
5. Speck in kleine Würfel **schneiden** e
6. mit fein gehackter Zwiebel **anrösten** c

a. *take out*
b. *season*
c. *brown lightly*
d. *halve*
e. *cut*
f. *add*

Kartoffelsalat mit Speck

1Pfd. gekochte Kartoffeln
50g Speck
1 Zwiebel
3 Esslöffel Essig
Salz
Pfeffer
4 Esslöffel Brühe

Kartoffeln in Scheiben schneiden. Warm halten. Etwas Speck in kleine Würfel schneiden und mit fein gehackter Zwiebel anrösten. Essig dazugeben und die Kartoffeln und den Speck mit Salz und Pfeffer abschmecken. Die heiße Fleischbrühe dazugeben.

Gefüllte Eier

Mandelkuchen

150 g Butter oder Margarine
200 g Zucker
1 Päckchen Vanillin-Zucker
5 Eier
3 Tropfen Bittermandelöl
100 g Weizenmehl
50 g Maisstärke
1 Teelöffel Backpulver

Aus den Zutaten einen Rührteig bereiten, dann 150 g Mandeln, gemahlen und 150 g Schokoladenstücke unterheben und alles in eine gefettete Kastenform füllen. Bei 175 Grad etwa 60-70 Minuten backen.

Gefüllte Eier

Hart gekochte Eier, nach Bedarf
Butter
Salz
fein gehackte Kräuter
(Thymian, Majoran,
Basilikum, Estragon)

Die Eier halbieren, die Dotter herausnehmen und in einer Schüssel mit der Butter, dem Salz und den fein gehackten Kräutern gut verrühren. Die Masse wieder in die Eihälften füllen.

4. Scan the lists of ingredients. How are most of the ingredients measured? How does that compare to recipes in the United States? *in grams rather than cups*

5. What ingredients will you need to make the deviled eggs? What do you think **Kräuter** means? (*Hint: look at the words in parentheses that follow.*)

6. What ingredients will you need to make **Kartoffelsalat**? How does this differ from the way you would make potato salad?

7. What steps will you need to follow to make the **Kartoffelsalat?**

8. What ingredients will you need to make the **Mandelkuchen**? What do you think **Bittermandelöl** is?

9. What cooking temperature is given for the cake? The baking temperature for electric ovens is 175°. This number is much lower than the usual temperature needed for baking cakes. How can you explain this? (Remember what you learned in **Kapitel 7** about how temperature is measured in German-speaking countries.)

10. What are the steps in making deviled eggs?

11. Assume you are in Germany, and you have been asked to bring your favorite food to a party, along with the recipe. Choose something that is not too complicated to make and write out the recipe.

5. eggs, butter, salt, chopped herbs; Herbs
6. potatoes, bacon, onion, vinegar, salt, pepper, broth
7. Slice potatoes. Brown bacon and onions. Add vinegar, salt, pepper, potatoes and broth.
8. butter or margarine, sugar, vanilla sugar, eggs, almond flavor, flour, cornstarch, baking powder, almonds, chocolate chips; almond flavor
9. given in Celsius
10. Cut eggs in half, take out yolks and mix them with other ingredients. Fill eggs with yolk mixture.

Übungsheft, S. 143, Ü. 24

Mehr Grammatikübungen

▣ internet
go.hrw.com
ADRESSE: go.hrw.com
KENNWORT:
WK3 BADEN-WUERTTEMBERG-12

Answers

Erste Stufe

Objectives Offering help and explaining what to do

1 Vor der Party gibt es so viel zu tun! Vervollständige die folgenden Anweisungen und schreib dabei die passende Form von **können** in die erste Lücke, das passende Possessivpronomen in die zweite Lücke und ein passendes Verb in die dritte Lücke. **(S. 337)**

Was können wir für euch tun?

1. Peter, du _____ für _____ Vater den Rasen _____ .
2. Heike, du _____ für _____ Mutter das Geschirr _____ .
3. Uwe und Eva, ihr _____ für _____ Opa den Müll _____ .
4. Klaus und Antje, ihr _____ für _____ Tante den Tisch _____ .
5. Hans und Grete, ihr _____ für _____ Oma einkaufen _____ .
6. Du und ich, wir _____ für _____ Kusine Staub _____ .

kannst; meinen; mähen

kannst; meine; spülen

könnt; meinen; sortieren

könnt; meine; decken

könnt; meine; gehen

können; meine; saugen

2 Es gibt so viel Arbeit, und deshalb hat Nicoles Mutter eine Arbeitsliste gemacht. Wer kann was für sie tun? Lies die Liste und schreib Nicoles Mutters Anweisungen. **(S. 337)**

BEISPIEL THOMAS   Garage aufräumen
Thomas, du kannst für mich die Garage aufräumen.

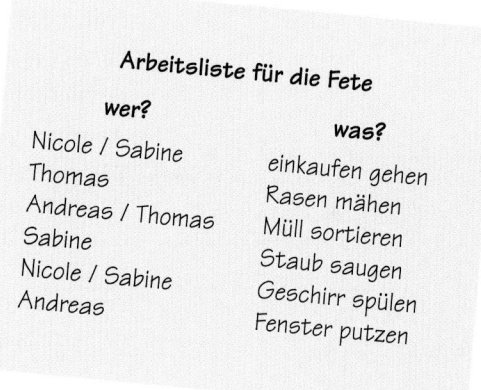

Arbeitsliste für die Fete

wer?

Nicole / Sabine
Thomas
Andreas / Thomas
Sabine
Nicole / Sabine
Andreas

was?

einkaufen gehen
Rasen mähen
Müll sortieren
Staub saugen
Geschirr spülen
Fenster putzen

1. Nicole und Sabine, _____ .   ihr könnt für mich einkaufen gehen
2. Thomas, _____ .   du kannst für mich den Rasen mähen
3. Andreas und Thomas, _____.   ihr könnt für mich den Müll sortieren
4. Sabine, _____.   du kannst für mich Staub saugen
5. Nicole und Sabine, _____ .   ihr könnt für mich das Geschirr spülen
6. Andreas, _____ .   du kannst für mich die Fenster putzen

3 Du sagst zuerst einem Freund, was er tun soll. Danach sagst du zwei Freunden dasselbe. Schreib also das erste Mal den **du**-Imperativ in die Lücken, das zweite Mal den **ihr**-Imperativ. (S. 337)

1. _____ bitte zuerst den Müll und _____ danach den Rasen! Sortier; mäh | Sortiert; mäht
2. _____ bitte einkaufen und _____ Milch, Brot und Obst! Geh; kauf | Geht; kauft
3. _____ bitte zuerst die Fenster und _____ danach Staub! Putz; saug | Putzt, saugt
4. _____ bitte das Geschirr und _____ dann den Tisch! Spül; deck | Spült; deckt
5. _____ doch zu Hause und _____ ein Buch! Bleib; lies | Bleibt; lest
6. _____ mit ins Café Freizeit und _____ einen Apfelsaft! Komm; trink | Kommt; trinkt

4 Jeder weiß etwas. Schreib die folgenden Fragen und Sätze ab und schreib dabei die korrekte Form von **wissen** in die erste Lücke und eine passende Verbform in die zweite Lücke. (S. 340)

1. Herbert, _____ du, wann unser Deutschlehrer Geburtstag _____ ? weißt; hat
2. Wer _____ , wann der Namenstag von Erika _____ ? weiß; ist
3. Eva und Jörg, _____ ihr, wie der Ahmet zur Schule _____ ? wisst; kommt
4. Wir _____ nicht, wer heute Abend eine Fete _____ . wissen; hat
5. Ich _____ , was ich meinem Opa zum Geburtstag _____ . weiß; schenke
6. Meine Eltern _____ , dass ich gern Gruselromane _____ . wissen; lese

5 Du sagst verschiedenen Erwachsenen *(various adults),* was sie tun sollen. Schreib den **Sie**-Imperativ in die Lücken. (S. 340)

1. _____ nicht diesen Liebesroman! Er ist viel zu schmalzig. Lesen Sie
2. _____ die Brötchen lieber beim Bäcker! Dort sind sie immer frisch. Kaufen Sie
3. _____ Ihrer Großmutter einen Blumenstrauß! Sie hat Blumen gern. Schenken Sie
4. _____ doch mal über Mode und nicht immer über Politik! Sprechen Sie
5. _____ doch mal Schach und nicht immer Karten! Spielen Sie
6. _____ doch mal Orangensaft und nicht immer nur Apfelsaft! Trinken Sie

---

Zweite Stufe

Objectives Making plans and inviting someone to come along; talking about clothing; discussing gift ideas

6 Du und deine Freunde, ihr wollt heute so viel tun. Aber zuerst müsst ihr die Arbeiten fertig machen, die ihr angefangen habt. Schreib die folgenden Sätze ab und schreib dabei die richtige Form von **wollen** in die erste Lücke und die richtige Form von **müssen** in die zweite Lücke. (S. 342)

1. Peter, _____ du ins Kino gehen? — Ja, aber zuerst _____ ich Staub saugen. willst; muss
2. _____ ihr Schach spielen? — Klar, aber zuerst _____ wir alles aufräumen. Wollt; müssen
3. Karl _____ ins Café gehen, aber zuerst _____ er den Hund füttern. will; muss
4. Die Kinder _____ lesen, aber zuerst _____ sie das Zimmer aufräumen. wollen; müssen
5. Ich _____ mit Peter Tennis spielen, aber er _____ zuerst einkaufen gehen. will; muss
6. Eva und Kurt, _____ ihr Musik hören, oder _____ ihr nach Hause gehen? wollt; müsst

Mehr Grammatikübungen

Answers

CD-ROM
DISC 3

go.hrw.com

WK3 BADEN-WUERTTEMBERG-12

7 Du fragst eine Freundin, was du für sie und ihre Familie tun kannst. Schreib die folgenden Fragen ab und schreib dabei die richtige Form von **dein** in die erste Lücke und das richtige Personalpronomen in die zweite und dritte Lücke. (S. 345)

1. _____ Bruder, wie heißt _____ ? Was kann ich für _____ tun?   *Dein; er; ihn*
2. _____ Schwester, wie heißt _____ ? Was kann ich für _____ tun?   *Deine; sie; sie*
3. _____ Opa, wie heißt _____ ? Was kann ich für _____ tun?   *Dein; er; ihn*
4. _____ Großmutter, wie heißt _____ ? Was kann ich für _____ tun?   *Deine; sie; sie*
5. _____ Kusine, wie heißt _____ ? Was kann ich für _____ tun?   *Deine; sie; sie*
6. _____ Cousin, wie heißt _____ ? Was kann ich für _____ tun?   *Dein; er; ihn*

8 Was schenkst du? Du fragst einen Freund, was er seinen Familienmitgliedern schenkt. Schreib die folgenden Fragen und Antworten ab und schreib dabei die richtige Form von **dein** in die erste Lücke, die richtige Form von **mein** in die zweite Lücke und das richtige Pronomen in die dritte Lücke. (S. 345)

1. Was schenkst du _____ Oma?   _____ Oma? Ich schenke _____ ein Buch.   *deiner; Meiner; ihr*
2. Was schenkst du _____ Opa?   _____ Opa? Ich schenke _____ Pralinen.   *deinem; Meinem; ihm*
3. Was gibst du _____ Kusine?   _____ Kusine? Ich gebe _____ eine Uhr.   *deiner; Meiner; ihr*
4. Was gibst du _____ Cousin?   _____ Cousin? Ich gebe _____ ein Poster.   *deinem; Meinem; ihm*
5. Was kaufst du _____ Mutti?   _____ Mutti? Ich kaufe _____ Parfüm.   *deiner; Meiner; ihr*
6. Was kaufst du _____ Vati?   _____ Vati? Ich kaufe _____ einen Roman.   *deinem; Meinem; ihm*

Dritte Stufe

Objectives Describing people and places; saying what you would like and whether you do or don't want more; talking about what you did

9 Du schaust mit einer Freundin das Familienalbum an und sprichst über deine Familienmitglieder. Schreib den folgenden Absatz ab und schreib dabei die richtigen Possessivpronomen und Pronomen in die Lücken. (S. 346)

Den Mann hier, kennst du _____ ? Das ist _____ Vater. _____ ist 40   *ihn; mein; Er*

Jahre alt. _____ hat braune Haare und grüne Augen. Ich habe _____   *Er; ihn*

sehr gern. _____ spielt immer Ball mit mir. Am Samstag hat _____   *Er; er*

Geburtstag und ich schenke _____ Blumen, weil _____ Blumen so   *ihm; er*

gern hat. Die Frau hier ist _____ Oma. _____ ist schon 70 Jahre alt.   *meine; Sie*

_____ hat graue Haare und _____ hat eine Brille. Ich habe _____   *Sie; sie; meine*

Oma gern. Nächste Woche hat _____ Oma Namenstag, und ich   *meine*

schenke _____ Pralinen zum Namenstag und vielleicht gebe ich   *ihr*

_____ auch einen Blumenstrauß.   *ihr*

10 Auf einer Party bietet man den Gästen mehr zu essen und zu trinken an. Aber alle sagen nein. Schreib die folgenden Fragen und Antworten ab und schreib dabei die richtige Form von **möchte** in die erste Lücke und die richtige Form von **kein** in die zweite Lücke. (S. 348)

1. Claudia, _____ du noch Kuchen? — Nein, danke, _____ Kuchen mehr.   möchtest; keinen
2. Frau Bär, _____ Sie noch Obst? — Nein, danke, _____ Obst mehr.   möchten; kein
3. _____ ihr noch Milch? — Nein, danke, _____ Milch mehr.   Möchtet; keine
4. _____ die Kinder noch Leberkäs? — Nein, danke, _____ Leberkäs mehr.   Möchten; keinen
5. Wer _____ noch Saft? — Nein, danke, _____ Saft für mich.   möchte; keinen
6. _____ du noch ein Wurstbrot? — Nein, danke, _____ Wurstbrot mehr.   Möchtest; kein

11 Du hast eine kleine Wohnung und brauchst verschiedene Möbel und Geräte. Du gehst in ein Geschäft, und fragst den Verkäufer nach den Dingen, die links abgebildet sind. (S. 348)

1. – Wie teuer ist _____ _____ ?
   – _____ kostet 200 Euro.
   – Ich suche _____ _____ für ungefähr 120 Euro.
   – Für 120 Euro finden Sie _____ _____ . Bestimmt nicht!

   Teppich

   der; Teppich
   Er
   einen; Teppich
   keinen; Teppich

2. – Wie teuer ist _____ _____ ?
   – _____ kostet 150 Euro.
   – Ich suche _____ _____ für ungefähr 80 Euro.
   – Für 80 Euro finden Sie _____ _____ . Bestimmt nicht!

   Couch

   die; Couch
   Sie
   eine; Couch
   keine; Couch

3. – Wie viel kostet _____ _____ ?
   – _____ kostet 300 Euro.
   – Ich suche _____ _____ für ungefähr 200 Euro.
   – Für 200 Euro finden Sie _____ _____ . Bestimmt nicht.

   Ofen

   der; Ofen
   Er
   einen; Ofen
   keinen; Ofen

4. – Wie teuer ist _____ _____ ?
   – _____ kostet 50 Euro.
   – Ich suche _____ _____ für ungefähr 30 Euro.
   – Für 30 Euro finden Sie _____ _____ . Bestimmt nicht!

   Handy

   das; Handy
   Es
   ein Handy
   kein; Handy

5. – Wie teuer ist _____ _____ ?
   – _____ kostet 700 Euro.
   – Ich suche _____ _____ für ungefähr 200 Euro.
   – Für 200 Euro finden Sie _____ _____ . Bestimmt nicht!

   der; Computer
   Er
   einen; Computer
   keinen; Computer

   Computer

Anwendung

CD-ROM
DISC 3

internet
ADRESSE: go.hrw.com
KENNWORT:
WK3 BADEN-WUERTTEMBERG-12

The CD-ROM Tutor offers guided recording and writing activities to accompany the **Anwendung.** These activities are designed to practice students' oral and written communication skills and to review material from each chapter.

1 You will hear five different conversations taking place at Martin's party. Listen and decide which of the five topics below belongs with which conversation. Script on p. 331H

CD 12 Tr. 15

a. Filme   **b.** Musik   **c.** Essen   **d.** Sport   **e.** Schule

a-4; b-3; c-1; d-2; e-5

2 Wer ist deine Lieblingsperson? Schreib alles über deine Lieblingsperson in dein Notizbuch. Wer ist diese Person? Wie alt ist sie? Wo wohnt sie? Wie sieht diese Person aus? Was macht diese Person in der Freizeit? Was für Interessen hat sie?

3 Du gehst bald zu einem Familientreffen (*family reunion*). Du willst den Verwandten etwas schenken. Was schenkst du ihnen? Zum Beispiel, was schenkst du deinem Onkel? Und deiner Kusine? Erzähl es deinem Partner! Danach sagt er dir, was er schenkt.

4 You are taking a day trip to Stuttgart and would like to visit some interesting places. Go to the information center and find out how to get to the following places. Your partner will give you directions at the information counter.

1. ins Theater in der Altstadt   **3.** zum Alten Schloss

2. zum Rathaus   **4.** zur tri-bühne

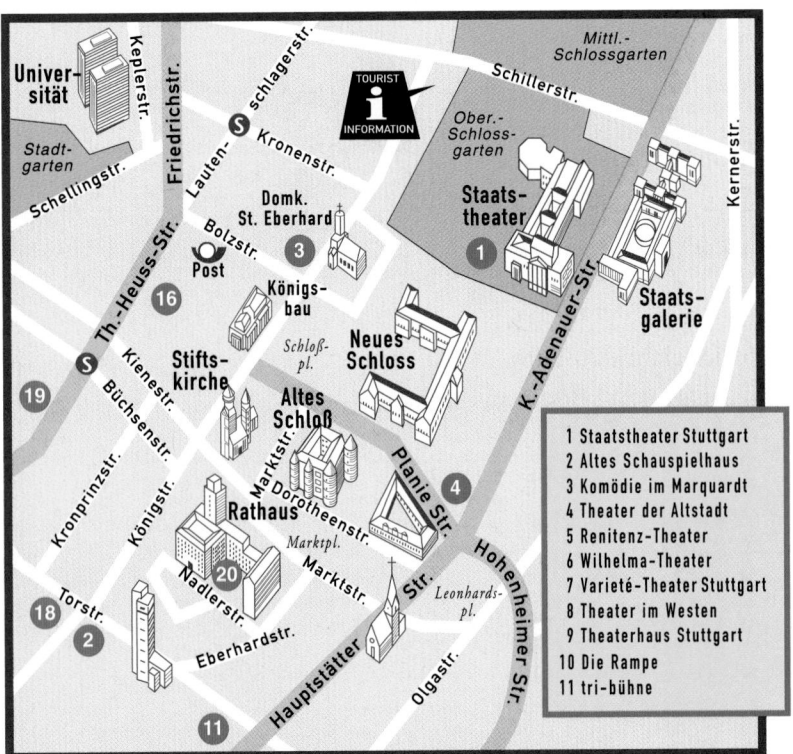

1 Staatstheater Stuttgart
2 Altes Schauspielhaus
3 Komödie im Marquardt
4 Theater der Altstadt
5 Renitenz-Theater
6 Wilhelma-Theater
7 Varieté-Theater Stuttgart
8 Theater im Westen
9 Theaterhaus Stuttgart
10 Die Rampe
11 tri-bühne

1. Nach rechts und wieder rechts in die Schillerstr. Die erste Straße rechts und geradeaus bis zur Planie Str. und dort rechts.
2. Links herunter. Die fünfte Straße links, dann geradeaus. Rechts in die Eberhardstr., dann noch mal rechts.
3. Links herunter. Danach die vierte Straße links. Dann rechts in die Marktstr. und die erste Straße links.
4. Nach rechts und wieder rechts in die Schillerstr. Die erste Straße rechts und immer geradeaus bis zur Torstr., dann rechts.

5 Zum Schreiben

Klaus, your school's exchange student from Germany, returned home just before the surprise party to celebrate John's birthday and the end of school. Write a letter telling him all about the party. In your letter, tell Klaus who did chores to help out before the party, who could not come and why, who brought which gift, what there was to eat and drink, and describe any comical birthday cards guests brought.

> **Schreibtipp Combining sentences** is a good way to improve your paragraphs. Short, choppy sentences tend to break up the reader's thoughts. If you use words like "and," "but," and "because," your ideas will flow more naturally.

Prewriting

Make lists of chores that need to be done before a party, of food and drink necessary for a party, of gifts one might bring for a birthday, and of reasons for which one might not be able to attend a party.

Writing

For your first draft, use the writing strategies you've practiced this year. Think about what verbs and grammar structures you will need to describe party activities. Ask your teacher if you are uncertain about a grammar point. Combine sentences to give your paragraphs a natural flow. In describing a chain of events, such as what was done first, later and last during the party preparation, the terms **zuerst, dann, danach,** and **zuletzt** are helpful. End with a conclusion summing up the party.

Revising

- Reread your letter several times, listening for confusing statements and awkward wording. Check over spelling and grammar, make changes, then read your letter aloud.

- Set the letter aside and go back to it later. Reread it again, then switch letters with a classmate and check the strengths and weaknesses of each other's paper.

- Read the conclusion. Does it review or summarize the main idea? Proofread your letter once more for spelling and grammar errors, making any corrections necessary.

- Revise your letter and submit it to your teacher.

6 Rollenspiel

Everyone writes the name of the store that he or she created in Activity 16 on page 345 on a slip of paper and puts it into a small box. Draw out five stores. The people whose stores were chosen will line up at the front of the class with their store windows and play the **Verkäufer.** Bring in old clothing for the customers to try on. The rest of the class will divide into pairs and take turns visiting the stores on the **Einkaufsstraße.** When you are finished, draw more store names and continue your shopping spree. Remember to ask the salesperson about color and price. Try the clothes on and discuss the fit. Comment on your friend's clothing when he or she tries something on.

Kann ich's wirklich?

Can you offer help and explain what to do? (p. 337)

1 How would you offer to help a classmate do some chores around the house?
Kann ich etwas für dich tun? Was kann ich für dich tun?

2 How would he or she respond if he or she needed you to
a. pick up clothes *a. Du kannst für mich die Klamotten aufräumen.*
c. go to the store *c. Du kannst für mich einkaufen gehen.*
b. clean the windows
d. buy some tomatoes
b. Du kannst für mich die Fenster putzen. *d. Du kannst für mich Tomaten kaufen.*

Can you ask directions and say where something is located? (p. 339)

3 How would you tell a classmate how to get to school from your house? How would you tell him or her where your school is located?

Can you make plans and invite someone to come along? (p. 342)

4 How would your friend invite you to go to a concert at 8:30 on Saturday evening? How would you respond if
a. you accept *Answers may vary. Some examples:* *Kommst du mit?*
Ich will um halb neun ins Konzert gehen. *Ja, gern! / Das geht leider nicht; denn ich gehe um 8 Uhr ins Kino.*
b. you decline because you're going to a movie at 8:00

Can you talk about clothes in a clothing store? (p. 344)

5 Write a conversation you would have with a salesperson in a clothing store. Talk about particular items of clothing, price, color, fit, and make some comments about how the clothing looks on you. *Answers will vary.*

Can you discuss gift ideas? (p. 345)

6 How would you tell a classmate what you plan to give two family members for their birthdays?
Answers will vary. Some examples: Ich schenke meinem Bruder eine CD. Ich schenke meiner Mutter ein Buch.

Can you describe people and places? (p. 346)

7 How would you describe your partner: how he or she looks, his or her interests, and where he or she lives? *Answers will vary.*

8 How would you describe your living room and your kitchen?
Answers will vary.

Can you say what you would like and that you do or don't want more? (p. 347)

9 How would you say that you do or don't want more of the following items?
a. eine Semmel *a. Ich möchte noch eine Semmel. Nein danke! Keine Semmel mehr.*
c. ein Apfelsaft *c. Ich möchte noch einen Apfelsaft. Nein danke! Keinen Apfelsaft me[hr]*
b. ein Apfel
d. ein Käsebrot *d. Ich möchte noch ein Käsebrot. Ne[in] danke! Kein Käsebrot mehr.*
b. Ich möchte noch einen Apfel. Nein danke! Keinen Apfel mehr.

Can you talk about what you did? (p. 349)

10 How would a friend ask you what you did last weekend? How would you respond, telling where you were, what you bought, what movies you saw, or what books you read? *Answers may vary. Examples: Was hast du am Wochenende gemacht? Ich war in der Innenstadt. Ich habe Bücher gekauft. Am Sonntag habe ich „Contact" gesehen. Am Abend habe ich „Idoru" gelesen.*

Erste Stufe

Ingredients for a recipe

das Salz	salt
das Öl	oil
die Zwiebel, -n	onion

die Zitrone, -n	lemon
der Zimt	cinnamon
das Butterschmalz	shortening
der Salat, -e	salad

Zweite Stufe

Making plans

die Stadt besichtigen	to visit the city
in den Park gehen	to go to the park
in den Zoo gehen	to go to the zoo
Schlittschuh laufen	ice skate
joggen	to jog
ein Brettspiel spielen	to play a board game

Talking about clothing

die Seide	silk
aus Seide	made of silk
die Baumwolle	cotton
aus Baumwolle	made of cotton
das Leder	leather
aus Leder	made of leather
gestreift	striped
gepunktet	polka-dotted

Dritte Stufe

 p. 331X

Describing places

im Wohnzimmer	in the living room
das Sofa, -s	sofa
der Tisch, -e	table
aus Holz	made of wood
aus Kunststoff	made of plastic
die Lampe, -n	lamp

der Teppich, -e	carpet
der Sessel, -	armchair
die Küche, -n	kitchen
in der Küche	in the kitchen
der Esstisch, -e	dining table
der Kühlschrank, ¨e	refrigerator

der Herd, -e	stove
der Ofen, ¨	oven
das Spülbecken, -	sink
rund	round
eckig	with corners
modern	modern

Reference Section

▶ **Summary of Functions** R3

▶ **Additional Vocabulary** R9

▶ **Grammar Summary** R15

▶ **Guide to Pronunciation Features** R27

▶ **German-English Vocabulary** R29

▶ **English-German Vocabulary** R47

▶ **Grammar Index** R55

▶ **Acknowledgments and Credits** R59

Summary of Functions

Functions are probably best defined as the ways in which you use a language for specific purposes. When you find yourself in specific situations, such as in a restaurant, in a grocery store, or at school, you will want to communicate with those around you. In order to do that, you have to "function" in the language so that you can be understood: you place an order, make a purchase, or talk about your class schedule.

Such functions form the core of this book. They are easily identified by the boxes in each chapter that are labeled SO SAGT MAN DAS! These functions are the building blocks you need to become a speaker of German. All the other features in the chapter—the grammar, the vocabulary, even the culture notes—are there to support the functions you are learning.

Here is a list of the functions presented in this book and the German expressions you will need in order to communicate in a wide range of situations. Following each function is the chapter and page number where it was introduced.

Socializing

Saying hello Ch. 1, p. 21
Guten Morgen!
Guten Tag!
Morgen! ⎱
Tag! ⎰ *shortened forms*
Hallo! ⎱
Grüß dich! ⎰ *informal*

Saying goodbye Ch. 1, p. 21
Auf Wiedersehen!
Wiedersehen! *shortened form*
Tschüs! ⎱
Tschau! ⎰ *informal*
Bis dann! ⎰

Offering something to eat and drink Ch. 3, p. 74
Was möchtest du trinken?
Was möchte (*name*) trinken?
Was möchtet ihr essen?

Responding to an offer Ch. 3, p. 74
Ich möchte (*beverage*) trinken.
Er/Sie möchte im Moment gar nichts.
Wir möchten (*food/beverage*), bitte.

Saying please Ch. 3, p. 76
Bitte!

Saying thank you Ch. 3, p. 76
Danke!
Danke schön!
Danke sehr!

Saying you're welcome Ch. 3, p. 76
Bitte!
Bitte schön!
Bitte sehr!

Giving compliments Ch. 5, p. 139
Der/Die/Das (*thing*) sieht (*adjective*) aus!
Der/Die/Das (*thing*) gefällt mir.

Responding to compliments Ch. 5, p. 139
Ehrlich?
Wirklich?
Nicht zu (*adjective*)?
Meinst du?

Starting a conversation Ch. 6, p. 161
Wie geht's? ⎱ *Asking how someone is*
⎰ *doing*

Wie geht's denn? ⎱
Sehr gut!
Prima!
Danke, gut!
Gut!
Danke, es geht.
So lala. ⎰ *Responding to **Wie geht's?***
Nicht schlecht.
Nicht so gut.
Schlecht.
Sehr schlecht.
Miserabel. ⎰

Making plans Ch. 6, p. 166
Was willst du machen?   Ich will (*activity*).
Wohin will (*person*) gehen?   Er/Sie will in(s)
(*place*) gehen.

Ordering food and beverages Ch. 6, p. 170

Was bekommen Sie?	Ich bekomme (food/beverage).
Ja, bitte?	
Was essen Sie?	Ein(e)(n) (food), bitte.
Was möchten Sie?	Ich möchte (food/beverage), bitte.
Was trinken Sie?	Ich trinke (beverage).
Was nimmst du?	Ich nehme (food/beverage).
Was isst du?	Ich esse (food).

Talking about how something tastes Ch. 6, p. 172

Wie schmeckt's?	Gut!
	Prima!
	Sagenhaft!
	Der/die/das (food/beverage) schmeckt lecker!
	Der/die/das (food/beverage) schmeckt nicht.
Schmeckt's?	Ja, gut!
	Nein, nicht so gut.
	Nicht besonders.

Paying the check Ch. 6, p. 172

Hallo!
Ich will/möchte zahlen.
Das macht (zusammen) (total).
Stimmt schon!

Extending an invitation Ch. 7, p. 194; Ch. 11, p. 313

Willst du (activity)?
Wir wollen (activity). Komm doch mit!
Möchtest du mitkommen?
Ich habe am (day/date) eine Party. Ich lade dich ein. Kannst du kommen?

Responding to an invitation Ch. 7, p. 194; Ch. 11, p. 313

Ja, gern!
Toll! Ich komme gern mit!   } accepting
Aber sicher!
Natürlich!
Das geht nicht.   } declining
Ich kann leider nicht.

Expressing obligations Ch. 7, p. 194

Ich habe keine Zeit. Ich muss (activity).

Offering help Ch. 7, p. 199

Was kann ich für dich tun?   } asking
Kann ich etwas für dich tun?
Brauchst du Hilfe?
Gut! Mach ich!   agreeing

Asking what you should do Ch. 8, p. 222

Was soll ich für dich tun?	Du kannst für mich (chore).
Wo soll ich (thing/things) kaufen?	Beim (Metzger/Bäcker). In der/Im (store).
Soll ich (thing/things) in der/im (store) kaufen?	Nein, das kannst du besser in der/im (store) kaufen.

Telling someone what to do Ch. 8, p. 223

Geh bitte (action)!
Geht (thing/things) holen, bitte!

Getting someone's attention Ch. 9, p. 250

Verzeihung!
Entschuldigung!

Offering more Ch. 9, p. 258

Möchtest du noch etwas?
Möchtest du noch ein(e)(n) (food/beverage)?
Noch ein(e)(n) (food/beverage)?

Saying you want more Ch. 9, p. 258

Ja, bitte. Ich nehme noch ein(e)(n) (food/beverage).
Ja, bitte. Noch ein(e)(n) (food/beverage).
Ja, gern.

Saying you don't want more Ch. 9, p. 258

Nein, danke! Ich habe keinen Hunger mehr.
Nein, danke! Ich habe genug.
Danke, nichts mehr für mich.
Nein, danke, kein(e)(n) (food/beverage) mehr.

Using the telephone Ch. 11, p. 310

Hier (name).
Hier ist (name).
Ich möchte bitte (name) sprechen.
Kann ich bitte (name) sprechen?   } starting a conversation
Tag! Hier ist (name).
Wiederhören!
Auf Wiederhören!   } ending a conversation
Tschüs!

Talking about birthdays Ch. 11, p. 314

Wann hast du Geburtstag?	Ich habe am (date) Geburtstag. Am (date).

Expressing good wishes Ch. 11, p. 314

Alles Gute zu(m)(r) (occasion)!
Herzlichen Glückwunsch zu(m)(r) (occasion)!

Exchanging Information

Asking someone his or her name and giving yours Ch. 1, p. 22

Wie heißt du?	Ich heiße (name).
Heißt du (name)?	Ja, ich heiße (name).

Asking and giving someone else's name Ch. 1, p. 22

Wie heißt der Junge?	Der Junge heißt (name).
Heißt der Junge (name)?	Ja, er heißt (name).
Wie heißt das Mädchen?	Das Mädchen heißt (name).
Heißt das Mädchen (name)?	Nein, sie heißt (name).

Asking and telling who someone is Ch. 1, p. 23

Wer ist das?   Das ist der/die (name).

Asking someone his or her age and giving yours Ch. 1, p. 25

Wie alt bist du?	Ich bin (number) Jahre alt.
	Ich bin (number).
	(Number).
Bist du schon (number)?	Nein, ich bin (number).

Asking and giving someone else's age Ch. 1, p. 25

Wie alt ist der Peter?	Er ist (number).
Und die Monika? Ist sie auch (number)?	Ja, sie ist auch (number).

Asking someone where he or she is from and telling where you are from Ch. 1, p. 28

Woher kommst du?	Ich komme aus (place).
Woher bist du?	Ich bin aus (place).
Bist du aus (place)?	Nein, ich bin aus (place).

Asking and telling where someone else is from Ch. 1, p. 28

Woher ist (person)?	Er/sie ist aus (place).
Kommt (person) aus (place)?	Nein, sie kommt aus (place).

Talking about how someone gets to school Ch. 1, p. 30

Wie kommst du zur Schule?	Ich komme mit der/dem (mode of transportation).
Kommt Ahmet zu Fuß zur Schule?	Nein, er kommt auch mit der/dem (mode of transportation).
Wie kommt Ayla zur Schule?	Sie kommt mit der/dem (mode of transportation).

Talking about interests Ch. 2, p. 48

Was machst du in deiner Freizeit?	Ich (activity).
Spielst du (sport/instrument/game)?	Ja, ich spiele (sport/instrument/game).
	Nein, (sport/instrument/game) spiele ich nicht.
Was macht (name)?	Er/Sie spielt (sport/instrument/game).

Saying when you do various activities Ch. 2, p. 55

Was machst du nach der Schule?	Am Nachmittag (activity).
	Am Abend (activity).
Und am Wochenende?	Am Wochenende (activity).
Was machst du im Sommer?	Im Sommer (activity).

Talking about where you and others live Ch. 3, p. 73

Wo wohnst du?	Ich wohne in (place).
	In (place).
Wo wohnt der/die (name)?	Er/Sie wohnt in (place).
	In (place).

Describing a room Ch. 3, p. 79

Der/Die/Das (thing) ist alt.
Der/Die/Das (thing) ist kaputt.
Der/Die/Das (thing) ist klein, aber ganz bequem.
Ist (thing) neu?   Ja, er/sie/es ist neu.

Talking about family members Ch. 3, p. 82

Ist das dein(e) (family member)?	Ja, das ist mein(e) (family member).
Und dein(e) (family member)? Wie heißt er/sie?	Er/Sie heißt (name).
Wo wohnen deine (family members)?	In (place).

Describing people Ch. 3, p. 84

Wie sieht (person) aus?   Er/sie hat (color) Haare und (color) Augen.

Talking about class schedules Ch. 4, p. 106

Welche Fächer hast du?	Ich habe (classes).
Was hast du am (day)?	(Classes).
Was hat die Katja am (day)?	Sie hat (classes).
Welche Fächer habt ihr?	Wir haben (classes).
Was habt ihr nach der Pause?	Wir haben (classes).
Und was habt ihr am Samstag?	Wir haben frei!

Using a schedule to talk about time Ch. 4, p. 107

Wann hast du (class)?	Um (hour) Uhr (minutes).
Was hast du um (hour) Uhr?	(Class).
Was hast du von (time) bis (time)?	Ich habe (class).

Sequencing events Ch. 4, p. 109

Welche Fächer hast du am (day)?	Zuerst hab ich (class), dann (class), danach (class) und zuletzt (class).

Talking about prices Ch. 4, p. 115

Was kostet (thing)?	Er/Sie kostet nur (price).
Was kosten (things)?	Sie kosten (price).
Das ist (ziemlich) teuer!	
Das ist (sehr) billig!	
Das ist (sehr) preiswert!	

Pointing things out Ch. 4, p. 116

Wo sind die (things)?	Schauen Sie!
	Dort!
	Sie sind dort drüben!
	Sie sind da hinten.
	Sie sind da vorn.

Expressing wishes when shopping Ch. 5, p. 134

Was möchten Sie?	Ich möchte ein(e)(n) (thing) sehen, bitte.
	Ich brauche ein(e)(n) (thing).
Was bekommen Sie?	Ein(e)(n) (thing), bitte.
Haben Sie einen Wunsch?	Ich suche ein(e)(n) (thing).

Describing how clothes fit Ch. 5, p. 137

Es passt prima.
Es passt nicht.

Talking about trying on clothes Ch. 5, p. 143

Ich probiere den/die/das (item of clothing) an.
Ich ziehe den/die/das (item of clothing) an.

If you buy it:	*If you don't:*
Ich nehme es.	Ich nehme es nicht.
Ich kaufe es.	Ich kaufe es nicht.

Telling time Ch. 6, p. 162

Wie spät ist es jetzt?	Es ist (time).
Wie viel Uhr ist es?	Es ist (time).

Talking about when you do things Ch. 6, p. 162

Wann gehst du (activity)?	Um (time).
Um wie viel Uhr (action) du?	Um (time).
Und du? Wann (action) du?	Um (time).

Talking about how often you do things Ch. 7, p. 198

Wie oft (action) du?	(Einmal) in der Woche.
Und wie oft musst du (action)?	Jeden Tag. Ungefähr (zweimal) im Monat.

Explaining what to do Ch. 7, p. 199

Du kannst für mich (action).

Talking about the weather Ch. 7, p. 203

Wie ist das Wetter heute?	Heute regnet es. Wolkig und kühl.
Wie ist das Wetter morgen?	Sonnig, aber kalt.
Regnet es heute?	Ich glaube schon.
Schneit es am Abend?	Nein, es schneit nicht.
Wie viel Grad haben wir heute?	Ungefähr 10 Grad.

Talking about quantities Ch. 8, p. 226

Wie viel (food item) bekommen Sie?	500 Gramm (food item). 100 Gramm, bitte.

Asking if someone wants anything else Ch. 8, p. 227

Sonst noch etwas?
Was bekommen Sie noch?
Haben Sie noch einen Wunsch?

Saying that you want something else Ch. 8, p. 227

Ich brauche noch ein(e)(n) (food/beverage/thing).
Ich bekomme noch ein(e)(n) (food/beverage/thing).

Telling someone you don't need anything else Ch. 8, p. 227

Nein, danke.
Danke, das ist alles.

Giving a reason Ch. 8, p. 230

Jetzt kann ich nicht, weil ich (reason).
Es geht nicht, denn ich (reason).

Saying where you were Ch. 8, p. 231

Wo warst du heute Morgen? Ich war *(place)*.
Wo warst du gestern? Ich war *(place)*.

Saying what you bought Ch. 8, p. 231

Was hast du gekauft? Ich habe *(thing)* gekauft.

Talking about where something is located
Ch. 9, p. 250

Verzeihung, wissen Sie, wo
der/die/das *(place)* ist? In der Innenstadt.
Am *(place name)*.
In der *(street name)*.

Wo ist der/die/das *(place)*? Es tut mir Leid. Das weiß ich nicht.

Entschuldigung! Weißt du,
wo der/die/das *(place)* ist? Keine Ahnung! Ich bin nicht von hier.

Asking for directions Ch. 9, p. 254

Wie komme ich zu(m)(r) *(place)*?
Wie kommt man zu(m)(r) *(place)*?

Giving directions Ch. 9, p. 254

Gehen Sie geradeaus bis zu(m)(r) *(place)*.
Nach rechts/links.
Hier rechts/links.

Talking about what there is to eat and drink
Ch. 9, p. 257

Was gibt es hier
zu essen? Es gibt *(foods)*.
Und zu trinken? Es gibt *(beverage)* und auch *(beverage)*.

Talking about what you did in your free time
Ch. 10, p. 292

Was hast du *(time
phrase)* gemacht? Ich habe
(person/thing) gesehen.
(book, magazine, etc.)
gelesen.
mit *(person)* über *(subject)*
gesprochen.

Discussing gift ideas, Ch. 11, p. 318

Schenkst du *(person)*
ein(e)(n) *(thing)*
zu(m)(r) *(occasion)*? Nein, ich schenke
ihm/ihr ein(e)(n)
(thing).

Was schenkst du *(person)*
zu(m)(r) *(occasion)*? Ich weiß noch nicht.
Hast du eine Idee?

Wem schenkst du
den/die/das *(thing)*? Ich schenke *(person)*
den/die/das *(thing)*.

Expressing Attitudes and Opinions

Asking for an opinion Ch. 2, p. 57; Ch. 9, p. 260

Wie findest du *(thing/activity/place)*?

Expressing your opinion Ch. 2, p. 57;
Ch. 9, p. 260

Ich finde *(thing/activity/place)* langweilig.
(Thing/Activity/Place) ist Spitze!
(Activity) macht Spaß!
Ich finde es toll, dass ...
Ich glaube, dass ...

Agreeing Ch. 2, p. 58; Ch. 7, p. 199

Ich auch!
Das finde ich auch!
Stimmt!
Gut! Mach ich!

Disagreeing Ch. 2, p. 58

Ich nicht!
Das finde ich nicht!
Stimmt nicht!

Commenting on clothes Ch. 5, p. 137

Wie findest du den/die/
das *(clothing item)*? Ich finde ihn/sie/es
(adjective).
Er/Sie/Es gefällt mir
(nicht).

Expressing uncertainty, not knowing
Ch. 5, p. 137; Ch. 9, p. 250

Ich bin nicht sicher.
Ich weiß nicht.
Keine Ahnung!

Expressing regret Ch. 9, p. 250

Es tut mir Leid.

Expressing Feelings and Emotions

Asking about likes and dislikes Ch. 2,
p. 50; Ch. 4, p. 110; Ch. 10, p. 282

Was *(action)* du gern?
(Action) du gern?
Magst du *(things/activities)*?
Was für *(things/activities)* magst du?

Expressing likes Ch. 2, p. 50; Ch. 4, p. 110; Ch. 10, p. 282

Ich *(action)* gern.
Ich mag *(things/activities)*.
(Thing/Activities) mag ich (sehr/furchtbar) gern.

Expressing dislikes Ch. 2, p. 50; Ch. 10, p. 282

Ich *(action)* nicht so gern.
Ich mag *(things/action)* (überhaupt) nicht.

Talking about favorites Ch. 4, p. 110

Was ist dein
  Lieblings*(category)*?   Mein Lieblings*(category)*
                            ist *(thing)*.

Responding to good news Ch. 4, p. 112

Toll!
Das ist prima!
Nicht schlecht.

Responding to bad news Ch. 4, p. 112

Schade!
So ein Pech!
So ein Mist!
Das ist sehr schlecht!

Expressing familiarity Ch. 10, p. 284

Kennst du
  (person/place/thing)?   Ja, sicher!
                            Ja, klar! or
                            Nein, den/die/das
                            kenne
                              ich nicht.
                            Nein, überhaupt nicht.

Expressing preferences and favorites
Ch. 10, p. 285

(Siehst) du gern ...?   Ja, aber ... (sehe) ich
                          lieber.
                        Und am liebsten (sehe)
                          ich ...

(Siehst) du lieber
  ... oder ...?   Lieber ... Aber am liebsten
                          (sehe) ich ...

Was (siehst) du
  am liebsten?   Am liebsten (sehe) ich ...

This list includes additional vocabulary that you may want to use to personalize activities. If you can't find the words you need here, try the German–English and English–German vocabulary sections beginning on page R29.

Sport und Interessen
(Sports and Interests)

angeln	*to fish*
Baseball spielen	*to play baseball*
Brettspiele spielen	*to play board games*
fotografieren	*to take photographs*
Gewichte heben	*lift weights*
Handball spielen	*to play handball*
joggen	*to jog*
kochen	*to cook*
malen	*to paint*
Münzen sammeln	*to collect coins*
nähen	*to sew*
Rad fahren	*to ride a bike*
reiten	*to ride (a horse)*
Rollschuh laufen	*to roller-skate*
segeln	*to sail*
Skateboard fahren	*to ride a skateboard*
Ski laufen	*to (snow) ski*
stricken	*to knit*
Tischtennis spielen	*to play table tennis*
Videospiele spielen	*to play video games*

Instrumente *(Instruments)*

die Blockflöte, -n	*recorder*
das Cello (Violoncello), -s	*cello*
die Flöte, -n	*flute*
die Geige, -n	*violin*
die Harfe, -n	*harp*
die Klarinette, -n	*clarinet*
der Kontrabass, ¨e	*double bass*
die Mandoline, -n	*mandolin*
die Mundharmonika, -s	*harmonica*
die Oboe, -n	*oboe*
die Posaune, -n	*trombone*
das Saxophon, -e	*saxophone*
das Schlagzeug, -e	*drums*
die Trompete, -n	*trumpet*
die Tuba, (pl) Tuben	*tuba*

Getränke *(Beverages)*

die Limo, -	*lemon-flavored drink*
ein Glas Milch	*a glass of milk*
ein Glas Tee	*a glass of tea*
eine Tasse, -n Kaffee	*a cup of coffee*

Speisen *(Foods)*

die Ananas, -	*pineapple*
der Apfelstrudel, -	*apple strudel*
die Banane, -n	*banana*
die Birne, -n	*pear*
der Chip, -s	*potato chip*
der Eintopf	*stew*
die Erdbeere, -n	*strawberry*
die Erdnussbutter	*peanut butter*
das Gebäck	*baked goods*
die Gurke, -n	*cucumber*
die Himbeere, -n	*raspberry*
der Joghurt, - *or* Jogurt	*yogurt*
die Karotte, -n	*carrot*

die Marmelade, -n	*jam, jelly*
die Mayonnaise	*mayonnaise*
die Melone, -n	*melon*
das Müsli	*muesli (cereal)*
die Nuss, ⸚e	*nut*
die Orange, -n	*orange*
das Plätzchen, -	*cookie*
die Pommes frites (pl)	*french fries*
der Spinat	*spinach*
die Zwiebel, -n	*onion*

Möbel *(Furniture)*

das Bild, -er	*picture*
der Computer, -	*computer*
die Lampe, -n	*lamp*

der Sessel, -	*armchair*
das Sofa, -s	*sofa*
der Teppich, -e	*carpet, rug*
der Tisch, -e	*table*
der Vorhang, ⸚e	*curtain*

Familie *(Family)*

der Halbbruder, ⸚	*halfbrother*
die Halbschwester, -n	*halfsister*
der Stiefbruder, ⸚	*stepbrother*
die Stiefmutter, ⸚	*stepmother*
die Stiefschwester, -n	*stepsister*
der Stiefvater, ⸚	*stepfather*

Fächer *(School Subjects)*

Algebra	*algebra*
Band	*band*
Chor	*chorus*
Französisch	*French*
Hauswirtschaft	*home economics*
Informatik	*computer science*
Italienisch	*Italian*
Japanisch	*Japanese*
Orchester	*orchestra*
Russisch	*Russian*
Spanisch	*Spanish*
Sozialkunde	*social studies*
Werken	*shop*
Wirtschaftskunde	*economics*

Kleidungsstücke *(Clothing)*

der Anzug, ⸚e	*suit*
der Badeanzug, ⸚e	*swimsuit*
der Blazer, -	*blazer*
das Halstuch, ⸚er	*scarf*
der Handschuh, -e	*glove*
der Hut, ⸚e	*hat*
die Krawatte, -n	*tie*
der Mantel, ⸚	*coat*
die Mütze, -n	*cap*
die Sandalen (pl)	*sandals*
der Schal, -s	*shawl*
die Strumpfhose, -n	*panty hose*
die Weste, -n	*vest*

R10

Farben (Colors)

beige	*beige*
bunt	*colorful*
gepunktet	*polka-dotted*
gestreift	*striped*
golden	*gold*
lila	*purple*
orange	*orange*
rosa	*pink*
silbern	*silver*
türkis	*turquoise*

Hausarbeit (Housework)

das Auto polieren	*to polish the car*
das Auto waschen	*to wash the car*
den Fußboden kehren	*to sweep the floor*
den Müll wegtragen	*to take out the trash*
putzen	*to clean*

Staub wischen	*to dust*
sauber machen	*to clean*
die Wäsche waschen	*to do the laundry*
trocknen	*to dry*
aufhängen	*to hang*
legen	*to fold*
bügeln	*to iron*
einräumen	*to put away*

Haustiere (Pets)

die Eidechse, -n	*lizard*
der Fisch, -e	*fish*
der Frosch, ⸚e	*frog*
der Hamster, -	*hamster*
der Hase, -n	*hare*
der Kanarienvogel, ⸚	*canary*
die Maus, ⸚e	*mouse*
das Meerschweinchen, -	*guinea pig*
der Papagei, -en	*parrot*
das Pferd, -e	*horse*
die Schildkröte, -n	*turtle*

die Schlange, -n	*snake*
das Schwein, -e	*pig*
der Vogel, ⸚	*bird*

Wetter (Weather)

feucht	*damp*
gewittrig	*stormy*
halbbedeckt	*partly cloudy*
heiter	*bright*
kühl	*cool*
neblig	*foggy*
nieslig	*drizzly*
trüb	*murky*
windig	*windy*

Computer (Computer)

abrufen (die E-mail abrufen) (sep)	*to check the e-mail*
Bildschirm, der	*screen*
CD-ROM, die	*CD-ROM disc*
CD-ROM Laufwerk, das	*CD-ROM drive*
Computer, der	*computer*

E-mail, die	*e-mail*
Eingabemarke, die	*cursor*
Eingabetaste, die	*return key*
einloggen (sep)	*to log on*
entfernen	*to delete*
Entferntaste, die	*delete key*
Festplatte, die	*hard drive*
herunterladen (sep)	*to download*
Internet, das	*Internet*
Lesezeichen, das	*bookmark*
Maus, die	*mouse*

Modem, das	*modem*
Monitor, der	*monitor*
Netz, das (das Internet)	*Internet*
neu starten	*to reboot, restart*
speichern	*to save*
suchen	*to search*
Suchmaschine, die	*search engine*
surfen (im Internet surfen)	*to surf (the Net)*
Tastatur, die	*keyboard*

Zentraleinheit, die	*CPU (central processing unit)*
ziehen (auf Symbole)	*to drag*

In der Stadt (Places around Town)

die Brücke, -n	*bridge*
die Bücherei, -en	*library*
der Flughafen, (pl) Flughäfen	*airport*

das Fremdenverkehrsamt, (pl) Fremdenverkehrsämter	*tourist office*
der Frisiersalon, -s	*beauty shop*
das Krankenhaus, (pl) Krankenhäuser	*hospital*
der Park, -s	*park*
die Polizei	*police station*
der Zoo, -s	*zoo*

Zum Diskutieren (Topics to Discuss)

die Armut	*poverty*
die Gesundheit	*health*
der Präsident	*the president*
die Politik	*politics*
die Reklame	*advertising*
die Umwelt	*the environment*
das Verbrechen	*crime*
der Wehrdienst	*military service*
der Zivildienst	*alternate service*

Geschenkideen (Gift Ideas)

das Bild, -er	*picture*
die Kette, -n	*chain*
der Ohrring, -e	*earring*
die Puppe, -n	*doll*
das Puppenhaus. ¨er	*dollhouse*
der Ring, -e	*ring*
... aus Silber	*made of silver*
... aus Gold	*made of gold*
die Schokolade	*chocolate*
das Spielzeug, -e	*toy*

ERDKUNDE *(GEOGRAPHY)*

Here are some terms you will find on German-language maps:

Länder *(States)*

Most of the states in the United States (**die Vereinigten Staaten**) have the same spelling in German that they have in English. Listed below are those states that have a different spelling.

Kalifornien	*California*
Neumexiko	*New Mexico*
Nordkarolina	*North Carolina*
Norddakota	*North Dakota*
Südkarolina	*South Carolina*
Süddakota	*South Dakota*

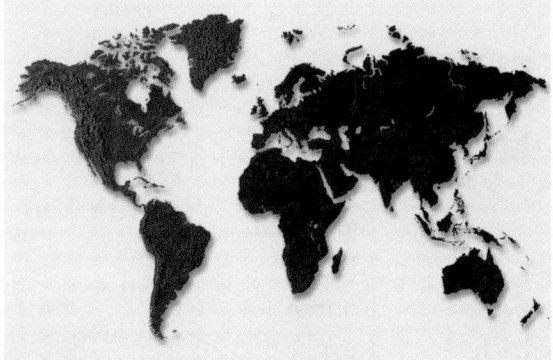

Staaten *(Countries)*

Ägypten	*Egypt*
Argentinien	*Argentina*
Brasilien	*Brazil*
Indien	*India*
Indonesien	*Indonesia*
Kanada	*Canada*
Mexiko	*Mexico*
Russland	*Russia*
die Vereinigten Staaten	*The United States*

Kontinente *(Continents)*

Afrika	*Africa*
die Antarktis	*Antarctica*
Asien	*Asia*
Australien	*Australia*
Europa	*Europe*

Nordamerika	*North America*
Südamerika	*South America*

Meere *(Bodies of Water)*

der Atlantik	*the Atlantic*
der Golf von Mexiko	*the Gulf of Mexico*
der Indische Ozean	*the Indian Ocean*
das Mittelmeer	*the Mediterranean*
der Pazifik	*the Pacific*
das Rote Meer	*the Red Sea*
das Schwarze Meer	*the Black Sea*

Geographical terms

der Breitengrad	*latitude*
die Ebene, -n	*plain*
der Fluss, ¨e	*river*
das ... Gebirge	*the ... mountains*
die Grenze, -n	*border*
die Hauptstadt, ¨e	*capital*
der Kontinent, -e	*continent*
das Land, ¨er	*state*
der Längengrad	*longitude*
das Meer, -e	*ocean, sea*
der Nordpol	*the North Pole*
der See, -n	*lake*
der Staat, -en	*country*
der Südpol	*the South Pole*
das Tal, ¨er	*valley*

DEUTSCHE NAMEN *(GERMAN NAMES)*

Some German names are listed in the **Vorschau,** but here are some additional ones that you will hear when you visit a German-speaking country.

Mädchen *(girls)*

Andrea	Elke	Jutta
Angela, Angelika	Erika	Karin
Anja	Eva	Katharina
Anna	Gabriele (Gabi)	Katja
Anneliese	Gertrud (Trudi(e))	Katrin
Annette	Gisela	Kirstin
Antje	Grete	Liselotte (Lotte)
Barbara	Gudrun	Marie
Bärbel	Hannelore	Marta
Beate	Heidi/ Heidemarie	Martina
Birgit	Heike	Meike
Brigitte	Helga	Michaela
Britta	Hilde	Monika
Christa	Hildegard	Nicole
Christiane	Ilse	Petra
Christine	Ina	Regina
Claudia	Inge	Renate
Connie	Ingrid	Roswitha
Cordula	Irmgard	Rotraud
Dorothea	Jennifer	Sabine
Dorothee	Julie	Sara
Elfriede		Silke
Elisabeth (Lisa)		Simone
		Stephanie
		Susanne
		Silvia
		Tanja
		Ulrike (Uli)
		Ursel
		Ursula (Uschi)
		Ute
		Veronika
		Waltraud

Jungen *(boys)*

Alexander	Heinz	Rainer (Reiner)
Andreas	Heinz-Dieter	Ralf
Axel	Helmar	Reinhard
Bernd(t)	Helmut	Reinhold
Bernhard	Ingo	Rolf
Bruno	Jan	Rudi
Christian	Jens	Rüdiger
Christoph	Joachim	Rudolf
Daniel	Jochen	Sebastian
Detlev(f)	Johann	Stefan (Stephan)
Dieter	Johannes	Thomas
Dietmar	Jörg	Udo
Dirk	Josef	Ulf
Eberhard	Jürgen	Ulrich (Uli)
Erik	Karl	Uwe
Felix	Karl-Heinz	Volker
Frank	Klaus	Werner
Franz	Konrad	Wilhelm (Willi)
Friedrich	Kurt	Wolfgang
Fritz	Lars	
Georg	Lothar	
Gerd	Lutz	
Gerhard	Manfred	
Gottfried	Markus	
Gregor	Martin	
Günter	Mathias	
Gustav(f)	Max	
Hannes	Michael	
Hans	Norbert	
Hans-Georg	Otto	
Hans-Jürgen	Patrick	
Hartmut	Paul	
Hauke	Peter	
Heinrich	Philipp	

NOUNS AND THEIR MODIFIERS

In German, nouns (words that name a person, place, or thing) are grouped into three classes or genders: masculine, feminine, and neuter. All nouns, both persons and objects, fall into one of these groups. There are words used with nouns that signal the class of the noun. One of these is the definite article. In English there is one definite article: *the*. In German, there are three, one for each class: **der, die,** and **das**.

THE DEFINITE ARTICLE

SUMMARY OF DEFINITE ARTICLES

	Nominative	Accusative	Dative
Masculine	der	den	dem
Feminine	die	die	der
Neuter	das	das	dem
Plural	die	die	den

When the definite article is combined with a noun, a noun phrase is formed. Noun phrases that are used as subjects are in the nominative case. Nouns that are used as direct objects or the objects of certain prepositions (such as **für**) are in the accusative case. Nouns that are indirect objects, the objects of certain prepositions (such as **mit, bei**), or the objects of special verbs that you will learn about in Level 2, are in the dative case. Below is a summary of the definite articles combined with nouns to form noun phrases.

SUMMARY OF NOUN PHRASES

	Nominative	Accusative	Dative
Masculine	der Vater der Ball	den Vater den Ball	dem Vater dem Ball
Feminine	die Mutter die Kassette	die Mutter die Kassette	der Mutter der Kassette
Neuter	das Mädchen das Haus	das Mädchen das Haus	dem Mädchen dem Haus

THE INDEFINITE ARTICLE

Another type of word that is used with nouns is the *indefinite article:* **ein, eine, ein** in German, *a, an* in English. There is no plural form of **ein**.

SUMMARY OF INDEFINITE ARTICLES

	Nominative	Accusative	Dative
Masculine	ein	einen	einem
Feminine	eine	eine	einer
Neuter	ein	ein	einem
Plural	—	—	—

THE NEGATING WORD **KEIN**

The word **kein** is also used with nouns and means *no, not,* or *not any.* Unlike the **ein-** words, **kein** has a plural form.

	Nominative	Accusative	Dative
Masculine	kein	keinen	keinem
Feminine	keine	keine	keiner
Neuter	kein	kein	keinem
Plural	keine	keine	keinen

THE POSSESSIVES

These words also modify nouns and tell you *whose* object or person is being referred to (*my* car, *his* book, *her* mother). These words have the same endings as **kein**.

SUMMARY OF POSSESSIVES

	Before Masculine Nouns			Before Feminine Nouns		Before Neuter Nouns		Before Plural Nouns	
	Nom	Acc	Dat	Nom & Acc	Dat	Nom & Acc	Dat	Nom & Acc	Dat
my	mein	meinen	meinem	meine	meiner	mein	meinem	meine	meinen
your	dein	deinen	deinem	deine	deiner	dein	deinem	deine	deinen
his	sein	seinen	seinem	seine	seiner	sein	seinem	seine	seinen
her	ihr	ihren	ihrem	ihre	ihrer	ihr	ihrem	ihre	ihren

Other possessive adjectives that you will learn more about in Level 2 are:

unser	*our*
euer	*your* (informal, plural)
ihr	*their*
Ihr	*your* (formal)

NOUN PLURALS

Noun class and plural forms are not always predictable. Therefore, you must learn each noun together with its article (**der, die, das**) and with its plural form. As you learn more nouns, however, you will discover certain patterns. Although there are always exceptions to these patterns, you may find them helpful in remembering the plural forms of many nouns.

Most German nouns form their plurals in one of two ways: some nouns add endings in the plural; some add endings and/or change the sound of the stem vowel in the plural, indicating the sound change with the umlaut (¨). Only the vowels **a, o, u,** and the diphthong **au** can take the umlaut. If a noun has an umlaut in the singular, it keeps the umlaut in the plural. Most German nouns fit into one of the following five plural groups.

1. Nouns that do not have any ending in the plural. Sometimes they take an umlaut.
   NOTE: There are only two feminine nouns in this group: **die Mutter** and **die Tochter**.

der Bruder, die Brüder	der Schüler, die Schüler	das Fräulein, die Fräulein
der Lehrer, die Lehrer	der Vater, die Väter	das Mädchen, die Mädchen
der Onkel, die Onkel	die Mutter, die Mütter	das Poster, die Poster
der Mantel, die Mäntel	die Tochter, die Töchter	das Zimmer, die Zimmer

2. Nouns that add the ending **-e** in the plural. Sometimes they also take an umlaut. **NOTE:** There are many one-syllable words in this group.

der Bleistift, die Bleistifte	der Sohn, die Söhne	das Jahr, die Jahre
der Freund, die Freunde	die Stadt, die Städte	das Spiel, die Spiele

3. Nouns that add the ending **-er** in the plural. Whenever possible, they take an umlaut, i.e., when the noun contains the vowels **a, o,** or **u,** or the diphthong **au.** **NOTE:** There are no feminine nouns in this group. There are many one-syllable words in this group.

das Buch, die Bücher	das Haus, die Häuser
das Fach, die Fächer	das Land, die Länder

4. Nouns that add the ending **-en** or **-n** in the plural. These nouns never add an umlaut.
   NOTE: There are many feminine nouns in this group.

der Herr, die Herren	die Klasse, die Klassen	die Tante, die Tanten
der Junge, die Jungen	die Karte, die Karten	die Wohnung, die Wohnungen
die Briefmarke, die Briefmarken	der Name, die Namen	die Zahl, die Zahlen
die Familie, die Familien	der Vetter, die Vettern	die Zeitung, die Zeitungen
die Farbe, die Farben	die Küche, die Küchen	
die Frau, die Frauen	die Schwester, die Schwestern	

   Feminine nouns ending in **-in** add the ending **-nen** in the plural.

die Freundin, die Freundinnen	die Verkäuferin, die Verkäuferinnen
die Lehrerin, die Lehrerinnen	

5. Nouns that add the ending **-s** in the plural. These nouns never add an umlaut. **NOTE:** There are many words of foreign origin in this group.

der Kuli, die Kulis	das Auto, die Autos
die Kamera, die Kameras	das Hobby, die Hobbys

SUMMARY OF PLURAL ENDINGS

Group	1	2	3	4	5
Ending:	-	-e	-er	-(e)n	-s
Umlaut:	sometimes	sometimes	always	never	never

PRONOUNS

PERSONAL PRONOUNS

	Nominative	Accusative	Dative
Singular			
1st person	ich	mich	mir
2nd person	du	dich	dir
3rd person *m.*	er	ihn	ihm
3rd person *f.*	sie	sie	ihr
3rd person *n.*	es	es	ihm
Plural			
1st person	wir	uns	uns
2nd person	ihr	euch	euch
3rd person	sie	sie	ihnen
you (formal, sing. & pl.)	Sie	Sie	Ihnen

DEFINITE ARTICLES AS DEMONSTRATIVE PRONOUNS

The definite articles can be used as demonstrative pronouns, giving more emphasis to the sentences than the personal pronouns **er, sie, es.** Note that these demonstrative pronouns have the same forms as the definite articles:

Wer bekommt *den* Cappuccino? *Der* ist für mich.

	Nominative	Accusative
Masculine	der	den
Feminine	die	die
Neuter	das	das
Plural	die	die

INTERROGATIVES

INTERROGATIVE PRONOUNS

	People		Things	
Nominative	**wer?**	*who?*	**was?**	*what?*
Accusative	**wen?**	*whom?*	**was?**	*what?*
Dative	**wem?**	*to, for whom?*		

Grammar Summary

OTHER INTERROGATIVES

wann?	*when?*	**wie viele?**	*how many?*	**welche?**	*which?*		
warum?	*why?*	**wo?**	*where?*	**was für (ein)?**	*what kind of (a)?*		
wie?	*how?*	**woher?**	*from where?*	(eine)			
wie viel?	*how much? how many?*	**wohin?**	*to where?*	(einen)			

WORD ORDER

POSITION OF VERBS IN A SENTENCE

The conjugated verb is in **first** *position in:*	*yes/no questions (questions that do not begin with an interrogative)* **Trinkst du Kaffee?** **Spielst du Tennis?** **Möchtest du ins Konzert gehen?** *both formal and informal commands* **Kommen Sie bitte um 2 Uhr!** **Geh doch mit ins Kino!**
The conjugated verb is in **second** *position in:* *The conjugated verb is in* **second** *position and the infinitive or past participle is* **final** *in:*	*statements with normal word order* **Wir spielen heute Volleyball.** *statements with inverted word order* **Heute spielen wir Volleyball.** *questions that begin with an interrogative* **Wohin gehst du?** **Woher kommst du?** **Was macht er?** *statements with modals* **Ich möchte heute ins Kino gehen.** *statements in conversational past* **Ich habe das Buch gelesen.**
The conjugated verb is in **final** *position in:*	*clauses following the verb* **wissen** **Ich weiß, wo das Hotel ist.** *clauses that begin with* **weil** *or* **dass** **Ich gehe nicht ins Kino, weil ich kein Geld habe.** **Ich glaube, dass er Rockmusik gern hört.**

NOTE: In Level 2 you will learn more about word order in clauses with modals and verbs with separable prefixes:

> Ich komme morgen nicht, weil ich zu Hause helfen muss.
> Ich weiß nicht, wer heute Morgen angerufen hat.

POSITION OF **NICHT** IN A SENTENCE

To negate the entire sentence, as close to end of sentence as possible:	Er fragt seinen Vater		nicht.
Before a separable prefix:	Ich rufe ihn	nicht	an.
Before any part of a sentence you want to negate, contrast, or emphasize:	Er kommt	nicht	heute. (Er kommt morgen.)
Before part of a sentence that answers the question **wo?**	Ich wohne	nicht	in Berlin.

VERBS

PRESENT TENSE VERB FORMS

		Regular	-eln Verbs	Stem Ending with t/d	Stem Ending with s/ß
INFINITIVES		spiel -en	bastel -n	find -en	heiß -en
PRONOUNS		stem + ending	stem + ending	stem + ending	stem + ending
I	ich	spiel -e	bastl -e	find -e	heiß -e
you	du	spiel -st	bastel -st	find -est	heiß -t
he *she* *it*	er sie es	spiel -t	bastel -t	find -et	heiß -t
we	wir	spiel -en	bastel -n	find -en	heiß -en
you (plural)	ihr	spiel -t	bastel -t	find -et	heiß -t
they	sie	spiel -en	bastel -n	find -en	heiß -en
you (formal)	Sie	spiel -en	bastel -n	find -en	heiß -en

NOTE: There are important differences between the verbs in the above chart:

1. Verbs ending in **-eln** (**basteln, segeln**) drop the **e** of the ending **-eln** in the **ich**-form: **ich bastle, ich segle** and add only **-n** in the **wir-, sie-,** and **Sie**-forms. These forms are always identical with the infinitive: **basteln, wir basteln, sie basteln, Sie basteln.**

2. Verbs with a stem ending in **d** or **t**, such as **finden**, add an **e** before the ending in the **du**-form (**du findest**) and the **er-** and **ihr**-forms (**er findet, ihr findet**).

3. All verbs with stems ending in an **s**-sound (**heißen** or **müssen**) add only -**t** in the **du**-form: **du heißt, du musst.**

VERBS WITH A STEM-VOWEL CHANGE

There are a number of verbs in German that change their stem vowel in the **du-** and **er/sie-** forms. A few verbs, such as **nehmen** (*to take*), have a change in the consonant as well. You cannot predict these verbs, so it is best to learn each one individually. They are usually irregular only in the **du-** and **er/sie-** forms.

	e → i			e → ie		a → ä	
	essen	geben	nehmen	lesen	sehen	fahren	einladen
ich	esse	gebe	nehme	lese	sehe	fahre	lade ein
du	isst	gibst	nimmst	liest	siehst	fährst	lädst ein
er, sie	isst	gibt	nimmt	liest	sieht	fährt	lädt ein
wir	essen	geben	nehmen	lesen	sehen	fahren	laden ein
ihr	esst	gebt	nehmt	lest	seht	fahrt	ladet ein
sie	essen	geben	nehmen	lesen	sehen	fahren	laden ein
Sie	essen	geben	nehmen	lesen	sehen	fahren	laden ein

SOME IMPORTANT IRREGULAR VERBS: **HABEN, SEIN, WISSEN**

	haben	sein	wissen
ich	habe	bin	weiß
du	hast	bist	weißt
er, sie	hat	ist	weiß
wir	haben	sind	wissen
ihr	habt	seid	wisst
sie	haben	sind	wissen
Sie	haben	sind	wissen

MODAL (AUXILIARY) VERBS

The verbs **können, müssen, sollen, wollen, mögen** (and the **möchte**-forms) are usually used with an infinitive at the end of the sentence. If the meaning of that infinitive is clear, it can be left out: **Du musst sofort nach Hause!** (**Gehen** is understood and omitted.)

	können	müssen	sollen	wollen	mögen	möchte
ich	kann	muss	soll	will	mag	möchte
du	kannst	musst	sollst	willst	magst	möchtest
er, sie	kann	muss	soll	will	mag	möchte
wir	können	müssen	sollen	wollen	mögen	möchten
ihr	könnt	müsst	sollt	wollt	mögt	möchtet
sie	können	müssen	sollen	wollen	mögen	möchten
Sie	können	müssen	sollen	wollen	mögen	möchten

VERBS WITH SEPARABLE PREFIXES

Some verbs have *separable prefixes:* prefixes that separate from the conjugated verbs and are moved to the end of the sentence.

	Infinitive: aussehen
ich sehe ... aus	Ich sehe heute aber sehr schick aus!
du siehst ... aus	Du siehst heute sehr fesch aus!
er/sie/es sieht ... aus	Sieht sie immer so modern aus?
	Sieht dein Zimmer immer so unordentlich aus?
wir sehen ... aus	Wir sehen heute sehr lustig aus.
ihr seht ... aus	Ihr seht alle so traurig aus.
sie sehen ... aus	Sie sehen sehr schön aus.
Sie sehen ... aus	Sie sehen immer so ernst aus.

Here are the separable-prefix verbs you learned in Level 1.

abheben	anziehen	einkaufen
abräumen	auflegen	einladen
anprobieren	aufräumen	einstecken
anrufen	aussehen	mitkommen

COMMAND FORMS

Regular Verbs	gehen	kommen
Persons you address with **du** (singular) with **ihr** (plural) with **Sie** (sing & pl)	Geh! Geht! Gehen Sie!	Komm! Kommt! Kommen Sie!

Separable-prefix Verbs	mitkommen	anrufen	einladen	anziehen	ausgehen
	Komm mit! Kommt mit! Kommen Sie mit!	Ruf an! Ruft an! Rufen Sie an!	Lad ein! Ladet ein! Laden Sie ein!	Zieh an! Zieht an! Ziehen Sie an!	Geh aus! Geht aus! Gehen Sie aus!

Stem-changing Verbs	essen	nehmen	geben	sehen	fahren
	Iss! Esst! Essen Sie!	Nimm! Nehmt! Nehmen Sie!	Gib! Gebt! Geben Sie!	Sieh! Seht! Sehen Sie!	Fahr! Fahrt! Fahren Sie!

Note: The vowel changes **e → i** and **e → ie** are maintained in the **du**- form of the command. The umlaut vowel change **a → ä** does not occur in the command form.

EXPRESSING FUTURE TIME

You can use the present tense with a time expression to talk about events that will take place in the future:

Wir fahren morgen nach Berlin.

Am Wochenende besuche ich meine Großeltern.

PAST TENSE VERB FORMS

In this book, you learned the following verbs to express past time:

Weak Verbs		Strong Verbs	
Present Tense Form	**Past Tense Form**	**Present Tense Form**	**Past Tense Form**
Er macht das. Sie kauft das.	Er hat das gemacht. Sie hat das gekauft.	Er spricht oft. Sie sieht das nicht. Du liest gern.	Er hat oft gesprochen. Sie hat das nicht gesehen. Du hast gern gelesen.

In addition you learned the simple past form of the verb **sein**:

THE SIMPLE PAST OF SEIN

ich	war
du	warst
er, sie	war
wir	waren
ihr	wart
sie	waren
Sie (formal)	waren

THE CONVERSATIONAL PAST

In Level 2 you will learn more about how to express past events. In general, German verbs are divided into two groups: weak verbs and strong verbs. Weak verbs usually follow a regular pattern, as do the English verb forms *play, played, has played*. In German, weak verbs add a **ge-** and a **-t** to the verb stem to form the past participle. Strong verbs usually have irregularities, like the English verb forms *run, ran, has run* and *go, went, has gone*. Look at the past tense verb forms chart above and compare the present tense forms of the verbs on the left with the past tense forms on the right. As a rule of thumb, verbs that are irregular (stem-changing verbs) in the present tense are irregular, or strong, in the past tense.

In Level 1 you have learned that **haben** is used as the helping verb with the past participle. In Level 2 you will also learn some verbs that use **sein** as their helping verb, such as the verb **gehen** in the following example:

Ich gehe oft ins Kino.   **Ich bin gestern ins Kino gegangen.**

PRINCIPAL PARTS OF THE VERBS PRESENTED IN LEVEL 1*

This list includes all verbs included in the **Wortschatz** sections of this textbook. Both strong and weak verbs, including verbs with separable prefixes, stem-vowel changes, and other irregularities, are listed. Though most of the verbs in this list form the conversational past with **haben**, a few of the verbs you have learned take **sein** in the present perfect tense. You will work with these verbs and learn more about them in Level 2.

STRONG VERBS

Infinitive	Present (stem-vowel change and/or separable prefix)	Past Participle	Meaning
abheben	hebt ab	abgehoben	to lift (the receiver)
anrufen	ruft an	angerufen	to call up
anziehen	zieht an	angezogen	to put on (clothes)
aussehen	sieht aus	ausgesehen	to look, appear
bekommen	bekommt	bekommen	to get, receive
einladen	lädt ein	eingeladen	to invite
essen	isst	gegessen	to eat
fahren	fährt	(ist) gefahren	to drive, ride
finden	findet	gefunden	to find
geben	gibt	gegeben	to give
gefallen	gefällt	gefallen	to like, be pleasing to
gehen	geht	(ist) gegangen	to go
gießen	gießt	gegossen	to pour; to water
haben	hat	gehabt	to have
heißen	heißt	geheißen	to be called
helfen	hilft	geholfen	to help
kommen	kommt	(ist) gekommen	to come
lesen	liest	gelesen	to read
mitkommen	kommt mit	(ist) mitgekommen	to come along
nehmen	nimmt	genommen	to take
scheinen	scheint	geschienen	to shine
schreiben	schreibt	geschrieben	to write
schwimmen	schwimmt	(ist) geschwommen	to swim
sehen	sieht	gesehen	to see
sein	ist	(ist) gewesen	to be
sprechen	spricht	gesprochen	to speak
trinken	trinkt	getrunken	to drink
tun	tut	getan	to do
wissen	weiß	gewusst	to know

*The past participles in this chart are for reference only. Most of them will be taught in Level 2.

WEAK VERBS

abräumen	räumt ab	abgeräumt	*to clear away*
anprobieren	probiert an	anprobiert	*to try on*
auflegen	legt auf	aufgelegt	*to hang up (receiver)*
aufräumen	räumt auf	aufgeräumt	*to pick up/clean room*
basteln	bastelt	gebastelt	*to do arts and crafts*
besichtigen	besichtigt	besichtigt	*to sightsee*
besuchen	besucht	besucht	*to visit*
brauchen	braucht	gebraucht	*to need*
decken	deckt	gedeckt	*to set (the table)*
füttern	füttert	gefüttert	*to feed*
einkaufen	kauft ein	eingekauft	*to shop*
einstecken	steckt ein	eingesteckt	*to insert (coin)*
glauben	glaubt	geglaubt	*to believe*
holen	holt	geholt	*to get*
hören	hört	gehört	*to hear*
kaufen	kauft	gekauft	*to buy*
kennen	kennt	*gekannt	*to know*
kosten	kostet	gekostet	*to cost*
machen	macht	gemacht	*to do or make*
mähen	mäht	gemäht	*to mow*
meinen	meint	gemeint	*to think, be of the opinion*
passen	passt	gepasst	*to fit*
putzen	putzt	geputzt	*to clean*
regnen	regnet	geregnet	*to rain*
sagen	sagt	gesagt	*to say*
sammeln	sammelt	gesammelt	*to collect*
schauen	schaut	geschaut	*to look (at)*
schenken	schenkt	geschenkt	*to give (a gift)*
schmecken	schmeckt	geschmeckt	*to taste*
sortieren	sortiert	sortiert	*to sort*
spielen	spielt	gespielt	*to play*
spülen	spült	gespült	*to wash dishes*
suchen	sucht	gesucht	*to look for*
tanzen	tanzt	getanzt	*to dance*
telefonieren	telefoniert	telefoniert	*to call (on the phone)*
verbringen	verbringt	*verbracht	*to spend time*
wählen	wählt	gewählt	*to dial*
wandern	wandert	(ist) gewandert	*to hike*
wohnen	wohnt	gewohnt	*to live*
zahlen	zahlt	gezahlt	*to pay*
zeichnen	zeichnet	gezeichnet	*to draw*

*Although weak, these verbs have a vowel change in the past participle.

Learning to pronounce new and different sounds can be one of the most challenging aspects of learning a new language. You must first learn to hear new sounds. Then you have to learn to use your tongue, lips, jaw, and facial muscles in new ways to produce the sounds. Pronunciation can also be a very important aspect of learning a language; poor pronunciation can often interfere with communication. Although it is not necessary to learn to speak "like a native," it is important that you learn to make the sounds in order to communicate clearly and effectively.

The pronunciation features treated in this book are intended to be as helpful as possible. The descriptions of the German sound system used throughout this book focus on spelling and how different letters or letter combinations are usually pronounced. The **Aussprache** sections are meant to familiarize you with the German sound system, to help you recognize individual sounds when they occur, and to enable you to "sound out" new words and pronounce them correctly. Luckily, in German there is a much closer relationship between spelling and pronunication than there is in English. There are, of course, exceptions, and for the most conspicuous ones, we have provided examples to remind you that these pronunciation rules are usually true, but not always.

Whenever possible, a familiar sound in an English word is compared to the German sound being introduced. All German sounds are designated by boldfaced print, and all English sounds are designated by italics. For sounds not occurring in English, we have provided brief descriptions of how to produce the sounds. In general, German vowels require more tension in the facial muscles and less movement of the tongue than English. The vowels usually do not glide, which means the sounds are more pure or continuous.

The thought of learning a whole new sound system might be intimidating at first, but practice will be your key to success. Here are some hints that might make learning pronunciation seem a little easier:

Don't be afraid to guess the pronunciation of an unfamiliar German word!

In general, German words are pronounced just like they are written. By looking at the spelling of a German word, you can often guess the pronunciation. Regardless of whether you are dealing with a short word, like **Katze,** or a much longer word, such as **Donaudampfschifffahrtsgesellschaftskapitän,** you should be able to sound out the word using the spelling as a guide.

Don't be afraid to make pronunciation mistakes!

Learning a foreign language takes time, and you are going to make some mistakes along the way. Making German sounds requires the use of different facial muscles and, just like riding a bike, it takes practice to get it right.

Pronunciation and dictation exercises are found at the end of the **Dritte Stufe** in each chapter. The symbols within slashes below, for example /e/, are from the *International Phonetic Alphabet* and represent sounds.

CHAPTER PAGE	LETTER/ COMBINATION	IPA SYMBOL	EXAMPLE
Ch. 1 p. 33	the long vowel **ä**	/e/	Mädchen
	the long vowel **e**	/e/	zehn
	the long vowel **ü**	/y/	Grüß
	the long vowel **ö**	/ø/	hören
	the letter **w**	/v/	wer
	the letter **v**	/f/	vier
Ch. 2 p. 59	the vowel combination **ie**	/i/	spielen
	the diphthong **ei**	/ai/	schreiben
	the letter **j**	/j/	Junge
	the letter **z**	/ts/	zur
Ch. 3 p. 85	the long vowel **o**	/o/	Obst
	the long vowel **u**	/u/	Stuhl
	the letter **s**	/z/	sieben
	the letter **s**	/s/	Preis
	the letters **ss**	/s/	müssen
	the letter **ß**	/s/	Straße
Ch. 4 p. 117	the diphthong **eu**	/ɔy/	teuer
	the diphthong **äu**	/ɔy/	Verkäufer
	the diphthong **au**	/au/	bauen
	the final **b**	/p/	gelb
	the final **d**	/t/	Rad
	the final **g**	/k/	sag
Ch. 5 p. 145	the short vowel **i**	/ɪ/	schick
	the short vowel **ä**	/ɛ/	lässig
	the short vowel **e**	/ɛ/	Bett
	the long vowel **a**	/a/	haben
	the letter combination **sch**	/ʃ/	Schule
	the letter combination **st**	/ʃt/	Stiefel
	the letter combination **sp**	/ʃp/	Spitze
Ch. 6 p. 173	the letter combination **ch**	/ç/	ich
	the letter combination **ch**	/x/	doch
	the letter **r**	/r/	rund
	the final **er**	/ɐ/	super

CHAPTER PAGE	LETTER/ COMBINATION	IPA SYMBOL	EXAMPLE
Ch. 7 p. 205	the short vowel **o**	/ɔ/	wolkig
	the short vowel **u**	/ʊ/	uns
	the letter **l**	/l/	Lehrer
	the letter combination **th**	/t/	Mathe
	the letter combination **pf**	/pf/	Pfennig
Ch. 8 p. 233	the short vowel **ö**	/œ/	können
	the short vowel **ü**	/Y/	Stück
	review diphthong **ei**	/ai/	Eier
	review vowel combination **ie**	/i/	wieder
	review letter **z**	/ts/	Zeit
Ch. 9 p. 261	review long vowel **ü**	/y/	für
	review long vowel **ö**	/ø/	blöd
	review letter **s**	/z/	Senf
	review letter **s**	/s/	es
	review letters **ss**	/s/	besser
	review letter **ß**	/s/	Spaß
Ch. 10 p. 293	review short vowel **o**	/ɔ/	Onkel
	review long vowel **o**	/o/	Oma
	review short vowel **u**	/ʊ/	Gruppe
	review long vowel **u**	/u/	Musik
	review combination **ch**	/ç/	Pech
	review combination **ch**	/x/	Buch
Ch. 11 p. 321	review **r**	/r/	Bruder
	review **er**	/ɐ/	meiner
	review long vowel **a**	/a/	Vater
	review diphthong **eu**	/ɔy/	heute
	review diphthong **äu**	/ɔy/	Verkäufer
	review diphthong **au**	/au/	Strauß
Ch. 12 p. 349	review letter **w**	/v/	weiß
	review letter **v**	/f/	viel
	review letter **j**	/j/	Juli
	review short vowel **ä**	/ɛ/	hässlich
	review short vowel **e**	/ɛ/	Sessel
	review long vowel **ä**	/e/	Käse
	review long vowel **e**	/e/	dem

This vocabulary includes almost all words in this textbook, both active (for production) and passive (for recognition only). Active words and phrases are practiced in the chapter and are listed in the **Wortschatz** section at the end of each chapter. You are expected to know and be able to use active vocabulary. An entry in black, heavy type indicates that the word or phrase is active. All other words—some in the opening dialogs, in exercises, in optional and visual material, in the **Landeskunde, Zum Lesen** and **Kann ich's wirklich?** sections—are for recognition only. The meaning of these words and phrases can usually be understood from the context or may be looked up in this vocabulary.

With some exceptions, the following are not included: proper nouns, forms of verbs other than the infinitive, and forms of determiners other than the nominative.

Nouns are listed with definite article and plural form, when applicable. The numbers in the entries refer to the chapter where the word or phrase first appears or where it becomes an active vocabulary word. Vocabulary from the preliminary chapter is followed by a page reference only. Vocabulary from the location openers is followed by a "Loc" and the chapter number directly following the location spread.

The following abbreviations are used in this vocabulary: adj (adjective), pl (plural), pp (past participle), sep (separable-prefix verb), sing (singular), and conj (conjunction).

A

ab *from, starting at,* 4; ab und zu *now and then,* 10
der Abend, -e *evening,* 2; **am Abend** *in the evening,* 2; jeden Abend *every evening,* 10
der Abendhauch *evening breeze,* 10
abends *evenings,* 6
der Abenteuerfilm, -e *adventure movie,* 10
aber *but,* 3; **Aber sicher!** *Sure!,* 11
die Abfahrt, -en *departure,* 6
abgelegen *remote,* 6
abheben (sep) *to pick up,* 11;
den Hörer abheben *to pick up the receiver,* 11
das Abitur, -e *final examination in high school,* 4
abräumen (sep) *to clean up, clear off,* 7; **den Tisch abräumen** *to clear the table,* 7
der Absatz, ⁀e *paragraph,* 11
abschmecken (sep) *to taste,* 12
abschreiben *to copy,* 8
die Abschrift, -en *transcript,* 8
die Abteilung, -en *section,* 9
abwaschen (sep) *to wash dishes,* 12
Ach Oh!, 2; **Ach ja!** *Oh yeah!,* 1; Ach so! *Oh, I see!,* 1; Ach was! *Give me a break!,* 5; Ach wo! *Oh no!,* 4
acht *eight,* 1
achten *to pay attention (to),* 9
Achtung! *Attention!,* 6
achtzehn *eighteen,* 1

achtzig *eighty,* 3
der Ackerbau *agriculture,* Loc 4
der Actionfilm, -e *action movie,* 10
actionsgeladen *full of action,* 10
addieren *to add,* 8
das Adressbuch, ⁀er *address book,* 11
der Affe, -n *ape, monkey,* 10
ähnlich *similar,* 11
die Ahnung: **Keine Ahnung!** *I have no idea!,* 9
das Akkordeon, -s *accordion,* 10
aktiv *active,* 12
die Aktivität, -en *activity,* 7
aktuell *current,* 10
akzeptieren *to accept,* 7
die Algebra *algebra,* 4
alle *all, everyone,* 2
allein *alone,* 8
aller *of all,* 8
allerdings *admittedly,* 7
alles *everything,* 2; **Das ist alles.** *That's all.* 8; Alles klar! *O.K.!,* 10; **Alles Gute zum Geburtstag!** *Best wishes on your birthday!,* 11; **Alles Gute zum Muttertag!** *Happy Mother's Day!,* 11
allgemein *general,* 4; im Allgemeinen *in general,* 10
alltäglich *daily,* 8
allzu *overly,* 10
der Alptraum, ⁀e *nightmare,* 10
als *as,* 6; als letzter *the last,* 12
also *well then,* 2; Also, auf geht's! *Well, let's go!,* 9; **Also, einfach!** *That's easy.* 1
alt *old,* 3; **Wie alt ...?** *How old ...?,* 1

älter *older,* 3
das Altpapier *recycled paper,* 7
die Altstadt, ⁀e *historical part of downtown,* 12
das Alter: in deinem Alter *your age,* 9
das Aluminium *aluminum,* 7
am=an dem *at the,* 2; **am ...platz** *on ... Square,* 9; **am Abend** *in the evening,* 2; **am ersten (Juli)** *on the first (of July),* 11; **am liebsten** *most of all,* 10; Am liebsten sehe ich Krimis. *I like detective movies the best.,* 10; **am Montag** *on Monday,* 4; **am Nachmittag** *in the afternoon,* 2; **am Wochenende** *on the weekend,* 2
der Amerikaner, - *American (male),* 9
die Amerikanerin, -nen *American (female),* 9
amerikanisch *American (adj),* 8
die Ampel, -n *traffic light,* 9; an der Ampel *at the traffic light,* 9; **bis zur Ampel** *until you get to the traffic light,* 9
amtlich *official,* 9
an *to, at,* 4; an der Ampel *at the traffic light,* 9; ansonsten *otherwise,* 11; an welchem Tag? *on which day?,* 11
die Ananas, - *pineapple,* 8
anbieten, *to offer,* 8
das Andenken, - *souvenir,* 11
andere *other,* 2
ändern *to change,* 9
anerkannt *recognized,* 4
anfallen (sep): alles was anfällt *anything that comes up,* 12

der Anfänger, - *beginner*, 4
angefangen (pp) *started*, 7
angeln *to fish*, 10
ankommen: es kommt darauf an *it depends on*, 12
der Anlass, ⸚e *occasion*, Loc 7
anprobieren (sep) *to try on*, 5
anrösten (sep) *to brown*, 12
anrücken *to advance*, 10
anrufen (sep) *to call* (phone), 11; Ruf mal an! *Give me a call!*, 11
anschauen (sep) *to look at*, 6
ansehen (sep) *to look at*, 9
ansonsten *otherwise*, 11
anstrengend *exhausting*, 7
die Antwort, -en *answer*, 1
antworten *to answer*, 2
der Anwalt, ⸚e *lawyer*, 10
die Anweisung, -en *instruction*, 9
die Anwendung, -en *application*, 1
die Anzeige, -n *ad*, 10
anziehen (sep) *to put on, wear*, 5
der Anzug, -e *suit*, 5
der Apfel, ⸚e *apple*, 8
der Apfelkuchen, - *apple cake*, 6
das Apfelküchle, - *(see p. 298)*, 12
der Apfelsaft, ⸚e *apple juice*, 3; **ein Glas Apfelsaft** *a glass of apple juice*, 3
der Apfelstrudel, - *apple strudel*, 8
der Apparat, -e *telephone*, 11
die Applikation, -en *appliqué*, 5
das Apricot *apricot (color)*, 5
der April *April*, 7
das Aquarium, die Aquarien, *aquarium*, 10
die Arbeit *work*, 7
die Arbeitslehre, -n *work-study class*, 4
die Arbeitsliste, -n *work list*, 12
der Architekt, -en *architect*, 4
ärgerlich *annoying*, 6
die Arie, -n *aria*, 11
die Armbanduhr, -en *wristwatch*, 11
der Ärmel, - *sleeve*, 5
aromatisch *aromatic*, 9
der Artikel, - *article*, 8
die Asche, -n *ash*, 10
der Aschermittwoch *Ash Wednesday*, 9
der Ast, ⸚e *branch*, 8
die Atmosphäre, -n *atmosphere*, 4
das Attentat, -e *assassination*, 10
auch *also*, 1; **Ich auch.** *Me too.*, 2
auf *on; to*, 1; Also, auf geht's! *Well, let's go!*, 9; **auf dem Land** *in the country*, 3; auf dem Weg *on the way*, 6; auf der Straße *on the street*, 9; auf einer Fete *at a party*, 12; auf Englisch *in English*, 10; auf Schritt und Tritt *all the time*, 10; **Auf Wiederhören!** *Goodbye! (on the telephone)*, 11; **Auf Wiedersehen!** *Goodbye!*, 1; auf Deutsch *in German*, 9; auf der rechten Seite *on the right (hand) side*, 9
aufdringlich *pushy*, 7
der Aufdruck, -e *design*, 5

auffällig *conspicuous*, 9
die Aufgabe, -n *task*, 7
aufhängen (sep) *to hang up*, 12; die Wäsche aufhängen *to hang up the laundry*, 7
aufhören (sep) *to stop*, 3
auflegen (sep) *to hang up (the telephone)*, 11; **den Hörer auflegen** *to hang up (the receiver)*, 11
die Aufnahme, -n *admittance*, 2
aufpassen: **Pass auf!** *Watch out!*, 6; **Passt auf!** *Pay attention!*, p. 8
aufräumen (sep) *to clean up*, 7; **mein Zimmer aufräumen** *to clean my room*, 7; **meine Klamotten aufräumen** *to pick up my clothes*, 7
der Aufschnitt *cold cuts*, 8
aufschreiben *to write down*, 7
aufspüren *to track down*, 10
das Auge, -n: *eye*; **blaue (braune, grüne) Augen** *blue (brown, green) eyes*, 3
der August *August*, 7
aus *from*, 1; *made of*, 9; **aus Baumwolle** *made of cotton*, 12; **aus Holz** *made of wood*, 12; **aus Kunststoff** *made of plastic*, 12; **aus Leder** *made of leather*, 12; **aus Seide** *made of silk*, 12
ausarbeiten *to work out*, 7
ausbacken (sep) *to bake until done*, 12
der Ausdruck, ⸚e *expression*, p. 8
ausgeben (sep) *to spend (money)*, 8
ausgehen (sep) *to go out*, 11
die Auskunft, ⸚e *information*, 4
das Ausland *foreign country*, 11
der Ausländer, - *foreigner*, 9
das Auslandsgespräch, -e *international telephone call*, 11
ausleihen (sep) *to rent*, 10
auspacken (sep) *to unpack*, 8
ausräumen (sep) *to clean, clear out*, 12; den Geschirrspüler ausräumen *to unload the dishwasher*, 12
ausreichend *sufficient, passing (grade)*, 4
ausruhen (sich) *to rest* Loc 7
die Aussage, -n *statement*, 9
aussehen (sep) *to look like, to appear*, 3; **der Rock sieht ... aus.** *The skirt looks…*, 5; **er/sie sieht aus** *he/she looks like*, 5; **Wie sieht er aus?** *What does he look like?*, 3; **Wie sehen sie aus?** *What do they look like?*, 3
außerdem *in addition*, 7
außerhalb *outside of*, 6
aussprechen (sep) *to pronounce*, 1; richtig aussprechen *to pronounce correctly*, 1
die Ausstellung, -en *exhibit*, 10
aussuchen, (sich) *to select, pick*, 8
austauschen *to exchange*, 7

der Austauschschüler, - *exchange student*, 9
die Auswahl *selection*, 11
auswählen (sep) *to select*, 4
auswandern *to emigrate*, 11
das Auto, -s *car*, 1; Auto fahren *to drive (a car)*, 9; **mit dem Auto** *by car*, 1

backen *to bake*, 8
der Bäcker, - *baker*, 8; **beim Bäcker** *at the baker's*, 8
die Bäckerei, -en *bakery*, 8
das Backpulver *baking powder*, 12
das Bad, ⸚er *pool*, 12
baden *to swim*, 6; **baden gehen** *to go swimming*, 6
der Badepark, -s *park with swimming facilities*, 12
der Bahnhof, ⸚e *train station*, 9
bald *soon*, 11
der Ball, ⸚e *ball*, 12
das Ballett, -e *ballet*, 10
der Ballon, -s *balloon*, 11
banal *trivial*, 10
die Banane, -n *banana*, 3
die Bank, -en *bank*
der Baseball *baseball*, 2
basieren (auf) *to be based on*, 4
das Basilikum *basil*, 12
das Basisstück, -e *basic item*, 5
der Basketball, ⸚e *basketball*, 2
basteln *to do crafts*, 2
bauen *to build*, 5
das Bauernbrot, -e *(coarse) brown bread*, 8
das Bauernhaus, ⸚e *farm house*, Loc 10
die Baumwolle *cotton*, 12; **aus Baumwolle** *made of cotton*, 12
die Baustelle, -n *construction site*, 10
bayrisch *Bavarian (adj)*, 9
beantworten *to answer*, 9
der Becher, - *cup*, 6
der Bedarf *need*, 12
bedeckt *cloudy*, 7
bedeuten *to mean*, 10; Was bedeutet ...? *What does…mean?*, p. 8
bedeutend *important*, Loc 7
bedruckt *printed*, 5
befriedigend *satisfactory (grade)*, 4
beginnen *to begin*, 11
begleiten *to accompany*, 9
begonnen (pp) *begun*, 10
begreifen *to understand*, 10
begrüßen *to greet*, 1
behalten *to keep*, 6
behutsam *cautious*, 10

bei *at,* 1; bei meinen Freunden *at my friends',* 10; **beim Bäcker** *at the baker's,* 8; **beim Metzger** *at the butcher's,* 8; **Hier bei ...** *The ...residence.,* 11

beide *both,* 5

beim=bei dem *at the,* 2

das Beispiel, -e *example, model,* p. 5; zum Beispiel *for example,* 10

der Bekannte *acquaintance (male),* 7

bekannt (für) *known (for),* Loc, 7

bekommen *to get, to receive,* 5; **ich bekomme ...** *I'll have...,* 6; **Was bekommen Sie?** *What would you like?,* 5; *What will you have?* 6

belegen: mit Tomaten belegen *to top with tomatoes,* 8

beliebt *popular,* Loc 4

die Belletristik *fiction,* 10

bemalt *painted,* 11

die Bemerkung, -en *remark,* 4

benehmen (sich) *to behave,* 11

benutzen *to use,* 9

Benutzung, -en *use,* 4

bequem *comfortable,* 3

beraten *to consult,* 11

die Beratung, -en *advice,* 11

bereit *ready,* 10

bereiten *to prepare,* 12

der Berg, -e *mountain,* 10

der Bericht, -e *report,* 10

berichten, *to report,* 7

der Berliner, - *here: jelly-filled roll,* 9

die Berliner (pl) *residents of Berlin,* 9

berufsorientiert *career-oriented,* 4

berühmt *famous,* Loc 7

beschäftigt *occupied, busy,* 8

beschäftigt sein *to be busy,* 8

beschattet *tailed, shadowed,* 10

beschreiben *to describe,* 9

die Beschreibung, -en *description,* 12

besetzt *busy* (telephone), 11

besichtigen *to visit, to sightsee,* 9; **die Stadt besichtigen** *to visit the city,* 12

besonder *special,* 7

besonders *especially,* 8; **Nicht besonders.** *Not really.* 6; **besonders gern** *especially like,* 10

besprechen *to discuss,* 11

besser *better,* 8

best *best,* 1

bestimmt *certainly, definitely,* 5

bestimmt *definite,* 8

bestreuen *to sprinkle,* 8

der Besuch *visit,* Loc 10

besuchen *to visit,* 2; **Freunde besuchen** *to visit friends,* 2

besuchen (eine Schule) *to attend,* Loc 7

der Betrag, ⁝e *amount,* 11

das Bett, -en *bed,* 3; **das Bett machen** *to make the bed,* 7

die Bettwäsche *bed linen,* 9

die Beurteilung, -en *evaluation,* 4

der Beutel, - *bag,* 8

bevor *before,* 2

bewohnbar *inhabitable,* 3

die Bewölkung *cloudiness,* 7

bieten *to offer,* 4

bieten: anbieten (sep) *to offer,* 7

das Bild, -er *picture,* 11

billig *cheap,* 4

bin: ich bin *I am,* 1

die Biologie (Bio) *biology,* 4

die Biologielehrerin, -nen *biology teacher (female),* 1

die Birne, -n *pear,* 8

bis *until,* 1; Bis bald! *See you soon!,* 9; **Bis dann!** *Till then! See you later!,* 1; **bis zum ...platz** *until you get to ... Square,* 9; **bis zur ...straße** *until you get to ... Street,* 9; **bis zur Ampel** *until you get to the traffic light,* 9

bisschen: ein bisschen *a little,* 5; **ein bisschen mehr** *a little more,* 8;

bist: du bist *you are,* 1

bitte *please,* 3; Bitte? *Excuse me?,* 1; **Bitte (sehr, schön)!** *You're (very) welcome!,* 3; **Bitte?** *Yes? Can I help you?,* 5

das Bittermandelöl, -e *almond flavor,* 12

blättrig *flaky,* 8

blau *blue,* 3; **in Blau** *in blue,* 5

bleiben *to stay,* 7

der Bleistift, -e *pencil,* 4

der Blick, -e *view,* Loc 7

blöd *dumb,* 2

blond *blonde,* 3

bloß *only,* 4

der Blouson, -s *short jacket,* 5

die Blume, -n *flower,* 7; **die Blumen gießen** *to water the flowers,* 7

das Blumengeschäft, -e *florist shop,* 8

der Blumenkohl *cauliflower,* 8

der Blumenstrauß, ⁝e *bouquet of flowers,* 11

die Bluse, -n *blouse,* 5

blutig *bloody,* 10

die Bockwurst, ⁝e *smoked and cooked sausage,* 6

die Bowle, -n *punch,* 12

braten *to roast,* 8

die Bratkartoffeln (pl) *fried potatoes,* 6

die Bratwurst, ⁝e *bratwurst,* 8

brauchen *to need,* 5; **ich brauche ...** *I need...,* 5; **ich brauche noch ...** *I also need...,* 8

die Brauerei, -en *brewery,* 7

braun *brown,* 3; **in Braun** *in brown,* 5

das Brettspiel, -e *board game,* 2; **ein Brettspiel spielen** *to play a board game,* 12

die Brezel, -n *pretzel,* 8

die Brezenstange, -n *pretzel stick,* 8

der Brief, -e *letter,* 2

die Briefmarke, -n *stamp,* 2; **Briefmarken sammeln** *to collect stamps,* 2

die Brille, -n *a pair of glasses,* 3

bringen *to bring,* 1

das Brot, -e *bread,* 8; **Ich habe Brot gekauft.** *I bought bread.,* 8

das Brötchen, - *hard roll,* 8

die Brücke, -n *bridge,* 10

der Bruder, ⁝ *brother,* 3

die Brühe, -n *broth,* 12

brutal *brutal, violent,* 10

brutalste *the most brutal,* 10

das Buch, ⁝er *book,* 4

die Buchhandlung, -en *bookstore,* 10; buchstabieren *to spell,* 1

bügeln *to iron,* 7

der Bummel *stroll,* 9

das Bundesland, ⁝er *federal state* (German), 1

bunt *colorful,* 6

der Buntstift, -e *colored pencil; crayon,* 11

der Bürgerkrieg, -e *civil war,* 10

das Bürgertelefon *help line,* 11

der Bus, -se *bus,* 1; **mit dem Bus** *by bus,* 1

die Butter *butter,* 8

das Butterschmalz *shortening,* 12

das Café, -s *café,* 6; **in ein Café/ins Café gehen** *to go to a/the café,* 6

der Cappuccino, -s *cappuccino,* 6

die CD, -s *compact disc,* 11

der Cent, - *cent (smallest unit of the euro; 1/100th of a euro),* 4

der Champignon, -s *mushroom,* 8

die Chance, -n *chance,* 10

Chanukka *Hanukkah,* 11; **Frohes Chanukka-Fest!** *Happy Hanukkah!,* 11

charmant *charming,* 3

Chemie (die) *chemistry,* 4

chic *smart (looking),* 12

der Chor, ⁝e *choir,* 4

die Clique, -n *clique,* 10

der Club, -s *club,* 2

die Cola, -s *cola,* 3

die Comics (pl) *comic books,* 2; **Comics sammeln** *to collect comics,* 2

der Computer, - *computer,* 3

die Couch, -en *couch,* 3

der Cousin, -s *cousin (male),* 3

die Currywurst, ⁝e *curry sausage,* 6

D

da *there*, 1; da drüben *over there*, 4; **da hinten** *there in the back*, 4; **da vorn** *there in the front*, 4
dabei *with*, 4
dabei *at the same time*, 8
das Dach, ⸚er *roof*, Loc 7
dafür *for it*, 5
dahin *there*, 10
der Dalmatiner, - *Dalmatian*, 10
die Dame, -n *lady*, 5
damenhaft *ladylike*, 5
damit *with it; so that*, 7
danach *after that*, 4
Danke! *thank you!*, 3; **Danke (sehr, schön)!** *Thank you (very much)!*, 3
dann *then*, 4
darauf *on it*, 7
darüber *about it*, 5
das *the* (n); *that*, 1; **Das ist ...** *That's...*, 1; **Das ist alles.** *That's all.*, 8; **Das sind...** *These are...* (with plurals), 3
dass *that* (conj), 9; **ich finde es gut/schlecht, dass ...** *I think it's good/bad that...*, 9; **ich finde, dass ...** *I think that...*, 9; ich glaube, dass ... *I think that...*, 9
dasselbe *the same*, 11
dauern *to last*, 9
davor *in front*, Loc 10
dazugeben *to add*, 12
decken: den Tisch decken *to set the table*, 7
deftig *hearty*, 6
dein *your*, 3; **deinem Vater** *to, for your father*, 11; **deiner Mutter** *to, for your mother*, 11
dem *the* (masc, neuter, dat case), 11
den *the* (masc, acc case), 5
denken *to think*, 3
denn (particle), 1; 6
denn *because, for* (conj), 8
der *the* (m), 1; *to the* (fem, dat case), 11
des *of the*, 4
desillusioniert *disillusioned*, 10
deutsch *German* (adj), 9
Deutsch *German* (language), p. 4; (school subject), 4; **Ich habe Deutsch.** *I have German.*, 4
der Deutsche, -n *German (male)*, 2
die Deutsche *German (female)*, 2
die Deutschen (pl) *German people*, 2
Deutschland (das) *Germany*, 1
der **Deutschlehrer, -** *German teacher (male)*, 1
die **Deutschlehrerin, -nen** *German teacher (female)*, 1
der **Dezember** *December*, 7
dich *you* (acc), 7

die *the*, 1
der Dieb, -e *thief*, 10
dienen *to serve*, 9
der **Dienstag** *Tuesday*, 4
dienstbereit *ready for service*, 9
dies- *this, these*, 2
diesmal *this time*, 10
das Diktat, -e *dictation*, 1
der Dinosaurier, - *dinosaur*, 10
die Diplomatie *diplomacy*, 4
dir *to you*, 3
direkt *direct(ly)*, 6
der Dirigent, -en *conductor (music)*, 6
die **Disko, -s** *disco*, 6; **in eine Disko gehen** *to go to a disco*, 6
diskutieren *to discuss*, 10
DM = Deutsche Mark *German mark* (former monetary unit)
doch (particle), 6
Doch! *Oh yes!*, 2
der **Donnerstag** *Thursday*, 4
donnerstags *Thursdays*, 6
doof *dumb*, 10
dort *there*, 4; **dort drüben** *over there*, 4;
dorthin *there*, 9
die Dose, -n *can*, 7
das Dotter, - *egg yolk*, 12
dramatisch *dramatic*, 10
drei *three*, 1
dreimal *three times*, 7
dreißig *thirty*, 3
dreiundzwanzig *twenty-three*, 3
dreizehn *thirteen*, 1
der Drill -s *drill*, 10
drin *in it*, 9
dritte *third*, 8
der Druck: jemanden unter Druck setzen *to put pressure on somebody*, 10
du *you* (sing), 2
dumm *dumb, stupid*, 10
dunkel *dark*, 10
dunkelblau *dark blue*, 5; **in Dunkelblau** *in dark blue*, 5
durch *through*, 9; *divided by*, 3
der Dummschwätzer *silly prattler*, 10
die Dunkelheit *darkness*, 10
die Durchschnittstemperatur, -en *average temperature*, 9
der Durst *thirst*, 6

E

eben (particle), 5
ebenso...wie *just as...as*, 10
ebenso wie *as well as*, Loc 10
echt *real, really*, 5
echt super! *great!*, 1
eckig *with corners*, 12
ehemalig *former*, 9
ehrlich *honestly*, 5

das **Ei, -er** *egg*, 8; gefüllte Eier *deviled eggs*, 12
der Eierkuchen, - *pancake* 9
eigen *own* (adj), 10
eigentlich *actually*, 5
die Eigentumswohnung, -en *condominium*, 3
ein *a, an*, 3; **ein paar** *a few*, 3; **eine Eins (Zwei, Drei, Vier, Fünf, Sechs)** (German grades), 4
einbiegen (in eine Straße) *to turn onto (a street)*, 9
einen *a, an* (masc, acc case), 5; **Einen Pulli in Grau, bitte.** *A sweater in gray, please.*, 5
einfach *simple, easy*, 1; **Also, einfach!** *That's easy!*, 1
das Einfamilienhaus, ⸚er *single-family house*, 3
einfarbig *solid color*, 5
eingeladen (pp) *invited*, 11
eingelegt (pp): eine Mittagspause einlegen *to take a lunch break*, 9
einige *some*, 9
die Einheit, -en *unit*, 10
der Einkauf, ⸚e *purchase*, 8
einkaufen *to shop*, 8; **einkaufen gehen** *to go shopping*, 8
der Einkäufer, - *shopper*, Loc 7
der Einkaufsbummel *shopping trip*, 8
das Einkaufszentrum, die Einkaufszentren *shopping center*, 6; ins Einkaufszentrum gehen *to go to the shopping center/mall*, 6
der Einkaufszettel, - *shopping list*, 8
der Einklang, ⸚e *unison, harmony*, 8
einladen (sep) *to invite*, 11; **er/sie lädt ... ein** *he/she invites*, 11
die Einladung, -en *invitation*, 11
einmal *once*, 7
eins *one*, 1; **eine Eins** *an A*, 1
die Einschreibung, -en *registration*, 4
einsetzen *to insert*, 8
der Eintritt, -e *admission*, 4
einundzwanzig *twenty-one*, 3
einverstanden *agreed*, 8
der Einwohner, - *inhabitant*, Loc 4
die Einwohnerzahl, -en *population*, 1
einzeln *single, individual*, 7
der Einzelpassagier, -e *individual passenger*, 9
einzigartig *unique*, Loc 10
das **Eis** *ice cream*, 6; *ice*, 7; **ein Eis essen** *to eat ice cream*, 6
der **Eisbecher, -** *a dish of ice cream*, 6
das Eiscafé, -s *ice cream parlor*, 8
die Eissporthalle, -n *skating rink*, 12
das Ekel, - *nasty person*, 10
EL=Esslöffel *tablespoon*, 8
die Elektronik *electronics*, 7
die Elektrotechnik *electrical engineering*, Loc 10
elf *eleven*, 1
eloquent *eloquent*, 10
die **Eltern** (pl) *parents*, 3

R32

der Emmentaler *Emmentaler (cheese)*, 12
emotional *emotional*, 10
das Ende *end*, 5
Ende: zu Ende schreiben *to finish writing*, 7
endgültig *final*, 10
eng *tight*, 5
engagiert *occupied*, 10
der Engel, - *angel*, 10
die Engländer (pl) *English people*, 1
der Engländer, - *English person (male)*, 9
die Engländerin, -nen *English person (female)*, 9
Englisch *English (adj)*, 4; auf Englisch *in English*, 10
Englisch *English (school subject)*, 4; *(language)*, 9
entfernt *away*, Loc 7
entführen *to carry off*, 6
entscheiden *to decide*, 9; sie entscheidet sich für *she decides on*, 11
die Entscheidung, -en *decision*, 10
entschließen *to decide*, 9
Entschuldigung! *Excuse me!*, 9
er *he*, 2; *it*, 3
die Erdbeere, -n *strawberry*, 8
das Erdbeereis *strawberry ice cream*, 9
der Erdbeerkuchen, - *strawberry cake*, 8
die Erdkunde *geography*, 4
die Erdnussbutter *peanut butter*, 8
die Erfrischung *refreshment*, 6
erfüllen *to fulfill*, 7
ergänzen *to complete*, 9
erkennen *to recognize*, 10
erklären *to explain*, 5
erleben *to experience*, 9
erledigen *to accomplish*, 9
ermittelt von *compiled by*, 10
der Ernährungsexperte, -n *nutrition expert*, 8
der Ernst *seriousness*, 10; im Ernst? *seriously?*, 10
erst *first*, 6
ersten: am ersten (Juli) *on the first (of July)*, 11
erteilen *to give*, 4
erwarten *to expect*, 12
erwecken *to awaken*, 10
erweisen *to grant*, 10
die Erweiterung, -en *expansion*, 9
erzählen *to tell*, 10; Erzähl weiter! *Keep on talking!*, 10
es *it*, 3
essen *to eat*, 3; **er/sie isst** *he/she eats*, 6
der Essig *vinegar*, 12
der Esslöffel, - *tablespoon*, 8
der Esstisch, -e *dining table*, 12
der Estragon *tarragon*, 12
etwa *approximately*, 12
etwas *something*, 7; **Sonst noch etwas?** *Anything else?*, 8

etwas: etwas zum Anziehen *something to wear*, 9; etwas zum Essen *something to eat*, 9
euch *you* (pl, acc case), 7
der Euro, - *euro (the national currency of most European countries)*, 4
europäisch *European (adj)*, 10
die Europareise, -n *trip to Europe*, 11
exclusiv *exclusive*, 10

das Fach, ⁻er *school subject*, 4
der Fächer, - *fan*, 11
der Fachlehrer, - *subject teacher*, 4
die Fachsprache, -n *technical lingo*, 12
fahren *to go, ride, drive (using a vehicle)*, 9; **er/sie fährt** *he/she drives*, 9; Auto fahren *to drive (a car)*, 9; in die Stadt fahren *to go downtown (by vehicle)*, 11; wir fahren Rad *we're riding bikes*, 10
der Fahrpreis, -e *fare*, 4
die Fahrpreisermäßigung, -en *reduced fare*, 4
das Fahrrad, ⁻er *bicycle*, 7
die Fahrt, -en *drive* 2
falsch *false*, 11
falsch *wrong*, 10
die Familie, -en *family*, 3
die Familienkomödie, -n *family comedy*, 10
das Familienmitglied, -er *family member*, 11
das Familientreffen, - *family reunion*, 12
Fang mit ... an! *Begin with...*, 9
das Fantasybuch, ⁻er *fantasy book*, 10
der Fantasyfilm, -e *fantasy film*, 10
der Fantasyroman, -e *fantasy novel*, 10
die Farbe, -n *color*, 5; Wir haben das in allen Farben. *We have that in all colors.*, 5
der Fasching *carnival*, 9
die Fassade, -n *facade*, 8
fast *almost*, 12
faul *lazy*, 7
faulenzen *to be lazy; to take it easy*, 6
die Faustregel, -n *rule of thumb*, 8
der Februar *February*, 7
fehlen *to be missing*, 4; Was fehlt hier? *What's missing?*, 5
fehlend- *missing*, 11
feiern *to celebrate*, 11
der Feiertag, -e *holiday*, 11
feiertags *holidays*, 10
fein gehackt *finely chopped*, 12
das Feinkosthaus, ⁻er *delicatessen*, 9
die Feinmechanik *precision mechanics*, Loc 10

das Fenster, - *window*, p. 8; die Fenster putzen *to clean the windows*, 7
die Ferien (pl) *vacation*, 1
das Ferngespräch, -e *long distance call*, 11
das Fernsehen *television*, 2; Fernsehen schauen *to watch television*, 2; im Fernsehen *on television*, 5
der Fernsehkoch, ⁻e *television chef*, 8
die Fernsehsendung, -en *television show*, 9
fertig *finished*, 7
fertig machen *to finish*
fesch *stylish, smart*, 5
das Fest, -e *festivity*, 11
festlich *festive*, Loc 7
die Fete, -n *party*, 5; auf einer Fete *at a party*, 12
feurig *fiery*, 6
der Film, -e *movie*, 10; **einen Film sehen** *to see a movie*, 6
die Filmart, -en *type of movie*, 10
der Filmkritiker, - *film critic*, 10
der Filmverleih, -e *movie rental*, 10
der Filzschreiber, - *felt-tip pen*, 11
finden *to think of, to find*, 2; **Das finde ich auch.** *I think so, too.*, 2; **Das finde ich nicht.** *I disagree.*, 2; **ich finde es gut/schlecht, dass ...** *I think it's good/bad that...*, 9; **ich finde (Tennis) ...** *I think (tennis) is...*, 2; **Ich finde den Pulli stark!** *The sweater is awesome!*, 5; Ich finde es toll! *I think it's great!*, 9; **Wie findest du (Tennis)?** *What do you think of (tennis)?*, 2
die Firma, die Firmen *firm, company*, 9
der Fisch, -e *fish*, 8
die Fläche, -n *surface, area*, Loc 4
das Fladenbrot *pita bread*, 6
die Flasche, -n *bottle*, 7
das Fleisch *meat*, 8
die Fleischbrühe, -n *meat broth*, 12
die Fliese, -n *tile*, 12
die Floßfahrt, -en *rafting trip*, 9
die Flöte, -n *flute*, 2
das Fluchtstück, -e *flight scene*, 10
der Fluss, ⁻e *river*, Loc 4
folgen *to follow*, 7
folgende *following*, 9
Folgendes *the following*, 7
die Folgezeit, -en *following period*, 9
die Form, -en *form*, 5
der Fortgeschrittene, -n *advanced person*, 4
das Foto, -s *photo*, 3
das Fotoalbum, die Fotoalben *photo album*, 3
das Fotogeschäft, -e *photo store*, 9
die Frage, -n *question*, 1
fragen *to ask*, 9
Französisch *French (school subject)*, 4
Frau *Mrs.*, 1
die Frau, -en *woman*, 3
frei: Wir haben frei. *We are off (out of school).*, 4

die Freiheit, -en *liberty*, 10
freilich *of course*, 9
der Freitag *Friday*, 4
freitags *Fridays*, 6
freiwillig *voluntary*, 7
der Freiwillige, -n *volunteer*, 4
die Freizeit *free time, leisure time*, 2
das Freizeitinteresse *free time interest*, 12
der Freizeitpark, -s *amusement park*, 10
das Freizeitvergnügen, - *enjoyment of leisure time*, 12
die Fremdsprache, -n *foreign language*, 4
die Freude, -n *joy, happiness*, 11
freuen *to be happy, glad*, 7; **Freut mich!** *It's a pleasure!*, 8; Sie freut sich darüber. *She is happy about it.*, 11; wir freuen uns *we're very happy, pleased*, 12
der Freund, -e *friend (male)*, 2; **Freunde besuchen** *to visit friends*, 2
der Freundeskreis, -e *peer group*, 9
die Freundin, -nen *friend (female)*, 1
freundlich *friendly*, 9
frisch *fresh*, 8
fritieren *to fry*, 8
froh *happy*, 11
fröhlich *happy, cheerful*, 11
die Frucht, ⸚e *fruit*, 8
das Fruchteis *ice cream with fruit*, 6
der Frühling *spring* (season), 2; **im Frühling** *in the spring*, 2
das Frühstück *breakfast*, 6
der Fußgänger, - *pedestrian*, 9
führen *to lead*, 12
füllen *to fill*, 12
fünf *five*, 1
fünfundzwanzig *twenty-five*, 3
fünfzehn *fifteen*, 1
fünfzig *fifty*, 3
für *for*, 7
Für wen? *For whom?*, 7
furchtbar *terrible, awful*, 5; **furchtbar gern haben** *to like a lot*, 10
fürs=für das *for the*, 2
der Fuß, ⸚e *foot*, 1; **zu Fuß** *on foot*, 1
der Fußball *soccer*, 2; **Ich spiele Fußball.** *I play soccer.*, 2
der Fußgänger, - *pedestrian*, 9
die Fußgängerzone, -n *pedestrian area*, Loc 7
füttern *to feed*, 7; **die Katze füttern** *to feed the cat*, 7

der Gamsbart, ⸚e *chamois beard*, Loc 7
ganz *really, quite*, 3; *not broken*, 4; *whole*, 9; die ganze Zeit *the whole time*, 12; Ganz einfach! *Quite simple!*, 9; **Ganz klar!** *Of course!*, 4
gänzlich *completely*, 9
die Ganztagsschule, -n *all-day school*, 4
gar (particle), 3; **gar nicht gern** *not to like at all*, 10
die Garantie, -n *guarantee, warranty*, 5
die Garderobe, -n *wardrobe*, 5
der Garten, ⸚ *yard, garden*, 9
der Gast, ⸚e *guest*, 12
die Gastmutter, ⸚ *host mother*, 8
der Gastgeber, - *host*, 12
die Gaudi *fun*, 9
das Gebäude, - *building*, Loc 7
geben *to give*, 11; **er/sie gibt** *he/she gives*, 11; **es gibt ...** *there is /are ...*, 9; **Was gibt es hier zu essen?** *What is there to eat here?*, 9; Was gibt's? *What's up?*, 1
geboren *born*, 4
der Gebrauch, ⸚e *practice*, 10; *use, operation*, 11
gebrauchen *to use*, 8
gebrüht *simmered*, 8
gebucht *booked*, 9
gebunden *bound*, 10
das Geburtsdatum (pl -daten) *date of birth*, 4
die Geburtsstadt, ⸚e *place of birth*, 6
der Geburtstag, -e *birthday*, 11; **Alles Gute zum Geburtstag!** *Best wishes on your birthday!*, 11; **Herzlichen Glückwunsch zum Geburtstag!** *Best wishes on your birthday!*, 11; **Ich habe am ... Geburtstag.** *My birthday is on...*, 11
das Geburtstagsgeschenk, -e *birthday present*, 8
die Geburtstagskarte, -n *birthday card*, 11
der Geburtstagskuchen, - *birthday cake*, 12
das Gedächtnis, -se *memory*, 10
gefährdet *endangered*, 11
gefahren (pp) *driven, gone*, 10
gefährlich *dangerous*, 9
gefallen *to be pleasing, to like*, 5; **Er/Sie/Es gefällt mir.** *I like it.*, 5; **Sie gefallen mir.** *I like them.*, 5
gefettet *oiled*, 12
gefühlvoll *full of feeling*, 10
gefüllt *filled*, 12
gegeben *given, supplied*, 10
die Gegend: in der Gegend von *in the vicinity of*, Loc 10
gegenseitig *reciprocal(ly)*, 5
das Gegenteil, -e *opposite*, 4
gegessen (pp) *eaten*, 9
gehackt *chopped*, 8
gehen *to go*, 2; **Das geht nicht.** *That won't work.*, 7; **Es geht.** *It's okay.*, 6; **nach Hause gehen** *to go home*, 3; Geht er noch? *Is it still working?*, 4; **Wie geht's (denn)?** *How are you?*, 6
gehören (zu) *to belong (to)*, Loc 7

der Geist, -er *ghost*, 10
gekauft (pp) *bought*, 8; **Ich habe Brot gekauft.** *I bought bread.*, 8; **Was hast du gekauft?** *What did you buy?*, 8
geknotet *knotted*, 5
gekocht *cooked*, 12
gelb *yellow*, 4; **in Gelb** *in yellow*, 5
gelten als *to be considered as*, 10
das Geld *money*, 4
gelesen (pp) *read*, 10; **Was hast du gelesen?** *What did you read?*, 10
gemacht (pp) *done*, 10; **Was hast du am Wochenende gemacht?** *What did you do on the weekend?*, 10
gemahlen *ground*, 12
gemalt *painted*, 11
gemeinsam *common*, 11
gemischt *mixed*, 8
das Gemüse *vegetables*, 8; **im Obst- und Gemüseladen** *at the produce store*, 8
der Gemüseladen, ⸚ *produce store*, 8
genau *exact(ly)*, 6; genauer lesen *reading for detail*, 6
genießen *to enjoy*, 6
genug *enough*, 9; **Ich habe genug.** *I have enough.*, 9
geöffnet *open*, 6
gepunktet *polka-dotted*, 12
gerade *just*, 8
geradeaus *straight ahead*, 9; **Fahren Sie geradeaus!** *Drive straight ahead.*, 9
das Gericht, -e *dish* (food), Loc 4; *court*, 10
das Gerichtsdrama, -en *courtroom drama*, 10
gern (machen) *to like (to do)*, 2; **gern haben** *to like*, 4; **Gern geschehen!** *My pleasure!*, 9; **Ja, gern!** *Sure!*, 11; **nicht gern (machen)** *to not like (to do)*, 2; **nicht so gern** *not to like very much*, 2; Siehst du gern Horrorfilme? *Do you like to watch horror movies?*, 10; **besonders gern** *especially like*, 10
gesagt (pp) *said*, 10
gesalzen *salted*, 8
der Gesangunterricht *singing lesson*, 4
das Geschäft, -e: ein Geschäft machen *to make a deal*, 7
geschehen: **Gern geschehen!** *My pleasure!*, 9
das Geschenk, -e *gift*, 11
die Geschenkidee, -n *gift idea*, 11
der Geschenkladen, ⸚ *gift shop*, 11
die Geschenkliste, -n *gift list*, 11
die Geschenkwaren (pl) *gifts*, 9
die Geschichte *history*, 4
geschickt *clever, talented*, 12
das Geschirr (pl) *dishes*, 7; **das Geschirr spülen** *to wash the dishes*, 7

der Geschirrspüler, - *dishwasher*, 12; den Geschirrspüler ausräumen *to unload the dishwasher*, 12

geschlossen *closed*, 10

der Geschmack *taste*, 8

die Geschwister (pl) *brothers and sisters*, 3

gesehen (pp) *seen*, 10; **Was hast du gesehen?** *What did you see?*, 10

gesetzt: unter Druck gesetzt werden *to be put under pressure*, 10

das Gespräch, -e *dialogue, conversation*, 7; *phone call*, 11

die Gesprächsnotiz, -en *message*, 11

gesprochen (pp) *spoken*, 10; **Worüber habt ihr gesprochen?** *What did you (pl) talk about?*, 10; Worüber sprichst du mit deinen Freunden? *What do you talk about with your friends?*, 10

die Geste, -n *gesture*, 7

gestern *yesterday*, 8; **gestern Abend** *yesterday evening*, 8;

gestreift *striped*, 12

gesund *healthy*, 8

das Getränk, -e *beverage*, 11

gewachsen *grown*, 8

gewährleisten *to guarantee*, 4

gewinnen *to win*, 2

das Gewitter, - *thunderstorm*, 7

gewöhnlich *usually*, 11

das Gewürz, -e *spice*, 8

gewürzt *spiced*, 8

gießen *to water*, 7; **die Blumen gießen** *to water the flowers*, 7

die Gitarre, -n *guitar*, 2

Gitarrenklänge *guitar music*, 6

gitterförmig *latticed*, 8

das Glas, ̈ er *glass*, 3; **ein Glas Apfelsaft** *a glass of apple juice*, 3; **ein Glas (Mineral)Wasser** *a glass of (mineral) water*, 3; **ein Glas Tee** *a glass of tea*, 6

die Glatze, -n *bald head*, 3; **eine Glatze haben** *to be bald*, 3

glauben *to believe*, 2; **ich glaube** *I think*, 2; ich glaube, dass ... *I think that...*, 9; Ich glaube schon. *I believe so.*, 7

gleich *equal*, 3; *same*, 10

das Gleis, -e *track*, 6

die Globalisierungsfalle, -n *pitfall of globalization*, 10

die Glocke, -n *bell*, 9

das Glück *luck*, 4; **So ein Glück!** *What luck!*, 4

der Glücksklee *clover* (symbol for good luck), 11

das Glücksschwein, -e *good luck pig* (symbol for good luck), 11

das Gold *gold*, 10

das Golf *golf*, 2

der Grad *degree(s)*, 7; **zwei Grad** *two degrees*, 7; **Wie viel Grad haben wir?** *What's the temperature?*, 7

das Gramm *gram*, 8

grau *gray*, 3; **in Grau** *in gray*, 5

grausam *cruel*, 10

die Grenze, -n *border*, 11

Griechenland (das) *Greece*, 8

die Griechin, -nen *Greek (female)*, 4

der Grill *barbecue*, 9

das Grillfest, -e *BBQ party*, 6

groß *big*, 3

die Größe, -n *size*, 5

die Großeltern (pl) *grandparents*, 3

die Großmutter (Oma), ̈ *grandmother*, 3

der Großvater (Opa), ̈ *grandfather*, 3

grün *green*, 3; **in Grün** *in green*, 5

das Grundstück, -e *piece of land*, 3

grüner *greener*, 8

die Gruppe, -n *group*, 10

der Gruselroman, -e *horror novel*, 10

der Gruß, ̈ e *greetings*; liebe Grüße *(many) kind regards; love*, 1

grüßen: **Grüß dich!** *Hi!*, 1

gucken *to watch*, 2

gültig *valid*, 4

die Gültigkeit *validity*, 6

günstig *advantageous, low-priced*, 4

die Gurke, -n *cucumber*, 8

der Gurkensalat, -e *cucumber salad*, 12

der Gürtel, - *belt*, 5

gut *good*, 4; **Gut!** *Good! Well!*, 6; **Gut! Mach ich!** *Okay, I'll do that!*, 7; **Alles Gute!** *Best wishes!*, 11

der Gutschein, -e *gift certificate*, 11

das Gymnasium, die Gymnasien *(German secondary school)*, 4

das Gyros *gyros*, 9

das Haar, -e *hair*, 3

haben *to have*, 4; **er/sie hat** *he/she has*, 4; **gern haben** *to like*, 4; **Haben Sie das auch in Rot?** *Do you have that also in red?*, 5

das Hackfleisch *ground meat*, 8

der Haferbrei *oatmeal*, 9

das Hähnchen, - *chicken*, 8

halb *half*, 6; **halb (eins, zwei, usw.)** *half past (twelve, one, etc.)*, 6

halb bedeckt *partly cloudy*, 7

der Halbbruder, ̈ *half brother*, 3

halbieren *to halve*, 12

das Halbjahr, -e *half a year*, 4

die Halbschwester, -n *half sister*, 3

die Hälfte, -n *half*, 12

Hallo! *Hi! Hello!*, 1

der Hals, ̈ e *neck*, 8

das Halstuch, ̈ er *scarf*, 11

halt (particle), 6

halten *to hold*, 7

der Hamster, - *hamster*, 7

handvermittelt *operator-assisted*, 11

das Handy, -s *cell phone*, 11

der Handball *handball*, 2

die Harmonielehre, -n *harmonics class*, 4

hart gekocht *hard-boiled*, 12

das Hasenfutter *rabbit food*, 8

hassen *to hate*, 9

hässlich *ugly*, 3

der Hauptbahnhof, ̈ e *main train station*, 4

hauptsächlich *mainly*, 6

die Hauptstadt, ̈ e *capital*, 1

das Hauptwort, -er *noun*, 11

das Haus, ̈ er *house*, 3; zu Hause sein *to be at home*, 6; **nach Hause gehen** *to go home*, 3; **zu Hause helfen** *to help at home*, 7

die Hausarbeit, -en *chores*, 7

die Hausaufgaben (pl) *homework*, 2; **Hausaufgaben machen** *to do homework*, 2

der Haushalt, -e *household*, 7

das Haustier, -e *pet*, 3

die Hauswirtschaft *home economics*, 4

He! *Hey!*, 2

das Heft, -e *notebook*, 4

heiß *hot*, 7

heißen *to be called*, 1; **er heißt** *his name is*, 1; **ich heiße** *my name is*, 1; **sie heißt** *her name is*, 1; **Wie heißt das Mädchen?** *What's the girl's name?*, 1; **Heißt sie …?** *Is her name …?*, 1; **Wie heißt der Junge?** *What's the boy's name?*, 1; **Wie heißt du?** *What's your name?*, 1

heiter *clear*, 7

der Held, -en *hero*, 10

helfen *to help*, 7; **zu Hause helfen** *to help at home*, 7

hell *light*, 5

hellblau *light blue*, 5; **in Hellblau** *in light blue*, 5

hellgrau *light gray*, 5

hellgrün *light green*, 5

das Hemd, -en *shirt*, 5

herausnehmen *to take out*, 12

der Herbst *fall (season)*, 2; **im Herbst** *in the fall*, 2

der Herd, -e *stove*, 12

Herr *Mr.*, 1

das Herz, -en *heart*, 10

das Herz: im Herzen *in the heart of*, Loc, 7

herzhaft *hearty*, 8

herzlich: Herzliche Grüße! *Best regards!*, 1; Herzlich willkommen bei uns! *Welcome to our home!*, 12; **Herzlichen Glückwunsch zum Geburtstag!** *Best wishes on your birthday!*, 11

heute *today*, 4; **heute Morgen** *this morning*, 8; **heute Nachmittag** *this afternoon*, 8; **heute Abend** *tonight, this evening*, 7

die Hexe, -n *witch*, Loc 10

das Hexenwegle *Witches' Walk*, Loc 10

hier *here*, 3; **Hier bei ...** *The...
residence.*, 11; **Hier ist ...** *This is...*,
11; hier vorn *here in front*, 5
hierher *over here*, 11
die Hilfe, -n *help*, 7
hin *to*, 8
hinten *back there*, 4; **da hinten**
there in the back, 4
hinter *after*, 7
der Hintergrund: im Hintergrund *in
the background*, Loc 7
das Hobbybuch, ̈er *hobby book*, 10
hoch *high*, 10
hochbegabt *very talented*, 10
die Hochdruckzone, -n *high-pressure
area*, 7
hoffen *to hope*, 9
der Höhepunkt, -e *highlight*, 9
holen *to get, fetch*, 8
das Holz *wood*, 12; **aus Holz** *out of
wood*, 12
die Holzbauten (pl) *wooden
construction*, Loc 10
hölzern *wooden*, 9
der Honig *honey*, 8
hören *to hear*, 1; **Hör gut zu!**
Listen carefully, p. 6; Hört zu!
Listen!, p. 8; **Musik hören** *to
listen to music*, 2
der Hörer, - *receiver*, 11; **den Hörer
abheben** *to pick up the
receiver*, 11; **den Hörer auflegen**
to hang up (the telephone), 11
der Horrorfilm, -e *horror movie*, 10
die Hose, -n *pants*, 5
das Hotel, -s *hotel*, 9
hübsch *pretty*, 5
das Hufeisen, - *horseshoe*, 11
der Hund, -e *dog*, 3
hundert *a hundred*, 3
der Hunger *hunger*, 9

ich *I*, 2; **Ich auch.** *Me too.*, 2; **Ich
nicht.** *I don't.; Not me.*, 2
die Idee, -n *idea*, 9
die Idylle, -n *idyll*, 10
ihm *to him, for him* (masc, neuter,
dat case), 11
ihn *it, him* (masc, acc case), 5
ihnen *them* (pl, dat case), 12
Ihnen *you* (formal, dat case), 5
ihr *her* (poss adj), 3
ihr *their* (poss adj), 2
ihr *to her, for her* (fem, dat case), 11
ihr *you* (pl, subj pron), 2
im=in dem *in the*, 1; im Fernsehen
on television, 5; **im Frühling** *in
the spring*, 2; **im Herbst** *in the
fall*, 2; **im Januar** *in January*, 7;
im Kino *at the movies*, 10; im
Konzert *at the concert*, 10;

(einmal) im Monat *(once) a
month*, 7; **im Sommer** *in the
summer*, 2; **im Supermarkt** *at the
supermarket*, 8; **im Winter** *in the
winter*, 2
der Imbissstand, ̈e *snack stand*, 6
die Imbissstube, -n *snack bar*, 9
immer *always*, 7
in *in*, 1; **in Blau** *in blue*, 5; **in
Braun** *in brown*, 5; **in Gelb** *in
yellow*, 5; **in Grau** *in gray*, 5; **in
Grün** *in green*, 5; **in Hellblau** *in
light blue*, 5; **in Rot** *in red*, 5; **in
Schwarz** *in black*, 5; **in Weiß** *in
white*, 5
der Individualist, -en *individualist*, 9
die Industrie, -n *industry*, Loc 4
die Informatik *computer science*, 4
die Information, -en *information*, 10
der Ingenieur, -e *engineer*, 10
das Inlandsgespräch, -e *domestic
telephone call*, 11
die Innenstadt, ̈e *downtown*, 5; **in der
Innenstadt** *in the city,
downtown*, 9
ins=in das *in the, into the*, 2; *to the*,
6
die Insel, -n *island*, Loc 4
insgesamt *all together*, 8
das Instrument, -e *instrument*, 2
inszenieren *to direct*, 10
intelligent *intelligent*, 10
die Intelligenz *intelligence*, 10
interessant *interesting*, 2
das Interesse, -n *interest*, 2; **Hast du
andere Interessen?** *Do you have
any other interests?*, 2
interessieren *to interest*, 10
das Internet *Internet*, 2
irgend- *any*, 11
irgendetwas *anything*, 6
irgendwann *anytime*, 11
irgendwelch- *some*, 8
irgendwie *somehow*, 8
der Irrtum, ̈er *error*, 10
ist: er/sie/es ist *he/she/it is*, 1; **sie ist
aus** *she's from*, 1
Italien (das) *Italy*, 3

ja *yes*, 1; **Ja klar!** *Of course!*, 1
die Jacke, -n *jacket*, 5
jäh *sudden*, 10
das Jahr, -e *year*, 1; **Ich bin ... Jahre alt.**
I am...years old., 1
der Januar *January*, 7; **im Januar** *in
January*, 7
die Jeans, - *jeans*, 5
die Jeans-Tasche, -n *denim school bag*,
4
jed- *every*, 5; jeden Abend *every
evening*, 10; **jeden Tag** *every day*, 7

jeder: jeder von euch *each of you*, 8
jederzeit *anytime*, 4
jeglich- *any*, 8; jeglicher Art *every
kind*, 9
jetzt *now*, 1
joggen *to jog*, 12
der Jogging-Anzug, ̈e *jogging suit*, 5
der Joghurt (Jogurt) *yogurt*, 8
das Joghurteis *frozen yogurt*, 8
die Jugend *youth*, 10
der Jugendclub, -s *youth club*, 9
der Jugendliche, -n *young adult*, 7
das Jugendzentrum, die Jugendzentren
youth center, 12
der Juli *July*, 7
jung *young*, 10
der Junge, -n *boy*, 1
der Juni *June*, 7

der Kaffee *coffee*, 8; **eine Tasse Kaffee**
a cup of coffee, 6
der Kaiser, - *emperor*, 6
der Kaiserschmarren *(Austrian and
southern German dish)*, 8
das Kalb, ̈er *veal*, 8
der Kalender, - *calendar*, 11
die Kalorie, -n *calorie*, 8
kalt *cold*, 7
die Kammer, -n *chamber*, 10
der Kampf, ̈e *struggle*, 10
der Kanal, ̈e *canal*, Loc 4
das Kaninchen, - *rabbit*, 7
das Kännchen, - *small (coffee) pot*, 6
die Kanzlei, -en *law office*, 10
das Kapitel, - *chapter*, 1
kaputt *broken*, 3
die Kapuze, -n *hood (of coat)*, 5
die Karte, -n *card*, 2
das Kartenspiel, -e *card game*, 2
die Kartoffel, -n *potato*, 8
der Kartoffelsalat, -e *potato salad*, 12
der Käse, - *cheese*, 8
das Käsebrot, -e *cheese sandwich*, 6
der Käsekuchen, - *cheese cake*, 6
die Kasse, -n *cashier*, 10
die Kassette, -n *cassette*, 4
die Kastagnette, -n *castanet*, 11
der Kasten, ̈ *box, container*, 9;
word box, 10
die Kastenform, -en *bread pan*, 12
die Katze, -n *cat*, 3; **die Katze füttern**
to feed the cat, 7
kaufen *to buy*, 5
das Kaufhaus, ̈er *department store*, 5
die Kavallerie, -n *cavalry*, 10
kegeln *to bowl*, 10
kein *no, none, not any*, 9; **Ich habe
keine Zeit.** *I don't have time.*, 7;
Ich habe keinen Hunger mehr.
I'm not hungry any more., 9;
kein(en) ... mehr *no more...*, 9;

Kein Problem! *No problem!*, 11; **Keine Ahnung!** *I have no idea!*, 9; Nein danke, keinen Kuchen mehr. *No thanks. No more cake.*, 9; **Ich möchte kein(e)(en) ... mehr.** *I don't want another….*, 9

der Keks, -e *cookie*, 3; **ein paar Kekse** *a few cookies*, 3

der Kellner, - *waiter*, 6

kennen *to know, be familiar or acquainted with*, 10

kennen lernen *to get to know*, 12

die Kerze, -n *candle*, 11

das Kilo=Kilogramm, - *kilogram*, 8

das Kind, -er *child*, 8

der Kindergarten ⸚ *kindergarten*, 4

der Kinderhort, -e *day-nursery*, 7

die Kinderkirche *Sunday school*, 8

das Kino, -s *cinema*, 6; im Kino *at the movies*, 10; **ins Kino gehen** *to go to the movies*, 6

die Kinokarte, -n *movie ticket*, 9

das Kinoprogramm, -e *movie guide*, 10

die Kirche, -n *church*, 9

die Kirschtorte, -n *cherry cake*, Loc 10

die Kiwi, -s *kiwi*, 8

die Klammer, -n *parenthesis*, 8

die Klamotten (pl) *casual term for clothes*, 5; **meine Klamotten aufräumen** *to pick up my clothes*, 7

Klar! *Sure!* 2; *Clear!*, 9; Alles klar! *O.K.!*, 10; **Ja, klar!** *Of course!*, 1

die Klasse, -n *grade level*, 4

Klasse! *Great! Terrific!*, 2

die Klassenarbeit, -en *test, exam*, 4

der Klassenkamerad, -en *classmate*, 3

das Klassenzimmer, - *classroom*, p. 8

der Klassiker, - *classicist*, 11

klassisch *classical*, 10

das Klavier, -e *piano*, 2; **Ich spiele Klavier.** *I play the piano.*, 2

die Klavierschule, -n *piano school*, 4

das Kleid, -er *dress*, 5

klein *small*, 3

kleiner *smaller*, 8

die Kleinigkeit, -en *small thing*, 11

klug *clever*, 9

knackig *crispy, firm*, 7

die Knoblauchzehe, -n *garlic clove*, 8

der Knochen, - *bone*, 8

kochen *to cook*, 2

der Kochschinken *baked ham*, 6

kommen *to come*, 1; **er kommt aus** *he's from*, 1; **ich komme** *I come*, 1; **ich komme aus** *I'm from*, 1; **Komm doch mit!** *Why don't you come along?*, 7; Komm mit nach ... *Come along to...*, 1; es kommt ganz darauf an *it really depends*, 12; **sie kommen aus** *they're from*, 1; **sie kommt aus** *she's from*, 1; **Wie komme ich zum (zur) ... ?** *How do I get to...?*, 9; **Wie kommst du zur Schule?** *How do you get to school?*, 1; Wie kommt man dahin? *How do you get there?*, 9

die Komödie, -n *comedy*, 10

der Komponist, -en *composer*, 11

die Konditorei, -en *pastry shop*, 8

die Konjunktion, -en *conjunction*, 8

können *to be able to*, 7; **Kann ich bitte Andrea sprechen?** *Could I please speak with Andrea?*, 11; Kann ich's wirklich? *Can I really do it?*, 1; **Was kann ich für dich tun?** *What can I do for you?*, 7; **Kann ich etwas für dich tun?** *Can I do something for you?*, 7

der Kontakt: Kontakt knüpfen *to establish contact*, 10

das Kontingent, -e *allotment*, 9

das Konzert, -e *concert*, 6; im Konzert *at the concert*, 10; **ins Konzert gehen** *to go to a concert*, 6

der Kopf, ⸚e *head*, 1

der Kopfsalat, -e *head lettuce*, 8

die Kopie, -n *copy, imitation*, 5

der Korb, ⸚e *basket*, 7

kosten *to cost*, 4; **Was kostet ... ?** *How much does...cost?*, 4

köstlich *delicious*, 8

das Kotelett, -s *cutlet*, 8

die Kräuter (pl) *herbs*, 12

der Krautsalat, -e *cabbage salad*, 12

kreativ *creative*, 7

kriegen *to get*, 10

der Kriegsfilm, -e *war movie*, 10

der Krimi, -s *detective movie*, 10; *detective novel*, 10; *crime drama*, 10

der Krug, ⸚e *jug*, 12

die Kruste, -n *crust*, 8

die Küche, -n *kitchen*, 12; **in der Küche** *in the kitchen*, 12

der Kuchen, - *cake*, 3; **ein Stück Kuchen** *a piece of cake*, 3

die Kuckucksuhr, -en *cuckoo clock*, 12

die Kugel, -n *scoop (of ice cream)*, 6

kühl *cool*, 7

kühler *cooler*, 7

der Kühlschrank, ⸚e *refrigerator*, 12

der Kuli, -s *ballpoint pen*, 4

kulinarisch *culinary*, 6

die Kultur, -en *culture*, 10

kulturell *cultural*, 10

der Kümmel *caraway*, 8

die Kunst, ⸚e *art*, 4

der Kunststoff, -e: aus Kunststoff *out of plastic*, 12

der Kurpark, -s *spa park*, 12

kurz *short*, 3

die Kusine, -n *cousin (female)*, 3

lachen *to laugh*, 11

der Laden, ⸚ *store*, 8; **im Obst- und Gemüseladen** *at the produce store*, 8

die Lampe, -n *lamp*, 12

das Land, ⸚er *country*, 3; **auf dem Land** *in the country*, 3

die Landeshauptstadt, ⸚e *state capital*, Loc 4

die Landschaft *environment*, Loc 10

lang *long*, 3

länger *longer*, 7

der Langlauf *cross-country*, 9

langweilig *boring*, 2

lässig *casual*, 5

die Last, -en *burden*, 7; die Last abnehmen *to take away a burden*, 7

das Latein *Latin*, 4

laufen *to run*, 2; Rollschuh laufen *to roller skate*, 9; **Schlittschuh laufen** *to ice skate*, 12

das Leben, - *life*, 10

leben *to live*, 10

die Lebensmittel (pl) *groceries*, 8

die Leber *liver*, 9

der Leberkäs (see p. 257), 9

lecker *tasty, delicious*, 6

das Leder *leather*, 12; **aus Leder** *made of leather*, 12

die Lederjacke, -n *leather jacket*, 5

die Lederhose, -n *leather pants*, Loc 7

legen *to put, lay*, 8

leger *casual*, 5

der Lehrer, - *teacher (male)*, 1

die Lehrerin, -nen *teacher (female)*, 1

leicht *easy*, 10

das Leichtkraftrad, ⸚er *light motorcycle*, 1

Leid: **Es tut mir Leid.** *I'm sorry.*, 9

das Leiden, - *suffering*, 10

leider *unfortunately*, 7; **Ich kann leider nicht.** *Sorry, I can't.*, 7

das Leinen *linen*, 5

der Leistungskurs, -e *accelerated course*, 4

leiten *to manage*, 11

die Lektüre, -n *reading*, 10

lernen *to study, learn*, 8

` **lesen** *to read*, 10; **er/sie liest** *he/she reads*, 10; richtig lesen *to read correctly*, 1

der Leserbrief, -e *letter to the editor*, 9

der Lesetrick, -s *reading trick*, 1

letzt *last*, 8; **letzte Woche** *last week*, 8; **letztes Wochenende** *last weekend*, 8

die Leute (pl) *people*, 9

das Lexikon, die Lexika *dictionary*, 10

das Licht, -er *light*, p. 8

lieb *nice*, 7

die Liebe *love*, 10

liebenswert *lovable*, 10

lieber (mögen) *to prefer*, 10; Ich sehe Komödien lieber. *I like comedies better.*, 10

Liebe(r) ... *Dear...*, 1

der Liebesfilm, -e *romance*, 10

der Liebesroman, -e *romance novel*, 10

der Liebling, -e *favorite*, 10

Lieblings- *favorite*, 4

das Lieblingsbuch, ¨er *favorite book*, 4
das Lieblingsessen, - *favorite food*, 4
der Lieblingsfilm, -e *favorite movie*, 4
das Lieblingsinstrument, -e *favorite instrument*, 4
liebsten: am liebsten *most of all*, 10
das Lied, -er *song*, 10
liegen *to lie, be located*, 1; liegen bleiben *to stay in bed*, 4
lila *purple*, 5
die Limo, -s (Limonade, -n) *lemon drink*, 3
link- *left*, 10; **nach links** *to the left*, 9; auf der linken Seite *on the left (side)*, 9
der Linseneintopf, ¨e *lentil soup*, 9
der Lippenpflege-Stift, -e *lip-care stick*, 11
die Liste, -n *list*, 7
der Liter, - *liter*, 8
locker *loose, loose-fitting*, 5
logisch *logical*, 4
los: Los geht's! *Let's start!*, 1; Was ist los? *What's happening?*, 5
die Lücke, -en *blank, space*, 8
lukullisch *sumptuous*, 6
die Lust: Lust haben *to feel like*, 7
lustig *funny*, 10
lustigste *funniest*, 10

machen *to do*, 2; **Das macht (zusammen) ...** *That comes to...*, 6; **Gut! Mach ich!** *Okay, I'll do that!*, 7; **Machst du Sport?** *Do you play sports?*, 2; Macht nichts! *It doesn't matter!* 4; **die Hausaufgaben machen** *to do homework*, 2
das Mädchen, - *girl*, 1
mähen *to mow*, 7; **den Rasen mähen** *to mow the lawn*, 7
die Mahlzeit, -en *meal*, 8
der Mai *May*, 7; **im Mai** *in May*, 7
der Maibaum, ¨e *maypole*, Loc 7
die Maisstärke *corn starch*, 12
der Majoran *marjoram*, 12
mal *(particle)*, 6; *(short for* **einmal***) once*, 9
malen *to paint*, 2
man *one, you (in general), people*, 1
manchmal *sometimes*, 7
die Mandel, -n *almond*, 12
der Mandelkuchen, - *almond cake*, 12
mangelhaft *unsatisfactory (grade)*, 4
der Mann, ¨er *man*, 3
die Männertracht, -en *local custom for men*, Loc 7
der Mantel, ¨ *coat*, 5

die Maracuja, -s *passion fruit*, 8
die Margarine *margarine*, 12
der Marienkäfer, - *ladybug*, 11
die Mariensäule *St. Mary's Column*, Loc 7
die Mark, - *mark (former German monetary unit)*
das Markenprodukt, -e *trademarked product*, 5
der Markt, ¨e *market*, 6
der Marktplatz, ¨e *market square*, 9
der Marktplatz, ¨e *outdoor market*, 8
die Marmelade, -n *jam, jelly*, 8
der März *March*, 7; **im März** *in March*, 7
der Maschinenbau *machine building industry, mechanical engineering*, Loc 10
die Masse, -n *mass*, 12
die Mathearbeit, -en *math test*, 4
die Mathematik (Mathe) *math*, 4
die Matheprüfung, -en *math exam*, 6
Mau-Mau *(card game)*, 2
die Mauer, -n *wall*, 12
die Maultaschen (pl) *(Southern German dish)*, 9
maurisch *Moorish*, 12
die Maus, ¨e *mouse*, 7
das Meer, -e *ocean*, 6
das Meerschweinchen, - *guinea pig*, 7
das Mehl *flour*, 8
mehr *more*, 2; **Ich habe keinen Hunger mehr.** *I'm not hungry anymore.*, 9
mehr *more*, 8
die Mehrwegflasche, -n *refund bottle*, 7
mein *my*, 3; **meinem Vater** *to, for my father*, 11; **meiner Mutter** *to, for my mother*, 11
meinen: **Meinst du?** *Do you think so?*, 5
die Meinung, -en *opinion*, 2
meisten *most*, 9
meistens *mostly*, 5
die Melone, -n *melon*, 3
der Mensch, -en *person*, 7; Mensch! *Oh man!*, 2
das Messer, - *knife*, 10
der Metzger, - *butcher*, 8; **beim Metzger** *at the butcher's*, 8
die Metzgerei, -en *butcher shop*, 8
mich *me*, 7
die Milch *milk*, 8
mild *mild*, 8
militärisch *military*, 10
die Million, -en *million*, 7
das Mineralwasser *mineral water*, 3
minus *minus*, 3
die Minute, -n *minute*, 8
mir *to me*, 3
miserabel *miserable*, 6
der Mist: **So ein Mist!** *Darn it!*, 2; *That stinks! What a mess!*, 4
mit *with, by*, 1; **mit Brot** *with bread*, 6; **mit dem Auto** *by car*, 1; **mit dem Bus** *by bus*, 1; **mit dem Moped** *by moped*, 1; **mit dem**

Rad *by bike*, 1; **mit der U-Bahn** *by subway*, 1; **mit Senf** *with mustard*, 9; **mit Zitrone** *with lemon*, 6
mitarbeiten (sep) *to work with*, 7
mitgebracht (pp) *brought with*, 12
das Mitglied, -er *member*, 10
die Mithilfe *cooperation*, 7
mitkommen (sep) *to come along*, 7
mitnehmen (sep) *to take with*, 10
der Mitschüler, - *classmate (male)*, 1
die Mitschülerin, -nen *classmate (female)*, 1
mitspielen (sep) *to join in, to cooperate*, 1
der Mittag, -e *noon*, 8
die Mittagspause, -n *midday break*, 9
der Mittagstisch, -e *lunch*, 4
mitteilen *to tell*, 7
die Mitternacht *midnight*, 10
mittler- *middle*, 6
der Mittwoch *Wednesday*, 4; **am Mittwoch** *on Wednesday*, 4
mitverantwortlich *jointly responsible*, 10
die Möbel (pl) *furniture*, 3
möchten *would like to*, 3; **Ich möchte ... sehen.** *I would like to see...*, 5; **Was möchtest du essen?** *What would you like to eat?*, 3; **Ich möchte noch ein(e) (en) ...** *I'd like another....*, 9; **Ich möchte kein(e)(en) ... mehr.** *I don't want another....*, 9
die Mode, -n *fashion*, 10
das Modegeschäft, -e *clothing store*, 5
der Modekenner, - *fashion expert*, 5
modern *modern*, 12
modisch *fashionable*, 5
mogeln *to cheat*, 2
mögen *to like, care for*, 10
möglich *possible*, 4
möglichst ... *as...as possible*, 12
der Moment, -e *moment*, 3; **Einen Moment, bitte!** *Just a minute, please.*, 11; **im Moment gar nichts** *nothing at the moment*, 3
der Monat, -e *month*, 7; **(einmal) im Monat** *(once) a month*, 7
das Monster, - *monster*, 1
der Montag *Monday*, 4; **am Montag** *on Monday*, 4
das Moped, -s *moped*, 1; **mit dem Moped** *by moped*, 1
morgen *tomorrow*, 1
der Morgen, - *morning*, 2; **Guten Morgen!** *Good morning!*, 1; **Morgen!** *Morning!*, 1
die Mühle, -n *mill*, Loc 10
der Müll *trash*, 7; **den Müll sortieren** *to sort the trash*, 7
der Mülleimer, - *trash can*, 12
die Münchner (pl) *residents of Munich*, 9
mündlich *oral*, 4
die Münze, -n *coin*, 11; **Münzen**

einstecken *to insert coins*, 11
das Münztelefon, -e *coin phone*, 11
das Murmeltier, -e *groundhog*, 10
das Museum, die Museen *museum*, 9
die Musik *music*, 2; **klassische Musik** *classical music*, 10; **Musik hören** *to listen to music*, 2
die Musikstätte, -n *music hall*, Loc 7
das Musikprogramm, -e *music program*, 10
das Müsli *muesli*, 8
müssen *to have to*, 7; **ich muss** *I have to*, 7
die Mutter, ∵ *mother*, 3
der Muttertag *Mother's Day*, 11; **Alles Gute zum Muttertag!** *Happy Mother's Day!*, 11
die Mutti *mom*, 3
die Mütze, -n *cap*, 10

Na? *Well?*, 2; Na ja. *Oh well*, 5; na dann *well then*, 9; Na klar! *Of course!*, 5
nach *after*, 2; **nach der Schule** *after school*, 2; **nach links** *to the left*, 9; **nach rechts** *to the right*, 9; **nach der Pause** *after the break*, 4; **nach Hause gehen** *to go home*, 3
die Nachbarschaft *neighborhood*, 8
nacherzählen *to retell*, 3
nachfolgend- *following*, 7
nachher *later, afterwards*, 3
die Nachhilfe *tutoring*, 7
die Nachhilfestunde, -n *tutoring lesson*, 7
der Nachmittag, -e *afternoon*, 2; **am Nachmittag** *in the afternoon*, 2
nächste *next*, 6; **die nächste Straße** *the next street*, 9; **nächste Woche** *next week*, 11
die Nacht, ∵e *night*, 6
die Nähe: **in der Nähe** *nearby*, 3
der Name, -n *name*, 1
der Namenstag, -e *name day*, 11
närrisch *foolish*, 9
nass *wet*, 7
Natürlich! *Certainly!*, 11
der Nebensatz, ∵e *clause*, 8
nehmen *to take*, 5; **er/sie nimmt** *he/she takes*, 5; **ich nehme ...** *I'll take...*, 5; Nehmt ein Stück Papier! *Take out a piece of paper.*, p. 8
nein *no*, 1
nennen *to name*, 5
nett *nice*, 2
neu *new*, 3
neuerdings *lately*, 1
neun *nine*, 1
neunundzwanzig *twenty-nine*, 3
neunzehn *nineteen*, 1
neunzig *ninety*, 3

neuste *newest*, 10
nicht *not*, 2; **Nicht besonders.** *Not really.*, 6; **nicht gern haben** *to dislike*, 4; **nicht schlecht** *not bad*, 4; **Ich nicht.** *I don't.*, 2; **Nicht zu lang?** *Not too long?*, 5
nichts *nothing*, 2; **Nichts, danke!** *Nothing, thank you!*, 3; **Nichts mehr, danke!** *Nothing else, thanks!*, 9
nie *never*, 7
niederländisch *Dutch*, 11
noch *yet, still*, 2; **Haben Sie noch einen Wunsch?** *Would you like anything else?*, 8; **Ich brauche noch ...** *I also need...*, 8; **Möchtest du noch etwas?** *Would you like something else?*, 9; **noch ein** *more, another*, 9; **Noch einen Saft?** *Another glass of juice?*, 9; **Noch etwas?** *Anything else?*, 9; **Ich möchte noch ein(e)(en) ...** *I'd like another...*, 9
noch einmal *once again*, 10
nördlich (von) *north (of)*, Loc 10
normalerweise *usually*, 10
Notizen machen *to take notes*, 8
die Note, -n *grade*, 4
das Notizbuch, ∵er *notebook*, 1
der November *November*, 7; **im November** *in November*, 7
die Nudelsuppe, -n *noodle soup*, 6
null *zero*, 1
die Nummer, -n *number*, 1
nummeriert *numbered*, 7
nun *now*, 6
nur *only*, 4
nützlich *useful*, 11

ob *whether* (conj), 9
oben *upstairs; up there*, 3
oberflächlich *superficial*, 10
obig *above*, 11
das Obst *fruit*, 3
der Obst- und Gemüseladen, ∵ *fresh produce store*, 8; **im Obst- und Gemüseladen** *at the produce store*, 8
der Obstkuchen, - *fruit cake*, 8
der Obstsalat, -e *fruit salad*, 8
obwohl *although* (conj), 7
oder *or*, 1
der Ofen, ∵ *oven*, 12
öffentlich *public*, 9
öffnen: Öffnet eure Bücher auf Seite ... ! *Open your books to page...*, p. 8
oft *often*, 2
ohne *without*, 5
Oje! *Oh no!*, 6
der Oktober *October*, 7; **im Oktober** *in October*, 7

das Öl, -e *oil*, 12
die Oma, -s *grandmother*, 3
der Onkel, - *uncle*, 3
der Opa, -s *grandfather*, 3
die Oper, -n *opera*, 10
die Optik *optics*, Loc 10
die Orange, -n *orange*, 3
der Orangensaft *orange juice*, 3
das Orchester, - *orchestra*, 4
ordnen *to order, put in the right sequence*, 7
Ordnung: in Ordnung, *O.K.*, 11
organisieren *to organize*, 11
die Originalfassung, -en *original version*, 10
der Ort, -e *place, location*, 9
der Ort, -e *site*, 9
das Ortsgespräch, -e *local call*, 11
das Optikunternehmen *optical industry*, Loc 10
das Ostern *Easter*, 11; **Frohe Ostern!** *Happy Easter!*, 11
Österreich (das) *Austria*, 1
österreichisch *Austrian* (adj), 9

das Paar, -e *pair*, 5; **paar: ein paar** *a few*, 3
das Päckchen, - *packet*, 12
das Paddel, - *paddle*, 12
die Pailletten (pl) *beads*, 5
das Papier *paper*, p. 8
der Paprika *bell pepper, paprika*, 8
das Parfüm, -e *perfume*, 11
der Park, -s *park*, 12; **in den Park gehen** *to go to the park*, 12
das Partizip *past participle*, 10
der Partner, - *partner (male)*, p. 7
die Partnerin, -nen *partner (female)*, 6
die Party, -s *party*, 11
der Passant, -en *passerby*, 9
passen *to fit*, 5; **der Rock passt prima!** *The skirt fits great!*, 5; Was passt zusammen? *What goes together?*, 1; aufpassen: Passt auf! *Pay attention!*, p. 8; **Pass auf!** *Watch out!*, 6
passend- *suitable*, 7
passen zu *to go with*, 7
passieren: Was passiert hier? *What's happening here?*, 1
die Pastellfarben (pl) *pastel colors*, 5
der Patient, -en *patient*, 10
die Pause, -n *break*, 4; **nach der Pause** *after the break*, 4
das Pech *bad luck*, 4; **So ein Pech!** *Bad luck!*, 4
die Perle, -n *bead*, 5
die Person, -en *person*, 3
persönlich *personally*, 11
der Pfadfinder, - *(similar to Boy Scout)*, 6

die Pfarrkirche, -n *parish church,* 9
Pfd.=Pfund (das) *pound,* 8
der Pfeffer *pepper,* 12
der Pfennig, - (smallest unit of the former German currency; 1/100 of a mark)
die Pflanze, -n *plant,* 11
die Pflaume, -n *plum,* 8
pflegen *to do regularly,* 9
die Pflicht, -en *duty,* 7
der Pflichtunterricht *mandatory class,* 4
das Pfund, - (Pfd.) *pound,* 8
phantasievoll *imaginative,* 10
phantastisch *fantastic,* 3
Physik (die) *physics,* 4
die Physikerin, -nen *physicist(f),* 4
pikant *spicy,* 8
der Pilz, -e *mushroom,* 6
die Pizza, -s *pizza,* 6
der Plan, ⸚e *plan,* 6
planen *to plan,* 6
die Planung, -en *planning,* 10
das Plastik *plastic,* 7
der Platz, ⸚e *place, spot,* 1; **am ...platz** *on ... Square,* 9; **bis zum ...platz** *until you get to ... Square,* 9
der Platz *space,* 8
der Pokalsieg, -e *victory,* 9
die Politik *politics,* 10
die Pommes frites, - *French fries,* 9
populär *popular,* 11
populärste *most popular,* 11
das Portemonnaie, -s *wallet,* 8
die Portion, -en *portion,* 12
die Post *post office,* 9
das Poster, - *poster,* 11
die Postkarte, -n *postcard,* 1
die Praline, -n *fancy chocolate,* 11
der Präsident, -en *president,* 9
der Preis, -e *price,* 4
das Preisplakat, -e *poster with prices,* 8
preiswert *reasonably priced,* 4; **Das ist preiswert.** *That's a bargain.,* 4
Prima! *Great!* 1; Prima Idee! *Great idea!,* 7
die Prise, -n: eine Prise Salz *a pinch of salt,* 12
privat *private,* 10
die Probestunde, -en *practice hour,* 4
probieren *to try* (with foods), 9
das Problem, -e *problem,* 8
der Produzent, -en *producer,* 10
das Pronomen, - *pronoun,* 8
Prost! *Cheers!,* 12
das Prozent, - *percent,* 5
die Prüfungsvorbereitung, -en *preparation for a test,* 7
Pst! *Ssh!,* 12
der Pulli, -s (Pullover, -) *pullover, sweater,* 5
pur *pure,* 8
das Putenschnitzel, - *turkey cutlets,* 8
putzen *to clean,* 7; **die Fenster putzen** *to wash the windows,* 7
das Putzmittel, - *cleaning agent,* 7

Q

der Quadratkilometer, - *square kilometer,* 1
qualifiziert *qualified; competent,* 4
die Qualität *quality,* 5
der Quark (milk product), 8
Quatsch! *Nonsense!,* 7

R

die Rache *revenge,* 10
das Rad, ⸚er *bike,* 1; *wheel,* 10; **mit dem Rad** *by bike,* 1; Wir fahren Rad. *We're riding bikes.,* 10
radeln *to ride a bike,* 7
Rad fahren *to ride a bike,* 2
der Radiergummi, -s *eraser,* 4
das Radieschen, - *radish,* 8
das Radio, -s *radio,* 11
der Radio-Meteorologe, -n *meteorologist,* 11
der Rand, ⸚er *edge,* 7
der Rasen, - *lawn,* 7; **den Rasen mähen** *to mow the lawn,* 7
raten: Rate! *Guess!,* 2; Rate mal! *Guess!,* 1
das Rathaus, ⸚er *city hall,* 9
der Rathausturm, ⸚e *City Hall Tower,* Loc 7
die Raumfahrtindustrie *space industry,* Loc 7
das Rautenmuster *diamond pattern,* Loc 7
die Realschule, -n *secondary school,* 4
der Rechner, - *calculator,* 4
das Recht: Du hast Recht! *You're right!,* 4
rechts: nach rechts *to the right,* 9
die Rechtschreibung *spelling,* 8
reden *to talk,* 5
reduziert *reduced,* 5
das Regal, -e *bookcase,* 3
die Regalreihe, -n *row of shelves,* 11
die Regel, -n *rule,* 2
regelmäßig *regularly,* 7
der Regen *rain,* 7
die Regie *stage-direction* (of a film), 10
regnen: Es regnet. *It's raining.,* 7
regnerisch *rainy,* 7
das Reich, -e *empire,* 6
reich *rich,* 8
die Reihe, -n *row,* 10
der Reim, -e *rhyme,* 11
rein *pure,* 6
das Reisebüro, -s *travel agency,* 9
reiten *to ride horseback,* 2
das Reitturnier, -e *riding tournament,* 12

reizvoll *charming,* Loc 10
die Religion, -en *religion* (school subject), 4
das Relikt, -e *relic,* 10
das Restaurant, -s *restaurant,* 9
der Restbetrag *change,* 11
richtig *correct(ly),* 1; *right,* 10
die Richtung, -en *direction,* 7
riechen *to smell,* 8
Riesen- *gigantic,* 8
der Rock, ⸚e *skirt,* 5
die Rolle, -n *role,* 9
der Rollschuh, -e *roller skate,* 2; Rollschuh laufen *to roller-skate,* 9; ich laufe Rollschuh *I roller-skate,* 9
die Rollschuhbahn, -en *roller-skating course,* 9
der Roman, -e *novel,* 10
der Rosenkohl *Brussels sprouts,* 9
die Rosine, -n *raisin,* 8
die Rostbratwurst, ⸚e *roasted sausage,* 6
rot *red,* 3; **in Rot** *in red,* 5
die Rückgabe *refund,* 11
Ruhe! *Quiet!,* 4
der Ruhetag, -e *day of rest,* 6
der Rührteig, -e *batter,* 12
rund *round,* 12
runter *down,* 3

S

das Sachbuch, ⸚er *non-fiction book,* 10
die Sache, -n *thing, item,* 5
der Saft, ⸚e *juice,* 3
saftig *juicy,* 6
der Saftstand, ⸚e *juice stand,* 9
sagen *to say,* 2; **Sag, ...** *Say...,* 1; **Sag mal ...** *Say...,* 2; so sagt man das *here's how you say it,* 1; Was sagst du dazu? *What do you say to that?,* 9; **Was sagt der Wetterbericht?** *What does the weather report say?,* 7; Wie sagt man ... auf Deutsch? *How do you say...in German?,* p. 8
sagenhaft *great,* 6
sagte *said,* 10
die Sahne *cream,* 8
die Saison, -s *season,* 5
der Salat, -e *lettuce,* 8; *salad,* 12
das Salz *salt,* 12
sammeln *to collect,* 2; **Comics sammeln** *to collect comics,* 2; **Briefmarken sammeln** *to collect stamps,* 2
der Samstag *Saturday,* 4; **am Samstag** *on Saturdays,* 4
der Sänger, - *singer (male),* 10
die Sängerin, -nen *singer (female),* 10
der Satz, ⸚e *sentence,* 1; Sätze bauen *to form sentences,* 1

sauber *clean*, Loc 7
sauber machen *to clean*, 12
sauberer *cleaner*, 7
sauer *annoyed*, 2
säuerlich *sour*, 12
saugen: Staub saugen *to vacuum*, 7
das **Schach** *chess*, 2
Schade! *Too bad!*, 4
die Schale, -n *serving dish*, 8
schätzen *to value*, 10
schauen *to look*, 2; **Schau!** *Look!*, 4; Schau mal! *Take a look!*, 1; **Schauen Sie!** (formal) *Look!*, 4; Schaut auf die Tafel! *Look at the board!*, 12; **Fernsehen schauen** *to watch television*, 2
der Schauer, - *(rain) shower*, 7
das Schaufenster, - *store window*, 12
der **Schauspieler**, - *actor*, 10
die **Schauspielerin, -nen** *actress*, 10
die Scheibe, -n *slice*, 8
scheinbar *seeming*, 10
scheinen *to shine*, 7; **Die Sonne scheint.** *The sun is shining.*, 7
schenken *to give (a gift)*, 11; **Schenkst du deinem Vater einen Kalender zum Geburtstag?** *Are you giving your father a calendar for his birthday?*, 11; **Was schenkst du deiner Mutter?** *What are you giving your mother?*, 11
scheußlich *hideous*, 5
schick, chic *smart (looking)*, 5
schimpfen *to complain*, 7
der Schinken *ham*, 6
das Schlagzeug *drums; percussion*, 2
schlecht *bad(ly)*, 4
der Schlittschuh, -e *ice skate*, 12; **Schlittschuh laufen** *to ice-skate*, 12
das Schloss, ̈er *castle*, Loc 1
schmalzig *corny, mushy*, 10
schmecken: **Schmeckt's?** *Does it taste good?*, 6; **Wie schmeckt's?** *How does it taste?*, 6
der **Schmuck** *jewelry*, 11
der **Schnee** *snow*, 7
schneiden *to cut*, 8
schneien: **Es schneit.** *It's snowing.*, 7
schnell *fast*, 7
das Schnitzel, - *cutlet*, 9
die Schokolade, -n *chocolate*, 11
das Schokoladeneis *chocolate ice cream*, 6
die Schokoladenstücke (pl) *pieces of chocolate*, 12
schon *already*, 1; schon bekannt *already known*, 2; Schon gut! *That's okay!*, 1
schon: schon lange nicht *not in a long time*, 8
schön *pretty, beautiful*, 3
schöner *more beautiful, prettier*, 5
schönste *most beautiful*, 5
der Schornsteinfeger, - *chimney sweep*, 11

der **Schrank**, ̈e *cabinet*, 3
schreiben *to write*, 2; richtig schreiben *to write correctly*, 1; schreib ... ab *copy*, 8 Schreibt euren Namen! *Write your names.*, p. 8; Schreib ... auf! *Write down...!*, 12 schreib ...um *rewrite*, 8
der **Schreibtisch, -e** *desk*, 3
das Schreibwarengeschäft, -e *stationery store*, 11
der Schreibwarenladen, ̈ *stationery store*, 4
schriftlich *written*, 4
der Schritt, -e *step*, 10; auf Schritt und Tritt *all the time*, 10
die **Schule, -n** *school*, 4; **nach der Schule** *after school*, 2; **Wie kommst du zur Schule?** *How do you get to school?*, 1
der Schüler, - *pupil, student (male)*, 3
der Schülerausweis, -e *student I.D.*, 4
die Schülergruppe, -n *group of students*, 9
der Schulhof, ̈e *schoolyard*, 4
das Schuljahr, -e *school year*, 4
die Schulklasse, -n *class, grade*, 1
die **Schulsachen** (pl) *school supplies*, 4
die **Schultasche, -n** *schoolbag*, 4
die Schulter, -n *shoulder*, 8
der Schulverbund, ̈e *school administration*, 4
der Schulzweig, -e *school branch*, 4
die Schüssel, -n *bowl*, 12
der Schutz *protection*, 11
der Schutzumschlag, ̈e *dust jacket (on a book)*, 10
schwach *weak*, 7
schwarz *black*, 3; **in Schwarz** *in black*, 5
der Schwarzwald *Black Forest*, Loc 10
das Schwein, -e *pig*, 8
der Schweinebraten, - *pork roast*, 8
das Schweineschnitzel, - *pork cutlet*, 9
die Schweinshaxe, -n *pork shank*, Loc 7
das Schweinswürstel, - *little pork sausage*, 12
schwer *difficult, hard*, 11
die **Schwester, -n** *sister*, 3
das **Schwimmbad**, ̈er *swimming pool*, 6; **ins Schwimmbad gehen** *to go to the (swimming) pool*, 6
schwimmen *to swim*, 2
der **Sciencefictionfilm, -e** *science fiction movie*, 10
der **Sciencefictionroman, -e** *science fiction novel*, 10
sechs *six*, 1
sechsundzwanzig *twenty-six*, 3
sechzehn *sixteen*, 1
sechzig *sixty*, 3
der See, -n *lake*, Loc 4
segeln *to go sailing*, 2
sehen *to see*, 10; Am liebsten sehe ich Krimis. *I like detective movies the best.*, 10; **er/sie sieht** *he/she sees*, 10; **einen Film sehen** *to see a movie*, 6

die Sehenswürdigkeit, -en *popular sight*, 9
sehenswert *worth seeing*, 9
sehr *very*, 2; **Sehr gut!** *Very well!*, 6
seid: ihr seid *you (pl) are*, 1
die **Seide, -n** *silk*, 12; **aus Seide** *made of silk*, 12
sein *to be*, 1; **er ist** *he is*, 1; **er ist aus** *he's from*, 1; **ich bin aus** *I am from*, 1; **sie sind** *they are*, 1; **sie sind aus** *they're from*, 1; **du bist** *you are*, 1
sein *his*, 3
seit *since, for*, 10
die Seite, -n *page*, 6; *side*, 9; auf der rechten Seite *on the right (hand) side*, 9
selber *myself*, 7
selbst *yourself*, 7
das Selbstgemachte *homemade item*, 11
selten *seldom*, 7
die **Semmel, -n** *roll*, 8
der **Senf** *mustard*, 6; **mit Senf** *with mustard*, 9
sensationell *sensational*, 10
separat *separate*, 7
der **September** *September*, 7
der **Sessel**, - *armchair*, 12
setzen *to sit down*, 6; Setzt euch! *Sit down!*, p. 8
setzen (sich) *to sit*, 9
setzen: setz ...ein *insert*, 8
die **Shorts** *pair of shorts*, 5
sich *oneself*, 5
Sicher! *Certainly!*, 3; **Ich bin nicht sicher.** *I'm not sure.*, 5
sichern *to secure*, 9
sie *she*, 2
sie (pl) *they*, 2
Sie *you* (formal), 2
sie *it* (with objects), 3
sie (pl) *they* (with objects), 3; *them* (with objects), 5
sieben *seven*, 1
siebenundzwanzig *twenty-seven*, 3
siebzehn *seventeen*, 1
siebzig *seventy*, 3
sind: sie sind *they are*, 1; **Sie** (formal) **sind** *you are*, 1; **wir sind** *we are*, 1
singen *to sing*, 10
sinnvoll *meaningful*, 11
die Sitte, -n *custom*, 10
der Sitz, -e *location*, Loc 7
sitzen *to be sitting*, 10
Skat (German card game), 2
Ski laufen *to ski*, 2
skurrilste *most ludicrous*, 10
so *so, well, then*, 2; so groß wie *as big as*, 6; **so lala** *so so*, 6; so oft wie möglich *as often as possible*, 10; so sagt man das *here's how you say it*, 1
sobald *as soon (as)*, 10
die **Socke, -n** *sock*, 5
das **Sofa, -s** *sofa*, 12

der Sohn, ⸚e *son*, 10
  sollen *should, to be supposed to*, 8
der Sommer *summer*, 2; **im Sommer** *in the summer*, 2
  sommerleicht *summery (clothing)*, 5
das Sonderangebot, -e *sale*, 4
  sondern *but*, 5
der Sonderpreis, -e *special price*, 6
die Sonne *sun*, 7
  sonnig *sunny*, 7
der Sonntag *Sunday*, 4
  sonntags *Sundays*, 8
  sonst *otherwise*, 2; **ansonsten** *otherwise*, 11; **Sonst noch etwas?** *Anything else?*, 8
die Sorge, -n *worry*, 8
  sorgen *to care (for), to take care of*, 6
  sorgen (sich) *to worry*, 10
  sortieren *to sort*, 7; **den Müll sortieren** *to sort the trash*, 7
  sowie *as well as*, Loc 7
  sowieso *anyway*, 5
die Sozialkunde *social studies*, 4
die Spalte, -n *column*, 10
  Spanien (das) *Spain*, 8
  Spanisch *Spanish* (class), 4; (language), 10
  spannend *exciting, thrilling*, 10
der Spargel *asparagus*, 8
  sparsam *thrifty*, 7
der Spaß *fun*, 2; **Hat es Spaß gemacht?** *Was it fun?*, 10; **(Tennis) macht keinen Spaß.** *(Tennis) is no fun.*, 2; **(Tennis) macht Spaß.** *(Tennis) is fun.*, 2; **Viel Spaß!** *Have fun!*, 9
  spät *late*, 6; **Wie spät ist es?** *What time is it?*, 6
  später *later*, 2
das Spätprogramm, -e *late show*, 10
das Spatzenbrett, -er (cutting board to make **Spätzle**), 12
die Spätzle (pl) (see p. 338), 12
der Speck *bacon*, 12
die Speisekarte, -n *menu*, 6
  spektakulärste *most spectacular*, 10
die Spezialität, -en *specialty*, 9
das Spiel, -e *game*, 10
  spielen *to play*, 2; **Ich spiele Fußball.** *I play soccer.*, 2; **Ich spiele Klavier.** *I play the piano.*, 2; **Spielst du ein Instrument?** *Do you play an instrument?*, 2
der Spieler, - *player*, 12
der Spießbraten, - *roast*, 6
der Spinat *spinach*, 9
  Spitze! *Super!*, 2
die Spitzenqualität *top quality*, 8
  sponsern *to sponsor*, 10
  spontan *spontaneous(ly)*, 9
der Sport *sports*, 2; *physical education*, 4; **Machst du Sport?** *Do you play sports?*, 2
die Sportanlage, -n *sports arena*, Loc 7
die Sportart, -en *type of sport*, 9

das Sportgymnasium, -ien *secondary school with stress on sports*, 4
die Sporthalle, -n *indoor gym*, 6
  sportlich *sporty*, 5
die Sportmode *sportswear*, 9
  spottbillig *dirt-cheap*, 11
die Sprache, -n *language*, 5
  sprechen: sprechen über *to talk about, discuss*, 10; **er/sie spricht über** *he/she talks about*, 10; **Kann ich bitte Andrea sprechen?** *Could I please speak with Andrea?*, 11
  sprengen *to blow up*, 9
das Spülbecken, - *sink*, 12
  spülen *to wash*, 7; **das Geschirr spülen** *to wash the dishes*, 7
die Spülmaschine, -n *dishwasher*, 12; **die Spülmaschine ausräumen** *to unload the dishwasher*, 12
  staatlich anerkannt *state-recognized*, 4
die Stadtkarte, -n *city map*, 9
die Stadt, ⸚e *city*, 9; **in der Stadt** *in the city*, 3; **in die Stadt fahren** *to go downtown (by vehicle)*, 11; **in die Stadt gehen** *to go downtown*, 6
die Stadtfahne, -n *city flag*, Loc 7
das Stadtmuseum *city museum*, 9
der Stadtplan, ⸚e *city map*, 9
der Stadtteil, -e *part of the city*, 9
der Standort, -e *location*, 12
  stark *great, awesome*, 5
  stattfinden: findet statt *takes place*, Loc 7
  stattgefunden (pp) *took place*, Loc 7
der Staub *dust*, 7; **Staub saugen** *to vacuum*, 7
  stehen: Steht auf! *Stand up!*, p. 8; **Wie steht's mit dir?** *How about you?*, 10
  stehen (vor) *to stand (in front of)*, 9
der Stehimbiss, -e *fast-food stand*, 9
  stellen *to put*, 10
  Stellung beziehen *move into a position*, 10
die Stereoanlage, -n *stereo*, 3
der Stiefbruder, ⸚ *stepbrother*, 3
der Stiefel, - *boot*, 5
die Stiefmutter, ⸚ *stepmother*, 3
die Stiefschwester, -n *stepsister*, 3
der Stiefvater, ⸚ *stepfather*, 3
der Stil, -e *style*, 10
  stimmen *to be correct*, 3; **Stimmt (schon)!** *Keep the change.*, 6; **Stimmt!** *That's right! True!*, 2; **Stimmt nicht!** *Not true!; False!*, 2
  stimmungsvoll *full of atmosphere*, 6
das Stirnband, ⸚er *headband*, 5
das Stockwerk, -e *floor*, 9
die Straße, -n *street*, 9; **auf der Straße** *on the street*, 9; **bis zur ...straße** *until you get to ... Street*, 9; **die erste (zweite, dritte) Straße** *the first (second, third) street*, 9; **in der ...straße** *on ... Street*, 3

das Straßenlokal, -e *street restaurant*, Loc 7
das Streichorchester, - *string-orchestra*, 6
der Streifen, - *stripe*, 5
  streng *strict*, 7
das Strickkleid, -er *knit dress*, 5
der Strumpf, ⸚e *stocking*, 5
das Stück, -e *piece*, p. 8; **ein Stück Kuchen** *a piece of cake*, 3
das Stückchen, - *small piece*, 8
das Studium, die Studien *study*, 4
die Stufe, -n *level*, 1
der Stuhl, ⸚e *chair*, 3
die Stunde, -n *hour*, 9
der Stundenplan, ⸚e *class schedule*, 4
  suchen *to look for, search for*, 5; **ich suche ...** *I'm looking for...*, 5
der Süden *south*, 7
  super *super*, 2
der Supermarkt, ⸚e *supermarket*, 8; **im Supermarkt** *at the supermarket*, 8
  surfen *to surf*, 2
  süß *sweet*, 8
die Süßigkeit, -en *sweets*, 11
die Süßspeise, -n *dessert*, 9
das Süßwarengeschäft, -e *candy store*, 11
die Szene, -n *scene*, 9

die Tafel, -n *(chalk)board*, p. 8; **Geht an die Tafel!** *Go to the board*, p. 8
der Tag, -e *day*, 2; **eines Tages** *one day*, 10; **Guten Tag!** *Hello!*, 1; **Tag!** *Hello!*, 1; **jeden Tag** *every day*, 7; **täglich** *daily*, Loc 7
der Tagesverlauf *duration of the day*, 7
  täglich *daily*, 10
die Tante, -n *aunt*, 3
  tanzen *to dance*, 2; **tanzen gehen** *to go dancing*, 6
das Taschengeld *pocket money*, 7
der Taschenrechner, - *pocket calculator*, 4
die Tasse, -n *cup*, 3; **eine Tasse Kaffee** *a cup of coffee*, 6
die Taucherausrüstung, -en *scuba gear*, 11
  tauschen *to switch, trade*, 9; **Tauscht die Rollen aus!** *Switch roles.*, 8
die Technik *technology*, 4
der Tee *tea*, 3; **ein Glas Tee** *a (glass) cup of tea*, 6, **eine Tasse Tee** *a cup of tea*, 3
der Teelöffel (TL) *teaspoon*, 8
der Teig *dough*, 8
der Teil, -e *part*, 9

teilweise *partly,* 12
das Telefon, -e *telephone,* 11
    telefonieren *to call,* 11
die Telefonkarte, -n *phone card,* 11
die Telefonnummer, -n *telephone number,* 11
die Telefonzelle, -n *telephone booth,* 11
das Telegramm, -e *telegram,* 11
der Teller, - *plate,* 11
der Temperaturanstieg, -e *rise of temperature,* 7
    Tennis *tennis,* 2
der Teppich, -e *carpet,* 12
der Termin, -e *appointment,* 9
    teuer *expensive,* 4
der Teufel, - *devil,* 10
der Text, -e *text,* 12
das Theater, - *theater,* 9; ins Theater gehen *to go to the theater,* 12
das Theaterstück, -e *(stage) play,* 10
das Thema, die Themen *topic,* 10
    Thüringen (das) *Thuringia,* 1
der Thymian *thyme,* 12
der Tibeter, - *Tibetan,* 10
der Tiefstwert, -e *minimum value,* 7
das Tier, -e *animal,* 7
die Tierschutzorganization, -en *organization that protects animals,* 11
der Tisch, -e *table,* 7; **den Tisch abräumen** *to clear the table,* 7; **den Tisch decken** *to set the table,* 7
das Tischtennis *table tennis,* 2
der Titel, - *title,* 10
    Tja ... *Hm...,* 2
die Tochter, ⸚ *daughter,* 10
    tödlich *deadly,* 10
die Toilette, -n *toilet,* 12
    toll *great, terrific,* 2; **Ich finde es toll!** *I think it's great!,* 9
die Tomate, -n *tomato,* 8
das Tor, -e *gate,* 12
die Torte, -n *layer cake,* 8
der Tote, -n *deceased person,* 10
die Touristenattraktion *tourist attraction,* Loc 10
die Tracht, -en *local costume,* Loc 7
    traditionsreich *rich in tradition,* Loc 10
das Training *training,* 1
die Traube, -n *grape,* 8
der Traumjob, -s *dream job,* 10
    traurig *sad,* 10
    traurigste *saddest,* 10
der Treff *meeting place,* 10
    treffen *to meet,* 9
der Treffpunkt, -e *meeting place,* 6
    treiben: Ich treibe Sport. *I do sports.,* 9
    treu *loyal,* 10
der Treuhänder, - *trustee,* 10
der Trimm-dich-Pfad, -e *fitness trail,* 2
    trinken *to drink,* 3
    trocken *dry,* 7
die Trompete, -n *trumpet,* 2

der Tropfen, - *drop,* 12
    trotzdem *nevertheless,* 5; *in spite of it,* 7
    trüb *overcast,* 7
    Tschau! *Bye! So long!,* 1
    Tschüs! *Bye! So long!,* 1
das T-Shirt, -s *T-shirt,* 5
    tun *to do,* 7; **Es tut mir Leid.** *I'm sorry.,* 9
die Tür, -en *door,* p. 8
    turbulent *turbulent,* 10
die Türkei *Turkey,* 1
der Turnschuh, -e *sneaker, athletic shoe,* 5
    tust: du tust *you do,* 9
die Tüte, -n *bag,* 5
    typisch *typical,* Loc 7

die U-Bahn=Untergrundbahn *subway,* 1; **mit der U-Bahn** *by subway,* 1
die U-Bahnstation, -en *subway station,* 9
    üben *to practice,* p. 9
    über *about,* 4
    überall *all over the place,* Loc 7
    überhaupt: überhaupt nicht *not at all,* 5; **überhaupt nicht gern** *strongly dislike,* 10
    überließ *left (to someone else),* 10
    überquellen *to overflow,* 9
die Überraschung, -en *surprise,* 12
die Übersetzung, -en *translation,* 11
    übertreffen *to outdo, surpass,* 5
    übertrieben (pp) *exaggerated,* 11
    überwachen *to supervise,* 4
    übrigens *by the way,* 3
die Übung, -en *exercise,* 11
    Uhr *o'clock,* 1; **um 8 Uhr** *at 8 o'clock,* 4; **um ein Uhr** *at one o'clock,* 6; **Wie viel Uhr ist es?** *What time is it?,* 6
die Uhrzeit *time (of day),* 6
    um *at,* 1; *around,* 9; **um 8 Uhr** *at 8 o'clock,* 4; **um ein Uhr** *at one o'clock,* 6; **Um wie viel Uhr?** *At what time?,* 6
die Umfrage, -n *survey,* 1
    umgeben *to surround,* 10
    umhören (sep)(sich) *to listen around,* 7
die Umrechnungstabelle, -n *conversion table,* 5
    umsteigen (sep) *to change lines (on a bus, subway, etc.),* 4
    umtauschen *to exchange,* 9
die Umwelt *environment,* 10
    unbedingt *absolutely,* 11
    unbequem *uncomfortable,* 3
    und *and,* 1
    unfreundlich *unfriendly,* 11

Ungarn (das) *Hungary,* 2
    ungefähr *about, approximately,* 7
    ungenügend *unsatisfactory (grade),* 4
    ungewöhnlich *unusual,* 12
    unheimlich *incredibly, incredible,* 8
die Uni, -s (Universität, -en), *university,* 2
    unlogisch *illogical,* 4
die Unordnung *disorder,* 8
    unregelmäßig *irregularly,* 8
    uns *us,* 7
    unschlagbar *unbeatable,* 8
    unser *our,* 4
    unten *below, downstairs,* 8
    unter *below, under,* 8
    unterbrechen *to interrupt,* 10
    unterhalten *to entertain,* 11
    unterheben *to fold in,* 12
die Unterrichtsveranstaltung, -en *school-sponsored activity,* 4
    unterschiedlich *different,* 7
die Unterschrift, -en *signature,* 4
    unterstützen *to support,* 10
    unterwegs *on the way,* 10
das Urteil, -e *verdict,* 10
    usw. = und so weiter *etc., and so forth,* 10

die Vanille *vanilla,* 6
das Vanilleeis *vanilla ice cream,* 6
der Vater, ⸚ *father,* 3; **deinem Vater** *to, for your father,* 11; **meinem Vater** *to, for my father,* 11
der Vatertag *Father's Day,* 11; **Alles Gute zum Vatertag!** *Happy Father's Day!,* 11
    verabreden *to make a date,* 6
die Veranstaltung, -en *event,* 10
das Verb, -en *verb,* 7
    verbringen *to spend (time),* 10; **Wie verbringst du deine Freizeit?** *How do you spend your free time?,* 10
    verdienen *to earn,* 7
    verdünnt *diluted,* 12
    veredeln *to refine,* 8
der Verein, -e *club,* 9
    verfeinern *to improve,* 8
    Verfügung: zur Verfügung haben *to have at one's disposal,* 11
die Vergangenheit *past tense,* 8
    vergessen *to forget,* 7; vergiss nicht *don't forget,* 7
    vergleichen *to compare,* 11
das Vergnügen, - *pleasure,* 10
die Vergünstigung, -en *benefit, discount,* 10
der Verkauf *sale,* 6
der Verkäufer, - *sales clerk (male),* 4

die Verkäuferin, -nen *sales clerk (female),* 4

der Verlag, -e *publishing house,* 7

verlangen *to ask for, to demand,* 7

verlaufen (sich) *to go the wrong way,* 9

verlegt: auf (time expression) verlegt *postponed until,* 6

verlieren *to lose,* 2

verloren *lost,* 9

vermeiden *to avoid,* 7

verrühren *to blend,* 12

der Vers, -e *verse,* 11

verschenkt *given away,* 11

verschieden *different,* 11

verschieden *various,* Loc 7; *different,* 9

verschollen *missing,* 10

versteckt: versteckte Sätze *hidden sentences,* 1

versuchen *to try,* 10

verteilen *to distribute,* 8

der Vertrag, ⁀e *contract,* 10

vervollständigen *to complete,* 8

der Verwandte, -n *relative (male),* 11

die Verwandte, -n *relative (female),* 11

die Verwandten (pl) *relatives,* 11

verwenden *to use,* 10

verwerten: wieder verwerten *to recycle,* 7

verzaubern *to transform into,* 10

Verzeihung! *Excuse me!,* 9

das Video, -s *videocassette,* 10

das Videospiel, -e *video game,* 2

die Viehzucht *cattle raising,* Loc 4

viel *a lot, much,* 2; Viel Spaß! *Have fun!,* 9; **viel zu** *much too,* 5; **viele** *many,* 2; viele Grüße *best regards,* 9; **Vielen Dank!** *Thank you very much!,* 9

die Vielfalt *diversity,* 5

vielleicht *probably,* 11

vier *four,* 1

viermal *four times,* 7

das Viertel, - *quarter,* 6; **Viertel nach** *a quarter after,* 6; **Viertel vor** *a quarter till,* 6

vierundzwanzig *twenty-four,* 3

vierzehn *fourteen,* 1

vierzig *forty,* 3

der Vogel, ⁀ *bird,* 7

volkstümlich *popular,* 9

die Volksschule, -n *elementary school,* 4

Volleyball *volleyball,* 2

das Vollkornbrot *whole-grain bread,* 8

die Vollkornsemmel, -n *whole-grain roll,* 9

der Vollstrecker, - *executioner,* 10

vom=von dem *from the,* 8

von *of,* 1; *from,* 3; **von 8 Uhr bis 8 Uhr 45** *from 8:00 until 8:45,* 4

vor *before,* 1; *in front of,* 9; vor allem *especially,* 9; **zehn vor ...** *ten till...,* 6

voraus *in advance,* 9

vorbeigehen (sep) *to go by,* 7

vorbeigekommen (pp) *came by,* 8

vorbeikommen (sep) *to come by,* 9

vorbereiten (sep) *to prepare,* 12

die Vorbereitung, -en *preparation,* 12

vorgestern *day before yesterday,* 8

die Vorhersagekarte, -n *weather-forecasting map,* 7

der Vormittag *before noon,* 2

vorn *ahead,* 4; hier vorn *here in front,* 5; **da vorn** *there in the front,* 4

der Vorort, -e *suburb,* 3; **ein Vorort von** *a suburb of,* 3

der Vorschlag, ⁀e *suggestion,* 12

vorstellen (sep) *to introduce,* 1

die Vorstellung, -en *introduction, presentation,* 10

die Vorwahlnummer, -n *area code,* 11

die Vorzeit, -en *prehistory,* 10

wählen *to choose,* 9; **die Nummer wählen** *to dial the (telephone) number,* 11

das Wahlpflichtfach, ⁀er *required elective,* 4

Wahnsinn! *Crazy!,* 11

wahnwitzigste *maddest,* 10

wahr *true,* 11

während *while,* 6

die Wahrheit *truth,* 10

wahrscheinlich *probably,* 11

das Wahrzeichen, - *symbol, emblem,* Loc 7

der Walnusskern, -e *walnut,* 8

wandern *to hike,* 2

wann? *when?,* 2; **Wann hast du Geburtstag?** *When is your birthday?,* 11

das Wappen, - *coat of arms,* Loc 7

war: ich war *I was,* 8; **Ich war beim Bäcker.** *I was at the baker's.,* 8

die Ware, -n *ware,* 5; *merchandise,* 8

waren: wir waren *we were,* 8; **sie waren** *they were,* 8; **Sie** (formal) **waren** *you were,* 8

warm *warm,* 7; warm halten *to keep warm,* 12

die Warmluft *warm air,* 7

warst: du warst *you were,* 8; **Wo warst du?** *Where were you?,* 8

wart: ihr wart *you (plural) were,* 8

warten *to wait,* 2; ich warte auf *I'm waiting for,* 10

warum? *why?,* 7

was? *what?,* 2; Was ist los? *What's up?,* 4; Was gibt's? *What's up?,* 1; Was ist das? *What is that?,* p. 8; **Was noch?** *What else?,* 2

was für? *what kind of?,* 10; **Was für Filme magst du gern?** *What kind of movies do you like?,* 10; **Was für Musik hörst du gern?** *What kind of music do you like?,* 10

die Wäsche *laundry,* 12; die Wäsche aufhängen *to hang up the laundry,* 7

die Waschmaschine, -n *washing machine,* 12

das Wasser *water,* 3; **ein Glas (Mineral)Wasser** *a glass of (mineral) water,* 3

wasserscheu *afraid of water,* 12

Wasserski *(das) waterski,* 4

der Wecken, - *roll,* 8

weder...noch *neither...nor,* 10

weg *away,* 7

der Weg, -e: den Weg zeigen *to give directions,* 9

wegbringen (sep) *to take away,* 7

weggebracht (pp) *taken away,* 7

der Weichkäse *soft cheese,* 8

das Weihnachten *Christmas,* 11; **Fröhliche Weihnachten!** *Merry Christmas!,* 11

weil *because* (conj), 8

weiß *white,* 3; **in Weiß** *in white,* 5

die Weißwurst, ⁀e *(southern German sausage specialty),* 9

weit *far,* 3; *wide,* 5; **weit von hier** *far from here,* 3

weiter *farther,* 7

weiterhin *further on,* 7

das Weizenmehl *wheat flour,* 12

welch- *which,* 4; an welchem Tag? *on which day?,* 11; **Welche Fächer hast du?** *Which subjects do you have?,* 4

die Welt *world,* 8

der Weltkrieg, -e *world war,* 9

das Weltmeer, -e *ocean,* 11

wem? *whom, to whom?, for whom?,* 11

wen? *whom?,* 7; Wen lädst du ein? *Whom are you inviting?,* 12

wenden *to turn (to),* 9

wenig *few,* 7

weniger *less,* 8

wenn *when, if* (conj), 5

wer? *who?,* 1; **Wer ist das?** *Who is that?,* 1

werben *to advertise,* 8

die Werbung *advertisement,* 4

werden *to become,* 5

Werken (das) *shop (school subject),* 4

der Wert, -e *value,* 7

die Weste, -n *vest,* 5

der Western, - *western (movie),* 10

das Wetter *weather,* 7; **Wie ist das Wetter?** *How's the weather?,* 7

der Wetterbericht, -e *weather report,* 7

der Wetterdienst *weather service,* 7

die Wetterkarte, -n *weather map,* 7

wichtig   *important*, 7
wie?   *how?*, 1; **Wie alt bist du?** *How old are you?*, 1; **Wie bitte?** *Excuse me?*, 8; **Wie blöd!** *How stupid!*, 4; **wie oft?** *how often?*, 7; **wie viel?** *how much?*, 8; **Wie viel Grad haben wir?** *What's the temperature?*, 7; **Wie viel Uhr ist es?** *What time is it?*, 6
wieder   *again*, 9; wieder verwertet *reused*, 7
Wiederhören   *Bye!* (on the telephone), 11; **Auf Wiederhören!** *Goodbye!* (on the telephone), 11
Wiedersehen!   *Bye!*, 1; **Auf Wiedersehen!** *Goodbye!*, 1
wiegen   *to weigh*, 8
das **Wiener (Würstchen)**, -   *sausage*, 6
willig   *willing*, 10
willkommen: Herzlich willkommen bei uns!   *Welcome to our home!*, 12
windig   *windy*, 7
der **Winter**   *winter*, 2; **im Winter** *in the winter*, 2
wir   *we*, 2
wird   *becomes*, 7
wirklich   *really*, 5
die **Wirkung**, -en   *effect*, 8
die **Wirtschaftsschule**, -n   *business school*, 4
wischen   *to mop*, 12
wissen   *to know* (a fact, information, etc.), 9; **Das weiß ich nicht.** *That I don't know.*, 9; **Ich weiß nicht.** *I don't know.*, 5; **Weißt du noch?** *Do you still remember?*, 7; **Weißt du, wo das Museum ist?** *Do you know where the museum is?*, 9
witzig   *funny*, 10
wo?   *where?*, 1
wobei   *in doing so, in the process of*, 7
die **Woche**, -n   *week*, 6; **(einmal) in der Woche** *(once) a week*, 7
das **Wochenende**, -n   *weekend*, 2; **am Wochenende** *on the weekend*, 2
die **Wochenendheimfahrerin**, -nen   *student (female) who goes home on weekends*, 3
woher?   *from where?*, 1; **Woher bist du?** *Where are you from?*, 1; **Woher kommst du?** *Where are you from?*, 1
wohin?   *where (to)?*, 6; **Wohin geht's?** *Where are you going?*, 7
das **Wohlbefinden**   *well-being*, 8
das **Wohlergehen**   *welfare*, 8
wohnen   *to live*, 3; **Wo wohnst du?** *Where do you live?*, 3

die **Wohnung**, -en   *apartment*, 3
das **Wohnzimmer**, -   *living room*, 12; **im Wohnzimmer** *in the living room*, 12
der **Wolf**, ̈-e   *wolf*, 12
wolkenlos   *cloudless*, 7
wolkig   *cloudy*, 7
wollen   *to want (to)*, 6
die **Wollwurst**, ̈-e   (southern German sausage specialty), 8
das **Wort**, ̈-er   *word*, 2
das **Wörterbuch**, ̈-er   *dictionary*, 4
der **Wortschatz**   *vocabulary*, 1
die **Wortstellung**   *word order*, 8
worüber?   *about what?*, 10; **Worüber habt ihr gesprochen?** *What did you* (pl) *talk about?*, 10; **Worüber sprichst du mit deinen Freunden?** *What do you talk about with your friends?*, 10
wunderbar   *wonderful*, 4
der **Wunsch**, ̈-e   *wish*, 5; **Haben Sie einen Wunsch?** *May I help you?*, 5; **Haben Sie noch einen Wunsch?** *Would you like anything else?*, 8
würde   *would*, 10
würdest: du würdest   *you would*, 7
der **Würfel**, -   *cube*, 12
die **Wurst**, ̈-e   *sausage*, 8
das **Wurstbrot**, -e   *bologna sandwich*, 6
das **Würstchen**, -   *sausage link*, 9
das **Wüten**   *raging*, 10

Z

zahlen   *to pay*, 6; **Hallo! Ich möchte/will zahlen!** *The check please!*, 6
die **Zahlen** (pl)   *numbers*, p. 9
die **Zahnbürste**, -n   *toothbrush*, 11
zart   *tender*, 8
z.B.=zum Beispiel   *for example*, 10
zehn   *ten*, 1
der **Zeichenblock**, ̈-e   *sketch pad*, 11
die **Zeichenerklärung**,   -en *list of conventional signs*, 7
das **Zeichentrickabenteuer**, -   *cartoon adventure*, 10
zeichnen   *to draw*, 2
die **Zeichnung**, -en   *drawing*, 6
zeigen   *to show*, 3; den Weg zeigen *to give directions*, 9
die **Zeile**, -n   *line*, 11
die **Zeit**   *time*, 4; die ganze Zeit *the whole time*, 12; **Ich habe keine Zeit.** *I don't have time.*, 7

die **Zeitschrift**, -en   *magazine*, 10
die **Zeitung**, -en   *newspaper*, 10
das **Zentrum**   *center*, Loc 7
das **Zeug**   *stuff*, 4
das **Zeugnis**, -se   *report card*, 4
das **Ziel**, -e   *goal*, 2
ziemlich   *rather*, 4
das **Zimmer**, -   *room*, 3; **mein Zimmer aufräumen** *to clean my room*, 7
der **Zimt**   *cinnamon*, 12
die **Zitrone**, -n   *lemon*, 12; **mit Zitrone** *with lemon*, 6
der **Zitronensaft**, ̈-e   *lemon juice*, 8
die **Zivilisation**, -en, *civilization*, 10
der **Zoo**, -s   *zoo*, 12; **in den Zoo gehen** *to go to the zoo*, 12
zu   *too*, 5; *to*, 7; **zu Fuß** *on foot*, 1; zu Hause *at home*, 3; **zu Hause helfen** *to help at home*, 7; zu Hause sein *to be at home*, 6
die **Zubereitung**, -en   *preparation (of food)*, 8
der **Zucker**   *sugar*, 8
zuerst   *first*, 4
der **Zug**, ̈-e   *train*, 4
zuhören (sep)   *to listen*, p. 6
zuletzt   *last of all*, 4
zum = zu dem   *to the*, 2; zum Beispiel *for example*, 10
zur = zu der   *to the*, 1
zurechtkommen (mit) (sep)   *to do well with*, 4
zurück   *back*, 4
zurückbekommen (sep)   *to get back*, 4
zurückkommen (sep)   *to come back*, 12
zusammen   *together*, 2
zusammenlegen (sep)   *to fold (the wash)*, 12
zusammentun (sep)   *to join*, 11
zusätzlich   *additional*, 4
der **Zuschauer**, -   *viewer*, 7
die **Zutaten** (pl)   *ingredients*, 8
zwanzig   *twenty*, 1
zwei   *two*, 1
zweimal   *twice*, 7
zweite   *second*, 4; **am zweiten...** *on the second...*, 11
zweiundzwanzig   *twenty-two*, 3
die **Zwiebel**, -n   *onion*, 12
zwischen   *between*, 9
zwölf   *twelve*, 1
zynisch   *cynical(ly)*, 5

This vocabulary includes all of the words in the **Wortschatz** sections of the chapters. These words are considered active—you are expected to know them and be able to use them.

Idioms are listed under the English word you would be most likely to look up. German nouns are listed with definite article and plural ending, when applicable. The number after each German word or phrase refers to the chapter in which it becomes active vocabulary. To be sure you are using the German words and phrases in the correct context, refer to the chapters in which they appear.

The following abbreviations are used in the vocabulary: sep (separable-prefix verb), pl (plural), acc (accusative), dat (dative), masc (masculine), and poss adj (possessive adjective).

a, an *ein(e)*, 3
about *ungefähr*, 7
action movie *der Actionfilm, -e*, 10
actor *der Schauspieler, -*, 10
actress *die Schauspielerin, -nen*, 10
adventure movie *der Abenteuerfilm, -e*, 10
after *nach*, 2; **after school** *nach der Schule*, 2; **after the break** *nach der Pause*, 4
after that *danach*, 4
afternoon *der Nachmittag, -e*, 2; **in the afternoon** *am Nachmittag*, 2
again *wieder*, 9
along: Why don't you come along! *Komm doch mit!*, 7
already *schon*, 1
also *auch*, 1; **I also need...** *ich brauche noch ...*, 8
always *immer*, 7
am: I am *ich bin*, 1
and *und*, 1
another *noch ein*, 9; **I don't want any more....** *Ich möchte kein(e)(en) ... mehr.*, 9; **I'd like another....** *Ich möchte noch ein(e)(en) ... ,* 9
anything: Anything else? *Sonst noch etwas?*, 8
appear *aussehen (sep)*, 5
apple *der Apfel, ∺*, 8
apple cake *der Apfelkuchen, -*, 6
apple juice *der Apfelsaft, ∺*, 3; **a glass of apple juice** *ein Glas Apfelsaft*, 3
approximately *ungefähr*, 8
April *der April*, 7
are: you are *du bist*, 1; (formal) *Sie sind*, 1; (pl) *ihr seid*, 1; **we are** *wir sind*, 1
armchair *der Sessel, -*, 12
art *die Kunst*, 4
at: at 8 o'clock *um 8 Uhr*, 4; **at one o'clock** *um ein Uhr*, 6; **at the**

baker's *beim Bäcker*, 8; **at the butcher's** *beim Metzger*, 8; **at the produce store** *im Obst- und Gemüseladen*, 8; **at the supermarket** *im Supermarkt*, 8; **At what time?** *Um wie viel Uhr?*, 6
August *der August*, 7
aunt *die Tante -n*, 3
Austria *Österreich*, 1
awesome *stark*, 5; **The sweater is awesome!** *Ich finde den Pulli stark!*, 5
awful *furchtbar*, 5

bad *schlecht*, 4; **badly** *schlecht*, 6; **Bad luck!** *So ein Pech!*, 4
baker *der Bäcker, -*, 8; **at the baker's** *beim Bäcker*, 8
bakery *die Bäckerei, -en*, 8
bald: to be bald *eine Glatze haben*, 3
ballpoint pen *der Kuli, -s*, 4
bank *die Bank, -en*, 9
bargain: that's a bargain *das ist preiswert*, 4
basketball *Basketball*, 2
be *sein*, 1; **I am** *ich bin*, 1; **you are** *du bist*, 1; **he/she is** *er/sie ist*, 1; **we are** *wir sind*, 1; (pl) **you are** *ihr seid*, 1; (formal) **you are** *Sie sind*, 1; **they are** *sie sind*, 1
be able to *können*, 7
be called *heißen*, 1
beautiful *schön*, 3
because *denn, weil*, 8
bed *das Bett, -en*, 3; **to make the bed** *das Bett machen*, 7
believe *glauben*, 9
belt *der Gürtel, -*, 5
best: Best wishes on your birthday! *Herzlichen Glückwunsch zum Geburtstag!*, 11

better *besser*, 8
big *groß*, 3
bike *das Fahrrad, ∺er*, 1; **by bike** *mit dem Rad*, 1
biology *Bio (die Biologie)*, 4
biology teacher (female) *die Biologielehrerin, -nen*, 1
birthday *der Geburtstag, -e*, 11; **Best wishes on your birthday!** *Herzlichen Glückwunsch zum Geburtstag!*, 11; **Happy Birthday!** *Alles Gute zum Geburtstag!*, 11; **My birthday is on....** *Ich habe am ... Geburtstag.*, 11; **When is your birthday?** *Wann hast du Geburtstag?*, 11
black *schwarz*, 3; **in black** *in Schwarz*, 5
blond *blond*, 3
blouse *die Bluse, -n*, 5
blue *blau*, 3; **blue (brown, green) eyes** *blaue (braune, grüne) Augen*, 3; **in blue** *in Blau*, 5
board game *das Brettspiel, -e*, 12
bologna sandwich *das Wurstbrot, -e*, 6
book *das Buch, ∺er*, 4
bookcase *das Regal -e*, 3
boot *der Stiefel, -*, 5
boring *langweilig*, 2
bought *gekauft*, 8; **I bought bread.** *Ich habe Brot gekauft.*, 8
bouquet of flowers *der Blumenstrauß, ∺e*, 11
boy *der Junge, -n*, 1
bread *das Brot, -e*, 8
break *die Pause, -n*, 4; **after the break** *nach der Pause*, 4
broken *kaputt*, 3
brother *der Bruder, ∺*, 3; **brothers and sisters** *die Geschwister (pl)*, 3
brown *braun*, 3; **in brown** *in Braun*, 5
brutal *brutal*, 10
bus *der Bus, -se*, 1; **by bus** *mit dem Bus*, 1
busy (telephone) *besetzt*, 11
but *aber*, 3

butcher shop *die Metzgerei, -en,* 8; **at the butcher's** *beim Metzger,* 8
butter *die Butter,* 8
buy *kaufen,* 5; **What did you buy?** *Was hast du gekauft?,* 8
by: by bike *mit dem Rad,* 1; **by bus** *mit dem Bus,* 1; **by car** *mit dem Auto,* 1; **by moped** *mit dem Moped,* 1; **by subway** *mit der U-Bahn,* 1
Bye! *Wiedersehen! Tschau! Tschüs!,* 1; (on the telephone) *Wiederhören!,* 11

C

cabinet *der Schrank, ⸚e,* 3
café *das Café, -s,* 6; **to the café** *ins Café,* 6
cake *der Kuchen, -,* 3; **a piece of cake** *ein Stück Kuchen,* 3
calendar *der Kalender, -,* 11
call *anrufen* (sep), *telefonieren,* 11
can *können,* 7
capital *die Hauptstadt, ⸚e,* 1
car *das Auto, -s,* 1; **by car** *mit dem Auto,* 1
card *die Karte, -n,* 2
care for *mögen,* 10
carpet *der Teppich, -e,* 12
cassette *die Kassette, -n,* 4
casual *lässig,* 5
cat *die Katze, -n,* 3; **to feed the cat** *die Katze füttern,* 7
cell phone *das Handy, -s,* 11
cent *der Cent, -,* 4
Certainly! *Natürlich!,* 11; *Sicher!,* 3
chair *der Stuhl, ⸚e,* 3
change: Keep the change! *Stimmt (schon)!,* 6
cheap *billig,* 4
check: The check please! *Hallo! Ich möchte/will zahlen!,* 6
cheese *der Käse, -,* 8
cheese sandwich *das Käsebrot, -e,* 6
chemistry *(die) Chemie,* 4
chess *das Schach,* 2
chicken *das Hähnchen, -,* 8
Christmas *das Weihnachten, -,* 11; **Merry Christmas!** *Fröhliche Weihnachten!,* 11
church *die Kirche, -n,* 9
cinnamon *der Zimt,* 12
cinema *das Kino, -s,* 6
city *die Stadt, ⸚e,* 9; **in the city** *in der Stadt,* 3
city hall *das Rathaus, ⸚er,* 9
class schedule *der Stundenplan, ⸚e,* 4
classical music *klassische Musik,* 10
clean: to clean the windows *die Fenster putzen,* 7; **to clean up my room** *mein Zimmer aufräumen* (sep), 7

clear: to clear the table *den Tisch abräumen* (sep), 7
clothes (casual term for) *die Klamotten* (pl), 5; **to pick up my clothes** *meine Klamotten aufräumen* (sep), 7
cloudy *wolkig,* 7
coffee *der Kaffee,* 8; **a cup of coffee** *eine Tasse Kaffee,* 6
coin *die Münze, -n,* 11
cold *kalt,* 7
cold cuts *der Aufschnitt,* 8
collect *sammeln,* 2; **to collect comics** *Comics sammeln,* 2; **to collect stamps** *Briefmarken sammeln,* 2
color *die Farbe, -n,* 5
come *kommen,* 1; **I come** *ich komme,* 1; **That comes to....** *Das macht (zusammen) ... ,* 6; **to come along** *mitkommen* (sep), 7
comedy *die Komödie, -n,* 10
comfortable *bequem,* 3
comics *die Comics,* 2; **to collect comics** *Comics sammeln,* 2
computer *der Computer, -,* 3
computer science *die Informatik,* 4
compact disc *die CD, -s,* 11
concert *das Konzert, -e,* 6; **to go to a concert** *in ein Konzert gehen,* 6
cookie *der Keks, -e,* 3; **a few cookies** *ein paar Kekse,* 3
cool *kühl,* 7
corners: with corners *eckig,* 12
corny *schmalzig,* 10
cost *kosten,* 4; **How much does... cost?** *Was kostet ... ?,* 4
cotton *die Baumwolle,* 12; **made of cotton** *aus Baumwolle,* 12
couch *die Couch, -en,* 3
country *das Land, ⸚er,* 3; **in the country** *auf dem Land,* 3
cousin (female) *die Kusine, -n,* 3; **cousin (male)** *der Cousin, -s,* 3
crime drama *der Krimi, -s,* 10
cruel *grausam,* 10

D

dance *tanzen,* 2; **to go dancing** *tanzen gehen,* 6
dancing *das Tanzen,* 2
dark blue *dunkelblau,* 5; **in dark blue** *in Dunkelblau,* 5
Darn it! *So ein Mist!,* 2
day *der Tag, -e,* 1; **day before yesterday** *vorgestern,* 8; **every day** *jeden Tag,* 7
December *der Dezember,* 7
definitely *bestimmt,* 5
degree *der Grad, -,* 7
Delicious! *Lecker!,* 6
desk *der Schreibtisch, -e,* 3

detective movie *der Krimi, -s,* 10
detective novel *der Krimi, -s,* 10
dial *wählen,* 11; **to dial the number** *die Nummer wählen,* 11
dictionary *das Wörterbuch, ⸚er,* 4
different *verschieden,* 11
dining table *der Esstisch, -e,* 12
directly *direkt,* 4
disagree: I disagree. *Das finde ich nicht.,* 2
disco *die Disko, -s,* 6; **to go to a disco** *in eine Disko gehen,* 6
dishes *das Geschirr,* 7; **to wash the dishes** *das Geschirr spülen,* 7
dislike *nicht gern haben,* 4; **strongly dislike** *überhaupt nicht gern,* 10
do *machen,* 2; *tun,* 7; **do crafts** *basteln,* 2; **do homework** *die Hausaufgaben machen,* 2; **Do you have any other interests?** *Hast du andere Interessen?,* 2; **Do you need help?** *Brauchst du Hilfe?,* 7; **Do you play an instrument?** *Spielst du ein Instrument?,* 2; **Do you play sports?** *Machst du Sport?,* 2; **Do you think so?** *Meinst du?,* 5; **Does it taste good?** *Schmeckt's?,* 6; **What did you do on the weekend?** *Was hast du am Wochenende gemacht?,* 10
dog *der Hund, -e,* 3
done *gemacht,* 10
downtown *die Innenstadt,* 9; **to go downtown** *in die Stadt gehen,* 6
draw *zeichnen,* 2
dress *das Kleid, -er,* 5
drink *trinken,* 3
drive *fahren,* 9; **he/she drives** *er/sie fährt,* 9
dry *trocken,* 7
dumb *blöd,* 2; *doof, dumm,* 10

E

Easter *das Ostern, -,* 11; **Happy Easter!** *Frohe Ostern!,* 11
easy *einfach,* 1; **That's easy!** *Also, einfach!,* 1
eat *essen,* 3; **he/she eats** *er/sie isst,* 6; **to eat ice cream** *ein Eis essen,* 6
egg *das Ei, -er,* 8
eight *acht,* 1
eighteen *achtzehn,* 1
eighty *achtzig,* 3
eleven *elf,* 1
enough *genug,* 9
environment *die Umwelt,* 10
eraser *der Radiergummi, -s,* 4
especially *besonders,* 6; **especially like** *besonders gern,* 10
euro *der Euro, -,* 4

evening *der Abend*, 1; **in the evening** *am Abend*, 2
every: every day *jeden Tag*, 7
exciting *spannend*, 10
Excuse me! *Entschuldigung!, Verzeihung!*, 9
expensive *teuer*, 4
eye *das Auge, -n*, 3; **blue (brown, green) eyes** *blaue (braune, grüne) Augen*, 3

fall *der Herbst*, 2; **in the fall** *im Herbst*, 2
family *die Familie, -n*, 3
fancy chocolate *die Praline, -n*, 11
fantasy novel *der Fantasyroman, -e*, 10
far *weit*, 3; **far from here** *weit von hier*, 3
fashion *die Mode*, 10
father *der Vater, ∸*, 3; **to, for your father** *deinem Vater*, 11; **to, for my father** *meinem Vater*, 11
Father's Day *der Vatertag*, 11; **Happy Father's Day!** *Alles Gute zum Vatertag!*, 11
favorite *Lieblings-*, 4
February *der Februar*, 7
feed *füttern*, 7; **to feed the cat** *die Katze füttern*, 7
fetch *holen*, 8
few: a few *ein paar*, 3; **a few cookies** *ein paar Kekse*, 3
fifteen *fünfzehn*, 1
fifty *fünfzig*, 3
first *erst-*, 11; **first of all** *zuerst*, 4; **on the first of July** *am ersten Juli*, 11; **the first street** *die erste Straße*, 9
fit *passen*, 5; **The skirt fits great!** *Der Rock passt prima!*, 5
five *fünf*, 1
flower *die Blume, -n*, 7; **to water the flowers** *die Blumen gießen*, 7
foot: on foot (I walk) *zu Fuß*, 1
for *für*, 7; *denn* (conj), 8
forty *vierzig*, 3
four *vier*, 1
fourteen *vierzehn*, 1
for whom? *für wen?*, 8
free time *die Freizeit*, 2
fresh *frisch*, 8
fresh produce store *der Obst- und Gemüseladen, ∸*, 8
Friday *der Freitag*, 4
friend (male) *der Freund, -e*, 1; **(female)** *die Freundin, -nen*, 1; **to visit friends** *Freunde besuchen*, 2
from *aus*, 1; *von*, 4; **from 8 until 8:45** *von 8 Uhr bis 8 Uhr 45*, 4
from where? *woher?*, 1; **I'm from** *ich bin (komme) aus*, 1; **Where are**

you from? *Woher bist (kommst) du?*, 1
front: there in the front *da vorn*, 4
fruit *das Obst*, 8; **a piece of fruit** *Obst*, 3
fun *der Spaß*, 2; **(Tennis) is fun.** *(Tennis) macht Spaß.*, 2; **(Tennis) is no fun.** *(Tennis) macht keinen Spaß.*, 2
funny *lustig*, 10
furniture *die Möbel* (pl), 3

garden(s) *der Garten, ∸*, 9
geography *die Erdkunde*, 4
German mark (former German monetary unit) *DM = Deutsche Mark*, 4
German teacher (male) *der Deutschlehrer, -*, 1; **(female)** *die Deutschlehrerin, -nen*, 1
Germany *Deutschland*, 1
get *bekommen*, 4; *holen*, 8
gift *das Geschenk, -e*, 11
gift idea *die Geschenkidee, -n*, 11
girl *das Mädchen, -*, 1
give *geben*, 11; **he/she gives** *er/sie gibt*, 11
give (a gift) *schenken*, 11
glass *das Glas, ∸er*, 3; **a glass (cup) of tea** *ein Glas Tee*, 6; **a glass of (mineral) water** *ein Glas (Mineral)Wasser*, 3; **a glass of apple juice** *ein Glas Apfelsaft*, 3
glasses: a pair of glasses *eine Brille, -n*, 3
go *gehen*, 2; **to go home** *nach Hause gehen*, 3
golf *Golf*, 2
good *gut*, 4; **Good!** *Gut!*, 6
Good morning! *Guten Morgen! Morgen!*, 1
Goodbye! *Auf Wiedersehen!*, 1; (on the telephone) *Auf Wiederhören*, 11
grade *die Note, -n*, 4
grade level *die Klasse, -n*, 4
grades: a 1, 2, 3, 4, 5, 6 *eine Eins, Zwei, Drei, Vier, Fünf, Sechs*, 4
gram *das Gramm, -*, 8
grandfather *der Großvater (Opa), ∸*, 3
grandmother *die Großmutter (Oma), ∸*, 3
grandparents *die Großeltern* (pl), 3
grape *die Traube, -n*, 8
gray *grau*, 3; **in gray** *in Grau*, 5
Great! *Prima!*, 1; *Sagenhaft!*, 6; *Klasse! Toll!*, 2
green *grün*, 3; **in green** *in Grün*, 5
groceries *die Lebensmittel* (pl), 8
ground meat *das Hackfleisch*, 8
group *die Gruppe, -n*, 10

guitar *die Gitarre, -n*, 2
gyros *das Gyros, -*, 9

hair *die Haare* (pl), 3
half *halb*, 6; **half past (twelve, one, etc.)** *halb (eins, zwei, usw.)*, 6
hang up (the telephone) *auflegen* (sep), 11
Hanukkah *Chanukka*, 11; **Happy Hanukkah!** *Frohes Chanukka-Fest!*, 11
have *haben*, 4; **he/she has English** *er/sie hat Englisch*, 4; **I have German.** *Ich habe Deutsch.*, 4; **I have no classes on Saturday.** *Am Samstag habe ich frei.*, 4; **I'll have...** *Ich bekomme ...*, 6
have to *müssen*, 7; **I have to** *ich muss*, 7
he *er*, 2; **he is** *er ist*, 1; **he's from** *er ist (kommt) aus*, 1
hear *hören*, 2
Hello! *Guten Tag! Tag! Hallo! Grüß dich!*, 1
help *helfen*, 7; **to help at home** *zu Hause helfen*, 7
her *ihr* (poss adj), 3; **her name is** *sie heißt*, 1
hideous *scheußlich*, 5
hike *wandern*, 2
him *ihn*, 5
his *sein* (poss adj), 3; **his name is** *er heißt*, 1
history *die Geschichte*, 4
hobby book *das Hobbybuch, ∸er*, 10
holiday *der Feiertag, -e*, 11
homework *die Hausaufgabe, -n*, 2; **to do homework** *Hausaufgaben machen*, 2
honestly *ehrlich*, 5
horror movie *der Horrorfilm, -e*, 10
horror novel *der Gruselroman, -e*, 10
hot *heiß*, 7
hotel *das Hotel, -s*, 9
how much? *wie viel?*, 8; **How much does... cost?** *Was kostet ... ?*, 4
how often? *wie oft?*, 7
how? *wie?*, 1; **How are you?** *Wie geht's (denn)?*, 6; **How do I get to...?** *Wie komme ich zum (zur) ... ?*, 9; **How do you get to school?** *Wie kommst du zur Schule?*, 1; **How does it taste?** *Wie schmeckt's?*, 6; **How old are you?** *Wie alt bist du?*, 1; **How's the weather?** *Wie ist das Wetter?*, 7

hunger *der Hunger*, 9
hungry: I'm hungry. *Ich habe Hunger.*, 9; **I'm not hungry any more.** *Ich habe keinen Hunger mehr.*, 9

I *ich*, 2; **I don't.** *Ich nicht.*, 2
ice *das Eis*, 7
ice cream *das Eis*, 6; **a dish of ice cream** *ein Eisbecher*, 6
ice-skate *Schlittschuh laufen*, 12
idea: I have no idea! *Keine Ahnung!*, 9
imaginative *phantasievoll*, 10
in *in*, 2; **in the afternoon** *am Nachmittag*, 2; **in the city** *in der Stadt*, 3; **in the country** *auf dem Land*, 3; **in the evening** *am Abend*, 2; **in the fall** *im Herbst*, 2; **in the kitchen** *in der Küche*, 12; **in the living room** *im Wohnzimmer*, 12; **in the spring** *im Frühling*, 2; **in the summer** *im Sommer*, 2; **in the winter** *im Winter*, 2
insert *einstecken*, 11; **to insert coins** *Münzen einstecken* (sep), 11
instrument *das Instrument, -e*, 2; **Do you play an instrument?** *Spielst du ein Instrument?*, 2
interest *das Interesse, -n*, 2; **Do you have any other interests?** *Hast du andere Interessen?*, 2
interesting *interessant*, 2
Internet *das Internet*, 2
invite *einladen* (sep), 11; **he/she invites** *er/sie lädt ... ein*, 11
is: he/she is *er/sie ist*, 1
it *er, es, sie*, 3; *ihn*, 5

jacket *die Jacke, -n*, 5
January *der Januar*, 7; **in January** *im Januar*, 7
jeans *die Jeans, -*, 5
jewelry *der Schmuck*, 11
jog *joggen*, 12
jogging suit *der Jogging-Anzug, ⸚e*, 5
juice *der Saft, ⸚e*, 3
July *der Juli*, 7
June *der Juni*, 7
just: Just a minute, please. *Einen Moment, bitte!*, 11

keep: Keep the change! *Stimmt (schon)!*, 6
kilogram *das Kilo, -*, 8
kitchen *die Küche, -n*, 12; **in the kitchen** *in der Küche*, 12
know (a fact, information, etc.) *wissen*, 9; **I don't know.** *Ich weiß nicht.*, 5
know (be familiar or acquainted with) *kennen*, 10

L

lamp *die Lampe, -n*, 12
last *letzt-*, 8; **last of all** *zuletzt*, 4; **last week** *letzte Woche*, 8; **last weekend** *letztes Wochenende*, 8
Latin *Latein*, 4
lawn *der Rasen, -*, 7; **to mow the lawn** *den Rasen mähen*, 7
layer cake *die Torte, -n*, 8
leather *das Leder*, 12; **made of leather** *aus Leder*, 12
left: to the left *nach links*, 9
lemon *die Zitrone, -n*, 12
lemon drink *die Limo, -s*, 3
lettuce *der Salat*, 8
light blue *hellblau*, 5; **in light blue** *in Hellblau*, 5
like *gern haben*, 4; *mögen*, 10; **I like it.** *Er/Sie/Es gefällt mir.*, 5 **I like them.** *Sie gefallen mir.*, 5; **like an awful lot** *furchtbar gern*, 10; **not like at all** *gar nicht gern*, 10; **not like very much** *nicht so gern*, 2
like (to do) *gern (machen)*, 2; **to not like (to do)** *nicht gern (machen)*, 2
listen (to) *hören*, 2; *zuhören*, p. 6
liter *der Liter, -*, 8
little *klein*, 3; **a little** *ein bisschen*, 5; **a little more** *ein bisschen mehr*, 8
live *wohnen*, 3
living room: in the living room *im Wohnzimmer*, 12
long *lang*, 3
look *schauen*, 2; **Look!** *Schauen Sie!*, 4
look for *suchen*, 5; **I'm looking for** *ich suche*, 5
look like *aussehen* (sep), 5; **he/she looks like** *er/sie sieht ... aus*, 5; **The skirt looks....** *Der Rock sieht ... aus.*, 5; **What do they look like?** *Wie sehen sie aus?*, 3; **What does he look like?** *Wie sieht er aus?*, 3
lot: a lot *viel*, 2
luck: Bad luck! *So ein Pech!*, 4; **What luck!** *So ein Glück!*, 4

made: made of cotton *aus Baumwolle*, 12; **made of leather** *aus Leder*, 12; **made of plastic** *aus Kunststoff*, 12; **made of silk** *aus Seide*, 12; **made of wood** *aus Holz*, 12
magazine *die Zeitschrift, -en*, 10
make *machen*, 2; **to make the bed** *das Bett machen*, 7
man *der Mann, ⸚er*, 3
many *viele*, 2
March *der März*, 7
market square *der Marktplatz, ⸚e*, 9
math *Mathe (die Mathematik)*, 4
may: May I help you? *Haben Sie einen Wunsch?*, 5
May *der Mai*, 7
maybe *vielleicht*, 11
me *mich*, 7; **Me too.** *Ich auch.*, 2
meat *das Fleisch*, 8
mess: What a mess! *So ein Mist!*, 4
milk *die Milch*, 8
mineral water *das Mineralwasser*, 3
minute: Just a minute, please. *Einen Moment, bitte.*, 11
miserable *miserabel*, 6
modern *modern*, 12
moment *der Moment, -e*, 3
money *das Geld*, 4
month *der Monat, -e*, 7
moped *das Moped, -s*, 1; **by moped** *mit dem Moped*, 1
more *mehr*, 9
morning *der Morgen*, 1; **Morning!** *Morgen!*, 1
most of all *am liebsten*, 10
mother *die Mutter, ⸚*, 3
Mother's Day *der Muttertag*, 11; **Happy Mother's Day!** *Alles Gute zum Muttertag!*, 11
movie *der Film, -e*, 10; **to go to the movies** *ins Kino gehen*, 6
movie theater *das Kino, -s*, 6
mow *mähen*, 7; **to mow the lawn** *den Rasen mähen*, 7
Mr. *Herr*, 1
Ms. *Frau*, 1
much *viel*, 2; **much too** *viel zu*, 5; **very much** *sehr gern*, 10
museum *das Museum, die Museen*, 9
music *die Musik*, 2; **to listen to music** *Musik hören*, 2
mustard *der Senf*, 6; **with mustard** *mit Senf*, 6
my *mein*, 3; **my name is** *ich heiße*, 1; **to, for my father** *meinem Vater*, 11 **to, for my mother** *meiner Mutter*, 11

N

name *der Name, -n,* 1; **her name is** *sie heißt,* 1; **his name is** *er heißt,* 1; **my name is** *ich heiße,* 1; **What's the boy's name?** *Wie heißt der Junge?,* 1; **What's the girl's name?** *Wie heißt das Mädchen?,* 1; **What's your name?** *Wie heißt du?,* 1
nearby *in der Nähe,* 3
need *brauchen,* 5; **I need** *ich brauche,* 5
never *nie,* 7
new *neu,* 3
newspaper *die Zeitung, -en,* 10
next: the next street *die nächste Straße,* 9; **next week** *nächste Woche*
nine *neun,* 1
nineteen *neunzehn,* 1
ninety *neunzig,* 3
no *kein,* 9; **No more, thanks!** *Nichts mehr, danke!,* 9
non-fiction book *das Sachbuch, ⁻er,* 10
none *kein,* 9
noodle soup *die Nudelsuppe, -n,* 6
not *nicht,* 2; **not at all** *überhaupt nicht,* 5; **not like at all** *gar nicht gern,* 10; **Not really.** *Nicht besonders.,* 6; **Not too long?** *Nicht zu lang?,* 5
not any *kein,* 9
notebook *das Notizbuch, ⁻er,* 1; *das Heft, -e,* 4
nothing *nichts,* 3; **nothing at the moment** *im Moment gar nichts,* 3; **Nothing, thank you!** *Nichts, danke!,* 3
novel *der Roman, -e,* 10
November *der November,* 7
now *jetzt,* 1; *nun,* 6
number *die (Telefon)nummer, -n,* 11; **to dial the number** *die Nummer wählen,* 11

O

o'clock: at 8 o'clock *um 8 Uhr,* 4; **at one o'clock** *um ein Uhr,* 6
October *der Oktober,* 7
Of course! *Ja klar!,* 1; *Ganz klar!,* 4
often *oft,* 2
Oh! *Ach!,* 1; **Oh yeah!** *Ach ja!,* 1
oil *das Öl,* 12
Okay! I'll do that! *Gut! Mach ich!,* 7; **It's okay.** *Es geht.,* 6
old *alt,* 3; **How old are you?** *Wie alt bist du?,* 1
on: on ... Square *am ...platz,* 9; **on ... Street** *in der ...straße,* 3; **on foot (I walk)** *zu Fuß,* 1; **on Monday** *am Montag,* 4; **on the first of July**

am ersten Juli, 11; **on the weekend** *am Wochenende,* 2
once *einmal,* 7; *mal,* 9; **once a month** *einmal im Monat,* 7; **once a week** *einmal in der Woche,* 7
one *eins,* 1
one hundred *hundert,* 3
onion *die Zwiebel, -n,* 12
only *bloß, nur,* 4
opera *die Oper, -n,* 10
or *oder,* 1
orange juice *der Orangensaft, ⁻e,* 3
other *andere,* 2
oven *der Ofen, ⁻,* 12
over there *dort drüben,* 4; **over there in the back** *da hinten,* 4
overcast *trüb,* 7

P

pants *die Hose, -n,* 5
parents *die Eltern (pl),* 3
park *der Park, -s,* 12; **to go to the park** *in den Park gehen,* 12
party *die Party, -s,* 11
pencil *der Bleistift, -e,* 4
people *die Leute (pl),* 9
perfume *das Parfüm, -e,* 11
pet *das Haustier, -e,* 3
phone card *die Telefonkarte, -n,* 11
physical education *der Sport,* 4
physics *(die) Physik,* 4
piano *das Klavier, -e,* 2; **I play the piano** *Ich spiele Klavier.,* 2
pick up *aufräumen (sep),* 7; **to pick up my clothes** *meine Klamotten aufräumen,* 7; **to pick up the telephone** *abheben (sep),* 11
piece *das Stück, -e,* 3; **a piece of cake** *ein Stück Kuchen,* 3; **a piece of fruit** *Obst,* 3
pizza *die Pizza, -s,* 6
plastic *der Kunststoff, -e,* 12; **made of plastic** *aus Kunststoff,* 12
play *spielen,* 2; **I play soccer.** *Ich spiele Fußball.,* 2; **I play the piano.** *Ich spiele Klavier.,* 2; **to play a board game** *ein Brettspiel spielen,* 12
please *bitte,* 3
pleasure: My pleasure! *Gern geschehen!,* 9
pocket calculator *der Taschenrechner, -,* 4
politics *die Politik,* 10
polka-dot *gepunktet,* 12
post office *die Post,* 9
poster *das Poster, -,* 11
potato *die Kartoffel, -n,* 8
pound *das Pfund, -,* 8
prefer *lieber (mögen),* 10
pretty *hübsch,* 5; *schön,* 3
pretzel *die Brezel, -n,* 8

probably *wahrscheinlich,* 11
produce store *der Obst- und Gemüseladen, ⁻,* 8; **at the produce store** *im Obst- und Gemüseladen,* 8
Pullover *der Pulli, -s,* 5
put on *anziehen (sep),* 5

Q

quarter: a quarter after *Viertel nach,* 6; **a quarter to** *Viertel vor,* 6

R

railroad station *der Bahnhof, ⁻e,* 9
rain *der Regen,* 7; **It's raining** *Es regnet.,* 7
rainy *regnerisch,* 7
rather *ziemlich,* 4
read *lesen,* 10; **he/she reads** *er/sie liest,* 10; **What did you read?** *Was hast du gelesen?,* 10
really *ganz,* 3; *echt,* 5; **Not really.** *Nicht besonders.,* 6
receive *bekommen,* 4
receiver *der Hörer, -,* 11
red *rot,* 3; **in red** *in Rot,* 5
refrigerator *der Kühlschrank, ⁻e,* 12
religion *die Religion, -en,* 4
report card *das Zeugnis, -se,* 4
residence: The ... residence *Hier bei ... ,* 11
right: to the right *nach rechts,* 9
roll *die Semmel, -n,* 8
romance *der Liebesfilm, -e,* 10; **romance novel** *der Liebesroman, -e,* 10
room *das Zimmer, -,* 3; **to clean up my room** *mein Zimmer aufräumen (sep),* 7
round *rund,* 12

S

sad *traurig,* 10
salad *der Salat, -e,* 12
salt *das Salz,* 12
Saturday *der Samstag,* 4
sausage *die Wurst, ⁻e,* 8
say *sagen,* 1; **Say!** *Sag mal!,* 2; **What does the weather report say?** *Was sagt der Wetterbericht?,* 7

school   *die Schule, -n,* 4; **after school**   *nach der Schule,* 2;   **How do you get to school?**   *Wie kommst du zur Schule?,* 1
school subject   *das Fach, ̈-er,* 4
school supplies   *die Schulsachen* (pl), 4
schoolbag   *die Schultasche, -n,* 4
science fiction movie   *der Sciencefictionfilm, -e,* 10
science fiction novel   *der Sciencefictionroman, -e,* 10
search (for)   *suchen,* 4
second   *zweit-,* 11; **the second street**   *die zweite Straße,* 9
see   *sehen,* 10; **he/she sees**   *er/sie sieht,* 10; **See you later!**   *Bis dann!,* 1; **to see a movie**   *einen Film sehen,* 6; **What did you see?**   *Was hast du gesehen?,* 10
sensational   *sensationell,* 10
September   *der September,* 7
set   *decken,* 7; **to set the table**   *den Tisch decken,* 7
seven   *sieben,* 1
seventeen   *siebzehn,* 1
seventy   *siebzig,* 3
she   *sie,* 2; **she is**   *sie ist,* 1; **she's from**   *sie ist (kommt) aus,* 1
shine: the sun is shining   *die Sonne scheint,* 7
shirt   *das Hemd, -en,* 5
shop   *einkaufen* (sep), 8; **to go shopping**   *einkaufen gehen,* 8
short   *kurz,* 3
shortening   *das Butterschmalz,* 12
shorts: pair of shorts   *die Shorts, -,* 5
should   *sollen,* 8
silk   *die Seide,* 12; **made of silk**   *aus Seide,* 12
singer (female)   *die Sängerin, -nen,* 10
singer (male)   *der Sänger, -,* 10
sink   *das Spülbecken, -,* 12
sister   *die Schwester, -n,* 3; **brothers and sisters**   *die Geschwister* (pl), 3
six   *sechs,* 1
sixteen   *sechzehn,* 1
sixty   *sechzig,* 3
size   *die Größe, -n,* 5
skirt   *der Rock, ̈-e,* 5
small   *klein,* 3
smart (looking)   *fesch, schick, chic,* 5
snack bar   *die Imbissstube, -n,* 9
sneaker   *der Turnschuh, -e,* 5
snow   *der Schnee,* 7; **It's snowing**   *Es schneit.,* 7
so   *so,* 2; **So long!**   *Tschau! Tschüs!,* 1; **so so**   *so lala,* 6
soccer   *der Fußball,* 2; **I play soccer.**   *Ich spiele Fußball.,* 2
sock   *die Socke, -n,* 5
soda: lemon-flavored soda   *die Limo, -s (die Limonade, -n),* 3
sofa   *das Sofa, -s,* 12
something   *etwas,* 7
sometimes   *manchmal,* 7
song   *das Lied, -er,* 10
soon   *bald,* 11

sorry: I'm sorry.   *Es tut mir leid.,* 9; **Sorry, I can't.**   *Ich kann leider nicht.,* 7
sort   *sortieren,* 7; **to sort the trash**   *den Müll sortieren,* 7
spend (time)   *verbringen,* 10
sports   *der Sport,* 2; **Do you play sports?**   *Machst du Sport?,* 2
spring   *der Frühling,* 2; **in the spring**   *im Frühling,* 2
square   *der Platz, ̈-e,* 9; **on ... Square**   *am ...platz,* 9
stamp   *die Briefmarke, -n,* 2; **to collect stamps**   *Briefmarken sammeln,* 2
state: German federal state   *das Bundesland, ̈-er,* 1
stereo   *die Stereoanlage -n,* 3
stinks: That stinks!   *So ein Mist!,* 4
store   *der Laden, ̈-,* 8
storm   *das Gewitter, -,* 7
stove   *der Herd, -e,* 12
straight ahead   *geradeaus,* 9
street   *die Straße, -n,* 9; **on ... Street**   *in der ...straße,* 3
striped   *gestreift,* 12
stupid   *blöd,* 5
subject (school)   *das Fach, ̈-er,* 4; **Which subjects do you have?**   *Welche Fächer hast du?,* 4
suburb   *der Vorort, -e,* 3; **a suburb of**   *ein Vorort von,* 3
subway   *die U-Bahn,* 1; **by subway**   *mit der U-Bahn,* 1
subway station   *die U-Bahnstation, -en,* 9
sugar   *der Zucker,* 8
summer   *der Sommer,* 2; **in the summer**   *im Sommer,* 2
sun   *die Sonne,* 7; **the sun is shining**   *die Sonne scheint,* 7
Sunday   *der Sonntag,* 4
sunny   *sonnig,* 7
Super!   *Spitze!, Super!,* 2
supermarket   *der Supermarkt, ̈-e,* 8; **at the supermarket**   *im Supermarkt,* 8
supposed to   *sollen,* 8
Sure!   *Aber sicher!, Ja, gern!,* 11
sure: I'm not sure.   *Ich bin nicht sicher.,* 5
surf   *surfen,* 2
sweater   *der Pulli, -s,* 5
swim   *schwimmen,* 2; **to go swimming**   *baden gehen,* 6
swimming pool   *das Schwimmbad, ̈-er,* 6; **to go to the (swimming) pool**   *ins Schwimmbad gehen,* 6

T

T-shirt   *das T-Shirt, -s,* 5
table   *der Tisch, -e,* 12; **to clear the**

table   *den Tisch abräumen* (sep), 7; **to set the table**   *den Tisch decken,* 7
take   *nehmen,* 5; **he/she takes**   *er/sie nimmt,* 5; **I'll take**   *ich nehme,* 5
talk about   *sprechen über,* 10; **he/she talks about**   *er/sie spricht über,* 10 **What did you** (pl) **talk about?**   *Worüber habt ihr gesprochen?,* 10
taste   *schmecken,* 6; **Does it taste good?**   *Schmeckt's?,* 6; **How does it taste?**   *Wie schmeckt's?,* 6
Tasty!   *Lecker!,* 6
tea   *der Tee,* 6; **a glass (cup) of tea**   *ein Glas Tee,* 6
teacher (male)   *der Lehrer, -,* 1; **(female)**   *die Lehrerin, -nen,* 1
telephone   *das Telefon, -e, der Apparat, -e,* 11; **pick up the telephone**   *abheben* (sep), 11
telephone booth   *die Telefonzelle, -n,* 11
telephone number   *die Telefonnummer, -n,* 11
television   *das Fernsehen,* 2; **to watch TV**   *Fernsehen schauen,* 2
temperature: What's the temperature?   *Wie viel Grad haben wir?,* 7
ten   *zehn,* 1
tennis   *Tennis,* 2
terrible   *furchtbar,* 5
terrific   *Klasse, prima, toll,* 2
thank   *danken,* 3; **Thank you (very much)!**   *Danke (sehr, schön)!,* 3; *Vielen Dank!,* 9; **Thank you!**   *Danke!,* 3
that   *dass* (conj), 9; **That's all.**   *Das ist alles.,* 8; **That's...**   *Das ist ...,* 1
the   *das, der, die,* 1; *den* (masc, acc), 5; *dem* (masc, neuter, dat), 11
theater   *das Theater, -,* 9
then   *dann,* 4
there   *dort,* 4
There is/are...   *Es gibt...,* 9
they   *sie,* 2; **they are**   *sie sind,* 1; **they're from**   *sie sind (kommen) aus,* 1
think   *denken,* 3; **Do you think so?**   *Meinst du?,* 5; **I think**   *ich glaube,* 2; **I think (tennis) is...**   *Ich finde (Tennis) ... ,* 2;   **I think so too.**   *Das finde ich auch.,* 2; **I think it's good/bad that....**   *Ich finde es gut/schlecht, dass ...,* 9; **I think that...**   *Ich finde, dass ...,* 9 **What do you think of (tennis)?**   *Wie findest du (Tennis)?,* 2
third   *dritte,* 9
thirteen   *dreizehn,* 1
thirty   *dreißig,* 1
this: this afternoon   *heute Nachmittag,* 8; **This is...**   *Hier ist ...* (on the telephone), 11; **this morning**   *heute Morgen,* 8
three   *drei,* 1
three times   *dreimal,* 7
thrilling   *spannend,* 10
Thursday   *der Donnerstag,* 4

tight *eng*, 5
till: ten till two *zehn vor zwei*, 6
time *die Zeit*, 4; **At what time?** *Um wie viel Uhr?*, 6; **I don't have time.** *Ich habe keine Zeit.*, 7; **What time is it?** *Wie spät ist es?, Wie viel Uhr ist es?*, 6
to, for her *ihr*, 11
to, for him *ihm*, 11
today *heute*, 4
tomato *die Tomate, -n*, 8
tomorrow *morgen*, 7
tonight *heute Abend*, 7
too *zu*, 5; **Too bad!** *Schade!*, 4
tour *besichtigen*, 12; **to tour the city** *die Stadt besichtigen*, 12
train station *der Bahnhof, ̈-e*, 9
trash *der Müll*, 7; **to sort the trash** *den Müll sortieren*, 7
true: Not true! *Stimmt nicht!*, 2; **That's right! True!** *Stimmt!*, 2
try *probieren*, 9
try on *anprobieren* (sep), 5
Tuesday *der Dienstag*, 4
twelve *zwölf*, 1
twenty *zwanzig*, 1
twenty-one *einundzwanzig*, 3; (see p. 83 for numbers 21-29)
twice *zweimal*, 7
two *zwei*, 1

ugly *hässlich*, 3
uncle *der Onkel, -*, 3
uncomfortable *unbequem*, 3
unfortunately *leider*, 7; **Unfortunately I can't.** *Leider kann ich nicht.*, 7
until: from 8 until 8:45 *von 8 Uhr bis 8 Uhr 45*, 4; **until you get to ... Square** *bis zum ...platz*, 9; **until you get to ... Street** *bis zur ...straße*, 9; **until you get to the traffic light** *bis zur Ampel*, 9
us *uns*, 7

vacuum *Staub saugen*, 7
vegetables *das Gemüse*, 8
very *sehr*, 2; **Very well!** *Sehr gut!*, 6
videocassette *das Video, -s*, 10
violent *brutal*, 10
visit *besuchen*, 2; **to visit friends** *Freunde besuchen*, 2
volleyball *Volleyball*, 2

want (to) *wollen*, 6
war movie *der Kriegsfilm, -e*, 10
warm *warm*, 7
was: I was *ich war*, 8; **I was at the baker's.** *Ich war beim Bäcker.*, 8; **he/she was** *er/sie war*, 8
wash *spülen*, 7; **to wash the dishes** *das Geschirr spülen*, 7
watch *schauen*, 2; **to watch TV** *Fernsehen schauen*, 2; **Watch out!** *Pass auf!* 6
water: to water the flowers *die Blumen gießen*, 7
water *das Wasser*, 3; **a glass of (mineral) water** *ein Glas (Mineral)Wasser*, 3
we *wir*, 2
wear *anziehen* (sep), 5
weather *das Wetter*, 7; **How's the weather?** *Wie ist das Wetter?*, 7; **What does the weather report say?** *Was sagt der Wetterbericht?*, 7
Wednesday *der Mittwoch*, 4
week *die Woche, -n*, 7
weekend *das Wochenende, -n*, 2; **on the weekend** *am Wochenende*, 2
weigh *wiegen*, 8
were: Where were you? *Wo warst du?*, 8; **we were** *wir waren*, 8; **they were** *sie waren*, 8; **you** (pl) **were** *ihr wart*, 8; **you** (formal) **were** *Sie waren*, 8
western (movie) *der Western, -*, 10
wet *nass*, 7
what? *was?*, 2; **What can I do for you?** *Was kann ich für dich tun?*, 7; **What else?** *Noch etwas?*, 9
what kind of? *was für?*, 10; **What kind of movies do you like?** *Was für Filme magst du gern?*, 10; **What kind of music do you like?** *Was für Musik hörst du gern?*, 10; **What will you have?** *Was bekommen Sie?*, 6
What's there to eat? *Was gibt's zu essen?*, 9
when? *wann?*, 2
where? *wo?*, 1; **Where are you from?** *Woher bist (kommst) du?*, 1
where (to)? *wohin?*, 6
which *welch-*, 4
white *weiß*, 3; **in white** *in Weiß*, 5
who? *wer?*, 1; **Who is that?** *Wer ist das?*, 1
whole-grain roll *die Vollkornsemmel, -n*, 9
whom *wen*, 7; *wem*, 11
whom? (to whom? for whom?) *wem?*, 11

why? *warum?*, 8; **Why don't you come along!** *Komm doch mit!*, 7
wide *weit*, 5
window *das Fenster, -*, 7; **to clean the windows** *die Fenster putzen*, 7
winter *der Winter*, 2; **in the winter** *im Winter*, 2
with *mit*, 6; **with bread** *mit Brot*, 6; **with corners** *eckig*, 12; **with lemon** *mit Zitrone*, 6; **with mustard** *mit Senf*, 9
woman *die Frau, -en*, 3
wood: made of wood *aus Holz*, 12
work: That won't work. *Das geht nicht.*, 7
would like (to) *möchten*, 3; **I would like to see....** *Ich möchte ... sehen.*, 5; **What would you like to eat?** *Was möchtest du essen?*, 3; **What would you like?** *Was bekommen Sie?*, 5; **Would you like anything else?** *Haben Sie noch einen Wunsch?*, 8
wristwatch *die Armbanduhr, -en*, 11
write *schreiben*, 2

year *das Jahr, -e*, 1; **I am...years old.** *Ich bin ... Jahre alt.*, 1
yellow *gelb*, 5; **in yellow** *in Gelb*, 5
yes *ja*, 1; **Yes?** *Bitte?*, 5
yesterday *gestern*, 8; **yesterday evening** *gestern Abend*, 8; **the day before yesterday** *vorgestern*, 8
you *du*, 2; **you are** *du bist*, 1; (pl) **you are** *ihr seid*, 1; (formal) **you are** *Sie sind*, 1
you (formal) *Sie*, 2
you (plural) *ihr*, 2
you (pl, acc pronoun) *euch*, 7
you (acc pronoun) *dich*, 7
you're (very) welcome! *Bitte (sehr, schön)!*, 3
your *dein*, 3; **to, for your father** *deinem Vater*, 11; **to, for your mother** *deiner Mutter*, 11

zoo *der Zoo, -s*, 12; **to go to the zoo** *in den Zoo gehen*, 12

Page numbers in boldface type refer to **Grammatik** and **Ein wenig Grammatik** presentations. Other page numbers refer to grammar structure presented in **So sagt man das!, Sprachtipp, Lerntrick, Wortschatz,** and **Landeskunde** sections. Page numbers beginning with R refer to the Grammar Summary in this Reference Section.

A

aber: 79; *see also* conjunctions
abräumen: **196,** R22; *see also* separable-prefix verbs
accusative case: 134; definite article **135;** noun phrase in **135;** indefinite article **135, 171, 258;** third person pronoun singular **140;** third person pronoun singular and plural **200;** first and second person pronoun singular and plural **200;** the interrogative pronoun **wen 200;** following **für** 199, **200,** 337; following **es gibt** 257; **kein** 258, **259;** *see also* R15, R16, R18; direct object
adjectives: whether you enjoy something 57; describing a room 79; describing people 84; talking about weather 202; talking about movies and books 290
am liebsten: 285
anprobieren: present tense forms of **143,** R22; *see also* separable-prefix verbs
anziehen: present tense forms of **143,** R22; *see also* separable-prefix verbs
article: **24, 76, 78, 135, 258;** *see also* definite article, indefinite article
aufräumen: 196, R22; *see also* separable-prefix verbs
aussehen: present tense forms of **143,** R21, R22; *see also* separable-prefix verbs
auxiliary: **75, 166, 195, 199, 223, 282;** see also modal auxiliary verbs

C

case: **135, 319;** *see also* nominative case, accusative case, dative case
class: definition of 24
clauses: **230, 250;** *see also* dependent clauses
command forms: **du**-commands 223, **224, 255,** 337, R22; **ihr**-commands 223, **224, 255,** 337, R22; **Sie**-commands 336, **255,** R22
comparisons: **285;** *see also* **lieber, am liebsten**
conjugations: *see* present tense; present perfect
conjunctions: **und** 29; **aber** 79; **denn** and **weil** 230; **dass 260;** *see also* expressions
connecting words: 29, 79, 230, 260; *see also* conjunctions
contractions: **zum, zur** 30, 254; **am** 55, 106; **ins,** 162, 165

D

dass: 260; *see also* conjunctions
dative case: 30, 55, 106, 318; introduction to **319;** following **mit 319;** interrogative pronoun **wem 319;** word order with **320;** third person pronouns 318, 319; *see also* R15; R16; R18; indirect object
definite article: 23; to identify class **24,** 78; nominative and accusative case **135,** 140; dative **319;** *see also* R15
denn: 230; *see also* conjunctions
dependent clauses: **wo** 250, R19; *see also* word order for **denn, weil,** and **dass**-clauses; *see also* clauses
direct object: definition of **135;** noun phrases as **135;** *see also* accusative case
direct object pronouns: **140, 200**
du-commands: 223, **224,** R22; see also command forms

E

ein: 74; nominative **74;** accusative 134, **135,** 170, **171, 258;** *see also* R16
ein-words: 74; **mein(e), dein(e) 82,** 83, 84; sein(e), ihr(e) 84; accusative **258,** 318; dative **319; kein 259;** *see also* R16
emphasis words: **denn, mal, halt, doch** 164; for **denn** *see also* conjunctions
endings: **48, 50, 52,** 82, 114, 231; *see also* plural formation of nouns, possessives, present tense verb endings, past tense, and infinitive
es gibt: 257
essen: 170; present tense forms of **171,** R21; *see also* stem-changing verbs
expressions: 29

F

fahren: present tense forms of 254, R21; **fahren** vs. **gehen** 255
first person: **ich, wir,** 26, 28, 50, 79; *see also* subject pronouns
formal form of address: 21, **52,** 116, 169, 250, 254, 255
forming questions: **23,** 28; *see also* questions and question words
für: preposition followed by accusative 199, **200,** 222, **337**
future: use of **morgen** and present tense for **203**

gefallen: 137, 144
gender: **24;** *see also* class
gern: 50, 282 285; with **haben** 110; compared to **lieber** and
    am liebsten 285

haben: present tense forms of 84, 106, **108;** with **gern** 110
helping verbs: *see* **haben** and **sein**

ihr-commands: **224,** R22; *see also* command forms
imperatives: **224;** *see also* command forms
indefinite article: **ein;** nominative **76;** accusative 76, 134, **135,**
    258, R16
indirect object: **318;** definition of, **319;** word order **320;** *see also*
    dative case
indirect object pronouns: **318;** definition of **319;** third person
    singular **319, 320**
infinitive: definition of **52;** in final position following modals
    166, 195, 196, 222, 342, R20–R22; *see also* word order
interrogatives: **23,** 28; *see also* questions and question words
interrogative pronouns: nominative form **wer** 23; accusative
    form **wen 200;** dative form **wem** 318, **319;** *see also* R18
irregular verbs: **26, 170, 255, 285, 291;** *see also* present tense
    and stem-changing verbs

kein: negation 258, **259,** R16
können: present tense of **199,** R21; *see also* modal auxiliary
    verbs

lesen: present tense forms of **291,** R21
lieber: 285
Lieblings-: 110

möchte-forms: 74; present tense **75,** 134,
    170, **171,** R21; *see also* modal auxiliary verbs
modal auxiliary verbs: 74; **möchte**-forms **75,** 134, 166, R21;
    wollen 166, 194, R21; **müssen 195,** R21; **können 199,**
    222, R21; **sollen** 222, **223,** R21; **mögen 282,** R21

mögen: present tense forms of **282,** R21; *see also* modal
    auxiliary verbs
morgen: 203; *see also* future
müssen: 194; present tense forms of **195,** R21; *see also* modal
    auxiliary verbs

near future: **203;** *see also* future
nehmen: 143; present tense forms of **144, 171,** R21; *see also*
    stem-changing verbs
nicht: 58
noch ein: 258
nominative case: interrogative pronoun
    wer 23; ein and **mein 82;** definition of
    135; indefinite article **135;** noun phrase in **135;** personal
    pronoun in **140;** *see also* subject
noun phrases: masculine, feminine, neuter **24;** as subject and
    direct object **135,** R15; *see also* definite article, accusative,
    dative, nominative
nouns: classes/genders of **24,** R15; plural of **114,** 115, 116, R17
numbers: 25, 83

object pronouns: **140, 200, 319, 320;** *see also* direct object
    pronouns and indirect object pronouns

past participle: 292, 343, R23, R24
past tense of: **sein 231,** R23
personal pronouns: **26,** 50, 79, **140, 200, 319;** *see also* pronouns
plural formation of nouns: **114,** 115, 116, R17
possessives: **mein(e), dein(e),** nominative **82; sein(e), ihr(e)**
    83; accusative **258;** dative **345;** *see also* R16
prefix: **Lieblings- 110;** *see also* separable prefixes
preposition: **aus** 28; **für** 199, **200; über,** use with **sprechen 291,**
    292; mit 30, **319**
present perfect: 292, 349, R24
present tense: definition of **52;** of **sein** 26; of **spielen** 52; of
    the **möchte**-forms **75;** of **haben** 108; of **anziehen** 143;
    of **nehmen, aussehen** 144; of **wollen** 166; of **essen** 171;
    of **müssen** 195; of **können** 199; of **sollen** 223; of **wissen**
    250; of **mögen** 282; of **sehen** 285; of **lesen, sprechen**
    291; *see also* R20–R22; present tense verb endings; verbs
present tense verb endings: **48, 50, 52;** verbs with stems ending
    in **d, t,** or **n 57;** verbs with stems ending in **-eln 58;** *see*
    also R20; present tense; stem-changing verbs; verbs
pronouns: 22, 25, 48; personal pronouns singular **26,** 115;
    personal pronouns plural **50;** class/gender **79,** 137; third
    person singular, accusative **140;** first and second person,
    accusative **200;** dative **319, 320;** *see also* R18; direct object
    pronouns, indirect object pronouns, subject pronouns,
    and personal pronouns

question words/interrogatives: **wie** 22, **23,** 25, 30, 57, 84, 161, 162, 254; **wer 23; woher 23,** 28; **was** 48, 50, 55, 74, 115, 134, 170; **wo 23,** 73, 116; **wann** 107, 164, 314; **worüber 291; wem 319;** *see also* R18

questions: 22; asking and answering questions **23;** questions beginning with a verb **23;** questions beginning with a question word **23;** questions anticipating a yes or no answer **23;** *see also* word order

second person: **du, ihr, Sie** (formal singular and plural), *see* subject pronouns

sehen: present tense forms of **285,** R21

sein: 25; present tense forms of **26,** R21; simple past tense forms of **231,** R23

separable prefixes: **an, aus 143, 144; auf, ab, mit 196; ein** 313; placement of **143, 196**

separable-prefix verbs: definition of **143; anziehen, anprobieren 143; aussehen 143, 144; aufräumen, abräumen, mitkommen 196; abheben, anrufen, auflegen, einstecken** 309; **einladen** 313; *see also* R22

sequencing: 109

Sie-commands: 116, 254, **255;** *see also* command forms

sollen: 222; present tense forms of **223,** R21; *see also* modal auxiliary verbs

sprechen: present tense forms of **291;** with **über** 291, R21

stem-changing verbs: **nehmen, aussehen 144; essen** 170, **171; fahren 255; sehen 285; lesen, sprechen 291;** *see also* R21; present tense verb endings

subject: 25, **135;** placement of **56;** *see also* nominative case

subject pronouns: 22, 25, **26,** 28, 48; plurals **50, 79;** as opposed to direct object pronouns **140**

subordinating conjunctions: **denn, weil** 230; *see also* word order

superlatives: suffix -**ste** 287

time expressions: 55, 106, 107, 198, 199; **morgen 203;** *see also* word order

third person: **er, sie, sie** (plural), **Sie** (plural formal) **26,** 28, 48, 79; *see also* subject pronouns

und: 29; *see also* conjunctions

verbs: with separable prefixes, **anziehen, anprobieren, aussehen 143; aufräumen, abräumen, mitkommen 196; einladen** 313; with vowel change in the **du-** and **er/sie**-form, **nehmen, aussehen 144; essen** 170, **171; fahren 255; sehen 285; lesen, sprechen 291;** *see also* R20–R22; present tense and present tense verb endings

verb-final position: in **weil**-clauses **230;** in clauses following **wissen 250,** in **dass**-clauses **260;** *see also* R19

verb-second position: 55, **56, 167**

weil: **230;** *see also* conjunctions

wissen: present tense forms of, word order following **250,** R19, R21; **wissen** vs. **kennen 284**

wo: 23, 73, 116

woher: 28

wollen: present tense forms of **166,** R21; *see also* modal auxiliary verbs

word order: 22; questions beginning with a verb **23;** questions beginning with a question word **23,** 55; verb in second position **54;** with separable prefix verbs **143;** using modals **166, 167, 199, 222, 342;** in **denn-** and **weil**-clauses **230;** verb-final in clauses following **wissen 250;** verb-final in **dass**-clauses **260;** with dative case **320;** *see also* R19; infinitive; questions

worüber: 291

Grammar Index

ACKNOWLEDGMENTS *(continued from page ii)*

Bertelsmann Club: Advertisement and front cover, "Die Firma," from *Bertelsmann Club,* March 1993, p. 9.

C & A Mode Düsseldorf: Adapted advertisement, "C & A: SCHNUPPER PREISE," from *Süddeutsche Zeitung,* March 1992, p. 18.

Deike-Press-Bilderdienst: Game, "Skat," from *Südwest Presse: Schwäbisches Tagblatt,* Tübingen, July 1990. Copyright © 1990 by Deike Press, Germany.

Winfred Epple: Advertisement, "Gute Laune," by Wertobjekte Immobilien Epple (WIE) from *Südwest Presse: Schwäbisches Tagblatt,* Tübingen, July 14, 1990.

Die Gilde Werbeagentur GmbH: Advertisement, "Das neue Plantaris."

Dr. Rudolf Goette GmbH: Advertisements, "Dienstag, 26. Januar" and "Dienstag, 25. Mai," from *Pro-Arte: Konzerte '93.*

Gräfe und Unzer Verlag, München: "Dallmayr," "Das Wetter" (weather chart), "Der besondere Tip," "Englischer Garten," "Januar Fasching," "Ludwig Beck," "Medizinische Versorgung," "Olympiapark," and "Peterskirche" by H. E. Rübesamen from *Merian live-München,* pp. 30–31, 39, 45, 79, 80, 95, 112, 119 and 120. Copyright © 1993 by Gräfe und Unzer Verlag, München.

Händle & Partner: Advertisement, "Der mit dem Wolf tanzt," from *1. Ludwigsburger: Sommernachts Open Air-Kino,* text by Frank Schneider, illustration by Gernot Händle.

München Hilton Hotel: Advertisement, "Kulinarische Highlights im München City Hilton," (retitled "Hamburg Kulinarische Highlights".)

Immobilien: Advertisement, "Immobilien T. Kurcz," from *Südwest Presse: Schwäbisches Tagblatt,* July 14, 1990.

Institut Rosenberg: Advertisement, "Institut Rosenberg," from *Süddeutsche Zeitung,* July 10–11, 1993, p. 40.

IVT - Immobiliengesellschaft der Volksbank Tübingen mbH & Co., Grundstücks-KG.: "Auf dem Lande" and "2-Zi.-Eigentumswohnung" from "Immobilienverbund-Volksbanken Raiffeisenbanken" from *Südwest Presse: Schwäbisches Tagblatt,* Tübingen, July 14, 1990.

Jahreszeiten Verlag GmbH: "DAS WEISSE HEMD" from *Petra,* May 1992. p. 52.

K + L Ruppert GmbH: Advertisement, "Kurz und Gut!" and "Qualitäts-Garantie."

Karsten Jahnke Konzertdirektion GmbH: Advertisement of upcoming concert tours from *Konzerte: Karsten Jahnke präsentiert Konzertübersicht 1993,* no. 248.

Emil Kriegbaum GmbH & Co. KG: Advertisement, "Stark Reduziert!," from *Südwest Presse: Schwäbisches Tagblatt,* Tübingen, June 27, 1990.

Liberty Diskothek Café: Advertisement, "Liberty Diskothek Café," from *in münchen,* no. 30/31, July 25–August 7, 1991.

Messe Stuttgart Kongress-U. Tagungsbüro. "Hanns-Martin-Schleyer-Halle" from *Veranstaltungskalender der Messe Stuttgart: Programm,* March 1992.

Müller Brot: Advertisements, "Der Mensch ist, wie er ißt" and "HOTLINE."

OK-PUR: From "MTV News" and "OK-PUR TAGESTIP: The Romeos" from *OK-PUR,* June 22, 1993.

QUICK Verlag GmbH: Advertisement, "Milchbars," from *QUICK,* August 8, 1991, no. 33. Copyright © 1991 by QUICK Verlag GmbH.

Dr. Rall GmbH, Reutlingen: Advertisement, "Tübingen-Lustnau am Herrlesberg," from *Südwest Presse: Schwäbisches Tagblatt,* Tübingen, July 14, 1990.

Sator Werbe-Agentur: Advertisement, "Bahrenfelder Forsthaus," from *Hotels und Restaurants 93/94,* D-22761 Hamburg Das Tor zur Welt.

Hartmut Schmid: Game, "Schach," from *Südwest Presse: Schwäbisches Tagblatt,* Tübingen, July 13, 1990.

Schwäbisches Tagblatt: Advertisement, "UNI Sommerfest," from *Südwest Presse: Schwäbisches Tagblatt,* Tübingen, June 23, 1990.

Spar Öst. Warenhandels-AG: From flyer, "Spar Supermarkt: NEUERÖFFNUNG, July 1, 1993."

Stadt Bietigheim-Bissingen: Captions from *Stadt Bietigheim-Bissingen.*

Stuttgart - Marketing GmbH: Captions from *Stuttgart.*

Südwest Presse, Tübingen: Advertisement, "Eninger Hot Jazz Festival," from *Schwäbisches Tagblatt,* Tübingen, June 23, 1990.

Tiefdruck Schwann-Bagel GmbH: Adaption of advertisement, "Hobby" from *JUMA Das Jugendmagazin,* 2/90, February 1990, p. 47. Advertisement, "Mode '91" from *JUMA Das Jugendmagazin,* 3/91, July 1991, p. 31. Caption from "Polo mit Eskimorolle" from *JUMA Das Jugendmagazin,* 1/92, January 1992, pp. 2–3. "Geschenke,"

"Hallo Heiko!," "Hallo Sven!," "Hallo Tina!," "Im Geschenkladen sucht," "Im Supermarkt läuft Ben," "Stefan wird im Schreibwarengeschäft," and "Wem hilfst du?" from *JUMA Das Jugendmagazin,* 2/93, April 1993, pp. 21, 23, 38, 39, 40 and 42.

Tourismus-Zentrale Hamburg GmbH: Advertisement, "Tag u. Nacht," from *Hotels und Restaurants 93/94,* Hamburg Das Tor zu Welt.

United International Pictures GmbH: Advertisement, "Jurassic Park," from *Kino Magazin,* February 1993.

Verlag J.C.B. Mohr (Paul Seibeck) Tübingen: Advertisement, "Wohnung," from *Südwest Presse: Schwäbisches Tagblatt,* Tübingen, July 14, 1990.

Zeiler Möbelwerk GmbH & Co. KG, D-97475 Zeil am Main: Advertisement, "Best in Germany—Best in America (allmilmö®)," from *Metropolitan Home®,* Special Edition, The Best of Winners!, Fall 1991, p. 9.

PHOTOGRAPHY CREDITS

Abbreviations used: (t) top, (c) center, (b) bottom, (l) left, (r) right, (bckgd) background, (i) inset.

All photographs by George Winkler/Holt, Rinehart and Winston, Inc. except:

Border images: Victoria Smith/HRW Photo.

TABLE OF CONTENTS: Page vii (bl), Michelle Bridwell/Frontera Fotos; ix (bl), Victoria Smith/HRW Photo; xi (tl), Michelle Bridwell/Frontera Fotos; xviii (t), Michelle Bridwell/Frontera Fotos; xxi (br), ©European Communities; xxii (bl), Helga Lade/Peter Arnold, Inc.; xxiii (br), Helga Lade/Peter Arnold, Inc.

Preliminary Chapter: Page 1 (cl, tl), Westlight/CORBIS; 1 (br), Bernard Silberstein/FPG International; 4 (tl), DPA/IPOL; 4 (cl), Robert Young Pelton/Westlight/Corbis; 4 (bl), Dallas & John Heaton/Westlight/Corbis; 4 (br), J. Zuckerman/Westlight/Corbis; 4 (tr), Digital imagery® copyright 2003 PhotoDisc, Inc.; 5 (tl), Bettman Archive/Corbis; 5 (tr), AP/Wide World Photos; 5 (tc), Bettman Archive/Corbis; 5 (cl), HRW Photo; 5 (bl), Archive Photos; 5 (cr), AP/Wide World Photos; 9 (all), Victoria Smith/HRW Photo; 10 (bc), AP/Wide World Photos; 10 (tl, cl), Digital imagery® copyright 2003 PhotoDisc, Inc.; 10 (cr), Corbis Images; 11 (bl, bc), Michelle Bridwell/Frontera Fotos.

UNIT ONE: Page 12-13 (all), Jose Fuste Raga/The Stock Market; 14 (tr), Helga Lade/Peter Arnold, Inc.

Chapter One: Page 20 (br), Michelle Bridwell/Frontera Fotos; 21 (bl, cl), Michelle Bridwell/Frontera Fotos; 21 (cr), Viesti Collection, Inc.; 21 (br), Michelle Bridwell/Frontera Fotos; 34-35 (bkgd), Courtesy of Lufthansa German Airlines; 35 (bl), Corbis Images; 36 (c), Michelle Bridwell/Frontera Fotos.

Chapter Two: Page 47 (bl), EyeWire, Inc. Image Club Graphics ©1998 Adobe Systems, Inc.; 47 (bc, br), Digital imagery® copyright 2003 PhotoDisc, Inc.; 48 (tl, tr, cl, br, bl), Digital imagery® copyright 2003 PhotoDisc, Inc.; 51 (l, cl, c, cr), Digital imagery® copyright 2003 PhotoDisc, Inc.; 51 (bcr), John Langford/HRW Photo; 51 (bl), ©1997 Radlund & Associates for Artville; 51 (bcl), Sam Dudgeon/HRW Photo; 51 (r), Digital imagery® copyright 2003 PhotoDisc, Inc.; 51 (bc), Corbis Images; 53 (l, cl, cr, r), Michelle Bridwell/Frontera Fotos; 53 (br), Sam Dudgeon/HRW Photo; 53 (inset), Michelle Bridwell/HRW Photo; 60 (tr), Digital imagery® copyright 2003 PhotoDisc, Inc.; 62 (cr), Michelle Bridwell/Frontera Fotos; 65 (tl, tc, tr), Viesti Collection, Inc.

Chapter Three: Page 73 (c, bl, bc, cr), Michelle Bridwell/Frontera Fotos; 73 (br), Viesti Collection, Inc.; 74 (tl), Richard Hutchings/PhotoEdit; 74 (tcl, tcr), Viesti Collection, Inc.; 75 (tcl, tl), Corbis Images; 75 (bl, bcl), Victoria Smith/HRW Photo; 75 (tcr), ©Stockbyte; 75 (tr), composite - apple (Corbis Images); cherries, banana and pear (Digital Imagery® copyright 2003 PhotoDisc, Inc.; 75 (bcr), Victoria Smith/HRW Photo; 76 (l, cll, cl), Corbis Images; 76 (c, cr), Victoria Smith/HRW Photo; 76 (r), ©Stockbyte; 80 (cl, c, cr, bl), Courtesy of Scandinavia Contemporary Interiors; 80 (bc), Michelle Bridwell/Frontera Fotos; 80 (br), Digital imagery® copyright 2003 PhotoDisc, Inc.; 81 (tl, tr, cl, c, cr, br), Viesti Collection, Inc.; 81 (bl, bc), Michelle Bridwell/Frontera Fotos; 93 (tl, tc, tr, bl, cl, cr, br), Michelle Bridwell/Frontera Fotos.

UNIT TWO: Page 96-97 (all), Helga Lade/Peter Arnold, Inc.; 98 (tr, cr, b), Helga Lade/Peter Arnold, Inc.

Chapter Four: Page 114 (tl, tcl, tcr, tr, cl, c, cr), Victoria Smith/HRW Photo; 115 (tl, tcl, tcr, tr), Michelle Bridwell/Frontera Fotos; 115 (b), ©European Communities; 122 (c), Victoria Smith/HRW Photo; 123 (b), ©European Communities; 124 (bl, br), Victoria Smith/HRW Photo.

Chapter Five: Page 133 (tl, tc, tr, cl, c, cr, bl), Victoria Smith/HRW Photo; 140 (br), Victoria Smith/HRW Photo; 140 (inset), Sam Dudgeon/HRW Photo; 141 (cl, cr, b), Michelle Bridwell/Frontera Fotos; 143 (tl, tcl, tcr, tr), Michelle Bridwell/Frontera Fotos; 149 (tr, cr), Victoria Smith/HRW Photo; 150 (br, cl, cr), Victoria Smith/HRW Photo; 152 (br), David Vance Associates/The Image Bank.

Chapter Six: Page 171 (tl, tcl, tcr), Victoria Smith/HRW Photo; 171 (tr), Michelle Bridwell/HRW Photo; 171 (cl), Digital imagery® copyright 2003 PhotoDisc, Inc.; 171 (ccl, ccr, cr), Victoria Smith/HRW Photo; 178 (cr), Michelle Bridwell/HRW Photo; 178 (bc), Victoria Smith/HRW Photo; 179 (cr), Victoria Smith/HRW Photo.

UNIT THREE:

Chapter Seven: Page 193 (tl, tcr, cl, clc, crc), Michelle Bridwell/Frontera Fotos; 193 (br), Viesti Collection, Inc.; 201 (tl, tr, cl, cr, bl, br), Digital imagery® copyright 2003 PhotoDisc, Inc.; 203 (cr), Viesti Collection, Inc.; 203 (cl), Tony Freeman/PhotoEdit; 203 (cr), Dennis MacDonald/PhotoEdit; 203 (bl), Vic Bider/PhotoEdit; 203 (bc), David Young-Wolff/PhotoEdit; 207 (tl), Viesti Collection, Inc.; 207 (bl), Michelle Bridwell/Frontera Fotos; 212 (bl), David Madison/Duomo Photography; 212 (clc, bc), Michelle Bridwell/Frontera Fotos.

Chapter Eight: Page 221 (tl, tc, tcr, tr, tlb, tcb), Michelle Bridwell/Frontera Fotos; 221 (crc, cr), Sam Dudgeon/HRW Photo; 221 (bl, blc, bc, bcr, br, tr), Viesti Collection, Inc.; 226 (tl, cl), Victoria Smith/HRW Photo; 226 (bc), Digital imagery® copyright 2003 PhotoDisc, Inc.; 226 (tr), Victoria Smith/HRW Photo; 226 (cr), ©PhotoSpin, Inc.; 226 (bc), Victoria Smith/HRW Photo; 236 (tr), Sam Dudgeon/HRW Photo; 236 (cr), Michelle Bridwell/Frontera Fotos; 237 (b), ©PhotoSpin, Inc.; 238 (tr), Digital imagery® copyright 2003 PhotoDisc, Inc.

Chapter Nine: Page 254 (tr, bl), Michelle Bridwell/Frontera Fotos; 260 (tr), Thomas Kanzler/Viesti Collection, Inc.; 265 (c), Michelle Bridwell/Frontera Fotos.

UNIT FOUR: Page 272-273 (all), S.K./Helga Lade/Peter Arnold, Inc.; 274 (c), S.K./Helga Lade/Peter Arnold, Inc.

Chapter Ten: Page 281 (c, cr), Everett Collection; 281 (tl, tc, tr, cl, bl, bc, br), Motion Picture & Television Photo Archive; 283 (bl), Marco Shark/Shark Images Photography; 287 (tl), ©2003/Kennan Ward/Adventure Photo & Film; 288 (c), Michelle Bridwell/Frontera Fotos; 291 (tl, tr, cr, br), Michelle Bridwell/Frontera Fotos; 296 (bc), Motion Picture & Television Photo Archive; 297 (bl), Motion Picture & Television Photo Archive.

Chapter Eleven: Page 304-305 (all), Michelle Bridwell/Frontera Photos; 309 (bcl), Sam Dudgeon/HRW Photo; 309 (bcr), Digital imagery® copyright 2003 PhotoDisc, Inc.; 311 (cl), Sam Dudgeon/HRW Photo; 317 (tr, cl), Michelle Bridwell/Frontera Fotos; 317 (clc), Viesti Collection, Inc.; 317 (c), Michelle Bridwell/Frontera Fotos; 317 (crc), Viesti Collection, Inc.; 317 (cr, bl, bc, br, tl, tr, cr, tr, cl, c, tc), Michelle Bridwell/Frontera Fotos; 324 (b), Sam Dudgeon/HRW Photo; 325 (tr), Michelle Bridwell/Frontera Fotos; 326 (bl, bc, br), Michelle Bridwell/Frontera Fotos; 328 (tl, c, bl), Michelle Bridwell/Frontera Fotos.

Chapter Twelve: Page 340 (bl), Michelle Bridwell/Frontera Fotos; 340 (bc), Viesti Collection, Inc.; 343 (tr), Michelle Bridwell/Frontera Fotos; 350 (tr, br), Michelle Bridwell/Frontera Fotos; 350 (c), Digital imagery® copyright 2003 PhotoDisc, Inc.; 351 (tl), Michelle Bridwell/Frontera Fotos; 351 (bl), Digital imagery® copyright 2003 PhotoDisc, Inc.; 351 (c), Corbis Images; 355 (cr), Michelle Bridwell/Frontera Fotos; 355 (br), Sam Dudgeon/HRW Photo.

Reference Section: Page R9 (tl, tc), Digital imagery® copyright 2003 PhotoDisc, Inc.; R9 (tr), EyeWire, Inc. Image Club Graphics ©1998 Adobe Systems, Inc.; R9 (c), Randal Alhadeff/HRW Photo; R9 (cr, brt, bc), Digital imagery® copyright 2003 PhotoDisc, Inc.; R9 (br), Corbis Images; R10 (tl), Corbis Images; R10 (tr), EyeWire, Inc.; R10 (cl, c), Scott Van Osdol/HRW Photo; R10 (br), Digital imagery® copyright 2003 PhotoDisc, Inc.; R11 (cr), Corbis Images; R11 (tl, tr, cl, c, bl, br), Digital imagery® copyright 2003 PhotoDisc, Inc.; R12 (tl, cl), Digital imagery® copyright 2003 PhotoDisc, Inc.; R12 (br), ©Stockbyte; R12 (bc), Sam Dudgeon/HRW Photo; R12 (bl), Corbis Images; R13 (cl), © Digital Vision; R13 (br), Corbis Images; R14 (bl, br), Michelle Bridwell/Frontera Fotos.

ILLUSTRATION AND CARTOGRAPHY CREDITS

Abbreviated as follows: (t) top, (b) bottom, (l) left, (r) right, (c) center.

All art, unless otherwise noted, by Holt, Rinehart & Winston.

Preliminary Chapter: Page xxii, MapQuest.com; 2, MapQuest.com; 3, MapQuest.com; 6, Holly Cooper; 8, Tom Rummonds.

Chapter One: Page 12, MapQuest.com; 22 (t), George McLeod; 22 (cr), Holly Cooper; 23, George McLeod; 30, George McLeod; 39, Tom Rummonds.

Chapter Two: Page 47 (c) Gail Piazza; 47 (b), Eduard Böhm; 48, Eduard Böhm; 51 (l), George McLeod; 51 (r), Eduard Böhm; 55, Gail Piazza; 64, Holly Cooper.

Chapter Three: Page 74, George McLeod; 78, George McLeod; 81, Holly Cooper; 84, Gail Piazza; 92, Tom Rummonds.

Chapter Four: Page 96, MapQuest.com; 105, Holly Cooper; 107, Holly Cooper; 108, Gail Piazza; 114, Eduard Böhm; 116, George McLeod; 121, Holly Cooper; 124, Eduard Böhm.

Chapter Five: Page 136, Holly Cooper; 137, Holly Cooper; 138, Tom Rummonds; 139, Tom Rummonds; 144, Holly Cooper; 145, Holly Cooper; 152, Holly Cooper; 154, Holly Cooper.

Chapter Six: Page 161 (c), Tom Rummonds; 161 (b), Holly Cooper; 162, Leslie Kell; 164, George McLeod; 165, Tom Rummonds; 172, Holly Cooper; 173, Holly Cooper; 180, Holly Cooper.

Chapter Seven: Page 184, MapQuest.com; 194, George McLeod; 195 (t), Holly Cooper; 195 (b), Eduard Böhm; 199, Tom Rummonds; 200, Tom Rummonds; 201 (t), George McLeod; 204, Tom Rummonds; 214, Holly Cooper.

Chapter Eight: Page 223, Holly Cooper; 224, Tom Rummonds; 232, Tom Rummonds.

Chapter Nine: Page 249, John Wilson; 251 (t), John Wilson; 251 (c), George McLeod; 253 (c), Riki Rushing; 253 (b), Leslie Kell; 256, Holly Cooper; 259, Eduard Böhm; 270, John Wilson.

Chapter Ten Page 272, MapQuest.com; 286, Eduard Böhm.

Chapter Eleven: Page 309, Tom Rummonds; 310, Tom Rummonds; 314, Eduard Böhm; 315 (c), Mike Krone; 315 (b), Eduard Böhm; 320, Mike Krone; 328, George McLeod; 330, Mike Krone.

Chapter Twelve: Page 338 (bl, br), Eduard Böhm; 339, Mike Krone; 342, George McLeod; 344, Holly Cooper; 345 (t), Holly Cooper; 345 (b), Eduard Böhm; 347, Eduard Böhm; 356, Riki Rushing.